PRICE GUIDE TO

COUNTRY

ANTIQUES & COLLECTIBLES

FOURTH EDITION

Dana G. Morykan

D0595619

HOUSE OF COLLECTIBLES

THE BALLANTINE PUBLISHING GROUP • NEW YORK

Copyright ©1999 by Rinker Enterprises, Inc.

House of Collectibles and the HC colophon are trademarks of Random House, Inc.

Published by: House of Collectibles
The Ballantine Publishing Group
201 East 50th Street
New York, New York 10022

Distributed by The Ballantine Publishing Group, a division of Random House, Inc., New York, and simultaneously in Canada by Random House of Canada Limited, Toronto.

www.randomhouse.com/BB/

Manufactured in the United States of America

ISSN: 1522–5135

ISBN: 0–676–60165–0

Cover design by Cathy Colbert

Fourth Edition: February 1999
10 9 8 7 6 5 4 3 2 1

CONTENTS

ACKNOWLEDGMENTS

Family is the heart of Country and the Rinker Enterprises family is the heart of this book. While my name appears on the title page as author, it is a team effort.

In the Acknowledgments of the *Third Edition*, Harry L. Rinker noted my increased role in preparing this title. Recognizing that I made an even greater contribution to this edition, Harry decided to step aside as co–author. I express my deepest thanks to him for giving me a book of my own and his continuing confidence and support.

Dena George, my twin sister, joined the Rinker Enterprises staff between the publication of the third and fourth editions of this book. Her expertise is responsible for the quality of the scanned images that appear in this edition. Kathy Williamson provided invaluable help with the new listings. Nancy Butt verified and updated the references and other information that appears in the category introductions. Virginia Reinbold and Richard Schmeltzle provided support services.

Purchasers of earlier editions of this book will note two significant changes between this and previous editions. First, the book has returned to its smaller format, a size that makes it easier to carry into the field. Second, Random House's House of Collectibles has replaced Wallace–Homestead as the title's publisher. It is great to be a New York author. Special thanks to Tim Kochuba, General Manager of House of Collectibles, for accepting the title, to Randy Ladenheim–Gil for her skilled editorial talents, and to Alex Klapwald for his technical support throughout the production process.

Country people share. A general thanks to all those who shared their information, thoughts, and photographs. Auction houses, collectors, collectors' clubs, dealers, manufacturers and trade periodicals never hesitated to answer yes when I requested their help.

I wish this book were perfect. I am not naive enough to think it is. However, I can assure you that it improves upon its predecessors and is the foundation upon which its successors will be built. You can help to make it even better by sending suggestions, positive or critical, to *Price Guide to Country Antiques & Collectibles*, 5093 Vera Cruz Road, Emmaus, PA 18049. Every idea received is carefully considered.

It is my fondest hope that this book makes Country come alive for you. While Country is a look, it is also a state of mind. Country is harmony, tranquility and a leisurely pace. May you enjoy all these attributes from the Country objects that surround you.

Finally, a very special thanks to my husband, Ray, and to my children, Kristen and Zack. Antiques and collectibles is not a nine–to–five occupation, especially for an author. Their enthusiasm and support ensures that time spent working at home never interferes with the quality of our family life.

5093 Vera Cruz Road
Emmaus, PA 18049

Dana G. Morykan
November 1998

INTRODUCTION

Welcome to the fourth edition of *Country Antiques & Collectibles.* You will note a significant difference between this fourth edition and its Country cousins, the first three editions. Dana Morykan, co–author of the first three editions, has assumed full responsibility as the book's author, releasing Harry Rinker to develop several new projects in the antiques and collectibles field. House of Collectibles, part of Random House's Ballantine Publishing group, is the title's new publisher. Country has arrived. It is now part of the New York scene. Finally, the reproduction craftspersons and manufacturers references have been dropped in favor of more object listings and prices. Previous readers have asked for this, and we have responded.

This fourth edition of *Country Antiques & Collectibles* contains all the traditional features of the previous editions—category introductions featuring history, references, periodicals, collectors' clubs, museums, reproduction alerts, and detailed, accurate listings. Yet, it is more than the sum of these parts.

The book focuses on a "style" rather than group of objects. Country is a look, a decorating style. Many individuals do not collect Country. They decorate their living room, kitchen, bedroom, and often their entire house in Country. While the focus of this look changes continuously, Country has been the dominant American decorating style for decades. It will remain so well into the 21st century.

DEFINING COUNTRY

For the purpose of this book, Country includes those objects that were part of nineteenth and early twentieth century rural life. The agrarian community included farm and village. Objects from both are included.

Country is part of Americana. Its objects reflect how a major portion of our country's population lived. This book documents Country's legacy.

Limiting Country to American objects is shortsighted. In the 1980s Country collectors expanded their horizons and discovered English Country and French Country. You will find categories relating to each throughout the book.

There is a strong link between Country and folk art. Many so–called folk art items originated in rural America. Many Country categories, e.g., quilts, have been appropriated by folk art collectors and made part of their movement. This book is concerned only with the objects themselves. If an object is Country in origin, it belongs in this book. Hence, you will find a fair amount of "folk art" within these pages.

Throughout the 1970s and early 1980s collectors, dealers, and decorators stressed the informal, generic side of Country. In the mid–1980s they discovered that Country had a formal side. *Country Antiques & Collectibles* has carefully blended the formal and informal. As a result, some categories and listings may challenge your understanding of what does and does not constitute Country.

On the national level Country returned to its Early American roots in the early 1990s. While some listings reflect this shift, this book's principal focus is on Country as it was defined during the 1970s and 1980s.

Each of us defines Country differently. In a way this reflects the diversity and independent frame of mind that is so much a part of Country. Country continually evolves. Each new edition of this book reflects those changes.

FINDING COUNTRY

Country is everywhere. You will find objects that are part of Country at virtually every craft show, flea market, mall, shop, or show that you visit. This is due to Country's modern eclecticism and its dualistic nature—formal and informal.

In the past two decades a number of "Country" shows and flea markets have developed with a strong Country emphasis. The following list will help you locate them. Because some of the show dates shift, the list is organized by promoter. Check with the promoter for the exact dates of their next Country event.

Jim Burk (3012 Miller Road, Washington Boro, PA 17582; 717-397-7209). Check the dates for his shows held at the York County Fairgrounds, York, PA, and Franklin and Marshall College, Lancaster, PA.

Ronald Cox (1830 South Muessing Road, Indianapolis, IN 46239; 317-891-1270). The Hoosier Antiques Exposition is held at the Indiana State Fairgrounds, Indianapolis, IN, in early April and mid–September.

Steve Jenkins (PO Box 580, Fishers, IN; 317-598-0012). Crutcher Antiques Show & Sale, Indiana State Fairgrounds, Indianapolis, IN, held in mid–April and mid–October.

Bruce and Vivalyn Knight (PO Box 2429, Springfield, OH 45501; 513-325-0053). The Springfield Antiques Show & Flea Market is held at the Clark County Fairgrounds, Springfield, OH, on the third weekend of the month, year round, excluding July. The December market is held the second weekend of the month.

Richard E. Kramer (427 Midvale Avenue, St. Louis, MO 63130; 800-862-1090). Kramer's Heart of Country show held at the Opryland Hotel in Nashville, TN, in early spring each year is the bellwether Country show in America. Also check out Home in Indiana held in Indianapolis in early fall.

Maine Antique Dealers Association (Contact: Nancy Prince, PO Box 604, North Turner, ME 04266; 207-224-7823). Held in mid–July at the University of New England's Campus Center, Biddeford, ME.

Helen Robinson (PO Box 549, St. Charles, IL 60174; 603-377-2252). Kane County Antiques Flea Market is held at the Kane County Fairgrounds, St. Charles, IL, the first Sunday of every month and the preceding Saturday.

Sandwich Antiques Market (1510 North Hoyne, Chicago, IL 60622; 773-227-4464). The Sandwich Antiques Market is held at The Fairgrounds, Sandwich, IL, one Sunday each month from May through October.

Sha–Dor Shows (PO Box 12069, Silver Spring, MD 20908; 301-924-5002). Check out the Washington, DC, Antiques Fairs held at DC Armory, Washington, DC.

If the Midwest and Plains states are the "heart" of country, Indianapolis, Indiana, is its capital. Almost every weekend there is a show in or around Indianapolis with a strong Country appeal. Malls in the surrounding area also heavily emphasize Country.

There are many regional Country–theme antiques shows. Some communities such as New Oxford, Pennsylvania, and Fairhaven, Ohio, turn their entire town into an outdoor antiques festival one or more times a year. All these shows and antiques festivals advertise in the leading trade papers. Attend as many as possible.

Do not overlook contemporary craft shows. State and regional craft shows abound. Check with your local Council of the Arts to determine the date and location of the shows nearest you.

Finally, one auction house deserves special attention—Garth's Auctions, Inc. (PO Box 369, Delaware, OH 43015). An annual subscription to its catalogs is a must for any serious Country collector.

ORGANIZATION OF THE BOOK

General Approach: This book treats Country topically. In order to do this, a twofold approach was used in selecting the major categories—(1) general collecting topics, e.g., furniture, and (2) phases of agrarian life, e.g., the barn. This corresponds with how you collect and deal with Country.

This approach is workable because of the book's strong index. Use it to find the correct location of the Country item you seek.

History: This section provides historical background, describes how objects were made, identifies who are or were the leading manufacturers, and notes variations of form and style.

Whenever possible, we place objects in a social context—how they were used, for what purposes, etc. We also show how the objects fit within a Country decorating scheme. An object's decorative use is just as much a part of its history as its utilitarian use. Where appropriate, we have added collecting hints, e.g., where cross–category collecting and outside factors affect pricing.

References: A few general references are listed to encourage collectors to learn more about their objects. Included are author, title, most recent edition, publisher (if published by a small firm or individual, we have indicated "published by author"), and a date of publication.

Finding these books may present a bit of a problem. The antiques and collectibles field is blessed with a dedicated core of book dealers who stock these specialized publications. You may find them at flea markets, antiques shows, and through their advertisements in leading publications in the field. Many dealers publish annual or semi–annual catalogs. Ask to be put on their mailing lists. Books go out of print quickly, yet many books printed over twenty–five years ago remain the standard work in a field. Also, haunt used book dealers for reference material.

No one involved in the antiques and collectibles field should be without a copy of David Maloney, Jr.'s *Maloney's Antiques and Collectibles Resource Directory.* This indispensable reference source is currently in its fourth edition.

Collectors' Clubs: Collectors' clubs add vitality to any collecting field. Their publications and conventions produce knowledge which often cannot be found anywhere else. Many of these clubs are short lived; others are so strong that they have regional and local chapters. Support those clubs that match your collecting interest.

Periodicals: The Country field is served by a wealth of general and specific publications. You need to be aware of the following:

American Country Collectibles, Goodman Media Group/GCR Publishing Group, 1700 Broadway, New York, NY 10019.

Country, Reiman Publications, 5400 South 60th Street, Greendale, WI 53129.

Country Accents, Goodman Media Group/GCR Publishing Group, 1700 Broadway, New York, NY 10019.

Country Almanac, Harris Publications, 1115 Broadway, New York, NY 10010.

Country Collectibles, Harris Publications, 1115 Broadway, New York, NY 10010.

Country Folk Art, 8393 East Holly Road, Holly, MI 48442.
Country Home, Meredith Corporation, 1716 Locust Street, Des Moines, IA 50309.
Country Living, Hearst Corporation, 224 West 57th Street, New York, NY 10019.
Country Sampler, Sampler Publications, 707 Kautz Road, St. Charles, IL 60174.
Country Woman, Reiman Publications, 5400 South 60th Street, Greendale, WI 53129.
Early American Homes, Cowles Enthusiastic Media, Inc., 6405 Flank Drive, Harrisburg, PA 17112.
Farm and Ranch Living, Reiman Publications, 5400 South 60th Street, Greendale, WI 53129.
Martha Stewart Living, EVP Publishing Group, 20 West 43rd Street, New York, NY 10036.

Regional papers from New England, the Middle Atlantic, and Midwest stress Country more heavily than regional papers from other parts of the country. A complete list of these papers is found in this book's introductory material.

Museums: The best way to study a specific field is to see as many documented examples as possible. For this reason, we have listed museums where significant collections are on display. We especially recommend visiting state and regional farm museums.

Reproduction Alert: Reproductions (exact copies) and copycats (stylistic copies) are a major concern. Unfortunately, many of these items are unmarked. Newness of appearance is often the best clue to spotting them. Where "Reproduction Alert" appears, a watchful eye should be kept within the entire category.

Reproductions are only one aspect of the problem. Outright fakes (objects deliberately meant to deceive) are another. Be especially alert for fakes in categories where Country and folk art come together.

Listings: We have attempted to make the listings descriptive enough so the specific object can be identified. Most guides limit their descriptions to one line, but not us. We focus primarily on items that are actively sold in the marketplace. Nevertheless, some harder–to–find objects are included in order to demonstrate the market spread.

PRICE NOTES

Most prices within Country categories are relatively stable. This is why we use a one–price system. Pricing is based on an object being in very good condition. If otherwise, we note this in the description. It would be ideal to suggest that mint or unused examples of all objects exist. Objects from the past were used, whether glass, ceramics, metal, or wood. Because of this use, some normal wear must be expected.

As the number of special interest collectors grows, a single object may appeal to more than one buyer, each of whom has his own "price" in mind. In preparing prices for this guide we look at the object within the category being considered and price it as though an individual who collects actively within that category were buying it.

Some Country objects have regional interest. However, a national price consensus has formed as a result of the publication of specialized price guides, collectors' club newsletters, and magazines and newspapers. Regional pricing is discounted in favor of a more general national consensus.

RESEARCH

Collectors of Country deserve credit for their attention to scholarship and the skill by which they have assembled their collections. This book attests to how strong and encompassing the Country market has become through their efforts.

We obtain our prices from many key sources—dealers, publications, auctions, collectors, and field work. The generosity with which dealers have given advice is a credit to the field. Everyone recognizes the need for a guide that is specific and has accurate prices. We study newspapers, magazines, newsletters, and other publications in the collectibles and antiques field. All are critical to understanding what is available in the market.

Our staff is constantly in the field—from Massachusetts to Florida, Pennsylvania to California. This book incorporates information from hundreds of auction catalogs generously furnished by the firms listed in the Auction House section. Finally, private collectors have worked closely with us, sharing their knowledge of price trends and developments unique to their specialties.

BUYER'S GUIDE, NOT SELLER'S GUIDE

Country Antiques & Collectibles is designed to be a buyer's guide, a guide to what you would have to pay to purchase an object on the open market from a dealer or collector. It is not a seller's guide to prices. People frequently make this mistake and are deceiving themselves by doing so.

If you have an object in this book and wish to sell it, you should expect to receive approximately 35 to 40 percent of the values listed. If the object cannot be resold quickly, expect to receive even less. The truth is simple. Knowing to whom to sell an object is worth 50% or more of its value. Buyers are very specialized; dealers work for years to assemble a list of collectors who will pay top dollar for an item.

Examine your piece as objectively as possible. If it is something from your childhood, try to step back from the personal memories in evaluating its condition. As an antiques appraiser, I spend a great deal of my time telling people their treasures are not rare, but items readily available in the marketplace.

In respect to buying and selling a simple philosophy is that a good purchase occurs when both the buyer and seller are happy with the price. Don't look back. Hindsight has little value in the collectibles field. Given time, things tend to balance out.

COMMENTS INVITED

Country Antiques & Collectibles is a major effort to deal with a complex field. Our readers are encouraged to send their comments and suggestions to Dana Morykan, c/o Rinker Enterprises, 5093 Vera Cruz Road, Emmaus, PA 18049.

COUNTRY IN THE 21ˢᵀ CENTURY

After a period of prolonged tranquility from the mid–1970s through the late 1980s, best identified by the dominance of a Country look that drew its inspiration from the nineteenth and early twentieth century rural Midwest, Country has experienced several major stylistic changes within a relatively short period of time.

In the past decade, Country has followed a course that saw it change from its Midwest emphasis to International Country to Early American Formal Country to its present day diverse blend of frill and function. Country in the late 1990s is heavily influenced by the interior decorator. It is as much about pattern as object. Country's earlier association with the rigors of pioneer life, exemplified by the broad axe, spinning wheel, and Kentucky long rifle, has evolved to take on a more genteel air, dominated by a look that is almost exclusively female.

COUNTRY'S EVOLUTION

Prior to World War II—in fact through the 1950s—American Country and Early American were synonymous. A Country kitchen or den contained a large open–hearth fireplace with a wood–carved mantel, spider–legged cast iron cooking utensils, trestle table, spinning wheel, and appropriate accessories. Living and bedrooms consisted of a mix of semi–formal Chippendale and Federal pieces with an occasional rustic piece, e.g., a table–chair, thrown in for good measure.

The Early American style is rooted in the prosperous, small, inland coastal villages of the eighteenth and early nineteenth centuries. It is an East Coast style with a heavy New England presence, typified by historic sites such as Old Sturbridge Village and Historic Deerfield in Massachusetts and Colonial Williamsburg in Virginia. Each site represents a community that has won the struggle with the frontier and is now ready to reap the rewards, i.e., settle down and enjoy the good times.

In the 1960s the dominance of the Early American style was challenged. The social activism of the era stressed a more simplistic, back–to–nature approach. A major handcraft revival occurred. Influenced by Foxfire and similar projects, Country headed for America's backwoods and mountain valleys.

By the mid–1960s America was deeply engrossed in the preparation for America's Bicentennial. A decision was made to concentrate activities on the local, not national level. America would celebrate all of its history, not just the 150–year period leading up to the American Revolution. As a result the nineteenth century, not the eighteenth century, became the focal point for Midwest, Plains, Southwest, and West Coast celebrations.

A new Country look was born. Country of the late 1960s through the mid–1980s was rooted in the American heartland of the Midwest of the late nineteenth and early twentieth centuries. Country and the rural farmstead became one. The agrarian myth became reality.

A sense of excitement and experimentation swept through Country. Country enjoyed a renewed youthful exuberance. The style was free and open to a vast amount of interpretation. Country was eclectic. There was no emphasis on period, i.e., everything in a room belonging to one fixed historical time period. Country became whatever anyone wanted to make it.

The primitive look—weather–beaten, time tested, and true—dominated the era. This was Country before the advent of electricity and indoor plumbing. It was a Country style rooted in the earth, its colors linked to nature's seasons.

Emphasis was placed on objects that were handmade, the cruder the better, rather than mass produced in a factory. The barn, barnyard, field, back porch, and kitchen provided the most favored objects. This Country look stressed the never–ending struggle with nature. The struggle itself was the important thing, not its success or failure.

In the 1970s a kinship was forged between Country and folk art. It is no surprise that Country and folk art evolved at the same time. However, where folk art is aesthetic (at least this is what its collectors and dealers would have one believe), Country is utilitarian. Both celebrate life, particularly the life of the "average" American. Where folk art emphasizes the individual, Country adds the tempering element of community.

The linkage between Country and folk art served both movements in good stead in the 1970s and early 1980s. It proved disastrous to Country when the folk art market collapsed in the late 1980s. Overexposure, overpricing, numerous fakes and forgeries, and the recession are reasons folk art fell on hard times. Unfortunately, folk art dragged 1980s contemporary Country down with it. While folk art is not the sole reason for the shift in emphasis within Country, it is a major one.

As the 1970s ended, interior decorators and Country magazines stole control of Country from the antiques community. Country became the foremost decorating style in America. Country collecting was now in the hands of individuals whose survival relied on continual change. One year ducks and redware were in, the next they were out. Country lost its sense of long–term continuity.

The effect on Country has been profound. In the first half of the 1980s the interior decorating community linked Country to the prosperous look of late nineteenth–century Victorian America. Just as collectors became comfortable with the transition, decorators shifted emphasis to International Country, a diverse approach that includes the English rural gentry look, the bleached look of the Mediterranean, and/or rural Scandinavian. Country went International just as the recession of the late 1980s struck.

The recession drove the interior decorators from the market. They abandoned ship, leaving Country to sink or swim by itself. Leadership fell to the periodicals. They brought Country full circle. The Early American look returned. Country became formal and urbane. Many collectors felt betrayed.

The dominance of the Early American style profoundly affected Country. Its formal emphasis required the acquisition of high–design style handcrafted or mass–produced period pieces. Decorating in Country became expensive. Affordability was a major key to Country's longstanding dominance as America's leading decorating style. When prices for semi–formal corner cupboards and hutches topped the $5,000 plus mark, high–end Country moved beyond the reach of the average collector. As period pieces became more expensive, individuals interested primarily in the Country look turned to reproductions, copycats, and fantasy items, which often sell for 50 percent or less than the cost of a period piece.

The handcraft and gift community responded by shifting its emphasis from the primitive to the formal and from the 1875–1915 period to the years 1760–1840. Country gift shows of the late 1990s are very different from those of the late 1980s. The number of individually handcrafted products has diminished. Many craftspersons became members of commercial business consortiums.

Had the changes in Country ended at this point, all would have been well. Traditional Country experienced a major resurgence in America's heartland. Country returned to its roots, not those of a region's settlement but those of its first prosperity. This Country is well–to–do and established.

However, in the early 1990s the interior decorator and individuals desiring Country pieces for use as decorative accents returned to the Country scene with a vengeance. Their desires varied greatly from those of the traditionalists.

One look at the illustrations in Country periodicals confirms this fact. Decorators have moved Country inside the home. Forget the Country store with its shelves of merchandise and advertising signs. Forget the field and barn. While the kitchen is still the focal point of Country life, today's Country magazine is just as likely to illustrate a bedroom, dining room, or living room picture to make a point.

The contemporary Country home combines styles and forms from room to room in a hodgepodge manner. The Country kitchen is characterized by clean lines and a bright, cheerful atmosphere. Yellow ware bowls, blue and white swirled graniteware coffeepots, and scrubbed pine furniture is the favored look. In the bedroom, fussy floral patterned wallpaper and fabrics with a strong Victorian feel are everywhere. White–patterned ironstone china, chintz–patterned linens, and late nineteenth–century style furniture complete the appointments. Early American formal, dominated by Queen Anne and Chippendale style furniture, reigns supreme in the living room.

It is difficult to find one word to describe the Country look of the mid–1990s. Mixed messages sent by Country style magazines is the reason. A magazine's interpretation of Country is contingent upon where its editor lives. New York City Country is very different from Iowa Country. New York Country has reached the point where one can look at some illustrations and ask, "What has this to do with Country?"

Based on this, perhaps "confused" is the best word to use to describe Country as it enters the 21st century. Since it is unlikely to find favor with traditional Country collectors or interior decorators, let's go with "comfortable" Country, recognizing its definition relies heavily on personal taste, until a better term arises.

STATE OF THE MARKET

Prices for Country antiques and collectibles have been stable for over a decade. Do not assume that a stable market is a dead market. Country is selling actively and well. As Country enters the 21st century, its secondary resale market is strong and likely to remain so well into the future. There is nary a storm cloud on the horizon.

In any stable market, individual categories will be running hot or cooling off. Country is no exception. As with other antiques and collectibles collecting categories, Country categories respond continually to the shifting trends in the collector and decorator marketplaces. Trendiness is as much a fact of life in Country as it is elsewhere.

Several major changes have occurred in the dinnerware sector. Busy embossed patterns with animal, flower, and fruit decorative motifs have yielded to bright, solid colored patterns featuring simple geometric designs. Homer Laughlin's Fiesta has regained lost market share. Bauer's Ring ware and Shawnee's Valencia patterns are other favorites of the moment.

Blue and white English Staffordshire transfer patterns from leading twentieth century manufacturers such as Johnson Bros. and Royal Staffordshire are perfect complements to the Early American and formal Country dining rooms. Some red and polychrome transfer patterns, e.g., Johnson Bros.' Chippendale, Friendly Village, Heritage Hall, and Old English Countryside, also enjoy strong appeal. Inexpensive and moderately expensive 1920s and 30s period dinnerware from Harker, Homer Laughlin, and other American ceramic manufacturers are experiencing a lull.

The revival of yellow ware is the big news in the utilitarian ceramics sector. It is the age of the banded yellow ware mixing bowl. Watt's apple patterned wares are holding their own, albeit no longer No. 1 in desirability. Although molded earthenware, such as the blue and white or green glazed redware, and stoneware products appear regularly in Country periodical illustrations, prices within the category remain stable. Keep an eye open for a possible jump in secondary market values.

Eighteenth– and nineteenth–century redware remains conspicuously absent from the market. The one exception is New England, proof again that regional markets still have an impact on value within Country. Cobalt blue decorated stoneware, particularly from Pennsylvania makers such as Cowden & Wilcox, has shown surprising auction strength recently.

The use of chintz patterns has leveled. Although still a popular bedroom textile or ceramic accessory pattern, its use elsewhere in the home has diminished. In many instances, it has disappeared completely.

In any market analysis, as much can be learned from what is missing than from what one sees. Country store memorabilia and Country farm collectibles, e.g., cranberry scoops and singletrees, are no longer part of Country's mainstream. Country advertising is plagued with an overabundance of advertising reproductions (exact copies), copycats (stylistic copies), and fantasy items (new forms, shapes, and patterns that did not exist historically). The advent of the large commercial farm and decline of the family farm has greatly reduced the number of young Country collectors who would recognize a singletree.

Country without animals? Unthinkable! Not if you spend time looking through the current Country literature. With the exception of figural cookie jars and planters, animal images are minimal. Cows have fared better than the rest. There are still a few around. Chickens, ducks, pigs, roosters, and other barnyard residents are in short supply. Country seems somehow incomplete without our barnyard friends. Hopefully, their 21st century revival will emphasize their Country contributions rather than their decorator or folk art appeal.

Country appears to be rediscovering its more traditional roots as it enters the 21st–century. Classic pieces, i.e., historical forms, shapes, and patterns, are featured more prominently in Country periodicals. These are "blue chip" Country—ceramics (Majolica and historic Staffordshire), furniture (primitive, generic, and Shaker), glass (flasks and kerosene/oil lamps), metals (copper and pewter), and textiles (coverlets, quilts, and samplers). This trend is stronger in the Midwest and Plains than on either coast. Look for its continued outward spread.

Folk art continues to be estranged from Country. Many hope the separation will result in a permanent divorce. Hard–to–detect fakes and obvious market value manipulation are the primary reasons.

Recent reproductions, especially ceramics, continue to plague the Country market. Each new batch of Roseville reproductions is better than its predecessor. It will soon be impossible to tell the new pieces from their period counterparts. Reproductions, copycats, and fantasy pieces have appeared in several art pottery categories, e.g., Grueby, Fulper, Rookwood, and Teco. Problems also exist in several paper categories, e.g., advertising, calendars, and prints.

What about Country and the Internet? At the moment, only contemporary Country, newly made mass–produced and craft articles, has found a ready home on the Internet. Internet sites are more focused on mainstream antiques and collectibles. Based on developments within these other markets, Country is well served by its slow introduction into the Internet marketplace. Further, Country is a unique American look. The Internet's international focus is another reason why the transition to cyberspace will take longer for Country than other antiques and collectibles categories. Besides, Country is down–to–earth. A horse–drawn buggy is far more at home travelling beneath the Milky Way than through it.

AUCTION HOUSES

The following auctioneers and auction companies generously supply Rinker Enterprises, Inc., with copies of their auction lists, press releases, catalogs and illustrations, and prices realized.

If you would like to be included on this list, write or phone Rinker Enterprises at 5093 Vera Cruz Road, Emmaus, PA 18049; (610) 965-1122.

Action Toys, PO Box 102, Holtsville, NY 11742; (516) 563-9113; Fax: (516) 563-9182.

Sanford Alderfer Auction Co., Inc., 501 Fairgrounds Road, PO Box 640, Hatfield, PA 19440; (215) 393-3000; e mail: auction@alderfercompany.com; web: http://www.alderfercompany.com.

American Social History and Social Movements, 4025 Saline Street, Pittsburgh, PA 15217; (412) 421-5230; Fax: (412) 421-0903.

Arthur Auctioneering, RD 2, Box 155, Hughesville, PA 17737; (800) ARTHUR 3.

Aston Macek, 154 Market Street, Pittston, PA 18640; (717) 654-3090.

Auction Team Köln, Breker – Die Spezialisten, Postfach 50 11 19, D-50971, Köln, Germany; Tel: 0221/38 70 49; Fax: 0221/37 48 78; Jane Herz, International Rep USA (941) 925-0385; Fax: (941) 925-0487.

Bill Bertoia Auctions, 1881 Spring Road, Vineland, NJ 08361; (609) 692-1881; Fax: (609) 692-8697; e mail: bba@ccnj.net; web: http://bba.ccnj.net.com.

Butterfield & Butterfield, 220 San Bruno Avenue, San Francisco, CA 94103; (415) 861-7500; Fax: (415) 861-8951; web: http://www.butterfields.com.

Butterfield & Butterfield, 7601 Sunset Boulevard, Los Angeles, CA 90046; (213) 850-7500; Fax: (213) 850-5843; web: http://www.butterfields.com.

Butterfield, Butterfield & Dunning's, 755 Church Road, Elgin, IL 60123; (847) 741-3483; Fax: (847) 741-3589; web: http://www.butterfields.com.

Cards From Grandma's Trunk, The Millards, PO Box 404, Northport, IN 49670; (616) 386-5351.

Christie's, 502 Park Avenue at 59th Street, New York, NY 10022; (212) 546-1000; Fax: (212) 980-8163; web: http://www.christies.com.

Christie's East, 219 East 67th Street, New York, NY 10021; (212) 606-0400; Fax: (212) 737-6076; web: http://www.christies.com.

Christmas Morning, 1806 Royal Lane, Dallas, TX 75229-3126; (972) 506-8362; Fax: (972) 506-7821.

Cobb's Doll Auctions, 1909 Harrison Road, Johnstown, OH 43031-9539; (740) 964-0444; Fax: (740) 927-7701.

Collectors Auction Services, RR 2, Box 431 Oakwood Road, Oil City, PA 16301; (814) 677-6070; Fax: (814) 677-6166.

Collector's Sales and Service, PO Box 4037, Middletown, RI 02842; (401) 849-5012; Fax: (401) 846-6156; web: www.antiquechina.com; e mail: collectors@antiquechina.com.

Copake Auction, Box H, 226 Route 7A, Copake, NY 12516; (518) 329-1142; Fax: (518) 329-3369.

Dawson's, 128 American Road, Morris Plains, NJ 07950; (973) 984-6900; Fax: (973) 984-6956; web: http://idt.net/-dawson1; e mail: dawson1@idt.net.

Dixie Sporting Collectibles, 1206 Rama Road, Charlotte, NC 28211; (704) 364-2900; Fax: (704) 364-2322; web: http://www.sportauction.com; e mail: gun1898@aol.com.

William Doyle Galleries, Inc., 175 East 87th Street, New York, NY 10128; (212) 427-2730; Fax: (212) 369-0892; web: www.doylegalleries.com.

Dunbars Gallery, 76 Haven Street, Milford, MA 01757; (508) 634-8697; Fax: (508) 634-8698; e mail: dunbar2bid@aol.com.

Early Auction Co., Roger and Steve Early, 123 Main Street, Milford, OH 45150; (513) 831-4833; Fax: (513) 831-1441.

Etude Tajan, 37, Rue de Mathurins 75008, Paris, France; Tel: 1-53-30-30-30; Fax: 1-53-30-30-31; web: http://www.tajan.com; e mail: tajan@worldnet.fr.

Ken Farmer Auctions & Estates, LLC, 105A Harrison Street, Radford, VA 24141; (540) 639-0939; Fax: (540) 639-1759; web: http://kenfarmer.com.

Fink's Off the Wall Auction, 108 East 7th Street, Lansdale, PA 19446; (215) 855-9732; Fax: (215) 855-6325; web: http://www/finksauctions.com; e mail: lansbeer@finksauction.com.

Flomaton Antique Auction, 277 Old Highway 31, Flomaton, AL 36441.

Frank's Antiques, Box 516, Hilliard, FL 32046; (904) 845-2870; Fax: (904) 845-4000.

Frasher's Doll Auctions, Inc., Route 1, Box 142, Oak Grove, MO 64075; (816) 625-3786; Fax: (816) 625-6079.

Garth's Auction, Inc., 2690 Stratford Road, PO Box 369, Delaware, OH 43015; (614) 362-4771; Fax: (614) 363-1064.

Glass-Works Auctions, PO Box 180, East Greenville, PA 18041; (215) 679-5849; Fax: (215) 679-3068; web: http://www.glswrk-auction.com.

Greenberg Auctions, 7566 Main Street, Sykesville, MD 21784; (401) 795-7447.

Marc Grobman, 94 Paterson Road, Fanwood, NJ 07023-1056; (908) 322-4176; web: mgrobman@worldnet.att.net.

Gypsyfoot Enterprises, Inc., PO Box 5833, Helena, MT 59604; (406) 449-8076; Fax: (406) 443-8514; e mail: gypsyfoot@aol.com.

Hakes' Americana and Collectibles, PO Box 1444, York, PA 17405; (717) 848-1333; Fax: (717) 852-0344.

Gene Harris Antique Auction Center, Inc., 203 South 18th Avenue, Marshalltown, IA 50158; (515) 752-0600; Fax: (515) 753-0226; e mail: ghaac@marshallnet.com.

Norman C. Heckler & Co., Bradford Corner Road, Woodstock Valley, CT 06282; (860) 974-1634; Fax: (860) 974-2003.

The Holidays Auction, 4027 Brooks Hill Road, Brooks, KY 40109; (502) 955-9238; Fax: (502) 957-5027.

Horst Auction Center, 50 Durlach Road, Ephrata, PA 17522; (717) 859-1331.

Michael Ivankovich Antiques, Inc., PO Box 2458, Doylestown, PA 18901; (215) 345-6094; Fax: (215) 345-6692; e mail: wnutting@comcat.com.

Jackson Auction Co., 2229 Lincoln Street, Cedar Falls, IA 50613; (319) 277-2256; Fax: (319) 277-1252; web: http://jacksonauction.com.

James D. Julia, Inc., PO Box 830, Fairfield, ME 04937; (207) 453-7125; Fax: (207) 453-2502.

Gary Kirsner Auctions, PO Box 8807, Coral Springs, FL 33075; (954) 344-9856; Fax: (954) 344-4421.

Charles E. Kirtley, PO Box 2273, Elizabeth City, NC 27906; (919) 335-1262; Fax: (919) 335-4441; e mail: ckirtley@erols.com.

Henry Kurtz, Ltd., 163 Amsterdam Avenue, Suite 136, New York, NY 10023; (212) 642-5904; Fax: (212) 874-6018.

Lang's Sporting Collectables, Inc., 31R Turtle Cove, Raymond, ME 04071; (207) 655-4265.

Los Angeles Modern Auctions, PO Box 462006, Los Angeles, CA 90046; (213) 845-9456; Fax: (213) 845-9601; web: http://www.lamodern.com; e mail: peter@lamodern.com.

Howard Lowery, 3812 West Magnolia Boulevard, Burbank, CA 91505; (818) 972-9080; Fax: (818) 972-3910.

Mad Mike, Michael Lerner, 32862 Springside Lane, Solon, OH 44139; (216) 349-3776.

Majolica Auctions, Michael G. Strawser, 200 North Main, PO Box 332, Wolcottville, IN 46795; (219) 854-2859; Fax: (219) 854-3979.

Manion's International Auction House, Inc., PO Box 12214, Kansas City, KS 66112; (913) 299-6692; Fax: (913) 299-6792; web: www.manions.com; e mail: collecting@manions.com.

Ted Maurer, Auctioneer, 1003 Brookwood Drive, Pottstown, PA 19464; (610) 323-1573; web: www.maurerail.com.

Wm Morford, RD 2, Cazenovia, NY 13035; (315) 662-7625; Fax: (315) 662-3570; e mail: morf2bid@aol.com.

Muddy River Trading Co., Gary Metz, 263 Key Lakewood Drive, Moneta, VA 24121; (540) 721-2091; Fax: (540) 721-1782.

New England Absentee Auctions, 16 Sixth Street, Stamford, CT 06905; (203) 975-9055; Fax: (203) 323-6407; e mail: neaauction@aol.com.

New England Auction Gallery, Box 2273, West Peabody, MA 01960; (508) 535-3140; Fax: (508) 535-7522; web: http://www.oldtoys.com.

Norton Auctioneers of Michigan, Inc., Pearl at Monroe, Colwater, MI 49036-1967; (517) 279-9063; Fax: (517) 279-9191; e mail: nortonsold@juno.com.

Nostalgia Publications, Inc., 21 South Lake Drive, Hackensack, NJ 07601; (201) 488-4536.

Richard Opfer Auctioneers, Inc., 1919 Greenspring Drive, Timonium, MD 21093; (410) 252-5035; Fax: (410) 252-5863.

Ron Oser Enterprises, PO Box 101, Huntingdon Valley, PA 19006; (215) 947-6575; Fax: (215) 938-7348; web: members.aol.com/ronoserent.

Pacific Book Auction Galleries, 139 Townsend Street, 4th Floor, San Francisco, CA 94108; (415) 989-2665; Fax: (415) 989-1664; web: www.nbn.com/pba; e mail: pba@slip.net.

Past Tyme Pleasures, 101 First Street, Suite 404, Los Altos, CA 94022; (510) 484-4488; Fax: (510) 484-2551.

Pettigrew Auction Co., 1645 South Tejon Street, Colorado Springs, CO 80906; (719) 633-7963; Fax: (719) 633-5035.

Phillips Ltd., 406 East 79th Street, New York, NY 10021; (800) 825-2781; Fax: (212) 570-2207; web: http://www.phillips-auctions.com.

Postcards International, PO Box 5398, Hamden, CT 06518; (203) 248-6621; Fax: (203) 248-6628; web: csmonline.com/postcardsint/; e mail: postcrdint@aol.com.

Poster Mail Auction Co., PO Box 133, Waterford, VA 20197; (703) 684-3656; Fax: (540) 882-4765.

Provenance, PO Box 3487, Wallington, NJ 07057; (201) 779-8785; Fax: (212) 741-8756.

David Rago Auctions, Inc., 333 North Main Street, Lambertville, NJ 08530; (609) 397-9374; Fax: (609) 397-9377.

Lloyd Ralston Gallery, 109 Glover Avenue, Norwalk, CT 06850; (203) 845-0033; Fax: (203) 845-0366.

Red Baron's, 6450 Roswell Road, Atlanta, GA 30328; (404) 252-3770; Fax: (404) 257-0268; e mail: rbarons@onramp.net.

Remmey Galleries, 30 Maple Street, Summit, NJ 07901; (908) 273-5055; Fax: (908) 273-0171; e mail: remmeyauctiongalleries@worldnet.att.net.

L. H. Selman Ltd., 761 Chestnut Street, Santa Cruz, CA 95060; (800) 538-0766; Fax: (408) 427-0111; web: http://paperweight.com; e mail: selman@paperweight.com.

Skinner, Inc., Bolton Gallery, 357 Main Street, Bolton, MA 01740; (978) 779 6241; Fax: (978) 350-5429.

Slater's Americana, 1535 North Tacoma Avenue, Suite 24, Indianapolis, IN 46220; (317) 257-0863; Fax: (317) 254-9167.

Smith & Jones, Inc., 12 Clark Lane, Sudbury, MA 01776; (978) 443-5517; Fax: (978) 443-2796.

R. M. Smythe & Co., Inc., 26 Broadway, Suite 271, New York, NY 10004-1701; (800) 622-1880; Fax: (212) 908-4047.

Sotheby's, 1334 York Avenue at 72nd Street, New York, NY 10021; (212) 606-7000; web: http://www.sothebys.com.

Steffen's Historical Militaria, PO Box 280, Newport, KY 41072; (606) 431-4499.

Susanin's, Gallery 228 Merchandise Mart, Chicago, IL 60654; (312) 832-9800; Fax: (312) 832-9311; web: http://www.theauction.com.

Swann Galleries, Inc., 104 East 25th Street, New York, NY 10010; (212) 254-4710; Fax: (212) 979-1017.

Theriault's, PO Box 151, Annapolis, MD 21404; Fax: (410) 224-2515.

Tool Shop Auctions, Tony Murland, 78 High Street, Needham Market, Suffolk, 1P6 8AW England; Tel: 01449 722992; Fax: 01449 722683; web: http://www/toolshop.demon.co.uk; e mail: tony@toolshop.demon.co.uk.

Toy Scouts, 137 Casterton Avenue, Akron, OH 44303; (330) 836-0668; Fax: (330) 869-8668.

Tradewinds Auctions, PO Box 249, 24 Magnolia Avenue, Manchester–by–the–Sea, MA 01944; (978) 768-3327; Fax: (978) 526-3088.

James A. Vanek, 7031 NE Irving Street, Portland, OR 97213; (503) 257-8009.

Victorian Images, PO Box 284, Marlton, NJ 08053; (609) 953-7711; Fax: (609) 953-7768.

Tom Witte's Antiques, PO Box 399, Front Street West, Mattawan, MI 49071; (616) 668-4161; Fax: (616) 668-5363.

York Town Auction, Inc., 1625 Haviland Road, York, PA 17404; (717) 751-0211; Fax: (717) 767-7729.

PERIODICALS

Rinker Enterprises receives the following general and regional periodicals. Periodicals covering a specific collecting category are listed in the introductory material for that category.

NATIONAL MAGAZINES

Antique Trader's Collector Magazine & Price Guide, PO Box 1050, Dubuque, IA 52004-1050; (800) 334-7165; web: traderpubs@aol.com.

Antiques & Collecting Magazine, 1006 South Michigan Avenue, Chicago, IL 60605; (800) 762-7576; Fax: (312) 939-0053; e mail: lightnerpb@aol.com.

Collectors' Eye, Woodside Avenue, Suite 300, Northport, NY 11768; (516) 261-4100; Fax: (516) 261-9684.

Collectors' Showcase, 7134 South Yale Avenue, Suite 720, Tulsa, OK 74136; (888) 622-3446.

Country Accents Collectibles, Flea Market Finds, GCR Publishing Group, Inc., 1700 Broadway, New York, NY 10019; (800) 955-3870.

NATIONAL NEWSPAPERS

Antiques and the Arts Weekly, The Bee Publishing Company, PO Box 5503, Newtown, CT 06470-5503; (203) 426-8036; Fax: (203) 426-1394; web: http://www.thebee.com; e mail: editor@thebee.com.

The Antique Trader Weekly, PO Box 1050, Dubuque, IA 52004-1050; (800) 334-7165; Fax: (800) 531-0880; web: http://www.csmonline.com; e mail: traderpubs@aol.com.

Antique Week (Central and Eastern Editions), 27 North Jefferson Street, PO Box 90, Knightstown, IN 46148; (800) 876-5133; Fax: (800) 695-8153; web: http://www.antiqueweek.com; e mail: antiquewk@aol.com.

Collectors News, 506 Second Street, PO Box 156, Grundy Center, IA 50638; (800) 352-8039; Fax: (319) 824-3414; web: http://collectors-news.com; e mail: collectors@collectors-news.com.

Maine Antique Digest, 911 Main Street, PO Box 1429; Waldoboro, ME 04572; (207) 832-4888; Fax: (207) 832-7341; web: http://www.maineantiquedigest.com; e mail: mad@maine.com.

Warman's Today's Collector, Krause Publications, 700 East State Street, Iola, WI 54990; (800) 258-0929; Fax: (715) 445-4087; web: www.krause.com; e mail: todays_collector@krause.com.

REGIONAL NEWSPAPERS

NEW ENGLAND

MassBay Antiques, 2 Washington Street, PO Box 192, Ipswich, MA 01938; (508) 777-7070.

New England Antiques Journal, 4 Church Street, PO Box 120, Ware, MA 01082; (800) 432-3505; Fax: (413) 967-6009; e mail: visit@antiquesjournal.com.

New England Collectibles, PO Box 546, Farmington, NH 03835-0546; (603) 755-4568; Fax: (603) 755-3990.

New Hampshire Antiques Monthly, PO Box 546, Farmington, NH 03835-0546; (603) 755-4568; Fax: (603) 755-3990.

Unravel the Gavel, 9 Hurricane Road, #1, Belmont, NH 03220; (603) 524-4281; Fax: (603) 528-3565; web: http://www.the–forum.com/gavel; e mail: gavel96@aol.com.

MIDDLE ATLANTIC STATES

American Antique Collector, PO Box 454, Murrysville, PA 15668; (412) 733-3968; Fax: (412) 733-3968.

New York City's Antique News, PO Box 2054, New York, NY 10159-2054; (212) 725-0344; Fax: (212) 532-7294.

Northeast Journal of Antiques & Art, 364 Warren Street, Hudson, NY 12534; (800) 836-4069; Fax: (518) 828-9437.

Renninger's Antique Guide, PO Box 495, Lafayette Hill, PA 19444; (610) 828-4614; Fax: (610) 834-1599.

Treasure Chest, PO Box 245, North Scituate, RI 02857-0245; (800) 557-9662; Fax: (401) 647-0051.

SOUTH

The Antique Finder Magazine, PO Box 16433, Panama City, FL 32406-6433; (850) 236-0543; Fax: (850) 914-9007.

Antique Gazette, 6949 Charlotte Pike, Suite 106, Nashville, TN 37209; (800) 660-6143; Fax: (800) 660-6143.

The Antique Shoppe, PO Box 2175, Keystone Heights, FL 32656; (352) 475-1679.

The Antique Shoppe of the Carolinas, PO Box 640, Lancaster, SC 29721; (800) 210-7253; Fax: (803) 283-8969.

Carolina Antique News, PO Box 241114, Charlotte, NC 28224; (704) 553-2865.

Cotton & Quail Antique Trail, 205 East Washington Street, PO Box 326, Monticello, FL 32345; (800) 757-7755; Fax: (850) 997-3090.

The MidAtlantic Antiques Magazine, Henderson Newspapers, Inc., 304 South Chestnut Street, PO Box 908, Henderson, NC 27536; (919) 492-4001; Fax: (919) 430-0125.

The Old News Is Good News Antiques Gazette, 41429 West I-55 Service Road, PO Box 305, Hammond, LA 70404; (504) 429-0575; Fax: (504) 429-0576; e mail: gazette@i–55.com

Second Hand Dealer News, 18609 Shady Hills Road, Spring Hill, FL 34610; (813) 856-9477.

Southern Antiques, PO Drawer 1107, Decatur, GA 30031; (888) 800-4997; Fax: (404) 286-9727.

20th Century Folk Art News, 5967 Blackberry Lane, Buford, GA 30518; (770) 932-1000; Fax: (770) 932-0506.

MIDWEST

The American Antiquities Journal, 126 East High Street, Springfield, OH 45502; (800) 557-6281; Fax: (937) 322-0294.

The Antique Collector and Auction Guide, Weekly Section of *Farm and Dairy,* PO Box 38, Salem, OH 44460; (330) 337-3419; Fax: (330) 337-9550.

Antique Review, PO Box 538, Worthington, OH 43085; (614) 885-9757; Fax: (614) 885-9762.

Auction Action News, 1404¹/₂ East Green Bay Street, Shawano, WI 54166; (715) 524-3076; Fax: (800) 580-4568.

Auction World, 101 12th Street South, Box 227, Benson, MN 56215; (800) 750-0166; Fax: (320) 843-3246.

The Collector, 204 South Walnut Street, PO Box 148, Heyworth, IL 61745-0148; (309) 473-2466; Fax: (309) 473-3610.

Collectors Journal, 1800 West D Street, PO Box 601, Vinton, IA 52349-0601; (319) 472-4763; Fax: (816) 474-1427; web: http://discoverypub.com/kc.

Discover Mid–America, 400 Grand, Suite B, Kansas City, MO 64106; (800) 899-9730.

Great Lakes Trader, 132 South Putnam Street, Williamston, MI 48895; (800) 785-6367; Fax: (517) 655-5380; web: gltrader@aol.com.

The Old Times, PO Box 340, Maple Lake, MN 55358; (800) 539-1810; Fax: (320) 963-6499; e mail: oldtimes@lkdllink.net.

Three Trails Emporium, PO Box 459, Independence, MO 64051; (816) 254-8600; web: examiner.net.

Yesteryear, PO Box 2, Princeton, WI 54968; (920) 787-4808; Fax: (920) 787-7381.

SOUTHWEST

The Antique Traveler, PO Box 656, 109 East Broad Street, Mineola, TX 75773; (903) 569-2487; Fax: (903) 569-9080.

Arizona Antique News, PO Box 26536, Phoenix, AZ 85068; (602) 943-9137.

Auction Weekly, PO Box 61104, Phoenix, AZ 85082; (602) 994-4512; Fax: (800) 525-1407.

WEST COAST

Antique & Collectables, 500 Fensler, Suite 205, PO Box 12589, El Cajon, CA 92022; (619) 593-2930; Fax: (619) 447-7187.

Antique Journal, 1684 Decoto Road, Suite 166, Union City, CA 94587; (510) 791-8592; Fax: (510) 523-5262.

Antiques Today, Kruse Publishing, 977 Lehigh Circle, Carson City, NV 89705; (800) 267-4602; Fax: (702) 267-4600.

Old Stuff, VBM Printers, Inc., 336 North Davis, PO Box 1084, McMinnville, OR 97128; (503) 434-5386; Fax: (503) 472-2601; e mail: bnm@pnn.com.

The Oregon Vintage Times, 856 Lincoln #2, Eugene, OR 97401; (541) 484-0049; e mail: venus@efn.org; web: www.efn.org/~venus/antique/antique.html.

West Coast Peddler, PO Box 5134, Whittier, CA 90607; (562) 698-1718; Fax: (562) 698-1500.

INTERNATIONAL NEWSPAPERS

AUSTRALIA

Carter's Homes, Antiques & Collectables, Carter's Promotions Pty. Ltd., Locked Bag 3, Terrey Hills, NSW 2084, Australia; Tel: (02) 9450 0011; Fax: (02) 945-2532; e mail: carters@magna.com.au.

CANADA

Antique Showcase, Trojan Publishing Corp., 103 Lakeshore Road, Suite 202, St. Catherine, Ontario, Canada L2N 2T6; (905) 646-0995; web: http://www.vaxxine.com/trojan/; e mail: bret@trojan.com.

Antiques and Collectibles Trader, PO Box 38095, 550 Eglinton Avenue West, Toronto, Ontario, Canada M5N 3A8; (416) 410-7620.

The Upper Canadian, PO Box 653, Smiths Falls, Ontario, Canada K7A 4T6; (613) 283-1168; Fax: (613) 283-1345; e mail: uppercanadian@recorder.ca.

ENGLAND

Antique Trade Gazette, 17 Whitcomb Street, London WC2I I 7PL, England.

ABBREVIATIONS

4to = 8 x 10"
8vo = 5 x 7"
12mo = 3 x 5"
ADS = autograph document signed
adv = advertising or advertisement
ALS = autograph letter signed
AOG = all over gold
AP = album page signed
AQS = autograph quotation signed
C = century
c = circa
cal = caliber
cov = cover or covered
CS = card signed
d = deep or diameter
dec = decorated or decoration
dj = dust jacket
dwt = penny weight
DS = document wigned
ed = edition
emb = embossed
ext = exterior
FDC = first day cover
FH = flat handle
folio = 12 x 16"
ftd = footed
gal = gallon
ground = background
h = height
HH = hollow handle
hp = hand painted
illus = illustrated, illustration, or
    illustrator

imp = impressed
int = interior
irid = iridescent
j = jewels
l = length
lb = pound
litho = lithograph or lithographed
LS = letter signed
mfg = manufactured, manufacturer, or
    manufacturing
mkd = marked
opal = opalescent
orig = original
oz = ounce
pat = patent
pc(s) = piece or pieces
pp = pages
pkg = package or packaging
pr = pair
PS = photograph signed
pt = pint
qt = quart
rect = rectangular
sgd = signed
SP = silver plated
sq = square
TLS = typed letter signed
unmkd = unmarked
unsgd = unsigned
Vol = Volume
vols = volumes
w = width
# = number

COUNTRY BARN

If the Country kitchen is the farm's social center, the barn is the farm's work center. The barn and its supporting structures differ from region to region. Great bank barns are the dominant barn type in Pennsylvania. The lower level housed the animals, the upper level provided equipment storage and the lofts and attached silo stored feed. Support buildings, e.g., corn cribs, chicken houses, and storage sheds, completed the farm setting.

Much of farm labor is seasonal in nature and requires specific equipment designed for the task at hand. In many instances, equipment usage is limited to a few days or weeks per year. As a result, farm equipment spends most of its time in storage.

Like most individuals, farmers tend to fill up space when it is available. Space makes savers. Farmers and individuals in rural communities are driven to saving by two key philosophies: (1) it's too good to throw out and (2) I'll never know when I will need it. It is primarily for these reasons that corners and lofts of barns are treasure–troves for the Country collector.

The Country barn and out buildings required continual maintenance, usually drawing the farmer's attention outside the planting and harvesting seasons. An individual farmer's worth in the community was judged by how he maintained his buildings, equipment, and animals. The condition of the barn was a fair judge of the value of the farm.

The barn also had a developmental and social role. It was a gigantic playground, often an amusement park, for farm youngsters. The hay loft could be a medieval castle one moment, a frontier fort the next. Sneaking behind the barn was a common means of escaping the watchful eyes of parents.

No farm youngster needs a school course on sex education. One learns at a very early age the role of the bull, rooster, and serum injection. The privacy of the barn provides a haven for young lovers. Little wonder there is a strong tradition in rural America of shotgun weddings.

Removing the equipment from the barn created a social hall for functions ranging from an extended family meal to a hoe–down. Social gatherings were extremely important in rural America where the nearest neighbor may be a quarter to half a mile down the road.

Farm museums take pride in their period barn recreations. Since almost every state has one or more farm museums, locating an example should not prove difficult. The fun is to visit a Midwest farm museum shortly after visiting a New England farm museum. One quickly develops an appreciation for the development and differences in farm technology over time and as American agriculture moved west.

References: Terri Clemens, *American Family Farm Antiques,* Wallace–Homestead, Krause Publications, 1994; Joan and David Hagan, *The Farm: An American Living Portrait,* Schiffer Publishing, 1990; R. Douglas Hurt, *Agricultural Technology in the Twentieth Century,* Sunflower University Press, 1991; Kathryn McNerney, *Primitives: Our American Heritage, First Series* (1979, 1996 value update), *Second Series* (1987, 1996 value update), Collector Books; Stanley Schuler, *American Barns: In a Class By Themselves,* Schiffer Publishing; *Stable & Barn Fixtures Manufactured by J. W. Fiske Iron Works,* Apollo Books, 1987; C. H. Wendel, *Encyclopedia of American Farm Implements,* Krause Publications, 1997.

Periodical: *Farm Antique News,* 812 North 3rd Street, Tarkio, MO 64491.

Museum Directory: Farm Museum Directory, PO Box 328, Lancaster, PA 17608.

Museums: Billings Farm & Museum, Woodstock, NY; Carroll County Farm Museum, Westminster, MD; Landis Valley Farm Museum, Lancaster, PA; Living History Farms, Urbandale, IA; National Agricultural Center & Hall of Fame, Bonner Springs, KS; Never Rest Museum, Mason, MI; New York State Historical Assoc and The Farm Museum, Cooperstown, NY; Ontario Agricultural Museum, Milton, Ontario, Canada.

ANIMAL RELATED

When one thinks farm, one thinks animals. Even grain farmers keep a few animals. The domestication of animals and development of agriculture are two of the most important steps in the evolution of humankind.

During the twentieth century many of the hand tasks associated with animals were mechanized. Two transitions that I witnessed as a young boy were the switching of a dairy farm from hand milking to mechanical milking and a chicken farm from nests to individual wire cages. The Country collector is not fascinated by these "newfangled" devices. They prefer a simpler(?) time when there was one to one contact between farmer and animal. The image is highly myth oriented, but it persists.

Collectors focus on three types of animal related objects—(1) those used in the care and feeding of animals, (2) those involved in the use of the animal, and (3) those linked to an animal's food value. In almost every instance, the collector wants an object that shows signs of wear, but yet is in good enough condition to display.

The care and feeding category ranges from grain scoops to chicken feeds. Look for objects that contain elaborate stenciling, decoration, and manufacturer information, and/or have an unusual form. Do not overlook veterinarian products.

Animals paid for their keep by working or producing a salable product, in some instances, both. The popularity of animal working gear is very craze oriented. One year ox yokes are in vogue, another year animal harnesses prove popular. Many of these objects do not display well, making this material the least popular of the animal related collectibles.

The most popular category is items involved with processing animal products or involving the butchering of animals. Hog scrapers, milking stools, sheep shears, and egg crates are just a few of the popular items found in most Country decorating schemes. A single type of object is often found in dozens of variations, creating the opportunity for an unusual specialized collection.

Since many individuals utilizing a Country decor did not grow up in a farming environment, it is not unusual to find objects whose use is uncertain among the items displayed. These "what's–its" make excellent conversation pieces.

Few Country collectors attempt to recreate a barn or equipment shed environment. Instead, animal related items are used indoors and out primarily as decorative accents. A set of harnesses makes an attractive wall display. A stoneware chicken feeder finds a welcome home among a display of stoneware crocks and jugs. A pig carrier with a piece of glass on top functions well as a coffee table. A cast iron scalding kettle serves in the front yard as a planter.

The use of animal related objects in interior and exterior decorating is due in part to the image that they convey of hard, but highly productive work. Metal objects develop a dark, smooth patina; wood implements have a weathered, worn smooth look. They evoke a strong sense of the unending commitment that a farmer must make.

Reference: Robert Rauhauser, *Hog Oilers Plus: An Illustrated Guide,* published by author, 1996.

Bit, eagle, mkd "G.S. Garcia" $700
Branding Iron, set of 4, numbered 1, 2, 3, and 5, wrought iron, pre–1900,
   30" l 50
Bridle Rosette, price for pair 50
Chicken Feeder, tin 15
Chicken Fountain, stoneware, unmkd, 1 gal 65
Cow Bell, sheet copper, 6" h 30
Cream Separator, painted tin body, wood legs, brass spigot 75
Egg Candler, tin, kerosene burner, mica window, 8" h 25
Egg Crate, wood frame, wire egg holders 35
Feed Bag, homespun, stenciled "S. Kruger," 21 x 58" 50
Feed Box, wood, homemade, 20" l 30
Goat Yoke, single, wood, bentwood bow 20
Harness Strap, leather, 4 decorative brasses, 10" l 45
Hitching Post, black jockey, cast aluminum, old worn repaint, 31" h 250
Hobbles, sideline type, chain and leather 75
Hog Scraper, tin, circular blade, 6½" h 20
Hoof Trimmer, iron 75
Horse Blanket, 1 side black, other side mottled brown 60
Horse Collar, leather covered wood, brass trim 125
Incubator, wood cabinet, 39" h 75
Lasso, horsehair, rawhide covered tips, 1890s 250
Milking Pail, tin, wire bail handle, 2 gal 60
Milking Stool, oak, splayed base 50
Milk Skimmer, punched tin, hanging loop, c1800 35
Riata, braided rawhide 150
Rug, horsehide, 48 x 72" 175
Saddle, McClelland type, large fenders, early 1900s 600
Saddle Blanket, Navajo, early 1900s 850

Left: Cream Separator, De Laval, cast iron, 48" h, $225.

Center: Saddle, 2–tone leather, horse motif, $285. Photo courtesy Collectors Auction Services.

Right: Sheep Bell, brass, leather strap, $30.

Saddle Stand, pine, red wash **65**
Scalding Kettle, cast iron, 2 handles, 30" d **350**
Sheep Shears, wrought iron **40**
Singletree, wood and iron **35**
Sleigh Bells, leather strap, 27 nickel plated steel bells, graduated sizes, worn
    plating, 80" l **135**
Sleigh Bells, worn leather strap, 48 nickel plated bells, all bells same size,
    tug hook, 84" l **200**
Spurs, pr, steel chains **125**
Tether Weight, cast iron, black, 20 lbs **30**
Trough, cast iron, 45" l **25**

DAIRY COLLECTIBLES

Hervey Thatcher is recognized as the father of the glass milk bottle. By the early 1880s glass milk bottles appeared in New York and New Jersey. A. V. Whiteman had a milk bottle patent as early as 1880. Patents reveal much about early milk bottle shape and manufacture. Not all patentees were manufacturers. Many individuals engaged others to produce bottles under their patents.

The Golden Age of the glass milk bottle is 1910 to 1950. Leading manufacturers include Lamb Glass Co. (Mt. Vernon, Ohio), Liberty Glass Co. (Sapulpa, Oklahoma), Owens–Illinois Glass Co. (Toledo, Ohio), and Thatcher Glass Co. (New York).

Milk bottles can be found in the following sizes: gill (quarter pint), half pint, 10 ounces (third quart), pint, quart, half gallon (two quart), and gallon.

Paper cartons first appeared in the early 1920s and 30s and achieved popularity after 1950. The late 1950s witnessed the arrival of the plastic bottle. A few dairies still use glass bottles today, but the era has essentially ended.

Many factors influence the price—condition of the bottle, who is selling, the part of the country in which the sale is transacted, and the amount of desire a buyer has for the bottle. Every bottle does not have universal appeal. A sale of a bottle in one area does not mean that it would bring the same amount in another locale. For example, a rare Vermont pyro pint would be looked upon as only another "pint" in Texas.

A painted milk can, often with a regional folk art design, is a commonly used Country decorative accent. When used on the farm, milk cans contained little or no decoration. "Folk Art" milk can painters pay between five and ten dollars for a plain can depending on size and condition. There are milk can collectors, but their number is few, thus keeping prices low.

References: Leigh and Jeff Giarde (eds), *The Complete, Authentic and Unabridged Milk House Moosletter, Vol. 1,* published by editors, 1993; Don Lord, *California Milks,* published by author; John Tutton, *Udder Delight* (1980), *Udderly Beautiful: A Pictorial Guide to the Pyroglazed or Painted Milkbottle* (1996), published by author.

Newsletters: *Creamers,* PO Box 11, Lake Villa, IL 60046; *The Udder Collectibles,* HC 73 Box 1, Smithville Flats, NY 13841.

Collectors' Clubs: Cream Separator Assoc, Route 3, Box 189, Arcadia, WI 54612; National Assoc of Milk Bottle Collectors, Inc, 4 Ox Bow Road, Westport, CT 06880.

Museums: Billings Farm Museum, Woodstock, VT; New York State Historical Assoc and Farmers Museum, Cooperstown, NY; Southwest Dairy Museum, Arlington, TX.

Bottle, baby top, "E. M. Dwyer Dairy, Weymouth" on front, same reverse, red, square qt 65

Bottle, baby top, "Greenleaf Dairy, Petersburg, Va." and 2 maple leaves on front, same reverse, green, square qt 55

Bottle, baby top, "Honicker's Dairy" on front, same reverse, emb, base emb "St. Clair, Pa.," round pt 55

Bottle, cream top, "Cloverdale Farms" on front, "Milk Is Your Best Food Buy" on reverse, red, square qt, small dacro–style top 17

Bottle, cream top, "McAdams Dairy Products, J. F. McAdams & Bros" on front, "Producers, Processors, Distributors" with cow, tank, and home on reverse, orange, round qt, round bulb 24

Bottle, cream top, "Round Top Farms, Quality Dairy Products, Pasteurized" on front, "Our Milk Room Where Cleanliness Prevails" with large milk room graphic on reverse, Maine seal, green, round qt 25

Bottle, dairy creamer, "Anthony's Cream," red, blank reverse, round, 1/2 oz . . . 25

Bottle, dairy creamer, "Darts' Dairy, Manchester, Conn.," orange, same reverse, round, 3/4 oz 28

Bottle, dairy creamer, "Olds Dairy," maroon, blank reverse, round, 3/4 oz 20

Bottle, dairy creamer, "Price Dairy," red, same reverse, round, 3/4 oz 24

Bottle, dairy creamer, "Purity Maid Products Co," blue, same reverse, round, 3/4 oz 20

Bottle, dairy creamer, "Rosebud Creamery," maroon, blank reverse, square, 3/4 oz 18

Bottle, dairy creamer, "Shamrock Dairy," green, same reverse, round, 1/2 oz . . 20

Bottle, gill, "Bezanilla Dairy, Carthage, NY, Better Milk" with baby in center on front, orange pyro, "Drink Bezanilla Dairy Milk" on reverse 22

Bottle, gill, "Delchester Farms, Edgemont, PA," emb 15

Bottle, gill, "Vale Edge Dairy, Franklin P. Gray," emb 23

Bottle, 1/4 pt, "C.A. Dorr Dairy, Watertown, NY," orange pyro, "Milk Is Nature's Most Perfect Food" with children, cow, and barn on reverse 25

Bottle, 1/4 pt, "Dunn Bros. Dairy, Howell, Mich," emb 26

Bottle, 1/4 pt, "Hassenteufel Dairy, Raritan Township," emb 22

Bottle, 1/4 pt, "H.J. Whitmore, Clayton, NY," orange pyro, "Thousand Island Dairy" cow in pasture scene on reverse 28

Bottle, 1/4 pt, "H.P. Fairchild, Lyons Falls, NY," emb 26

Bottle, 1/4 pt, "Spencer Milk Co., Sidney, NY," emb 18

Bottle, 1/2 pt, "Borden's" with Elsie head in wreath, red, same reverse, square . 6

Left: Bottle, 1/2 pt, emb "Bangor Sanitary Dairy, Bangor, PA," $12.

Right: Bottle, qt, clear, emb "Producer's Milk Co.," c1915, 9 1/2" h, $15.

Bottle, ½ pt, "D.M. McPherson, Gloucester, Mass," orange, same reverse ... 12
Bottle, ½ pt, "Gagnon & Son Dairy, Nashua, New Hampshire," orange, square, squat 8
Bottle, ½ pt, "Mid Valley Farm Dairy" with 2 children, green, square 6
Bottle, ½ pt, "Morgan's Meadow Brook Farm, Troy, NY," red, round 7
Bottle, ½ pt, "Smith's Dairy Farm, Erie, PA," maroon, round 7
Bottle, ½ pt, "S.O. Sargent, Milk From Federally Tested Cows, Concord, NH," on front, "Pine Hill Farm, Ayshire Milk Raw & Pasteurized" on reverse, red, round 16
Bottle, pt, tall round, "A.G. Dorr Dairy, Watertown, NY," orange, seated baby reaching up on reverse 12
Bottle, pt, tall round, "Dellinger Dairy Farm, Jeffersonville, Ind" on front in black with orange outline and dotted orange ground, "Jeffersonville's Only Gold Medal Herd" in orange with black cow on reverse 30
Bottle, pt, tall round, "Realicious Cooperative Dairies, Phone 201" on front, green, "Prepared And Ready For Orders! Are You?" with saluting soldier on reverse 20
Bottle, pt, tall round, "Schlichting's Dairy & Berry Farm, Sheboygan Falls, Wis" on front in orange with blue outline, "Vitality, From Farm To You" with 2-color farm scene on reverse 35
Bottle, pt, tall round, "Zenda Farms, Golden Guernsey, Clayton, NY," store banner on neck, orange, "Zenda Farms, Clayton, New York" on reverse ... 15
Bottle, qt, short round, "Alamito, Omaha's Pioneer Dairy" with covered wagon in orange and maroon on front, "Perfectly Pasteurized, Always Delicious" in maroon on reverse 65
Bottle, qt, short round, "Gill Bros. Ice Cream, Chestertown, Md." on front, red, "Once I Met A Little Girl, Whose Skin Was Fine As Silk, For Every Day Beside Her Plate, There Was A Glass of Gill Bros. Milk" with castle and cottage scene on reverse 40
Bottle, qt, short square, Borden's, "Elsie" with Elsie head in wreath, red 18
Bottle, qt, short square, "Gulf Hill Farms, Country Fresh Milk," cow's head, orange 6
Bottle, qt, short square, "Irwin's Dairy Inc. Camp Hill Pa.," red and orange printing all 4 sides 7
Bottle, qt, short square, "Rickett's Dairy," amber 12
Bottle, qt, tall round, "Ben Jansing Farm Dairy, Licking Pike, Newport, KY" on front, red, "Yes Sir!, It's Good For Grown–Ups Too" with family drinking milk on reverse 25
Bottle, qt, tall round, "Capitol Dairies Inc." with large Capitol dome, emb ... 12
Bottle, qt, tall round, "Diamond Farm Dairy, Pueblo, Colo." in diamond on front, "Reach For Diamond Farm Milk, Taste The Difference" with "Diamond Farm" in black and rest in red on reverse 60
Bottle, qt, tall round, "Farmer's Delight Dairy, Phone GGW1, Leechburg, Pa." on front, orange, "It's Pasteurized" on reverse 20
Bottle, qt, tall round, "Gefke Dairy, Oregon, Wis" with large cow on front, black, "Farmer Producer to City Consumer" with farm, delivery truck and home on reverse 35
Bottle, qt, tall round, "Highland Dairy Company" with kilted bagpipe player, orange 18
Bottle, qt, tall round, "Horne's Dairy, Milk at It's Best, Skowhegan, Maine" on front, yellow, "Fresh From the Farm" and barnyard on reverse 18

Bottle, qt, tall round, "Middletown Cremi–Rich" on front, brown, "Middletown Milk & Cheese Co. Inc." on reverse 18

Bottle, qt, tall round, "Try Our Butter, There's None Better, Phone 8783, Salem, Ore." in orange with large green "Curly's" in center on front, "Ask For Curly's Famous Buttermilk" in orange with green churn on reverse 50

Bottle, qt, tall square, "Fitchett Bros. Dairy, Poughkeepsie, N.Y.," orange 8

Bottle, qt, tall square, "Martin Farms, Rochester, Vt." with cow's face, orange . 7

Bottle, qt, tall square, "Polk County Co–Op Dairies, Winter Haven, Fla.," red . 15

Bottle, qt, tall square, "Schramm Cry. Co., Farmington, Mo." with clove leaf, green 8

Bottle, qt, tall square, "Tarbell Guernsey Milk, Smithville Flats, New York," black and orange 12

Bottle, sour cream/cottage cheese, wide mouth, "Ideal Farms, Augusta, Ga., Golden Guernsey, The World's Finest Milk" on front, orange, "Ideal Farms, N. Haledon, N.J." on reverse, qt 18

Bottle, sour cream/cottage cheese, wide mouth, "Queensboro Farm Products Inc" with cow on front, maroon, same reverse, pt 10

Bottle, sour cream/cottage cheese, wide mouth, "Sodus Sour Cream, since 1894" on front, blue, same reverse, pt 10

Bottle, war slogan, "Cole Farm Dairy, Biddeford, Me." on front, maroon, "Milk The First Line Of Health Defense" in shield on reverse, round ⁵⁄₈ pt .. 15

Bottle, war slogan, "Dublin Coop. Dairies, Milk & Cream" on front, red, "You Owe It To Your Country, Buy War Bonds" with Uncle Sam's hand on reverse, round pt 18

Bottle, war slogan, "Norwalk Pure Milk Inc. Norwalk, O." on front, orange, "War Bonds For Victory, Milk For Strength" with bust of Uncle Sam holding glass of milk on reverse, tall round qt 60

Dairy Coupon Book, Cloverleaf Jersey Dairy, Helena, MT, blue 3

Dairy Coupon Book, Jersey Gold Creameries, Shreveport, LA, green 3

Dairy Scale, Chatillon Milk Scale, 8" brass dial, 150 lbs 50

Dairy Scale, Pelouze, white enamel on brass 65

Dairy Token, Blue Valley Dairy, 1 pt milk, brass 2

Dairy Token, Palmiter Dairy, 1 qt milk, brass 2

LIGHTNING RODS

Lightning rod balls and pendants are the ornamental portion of lightning rod systems typically found on the roofs of barns and rural houses from the 1840s to 1930s. The glass balls and pendants served only aesthetic purposes and did not contribute to the operation of the lightning rod system.

Glass balls ranged in color from the common white milk glass and blue milk glass to clear. Some clear glass has turned shades of sun colored amethyst (SCA) through exposure to the sun. Other colors include shades of amber, cobalt, green, and red to the rarer colors of pink, orange, yellow, and marbleized slag. Mercury colored balls were created by silvering the interior surface of balls of different colors to produce silver, gold, cobalt, red, and green mercury colors. Lightning rod balls were colored using several different glass making techniques—flashing, casing, and solid colors.

There are thirty–four standard shapes or styles of lightning rod balls. Some were made exclusively by a single glass maker; others were made by several. Value depends on design, color, locality, and condition. Obviously, the scarcer patterns are more valuable and higher in price. Since some lightning rod balls closely resemble lamp parts whose collars often are ground, it is best to avoid any ball that has a ground or etched collar.

White and blue milk glass balls are the most common and usually the least expensive. Prices escalate by color beginning with sun color amethyst, amber, and red. The rare colors of orange, pink, and yellow are at the top of the scale. Mercury balls are higher priced than the clear versions from which they were made.

Pendants were generally installed in sets of four, one dangling from each arm extending from a lightning rod. A metal hook or loop attached to a metal cap held the pendant in place. Rust and the elements often caused the hook or cap to fail, resulting in the loss of a pendant. Cold weather could crack a pendant if water worked its way inside.

Pendants measure 5½" high including cap and hook, 4½" not including cap and hook. They are approximately 3" wide and teardrop shaped. Collectors prefer pendants in mint condition. Loss of the metal loop fastened to the cap or the cap itself reduces value.

Reference: Mike Bruner and Rod Krupka, *The Complete Book of Lightning Rod Balls,* published by authors, 1982.

Newsletter: *The Crown Point,* 2615 Echo Lane, Ortonville, MI 48462.

Reproduction Alert: Reproductions of the Thompson ball have been found in five colors: white milk glass, amber, cobalt, blue–green, and red. Some rarer colored balls may have been reproduced using period molds.

Ball, Chestnut, green milk glass	**$60**
Ball, Chestnut, silver mercury	**250**
Ball, D & S, green	**275**
Ball, D & S, sun colored amethyst	**15**
Ball, D & S, white milk glass	**15**
Ball, Diddie Blitzen, clear	**40**
Ball, Doorknob, slag	**400**
Ball, Doorknob, sun colored amethyst	**75**
Ball, Electra Cone, clear	**75**
Ball, Electra Cone, flashed blue over clear	**90**
Ball, Electra Cone, white milk glass	**10**
Ball, K–Ball, blue milk glass	**40**
Ball, Mast, white milk glass	**80**
Ball, Moon & Star, amber	**50**
Ball, Moon & Star, gold mercury	**300**
Ball, Moon & Star, white milk glass	**10**
Ball, National Belted, silver mercury	**375**
Ball, National Round, sun colored amethyst	**100**
Ball, National Round, white milk glass	**20**
Ball, Onion, dark blue milk glass	**125**
Ball, Patent '77, gold mercury	**325**
Ball, Patent '77, sun colored amethyst, 3½"	**85**
Ball, Patent '77, sun colored amethyst, 4"	**125**
Ball, Plain Round, amber, 3½"	**95**
Ball, Plain Round, amber, 5½"	**20**
Ball, Plain Round, blue milk glass, 4¾"	**25**
Ball, Plain Round, dark blue milk glass, 4½"	**65**

Left: Hawkeye,
white milk glass,
5¹/₄ x 4¹/₄", $20.

Right: Swirl, amber,
5³/₄ x 5", $45.

Ball, Plain Round, dark green, 4¹/₂"	350
Ball, Plain Round, root beer, 4¹/₂"	15
Ball, Plain Round, 7-Up green, 4¹/₂"	150
Ball, Plain Round, sun colored amethyst, 3¹/₂"	20
Ball, Plain Round, sun colored amethyst, 4¹/₂"	20
Ball, Plain Round, vaseline, 5"	15
Ball, Plain Round, white milk glass, 4¹/₂"	15
Ball, Plain Round, white milk glass, 5"	12
Ball, Pleat Pointed, red, 3¹/₂"	200
Ball, Pleat Pointed, root beer, dated	425
Ball, Pleated Round, cobalt blue	75
Ball, Pleated Round, 7–Up green	115
Ball, Quilt Flat, sun colored amethyst	60
Ball, Quilt Flat, teal	400
Ball, Quilt Raised, red	300
Ball, Quilt Raised, white milk glass	50
Ball, Ribbed Grape, green–gray	400
Ball, Ribbed Grape, red	325
Ball, S Company, blue milk glass	50
Ball, Shinn Belted, blue milk glass	45
Ball, Shinn Belted, sun colored amethyst	55
Ball, Shinn System, white milk glass	25
Ball, SLR Co, cobalt blue, wide collar, no em	75
Ball, SLR Co, flashed red, wide collar, no em	125
Ball, SLR Co, root beer, narrow collar	350
Ball, SLR Co, sun colored amethyst, narrow collar	1,450
Ball, Swirl, blue milk glass	70
Ball, Thompson, cobalt blue	70
Ball, Thompson, teal	50
Directional, aluminum	65
Pendant, Acorn, flashed red	175
Pendant, Hawkeye, red	375
Pendant, Quilt Flat, sun colored amethyst	225
Pendant, Ribbed and Paneled, flashed red	175
Stand, scroll, 3 legs, wood base	100
Stand, twisted rods, wood base, refinished	20

TOOLS & EQUIPMENT

The self–reliant aspect of agrarian life required that its members were builders, mechanics, and providers all rolled into one. Farmers and homesteaders were generalists, capable of performing many specialized tasks. In addition, the urgency of time and the state of finances often required "doing things yourself now."

As a result, most rural households and farms contained a wide variety of equipment and tools. Much of the equipment was specialized, designed to perform a specific task such as a corn dryer or stitching horse. Tools were used to keep the equipment in repair, e.g., a hoopsetter or oilstone, or in partnership with the individual to perform a task, e.g., ax or saw.

Equipment and tools are one of the four principal criteria by which others judged individuals in the agrarian environment. The other three are land, buildings, and stock. Most equipment and tools were designed to last for generations, provided they received adequate care and proper use. On most farmsteads, the vast majority of equipment and tools will have been acquired through the secondary market, i.e., passed down through the family or purchased at a farm auction.

Initially farm tools and equipment were made by local craftsmen—the blacksmith, wheelwright, or the farmer himself. Product designs varied greatly. In a large number of instances, the reason a specific tool or piece of equipment was made has been lost. Many collections contain one or more of these "what's–its."

The industrial age and the "golden age" of American agriculture go hand in hand. By 1880–1900 manufacturers saw the farm market as an important source of sales. Farmers demanded quality products capable of withstanding hard use. While Stanley is the most recognized and collected manufacturer, collectors have not ignored the thousands of other firms who concentrated on making equipment and tools for the agrarian community.

In the 1940s urban growth began to draw attention away from the rural areas and consolidation of farms took place. Bigger machinery was developed. Post–World War II farm tools and equipment are just beginning to attract the attention of collectors.

Within the Country community, equipment and tools serve primarily as furniture pieces and wall hangings. Few pieces are displayed in context. Decorators like pieces made wholly or partly of wood with signs of heavy use.

Tool collectors are a breed unto themselves. Although they are found at country auctions, they do much of their trading and buying through the mail, via phone, or at specialized shows and meets. Regional and state collectors' clubs include the Mid–West Tool Collectors Association (808 Fairway Drive, Columbia, MO 65201) and the Ohio Tool Collectors Association (PO Box 261, London, OH 43140).

References: Ronald S. Barlow, *The Antique Tool Collector's Guide to Value, Third Edition,* Windmill Publishing Company, 1991; *The Catalogue of Antique Tools,* Martin J. Donnelly Antique Tools, (1997); Kenneth L. Cope, *American Machinist's Tools: An Illustrated Dictionary of Patents,* Astragal Press, 1993; Kenneth L. Cope, *Makers of American Machinist Tools: A Historical Directory of Makers and Their Tools,* Astragal

Press, 1993; R. Douglas Hurt, *American Farm Tools From Hand–Power to Steam Power,* Sunflower University Press, 1982; Herbert P. Kean and Emil S. Pollak, *A Price Guide to Antique Tools,* Astragal Press, 1992; Herbert P. Kean and Emil S. Pollak, *Collecting Antique Tools,* Astragal Press, 1990; Kathryn McNerney, *Antique Tools: Our American Heritage,* Collector Books, 1979, 1996 value update; Jim Moffet, *American Corn Huskers: A Patent History,* Off Beat Books, 1994.

Emil and Martyl Pollak, *A Guide to American Wood Planes and Their Makers, Second Edition,* Astragal Press, 1991; Emil and Martyl Pollak, *Prices Realized on Rare Imprinted American Wooden Planes, 1979–1992,* Astragal Press, 1993; *A Price Guide to Keen Kutter Tools,* L–W Book Sales, 1993 values; R. A. Salaman, *Dictionary of Tools,* Charles Scribner's Sons, 1974; John Walter, *Antique & Collectible Stanley Tools: A Guide to Identity and Value, Second Edition,* Tool Merchant, 1996; John Whelan, *The Wooden Plane: Its History, Form, and Function,* Astragal Press, 1993; Jack P. Wood, *Early 20th Century Stanley Tools: A Price Guide,* L–W Book Sales, 1992, 1996 value update; Jack P. Wood, *Town–Country Old Tools and Locks, Keys and Closures,* L–W Books, 1990, 1997 value update.

Periodicals: *Stanley Tool Collector News,* 208 Front Street, PO Box 227, Marietta, OH 45750; *The Fine Tool Journal,* 27 Fickett Road, Pownal, ME 04069; *Tool Ads,* PO Box 33, Hamilton, MT 59840.

Newsletter: *Plumb Line,* 10023 St Clair's Retreat, Fort Wayne, IN 46825.

Collectors' Clubs: Early American Industries Assoc, 167 Bakersville Road, South Dartmouth, MA 02748; Early American Industries Assoc–West, 8476 West Way Drive, La Jolla, CA 92038; International Society of Antique Scale Collectors, 176 West Adams Street, Suite 1706, Chicago, IL 60603; Tool Group of Canada, 7 Tottenham Road, Toronto, Ontario, M3C 2J3, Canada.

Museums: American Precision Museum Assoc, Windsor, VT; Bucks County Historical Society, Mercer Museum, Doylestown, PA; Landis Valley Farm Museum, Lancaster, PA; Shelburne Museum, Shelburne, VT; World O'Tools Museum, Waverly, TN.

Apple Picker, wire cage, wood handle	$25
Bellows, blacksmith's, painted	250
Bit Stock, primitive, hand wrought, beech, hardwood head, 4" throw, 3¼" d head, 18½" l	200
Bow Saw, primitive, hand wrought, ash, 12 x 23"	25
Broad Ax, Hopkins & Co, Hartford, wood handle, "Warranted Cast Steel," 8½" w	75
Buck Saw, 30" blade	25
Buggy Wrench, brace style, ratchet positioned	75
Chisel, primitive, hand wrought, hardwood handle, 2" w, 16" l	18
Cobbler's Bench, NH, early 19th C	600
Corn Dryer, wrought iron	20
Corn Husking Peg, hand carved, c1900, 5" l	30
Corn Sheller, wood case with red wash, iron gears, hand crank, 34" h	75
Cranberry Scoop, wood and tin, eighteen fingers, early 20th C	200
Draw Knife, hand wrought by blacksmith, miniature, 8" w	20
Felling Ax, Rockaway pattern	15
Goosewing Ax, Stahler	300
Grain Cradle, 4 fingers, 41" l	65
Grain Shovel, wood, 48½" l	75

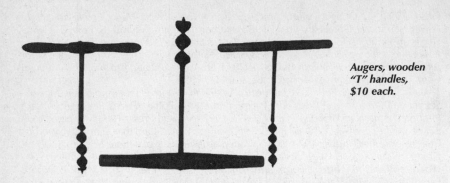

Augers, wooden "T" handles, $10 each.

Hammer, J Vigeant, Marlboro, MA, #1, double headed shoe hammer, patented Jan 7, 1868, graphic, 12" l   75

Hammer, Stanley Rule & Level, carpenter's bell faced claw hammer, sweetheart trademark, c1920s, 13" l   45

Hammer, unmkd "Goat Head" hammer, brass, promotional item, orig red paint and turned handle, 8½" l   175

Harrow, mule–drawn, arrow shaped, wood frame, iron spikes   30

Hatchet, hewing, flat side, 8" edge   15

Hay Fork, PA, metal prongs, wood fork and handle, maker's initials   140

Hay Rake, wood, 50" l   35

Hide Scraper, hand wrought, shaped rosewood handles and cover, 6" w blade, 11" l handle and cover   100

Hoof Rest, hand wrought by blacksmith, iron, 3 splayed legs, 2" d rest, 20" h   40

Ice Tongs, wrought iron, double handle, 26" l   50

Level, L L Davis, Springfield, MA, inclinometer, filigree casting with gold pinstriping and highlights, japan finish, 1867 patent, 18" l 1,150

Level, New Britain Hardware Co, patent bench level, copper flash finish, patented Mar 28, 1916, 15" l   85

Level, Peerless Level & Tool Co, "The Levelette," mahogany, curved vial, bright yellow decal, 3" l   35

Level, Stratton Bros, Greenfield, MA, bench level, nickel plated, solid brass body, 3½" l   450

Level, unmkd, Brazilian rosewood, brass plates and binding, clear brushed lacquer finish, 7½" l   150

Level and Plumb, hand wrought, mahogany and brass, 43" l stylized arrow carved on 1 side, 48" l   15

Lodge Axe, wood, gold, green, and red repaint, blade mkd "Blue Grass," varnished handle, 47½" l   150

Mortising Ax, double blade   50

Nail Header, hand wrought by blacksmith, 13¾" l   40

Plane, Casey and Co, Auburn, NY, #105, boxed bead molding plane, 9½" l . .   25

Plane, Hayden, Syracuse, NY, adjustable patent beveling plane, patented April 1848, 16" l 1,800

Plane, John Briscoe, Birmingham, England, quarter round molding plane, c1785, 9¾" l   150

Plane, Shiverick & Malcom, Brooklyn, NY, handled stair plane, movable fence, 9" l **600**
Plane, Stanley, #3, smooth plane, type 15, 1931–32 . . . . **45**
Plane, Stanley, #5, jack plane, type 6, 1888–92 . . . . **20**
Plane, Stanley, #7C, router plane, 3 irons, fence, and throat closing attachment **60**
Plane, Stanley, #43, Millers Patent plow plane **200**
Plane, Stanley, #444, dovetail plane, missing sample block and instructions, with orig dovetailed box and label **950**
Plane, Stanley, #G4, gauge smooth plane **110**
Plane, unmkd, block plane, carriage maker's, tapered, 8" l **20**
Plane, unmkd, panel plane, beech, ornate handle, 3" w double iron and adjustable fence, 15¼" l **75**
Plumb Bob, C L Berger & Sons, Boston, MA, surveyor's, brass, 3" l **60**
Plumb Bob, Keuffel & Essor Co, NY, #83 0036, surveyor's, brass, orig green box, 5" l **65**
Plumb Bob, L S Starrett Co, Athol, MA, surveyor's, cast iron, orig box, 3¼" l . . **85**
Rake, wood, twelve prongs, 3 graduating semi–circular braces, c1850, 77" l . **125**
Reaping Hook, hand held, hand forged blade, wood handle, sgd, c1870 . . . . **100**
Rip Saw, Atkins **25**
Rule, D Annis, early board measure rule, eagle logo, c1820–30, 24" l **350**
Rule, Esborn Lumber Corp, NY, adv hook rule with lumber scales, adv on reverse, 24" l **75**
Rule, Kerby & Bro, NY, horse measure rule with integral level, 80" l **1,000**
Rule, unmkd, circular yard rule, boxwood, 36" l **75**
Sap Spout, carved wood **10**
Scale, Fairbanks, grain, brass, bushel **275**
Scale, Forschner, spring balance, brass, hanging **75**
Scale, Hanson Viking, spring balance, #8910, steel, painted green, 1 to 100 lbs **40**
Scale, Jiffyway, egg grading, brass **95**
Scale, Oak Manufacturing Co, egg grading **15**
Scale, Ohaus, grain, brass **250**
Scale, PS & T Warranted, balance, brass front, patented July 8, 1889, 0 to 50 lbs **35**
Scale, Winchester, grain, brass, hanging, bushel **200**
Screwdriver, brass handle inlaid with ebony and red Bakelite, 9½" l **10**
Schnitzelbank, cooper's bench, hand hewn oak, 62" l, 37" h **125**
Scythe, wood handle, hand forged blade **40**
Seed Planter, wood, black stenciled eagle and label "Norcross & Boynton, Makers, Monmouth, Me. Patent Applied For," 39½" h **150**
Sickle, wood handle, iron blade, 21" l **20**
Spoke Shave, Stanley #66 . . . . **10**
Stitching Horse, hickory, wood screw vise, mortised, hand made, c1840 . . . . **150**
Tool Tray, pine, square nail construction, cutout handle, 29½" l, 12" w, 8½" h **50**
Traveler, iron, hand wrought, primitive, wooden handle, 7" d wheel, 11½" l . . **40**
Traveler, wood, hand wrought, 8" d wheel, 14" l **125**
Two–Man Saw, cross cut timber, 72" l **20**
Wagon Brace, metal **15**

Left: Egg Grading Scale, Farm Master, black, red, and yellow, $50.

Right: Tobacco Chopper, bentwood, curved blade, Shaker style, $165. Photo courtesy James D. Julia.

Wheelbarrow, wood, iron wheel and braces, removable sides, sgd **75**
Whetstone Wreath, primitive, cow horn, hook for fitting on belt, 8½" l **35**

WEATHER VANES

A weather vane indicates wind direction. The earliest known examples were found on late seventeenth–century structures in the Boston area. The vanes were hand craft-ed of wood, copper, or tin. By the last half of the nineteenth century, weather vanes adorned farms and houses throughout the nation. Mass–produced vanes of cast iron, copper, and sheet metal were sold through mail order catalogs or at country stores.

In addition to being functional, weather vanes were decorative. Popular forms include horses, Indians, leaping stags, and patriotic emblems. Church vanes were often in the form of a fish or cock. Buildings in coastal towns featured ships or sea creatures. Occasionally a vane doubled as a trade sign.

The champion vane is the rooster. In fact, the name weathercock is synonymous with weather vane. The styles and patterns are endless. Weathering can affect the same vane differently. For this reason, patina is a critical element in collecting vanes.

The two principal forms are silhouette and three dimensional vanes. Silhouette vanes are extremely fragile. Most examples have been repaired with some form of reinforcing strap.

Sportsmen and others frequently used weathervanes for target practice. Bullet holes decrease the value of a vane. Filled holes usually can be detected with a black light.

References: Robert Bishop and Patricia Coblentz, *A Gallery of American Weathervanes and Whirligigs,* E. P. Dutton, 1981; Ken Fitzgerald, *Weathervanes and Whirligigs,* Clarkson N. Potter, 1967; Steve Miller, *The Art of the Weathervane,* Schiffer Publishing, 1984.

Museum: Heritage Plantation of Sandwich, Sandwich, MA.

Reproduction Alert: Reproductions of early models exist, are being aged, and sold as originals. Check provenance and get a written guarantee from any seller.

In the early 1980s the market was flooded with silhouette vanes manufactured in Haiti. These vanes are made from old drums and lack the proper supporting strapwork of an older vane.

Arrow, bow tie, tin, wrought iron **$65**
Arrow, crescent moon tail, 4 rods, 2 stars, wrought iron **500**
Arrow, glass tail, wrought iron arrow, Barnett, block lettering, cobalt blue ... **225**
Arrow, glass tail, wrought iron arrow, Barnett, script lettering, cobalt blue ... **385**
Arrow, glass tail, wrought iron arrow, Barnett, script lettering, red **175**
Arrow, glass tail, wrought iron arrow, fleur–de–lis, large, 24" **100**
Arrow, glass tail, wrought iron arrow, fleur–de–lis, small **100**
Arrow, glass tail, wrought iron arrow, hearts and balls, 24" **200**
Arrow, glass tail, wrought iron arrow, horse, etched, red, weighted front **500**
Arrow, glass tail, wrought iron arrow, Kretzer, red, large, 24" **45**
Arrow, glass tail, wrought iron arrow, Kretzer, transparent green, sticker **275**
Arrow, glass tail, wrought iron arrow, kite tail, red, large etched daisy **325**
Arrow, glass tail, wrought iron arrow, kite tail, transparent green **175**
Arrow, glass tail, wrought iron arrow, star in diamond, red **135**
Arrow, Robbins Co, aluminum **25**
Arrow, Scott Detroit, aluminum **250**
Arrow, Security, bow tie with tail, wrought iron **185**
Arrow, Shinn, aluminum **125**
Arrow, SLR Co, wrought iron, blue milk glass ball **450**
Arrow, SLR Co, wrought iron, cobalt blue ball, wire star front **350**
Arrow, tin tail, plain, wrought iron, 24" l **40**
Automobile, gilded sheet copper, full bodied car on 4 wire wheels, retains traces of orig gilding, mounted on rod and black metal base, early 20th C, 13" h, 31" l **7,000**
Banner, wrought iron and sheet iron, banner form pointer pierced with date "1668," swivels on spirally fluted shaft surmounted by scrolling device and stylized corkscrew finial, 42½" h **2,500**
Bull, full bodied, copper and zinc, 25½" l **3,000**
Butterfly, sheet metal, late 19th C, 23" h, 16½" l **1,500**
Cow, molded copper, cast zinc head, traces of gilt, greenish patina, 17½" h plus modern base **3,850**
Dove, sheet iron, painted and gilded, folk art design, c1860, 23" h **2,750**
Duck, sheet metal, hollow, 36" l **275**
Eagle, molded and gilded copper, perched on orb, spread wings, arrow below, cast iron directionals, regilded, 23½" w wingspan **1,150**
Eagle, molded copper, perched on orb, folded wings, molded, arrow below, 29" l **450**
Eagle, molded copper, silver paint over orig gilding, spread wings, open beak, large ornate arrow below orb, bullet hole through neck, JW Fiske Co, NY, late 19th C, 49½" w wingspan **3,500**
Fish, molded copper, detailed scales and fins, c1900, 38" l **5,500**
Fish, sheet iron, silhouette, dorsal fins and tail, drilled eye hole, cut mouth, rod standard mount on driftwood steeple base, 19th C, 33½" h, 11½" l ... **1,500**
Fish, wood, primitive, gray patina, spire standard, 67" h **425**
Horse, Black Hawk, trotting, molded copper, swell bodied figure with molded mane, neck veins and tail detail, weathered to allover verdigris, mounted on rod and black metal base, Harris & Co, Boston, MA, third quarter 19th C, 22" h, 33" l **3,500**

Left: Cow, sheet metal silhouette, rod standard, 16" l, $550.

Right: Eagle on Arrow, JW Fiske Co, bullet hole in neck, $4,025. Photo courtesy James D. Julia.

Horse, Dexter, molded copper, 33" l **825**

Horse, Hackney, molded and gilded copper, swell bodied figure of trotting horse with molded tail detail and ridged sheet copper mane, covered in gilding with traces of yellow polychrome, mounted on rod, attributed to JW Fiske & Co, NY, c1893, 18" h, 25½" l **4,325**

Horse, molded copper and zinc, full bodied figure in running pose, molded tail and mane detail, cast zinc head and ears, retains traces of orig gilding, mounted on rod and later black metal base, 27¾" h, 34" l **5,750**

Horse, Index, molded copper and zinc, swell bodied figure with molded zinc head, man, and forequarters, molded copper ears, legs, and hind quarter, ridged sheet copper tail, mounted on rod and black metal base, J Howard & Co, West Bridgewater, MA, late 19th C, 22¼" h, 30¼" l **20,000**

Horse, prancing, wood, carved and painted, old weathered white paint, modern base, 1900s, 24" h **100**

Horse, pulling sulky, molded copper, full bodied horse with sheet copper ears, full bodied driver wearing cap and holding wire reins, mounted on rod above directionals and orb, repaired, 20" h, 34½" l **2,875**

Horse, running, cast iron, full bodied figure, c1900, 30" h, 23½" l **2,750**

Horse, running, cast zinc, traces of orig gilt, fitted with threaded pipe, no directionals, 54" l, 23" h **1,750**

Horse, running, molded and gilded copper and zinc, molded zinc head, neck, and forequarters, incised and molded eye detail, cut and crinkled repoussé sheet copper mane and tail, sheet copper ears, traces of worn orig gilding, mounted on rod and black metal base, J Howard & Co, West Bridgewater, MA, third quarter 19th C, 19" h, 37½" l **21,850**

Horse, silhouette, carved and painted pine, white horse carved from single pc of pine, black mane, bridle, tail, and hoofs, fitted with sheet metal reins, probably PA, 19th C, 18" h, 28" l **1,950**

Indian Chief, molded copper, Mashamoquet, full bodied, shaggy pony tail, short skirt, repoussé detail, drawing bow and arrow, standing on arrow headed rod on rockwork, c1850, 37" l, 35" h **8,000**

Indian In Canoe, primitive, heavy galvanized sheet steel, modern base with rod, 51" h, 39" l **200**

Indian Warrior on Horseback, zinc, silhouette, scalloped headdress, holding molded bow with twisted wire bow string, flat horse with molded neck, punchmark outlining, rod mounting, 19th C, 27½" h, 35½" l **6,750**

Logger, sheet metal, silhouette, man pushing 3 logs, traces of polychrome paint, 19th C, 28" h, 35" l **625**

Moose, zinc and copper, silhouette, wood base, 20th C, 28½" h, 39" l 350
Peacock, wood and wire, silhouette, painted, early 20th C, 14" h, 49" l 950
Plow, copper and cast zinc, rod mounting, black metal base, c1860, 23" h,
  42" l 5,500
Quill Pen, molded copper, polychrome painted, repoussé feathers, rod
  mounting, black metal base, 19th C, 33" l 10,000
Rooster, fighting cock, molded copper, 24" l 450
Rooster, molded and gilded copper, swell bodied figure with molded feath-
  er and eye detail, ridged sheet copper tail and comb, and sheet copper
  wattle, traces of orange polychrome and orig gilding, standing on arrow
  above orb and letter directionals, wood base, third quarter 19th C,
  23¾" h, 20" l 2,500
Rooster, molded copper, swell bodied figure with ridged sheet copper tail,
  rod mounting on wood base, 18" h, 19" l 1,000
Rooster, silhouette, primitive, sheet iron, 14" h 300
Sailboat, primitive, iron, riveted blacksmith construction, traces of red and
  black paint, modern standard, 20½" h 250
Schooner, wood, carved and painted, tin sails, wire rigging, 20th C, 31" l . . .1,250
Scroll, gilded copper, zinc, and iron, 19th C, 55" w, 7" d, 47" h 1,000
Setter, molded and gilded copper, swell bodied figure standing at point,
  molded sheet copper ears, molded tail and fur detail, traces of yellow
  paint, mounted on rod and black metal base, regilded, JW Fiske & Co, NY,
  late 19th C, 14" h 7,000
Sheep, molded copper, verdigris surface, repaired bullet holes, early 20th C,
  28½" l 4,250
Squirrels, molded copper, swell bodied figures of 2 squirrels facing each
  other, eye and fur detail and bushy tails, 1 holding acorn, other lunging
  for acorn at center, squirrels perched on arrow directional, weathered to
  allover verdigris, 35" h, 94½" l 6,900
Stag, leaping, molded and gilded copper and zinc, swell bodied figure,
  forelegs tucked, rear legs extended, cast zinc head, ears, and antlers,
  molded copper upturned tail, orig gilding, mounted on rod and black
  metal base, JW Fiske & Co, NY, third quarter 19th C, 22" h, 26" l 18,500

Left: Horse and Jockey, molded full–bodied figure, $2,500.
Right: Locomotive, sheet metal, 19th C, $7,700. Photo courtesy James D. Julia.

WINDMILL WEIGHTS

Windmills were an important fixture on the early prairie landscape of the Midwest. They pumped underground water for crops, household use, livestock, and steam locomotives.

Windmill weights counterbalanced the weight of the large wind wheels which could measure as much as thirty feet in diameter. They were located at the end of the arm that ran back from the hub of the wind wheel. Although simple geometric shapes such as circles and rectangles were used, many of the weights were figural. Weight varied from ten to two hundred pounds. Windmill weights were painted to match the color of the windmill. Black was common. Blue, green, and red also were popular.

Most windmill weights were manufactured in the Midwest between 1880 and the 1920s. Leading manufacturers include the Dempster Mill Manufacturing Company (Beatrice, Nebraska), Elgin Wind Power and Pump Company (Elgin, Illinois), and Fairbury Windmill Company (Fairbury, Nebraska).

In the early 1980s windmill weights joined weather vanes as a darling of the folk art set. Although cast in molds and mass produced, windmill weights were elevated from utilitarian objects to objets d'art. In 1985 the Museum of American Folk Art sponsored a traveling exhibition on windmill weights.

References: Rick Nidey and Don Lawrence, *Windmill Weights: Pictured – Identified*, published by authors, 1996; Milton Simpson, *Windmill Weights*, Johnson & Simpson, 1985; Donald E. Sites, *Windmills and Windmill Weights*, published by author.

Newletter: *Windmillers' Gazette*, PO Box 507, Rio Vista, TX 76093.

Museum: Volendam Windmill Museum, Milford, NJ.

Reproduction Alert: Doug Clemence (Treasure Chest, 436 N Chicago, Salina, KS 67401) sells unpainted reproductions of the small chicken, Hummer #184 chicken with long shaft, Hummer #184 chicken with short shaft, "barnacle eye" chicken, short– tail horse, buffalo, and squirrel. Reproductions of the BOSS bull, Fairbury flat bull (#17 in Sites' book), long–tail horse, and a chicken with five tail feathers (#41 in Sites' book) have also been spotted.

New castings often have a finely granulated orange colored rust, which can be hidden by new paint, and rough casting edges. Modern reproductions often are done with pot metal, rather than cast iron. Finally, reproduction surfaces are rough and grainy, not weathered and smooth.

Bobtail Horse, Dempster Mill Mfg Co, Beatrice, NE, old black paint, 17" l, 16½" h	$385
Buffalo, Dempster Mill Mfg Co, Beatrice, NE, painted, 16" l	500
Bull, Dempster Mill Mfg Co, Beatrice, NE, mkd "BOSS," 18 lbs	700
Bull, Fairbury Windmill Co	650
Bull, Simpson Windmill and Machine Co, Hanchett, bolted halves	500
Crescent Moon, Fairbanks Morse Co, mkd "ECLIPSE," 1900, 27 lbs, 10" l	150
Halladay Star, US Wind Engine and Pump Co, 5 points, stripped, 1890s, 14½" h	400
Rooster, Elgin Wind Power and Pump Co, Elgin, IL, Hummer, 13½" h plus wood base	600
Rooster, Elgin Wind Power and Pump Co, Elgin, IL, rainbow tail, painted	950
Squirrel, Elgin Wind Power and Pump Co, Elgin, IL, dark tan paint, 17½" h	1,650
W, Althouse Wheeler Co, Waupun, WI, stripped, 16" l	350

COUNTRY STORE

The country store is the heart of rural America. Its functions are multifold—supplies, equipment, drugstore, post office, bank, accounting and bookkeeping services, meeting place, transportation center, information source, and social arbiter. Although the famed "general" store has gradually been replaced by shopping centers and mini–malls, many Americans still have fond memories of spending time around a pot-bellied woodstove.

One's first country store image is generally the vivid advertising, from broadsides to products, that graced the counters, shelves, and walls. The countertop equipment is remembered next, followed by promotional giveaways, some failing to survive because they were consumable. These are recapturable memories. The individuals, smells, clutter, and grime that were a part of the setting are in the distant past. Most museums and private collection re–creations are much too clean and orderly.

Re–creating a complete turn–of–the–century country store has been a popular goal of collectors and museums since the 1920s. It was common to buy the entire contents of a country store that was going out of business as a collection base. The advertising craze that started in the 1970s put an end to this practice. Sellers quickly realized that they could obtain far more for their objects by selling them one at a time, rather than in a lot. Rapidly escalating prices, especially for store equipment, makes re–creating a complete turn–of–the–century store in the 1990s a very expensive proposition.

For this reason, collectors have begun to focus on re–creating Depression era and post–World War II country stores, recognizing that they were very different from their early 1900s counterparts. This corresponds with the new found interest at farm museums in mid–twentieth century farming technology and life.

References: Douglas Congdon–Martin, *Drugstore and Soda Fountain Antiques,* Schiffer Publishing, 1991; Douglas Congdon–Martin, *Country Store Antiques: From Cradles to Caskets,* Schiffer Publishing, 1991; Douglas Congdon–Martin, *Country Store Collectibles,* Schiffer Publishing, 1990; Patricia McDaniel, *Drugstore Collectibles,* Wallace–Homestead, 1994; Don and Carol Raycraft, *American Country Store,* Wallace–Homestead, Krause Publications, 1994; David L Wilson, *General Store Collectibles: An Identification and Value Guide,* Collector Books, 1994, 1997 value update.

ADVERTISING

The earliest advertising in America is found in colonial newspapers and printed broadsides. A large number of the advertisements are rural in nature, often accompanied by a farm related vignette. Rural newspapers were in place by the early nineteenth century.

By the mid–nineteenth century manufacturers began to examine how a product was packaged. They recognized that the package could convey a message and serve as a source of identification, thus selling more product. The package logo also could be used effectively in pictorial advertising.

The advent of the high speed, lithograph printing press led to regional and national magazines, resulting in new advertising markets. The lithograph press also brought the element of vivid colors into the advertising spectrum.

Although the "general" store remained a strong force in rural and small town America into the 1950s, it changed with the times. Specialized departments were created. Some product lines branched off as individual stores. The amount and variety of product increased significantly, as did the advertising to go with it.

By 1880 advertising premiums, such as calendars and thermometers, arrived upon the scene. Country store merchants were especially fond of these giveaways. Diecut point–of–purchase displays, wall clocks, and signs were introduced and quickly found their way onto walls and shelves.

Advertising continued to respond to changing opportunities and times. The advertising character developed in the early 1900s. By the 1950s the star endorser was established firmly as an advertising vehicle. Advertising became a big business as specialized firms, many headquartered in New York City, developed to meet manufacturers' needs. Today television programs frequently command well over one hundred thousand dollars a minute for commercial air time.

Many factors affect the price of an advertising collectible—the product and its manufacturer, the objects or persons used in the advertisement, the period and aesthetics of design, the designer and/or illustrator, and the form the advertisement takes. Add to this the continued use of advertising material as decorative elements in bars, restaurants, and other public places. The interior decorator purchases at a very different price level than the collector.

In truth, almost every advertising item is sought by a specialized collector in one or more collectible areas. The result is a divergence in pricing, with the price quoted to an advertising collector usually lower than that to a specialized collector, a category into which country store advertising collectors fall.

References: A. Walker Bingham, *The Snake–Oil Syndrome: Patent Medicine Advertising,* Christopher Publishing House, 1994; Dave Cheadle, *Victorian Trade Cards: Historical Reference & Value Guide,* Collector Books, 1996; Terri Clemens, *American Family Farm Antiques,* Wallace–Homestead, Krause Publications, 1994; Douglas Congdon–Martin, *America for Sale: A Collector's Guide to Antique Advertising,* Schiffer Publishing, 1991; Sharon and Bob Huxford, *Huxford's Collectible Advertising, Second Edition* (1995), *Third Edition* (1997), Collector Books.

Robert Joy, *The Trade Card in Nineteenth–Century America,* University of Missouri Press, 1987; Ray Klug, *Antique Advertising Encyclopedia, Vol 1* (1978, 1993 value update), *Vol 2* (1985), L–W Book Sales; Dawn E. Reno, *Advertising: Identification and Price Guide,* Avon Books, 1993; Louis Storino, *Chewing Tobacco Tin Tags: 1870–1930,* Schiffer Publishing, 1995; B. J. Summers, *Value Guide to Advertising Memorabilia,* Collector Books, 1994; Jean Williams Turner, *Collectible Aunt Jemima: Handbook and Price Guide,* Schiffer Publishing, 1994.

Periodicals: *Paper and Advertising Collector (P.A.C.),* PO Box 500, Mount Joy, PA 17552; *P.C.M. (Paper Collectors' Marketplace),* PO Box 128, Scandinavia, WI 54977.

Collectors' Clubs: Antique Advertising Assoc of America, PO Box 1121, Morton Grove, IL 60053; Campbell Soup Collectors Club, 414 Country Lane Ct, Wauconda, IL 60084; The Ephemera Society of America, Inc, PO Box 95, Cazenovia, NY 13035; Inner Seal Club (Nabisco), 4585 Saron Drive, Lexington, KY 40515; Porcelain Advertising Collectors Club, PO Box 381, Marshfield Hills, MA 02051; Trade Card Collector's Assoc, 3706 South Acoma Street, Englewood, CO 80110.

Museums: American Advertising Museum, Portland, OR; Museum of Transportation, Brookline, MA; National Museum of American History and Warsaw Collection of Business Americana, Smithsonian Institution, Washington, DC.

Advertising Trade Card, Buffalo Scale Co, "Illustrated History of the Scale Business" **$30**

Advertising Trade Card, Carter's Iron Pills, Liver Pills and Back Ache Plasters, 3 children **45**

Advertising Trade Card, Chadwick's Spool Cotton, boy balancing on spool . . . **30**

Advertising Trade Card, Columbia Bicycles, light orange, black image of cyclists **50**

Advertising Trade Card, Dusky Diamond Soap, 2 men painting **15**

Advertising Trade Card, Eagle Stove Polish, woodcut, black and white **20**

Advertising Trade Card, Estey Organs, factory scene **12**

Advertising Trade Card, Everit's Horse Remedies, horse treatments **65**

Advertising Trade Card, Geo Thompson Ornamental Printing, young boys running print shop, red lettering, gold border **150**

Advertising Trade Card, Hygienic Kalsomine, Uncle Sam **30**

Advertising Trade Card, Lautz Soap, patriotic boy **25**

Advertising Trade Card, Liebig Mfg Co Fertilizers, factory **45**

Advertising Trade Card, Radiant Home Stove, man shielding face from heat . . **50**

Advertising Trade Card, Standard Laundry Soap, black and white **75**

Advertising Trade Card, Standard Sewing Machine, rotary shuttle used as bicycle **12**

Banner, Planters Peanuts, paper, Mr Peanut pushing loaded cart, "Planters Mr Peanut Sale, Stock up now and Save!, Planters taste so–o–o good!," 1950s, 15" h, 36" w **175**

Bill Hook, Breakfast Cheer Coffee, litho celluloid, oval button with product image, 6³/₄" h **85**

Bill Hook, Ceresota Flour, rect, litho cardboard, Ceresota boy, "Prize Bread Flour," 5¹/₂" h **45**

Blotter, H Gamse & Bros, Food Products Labels of Quality, multicolor, Apr 1923 calendar **20**

Blotter, JI Case Threshing Machine Co, Racine, WI, multicolor, c1920 . . . . **25**

Blotter, William H Geer Co, Hudson St, NY, canned good, multicolor, c1900 . **40**

Booklet, Calumet Baking Powder, "Want Book," boy standing atop large baking powder tin, 8³/₄" h **15**

Booklet, Jell-O, Genesee Pure Food Co, Leroy, NY, 14 pp, ©1920 . . . . **20**

Broadside, COD Clothing, dated Nov 1, 1879, 12 x 4¹/₂" **125**

*Left: Activity Book, **The Adventures of Ceresota**, by Marshall Whitlach, color litho cov and illus, 1912, 44 pp, 8 x 6", $50.*

Right: Advertising Trade Card, Buckeye Forge Pumps, 6 x 3¹/₂", $15.

Broadside, Geo W Smith, Dry Goods, Groceries, Provisions, Mattawamkeag, ME, black and white, dry goods store illus **275**

Broadside, Splendid Millinery Goods, clothing adv, dated Sep 27, 1865, 10 x 7" **120**

Broom Holder, Wilbur's Cocoa, diecut litho tin, product tin, multicolor, 6¾" h **225**

Calendar, Collins Baking Co, Buffalo, NY, emb, girl sitting in wicker chair, holding St Bernard puppy, mother dog standing nearby, floral border, small pad at lower right corner, 1911 . . . . **150**

Calendar, Libby, McNeill & Libby Corned Beef, litho, red lettering, smiling girl holding flower, corned beef can beside calendar pad at bottom, green ground, 1905, 11" w, 16½" h **50**

Calendar, Sharples Separator Co, West Chester, PA, Tubular and Jersey Cream Separators, milkmaid holding pail, standing beside separator, cow peering through open window, full pad, 1912, 7" w, 13¾" h **100**

Calendar, Singer Sewing Machines, litho tin holder, red "S" logo with "Singer Sewing Machines" and "For Every Stitching Operation," litho cardboard date cards, 18½" h **365**

Calendar, United States Cream Separators, Vermont Farm Machine Co, Bellows Falls, VT, woman leaning against stone wall, cows in background, inset of cream separator, 1910, 20" w, 30" h **225**

Clock, Calumet Baking Powder, wood case, molded top, glazed front, gold lettering "Time To Buy Calumet Baking Powder 'Best by Test'," shaped and bracketed base, 38" h, 18" w **350**

Clock, Coca–Cola, wood case, cove molded top, glazed front, gold hands and lettering "Coca–Cola In Bottles," shaped and bracketed base, new lettering, 34½" h, 18" w **275**

Clock, Duquesne Pilsener Beer, round, reverse glass face, man holding glass of beer, red, gold, and blue, c1955, 14½" d **50**

Clock, Ever–Ready Safety Razor, emb painted tin, rect case, shaving man image on clock face, gold and black lettering "Eight Day Clock," instructions painted on back, 18" h, 12½" w **850**

Clock, None–Such Mince Meat Pumpkin and Squash, emb paper litho in pie tin, pumpkin image, "Like Mother Used to Make," 9½" h **1,075**

Display, Bickmore's Gall Cure, diecut cardboard, repair to horses's ears, $250. Photo courtesy Collectors Auction Services.

Clock, Jolly Tar, USG Harness Oil, $1,050.

Clock, Oilzum Motor Oil, round, glass front, man's head wearing driving
cap and goggles, orange, black, and white, 14½" d **1,500**

Clock, Red Goose Shoes, illuminated, round, Red Goose image, Telechron,
late 1930s/early 1940s **400**

Clock, Sauer's Flavoring Extracts, wood case, face mkd "New Haven
U.S.A.," reverse painted and lettered door with awards and "Highest
American and European Awards for Sauer's Flavoring Extracts, Best by
Every Test, Purity, Strength," 42¼" h **1,700**

Cookbook, Ceresota Flour, Northwestern Consolidated Milling Co,
Minneapolis, MN, loaf of bread and other baked goods in rect above oval
vignette with Ceresota boy, litho paper covers, 8¾" h **18**

Display, Armour Cloverbloom Butter, diecut litho cardboard, girl in overalls
eating buttered bread and holding tethered calf, "fresh – as all outdoors,"
multicolor, 1930s, 28" w, 40" h **235**

Display, Brookfield Eggs, litho cardboard, standup, bunny wearing clothes
and carrying pkg of eggs, 11" h **200**

Display, Campbell's Soup, diecut cardboard, Campbell Kid, standup **15**

Display, Dazey Butter Churn, diecut litho cardboard, housewife with butter
churn, 27 x 22" **195**

Display, Dr Morse's Indian Root Pills, diecut litho cardboard, Indians scene,
42 x 27" **375**

Display, Duco Paint, DuPont, diecut cardboard, standup, woman painting
dropleaf table, offering paint brush, "You try DUCO — It's so Easy,"
c1930, 38" h, 28" w **200**

Display, Flower Seeds, diecut cardboard standup, slots hold flower and vegetable seed packets, "The Loveliest Garden can be yours easily—eco-
nomically with these Flower Seeds, 10¢, Plan Your Garden Now!," new
old stock, 41" h, 24" w **150**

Display, Mohawk Carpet, Indian boy standing on tree stump beating drum,
"Carpet Craftsmanship from the Looms of Mohawk," automated, c1948,
23" h **285**

Display, Occident Flour, tin, 6 stages of wheat processing, encapsulated
wheat and flour samples, flour bag in upper corners, blue and white let-
tering, c1935, 14" w, 9" h **350**

Display, Peters Cartridge Co, diecut cardboard, standup, hunter with rifle
and dog, large shell with "Shoot PETERS and be Sure," product images
below, 1930s, 28" w, 47" h **600**

Display, Snow King Baking Powder, diecut litho cardboard, Santa in reindeer–drawn sleigh, "Use Snow King Baking Powder, One Trial
Convinces," c1900, 28" w, 17" h **225**

Display, Swing's Coffee, black man seated atop Swing's Coffee box, automated, when activated man pours cup of coffee from white and red
enamel coffeepot into cup, moves lips, raises eyebrows, rolls eyes, and
drinks coffee which disappears into tube in cup and reappears in coffee-
pot, c1925, 29 x 17½ x 15½" **2,250**

Door Bar and Handle, Salada Tea, porcelain, red lettering, white ground,
"Delicious 'Salada' Tea Flavors," 3¼" h, 3½" w **25**

Door Bar and Handle, Sunbeam Bread, adjustable, bread loaf shape handle,
1950s, 15" h, 30" w **275**

Door Push, Ken–L Ration Dog Food, porcelain, dog's head, "Ken–L, Biskit,
Ration, Ken–L Meal," blue ground, 1950s **425**

Door Push, Kool Cigarettes, porcelain, cigarette pack, green and white
ground, "They're So Refreshing!" **60**
Door Push, L & M Cigarettes, porcelain, cigarette pack, blue and white
ground, "Friendly Flavor...your taste comes alive!," 1960s **60**
Door Push, Old Gold Cigarettes, porcelain, dancing cigarette packs, "For a
Treat...Old Gold Cigarettes, Regular and King Size," red ground **125**
Door Push, 7–Up, aluminum, "Come in, 7Up (in button)...likes you," white
ground, 1940s **85**
Door Push, Sunbeam Batter Whipped Bread, enameled steel, bread loaf,
side mounting bars, 1950s, 18" w, 9" h **275**
Fan, hand held, diecut litho cardboard, stick handle, 20 Mule Team Borax,
Borax Bill Jr holding product with mule team in background, reverse has
caricature mule wearing apron and scrubbing laundry, c1900, 8" w, 9" h . .   **275**
Fan, hand held, diecut litho cardboard, stick handle, 20 Mule Team Borax,
little girl carrying doll and product to bathtub, product images on reverse,
c1911, 9" d **150**
Fan Hanger, litho cardboard, double sided, JP Alley's 5¢ Hambone Cigars,
caricature black man flying airplane, 7" d **120**
Fan Hanger, litho cardboard, double sided, Juicy Apple Gum, apple shaped,
12³/₄" h **350**
Fan Hanger, litho cardboard, double sided, Keds Shoes, well–dressed man
wearing Keds, beach and sunbathers in background, "Perfected Rubber
Soled Canvas Shoes," woman's image on reverse, 9¹/₄" h **95**
Marquee, painted wood, "Dr. Lesure's Warranted Veterinary Medicines,"
15³/₄" l **300**
Match Holder, Adriance Farm Machinery, litho tin, rect back panel with corn
binder image, 5" h **475**
Match Holder, Allyn & Blanchard Coffee, diecut litho tin, "Our Coffee and
Spices are of our own importation and are The Best," sepia tones, match
holder is spice tin, 7" h **325**
Match Holder, Born Steel Range, litho tin, rect back panel with stove image,
5" h **415**
Match Holder, Buster Brown Bread, diecut litho tin, Buster Brown, Tige, and
other children at table, 7" h **1,050**
Match Holder, Ceresota Flour, emb diecut litho tin, Ceresota boy atop bar-
rel, orig box with missing lid, 6¹/₂" h **500**

*Left: Fan Hanger,
Salada Tea, double
sided, 7¹/₂ x 11", $8.*

*Right: Match Holder,
Old Judson, JC
Stevens, tin, 5" h,
$120.*

Match Holder, Ceresota Flour, litho tin, rect back panel with Ceresota boy sitting on bench cutting slice from large loaf of bread, 5" h 365

Match Holder, Chef Spices, litho tin, rect back panel with chef holding spoon, 5" h 1,700

Match Holder, Columbia Mill Co, emb diecut litho tin, Columbia image, 6" h 875

Match Holder, De Laval Cream Separators, emb diecut litho tin, replica cream separator, orig box with missing lid, 6¼" h 375

Match Holder, Dutch Boy Paints, emb diecut litho tin, Dutch Boy image, 6½" h 650

Match Holder, Holsum Bread, litho tin, rect back panel with loaf of bread, "The Sanitary Bread, Made Clean — Kept Clean," 5" h 175

Match Holder, Keybrand Shoes, litho tin, rect back panel with shoe image, black, white, and brown, 5" h 200

Match Holder, Kirkman's Borax Soap, diecut litho tin, woman scrubbing wash at washtub, "For Laundry Work, Save the Wrappers for Premiums," 7" h 6,250

Match Holder, Miller Range & Furnace Co, litho tin, figural stove with hinged top burner surface, dated 1888, 5" h 575

Match Holder, Milwaukee Harvesting Machines, litho tin, rect back panel with farmer "holding" match holder depicted as basket, 5½" h 375

Match Holder, Mother's Worm Syrup, diecut litho tin, mother spoon feeding worm syrup to her children, "Good as Honey, Children Eat It on Their Bread," 6¾" h 1,000

Match Holder, New Process Gas Range, litho tin, hanging, stove image, red ground, gold lettering, 3¼" h 110

Match Holder, Reliance Baking Powder, diecut litho tin, woman baking at kitchen table, child watching, sepia tones, match holder is baking powder tin, 5¾" h 465

Match Holder, Rex Flintkote Roofing, litho tin, rect back panel with barn image, 5" h 385

Match Holder, Topsy Hosiery, litho tin, rect back panel with woman at beach wearing bathing costume complete with stockings, 5" h 1,150

Match Holder, Universal Stoves and Ranges, litho tin, rect back panel with globe in wreath, 5" h 265

Match Striker, Bull Dog Cut Plug, diecut litho tin, red bull dog, "Won't Bite," 6¾" h 1,900

Match Striker, JL Clark, litho tin, oval, adv tin pkg with "JL Clark Mfg Co Makers Of Decorated Tin Cans & Boxes," 4¾" h 70

Needle Threader, J & P Coats, litho tin, spool shaped, red and yellow, instructions on reverse, 1½" h 35

Pocket Mirror, Angelus Marshmallows, Chicago, IL, "Mirror Free With Package Angelus Marshmallows Or Mailed For 3–2¢ Stamps, Ask Your Dealer," angel holding horn and pkg, multicolor, oval, 46 x 71mm 30

Pocket Mirror, Cedarburg Milk Co, celluloid, round, red and black, mother, baby, and milk bottle, "Three Klos Friends" 125

Pocket Mirror, Ceresota Flour, "Prize Bread Flour of the World," young boy cutting from loaf of bread, multicolor, round, 53mm 25

Pocket Mirror, Copper–Clad, "The World's Greatest Range Lined With Pure Copper Where Other Ranges Rust Out," blue and orange, oval, 70mm 28

Left: Paperweight, Knox Stove Works, cast iron, "A Whale of a Stove," 3³/₄" l, $45.
Right: Pinback Button, Swift's Premium Hams and Bacon, 1¹/₄" d, $25.

Pocket Mirror, Fleischmann's Yeast, "For Perfect Baking, Makes Good Bread," young lady wearing bonnet, multicolor, round, 55mm **150**

Pocket Mirror, John Deere, "'Ohio' Silo Filler, Stands For Best—See For Yourself," machine, green and yellow, oval **85**

Pocket Mirror, Johnson Hat Co, caricature man in black face, multicolor, round, 55mm **45**

Pocket Mirror, Merode Hand–Tailored Knit Underwear, "Women's, Children's, Men's, Infants'," lady wearing undergarment, sepia tone, rect, 70mm **45**

Pocket Mirror, Morton's, "The Perfect Salt At Last," inverted salt box, white and blue, round, 44mm **45**

Pocket Mirror, "There Is Something To See Along The Frisco Line," train in landscape, multicolor, round, 53mm **90**

Pocket Mirror, Tomson's Borax Soap, celluloid, round, soap box, red lettering, white ground, "Save Wrappers for Premiums" **30**

Postcard, Cherry Smash, black servant serving Cherry Smash to George and Martha Washington at Mount Vernon **100**

Postcard, Crubro Apple Butter, "Our new apple butter package," product image, Cruikshank Bros Co, Pittsburgh **50**

Postcard, Dinah Black, foldout, black mammy wearing red bandanna, white ground, "Let Dinah Black tell you the story," 1930, 3¹/₂" h, 5" w **45**

Postcard, Gold Medal Flour, lighthouse, adv for free cookbook from Washburn–Crosby Co, Minneapolis, c1905 .... **45**

Postcard, Kellogg's Corn Flakes, "Circumstances Alter Faces," happy and sad faces, cereal box, WK Kellogg Co **35**

Postcard, Star Vestibule Storm Front, storm shields for horse–drawn carriages, snowy Christmas scene with horse–drawn carriage **35**

Poster, Aultman & Taylor Farm Machinery, barnyard scene, 36 x 14¹/₂" **350**

Poster, Barker's Liniment, farm animals by river, 30 x 24" **525**

Poster, Bond Bread, roll–down, girl watering Easter lilies, bread loaf, "Easter Greetings, Bond," 1930s–40s, 38" h, 13" w **110**

Poster, Chase & Sanborn's Teas, litho, metal border, 27 x 21" **50**

Poster, Dunlap's Seeds, litho **175**

Poster, Harvesting Machine, US map with starred manufacturing locations, threshers and agriculture implements on border, 58½ x 39½" 350

Poster, Hazlett's Livery, multicolor, metal border, wood frame, 19 x 14" 275

Poster, Hercules Powder Co, outdoor scene with hunter holding puppy, "Next Year, Young Fellow," dog watching, Arthur D Fuller artist, c1930, 12" w, 20" h 125

Poster, International Poultry Food, litho, multicolor, wood frame, 27 x 20" ... 200

Poster, International Stock Food, litho, multicolor, cattle yard, wood frame, 27 x 21" 150

Poster, Ivory Soap, paper with linen backing, "Ivory Soap, It Floats," 17" h, 56½" w 40

Poster, Lakeside Maple Syrup, horse–drawn sleigh passing winter workers tapping maple trees, skater in background, 19½ x 13" 850

Poster, Rice's Seeds, farm girl and man looking at produce, 20 x 28" 1,000

Poster, Runkel Cocoa, couple sampling breakfast cocoa, child holding product, 18 x 24" 700

Poster, Yeast Foam, delivery boy handing woman product, child holding doll in background, metal strip borders, 12 x 17½" 450

Salesman's Sample, boots, leather, 4½" h 100

Salesman's Sample, curtain stretcher, Quaker, 26" l, 17" h 50

Salesman's Sample, fence, Pace Fence Co, chicken wire, cast metal base, 11 x 6 x 1" 75

Salesman's Sample, furnace, gas boiler, cast iron and brass, orig paint, 3 x 10½" 450

Salesman's Sample, gate, wood and metal, 18" l, 10½" h 200

Salesman's Sample, harness, leather, 5 x 6" 225

Salesman's Sample, Hoosier–style cabinet, Cass, oak, 13¾" w, 15½" h 350

Salesman's Sample, loom, wood, "Miniature Loom" paper label, "NRA" (National Recovery Act) ink stamp, 9½" w, 15½" d, 12½" h 25

Salesman's Sample, ox yoke and buggy undercarriage, 18" l 75

Salesman's Sample, pitchfork, True Temper Pitchfork, wood and cast iron, 30" l 350

Salesman's Sample, plow, cast iron, painted, 13" l 125

Salesman's Sample, post hole digger, wood and brass, 3 x 29" 225

Salesman's Sample, stove, Karr, blue enameled steel and nickel plated cast iron, 14 x 21 x 9" 4,500

Salesman's Sample, stove, Quick Meal, cast iron, includes pots and pans, 17 x 26 x 16" 1,250

Salesman's Sample, table, drop leaf, walnut, round leaves, turned legs, 9¼" h 175

Salesman's Sample, thrasher, wood and tin, 19" l, 9" h 115

Salesman's Sample, windmill, Model 12B, Aero Mfg Co, aluminum, 16¾" h .. 150

Salesman's Sample, wringer washer, Gem, cast iron and wood, 16" h 100

Salesman's Sample, wringer washer, Lovell Mfg Co, Erie, PA, 8" h 40

Sign, Aunt Jemima Flour, porcelain, curved corner sign, Aunt Jemima image, 22" h, 18" w 4,500

Sign, Borden's Milk and Cream, enameled steel, double sided flange, white and blue lettering, brown and white ground, Elsie in center, "If It's Borden's, It's Got To Be Good," 20" w, 12" h 475

Sign, Borden's Sun State Dairy, tin, diamond shaped, Elsie logo above red lettering, white ground, yellow border stripe, 1950s, 12" sq 175

Sign, Bull Frog Shoe Polish, litho tin, rect, double sided, seated bullfrog looking sideways at lettering, red moon in background, black ground, "Bull
Frog Shoe Polish, 5¢, Black or Tan," 13" h, 17³/₄" w **4,500**

Sign, Bunny Bread, emb diecut tin, bread loaf shape, 1950s–60s, 28" h,
52" w **300**

Sign, Carnation Milk, tin over cardboard, product image, blue ground,
1950s, 18" h, 12" w **195**

Sign, Coble Milk, emb tin, large milk carton, smaller cartoon carton saying
"Reach For Me!," 1953, 15" h, 24" w **300**

Sign, Collins Axes, emb litho cardboard, ax head and globes, "The Axes of
the World are Collins, 'The Best is the Cheapest'," 20" h **60**

Sign, De Laval Cream Separators, litho tin, center vignette with close–up of
milkmaid and cow, 4 background pictures each with milkmaid, cow, and
cream separator in foreign country setting, ornate gilt frame, 40¹/₂" h,
29¹/₂" w **3,000**

Sign, De Laval Cream Separators, porcelain, double sided flange, rect, cream
separator image, white ground, "Local Agency," 1905–15, 26" h, 18" w . . . **450**

Sign, De Laval Cream Separators, porcelain, rect, navy blue ground, yellow
letters and border, "We Use The De Laval Cream Separator," 1920s,
12" w, 10" h **175**

Sign, Donald Duck Bread, tin, Donald Duck's head and loaf of bread, "Oven
Fresh Flavor," 1940s–50s, 30" h, 39" w **350**

Sign, Donnell's De Luxe Ice Cream, porcelain, double sided, white ground,
dark blue and red lettering, 1920s boy and girl sharing large sundae, "The
Aristocrat of Ice Creams," c1920, 24" w, 16" h **400**

Sign, EC Simmons Fine Fishing Tackle, oilcloth, catfish, sunfish, and brook
trout, green, black, and red on white ground, c1915, 18" h, 36" w **250**

Sign, Harvest Horse Feed, tin, horse head in circle, orange ground, "Lower
Your Feed Cost, Harvest Horse Feed, For Sale By...," 19¹/₂" h, 14" w **275**

Sign, Hire's Root Beer, diecut tin, bottle shaped, multicolor, c1950s, 6" w,
22" h **175**

Sign, Kellogg's Corn Flakes, diecut litho cardboard, standup, farm girls wearing bonnet, ears of corn, bowl of cereal, and cereal box, ©1948, 40" h,
35" w **95**

*Left: Sign, Pflueger Fishing
Tackle, standup, Zane Grey
testimonials on reverse, 1926,
22 x 28", $550.* Photo courtesy
Lang's Sporting Collectables.

*Right: Thermometer,
Indianapolis Indian Gloves,
wood, paint chips and soiling,
10⁵/₈" h, 4" w, $100.* Photo
courtesy Collectors Auction
Services.

Sign, Kellogg's Toasted Corn Flakes, litho sheet steel, double sided flange, bonneted baby peering from hooded carriage at cereal box, 19½" h, 13½" w **3,750**

Sign, Kow Kare, enameled steel, flange, product images, "Sold Here," 12" w, 9" h, 1½" d **200**

Sign, Leaf Chewing Gum, emb tin, product image, yellow ground, "Leaf, The Flavor Lingers Longer," 1940s–50s, new old stock **325**

Sign, Libby's Rolled Ox Tongues, litho paper under glass, girl standing by chair with tin can on seat, 30¾" h **465**

Sign, Life Savers, porcelain, rect, roll of Pep–O–Mint Life Savers, "Real Life Savers, 'Always good taste'," red and white lettering, black ground, 1920s, 60" h, 27" w **2,100**

Sign, Mayo's Plug, porcelain, rect, crowing rooster on tobacco pkgs, "Smoking Cock O–The Walk," 1910s–20s, 13" h, 6½" w **1,000**

Sign, Merita Bread, porcelain, rect, Lone Ranger and Silver above large loaf of bread, 1955, 24" w, 36" h **350**

Sign, Morton's Salt, porcelain, rect, white and red lettering, black ground, red and white border, "We Sell Morton's Salt, Blocks–Barrels–Bags–Packages, The Best Grades for Every Purpose, Osage Flour & Feed Co," 17½" h, 47½" w **235**

Sign, Oh Boy Gum, tin, boy holding sticks of gum while elf whispers in his ear, black ground, "1¢, It's Pure!," 1920s–30s, 15" h, 7" w **325**

Sign, Old Dutch Cleanser, porcelain, rect, product image, "We Sell, Large Sifter Can 10¢," stamped "Ingraham Richardson," 14" w, 20" h **475**

Sign, Oshkosh J&G RR Suits Union Made, reverse painted under glass, rect, oil man image, framed, 18½" h, 48¼" w **4,175**

Sign, Palmolive Soap, tin, man, woman, and bar of soap, yellow ground, red lettering "Palmolive's Beauty Plan brings you a younger–looking skin from head to toe," 1940s, 14" h, 28" w **400**

Sign, Park & Pollard Co Feeds, emb tin, "Lay or Bust," chickens in open meadow, multicolor, framed, 1920–30 . . . . **950**

Sign, Peter Rabbit Safety Pins, paper, rect, upper image of girl and rabbits, lower image of dancing rabbits, framed, 6½" h, 10½" w **300**

Sign, Pippins 5¢ Cigars, emb litho tin, apple image, 21" l **275**

Sign, Purity Pasteurized Ice Cream, porcelain, double sided, calla lily, c1920s, 37" w, 27" h **475**

Sign, Rhinelander Butter, tin over cardboard, product pkgs, dark blue ground, "We Sell A Lot of Rhinelander Butter, Pound & ½ Pound Cartons," new old stock, 9" h, 13" w **140**

Sign, Richardson Root Beer, diecut tin, overflowing barrel, "Rich in Flavor," 20" w, 26" h **125**

Sign, Roth's Hy–Quality Coffee, diecut paper litho on cardboard, hanging, 1–sided, woman with cup of coffee sitting on swing suspended from sign, 36¼" h **1,000**

Sign, Silk Hosiery, figural shapely leg mirror with acid etched lettering, hanging, 13" h **685**

Sign, Simpson Spring Beverages, emb tin, rect, dark green and red ground, dark green and white lettering, "Best of All," lists flavors including "Russet Cider" and "Nerve Tonic," 14" w, 20" h **300**

Sign, Singer Sewing Machines, porcelain, flange, early seamstress logo, white lettering and stars on large red "S," dark green ground, 1920s, 12" w, 19" h **950**

Sign, Sunbeam Bread, enameled, Sunbeam girl, "Reach For Sunbeam Energy–Packed Bread," red ground, 1953, 55" h, 19" w **675**

Sign, Victory Cigars, litho cardboard, rect, hanging, double sided ornate lettering, "Smoke Victory 5¢," 6³/₄" l **45**

Sign, Walk–Over Shoes, litho on sheet steel, double sided flange, well-dressed man and large shoe in oval frame, 19¹/₂" h, 13¹/₂" w **650**

Sign, Waterman's Ideal Fountain Pen, porcelain, rect, black ground, "Selection" above, "Service" below, and "Ideal" superimposed over globe in center, orig wood frame, 20" w, 8" h **275**

Sign, Welch's Grape Juice, tin over cardboard, juice bottle, "Drink A Bunch of Grapes from Welch Juniors, 10¢," purple ground, orig easel and string hanger on back, 1930s, 6" h, 9" w **200**

Sign, Wonder Bread, diecut tin, bread loaf shape, 1950s, 30" h, 42" w **185**

Sign, Wrigley's Gum, tin over cardboard, 4 gum pkgs, black ground, "Wrigley's Delicious Lasting Flavors," 1920s, 7" h, 11" w **250**

Store Card, Laflin & Rand Powder, litho, boy holding rifle and "bagged" quail and grouse, hunting dog in background, "Shot with Laflin & Rand Powder," ©1903 American Litho Co, NY, 8" w, 12" h **200**

Thermometer, Arbuckles' Coffee, litho tin, wood back, rect, red and yellow, product image, 19¹/₄" h **650**

Thermometer, CE Hidlebaugh Saddlery Co, wood, stenciled lettering, 47" h . . **200**

Thermometer, Clark Bar, painted wood, candy bar on clock above "4PM 'Clark Bar o'Clock,' Clark Bar, Join The Millions In This Mid–Afternoon Candy Delight," 19" h **350**

Thermometer, Coca–Cola, bottle shaped, diecut, 1956 . . . . **125**

Thermometer, Coca–Cola, rect, masonite, Coke button above soda bottle, green ground, "Drink Coca–Cola, Thirst knows no season," c1942 . . . . **325**

Thermometer, Dr Pepper, tombstone shaped, red and white ground, red, white, and black lettering, "Hot Or Cold, Enjoy the Friendly 'Pepper–Upper,' Dr Pepper," 1950s, 16" h, 6¹/₂" w **175**

Thermometer, ExLax, The Chocolate Laxative, porcelain, black lettering, 36" h **125**

Thermometer, Folger's Coffee, tin, red and black product image, white ground, 9" d **225**

Thermometer, Hills Bros Coffee, porcelain and wood, trademark man in yellow robe drinking coffee, red ground, white lettering, 20³/₄" h **350**

Thermometer, Joan of Arc Red Kidney Beans, wood, painted and stenciled, white ground, 15" h **50**

Thermometer, Mail Pouch Tobacco, metal, bull's eye and product pkgs, dark blue ground, "Chew Mail Pouch Tobacco, Treat Yourself to the Best," 39" h, 8¹/₂" w **90**

Thermometer, Mission Orange, vertical panel, soda bottle, white ground, 1950s, 17" h, 5" w **150**

Thermometer, Northrup, King & Co, Clover and Alfalfa Seed, steel, black lettering, yellow ground, 27" h **100**

Thermometer, Orange Crush, vertical oval shape, brown soda bottle, "Get the 'Happy Habit,' Krinkly Brown Bottle Protects 'Luscious Orange Flavour'," 1930s–40s, 19" h, 6" w **175**

Thermometer, Pepsi–Cola, vertical rect, vintage soda bottle, blue ground, white rim, "Bigger, Better," late 1930s/early 1940s, 16" h, 6½" w **400**
Thermometer, Rock Island Plow Co, wood, imp letters, "Better Farm Implements," lacquered finish, 21" h **100**
Thermometer, Sauer's Vanilla, painted wood, product box replica, 8" h **300**
Thermometer, Singer Sewing Machines, vertical rect, porcelain, large "S" and woman sewing logo at top, sewing machine below, white ground, convex surface, porcelain bulb cover, 35" h, 7" w **2,500**
Tip Tray, litho tin, Cottolene, woman and young girl picking cotton, "The source of Cottolene, Best for Shortening — Best for Frying," 4¼" d **100**
Tip Tray, litho tin, Fairy Soap, little girl sitting atop bar of soap, 4¼" d **120**
Tip Tray, litho tin, Pippins 5¢ Cigar, apple shaped, 5½" l **230**
Tray, Hick's Capudine Liquid, litho tin, 2 angels holding product box, "It's Liquid—Prompt Results, 10, 25 and 50 cts A Bottle," 10" d **325**
Tray, Jersey–Creme, litho tin, woman with chin resting on hands, drink on table in front of her, "The Perfect Drink, At Founts, In Bottles," 12" d **325**

CATALOGS

Catalogs played an important role in country living. First, they broadened the farmer's knowledge of what was available beyond his local community. Second, they provided a means of keeping abreast of changing technology. Finally, they decreased the sense of isolation that is part of farming.

Catalogs serve as excellent research sources. The complete manufacturing line of a given item is often described and pictured in a wide variety of styles, colors, etc. Catalogs provide an excellent method to date objects.

Many old catalogs are reprinted for use by collectors as an aid to identification of items within their collecting interest, e.g., reprints of Heisey and Hubley catalogs. The photocopy machine also contributes to the distribution of information among friends.

References: Ron Barlow and Ray Reynolds, *The Insider's Guide to Old Books, Magazines, Newspapers, Trade Catalogs,* Windmill Publishing, 1995; Terri Clemens, *American Family Farm Antiques,* Wallace–Homestead, Krause Publications, 1994; Norman E. Martinus and Harry L. Rinker, *Warman's Paper,* Wallace–Homestead, Krause Publications, 1994.

Albany Foundry Co, Albany, NY, 1926, undercoated gray iron castings, door knockers, candlesticks, lamp bases, bookends, decorative door stops, candle sconces, andirons, etc, 20 pp, 6¾ x 9" **$75**
American Seeding Machine Co, Richmond, IN, c1924, corn planters, drills, fertilizer disc planters, 1 row corn drills, fertilizer hoes and drills, etc, 16 pp, 7¾ x 9¾" **25**
Behr–Manning Corporation, Troy, NY, 1934, "How To Sharpen," for farmer, mechanic, handyman, and student, Norton Pike products, bench and India stones, India files, gouge slip, auger bit stone, stroppers, scythe stones, grinders, etc, illus, 48 pp, 3¼ x 5¾" **18**
Butler Brothers, New York, NY, 1932, "Our Drummer," August home goods, school goods, lighting fixtures, store needs, beds and bedding, furniture, plumbing accessories, auto supplies, hardware, tools, misc kitchen needs, wash day items, enamel ware, kitchen wares, etc, 196 pp, 9¼ x 13¼" **35**

Co–Operative Foundry Co, Rochester, NY, c1920, enameled Red Cross combination ranges, Red Cross Welcome with high shelf, with high closet, with elevated baking and broiling ovens, with gas water heater attachment, Red Cross Popular with high closet, with high shelf, etc, 16 pp, 4¹/₂ x 6³/₄" **15**

Cray Brothers, Cleveland, OH, 1899, carriage and wagon materials, forges, bellows, blacksmith tools, horse shoes, nails, springs, bolts and nuts, carriage steps, fifth wheels, leather dashes, carriage lamps, buggy tops, etc, 104 pp, 5¹/₂ x 8¹/₂" **65**

CR Hood Studio, Boston, MA, 1928, illus brochures laid–in, Early American reproductions of chairs, tables, dressers, chiffrobes, chests, beds, dining room, hall, and living room furniture, 42 illus, 12 pp, 6 x 9" **20**

Dorries Saddlery Co, Inc, no date, harness and strap work, collars, team bridles, cheeked blinds, throat latches, buggy overchokes, halters, whips, saddles, etc, 48 pp, 9 x 12" **45**

Everett & Small, Boston, MA, c1895, garden seed drill, Matthew's Improved drill and cultivator, Eclipse horse hoe, wheel hob, hand cultivator, seed drill, and cultivator, 12 pp, 3¹/₄ x 5³/₄" **18**

Gilson Manufacturing Co, Port Washington, WI, 1926, drills and attachments for garden tractors laid–in, Bolens Hi-Boy tractors, models 24–30, 30–36, and 30–43 with pictures of tractors, light horse type tools, seeder equip, wheel hoe tools, etc, 12 pp, 6 x 9" **32**

Hagerstrom Metalcraft, Wheeling, IL, c1935, Towncrier line for use on weather vanes or house signs, 18 illus, 6 pp, 5¹/₂ x 8¹/₄" **18**

Household Patent Co, Norristown, PA, 1930, decorative signs, boot scrapers, weather vanes, etc, 8 pp, 6 x 9" **24**

Howe Scale Co, St Louis, MO, c1899, No. 35, agate scales, Vermont counter, Union or Family, grocer, Ball scale for candy, Troemner Agate package, Chatillon candy, single dial computing, Pennsylvania automatic computing, etc, 47 illus, 40 pp, 4¹/₄ x 7¹/₂" **100**

Left: DM Ferry & Co Seed Annual, color plates, 1882, 168 pp, 5³/₄ x 8³/₄", $40.

Center: The Larkin Plan, No. 79, Spring and Summer 1918, 188 pp, 8 x 11", $45.

Right: Lincoln Chair and Novelty Co, 1932–33, sepia photo illus, 32 pp, 9 x 12", $45.

Huntley, Cranson & Hammon, Silver Creek, NY, 1889, Cranson and Monitor grain and corn cleaning and buckwheat machinery scouring, polishing, and separating machines with magnetic attachment, corn shellers, corn scouring, etc, 48 pp, 6 x 9"   38

International Harvester, Chicago, IL, 1920, Primrose cream separators with color picture, cutaway view pointing out various parts, cuts of parts, etc, 24 pp, 38³/₄ x 11³/₄"   24

JS & HC Starr, Decatur, IL, c1900, 15th year, price list laid–in, vehicles for wholesale dealers, cut under runabout auto seat, buggy with bike axles, open buggy, stick, or panel seat, bike wagons, surreys, farmer's spring wagon, pony wagons and carts, etc, 42 pp, 5¹/₂ x 8¹/₂"   75

Mayer & Grosh Cutlery Co, Toledo, OH, c1900, price list No. 18, hand forged, razor steel pocket cutlery, razors, shears, pruning shears, scissors, clippers, fishing tackle, chains, locks, whistles, tools, butcher knives, axes, hatchets, etc, 80 pp, 5³/₄ x 8³/₄"   45

Milk Pan Co, New York, NY, 1877, Monitor porcelain lined milk pan mfg by New York State Monitor Milk Pan Co, letter to dairymen, testimonials, illus, 8 pp, 3³/₄ x 6", 6 x 14³/₄" sheet folded as issued   10

Nash & Bro, Millington, NJ, 1884, ACME pulverizing harrow, clod crusher and leveler, Model #6 and #7 double gangs for 2 horses, Model #8 double gang for 4 horses, Model #9 double gang for 6 horses, parts, testimonials, etc, 48 pp, 5 x 9"   50

National Band & Tag Co, Newport, KY, 1932, No. 32R, envelope of 5 leg bands laid–in plus pamphlets, poultry, game bird, pigeon leg, and wing bands, master seal, spiral, aluminum leg bands, adjustable bands, cinch and sure cinch bands, numbering machines, etc, 33 pp, 5¹/₂ x 8¹/₂"   20

National Miller, Chicago, IL, 1927, hard cover completely indexed Consolidated Grain Milling catalogs, equipment, supplies, construction for flour, feed, and cereal mills, flour warehouses, and grain elevators, illus adv for each company, 288 pp, 8¹/₂ x 11¹/₂"   24

Naylon–Pierson–Hough Co, Detroit, MI, c1922, No. 12, Peer–Ho horse supplies, harnesses for single or team, harness blinds, bridle fronts, straps, collars, traces, saddles, etc, 144 pp, 8¹/₂ x 10³/₄"   38

New Jersey Fence Co, Burlington, NJ, 1926, HR Lindabury & Sons Owners & Mfgrs of interwoven snow fences, picket and wire fencing, lawn and farm fence, sun screens for nurseries and corn cribs, illus of hurdle, snow, lawn and farm, colonial bungalow fences, etc, and gates, 14 pp, 6¹/₄ x 9" . .   35

Oakes Manufacturing, Tipton, IN, 1932, No. 40, poultry equip, flock feeders, feeder troughs, grit and shell boxes, mash hoppers, chick feeders, waterers, warm thermo fountains, incubators and brooders, brooder stoves, brood coops, tanks, etc, 68 pp, 8 x 10"   18

Peninsular Stove Co, Chicago, IL, early 1900, "Model Kitchens," 21 cuts of stoves, some in kitchen environments, steel ranges for wood or coal, Electro Peninsular steel ranges, Modern and Advance steel ranges, 16 pp, 4¹/₂ x 6"   35

Putnam Nail Co, Boston, MA, 1891, circular of Putnam hot forged hammer pointed government standard horseshoe nail with illus of 22 nails, 7 defective nails from horses feet, and 2 cuts of horses feet, 8 pp, 3¹/₄ x 5³/₄", 5³/₄ x 12³/₄" sheet folded as issued   25

Rome Sporting Goods Mfg, Rome, NY, c1929, snowshoe sandals, ski bindings, axe and knife sheaths, cartridge carrier, carry straps, live decoy duck collars, leather rod belts, camp packs, gun and rifle covers, holsters, clothing, archery goods, etc, 30 pp, 5³/₄ x 8³/₄" **30**

Royal Mfg Co, Toledo, OH, 1929, No. 7, poultry and hatchery supplies, oil and coal brooders and stoves, chick hoppers, troughs, fountains, buttermilk feeders, electric fountains and heaters, trap nests and fronts, brooder houses, storage brooders, etc, 48 pp, 6¹/₄ x 9" **12**

Sears, Roebuck & Co, Chicago, IL, 1915, Jan and Feb, 7th annual sale of white goods, linens, curtains, suiting, stoves, bedding, pianos, kitchen cabinets, floor coverings, farm tools and implements, window shades, work clothes, women's clothes, shoes, etc, 150 pp, 8¹/₂ x 11" **55**

Selby, Starr & Co, Peoria, IL, 1889, for sale by Rouse, Hazard & Co, Peoria, Perfection weigher used by farmers for weighing and disposing of grain from threshing machines, 5 illus, comments, testimonials, etc, 16 pp, 5¹/₂ x 7¹/₂" **40**

Singer Manufacturing Co, New York, NY, c1870, pictures 9 different Singer sewing machines, 16 pp, 3¹/₄ x 5¹/₂", 11 x 12¹/₂" sheet folded as issued **28**

Todhunter, New York, NY, c1929, weather vanes, 2 pp, 8¹/₂ x 11" **20**

Wm Henry Maule, Philadelphia, PA, 1888, Maule's Catalogue of roses, flowering plants, bulbs, etc with large cuts of plants, flowers, hybrid roses, bulbs, misc collections, small fruits and berries, hardy vines and creepers, ornamental grasses, basket plants, etc, 16 pp, 8 x 10³/₄" **30**

FIXTURES

When a building was built specifically as a country store building, it was customary to build in shelving, cabinets, and counters. Much of the interior architecture was utilitarian, not ornately decorative or elaborately trimmed. A surprising number of these buildings survive. Attempting to remove and relocate these fixtures poses a major problem.

The key merchandising technique utilized by the country store was open storage. Glass cases, visible from front, top, and sides and with a back featuring a stepped shelf interior, were common. The main counter was the exception, usually containing a plank board top and solid side with shelves or bins accessible only from the back.

The main counter usually contained several small and medium size, special purpose glass cabinets. The three most prevalent uses were candy, cheese, and notions. In addition, companies, especially thread companies, provided the country store merchant with cabinets designed to store, promote, and sell their product. Many of these featured brightly lithographed tin fronts.

In addition to the fixed pieces, the country store was home to a host of other point–of–purchase display units, ranging from the cracker barrel to the broom rack. Large floor bins held coffee, flour, and grains. Many of these contained stenciled advertisements.

The country store counter top was home to a number of items that supplemented the counters and larger display units. Attractive lithograph tin bins housed products ranging from coffee and tea to spices and tobacco. The cast iron decorative elements on cash registers turned them into stylish works of art. Coffee grinders, glass jars, paper dispensers, and string holders are just a few of the additional items that can be found.

The Country store collector competes with the advertising tin collector and specialized theme collector for much of this material. Since the vast majority was mass produced and used in a variety of settings other than the country store, Country store collectors place a premium on pieces with a country store provenance.

The universal country store look is eclectic. Occasionally a merchant remodeling his store would install a matched set of counters, cabinets, and shelves. These matched sets bring a handsome premium when sold. However, carefully check the provenance of any matched set offered. The same fixtures would be used in a jewelry or small department store. Country store collectors prefer a country store provenance.

Keep your eyes open for photographs of country store interiors. They are important research sources for collectors and museums. Value ranges from $5 to $25. Add 10–25% if the store and town are identified and the photograph dated.

References: Henry Bartsch and Larry Sanchez, *Antique Cash Registers, 1880–1920: The Yellow Book,* published by authors, 1987; Steve Batson, *Country Store Counter Jars and Tins,* Schiffer Publishing, 1997; Richard Crandall and Sam Robins, *The Incorruptible Cashier, Volume I: The Formation of an Industry, 1876–1890* (1988) and *Volume II: The Brass Era, 1888–1915* (1991), Vestal Press; Joseph Edward MacMillan, *The MacMillan Index of Antique Coffee Mills,* Cherokee Publishing, 1995.

Collectors' Club: Assoc of Coffee Mill Enthusiasts, 5941 Wilkerson Road, Rex, GA 30273.

Museums: Arbuckles' Coffee Museum, Cedar Rapids, IA; John Conti Coffee Museum, Louisville, KY.

Apothecary Chest, 9 drawers, pine, applied lid and base moldings, dovetailed drawers with turned pulls, turned feet, some repairs to drawers, 20³/₄" w, 23³/₄" h **$1,150**
Apothecary Chest, 14 drawers, pine, dovetailed case and drawers, 3 graduated rows of 4 small drawers over 2 long graduated drawers, some drawers with dividers, turned wood knobs, brown and white paint over orig green, 37¹/₄" w, 13" d, 31" h **1,650**
Apothecary Chest, 24 drawers, refinished pine and poplar, wire nail construction, wood pulls, backboards replaced, early 20th C, 29" w, 32" h **550**
Apothecary Chest, 41 drawers, Shaker type, blue over red paint, dovetailed case and drawers, angled dividers in drawers, graduated drawer construction with 11 over 9 over 8 over 7 over 6 drawers, small metal ring pulls, 90" w, 11" d, 41¹/₄" h **5,750**
Bag Holder, red paint, black stenciled dec, cast iron string holder on top, 20¹/₄" h **785**
Bag Holder, Snow King Baking Powder, countertop, bag racks flanked by diecut tin side panels depicting baking powder tins, 16¹/₂" h **1,500**
Bag Holder, Tulip Soap adv, 3–panel tin sign adv "C.L. Jones & Co. Tulip Soap For Sale Here" resting on cast iron base with wire rods for holding bags and cast iron cup string holder in center, hanging chain, 15" h **2,300**
Barrel, wood hinged top with glass panel, grapevine band around body, 1 side panel cracked, 28³/₄" h **175**
Bin, Blanke's Coffee, litho and painted tin, woman on horse image, "Always Uniform, Always The Best," replaced lid, 24³/₄" h **650**
Bin, Lion Coffee, stained wood, litho labels, recessed panel sides, lion–drawn chariot on lift lid, lion's head on front panel, 32¹/₄" h **500**

Bin, WF McLaughlin & Co, tin, 3 compartments, "'Blended for Flavor' Coffees, Kept fresh by McLaughlin, Coffee Service," 26½" h **285**

Bin, White Oak Coffee, tin, "Imported for Oakford & Fahnestock," 17½" h, 18" w, 14" d **115**

Cabinet, AC Spark Plugs, oak frame, single shelf, worn white label "AC the Standard Spark Plug of America," 34¾" h **325**

Cabinet, AW Co Braid, wood, tambour front door retracts into case, stenciled label on door, 12½" h **60**

Cabinet, Cattarausus Cutlery Co, square wood frame, shaped crests with stenciled labels, glass side panels, revolving interior with 3 tiers and hooks to hang scissors, 30" h **1,000**

Cabinet, Clark's O N T Spool Cotton, walnut, 2 long drawers with reverse painted glass panel drawer fronts, 22" w, 7½" h **450**

Cabinet, Clark's O N T Spool Cotton, wood, 5 long drawers over 2 short drawers, ruby glass drawer front panels, brass dec knobs, 29¼" l **2,300**

Cabinet, Colgan's Gum, wood, glass front with acid etched lettering, brass mfg tag at bottom, 17½" h **1,650**

Cabinet, Daggett & Ramsdell's Perfect Cold Cream, litho tin, countertop display, long–haired woman gazing at hourglass, product pkg on right, "The Kind That Keeps," 10½" h **1,425**

Cabinet, Diamond Dyes, wood, emb multicolor litho tin door panel with children decorating Maypole, "It's Easy To Dye With Diamond Dyes," 29½" h **2,975**

Cabinet, Diamond Dyes, wood, emb multicolor litho tin door panel with children playing on lawn, steps and mansion in background, "The Standard Package Dyes of the World," 24¼" h **1,100**

Cabinet, Diamond Dyes, wood, emb multicolor litho tin door panel with children playing with hot air balloon, "The Standard Package Dyes of the World," labeled cubicles inside, 24¼" h **1,275**

Cabinet, Christie's Biscuits, ash, 16 compartments each with glass pane and label, c1900, 54" h, 47" w, 12½" d, $1,250.

*Cabinet, Dexter Fine Yarn, oak,
4 drawers, 18³/₄" h, 17¹/₈" w, 16" d,
$650.*

Cabinet, Diamond Dyes, wood, emb multicolor litho tin door panel with
fairy surrounded by vignettes of people engaged in various activities,
cherubs at top center, image by Wells and Hope Co, 30¹/₂" h 2,525
Cabinet, Diamond Dyes, wood, emb multicolor litho tin door panel with little girl within diamond frame surrounded by flowers, feathers, and bird's
nest, "The Diamond Dyes for Domestic and Fancy Dyeing," 20" h 1,425
Cabinet, Diamond Dyes, wood, emb multicolor litho tin door panel with
woman dyeing clothing, "It's Easy to Dye with Diamond Dyes," 29¹/₂" h . . .2,650
Cabinet, Dispensing Department, carved cherry wood, center section with
broken arch pediment, urn finial, molded cornice, reverse painted under
glass label, mirror panel, flanked by wood shelving units with glass fronts
on either side, 70" l 2,750
Cabinet, Dr Daniel's Veterinary Medicines, oak, emb multicolor litho tin
door panel with bust of Dr Daniel's above product pkgs and list of prices,
26³/₄" h 2,875
Cabinet, Dr Lesure's Famous Remedies, wood, emb multicolor litho tin door
panel with horse head, 26³/₄" h 4,500
Cabinet, Dy–O–La Dyes, wood case, 2–sided, tin panels front and back with
"Dy–O–La Dyes, One Dye For All Goods," complete with dyes in inside
compartments, 17¹/₄" h, 13" w, 8" d 145
Cabinet, Eureka Spool Silk, carved and chip carved wood frame, gallery top,
pullout spool shelves, drawer in base, 37" h 2,750
Cabinet, German Household Dyes, wood, paper litho label with fox head in
starburst on door front, 3 interior shelves, 23³/₄" h 450
Cabinet, Humphreys' Specifics, wood, corner cabinet, emb multicolor litho
tin door panel with vignette of nude and lion, "The Mild Power Cures,
Homeopathic," 27³/₄" h 2,325
Cabinet, John J Clark's Spool Cotton, oak, 2 drawers, pop–up lid, decal
labels on drawer fronts, 12" h, 20" w, 16" d 700
Cabinet, May's Seeds, wood, revolving, 3 sides with open columns to display seed packets, 1 side opens to reveal shelves, decals on all 4 corners,
complete with seed packets, 23" h 2,000
Cabinet, P Lorillard & Co Tobacco, wood, spindled gallery top with gingerbread tablet, 2 glass doors with acid etched labels, stenciled labels, two
drawers below, brass fixtures, 43" h 6,500

Left: Cash Register, National, model #323, replaced face plate and top plate, $750.

Right: Cigar Cutter, Don Equestro Havana Cigars, cast metal, oval mirror, 8½" h, 8" w, $135.

Cabinet, Pratts Veterinary Remedies, wood case, stenciled label "Pratt Food Co., Philadelphia, PA," tin door panel with adv and product pkgs, 33" h, 16½" w 465

Cabinet, Putnam Fadeless Dyes, wood, lift lid with litho vignette of General Putnam on horseback being pursued by Redcoats, litho paper label under lid, with dye envelopes, 20" l 375

Cash Register, National, brass, marble shelf, emb front lift top panel, orig "Gilbertson & Son" marquee, 23" w, 19½" d, 16" h 225

Cash Register, National, candy store model, brass, marble, glass and wood, 20½" h 1,425

Cash Register, National, nickel finish, emb case, "The Amount of your Purchase" marquee, restored, c1893, 18" h, 8½" w, 15" d 1,000

Cash Register, National, No. 317, brass, "Amount Purchased" marquee, 21" h, 10" w, 16" d 500

Cigar Cutter, Silas Pierce & Co's Nine Cigar, blue glass globe and lighter font above circular cast iron base, key wound cutter, match striker on base 650

Cigar Cutter, Sir Roger de Coverley Cigar, key wound, cast iron, coal oil lighter font and wick holders attached to ornate cutter, paper label under glass plate, 9½" h, 5" w, 12" d 275

Coffee Grinder, Enterprise, painted and stenciled cast iron, 12" h 745

Coffee Grinder, Enterprise, painted cast iron, emb lettering, red ground, stenciled and pinstriped, 68" h 4,175

Coffee Grinder, Golden Rule, wall mounted, painted and emb cast iron, wood, and glass, 16½" h 465

Coffee Grinder, Hoffmann's Old Time Roasted Coffee, cast iron and wood, crank handle, litho tin front plate with old woman holding cup, 13½" h ... 1,325

Coffee Grinder, Lane Brothers, No. 15, emb lid, decals on sides and tin box, 29½" h, 19½" d wheel 2,875

Coffee Grinder, National Specialty Mfg Co, Philadelphia, PA, painted green, gilt details, wood base with drawer, 13" h 875

Cooler, Coca–Cola, Westinghouse style, metal, red, lift lid, 1930s, 26" w, 34" h 775

Cooler, Ward's Orange–Crush Filling Station, wood, zinc lining, stenciled label, 1910s–20s, 34" l, 19" d, 33" h 375

Cupboard, walnut and cherry, old mustard yellow paint, paneled back with scalloped brackets, 2 drawers above 2 pairs of raised panel cupboard doors, base molding, drawers rebuilt, some edge damage and age cracks, 86" w, 15" d, 56½" h **2,100**

Dispenser, Cherry Smash Fountain Syrup, clear glass funnel section on white milk glass base with red lettering "Drink Cherry Smash," complete with 1 gal clear glass jug with inverted paper label, 19" h . . . . ; **475**

Dispenser, Coffee Beans, wall mount, half round cylinder, brass case, glass window, measuring spout, 41" l **200**

Dispenser, Green River, trophy shape, clear glass body, metal lid, handles, and pedestal base, 15" h **200**

Dispenser, Liberty Root Beer, oak barrel, orig decals, metal spigot, 1920s, 24" h **350**

Dispenser, Maxwell House Ice Tea, ceramic, barrel shape, emb lettering, 12½" h **350**

Dispenser, Middleby Root Beer, stein shape, amber glass, Bakelite base, 16" h **275**

Dispenser, Mission Orange, emb amber glass barrel, flaring pedestal base, orig decals, 14" h **225**

Dispenser, Monarch Pickles, sheet metal, litho lion logo, 4 removable ceramic containers with octagonal glass lids, 43" l **825**

Dispenser, Richardson's Liberty Root Beer, ceramic, barrel on tree stump **500**

Dispenser, Yeast Foam, litho tin, hanging, product pkgs design on inside with 5 litho cardboard boxes, 27¾" h **375**

Display Case, Bachrach Collar Buttons, brass frame, glass panels, dome top pivots back to reveal fitted interior compartments for collar buttons, orig tiger striping on brass, metal tag in back "Pat'd July 12, 1910 Sampson Bachrach," 9½" h, 14" d **2,000**

Display Case, Black Diamond Musical Instrument Strings, tin, glass front, product pkgs and "Black Diamond, The World's Best Strings for all Musical Instruments," 20" h, 19½" w, 10" d **115**

Display Case, Eveready Flashlight Batteries and Mazda Lamps, countertop, tin, glass top, hand loading vintage flashlight on front, light bulb and batteries pictured on sides, 11½" h **235**

Display Case, Ever–Ready Shaving Brushes, countertop, tin, depicts oversized shaving brush at left and trademark bald man shaving lathered face on right, brushes displayed behind window, 12" h, 15" w **1,100**

Display Case, FJ Robert's Razor Cutlery, countertop, curved front glass with acid etched label and "Best in the World," metal label "Farley & Hoffman of New York," 10½" h, 22" w, 16" d **1,600**

Display Case, King Collar Buttons, oak, painted label on glass front, 8¾" h, 9¾" w **125**

Display Case, Life Savers, tin, holds 4 flavors, Life Saver candies and flavors on marquee, 9½" h, 12½" w, 9" d **900**

Display Case, Mapacuba Cigars, countertop, wood grained tin humidor, marquee top, slanted glass lid, 16½" h, 22" d **285**

Display Case, Mother's Bread, oak frame, glass panels, gallery top, acid etched labels on front panels "For Goodness Sake Eat Mother's Bread," rear opening, 39" h, 50½" w, 27" d **575**

Display, Rice's Seeds, wood and metal, folding, 36 seed slots, tin sign on front, paint loss and fading to sign, c1909, $325. Photo courtesy Collectors Auction Services.

Display Case, Munyon's Homoeopathic [sic] Home Remedies, tin, slant top, 3 drawers, Munyon's image on lid declares "I would rather preserve the health of the nation than be its ruler," 12" h, 15" w, 13½" d **1,000**

Display Case, Primley's Chewing Gum, oak frame, curved glass front with acid etched "J. P. Primley's California, Fruit and Pepsin Chewing Gum," glass quarter round side panels, int mirrored back, 18¼" l **575**

Display Case, Shredded Wheat, clear glass rect cover with emb "Shredded Wheat" on wood base, shredded wheat inside, 11¾" h **3,750**

Display Case, Slidewell Collars, oak frame, glass side panels and top, decal labels, with collars, 25¼" h **2,750**

Display Case, Totem Cigars, countertop, tin, holds box of Waitt & Bond's Totem 5¢ Cigars, lift–up glass door, mfg by HD Beach Co, 14¾" h **725**

Display Case, Ward's Cake, tin frame, tin and glass panels, tin panels with images of pound cake, 5 children in vintage dress around table eating Ward's cake, and little girl offering slice of cake to 3 other children, ©1920 HD Beach Co, 20¼" h, 17" w, 13" d **2,600**

Display Rack, Beech–Nut Chewing Gum, countertop, diecut tin, 4 shelves, flip–up marquee, 15" h, 6½" w, 6¾" d **775**

Display Rack, collars, countertop, pair of plaster heads on turned wood pedestal stands modeling miniature collars, 14" h **1,750**

Display Rack, Heinz Strained Foods, wire rack, tin marquee with baby image and "Babies Need Heinz Strained Foods," 14" h, 19" w **225**

Display Rack, Kabo Bust Perfector, countertop, torso models lady's under-garment, turned wood pedestal base, 28" h **575**

Display Rack, Lion Collars, countertop, wood rack holds 6 collars, 29" h **225**

Display Rack, postcards, wood, revolving, 12" h **35**

Fire Extinguisher, Manville, tubular, litho tin, red, black, and gold, 22" h **175**

Grabber, Babbit's Soap, wood handle with engraved logo, steel handle and grabber, 50" l **75**

Lamp, hanging, Bradley & Hubbard, brass, painted tin shade, glass chimney, emb font, 28½" h **385**

Mannequin, Stockman, Paris, child size **375**

Mirror, countertop model, brass, swiveling oval mirror plate with beveled edge and reverse under glass label "Henderson Corsets, Favorites of the Fair Sex," pedestal base, 24½" h **635**

Peanut Warmer, Uncle Sam Peanuts, tin, glass front panel, stenciled labels, dated 1885, 21½" h **750**

Postmaster's Desk, Moore's patent, unsgd, walnut, poplar secondary wood, paneled construction, spindled gallery top, 2 hinged sections roll open to reveal fitted interior with pullout writing surface, pigeon holes, drawers, cardboard pullout files, and "Letter" slot with interior compartment with door, 3 drawers over writing shelf replaced, gallery has some edge damage, 42" w, 27¼" d closed size, 61¾" h **5,000**

Scale, Central Scientific Co, analytical balance scale, mahogany case, 17½" h **180**

Scale, Jacobs, Brooklyn, NY, hardware scale, 8" dial, 20 lbs, scoop type weighing pan, suspension chains **50**

Scale, National Store Specialty Co, candy scale, 4 lb, nickel plated cast iron, ftd base, 14" h **275**

Scale, Purina, red, red and white checkered top, blue and cream bottom, metal pan, "Purina Feed Saver and Cow Culler" adv **100**

Scale, Royal Crown Cola, platform scale, figural soda bottle, red and yellow label, drop coins in yellow bottle cap, 1950s, 45½" h **2,250**

Left: Display Case, Boye Needle Co Rotary Needle Case, Chicago, holds tubes of needles and shuttles, metal, last patent date July 9, 1907, 16" d, $75.

Right: Scale, metal, "Patented Oct 29th 1912," 8½" h, 6½" w, $20. Photo courtesy Collectors Auction Services.

Scale, Watling Fortune Scale, Watling Scale Co, Chicago, IL, platform scale, porcelain, more than 2,000 different response cards with fortunes, dreams, and quiz questions, c1935, 66" h **235**

Showcase, boots, nickel over wood frame, top with 2 shelves and glass front panel, bottom section with curved glass front, 33½" h **850**

Showcase, floor model, wood frame, beveled glass top, glass sides and front, sliding glass doors in back, 60" l **225**

String Holder, Es–Ki–Mo Rubbers, double sided litho sheet steel sign with center cutout to hold spool of string, rubber boot hanger, "Ask For Es–Ki–Mo Rubbers, Winch Brothers Company Distrubuters [sic]," 19¾" h, 17¼" w **4,500**

String Holder, J & P Combs, glazed pottery, circular dish shape with hole in side for string, 5" h **185**

String Holder, Mail Pouch Tobacco, 2–sided hanging tin sign, spool of string mounts on top, mail pouch slides up side of sign when string is pulled, HD Beach Co litho, patent date Mar 8, 1908, 19½" h, 15" w **2,750**

String Holder, Post Toasties, tin, 11½" d **725**

String Holder, Pretzel Tobacco, cutout wood, stenciled lettering, shelf at top holds ball of string, 45¼" h **385**

String Holder, Red Goose Shoes, painted cast iron, figural red goose, yellow lettering, green base, 14½" l **475**

String Holder, Walker's King of Soaps, cast iron, countertop, beehive shape, 4½" h **250**

Tape Dispenser, litho tin, donut shaped, Christmas motif with holly branches and "Scotch Cellulose Tape, Requires No Moistening, Christmas Utility Roll," 2¼" h **150**

Telephone, Automatic Electric Company Pay Phone, candlestick phone type receiver, speaker horn, cylinder dial, 18" h **285**

Tobacco Cutter, Enterprise, emb cast iron, stenciled, countertop model, 17" l **50**

Tobacco Plug Maker, wood frame box and mallet, 18¼" h **110**

Vending Machine, Caille Gumball Vendor, ornate emb cast iron case, "1¢ Ball–Gum 1¢, Your Fortune in Gum," 18" h **750**

Vending Machine, Cent–A–Smoke, Marshall Supply Co, speckled paint finish, c1930, 9" h **325**

Vending Machine, Knapsack Matches, United Machine Supply Co, octagonal, clockwork mechanism, front glass panel instructs customer to "Drop One Cent In Slot," label painted on 7 sides, repainted, c1902, 11" h **2,750**

Vending Machine, Parker Pencil Co, aluminum case, "Our Library Booster Pencils" emb on front, "Patd. March 3, 1927," repainted, 11" h **1,500**

Vending Machine, Ramado Cigarettes, National Cigarette Co, glass dome, orig paint and decals, patented Oct 26, 1909, 12" h **1,375**

Vending Machine, Silver King Hot Nut, aluminum, ruby hobnail glass dome flashes on top, repainted base, c1947, 15½" h **250**

Vending Machine, The Honest Clerk Cigars, Jackson Supply Co, painted cast iron, sides emb with filigree and name, c1905, 14" h **3,300**

Vending Machine, Wilbur's Chocolate, National Vending Co, glass dome, metal base, single column, decal label, 1904, 14½" h **5,225**

Vending Machine, Zeno Chewing Gum, porcelain, black lettering, yellow ground, clockwork mechanism dispenses stick gum, last patent date May 5, 1908, 17" h **500**

PACKAGING

Factory processed food revolutionized life in the second half of the nineteenth century. Although it would be several decades before the majority of the food that constituted an American's daily diet would be "store bought" and not "fresh," factory processed food was eagerly embraced by most Americans.

The number of factory processed food products was limited initially. Manufacturers quickly realized that packaging was the key to sales and the development of brand loyalty. The evolution of processed food also corresponded to the golden age of American lithography. The country store's shelves were lined with brightly colored lithographed paper and tin packages.

Unlike their historical antecedents whose shelves contained several dozen of each item, few country store collectors have more than one example of a product on their shelves. Cost is the prohibiting factor.

Although condition and scarcity are two important value considerations, the pizzazz of the piece is the most critical value element. Many packages contain images that cross over into other collecting categories, e.g., a movie star collector is as strong or stronger a competitor than a country store collector for a Jackie Coogan Peanut Butter pail.

References: Al Bergevin, *Drugstore Tins and Their Prices,* Wallace–Homestead, Krause Publications, 1990; Al Bergevin, *Food and Drink Containers and Their Prices,* Wallace–Homestead, 1978; Al Bergevin, *Tobacco Tins and Their Prices,* Wallace–Homestead, 1986; Douglas Congdon–Martin, *Tobacco Tins: A Collector's Guide,* Schiffer Publishing, 1992; Fred Dodge, *Antique Tins: Identification and Values,* Collector Books, 1995, 1997 value update; M. J. Franklin, *British Biscuit Tins 1868–1939: An Aspect of Decorative Packaging,* Schiffer Publishing, 1979; Vivian and Jim Karsnitz, *Oyster Cans,* Schiffer Publishing, 1993; Robert and Harriet Swedberg, *Tins 'N Bins,* Wallace–Homestead, 1985; David Zimmerman, *The Encyclopedia of Advertising Tins: Smalls & Samples,* published by author, 1994.

Collectors' Club: Tin Container Collectors Assoc, PO Box 440101, Aurora, CO 80044.

Barrel, wood, grapevine bands, glass panel in wood hinged top, unmkd, 28³/₄" h **$175**

Bin, Adams Pepsin Gum, litho tin, rect, red and black on yellow ground, product pkgs, 6" h **450**

Bin, All Nations Chewing Tobacco, litho tin, rect, red, black, and yellow, 11¹/₂" l **525**

Bin, American Sodas, tin, paper label, Uncle Sam holding biscuits, 11¹/₂" h . . **35**

Bin, Cream of Tartar, litho tin, square, woman's portrait in oval, gold and black on red ground, 8¹/₄" h **125**

Bin, Cremo Cigars, litho tin, rect, black lettering, brown ground, image on inside top of lid, 13⁷/₈" l **60**

Bin, English Breakfast Tea, stenciled and litho tin, woman and begging dogs in oval on front, gold on black ground, 19¹/₄" h **600**

Bin, Game Fine Cut Tobacco, litho tin, rect, quail, multicolor, 11¹/₄" l **600**

Bin, Henry Horner & Co Coffee, litho tin, building shape, slanting roof lid, "Happy Home Mills," 15" h **400**

Bin, Honest Scrap, litho tin, rect, dog, cat, and product pkg, multicolor on red ground, 18" l **3,075**

Left: Box, Greer's "Moo Girl" Butter, 1 lb, ©1925, $3.
Right: Canister, Nationwide Rolled Oats, 9¹/₂" h, 5¹/₄" d, $10.

Bin, Jas McClurg & Co's Crackers, painted and stenciled tin, glass front, rect, 11¹/₂" h **300**

Bin, Mail Pouch Tobacco, litho tin, rect, white and yellow lettering, black ground, contains 3 pack of tobacco, 13¹/₂" l **135**

Bin, McCormick's Tea, litho tin, round, glass panel in lid, 8¹/₂" h **85**

Bin, Old Glory Coffee, litho tin, dome top, "Mocha & Java Flavored," 13¹/₄" h **650**

Bin, Parke's Dry Roast Coffee, litho tin, rect, dome top, red, yellow, and black, 20¹/₂" h **1,500**

Bin, Scull's Sterling Coffee, stenciled and litho tin, rect, dome top, butler serving coffee on lid, woman with coffee grinder on front, red and black on white ground, 21¹/₂" h **1,000**

Bin, Sure Shot Tobacco, litho tin, rect, Indian drawing bow, red, black, and white, hinged lid, 15¹/₄" l **875**

Bin, Weyman's Cutty–Pipe Chewing and Smoking Tobacco, litho tin, square, red, green, and white, product image, round lid, 12³/₄" h **350**

Bin, Yucatan Gum, litho tin, rect, red and black on yellow ground, product pkgs, 6" h **425**

Box, Altoona Steam Bakery, wood, litho paper label on front, train with buildings in background, 22" h **415**

Box, American Biscuit & Mfg Co, wood, litho paper label, parrot, 10¹/₂" l **75**

Box, Bixby Best Blacking, wood, dovetailed, litho paper label inside lid, kids shining shoes, 12" l **70**

Box, Blanke's Coffee, wood, stenciled labels on 4 sides, 20¹/₄" h **185**

Box, Bossie's Best Brand Butter, cardboard, 1 lb **5**

Box, Bromo Seltzer, wood, stenciled labels, 9¹/₂" l **175**

Box, Duryea's Stain Gloss Starch, wood, dovetailed, stenciled labels, litho paper label under lid and 1 end, 10¹/₄" l **165**

Box, Dwight's Soda, wood, dovetailed, litho paper label front, cow image, stenciling on 3 sides and bottom, no lid, 15¹/₂" l **200**

Box, Dwinell–Wright Coffee, wood, litho paper labels on front, back, and top, factory scene, 21" h **135**

Box, Fairbank's Gold Dust Washing Powder, litho cardboard, rect, Gold Dust
Twins image, orig contents, 8¾" h   110
Box, Fairbank's Pure White Floating Soap, wood, stenciled labels, litho
paper label under lid, 17" l   230
Box, Foley's Honey and Tar Compound, wood, dovetailed, stenciled labels,
24¼" l   65
Box, Grandma's Borax Powder Soap, litho cardboard, red, black, and cream,
8¼" l   60
Box, Hood's Sarsaparilla, wood, dovetailed, stenciled labels, 14" h   65
Box, Hope Biscuit Works, wood, litho paper labels on front and under lid,
21¼" l   145
Box, India Mills Spice, wood, dovetailed, litho paper label front, stenciled
back, no lid, 7¾" l   45
Box, Jersey Coffee, wood slat construction, stenciled labels, partial paper
label on top, 29½" l   165
Box, John H Woodbury's Facial Soap, litho cardboard, 3 soap bars, green
and cream   50
Box, Kingsbury Toys, wood, dovetailed, stenciled labels, "No. 8823 Auto-
matic Fire Station," no lid, 10¾" h   200
Box, Kingsford's Silver Gloss Starch, wood, dovetailed, green stenciled
labels, litho paper end label, 11½" l   100
Box, Kow–Kure, wood, dovetailed, litho paper label, 12¼" h   60
Box, Lenox Soap, Proctor & Gamble, wood, dovetailed, litho paper label
front, stenciling 3 sides, hand holding bar of soap, 11¼" l   40
Box, Log Cabin Brownies, litho cardboard, log cabin shape, Palmer Cox
brownies around 4 sides, 2¼" h   195
Box, Lydia E Pinkham's Vegetable Compound, wood, dovetailed, stenciled
labels, 9¾" h   50
Box, Magnolia Brand Condensed Milk, wood, stenciled letters, 13" h   35
Box, Marksman Cigars, litho cardboard, 2 men shooting guns, 5" l   25
Box, Mason's Blacking, wood, dovetailed, litho paper labels on front and
under lid, shoeshine boys and large boot, 11¼" l   150
Box, Robinson Bros Crackers and Fine Cakes, wood, litho paper labels on
front and 1 side, factory and eagle vignettes, 23½" l   175
Box, Royal Baking Powder, wood, dovetailed, litho paper label on 1 end,
baking powder tin, stenciling on 3 sides, no lid, 11½" l   80
Box, Skabcura Liquid Sheep Dip, wood, stenciled labels, 6¼" h   100
Box, Slade's Mustard, wood, litho paper labels, red, white, and blue, 20" l . . .   60
Box, Stickney & Poor's Mustard, wood, dovetailed, litho paper labels on
front and under lid, fireside scene, 14¾" l   185
Box, Van Houten's Cocoa, wood, litho paper label, stamped lettering, 10" h . .   75
Box, Warner's Safe Yeast, wood, dovetailed, c1900, 7" h   40
Box, Washington Crisps Toasted Corn Flakes, litho cardboard, Washington
portrait in oval, red and white striped background, 9" h   100
Box, Winan Bros Indian Cure, wood, stenciled labels, 12¼" l   65
Box, WJ Sands & Sons Biscuits and Crackers, wood, litho paper labels on
front, 1 side, and under lid, lid unattached, 21¼" l   45
Canister, cylindrical, Blue–Jay Corn Plasters, litho tin, woman applying plas-
ter, 6" l   50
Canister, cylindrical, Franklin Coffee, litho tin, Ben Franklin portrait, "Flour"
on reverse, red, gold, and white, 9" h   745

Canister, cylindrical, Hoosier Poet Brand Rolled Oats, cardboard, 7½" h   60

Canister, cylindrical, Mother's Crushed Oats, cardboard, mother and child, 7¼" h   25

Canister, cylindrical, Scotch Brand Oats, cardboard, Scotsman, 7¼" h   35

Canister, cylindrical, Universal Coffee, litho tin, Uncle Sam and sunrise, multicolor, red lid with finial, 7" h   145

Canister, cylindrical, Wheat Sheaf Coffee, litho tin, wheat fields and farming scenes, finial lid, 6½" h   175

Jar, clear glass, Bunte, 10 sided, emb "Bunte," glass stopper lid, 12" h   50

Jar, clear glass, Kis–Me Gum, square with beveled corners, emb "Kis–Me Gum" on 1 side, "Kis–Me Gum Co. Louisville, KY" other side, glass stopper lid, 11" h   150

Jar, clear glass, Lutted's S.P. Cough Drops, log cabin shape, glass lift–off roof lid, emb "Lutted's S.P. Cough Drops" on roof, 7" l   200

Jar, clear glass, Planters Peanuts, angled top, front emb "Planters," Planters Salted Peanuts decal each side, Mr Peanut on tin threaded lid, 8½" h   150

Jar, clear glass, Planters Peanuts, barrel shape, front and back emb with Mr Peanut running toward trademark Mr Peanut leaning on cane, glass lid emb "Planters" on 2 sides, figural peanut finial, 12½" h   200

Jar, clear glass, Planters Peanuts, paneled side with emb "Planters Peanuts" all 4 sides, paper label with Mr Peanut and 5¢ peanut bag, figural peanut finial on glass lid, 12½" h   185

Jar, clear glass, Planters Peanuts, square, emb lettering and Mr Peanut decal all 4 sides, metal threaded lid, 8¼" h   300

Jar, clear glass, Price's Toilet Soap, cov and bowl etched "Price's Toilet Soaps," red paint over etching on glass lid, 7" d   200

Jar, clear glass, Schepp's Cocoanut, emb lettering on glass lid with ball finial, 6¾" h   275

Jar, clear glass, Squirrel Brand Salted Nuts, urn shape, emb trademark squirrel and "Squirrel Brand Salted Nuts," partial paper label on back, glass lid, 14" h   85

Milk Can, Union Leader Cut Plug, eagle, red, 9" h   325

Package, Brownie Tobacco, litho paper, brownie image, black and white, orig seal and contents, 5" h   165

Pail, bail handle, A Bailey, York, PA, litho tin, tapered sides, "Merry Christmas and Happy New Year," Santa and holly, red, gold, green, and black, 3½" h   275

Pail, bail handle, Bayle Peanut Butter, litho tin, straight sides, Boy Scout and Girl Scout, multicolor, 3¼" h   230

Pail, bail handle, Beaver Brand Peanut Butter, litho tin, slanted sides with opening narrower than base, beaver and leaves, gold and black, 3½" h . . .1,050

Pail, bail handle, Big Sister Peanut Butter, litho tin, tapered sides, Halloween images, multicolor, 3½" h   300

Pail, bail handle, Campbell Brand Coffee, litho tin, straight sides, camels in desert, red, yellow, and black, emb lettering on lid, 8" h   150

Pail, bail handle, CF Gunther, litho tin, tapered sides, "Wishing You A Merry Christmas and a Happy New Year," trumpeting angels, dated 1901–02, 3¼" h   165

Pail, bail handle, College Hill Booster's Club, litho tin, tapered sides, "Merry Christmas and Happy New Year," Victorian Santa in sleigh and reindeer, multicolor, 3½" h   415

Pail, bail handle, C P C (California Peanut Co) Peanut Butter, litho tin, tapered sides, over 30 comic images on sides and back including black man, cops and robbers, and kids, multicolor on gold, 3½" h   465

Pail, bail handle, Fairyland Peanut Butter, litho tin, straight sides, classroom with children and teacher, multicolor, 3¼" h   550

Pail, bail handle, Ground Hog Brand Lard, litho tin, straight sides, ground hog, red, black, and gold, 4½" h   150

Pail, bail handle, Jackie Coogan Peanut Butter, litho tin, straight sides, 2 Jackie Coogan portraits, blue ground, emb directions on lid, 3¾" h 1,150

Pail, bail handle, Jolly Time Hulless Pop Corn, litho tin, straight sides, scenes of children with popcorn, multicolor on red ground, 4½" h   215

Pail, bail handle, Lovell & Covel Candy, litho tin, tapered sides, 4 historic scenes, multicolor, 3" h   165

Pail, bail handle, Lovell & Covel Candy, litho tin, tapered sides, 4 Peter Cottontail scenes, 3" h   350

Pail, bail handle, Mammy's Favorite Coffee, litho tin, straight sides, Mammy, red, gold, and black, 10¾" h   415

Pail, bail handle, Nigger Hair Tobacco, litho tin, straight sides, gold ground, native with ear and nose rings, 6½" h   415

Pail, bail handle, Otto Lindner, litho tin, tapered sides, "Merry Christmas," pig and vines, 3¼" h   110

Pail, bail handle, Our Little Friends, litho tin, tapered sides, "Merry Christmas," Santa's sleigh and reindeer silhouette, red, black, and white, dated 1924, 3½" h   575

Pail, bail handle, Pan Work Candy, litho tin, tapered sides, elves' workshop, multicolor on gold, 3¼" h   550

Pail, bail handle, Pickaninny Brand Peanut Butter, litho tin, tapered sides, pickaninny, red, gold, and black, 3½" h   310

Pail, bail handle, Planters Peanut Butter, litho tin, straight sides, Mr Peanut engaged in various activities including playing band instruments and performing airplane stunts, brown, yellow, blue, white, and black, 3¾" h 1,100

Pail, bail handle, Salted Peanuts, litho tin, tapered sides, Jackie Coogan portrait, classroom image on sides and back, yellow, black, and gold, emb lettering on lid, 3½" h   200

Left: Seed Packet, Early Alaska Peas, Card Seed Co, 3¼ x 5", $5.

Right: Tin, Crisco, blue lettering on white ground, scratches, rust, and dents, 50 lbs, 15½" h, 12½" d, $70. Photo courtesy Collectors Auction Services.

Pail, bail handle, Teddie Peanut Butter, litho tin, tapered sides, peanut and peanut field, 8" h **230**

Pail, bail handle, Wilson's Peanut Butter, litho tin, straight sides, Old Woman and the Shoe, multicolor, 3" h **550**

Store Can, cylindrical, Sweet Burley Tobacco, litho tin, red and gold, 10¾" h **240**

Store Can, cylindrical, Sweet Cuba Tobacco, litho tin, black and gold, 10¾" h **130**

Store Can, Tiger Chewing Tobacco, "5 Cent Packages," litho tin, tiger head, red and gold, 11" h **300**

Tin, ACME Coffee, litho tin, cylindrical, flowers, red and white polka dot band, coffee pot and cup on reverse, 6" h **130**

Tin, Apache Trails Cigars, litho tin, cylindrical, Apache on horseback, arrowhead side panels, multicolor, 5¾" h **965**

Tin, Baker & Co's Breakfast Cocoa, sample, litho tin, cylindrical, yellow, 1¾" h **95**

Tin, Blue Parrot Coffee, litho tin, cylindrical, blue parrot on branch, yellow ground, white lettering, metal threaded lid, 6" h **5,500**

Tin, Buffalo Brand Fancy Salted Peanuts, litho tin, cylindrical, buffalo, red and gold, 9½" h **195**

Tin, Bunker Hill Coffee, litho tin, cylindrical, Bunker Hill monument, multicolor, 6" h **185**

Tin, Bunnies Salted Peanuts, litho tin, cylindrical, dressed rabbit holding product, red, yellow, white, and black, 11¼" h **550**

Tin, Campfire Supreme Marshmallows, litho tin, round, evening camp scene multicolor, 7¾" d **110**

Tin, Checker Strawberry Jam, litho tin, cylindrical, red strawberries, black and white checkerboard ground, 4¾" h **175**

Left: Tin, Peachey Double Cut Tobacco, red, green, and yellow, striker on bottom, 4" h, 2¹/₂" w, $75. Photo courtesy Collectors Auction Services.

Center: Tin, Royal Baking Powder, paper label, red ground, 4" h, 2³/₈" d, 6 oz, $25. Photo courtesy Ray Morykan Auctions.

Right: Tin, Towle Log Cabin Syrup, sample size, 1¹/₂ oz, $375.

Tin, Continental Cubes, litho tin, kidney shape, General Washington, no lid,
7½" h **225**

Tin, Davis Baking Powder, sample, litho tin, cylindrical, red and yellow,
1¾" h **50**

Tin, Dr Hand's Chafing Powder, litho tin, cylindrical, Victorian design with
hands and flowers, 4" h **450**

Tin, Dr Johnson's Educator Crackers, litho tin, square, wheat stalks, 5¾" h ... **50**

Tin, Dr Le Gear's Antiseptic Healing Powder, sample, litho paper, tin top and
bottom, man, horse, and fence, red, white, and black, 2" h **60**

Tin, Droste's Cocoa, sample, litho tin, square, Dutch man and woman, 2" h .. **90**

Tin, Dr Wernet's Powder for False Teeth, sample, litho tin, oval, hands applying tooth powder to false teeth, red, black, and white, 2¼" h **60**

Tin, Duff's Peanut Butter, sample, litho paper over tin, cylindrical, peanut
plants, red and yellow, 1¾" h **200**

Tin, Eagle Brand Coffee, litho tin, eagle, multicolor, threaded lid, 6" h **465**

Tin, Family Tea, litho tin, cylindrical, Victorian design, stag, red and black,
8¾" h **145**

Tin, Fort Pitt Coffee, litho tin, cylindrical, fort, red and gold, 5½" h **365**

Tin, Giant Salted Peanuts, litho tin, cylindrical, giant, red and yellow,
11¼" h **305**

Tin, Great American Tea Company, litho, Victorian stencil design, gold and
black, 7¾" h **110**

Tin, Griffing's Lunch Cocoa, litho tin, rect, flowers, yellow and black, 13" h .. **120**

Tin, Handsome Dan Mixture, litho tin, rect, Boston terrier, black and white .. **165**

Tin, Harmony Carnation Talc, sample, litho tin, oval, carnation, red and
gold, 2¼" h **120**

Tin, Hoosier Boy Coffee, litho paper on tin, cylindrical, boy whitewashing
fence, multicolor, 6" h **175**

Tin, Instant Postum, sample, litho tin, oval, breakfast table, red, white, and
blue, 2" h **45**

Tin, Klein's Cocoa, sample, litho tin, rect, parrot, 1¾" h **200**

Tin, Loyl Coffee, litho tin, cylindrical, flying eagle, multicolor, threaded lid,
6¼" h **175**

Tin, Mammoth Salted Peanuts, litho tin, cylindrical, mammoth, black and
white, 11¼" h **295**

Tin, Mennen's Toilet Talcum, litho tin, cylindrical, man with handlebar
mustache, red, gold, and white, matching lid, 4" h **265**

Tin, Monarch Cocoa, sample, litho tin, square, lion head logo on all 4 sides,
multicolor, 3" h **80**

Tin, Nestle's Food, sample, litho tin, cylindrical, black and white, 1¾" h **75**

Tin, Old Bond 5¢ Cigars, litho tin, rect, George Washington portrait, 6" l **110**

Tin, Police Foot Powder, litho tin, oval, vintage policeman, red, gold,
black, and white, 4½" h **500**

Tin, Postum Cereal, sample, litho tin, oval, red, white, and black, 1¾" h **28**

Tin, Powow Brand Salted Peanuts, litho tin, cylindrical, Indian chief head,
red, white, and dark green, 8½" h **350**

Tin, Pure Gold Coffee, litho tin, cylindrical, Victorian design, moose, green
and black, 9" h **300**

Tin, Rawleigh's Baking Powder, sample, litho tin, cylindrical, red, 1½" h **200**

Tin, Red Turkey Coffee, litho tin, cylindrical, turkey, red, black, and white,
5¾" h **250**

Tin, Rexall Baby Talc, litho tin, oval, baby, multicolor, 4½" h **415**

Tin, Rex Anti–Slip Brake Wafers, sample, litho tin, cylindrical, man pointing at wheel, white, red, and black, 2¼" h **85**

Tin, Rockwood's Decorettes, sample, litho tin, rect, decorated cake, red, white, and blue, 2" h **95**

Tin, Rooster Snuff, sample, litho paper label, cylindrical, crowing rooster, red, black, and yellow, 1" h **95**

Tin, Runkel's Cocoa, sample, litho tin, rect, red, white, and black, 1½" h **120**

Tin, Shaker Table Salt, sample, litho paper over tin, cylindrical, different image on 3 panels, red and yellow, 2" h **65**

Tin, Sunshine Coffee, litho tin, cylindrical, child with umbrella, blue ground, 6" h **200**

Tin, Swansdown Coffee, litho tin, cylindrical, swan, multicolor on yellow ground, 6¼" h **235**

Tin, Swell Blend Coffee, litho tin, steamship, multicolor, 6" h **230**

Tin, Syke's Comfort Powder, litho tin, oval, 2 children on front, nurse on reverse, multicolor on black, 4½" h **325**

Tin, Tac–Cut Coffee, litho tin, cylindrical, hen, red and white, 5¾" h **400**

Tin, Towle's Log Cabin Syrup, litho tin, cabin shape, woman at window, bear at door saying "Wonder if they'll give me some, huh?," multicolor, 3¾" l . . **230**

Tin, Turkey Coffee, litho tin, cylindrical, turkey, red, green, and white, 10½" h **650**

Tin, Vanko Cigars, litho tin, rect, emb, horse head, 5½" h **45**

Tin, Vantine's Sana–Dermal Baby Talc, litho tin, oval, mother and baby, multicolor, 4½" h **385**

Tin, Vick's Vaporub, sample, litho tin, round, product box and bottle image on front, woman and label on reverse, red, white, and blue, 2" d **45**

Tin, Voegele's Dainty Specialties, litho tin, cylindrical, Dutch boy and girl, red, white, and black, 11¼" h **165**

Tin, Watkin's Baking Powder, sample, litho tin, cylindrical, woman holding plate of muffins, red and yellow, 2½" h **95**

Tin, Webster's Coffee, litho tin, cylindrical, woman pouring coffee, multicolor on yellow ground, 6" h **385**

Tin, Wells, Richardson & Co, litho tin, square, farmer and cow, yellow and brown, 10¼" h **185**

Tin, WGY Coffee, litho tin, cylindrical, coffee pot, multicolor, 6¼" h **85**

Tin, White Goose Coffee, litho tin, goose, multicolor on red ground, 6" h **375**

Tin, Wild Cherry Sweet Scotch Snuff, sample, litho paper over tin, cylindrical, cherries and leaves, multicolor, 1¾" h **85**

Tin, William's Baby Talc, litho tin, oval, baby, multicolor, 5" h **550**

Tin, Winchester After Shave Talc, litho tin, oval, hunter and dog, multicolor on red, 4¾" h **185**

Tin, Wood Hydraulic Hoists, sample, litho celluloid band over tin, cylindrical, vintage truck, black and white, 1¼" h **75**

FOLK ART

Although there was a folk art consciousness among a few collectors and museum professionals prior to the 1960s, it was largely ignored by most collectors and dealers. All that changed in the late 1960s and early 1970s as museum exhibits and other events leading up to the celebration of the American Bicentennial seized upon folk art as the popular art of the American people.

The definition of what constitutes folk art is still being vigorously debated among collectors, dealers, museum curators, and scholars. Some want to confine folk art to non–academic, handmade objects. Others are willing to include manufactured material. In truth, the term is used to cover objects ranging from crude drawings by obviously untalented children to academically trained artists' paintings of "common" people and scenery.

Since this book wishes to avoid this brouhaha altogether, it has adopted the widest definition possible. If one or more groups within the field have deigned a category or item as part of the folk art movement, it is listed. Since the Country community tends to emphasize the primitive, naive, and painted over the more formal, these pieces are more heavily weighted in the listings.

A major development in the folk art renaissance of the 1970s was the revival of the folk art craftsperson. Across the United States individuals and manufacturers began to copy pieces from the past, often using the same tools and techniques to produce them as was done originally. You will find more craftspersons and manufacturers listed in this section of the book than any other.

Collect pieces from individuals and manufacturers who are introducing new design and form in the vocabulary of their chosen category, rather than on those who merely copy the past. These pieces have potential long–term value. While exact copies have immediate and decorative value, they will be the least sought examples in the future.

Because so many objects are being copied exactly, collectors and dealers have been fooled by them. This resulted in a slowing down of the folk art market in the late 1980s. Reproductions, copycats, and fantasy folk art pieces continue to grow in numbers. Until all these forms are documented with detailed information as to how to distinguish them from the original, the folk art market will remain a perilous place.

In addition to being plagued with the problem of confusing contemporary copies, the folk art market is subject to hype and manipulation. Weather vanes, cigar store figures, and quilts are just a few of the categories that were actively hyped and manipulated in the 1970s and 80s. Neophyte collectors are encouraged to read Edie Clark's "What Really Is Folk Art?" in the December 1986 *Yankee*. Clark's article provides a refreshingly honest look at the folk art market.

Finally, the folk art market is extremely trendy and fickle. What is hot today can become cool and passé tomorrow. Late nineteenth–century quilts are cool, twentieth–century quilts such as the Double Wedding Ring are hot. Whirligigs are cool, painted firemen's hats are hot.

Finally, in the 1980s, the American market began to look seriously at European material that closely resembled American folk art forms. Much was brought into the United States and sold. By the second and third transaction, many European pieces wound up with an American attribution. Today's folk art collector needs a thorough background in both American and European folk art to collect effectively.

All in all, collecting folk art is not for the weak–of–heart or the cautious investor.

References: Kenneth L. Ames, *Beyond Necessity: Art in the Folk Tradition,* W W Norton, 1977; Robert Bishop and Judith Rieter Weissman, *Folk Art: The Knopf Collectors' Guides to American Antiques,* Alfred A. Knopf, 1983; *Country Living Magazine, Living With Folk Art,* Hearst Books, 1994; Jean Lipman and Alice Winchester, *The Flowering of American Folk Art 1776–1876,* Penguin Books, 1977; Beatrix T. Rumford and Carolyn J. Weekley, *Treasures of American Folk Art From the Abby Aldrich Rockefeller Folk Art Center,* Little, Brown and Company, 1989; Shenandoah Valley Folklore Society, *Folk and Decorative Art of the Shenandoah Valley,* Shenandoah Valley Folklore Society, 1993.

Periodicals: *Folk Art,* Museum of American Folk Art, 61 West 62nd Street, New York, NY 10023; *Journal of the Early Southern Decorative Arts,* Museum of Early South Decorative Arts, PO Box 10310, Winston–Salem, NC 27108.

Collectors' Clubs: American Folk Art Society, 597 Chippendale Avenue, Simi Valley, CA 93065; Folk Art Society of America, PO Box 17041, Richmond, VA 23226.

Museums: Abby Aldrich Rockefeller Folk Art Center, Williamsburg, VA; Albany Institute of History & Art, Albany, NY; Bayou Bend Collection & Gardens, Houston, TX; Boston Museum of Fine Arts, Boston, MA; Bucks County Historical Society, Doylestown, PA; Cooper–Hewitt Museum, New York, NY; Crafts & Folk Art Museum, Los Angeles, CA; Daughters of the American Revolution Museum, Washington, DC; Fruitlands Museum, Harvard, MA; Historical Society of PA, Philadelphia, PA.

Landis Valley Farm Museum, Lancaster, PA; Museum of American Folk Art, New York, NY; Museum of Early Southern Decorative Arts, Winston–Salem, NC; Museum of International Folk Art, Santa Fe, NM; National Museum of American History, Washington, DC; New–York Historical Society, New York, NY; New York State Historical Assoc and The Farmer's Museum, Cooperstown, NY; PA Academy of Fine Arts, Philadelphia, PA; Yale University Art Gallery, New Haven, CT.

CARVINGS

Carving and whittling was a common pastime in rural America. In many cases, the end product was a whimsical item or simply a pile of shavings. Skills varied tremendously.

Figures, especially those used for store displays and ship's mastheads, were professionally done. Better local carvers developed a regional reputation. Few carvers trained a successor. Nonetheless, earlier works are known to have influenced later generations, e.g., Schimmel's influence on Mountz.

Much of the "folk" carving in modern collections dates from the last half of the nineteenth through the first half of the twentieth centuries. Age is not as critical a factor in this sector as in other "folk art" categories. Identification of the carver is critical to value. Since many of the pieces are unsigned, identification is done primarily by attribution. Many attributions are loosely made and should be questioned.

Modern folklorists, such as Bishop and Hemphill, have been instrumental in the identification and promotion of contemporary carvers. Recent auction results have proven that much of the value attributed to these pieces is speculative.

References: Robert Bishop, *American Folk Sculpture,* E. P. Dutton, 1974; Catherine Dike, *Canes in the United States: Illustrated Mementoes of American History, 1607–1953,* Cane Curiosa Press, 1994, Jack T. Ericson, *Folk Art in America: Painting and Sculpture,* Mayflower Books, 1979; Herbert W Hemphill, *Folk Sculpture U.S.A.,* Universe Books, 1976; Jean Lipman, *American Folk Art in Wood, Metal, and Stone,*

Dover Publications, 1972; Richard and Rosemarie Machmer, *Just For Nice: Carving and Whittling Magic of Southeastern Pennsylvania,* Historical Society of Berks County (PA), 1991; George H. Meyer, *American Folk Art Canes: Personal Sculpture,* Sandringham Press, Museum of American Folk Art and University of Washington Press, 1992; Francis H. Monek, *Canes Through the Ages,* Schiffer Publishing, 1995; Jeffrey B. Snyder, *Canes: From the Seventeenth to the Twentieth Century,* Schiffer Publishing, 1993; John J. Stoudt, *Early Pennsylvania Arts and Crafts,* A. S. Barnes and Co, 1964.

Newsletter: *The Cane Collector's Chronicle,* 2515 Fourth Avenue #405, Seattle, WA 98121.

Reproduction Alert: Fakes, pieces deliberately meant to deceive, abound. In the early 1970s, Harry L. Rinker visited a York County carver who was aging a garage full of Schimmel copies. I believe several of these have entered the market in the intervening years as Schimmel originals.

The August 1991 issue of *Maine Antique Digest* contained the article "Jacob Joyner: Mississippi Wood Carver or The Man Who Never Was?" by David Hewitt. An entire school of carvings, sold by some of America's most prominent folk art dealers and purchased by some of America's leading collectors, turned out to be forgeries. There are many who question whether the Joyner incident is an isolated example.

Calabash Pipe, hardwood, alligatored varnish finish, animal head, cross-
hatching, rope carving, and human hand detail, horn fittings, 18" l **$225**
Cane, alligator head handle, gaping mouth, brass tack eyes, bone teeth,
hand pegged onto hardwood shaft, metal ferrule, c1900, 35¾" l **250**
Cane, bird in hand handle, dogwood, curved handle carved with hand holding bird, tapered shaft, "Schtockschnitzler" Simmons, PA, c1900, 35" l **1,375**
Cane, black man's head handle, glass eyes, wearing round brown hat, thin
malacca shaft with swirled dark stain dec, metal ferrule, c1880, 35¾" l . . . **625**
Cane, carp handle, carved carp lying on its side, glass eyes, 1" silver collar,
mahogany shaft with brass ferrule, 35¾" l **550**
Cane, Civil War reconciliation, burnished brass ball knob, dark stained
hardwood shaft carved with owners' initials "W.B.L." and harp, Victorian
man smoking Indian peace pipe, foliage and flowers, 2 clasped hands
mkd "North" and "South" on cuffs, fish, alligator attacking dove, 34" l **825**
Cane, dog handle, dogwood, high relief figure of reclining dog, tapered shaft
carved at top with squirrel holding nut, initialed "AK," metal tip, attributed
to Adam Krauss, Montgomery County, PA, c1900, 32¼" l **350**
Cane, duck head handle, dogwood, inset glass eyes, tapered shaft, metal tip,
PA, c1900, 35" l **700**
Cane, folk art, carved from single pc of hickory, bark handle, shaft carved in
high relief with kangaroo head, kangaroo, elephant, flying goose, prong
horn deer, rhino, oak leaves, alligator, coiled rattlesnake, padlock, male
lion, pelican, gar fish, rabbit head, camel, jackknife, frog, tiger, running
doe, flying duck, antelope, full-bodied owl standing on coffeepot, and
hatch, sgd in ink on coffeepot "Trade Mark, R. M. Foster, Sparta, Mo.,"
lead ferrule, late 19th C, 33½" l **2,250**
Cane, goat handle, dogwood, curved handle carved with goat leaping
through barrel, dog leaping through other end clutching box, bearded
gentleman seated astride keg fitted with metal spigot and holding bottle
and glass, eyes and buttons detailed with colored glass beads, tapered
shaft, sgd "Bally Carver," R Heinz, Berks County, PA, c1900, 37" l **575**

Cane, knopped handle, dogwood, tapered shaft carved in relief with band of stars, 2 horses, American eagle over scrolled banner with stars, stag, and rearing stallion, PA, c1900, 29³/₄" l **1,275**

Cane, Masonic, carved from single pc of chestnut, fist clutching ball handle, carved octagonal band with Masonic incised signs, dated in block letters "August 1888," encircling snake with burned dec twist down remainder of shaft, 37¹/₂" l **350**

Cane, puzzle, handle is carved cage enclosing 2 wooden balls, plain shaft with bark, spike ferrule, 35" l **60**

Diorama, ship, wood, paper, cellophane, and string, painted, flying American flag, 6⁵/₈" h, 9 ⁷/₈" l **100**

Figure, American eagle, carved pine and gesso, stylized figure with out-spread wings and head turned to left, scored and layered wing detail and crosshatched body, US shield hung from neck, painted dark brown with traces of red, white, and blue, Wilhelm Schimmel, Cumberland Valley, PA, c1870, 10¹/₄" h, 17¹/₄" l **38,000**

Figure, bird, pine, stylized figure with long tail perched on tree trunk fash-ioned from branches, painted with red, green, and yellow markings on cream ground, wire legs, mounted on split log base, PA, late 19th/early 20th C, 13¹/₂" h **2,300**

Figure, bird, stylized, carved wing and head detail, serrated tail, painted green and brown, wire legs, dome square base, the Deco–Tex Carver, PA, 20th C, 2³/₄" h **1,000**

Figure, bird on stump, stylized, carved beak, eye, wing, and tail detail, paint-ed red with black wings and head, wire legs, "Schtockschnitzler" Simmons, PA, c1900, 7" h **5,475**

Figure, black man and woman, articulated limbs, cloth costumes, poly-chrome paint, 9¹/₄" h, price for pair **225**

Figure, bust of man with hat, polychrome paint and varnish, 6⁷/₈" h **300**

Figure, chariot, pulled by giraffe–like animals, polychrome paint, base sgd "Hand carved by Rev. A. W. Wentworth," 10³/₄" l **275**

Figure, dog, pine, stylized reclining figure with head forward, mouth open, tongue out, and tail curved around to side, painted dark brown, black, and red, scored fur detail, rect base, late 19th C, 2³/₄" h **1,150**

Figure, eagle, stylized, standing erect with head up, wings out to sides, and tail down, carved feather detail, green glass eyes, painted black, white, and yellow, standing on shaped brown base, initialed "S.P." (Stephen Polaha), Reading, PA, 20th C, 15¹/₂" h **635**

Figure, elk, standing figure with head up and turned slightly to left and ears pricked, painted mottled brown and black, mounted on later rect wood base, John Reber, Germansville, PA, early 20th C, 13¹/₂" h **9,775**

Figure, gooney bird, pine, stylized, chip carved wings, long legs, painted black with orange, blue, and yellow details, standing on rect base, PA, early 20th C, 6³/₈" h **525**

Figure, greyhound with rabbit, painted red–brown over white with black spots, green base, 11" l **925**

Figure, hackney horse, standing chestnut horse with right front leg raised, carved details, glass eyes, mounted on black wood base, Henry Turner, VT, c1880, 15¹/₂" h, 18" l **79,500**

Figure, Indian, pine, primitive, standing figure with rope hair and headdress, stained red, probably OH, 74" h **1,435**

*Staff,
heart–in–hand
"Odd Fellows,"
carved and
painted, $1,100.*
Photo courtesy
Aston Macek.

Figure, Indian brave, standing figure with right hand raised above head, left
   hand holding knife, wearing single feather headband, bear tooth neck-
   lace, arm bracelet, buckskin pants, and moccasins, blanket draped over
   shoulder, platform base   800
Figure, Indian medicine man, pine with horsehair and painted fabric, carved
   and polychromed wood feather headdress, carved wood bow, quiver fitted with individually carved arrows, and tomahawk, painted, late 19th C,
   66½" h 20,750
Figure, lamb, carved walnut, alligatored finish, rect base, 6½" l   325
Figure, lion, stylized figure standing foursquare with tail back, carved mane
   detail, inset glass eyes, sgd and dated "Paul Tyson '76, #72," Royersford,
   Montgomery County, PA, 13¼" l 1,500
Figure, pig dog, painted gray over pink with black trim, 20th C, 13" l   175
Figure, poodle, carved and gesso, stylized figure standing foursquare with
   tail extended back, crosshatched fore–section, clutching stick in jaws,
   painted ocher, red, black, and green, Wilhelm Schimmel, Cumberland
   Valley, PA, c1880, 3¾" h, 6¼" l 13,800
Figure, rooster, pine, full bodied figure with head up and tail fanned, chip
   carved wing and tail, painted red, black, yellow, green, white, orange, and
   brown, standing on dome mound, Schoharie County, NY, 10" h 1,375
Figure, soldier, articulated arms, painted blue, black, white, mustard yellow,
   and red, 19th C, 17" h 8,250
Figure, squirrel, sitting on tree stump, brown stain, 20th C, 5" h   30
Figure, tree, wire nail construction, chip carved with heart center, lyre arms
   with 3 perched and 4 flying birds, alligatored green and yellow painted
   tree, black with salmon pink and yellow with black birds, 20th C, 27" h . .2,525
Figure, 2 men, pink, crudely carved stylized standing figures with articulated arms, wearing caps, painted red, white, and blue–gray, mounted on
   later painted wood stands, Lebanon County, PA, late 19th/early 20th C,
   7¼" h, price for pair   85
Figure, Uncle Sam, standing figure wearing top hat, blue swallowtail coat
   with white stars and flying tails, pink vest, striped pants, black shoes, and
   gray stirrups, holding fabric American flag, yellow pyramid base, late
   19th/early 20th C, 17¼" h 12,500
Figure, woman, primitive, wearing long skirt, articulated arms, old worn
   patina, 7¼" h   325
Figure, woman with cane, worn black paint, brown varnish finish, 9¾" h   425

Group, bird tree, stylized tree with tapered trunk and 5 horizontal limbs on which are perched 11 birds with incised wing and beak detail and nail head eyes, 4 stylized leaf from feet, painted dark brown, Stephen Deady, Galina, IL, late 19th C, 24¼" h 18,500

Group, fox hunting group, 5 hunters on horseback, 12 hounds, male holding fox, snake, raccoon, and 2 birds in tree, mounted on rect base, painted, George D Wolfskill, Fivepointville, Lancaster County, PA, early 20th C...27,500

Group, guinea hens, 3 stylized guinea hens, chip carved feather detail, perched on 3 branches on domed base, PA, late 19th C, 14¼" h 1,725

Masthead, young woman with right arm across chest to left shoulder, repainted, found on Martha's Vineyard Island, mid–19th C, 47½" h 17,000

Model, Brig Truxton, painted, 20th C, 16" l 525

Model, engine and tender Cornwall, painted, late 19th/early 20th C, 40" l, 17½" h 1,100

Model, Flying Cloud of Boston, painted, fully rigged, labeled "by E. F. Tanner," glass case, 20th C, 91" l 3,250

Model, M.M.F. Emileo, class model for pond racing, painted hull, paper label on cradle with name and "on Lowell St., Peabody, Mass," New England, early 20th C, 50" l, 76" h 1,600

Model, whale boat, painted, fully rigged sails, tubs of line and harpoons, mounted on display stand, 20th C, 18½" l 950

Panorama, street scene, pine, rect panel with various carved wood figures including policeman, mother and daughter, dog, 7 men, and newspaper boy waiting near back steps of theater, sgd and dated "C. W. Ladd, The Jail Carvers, Berks County Prison, Pennsylvania, 1914," 9" h, 19" l 1,500

Pilot House Figure, Columbia, half round, relief carved, golden tresses, corkscrew curls, draped robes, holding gold sphere in left hand and elongated US shield in right, stars and stripes on shield, pendant spray of wheat sheaves at her side, mid–19th C, 22½" w, 64" h 24,500

Plaque, eagle, flying with head down and turned to right, clutching shield with stars and stripes in 1 talon, arrows in other, traces of paint, varnished, in the style of Bellamy, 20th C, 44" w 935

Plaque, fish, cardboard fins, painted, mounted on old raised panel board, 11¼" h, 14¾" l 300

Plaque, Indian head, walnut, round, bust–length profile of male Indian, punchwork background, 19th C, 10" d 60

Wall Bracket, bowed shelf above spreadwing eagle perched on rocky crag, backed by shaped and molded panel, gilded and painted, c1820, price for pair 2,500

DECOYS

Carved wooden decoys, used to lure ducks and geese to the hunter, have become widely recognized as an indigenous American folk art form in the past several years.

Many decoys are from the 1880–1930 period when commercial gunners commonly hunted using rigs of several hundred decoys. Many fine carvers also worked through the 1930s and 1940s.

The value of a decoy is based on several factors: (1) fame of the carver, (2) quality of the carving, (3) species of wild fowl—the most desirable are herons, swans, mergansers, and shorebirds, and (4) condition of the original paint.

The inexperienced collector should be aware of several facts. The age of a decoy, per se, is usually of no importance in determining value. Since very few decoys were ever signed, it will be quite difficult to attribute most decoys to known carvers. Anyone who has not examined a known carver's work will be hard pressed to determine if the paint on one of his decoys is indeed original.

Repainting severely decreases a decoy's value. In addition, there are many fakes and reproductions on the market and even experienced collectors are occasionally fooled.

Decoys listed below are of average wear unless otherwise noted.

References: Joel Barber, *Wild Fowl Decoys,* Dover Publications, 1954; Joe Engers (general ed), *The Great Book of Wildfowl Decoys,* Thunder Bay Press, 1990; Henry A. Fleckenstein, Jr., *American Factory Decoys,* Schiffer Publishing; Ronald J. Fritz, *Michigan's Master Carver Oscar W. Peterson, 1887–1951,* Aardvark Publications, 1988; Gene and Linda Kangas, *Decoys: A North American Survey,* Hillcrest Publications, 1983; Linda and Gene Kangas, *Collector's Guide to Decoys,* Wallace–Homestead, Krause Publications, 1992; Carl F. Luckey, *Collecting Antique Bird Decoys and Duck Calls: An Identification & Value Guide, Second Edition,* Books Americana, Krause Publications, 1992; William Mackey, Jr., *American Bird Decoys,* E. P. Dutton, 1965.

Periodicals: *Decoy Hunter Magazine,* 901 North 9th, Clinton, IN 47842; *Decoy Magazine,* PO Box 277, Burtonsville, MD 20866; *North American Decoys,* PO Box 246, Spanish Fork, UT 84660; *Wildfowl Art,* Ward Foundation, PO Box 3416, Salisbury, MD 21802; *Wildfowl Carving & Collecting,* 500 Vaughn Street, Harrisburg, PA 17110.

Museums: Havre de Grace Decoy Museum, Harve de Grace, MD; Heritage Plantation of Sandwich, Sandwich, MA; Museums at Stony Brook, Stony Brook, NY; Peabody Museum of Salem, Salem, MA; Refuge Waterfowl Museum, Chincoteague, VA; Shelburne Museum, Shelburne, VT; Ward Museum of Wildfowl Art, Salisbury, MD.

Bald Pate, Ken Burrell, London, Ontario, Canada, initialed "W.B.," orig
    paint, glass eyes, 12¼" l, price for pair **$40**
Black Breasted Plover, Mason Decoy Factory, Chicago, IL, solid, tack
    eyes, nail bill, orig paint, c1890 .... **1,150**
Black Duck, Gene Sullivan, Salisbury style, orig paint **400**
Black Duck and Pintail Duck, Ralph Malpage, Ontario, Canada, unsgd, orig
    paint, glass eyes, 17" l black duck, 22" l pintail duck, price for pair **150**
Bluebill, Jobes, Harry, Aberdeen, MD, sgd "Capt Harry Jobes," orig paint,
    19½" l, price for mated pair **150**
Bluebill, Waubaushene, Harold Dinham, Ontario, Canada, sgd, orig paint,
    glass eyes, 13" l, price for pair **75**
Bluebill Drake, Hodgman, Dave, Niles, MI, carved wing detail, orig paint,
    glass eyes, 14" l **55**
Bluebill Drake, Nichol, Addie, Smith Falls, Ontario, professionally restored .. **275**
Bluebill Drake, Saginaw Bay area, old working repaint, glass eyes, 13¼" l ... **40**
Bluebill Hen, Irving Miller, MI, orig paint, glass eyes, 11½" l **150**
Blue Goose and Canada Goose, Ralph Malpage, Ontario, Canada, unsgd,
    orig paint, glass eyes, 23" l blue goose, 21½" l Canada goose,
    price for pair **90**

Bluewing Teal Drake, Joseph Serigny, LA, carved cypress root, raised
detail and tail feathers, orig paint **225**

Bluewing Teal Hen, Charles Spiron, Winston Salem, NC, raised detail,
branded name on bottom **200**

Brandt, Willima Goenne, King City, CA, branded "WRG," orig paint,
glass eyes, 21" l **60**

Broadbill Drake, Barnegat Bay Decoy Co, Point Pleasant, NJ, orig paint **200**

Bufflehead Drake, hollow, low head, orig paint, c1900 .... **700**

Canada Goose, Castle, John, Birmingham, MI, unsgd, blue–black stain, glass
eyes, 25½" l **200**

Canada Goose, Lincoln, Joe, Accord, MA, branded "Bradford," solid, carved
bill detail, orig paint, glass eyes, weight removed, c1915 .... **3,735**

Canada Goose, Long Island area, sleeper, primitive, weathered paint, glass
eyes, 20½" l **350**

Canada Goose, Smith, Miles, Marine City, MI, sgd, hollow with open bottom, orig paint with stamped feather design, glass eyes, 17¾" l **60**

Canvasback Drake, Alex Meldrum, Marine City, MI, unsgd, hollow
block, old working repaint, glass eyes, 16¾" l **160**

Curlew, Accomac, VA, solid, sickle bill, weathered orig paint, c1900 .... **1,150**

Curlew, Nichols, Fred, Lynn, MA, solid, carved wing detail, orig paint, shoe
button eyes added at later date, inscribed "Willet, Thomas Gelston,
Quogue, L.I." on underside, bill probably replaced, 1870–80 .... **4,600**

Curlew, Sprague, Jonas, Beach Haven, NJ, solid, carved eye detail, orig paint,
orig sickle bill, 1870–80 .... **4,900**

Dowitcher, Mason Decoy Factory, Chicago, IL, solid, orig paint, glass
eyes, nail bill, c1890 .... **1,275**

Greater Yellowlegs, Noah Sterling, Crisfield, MD, solid figure with beetle head, orig paint, wire legs, wood bill replaced, c1880 .... **3,500**

Green Wing Teals, Ken Burrell, London, Ontario, Canada, unsgd, orig
paint, glass eyes, 14¼" l, price for pair **80**

Loon, Byron Bruffee, orig paint, name stamped on base **350**

Mallard Drake, Duck Creek Hunt Club, Lake Erie, Ontario, Canada, old
working repaint, tack eyes, 17½" l **85**

Merganser Drake, James Sprankle, NY, hooded, sgd on bottom **200**

Owl, Souler Swicher, Decatur, IL, confidence decoy, papier–mâché, orig
paint, 4 glass eyes, 14¼" h **125**

Pintail Drake, Lou Reineri, VA, flying posture, c1960s **325**

Pintail Hen, Mike Bonnet, WI, preener, Illinois River style, orig paint,
glass eyes, 13½" l **200**

Redbreasted Merganser, Harry Conklin, NJ, orig paint, price for mated
pair **1,250**

Redhead Drake, Crowell, A Elmer, East Harwich, MA, solid, carved bill,
crossed wing tips and tail detail, glass eyes, c1910 .... **575**

Redhead Drake, Meldrum, Alex, Marine City, MI, sgd "Alex C. Meldrum
Made in 1920," hollow block, old working repaint, glass eyes, 16¾" l **195**

Robin Breasted Snipe, Long Island, solid, carved wing and tail detail,
orig paint, bill replaced, c1880 .... **450**

Ruddy Turnstone, NJ, solid, orig paint, carved initials "F.D.B." on underside, bill repaired and possibly replaced, last quarter 19th C **700**

Sanderling, probably VA, solid, repainted, c1880 .... **700**

Seagull, Nantucket, MA, solid, carved wing and eye detail, orig paint, c1930 . **350**

Seagull, Ward Bros, Crisfield, MD, hollow, head turned to left, carved bill
  detail, orig paint, glass eyes, inscribed "Made by Steve, Painted by Lem,
  Ward Bro, 1966, Crisfield, Md., Lem Ward, Steve Ward" **1,025**
Widgeon Drake, Dave Hodgman, Niles, MI, orig paint, glass eyes,
  14³/₄" l **275**
Willet, southern NJ, flattened solid figure, carved wing detail, orig paint,
  nail bill, shoe–button eyes, c1880 . . . . **575**
Yellowlegs, Dodge Decoy Co, Detroit, MI, solid, traces of orig paint,
  tack eyes, nail bill, c1890 . . . . **1,050**

FRAKTUR

Fraktur, the calligraphy associated with the Pennsylvania Germans, is named for
the elaborate first letter found in many of the hand–drawn examples. Throughout its
history printed, partially printed hand–drawn, and fully hand–drawn works existed
side by side. Frakturs often were made by the school teachers or ministers living in
rural areas of Pennsylvania, Maryland, and Virginia. Many artists are unknown.

Fraktur exists in several forms—geburts and taufschein (birth and baptismal certificates), vorschrift (writing example, often with alphabet), haus sagen (house blessing),
bucherzeichen (bookplates), bookmarks, rewards of merit, illuminated religious text,
valentines, and drawings. Although collected for decoration, the key element in fraktur is the text.

Fraktur prices rise and fall along with the American folk art market. The key market place is Pennsylvania, the Middle Atlantic states, and Ontario, Canada.

References: Michael S. Bird, *Ontario Fraktur: A Pennsylvania–German Folk Tradition
in Early Canada*, M. F. Feheley Publishers, 1977; Donald A. Shelley, *The Fraktur–
Writings of Illuminated Manuscripts of the Pennsylvania Germans*, Pennsylvania
German Society, 1961; Frederick S. Weiser and Howell J. Heaney (compilers), *The
Pennsylvania German Fraktur of the Free Library of Philadelphia*, two–volume set,
Pennsylvania German Society, 1976.

Museum: Free Library of Philadelphia, Philadelphia, PA.

HAND DRAWN

Birth and Baptismal Certificate (Geburts und Taufschein), Bentz, Samuel,
  Lancaster County, PA, 1828, attributed to watercolor and ink, central
  inscribed birth record of Mary Beck, born to Jacob and Catherine Beck on
  October 6, 1790, enclosed on 3 sides by floral and striped band with
  checkerboard corners and shoulders, embellished above by 2 flowers
  flanking striped sphere enclosed by similar striped and checkerboard sur-
  round, 9 ³/₄" h, 8" w **$11,270**
Birth and Baptismal Certificate (Geburts und Taufschein), Bentz, Samuel,
  Lancaster County, PA, 1836, watercolor on paper, clock face and paired
  striped spheres, inscribed "Amos Good (son of Henry Good and his Wife
  Anna born Stirk) was born February 8th in the year of our Lord 1836," 9¹/₂
  x 7¹/₂" **3,165**
Birth and Baptismal Certificate (Geburts und Taufschein), Berks County (PA)
  artist, 1784, pen and ink and watercolor on paper, winged angels, paired
  birds and mermaids, certificate for Frederick Heverling, 12¹/₄ x 15¹/₂" **2,100**

Birth and Baptismal Certificate (Geburts und Taufschein), Brechall, Martin, 1808, pen and ink and watercolor on paper, paired tulips and red and yellow blossoms, certificate for Lea Claus, sgd and dated "Martin Brechall, Linn Township, Northampton County, March 7, 1808," 8 x 13¼" **1,050**

Birth and Baptismal Certificate (Geburts und Taufschein), Daly, George W, 1829, pen and ink on woven paper, black and red, geometric border with "Esther Fisher" in semicircle around house and "Was Born Adomino, MDCCC, Eaton, P. Co. Ohio," gilded frame, 9½ x 11½" **1,000**

Birth and Baptismal Certificate (Geburts und Taufschein), Durham Township, Bucks County (PA) artist, attributed to, 1823, watercolor and ink, central rect yellow and red bordered reserve inscribed with record of Hannah Hefler born October 17, 1815, in Haycock Township, Bucks County to Jacob and Sarah Hefler, below trapezoidal red and yellow bordered reserve centering above green, red, and yellow geometric decorated urn issuing similarly colored flowers and flanked by green, red, and yellow songbirds, whole flanked by red, yellow, and green geometric decorated urns issuing oversized and stylized tulips, flowers, buds, and leaves above squared red bordered reserves inscribed with religious verses and "Bucks County, March the 21st 1823," 7¾" h, 12⅝" w **1,950**

Birth and Baptismal Certificate (Geburts und Taufschein), Hoevelmann, Arnold, early 19th C, pen and ink and watercolor on paper, military gentleman wearing red coat and cocked hat and carrying sword, certificate for Wilhelm Heiges, born Nov 5, 1787, in York County, PA, 11 x 15" **20,700**

Birth and Baptismal Certificate (Geburts und Taufschein), Huth, Adam, Lebanon County, PA, attributed to, 1823, watercolor and ink, record of birth of Phillip Schaeffer on August 13, 1823, in Lebanon Township, Lebanon County in center enclosed in yellow, red, and green sawtooth diamond rect surround, embellished above with similarly colored flower, flying angels, and central bursting rosette, flanked on either side by red, yellow, and green oversized tulips issuing smaller buds and hanging berry bunches and centering a taupe colored urn issuing yellow and red flowers, 12½" h, 15½" w **5,750**

Birth and Baptismal Certificate (Geburts und Taufschein), Ohio artist, pen and ink and watercolor on laid paper, multicolored floral wreath with 2 birds surrounding rect text block with heart in each corner, red, blue, yellow, and green, records 1781 birth, back inscribed "Ballia County, Ohio Addison Township...," matted, unframed, 8 x 12" **775**

Birth and Baptismal Certificate (Geburts und Taufschein), Otto, Daniel, "The Flat Tulip Artist," 1805, watercolor on paper, paired green and red parrots, yellow, red, and green blossoms, and red heart, certificate for Katherine Schudern, Mahonoy Township, PA, Daniel Otto "The Flat Tulip Artist," 7½ x 6¼" **8,050**

Birth and Baptismal Certificate (Geburts und Taufschein), Peterman, Daniel, 1860, watercolor and ink, text flanked by 2 standing women and above by green, yellow, orange, blue, red, and white flowers, tulips, and birds, records November 22, 1860, birth of Allas Scha to Dephraim A. and Maria (Sterner) Scha in Carroll County, MD, sgd below "Made by Daniel Peterman, Shrewsbury T., York C., P.A.," 13¾" h, 11¾" w **4,825**

Birth and Baptismal Certificate (Geburts und Taufschein), Peterman, Daniel, 1862, pen and ink, pencil, and watercolor on woven paper, birds, stylized

flowers, and 2 standing women, records 1862 birth of Levy Altland in York
County, PA, sgd "Made by Daniel Peterman, Jr. S.T.Y.C.P.," 13¼ x 10¾" . . . **2,875**
Birth and Baptismal Certificate (Geburts und Taufschein), Portzline, Francis,
1802, watercolor and ink, red and yellow heart inscribed with birth
record of George Portzline, son of Frantz [sic] and Sabina (Heigel)
Portzline on June 2, 1802, flanked on either side by large red birds with
red and yellow wings, yellow singing bird with red and yellow wings,
large green birds with red heads, yellow and green wings, and yellow and
red tails perched on thick green vine with yellow flowers, centered above
and below by black, red, and yellow heart–petalled rosette, inscribed baptismal verse at center bottom, 12¾" h, 15½" w **6,325**
Birth and Baptismal Certificate (Geburts und Taufschein), Speyer, Georg
Friedrich (PA), attributed to, 1786, central black and red banded reserve
inscribed with birth record of John Jacob Miller on July 6, 1786, in
Langenschwamm Township in Berks County and dec on each side with
red, black, and brown fans, tulips, and stylized flowers, all enclosed in
conforming border of meandering red, black, yellow, and brown scrolling
leaves, tulips, stylized flowers, fans, and striped triangles within red and
black border, 13" h, 16" w **3,675**
Birth and Baptismal Certificate (Geburts und Taufschein), Stony Creek artist,
1815, watercolor on paper, red and green blossoms and stars, certificate
for Anna Bachman, 6⅜ x 8" **1,955**
Birth and Baptismal Certificate (Geburts und Taufschein), unknown artist,
1806, pen and ink and watercolor on paper, 4 red, yellow, and black
tulips with fans and scrolls, certificate for Anna Bauer, 7 x 12½" **7,475**
Birth and Baptismal Certificate (Geburts und Taufschein), unknown artist,
1816, pen and ink and watercolor on paper, red and yellow blossoms on
pale green vines, certificate for Christian Heft, Springfield Township,
Bucks County, PA, dated March 10, 1816, 7¾ x 12½" **2,875**
Birth and Baptismal Certificate (Geburts und Taufschein), unknown artist,
19th C, pen and ink on woven paper, brown, black, and green with flourishes, German inscription "Maria Grager, 1850, born June 4th, AD 1833
in State of Ohio," framed, 6½ x 9½" **825**
Birth and Baptismal Certificate (Geburts und Taufschein), Young, Henry,
attributed to, 1846, watercolor and ink, text recording birth of John
William Hull, born February 12, 1846, in Lamar Township, Clinton
County centered at top above standing profiles of facing man and woman
with potted flowers on stand between them, 10" h, 7¾" w **2,525**
Bookplate (Bucherzeichen), Kolb, Andreas (PA), attributed to, 1797, watercolor and ink, heart with green hatch striped and red polka dot dec border inscribed "This New Testament belongs to Elizabeth Scheimer...25th
day March...1797, in Upper Milford Township, Northampton" and issuing stylized brown leaves with peach and red flowers and buds, all above
2 brown buds and enclosed in rope twist banded border of alternating yellow and taupe with red corner blocks, 6⅝" h, 3⅝" w **5,975**
Bookplate (Bucherzeichen), Montgomery County (PA) Artist, 19th C, watercolor on paper, blue and yellow birds around red, green, and yellow blos-
soming trees, 3⅜ x 5¾" **550**
Bookplate (Bucherzeichen), Plumstead Township Artist, Bucks County, PA,
attributed to, 1828, watercolor and ink, upper half centering stylized
brown, red, and yellow flower with double petals embellished with line

dec above tapering stem embellished with alternating scroll dec and flanked by 2 smaller similar flowers over translated inscription "This song-book belongs to Susanna Meyer in Hill Township 1828," all within red, yellow, and brown striped and dec surround, 6¼" h, 3½" w **3,000**

Bookplate (Bucherzeichen), unknown artist, 1790, pen and ink and water-color on laid paper, tulips and heart in red, yellow, and black, inscribed "Barbara Hallern 1790," Berks County, PA, framed, 6⅞ x 5⅜" **1,500**

Bookplate (Bucherzeichen), unknown artist, 1804, southeastern PA, proba-bly Bucks County, watercolor and ink, rect page with red and yellow geo-metric line border, similarly colored leafy spandrels centering brown, yel-low, and squiggle–and–dot dec surround inscribed within "This New Song Book Belongs to Johannes Kreundig...," above similarly dec smaller cir-cular enclosure dated "12th February 1804," and surmounted by red and yellow dot and hatch dec tulip on brown and yellow stepped base, 6⅜" h, 3⅜" w **1,100**

Bookplate (Bucherzeichen), unknown artist, 1814, southeastern PA, water-color and ink, red, green, and yellow sawtooth diamond border enclosing banded register of red, green, and yellow flowers above red, green and yellow fraktur written inscription "This book Belongs to me, Anna Oberholzer" over a red, green, and mustard yellow bordered chevron with angels and further dated inscription, whole embellished with mean-dering red, green, and yellow flowering and vines, 6⅜" h, 3½" w **4,600**

Bookplate (Bucherzeichen), unknown artist, 1821, Schwenkfelder style, PA, watercolor and ink, rect bordered page in 2 registers, top centering fruit-ed tree flanked by scrolling flowers above grazing animals, bottom cen-tering verses of Psalms 1:3 above "In the year of the Lord 1821, the 23rd...," together with its book "Kurze Fragen Ueber die Christliche Glaubens–Lehre..." published Philadelphia, 1784, 6" h, 3½" w **4,600**

Bookplate (Bucherzeichen), unknown artist, 1830, pen, ink, pencil, and watercolor on woven paper, red, orange, blue, olive, and yellow stylized flowers with "1830," PA German text, framed, 9 x 6½" **650**

Drawing, Dieterly, Elizabeth, Bedminster Township, Bucks County, PA, attributed to, 1830, watercolor and ink, central stylized flower with alter-nating yellow dappled petals and elongated blue petals with red termini and green leaves on a stylized yellow stem issuing green buds and yellow, red, and black strawberries, brown triangular base, bounded vertically on each side by red and blue striped border, 7¾" h, 3¾" w **2,750**

Drawing, Dieterly, Elizabeth, Bedminster Township, Bucks County, PA, attributed to, second quarter 19th C, watercolor and ink, red bird with yel-low wing and blue tail and beak perched on yellow stem bursting with yellow, red, and blue flowers, tulips, and green leaves, 6" h, 4" w **4,375**

Drawing, Durham Township Artist, Bucks County, PA, 1823, watercolor and ink, central striped urn issuing tulips and flowers above striped plinth inscribed "Liberty is the life of the world and tyranny is its death," flanked by scrolling vines issuing flowers, strawberries, and buds, heralded above by 2 spreadwing dappled and shielded eagles clutching unfurled banner inscribed "Pluribus Unium" [sic], brown striped ground inscribed "Durham Tps., Bucks County...April the 9th 1823," 10" h, 7⅞" w **46,000**

Drawing, Ellinger, David, c1950, pen and ink and watercolor on paper, red, yellow, and black fantailed rooster beneath arched tulip, 4¼ x 3¾" **750**

Drawing, Englehard, attributed to, 1836, pen and ink and watercolor on cut paper, commemorates George Zoller, depicted as civilian, soldier, and as a married man with his wife, red, green, and yellow, 16 x 13" **1,950**

Drawing, Gerhart, George, attributed to, first quarter 19th C, watercolor and ink, owl with ocher head, red beak, eyes, and horns, red, black, and yellow dapple body, and black dec wing on branch issuing black, yellow, and red leaves, page embellished with yellow, black, and red rosettes and yellow and red leafy branch, red squiggle border, 6½" h, 4½" w **46,000**

Drawing, Gerhart, George, attributed to, 1826, watercolor and ink, central bursting red, black, and mustard stylized flower emanating from similar colored stylized leafy base above red rect reserve inscribed "1826" and surrounded by similar red, black, and mustard flowers and rosettes, enclosed in red squiggle border, 4⅞" h, 3⅞" w **1,150**

Drawing, Gerhart, George, attributed to, 1837, watercolor and ink, rect, upper half central stylized green, red, and yellow flower with striped stem issuing brown and yellow leaves flanked by 2 stylized striped and dappled red, yellow, and green opposing birds each facing a scrolling red, yellow, and green foliate vine, lower half with striped and dappled brown and red divide above a horizontal register inscribed "Catherine Hillegas, February 19th 1836, Made by Geo. Gerhart," all within a striped and dappled brown and red border, 6½" h, 4" w **27,600**

Drawing, Gottschall Family, attributed to, early 19th C, pen and ink and watercolor on paper, red, green, and black interlaced calligraphic figure 8 with 4 angel heads in corners, 9½ x 7⅛" **3,750**

Drawing, Peterman, Daniel, attributed to, c1838, watercolor on paper, paired birds, elegant ladies, and basket of blossoms, inscribed "The Birds of Paradise in all their Joys" across top, "A walk in the garden by two 2 sisters" lower left, and "A Christmas gift for Miss Mary Ann Rickert. Presented by M. Palmer December the 23rd 1838" lower right, 13¾ x 16¾" **13,800**

Drawing, Rockhill Township Artist, Bucks County, PA, attributed to, second quarter 19th C, watercolor and ink, red bird with yellow wing and beak and blue tail perched on curved branch with green leaves and 3 yellow, blue, and red flowers, enclosed in red band border, 3¾" h, 3" w **2,075**

Hand Drawn, drawings, Southeastern PA artist, possibly Bucks County, 1820–50, red, yellow, and green, price for pair, $3,450. Photo courtesy Christie's New York.

Drawing, School of George Gerhart, Bucks County, PA, mid–19th C, watercolor and ink, central tapering red and black diamond dec stem embellished with red and brown leaves below 2 segmented double–petaled red, brown, and yellow flowers, flanked on either side by yellow and red striped birds with brown wings and heads and stylized tails, geometric dec border, 6" h, 4¼" w **9,200**

Drawing, School of Johann Adam Eyer, probably Bucks County, PA, 1825, watercolor and ink, rect page centering profile of walking man wearing hat and coat flanked by oversized stylized tulips in blue, red, and yellow all above red and yellow dappled divide over "Sophia Gross" and "1825," all within conforming red and yellow sawtooth and scrolling surround, 6" h, 3¾" w **34,500**

Drawing, unknown artist, 1804, Schwenkfelder style, Bucks County, PA, rect, elaborate multiple bordered red, black, and yellow pinwheel flanked above and below by similarly colored rosette and open tulip dec heart inscribed "1804," surrounded on either side by highly dec yellow, red, and black framed pinwheel on scrolled ground issuing lush red, yellow, blue, black, and striped leaves, all above solid black band inscribed "Judiah Andersin," 9⅜" h, 7¼" w **16,100**

Drawing, unknown artist, 1820–50, southeastern PA, red bird with yellow wings perched on leafy vine with yellow, red, and green upright and pendant flowers, enclosed in rect border of red, yellow, and green bands and corner blocks, 5⅝" h, 2¾" w, price for pair **3,450**

Drawing, unknown artist, 1838, watercolor on paper, orange, red, and brown trumpeting angel, inscribed "Fredericksburg, Lebanon County, Penna. February 22nd, 1838, Washington Birthday, Fredericksburg, Lebanon, PA 1838" on verso, 4¼ x 2¾" **1,035**

Drawing, Weisel, Samuel, Bedminster and Hilltown Townships, Bucks County, PA, 1840, instructional, watercolor and ink, central clover shape comprised of intersecting compass drawn circles and cords, overlapping segments colored in green, white, red, brown, yellow, and black, all above ink inscribed set of instructions on how to make oil paint, 7¾" h, 6¼" w **2,075**

Hand Drawn, writing example (vorschrift), Christian Friederich Helener, dated 1830, copy book with cardboard cov and several illuminated pages, fraktur alphabets, and writing exercises, 6¾ x 8⅜", **$1,495.** Photo courtesy Sotheby's.

Marriage Certificate, school of Daniel Schumacher, 1777, paired red, yellow, and green birds flanking arch with crown, certificate for Johannes Haber and Elisabeth Stimmes, Windsor Township, Berks County, PA, 8 x 12½" 1,050

Reward of Merit, unknown artist, c1800, pen and ink and watercolor on paper, red, yellow, and blue–tailed bird perched on flowering branch, 3⅜ x 3⅛" 1,100

Reward of Merit, unknown artist, early 19th C, pen and ink and watercolor on paper, red and yellow birds and green and yellow pinwheel flower, 4⅛ x 3¼" 350

Songbook, David Kiestand, Macungie Township, Lehigh County, PA, dated February 8, 1823, marbled covers, leather binding, several handwritten and calligraphic pages with illuminated bookplate, 4⅛ x 6¾" 1,375

Writing Example (Vorschrift), Gerhart, George, Rockhill Township, Bucks County, PA, c1820, watercolor and ink, brown, red, yellow, blue, and green scrolling floral and foliate embellished fraktur writing in 2 horizontal registers above inscription of Psalm 128 and red, yellow, and blue bordered reserve centering brown and red dappled bird with black head, red wings, and blue tail perched on scrolling brown stem with brown and red leaves terminating in yellow, red, blue, and brown bursting flower, 7¾" h, 12½" w 6,325

Writing Example (Vorschrift), unknown artist, 1779, pen and ink and watercolor on paper, paired birds and strapwork lettering in red, green, and yellow, "Go Out My Heart," 8½ x 13⅛" 4,000

Writing Example (Vorschrift), unknown artist, late 18th/early 19th C, Bucks County, PA, watercolor and ink, rect page bound by conforming geometric border in red, green, black, and yellow enclosing similarly colored fraktur–written introductory text embellished with scrolling flowering and budding vines above further inscription 11,500

Writing Example (Vorschrift), unknown artist, 1834, Upper Milford Township, Lehigh County, PA, watercolor and ink, top and left borders with diamond banded geometric bands in green, red, yellow, and blue, enlarged foliate and floral dec fraktur lettering over 3 horizontal registers including 1 inscribed "Exhortation on the Youth," inscribed "John Mack" in lower left corner below blossoming garland, 8¼" h, 12¾" h 10,350

Writing Example (Vorschrift), unknown artist, first quarter 19th C, Bucks County, PA, watercolor and ink, executed in 3 horizontal registers, top in large fraktur lettering embellished with red, yellow, green, and blue diamonds, birds, leaves, and flowers above second smaller single line inscription over fully scripted verse followed by numeric and alphabetical band flanked at each lower corner by red frame with green bird with red head and wings and yellow tail perched on tulip vine, 8" h, 13" w 18,400

PRINTED FORM

Birth and Baptismal Certificate (Geburts und Taufschein), Krebs, Friederich, scrivener, 1799, watercolor dec, central printed heart inscribed with birth record of Johannes Ries, Paxton Township, Dauphin County, PA, flanked by 2 small printed hearts with text and watercolor dec paired parrots, stylized flowers, vining tulips, and sun faces, flanked above with crown and below with urn, printed by Gottlieb Jungmann, Reading, Friedrich Krebs imprint, dated "August 28, 1799," 13" h, 15⅞" w $2,185

Birth and Baptismal Certificate (Geburts und Taufschein), Krebs, Friederich, scrivener, 1800, watercolor dec, central printed heart inscribed with birth record of Henrich Ott, Bucks County, Bedminster Township, PA, flanked by 2 red and green parrots, tulips, sun faces, and crown, 12" h, 15" w **975**

Birth and Baptismal Certificate (Geburts und Taufschein), Krebs, Friederich, scrivener, 1803, watercolor, ink, and tinfoil dec, printed heart enclosing printed and inscribed birth record of Lydia Vogel, born 18 April 1803 to Abraham and Maria Margret (Fuchs?) Vogel of Nazareth Township in Northampton County, PA, surrounded by printed and inscribed hearts, watercolor painted flowers and crowns, and applied tinfoil cutout figures, 13" h, 16" w **575**

Birth and Baptismal Certificate (Geburts und Taufschein), Speyer, Frederick, scrivener, 1789, printed central heart inscribed with birth record for Sarra Grill, Lehigh County, PA, surrounded by watercolor dec paired angels, parrots, blossoms, and mermaids, 13" h, 16" w **1,375**

Birth and Baptismal Certificate (Geburts und Taufschein), unknown scrivener, 1796, watercolor dec, central printed heart inscribed with birth record of John Moll, son of John and Elizabeth (Nuysart) Moll in Allentown, Northampton (Lehigh) County on November 13, 1796, surrounded by printed and green, red, yellow, and peach watercolor dec scrolling foliate flowers, stars, birds, stylized leaves, and leaping deer, form printed by John Baumann, Ephrata, Lancaster County, PA, 12¼" h, 15¼" w **750**

Birth and Baptismal Certificate (Geburts und Taufschein), unknown scrivener, 1801, printed heart in black, floral designs with birds and parrots, printed in red with watercolor in yellow, red, 2 shades of green, and blue, records 1801 birth in Dauphin County, penciled–in English translation of PA German text, 17¼ x 21¼" **500**

Birth and Baptismal Certificate (Geburts und Taufschein), unknown scrivener, 1809, watercolor dec, central printed heart inscribed with birth record of Joseph Raub, Berks County, Bern Township, PA on July 8, 1809, surrounded by printed and watercolor dec scrolling foliate flowers, stars, birds, stylized leaves, and leaping deer, form printed by S Baumann, 12" h, 15" w **450**

Birth and Baptismal Certificate (Geburts und Taufschein), unknown scrivener, c1840, watercolor dec, central frame with large flower and birth record flanked by paired angels above trees each with 2 perched birds, shielded eagle clutching arrows and olive branch above, potted flowers and small trees below, form printed by John T Hanzsche, No. 30 Market St, Baltimore, MD, 14⅞" h, 12⅛" w **300**

Birth and Baptismal Certificate (Geburts und Taufschein), unknown Scrivener, c1840, watercolor dec, Lord's Supper theme, printed by C F Egelmann, Reading, PA, 11" h, 9" w **225**

Birth and Baptismal Certificate (Geburts und Taufschein), unknown scrivener, c1860, birth and baptismal text centered within elaborate scrolling border with winged angels and 4 vignettes depicting various stages of life, color form engraved by Hobarth Sebald and published by Ignatius Kohler, Philadelphia on woven paper, 13¼" h, 10⅜" w **75**

Birth and Baptismal Certificate (Geburts und Taufschein), unknown scrivener, c1860, watercolor dec, unfurled banner above open Bible, center frame for birth record flanked by paired angels, 2 birds perched on vining branch below, form printed by J S Dreisbach, Bath, PA, 16¾" h, 13⅝" w . . **150**

House Blessing (Haus–Segen), Krebs, Friedrich (PA), attributed to, 1785, watercolor dec, vertical rect page with central red, yellow, and blue flower and shell edge dec heart enclosing printed house blessing, whole surrounded by 12 individual green and red outlined printed blessings, page dec with red, yellow, blue, and green stylized flowers, buds, and leaves, meandering green and red base, 16" h, 13" w   700

House Blessing (Haus–Segen), unknown scrivener, 3 text blocks with sawtooth borders, 3 angels, 2 birds, flowers, leaves, and fruit, orange, green, blue, yellow, brown, and black, form printed by Johann Ritter, Reading, PA, repaired and rebacked on cloth, 15½" h, 11¾" w, old stenciled frame 18¼" h, 14⅜" w   500

LAWN ORNAMENTS

It was common to find a cast iron bench under a large tree, often a willow, or ornamental statue as part of a farmyard setting. Farmers enjoyed relaxing in the outdoors as much as working. Ornamental pieces also were used in garden and entrance settings.

Most lawn ornaments were cast from metal or concrete. Often they were painted to provide protection from the elements. Finding an example with original paint is unusual. Hitching posts are a favorite form among collectors.

The 1980s witnessed a renewed collecting interest in lawn ornaments and accessories, due in part to the Victorian decorating craze. Prices rose dramatically. Often outside ornaments became part of inside decorating schemes.

Many individuals failed to realize that excellent reproductions and copycats of nineteenth–century examples were made in the 1930s and 1940s by a number of firms, e.g., Virginia Metalcrafters. Ruth Webb Lee's "Ironworks" chapter in *Antique Fakes & Reproductions: Enlarged and Revised, Seventh Edition* (Lee Publications: 1950) is well worth reading.

Reference: J. P. Whyte's Pyghtle Works (Bedford England), *Garden Furniture,* Apollo Books, 1987.

Bell and Yoke, cast iron, painted black $75

Birdhouse, airplane shape, sheet metal and wood, stylized airplane with sheet metal body pierced with hole on 1 side above perch, sheet metal wheels and tail, wood propeller, traces of green and white paint, mounted on red painted wood stand, 7" h, 26" l   500

Birdhouse, seacoast house shape with mansard roof and cupola, wood, good detail with old red, gray, blue, white, and green paint, found in Kittery, ME, 24" h 1,815

Chairs, wood slat seats, painted black and white, each with different back, anvil, initials, and "1931," 36" h, price for set of 3   700

Fencing, cast iron, single panel, 3 posts, extra finials and hardware   225

Garden Chairs, cast iron, vintage design, white repaint, 14" h seat, 27¼" h, price for set of 4   200

Garden Settee, cast iron, vintage design, stripped, 38" l   250

Garden Stake, wood cutout, painted, black boy fishing, c1950, 28" h   60

Garden Table, round reticulated top, 4 scrolled legs, old white repaint, 40" d, 26" h   110

Garden Urns, cast iron, with ears, labeled "The Kramer Bros Fdy Dayton, O,"
old dark blue repaint, 31" h, price for pair **650**

Gate, wood, picket, painted gray, New England, 19th C, 35¼" w, 49" h **200**

Hitching Post, cast iron, dog, seated on its haunches with head up and ears
pricked, cast in the round, traces of worn white, gray, and brown polychrome paint, mounted on rect base, 19th C, 24" h **3,500**

Hitching Post, cast iron, horse head finial, fluted tapered standard with lion's
masks and acanthus leaves at base above octagonal plinth, cast in the
round, traces of worn blue–green paint, mounted on tapered rect black
wood base, 19th C, 48" h **3,500**

Hitching Post, cast iron, jockey, black features, holding ring, standing on
square plinth base, polychrome repaint, 37½" h **350**

Kettle, cast iron, bail handle, 28" d **85**

Lawn Ornament, begging squirrel, wood cutout, painted, wearing high col-
lared shirt and checkered pants **100**

Lawn Ornament, jockey, sheet metal, articulated arm, painted green, yellow,
and pink, mounted on rod, 12½" h **250**

Lawn Ornament, turtle, wood cutout, painted, standing upright, wearing top
hat, modern steel base, 25½" h **85**

Planter, tulip shape, cast iron, worn green paint, 8½" h **50**

Planter, urn shape, cement, painted white, square base, 24" h **20**

Planter, signal cannon, cast iron, ornate, painted black, 17⁴⁄₄" l **400**

Statue, dog, cast iron, painted, long thin tail, 19th C, 40" l, 28½" h **3,000**

Statue, rabbit, cast iron, full bodied, seated, painted white, 12" h **385**

Statue, stags, cast iron, full bodied standing figures modeled with heads up
and turned slightly right, cast fur detail, rect base, second half 19th C,
59½" h, 46½" l, price for pair **8,000**

Sundial, lead, 9¼ x 9¼" **100**

Wagon Wheel, wood, metal hub, painted white **50**

Water Pump, cast iron, painted black **50**

*Left: Lawn Jockey, hollow cast iron, red, white, and black, White
Oak Foundry, Peapack, NJ, 47" h, 20" w, $880.* Photo courtesy
Collectors Auction Services.

*Right: Garden Statue, dog, cast iron, painted, America, 19th C,
49" l, 28½" h, $3,025.* Photo courtesy Skinner, Inc., Boston, MA.

PAINTINGS & DRAWINGS

Four major types of paintings and drawings play important roles in the agrarian community—portraits, town and homestead views, landscapes, and student artwork. Each provides a valuable record of the past. Their highly personal nature was both a plus and minus. Because many had strong family connections, they were handed down from generation to generation. However, as tastes changed or individuals moved, the importance often diminished. As a result there are often more paintings and drawings found in a rural homestead's attic than hanging on the walls.

The individual portrait helped preserve the sense of family continuance. The portraitist survived in rural America until the end of the nineteenth century. The talents of the artists varied widely. However, a portrait by a less skilled artist was better than no portrait at all. Today knowing the name of the subject, date of the painting, and identity of the artist are value pluses when examining any work. By 1900 the camera replaced the portrait artist. It is worth noting that many late nineteenth and early twentieth century photographs meant to hang on the wall duplicated the size and poses of early oil and watercolor portraits.

Farm homestead and townscapes were done in fewer numbers. They are valued not only as works of art, but as historical documents. Many were done by amateurs and crudely drawn. A small majority were done by semi–professional and professional artists. Some of these artists have reached legendary status, e.g., the Pennsylvania Alms House painters of the mid–nineteenth century.

Rural America loved landscapes, evident by the large number of oils, watercolors, and prints that survive. Many are extremely large in size, meant to occupy the major portion of a wall in a rural parlor. Most were done by academically trained artists. Alas, the location, if painted from real life, has all too often been lost. Today the frame is often more valuable than the painting or watercolor that it contains.

Drawing was part of the curriculum in rural schools. Popular prints of the period and illustration plates in textbooks provided the inspiration for these aspiring artists. Although often crudely drawn, these artwork examples were displayed and saved by proud parents. Be careful not to confuse the work of children with that of the adult "folk" artist.

Many members of the rural community could not afford to purchase original works of art. Instead they relied on mass–produced etchings and prints that copied the works of popular painters of the period to decorate their walls. This is one of the most overlooked areas of collecting. Many examples sell for less than one hundred dollars.

There is no way a listing of less than several hundred paintings and drawings can accurately represent the breadth and depth of the folk paintings and drawings sold during the last few years. The listing merely serves as an introduction to the wealth of material that is part of this folk category.

The art community assigns a broad definition to folk painting and drawing. The itinerant limners of the colonial period are viewed as kin to Grandma Moses. In the 1970s and 1980s ethnicity was introduced as a key element in nineteenth and twentieth century examples.

In the final analysis, what constitutes a "folk" painting or drawing is a judgment call. Since attaching a "folk" attribution usually results in a significant increase in value, learn to question the motives of individuals making such an attribution.

References: The principal purpose of this section is to assist users in identifying and valuing their paintings. The section begins with general reference books on artist identification and folk paintings in particular. Price guide listings follow. Many specialized studies, such as Barbara and Lawrence Holdridge's *Ammi Phillips: Portrait of a Painter, 1788–1865* (Crown, 1969), exist. Check with the librarian at your local art museum for help in locating them.

Artist Dictionaries: Emmanuel Benezit, *Dictionnaire Critique et Documentaire des Peintres, Sculpteurs, Dessinateurs et Graveurs,* 10 volumes, *Third Edition,* Grund, 1976; Peter Hastings Falk, *Dictionary of Signatures & Monograms of American Artists,* Sound View Press, 1985; Mantle Fielding, *Dictionary of American Painters, Sculptors and Engravers,* Apollo Books, 1983; J. Johnson and A. Greutzner, *Dictionary of British Artists, 1880–1940: An Antique Collector's Club Research Project Listing 41,000 Artists,* Antique Collector's Club, 1976; Les Krantz, *American Artists, Facts on File,* 1985.

Folk Painting References: Robert Bishop, *Folk Painters of America,* E. P. Dutton, 1981; Mary Black and Jean Lipman, *American Folk Painting,* Clarkson N. Potter, 1966; C. Kurt Dewhurst, Betty MacDowell, and Marsha MacDowell, *Artists in Aprons: Folk Art by American Women,* E. P. Dutton, 1979; John and Katherine Ebert, *American Folk Painters,* Charles Scribner's Sons, 1975; Jack T. Ericson, *Folk Art in America: Painting and Sculpture,* Mayflower Books, 1979; Herbert W. Hemphill, Jr., and Julia Weissman, *Twentieth Century American Folk Art and Artists,* E. P. Dutton, 1974; Sidney Janis, *They Taught Themselves: American Primitive Painters of the 20th Century,* Dial Press, 1942; Jean Lipman and Tom Armstrong, *American Folk Painters of Three Centuries,* Hudson Hills Press, 1980; Beatrix T. Rumford, *American Folk Portraits: Paintings and Drawings From The Abby Aldrich Rockefeller Folk Art Center,* New York Graphic Society Books, 1981.

Price Guide References, Basic: *Art At Auction in America, 1995–1996 Edition,* Krexpress, 1996; William T. Currier (compiler), *Currier's Price Guide to American Artists 1645–1945 at Auction, Fourth Edition,* Currier Publications, 1994; Rosemary and Michael McKittrick, *The Official Price Guide to Fine Art, Second Edition,* House of Collectibles, 1993; Susan Theran, *Fine Art: Identification and Price Guide, Third Edition,* Avon Books, 1996.

Price Guide References, Advanced: *ADEC/Art Price Annual International,* Ehrmann; R. J. Davenport, *Davenport's Art Reference & Price Guide, 1997–98 Edition,* 2 Vols, Davenport Publishing, 1997; Peter Hastings Falk (ed), *Art Price Index International,* Sound View Press, 1997; Richard Hislop (ed), *The Annual Art Sales Index,* Weybridge, Surrey, England, Art Sales Index, Ltd, since 1969; Enrique Mayer, *International Auction Records,* Archer Fields, since 1967; Susan Theran (ed), *Leonard's Price Index of Art Auctions,* Auction Index, Inc, since 1980.

Museum Directories: American Art Directory, R. R. Bowker Co; American Assoc of Museums, The Official Museum Directory: United States and Canada, updated periodically.

Reproduction Alert: Unless you are thoroughly familiar with the artist, you are advised to have any folk painting that you are considering buying authenticated by an independent source. In Samuel Pennington's "The Folk Art Forger," an article about Robert Trotter's forgeries in the March 1990 *Maine Antique Digest,* he states: "No amount of money or hard time in prison, however, is likely to heal the scars his schemes inflicted on an industry that often all too readily absorbed his artistic frauds." Trotter is not the only art forger around; he just happened to get caught.

DRAWING

Brader, Ferdinand A (late 19th C), pencil on paper, The Property of John Willy, Alsace Town, Berks Co, man on horse in front lower left, barn with tractor and farmhouse with fenced yard in background, 21" h, 33¼" w . . . **$5,175**

Davis, Joseph H (1811–1865), watercolor, pen and ink, and pencil on paper, portrait of the Frost family, gentleman in black suit, little girl in orange dress, and lady in brown dress standing near grain painted table beneath wall clock, inscribed in ornamental calligraphy along bottom "James F. Frost, Born Oct. 24, 1802, Sarah Minerva Fanwood Frost, Born Sept. 23, 1832, Louisa N. Frost, Born July 7, 1811," 9¼" h, 15¼" w **10,925**

Highley, Omar M, pencil, watercolor, and charcoal on paper, primitive scene of homesteaders clearing land, sgd "Omar M. Highley Age 12, 1899," walnut molded frame with gilt liner, 21³/₄" h, 26⁴/₄" w **685**

Kitchen, pencil and graphite, landscape with mill, trees, and stream with rowboat, back sgd "Mrs. Kitchen," 15³/₈" h, 20⁷/₈" w **85**

Landes, Rudolph (Hilltown and New Britain Townships, Bucks County, PA 1784–1852), attributed to, watercolor and ink on paper, 2 intertwining preening parrots flanked by scrolling flowers and vines and crowned by sprouting foliage at juncture of necks, red, brown, black, and yellow, c1814, 7³/₄" h, 6½" w **99,300**

Lanham, J W, pen and ink, flowers and 5 birds inside circular design, small pointing hands, black, blue, and brown, sgd at bottom, mahogany veneer frame, 14¼" h, 12¼" w **125**

School of George Gerhart (Bucks County, PA mid–19th C), watercolor and ink on paper, central tapering red and black diamond dec stem embellished with red and brown leaves below 2 segmented double petaled red, brown, and yellow flowers, stem flanked on either side by yellow and red striped birds with brown wings and heads and stylized tails, geometric dec border, 6" h, 4¼" w **9,200**

Unknown Artist, brother and sister, pencil and watercolor on paper, primitive, young boy hugging sister, brown, orange, blue, and yellow, 8³/₁₆" h, 6³/₈" w, mahogany veneer beveled frame 10½" h, 9½" w **135**

Unknown Artist, eagle with flowers and "1822," pen and ink on woven paper, primitive, old beveled red frame, stains, 7³/₄" h, 9¼" w **525**

Unknown Artist, farm and residence of Abraham Benson, Liberty Tp. Hancock, Co. O 1882, pen and ink and pencil on paper, detailed aerial view, 8" h, 15" w, worn frame 9½" h, 16½" w **1,375**

Unknown Artist, patriotic theme, pencil and charcoal, folksy scene of man with trumpet backed up by all–girl band, stage and American flags in background, red, white, and blue rope carved frame, 23" h, 19½" w **2,000**

MINIATURE PORTRAIT

Crosse, regal lady, painted on celluloid ivory, sgd "Crosse," ornate gilt brass frame, 8³/₄" h, 6" w **$325**

Smart, Patrick Henry, painted on celluloid ivory, bust with red drape, sgd on back of frame "...Smart," 8¼" h, 7½" w **175**

Unknown Artist, woman, painted on porcelain, wearing white dress, gilded brass frame, 5⁷/₈" h, 5" w **175**

Unknown Artist, young girl, painted on ivory, blonde hair, red dress, gold filled case with pin back and loop for pendant with chain, memorial inscription "Maria Antoinette Brooks, Died May 2nd, 1847, Aged 3 years, 17 days," 2" h **450**

PAINTING

Bard, James (1815–1897), oil on board, Horse Jack of Woodbridge, NJ, inscribed, sgd, and dated "Horse Jack of Woodbridge, N.J.; This Picture the Property of Charles Drake — Presented by James Bard the Artist, N.Y. 1871" along bottom, 8½" h, 11¾" **$85,000**

Bard, James and John (1815–1897 and 1815–1856), oil on canvas, Steamboat Alida, 29" h, 49" w **85,000**

Black, John, pen and ink and watercolor on woven paper, landscape, house, 2 trees, sky with 3 bird's head clouds, brown, red, yellow, black, and green, artist sgd, mahogany veneer beveled frame, 11" h, 9" w **1,550**

Brunner, Hattie K. (1890–1982), watercolor and gouache on paper, Country Snow Scene, winter landscape with covered bridge, train, houses, horse–drawn sleigh, and skaters on frozen pond, sgd and dated "Hattie K. Brunner '70" in lower right, 18" h, 26" w **9,200**

Clough, C L (New York 1824–1901), oil on canvas, landscape with cattle in stream, sgd by artist, repaired and rebacked, gilt frame, 19" h, 23" w . . . **1,550**

Davison, Austin (died 1993), oil on masonite, paired doves, tulips, and blossoms within heart surround, rendered for The Index of American Design, The Pennsylvania Area, 16" h, 20⅛" w **450**

DeBlois, Francois B, oil on canvas, "Looking Throughout the Orchard 1881," landscape, sgd by artist, gilt frame, 16¼" h, 22¾" w **1,875**

DeVoss, oil on canvas, landscape with cottage and river, sgd, 24" h, 36" w . .   **135**

Ehrlinger, F J, oil on canvas, winter landscape with white bearded black man and dog, sgd and dated "F.J. Ehrlinger 1894," unsgd landscape on canvas back, 20¾" h, 15¾" w; old gilt frame 22¾" h, 18⅝" w **450**

Ellinger, David (20th C), oil on canvas laid on board, White Washing, farmer white washing stone wall, large barn with hex signs in background, sgd "D. Ellinger" lower left, "White Washing" on verso, 18⅛" h, 22" w **4,025**

English, Frank F (1854–1922), watercolor on paper, Haying in a Pennsylvania Farm, rural landscape with farmhouse, hay field, and team of horses, sgd "F.F. English" lower right, 16½" h, 30½" w **1,725**

Eshelman, Frank (1874–1959), oil on canvas, view of the David Moll farm, north of the present Hamburg area middle school, PA, 21½" h, 30¼" w . . . **1,850**

Freeman, Agatha C, oil on canvas, landscape with village and ducks in stream, sgd on stretcher "Agatha C. Freeman, Jan. 31st 1893," gilt frame, 11" h, 17¼" w **400**

Gates, E A, oil on canvas, landscape with road and trees, black, white, and gray with yellow and green, sgd by artist, framed, 24¾" h, 34¾" w **75**

Grinvald, A, watercolor on paper, Village Scene with Horse and Buggy, sgd and dated "A. Grinvald 1859" lower right, 19¾" h, 27¼" w **3,450**

Kollner, Augustus (1812–1906), attributed to, watercolor on paper, topographical farm scene, 13¼" h, 17½" w **3,450**

Maentel, Jacob (1763–1863), watercolor on paper, full–length profile portrait of brown haired young lady wearing long lavender gown with white ruffled collar and turquoise sash and holding sprig of pink roses, orig frame and glass, c1830, 9" h, 6⅞" w **4,885**

Malton, watercolor on paper, landscape with town, river, and cows, sgd "Malton 1823," rosewood veneer frame with gilt liner, 19³/₈" h, 23³/₈" w . . . **1,050**

Mays, Anna, oil on canvas, Woman's Sanitary Corp, primitive Civil War scene of women caring for wounded soldiers, tents and American flag in background, titled and labeled "Painted by Anna Mays, Arcanum, OH," on frame backing, cleaned, 22" h, 18" w, frame 23¹/₄" h, 19¹/₄" w **5,275**

Montgomery, Alfred (Los Angeles, CA 1857–1922), oil on canvas, hanging game bird, sgd "Alfred Montgomery 1872," 2 old patches and restoration, 24" h, 20" w, gilt frame 26³/₄" h, 22³/₄" w **100**

Nye, Emily, watercolor on paper, flower, red, yellow, and green, 2⁷/₈" h, 3³/₄" w, wood frame 4" h, 4³/₄" w **275**

Rank, W (20th C), oil on velvet, Horse and Sulky, sgd lower right, 10¹/₈" h, 14" w **490**

Schroeder, G Eugene, oil on canvas, His Sunset, landscape with Indian, sgd, dated, and titled on back "His Sunset, orig. comp. By G. Eugene Schroeder, 1923," 22¹/₂" h, 18" w, gilt frame 28¹/₄" h, 24" w **875**

Shaylor, HW (20th–C American artist), watercolor on paper, 2 men in boat Pollywog, sgd by artist, both men and Lake Cabbosseeantee, ME, identified on back, matted and framed, 13³/₄" h, 16¹/₂" w **110**

Sheets, oil on cardboard, patriotic scene, primitive, soldier in Revolutionary War uniform beside lake with pine trees, American flag like sky, back mkd "This picture was painted by Mr. Sheets before he got shot by a German, Dec. 31, 1917," framed, 14" h, 18¹/₂" w **75**

Strohl, Clifford (born 1893), oil on board, The Blacksmith Shop, 18¹/₂" h, 24¹/₂" w **250**

Topping, James, oil on canvas, sgd by artist, gilt frame, 26" h, 28¹/₂" w **525**

Unknown Artist, Bethesda Chapel, church scene, oil on cardboard, primitive, gilt frame, 13¹/₄" h, 18¹/₂" w **385**

Unknown Artist, country landscape, oil on academy board, primitive, house and out buildings, back inscribed "Presented to the West Grammar School by R.M. Deblors," cleaned, old gilt frame, 12¹/₂" h, 15¹/₂" w **275**

Unknown Artist, floral design, watercolor on paper, braided hair attachments, matted and framed, 7⁵/₈" h, 5⁵/₈" w **25**

Unknown Artist, homestead, oil on academy board, primitive, framed, 1¹/₂" h, 24" w, frame 21" h, 26¹/₂" w **250**

Painting, V P Anderson, American, oil on canvas, Feeding Time in the Barn, sgd, 14 x 20", $2,955. Photo courtesy Sotheby's.

Unknown Artist, horse and dog, watercolor and pencil on paper, brown and black, matted and framed, 13¼" h, 17¼" w **110**

Unknown Artist, landscape, oil on poplar board, old man and dog beside cabin, revarnished, gilt frame, 14¼" h, 18¼" w **765**

Unknown Artist, landscape with cows in stream and fisherman, oil on artist board, gilt frame, 12" h, 16" w **225**

Unknown Artist, portrait, oil on tin, primitive, young woman wearing red dress, orig paper label with ink inscription on back "Portrait of Cornelia D. Seward painted when 10 or 11 years of age," mahogany veneer beveled frame, 6¾" h, 5¼" w **350**

Unknown Artist, portrait, watercolor on paper, man wearing blue frock coat, red and black painted handmade frame, inletted irregular pc of old glass, 5" h, 4¼" w **325**

Unknown Artist, portrait, watercolor on paper, young woman wearing blue dress and white bonnet, matted, old gilt frame, 5⅞" h, 5⅛" w **350**

Unknown Artist, Sacketts Harbor, NY, oil on wood panel, later inscription "Capt. Haas 1812, Sacketts Harbor, NY" on verso, 13½" h, 18" w **5,450**

Unknown Artist, still life of watermelons and peach, oil on canvas, 17¾" h, 23¾" w, worn gilt frame 20¾" h, 26¾" w **1,375**

Unknown Artist, still life with fruit in basket, oil on academy board, gilded frame, 26¾" h, 20½" w **250**

Unknown Artist, 2 chickens, watercolor on paper, primitive, black chickens, stains, uneven edges, short tear, old frame with red and black repaint, 11½" h, 18" w **465**

Waldron, James MK (1909–1974), watercolor on paper, Farm at Warwick Mill, sgd and dated "James M.K. Waldron, 1973" and titled "Farm at Warwick Mill" lower right, 14" h, 21" w **315**

Walker, Harold, watercolor on paper, landscape, matted and framed, 20" h, 25" w **100**

Wendell, Oscar, watercolor and oil on canvas, primitive, soldiers, American flag, cannons and "Brooklyn Navy Yard Marines New York City," red, blue, white, and gold, sgd and dated on back "Oscar Wendell, Dec. 1, '89," beveled frame, 11" h, 14" w **325**

Wysocki, Charles (born 1928), oil on canvas, Barn Dance, 30" h, 36" w **10,350**

REVERSE PAINTING ON GLASS

Unknown Artist, portrait, woman wearing red and white dress and plumed hat, 7" h, 4½" w **$165**

Unknown Artist, winter landscape, country house, gilt frame, 10½" h, 12½" w   **75**

SCHERENSCHNITTE

Scherenschnitte, translated as scissor–cut, is the art of decorative paper cutting. It was brought to America by German–speaking immigrants.

Scherenschnitte is found in two basic forms—complete picture and supplemental decoration. While a silhouette is technically a scissor–cutting, the term is generally reserved for full size pictures of landscape and forest scenes. As a decorative element, scherenschnitte is found on objects such as birth certificates, marriage certificates, memorial pictures, and valentines.

The term "scherenschnitte" is generally reserved for examples cut in the late eighteenth and early nineteenth centuries. Some were cut of gilded paper. Most were mounted against a contrasting color cloth or paper background.

Scissor–cutting is a continuing tradition, although late nineteenth– and early twentieth–century Victorian works do not command the same value as early examples. In Europe the tradition is especially strong in Slavic regions. Many of these examples have worked their way into the American market.

Finally, some contemporary scherenschnitte artists are experimenting with cutting techniques other than scissors, e.g., lasers. When buying a contemporary example make certain that you know how the piece was cut.

Birth Certificate, watercolor and ink dec, fraktur written birth and baptismal announcement of Esther Guthart, daughter of Friedrich and Maria (Schaffner) Guthart in Exeter Township, Berks County, November 22, 1803 within conforming rect border with cutwork vining flowers and heart corners in red, yellow, and buff, attributed to Wilhelmus Antonius Faber (1790–1818), PA, 7³/₄" h, 12³/₄" w **$1,000**

Card, cut work, people, animals, and hearts **3,500**

Picture, circular design with birds, hearts, and flowers, scissor–cut and pin-pricked white paper, mahogany veneer beveled frame, 16¹/₂ x 13¹/₈" **415**

Picture, collection of 25 individual designs including horse–drawn vehicles, trees, birds, and flowers, scissor–cut white paper mounted on black ground cloth, shadow box frame, 22¹/₄ x 18¹/₂" **575**

Picture, landscapes, 1 with church, mill, houses, animals, and trees, other with manor house, swan pond, outbuildings, gate, animals, and trees, scissor–cut white paper on turquoise blue paper ground, 19th C, 11¹/₂ x 16", price for pair **1,100**

Picture, vignettes, "Man's Abuse of Animals" and "The Hunted's Revenge," first grouping illus abuse by man of animals in hunting, farming, and playing, second grouping depicts hunted birds and deer stringing up their persecutors, green paper ground, 19th C, 7³/₄ x 9", price for pair **875**

Valentine, 8–point star, surrounded by 8 hearts and birds on vines, heart border, verses inscribed on all hearts, scissor–cut white paper, c1840, 14³/₄ x 15" **1,000**

Valentine, 16–point star, surrounded by 8 hearts, verses inscribed on hearts, busts of 19th–C garbed man and woman over each heart, pairs of birds flanking small heart in each corner, scissor–cut white paper, dated 1850, 14³/₄ x 15" **1,200**

Valentine, circular, watercolor and ink dec, conforming scalloped center painted white, red, blue, and green and inscribed with 8 numbered romantic verses, within 8–pointed rosette dec with blue, red, and green painted tulips and lovebirds, bound in conforming red, green, and blue cut rosette guilloche, southeastern PA, first quarter 19th C, 13" d **2,300**

Valentine, circular with hex sign type cuttings, hearts and other borders, pen and ink inscription, scissor–cut white paper mounted on olive green ground, dated 1842, 13" d **2,000**

Valentine, hexagonal motif, watercolor and ink dec, central flowering blossom within wreath of red, blue, green, and yellow leafy buds surrounded by 6 numbered and attached hearts, each outlined in red, blue, and green, dec with a tulip, and inscribed with romantic sentiment, southeastern PA, early 19th C, 12¹/₈" h, 10¹/₄" w **1,275**

SEWER TILE ART

The sewer tile factories in the area of eastern Ohio, near Akron, produced utilitarian objects made of clay. These companies made a number of advertising giveaways featuring miniature examples of their products or decorative items such as plaques, paperweights, and horseshoes. At day's end workers fashioned leftover clay into a myriad of objects for personal enjoyment. Molds also were available, and miscellaneous figures from cats to pigs were made.

Although sewer tile materials date from the 1800s to the 1950s, the golden age of this folk art form dates from 1900 to 1940. Emphasis is on the hand sculpted pieces. Research has identified many of the artisans who produced these materials.

Since pieces are highly individualistic, artistic consideration is a large factor in determining price. Damage causes serious problems for the collector. One of a kind items need to be carefully restored if damaged. Collectors prefer items in very good or better condition. Prices do fluctuate; the market is still seeking a level of stability. Whenever a collecting category attracts the folk art collectors; it is difficult to find an accurate pricing level. Design, style, and even the whimsical nature of the piece determine the price, as well as how much the collector is willing to pay.

Reference: Jack E. Adamson, *Illustrated Handbook of Ohio Sewer Pipe Folk Art,* privately printed, 1973.

Bank, pig, seated, incised "To Pat my Godfather," 9¼" h **$225**
Bank, pig, standing upright, wearing bow tie and pants, 8³/₈" h **175**
Bank, pig, standing upright, wearing hat, bow tie, and jacket, incised "W.S.,"
  8⁷/₈" h **65**
Bank, pig, standing upright, wearing hat, neckerchief, and clothing, initialed
  "E.D.," 8³/₄" h **165**
Birdhouse, cylindrical, tooled bark surface, 8½" h **550**
Candelabra, scrolling branches with applied flowers, birds, and leaves, some
  color mixed in clear glaze, 12³/₈" h **75**
Figure, bulldog puppy, seated, rect base, 3³/₄" h **150**
Figure, bullfrog, 7" l **100**
Figure, cat, seated, 7" h **165**
Figure, dog, seated, Staffordshire type, free standing front legs, 10¼" h **225**
Figure, lion battling serpent, realistically modeled, rect base, 11" l, 8" h **225**
Figure, owl, looking to right, feather detail, incised "Tim Gibson," 8¼" h **135**
Figure, raccoon, crouching, white slip details and striped tail, green painted
  eyes, incised initials "J.C.," 15" l **165**
Figure, raccoon, crouching on log, incised "Chuck Miburn," 13" l **235**
Figure, squirrel, climbing, drilled holes for nailing to tree, incised "E.A.,"
  7½" h **150**
Figure, squirrel eating nut, yellow slip eye, incised "CM1980," 6³/₄" h **25**
Figure, squirrel holding nut, initialed "E.D.," 9" h **55**
Jar, ovoid, molded Art Deco designs, 19" h **55**
Lamp, tree with 4 stumps, lion, and reclining naked lady in front, base
  incised "J.W. Moore, June 10, 1926, Uhrichsville, O. Evans Pipe Co.,"
  13³/₄" h **2,650**
Lamp, vine–wrapped tree, bird's eggs in knothole, incised "Made by Earl F.
  Page," 23½" h **550**
Planter, basket, rect, tooled bark finish, 10" h **225**

Planter, box, square, molded, applied and tooled surface, 4 bracket legs with
base stretcher, 9 x 9" sq, 11½" h 335
Planter, tree stump, reserve on side with inscription "Mark Milliken, born
July 1823, Died June 22, 1879, Joanna his wife born Aug. 27, 1825, Died
Jan. 25, 1908," 22½" h 335
Umbrella Stand, ovoid, Art Deco designs around shoulder, 18½" h 75

SILHOUETTES

Silhouettes (shades) are shadow profiles, produced by hollow cutting, mechanical
tracing, or painting. They were popular in the eighteenth and nineteenth centuries.

The name came from Etienne de Silhouette, a French Minister of Finance, who
tended to be tight with money and cut "shades" as a pastime. In America the Peale
family was one of the leading silhouette makers. An impressed stamp marked "PEALE"
or "Peale Museum" identifies their work.

Silhouette portraiture lost popularity with the introduction of the daguerreotype
prior to the Civil War. In the 1920s and 30s a brief revival occurred when tourists to
Atlantic City and Paris had their profiles cut as souvenirs.

References: Shirley Mace, *Encyclopedia of Silhouette Collectibles On Glass*, Shadow
Enterprises, 1992; Blume J. Rilken, *Silhouettes in America, 1790–1840, A Collectors'
Guide*, Paradigm Press, 1987.

Museums: Essex Institute, Salem, MA; National Portrait Gallery, Washington, DC.

Bust, Abraham Lincoln, reverse painted glass, inscribed "Abraham Lincoln,"
ogee bird's-eye frame with gilded liner, 8" h, 7¼" w $165
Bust, Andrew Jackson, cut black paper with gilt and black ink, inscribed
"Andrew Jackson, President of the United States," minor foxing, ogee
bird's eye frame with gilded liner, 9⅞" h, 8⅞" w 800
Bust, couple, man and woman, hollow cut, emb "Peale Museum" labels,
framed together, eglomise glass, gilt frame, 11¼" h, 13¼" w 90
Bust, couple, man and woman, ink and ink wash on paper, stains, walnut
frame, 6½" h, 4¼" w, price for pair 450
Bust, gentleman, black and gilt on plaster, miniature, sgd "Miers," gutta per-
cha frame, 2⅞" h 900
Bust, gentleman, hollow cut, black paper backing, stains, old black painted
turned round frame, 5⅛" d 135
Bust, gentleman, hollow cut, ink detail, reverse painted glass backing, rect
wood frame with oval opening, 5¼" h, 4¼" w 195
Bust, gentleman, hollow cut with ink detail and white highlights on black
paper backing, emb "Davis Patent," oval brass frame, 4½" h, 3⅞" w 150
Bust, German couple, double silhouette, cut from paper with well executed
details in black, white, and shades of gray, old paper label on back identifying German couple and stating silhouettes were made on their wedding day in 1795, molded frame, 6⅝" h, 8⅞" w 775
Bust, lady, hollow cut with ink detail and blue crêpe bodice, black reverse
painted matte, old molded frame, wood frame backing mkd "Miss
Rosanna Taylor," 5⅝" h, 5" w 160
Bust, Major Zackary Taylor, cut black paper, stain at nose, inscribed "Major
Zackary Taylor, 1836," ebonized wood frame with gilded brass liner,
6⅝" h, 5⅞" w 415

Bust, mature woman, cut black paper with gilded highlights, labeled "Cut w/common scissors by Mr. W. Seville" on orig black lacquer frame with brass fittings, 6¼" h, 5" w **670**

Bust, military man, ink and watercolor, inscribed "F. Bishop 1815," probably not as old as date indicates, 10⅜" h, 8⅜" w **40**

Bust, military man, ink and watercolor, inscribed, "F. Collins 1824," probably not as old as date indicates, 8¾" h, 6¾" w **35**

Bust, William Lloyd Garrison, ink on paper with white highlights, sgd "Thos. Edwards, Boston 1837. Hon William Lloyd Garrison Abolitionist," minor stains, shadowbox frame, 8⅜" h, 6⅞" w **575**

Bust, woman, hollow cut head, brushed ink bodice, old black frame with gilt stenciling, 5¼" h, 4¼" w **325**

Bust, woman, hollow cut, wearing bonnet, black paper backing, water stain at bottom edge, later inscription on back of frame "Margret Ten Eyck Age 37, Hurley, N.Y.," 4" h, 3¼" w, emb brass frame 5⅛" h, 4½" w **225**

Bust, woman, ink and ink wash on paper, wearing bonnet, black lacquered frame with gilded liner and cut corners, 4½" h, 4¼" w **225**

Bust, woman, painted, black and white, sgd "Adolphe 1826," Maurier collection sticker on frame, 5¼" h, 4" w **55**

Bust, young man, cut from black paper, later inscription on back of frame "Jacobus Ten Eyck Age 19," 4" h, 3¼" w, emb brass frame 5¼" h, 4½" w . . **225**

Bust, young man, hollow cut, black cloth backing, eglomise glass and old black molded frame, 6" h, 5¼" w **135**

Bust, young man, hollow cut, faded black cloth backing, pencil inscription "March 25th, 1857," old black molded frame with gilded brass corner ornaments, 6½" h, 5½" w **165**

Bust, young man, hollow cut with ink detail and black cloth backing, emb "Herve" shadowbox frame, 6½" h, 5¾" w **300**

Bust, young woman, hollow cut, black backing, pen and ink inscription "Cut without hands by M.A. Honeywell," framed, 5" h, 4" w **325**

Bust, young woman, hollow cut, black cloth backing, stained paper, gilded frame, 6¾ x 6¾" **195**

Bust, young woman, hollow cut, ink detail, black paper backing, old rect gilt frame, 4⅛" h, 3¼" w **140**

Bust, young woman, reverse painted on glass, black lacquer frame with gilded brass fittings, emb label on hanger "Herve, Miniature Painter, 12 Cheapside," 5" h, 4⅛" w **165**

Full Length, child, cut black paper, simple watercolor background paper, unframed, 4½" h, 3½" w **250**

Full Length, Daniel Webster, cut black paper, scratched detail, labeled in pencil "DanL. Webster," shadowbox frame, 8½" h, 6½" w **165**

Full Length, girl, cut paper profile, holding bird in hand, sun hat resting off shoulders, ink wash background with fence and "Lydia Harris" and "Aug. Edouart fecit 1842," back of figure has ghost image of another silhouette and some pencil sketched lines done preliminary to finished cutout which may have been altered and reused by Edouart, 10⅞" h, 8⅞" w, shadowbox frame 14¼" h, 12¼" w **2,300**

Full Length, man reading book, cut black paper figure with ink detail background, sgd "Aug. Edouart fecit 1826," background faded and has edge tear, black touched up on figure, framed, 12⅛" h, 8¾" w **325**

Full Length, man sitting in chair, legs crossed, cut paper with gilded detail
    and inkwash ground, sgd "S. Metford fecit," old label on back identifies
    subject as Robert Bishop and artist as Samuel Metford, minor stains, ogee
    frame, 11¾" h, 9½" w **450**

Full Length, man sitting in chair, reading book, separate cut out candlestand,
    cut black paper, sgd "Aug. Edouart fecit 1828," age stains, 10" h, 9" w **1,200**

Full Length, man standing, 1 arm held back, other holding top hat at knee,
    cut black figure with white highlights, sgd "J. Blackburn, King St.
    Manchester, 1827," minor stains, 9⅜" h, 7" w **250**

Full Length, man standing, 1 arm resting at small of back, other holding top
    hat at knee, cut paper with gilt detail and simple inkwash ground, sgd "F.
    Frith" (Frederick Frith), oak veneer frame with gilded liner, 13¼" h,
    10⅝" w **325**

Full Length, man walking, wearing top hat and long coat, carrying walking
    stick, cut black paper with simple inkwash ground, sgd "Augustin Edouart
    fecit 1826," framed, 10⅜" h, 7" w **1,000**

Full Length, room setting, aristocratic family, reverse painted on glass, stand-
    ing man and child, seated woman, bust on pedestal, small stand with stat
    ue, other furniture and draping, black, red, and blue, old glass with some
    imperfections, probably late 19th C, bird's–eye maple ogee frame with
    gilded liner, 15" h, 19" w **475**

Full Length, youth, standing while reading book, cut black paper, gilt detail,
    emb label "Taken at the Hubard Gallery" (Master Hubard), framed,
    11¼" h, 8" w **635**

THEOREM

Theorem describes the creation of art through the use of stencils, one for each
color. As a form it was extremely popular in the early nineteenth century, especially in
New England and Pennsylvania. The technique was used by furniture manufacturers
as well as artists. However, when used by the antiques community, theorem means a
work of art executed as a watercolor on paper or oils on velvet or cloth.

Still lifes of fruits and flowers in bowls and vases were the most popular subject.
Many of the patterns were based upon examples in instruction manuals or popular
prints. Although some individuals cut their own stencils and mixed their own colors,
many of the young female academy students and women at home that painted theorems relied on pre–cut and ready mixed colors.

Dating theorems can often be accomplished by noting the style of the basket or
container used in the still life. Pressed glass compotes were first produced in the
1830s. Another aid is to note the stencil pattern and compare it with dated examples
found in carpets, fabrics (bedspreads, curtains, pillow shams, and tablecloths), and
floors. Patterns did cross over.

Two keys to value are design and originality. Add extra for the inclusion of animals,
such as a bird or butterfly. Most collectors assign a fifty percent premium to a watercolor on paper theorem. However, oils on velvet theorem often acquire a mellow
palette that is stunning.

Two contemporary theorem painters deserve special mention—David Ellinger
(active between 1940 and 1980) and William Rank. Ellinger's works appear on velvet,
cotton, and paper and are often confused with period examples. Not all his works are
signed. Rank's theorems are much more vivid in color than those of Ellinger.

Basket of Flowers, bird nest and mother bird feeding young, painted on velvet, red, blue, green, and brown, damage and holes in velvet upper left, beveled frame with old green paint, 15" h, 18" w **$250**

Basket of Fruit, oil on cardboard, blue, green, brown, pink, and red, white ground, unframed, 8" h, 10" w **110**

Basket of Fruit, watercolor on paper, initialed "A.E.M.," primitive, slightly trimmed, framed, 18½" h, 14½" w **225**

Basket of Fruit, watercolor on velvet, 10" h, 12" w **1,600**

Basket of Fruit and Foliage, shades of green, brown, blue, and red, beveled frame with orig red flame graining, minor stains, 13½" h, 16¾" w **1,750**

Basket of Roses and Other Flowers, painted on velvet, faded reds and yellows with olive green and blue, sgd under basket in blue "Leonora L. Kellogg," old tape label on ext of glass in bottom corner "painted on velvet by my grandmother L. Kellogg Barrows," matted and framed, 19" h, 22" w **500**

Bird, watercolor on paper, brown, yellow, and green, modern frame, 7¾" h, 5⅜" w **100**

Bowl of Flowers, watercolor, pencil, and mica on paper, yellow and red tulips, roses, chrysanthemums, and pansies, glittering bowl, c1830, 11¼" h, 8¾" w **1,500**

Bowl of Fruit, watercolor on paper, red, yellow, orange, green, and brown, ink inscription reads "Friendship, Laura M. Lord," fold lines, minor stains and tears, beveled frame with alligatored red and yellow paint, 10⅜" h ... **3,125**

Cherries, watercolor on paper, red, brown, and green, old beveled curly maple frame, 8" h, 7½" w **685**

Compote of Flowers, polychrome paints on velvet, small stains to lower background, 19th C, 23½" h, 17½" w **1,750**

Compote of Fruit, Mary Ellen Fuller, watercolor on paper, blue, green, yellow, brown, and red, minor fading and stains, damaged old gilt frame, 14" h, 16" w **1,650**

Cucumber, radish, and blossoms in green, red, and yellow, sgd "Marion L. Fowler," old gilt frame, 9" h, 11" w **475**

Horse, eagle, shield, and flag, watercolor and graphite on paper, 26½ x 20½" **3,000**

Landscape, watercolor on velvet, buildings, trees, and deer, red, yellow, green, brown, and blue, 13⅛ x 12¼" **5,000**

Parrot, watercolor on velvet, perched on grapevine and eating strawberries from overflowing basket of fruit, soft colors, 26 x 22" **3,100**

Roses and Morning Glories, faded colors, orig mahogany veneer frames, 8½" h, 8" w, price for pair **550**

Roses and Other Flowers, velvet ground, pink, green, blue, and yellow, old gilded frame, 8¼" h, 11½" w **475**

Stylized Tulips, with other flowers and foliage, painted on velvet, red, black, green, and yellow, inscribed on back edge "To Cora Lee from David Ellinger" (20th-C PA folk artist), framed, 16¾" h, 13½" w **200**

Vase of Flowers, watercolor on laid paper, sponged technique in red, blue, green, and yellow, pen and ink name and date in brown and green "Sarah Morrel 1857," stains, old beveled frame, 15¾" h, 11¾" w **275**

Vase of Flowers, watercolor on paper, pink, blue, yellow, green, and brown, creases and water stains, ¼" strip emb paper glued to edges, old gilt frame, 18¼" h, 14" w **350**

TRAMP ART

The making of tramp art was prevalent in the United States from 1875 to the 1930s. The majority of items were made by itinerant artists who left no record of their identities. They used wood from old cigar boxes and fruit and vegetable crates. The edges of items were chip carved and layered, creating the "Tramp Art" effect. Finished items usually were given an overall stain.

Reference: Clifford A. Wallach and Michael Cornish, *Tramp Art: One Notch At a Time,* published by authors, 1997.

Box, hinged lid, 9½" l **$100**
Box, multi–layered chip carved lid, paneled sides, secret compartment in lid, old label reads "Made by Gus C. Leyerle 10–30–57," 14½" l   80
Box, white porcelain buttons, worn finish, 10" l   150
Box, worn maroon velvet panels, gilded tin trim, missing lid mirror and int lining, 13½" l   125
Chest, pine, ovoid, 3 drawers, front, back, sides, and top mounted with stacked graduated rectangular chip carved panels, 4 tapered feet, painted green and red, stamped on 2 drawers and underside of top "Factory No. 664 1st Dis., State of Penna., Notice...," 11" h, 10" w, 9" d **2,185**
Chest of Drawers, miniature, 3 drawers, porcelain pulls, old alligatored finish, back labeled "I bought this July 2, 1955," old repairs to crest, 13" h . . .   150
Clock, portrait medallion below clock face, 27" h   500
Cosmetic Box, int mirror and red velvet lining, 10½" l   125
Cuckoo Clock, polychrome dec, birds perched on arched crest inscribed and cutout "Made in Brookfield, Mass, Aderlarl Courville," early 20th C, 21" h . **1,000**

Left: Picture Frame, star motif, notch carved, 26 x 20", $350.

Right: Box, painted and notch carved, early 20th C, $990. Photo courtesy Aston Macek.

Desk, miniature, pine, multi–layered chip carved stars, compasses, circles, and geometric shapes, slant–front hinged lid, blue paper lined int, 6 drawers, c1930, 21 x 15" **1,250**

Jewelry Box, poplar, bird finial, floral dec, carved name "Addie," 4 swing–out trays, center compartment, scrolled feet, old dark finish, 12¼" h   250

Magazine Rack, hanging, brass tack dec, dark finish, 15" w   125

Mirror, pine, multi–layered moons, circles, hearts, and geometric designs, c1930, 12¼" w, 20½" h **1,000**

Picture Frame, applied dec, hearts at corners with points extending outward, elongated diamond each side, late 19th C, 8 x 10" opening   300

Picture Frame, floral design, 4 rect slats overlapping at corners, early 20th C, 8½ x 10" opening   125

Picture Frame, star shaped, old brown paint, 9 x 10¾" opening   350

Sewing Box, frame top with pincushion, single drawer, dark finish, 9½" l   75

Wall Pocket, multi–layered strip dec, 11 x 16½"   150

WHIRLIGIGS

Whirligigs are a type of whimsical wind toy. Their origins are uncertain. Some claim that they began as a "Sabbath day toy" in Pennsylvania's German regions; others see them as a weather vane variation. In 1819 Washington Irving mentions whirligigs in his famous story "The Legend of Sleepy Hollow." Whirligigs enjoyed great popularity in the rural areas of New England, Middle Atlantic states, and the Midwest.

Whirligigs often contain more than one material in their construction. Wood and wire are the most commonly found. Since most were made by amateurs, a primitive appearance dominates. Single figures usually feature rotating paddle–like arms. Multi–figure examples employ a propeller that drives a series of gears and rods to make the figures move. The variety of subjects is endless.

Collectors place a premium on nineteenth–century examples, many of which featured three–dimensional figures. The use of plywood and silhouette figures are signs of a twentieth–century example.

Many whirligigs have been reproduced and faked. Since whirligigs were used outdoors, there should be strong evidence of weathering as well as wear where the movable parts rubbed against the body. Look for signs of rust and corrosion. Contemporary whirligig makers copy older designs. Placed outside, they can age quickly. Thus, relying solely on condition to date a whirligig is risky.

References: Robert Bishop and Patricia Coblentz, *A Gallery of American Weathervanes and Whirligigs,* E. P. Dutton, 1979; Ken Fitzgerald, *Weathervanes and Whirligigs,* Clarkson N. Potter, 1967.

Carousel, wood and tin, carved and painted, bicycle wheel base, horses, chariots, toy soldiers, red, white, and blue tin base and scalloped awning roof, topped by flag and brass lamp finial, 4 conical metal cups mounted under base catch wind and turn carousel, carved wood lamp base, c1900, 24" d, 51" h **$6,500**

Dewey Boy, carved and painted wood, paddle arms, c1900, 12" h   950

Dirigible, pine and tin, carved and painted, silhouette of man on wood rod suspended by thin metal wires from flattened cigar shaped balloon, green tin propellers and tail, early 20th C, 25½" l, 22½" h **4,125**

Dragonfly, wood, paddle wings, painted black, green, and orange, 13" l   170

Policeman, carved hat with tin bill and gold painted tin badge, dome tack eyes, polychrome body with 3 dome tack buttons and gold painted cutout tin badge, multiple paint layers, 20th C, 22" h, $440. Photo courtesy Jackson's Auctioneers and Appraisers.

Duck, wood, paddle wings, polychrome painted, 8" h **150**

George Washington on Horseback, pine, carved and painted, stylized figure wearing military uniform, dappled gray horse, cannon, red, white, and blue propeller, green base, figures move when activated, late 19th/early 20th C, 47½" l, 26¼" h **7,250**

Indian in Canoe, wood, dark–skinned figure wearing feathered headdress and white skirts, canoe paddles attached to arm baffles, green turned baluster and sphere base, late 19th/early 20th C, 16½" h **1,000**

Kicking Mule, wood, polychrome painted, 20th C, 48" l **275**

Man in Canoe, wood, comic figure with paddle arms, tack buttons, painted bright yellow, red, and blue, 15" l **110**

Sailor, pine, carved and painted, relief carved facial features, painted hair, blue hat with metal brim, navy blue short jacket with nail head buttons, white shirt and pants, relief carved fingers and thumbs, holding paddles, square black base, early 19th C, 14" h **40,000**

Scull, with 4 rowers, wood, weathered green, white, and black paint, 1 rower mkd "Harvard," one mkd "Yale," mounted on steel pole, 20th C, 43" h **225**

Soldier, wood, worn 2–tone blue paint, tin hat, belt, buttons, sword, and medal, Prince Albert Tobacco adv on hat, replaced applied facial features, 15¾" h plus old wood stool base **1,200**

Tandem Bicycle, painted iron and sheet iron, silhouette lady and gentleman smoking pipe, each with articulated legs, riding tandem bicycle with wire wheels, traces of green polychrome paint, mounted over arrow directional, missing propeller blades, 20" h, 45" l **1,500**

Two Men Sawing Wood, polychrome painted wood, propeller activated, 1 propeller vane replaced, 20th C, 43" l **85**

Uncle Sam, pine, standing bearded figure wearing painted metal hat, wool jacket, and velvet breeches, arms fitted with paddles, red painted baluster base, late 19th/early 20th C, 14⅝" h **865**

FURNITURE

The Country look divides into three major categories—primitive, vernacular, and formal. A typical rural home contained all three types. Primitive work benches, shelves, and cabinets were found in the pantry, back porch, wash area, and sheds. Vernacular furniture dominated the kitchen, guest bedrooms, and living room. The parlor and master bedroom were home to more formal pieces.

Not only was the country home an eclectic mixture of furniture types, styles were mixed as well. Pieces were passed down from generation to generation. Family heirlooms comprised much of a Country home's furnishings. Further, members of the agrarian community practiced thrift. Many household furnishings and equipment were bought second hand at country auctions.

Rural America was not isolated from the formal furniture styles of the large metropolitan areas. However, they worked their way slowly into the countryside. Further, only styles whose architecture conveyed ruggedness and a long–lasting quality were favored.

In the formal area, two major currents dominate the American furniture marketplace—furniture made in Great Britain and furniture made in the United States. American buyers continue to show a strong prejudice for objects manufactured in the United States. They will pay a premium for such pieces and accept them above technically superior and more aesthetic English examples.

Until the last half of the nineteenth century formal American styles were dictated by English examples and design books. Regional furniture, such as the Hudson River Valley [Dutch] and the Pennsylvania German styles, did develop. A less formal furniture, designated as vernacular, developed throughout the nineteenth and early twentieth centuries. Vernacular furniture deviates from the accepted formal styles and has a genre charm that many collectors find irresistible.

America did contribute a number of unique decorative elements to English styles. The American Federal period is a reaction to the English Hepplewhite period. American designers created furniture which influenced, rather than reacted, to world taste in the Gothic Revival style, Arts and Craft Furniture, Art Deco, and Modern International movement.

The following chart introduces you to the formal American design styles. Note that dates are approximate.

FURNITURE STYLES (APPROX. DATES)

William and Mary	1690–1730
Queen Anne	1725–1815
Chippendale	1755–1790
Federal	
Hepplewhite	1790–1810
Sheraton	1795–1815
Empire (Classical)	1805–1830
Victorian	
French Restauration	1830–1850
Gothic Revival	1840–1865
Rococo Revival	1845–1900
Naturalistic Revival	1850–1870
Louis XVI Revival	1850–1914

Elizabethan Revival 1850–1915
Neo–Greek Revival 1860–1885
Renaissance Revival 1860–1885
Eastlake 1870–1890
Art Furniture 1875–1914
Arts and Crafts 1885–1920
Art Nouveau 1896–1914
Art Deco 1925–1940
International Movement 1940–Present

American Country pieces, with the exception of Windsor chairs, stabilized and even dropped off slightly in value. This is due to two major market developments. First, the Country–designer look no longer enjoys the popularity it did during the American Bicentennial period in the late 1970s. Second, American decorators have focused more recently on the regional and European Country look.

Furniture is one of the few antiques fields where regional preferences are a factor in pricing. Victorian furniture is popular in New Orleans and unpopular in New England. Oak is in demand in the Northwest more so than in the Middle Atlantic states.

References: *American Manufactured Furniture, Furniture Dealers' Reference Book,* reprint by Schiffer Publishing 1988, 1996 value update; *American Wooden Chairs: 1895–1908,* Schiffer Publishing, 1997; Joseph T. Butler, *Field Guide to American Furniture,* Facts on File Publications, 1985; Eileen and Richard Dubrow, *American Furniture of the 19th Century, 1840–1880,* Schiffer Publishing, 1983; Eileen and Richard Dubrow, *Furniture Made in America, 1875–1905,* Schiffer Publishing, 1982, 1994 value update; Nancy Goyne Evans, *American Windsor Chairs,* Hudson Hills Press, 1996; Oscar Fitzgerald, *Four Centuries of American Furniture,* Wallace–Homestead, Krause Publications, 1995; Benno M. Forman, *American Seating Furniture, 1630–1730,* Winterthur Museum, W. W. Norton & Co, 1988; Jennifer George, *Collector's Guide to Oak Furniture: Identification & Values,* Collector Books, 1995; Heywood–Wakefield Co, *Antique Wicker From the Heywood–Wakefield Catalog,* Schiffer Publishing, 1994; *Indiana Cabinets With Prices,* L–W Book Sales, 1997; Myrna Kaye, *Fake, Fraud, Or Genuine, Identifying Authentic American Antique Furniture,* New York Graphic Society Book, 1987; William C. Ketchum, Jr., *American Cabinetmakers: Marked American Furniture, 1640–1940,* Crown Publishers, 1995; William C. Ketchum, Jr., *Furniture, Volume 2: Chest, Cupboards, Desks, & Other Pieces,* Knopf Collectors' Guides to American Antiques, Alfred A. Knopf, 1982.

Lew Larason, *Buying Antique Furniture: An Advisory,* Scorpio Publications, 1992; David P. Lindquist and Caroline C. Warren, *Colonial Revival Furniture With Prices,* Wallace–Homestead, Krause Publications, 1993; David P. Lindquist and Caroline C. Warren, *Victorian Furniture,* Wallace–Homestead, Krause Publications, 1995; Kathryn McNerney, *American Oak Furniture, Book I* (1984, 1994 value update), *Book II* (1994), Collector Books; Kathryn McNerney, *Primitives: Our American Heritage, First Series* (1979, 1996 value update), *Second Series* (1987, 1996 value update), Collector Books; Kathryn McNerney, *Victorian Furniture: Our American Heritage, Book I* (1981, 1997 value update), *Book II* (1997), Collector Books; Judith and Martin Miller, *Miller's Pine & Country Furniture Buyer's Guide,* Millers Publications, 1996; Milo M. Naeve, *Identifying American Furniture: A Pictorial Guide to Styles and Terms, Colonial to Contemporary, Second Edition,* American Assoc for State and Local History, 1989; George C. Neumann, *Early American Antique Country Furnishings: Northeastern America, 1650–1800's,* L–W Book Sales, 1984, 1996 reprint; Ellen M. Plante, *Country*

Furniture, Wallace–Homestead, Krause Publications, 1993; Michael Regan (ed), *American & European Furniture Price Guide,* Antique Trader Books, 1995; Harry L. Rinker, *Warman's Furniture,* Wallace–Homestead, 1993.

Marvin D. Schwartz, *Furniture: Volume 1: Chairs, Tables, Sofas & Beds,* Knopf Collector's Guides to American Antiques, Alfred A. Knopf, 1982; Herbert and Peter Schiffer, *Miniature Antique Furniture,* Schiffer Publishing, 1995; Tim Scott, *Fine Wicker Furniture, 1870–1930,* Schiffer Publishing, 1990; John G. Shea, *Making Authentic Country Furniture: With Measured Drawings of Museum Classics,* Dover, 1975, 1993 reprint; Robert W. and Harriett Swedberg, *American Oak Furniture, Style and Prices, Book I, Third Edition* (1992), Wallace–Homestead, Krause Publications; Robert W. and Harriett Swedberg, *Collector's Encyclopedia of American Furniture, Volume 1* (1990, 1996 value update), *Volume 2* (1992, 1996 value update), *Volume 3* (1994), Collector Books; Robert W. and Harriett Swedberg, *Furniture of the Depression Era,* Collector Books, 1987, 1996 value update; Norman Vandal, *Queen Anne Furniture,* The Taunton Press, 1990; Lyndon C. Veil, *Antique Ethnic Furniture,* Wallace–Homestead, 1983; Gerald W. R. Ward, *American Case Furniture,* Yale University Art Gallery, 1988; Velma Susanne Warren, *Golden Oak Furniture,* Schiffer Publishing, 1992; Derita Coleman Williams and Nathan Harsh, *The Art and Mystery of Tennessee Furniture,* Tennessee Historical Society, 1988.

There are hundreds of specialized books on individual furniture forms and styles. Two examples of note are: Monroe H. Fabian, *The Pennsylvania–German Decorated Chest,* Universe Books, 1978, and Charles Santore, *The Windsor Style in America, 1739–1830, Revised, Volumes I and II,* Running Press, 1992.

Clocks: Robert W. D. Ball, *American Shelf and Wall Clocks: A Pictorial History for Collectors,* Schiffer Publishing, 1992; Roy Ehrhardt, *Clock Identification and Price Guide, Book I* (revised 1979), *Book II* (1979), Heart of America Press; Roy Ehrhardt (ed), *The Official Price Guide to Antique Clocks, Third Edition,* House of Collectibles, 1985; Brian Loomes, *Brass Dial Clocks,* Antique Collectors' Club, 1997; Tran Duy Ly, *American Clocks: A Guide to Identification and Prices,* Arlington Book Co, 1989, 1991 value update; Rich Ortenburger, *Vienna Regulators and Factory Clocks,* Schiffer Publishing, 1990.

Museums and Libraries: Baker Furniture Library, Grand Rapids, MI; Ballantine House, Newark Museum, Newark, NJ; Bernice Bienenstock Furniture Library, High Point, NC; Colonial Williamsburg, Williamsburg, VA; Craftsman Farms Foundation, Inc, Morris Plains, NJ; Edison Institute, Dearborn, MI; Henry Ford Museum, Dearborn, MI; Grand Rapids Public Library, Grand Rapids, MI; International Home Furnishings Center, High Point, NC; Lyndhurst, Tarrytown, NY; Public Museum of Grand Rapids, Grand Rapids, MI; Reynold House Museum of American Art, Winston–Salem, NC; Rhode Island School of Design, Museum of Art, Providence, RI; The Bennington Museum, Bennington, VT; The Society for the Preservation of New England Antiquities, Boston, MA; Wadsworth Atheneum, Hartford, CT; Winterthur Museum, Winterthur, DE.

Reproduction Alert: Beware of the large number of reproductions. During the twenty–five years following the American centennial of 1876, there was a great revival in copying furniture styles and manufacturing techniques of earlier eras. These centennial pieces now are over one hundred years old. They confuse many dealers and collectors.

Note: Prices vary considerably on furniture. Shop around. Furniture is plentiful unless you are after a truly rare example. Examine all pieces thoroughly. Too many furniture pieces are bought on impulse. Turn furniture upside down; take it apart. The amount of repairs and restoration to a piece has a strong influence on price. Make certain you know about all repairs and changes before buying.

The prices listed below are "average" prices. They are only a guide.

BED

Jenny Lind, walnut, old finish, 68½" l side rails, 40" w, 42½" h **$175**

Pencil Post, birch, tapered posts with chamfered corners, shaped headboard, replaced side rails and canopy frame, 70" l, 50" w, 73" h **3,000**

Pencil Post, maple and pine, painted red, tapering and faceted head posts and foot posts, peaked pine headboard, New England, 1780–1800, 75½" l, 52¼" w, 83" h **4,885**

Quarter Tester, cherry, octagonal shaped posts, shaped headboard, acorn finials on foot posts, baluster turned legs, 59½" l, 78" h **1,500**

Rope, birch and pine, cannonball finials, turned posts, scrolled headboard, replaced side rails, 74" l, 53" w, 48" h **300**

Rope, cherry and poplar, cannonball finials, shaped head and foot boards, replaced side rails, refinished, 72½" l, 54" w, 48" h **425**

Rope, curly maple, bottle shaped finials, turned posts, shaped head and foot boards, turned tapered feet, refinished, footboard and side rails replaced, 74" l, 46" w, 52" h **1,250**

Rope, curly maple, mushroom and ball finials, turned posts, scrolled head board with turned crest, turned blanket rail, raised ball feet, 69" l, 53" w, 60" h **2,000**

Rope, grain painted, fancy turned posts with mushroom finials and raised ball feet, paneled head and foot boards with shaped crest, PA or OH, 19th C, 51½" w, 47½" h **1,500**

Left: Rope, turned posts, old red and black graining, red and gold stenciled floral dec, dec not original, 48" h, $450.

Right: Arts & Crafts, double size, tapered posts, spindles, orig finish, unmkd, 47½ x 57¼" *headboard, $3,000.* Photo courtesy David Rago Auctions.

Rope, maple, square posts with turned finials, curved molded edge headboard, orig rails, old refinishing, 70" l, 49" w **110**
Rope, poplar, flattened ball finials, turned posts, shaped head and foot
boards, old replaced side rails, gray repaint over earlier layers, 57" l,
42" w, 32½" h **175**
Rope, poplar, goblet finials, centering paneled headboard with turned and
scrolled detail, turned posts, turned legs, orig rails **775**
Rope, poplar, spool shaped finials, turned posts, shaped head and foot
boards, raised flattened ball feet, 73" l, 50" w, 47½" h **150**
Settle, pine, paneled back with applied molding at top, shaped ends, bench
folds out into bed, finish cleaned down to old red, minor repairs, 73½" w,
48¾" h **850**
Tall Post, bird's–eye maple and poplar, tester, massive ball turned posts with
mushroom finials, paneled headboard, ball feet, old refinishing, replaced
headboard, rails extended, age cracks in posts, replaced tester frame,
76" l, 53" w, 85" h **450**
Tall Post, cherry and mahogany, Empire, turned posts, paneled headboard
with broken arch and rosettes, repairs and edge cracks, 74" rails, 58" w,
90½" h on casters **700**
Tall Post, curly maple, turned posts with acorn finials, cherry blanket rail,
scrolled headboard, 55" w, 68¼" h **600**
Tall Post, mahogany, Chippendale, fluted tapered posts, shaped headboard,
cabriole legs, claw and ball feet, restored, MA, 76" l, 56¾" w, 81¾" h **4,000**
Tall Post, mahogany, Federal, reeded and waterleaf carved posts, arched
headboard, cylindrical tapering and incised legs with socket casters,
Salem, MA, 1790–1810, 78" l, 42" w, 65" h **1,375**
Tall Post, mahognay, Federal, tester, 2 fluted vasiform and ring turned posts,
2 plain posts, New England, c1800, 82" h **2,500**
Tall Post, mahogany, Federal, turned and reeded bulbous posts, highly
arched headboard, turned legs, old faded finish, rails replaced, headboard
altered to make bed narrower, 73" l, 44" w, 89½" h **1,750**

BENCH

Bucket, ash, mortised construction, rect top, 2 shelves, single board bootjack
ends, old varnish finish, OH, 37" w, 14" d, 32" h **$300**
High Back, armchair style, pine, paneled back, old green repaint,
16¾" h seat, 57½" h **1,100**
Hitchcock Style, gold dec, turned crest rail with 3 pillow blocks, arrow back
half spindles with double cornucopia slats, scrolled arms, turned legs and
stretchers, old black repaint, repairs, 77" l **775**
Mammy's, arrow back, black repaint with yellow striping, replaced baby
guard, repairs, 73" l **550**
Mammy's, Windsor, bamboo turnings, flat crest rail, double seat back with
16 turned spindles, scrolled arms, plank seat, flat board stretchers front
and back, rockers, refinished, holes in seat for baby guard plugged, 54" l .. **750**
Piano, oak, rounded corners on rect overhanging seat, straight skirt,
square tapered legs, flared feet, 39" w, 19" d, 21" h **150**
Porch, pine, plank top, shaped apron, bootjack ends, trestle stretcher, old
brown graining, minor wear and edge damage, 55½" l, 15½" d, 18" h **150**

Porch, pine, weathered top, cutout feet mortised through top, 2 diagonal
braces, age cracks, 14½ x 89½", 19½" h **110**

Porch, poplar, wire nail construction, mustard yellow repaint, edge damage,
age cracks, nailed repair, 60" l **300**

Settle, arrow back, poplar and hardwood, plank seat, highly refinished,
72" w **350**

Settle, arrow back, straight crest, tripartite back, scrolled arms, turned
tapered legs, refinished, repairs and replacements, 76" w **400**

Settle, arrow back, turned posts, arrow spindles, scrolled arms, plank seat,
turned legs, black repaint, 78" l **495**

Settle, arrow back, wide board crest, tripartite back with 21 arrow spindles,
scrolled arms, shaped seat, splayed base with 8 turned tapered legs and
wide board stretchers, refinished, repairs and replacements, 76" w **400**

Settle, decorated, brown and black striping, angel wing, fruit, and foliage
dec, gray–yellow ground, shaped crest, tripartite back with 3 fat vase
splats separated by turned spindles, scrolled arms, S–scrolled seat, turned
legs, flat board stretchers front and back, 80½" w **1,500**

Settle, decorated, polychrome stenciled birds and fruit on shaped 2–part
crest rail, turned half spindle back, shaped arms rolled plank seat, turned
legs and front stretchers, white and yellow striping on arms, seat, and turnings, dark ground, striping may be old repaint, 73" w **1,250**

Settle, paneled, yellow and green painted pine, ogival wings centering back
comprising 8 inset panels, scrolled arm supports centering rect seat, sides
forming feet, panels painted green on yellow ground, repairs, 1790–1830,
77" l **3,150**

Settle, paneled back, pine, shaped ends and arms, shoe feet, minor age
cracks, worn finish, 60½" w, 16" d, 55" h **2,500**

Settle, Windsor, step down crest, bamboo turnings, repaired plank seat,
77" l, 18" h seat, 36" h overall **1,050**

Sofa, oak, Mission style, reupholstered brown leather finish vinyl cushion,
78" l **350**

Water, pine, bootjack ends, old worn mustard yellow repaint, 30½" w,
11¾" d, 30" h **385**

Water, pine, rect overhanging top, bootjack ends, rect base shelf, single
board top, ends, and shelf, square nail construction, 48" w, 17½" d, 27" h . **250**

Water, pine and poplar, scalloped crest, shaped brackets, upper shelf with
3 bevel edged dovetailed drawers, shaped ends, open back with straight
backsplash, pair of paneled cupboard doors, cutout feet, refinished,
42" w, 18" d, 54" h **2,000**

Water, poplar, step back upper shelf with peaked crest and 2 dovetailed
drawers, shaped single board ends, base with open shelf, 2 paneled doors,
and cutout feet, cast iron pulls, old varnish finish, door latches replaced
with turnbuckles, 48" w, 15" d, 47½" h **1,250**

Water, poplar, three–quarter gallery, 2 shelves, bootjack ends, old worn olive
gray repaint, 48½" w, 14" d, 29" h **500**

Windsor, bowed back rail, 39 bamboo turned back spindles, scrolled arms,
turned arm supports, shaped seat, splayed base with bulbous turned legs
and H–form stretchers, old repaired split in 1 end of seat at arm post,
minor repairs, Philadelphia, PA, 72½" w, 16¼" h seat, 35" h overall **6,000**

BLANKET CHEST

Decorated, brown and yellow vinegar graining, bootjack ends, minor wear and edge damage, feet repaired on 1 end, 48½" w, 20½" d, 29¾" h **$750**

Decorated, brown comb graining over yellow ground, poplar, dovetailed case, large lidded till, scrolled apron 4 sides, dovetailed bracket feet, 47½" w, 23" d, 28" h **700**

Decorated, brown graining, 6 white tombstone reserves with tulips in green, red, yellow, and black, stars on ends, poplar, edge molded lid, dovetailed case, int till with lid, base molding, turned feet, 43¾" w, 18¾" d, 22½" h . . **1,425**

Decorated, brown graining on yellow ground, brown and green trim, pine, hinged rect lid, dovetailed case, walnut till with lid, turned feet, lock and key, cast butt hinges mkd "W. H. Carr, Phila," minor edge wear, hinge rail on lid restored, 49" w, 23" d, 27½" h **1,450**

Decorated, case front painted with pot filled with tulips and flowers in yellow, red, white, and black, centering "A.N. 1829," dark blue ground, pine, rect molded hinged lid opening to well with till, int of lid with attached watercolor on paper depicting spreadwing American eagle, shield, and "Be to God on High," molded base, bracket feet, 43" w, 17½" d, 17¼" h . **67,500**

Decorated, dark brown graining, pine, molded edge lid, dovetailed case, lidded till, base molding, turned feet 43" w, 21" d, 26" h **300**

Decorated, dark repaint with simple landscape in panel and flowers on frame and lid, poplar and chestnut, turned legs, repainted till, added lid braces and prop, Pennsboro, WV, 37" w, 18¾" d, 23" h **550**

Decorated, ocher and mustard putty dec, pine, 6–board construction, bracket feet, New England, c1820, 42" w, 17⅛" d, 22½" h **3,500**

Decorated, polychrome painted pots of tulips on 2 white front panels, dovetailed bracket feet with scrolled apron, 32" l **650**

Decorated, red and black graining, black trim, stenciled detail on feet, floral decal transfer facade, lid edge molding, reeded rim, dovetailed case with 2 drawers, bracket feet, pencil inscription on till lid "D.S. Yoder, Scalpland, Cumbria, Co. Pa. Apr. 10, 1882," damage to till lid, 1 hinge pin missing, 44¼" w, 20¼" d, 27¼" h **3,250**

Decorated, red and black graining over earlier dark brown finish, poplar, dovetailed case with relief carved arched front and end panels, lidded till, molded base, ogee bracket feet, yellow painted initials, date, and trim on panels, added underside braces to lid, repair to till lid, 48½" w, 22½" d, 29" h **2,000**

Decorated, red–brown flame graining, poplar, molded edge lid, dovetailed case, molded edge base, turned feet, till removed, 45¾" w, 20" d, 24" h . . . **1,250**

Decorated, red flame graining, pine and poplar, molded edge lid, paneled case with square corner posts, lidded till, turned ball feet, minor molding damage, 36¾" w, 18¼" d, 24¾" h **900**

Decorated, red graining, pine, hinged breadboard–type lid, dovetailed case with int till, turned feet, 38" w, 19" d, 24¼" h **750**

Decorated, red graining on light colored ground, pine and poplar, hinged rect lid, dovetailed case, int till with lid, turned feet, 43¼" l **450**

Decorated, red vinegar graining on yellow ground with black trim, poplar, molded edge lid, lidded till, dovetailed case, molded edge base, turned legs, orig porcelain escutcheon, 44" w, 22½" d, 24½" h **2,000**

Decorated, salmon graining, maple and pine, 2 false drawers, single base
drawer, MA, c1750, 41³/₄" w, 18" d, 34¹/₂" h **1,750**
Pine, gray wash over red, lid painted red, undersized lid with edge molding,
int till, bracket feet, age cracks, 28" l **175**
Pine, putty green paint, single drawer, New England, 42" w, 20" d, 32" h **1,000**
Pine, red stain, applied lid and base molding, dovetailed case with 2 dovetailed overlapping drawers and int till with lid, dovetailed bracket feet,
strap hinges and bear trap lock, refinished, 53" w, 23" d, 29¹/₂" h **500**
Pine, red wash, 6–board construction, wrought iron rose head nails, edge
damage to lid, early, 52" w, 19" d, 18" h **600**
Pine, 6–board construction, primitive, dovetailed case and till, refinished,
43¹/₂" l **125**
Poplar, edge molded lid, int till with lid, dovetailed case, molded base,
bracket feet, added side handles, missing lock, replaced hinges, hinge rail
restored, 50¹/₄" w, 23¹/₂" d, 26¹/₄" h **375**
Poplar and Pine, dovetailed case, till, molded base, bracket feet, wrought
iron strap hinges, refinished, glued repair to foot, 46" w, 20³/₄" d, 25" h ... **475**
Walnut, Country Chippendale, dovetailed case, lidded till, bracket feet,
added lid prop, refinished, 50" l **650**
Walnut, Country Chippendale, molded edge lid, int till, dovetailed case,
molded base, 2 dovetailed and cockbeaded drawers flanked by carved
rope twist quarter columns, ogee bracket feet, orig oval brasses, varnished
int, traces of red and yellow paint, minor repair to 1 foot, old faded refinishing, 44" w, 21³/₄" d, 28¹/₄" h **2,500**
Walnut, Country Sheraton, mortised and pinned construction, applied lid
edge molding, lidded till, paneled sides and ends, applied base molding,
high turned feet on casters, old mellow finish, KY or TN, 43¹/₂" w, 22" d,
31¹/₄" h **750**
Walnut and Poplar, Country Chippendale, molded edge lid, dovetailed case,
till with 3 dovetailed drawers, 3 dovetailed overlapping base drawers,
base molding, dovetailed ogee feet including center foot, wrought iron
strap hinges, old worn soft finish, feet replaced, some edge damage to
drawers, drawer pulls missing, 50" w, 22³/₄" d, 27³/₄" h **1,250**

BOOKCASE

Cherry, Chippendale, on frame, molded cornice, 3 glazed doors each with
10 panes, 3 short drawers in base, shaped bracket feet, 2 shaped center
feet, NY, c1800, 72" w, 19" d, 86¹/₂" h **$6,500**
Oak, Mission style, sectional, 4 graduated sections, hinged glass fronts,
Viking trademark Skandia Furniture Co, Rockford, IL **600**
Quarter Sawn Oak, sectional, 5 pcs, swelled ogee cornice, 3 graduated
bookcase sections with retractable glass doors, false drawer in base, brass
knobs, paper label "Manufactured by the Globe–Wernicke Co.,
Cincinnati, O," 34" w, 12" d, 47" h **650**
Walnut, Country Hepplewhite, poplar secondary wood, molded cornice,
glazed double doors each with 8 wavy glass panes, beaded door frames,
cloth lined int, 4 dovetailed overlapping drawers, slightly curved apron,
high cutout feet, old refinishing, replaced brasses, minor pieced repairs in
feet and cornice, 63" w, 12³/₄" d, 84¹/₄" h **4,750**

Left: Bookcase, oak, Mission, revolving, 4 sides, each fitted with 4 shelves, all within slat–form divisions, 4 legged base on casters, 24³/₄" w, 69⁵/₈" h, $1,250.

Right: China Cabinet, corner, quarter sawn oak, heart shaped, mirrored crest, pair of doors with curved glass, 4 glass shelves, hoof feet, $3,600.
Photo courtesy Jackson's Auctioneers & Appraisers.

CABINET

China, oak, bow front, back crest mirror with lions heads, curved glass ends, flat door, top int with mirrored back, wood shelves, claw feet on casters, 43" w, 72" h **$2,400**

China, oak, bow front, shaped top with molded back, rect center glazed door with single pane, convex glass wide panels flanked by scrolled columns, ogee bracket feet, 38" w, 58" h **650**

China, oak, Mission style, rect top with inset corner posts, 2 plain glazed doors, adjustable shelves, Lifetime Co, Grand Rapids, MI, 43" w, 14¹/₂" d, 57" h **750**

China, oak veneer, quarter sawn, flat cornice, 2 full–length glazed doors, int shelves, base molding, cabriole legs on casters, 40" w, 12" d, 63" h **575**

Kitchen, Hoosier, oak, 2 cabinet doors with built in spice racks, tilting flour bin, and pair of tambour sliding doors in top, pullout porcelain work surface, single cupboard door opening to pullout shelf and cutting board, 2 utility drawers and metal bread drawer in base, on casters, 1925, 41" w, 70" h **750**

Kitchen, Hoosier White Beauty, oak, 5 paneled doors in top with flour bin, spice racks, and sugar bin, pullout aluminum covered work surface, pullout cutting board, cutlery drawer, 2 utility drawers, bread drawer, and cupboard door with pullout shelf in base, paneled ends, on casters, c1915, 41" w, 71¹/₄" h **850**

Kitchen, McDougall, oak, upper section with 2 doors for storage and door with tilt–out flour bin, 2 narrow shelves above work surface, glass jar for sugar bin suspended by metal bracket, pullout porcelain work surface, pullout cutting board, large cutlery drawer, cupboard door, 2 short drawers and metal lined bread drawer, on casters, refinished, 1917 . . . . **1,000**

Kitchen, Napanee Dutch Kitchenette, oak, pair of cupboard doors with built in spice racks, cookbook holder, and bill hooks, above tambour sliding door with sugar bin and canister shelf, split cabinet door opening to flour bin with sifter, pullout porcelain work surface, pullout kneading board and chopping block, partitioned cutlery drawer, 2 cupboard doors opening to sliding wire and wood shelves and metal bread drawer, on casters, 1915 . . . . **900**

Kitchen, Sellers, oak frame, tall cupboard door with int shelf and flour bin, pair of cupboard doors with int shelf above tambour sliding door, pullout porcelain work surface, base with large cupboard door with int pullout cutting board and sliding wire rack shelf, 2 utility drawers, and metal bread drawer, on casters, refinished, 1920s, 48" w **1,000**

CANDLESTAND

Birch, Chippendale, oblong serpentine top above tapered urn standard, cabriole legs ending in peaked snake feet, orig finish, minor repair to lower section of standard, MA, c1780, 16½" w, 17" d, 27½" h **$7,500**

Birch, Country Hepplewhite, rect top with cut corners, turned column, simitar legs, refinished with traces of old red finish, some damage to legs where they join column, 1 leg nailed, stained top, 31¼" w, 13½" d, 26¼" h **250**

Birch, Hepplewhite, round single board top, turned column, tripod base, snake feet, refinished, 19½" d, 27" h **275**

Cherry, Chippendale, rect tray top with raised edge fitted on underside with dual-directionals drawer, tapered ring turned standard, cabriole legs ending in snake feet, CT, c1785, 18¼" w, 17⅝" d, 26½" h **3,165**

Cherry, Chippendale, square single board top with scalloped edge, turned column with simple chip carved dec, tripod base, snake feet, 15¾" sq, 26" h **2,500**

Cherry, Country Chippendale, square top, turned column, tripod base with snake feet, old soft finish, repairs, 2 feet ended out, patch and age cracks to top, 16½" sq, 27" h **500**

Cherry, Hepplewhite, square 2-board top with rounded corners, turned column, tripod base with snake feet, refinished, 16⅜" x 16½", 28" h **1,000**

Curly Maple, Hepplewhite, 2 board top with cutout ovolo corners, turned column, tripod base with spider legs, mellow refinishing, replaced top, 16" w, 15½" d, 26" h **950**

Curly Maple, octagonal top with applied gallery, turned 2-part laminated column, tripod base with snake feet, old finish, small crack in 1 leg at post, 1 section of gallery molding damaged, 14" w, 28½" h **1,750**

Curly Maple and Birch, Country Hepplewhite, elongated octagonal curly maple tilt top, birch tripod base with turned column and spider legs ending in spade feet, old mellow finish, age cracks in column, 1 leg repaired, New England, 20¼" w, 12½" d, 27½" h **450**

Mahogany, Chippendale, hinged round top tilting and revolving above birdcage support, flaring ring turned compressed ball standard, cabriole legs ending in bulbous snake feet, dark chocolate brown color, old dry surface, Philadelphia, PA, c1765, 20½" d, 28¾" h **36,800**

Mahogany, Country Federal, round top, turned column, cabriole legs, pad feet, refinished, top reset, RI, 1790–1800, 19½" d, 26" h **850**

Mahogany, Country Federal, tilt top, octagonal shaped top with band inlaid edge, tripod base with ring turned baluster column and spider legs, New England, 1800–15, 28½" h **750**

Mahogany, Federal, tilt top, clover shaped top, baluster and urn turned pedestal, tripartite base with arched legs, NY, 1800–10, 17¼" w, 23" d, 28¾" h **800**

Mahogany, Queen Anne, round dished top tilting and revolving above bird-cage support, compressed ball standard, cabriole legs ending in snake feet, lower section of standard repaired, patches to edges of top, Philadelphia, PA, c1760, 18¾" d, 26" h **3,165**

Maple, Country Chippendale, square 2–board top with rounded corners, turned column with chip carved dec, tripod base with snake feet, refinished, repairs to legs and column base, 16¾" sq, 27" h **650**

Maple, Federal, oblong top with rounded corners, ring turned urn form standard, cabriole legs ending in peaked snake feet, top inscribed with dates "1806" and "1896" in yellow paint, New England, c1805, 18" w, 17½" d, 28" h **450**

Maple, single board top with decorative cutout corners, turned column, tripod base with highly arched cutout feet, old dark reddish brown varnish stain, old repairs to column base, 1 leg loose, 17½" w, 16¼" d, 27¾" h ... **400**

Maple and Oak, William and Mary, round top, square flaring pedestal with chamfered corners, X–form base, later red paint, New England, 1700–50, 15" d, 30" h **1,050**

Painted Red, Country Queen Anne, octagonal molded top, tapered urn–form and ring turned standard, delicate faceted cabriole legs ending in snake feet, northeastern New England, 1750–75, 17½" d, 25½" h **24,000**

Walnut, Chippendale, round dished top, turned column, tripod base with snake feet, refinished, PA, c1770, 18¼" d, 27" h **1,250**

Walnut, round single board tilt top, turned column ending in 4 widely arched feet, old refinishing, repaired crack in top, 18" d, 26¼" h **250**

Walnut, turtle back top, turned column, tripod base with short cutout legs and snake feet, old worn green repaint, 2 legs with repaired breaks, 15¼" w, 15" d, 25¼" h **650**

Walnut and Cherry, Country Chippendale, round walnut top, cherry tripod base, turned column, padded snake feet, 18⅛" w, 17⅜" d, 25¼" h **500**

Walnut and Cherry, Country Federal, rect single board top with cut corners, turned column, tripod base, scrolled legs, 16¾ x 22" top, 29" h **275**

CHAIR

Arrow Back, dec, orig dark brown paint, yellow striping and floral dec on crest, some wear, 17½" h seat, 33¼" h overall, price for set of 6 ....**$1,500**

Banister Back, curly maple, shaped arched crest, block and baluster turned posts with urn shaped finials, 4 shaped vertical slats, rush seat, bulbous turned front stretcher, refinished, replaced seat, 44" h **550**

Banister Back, maple and hardwood, turned detail, old woven splint seat, refinished, 17" seat, 46" h overall **275**

Barrel Back, Federal, mahogany, arched bowed crest rail, upholstered back, shaped wings continuing to outscrolling arms, bowed seat rail, reeded square tapering legs with casters, MA, 1790–1810, 45" h **3,675**

Corner, shaped crest and arms, turned posts, shaped splats, double box stretchers, replaced rush seat, old worn black paint over earlier dark green, damaged seat, 33" h **650**

Dining, Country Empire, straight crest with stenciled rose dec, 5 turned spindles, arched back posts, scrolled seat, turned legs and front stretcher, ball feet, red flame graining and black ground with yellow striping, 33" h, price for set of 6 . . . . **1,500**

Dining, Country Queen Anne, dec hardwood, yoke crest, vasiform splat, rush seat, old black paint with gold striping and chinoiserie dec on splat, 42¾" h **250**

Dining, Country Queen Anne, yoke crest, vasiform splat, turned posts with flared finials, rush seat, turned legs and stretchers, old black repaint, replaced seat, wear and damage, Connecticut River Valley, 39¼" h **150**

Dining, Country Sheraton, hardwood and curly maple, turned arched crest rail, shaped center slat, narrow lower slat, heavily ring turned front legs and stretcher, tapered back legs with button feet, old mellow refinishing, price for pair **400**

Dining, Federal, carved mahogany, shield shaped splat centering carved plums and drapery swag above barrel, upholstered slip seat, molded arms terminating in carved rosettes, square tapering legs, NY, 1790–1810, 21½" w, 36¾" h **3,675**

Dining, Queen Anne, maple, carved, molded yoke form crest above baluster splat flanked by outscrolled arms, ring turned baluster form arm supports, trapezoidal slip seat with conforming frame, angular cabriole legs joined by turned H–form stretcher ending in square pad feet, repairs to crest at juncture with stiles, attributed to William Savery, Philadelphia, 1730–50 . . . . **23,000**

Left: Dining, Federal, mahogany, shield back with carved wheat sheaves, molded leaf carved arms, flowerhead terminals, square molded tapering legs, casters, $1,492. Photo courtesy Sotheby's.

Center: Desk, Arts & Crafts, Quaint Furniture, c1910, arched crest rail, 2 horizontal rails, wide vertical slat with 3 inlaid tulips, arched side stretchers, shaped front feet, branded mark, 16" w, 15" d, 38¼" h, $900.

Right: Ladder Back, Colonial Revival, Wallace Nutting, ball finials, sausage turned posts, 5 arched slats, rush seat, shaped arms, branded signature, price for pair, $500.

Left: Side Chair, Fancy Sheraton, New England, early 19th C, lyre–form splat, chamfered stiles, rush seat, button feet, stencil dec, price for set of 2 armchairs and 6 side chairs, $5,225.

Right: Side Chair, Hitchcock style, c1830, gold accents on ring turnings, swirl and grape leaf stenciled dec, price for set of 6, $1,000.

Left: Side Chair, Chippendale, walnut, PA, c1760, shaped crest, vasiform splat, trapezoidal slip seat, cabriole legs, trifid feet, $4,892. Photo courtesy Sotheby's.

Right: Side Chair, Arts & Crafts, L and JG Stickley, orig dark finish, replaced brown leather seat, loose joints, handcraft decal, 36 1/2 x 16 1/4 x 15 3/4", $150. Photo courtesy David Rago Auctions.

Left: Windsor, comb back, Philadelphia, c1760, painted black, polychrome dec, carved knuckle terminals, vase and reel turnings, shaped saddle seat, bulbous stretchers, $7,475.

Right: Windsor, bow back, old black repaint with yellow striping, molded rail, splayed base with bulbous bamboo turnings, 30 1/4" h, price for set of 6, $5,280.

Photos courtesy Sotheby's.

Dining, Queen Anne, maple, shaped yoke crest, curved back posts, vasiform splat, slip seat, cabriole legs, turned H–form stretcher, padded slipper feet, old refinish on underside of seat frame and bottoms of stretchers, minor repair to seat frame and 1 foot, 17½" h seat, 40" h overall **1,000**

Dining, Queen Anne style, armchair and 6 side chairs, shaped crest rail with carved ears, shaped splat, rush seat, block turned front posts, turned stretchers, slipper feet, armchair with scrolled arms, worn brown paint, 42¾" h, price for set of 7 . . . . **2,000**

Easy Chair, Chippendale, mahogany, reupholstered in silk brocade, Newport, RI, 1770–90, 15" h seat rail, 44½" h overall **11,000**

Hitchcock Style, yellow striping, polychrome floral dec slats, dark ground, balloon seats with old rush, turned legs, 34" h, price for pair   175

Ladder Back, hardwood, armchair and 4 side chairs, turned spire shaped finials, 4 arched graduated slats, rush seat, reddish varnish finish, armchair with scrolled arms, some replaced seats, 42¾" h, price for set of 5 . .   750

Ladder Back, oak, dark worn finish, early 20th C, 40¼" h, price for pair   120

Lolling, Hepplewhite, mahogany, inlaid, serpentine upholstered back, shaped arms, outline stringing on down curving arm supports and square tapered legs, yellow upholstered seat, casters, refinished, restored, New England, early 19th C, 18" h seat, 46" h overall **2,000**

Martha Washington, Chippendale style, mahogany frame, worn gold striped upholstery, worn finish, 38" h   150

Moravian, walnut and pine, tapered legs, refinished, 20½" h seat, 36¾" h overall   100

Morris, Mission, oak, adjustable back with curved crest rail and 4 narrower horizontal slats, shaped slanted arms with corbels, 5 vertical side slats, spring cushion seat, casters, Gustav Stickley brand mark, No. 369, refinished, c1912, 32½" w, 41½" h **5,000**

Office, oak, bow back, turned supports, pedestal base, woven cane back and seat, needs recaning   60

Overstuffed, mahogany frame, foliate carved apron, carved scrolling legs, animal paw front feet, new cut velvet floral upholstery, 36½" h, with matching ottoman   85

Side Chair, decorated, half spindle, rabbit ear posts, shaped crest, narrow slat, 4 turned half spindles, plank seat, turned legs and front stretcher, worn orig red and black graining with yellow and pale blue striping and stylized fruit and foliage dec, 17½" h seat, 32¼" h overall, price for set of 8   500

Side Chair, decorated, rabbit ear posts, stenciled crest, 4 turned spindles, shaped seat, bamboo turned legs, red and black with yellow striping, 17" h seat, 34" h overall   75

Windsor, bow back, bowed crest with spindles, turned posts, shaped arms and seat, splayed base, bulbous turned legs, H stretcher, 18½" h seat, 36½" h overall   475

Windsor, bow back, molded bow, 7 spindle back, saddle seat, splayed base with bamboo turnings, refinished, 36¾" h   175

Windsor, bow back, molded crest rail, 7 spindle back, saddle seat, splayed base with bamboo turned legs, H–form stretcher, refinished, traces of red paint on seat, age cracks, 15¾" h seat, 38" h overall   275

Windsor, brace back, arched molded crest and stiles centering 10 flaring spindles, shaped saddle seat, bold vase and reel turned legs joined by bulbous turned H–form stretchers, tapered feet, painted black over red and green, minor cracks in crest, 1 with old repairs to stiles and spindle, other with repairs to stretchers, c1785, price for pair **7,500**

Windsor, comb back, shaped crest, bowed crest rail, shaped arm rail, 5 spindle back, turned arm supports, saddle seat, splayed base with bulbous turned legs and H–form stretcher, worn old red repaint, repair in back edge of seat, arm rail with split at curve, 18" h seat, 48½" h overall **1,500**

Windsor, sack back, arched crest rail, spindle back, U shaped arm rail continuing to scrolled arms, canted baluster turned arm supports, oval saddle seat, splayed base with baluster turned legs, H–form stretcher, painted dark green, PA, c1780 ....**1,500**

Windsor, sack back, knuckle arm, old red varnish, New England, c1780, 28" h **3,850**

Windsor, wing back, Chippendale, shaped wings, outscrolled arms, upholstered with brass tack trim around bottom, molded front legs, straight stretchers, refinished, restored, PA, 1770–90, 17½" h seat, 48" h overall ...**2,750**

Windsor, wing back, Federal, mahogany, arched crest rail, upholstered back, shaped wings continuing to outscrolling arms and bowed seat rail, square molded legs joined by H–form stretcher, MA, 1790–1810, 47" h **12,650**

Windsor, wing back, Hepplewhite, mahogany, serpentine upholstered back flanked by shaped wings, outscrolled arms, upholstered seat, square tapering legs, straight stretchers, refinished, pumpkin colored 20th–C upholstery, New England, early 19th C, 17½" h seat, 46½" h overall **1,200**

Windsor, wing back, Queen Anne, walnut frame, arched upholstered crest flanked by ogival wings and outscrolled arms, loose cushion added to seat, cabriole legs joined by turned stretchers, ending in pad feet, old finish, Boston, MA, c1755 ....**15,000**

Writing, shaped crest, spindle back, scrolled arm, large leather–covered writing arm with 2 underside drawers, turned posts and legs, plank seat with drawer beneath, stretchers, gold striping, old black repaint, some edge damage, 1 drawer replaced, 17½" h seat, 47" h overall **250**

CHEST OF DRAWERS

Birch, Chippendale, pine secondary wood, rect top with edge molding, dovetailed case, 4 overlapping dovetailed drawers, ogee feet, replaced brasses, refinished, sanded top, 38" w, 36¾" h **$1,700**

Birch, Country Federal, rect top, 4 cockbeaded drawers, shaped apron continuing to French feet, oval brasses, restoration to back edge of top, New England, 1810–20, 41" w, 41½" h **1,250**

Cherry, Chippendale, chest on chest, molded cornice, dovetailed cases with 9 dovetailed overlapping drawers, bracket feet, refinished, replaced brasses, 35½" w, 19 x 38½" cornice, 73½" h **7,700**

Cherry, Chippendale, pine and poplar secondary wood, tall chest, molded cornice, dovetailed case with 10 overlapping drawers, high ogee feet, repairs to feet and backboards, replaced brasses, 38" w, 23 x 41¾" cornice, 65½" h **3,950**

Cherry, Country, rounded corner top, 2 short over 4 graduated long drawers, rounded corner stiles, solid ends, deeply scalloped apron, refinished, filled age cracks in ends, replaced brass pulls and escutcheons, 38¾" w, 18" d, 43¾" h **1,000**

Cherry, Country Empire, 4 dovetailed cockbeaded drawers, large projecting drawer supported on turned and rope carved pilasters, 3 recessed graduated drawers, turned feet and pulls, old worn finish, 42¼" w, 20" d, 47" h . **600**

Cherry, Country Hepplewhite, 4 graduated dovetailed drawers with line inlaid drawer fronts, extra deep top drawer over 3 graduated drawers, single board ends, shaped apron, cutout feet, refinished, replaced eagle brasses, edge damage, front feet replaced, drawer runner needs repair, 46¾" w, 20" d, 46" h **500**

Cherry, Country Hepplewhite, poplar secondary wood, tall chest, inlaid band below cove molded cornice, 5 short over 5 graduated long cockbeaded drawers, orig acorn brasses, band inlaid base, curved apron, straight cutout legs, inlaid diamond shield escutcheons, feet poorly ended out, edge damage, old repairs, 45¼" w, 23¾" d, 75" h **4,000**

Cherry, Country Sheraton, poplar secondary wood, shaped crest, 4 dovetailed drawers with applied edge beading, crossbanded walnut veneer and surface beading with inlaid diamond escutcheons, paneled ends, turned legs, refinished, split in 1 back post, 45½" w, 20" d, 41" h **650**

Cherry, Federal, curly maple and walnut veneer, single dovetailed long drawer above 3 dovetailed curved front drawers, turned column pilasters with leafy Ionic capitals, paneled ends, turned feet, replaced brasses, 45¼" w, 53" h **775**

Left: Sycamore, Queen Anne, chest on frame, molded cornice, 5 short drawers, 3 long graduated drawers, shaped skirt, cabriole legs, pad feet, frame restored, New England, 56" h, 38" w, 22" d, $3,162. Photo courtesy Sotheby's.

Right: Cherry, Chippendale style, tall chest, molded cornice, 6 graduated drawers, ogee bracket feet, RI, late 18th C, $4,250.

Cherry, Federal, 4 dovetailed drawers with applied edge beading, half turned columns, turned legs, old mellow refinishing, minor edge damage, $41^5/_8$ x $21^1/_2$" top, $46^1/_4$" h **550**

Cherry, Hepplewhite, walnut secondary wood, figured veneer panels and line inlay, square edge top with applied molding, 5 dovetailed drawers with applied molding, banding around base, French feet, replaced feet, backboards, top, and brasses, $37^3/_4$" w, $39^1/_4$" h **650**

Cherry, Queen Anne, lowboy, oblong top with scalloped sides above case with 1 long and 3 short drawers, center drawer carved with fan, cyma shaped skirt below continuing to cabriole legs ending in pad feet, old finish, CT, 1770, 36 x $21^1/_8$" top, $31^3/_4$" h **3,750**

Cherry, Sheraton, poplar secondary wood, curly maple facade, 7 dovetailed drawers arranged with 2 bonnet drawers and 2 small drawers, turned feet, turned burl knobs, $40^1/_4$" w, 20 x 42" top, $44^3/_4$" h **1,400**

Cherry and Curly Maple, Country Sheraton, poplar secondary wood, veneer drawer fronts, 4 dovetailed drawers with applied beading, reeded stiles, turned feet, incomplete feet, replaced brasses, refinished, 40" w, 37" h **825**

Cherry and Curly Maple, Hepplewhite, poplar secondary wood, mahogany veneer facade, 6 dovetailed drawers with applied edge beading, scrolled apron with inlaid banding, French feet, refinished, $45^1/_2$" w, $47^1/_4$" h **825**

Cherry and Poplar, Country, slightly overhanging rect top with molded edge, 2 short over 4 graduated long dovetailed drawers, shaped apron, cutout feet, repairs to top edge molding, front feet, and apron, replaced pulls, $40^3/_4$" w, $16^1/_2$" d, $41^1/_2$" h **500**

Curly Maple, Queen Anne, highboy, top with cove molded cornice, dovetailed case, and 5 graduated dovetailed overlapping drawers, base with

Left: Tiger Maple, Federal, bow front, oblong top with reeded edge, conforming case, 4 cockbeaded and graduated long drawers, shaped apron, French feet, New England, c1880, 40" h, $39^1/_2$" w, 21" d, $3,600.

Right: Walnut, Queen Anne, lowboy, rect top with canted corners, 3 drawers, cabriole legs, shell carved knees, trifid feet, top replaced, Delaware River Valley, c1760, 29" h, $34^1/_2$" w, 21" d, $19,550. Photo courtesy Sotheby's.

2 graduated dovetailed overlapping drawers, scrolled apron, cabriole legs, and padded duck feet, old mellow refinishing, replaced batwing brasses, CT, 38½" w, 20½" d, 73½" h 13,750

Curly Maple and Walnut, Country Sheraton, tall chest, walnut top, dovetailed drawers, 2 short drawers flanked by 2 bonnet drawers over 3 graduated long drawers, scalloped apron, turned feet, walnut edging on drawer fronts, old mellow refinishing, back boards replaced, top may be old replacement, replaced oval brasses, 43½" w, 22½" d, 50¾" h 1,750

Decorated, Hepplewhite style, birch, red and black flame graining, yellow and green striping, 4 dovetailed drawers, beaded frame, scalloped apron, cutout feet, turned wood pulls, emb brass escutcheons, 36⅜" h 3,500

Decorated, painted diamond and swirl pattern, single extra deep drawer over 3 graduated long drawers, cutout feet, turned wood pulls, PA, c1825, 44" w, 17" d, 41½" h 2,750

Mahogany, Queen Anne, block front, oblong thumb molded top with blocked front above conforming case with 4 graduated long drawers each with cockbeaded surrounds, molded blocked base continuing to bracket feet, orig brasses, lacks central pendant on skirt, patch to right side rear panel, minor repair to front left foot facing, Boston, MA, c1760, 35½" w, 19¾" d, 31½" h 31,000

Mahogany Veneer, Country Federal, bow front, conforming case with 4 cockbeaded long drawers, shaped bracket feet, oval brasses, refinished, New England, 1800–20, 38¾" w, 19¾" d, 40½" h 1,875

Maple, Chippendale, pine and poplar secondary wood, molded edge top, dovetailed case, 6 dovetailed overlapping drawers, bracket feet, replaced brasses, 36" w, 18½ x 38" top, 44¼" h 3,400

Maple, Country Chippendale, pine and poplar secondary wood, tall chest, molded cornice with secret drawer, 6 graduated overlapping dovetailed drawers, dovetailed case, high cutout dovetailed bracket feet, refinished, minor edge repairs, replaced brasses, 39¾" w, 20¾" d, 56½" h 4,500

Maple, Queen Anne, flat top highboy, 2 sections, upper section with molded cornice, 5 short over 4 long graduated molded drawers, center short drawer carved with fan, lower section with 1 long over 3 short molded drawers, center short drawer carved with fan, shaped skirt with acorn pendant continuing to angular cabriole legs ending in pad feet, most brasses orig, some patches to drawer lips, lacks 1 side knee return, 37½" w, 21" d, 77" 15,000

Maple, Queen Anne, highboy, top with molded cornice, dovetailed case, and 4 graduated dovetailed overlapping drawers, base with 2 graduated dovetailed long drawers, bottom drawer with 3 false fronts and carved sunburst, scalloped apron, cabriole legs, padded duck feet, deep honey colored finish, old brasses, 1 bail missing, minor repair to drawer overlap and feet, knee returns replaced, CT, 39¾" w, 20½" d, 72¾" h 10,000

Maple, Sheraton, bow front, slightly overhanging top, 4 drawers with bird's–eye maple veneer fronts, fluted three–quarter column stiles, scalloped skirt front and ends, ring turned tapered legs, ball feet, refinished, replaced turned wood pulls, northern New England, c1815, 44½" w, 18½" d, 43" h 1,450

Maple, tall chest, painted red, molded cornice, 6 graduated long drawers, eagle brasses, scalloped bracket feet, New England, c1780, 36" w, 17¾" d, 53" h 7,250

Pine, Country Empire, rect top with rounded corners, 4 graduated drawers with ogee fronts, rounded corner posts, block feet, refinished, age cracks in top, replaced pulls, repairs to feet, 36½" w, 22" d, 35½" h **400**

Poplar, Country Chippendale, tall chest, molded cornice, 2 short over 4 long graduated overlapping drawers, bracket feet, old medium brown refinishing, repairs to backboards, some edge damage, replaced feet and brasses, 38¾" w, 20¾" d, 55¾" h **1,250**

Quarter Sawn Oak, Mission, swivel mirror, 2 narrow short over 2 graduated long drawers, arched skirt, wood knobs, Stickley Brothers **950**

Walnut, Chippendale, flat top highboy, 2 sections, upper section with molded cornice above 5 short molded drawers above 3 long graduated molded drawers, flanked by fluted quarter columns, lower section with mid molding and 4 molded drawers, shaped skirt dec with large carved scallop shell and flanked by fluted quarter columns continuing to shell carved cabriole legs ending in claw and ball feet, oval brasses, PA, c1760, 42" w, 22¾" d, 76½" h **11,500**

Walnut, Country Hepplewhite, 4 graduated dovetailed drawers with applied edge beading and inlaid diamond escutcheons, scalloped apron, cutout feet, old worn refinishing, some edge damage, old repair, 39¾" w, 29¾" d, 41¼" h **1,000**

Walnut, Country Queen Anne, pine secondary wood, top with molded cornice, dovetailed case, and 8 dovetailed overlapping drawers, base with 3 dovetailed overlapping drawers, scalloped apron, and cabriole legs, orig engraved brasses, orig finish, 41¾" w, 22¾" d, 69¾" h **18,750**

Walnut, Queen Anne, oblong thumb molded top with notched front corners, single long drawer above 2 short drawers above 2 long molded graduated drawers, fluted quarter columns flanking drawers, molded base on tall ogee bracket feet, old finish, some repairs to feet, 1 foot with 4" replaced patch, Philadelphia, c1765, 38⅛" w, 22½" d, 33½" h **12,650**

Walnut and Cherry, Federal, poplar secondary wood, gallery with scrolled crest and turned side spindles, 4 dovetailed drawers with edge beading, paneled ends, high turned feet, clear glass pulls, old finish, damage to feet, 42¼" w, 20½" x 43¼" top, 52¼" h **600**

CHESTS, OTHER

Carpenter's, poplar, fitted int, age cracks, 48½" w, 22¾" d, 23" h **$195**

Chest Over Drawers, decorated, Queen Anne, pine, grain painted, molded lid, 2 false drawers over 2 working drawers, molded base, bracket feet, teardrop pulls, 34½" w, 17½" d, 36¼" h **1,500**

Chest Over Drawers, joined, rounded corners on rect cleated top, 3 raised panels on chest front, 2 long drawers with raised panel fronts, paneled sides, old refinish, western MA, 17th C, 41½" w, 19½" d, 43" h **4,500**

Dower's, dec and grain painted pine, edge molded lid, dovetailed case, till, dovetailed bracket feet, wrought iron strap hinges, yellow, black, and white polka dots, stylized potted flowers, eagles, names of couple, and date "September 21, 1826," red ground, faint signature inside lid, till lid and lock missing, feet repaired, lid molding replaced 1 end, lid dec very worn, dec on chest may be old repaint, PA, 47" w, 21" d, 22½" h **1,750**

Immigrant's, decorated, pine, paneled lid and ends, dovetailed case, iron bear trap lock and key, blue ground, red trim, polychrome flowers, name,

and date on light blue panels on front, traces of paint on lid panels, old
repairs, turned feet missing, iron strapping added to front and ends, 1820,
50½" w, 23" d, 21" h ..../............ **750**
Immigrant's, pine, iron bound, white painted label, blue ground, 31½" l **350**
Mule, cherry, Country Chippendale, 6 board type construction, lift lid with
applied edge molding, graduated dovetailed drawers with 2 false drawers
over 2 working drawers, wide edge beading, dovetailed bracket feet, refinished, replaced batwing brasses, minor repairs to feet, 44" w, 19½" d,
42½" h **2,250**
Mule, hardwood and pine, 6 board construction, lift lid with applied edge
molding, 2 dovetailed overlapping drawers, 2 false drawers, bracket feet,
replaced brasses, staple hinges, 35½" w, 17 x 37½" top, 41½" h **2,300**
Mule, pine, Country Chippendale, 6 board type construction, 2 false drawers over 3 graduated dovetailed overlapping working drawers, bracket
feet, old worn yellow grained repaint, 1 back foot facing incomplete,
locks removed, 39½" w, 19¾" d, 40¾" h **1,500**
Mule, pine, decorated, red striped graining, blue trim, molded edge top,
3 dovetailed overlapping drawers, cutout end feet, orig oval brasses, wear,
minor edge damage, 45" w, 18¼ x 48" top, 40¾" h **700**
Mule, pine, 6 board construction, old dark red paint, lift lid with int till,
2 dovetailed overlapping drawers, cutout feet, minor edge damage,
replaced brasses, till lid rehinged, 29¾" w, 16¾ x 31¼" top, 36¼" h **2,500**
Mule, pine, turned feet, 4 dovetailed drawers, replaced crest, 38" w, 42" h ... **325**
Spice, decorated, grain painted, William and Mary, single hinged door, int
drawers arranged as 2 over 3 over single base drawer, ball feet, molded
top and base, MA, early 18th C, 18¾" w, 12½" d, 18" h **10,500**
Spice, yellow pine, mortised and pinned construction, rect 2 board top,
10 dovetailed drawers, square posts extending to turned feet, old mellow
refinishing, age cracks in top, replaced turned wood pulls, southern states,
59¼" w, 25" d, 33½" h ..../.....**3,250**
Sugar, cherry, lift–off lid, dovetailed case with inlaid stars, lines, and circles,
large till, single dovetailed drawer in frame, square tapered legs, cutout
leg brackets, old finish, old repairs, replaced moldings, NC, 31¼" w,
15¾" d, 36" h **12,000**

CHILDREN'S FURNITURE

Armchair, dec, hardwood, orig red, white, and blue paint, patriotic stars and
stripes, replaced brown vinyl covered seat, 22½" h **$600**
Bed, maple and cherry, tall post, canopy, urn finials, turned and tapered
posts, shaped headboard, turned feet, restored, New England, 72¼" l,
38" w, 50" h **1,750**
Bench, settle, red repaint, weathered, repairs, Marietta, OH, 74" l **350**
Blanket Chest, 6 board construction, old blue paint, New England, 34" w,
15½" d, 20½" h **800**
Chair, arrow back, dec, polychrome fruit and flowers, brown repaint, 10"
seat, 23¾" h overall **165**
Chair, decorated, worn orig light green paint, black striping, gold stenciling,
and polychrome floral dec, 10¾" seat, 22" h overall **600**
Chair, ladder back, hardwood, worn woven splint seat, refinished **75**

Chair, Windsor, flat crest, rabbit ear posts, 3 arrow shaped spindles, shaped plank seat, bamboo turned legs, stretchers, black and red striping, red–brown flame graining on crest and seat, yellow ground, 17½" h seat, 29½" h overall **200**

Cradle, bentwood, oval bentwood basket, extended ornate scrolled supports, trestle base, c1900, 52" l, 36" h **750**

Cradle, cherry, Chippendale, 2 shaped flaring stiles mounted with brass carrying handles centering hanging bassinet, downswept legs ending in snake feet, minor burns, chips to base of bassinet, mid–Atlantic states, c1770, 38½" l, 30" d, 42" h **1,500**

Cradle, cherry, dovetailed, 4 cutout heart handles, wide shaped rockers, worn red paint, age cracks, nailed edge repairs, 42" l **350**

Cradle, cherry, Windsor, hooped bentwood ends with 3 turned spindles, upper and lower flat rails on sides joined by 10 short rods, pinned mortise construction, old green paint, nailed reinforcement to joints, some spindles are old replacements, 36" l **300**

Cradle, pine, hooded top, shaped sides, scrolled rockers, red, yellow, and green fruit border on brown ground, New England, c1830, 29" l, 19½" w, 28" h **750**

Cradle, pine, primitive, hardwood spindles, traces of old brown paint, 39" l . . **100**

Cradle, poplar, dovetailed, cutout and scrolled sides, heart cutouts in ends, scrolled rockers, old brown grained repaint, 40½" l **150**

Cradle, poplar, rounded hood, old green int paint, old ext refinishing, edge wear, renailing, 43" l **165**

Cradle, walnut, dovetailed, scrolled headboard, shaped sides and rockers, refinished, old replaced bottom, rockers reset, 39" l **300**

Cupboard, pine, top with pair of glazed doors, 4 drawers and bin in base, replaced plywood top, refinished, 32½" w, 14" d, 43" h **250**

Desk, hardwood and pine, wire nail construction, chip carved detail, 2 banks of 3 drawers, old dark varnish finish, 22¾" w, 8¾" d, 15½" h **375**

Left: High Chair, mule ear posts, 3 narrow slats, scrolled arms, ring turned posts and front stretchers, bulbous turned front posts, woven splint seat, $250.

Right: Kitchen Cabinet, Hoosier type, zinc work surface, 50" h, 28" w, $770. Photo courtesy Jackson's Auctioneers & Appraisers.

Desk, oak, roll top, C–roll, slightly overhanging rect writing surface, single drawer, square legs, stretchers at sides and back, turned wood pulls, 26" w, 16" d, 37" h 275

Desk, oak, slant front, arched crest, fall front writing flap with applied foliate moldings, single drawer, recessed base shelf, shaped bootjack ends with cutout tulip dec, turned wood pulls, 22" w, 11" d, 33" h 250

Dresser, cottage style, poplar, wire nail construction, high back mirror with shelves, 3 drawers, painted red with white striping, 23¹/₄" h 300

High Chair, bentwood, caned back panel and seat, stationary food tray, foot rest with punched board panel, outcurving legs, c1890 300

High Chair, decorated, salmon paint, white and black striping and polychrome floral dec with rose on crest, spindle back, plank seat, turned legs, PA, 36" h 700

High Chair, hardwood, ladder back, turned finials and posts, 3 shaped slats, rush seat, shaped foot rest, refinished, 38³/₄" h 350

High Chair, oak, pressed carved detail, cane back and seat, adjustable height, 39³/₄" h 275

High Chair, oak, stroller type, shaped crest rail with pressed arch, leaf, and fan dec, pressed foliate design on splat, turned stiles, hinged food tray, turned arm supports, caned seat, shaped foot rest, turned legs, ring turned stretchers, iron spoke wheels, 42" h 500

High Chair, oak, T–back, hinged bow front food tray, square arm supports, shaped seat, outcurving legs with ring and baluster turnings, rect foot rest, box stretchers, 39" h 200

High Chair, oak, turned and pressed detail, cane seat, adjustable base, cast iron wheels, refinished, 40" h 275

High Chair, Windsor, rod back, straight crest rail, open arms, saddle seat, splayed base with ring turned legs and stretchers, foot rest replaced, early 19th C 250

High Chair, Windsor, spindle back, flat crest rail, bamboo turned spindles, shaped plank seat with rolled front rail, splayed base, shaped foot rest, bamboo turned legs, orig yellow paint with olive green stencil dec and black striping, PA or OH, 24" h seat, 36¹/₂" h overall 1,000

Potty Chair, decorated, shaped crest with stenciled floral dec, 6 spindle back, scrolled arms, turned arm posts, shaped seat with round cutout, turned legs, old brown paint with black and yellow striping, door missing from compartment back, ironstone chamber pot, 39" h 75

Potty Chair, pine, high back with cutout handle in shaped crest, shaped sides and arms, scrolled apron, rockers, painted 150

Rocker, decorated, black and red graining, yellow striping, stenciled floral designs with eagle on crest, 24¹/₂" h 200

Rocker, decorated, green paint, yellow and gold striping, polychrome floral dec on crest, glued break and metal brace on separation in laminated back, 16¹/₂" h 195

Rocker, ladder back, turned posts with ball finials, 3 shaped slats, turned arms, splint seat, ring turned front posts, refinished, replaced seat, 25" h ... 150

Rocker, wicker, white repaint, replaced cane seat, 28" h 115

Rocker, Windsor, bamboo turnings, youth size, stepped crest, 5 spindle back, center spindle with dec tablet, shaped seat, splayed base, front stretcher with center tablet foot rest, shaped rockers, old yellowed white repaint with black and gold striping and foliage scrolls, 28¹/₂" h 275

CLOCK

Banjo, Aaron Willard type, presentation, mahogany, 8 day time only movement, gilt and rope turned moldings, applied lower balls and drop, brass side frets, painted metal dial, brass eagle and ball finial on molded pediment, lower glass with "Boston State House" painting, 36" h **$900**

Banjo, Howard, Model No. 1, wall regulator, simulated rosewood, mkd on movement "Howard Boston, Riggs," 12½" painted metal dial with subsidiary seconds, lower glass repainted, dial repainted or replaced, 50" l . . . **3,500**

Banjo, James Crofts, simulated rosewood, 8 day time only movement, brass side frets, painted metal dial, overpainted tablets, crack in 1 fret, dial sgd "James Crofts, Rochester, N.H.," 29" h **750**

Banjo, Model 5 type, simulated rosewood, 7½" painted metal dial with Breguet hands, black and gilt glasses, 28½" l **750**

Banjo, New Haven, miniature, mahogany, 8 day jeweled balance, silvered metal dial, brass eagle finial **95**

Banjo, Waterbury Willard No. 1, oak, 8 day weight driven movement, black and gold glasses with red accents, ball and spike finial, drop ending in acorn, porcelain dial, 43½" h **600**

Calendar, Ansonia Brass & Copper Co, rosewood veneer, 8 day time and strike movement, short drop case with turned finials, black and gold glass, painted metal dial with sweep calendar hand and month aperture, dial chipping and some paint loss on door, 26" h **550**

Kitchen, Ingraham "Mascot," walnut, 8 day time, strike, and alarm movement, case surmounted with cameo medallion on pediment and flanked with lion's heads on pillars, orig glass, fancy cast brass pendulum **400**

Kitchen, Waterbury "Nelson," walnut, 8 day time, strike, and alarm movement, fancy cast brass pendulum **250**

Mantel, A Stowell & Co, Boston, mahogany, 8 day time and strike movement, rect case, arched top, engraved face, Westminster chimes, key and pendulum, 12⅞" w, 18½" h **600**

Mantel, Junghans, mahogany, beehive case, 8 day, silvered dial, rear silent chime lever **175**

Mantel, Russell & Jones, marbleized wood, Tennessee marble columns, 8 day time movement, 5" dial, 10" h **175**

Mantel, Seth Thomas, mahogany, 8 day, brass dial with pierced overlay and silvered hour ring, subsidiary seconds, chime dials, fret sides, movement #113A **400**

Regulator, Ansonia Brass Clock Co, rosewood veneer, short drop, 8 day time only movement, painted metal dial, orig black and gold door glass, 25" h . **400**

Regulator, Ansonia Ionic, mahogany veneer, 8 day time and strike movement, painted metal dial with inset center, gilt tablet, fancy brass pendulum, 22" h **350**

Regulator, Boston Clock Co, cherry, 8 day time movement, painted case, 1880–90, 34" h **800**

Regulator, Gilbert No. 1, rosewood, 8 day time only weight driven movement, painted metal dial with subsidiary seconds, eglomise tablet **1,050**

Regulator, Little & Eastman Co, Boston, MA, quarter sawn oak, sgd 8 day time movement, c1890, 35¼" h **650**

Regulator, Riggs & Bro, grained softwood, octagonal with extended round drop, 8 day weight driven time only movement, 2 black and gold glasses, dial sgd "Riggs & Bro. Philada.," 33" l **1,000**

Left: Banjo, Aaron Willar, Boston, Federal style, circular white dial, black Roman numerals, eglomise panels within giltwood case, minor chips and losses, 19th C, 39¹/₄" h, $1,380. Photo courtesy Sotheby's.

Right: Shelf, Eli Terry & Sons, Plymouth, CT, stencil dec, 8 day, claw feet, $450.

Regulator, Seth Thomas, cherry, figure 8, 8 day time only movement, orig dial, tablet, and label, refinished, c1880, 28³/₄" h **900**

Regulator, Seth Thomas, mahogany, long drop, 8 day time only weight driven movement, painted metal dial with subsidiary seconds, repainted dial and case int, 35" l **750**

Regulator, unknown maker, mahogany veneer, turned and composition details, brass works, pendulum, 30" h **120**

Regulator, unknown maker, walnut veneer, octagonal, with pendulum and key, refinished, backboard renailed, minor veneer damage, 31³/₄" h **325**

Regulator, Waltham Clock Co, Waterbury, CT, oak, 8 day time and strike movement and half hour strike, regulator tablet, painted zinc dial, pendulum, 32" h **400**

Schoolhouse, hanging, Ingraham, pressed oak, 8 day time, strike, and calendar movement, c1900, 18³/₄" h **350**

Schoolhouse, hanging, Sessions Century Model, pressed oak, 8 day time, strike, and calendar movement, short drop, orig label, replaced calendar hand, Sessions Century model, c1900, 26¹/₂" h **450**

Schoolhouse, hanging, Seth Thomas Globe model, rosewood veneer, long drop, 8 day time only movement, orig label, c1875, 31¹/₂" h **725**

Schoolhouse, hanging, unknown maker, softwood, long drop, 8 day time and strike movement, octagonal, orig gilt and black molding, paper dial, 20" h **125**

Shelf, column, Forestville, mahogany, 8 day time and strike movement, carved fruit basket crest, painted wood dial, glasses with prints **375**

Shelf, column and splat, Atkins & Downs, mahogany, 8 day time and strike movement, painted wood dial, orig silvered tablet with central medallion, case with carved fruit basket crest and acanthus leaf columns, suppressed ball feet, 38" h **650**

Shelf, column and splat, Elisha Hotchkiss, mahogany, 8 day time and strike movement, eagle crest and acanthus leaf columns, painted wood dial, overpainted glasses, 39" h **500**

Shelf, column and splat, Henry C Smith, 30 hour wood time and strike movement, stenciled dec, painted wood dial, replaced tablet, repainted stenciling, ... 300

Shelf, column and splat, Jeromes & Darrow, mahogany veneer, wooden time and strike movement, stenciled black ½ columns, fruit basket carved crest, triple glazed door with mirrored center and orig eglomise tablet, painted wood dial, 40" h 450

Shelf, column and splat, Joseph Wells & Chauncey Boardman, 30 hour time and strike movement, detailed shell and leaf crest, acanthus leaf columns, paw feet, painted wood dial, mirrored panel, paint loss to dial, 35" h 325

Shelf, cottage style, Gilbert, rosewood, 30 hour time and strike movement, gilt medallion panel dec, painted metal dial 150

Shelf, cottage style, Terry & Andrews, rosewood, 8 day time and strike movement, painted metal dial, overpainted tablet 325

Shelf, miniature tall case, Mission, oak, 8 day time only movement, exposed pendulum, 15" h 100

Shelf, ogee, Chauncey Boardman, rosewood veneer, 30 hour time and strike movement, painted wood dial, orig tablet with eagle on shield 350

Shelf, ogee, New Haven, rosewood veneer, 30 hour time and strike movement, original glass with Greenwood Cemetery Entrance, overpainted metal dial 150

Shelf, pillar and scroll, E Terry & Sons, 30 hour time and strike movement, painted wood dial, ftd, replaced tablet, minor case restoration 1,200

Shelf, steeple, Ansonia Brass Co, rosewood veneer, 8 day time, strike, and alarm movement, painted metal dial, orig frosted tablet with gilt rose dec, minor veneer loss, Ansonia Brass Co 130

Shelf, steeple, Brewster & Ingraham, rosewood veneer, frosted and cut door glass, c1840, 19¼" h 375

Shelf, steeple, unknown maker, mahogany veneer, brass works, worn painted metal face, worn paper label, reverse painted transfer scene of "Washington's Rock, N.J.," some veneer damage, 20" h 175

Shelf, triple decker, Birge & Fuller, simulated rosewood graining, 8 day time and strike movement, painted wood dial, nice tablets, gilt fruit crest, half columns, ftd, 35" h 775

Study, pressed oak case with open well, weight driven, 8 day time and strike movement, porcelain dial with recessed center, Waterbury, 24" l 600

Tall Case, cherry, 8 day, broken arch top with inlaid rosettes and applied half column in center hood, painted dial with moon phase, case with chamfered corners, flat door inlaid in center with line inlay and "Joy," paneled base inlaid with bust of man, dial sgd "Caleb Davis (Woodstock, VA)," feet missing, glass missing in bonnet, 97" h 12,000

Tall Case, curly maple and tiger maple, dovetailed bonnet with freestanding columns, arched cornice with carved cherry fan ornament and brass ball and spire finials, chamfered corners and overlapping door in waist, cove molding between sections, dovetailed bracket feet, wag on the wall works with painted face, feet, cornice, finials, and top of curve on bonnet replaced, backed with wood to straighten warp, 90" h 5,600

Tall Case, mahogany, broken arch top hood, turned supports, 8 day, painted metal dial with moon phase, subsidiary seconds dial and calendar aperture, case with chamfered corners, beaded waist door, sunken molded panel in base, feet short, sgd "Daniel Oyster, Reading" on dial, 95" h 6,750

Tall Case, mahogany, hood with swan's neck crest, surmounted by 3 ball and steeple brass finials, arched glazed hinged door opening to white painted dial with phases of the moon, seconds, and calendar mechanism inscribed "John Parke Patterson, J P P," waisted case with shaped line inlaid door tympanum board above bookend inlaid panels flanked by fluted quarter columns, line inlaid base below raised on bracket feet, old finish, lacks finial plinths on hood, some losses to moldings, NJ, c1800, 19" w, 9³/₄" d, 95¹/₂" h 9,775

Tall Case, mahogany, Regency, 8 day, arched line inlaid hood with oak shaped and pierced applied fretwork, engraved brass dial with moon phase and silvered chapter ring, masked spandrels, calendar aperture, case with arched molded waist door flanked by fluted stiles, French bracket feet, dial sgd "H. Naylor, Thorton," 95" h 2,750

Tall Case, mahogany, Regency, 8 day, bonnet top with conch shell inlay, brass dial with moon phase, masked spandrels, subsidiary calendar dial, center with scroll and bird engraving, case with arched molded door, chamfered corners with ebony inlay, double line inlay on door and base, bracket feet, dial arch sgd "John Lawson, Bradford," 88" h 2,250

Tall Case, mahogany, Regency, 8 day, broken arch top with multiple line and checkered inlays, painted dial with moon phase with subsidiary seconds dial, shaped waist door with line inlay flanked by quarter columns, capital blocks with checkered inlay, blocks below columns with floral vase inlays, base with checkered cut corner inlay, bracket feet, dial sgd "W. Bellman Broughton," 93" h 2,750

Left: Dwarf Tall Case, mahogany, Victorian, swan's neck crest carved with florets, eglomise inset panel, arched clock face sgd "H. Kirk, Hanley," 2 train movement, fluted columns, double Gothic arched door flanked by fluted columns, imbricated base, later ogee bracket feet, panel cracked, late 19th C, 52¹/₂" h, 11¹/₂" w, 7¹/₂" d, $8,050.

Center: Tall Case, mahogany inlaid cherrywood, Chippendale, arched glazed door, painted face with moon phases, 2 train movement, seconds dial, waisted case, shaped crossbanded door, fluted quarter columns, outset base, bracket feet, restorations to bonnet, feet, and paint, PA, late 18th C, 90" h, 17¹/₂" w, 10" d, $7,475.

Photos courtesy Sotheby's.

Tall Case, pine, arched bonnet, surmounted by pierced fretwork plinths, glazed door below opening to white enameled dial inscribed in arch "Calvin Bailey Hanov. Mass. No. 100 1808" with Roman and Arabic numerals below, spandrels and arch dec with floral motifs in polychrome, waisted case below fitted with door within beaded surround and flanked by quarter columns on flaring base and tall bracket feet, patches to cornice, minor repairs to feet, Hanover, MA, c1810, 17" w, 10" d, 80" h **4,500**

Tall Case, pine, wooden works, worn painted face with American eagle and "Hoadley Plymouth," weights and pendulum, repaired hands, broken minute hand, replaced fretwork crest with turned finials, 91½" h **1,550**

Tall Case, quarter sawn oak, bonnet with molded cornice and fluted pilasters with gilded Corinthian capitals, inlaid star in door, brass works, engraved brass face, second hand, calendar movement, mkd "Geo White, Bristol," old finish, case and bonnet repaired, pendulum and chains replaced, 77¼" h **1,210**

Tall Case, tiger maple, Sheraton, 8 day, broken arch top, painted dial with scenic arch, wag movement, shaped door with mahogany banding under hood and base, sunken panel in base, turned feet, 96" h **7,250**

Tall Case, walnut, Queen Anne, 8 day, flat top, arched painted dial with rose dec, subsidiary seconds dial and calendar aperture, case with arched door, applied molded panel on base, bulbous feet, c1760, 87" h **3,250**

CUPBOARD

Chimney, decorated, walnut and poplar, old brownish yellow graining over earlier brighter yellow, simple cornice, single door with 4 recessed panels, int shelves, originally built–in cupboard, front edge moldings removed, OH, 26¾" w, 18¼" d, 83½" h **$500**

Chimney, pine, corner, 1 pc, open top, single board door, angled back, old finish, modern hinges, 24" w, 15" d, 84½" h **600**

Corner, butternut, 2 pc, scrolled cornice, perimeter molding, paneled doors, scrolled apron, inlaid diamond escutcheons, center scroll on cornice probably replaced, hinges replaced, 50" w, 91¼" h **1,650**

Corner, cherry, molded cornice with frieze, raised panel doors, scalloped apron, repairs, edge damage, wear, worn refinishing, 47" w, 52½" w cornice, 85" h **1,000**

Corner, cherry, 1–pc construction, molded cornice, paneled doors, scrolled bracket feet, refinished, cornice, feet, and hinges replaced, 50½" w, 81" h . . **1,500**

Corner, cherry, 2–pc construction, beveled cornice, pair of arched doors each with single pane of glass, pie shelf, 2 dovetailed drawers in base, paneled cupboard doors, orig cast iron latches and porcelain knobs, 54" w, 85" h **1,875**

Corner, cherry and poplar, molded poplar cornice, pair of doors each with 6 panes of glass, 2 dovetailed drawers, paneled cupboard doors, cutout feet, old varnish, edge damage to cornice, upper doors need to be reattached, 1 door missing hinges, 54½" w, 79" h **1,500**

Corner, cherry and poplar, 1 pc, brown grain painting, molded cornice, pair of doors each with 8 panes of old wavy glass, applied moldings, paneled cupboard doors, bracket feet, int with worn green repaint, some wear and edge damage, edge damage to cornice, 51" w, 86¼" h **2,300**

Corner, curly maple, Federal, 2 sections, upper section with molded cornice above light and dark contrasting inlaid tympanum, single hinged glazed mullioned door below opening to yellow painted shelved int, glazed panels dec with reverse paintings of stylized leaves and birds, lower section fitted with single long drawer above pair of paneled cupboard doors opening to shelves, shaped skirt, bracket feet, mellow old finish, small patch to upper right cornice molding and case, minor repair to 1 foot, PA, c1820, 38½" w, 23½" d, 89½" h 38,000

Corner, decorated, hanging, worn brown graining over red, 2 paneled doors with iron latches, wire nail construction, 26" w, 41½" h 675

Corner, pine, barrel back, crown molded cornice, open top with 2 shelves, pair of raised double panel doors, molded base, butterfly hinges, old dark patina, old repairs, edge damage, bottom boards and base molding replaced, repaired hinges are old replacements, 63" w, 75½" h 800

Corner, pine, hanging, molded cornice above double paneled hinged door opening to shelves, sides continuing to form scrolled pendant with 2 quarter–round shelves, orig wrought iron strap hinges, inked inscription on inside door "Eshelman Family Oley Vally [sic] PA," PA, 1750–70, 34" w, 24" d, 56" h 39,000

Corner, pine, hanging, wire nail construction, alligatored pale blue repaint, 13¼" w, 37¾" h 325

Corner, pine, 1 pc, green stain, molded cornice, serpentine shaped upper shelves, perimeter molding, paneled cupboard doors set in beaded frames, scalloped apron, 46¼" w, 80" h 4,125

Corner, pine, 1 pc, molded cornice with dentil frieze, pair of upper doors each with 6 panes of glass, wide applied waist molding, paneled cupboard doors, int painted light blue, bracket feet, old mellow refinishing, feet partially replaced, hardware replaced, 50½" w, 74½" h 1,425

Left: Corner, cherry, Federal, 2 sections, upper section with swan's neck cresting with stylized flowerhead terminals and ball finials, arched glazed door, lower section with molded waist over pair of paneled doors, shelved interior, bracket feet, PA, early 19th C, $7,475. Photo courtesy Sotheby's.

Right: Corner, cherry, Kentucky, molded cornice, paneled cupboard doors, $2,000.

Corner, pine, 2 pc, molded cornice, scalloped top rail, pair of glazed doors in top, 2 dovetailed drawers and 2 paneled doors in base, cutout feet, cast iron latches, brass and porcelain knobs, refinished, 56½" w, 61¾" w cornice, 86" h **1,500**

Corner, pine and poplar, 1 pc, molded cornice with Greek key detail, double doors in top each with 8 panes, shelved int with butterfly cutouts, paneled doors in base, applied perimeter moldings, 2 cracked and replaced glass panes, minor edge damage and pieced repair, refinished, 53" w cornice, 81¼" h **2,200**

Corner, poplar, Country Hepplewhite, arched top rail, cove molded cornice, single door top with 12 old glass panes, 2 dovetailed drawers, paneled base door, scalloped apron, French feet, dark varnish stain finish, replaced early cut glass knobs and brass amphora shaped key escutcheons, 41½" w, 44¾" w cornice, 86" h **3,500**

Corner, walnut, bonnet top, 2 sections, upper section with molded swan's neck crest centering 3 urn and flame finials, arched glazed mullioned door with scrolling stylized vine inlay, blue painted shelved int, lower section with 3 line inlaid small drawers above pair of line inlaid cupboard doors, molded base, ogee bracket feet, H hinges, finials replaced, repairs to tympanum board and pediment, PA, c1810, 39¾" w, 28" d, 58¾" h **7,475**

Corner, walnut, hanging, wire nail construction, scrolled detailed crest, paneled door, bracket feet with scrolling, damage to crest, glued repair, Lewis County, KY, 13¾" w, 5¼" d, 22" h **225**

Corner, walnut, 1–pc construction, molded cornice, paneled doors, 2 dovetailed drawers, chamfered details on rails and stiles, scalloped base, orig cast iron latch and porcelain knob, old varnish finish, 1 end of cornice molding has edge damage and needs to be reattached, glass knob fitted into keyhole of missing lock on top door, 48½" w, 92¼" h **1,000**

Dresser, pine, Federal, projecting molded cornice, scalloped and floral carved frieze, 3 open shelves with scalloped ends, rect top, single raised panel cupboard door, H–form hinges, second quarter 19th C, 58" w, 18½" d, 83" h **2,500**

Dresser, walnut, Eastlake, marble top, reconstructed top drawer, replaced pulls, 13½ x 27¼" top, 53" h **550**

Dutch, walnut, step back, ogee molded cornice, 2 upper doors with 6 glass panes each flanking center glazed stile with 3 panes, shelved int with plate rails and grooves and spoon racks, base with pie shelf above 3 short drawers over 2 double recessed panel doors, chamfered corners, bracket feet, refinished, replaced drawer slides and feet facing, 60" w, 19¼" d, 4¾" pie shelf, 86¼" h **8,800**

Jelly, cherry, walnut secondary wood, poplar door panels, 2 dovetailed drawers, cutout tapered feet, 43¼" w, 18½ x 44½" top, 55" h **875**

Jelly, decorated, poplar, brown burl grained door panels and drawer fronts, 2 nailed drawers over pair of raised panel doors, cutout feet, wood pulls, nailed repair to 1 door, 41" w, 14½" d, 54¼" h **500**

Jelly, decorated, yellow pine, primitive, painted yellow stylized trees and diamond latticework design on green ground, rough sawn wood, wire nail construction, single door with wood turnbuckle, cutout feet, found in barn in Catawba County, NC, 36" w, 17" d, 73" h **3,250**

Jelly, painted, primitive, single board doors with iron strap handles, gray top coat, layers of old paint, back boards repainted, 42" w, 18½" d, 44½" h ...**385**

Jelly, painted, 2–board door, cutout feet, worn bluish gray paint, 41½" w,
13¾" d, 27" h **400**

Jelly, pine, board and batten door, cutout feet, red painted int, repainted gray
ext, 35½" w, 12¼" d, 33" h **385**

Jelly, pine, Federal, shaped splashboard, straight front fitted with 2 small
drawers and pair of paneled doors, turned wood pulls, straight bracket
feet, c1800, 36" w, 19" d, 54" h **1,000**

Jelly, pine and poplar, primitive, dovetailed case, raised panel doors, cutout
feet, worn layers of red and gray paint, edge damage, age cracks, renailed,
missing cornice, 49⅝" w, 17½" d, 71" h **190**

Jelly, poplar, Country Empire, regionally known as a Jackson press, rect overhanging top, projecting dovetailed long drawer supported on half column
pilasters, 2 paneled cupboard doors, half turned feet, old worn red
repaint, 45" w, 21¼" d, 50½" h **350**

Jelly, walnut, Gothic panel doors, pine and poplar secondary wood, pressed
moldings, 3 dovetailed drawers, cutout feet, age cracks, repairs, MO,
50¼" h **675**

Jelly, walnut, molded cornice, single board top, pair of single board doors in
beaded frame, single dovetailed drawer, bracket feet, replaced turned
pulls and feet, 43¼" w, 19½ x 46¾" cornice, 60½" h **1,100**

Jelly, walnut, paneled doors, cutout feet, refinished, 42⅜" w, 56½" h **450**

Kas, pine, molded cornice, paneled doors set in beaded frames, open int
with cast iron hooks, solid ends, base molding, orig red paint, 64" w,
21½" d, 76¾" h **2,000**

Kas, pine, painted, break down, molded cornice, pair of paneled doors with
beaded frames, single board ends, molded edge base, cast iron hooks
inside, orig red paint, several hooks broken, 64" w, 21½" d, 76¾" h **2,000**

Linen Press, mahogany, 2 pc, top with molded cornice, 2 paneled doors, and
3 int drawers, base with 2 short over 3 long beaded edge drawers, shaped
skirt, and flaring French feet, small chips to front feet and skirt, brasses
replaced with turned wood pulls, New England, 1800–10, 54" w, 89" h ...**4,500**

Pewter, pine, 1 pc, open, red wash over worn paint, step back top with open
shelves, board and batten doors, base stiles, cutout feet, door and top
board replaced, 50" w, 16" d, 71" h **385**

Pewter, poplar, paint dec, 2 sections, upper with molded projecting cornice
above cyma shaped scalloped uprights centering 2 shelves with plate rails
and grooves pierced for cutlery, projecting lower section with 2 molded
drawers above pair of hinged paneled cupboard doors, molded base on
bracket feet, moldings painted green, rear feet replaced, 60½" w, 20½" d,
79¼" h **40,250**

Step Back, cherry, Country Sheraton, poplar secondary wood, 1 pc, triple
arched pediment with center broken arch with goosenecks above carved
oval sunbursts, pair of small paneled doors with carved oval sunbursts
flanked by banks of 5 graduated drawers and separated by applied half
turned columns, single shelf and secret compartment int, base with 4
dovetailed and cockbeaded graduated long drawers, figured walnut inlaid
stiles, short turned feet, secret compartment later addition, 1 front post
with poorly repaired break at foot, 41½" w, 19" d, 72½" h **4,500**

Step Back, decorated, brown flame graining, poplar, 2 pc, beveled cornice,
pair of glazed doors each with 6 old wavy glass panes, shelved int, pie

shelf, base with 2 nailed short drawers over pair of raised panel cupboard doors with molded center stile, simple cutout feet, bottom door has added brass thumb latch, some paint touch–up, 47" w, 19½" d, 84" h **3,500**

Step Back, pine, 1–pc construction, 2 tiered cornice, pair of paneled cupboard doors top and bottom, pie shelf, 2 short waist drawers, wood turnbuckle latches, refinished, age cracks in door panels, 44" w, 16" d **750**

Step Back, pine, 2–pc construction, dentil molded cornice, double doors in top, 2 nailed drawers and paneled doors in base, cutout feet, replaced cornice, backboard renailed, 47" w, 14½ x 50" cornice, 88½" h **550**

Step Back, poplar, 2 pc, cove molded cornice, pair of raised panel doors, shelved int, low pie shelf, base with center stack of drawers with 2 small drawers between 2 larger drawers, flanked by pair of raised panel cupboard doors, simple cutout feet, dovetailed case, mortised construction, turned pulls, some edge damage, nailed repair to 1 top stile at hinge, int with modern yellow paint, 55" w, 15½" d, 81½" h **3,000**

Step Back, walnut and poplar, beveled cornice, pair of paneled doors top and bottom set in beaded frames, high pie shelf, shelved int, deeply scalloped apron, high cutout feet, refinished, small repair to 1 corner of bottom door, base has some reconstruction, southern states, 48¼" w, 13¼" d, 79" h **1,750**

Utility, pine and hardwood, 2 full length doors with 3 recessed panels, 5–shelf int, bootjack ends, worn refinishing, 30" w, 14¾" d, 75" h **350**

Wall, butternut, molded cornice with rounded corners, paneled sides, high pie shelf, double doors with 6 panes of old wavy glass, 2 dovetailed drawers, paneled doors, scalloped apron, cutout feet, Rockingham drawer pulls, locks and surface mounted latches removed, cast iron escutcheons added, 1 drawer replaced, edge damage, repair, 47¾" w, 14¾ x 52" cornice, 19 x 49½" shelf, 88¼" h **1,875**

Wall, decorated, poplar, grain painted, 1 pc, 2 cupboard doors, 2 long drawers, bootjack ends, New England, 39" w, 17½" d, 39½" h **475**

Left: Sugar Chest, cherry, molded cornice, paneled doors, shelved int, lift lid over 2 drawers flanking center hinged door, Taylor County, KY, c1820, $11,000. Photo courtesy Green River Antiques Auctions.

Right: Linen Press, cherry, married, blind 2–door cupboard added to mid–19th C French Restauration chest of drawers with offset drawer above 3 graduated drawers flanked by bulbous and tapered turned columns, Kentucky, $3,900.

Wall, oak, molded cornice, pair of doors each with single glass pane, paneled doors in base, adjustable shelves, replaced hardware, 48" w, 16" d, 93³/₄" h **400**

Wall, pine, 1 pc, crown molded cornice, reeded frame, paneled doors, scrolled base, refinished, repairs, replaced cornice, 39³/₄" w, 15³/₄" d, 8³/₄" h **500**

Wall, pine, perimeter molding, single paneled door top and bottom, old refinishing, moldings partially replaced, 27¹/₂" w, 16¹/₄" d, 79" h **1,350**

Wall, pine and poplar, 1 pc, primitive, old green and red paint, 6 small shelves, age cracks in backboards, 10" w, 6" d, 41¹/₄" h **525**

Wall, poplar, 1 pc, single board cornice, 4 paneled doors, 2 nailed drawers, damage to base, nailed repair to back foot, edge damage to 1 drawer, red repaint, 40¹/₂" w, 20" d, 71" h **1,250**

Wall, walnut, hanging, molded cornice above paneled molded door with wrought iron rat's tail hinges opening to shelf, single molded drawer below, old finish, PA, c1760, 29" w, 12" d, 39" h **28,750**

Wall, walnut, 1 pc construction, stepped cornice, double doors each with 4 glass panes, paneled cupboard doors, cutout feet, backboards painted "G. W. Crum," old thumb latches, 47³/₄" w, 18³/₄ x 51³/₄" cornice, 86" h **1,000**

DAYBED

Cherry, block and baluster turned posts with urn finials, head and foot boards with 3 turned rails, tapered feet, orig rope rails, grayish blue ribbed upholstery back and seat cushions, board back added to support cushion, 72¹/₂" l **$500**

Cherry and Hardwood, shaped side rails slightly elevated at head end, dovetailed frame, shaped cutout feet on casters, 72" l, 24³/₄" w, 16" h **150**

Curly Maple, block and turned posts with triple ring turned finials, shaped walnut headboard, tick cushion, old mellow finish, 77" l, 24" w **500**

Curly Maple, turned posts and legs, webbed with canvas covering, 62¹/₂" l, 25" w, 31¹/₂" h **300**

Windsor, tripartite back, 3 rails over 18 half spindles, turned arms, baluster turned arm posts, upholstered seat cushion, foldout hinged sleeping area supported by 4 pinned legs, orig yellow paint with gold and black stenciled fruit and leaf dec, seat replaced, New England, 84" l, 26" w, 19¹/₂" h seat, 36¹/₂" h, 49¹/₂ x 80⁵/₈" open size **2,000**

DESK

Bookcase, cherry, Country Federal, molded broken scroll pediment, cast brass ball finials, pair of raised panel doors, shelved int, hinged writing flap, fitted int with small drawers and center prospect door, pullout slides, 4 graduated overlapping drawers, shaped skirt, French feet, refinished, replaced brasses, southern New England, early 19th C, 41¹/₂" w, 20¹/₄" d, 85¹/₂" h **$4,000**

Bookcase, oak, Larkin, bombé shaped cornice supported by beveled mirrored back panel and front columns with scrolled capitals, bowed top shelf, bowed bookcase with convex glass door panel, recessed beveled mirror over fall front writing flap, 3 graduated short drawers, column posts, scroll feet, turned wood pulls, 42" w, 14" d, 67" h **1,500**

Bookcase, oak, side by side, asymmetrical, shaped crest, full length book-case with glazed door, shelved int, square beveled mirror, paneled fall front writing flap, 3 overlapping short drawers, shaped apron, bracket feet, bail handle drawer pulls, 38" w, 14" d, 65" h **500**

Carpenter's, pine, painted red, rect top with lift lid, hinged slant front, pair of wainscoted cupboard doors, square feet on casters, 43" w, 19" d, 42" h . . **275**

Cylinder, burl walnut and mahogany, shaped pediment with carved flower-heads, pair of glazed cabinet doors, cylinder door enclosing writing sur-face over 2 doors, long drawer above recessed cupboard doors, shaped apron, 27" w, 22" d, 66" h **2,500**

Desk on Frame, butternut, Country Hepplewhite, dovetailed gallery with scrolled ends, slant top lift lid on dovetailed case, base stand with 2 dove-tailed short drawers and square tapered legs, turned pulls, refinished, repairs, reeded edge molding added to base, lid hinge broken, 20¼" w, 29½" d, 36" h **450**

Desk on Frame, pine, Country Hepplewhite, slant top desk compartment with wide early dovetailing, overlapping drop lid, fitted int with pigeon-holes with arched top baffles, base with single dovetailed drawer and square tapered legs, refinished, base reconstructed, lid replaced, 37¾" w, 19¾" d, 37¾" h **500**

Kneehole, walnut, poplar secondary wood, paneled construction, single paneled doors, 6 dovetailed drawers, turned feet, refinished, 49" w, 23½" d, 30" h **850**

Lady's, oak, fall front writing surface with applied moldings and carved dec, shaped mirrored back, 2 swelled drawers, cabriole legs, claw and ball feet, 29" w, 55" h **750**

Left: Roll Top, oak, Victorian, S–form roll, fitted int, paneled ends, double pedestal base with long center drawer flanked by banks of short drawers, 50" h, 54" w, 31" d, $1,200.

Right: Slant Front, walnut, Chippendale, int prospect door flanked by drawers and pigeon-holes, 3 long graduated drawers flanked by quarter columns, replaced ogee bracket feet, PA, c1770, 41" h, 40" w, 20½" d, $9,200. Photo courtesy Sotheby's.

Library, walnut, rect top with inset brown leather writing surface and gadrooned edge, straight front, single wide thumb molded drawer flanked by 4 small drawers, cabriole legs, claw and ball feet, brass bail handled pulls, 28½" w, 31½" d, 30½" h **800**

Parlor, quarter sawn oak veneer, brass gallery, molded rect top, applied C–scroll moldings on fall front writing flap, single drawer, shaped apron, cabriole legs, brass ring drop pulls, 26" w, 17" d, 38" h **600**

Roll Top, oak, C–curve, tambour sliding door, fitted int, single drawer over bracketed kneehole, pullout writing board over bank of 4 drawers, paneled ends, 36" w, 28" d, 44" h **1,250**

Roll Top, quarter sawn oak, S–curve, tambour sliding door, fitted int with prospect door, small drawers, shelves, and file slots, slightly overhanging desk top, center drawer and kneehole flanked by banks of drawers with pullout writing boards, paneled ends, 50" w, 34" d, 46" h **2,750**

School, pine, Country Hepplewhite, slant top lift lid, square tapered legs, old worn mellow refinishing, int corner braces added, hinges replaced, gallery removed, 25" w, 21" d, 31" h **150**

Schoolmaster's, decorated, old yellow paint graining over earlier red, low arched crest, slant top lift lid, nailed case, 1 int shelf, square tapered legs, 18½" w, 24¾" d, 34" h **250**

Schoolmaster's, pine, slant front, crest, drop down writing surface, red painted int with pigeonholes, base shelf, square tapered legs, replaced lid, repaired and restored, refinished, 33⅜" w, 20" d, 34¼" h **250**

Slant Front, birch and cherry, slant lid writing surface, fitted int with 3 pigeonholes and 4 drawers, 3 dovetailed overlapping drawers, bracket feet, refinished, 40" w, 18" d, 39" h **550**

Slant Front, cherry, Hepplewhite, lift lid, 2 int dovetailed drawers, mortised and pinned case, square tapered legs, refinished, missing lock, 24" w, 18" d, 32" h **500**

Slant Front, cherry, Hepplewhite, poplar secondary wood, hinged lid, 7 int dovetailed drawers and pigeonholes with scrolled brackets, 4 dovetailed long drawers with edge beading, scrolled apron, French feet, restored veneered facings on front feet and apron, front feet ended out **2,750**

Slant Front, curly maple, Chippendale, fold down lid, fitted int with pigeonholes, 11 dovetailed drawers with fan on top drawer, dovetailed case with 4 dovetailed overlapping drawers, ogee feet, feet replaced, drawer fronts repaired, hardware, lid hinges, and pigeonhole brackets replaced, 38¼" w, 20" d, 42¾" h **1,975**

Slant Front, maple, Chippendale, fitted int with pigeonholes and small drawers, drop front writing surface, pullout slides, 3 graduated drawers with bail handled pulls, bracket feet, refinished, New England, c1770, 36¼" w, 17¼" d, 44" h **4,000**

Slant Front, maple, Queen Anne, high back with whale's tail pediment, circular inlay, and rect beveled glass mirror, row of 5 small drawers, fitted int with valanced pigeonholes and drawers, 4 graduated drawers in base, bracket feet, New England, c1760, 35¼" w, 19" d, 66¾" h **10,000**

Slant Front, oak, Mission, gallery, fall front lid, fitted int, 2 long drawers, arched apron, round copper pulls, missing escutcheon plate, decal on lower side stretcher Lifetime Co, Grand Rapids, MI, Model No. 8548, c1910 . . . . **750**

Slant Front, pine, 1 pc, open shelf over 2 short drawers, hinged fold down writing surface, fitted int with pigeonholes, pullout slides, single board door in base, shaped apron, nut brown finish, reconstructed, 24" w, 16" d, 56½" h **750**

Slant Front, tiger maple, fall front lid, fitted int with leather writing surface, pullout slides, 4 graduated overlapping drawers, molded base, bracket feet, early 19th C, 36½" w, 17½" d, 41" h **4,000**

Slant Front, walnut, Country Formal, rect top, fall front lid, fitted int with 6 short drawers, 6 valanced pigeonholes, 2 fluted document drawers, and paneled prospect door opening to 3 drawers, 4 graduated long drawers below, ogee bracket feet, feet replaced, New England, 1800–15, 38½" w, 44½" h **2,000**

Slant Front, walnut, Country Sheraton, drop front writing surface, fitted int with pigeonholes, 9 small drawers with curly maple veneer fronts, and center door with bird's–eye maple veneer, dovetailed case with 3 graduated cockbeaded long drawers, reeded stiles, turned feet, 42" w, 21" d, 45" h **2,500**

Slant Front, walnut, paneled doors and fall front lid with fitted int pigeonholes and 2 drawers, single board ends, cutout feet with scalloped apron, Victorian cast iron door hinges on lid, old dark finish, 33¾" w, 18" d, 46" h **550**

Table Top, mahogany, folding, dovetailed construction, pop–up compartment, fitted int with pigeonholes and 4 dovetailed drawers, lift up writing surface with replaced green felt covering, old dark finish, folds to 10 x 16 x 22" **450**

DRY SINK

Decorated, brown flame graining, 1 pc, hutch top with peaked crest, 2 paneled doors, chamfered corner posts, 3 short drawers, shaped ends, and vertical board back, base with zinc lined well, pair of paneled cupboard doors, chamfered corner posts, and cutout feet, cast iron and brass thumb latches, white porcelain pulls, wire nail construction, damaged liner, 36" w, 19" d, 74¼" h **$1,750**

Butternut, removable lid, turned half columns, paneled doors, shaped skirt, refinished, 28½" h, 32" l, 18" d, $150.

Decorated, imitation oak graining over earlier red paint, shaped crest, overhanging well with zinc liner and single dovetailed drawer, pair of paneled cupboard doors, cutout feet, Lancaster County, PA, 45¾" w, 20½" d, 32¼" h plus crest **750**

Decorated, old worn red repaint with black brushed graining, poplar and walnut, black door panels over earlier dark blue, recessed well, pair of paneled doors flanking center stile, cutout feet, turnbuckle latches, 39¼" w, 19" d, 36" h **650**

Decorated, polychrome pineapples and feathery dec on red and green ground, pine, straight crest, 3 aligned drawers, horizontal random board back, shaped ends, base with drain board, single short drawer, open well, pair of paneled cupboard doors, 2 shelf int, and scalloped apron, turned wood pulls, some height loss, PA, 44" w, 17¼" d, 57½" h **825**

Decorated, red vinegar graining on yellow ground with sunbursts, fans, and X's, poplar, other secondary wood, open well, single dovetailed drawer, paneled doors, worn int shelf, well shaped bracket feet, 42" w, 19¼" d, 31¾" h **12,000**

Pine, board and batten doors, cutout feet, worn finish, replaced iron bolt latch, 56½" w, 21¼" d, 32" h **550**

Pine, central well flanked by 2 dovetailed drawers, pair of raised panel doors set in reeded frames, int and well painted blue, apron drop on center stile, cutout feet, ext with old mellow refinishing, 58¾" w, 22" d, 32" h **1,000**

Pine, flat cornice, shaped ends, single narrow shelf, rect well, pair of single board cupboard doors separated by center stile, straight apron, 39" w, 16" d, 51" h **750**

Pine, single shelf, well with applied edge molding, open base with cutout feet, worn blue paint, some restoration, 38¾" w, 17½" d, 30½" h **775**

Pine, straight crest, rect projecting tin lined well, pair of paneled cupboard doors separated by center stile, missing feet, 46" w, 25" d, 34" h **600**

Poplar, hutch top with shelf and 2 dovetailed drawers, zinc lined well, 2 dovetailed base drawers, pair of paneled doors, well shaped cutout feet, old dark finish, 61¾" w, 21½" d, 51" h **2,250**

Poplar, raised back with shelf, well, single dovetailed drawer, paneled doors, simple cutout feet, refinished, 54" w, 20" d, 42¾" h **525**

FIRE SCREEN

Cherrywood, Chippendale, surmounted by spiral twist finial, oval needlework panel below depicting mourning scene and standing lady near funereal urn, inscribed below "Artemisia," adjustable on rod, spirally fluted urn form standard below on stylized leaf carved cabriole legs ending in peaked snake feet, old finish, CT, c1790, 54¾" h **$9,250**

Mahogany, Chippendale, surmounted by ball finial, fire screen comprising needlework sampler dec with birds and illegible verse inscribed "Maryann Bragg 1810," hinged candle support below also sliding and adjustable on rod, urn form standard raised on cabriole legs ending in peaked snake feet, old and possibly orig finish, cracks to lower part of standard, 58¾" h **15,000**

Mahogany, Federal, rect frame enclosing silk–on–silk floral needlework panel and D–shaped adjustable hinged candleholder, both sliding on ring turned support surmounted by urn turned finial, arched legs, spade feet, MA, 1790–1810, 54" h **7,500**

FOOTSTOOL

Decorated, cherry, primitive village landscape on top, sponging, shaped aprons, bootjack ends, old repaint, 13½" w **$250**

Decorated, pine, old black paint and yellow striping, scrolled apron, bootjack ends, some damage, padded top recovered in old brown and white check homespun, 15" w, 8" d **250**

Decorated, pine, polychrome dec of 2 dogs, loving couple, and lovebirds on top, 2 dogs on 1 apron, green ground, rect top with diamond cutout handle, 14¼" w, 6½" d, 8" h **200**

Decorated, poplar, stylized floral design, red, green, and yellow on dark ground, rect top, splayed legs, dark varnish over orig finish, 13¾" w, 7" h .. **125**

Pine, book shaped top, cutout legs, old green paint, wear and edge damage, 15" w **300**

Upholstered, oval top, with floral design on hooked rag covering, red, olive, and gold on dark ground, brown fringe, dec base with red and yellow striping and yellow tree–like designs on each turned leg, green ground, bottom initialed "S.G.," worn fringe, some wear, 12½" w **375**

Upholstered, rect pine frame top with modern reupholstery, hardwood pencil post legs, old alligatored finish, 13½" w, 8½" d **30**

Windsor, pine, oval top, splayed base, turned legs, floral design, yellow striping, worn dark paint, 13" w, 7½" d, 8¾" h **135**

ICE BOX

Oak, Lapland Monitor, Ramey Refrigerator Co, Greenville, MI, double paneled full length door beside pair of paneled doors, paneled ends, straight apron, square feet, orig label, 35" w, 20" d, 48" h **$600**

Oak, Leonard Cleanable Refrigerator, white porcelain int, 35" w, 20½" d, 46¾" h **325**

Oak, North Pose, applied dec on paneled doors, paneled ends, bracket feet, metal tag, zinc lined, orig hardware, 25" w, 19" d, 55" h **500**

Oak, Victor, Challenge Refrigerator Co, Grand Haven, MI, single door with double raised panels, paneled ends, metal tag, zinc lined, orig hardware, 22" w, 15" d, 40" h **500**

MINIATURE

Bench, settle, decorated, double chair back, shaped crest rail, spindles, turned posts, legs, and stretchers, brown, white, and yellow fruit and foliage dec crests, yellow and brown striping, old green repainted ground, 1 back leg and stretcher poorly reglued, late 18th C, 26" l **$500**

Blanket Chest, decorated, poplar, brownish black ink graining on natural brown patina ground, hearts, diamonds, and initials "J. M. B." in rectangle on lid, inside of lid with pencil inscription "Patsy Lord, her trunk, Elizabeth Lord 28 Lawn Ave. Portland, Maine, owner of Patsy," wear, some edge damage, 5½ x 7 x 10½" **500**

Blanket Chest, decorated, poplar, reddish brown flame graining, molded lid, dovetailed case with lidded till, base molding, turned feet, 19¾" w **600**

Blanket Chest, pine, molded edge lid, paneled construction, turned feet, old dark reddish alligatored finish, 24½" w, 14½" d, 19" h **1,000**

Blanket Chest, pine and poplar, lid with applied edge molding, dovetailed
case, lidded till, molded base, shaped apron, bracket feet, presentation
inscription on till lid underside, 1 foot incomplete, damaged lid, repaired
hinge rail, 1 hinge reset, 24³/₄" l **400**

Chest of Drawers, cherry and curly maple, Country Sheraton, dovetailed
drawers, 2 short over 3 long graduated drawers with curly maple drawer
fronts and brass pulls, paneled ends, turned feet, refinished, replaced
pulls, repairs, back feet and top replaced, 14" w, 11" d, 17³/₄" h **800**

Chest of Drawers, curly maple, Hepplewhite style, slightly overhanging top,
4 dovetailed drawers with oval eagle brasses, scalloped apron, French
feet, 20¹/₄" w, 12" d, 22¹/₂" h **2,250**

Chest of Drawers, decorated, brown graining, yellow and red striping, polychrome floral dec, poplar, 2 step back handkerchief drawers, 3 long
drawers, scalloped apron, 23¹/₄" w, 13¹/₄" d, 25¹/₂" h **775**

Chest of Drawers, decorated, red–brown grain painting, pine, thumb molded top, 2 short over 2 long drawers, molded base, turned feet, wrought
nail construction, wood pulls, 13¹/₂" w, 7¹/₂" d, 17¹/₂" h **750**

Chest of Drawers, mahogany, Empire, poplar secondary wood, 3 dovetailed
drawers, S curve pilasters, scrolled feet, 13¹/₂" w, 7¹/₄" d, 13" h **500**

Chest of Drawers, mahogany, Federal, rect top above 3 long drawers, shaped
apron, bracket feet, orig flowerhead pulls, inside of backboard with pencil drawing of saber leg chair and inscription "Chair & Cabinet
Manufacturers Haskell & Card and Co., Lord & Dow Joiners Ship
Carpenters," upper drawer blade replaced, MA, possibly Salem, c1800,
16¹/₄" w, 8¹/₂" d, 13¹/₂" h **2,300**

Chest of Drawers, walnut and curly maple, poplar secondary wood, rect top,
3 dovetailed drawers, cutout feet, turned pulls, backboards replaced,
notch cut in back top edge, 13¹/₄" w, 12³/₄" d, 14¹/₂" h **350**

Cupboard, jelly, pine, paneled doors, 1 drawer, corner and edge molding,
turned front and tapered back feet, 20¹/₄" w, 9" d, 24¹/₂" h **400**

Cupboard, wall, decorated, red flame graining, pine, scrolled crest, molded
cornice, pair of paneled doors, adjustable int shelves, cutout feet, end pcs
of cornice molding missing, repaired crest, 18¹/₂" w, 8¹/₂" d, 24¹/₄" h **600**

Left: Blanket Chest, stenciled dec, sgd "JAW," $1,705. Photo courtesy Aston Macek.
Right: Table, burl walnut, 4¹/₂ x 5 x 9³/₄" l, $195.

Cupboard, wall, pine, molded cornice, open top shelf, paneled cupboard doors, dovetailed case, scalloped apron, dark finish, 21³/₄" w, 7" d, 22" h .. **300**

Desk, slant front, pine, mahogany fall front lid with pullout slides, 3 dovetailed drawers, old dark finish, old repairs, 10" w, 7¹/₄"d, 10¹/₂" h ... **250**

MIRROR

Convex, round gilded frame surmounted by eagle, early 20th C, 24" h **$250**

Decorated, beveled pine frame, orig black paint, gold stenciled designs in corners, 14" h, 18" w **275**

Decorated, old yellow and black repaint, on half columns with corner blocks, 12³/₄" h, 10³/₄" w **165**

Hall, oak, hanging, diamond shaped, applied beading on outer and inner edges, beveled mirror plate, 3 ornate iron double hat hooks at lower corners, 18" sq **250**

Scroll, cherry, Country Chippendale, scrolled crest and pendant, molded mirror frame, old glass, old finish, 8" h, 11" w **550**

Scroll, mahogany, Chippendale, refinished, 29³/₄" h, 17¹/₄" w **300**

Scroll, mahogany, Queen Anne, old dark finish, repaired break in top crest, 16¹/₄" h, 9⁵/₈" w **385**

Scroll, pine, Country Queen Anne, scrolled crest, molded frame, old dark finish, discolored and flaked orig glass, 14¹/₂" h, 8¹/₂" w **600**

Scroll, walnut, Country Chippendale, scrolled crest and pendant, old glass, old finish, 2 ears damaged, 18" h, 11³/₄" w **100**

Scroll, walnut, Country Queen Anne, scrolled crest and pendant, molded frame, old mirror plate with worn silvering, pendant scroll incomplete, 14¹/₂" h, 8³/₈" w **125**

Shaving, mahogany veneer, Federal, 5 dovetailed drawers, bowed center section, turned feet, scrolled apron, turned posts, mirror with old glass, 26¹/₂" w, 8³/₄" d, 24" h **400**

Shaving, pine and mahogany veneer, rect swivel mirror on plain square posts, bow front base with conforming dovetailed drawer, ball feet, 14¹/₂" w, 6³/₄" d, 16¹/₂" h **150**

Shaving, walnut and cherry, inlaid, turned posts, swivel mirror in inlaid frame, single dovetailed drawer, turned feet, old refinish, repairs, 17¹/₂" w, 7³/₄" d, 26" h **140**

PIE SAFE

Oak, flat cornice over 2 short drawers, pair of doors each with 3 punched tin panels, concentric circle and diamond design, paneled ends, French feet, 41" w, 15" d, 56" h **$600**

Pine, hanging, single door, 5 punched tin panels attached to form single large panel on door and back, dovetailed case, wrought iron hooks along end top edges, tin panels with concentric circles design, refinished, 39" w, 23¹/₂" d, 30¹/₄" h **400**

Pine, hanging, 2 doors, single full length panel on each side and door, punched concentric circle design, pegged construction, mortise and tenon joints, hand planed, PA, 36" w, 19¹/₂" d, 34³/₄" h **750**

Pine, on stand, 2 doors, 2 punched tin panels on each door and ends, punched diamond design with stylized tulip and stars, mortised and pinned frame, high square legs, NC, 42" w, 17" d, 60" h **1,500**

Pine, stepped gallery, cutout dec, rect cornice, pair of doors with screen panels, 3 int shelves, block feet, 30½" w, 15" d, 44" h 350

Pine, three-quarter gallery, shaped step down ends, 2 short drawers over 2 doors each with 3 punched tin panels, shaped apron, bracket feet, mellow refinishing, tin panels painted black, repairs and restoration, 42" w, 14" d, 57" h plus gallery 600

Poplar, hanging, gray, punched tin panels with circle, star, and flower designs, repainted, 28" w, 20¼" d, 34" h 575

Poplar, mortised rail construction, double doors, 12 punched tin panels with star and circle design, square corner posts, high feet, 40½" w, 18" d, 57½" h 825

Poplar, step back top, 2 pc, top with beveled cornice and 2 doors, 1 tin panel each door, base with 2 dovetailed drawers above pair of doors, 2 tin panels each door, square corner posts extend to tapered legs, 3 tin panels each end, punched diamond and concentric circle designs, int strips holding tins replaced, tin panels may be replacements, 44" w, 19½" d, 78" h . . 875

Poplar, 2 doors, 12 tin panels with punched star designs, single dovetailed drawer, square legs, refinished dark brown cherry color, some rust damage, 1 front leg and drawer front repaired, 39" w, 26½" d, 54" h 400

Walnut, poplar secondary wood, molded edge top, solid ends, double doors, 3 punched tin panels with heart and star design, single dovetailed drawer, 38½" w, 14½ x 40½" top, 58" h 1,000

Walnut, 2 doors, 3 punched tin panels each door and 3 each end, panels with circle and pinwheel design, slightly tapered legs are extensions of square corner posts, panels rusted and damaged, 1 front leg broken at tenon, 41¼" w, 18" d, 49¼" h 1,000

Yellow Pine, molded cornice, double top doors each with 2 punched tin panels, 2 dovetailed short drawers, pair of raised panel cupboard doors, paneled ends each with 2 upper and 1 lower punched tin panels and 1 raised panel at drawer level, corner posts extend to square legs, applied base molding, punched pinwheel design, minor repairs, replaced tins, GA, 43¼" w, 19½" d, 70¾" h 2,250

Yellow Pine, mortised construction, worn blue paint over green, 12 punched tin panels with compass star and circle designs, high feet, 19 x 39", 54¼" h 650

ROCKER

Banister Back, armchair, shaped crest, half arms, bulbous turnings, old red repaint, replaced woven fiber seat, 38¾" h $115

Bentwood, arched back with conforming caned panel, caned seat, broad sweeping supports, elongated S-form rockers, early 20th C 2,250

Country Chippendale, maple, shaped crest, pierced vasiform splat, turned posts, legs, and front stretcher, shaped arms, old rush seat, added rockers, old refinish, 40½" h 120

Country Windsor, crest with painted blue and yellow floral dec, spindle back, scrolled arms, plank seat, yellow striping on black ground, heavily alligatored repaint, 30¼" h 100

Ladder Back, scrolled slats and arms, half spindles, 43" h 200

Ladder Back, 3 shaped slats, turned finials and posts, scrolled arms, woven splint seat, shaped rockers, refinished, replaced seat, 39" h 150

Lady's, dec, shaped crest, 5 narrow turned spindles, scrolled arms, S–scroll seat, ring turned legs, worn and flaking orig red and black graining with yellow striping, 37" h **150**

Mission, oak, straight crest rail, 3 vertical slats, flat arms with rounded corners, 6 board seat, 26" h **175**

Platform, oak, applied leaf and vine dec on shaped crest, square posts, upholstered back panel, scrolled arms, baluster turned arm supports, overstuffed seat, platform base, on casters, 22" w, 38" h **225**

Pressed Back, oak, flower and bead design, straight crest rail, bulbous turned finials on tapered posts, 7 rod spindles, bentwood arms, splayed base with turned legs and box stretchers, 38" h **175**

Pressed Back, oak, Man of the North Wind design, shaped crest rail, ball finials on ring turned posts, 6 ring and baluster turned spindles, hip brackets, shaped seat, ring turned front legs and front stretchers, rod stretchers on ends and back, 39" h **200**

Windsor, armchair, worn mustard colored grained paint over earlier red, cutout clothespin crest, curved posts and spindles, scrolled arms, shaped seat, splayed base, bamboo turned legs, 43½" h **650**

Windsor, bow back, hooped crest rail, 7 tapered rods, U–shaped arm rail with knuckle hand holds, baluster turned arm posts, oval dished seat, splayed base, baluster turned legs, similarly turned H–form stretcher, repaired split in seat, arms ended out, rockers are later addition, 34" h **175**

Windsor, comb back, bamboo turnings, plain crest, spindled back, shaped seat, old worn refinishing, 38" h **135**

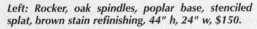

Left: Rocker, oak spindles, poplar base, stenciled splat, brown stain refinishing, 44" h, 24" w, $150.

Center: Rocker, Windsor, fan back, bamboo turnings, old black repaint, 29½" h, 22½" w, $425. Photo courtesy Ray Morykan Auctions.

Right: Secretary Bookcase, cherry, Chippendale, 2 sections, broken pediment bonnet, raised panel doors, thumbmolded writing surface, graduated drawers, bracket feet, fitted int, reduced in height, brasses replaced, New England, 18th C, 85" h, 36" w, $8,800.

SECRETARY BOOKCASE

Mahogany, Federal, 2 sections, upper section surmounted by giltwood wing-
spread eagle finial flanked by 2 brass urn finials, pair of hinged mullioned
doors opening to adjustable shelves and pigeonholes, lower section with
hinged baize lined writing flap above 4 graduated cockbeaded drawers
flanked by bellflower and dot inlaid stiles, tine inlaid square tapering legs,
orig finish, New England, c1805, 41¼" w, 31¾" d, 75" h $4,000

Pine and Poplar, cove molded cornice, raised panel door, lift top lid, fitted
int with 4 dovetailed drawers and pigeonholes, single dovetailed long
drawer, square tapered legs, replaced brasses and lock, 31¾" w, 25" d,
74¼" h 2,650

Tiger Maple, Chippendale, broken arch pediment with 3 urn and flame
finials, arched blind doors, inlaid slant top with fitted int consisting of
valanced pigeonholes, 12 drawers, and 2 document drawers, dovetailed
case with 4 long drawers, reeded quarter columns, and replaced bracket
feet, 38¼" w, 22½" d, 86½" h 20,000

Yellow Pine, primitive, 1 pc, chip carved detail, double glazed doors, fall
front writing surface with 2 drawers on each side, paneled cupboard
doors, bracket feet, orig cast iron hardware, old patina, feet and desk front
replaced, 38¼" w, 14" d, 68½" h 385

SETTEE

Decorated, Federal, yellow, green, and brown stenciled fruit dec on straight
crest rail, tripartite back with 3 splats, plank seat, ring turned tapered legs,
stretcher base, c1820, 75" w $750

Decorated, Sheraton, black, red, and gold shell and vintage dec crest,
pierced rail back, scrolled arms, turned arm supports, balloon shaped rush
seat, turned legs, outward curved feet, white ground, repainted 2,250

Walnut, Chippendale style, shaped crest rail, rolled arms and seat, salmon
upholstered back, seat, and sides, chamfered legs, 59" l 500

Windsor, arrow back, flat crest rail, 26 arrow shaped spindles, splayed base,
bamboo turned legs, double arrow shaped front stretchers, red and black
striping, red, green, and black floral dec, mustard ground, New England . .3,500

Windsor, rod back, 9 bamboo turned spindles, bamboo turned posts, arms,
and arm supports, shaped incised seat, splayed base with bamboo turned
legs, H–form stretcher with central tablet, refinished, repairs, New
England, early 19th C, 25" w, 10¼" h seat, 24" h overall 3,500

SHELVES

Corner, painted, 5 shelves, top 3 shelves graduated in size with stepped scalloped sides, bottom 2 shelves same size as third shelf, worn dark red
paint, late wire nail construction, 60" h $750

Corner, poplar, alligatored old varnish finish, applied sawtooth moldings,
35" w, 60" h 500

Crock, oak, 4 shelves, molded edges, scalloped legs, old green repaint,
39" w, 19" d, 43¾" h 375

Crock, pine, 2 shelves, wire nail construction, rect shelves with cove molded brackets, bootjack ends, old green paint, 34½" w, 12" d, 14½" h 350

Hanging, hardwood, 4 shelves, frame–like facade with half–turned pilasters, closed back, reddish brown stain ext, natural varnish int, 12$\frac{1}{4}$" w, 4$\frac{3}{4}$" d, 13$\frac{1}{4}$" h **50**

Hanging, oak, Mission style, 4 shelves, reticulated plank ends, D–shaped handles, exposed keyed tenons, 27$\frac{1}{4}$" w, 6$\frac{1}{4}$" d, 36" h **150**

Hanging, pine, 4 shelves, plate rack, plate bars on 2 center shelves, cutout ends, gray repaint, 68$\frac{1}{2}$" w, 11" d, 37" h **175**

Hanging, pine, 1 shelf, dovetailed drawer below, decorative cutout brackets, old red paint, 24$\frac{1}{4}$" w, 6$\frac{3}{4}$" d, 13" h **1,100**

Hanging, walnut, 3 scalloped shelves, turned posts and finials, refinished, 23$\frac{1}{2}$" w, 7$\frac{1}{4}$" d, 25$\frac{1}{2}$" h **125**

SIDEBOARD

Birch and Bird's–Eye Maple, Sheraton, server, scrolled crest, 4 dovetailed drawers, ring turned legs, turned feet, old mellow finish, replaced brasses with pretzel coiled snake, 29$\frac{3}{8}$" w, 17$\frac{1}{2}$" d, 36$\frac{1}{4}$" h **$825**

Cherry, Sheraton, huntboard, poplar secondary wood, reeded edge top, 4 dovetailed drawers with applied edge beading, reeded posts, slender turned legs, old mellow refinishing, replaced brasses, 39$\frac{5}{8}$" w, 18$\frac{1}{2}$ x 40$\frac{3}{4}$" top, 33$\frac{1}{8}$" h **2,750**

Cherry, Sheraton, poplar secondary wood, figured veneer and cross banding, 3 dovetailed drawers, 2 flat doors, 2 curved doors, turned and reeded legs, damage, repairs, 72" w, 23$\frac{1}{2}$" d, 51$\frac{1}{4}$" h **3,575**

Curly Maple, poplar secondary wood, scalloped crest, 3 dovetailed drawers, base shelf, turned legs and feet, turned curly maple pulls, light natural refinishing, 36$\frac{1}{2}$" w, 36$\frac{1}{2}$" h **4,000**

Decorated, Country Hepplewhite, pine, huntboard, mortised and pinned construction, rect top with applied edge molding and old gray over yellowed marbleized dec, pullout shelf between 2 dovetailed long drawers, square tapered legs, alligatored brown finish with black and gold painted dec, replaced pulls, molding around bottom edge of case replaced, 30$\frac{3}{4}$" w, 19$\frac{1}{2}$" d, 38" h **2,500**

Mahogany, Empire, poplar secondary wood, ogee molding below top edge molding, 3 dovetailed drawers, paneled doors, rounded pilasters, scrolled feet, added crest with pineapple finials, flame grain veneer, 48" w, 22" d, 41$\frac{1}{4}$" h plus crest **325**

Mahogany, Federal, inlaid, rect top, serpentine front, conforming line and striped inlay above conforming case, open central compartmented drawer embellished with line and diamonds inlay over 2 conforming doors with similar inlay flanked by large similarly inlaid doors, whole enclosed by inlaid reserves above conforming herringbone inlaid apron, cuffed square tapering legs with line and bellflower inlay, Baltimore, MD, 1790–1810, 65$\frac{1}{4}$" w, 24" d, 39$\frac{1}{2}$" h **13,800**

Mahogany, Hepplewhite, poplar secondary wood, inlaid with ebony stringing and banding, 6 dovetailed drawers with rectangles with invected corners, 4 doors with rounded medallions, square tapered legs, 79" w, 27$\frac{1}{4}$" d, 40$\frac{1}{2}$" h **6,500**

Oak, Empire style, rect molded top, 2 drawers, center section with glazed center door flanked by bowed glass end panels, demilune carved stiles, swelled base drawer, carved paw feet, 44" w, 38" h **500**

Oak, Mission style, 2 pcs, top with rect shelf supported by shaped brackets and rect beveled mirror plate flanked by outset étagère shelves, base with row of 2 drawers, 2 center drawers flanked by 2 glazed doors with geometric fretwork, single long base drawer, shaped apron, and paneled bootjack ends, 55" w, 18" d, 51" h 600

Pine, thumb molded rect top with rounded corners, 2 short drawers with molded edges, pair of paneled cupboard doors separated by center stile, scalloped apron, bracket feet, turned walnut drawer pulls 600

Pine and Poplar, plank top, splayed legs supporting 2 compartments, board and batten doors, red paint, late, 82³/₄" w, 18" d, 54" h 60

Quarter Sawn Oak, Naturalistic Revival, 2 pcs, applied moldings, top with center grotesque face flanked by gadrooned ram's horns and leafy dec, beveled mirror flanked by étagère shelves, shaped backboard, and ornate reeded and spiral turned columns, base with ovolo edges on overhanging rect top, 2 short drawers, single long drawer, 2 cupboard doors, paneled ends, and paw feet on casters, carved shell motif on short drawer fronts, wooden inverted shell pulls, applied conch shell dec on cupboard doors, applied scroll dec on top and bottom of stiles, 48" w, 24" d, 77" h 2,000

Yellow Pine, Federal, huntboard, rect top, 3 small drawers with wide early dovetailing, molding applied to top and bottom of apron, high square tapered legs, repairs to drawer fronts, SC, 52¹/₂" w, 25¹/₂" d, 42" h 4,750

SOFA

Cabriole, Country Formal, upholstered back and curving sides, loose seat cushion, carved mahogany square tapered legs with molded edges, straight front legs, curved back legs, MA or NY, 1790–1810, 80¹/₂" l $13,500

Camel Back, Chippendale, upholstered arched back, outscrolled arms, upholstered seat with loose cushion, mahogany square molded legs, stretchers, Philadelphia, PA, 1760–70, 97" l 2,250

Camel Back, Chippendale style, scrolled sides, loose seat cushion, carved mahogany base with square legs and box stretchers, pale gold floral damask upholstery, light stains, 85" l 850

Country, birch, curved back, rolled arms, turned legs, blue woven cloth, reupholstered, 84" l 825

Country, walnut, turned posts with acorn finials, slightly arched crest rail, upholstered cushion back and seat, turned arms and feet, ogee seat rail, old worn blue and white reupholstery, some edge damage, 77" l 500

Davenport, S A Cook & Co, Medina, NY, No. 1837–T, carved mahogany frame, serpentine crest rail, rolled arms, serpentine seat rail, padded slipper feet, scroll carved aprons, velour upholstery, 1910s, 81" l, $300.

Serpentine, Federal, carved mahogany frame, serpentine crest, downswept outward scrolling arms, conforming rect seat, serpentine front seat rail, 4 rosette carved and fluted square tapering legs with swelled feet, rear with squared stump legs, box stretchers, New England, 1790–1810, 91" l, 29" d, 38¾" h **4,375**

STAND

Drop Leaf, birch, Country Hepplewhite, rect top, 8" w leaves, nailed drawer, square tapered legs, turned pull, refinished, 25¾" w, 19½" d, 27¾" h .. **$125**

Drop Leaf, cherry, bird's–eye veneer drawer fronts, single board top, 9" w leaves with cutout corners, 2 graduated dovetailed drawers with turned wood pulls, boldly turned legs, raised ball feet, refinished, flange on 1 back leg chipped, 23¼" w, 15¼" d, 27¼" h **750**

Drop Leaf, walnut and curly walnut, single drawer with applied beveled edging, curved and tapered pencil post legs, age cracks, 22½" w with 8½" leaves, 30" h **500**

Night, cherry, Country, single board top, single dovetailed drawer, spool turned legs, reglued crack, 16" x 18" top, 28¾" h **190**

Night, cherry, Country Sheraton, rect 2 board top, single dovetailed drawer with turned wood pull, turned legs, old mellow refinish, 21¼" w, 20¾" d, 29¼" h **350**

Night, cherry, Country Sheraton, square overhanging 2–board top, dovetailed drawer with under lip pull, slender ring turned legs, raised ball feet, old worn red finish, worn and stained top, chip on back corner, edge damage to 1 front foot, PA, 16¾" sq, 30" h **650**

Night, cherry, Empire, 2 board top, ogee front, 2 dovetailed drawers, turned legs, 22⅞" w, 22½" d, 29½" h **550**

Night, cherry and curly maple, Country Sheraton, rect top, 2 graduated dovetailed drawers, turned legs, old mellow refinishing, repaired breaks in reattached top, replaced brass pull, 22" w, 18¼" d, 28½" h **875**

Night, cherry and curly maple, Sheraton style, poplar secondary wood, 2 dovetailed drawers, curly maple veneer stiles, turned and rope carved cherry legs, 17¼ x 19½" top, 29¾" h **2,225**

Night, curly maple, Hepplewhite, single dovetailed drawer, handmade, 12¾" x 13" top, 28¼" h **275**

Night, curly maple and walnut, Country Hepplewhite, 3 board rect top, dovetailed drawer with fiery opalescent lacy pull, square tapered legs with corner beading, drawer rebuilt, apron missing, 19½" w, 17½" d, 28" h **600**

Night, decorated, Sheraton, red flame grained pine, single board top with outset rounded corners, 2 dovetailed drawers, turned legs, raised ring turned feet, emb gilded brass pulls, 21¾" w, 17½" d, 28½" h **2,000**

Night, pine and poplar, 2 dovetailed drawers with ogee fronts, turned legs, refinished, replaced glass pulls, 15¾ x 21¾" top, 28½" h **175**

Night, poplar, single board top, mortised and pinned apron, splayed base with turned legs, dark finish with traces of old blue, PA, 17 x 17½" top, 28½" h **650**

Night, walnut, Country Empire, rect single board top with rounded corners, 2 dovetailed drawers, diamond shaped pearl inlays on drawers and rails, turned half columns applied to corner posts, block and turned legs, turned feet, curly maple pulls with inlaid diamonds, 1 pull replaced, 1 inlay missing, top flipped and reattached, 22" w, 19¾" d, 30" h **200**

Night, walnut, pine secondary wood, 2 board top, single dovetailed drawer, turned legs, 17³/₄ x 24" top, 29" h 200

Night, walnut, 2 drawers, turned legs, refinished, 19¹/₂" w, 26¹/₂" h 175

Night, walnut and poplar, Country Hepplewhite, rect 2 board top, mortised and pinned apron, pencil post legs, old dark finish, 20¹/₂" w, 19¹/₄" d, 28³/₄" h 150

Night, walnut and poplar, Country Sheraton, rect overhanging single board top, 2 dovetailed drawers, ring turned legs, turned feet, refinished, top reattached and probably replaced, 16³/₈" w, 19" h 275

Night, walnut and poplar, Hepplewhite, single board top, tapered pencil post legs, 18¹/₂ x 22" top, 27" h 110

Parlor, cherry and poplar, round 2 board top, splayed base with turned legs and ball feet, warped top, attributed to Zoar, OH, 24" d, 24" h 450

Pedestal, decorated, brown grain painting, round top, octagonal column, square base, some wear, age cracks in top, 15¹/₂" d, 31¹/₂" h 145

Pedestal, primitive, soft wood, round top, 4 board box type pedestal, shaped brackets, beveled base, old worn orange and blue repaint, 30" h 100

Plant, hardwood, square well with copper liner, cabriole legs, duck feet, 20th C, 30" h 200

Plant, mahogany veneer, 3 tier, solid mahogany frame with acanthus and reeded carving, bottom tier with flowerpot cutouts, outswept feet 100

Plant, oak, round top, turned and reeded baluster pedestal, circular base, 4 scroll feet, 12" d, 34" h 165

Plant, oak, square top, splayed base with ring and baluster turned legs, square medial shelf, 16" sq, 31" h 145

Sewing, Martha Washington style, mahogany, 3 drawers, shaped ends, ring turned legs, 1920, 28" w, 14" d, 29" h 125

Sewing, Priscilla type, painted red, dark trim, floral decal, turned rod handle, 1930, 13" w, 11" d, 25" h 50

Smoking, Mission, oak, square top, paneled cupboard doors and ends, plinth base, Charles Rohlfs, 1900, 30" w 900

Smoking, William and Mary style, walnut veneer, rect top, figured walnut veneer door, painted base, 18" w, 11" d, 30" h 125

Left: Nightstand, birch, curly maple, and mahogany, Federal, serpentine sided square top with ovolo corners, conforming frieze fitted with drawer, tapered reeded legs, minor losses to veneer, New England, c1810, 28¹/₄" h, 17¹/₂" sq, $1,725. Photo courtesy Sotheby's.

Right: Washstand, pine, spindle towel rods, cherry stain, 32" h, 22¹/₂" w, 13³/₄" d, $150.

Tilt Top, Country Hepplewhite, cherry and birch, single board tilt top with cutout corners, turned column, tripod base, cutout feet, turned column, refinished, 15" w, 18" d, 27" h **450**

Wash, decorated, brown graining, yellow ground, red, brown, and green striping, foliage and berries, lift lid, single drawer, single paneled door, scrolled base, 18¼ x 29" top, 29½" h **350**

Wash, grain painted, bowed high back with shelf, scalloped supports, rect top with outset corners, 2 drawers, bamboo legs, shaped medial shelf, New England, c1830, 39" w, 23" d, 46" h **450**

Wash, hardwood and softwood, Country Sheraton, three–quarter gallery with shaped ends, scalloped apron, turned posts, base shelf with drawer, turned feet, reddish repaint, reconstructed, 23½" w, 15½" d, 35" h **200**

Wash, mahogany, Hepplewhite, corner style, ebony line inlay, dovetailed gallery with small corner shelf, bowed top with bowl cutouts, center shelf with dovetailed drawer, trefoil bottom shelf, square outward curving legs, refinished, 25" w, 19" d, 41¾" h **985**

Wash, maple, rect molded top, harp shaped towel rack, swivel mirror with shell carved crest, ogee top drawer, serpentine shaped case with single cupboard door and 2 small drawers, 36" w, 76" h **400**

Wash, oak, Eastlake style, spoon carved dec, circles and incised lines on shaped backsplash, slightly overhanging top, single long drawer over paneled cupboard door and 2 graduated short drawers, acorn spoon carved designs and incised lines on drawer and door fronts, incised lines on stiles, brass bail handle pulls, 32" w, 19" d, 36" h **350**

Wash, oak, lyre shaped towel bar with applied feather moldings and molded base, serpentine shaped top with conforming long drawer above recessed paneled cupboard door and bank of 2 short drawers, shaped apron, square legs on casters, 34" w, 20" d, 53" h **400**

Wash, pine, Country Sheraton, three–quarter gallery with wide board crest and shaped ends, rect top with bowl cutout, turned posts, medial shelf with false drawer front, slender turned legs, refinished, 16½" w, 16¼" d, 30½" h plus gallery **200**

Wash, pine, scalloped splashboard with rounded corners on slightly overhanging top, single long drawer over pair of cupboard doors with tombstone shaped panels, shaped apron, bracket feet, turned wood pulls, 39" w, 15" d, 29" h **350**

Wash, pine, three–quarter gallery with shaped ends, square top with bowl cutout, square medial shelf with single drawer frieze, straight apron, square tapered legs, turned walnut pull, 14½" sq, 28½" h **250**

Wash, poplar, rect top, dovetailed three–quarter gallery with wide board crest and rounded corners, dovetailed drawer, block and baluster turned posts, base shelf, turned feet, stenciled label "Wm Brown, Successor to Brown & Tate, Manufacturer, Lawrenceburgh, Ind. Warranted" inside drawer, replaced porcelain pulls, 24½" w, 16½" d, 37¾" h plus gallery ... **400**

Wash, walnut, Hepplewhite, corner, line inlaid edges, arched dovetailed gallery, top shelf with bowl and accessory cutouts, medial shelf with dovetailed drawer flanked by false drawers, base shelf, square outcurving legs, refinished, drawer pull incomplete, 24½" w, 16" d, 41" h **575**

Work, cherry and maple, poplar secondary wood, curly maple veneer inserts on posts, 2 board top, 2 dovetailed drawers, solid bird's–eye maple drawer fronts, turned legs, 18 x 19", 29" h **715**

Work, hardwood and softwood, nailed apron, slender square tapered legs, top has wear and damage, old worn refinishing, 14¾ x 36" top, 27½" h . . . **135**

Work, walnut, Country Hepplewhite, removable 2 board top with cleated underside, single dovetailed drawer, square tapered legs, front has repaired split and some edge damage, 25½" w, 21¼" d, 29¼" h **900**

STOOL

Country Windsor, round top, splayed base with turned and tapered legs, double box stretchers, underside of seat branded "P. Mitchell," traces of old paint, 15¾" h **$100**

Mission, oak, rect top with spring cushion seat, legs with corbel supports, lower side stretcher, medial stretcher tenoned through side, 1910, 23" l, 17" d, 18" h **300**

Piano, oak, adjustable round seat on threaded rod, base with circular top, reeded bulbous pedestal, and splayed legs with reeded bulbous turnings, stretchers, and claw and glass ball feet, 12" d, 20" h **200**

Upholstered, mahogany, square top with floral upholstery, turned legs, box stretchers, turned feet, old dark finish, 17" sq, 20" h **125**

Windsor, red and black graining with yellow striping, worn bare round seat, glued splits, 13½" d, 13½" h **245**

Windsor, round seat, 3 turned legs joined by turned stretchers, worn green repaint, 15" d, 28½" h **775**

TABLE

Card, curly maple, Country Hepplewhite, yellow pine and poplar secondary wood, 2 board top with molded edge, single dovetailed drawer with molded edge, square tapered legs, 20¼ x 28" top, 29¾" h **$275**

Card, mahogany, Federal, radiating veneered demilune top with banded edge centering large demilune inlaid conch shell with green ground, conforming apron with 3 inlaid fields, geometric patterned inlaid edge on square tapering legs with interlacing bellflowers headed with oval floral medallion over cuffs, Baltimore, MD, 1790–1810, 36" w, 17⅞" d closed, 35⅞" d size, 29½" h, price for matched pair **22,500**

Card, mahogany, Hepplewhite, demilune, inlaid stringing, banding, bellflowers, flowers in oval medallions, 17½ x 35½" top, 28¾" h **2,000**

Card, walnut, Empire, swing top, turned legs, refinished, 17½ x 36" top, 30" h **300**

Dining, mahogany, extension, fluted columnar legs with capitals, 54 x 60" extends to 54 x 82", 26" h **1,200**

Dining, mahogany, Federal, inlaid, 3 sections, rect top, demilune ends, line inlaid edge above conforming line inlaid apron, square tapering line inlaid and cuffed legs, mid–Atlantic states, 1790–1810, 48¼" w, 117" d open, 29¾" h **9,250**

Dining, oak, Arts & Crafts, round table top with X–form stretcher meeting at square shelf, matching tuck–away chairs with triangular seats to form circle with table, orig finish, 38" d table, price for set **1,000**

Dining, oak, extension, round top, raised square beading on straight apron, turned pedestal base, 4 cabriole legs, carved paw feet on casters, 45" d, 30" h **850**

Dining, oak, extension, square top, incised lines on straight aprons, 5 reeded ring and ball turned legs, ball feet on casters, 42" sq, 30" h **450**

Dining, oak, extension, square top, straight apron, 5 rope turned legs with bulbous feet on casters, 3 leaves, 48" sq, 30" h **500**

Dining, oak, Mission, round overhanging top, wide apron, 5 tapered legs, recent shellac finish over orig medium brown color, Gustav Stickley, 48" d, 30½" h **1,000**

Dining, walnut, Chippendale, 2 thumb molded end drawers, square legs, block feet, PA, 1770–90, 49¼ x 52¼" top, 29¾" h **4,500**

Dressing, cherry, maple, and poplar, curly maple scrolled crest, 2 curly maple dovetailed drawers, turned legs, age cracks, refinished, 36¼" h **1,825**

Dressing, decorated, maple and hardwood, pine and chestnut secondary wood, red and black graining, black and yellow striping, removable top case with scrolled crest and 2 dovetailed drawers, mortised and pinned apron, single dovetailed long drawer in base, square tapered legs, 28" w, 20" d, 44¾" h **1,875**

Dressing, decorated, Sheraton, butternut and poplar, red and black graining, yellow striping, gold brushed and stenciled foliage designs, adjustable mirror with lyre posts, dovetailed top case with 2 dovetailed drawers, 2 dovetailed drawers in base, turned legs, 3 brass pulls replaced, NY, 37½" w, 20½" d, 57½" h **4,850**

Dressing, hardwood, curly maple drawer fronts, dovetailed gallery top, 2 dovetailed drawers, turned legs, replaced glass pulls, 30" w, 17½" d, 33" h **385**

Dressing, mahogany, Chippendale, rect molded top above single long and 3 short molded drawers flanked by molded quarter columns, shaped skirt carved with central scallop shell device continuing to cabriole legs ending in diminutive claw and ball feet, orig finish and brasses, Philadelphia, PA, c1780, 32½" w, 19⅝" d, 31" h **31,850**

Left: Bench, painted pine, multiple board top, seat section doubles as chest, trestle feet on casters, $3,300.

Right: Pembroke, cherry, Country Federal, shaped drop leaves, recessed frieze with end drawer, straight tapered legs, wavy X–form stretcher, 27½" h, 36" w, 20" d, $1,450.

Dressing, oak, adjustable side mirrors, arched center mirror, 2 small drawers, scalloped apron, high legs, cabriole front legs, straight back legs, 1925 .... **300**

Drop Leaf, ash, oval top with molded edge, turned legs, refinished, 26 x 42" top, four 11" w leaves **275**

Drop Leaf, cherry, Country, 2 board top, turned legs, pieced repair between boards and leaf, 19 x 38" top, 13³/₄" w leaves, 29³/₄" h **350**

Drop Leaf, cherry, Country Hepplewhite, square tapered legs, replaced top and corner blocks, refinished, 23 x 48" top, 12³/₄" leaves, 28¹/₂" h **300**

Drop Leaf, cherry, Sheraton style, rect top, 6 turned and rope carved legs, 49¹/₄ x 22" top, 23" w leaves, 26¹/₂" h **350**

Drop Leaf, cherry and birch, Country Sheraton, rect top, single rect 18¹/₂" w drop leaf, wide board apron, 2 dovetailed frieze drawers, turned and rope carved legs with brass casters, brass ring pulls, age cracks in top, 72 x 22³/₄" top, 28¹/₂" h **650**

Drop Leaf, cherry and maple, Queen Anne, demilune leaves, straight apron, square tapering slightly curving legs, slipper feet, New England, c1770, 45¹/₂ x 45" open top, 27¹/₂" h **1,750**

Drop Leaf, curly maple and pine, Hepplewhite, curly maple top, pine apron, square tapered birch legs, replaced hinges, warped leaves and top, 13¹/₄ x 42" top, 12" leaves, 27" h **825**

Drop Leaf, mahogany, Queen Anne, rect top, D–shaped leaves, cabriole legs, spade feet, Long Island, NY, c1770, 51¹/₂ x 40¹/₂" top, 28" h **4,500**

Drop Leaf, mahogany, Sheraton style, pine secondary wood, rect top with cut corners, single dovetailed drawer and leaves, turned legs, old finish, 12¹/₂ x 23¹/₂" top, 10³/₄" w leaves, 19" h **1,100**

Drop Leaf, maple and cherry, oak and pine secondary wood, scalloped aprons, square swing legs with fluting, 15¹/₂ x 48¹/₄" top, 15¹/₄" w leaves, 28" h **190**

Drop Leaf, pine and ash, gate leg, pine top, ash base, mortised and pinned construction, single board top, square tapered legs, 18 x 48" top, 14¹/₂" w leaves, 25³/₄" h **200**

Drop Leaf, walnut, Country Federal, rect leaves, single drawer, turned tapered legs, raised ball feet, refinished, PA, c1810, 44¹/₄" w open, 29³/₄" d, 29¹/₂" h **900**

Drop Leaf, walnut, Queen Anne, rect top with corner cutouts, scalloped apron, cabriole legs, drake feet, refinished, repairs, stained top, PA, 15¹/₂ x 47³/₄" top, 17" w leaves, 27¹/₂" h **4,500**

Farm, tiger maple and maple, Sheraton, rect 2 board top, 2 dovetailed drawers, turned legs, tapered feet, 48 x 28" top, 20" h **2,100**

Harvest, pine, rect overhanging 2 board top with applied edge molding, nailed apron, turned legs and feet, old brownish gray repaint, 105 x 29" top, 33¹/₄" h **600**

Harvest, pine and poplar, 2 board top, single drawer, square tapered legs, old brown grained repaint, 144 x 25¹/₂" top, 31" h **250**

Hutch, cherry, round cleated top, shaped ends, shoe feet, NY, 18th C, 29" d, 49¹/₂" h **3,000**

Hutch, maple, hinged oval top tilting to reveal well, shaped supports ending in shoe feet, traces of red stain, crack and patches to top, shoe feet worn, NY or New England, 1720–50, 42 x 36" top, 26" h **10,350**

Hutch, pine, removable 2 board top, box compartment, single board ends, shoe feet, layers of old worn reddish brown and blue paint, wear and age cracks, top boards warped, orig wrought iron nails with old renailing, 48 x 35" top, 27½" h **750**

Hutch, pine, 3 board top, lift lid, single board ends, worn yellow repaint, striping and stenciled design over earlier red, 33¼ x 51¾" top, 30" h **1,100**

Hutch, pine and maple, round top, straight ends, rect boxed seat, shoe feet, New England, late 18th C, 45¾" d, 27⅛" h **2,500**

Hutch, pine and poplar, rect 2 board pine top, hinged lid seat, poplar base with single board ends and cutout feet, old brown graining over orig red, 37 x 28" top, 28" h **1,250**

Library, mahogany, Mission, rect overhanging top, wide apron, massive square legs, base shelf, molded feet, George Washington Maher, Chicago, IL, 66 x 33" top, 36" h **3,000**

Library, quarter sawn oak, Mission style, rect top, 2 short drawers with triangular copper pulls, square legs, 3 vertical slats each side, side stretchers, medial shelf, applied tenons on legs and side stretchers, 50" w, 32" d, 30" h **500**

Parlor, oak, octagonal top, beaded apron, splayed base, slender spiral turned legs continuing to ring and baluster turnings, flattened ball feet, scalloped medial shelf, 26" w, 29" h **300**

Parlor, oak, square top, scalloped edge, conforming apron, splayed base with spiral, ring, and baluster turned legs, scalloped medial shelf with metal brackets, ball feet, 23" sq, 29" h **200**

Parlor, poplar, round 2 board top, square tapered legs with chamfered edge, old worn black paint, repaired crack and edge damaged top, 26¼" d, 26½" h **125**

Parlor, walnut, Victorian, burl veneer, white marble top, 20 x 31" top, 30½" h **450**

Pembroke, cherry, Country Sheraton, rect drop leaves, simple turned and tapered legs, ball feet, old red finish, minor edge damage, 40 x 17¼" top, 12½" w leaves, 28¾" h **500**

Pembroke, cherry and mahogany, Federal, pine and poplar secondary woods, drop leaf top with rounded corner leaves, single dovetailed drawer, turned and rope carved legs, 19½ x 40" top, 13" w leaves, 28½" h **385**

Pembroke, mahogany, Country Hepplewhite, inlaid, serpentine top and leaves, square tapered legs with corner beading, old worn finish, minor inlay damage, 35 x 16" top, 9¼" w leaves, 28½" h **2,000**

Pembroke, pine, Country Hepplewhite, rect top, square tapered legs, old dark natural finish on top, old red finish on base, top is old replacement, NY, 43¾ x 19¼" top, 12½" w leaves, 28½" h **300**

Sawbuck, pine, breadboard top, 3 board, red stain on base, old varnish finish, 30½ x 49½" top, 28¾" h **875**

Sawbuck, pine, cleated 2 board top, X–form legs with wide board stretchers, traces of old paint under red wash finish, age cracks in top, 31½ x 23" top, 20" h **450**

Sawbuck, pine and hardwood, single board breadboard top, old mellow refinishing, 1 end of cleat is ended out, 90 x 25" top, 29½" h **1,000**

Sawbuck, poplar, single board breadboard top, straight apron, X–form legs, orig dark mustard painted base, old natural finish top, VT, 43 x 21¼" top, 33¾" h **800**

Tavern, birch and pine, Chippendale, pine 2 board breadboard top, mortised and pinned apron with single dovetailed drawer, square chamfered legs, mortised and pinned stretcher, minor repairs, 26 x 41½" top, 28½" h **925**

Tavern, hardwood, Country Queen Anne, 2 board breadboard top, single overlapping drawer, turned legs, mortised and pinned stretchers, old worn finish, replaced batwing brass drawer pull, drawer joints loose, screws added to top, 41 x 26" top, 28" h **1,750**

Tavern, maple, Country Sheraton, rect overhanging top, single overlapping drawer with turned wood pull, turned legs, box stretcher base, turned feet, old refinish, restored, New England, 43½ x 29" top, 27" h **550**

Tavern, maple and pine, Chippendale, breadboard top, single dovetailed drawer, mortised and pinned apron; square molded legs joined by mortised and pinned stretchers, refinished, 26¼ x 35½" top, 28" h **165**

Tavern, oak, William and Mary style, oval top, recessed frieze, turned splayed legs, box stretcher, 34 x 25" top, 25" h **700**

Tavern, pine, Country Chippendale, oval 2 board top, deeply scalloped apron, splayed base, square legs with molded edge, top with natural finish and age cracks, layers of old paint on base, 31¾ x 24¾" top, 26½" h . . **1,750**

Tavern, pine and birch, Country Queen Anne, pine top, birch base, mortised and pinned construction, oval 2 board top, turned legs, red repaint, refinished, 23½ x 23½" top, 26¼" h **975**

Tavern, pine and maple, Queen Anne style, pine top, maple base, 2 board breadboard top, single dovetailed drawer, mortised and pinned apron, turned legs with molded detail joined by mortised and pinned stretchers, refinished, 28 x 42" top, 25¼" h **1,375**

Tavern, poplar, Country Hepplewhite, poplar breadboard top, red painted pine splayed base with reeded apron and square tapered legs, old breadboard top with edge damage, 31 x 23" top, 29¾" h **600**

Left: Tavern, tiger maple breadboard top, shaped apron, replaced drawer, 18th C, $715. Photo courtesy Aston Macek.

Right: Tea, mahogany, Chippendale, circular dished tilt top with piecrust edge, baluster turned birdcage support, fluted flaring compressed ball turned standard, cabriole legs, claw and ball feet, top and birdcage restored, patches and repairs, Philadelphia, c1760, 26¼" h, 32½" d, $6,900. Photo courtesy Sotheby's.

Tavern, walnut and cherry, Country, mortised and pinned construction, 2 board top with corner wings, apron, splayed base with chamfered legs, 31¾ x 32" top, 28¾" **1,000**

Tea, birch and maple, Country Queen Anne style, shaped 2 board porringer top with simple corner cutouts, mortised and pinned apron, slender turned legs, duck feet, refinished, 21½ x 29½" top, 26¾" h **1,650**

Tea, mahogany, Queen Anne style, poplar secondary wood, quatrefoil top, dovetailed drawer, shaped apron, turned tapered legs, duck feet, refinished, pieced repairs, repaired age cracks on top, 22 x 29¾" top, 25" h ...**3,025**

Tea, maple and cherry, Country Hepplewhite, round cherry tilt top, ample tripod base with turned column, spider legs, spade feet, 25" d, 28¾" h **550**

Work, bird's–eye maple, Sheraton, pine and poplar secondary wood, molded edge, 2 dovetailed drawers with fitted int, turned legs, old brass pulls, 17½ x 18" top, 30" h **825**

Work, curly maple, Country Chippendale, rect overhanging 2 board top with molded edge, dovetailed drawer, square molded legs, old refinishing, top reattached, reconstruction to drawer and parts of apron, 29½ x 20" top, 25½" h **900**

Work, decorated, poplar, removable rect top painted red, red paint grained apron with 2 dovetailed overlapping drawers, turned legs painted black, legs have plugged holes, 48 x 35¾" top, 28¼" h **1,000**

Work, hardwood and pine, Country Hepplewhite, rect overhanging 2 board top, wide board apron, splayed base, square tapered legs with molded corner beading, orange–red repainted base, slightly warped top, 33½ x 20" top, 28¼" h **500**

Work, mahogany, Federal, rect top, outset rounded corners, 3 cockbeaded drawers, ring turned engaged colonettes, reeded tapering legs, swelled feet on casters, MA, 1800–10, 20¾ x 16¼" top, 28¼" h **1,150**

Work, pine, Country Hepplewhite, removable overhanging 4 board top with rounded corners, mortised and pinned apron with dovetailed drawer, square tapered legs, refinished, traces of blue and white paint, 2 legs with edge damage, 1 leg with old nailed repair, 49 x 31" top, 29½" h **350**

Work, pine and maple, Country Hepplewhite, drop leaf with swing leg, single dovetailed drawer, square molded and tapered legs with inside chamfer, 25 x 47¾" top, 14¾" w leaf **875**

Work, pine and poplar, 4 board top, 2 drawers, turned legs, old blue repaint on base, wear, age cracks, and damage, 38½" x 67½" top, 28¾" h **350**

Work, poplar and ash, poplar 2 board top with reddish brown stain, ash base, 34¼ x 37¾" top, 29¼" h **165**

Work, walnut, Country Hepplewhite, overhanging 2 board breadboard top, mortised and pinned wide board apron with inlaid initials "A.H.," square tapered legs, worn and scrubbed finish, 34¾ x 25" top, 26½" h **450**

TRUNK

Dome Top, decorated, green and salmon putty dec, imperfections, New England, early 19th C, 23" w, 16½" d, 13¾" h **$500**

Dome Top, decorated, red and yellow graining, dovetailed, iron lock with shield shaped escutcheon, replaced hasp, edge damage, age cracks, 40¾" l **125**

Dome Top, decorated, red paint and black graining, poplar, iron lock with hasp, lift out tray and int covered with floral wallpaper, replaced hinges, 30" l 450

Dome Top, decorated, yellow ocher and burnt umber graining, minor surface mars, New England, 19th C, 30½" w, 15" d, 14" h 175

Flat Top, pine, rect hinged lid, dovetailed case, bail handles, bracket base, 36" w, 19" d, 22" h 200

WARDROBE

Decorated, red flame graining, pine and poplar, beveled cornice, single paneled door, cutout feet, worn varnish finish, top rail over door cracked, 44¼" w, 19¼" d, 79" h $400

Mahogany Veneer, chifferobe, 2 doors, 1 with int drawers, other side with rod for clothes, cabriole legs, labeled "Marvels Furniture Co., Jamestown, N. Y.," 39½" w, 20" d, 51½" h 225

Oak, arched pediment, with spoon carved dec, molded cornice, pair of double paneled cupboard doors, base drawer, 39" w, 16" d, 80" h 750

Oak, break down, molded cornice, applied scrolled dec on frieze, pair of paneled cupboard doors over 2 short base drawers, scalloped apron, square legs on casters, 43" w, 17" d, 83" h........................ 1,000

Painted, pine, Country, 1 pc, old dark red finish, peaked cornice with applied molding, pair of raised panel doors above single long drawer, single board ends, added shelf, edge and door damage, 43" w, 20" x 45" cornice, 82" h 425

Pine, break down, molded cornice, pair of paneled doors with molded frames, single base drawer, shaped apron, bracket feet, pegged construction, turned wood pulls, 46" w, 18½" d, 77½" h 750

Pine, molded cornice, raised panel doors, single drawer, base molding, int shelf and cast iron hooks, layers of old paint, edge damage, 1 end of molded cornice incomplete, 48" w, 19½" x 50¼" cornice, 84¾" h 165

Yellow Pine, molded cornice, 2 raised panel doors in molded frames, single board ends, bracket feet, old mellow refinishing, feet ended out, age cracks, some edge damage, moldings between doors replaced, some renailing, southern states, 52½" w, 20¼" d, 77" h 500

WICKER

Chair, barrel back, flat arms, round seat, skirt extends to ground with alternating closely woven panels and open oval rings, painted white $50

Chair, corner, photographer's, scrolled backrest, 3 spindles, square seat, scrolled apron, painted white 300

Chair, lounge, ornately dec asymmetrical back with curlicues, diamond work apron, painted white 800

Chaise Lounge, tightly woven crest continuing to braced armrests, 1 arm shorter, openwork back, tightly woven seat and seat rail, upholstered seat cushion, arched openwork skirt, wrapped tapered legs, white, 58" l, 35" w, 36" h 875

Fainting Couch, sleigh back, straight skirt, upholstered, painted white 150

Fernery, low, long rect well, closely woven arched skirt, braided trim, painted green 120

Rocker, Heywood–Wakefield, willow, reupholstered seat and back panel, minor wicker breaks, Heywood–Wakefield metal tags, 34 x 32 x 22", *$1,200.* Photo courtesy David Rago Auctions.

Footstool, round, tightly woven pattern radiating from center top and continuing to skirt with open weave edge, 4 wrapped outcurving ball turned legs with brackets, X–form stretchers, white, 16" d, 23" h **200**

Ottoman, rect, inverted U–shaped ends form handles and legs, padded top, painted white **150**

Parlor Suite, couch and chair, upholstered backs, cushion seats, rolled arms, arched aprons, natural finish **600**

Rocker, spider web back with oval above lyre, scrolled arms, spindled skirt, painted white **300**

Settee, high back with closely woven panels and openwork scrolled trim, rolled arms, arched apron, painted white **475**

Stand, 3 tier, posts topped with ball finials, open back and sides with spindles and curlicues, similarly dec apron, French feet, painted white **550**

Table, drop leaf, natural oak oval top, wicker base with gate legs and openwork panels, painted white **550**

Table, library, rect top with tightly woven covering, narrow projecting shelves either end, base shelf, wrapped legs, painted white **275**

Table, work, rect top, medial and base shelves, painted white **250**

Tea Cart, top shelf with openwork skirt, base shelf with straight skirt, spoked wheels, painted white **140**

Washstand, child's, porcelain enamel accessories, old white repaint, 12½ x 22" top, 31½" h **225**

ADIRONDACK & RUSTIC

The use of natural materials, ranging from tree branches to rattan, in furniture construction enjoyed great popularity in the latter half of the nineteenth century and first quarter of the twentieth century. The rustic look was found in cottage, porch, and some garden furniture.

It is extremely important to differentiate between rustic and primitive furniture. Although much rustic furniture appears primitive in form and construction, factory and craftsperson examples dominate. Among the catalogs in the collection at Rinker Enterprises is Rustic Furniture—Rustic Bird Houses of the Ye Olde Rustic Furniture Company of Philadelphia which advertises its products for "porches, lawns, summer homes, parks, country clubs, gardens, pavilions, theaters, hotels, dens, sanatoriums, etc."

One of the best known manufacturers of rustic furniture is the Old Hickory Furniture Company of Martinsville, Indiana, which celebrated its fortieth anniversary in 1931. Their "Pioneer" suite of porch furniture featured a chair, rocker, rocker settee, settee, stool, swing and chains, and table. Note the use of the term "Pioneer." Rustic furniture is sold as part of the Western as well as the Country look.

Adirondack furniture is a type of rustic furniture. It features a number of unusual designs and painted decoration. As a result, it became a darling of the folk art set in the 1980s. The collecting ardor for Adirondack furniture quickly cooled in the late 1980s when a large number of reproductions, copycats, and fakes arrived upon the scene. Beware of small end tables featuring a bird house motif.

References: Ralph Kylloe, *A History of the Old Hickory Chair Company and the Indiana Hickory Furniture Movement,* published by author, 1995; Ralph Kylloe, *Rustic Movement,* Gibbs–Smith, 1993; Ralph Kylloe (ed), *The Collected Works of Indiana Hickory Furniture Makers,* Rustic Publications, 1989; Victor M. Linoff (ed), *Porch, Lawn, and Cottage Furniture: Two Complete Catalogs, ca. 1904 and 1926,* Rustic Hickory Furniture Co., Dover Publications, 1991.

Museum: The Adirondack Museum, Blue Mountain Lake, NY.

Armchair, New York, log, stripped bark, painted dark green, straight crest,
 sloping arms, 19th C, 30¼" h **$200**
Bench, corner, cedar, straight upper rails, 3 posts, smooth planed 35 board
 seat, diamond shaped braces between upper and lower stretchers, c1915 . . **250**
Bench, garden, bark covered cedar, straight rails, geometric and random
 twig design back, twig braces, wide armrests with spindle supports,
 14 board seat, c1920 . . . . **275**
Bench, tennis, bark covered cedar, no back, X–form braces between front
 and back arm posts, 9 board seat **225**
Bookshelf, Jasper Hickory Furniture Co, Jasper, IN, spindled gallery and
 sides, 5 shelves with back rails, 1930s, 36" w, 12" d, 54" h **200**
Breakfront, pine, stripped bark, 4 doors, oak and walnut geometric wood
 facings, initials "J, O, H," and "N" above doors, 1875–1900, 87" w,
 94½" h **300**
Bunk Beds, arched rails with 3 spindles over fiber woven headboards and
 footboards, fiber woven side rails, woven diamond designs, on casters,
 detachable ladder, twin mattress size, 29" w, 68" h **500**
Chair, barrel back, Indiana Willow Products Co, Martinsville, IN, high
 square fiber woven back with rect headrest panel, open barrel shaped arm
 rails, splayed arm posts, fiber woven seat, box stretchers, 1948 . . . . **275**
Chest of Drawers, Indiana Willow Products Co, IN, rect overhanging top,
 5 drawers, paneled ends, square legs on casters, 1948, 39" w, 18" d,
 49" h **300**
Clothes Tree, State of Indiana Farm Industries, Putnamville, IN, hickory,
 8 pegs, 4 arched legs joined to column by stretchers, 1930s, 66" h **175**
Corner Cupboard, Old Hickory Furniture Co, Martinsville, IN, oak and hickory, spindled gallery, 2 glazed doors, int shelf, 2 paneled cupboard doors,
 ftd, dark oak finish, wooden pulls, 1930s, 20" w, 66" h **800**
Desk, Old Hickory Furniture Co, Martinsville, IN, hickory and oak, spindled
 gallery, oak top and 2 medial shelves each side, spindles on curved shelf
 supports, single drawer, dark oak finish, 1930s, 36" l, 24" w, 30¼" h **500**

Dining Chair, Indiana Hickory Furniture Co, hickory, woven seat, Paine
    Furniture Boston metal retailer's tag, price for set of 4 .... **800**
Divan, Old Hickory Furniture Co, Martinsville, IN, spindled back, arms, and
    base, wrapped woven splint crest rail, arms, and seat, checkered diamond
    design on cushions, 1930s, 64" l, 22" d, 18" h back **550**
Fainting Couch, Old Hickory Furniture Co, Martinsville, IN, raised curved
    backrest, continuous woven splint top reinforced with coil springs under
    weaving, 1930s, 29" w, 82" l **500**
Fernery, NY, twig, stripped bark, painted black and silver, 14" sq top **75**
Flower Box, bark covered cedar, 2 rows of 8 upright logs joined together,
    cutout rect well, 1910s, 8" d well, 33" l, 12" w **50**
Footstool, NY, blue and white cloth upholstered top, 13" w, 10½" d, 9" h **100**
High Chair, State of Indiana Farm Industries, Putnamville, IN, hickory,
    4 spindle back, rect food tray on hinged arms, woven splint seat, splayed
    base, shaped footrest, box stretchers, 1930s, 13" w seat, 14" d, 40" h **300**
Lawn Chair, bark covered cedar, straight rails, geometric and random twig
    designed back, twig braces, wide spindled arm rests, c1910 .... **300**
Magazine Rack, Old Hickory Furniture Co, Martinsville, IN, square oak top
    and 3 shelves, hickory legs, woven splint panels on sides and back, dark
    oak finish, 1930s **100**
Morris Chair, Old Hickory Furniture Co, Martinsville, IN, straight shawl rail,
    adjustable reclining woven splint back, 7 spindle arm supports each side,
    woven splint seat, box stretchers, 1912, 20" w seat, 21" d, 48" h **300**
Planter, NY, ftd, ornate orange and lime green paint dec, 51" l **475**
Porch Rocker, bark covered cedar, straight upper and lower rails, 5 straight
    spindles in back, 6 board seat, double box stretchers, 1910s, 40" h **250**
Porch Swing, Rustic Hickory Furniture Co, La Porte, IN, 3 rect woven splint
    panels in back, canted arm posts, woven splint seat, spindled skirt, 4 sus-
    pension chains, 60" l **300**
Rocker, Andrew Jackson style, Old Hickory Chair Co, Martinsville, IN, bark
    covered, continuous arms, woven splint back and seat, c1930, 20" w seat,
    18" d, 21" h **275**
Rocker, barrel back, Old Hickory Chair Co, Martinsville, IN, rect woven
    splint headrest above woven splint back and sides, woven splint seat, box
    stretchers, 17" w seat, 15" d, 47" h **250**
Rocker, child's, NY, black, red, and silver paint dec, 30" h **125**

*Settee, Old Hickory Furniture Co,
Martinsville, IN, hickory, double chair
back with woven splint panels and seat,
flared arm posts, 1930s, 22" h seat,
42" w, 19" d, $275.*

Settee, Indiana Willow Products Co, Martinsville, IN, double chair back, open barrel shaped arms, fiber woven back, sides, and seat with diamond designs, box stretchers, 1948, 42" w seat, 18" d **300**

Settee, Rustic Hickory Furniture Co, La Porte, IN, rocking, double barrel back, woven splint back curves around to sides, flared arm posts, woven seat, box stretcher base, 1913, 40" w seat, 16" d **400**

Side Chair, Rustic Hickory Furniture Co, IN, woven splint panel in square back, woven splint seat, box stretchers, 1904, 17" w seat, 15" d, 40" h **125**

Stand, corner whatnot, NY, oak and thornwood, stripped bark, 6 tiers, late 19th C, 55½" h **350**

Stand, pedestal, bark covered cedar, hexagonal top, tripod table top support and base, stretchers, 1910–20 . . . .   **125**

Stand, plant, Jasper Hickory Furniture Co, Jasper, IN, oak and hickory, square oak top, 4 legs, box stretchers at top and bottom joined by vertical spindles, 1930s, 16" sq, 21" h **100**

Standing Planter, bark covered cedar, 12 upright pickets form circular planter, tripod column, random logs form base, c1915 . . . .   **75**

Steamer Chair, Old Hickory Furniture Co, Martinsville, IN, woven splint back and seat, 12 x 24" writing table arm, spindled base, 1930s, 22" w, 48" d, 30" h **450**

Stool, Old Hickory Furniture Co, Martinsville, IN, woven splint saddle seat, 1930s, 18" w, 15" d, 15" h **75**

Table, drop leaf, Rustic Hickory Furniture Co, La Porte, IN, rect golden oak top, 11" leaves with rounded corners, splayed base, X–form stretchers, 1926, 33" w, 22" d, 31" h **200**

Table, gateleg, NY, oak and hickory, stripped bark, rect top with rounded corners, triangular leaves with rounded edges, thick legs, 22 spindles support 2 swing–out legs, cast iron hinges, c1915, 43½" w, 40" d, 33½" h **400**

Table, lamp, Old Hickory Furniture Co, Martinsville, IN, bark covered hickory and oak, octagonal oak top, splayed hickory legs, double stretchers, dark oak finish, c1932, 24" d, 30" h **250**

Table, tête–à–tête, bark covered cedar, 2 seats opening to opposite sides, straight rails, 4 spindles on backs and arms, 6 board seats, double stretchers front and back, 1910s **325**

Table, trestle, Old Hickory Furniture Co, Martinsville, IN, oak top, pinned trestle, hickory base, dark oak finish, 1930–35, 42" w, 24" d, 30" h **500**

ENGLISH COUNTRY

The role of the English gentry is glorified in fact and fiction. The concept of the "gentleman farmer" enjoys great popularity in America. Although American views about life in the English countryside are myth and idealistic oriented, their influence on American Country collecting is very strong.

Among early "antiques" collectors, there was a strong prejudice for things English. The concepts of England as the source for American design and that somehow English goods were simply superior resulted in English pieces occupying positions of prominence in many American collections.

English Country is found in both formal and vernacular styles. Formal was reserved for the manor house; vernacular suited the common folk and local tavern crowd. In the 1930s and 1940s English vernacular furniture from Welsh dressers to Windsor chairs was eagerly sought by American collectors. In the 1960s and 1970s emphasis was placed on things American. English Country vernacular lost favor.

The return to the formal look in the 1980s and the desire to replace the American Country look that evolved during the Bicentennial era resulted in the rediscovery of English Country by collectors and decorators. In essence, the market has come full circle. Pieces that were popular in the 1930s and 1940s are popular again in the 1990s.

The lack of adequate reference and decorating texts makes collecting English Country a hodgepodge operation. It is highly recommended that anyone wishing to focus on English Country travel to Great Britain and visit regional and local museums and historic sites.

References: Bernard D. Cotton, *The English Regional Chair,* Antique Collector's Club, 1990; David P. Lindquist and Caroline C. Warren, *English and Continental Furniture,* Wallace–Homestead, Krause Publications, 1994; Howard Pain, *The Heritage of Country Furniture: A Study in the Survival of Formal and Vernacular Styles From the United States, Britain, and Europe Found in Upper Canada, 1780–1900,* Van Nostrand Reinhold, 1978.

Reproduction Alert: A fair amount of English Country enters the American market via preassembled containers. Buyers should be aware that great liberties are taken in respect to rebuilding and reconstructing this furniture. Have any "period" piece authenticated by an expert.

Candlestand, Country Empire, tilt top, refinished cherry with figured wood
   veneer in pie shaped wedges on top, bulbous turned column,
   tripod base with simple scrolled legs, repairs, 18½" d, 29" h **$250**
Chair, Hepplewhite, mahogany, square back with 3 flat reeded spindles,
   white fabric covered slip seat, square tapered legs, H stretcher, old worn
   finish, seats recovered, 17¾" h seat, 34" h overall, price for set of 4 ...... **775**
Chair, ladder back, 6 graduated shaped slats, shaped arms, bulbous turned
   front legs and stretcher, paper rush seat, 14" h seat, 40" h overall **300**
Chair, Queen Anne, walnut, shaped crest rail and splat, flame stitch upholstered slip seats, shaped apron, cabriole legs with raised pad feet, old finish, seats are old replacements, repaired seat frame, 18" h seat, 38½" h,
   price for pair **1,500**
Chair, William and Mary Revival, walnut, tooled leather back with rampant
   lion motif and diamond shaped tacks above 6 half spindles, leather seat,
   turned legs, H–form stretchers, ball feet, 19th C, 18" h seat, 34" h, price
   for set of 4 .... **225**
Chair, Windsor, yew and hardwood, bow back, carved splat with center
   wheel flanked by 3 spindles each side, shaped arms and posts, shaped
   seat, splayed base, turned legs, old refinishing, repairs, 17½" h seat,
   34½" h **500**
Chair, Windsor style, low back, shaped crest and arms, 7 turned spindles,
   shaped seat, splayed base with stretchers, old finish, 31½" h, price for set
   of 3 .... **150**
Chaise Lounge, walnut with natural finish, double back with shaped crests
   and splats, cabriole legs with paw feet, upholstered in camel colored
   wool, high quality handmade reproduction, 35" d, 77" l **350**
Chest of Drawers, Chippendale, mahogany, pine and oak secondary wood,
   molded edge top, 2 short over 3 long graduated drawers with beveled

edges and original brasses, bracket feet, old finish, some edge damage and repairs, age cracks in ends, feet replaced, 35¾" w, 19¾ x 37" top, 36¼" h 2,000

Chest of Drawers, Chippendale, mahogany veneer, pine secondary wood, reeded edge top, 3 long graduated dovetailed drawers with applied edge beading, bracket feet, refinished, replaced oval brasses, filled–in cracks in veneer, 35⅞" w, 21½ x 36⅞" top, 36¼" h 650

Chest of Drawers, Chippendale, mahogany veneer, pine secondary wood, 2 short over 2 long graduated dovetailed drawers with applied edge beading, reeded base molding, bracket feet, old finish, repairs to feet, 35½" w, 20 x 36¾" top, 36" h 775

Chest of Drawers, Hepplewhite, mahogany veneer with banded inlay, 2 short over 3 long graduated dovetailed drawers with inlaid bone escutcheons and applied edge beading, banded columns on corners, shaped apron, French feet, replaced oval thistle brasses, 1 brass missing, wear, edge and veneer damage with some repair, 47¼" w, 21½ x 48" top, 42¼" h 650

Chest of Drawers, Hepplewhite, mahogany veneer with old finish, oak and pine secondary wood, reeded edge top, 2 short over 3 long graduated dovetailed drawers, cutout apron and feet, orig brasses, partially replaced locks, edge and veneer damage, 35¾" w, 36¼ x 16¼" top, 36¼" h 500

Chest of Drawers, Queen Anne, olive wood veneer with oyster burl inlay, mahogany and hardwood, pine and oak secondary wood, molded edge top, 4 graduated dovetailed long drawers with applied edge beading, bracket feet, replaced engraved brasses, replaced feet, age cracks and other repairs, 35½" w, 19¼ x 37¼" top, 41" h 2,750

Chest of Drawers, Queen Anne, walnut, highboy, burl veneer facade with herringbone banding on drawers, 2–pc construction, top with molded cornice, chamfered fluted corners with lamb's tongues, and 6 drawers, base with 3 drawers, scalloped apron, and cabriole legs with duck feet, repairs and brasses replaced, top is period, base is early–20th C replacement, 43" w, 67" h 2,200

Chest of Drawers, Queen Anne, walnut and walnut veneer, lowboy, rect overhanging top, 3 dovetailed drawers, shaped apron, turned legs, old bleached finish, insect damage, old repairs and restoration, age cracks, 19½ x 27" top, 27" h 1,200

Chest of Drawers, Queen Anne, walnut with inlay, highboy, molded cornice with hidden drawer, 2 short over 3 long graduated dovetailed overlapping drawers, 3 dovetailed overlapping drawers in base, shaped apron, carved cabriole legs, replaced brasses, minor repairs, refinished, 23¾ x 41½" cornice, 67" h 3,300

Chest of Drawers, Regency, figured mahogany and oak veneer with inlay, pine secondary wood, molded edge top, 2 short over 3 long graduated dovetailed drawers with applied edge beading, cutout feet and apron, ebonized turned pulls, 45¾" w, 21 x 46¾" top, 48" h 725

Chest on Chest, Hepplewhite, 2 pc, refinished mahogany veneer with inlay, pine secondary wood, molded cornice, 2 short over 3 long overlapping dovetailed drawers in upper section, 3 long overlapping dovetailed drawers in base, scalloped apron, high French feet, repaired veneer, age cracks, replaced brass pulls, 41" w, 21¾ x 46" cornice, 79" h 1,875

Left: Library Armchair, George III, mahogany, carved arm supports, square tapering molded legs, c1770, $6,900.

Right: Side Chair, George II, mahogany, carved crest, pierced splat, cabriole legs, claw and ball feet, mid–18th C, $1,150.

Photos courtesy Sotheby's.

Left: Chest of Drawers, George III, mahogany, bow front top over conforming case, dressing slide above cockbeaded drawers, shaped skirt, flared feet, early 19th C, 34¹/₂" h, 36¹/₂" w, 21¹/₂" d, $4,312. Photo courtesy Sotheby's.

Right: Corner Cupboard, Georgian, pine, molded cornice, glazed doors opening to shelved int, paneled doors, shaped apron, c1800, 92" h, 53" w, 23" d, $3,000. Photo courtesy Sotheby's.

Left: Candlestand, George II, carved mahogany, piecrust tilt top, acanthus carved standard, cabriole legs, claw and ball feet, mid–18th C, 27¹/₂" h, 24" d, $2,300. Photo courtesy Sotheby's.

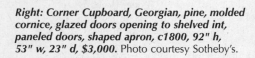

Clock, grandfather's, mahogany veneer with inlay and old finish, molding between sections, bonnet has broken arch pediment with molded goosenecks with brass rosettes, turned finials, and free standing columns, brass works with calendar movement and second hand, painted metal face with gold and black foliage scrolls, and mkd "A. Buchan, Perth," case with reeded quarter columns, missing feet, minor edge damage, replaced door, finials, and back edge trim, with weights and pendulum, 83" h 2,525

Corner Cupboard, architectural, 2 pc, pine with pickled finish, molded cornice, glazed double doors with fretwork on top, paneled cupboard doors in base, fluted column stiles, molded base, 20th C, 60" w cornice, 87" h . . 1,325

Corner Cupboard, hanging, oak, dentil molded cornice, inlaid floral medallion on single paneled door, molded base, minor edge damage, late 18th/early 19th C, 29" w at cornice, 40½" h . . . ./. 700

Corner Cupboard, hanging, oak, molded cornice, single paneled door with inlaid shell in almond medallion in center, molded base, brass H hinges, 23" w, 25" w at cornice, 39" h . . . .~. 1,500

Desk, Queen Anne, walnut veneer with inlaid banding, slant front lid with fitted int consisting of 8 dovetailed drawers, pigeonholes, 2 letter drawers, and center door flanked by half columns, pull out slides, shelf with sliding door with well, 2 short over 2 long dovetailed drawers, bracket feet, replaced oval brasses, repairs, 36¼" w, 9½" d, 39¾" h 3,000

Desk, roll top, oak with old finish, S–curve roll, fitted int with pigeonholes and 4 drawers, double pedestal base with center drawer and 4 drawers each side, paneled sides and back, pull out writing tablets, hardware mkd "Derby Desk, Leicester, Tanglesant & Sons, LTD," lid stuck in open position, 48" w, 30" d, 43½" h, 30" writing height 725

Desk Stand, oak, brass trim, paper compartment, single drawer, 2 clear cut ink wells, 10½" h 325

Gout Stool, hardwood with old brown stain, adjustable top with red leather upholstery, turned feet, labeled "Hospital Contacts Co. LTD.," 22" l 350

Huntboard, Queen Anne style, walnut, molded edge top, 3 dovetailed overlapping drawers, mortised and pinned frame, cabriole legs with padded duck feet, handmade reproduction, 18¾ x 71¾" top, 33½" h 500

Kettle Shelf, brass, reticulated top and apron, cabriole legs with flattened feet, small split in back top edge, 12½ x 14 x 13¾" h 250

Linen Press, mahogany, dentil molded cornice, dovetailed case with pair of recessed panel doors with shelved int, applied molding at stile, waist, and base, base with 2 short over single long cockbeaded drawer, paneled bracket feet, 46" w, 24" d, 70" h 3,650

Mirror, scroll, Chippendale, old finish, gilt and stylized Prince of Wales feather ornament liner with gold repaint, bottom crest repaired, replaced mirror glass, 29" h 325

Mirror, shaving, mahogany with old finish, oak secondary wood, swiveling beveled mirror in cross banded veneer frame, reeded posts, 4 dovetailed drawers, replaced feet, edge damage and repair, missing finials and 1 drawer pull, 23" w, 10¾" d, 25" h 75

Settle Bench, figured oak with refinishing, paneled construction, flat back with 3 doors for storage compartments, curved seat, conforming base with center drawer flanked by pair of short drawers either side, shaped arms, turned posts, some edge damage and age cracks, pieced repairs including 1 at corner of seat at post, 57" w, 26" d, 59" h 4,675

Shelves, mahogany, tiered, arched crest, 6 shelves with graduated depths, shaped ends, French feet, 20th C, 40" w, 12½" d at base, 60¼" h **715**

Sofa, Hepplewhite, carved mahogany frame with shaped crest rail continuing to arms and front legs, reupholstered in salmon velvet, old repairs to frame, 66" l **325**

Sofa Bed, Victorian, olive wood and mahogany frame with carved detail and figured veneer, scrolled back with raised center tablet with figured veneer, scrolled arms, pullout drawer with figured veneer front panels beneath seat, scrolled feet, burgundy velvet upholstery, 84" l **325**

Stand, Hepplewhite style, mahogany, pine secondary wood, square, gallery top with cutout handles, single door, square tapered legs, old finish, minor age cracks, 13 x 13" top, 28½" h **1,325**

Table, card, Chippendale, folding top supported by 2 back legs that extend with accordion folding apron, false drawer, cabriole legs with acanthus carving on knees and ball and claw feet, minor old pieced repairs, 17½ x 38" opens to 35 x 38", 27½" h **2,000**

Table, drop leaf, Queen Anne, mahogany, oval top, tapered swing legs with duck feet, dark finish, 17 x 54¼" top with 22" leaves, 28¼" h **1,600**

Table, gateleg, oak with old dark finish, oval drop leaf top, mortised and pinned stretcher base with turned and block legs, old repairs and restorations, age cracks in top, 16 x 45" with 19" leaves, 27¾" h **375**

Table, Pembroke, Chippendale, mahogany, drop leaves, single dovetailed drawer, cross stretcher with pierced carving, square molded corner legs with inside chamfer, old finish, repairs and edge damage, 18¼ x 27¾" top with 9¼" leaves, 28" h **575**

Table, pub, mahogany, round top, splayed triangular base with conforming apron and medial shelf, 3 triangular straight legs, minor repairs and age cracks, 28¾" d top, 27½" h, price for pair **1,000**

Left: Drop Leaf Table, George III, mahogany, rect top, spider leg base with ring turned columns, gates, and stretchers, last quarter 18th C, 28¼" h, 29½" open l, $1,500.

Right: Demilune Table, George I, mahogany, D–shaped top opens to well, frieze, tapering legs, pad feet, repairs, 27¾" h, 23¼" w, 23¾" d, $2,592. Photo courtesy Sotheby's.

Table, pub, oak, round tilt top, mortised frame, shoe feet, scrubbed finish, 38½" d, 26½" h 875

Table, tavern, oak, breadboard top, mortised apron and stretcher, turned legs, weathered age cracks in refinished top, old finish on base, 25½ x 37½" top, 26" h 450

Table, tea, Country Chippendale, mahogany, round 2 board tilt top, vasiform column, tripod base with snake feet, repaired break in base of column, top is probably old replacement, 20½" d, 28½" h 600

Washstand, Hepplewhite, corner, mahogany, dovetailed gallery with corner shelf, cutouts for bowl and accessories in curved top, conforming medial shelf with single dovetailed drawer, base shelf, square legs with outward curved feet, old worn finish with added varnish, minor damage and age cracks, 24" w, 31" h plus gallery, 41" h overall 450

FRENCH COUNTRY

Like its English counterpart, French Country furniture is found in formal and ver-nacular styles. Formal French Country tends toward the high style. Its American pop-ularity is confined to collectors and decorators living in metropolitan areas.

French vernacular pieces, especially the bleached examples from Southern France, were discovered by collectors and decorators in the mid–1980s. As the 1990s progress, their popularity appears to be waning. This is due in part to the large num-ber of reproductions, copycats, and fakes that flooded the American market.

French Canadian furniture is attracting strong attention among American Country collectors and decorators. It recently was revealed that a large amount of furniture that sold in the market from the 1960s through the 1980s as painted rural New England Country furniture was actually from the rural regions of French Canada.

References: Henri Algoud, Leon LeClerc, and Paul Baneat, *Authentic French Provincial Furniture From Provence, Normandy, and Brittany,* Dover Publications, 1993; Warren Johansson, *Country Furniture and Accessories From Quebec,* Schiffer Publishing, 1991; David P. Lindquist and Caroline C. Warren, *English and Continental Furniture,* Wallace–Homestead, Krause Publications, 1994; Howard Pain, *The Heritage of Country Furniture: A Study in the Survival of Formal and Vernacular Styles From the United States, Britain, and Europe Found in Upper Canada, 1780–1900,* Van Nostrand Reinhold, 1978.

Reproduction Alert.

Armoire, Louis Philippe, pine, projecting molded cornice, pair of paneled doors, paint int with shelves over 2 aligned drawers and 2 paneled cup-board doors, bracket feet, 52" w, 20" d, 98" h $2,000

Armoire, Second Empire, walnut, deeply molded cornice, single full length paneled door, chamfered and paneled ends, shaped block feet, 1860, 36" w, 22" d, 90" h 1,250

Bench, Louis XIV, refinished hardwood, triple seat caned back with carved crest rail, shaped arms, carved apron, cabriole legs carved with acanthus leaves at knees, three X–form stretchers, peach colored velvet cushion, 78" l 3,200

Bench, Louis XV style, window, fruitwood, scrolled voluted arms, cabriole legs, pale gray and dusty rose striped silk upholstery, 41½" w 375

Bookcase, Louis XV style, oak, thumb molded cornice, central grilled door, opposing foliate scroll carved frame on top and mid–section, grilled panels, plinth base, late 19th C, 60" w, 87" h **3,500**

Candlestand, Louis XVI style, mahogany, round top with pierced brass border, paneled column, shaped tripod base, 14½" d, 26½" h **1,250**

Chair, Louis XV style, carved hardwood frame with old dark finish, carved arms with padded rests, shaped apron, cabriole legs, padded scroll feet, velvet upholstery, matching footstool, 38½" h **275**

Chaise Lounge, Louis XV style, walnut, floral carved crest rail, shell carved seat rail, cabriole legs, yellow and ivory striped upholstered back and seat, price for pair **500**

Day Bed, Restauration, mahogany, slightly bowed rect upholstered back, upholstered seat, turned tapered legs, ball feet, crimson silk upholstery . . .   **600**

Footstool, Louis XVI style, walnut, petit point upholstered top **200**

Mirror, pier, Louis XV style, walnut, foliate pierced carved crest, scalloped beveled rect mirror plate surrounded by molded carved foliate dec, 34" w, 92" h **3,000**

Secretary Bookcase, Louis Philippe, walnut, molded cornice, single drawer, fall front writing surface, 3 drawers, turned feet, 40" w, 20" d, 65" h **1,500**

Settee, Louis XV, carved blonde wood frame, shaped crest rail, scrolled post, cabriole legs, muslin upholstered back and seat, minor edge damage, 51" l **1,500**

Sofa, Restauration, mahogany, asymmetrical shape, rolled ends, loose cushion seat, plain straight apron, turned legs, bell shaped feet, 66" w **750**

Table, dining, Louis XVI style, mahogany, round top with brass banding, straight tapered legs, brass toe caps, 54" w, 82" l extended, 27½" h **1,500**

Table, game, Louis XV style, oak, square top with shallow gallery, red leathered inset playing surface with gilt dec, scalloped apron, cabriole legs, 32¼" w, 28¾" h **2,000**

Cabinet, Provincial, Louis XV, inlaid fruitwood, wire paneled doors, shaped apron, scrolled feet, 73" h, 55" w, 18" d, $1,500.

*Stepback Cupboard, Louis Philippe, chestnut,
2 sections, top with molded cornice and pair
of raised panel doors, base with pair of short
drawers over pair of raised panel doors,
c1840, 97" h, 43" w, $1,750.* Photo courtesy
Sotheby's.

Table, sewing, Restauration, mahogany, square lift lid top, fitted int with
14 compartments, turned column with scrolled supports, square carved
base, 4 scrolled feet, c1830, 29¹/₄" h 1,750
Table, wine tasting, tilt top, refinished pine, round top, shoe feet, 42³/₄" d,
27" h 750
Table, writing, Louis Philippe, pine, rect top, paneled apron, reeded tapered
legs, 54¹/₂" w, 27¹/₂" d, 28" h 1,750

PENNSYLVANIA GERMAN

The first German settlers arrived in Pennsylvania in 1683. With Philadelphia as a
hub, they spread north, west (to Harrisburg, PA, then south), and east. The initial period of immigration ended in the 1740s at which time Pennsylvania communities dotted southeast Pennsylvania, the Shenandoah Valley from Hagerstown, Maryland, to the
Southern back country, and portions of Ontario, Canada.

The Germans brought with them a strong craft tradition. Next to Shaker,
Pennsylvania–German is the most widely collected form of American regional furniture. Although Pennsylvania–German painted furniture has received the most attention
in exhibit and print, there was also a strong tradition of unpainted formal pieces as
well.

Pennsylvania–German vernacular forms survived for centuries. One of the most
valuable reference sources is Henry Lapp's handbook. This book illustrates vernacular
forms made by Lapp well into the twentieth century.

Pennsylvania–German furniture was meant to be used and survive. Its sturdy construction and vertical lines make it easy to distinguish from other regional forms. Most
examples were made by furniture craftsmen. The Pennsylvania–German farmer as
maker of his own furniture is largely a myth.

References: Bernard Deneke, *Bauernmobel: Ein Handbuck Fur Sammler and Liebhaber*, Deutsche Taschenbuck Verlag, 1983; Monroe Fabian, *The Pennsylvania–German Decorated Blanket Chest*, Universe Books, 1978; Beatrice Garvan, *The Pennsylvania German Collection*, Philadelphia Museum of Art, 1982; Alan Keyser, Larry Neff, and Frederick S. Weiser (trans and eds), *The Accounts of Two Pennsylvania German Furniture Makers—Abraham Overholt, Bucks County, 1790–1833, and Peter Ranck, Lebanon County, 1794–1817*, Sources and Documents of the Pennsylvania Germans III, Pennsylvania German Society, 1978; Henry Lapp, *A Craftsman's Handbook*, Good Books, 1975; Marie Purnell Musser, *Country Chairs of Central Pennsylvania*, published by author, 1990.

Museums: Hershey Museum, Hershey, PA; Historical Society of Pennsylvania, Philadelphia, PA.

Bedstead, low post, maple and poplar, dark green and red painted, ball finials on turned posts centering pitched headboard and shaped foot board, tall turned tapering legs, early 19th C, 47½" w **$700**

Bedstead and Trundle, poplar, red stained, bed with ball finials above reel and vase turned supports centering shaped head and foot boards on tall tapering reel and vase turned legs ending in peg feet, trundle with ball finials and similar turnings centering head and foot boards on ball feet, Berne, Berks County, first half 19th C, 48" w bed **2,500**

Bench, pine, painted blue, horizontal crest above 18 flaring uprights, down-swept scrolling arms, plank seat fitted with 2 hinged panels opening to well, rect base and molded plinth, straight bracket feet, losses to foot fac-ings, paint chipped, Center County, 19th C, 79" l **4,000**

Blanket Chest, pine, allover blue swirl grain painting, hinged rect molded lid opening to well with till, base molding, bracket feet, c1810, 50" w, 19½" d, 23" h **12,750**

Blanket Chest, pine, paint dec, rect lid fitted on int with orig wrought iron heart strap hinges opening to well with till, front of case dec with 2 arched reserves flanked by balusters centering tulips and flowers, also centering inscription "Lisbeth Jacobisen, 1791," molded base, bracket feet, 49¼" w, 22" d, 25" h **3,150**

Blanket Chest, pine, paint dec, rect molded lid dec with two 8–point stars each flanked by blue and green bars, fitted int with lidded till, case dec with 3 painted domed panels each with scrolling foliate border, center panel with 2–handled black painted urn with incised signature "Seltzer" and 4 budded and blooming tulips, outer panels with black painted urns issuing red and blue flowers, 1 dated "1775," conforming molded base, bracket feet, Christian Seltzer (1749–1831), Jonestown, Lebanon County, 52" w, 23½" d, 22" h **9,200**

Blanket Chest, pine, painted blue, rect hinged lid opening to well, case with mid molding above 3 molded drawers, molded base, ogee bracket feet, moldings highlighted in red, orig brass pulls and escutcheon plate, c1785, 51" w, 22½" d, 27¾" h **5,175**

Blanket Chest, pine, polychrome dec, hinged rect lid opening to well and till with partially legible inscriptions on underside, case dec with 3 arched reserves flanked by and centering 4 pots of flowers and birds, center reserved dec with rampant unicorns and crown, flanking reserves depict-ing birds, tulips, and inverted hearts with riders on horseback wielding drawn swords and inscribed with date "1787," case sides depicting arched reserves with tulip filled pots, allover blue painted ground, molded base, straight bracket feet with central pendant, right top molding replaced, base molding and feet formed at later date from 18th–C painted architectural baseboard moldings, Windsor Township, Northern Berks County, 50" w, 22" d, 24" h **11,500**

Blanket Chest, pine, rect lid pegged on 3 sides with molded frame, int fitted with molded till, conforming case, 2 checkered astragal painted panels enclosing checkered flower pot issuing stylized tulips and leaves in red, black, green, and white centering astragal painted panel "Elisabetha, Blesin 1791," sides with similar dec, molded base, shaped bracket feet, red painted ground, orig wrought iron hinges, probably Berks County, 49³/₄" w, 21³/₄" d, 23⁷/₈" h **6,325**

Blanket Chest, pine and poplar, brown and blue vinegar graining with reserves on front, sides and lid, front has white heart with star flowers and "Johan Witmer 1799" in red and black, black molding and feet, dovetailed case with ogee feet and applied lid, case, and base molding, 2 overlapping dovetailed drawers, bear trap lock, wrought iron strap hinges, lidded till, secret compartment with 2 dovetailed drawers, minor wear and edge damage, paint wear primarily on lid, 51¹/₄" w, 23" d, 27" h **22,000**

Blanket Chest, pine and poplar, red and black grain painted, rect molded lid, int fitted with molded board till, case with applied molding below midsection over 2 thumb molded short drawers, molded base, shaped bracket feet, black grain painting on red ground, orig wrought iron hinges, brasses, and locks, 1800–20, 50" w, 22¹/₂" d, 28¹/₂" h **8,000**

Blanket Chest, poplar, grain and paint dec, rect top with molded edge open ing to well with till and 2 short drawers below, underside of lid inscribed "Thomas B. Reber Murall...1833 Thomas R. Reber January 16th 1837 C.D. Reber Feby 24–87 bought this chest at Uncle's sales for $3.85. Delivered to Addie May 14/03," case with mid molding and 2 short drawers, base molding below on splayed bracket feet, dec allover in tones of red and black simulating crotch mahogany, orig drawer pulls and brass escutcheons, repair to front left foot, 49¹/₂" w, 22" d, 27¹/₂" h, c1800 . . . . . .**3,150**

Chest of Drawers, pine, decorated, c1825, 41¹/₂" h, 44" w, 17" d, $2,750.

Blanket Chest, poplar, paint dec, rect lid paint dec in black and white on blue ground with five 12–pointed stars framed on 3 sides with red painted and molded edge, int fitted with lidded till, case with exposed dovetails and paint dec in white, red, yellow, and black on blue ground with "Dieses Kist Gehert Mir Barabara Staufern" over central 12–pitch star with initials "JF" above "1799" flanked by birds, flowers, unicorns, and stars, red painted molded base, ogee bracket feet, attributed to John Flory (1754–after 1824), Rapho Township, Lancaster County, 52³⁄₈" w, 24" d, 26¹⁄₈" h 24,150

Candlestand, Chippendale, maple, round tilt top revolving above birdcage support, baluster and reel turned standard, tripod base with downswept legs ending in slipper feet, metal brace applied to birdcage, c1800, 20¹⁄₂" d, 27¹⁄₂" h 3,500

Chair, Federal, fancy, floral dec, scrolling crest with pierced handhold, pierced baluster splat with paint dec basket containing budding and blooming roses edged in black, shaped plank seat, baluster, ring, and bamboo turned legs, turned box stretchers, mustard painted ground, 1830–50, price for pair 925

Chair, Federal, fancy, floral dec, shaped crest, baluster splat, raked and turned posts, shaped plank seat, turned legs joined by turned box stretchers, floral dec in red, green, white, and black with yellow and black detailing on mustard ground, 1830–50, 33" h, price for set of 6 4,600

Chair, Federal, fancy, paint and stencil dec, horizontal crest flanked by projecting stiles with 4 arrow form spindles, serpentine side bow front seat, turned tapering legs joined by stretchers, ball feet, dec with flowers and leafage with green highlights on yellow ground, Lehigh County, c1810 625

Chair, Federal, fancy, polychrome dec, shaped reverse scrolling crest, lyre form splat, turned stiles, trapezoidal cane seat, ring turned tapering legs joined by stretchers, ball feet, painted with bucolic landscapes in green, gray, and black tones on cream colored field, Philadelphia, c1820, price for set of 6 18,500

Chair, Federal, fancy, stencil dec, arched crest, tapering stiles centering vasiform splat, balloon form seat, ring turned tapering legs joined by stretchers, painted allover with fruit and flowers in tones of green, blue, and red with cream and gold highlights on brown field, c1855, price for set of 6   ..1,725

Chair, Federal, fancy, stencil dec, shaped crest on ring turned stiles, pierced vasiform splat, plank seat, ring turned tapering legs joined by stretchers, stenciled fruit and leafage dec in tones of green, red, and gold on red field, some dec worn slightly, c1850, price for set of 6 2,185

Chair, Federal, fancy, stencil dec, shaped crest on turned stiles centering stay–rail and 4 turned half spindles, plank seat, ring turned tapering legs joined by stretchers, stenciled fruit and foliage dec in tones of red and gold on green field, c1835, price for set of 6 4,000

Chest of Drawers, Chippendale, poplar, grain painted, rect top framed on 3 sides by molded overhang, 3 thumb molded short drawers above 3 graduated thumb molded long drawers flanked by canted corners with lamb's tongue termini, molded base with shaped knee returns and straight bracket feet, red on salmon grain painting with yellow detailing on upper and lower moldings and thumb moldings, late 18th C, 41¹⁄₂" w, 20¹⁄₈" d, 41³⁄₈" h 34,500

Chest of Drawers, Empire, cherrywood, painted and comb dec, rect molded top, 4 graduated cockbeaded drawers dec with squiggle and circular patterns, top drawer projects above lower 3 drawers flanked by engaged turned columns, similarly turned feet, 1830–50, 43" w, 21¼" d, 45⅞" h . . .**3,675**

Cupboard, corner, decorated, stippled yellow dec on dark green ground, 2 sections, molded and rope carved cornice above arched glazed door opening to painted and shelved int, pierced for cutlery, vine and tulip carved pilasters flanking door, projecting lower section with hinged scalloped paneled door, molded base on bracket feet, feet reduced in height, some patches to moldings and upper door refinished, 1790–1820, 48½" w, 21" d, 76" h **13,800**

Cupboard, corner, grain painted, late Federal, 2 sections, rect cornice with canted corners, glazed door opening to shelved int, lower section with conforming ovolo molding above 2 paneled doors enclosing shelved int, ovolo applied molding base, shaped skirt, reel turned feet, 1830–50, 43½" w, 24" d, 84½" h **12,650**

Cupboard, corner, grain painted, pine, late Federal, 2 sections, molded cornice with canted corners, case fitted with 2 double paneled doors opening to shelved int, lower section with conforming mid molding over conforming case fitted with 2 undulating short drawers above double paneled door opening to shelved int, shaped skirt, splayed French feet, all painted to simulate tiger maple and bird's–eye maple, 1830–40, 51" w, 24" d, 91" h **6,500**

Cupboard, Dutch, pine, black painted and polychrome dec, 2 sections, rect overhanging cornice above 2 glazed doors flanked by chamfered corners opening to 2 shelves pierced with spoon racks, case highlighted with blue, red, and yellow pinstriping, shelves similarly dec, projecting lower section with 3 frieze drawers, 2 raised panel cupboard doors flanked by chamfered corners, turned tapering feet, lower case highlighted with blue pinstriping, int shelf painted red, paint is later addition, 1810–40, 53" w, 20½" d, 86" h **4,475**

Cupboard, Dutch, poplar, red painted, 2 sections, overhanging molded cornice above 2 glazed doors opening to shelved int, projecting lower section with 3 short drawers and 2 raised panel cupboard doors, turned tapering legs ending in ball feet, orig Sandwich glass drawer pulls, c1840 .**16,100**

Cupboard, pewter, pine, blue, red, and buff painted, 2 sections, upper section with overhanging molded cornice and 2 open shelves flanked by scrolling sides, projecting base with molded edge, single long drawer, raised panel cupboard door opening to shelf, molded base, bun feet, possible restoration to mid molding, later paint dec, Lebanon County, second half 18th C, 48" w, 15¼" d, 79" h **1,150**

Cupboard, step back, pine, Federal, frontal molded cornice above rect case fitted with 2 glazed doors opening to shelved int, rect lower case fitted with 2 framed doors opening to shelved int, arched bracket feet, Berks County, 1815–40, 47½" w, 20¼" d, 84½" h **5,750**

Cupboard, step back, pine, Hepplewhite, grain painted, shaped sides terminating in scrolled volutes centering 2 shelves, rect case with applied molded edge over 2 raised panel doors with applied molding, molded base, shaped skirt, French feet, Lancaster County, 1810–30, 51¾" w, 15¾" d, 71" h **6,325**

Cupboard, step back, tiger maple, Federal, 2 sections, molded cornice, applied molding over 2 framed glazed doors opening to shelved int, chamfered and lamb's tongue embellished stiles resting within applied moldings of lower case, conforming lower case fitted with 3 drawers with incised beading, center drawer narrower than other 2, above 2 similarly incised and paneled doors centering double reeded center stile, flanked by chamfered and lamb's tongue embellished stiles, molded base with bracket feet, allover salmon and black grain painted dec, Delaware County, 1815–40, 62½" w, 19½" d, 82½" h **19,550**

Desk, shopkeeper's, maple and pine, hinged rect writing surface opening to int fitted with single short drawer and pigeonhole, frieze with single long drawer, turned flaring baluster–form legs, H–stretcher, ball feet, all orig including batwing brasses and escutcheons, c1780, 33" w, 25" d, 38" h . . .**3,500**

Rocker, Federal, polychrome dec, shaped reverse scrolling crest, caned back and seat, scrolling arms with spindle support, turned tapering legs joined by stretchers, painted with bucolic landscape in green, gray, and black tones on cream colored field, Philadelphia, c1820 . . . .**5,175**

Settee, Federal, polychrome dec, mustard painted, shaped tripartite crest on turned supports centering pierced baluster–form splats, downswept scrolling arms, plank seat, ring turned tapering legs joined by stretchers, dec in tones of yellow, red, and green with white and black highlights depicting fruit and flowers on ocher ground, Lehigh County, c1820, 75" l . .**1,100**

Table, farm, cherrywood, rect 3 board top with rounded corners, rect frame with molded apron fitted with 2 thumb molded short drawers, baluster and ring turned legs joined by flat molded box stretchers, reel and bun feet, early 19th C, 60" w, 33⅜" d, 29½" h **5,500**

Table, farm, pine and walnut, rect top with keyed dovetail chamfered battens, rect frame, ring and column turned legs, H–stretchers, frame painted red, Bucks County, first half 19th C, 79" w, 36½" d, 29¾" h **4,600**

Table, sawbuck, walnut, green painted, rect single board top above S–form supports joined by octagonal stretcher, Montgomery County, early 19th C, 43" w, 27" d, 27" h **865**

Table, tavern, pine and oak, rect top fitted with keyed and chamfered battens, rect case with thumb molded drawer, ring and baluster turned legs, molded box stretchers, reel turned feet, 1730–50, 31½" w, 18¼" d, 25" h . .**4,000**

Table, tavern, walnut, oval 3 board top with keyed battens, square frame fitted with thumb molded drawer, ring and baluster turned legs, straight molded box stretchers, reel and bun turned feet, early 19th C, 38¼" w, 27½" d, 30" h **6,325**

Table, tavern, walnut, rect top fitted with 2 keyed and chamfered battens, conforming frame with thumb molded drawer, ring and baluster turned legs, straight box stretchers, pad feet, early 19th C, 41½" w, 25½" d, 29" h **2,750**

Wardrobe, grain painted, ovolo and cove molded rect cornice, conforming case fitted with 2 paneled doors centering stile with applied molding, 2 cove molded short drawers, molded base, straight bracket feet, rag painted in brown on salmon ground, Lancaster County, 1800–20, 49¾" w, 19½" d, 77½" h **25,300**

GLASS

Glass serves two key functions in Country—utilitarian and decorative. Glass used in rural America was manufactured to last. Most pieces were thickly made and would last a long time when handled carefully. Glass had a permanence attached to it that was easily understood by the agrarian housewife.

Glass was recyclable. It could serve the same purpose over and over again. Every agrarian home had a place in the pantry or basement where jars and other glassware were stored awaiting reuse. Further, manufacturers of food products quickly realized the value placed upon glass by the agrarian housewife. Sales increased when prepackaged foods were placed in reusable glass.

The arrival of inexpensive glassware revolutionized country life. Storage possibilities increased considerably. Home canning became a seasonal activity. Inexpensive pattern glass added a touch of elegance to everyday life. The level of sanitation increased.

The country housewife classified her glassware in three categories: (1) storage vessels, (2) everyday glassware, and (3) special occasion glass. Glass storage vessels were limited until the arrival of the refrigerator. The most common glass storage vessel was the fruit jar. The fruit jar along with the cold cellar were the principal means of food storage in rural America until the arrival of electricity. Although some farmsteads had icehouses, most did not. Individuals living in towns fared better, albeit ceramic and tin storage dominated in an ice box.

Everyday glassware consisted primarily of drinking glasses and table accessories such as spoon holders and salt and pepper shakers. The kitchen and Depression era glasswares of the 1920 to 1950 period found favor among the rural housewife. It was colorful and affordable. Although more glass forms appeared throughout the house, the most heavily used items, e.g., dinner plates, still tended to be ceramic.

Glass played a major role in lighting. See the "Lighting" section for more detailed information.

Practicality aside, the agrarian housewife loved the decorative nature of glass. Leaded cut glass sparkled with brilliance on a dining room buffet. Shelves were installed in a kitchen window so light could reflect through a host of colored glasswares. A surprising amount of early American glass and flasks survived because they fulfilled this latter role.

References: Gary E. Baker, et al, *Wheeling Glass, 1829–1939: Collection of the Oglebay Institute Glass Museum,* 1994, distributed by Antique Publications; Corning Museum of Glass and the American Committee of the International Assoc for the History of Glass, *Glass Collections in Museums in the United States and Canada,* The Corning Museum of Glass, 1982; Harold Newman, *An Illustrated Dictionary of Glass,* Thames and Hudson, 1977; Mark Pickvet, *The Official Price Guide to Glassware,* House of Collectibles, 1995; Ellen Tischbein Schroy, *Warman's Glass, Second Edition,* Wallace–Homestead, Krause Publications, 1995; Jane Shadel Spillman, *Glass Tableware, Bowls & Vases, Vol 1, The Knopf Collectors' Guides to American Antiques,* Alfred A. Knopf, 1982; Jane Shadel Spillman, *Glass Bottles, Lamps & Other Objects, Vol 2, The Knopf Collectors' Guides to American Antiques,* Alfred A. Knopf, 1983; Kenneth Wilson, *American Glass 1760–1930: The Toledo Museum of Art,* 2 volumes, Hudson Hills Press and the Toledo Museum of Art, 1994.

Periodicals: *Antique Bottle & Glass Collector,* PO Box 180, East Greenville, PA 18041; *Glass Collector's Digest,* PO Box 553, Marietta, OH 45750; *The Daze,* PO Box 57, Otisville, MI 48463.

Museums: Bennington Museum, Bennington, VT; Bergstrom–Mahler Museum, Neenah, WI; Chrysler Museum, Norfolk, VA; Corning Museum of Glass, Corning, NY; Currier Gallery of Art, Manchester, NH; Glass Museum, Dunkirk, IN; Glass Museum Foundation, Redlands, CA 92373; High Museum of Art, Atlanta, GA; Huntingdon Galleries, Huntingdon, WV; Jones Museum of Glass & Ceramics, East Baldwin, ME 04024; Lightner Museum, St Augustine, FL; Museum of American Glass at Wheaton Village, Millville, NJ; Rockwell Museum, Corning, NY; Toledo Museum of Art, Toledo, OH.

BOTTLES

Bottle hunters know that a rural farmstead's dump and outhouse sites are prime locations for digging up a wealth of old bottles. The rural family used a wide variety of bottled products in the course of their daily activities.

In a society where daily bathing and use of deodorant did not become standard practice until well into the twentieth century, males as well as females used cologne or toilet water. It often was stored on bedroom bureaus or washstands in art glass and paint–decorated bottles similar to those found in the barber shop.

Rural America relied heavily on bitters and other types of patent medicines to fight illness and provide relief from a host of aches and pains. Bitters, often sold as a universal cure-all, was a remedy made from natural herbs and other ingredients usually mixed with a base that had a high alcohol content. Anyone could apply for a medicine patent, the first such patent being issued by the United States Patent Office in 1796. The only criteria was that the concoction not be poisonous.

Bitters and patent medicines were sold at the general store, through newspaper and magazine advertisements, and by "medicine show" barkers. Bitter and patent medicine almanac advertisements, broadsides, and trade cards make a wonderful secondary collection.

Manufacturers used a wide variety of bottle colors, shapes, and sizes to attract customers to their brand of bitters or patent medicine. Many bottles had the name of the "medicine" and/or manufacturer either impressed or in relief on their surface. Most were manufactured at glass plants in western Pennsylvania and Ohio.

In 1907 the Pure Food and Drug Act required that all medicines contain a label that accurately described the medicine's contents. This ended the bitters and patent medicine era. It also led to the era of established regional and national medicine brands, the bottles of which are highly collectible. Further, many of these medicines were sold in boxes with elaborate calligraphy and artwork.

Poison was used extensively in rural America for rodent control and other reasons. Manufacturers used shape (coffin), symbols (skull and crossbones), and raised letters (POISON) to identify poison bottles and prevent the accidental intake or misuse of their contents. John Howell of Newton, New Jersey, developed the first safety closure in 1866. It was not until the 1930s that the concept became popular.

Whiskey warmed the soul and also was used for medicinal purposes. The earliest whiskey bottles were hand blown or molded. The Biningers produced the first commercially manufactured whiskey bottles in the 1820s. By the 1860s, distillers utilized the cylindrical fifth shape.

The 1860s' E. G. Booz Old Cabin Whiskey amber bottle was the first embossed brand-name bottle. Folklore attributes the "booz" designation for whiskey to this bottle. Not true. "Booze" is a corruption of the sixteenth– and seventeenth–century words "bouse" and "boosy." It was mere coincidence that a Philadelphia manufacturer named Booz used the first embossed whiskey bottle. Beware, the E. G. Booz bottle has been reproduced more than a dozen times.

Barber, medicine, poison, and whiskey bottles are only the tip of the iceberg relative to the use of bottles in rural America. Ink and mineral (soda) bottles are other possible collecting categories.

Always emphasize condition. Do not buy bottles that are clouded or have other problems. Study the market before buying. Bottles that are scarce in one region may be plentiful in another. Beware of paying too much for commonly available examples.

References: Ralph and Terry Kovel, *The Kovels' Bottles Price List, Tenth Edition,* Crown Publishers, 1996; Jim Megura, *The Official Identification and Price Guide to Bottles, Eleventh Edition,* House of Collectibles, 1991; Michael Polak, *Bottles: Identification and Price Guide, Second Edition,* Avon Books, 1997; Carlo and Dorothy Sellari, *The Standard Old Bottle Price Guide,* Collector Books, 1989, 1997 value update.

Periodical: *Antique Bottle and Glass Collector,* PO Box 180, East Greenville, PA 18041.

Newsletter: *The Bitters Report,* PO Box 1253, Bunnell, FL 32110.

Collectors' Clubs: Federation of Historical Bottle Collectors, Inc, 88 Sweetbriar Branch, Longwood, FL 32750; Midwest Antique Fruit Jar & Bottle Club, PO Box 38, Flat Rock, IN 47234.

Museums: Hawaii Bottle Museum, Honolulu, HI; National Bottle Museum, Ballston Spa, NY; Old Bottle Museum, Salem, NJ.

Note: Consult *Maloney's Antiques & Collectibles Resource Directory,* by David J. Maloney, Jr., at your local library for regional bottle clubs.

Barber, clear, copper wheel cut "Checkerberry" lettering, smooth base, rolled lip, 1885–1925, 6⅝" h	**$75**
Barber, clear, raised rib pattern, cobalt blue coloration near smooth base, ground lip, 1885–1925, 7½" h	**325**
Barber, clear, red, white, and yellow overall splotch pattern, smooth base, tooled lip, 1885–1925, 9¼" h	**600**
Barber, cranberry, hobnail pattern, polished pontil, rolled lip, 1890–1920, 7⅛" h	**175**
Barber, opalescent clear, white swirled stripe pattern, smooth base, rolled lip, some light inside haze, 1885–1925, 9" h	**135**
Barber, opalescent cranberry, white Coinspot pattern, smooth base, rolled lip, 1885–1925, 6⅝" h	**625**
Barber, opalescent cranberry, white swirled stripe pattern, smooth base, rolled lip, 1885–1925, 8⅛" h	**650**
Barber, opalescent cranberry, white vertical stripe pattern, smooth base, rolled lip, 1885–1925, 7" h	**400**
Barber, opalescent cranberry frosted, white vertical stripes, melon ribbed, smooth base, rolled lip, 1885–1925, 6⅞" h	**185**
Barber, opalescent turquoise blue, Spanish Lace pattern, polished pontil, rolled lip, 1885–1925, 8⅛" h	**500**
Barber, turquoise blue, ribbed, smooth base, sheared lip, 1885–1925, 6¾" h	**70**
Barber, yellow with amber tone, Hobnail pattern, smooth base, rolled lip, 1885–1925, 7⅜" h	**75**

Bitters, 7–Up green, emb "Dr. Loew's Celebrated Stomach Bitters & Nerve Tonic, The Loew & Sons Co., Cleveland, O.," smooth base, tooled mouth, faint inside haze, 1890–1910, 9¼" h **150**

Bitters, amber, emb "Reed's Bitters," smooth base, applied double collar mouth, lady's leg neck, milky outside stain and ¼" iridescent bruise near neck, 1865–75, 12³/₈" h **125**

Bitters, aqua, "Poor Man's Family Bitters" on 99% orig wraparound label, smooth base, tooled lip, 1–cent tax stamp across lip, orig contents, 1885–95, 6³/₈" h **100**

Bitters, deep burgundy, figural ear of corn, "National Bitters," smooth base, applied mouth with ring, some external haze and wear, 1860–80, 12¼" h . . **675**

Bitters, deep yellow olive, cylindrical, "H M Crooke's Stomach Bitters," smooth base, applied sloping collared mouth, bulbous neck, chip on mouth filled with epoxy, light external haze, 1860–80, 10³/₈" h **1,100**

Bitters, golden yellow amber, emb "Dr. Campbells Scotch Bitters," strapside shape, smooth base, tooled mouth, light inside haze spots, 1880–90, ½ pt, 6¼" h **425**

Bitters, medium amber, "Baker's, Orange Grove, Bitters" label, emb "Baker's" on side, smooth base, applied sloping collar mouth, 95% orig label, 1860–70, 9½" h **375**

Bitters, medium amber, "Big Bill, Best, Bitters" label, smooth base, tooled mouth, 90% orig front label, 98% orig reverse label, 1900–10, 12" h **130**

Left: Bitters, light yellow amber with olive tone, "Old Dr. Townsend's Celebrated Stomach Bitters," flattened chestnut form, applied mouth with ring, pontil scar, 1840–60, 8½" h, $10,000. Photo courtesy Norman C. Heckler.

Center: Pattern and Blown, globular, medium golden amber, 24 ribs swirled to left, turned over collar, pontil, Zanesville, OH, 8³/₈" h, $385. Photo courtesy Collector's Sales and Service.

Right: Poison, figural coffin, medium amber, emb "Poison" on front and back and "Norwich" on smooth base, tooled lip, 1890–1910, 4⁷/₈" h, $850. Photo courtesy Glass–Works Auctions.

Bitters, medium yellow olive, figural fish, emb "The Fish Bitters," smooth base with emb "W.H. Ware Patent 1866," applied mouth, 1866–70, 11½" h **2,500**

Bitters, olive green, 8–sided, emb "Bryant's Stomach Bitters," pontil scarred base, applied sloping double collar mouth, lady's leg neck, dullness and some light scratching, 1857–60, 12" h **6,750**

Bitters, orange amber, oval with fluted shoulder, "Dr Gillmore's Laxative Kidney & Liver Bitters," smooth base, sloping collared mouth with ring, 1880–1900, 10⅛" h **110**

Bitters, orange amber, rect modified cabin shape, "Dr Bishop's WaHoo Bitters," smooth base, crudely applied square collared mouth, ¼" flat chip on mouth, some ext haze, 1860–80, 10⅛" h **425**

Bitters, yellow, figural ear of corn, emb "National Bitters" on front and "Patent 1867" on smooth base, applied mouth, 1867–75, 12⅝" h **1,000**

Bitters, yellow amber, 4–sided log cabin, emb "S.T. Drake's, 1860 Plantation, X Bitters, Patented 1862," smooth base, applied sloping collar mouth, 1862–70, 10⅜" h **80**

Bitters, yellow amber, Indian Queen figural, emb "Brown's Celebrated Indian Herb Bitters, Patented 1868," smooth base, rolled lip, shallow ⅜" chip on edge of skirt, 1868–75, 12¼" h **425**

Bitters, yellow amber, square with beveled corners, "Fulton M McRae Yazoo Valley Bitters," smooth base, applied sloping collared mouth, some light internal haze, 1870–90, 8⅝" h **160**

Bitters, yellow amber, triangular, "Morning Star Bitters," iron pontil mark, applied sloping collared mouth, flake on base corner, 1850–60, 11¾" h ... **160**

Ink, deep bluish aqua, semi–cottage shape, emb "Stuarts Ink – Made Only By Stuart & Harrison – Toledo Iowa," smooth base, applied mouth, 1860–70, 3⅛" h **200**

Ink, electric cobalt blue, 8–sided umbrella, unmkd, smooth base, tooled lip, 1875–85, 2¾" h **475**

Ink, medium emerald green, 8–sided umbrella, emb "Hover, Phila," pontil scarred base, rolled lip, tiny corner base flakes, 1845–55, ⅜" h **200**

Ink, medium sapphire blue, emb "Harrison's Columbian Ink," open pontil, applied mouth, 1845–55, 4⅛" h **500**

Ink, pale bluish aqua, barrel shape, emb "W.E. Bonney," "Bonney Writing Ink, Bost...," on 90% orig label, smooth base, partially rolled lip, 1855–65, 2⅝" h **90**

Medicine, amber, figural log, "Tippecanoe, H.H. Warner & Co." on 97% orig front label, emb "Tippecanoe" on reverse and "Pat. Nov. 20 83, Rochester N.Y." on smooth base, applied mouth, orig contents and tax stamp, 1875–95, 9" h **450**

Medicine, aqua, emb "U.F.M. & P.K. – Phila," 99% orig label reads "True University's Remedy, for the relief of Costive Bowels...," 6–sided, pontil scarred base, rolled lip, orig contents, 1835–45, 2⅛" h **130**

Medicine, clear, emb "Dr. L.E. Keeley's Double Chloride of Cold Cure for Neurasthenia, a Tested and Infallible Remedy, Discovered by Dr. L.E. Keeley, Dwight, Ills. – K.G.C., Lisle E. Keeley M.D.," smooth base, tooled mouth, 1890–1905, 5¾" h **400**

Medicine, deep aqua, emb "Turner's, Sarsaparilla, Buffalo N.Y.," smooth base, applied sloping collar mouth, highly whittled glass, 1855–65, 12¼" h **450**

Medicine, deep bluish aqua, emb "Dr. Kennedy's, Medical Discovery, Roxbury Mass," open pontil, applied sloping collar mouth, 1845–55, 8³/₄" h **125**

Medicine, deep cobalt blue, emb "The Bolton Drug Co., Improved Magnesia, Brooklyn," smooth base, tooled mouth, 1885–1900, 6³/₄" h **165**

Medicine, medium amber, inverted emb "Rohrer's, Expectoral, Wild Cherry Tonic, Lancaster, PA," smooth base, applied sloping double collar mouth, 1855–65, 10⁵/₈" h **225**

Medicine, yellowish olive amber, emb "Hampton's V Tincture, Mortimer & Mowbray, Balto," open pontil, applied mouth, 1845–55, 6¹/₄" h **1,200**

Pattern and Blown, amber, blown, globular, 24 swirled ribs with good impression, applied lip, stain, Zanesville, 9¹/₄" h **1,050**

Pattern and Blown, aqua, blown, globular, miniature, 20 swirled ribs, applied lip, Kent, 5³/₈" h **225**

Pattern and Blown, aqua, blown, globular, miniature, 30 ribs, applied lip, 5³/₈" h **300**

Pattern and Blown, aqua, blown, globular, 32 slightly swirled ribs, applied lip, handle, and foot, wear, 4³/₄" h **875**

Pattern and Blown, citron, blown, globular, 24 swirled ribs with good impression, applied lip, slight stain and shallow broken blisters, Zanesville, 7³/₄" h **9,100**

Pattern and Blown, deep bluish aqua, blown, globular, 24 swirled ribs, pontil scarred base, applied double collar mouth, minor inside base stain, Midwestern, 1820–30, 7⁷/₈" h **175**

Pattern and Blown, honey olive, blown, globular, 24 melon ribs with good impression, applied lip, minor wear and scratches, Zanesville, 8³/₈" h **550**

Pattern and Blown, honey olive, blown, globular, 24 swirled ribs, applied lip, minor wear, Zanesville, 7³/₄" h **1,300**

Pattern and Blown, honey olive, blown, globular, 25 melon ribs, applied lip, wear and scratches with star bruise at blister in side, Midwestern, 8" h **250**

Pattern and Blown, light sapphire blue, blown 3 mold, toilet water, pontil scarred base, flared lip, 1815–30, 5¹/₄" h **130**

Pattern and Blown, medium violet cobalt blue, blown 3 mold toilet water, pontil scarred base, rolled and flared lip, 1815–30, 5¹/₄" h **700**

Poison, cobalt blue, "Chester A. Baker, Boston" emb on front and "C.L.G. Co., Patent Applied For" on smooth base, tooled lip, 1890–1910, 5" h **300**

Poison, cobalt blue, lattice and diamond pattern, smooth base, tooled lip, orig emb "POISON" stopper, 1890–1910, 5¹/₂" h **100**

Poison, deep cobalt blue, "Poison, Bowman's Drug Stores, Poison" emb on front and "C.L.G. Co., Pat Appld For" on smooth base, tooled lip, overall light stain, 1890–1910, 2³/₄" h **175**

Poison, deep cobalt blue, "U.S.P.H.S." emb on smooth base, tooled lip, lattice and diamond pattern, bubbles and impurities swirl around bottle, gallon size, 1890–1910, 13¹/₄" h **1,750**

Poison, deep red amber, emb "Poison" on front and side, smooth base, tooled lip, "Lilly" on orig cork, 1890–1910, 10¹/₄" h **145**

Poison, medium cobalt blue, figural skull, emb "Poison" on skull forehead, "Pat Appl'd For" near base, and "Pat. June 26th 1894" on smooth base, tooled lip, neck professionally repaired, 1890–1910, 3⁵/₈" h **325**

Soda & Mineral Water, cobalt blue, emb "Seitz & Bro – Easton PA – Premium – Mineral – Waters," 8–sided, iron pontil, applied blob–type mouth, 1845–55, 7⁵/₈" h **250**

Soda & Mineral Water, deep cobalt blue, emb "A. Dearborn & Co, New York, Mineral Water, D, This Bottle is Never Sold," iron pontil, applied sloping collar mouth, ground imperfections and ¼" iridescent bruise on inside of lip, 1845–55, 7¼" h **85**

Soda & Mineral Water, deep emerald green, emb "G.A. Kohl, Lambertville, N.J.," iron pontil, applied sloping double collar mouth, 1845–55, 7⅛" h . .   **75**

Soda & Mineral Water, deep reddish amber, emb "Hennessey & Nolan, Albany, Ny – Hoxsie," smooth base, applied mouth, some letters are faint, 1855–70, pt, 6¾" h **80**

Soda & Mineral Water, deep sapphire blue, emb "Heiss, Philada – H, Union Glass Works, Philada," and 5–pointed star, iron pontil, applied sloping collar mouth, minor ground imperfections, 1845–55, 7⅜" h **85**

Soda & Mineral Water, medium blue–green, emb "P.Babb – Balto," iron pontil, applied sloping double collar mouth, 1845–55, 8¼" h **500**

Soda & Mineral Water, medium cobalt blue, emb "C. Lomax, Chicago" inside shield, iron pontil, applied blob–type mouth, shallow ⅛" flake on corner of base, 1845–55, 7¼" h **200**

Soda & Mineral Water, medium sapphire blue, emb "W.P. – Knicker – Bocker – Soda Water –164 18th St. N.Y. 1848," 10–sided, iron pontil, applied blob–type mouth, some ground imperfections, 1845–55, 7¾" h **145**

Soda & Mineral Water, medium yellowish amber, emb "Caladonia, Spring, Wheelock VT.," smooth base, applied sloping double collar mouth, ⁵/₈" l thin hairline crack on int shoulder, qt, 1865–75, 9½" h **190**

Soda & Mineral Water, orange amber, emb "M & J.S. Perrine, Importers, 37 North Front, Philada" on front and "Dyottville Glass Works Philada" on smooth base, applied sloping double collar mouth, whittled glass, qt, 1855–65, 8⅞" h **850**

Whiskey, aqua, figural pig, emb "Crescent" inside crescent moon and "Duffy, 124 Jefferson Street, Louisville, KY.," smooth base, ground lip, 1870–80, 7⁵/₈" l **1,800**

Whiskey, bluish aqua, "Old Hermitage Pure Rye Sour Mash Whisky, W.A. Gaines & Co., Frankfort, Kentucky" on 98% orig 3–sided wraparound label depicting riverfront scene, emb "H.B. Kirk & Co., Wine Merchant, New York, Estabd 1853," smooth base, tooled mouth, iridescent bruise on inside of lip, 1885–90, 7⅞" h **225**

Whiskey, clear, slight amethyst tint, figural pig, emb "Crescent" inside crescent moon and "Duffy, 124 Jefferson Street, Louisville, KY.," smooth base, ground lip, 1970–80, 7⁵/₈" l **700**

Whiskey, deep bluish aqua, emb "Geekie, 123 Baltimore St., MD," strapside shape, smooth base, applied mouth, mfg imperfection near base, 1870–80, 1 pt **140**

Whiskey, deep reddish puce amber, emb "R.B. Cutter, Pure Bourbon," pontil scarred base, applied mouth and handle, small chip on lower lip near handle, 1855–70, 8½" h **220**

Whiskey, medium yellowish amber, figural cabin, emb "E.G. Booz's, Old Cabin Whiskey, 120 Walnut St., Philadelphia," smooth base, applied sloping collar mouth, 1865–76, 7¾" h **2,250**

DEPRESSION GLASS

The country housewife welcomed utilitarian glassware for the country table. By the post–World War I period utilitarian glassware was readily available, durable, and inexpensive. Many patterns were produced in full table settings and often in a variety of colors.

When interest developed in collecting glass stemware and tableware from the post–World War I era in the early 1950s, a select group of patterns were classified as "Depression Glass." The label stuck. Unfortunately, such a designation contains more problems than it resolves.

First, many of the patterns were introduced long before the 1929 Depression. Second, many of the patterns continued in production long after the Depression ended. Third, the pattern selection was narrow, ignoring hundreds of patterns that were also produced during that period. Finally, antiques dealers used the "Depression Glass" label against these popular twentieth–century glass patterns. "Depression Glass" in their minds became that cheap junk that was sold in the five–and–dime or given away as premiums.

The Depression Era label continues to create more negatives than positives in the collecting of twentieth century glassware. It is time to abandon the concept. The dates simply are no longer meaningful as we move further and further away from the 1929 to 1940 period and glassware collecting interests expand into the 1950s and 60s.

A much better designation for this glassware is Twentieth–Century Utilitarian Household Glassware, a term used to cover mass–produced, mass–marketed glass manufactured from the 1920s through the present. The date is based on the assumption that for collecting purposes, the twentieth century actually started after World War I. Admittedly, the designation is a mouthful; but, it reflects the reality of the current collecting situation.

Such an approach puts the emphasis where it belongs—identity of major and minor patterns and allows prices to dictate which are the most desired. Collecting popularity is the key.

References: Gene Florence, *Collectible Glassware from the 40's, 50's, 60's: An Illustrated Value Guide, Fourth Edition,* Collector Books, 1998; Gene Florence, *The Collector's Encyclopedia of Depression Glass, Thirteenth Edition,* Collector Books, 1998; Gene Florence, *Elegant Glassware of the Depression Era, Seventh Edition,* Collector Books, 1995; Gene Florence, *Kitchen Glassware of the Depression Years, Fifth Edition,* Collector Books, 1995, 1997 value update; Gene Florence, *Very Rare Glassware of the Depression Era, Third Series* (1993), *Fourth Series* (1995), *Fifth Series* (1997), Collector Books; Ralph and Terry Kovel, *Kovels' Depression Glass & American Dinnerware Price List, Fifth Edition,* Crown Publishers, 1995; Carl F. Luckey, *An Identification & Value Guide to Depression Era Glassware, Third Edition,* Books Americana, Krause Publications, 1994; Hazel Marie Weatherman, *Colored Glassware of the Depression Era, Book 2,* published by author; Hazel Marie Weatherman, *1984 Supplement & Price Trends for Colored Glassware of the Depression Era, Book 1,* published by author, 1984.

Periodical: *The Daze,* PO Box 57, Otisville, MI 48463.

Collectors' Clubs: Canadian Depression Glass Club, 1026 Forestwood Drive, Mississaugua, Ontario, L5C 1GB Canada; National Depression Glass Assoc, Inc, PO Box 8264, Wichita, KS 67209; 20–30–40 Society, Inc, PO Box 856, La Grange, IL 60525.

Reproduction Alert: Send a self–addressed stamped business envelope to *The Daze* and request a copy of their glass reproduction list. It is one of the best bargains in the antiques business.

ADAM, JEANNETTE GLASS COMPANY, 1932–1934

Ashtray, green, 4⅝" d	$22
Cake Plate, ftd, green, 10" d	25
Cake Plate, ftd, pink, 10" d	27
Candlesticks, pr, pink	90
Coaster, green	18
Creamer, pink	25
Cup, pink	24
Dessert Bowl, green, 4¾" d	15
Dinner Plate, green, 9" d	27
Dinner Plate, pink, 9" d	30
Platter, oval, green, 11¾" l	27
Platter, oval, pink, 11¾" l	30
Platter, rect, green	30
Relish, 2 part, green, 8" l	27
Salad Plate, green, 7¾" d	15
Salt and Pepper Shakers, pr, pink	75
Saucer, pink	8
Sherbet, ftd, pink, 6" h	28
Sugar, cov, pink	45
Tumbler, green, 4½" h	28
Vegetable Bowl, green, 7¾" d	25

AMERICAN SWEETHEART, MacBETH–EVANS GLASS COMPANY, 1930–1936

Bowl, monax, 9" d	$75
Bowl, pink	65
Bread and Butter Plate, monax, 6" d	7
Cereal Bowl, pink	17
Cream Soup, monax, 4½" d	150
Cup and Saucer, monax	15
Cup and Saucer, pink	22
Dinner Plate, monax, 9¾" d	27
Platter, oval, monax	75
Platter, oval, pink	60
Vegetable Bowl, oval, monax, 11" l	85

BLOCK OPTIC (BLOCK), HOCKING GLASS COMPANY, 1929–1933

Bread and Butter Plate, green, 6" d	$3
Bread and Butter Plate, pink, 6" d	3
Bread and Butter Plate, yellow, 6" d	4
Cereal Bowl, green, 5¼" d	12
Creamer, ftd, yellow	15
Cup, green	6
Dinner Plate, green, 9" d	20
Dinner Plate, yellow, 9" d	45

Luncheon Plate, green, 8" d 5
Luncheon Plate, pink, 8" d 4
Luncheon Plate, yellow, 8" d 7
Sugar, ftd, yellow 12
Tumbler, ftd, pink, 9 oz 15
Tumbler, ftd, yellow, 9 oz 22

CAMEO (BALLERINA, DANCING GIRL), HOCKING GLASS COMPANY, 1930–1934

Bread and Butter Plate, green, 6" d $7
Bread and Butter Plate, yellow, 6" d 5
Butter dish, cov, green 225
Cake Plate, ftd, green 20
Candy Dish 65
Cereal Bowl, yellow 30
Creamer, green, 3¼" h 18
Cream Soup, green 75
Cup, yellow 10
Pitcher, green, 56 oz 50
Platter, oval, green 30
Relish, 3 part, green 25
Sherbet, green, 3⅛" h 15
Sugar, green, 3¼" h 20
Tumbler, ftd, yellow, 11 oz 60
Vase, green, 5¾" h 225
Vegetable Bowl, oval, green 30

CHERRY BLOSSOM, JEANNETTE GLASS COMPANY, 1930–1939

Berry Bowl, individual, green, 4¾" d $17
Berry Bowl, individual, pink, 4¾" d 20
Berry Bowl, master, green, 8½" d 45
Bowl, handled, pink, 9" d 65
Bread and Butter Plate, green, 6" d 7

Cherry Blossom, butter dish, cov, pink, 6" d, $75.

Cake Plate, ftd, pink 30
Creamer and Sugar, cov, green 60
Creamer and Sugar, cov, pink 50
Cup and Saucer, pink 35
Dinner Plate, pink, 9" d 25
Pitcher, flat, green, 42 oz 70
Pitcher, flat, pink, 42 oz 60
Platter, oval, green, 11" l 45
Platter, oval, pink, 11" l 50
Salad Plate, green, 7" d 22
Sherbet, green 20
Sherbet, pink 17

COLONIAL (KNIFE AND FORK), HOCKING GLASS COMPANY, 1934–1936

Berry Bowl, individual, green, 4½" d $17
Butter Dish, cov, clear 37
Cocktail, clear, 3 oz, 4" h 15
Creamer, green 25
Cup and Saucer, pink 17
Dinner Plate, green, 10" d 50
Goblet, 5¾" h 25
Grill Plate, pink, 10" d 27
Pitcher, with ice lip, clear, 54 oz 40
Platter, oval, green, 12" l 25
Sherbet, ftd, pink, 3⅜" h 12
Sugar, green, 4" h 12
Tumbler, flat, pink, 5 oz, 4" h 20
Vegetable Bowl, oval, green, 10" l 25

CUBE (CUBIST), JEANNETTE GLASS COMPANY, 1929–1933

Bowl, pink, 6½" d $12
Bread and Butter Plate, pink, 6" d 4
Butter Dish, cov, pink 70

Cube, creamer and sugar, pink, $20.

Candy Jar, cov, green 25
Candy Jar, cov, pink 27
Coaster, green 7
Creamer, large, green 10
Cup and Saucer, green 11
Dessert Bowl, green, 4½" d 8
Pitcher, pink 250
Powder Jar, cov, green 28
Powder Jar, cov, pink 27
Salad Plate, green, 8" d 10
Salt and Pepper Shakers, pr, green 32
Saucer, pink 3
Sherbet, ftd, pink 8
Tumbler, green, 9 oz, 4" h 70

DOGWOOD (APPLE BLOSSOM, WILD ROSE), MacBETH–EVANS GLASS COMPANY, 1929–1932

Berry Bowl, master, pink, 8½" d $55
Bowl, green, 10¼" d 275
Cake Plate, green, 13" d 125
Cake Plate, pink, 13" d 140
Cereal Bowl, pink, 5½" d 30
Creamer, green 55
Cup, monax 35
Cup and Saucer, green 45
Pitcher, dec, pink 180
Plate, green, 8" d 9
Plate, pink, 8" d 7
Salver, monax 20
Salver, pink 25
Saucer, green 10
Saucer, pink 5
Sherbet, pink 35
Tumbler, green, 10 oz, 4" h 85
Tumbler, pink, 10 oz, 4" h 40

FLORENTINE NO. 2 (POPPY NO. 2), HAZEL ATLAS GLASS COMPANY, 1932–1935

Ashtray, green, 5½" d $17
Berry Bowl, master, yellow, 8" d 32
Butter Dish, cov, clear 100
Butter Dish, cov, yellow 150
Candleholder, green 30
Candlesticks, pr, green 65
Candlesticks, pr, yellow 60
Candy Dish, green 120
Candy Dish, yellow 150
Comport, ruffled, clear, 3½" d 12
Creamer, ftd, clear 8

Creamer, green 12
Creamer, yellow 15
Cream Soup, green 15
Cup and Saucer, yellow 15
Custard Cup, clear 50
Custard Cup, yellow 80
Dinner Plate, green, 10" d 15
Gravy Boat and Underplate, yellow 90
Grill Plate, yellow 10
Parfait, ftd, yellow, 6" h 65
Pitcher, cone, clear 22
Pitcher, cone, yellow 30
Platter, green 17
Platter, yellow 22
Relish, 3 part, 10" l 35
Salad Plate, yellow, 8½" d 17
Salt and Pepper Shakers, pr, green 50
Salt and Pepper Shakers, pr, yellow 65
Sherbet, green 8
Sherbet, yellow 12
Sugar, ftd, clear 8
Sugar, ltd, green 12
Tumbler, ftd, clear, 3¼" h 13
Vegetable Bowl, cov, oval, yellow, 9" l 75

IRIS (IRIS AND HERRINGBONE), JEANNETTE GLASS COMPANY, 1928–1932; 1950s; 1970s

Berry Bowl, individual, beaded, clear, 4½" d $40
Butter Dish, cov, clear 50
Cup and Saucer, clear 30
Dinner Plate, clear, 9" d 50
Pitcher, clear 40
Pitcher, iridescent, 9½" h 40
Sandwich Plate, iridescent, 11¾" d 35
Sherbet, clear 30
Sugar, cov, iridescent 12
Vase, clear, 9" h 30

LACE EDGE (OPEN LACE, OLD COLONY), HOCKING GLASS COMPANY, 1935–1938

Butter Dish, cov, pink $70
Cereal Bowl, pink, 6½" d 20
Creamer and Sugar, pink 45
Cup and Saucer, pink 37
Dinner Plate, pink, 10½" d 25
Grill Plate, pink 22
Luncheon Plate, pink, 8¾" d 20
Platter, oval, pink 35
Relish, 3 part, pink, 10½" d 30
Salad Bowl, pink, 9½" d 30

Salad Plate, pink, 8¼" d 25
Saucer, pink 22
Sherbet, ftd, pink 85

MADRID, FEDERAL GLASS COMPANY, 1932–1939; INDIANA GLASS COMPANY, 1980s

Butter Dish, cov, amber $65
Cake Plate, amber, 11¼" d 18
Cookie Jar, cov, amber 50
Cream Soup, amber, 4¾" d 15
Cup and Saucer, amber 12
Luncheon Plate, amber, 8⅞" d 7
Platter, amber, oval, 11½" d 25
Salad Plate, amber, 7½" d 9
Salt and Pepper Shakers, pr, flat, amber, 3½" h 40
Tumbler, ftd, amber, 10 oz, 5½" h 25

MANHATTAN (HORIZONTAL RIBBED), ANCHOR HOCKING GLASS COMPANY, 1938–1943

Ashtray, clear, square $20
Candy Dish, ftd, pink 12
Cereal Bowl, handled, pink, 5¾" d 18
Coaster, clear 15
Dinner Plate, clear, 10¼" d 19
Fruit Bowl, ftd, pink, 9½" d 40
Sandwich Plate, 5 part, clear, 14" d 20
Sherbet, pink 15
Sugar, pink 10
Vase, clear, 8" h 20

MAYFAIR (OPEN ROSE), HOCKING GLASS COMPANY, 1931–1937

Butter Dish, cov, blue $275
Cake Plate, ftd, pink 30
Celery, divided, blue 65
Creamer, blue 80
Cup and Saucer, blue 27
Dinner Plate, pink 50
Fruit Bowl, scalloped rim, green, 12" d 35
Pitcher, blue, 6" h 150
Pitcher, pink, 6" h 60
Platter, oval, blue 75
Platter, oval, pink 32
Relish, 4 part, pink 40
Sandwich Server, center handle, blue 85
Sandwich Server, center handle, pink 45
Sherbet, flat, blue, 2¼" h 35
Vegetable Bowl, blue, 7" d 50

MODERNTONE, HAZEL ATLAS GLASS COMPANY, 1934–1942; LATE 1940s–EARLY 1950s

Berry Bowl, master, cobalt blue, 8" d	$65
Creamer and Sugar, amethyst	20
Creamer and Sugar, cobalt blue	37
Cream Soup, amethyst	17
Cream Soup, cobalt blue	25
Cup and Saucer, amethyst	12
Cup and Saucer, cobalt blue	20
Platter, amethyst, 12" d	40
Salt and Pepper Shakers, pr, cobalt blue	45
Sherbet, cobalt blue	20
Sugar, amethyst	12
Tumbler, cobalt blue, 5 oz	50

PRINCESS, HOCKING GLASS COMPANY, 1931–1935

Bowl, green, 9"d	$37
Bowl, yellow, 9" d	125
Cake Stand, ftd, green, 10" d	27
Cereal Bowl, yellow, 5" d	30
Creamer, yellow	20
Cup, green	12
Cup, yellow	20
Grill Plate, handled, green, 10½" d	15
Hat Shaped Bowl, green, 9½" w	40
Pitcher, yellow, 60 oz	75
Salad Bowl, octagonal, green, 9" d	45
Salt and Pepper Shakers, pr, green	55
Saucer, green	12
Sherbet, ftd, green	22
Sherbet, ftd, yellow	35
Tumbler, ftd, green, 13 oz, 5¼" h	37
Tumbler, ftd, yellow, 13 oz, 5¼" h	25
Vegetable Bowl, oval, green, 10" l	25
Vegetable Bowl, oval, yellow, 10" l	60

ROYAL RUBY, ANCHOR HOCKING GLASS COMPANY, 1938–1940

Ashtray	$10
Bowl, 4¾" d	8
Creamer and Sugar	15
Cup and Saucer	10
Dish, leaf shaped, handled, 6½" l	10
Pitcher, 3 qt	45
Salad Bowl, 11¾" d	35
Tumbler, 13 oz	14
Vase, 9" h	20

SANDWICH, INDIANA GLASS COMPANY, 1920s–EARLY 1930s

Bowl, green, 7" d **$125**
Creamer and Sugar, green 55
Cup, green 25
Juice Pitcher, green 200
Sugar, cov, green 25
Tumbler, juice, green 5

SHARON (CABBAGE ROSE), FEDERAL GLASS COMPANY, 1935–1939

Berry Bowl, individual, amber, 5" **$7**
Berry Bowl, individual, green, 5" 14
Bread and Butter Plate, amber, 6" d 5
Bread and Butter Plate, green, 6" d 8
Butter Dish, cov, amber 47
Butter Dish, cov, green 90
Cake Plate, ftd, pink, 11½" d 40
Candy Dish, cov, amber 45
Cereal Bowl, pink, 6" d 25
Creamer and Sugar, cov, amber 45
Cream Soup, green 55
Cup and Saucer, amber 12
Fruit Bowl, green, 10½" d 38
Salad Plate, pink, 7½" d 27
Salt and Pepper Shakers, pr, amber 37
Sherbet, ftd, amber 10
Sugar, green 18
Vegetable Bowl, oval, green, 9½" l 32

SWIRL (PETAL SWIRL), JEANNETTE GLASS COMPANY, 1937–1938

Candlesticks, pr, ultramarine **$45**
Cereal Bowl, ultramarine 13
Creamer, ftd, ultramarine 15
Dinner Plate, ultramarine 15

*Swirl, cup and saucer,
ultramarine, $25.*

Salad Bowl, ultramarine, 9" d   22
Salt and Pepper Shakers, pr, ultramarine   45
Sandwich Plate, ultramarine, 12" d   22
Sherbet, ultramarine   20
Tumbler, ftd, ultramarine, 9 oz   45
Vase, ftd, ultramarine, 8½" h....................................   23

EARLY AMERICAN GLASS

Early American glass covers glass made in America from the colonial period through the mid–nineteenth century. As such, it includes the early pressed glass and lacy glass made between 1827 and 1840.

Major glass producing centers prior to 1850 were: Massachusetts with the New England Glass Company and the Boston and Sandwich Glass Company; South Jersey; Pennsylvania with Stiegel's Manheim factory and Pittsburgh; and Ohio with Kent, Mantua, and Zanesville.

Early American glass was collected heavily during the 1920 to 1950 period, regaining some of its earlier popularity in the mid–1980s. In the Country movement, its role is largely as a decorative accessory.

Leading sources for the sale of early American glass are the mail auctions of Collector's Sales and Service and Glass Works Auctions and the auctions of Richard A. Bourne, Early Auction Company, Garth's, Norman C. Heckler & Company, and Skinners.

References: William E. Covill, *Ink Bottles and Inkwells,* 1971; Lowell Inness, *Pittsburgh Glass: 1797–1891,* Houghton Mifflin Co, 1976; George and Helen McKearin, *American Glass,* Crown Publishers, 1948; George and Helen McKearin, *Two Hundred Years of American Blown Glass,* Doubleday and Co, 1950; Helen McKearin and Kenneth Wilson, *American Bottles and Flasks,* Crown Publishers, 1978; Adeline Pepper, *Glass Gaffers of New Jersey,* Scribners, 1971; Jane S. Spillman, *American and European Pressed Glass,* Corning Museum of Glass, 1981; Kenneth Wilson, *New England Glass and Glassmaking,* Crowell, 1972.

Periodical: *China & Glass Quarterly,* PO Box 39, Portsmouth, RI 02871.

Collectors' Clubs: Early American Glass Traders, RD 5, Box 638, Milford, DE 19963; Glass Research Society of New Jersey, Wheaton Village, 1501 Glasstown Road, Millville, NJ 08332; The National Early American Glass Club, PO Box 8489, Silver Spring, MD 20907.

Museums: The Jones Museum of Glass & Ceramics, East Sebago, ME; New Bedford Glass Museum, New Bedford, MA; Sandwich Glass Museum, Sandwich, MA.

Bowl, green, blown, goblet shaped bowl, hollow stem, applied foot, 12⅞" h .   **$95**
Bowl, light green, blown, folded rim, applied foot, minor wear and scratch-
   es, Zanesville, 7¼" d, 4⅞" h **1,650**
Bowl, light green, blown, rim shaped, ftd, knop stem, 6¾" d, 7½" h **110**
Bowl, yellow, blown, flowerpot shape, folded lip, applied foot, 4⅞" h **125**
Canister, cov, clear, blown, cylindrical, 2 applied cobalt blue rings on jar,
   1 on lid, lid with cobalt finial on applied handle, 10" h **800**
Celery Vase, clear, flint, elaborately cut bowl with panels and diamonds,
   knop stem, star cut foot, minor wear and pinpoint rim flakes, Pittsburgh,
   9⅜" h **1,000**

Compote, clear, flint, bowl with cut diamond band and double band of almond shaped segments, baluster stem, unusual stepped foot, int wear and scratches, Pittsburgh, 8" d, 7" h **110**

Compote, clear, flint, bowl with 8 panels and eight sides with cut floral design, reverse baluster stem, applied foot, Pittsburgh, 4³/₄" d, 5" h **325**

Compote, clear, flint, bowl with folded lip and copper wheel engraved vintage design, hollow baluster stem, applied foot, Pittsburgh, 6¹/₂" d, 6¹/₄" h . . **85**

Compote, clear, flint, Loop and Petal pattern with bull's eyes on bowl, chips on foot, 10³/₄" d, 6¹/₂" h **250**

Compote, violet and amethyst, blown, swirled, applied stem and foot, 7¹/₂" d, 6¹/₂" h **775**

Creamer, aqua, blown, tooled lip, applied hollow handle, Zanesville, 4³/₄" h . **2,500**

Cruet, clear, flint, pillar mold, applied foot and hollow handle, pewter hinged lid, Pittsburgh, 10¹/₂" h **525**

Cuspidor, amber, blown, folded lip, similar witch ball cov, 6¹/₂" d, 4⁷/₈" h **110**

Decanter, amber, pillar mold, cut panels in neck, ribs with cut notches, star cut bottom, matching stopper, minor flakes, 11" h plus stopper **500**

Decanter, clear, blown 3 mold, Baroque, ribbed stopper, stain, 9" h **225**

Decanter, clear, blown 3 mold, swirled, emb "Brandy," matching stopper, light stain, 8¹/₂" h **500**

Decanter, clear, cased cranberry int, pillar mold, applied collar and bulbous lip, neck with cut panels, ribs with cut notches, wear and small flakes, chips on lip, 11¹/₄" h **4,175**

Decanter, deep amethyst, blown, octagonal with panels and ovals, applied lip, 10¹/₄" h **1,650**

Decanter, deep cobalt blue, blown, pillar mold, applied collar and handle, pewter jigger cap, 9³/₄" h **7,925**

Fire Grenade, medium cobalt blue, "Manf'd By Fire Extinguisher M'F'G. Co., Babcock Hand Grenade, Non–Freezing, 325–331 S. Des. Plaines St. Chicago," smooth base, ground lip, c1875–95, qt, 7¹/₂" h **1,300**

Fire Grenade, medium cobalt blue, "Rockford Kalamazoo Automatic and Hand Fire Extinguisher, Patent Applied For," smooth base, tooled mouth, c1890–1910, 11" h **425**

Left: Decanter, blown 3 mold, $375.

Right: Vase, light to medium amethyst, pressed, Circle and Ellipse, gauffered rim, hexagonal base, 1–pc construction, tiny bruise on 1 base point, mild roughness, New England, 1830–40, 7¹/₂" h, $300. Photo courtesy Collector's Sales and Service.

Fire Grenade, smoky grayish amethyst, "Hayward's Hand Fire Grenade – S.F. Hayward, 407 Broadway N.Y. – Patented Aug 8 1871," smooth base, tooled mouth, c1871–85, pt, 6¼" h **375**

Fire Grenade, yellow olive, "Hayward Hand Grenade Fire Extinguisher, No 407 Broadway New York," "Design H Patd" on smooth base, tooled mouth, c1875–90, pt, 6" h **750**

Flip, deep bluish aqua, 24 broken rib pattern swirled to left, pontil scarred base, Midwestern, c1820–30 . . . . **1,500**

Inkwell, aqua, blown, flattened ball shape, applied foot, 4½" d **550**

Inkwell, deep blue aqua, freeblown, pontil scarred base, sheared and tooled mouth, 1825–35, 3⅜" h **450**

Inkwell, deep cobalt blue, teakettle shape, smooth base, ground lip, shallow 3/16" chip on front of lip, 1880–90, 2" h **200**

Inkwell, deep sapphire blue, teakettle shape figural bust of Benjamin Franklin, smooth base, ground lip, orig brass neck band, 1875–95, 2⅞" h . . **2,000**

Inkwell, white milk glass, teakettle shape, smooth base, ground lip, orig sterling silver neck band and lid, 1875–95, 1⅝" h **325**

Jar, cov, clear, flint, pillar mold, bowl with 8 ribs, baluster stem, and wide foot, matching lid with applied finial, Pittsburgh, 17¾" h **1,275**

Milk Bowl, pale yellow, blown, folded rim, minor surface damage probably in the making, Zanesville, 9½" d, 3" h **2,100**

Mug, aqua, blown, straight tapered sides, applied handle, Zanesville, 5½" h . **1,150**

Mug, deep reddish amber, freeblown, tooled rim, applied handle, pontil scarred base, Midwestern, c1820–30 . . . . **4,100**

Nursing Bottle, aqua, blown, bubble filled glass with faint vertical ribs, sheared lip with pinpoints, paper sticker from "Knittle Collection," 6⅜" h . . **85**

Pan, medium amber, blown, folded rim, pontil scarred base, Midwestern, c1820–30, 6¼" d **1,100**

Pitcher, aqua, blown 3 mold, paneled crosshatched pattern, applied handle . . **7,500**

Pitcher, clear, flint, blown, applied ring at neck, applied hollow handle, Pittsburgh, 8⅜" h **385**

Pitcher, clear, flint, blown, tooled lip, applied foot and hollow handle, some wear at handle, Pittsburgh, 7½" h **225**

Pitcher, clear, flint, Cleat pattern, applied handle, 8¼" h **275**

Pitcher, clear, flint, molded rings, applied handle, polished pontil, 8¼" h **165**

Pitcher, clear, flint, pillar mold, applied handle, small open blister, Pittsburgh, 6½" h **400**

Pitcher, cobalt blue, blown, tooled lip, applied hollow handle, Pittsburgh, 7¾" h **4,200**

Pitcher, light green, blown, lily pad, applied foot and handle, wear and scratches, attributed to Ellenville, NY, 7¾" h **4,500**

Salt, deep bluish aqua, 24 vertical rib pattern, double ogee form, tooled flared–out rim, pontil scarred applied foot, Midwestern, c1820–30 . . . . . . **4,500**

Shot Glass, golden yellow amber, 6 sided, polished base, c1865–75, 2½" h . . **175**

Shot Glass, lime green, 6 sided, smooth base, c1865–75, 2" h **85**

Sugar Bowl, cov, aqua, blown, galleried bowl, lid with folded lip and applied finial, Zanesville, 5¾" h **5,500**

Sugar Bowl, cov, clear, flint, galleried bowl with copper wheel engraved flowers and foliage, baluster stem, applied foot, engraved band on lid, Pittsburgh, 8" h **2,500**

Sugar Bowl, cov, clear, flint, galleried bowl with strawberry diamonds and roundels with rays, knop stem, applied foot with cut star, lid has strawberry diamonds with fans and applied finial with cut rays, scratched number "39" on bowl, Pittsburgh **2,500**

Sugar Bowl, cov, clear, freeblown, tooled rim, applied foot with pontil scar, pontiled knop on lid, c1820–30, 6½" h **350**

Target Ball, amber, overall diamond pattern without center band, rough sheared mouth with V–shaped chip, American, c1880–90, 2⅝" d **550**

Target Ball, medium green, "For Hockeys Patent Trap," rough sheared lip, English, c1880–90, 2½" h **1,150**

Target Ball, medium yellow amber, blown 3 mold, rough sheared lip, American, c1880–90, 2⅝" d **85**

Target Ball, pale greenish aqua, "N.B. Glass Works Perth," allover diamond pattern with center band, sheared opening, flat bottom allows ball to stand upright, c1880–90, 2¾" d **100**

Target Ball, root beer amber, "From J.H. Johnston Great Western Gun Works, 169 Smithfield Street, Pittsburgh, PA. – Rifles Shotguns Revolvers Ammunition Fishing Tackle Choke Boring Repairing & C., Write For Price List," rough sheared lip, American, c1880–90, 2½" d **4,500**

Target Ball, yellow amber, "Bogardus's Glass Ball Pat'd Apr 10 1877," sheared opening, American, c1880–90, 2¾" d **500**

Taster, orangish amber, pontil scarred base, c1865–75, 2⅞" h **250**

Tumbler, aqua, blown, 16–rib broken swirl, attributed to Mantua, 4¼" h **375**

Tumbler, clear, blown 3 mold, some wear and stains, 3½" h **165**

Tumbler, deep cobalt blue, 8 sided, smooth base, c1865–75, 3¼" h **90**

Vase, amethyst, blown, 12 molded panels in base, flared lip, open blister, 8" h **5,500**

Vase, aqua, blown, lily pad, threaded neck, applied ear handles, applied tooled foot, small check at stone near base of 1 handle, tip of 1 handle gone, 8" h **325**

Vase, clear, flint, white looped bowl with applied second gather of clear glass and applied foot and stem, similar witch ball cov, Pittsburgh, 8¾" h, 5" d, 14" h with cov **2,650**

Pitcher, aquamarine with white loopings, freeblown, thick turned–over lip, applied round base and clear aqua handle with curled ending, large jagged solid pontil, crack across handle base, 8¼" h, $660.
Photo courtesy Collector's Sales and Service.

FLASKS

A flask is a container for liquids. Early American glass companies frequently formed them in molds which left a relief design on the front and/or back. Historical flasks with a portrait, building, scene, or name are the most desired.

Most flasks have a narrow neck. A chestnut flask is hand blown, small, and has a flattened bulbous body. The pitkin has a blown globular body with vertical ribs with a spiral rib overlay. Teardrop flasks are generally fiddle shaped and have a scroll or geometric design.

Dimensions can differ for the same flask because of variations in the molding process. Color is important, with scarcer colors demanding more money. Aqua and amber are the most common colors. Bottles with "sickness," an opalescent scaling which eliminates clarity, are worth much less.

Relief decorated flasks, especially those featuring patriotic or historical themes, are the most popular among Country collectors. Although aqua is the most common color, it is favored because of its ability to blend well into any Country decorating scheme.

References: Ralph and Terry Kovel, *The Kovels' Bottles Price List, Tenth Edition,* Crown Publishers, 1996; George and Helen McKearin, *American Glass,* Crown Publishers, 1948; Helen McKearin and Kenneth Wilson, *American Bottles and Flasks,* Crown Publishers, 1978; Jim Megura, *The Official Identification and Price Guide to Bottles, Eleventh Edition,* House of Collectibles, 1991; Michael Polak, *Bottles: Identification and Price Guide, Second Edition,* Avon Books, 1997; Carlo and Dorothy Sellari, *The Standard Old Bottle Price Guide,* Collector Books, 1989, 1997 value update.

Periodical: *Antique Bottle & Glass Collector,* PO Box 180, East Greenville, PA 18041.

Collectors' Clubs: Federation of Historical Bottle Collectors, Inc, 88 Sweetbriar Branch, Longwood, FL 32750; National Early American Glass Club, PO Box 8489, Silver Spring, MD 20907.

"BP & B," scroll, clear, pontil scarred base, sheared lip, Bakewell, Page, &
    Bakewell, Pittsburgh glasshouse, 1845–55, ½ pt **$900**
"Coffin & Hay, Hammonton," eagle and furled flag, pale smoky green, pon-
    til scarred base, sheared lip, 1825–35, qt **275**
Cornucopia and Urn, bluish aqua, open pontil, applied double collar
    mouth, 1825–35, pt **185**
Cornucopia and Urn, blue green, open pontil, sheared lip, Lancaster Glass
    Works, 1825–35, ½ pt **525**
Eagle and Grape Cluster, deep bluish aqua, pontil scarred base, sheared lip,
    1825–35, qt **150**
Eagle and Morning Glory, deep bluish aqua, open pontil, applied double
    collar mouth, 1825–35, pt **575**
Eagle With Banner, calabash, yellowish green, iron pontil, applied sloping
    collar mouth, 1855–65 .... **185**
"Flora Temple, Harness Trot 219¾," horse, deep bluish aqua, smooth base,
    applied mouth, Lockport, NY glasshouse, 1859, qt **650**
"For Our Country," eagle and furled flag, aqua, open pontil, sheared lip,
    1825–35, pt, 6¾" h **225**
Hunter and Fisherman, calabash, deep greenish aqua, pontil scarred base,
    applied sloping collar mouth, 1855–65 .... **100**

"Jenny Lind/Glass Works, S. Huffsey," Jenny Lind bust 1 side, glasshouse other side, calabash, deep yellow olive, pontil scarred base, applied sloping double collar mouth, 1855–60, 10½" h **2,500**

"Kensington/Union Co." Columbia 1 side, eagle other side, bluish aqua, pontil scarred base, sheared lip, 1820–30, pt **725**

"Louisville, Glass Works," scroll, deep bluish aqua, iron pontil, sheared lip, shallow ³/₁₆" chip on top of lip, 1835–45, qt **120**

"Louisville Ky Glass Works," eagle, bluish aqua, vertical rib pattern, smooth base, applied mouth, 1835–45, qt **185**

"Murdock & Cassel/Zanesville Ohio," deep greenish aqua, pontil scarred base, sheared lip, several small lip flakes, minor iridescent bruise in lip area, 1825–35, pt **1,800**

Scroll, deep olive amber, iron pontil, sheared lip, crude with internal fold of glass, 1845–55, pt **425**

Scroll, medium teal blue, open pontil, sheared lip, 1845–55, pt **1,650**

Scroll, medium yellow green, pontil scarred base, sheared lip, 1845–55, pt .. **1,400**

Scroll, moonstone with pink tint, pontil scarred base, sheared lip, 1845–55, pt **1,550**

Scroll, yellowish olive amber, open pontil, sheared lip, 1845–55, pt **475**

"Success To The Railroad," horse pulling cart, medium yellow olive, pontil scarred base, sheared lip, crude with many bubbles throughout and 1 partial open ³/₁₆" bubble on side, 1825–35, pt **475**

Sunburst, pale green, pontil scarred base, sheared lip, thin wispy ³/₈" l crack on medial rib, 1825–35, pt **300**

"The Father Of His Country/Dyottville Glass Works Philada, Gen. Taylor Never Surrenders" bust of Washington 1 side, bust of Taylor other side, medium cobalt blue, open pontil, sheared lip, qt **3,750**

"Union, F.A. & Co.," clasped hands and cannon, bluish aqua, iron pontil, sheared lip, 1860–70, ½ pt **425**

"Waterford," clasped hands 1 side, eagle with banner other side, yellow with olive tone, smooth base, applied square collar mouth, 1860–70, qt **1,200**

Left: Pitkin, olive green, Type II, 36 rib broken swirl to right, sheared mouth, tubular pontil, light ext spot wear, New England, 5⁵/₈" h, $357. Photo courtesy Collector's Sales and Service.

Right: Scroll, 2 stars, aqua, pontil, 2 qt, $450.

"Zanesville City Glass Works," deep greenish aqua, smooth base, applied
    mouth, 1870–80, pt **200**
"Zanesville City Glass Works," yellowish medium amber, strap–sided,
    smooth base, applied mouth, 1870–80, pt **600**
"Zanesville, Ohio, J. Shepard & Co," eagle and Masonic arch, deep bluish
    aqua, pontil scarred base, sheared lip, 1825–35, pt **350**
"Zanesville, Ohio, J. Shepard & Co," yellowish amber, pontil scarred base,
    sheared lip, 1825–35, pt **1,000**
"Zanesville, Ohio, J. Shepard & Co," yellowish amber upper half to reddish
    amber near base, pontil scarred base, wide flared out and rolled lip,
    1825–35, pt **1,800**
"Zanesville, Ohio, J. Shepard & Co," yellow olive, pontil scarred base,
    sheared lip, crude, several unmelted sand grain groupings in shoulder and
    neck, 1825–35, pt **2,750**

KITCHEN GLASS

The first quarter of the twentieth century brought inexpensive kitchen and table
products to center stage. Hazel Atlas, Hocking, McKee, U.S. Glass, and Westmoreland
were companies which led in the production of these items.

Utilitarian kitchen glassware complements Depression glass tablewares. Many
items were produced in the same colors and styles. Because the glass was molded,
added decorative elements included ribs, fluting, arches and thumbprint patterns.
Kitchen glassware was made thick to achieve durability, which resulted in forms which
were difficult to handle at times and often awkward aesthetically. After World War II,
aluminum products began to replace kitchen glassware.

Kitchen glassware was made in large numbers. Although collectors do tolerate
signs of use, they will not accept pieces with heavy damage. Many of the products
contain applied decals; these should be in good condition. A collection can be built
inexpensively by concentrating on one form such as canister sets, measuring cups,
reamers, etc.

References: Gene Florence, *Kitchen Glassware of the Depression Years, Fifth Edition,*
Collector Books, 1995, 1997 value update; Shirley Glyndon, *The Miracle in
Grandmother's Kitchen,* privately printed, 1983; Garry Kilgo, et al., *A Collectors Guide
to Anchor Hocking's Fire–King Glassware, Vol II,* K & W Collectibles Publisher, 1997;
April M. Tvorak, *Fire–King, Fifth Edition,* published by author, 1997; April M. Tvorak,
Pyrex Price Guide, published by author, 1992; Susan Tobier Rogove and Marcia Buan
Steinhauer, *Pyrex By Corning: A Collector's Guide,* Antique Publications, 1993; Mary
Walker, *Reamers—200 years* (1980, separate price guide) and *The Second Book, More
Reamers—200 Years* (1983), Muski Publishers.

Collectors' Clubs: Fire–King Collectors Club, 1406 East 14th Street, Des Moines, IA
50316; National Reamer Collectors Assoc, 47 Midline Ct, Gaithersburg, MD 20878.

Batter Bowl, jadeite, Hocking **$20**
Batter Bowl, opaque yellow, Hocking **80**
Batter Bowl, turquoise blue, Hocking **150**
Batter Bowl, white, Hocking, peach and grape dec **17**
Batter Jug, clear, cobalt blue cov, Paden City **75**
Batter Jug, forest green, New Martinsville **75**
Batter Jug, green transparent **130**

Batter Jug, jadeite, Jeannette 250
Batter Jug, pink, Cambridge 80
Batter Jug, red, McKee 80
Batter Set, black, Paden City 275
Batter Set, cobalt blue, New Martinsville 330
Batter Set, consists of batter jug, syrup, and tray, amber, New Martinsville ... 175
Beater Bowl, with beater, cobalt blue 90
Beater Bowl, with beater, delphite, Jeannette 75
Beater Bowl, with beater, green transparent, Jeannette 25
Beater Bowl, with beater, iridized 35
Beater Bowl, with beater, jadeite, Jeannette 30
Beater Bowl, with beater, pink 35
Beater Bowl, with beater, ultramarine 50
Butter Dish, cov, ¼ lb, amber, Federal 30
Butter Dish, cov, ¼ lb, clear frosted, Federal 15
Butter Dish, cov, ¼ lb, cobalt blue, Hazel Atlas, Crisscross pattern 90
Butter Dish, cov, ¼ lb, pink, Hazel Atlas, Crisscross pattern 35
Butter Dish, cov, 1 lb, amber, Federal 35
Butter Dish, cov, 1 lb, clear, Hazel Atlas, Crisscross pattern 20
Butter Dish, cov, 1 lb, cobalt blue, Hazel Atlas, emb "Butter Cover" on top .. 200
Butter Dish, cov, 1 lb, delphite, Jeannette, emb "Butter" on top 250
Butter Dish, cov, 1 lb, green clambroth, Hocking 75
Butter Dish, cov, 1 lb, green transparent, Hocking 30
Butter Dish, cov, 1 lb, jadeite, Jeannette, emb "Butter" on top 40
Butter Dish, cov, 1 lb, pink, Hazel Atlas, Crisscross pattern 40
Butter Dish, cov, 1 lb, seville yellow, McKee 65
Butter Dish, cov, 1 lb, ultramarine, Jeannette, Jennyware 150
Butter Dish, cov, 1 lb, white, Hazel Atlas, emb "Butter Cover" on top 25

Left: Canister, cov, clear, red, white, and yellow dec all around, Hocking, 4³/₄" d, 6" h, $25.
Right: Drum Pitcher, pink, Federal Glass Co, c1941, $30.

Butter Dish, cov, 1 lb, white, red ships dec, McKee 25
Butter Dish, cov, 2 lb, green transparent, Jeannette, emb "B" on top 150
Butter Dish, cov, 2 lb, pink, Jeannette, emb "B" on top 160
Canister, black lettering, screw–on lid 35
Canister, caramel, screw–on lid, 48 oz 90
Canister, clambroth, large, screw–on lid 40
Canister, clear, "Fleur–de–lis" and "Sugar" in black, screw–on lid 22
Canister, clear, stripe, 2 each red, white, and blue horizontal stripes, glass
    lid, 64 oz 15
Canister, clear, zipper design, emb "Coffee," screw–on lid 20
Canister, delphite, Jeannette, round, horizontal ribs, black lettering,
    screw–on lid, 40 oz 325
Canister, forest green, Owens–Illinois, ovoid, screw–on lid 50
Canister, green clambroth, Hocking, glass lid, 47 oz 45
Canister, jadeite, Jeannette, square, black lettering, glass lid, 5¹⁄₂" h, 48 oz ... 45
Cruet, clambroth, frosted, chicken decal 15
Cruet, green transparent, Hocking 20
Cruet, jadeite, "Vinegar" in black lettering 175
Cruet, pink, Hazel Atlas, clear stopper 45
Ice Bucket, black, Fenton 50
Ice Bucket, clear, Hocking, Ring pattern 15
Ice Bucket, cobalt blue, Cambridge 125
Ice Bucket, jade green, Fenton 40
Ice Bucket, pink, Paden City, Party Line 30
Knife, amber, Aer–Flo, 7¹⁄₂" l 150
Knife, amber, Dur–X, 3 leaf, 9¹⁄₄" l 130
Knife, amber, Rose Spray, 8¹⁄₂" l 175
Knife, amber, Stonex, 8¹⁄₄" l 175
Knife, blue, Dur–X, 3 leaf, 8¹⁄₂" l 28
Knife, blue, Dur–X, 5 leaf, 8¹⁄₂" l 20
Knife, blue, Vitex Glas, star, 9¹⁄₄" l 30
Knife, clear, Block, 8¹⁄₄" l 12
Knife, clear, Buffalo Knife, flowers, 9¹⁄₄" l 17
Knife, clear, Pinwheel 10
Knife, clear, Rose Spray, 8¹⁄₂" l 65
Knife, clear, Westmoreland, flowers, thumbguard, 9¹⁄₄" l 25
Knife, green, Aer–Flo, 7¹⁄₂" l 65
Knife, green, Buffalo Knife, leaves, 9¹⁄₄" l 40
Knife, green, Dur–X, 5 leaf, 8¹⁄₂" l 20
Knife, green, plain, 9¹⁄₄" l 35
Knife, green, Steel–ite 70
Knife, green, Westmoreland, flowers, thumbguard, 9¹⁄₄" l 200
Knife, pink, Block, 8¹⁄₄" l 35
Knife, pink, Dur–X, 3 leaf, 9¹⁄₄" l 27
Knife, pink, Steel–ite 90
Knife, pink, Vitex Glas, star, 8¹⁄₂" l 25
Knife, pink, white, Stonex, 8¹⁄₄" l 150
Ladle, Sauce, amethyst, round bottom 22
Ladle, Sauce, black, wedge handle 25
Ladle, Sauce, cobalt blue, etched, flat bottom 30
Ladle, Sauce, green clambroth, round bottom 20

Ladle, Sauce, ivory, Cambridge, flat bottom 25
Ladle, Sauce, pink, round bottom 12
Ladle, Sauce, red, triangular handle knob 35
Ladle, Sauce, vaseline, triangular handle knob 25
Ladle, Sauce, white, wedge handle 5
Ladle, Soup, amber 30
Ladle, Soup, black 85
Ladle, Soup, clear, black handle 30
Ladle, Soup, clear, red handle 50
Ladle, Soup, green 40
Ladle, Soup, white, black handle, measure on side of ladle 50
Ladle, Soup, white, Imperial 40
Match Holder, delphite, Jeannette, black lettering 75
Match Holder, jadeite, Jeannette, black lettering 35
Measuring Cup, dry, clear, Jeannette, 1/2 cup 25
Measuring Cup, dry, delphite, Jeannette, 1/2 cup 45
Measuring Cup, dry, jadeite, Jeannette, 1/4 cup 10
Measuring Cup, dry, pink, Jeannette, 1/3 cup 30
Measuring Cup, dry, ultramarine, Jeannette, 1/3 cup 35
Measuring Cup, liquid, 1 cup, amber, side spout 225
Measuring Cup, liquid, 1 cup, black, 2 spouts 750
Measuring Cup, liquid, 1 cup, caramel, 2 spouts 550
Measuring Cup, liquid, 1 cup, chalaine blue, 2 spouts 775
Measuring Cup, liquid, 1 cup, clear, Fry, 3 spouts 70
Measuring Cup, liquid, 1 cup, cobalt blue, Hazel Atlas, 3 spouts 375
Measuring Cup, liquid, 1 cup, pink, US Glass, slick handle 35
Measuring Cup, liquid, 1 cup, seville yellow, 2 spouts 175
Measuring Pitcher, blue, Fire–King, ftd, 2 spouts, 16 oz 25
Measuring Pitcher, clear, Empire Glass, 1 qt 20
Measuring Pitcher, clear, Hazel Atlas, 4 cup 15
Measuring Pitcher, clear, Hocking, ftd, ribbed, 2 cup 15
Measuring Pitcher, cobalt blue, ftd, 2 cup 150
Measuring Pitcher, custard, McKee, orange Dots pattern, 2 cup 35
Measuring Pitcher, delphite, green clambroth, Hocking, ftd, 2 cup 100
Measuring Pitcher, delphite, green frosted, Hazel Atlas, 4 cup 20
Measuring Pitcher, delphite, iridized carnival, 2 cup 40
Measuring Pitcher, delphite, McKee, ftd, 4 cup 25
Measuring Pitcher, delphite, Jeannette, Sunflower bottom, 2 cup 65
Measuring Pitcher, delphite, McKee, 2 cup 80
Measuring Pitcher, delphite, pink, US Glass, slick handle, 2 cup 40
Measuring Pitcher, delphite, red, fired on, Hazel Atlas, ftd, 2 cup 35
Measuring Pitcher, delphite, seville yellow, McKee, 2 cup 35
Measuring Pitcher, white, McKee, 2 cup, Black Diamond Check pattern 25
Measuring Pitcher, white, McKee, 2 cup, Red Ships dec 30
Measuring Pitcher, yellow, ftd, 2 cup 200
Measuring Pitcher with Reamer Top, amber, US Glass, 2 cup 275
Measuring Pitcher with Reamer Top, amber, US Glass, 4 cup 525
Measuring Pitcher with Reamer Top, amber, blue, US Glass, 2 cup 700
Measuring Pitcher with Reamer Top, clear, Morgantown, black handle and
  top, 2 cup 325

Measuring Pitcher with Reamer Top, clear, US Glass, dec, 2 cup **25**
Measuring Pitcher with Reamer Top, cobalt blue, Hazel Atlas, 2 cup **275**
Measuring Pitcher with Reamer Top, green, Hocking, ftd, 4 cup **35**
Measuring Pitcher with Reamer Top, green frosted, US Glass, 2 cup **25**
Measuring Pitcher with Reamer Top, pink, US Glass, Party Line, 4 cup **175**
Measuring Pitcher with Reamer Top, pink, Westmoreland, emb, 2 cup **150**
Measuring Pitcher with Reamer Top, turquoise, US Glass, 2 cup **100**
Measuring Pitcher with Reamer Top, white vitrock, Hocking, 2 cup **30**
Measuring Pitcher with Reamer Top, yellow, US Glass, 2 cup **275**
Milk Pitcher, clear, cobalt blue cov, Paden City **55**
Mixing Bowl, amber, US Glass, 8" d **25**
Mixing Bowl, black, McKee, 7³/₈" d **30**
Mixing Bowl, delphite, Jeannette, horizontal ribs, 5½" d **60**
Mixing Bowl, delphite, LE Smith, 7" d **50**
Mixing Bowl, green transparent, 6½" d **10**
Mixing Bowl, jadeite, Hocking, flower decal, 7½" d **15**
Napkin Holder, black, emb "NAR–O–FOLD" **125**
Napkin Holder, clear, LE Smith, horizontal ribs **40**
Napkin Holder, forest green **80**
Napkin Holder, green clambroth, emb "SERV–ALL" **150**
Napkin Holder, green transparent, emb "FAN FOLD" **120**
Napkin Holder, pink, Paden City, Party Line **125**
Napkin Holder, white, Ft Howard, emb "A HANDI–NAP" **50**
Reamer, amber, Fry **300**
Reamer, amber, Indiana **275**
Reamer, amber, Westmoreland, baby, 2 pc **175**
Reamer, black, McKee, grapefruit **1,000**

Left: Egg Beater and Measuring Cup, green, mkd "Handy Maid, Torrington, T & S," $35.
Photo courtesy Ray Morykan Auctions.

*Right: Water Set, pitcher and 12 tumblers, Hocking, #2078, Color Spiral II, red and white
stripes, mid–1930s, $85.*

Reamer, caramel, Sunkist 300
Reamer, chalaine blue, Sunkist 200
Reamer, clear, Hazel Atlas, Crisscross pattern, large 15
Reamer, clear, Westmoreland, flower decal, baby 40
Reamer, cobalt blue, Cambridge 2,500
Reamer, cobalt blue, Hazel Atlas, Crisscross pattern 275
Reamer, custard, grapefruit 600
Reamer, delphite blue, Jeannette, small 125
Reamer, green transparent, Hazel Atlas, tab handle 35
Reamer, jadeite, Saunders 1,400
Reamer, light gray, green cast, Sunkist 300
Reamer, pale green, Sunkist 300
Reamer, pink, Fry 50
Reamer, pink, Hazel Atlas, Crisscross pattern, lemon 300
Reamer, pink, Hazel Atlas, Crisscross pattern, orange 200
Reamer, pink, Jeannette, Jennyware 125
Reamer, pink, McKee 75
Reamer, seville yellow, Sunkist 65
Reamer, ultramarine, Jeannette, Jennyware 130
Reamer, white milk glass, Sunkist 20
Refrigerator Dish, cov, chalaine blue, 4 x 5" 50
Refrigerator Dish, cov, cobalt blue, Hazel Atlas, stacking, 4½ x 5", price for
    set of 2 90
Refrigerator Dish, cov, delphite, McKee, 4 x 5" 30
Refrigerator Dish, cov, green clambroth, Hocking, oval, 8" l 35
Refrigerator Dish, cov, green transparent, Jeannette, round, 9" d 35
Refrigerator Dish, cov, jadeite, wedge shaped 20
Rolling Pin, amber, light, blown 100
Rolling Pin, amethyst, blown 125
Rolling Pin, chalaine blue, blown 425
Rolling Pin, chalaine blue, McKee, shaker end 1,750
Rolling Pin, clambroth, wood screw-on handles 125
Rolling Pin, clear, cobalt blue screw-on handles 225
Rolling Pin, clear, mkd "Kardov Flour, Famous Self Rising," blown 55

Left: Batter Bowl, green transparent, Hocking, rough inner edge, 8⅞" d, 3¾" h, $25.
Right: Refrigerator Dish, cov, pink, Federal Glass Co, 8" sq, $35.

Rolling Pin, cobalt blue, blown 175
Rolling Pin, cobalt blue, handles attach to metal rod inside pin 450
Rolling Pin, custard, McKee, shaker top end, circular band opposite end 300
Rolling Pin, custard, mkd "Imperial Mfg. Co., Cambridge, Ohio," wood
    screw–on handles 150
Rolling Pin, delphite blue, McKee, shaker end 1,700
Rolling Pin, forest green, blown 125
Rolling Pin, green transparent, handles attach to wood dowel inside pin 400
Rolling Pin, jadeite, McKee, shaker end, circular band opposite end 375
Rolling Pin, peacock blue, dark, blown 200
Rolling Pin, peacock blue, handles attach to metal rod inside pin 275
Rolling Pin, pink, wood screw–on handles 425
Rolling Pin, pink, seville yellow, McKee, shaker end 300
Rolling Pin, white, mkd "Imperial Mfg. Co., Cambridge, Ohio," wood
    screw–on handles 50
Salt and Pepper Shakers, pr, amber, Sneath 50
Salt and Pepper Shakers, pr, black, roman arch, white "S" or "P" 50
Salt and Pepper Shakers, pr, blue, fired–on, Hocking 20
Salt and Pepper Shakers, pr, chalaine blue, McKee, square, black lettering ... 150
Salt and Pepper Shakers, pr, chalaine blue, McKee, square, emb 225
Salt and Pepper Shakers, pr, clambroth, emb, red lids 40
Salt and Pepper Shakers, pr, clear, Hazel Atlas, emb 45
Salt and Pepper Shakers, pr, clear, McKee, frosted 12
Salt and Pepper Shakers, pr, custard, McKee, roman arch, Dots pattern and
    green lettering 25
Salt and Pepper Shakers, pr, delphite, Basketweave pattern 25
Salt and Pepper Shakers, pr, delphite, Jeannette, square, black lettering 150
Salt and Pepper Shakers, pr, green, Owens–Illinois 7
Salt and Pepper Shakers, pr, green clambroth, Hocking, emb 90
Salt and Pepper Shakers, pr, jadeite, Art Deco pattern 30
Salt and Pepper Shakers, pr, jadeite, Jeannette, black lettering 35
Salt and Pepper Shakers, pr, jadeite, McKee, emb, square 90
Salt and Pepper Shakers, pr, opaque yellow, Hocking 35
Salt and Pepper Shakers, pr, pink, Hazel Atlas, emb 85
Salt and Pepper Shakers, pr, red, fired–on, McKee, roman arch 20
Salt and Pepper Shakers, pr, ultramarine, Jeannette, Jennyware 45
Salt and Pepper Shakers, pr, white, Hazel Atlas, Skating Dutch pattern 15
Salt and Pepper Shakers, pr, yellow, fired–on, Hocking 10
Salt Box, amber, Sneath 125
Salt Box, chalaine blue, McKee, metal lid 175
Salt Box, clear, emb "Salt" on front 15
Salt Box, clear, Flintex, emb "Salt" on front, glass lid 85
Salt Box, clear, Sneath 15
Salt Box, green transparent, Jeannette, round, emb "Salt" on lid, 6" d 175
Salt Box, green transparent, zipper pattern, round, wood lid incised "Salt" ... 125
Salt Box, jadeite, Jeannette, wood lid, black lettering 200
Salt Box, jadeite, McKee, metal lid 80
Salt Box, peacock blue 140
Salt Box, white, emb "Salt" on front 120
Salt Box, white, round, emb "Salt" on front 120
Spice Shaker, black, white lettering 25

Spice Shaker, blue, fired–on, Hocking **10**
Spice Shaker, chalaine blue, emb **125**
Spice Shaker, clear, blue Dutch boy dec, red lettering and lid, 16 oz **12**
Spice Shaker, custard, lady with apron dec, red lid **17**
Spice Shaker, custard, McKee, "Ginger" in black lettering **30**
Spice Shaker, delphite, Jeannette, round, horizontal ribs, "Paprika" in black
   lettering, 8 oz **100**
Spice Shaker, delphite, Jeannette, square, "Flour" in black lettering **75**
Spice Shaker, green, fired–on, Hocking **7.50**
Spice Shaker, green clambroth, Hocking, paneled, 8 oz **20**
Spice Shaker, green transparent, Sneath, square **45**
Spice Shaker, jadeite, Jeannette, round, horizontal ribs, "Flour" in black let-
   tering, 8 oz **12**
Spice Shaker, jadeite, Jeannette, square, "Flour" in black lettering **20**
Spice Shaker, opaque yellow, Hocking **15**
Spice Shaker, skokie green, McKee, roman arch, "Cinnamon" in black let-
   tering **35**
Spice Shaker, white, black cattail dec and lid **3**
Spice Shaker, white, Scottie dog **12**
Spice Shaker, yellow, fired–on, Hocking **5**
Sugar, amber, Paden City, pinched in **175**
Sugar, black **325**
Sugar, blue, "Monroe Mfg. Co., Elgin, Ill., Pat Pend.," liquid **225**
Sugar, clear, Hazel Atlas, metal flip top **10**
Sugar, clear, LE Smith, metal screw–on bottom **35**
Sugar, clear, "West Sanitary Automatic Sugar" **20**
Sugar, cobalt blue, Paden City **600**
Sugar, green transparent, green screw–in top **175**
Sugar, green transparent, Hocking **100**

Left: Reamer, white, 2 pc, measuring cup base, $12.

Right: Salt and Pepper Shakers, pr, clear, Hazel Atlas, Stripe #1164, 6 red stripes, red plastic lids, c1940, $10.

Sugar, green transparent, Lancaster, beehive, metal screw–on bottom **150**
Sugar, pink, Paden City, Party Line **100**
Sugar, pink, "Tilt–A–Spoon" on cap, ftd **250**
Sugar, ultramarine, Jeannette, bullet shape, screw–on bottom **225**
Sugar, yellow, Paden City, bullet shape **150**
Syrup Pitcher, amber, Cambridge **55**
Syrup Pitcher, amber, Imperial, slotted lid **70**
Syrup Pitcher, amber, Paden City, 8 oz **45**
Syrup Pitcher, black, Fenton **70**
Syrup Pitcher, Caribbean blue, Duncan & Miller **175**
Syrup Pitcher, clear, Duncan & Miller **70**
Syrup Pitcher, clear, Paden City, cobalt blue cov **55**
Syrup Pitcher, clear, US Glass, miniature **40**
Syrup Pitcher, Emerald–Glo, with liner **30**
Syrup Pitcher, forest green, New Martinsville **60**
Syrup Pitcher, green, Hazel Atlas **40**
Syrup Pitcher, green, Hocking, Swirl pattern **40**
Syrup Pitcher, green, Paden City **30**
Syrup Pitcher, pink, green knob and handle, pink liner **50**
Syrup Pitcher, pink, Hazel Atlas **50**
Syrup Pitcher, pink, Imperial, slotted lid **75**
Syrup Pitcher, pink, New Martinsville **50**
Syrup Pitcher, pink, Standard Glass **35**
Water Dispenser, clear, McKee, skokie green round top **50**
Water Dispenser, cobalt blue, LE Smith **375**
Water Dispenser, custard, McKee **125**
Water Dispenser, green clambroth, Sneath, clear round top **60**
Water Dispenser, light blue, LE Smith **225**
Water Dispenser, skokie green, McKee, 5¼" h **200**
Water Dispenser, white, McKee **100**

MILK GLASS

Milk glass enjoyed great popularity in rural America, beginning as a decorative accessory in parlors and dining rooms in the late Victorian period and ending as a utilitarian, everyday dining service in the 1940s and 50s.

Opaque white glass, commonly known as milk glass, enjoyed its greatest popularity in the period immediately following the turn of the century. Firms such as Atterbury, Challinor–Taylor, Flaccus, and McKee made a wide range of dinnerware, figural, household, kitchenware, and novelty forms. While the popularity of milk glass waned in the 1920s, several manufacturers continued to use it for their kitchenware and decorative novelty lines.

Milk glass enjoyed a brief renaissance extending from the early 1940s through the early 1960s. Fenton, Imperial, and Westmoreland renewed their production of milk glass. Fenton introduced Hobnail in 1940 and its Silvercrest line a few years later. Westmoreland revived Paneled Grape in the 1940s and launched Beaded Grape in the 1950s.

In 1945 John E. Kemple founded Kemple Glass Works, East Palestine, Ohio. The company only made milk glass. Kemple bought a number of the McKee molds from the Thatcher Glass Company shortly after it had purchased McKee. When fire destroyed the Kemple plant in 1956, the firm moved to Kenova, West Virginia. Its advertisements boasted, "Authentic Reproductions in Milk Glass—Made in the Original Molds." The Wheaton Company purchased Kemple's equipment and molds following the death of John Kemple in 1970.

The post–1940s milk glass of Fenton, Imperial, Kemple, and Westmoreland dominates today's marketplace. Post–1940 milk glass is very white in color. Milk glass from the turn of the century has a slight gray rather than a pure white tone.

References: E. McCamley Belknap, *Milk Glass*, Crown Publishers, 1949; Regis F. and Mary F. Ferson, *Today's Prices For Yesterday's Milk Glass*, privately printed, 1985; Regis F. and Mary F. Ferson, *Yesterday's Milk Glass Today*, published by authors, 1981; Myrna and Bob Garrison, *Imperial's Vintage Milk Glass*, published by authors, 1992; Everett Grist, *Covered Animal Dishes*, Collector Books, 1988; 1993 value update; S. T. Millard, *Opaque Glass, Fourth Edition*, Wallace–Homestead, 1975; Betty and Bill Newbound, *Collector's Encyclopedia of Milk Glass*, Collector Books, 1995, 1998 value update.

Collectors' Club: National Milk Glass Collectors Society, 46 Almond Drive, Hershey, PA 17033.

Note: Items listed are white unless otherwise noted.

Ashtray, grape leaf shape, Imperial, c1960	$8
Ashtray, trivet, Imperial, c1960	10
Basket, lace edge, Imperial, late 1950s, 8³/₄" l	40
Bone Dish, Fish and Shell	30
Bowl, Randolph, cov, Fostoria, 1950s, 9³/₄" x 8¹/₄"	35
Bowl, Scroll, Imperial, late 1950s, 8¹/₂" d	17
Box, cov, couch, orig green paint	180
Butter Dish, Lace & Dewdrop, Kemple, 6¹/₂" d, 6" h	40
Butter Dish, Strawberry	50
Cake Stand, floral dec and multicolored rings, hp, Challinor–Taylor, c1890s, 6" h, 9¹/₈" d	45
Cake Stand, Indiana, 1960s, 6³/₄" h, 10³/₈" sq	10
Candle Holders, pr, ball edge, Anchor Hocking, 1960s	7
Candle Holders, pr, Betsy Ross, open leaf edge, Fostoria	30
Candle Holders, pr, Imperial, double, 1930s	35
Candle Lamp, lighthouse, blue, 6¹/₄" h	250
Candlesticks, pr, dolphin, Westmoreland, 9¹/₄" h	70
Candlesticks, pr, English Hobnail, double, Westmoreland, 6¹/₄" h	70
Candlesticks, pr, Jewel & Dewdrop, Kemple	30
Cardholder, terrier	35
Cigar Jar, cigar bundle, naturalistic painting	250
Compote, basketweave, cov, Atterbury, c1880s, 10¹/₄" h, 8" d	85
Compote, Daisy and Button, petticoat edge, 6" h	25
Compote, Grape, LE Smith, 9³/₄ x 8¹/₄"	35
Compote, Jenny Lind, Challinor–Taylor, early 1890s, 8¹/₄ x 7³/₄"	95
Compote, Old Quilt, Westmoreland	25
Compote, open hand, Atterbury, c1880s, 8³/₄" h, 9¹/₈" d	80
Covered Dish, American Hen, "Patent Applied For," 6¹/₈" l	50
Covered Dish, boar's head, top and bottom mkd "Pat 1888," Atterbury, 9³/₈" l	1,800
Covered Dish, cabbage, Portieux, blue	40
Covered Dish, cannon on snare drum, Vallerysthal, small chip on bottom of base, 4¹/₂" d	90

Covered Dish, cat, Westmoreland, white head, blue body, white wide
ribbed base, 5½" l 45
Covered Dish, cat on drum, Portieux, blue, 4¾" d 75
Covered Dish, chick, basketweave base, 5¼" l 50
Covered Dish, chick and eggs, round lacy base, mkd "Patd Aug 6, 1889,"
chip on rim 225
Covered Dish, covered wagon, 5–ribbed frame, 6" l 190
Covered Dish, cow, oblong, relief design, orig paint, Vallerysthal, 7" l, 4¼" w 125
Covered Dish, cow, oval basketweave base, Kemple, 7¼" l 290
Covered Dish, crawfish finial, octagonal base, tab handles 200
Covered Dish, dog, half white, half blue, 5½" l 40
Covered Dish, dog, pointing, standing in grassy field, possibly Flaccus, 6⅝" l . 325
Covered Dish, dog on carpet, Vallerysthal 130
Covered Dish, dog on carpet, Vallerysthal, blue 225
Covered Dish, duck, swimming, Vallerysthal, blue, 6¼" l 140
Covered Dish, duck, wavy base, glass eyes, 8" l 60
Covered Dish, Easter egg, rabbit finial, 4¾" l........................ 225
Covered Dish, elephant, figural, black, 7½" l 70
Covered Dish, elephant, figural, walking 250
Covered Dish, English Hobnail, Westmoreland, 5½" h, 6¼" d 50
Covered Dish, fish, Challinor–Taylor, minor rim chip and stress cracks,
1880s 475
Covered Dish, fish, Vallerysthal 225
Covered Dish, fish, Vallerysthal, blue 425
Covered Dish, fox, lacy edged reticulated base, mkd "Patd Aug 6, 1889,"
Atterbury, 6⅜" l 125
Covered Dish, frog, figural, black, 5¾" l 300
Covered Dish, frog, figural, split rib base, 5½" l..................... 650
Covered Dish, hen on nest, basketweave base, Vallerysthal, pale amethyst,
6¾" l 70
Covered Dish, hen on nest, basketweave base, white with blue head, 5½" l .. 35

Left: Covered Dish, The American Hen, white, mkd "Patent Applied For," eggs mkd "Porto Rica/Cuba/Philippines," 6⅛" l, $100. Photo courtesy Gene Harris Auction Center.

Right: Basket Salt, white, Atterbury, July 21, 1874 patent date, 3¾" l, $25. Photo courtesy Ray Morykan Auctions.

Covered Dish, hen on nest, Challinor–Taylor, 8" l **100**
Covered Dish, hen on nest, chicks on base, probably Flaccus, 6¼" l **150**
Covered Dish, hen on nest, Westmoreland, 7½" l **125**
Covered Dish, hen on nest, Westmoreland, chocolate, 7½" l **300**
Covered Dish, jack rabbit, 6" l **350**
Covered Dish, lamb, octagonal base, blue cov, white head **45**
Covered Dish, lion, ribbed base, mkd "Pat'd Aug. 6, 1889" **210**
Covered Dish, lion, scroll base **35**
Covered Dish, melon, Vallerysthal, blue **80**
Covered Dish, monkey on grass mound, leaf and scroll base, 6¼" l **1,800**
Covered Dish, moose on egg, 5" l **575**
Covered Dish, owl **65**
Covered Dish, owl head on basket, Imperial, blue **50**
Covered Dish, peep and egg, 6½" h **160**
Covered Dish, Pekinese **400**
Covered Dish, pig on drum, pig finial, Portieux, 3" h **250**
Covered Dish, rabbit, mkd "Pat'd March 9, 1886," 6¼" l **260**
Covered Dish, rabbit, mule–eared, ribbed octagonal base, Westmoreland **55**
Covered Dish, rabbit, Portieux, 7" l **475**
Covered Dish, rabbit on egg, Vallerysthal, textured finish, 4¾" l **190**
Covered Dish, rabbit on eggs, 4½" l **75**
Covered Dish, salmon, oblong, 6" l **65**
Covered Dish, Santa on sleigh, figural **55**
Covered Dish, Santa on sleigh, facing backwards, Westmoreland, 5½" l **75**
Covered Dish, sheep, dome cov **350**
Covered Dish, snail on strawberry, some orig paint **175**
Covered Dish, stagecoach **175**
Covered Dish, swan, closed neck, blue, 5½" l **30**
Covered Dish, swan, open neck, 5½" l **90**
Covered Dish, swan, raised wing No. 2, orig paint and eyes, 9¾" l **225**
Covered Dish, swan, trunk with strap, 5½" l **25**
Covered Dish, turkey, figural, 7" h **180**
Covered Dish, turtle, figural, finial, octagonal base, tab handles **190**
Covered Dish, turtle, figural, knobby shell cov, 9½" l **240**
Covered Dish, turkey, figural, oval ribbed base, McKee **250**
Covered Dish, turtle, figural, snail on back, blue, 7½" l **600**
Creamer, Cherry Thumbprint, Westmoreland, 3½" h **17**
Creamer, Della Robbia, Westmoreland, 3" h **7**
Creamer, owl, orig eyes **25**
Creamer and Sugar, Betsy Ross, Fostoria, 1960s, 4" creamer, 3⅝" sugar **20**
Creamer and Sugar, cow and wheat, 4⅝" creamer, 3⅛ x 4⅞" sugar **175**
Creamer and Sugar, Grape, 3–toed, Imperial, 1960s **25**
Dish, heart shaped, Westmoreland, 3¾" l **12**
Egg Cup, chick, Westmoreland, 3½" h **15**
Egg Cup, kingfisher **10**
Figure, hen, Imperial, 4½" h **40**
Figure, jumping horse, Kemple **65**
Figure, rooster, LE Smith, 5¾" h **45**
Figure, Scottie, LE Smith, 5" h **40**
Fish Plate, clear border, "Pat'd Nov. 23, 1875," Atterbury, 9" w, 12⅞" l **1,700**
Fish Plate, "Pat. June 4th, 1872," 10¼" w, 14" l **40**

Fruit Bowl, Monroe, Fostoria, 1960s, 10⁵/₈" d 25
Goblet, Della Robbia, Westmoreland, 4⁷/₈" h 12
Goblet, Dewberry, Kemple, 6" h 15
Goblet, Jewel & Dewdrop, Kemple 20
Gravy Boat, plain 5
Honey Jar, beehive shape, beehive with vines, Vallerysthal, 5¹/₂" h 100
Honey Jar, beehive shape, Imperial, 4⁷/₈" h 35
Honey Jar, beehive shape, Jeannette, late 1950s, 4¹/₈" h 35
Jar, cov, Scottie, pink 45
Ladle, wooden handles, Cambridge, early 20th C, 14" l 55
Lady's Shoe, floral, blue, gold paint dec 15
Lamp, Acanthus, emb, 8¹/₄" h 250
Lamp, Beaded Panel, raised flowers, 15¹/₂" h 90
Lamp, Columbus, bearded, miniature 1,250
Lamp, Goddess of Liberty, clear frosted font, 11" h 360
Lamp, mantel dogs, pr, Atterbury, 5" h, 7" l 1,700
Lamp, scrollwork, cross–hatching, emb flower trim, ftd 100
Master Salt, flying fish, orig paint, 4⁵/₈" l 120
Master Salt, swan, head down, 3¹/₄" h, 5¹/₂" l 25
Master Salt, turtle, blue 70
Match Safe, Bible, blue 25
Match Safe, dog head 120
Match Safe, elf, hanging 210
Match Safe, Indian chief, hanging 60
Mug, bird and wheat 8
Mug, duck and swan, child's 20
Mug, Liberty Bell, child's, 2" h 50
Mustard Jar, log cabin, bank, orig paint and labels on bottom, Westmoreland . 100
Nappy, 3–toed, handled, Vallerysthal, blue 30
Pickle Dish, sheaf of wheat 12
Pin Dish, cov, lion, 4³/₄" x 3¹/₂" 10
Pin Tray, Indian maiden with headdress, 7" l 45
Pitcher, owl, glass eyes, Challinor–Taylor 200
Plaque, Lincoln, 8¹/₂" x 6³/₄" 130
Plate, Easter bunny and egg, orig bold border 50
Plate, Forget Me–Not, 7¹/₂" d 2
Plate, Grape, Imperial, c1960, 8³/₄" d 12
Plate, H–border, Atterbury, 1890, 7¹/₂" d 25
Plate, Roses, Imperial, c1960, 12" d 30
Plate, Scroll & Waffle, McKee, 1800s, 7¹/₄" d 17
Plate, row boat, "Patented Feb. 17th, 1874," 9¹/₂" l 15
Relish, apple, divided, Imperial, 1952, 9¹/₂ x 9" 30
Rolling Pin, wooden handles, Cambridge 60
Salt and Pepper Shakers, pr, blooming flower, Westmoreland, 4¹/₄" h 25
Salt and Pepper Shakers, pr, Paneled Scroll, 3³/₄" h 20
Salt and Pepper Shakers, pr, Quilted, with basket holder, Imperial, 1950s 30
Salt Box, hanging, emb, wooden lid, 6¹/₄" d, 5³/₄" h 100
Shaving Mug, Garfield memorial 155
Sugar, beehive, cov 80
Sugar, Betsy Ross, cov, Tiffin, 7" h 25
Sugar, fish, open, English, c1882 100

Sugar, Lace and Dewdrop, cov, Kemple, blue–painted   45
Syrup, corn with husk, 7½" h   60
Syrup, Grape, keyed lid, Imperial, c1960, 6¾" h   25
Syrup, Strawberry, 7" h   70
Toothpick Holder, bees in a basket   30
Toothpick Holder, boy with basket, Vallerysthal, blue   70
Toothpick Holder, heron in marsh, 3½" h   30
Toothpick Holder, Indian head, Challinor–Taylor, 1890s, 4¾" h   90
Toothpick Holder, monkey with hat   130
Toothpick Holder, owl with spread wings, Westmoreland, 3" h   17
Toothpick Holder, tight corset, orig dec   85
Tray, Diamond Grille, "Give us this day our daily bread," Atterbury, 12" l   50
Tray, Grape Cluster, Imperial, 1951, 6½ x 10"   25
Tray, lion, handled, 5" w, 9" l   15
Tray, Moses in the Bulrushes   50
Trinket Box, actress   35
Tumbler, actress head   25
Tumbler, scroll, mkd "From the Belknap Collection," Imperial, late 1950s   15
Tureen, sleigh, 5" h, 6" w, 9¼" l   40
Vase, Corn, gold paint, 4¼" h   10
Vase, Grape, lamp shaped, Imperial, 1950s, 7¼" h   20
Vase, hand holding cornucopia, early 1900s   45
Vase, Lily of the Valley, Westmoreland, 6" h   25
Vase, Zipper & Jewel, 7" h   12

PATTERN GLASS

Pattern glass often marked a country family's first introduction to utilitarian household glassware. Replacement of horn, tin, and wooden tableware occurred gradually. Initial glassware purchases often were reserved for Sundays, holidays, and special occasions.

Some patterns imitated cut glass patterns. It was common to find the two mixed together in a table setting. While clear (crystal) was the most popular color, colored lines were available in many patterns. It also was common practice to mix patterns, especially in accessory pieces.

Pattern glass is clear or colored glass pressed into one of hundreds of patterns. Deming Jarves of the Boston and Sandwich Glass Company invented the first successful pressing machine in 1828. By the 1860s glass pressing machinery had been improved, and mass production of good quality matched tableware sets began. The idea of a matched glassware table service (including goblets, tumblers, creamers, sugars, compotes, cruets, etc.) quickly caught on in America. Many pattern glass table services had numerous accessory pieces among which were banana boats, molasses cans, water bottles, etc.

Early pattern glass (flint) was made with a lead formula, giving it a ringing quality. During the Civil War lead became too valuable to be used in glass manufacturing. In 1864 Hobbs, Brockunier & Company, West Virginia, developed a soda lime (non–flint) formula. Pattern glass also was produced in colors, milk glass, opalescent glass, slag glass, and custard glass.

The hundreds of companies which produced pattern glass experienced periods of development, expansion, personnel problems, material and supply demands, fires, and mergers. In 1899 the National Glass Co. was formed as a combine of nineteen glass companies in Pennsylvania, Ohio, Indiana, West Virginia, and Maryland. U.S. Glass, another consortium, was founded in 1891. These combines resulted as an attempt to save small companies by pooling talents, resources, and patterns. Because of this pooling, the same pattern can be attributed to several companies.

Sometimes the pattern name of a piece was changed from one company to the next to reflect current fashion trends. U.S. Glass created the States series by issuing patterns named for a particular state. Several of these patterns were new issues, others were former patterns renamed.

References: Carl O. Burns, *Imperial Carnival Glass*, Collector Books, 1996; Bill Edwards, *The Standard Encyclopedia of Carnival Glass, Fifth Edition*, Collector Books, 1996; Bill Edwards, *The Standard Encyclopedia of Opalescent Glass, Second Edition*, Collector Books, 1997; Elaine Ezell and George Newhouse, *Cruets, Cruets, Cruets, Vol I* (1991), *Vol II* (1995), Antique Publications; William Heacock, *Encyclopedia of Victorian Colored Pattern Glass; Toothpick Holders from A to Z, Book 1, Second Edition*, (1976, 1992 value update); *Opalescent Glass from A to Z, Book 2* (1981); *Syrups, Sugar Shakers & Cruets from A to Z, Book 3* (1981); *Custard Glass from A to Z, Book 4* (1980); *U. S. Glass from A to Z, Book 5* (1980); *Oil Cruets from A to Z, Book 6* (1981); *Ruby Stained Glass from A to Z, Book 7* (1986); and, *More Ruby Stained Glass from A to Z, Book 8* (1987), Antique Publications; William Heacock, *1000 Toothpick Holders: A Collector's Guide*, Antique Publications, 1977; William Heacock, *Rare & Unlisted Toothpick Holders*, Antique Publications, 1984; William Heacock and William Gamble, *Encyclopedia of Victorian Colored Pattern Glass, Cranberry Opalescent from A to 7, Book 9*, Antique Publications, 1981; William Heacock, James Measell, and Berry Wiggins, *Dugan/Diamond: The Story of Indiana, Pennsylvania, Glass*, Antique Publications, 1993; William Heacock, James Measell, and Berry Wiggins, *Harry Northwood: The Early Years 1881–1900*, Antique Publications, 1990; William Heacock, James Measell, and Berry Wiggins, *Harry Northwood: The Wheeling Years 1901–1925*, Antique Publications, 1991.

Kyle Husfloen, *Collector's Guide to American Pressed Glass, 1825–1915*, Wallace–Homestead, Krause Publications, 1992; Bill Jenks and Jerry Luna, *Early American Pattern Glass—1850 to 1910: Major Collectible Table Settings with Prices*, Wallace–Homestead, Krause Publications, 1990; Bill Jenks, Jerry Luna, and Darryl Reilly, *Identifying Pattern Glass Reproductions*, Wallace–Homestead, 1993; Minnie Watson Kamm, *Pattern Glass Pitchers, Books 1 Through 8*, published by author, 1970, 4th printing; Mildred and Ralph Lechner, *The World of Salt Shakers, Second Edition*, Collector Books, 1992, 1996 value update; Ruth Webb Lee, *Early American Pressed Glass, 36th Edition*, Lee Publications, 1966; Ruth Webb Lee, *Victorian Glass, 13th Edition*, Lee Publications, 1944; Bessie M. Lindsey, *American Historical Glass*, Charles E. Tuttle Co, 1967; Mollie H. McCain, *The Collector's Encyclopedia of Pattern Glass*, Collector Books, 1982, 1996 value update; Marie McGee, *Millersburg Glass: As I Know It*, Glass Press, 1995; Alice Hulett Metz, *Early American Pattern Glass*, published by author, 1958; Alice Hulett Metz, *Much More Early American Pattern Glass*, published by author, 1965.

S. T. Millard, *Goblets I*, privately printed, 1938, reprinted, Wallace–Homestead, 1975; S. T. Millard, *Goblets II*, privately printed, 1940, reprinted Wallace–Homestead, 1975; John B. Murdock and Walter L. Adams, *Pattern Glass Mugs*, Antique Publications, 1995; Arthur G. Peterson, *Glass Salt Shakers: 1,000 Patterns*, Wallace–Homestead, 1970; Ellen T. Schroy, *Warman's Glass, Second Edition*, Wallace–Homestead, Krause Publications, 1995; Ellen T. Schroy, *Warman's Pattern Glass*, Wallace–Homestead, Krause Publications, 1993; Jane Shadel Spillman, *American and European Pressed Glass in the Corning Museum of Glass*, Corning

Museum of Glass, 1981; Ron Teal, Sr, *Albany Glass: Model Flint Glass Company of Albany, Indiana,* Antique Publications, 1997; Doris and Peter Unitt, *American and Canadian Goblets* (1994), *Vol II* (1994) For the Love of Glass Publishing; Peter Unitt and Anne Worrall, *Canadian Handbook, Pressed Glass Tableware,* Clock House Productions, 1983.

Collectors' Clubs: American Carnival Glass Assoc, 9621 Springwater, Miamisburg, OH 45342; Canadian Glass Assoc, 107 Montcalm Drive, Kitchner, Ontario N2B 2R4 Canada; Early American Glass Traders, RD 5, Box 638, Milford, DE 19963; Early American Pattern Glass Society, PO Box 340023, Columbus, OH 43234; International Carnival Glass Assoc, PO Box 306, Mentone, IL 46539; National Early American Glass Club, PO Box 8489, Silver Spring, MD 20907; National Toothpick Holder Collectors Society, PO Box 553, Marietta, OH 45750.

Museums: Corning Museum of Glass, Corning, NY; National Museum of Man, Ottawa, Ontario, Canada; Sandwich Glass Museum, Sandwich, MA; Schminck Memorial Museum, Lakeview, OR.

Reproduction Alert: Pattern glass has been widely reproduced.

Banana Boat, Fine Cut and Star, marigold carnival, 5" l	**$150**
Banana Boat, Heart with Thumbprint, clear	**80**
Banana Boat, Heart with Thumbprint, ruby stained	**125**
Barber Bottle, Heart with Thumbprint, clear	**115**
Berry Bowl, Holly Amber, individual, 4" d	**150**
Berry Bowl, Holly Amber, master, tiny rim flake, 9½" d	**300**
Bowl, Asters, marigold carnival	**60**
Bowl, Beaded Panel, marigold carnival, Imperial, 8" d	**45**
Bowl, Heart with Thumbprint, clear, scalloped, 10" d	**50**
Bowl, Heart with Thumbprint, clear, square, 9½"	**40**
Bowl, Heart with Thumbprint, ruby stained, scalloped, 10" d	**80**
Bowl, Heart with Thumbprint, ruby stained, square, 9½"	**95**
Bowl, Holly Amber, oval, 7½" l, 4½" w	**425**
Bowl, Holly Amber, round, 4" d	**175**
Bowl, Jumbo, cov, figural, frosted, molded shape of Jumbo wearing etched design blanket, trunk attached to base, c1883, 10½" h, 10¾" l	**660**
Bowl, Shell, green carnival, Imperial, 9" d	**75**
Butter Dish, cov, Heart with Thumbprint, clear	**125**
Butter Dish, cov, Heart with Thumbprint, ruby stained	**130**
Butter Dish, cov, Holly Amber, 5" h, 5" d	**950**
Butter Dish, cov, Holly Amber, 6½" h	**900**
Butter Dish, cov, Jumbo, frosted Jumbo finial, round, ring handles, pedestal base, round PT Barnum head, trunk separation	**330**
Butter Dish, cov, Jumbo, frosted Jumbo finial, square, blanket on back inscribed "JUMBO," 4–panel dome cov with tab handles, square base raised on 4 feet, minor chips	**1,700**
Butter Dish, cov, Old Abe, frosted and clear	**165**
Butter Dish, cov, Sheraton, pastel carnival, US Glass	**170**
Cake Plate, Double Dolphin, center handle, pastel carnival, Fenton	**85**
Cake Plate, Heart with Thumbprint, ruby stained, 9" d	**175**
Cake Stand, Heart with Thumbprint, clear, 9" d	**150**
Celery Vase, Garfield Drape, clear	**27**

Celery Vase, Heart with Thumbprint, clear 75
Celery Vase, Heart with Thumbprint, ruby stained 95
Celery Vase, Oasis, etched 55
Celery Vase, Paneled Forget–Me–Not, clear 40
Celery Vase, Pillar and Flute, purple carnival, Imperial 90
Celery Vase, Scroll and Cane Band, amber flashed 27
Compote, cov, Actress, frosted and clear, 11³/₄" h, 7" d 190
Compote, cov, Actress, frosted and clear, 12³/₄" h, 8" d 230
Compote, cov, Adonis, clear, 8" d 120
Compote, cov, Ashman, clear, 8" d 125
Compote, cov, Broken Column, clear, 7" d 175
Compote, cov, Cord Drapery, clear, high standard, 8" d 225
Compote, cov, Cut Log, clear, 5" d 65
Compote, cov, Daisy and Button with Crossbar, amber 35
Compote, cov, Dog, frosted and clear, 13" h, 8" d 195
Compote, cov, Feather, green, 8" d 550
Compote, cov, Grasshopper, clear 45
Compote, cov, Holly Amber, slight edge roughness on int of cov, 8" h 750
Compote, cov, Lion on Stump, frosted and clear, high standard, 13¹/₂" h,
    8" d 255
Compote, cov, Paneled Forget–Me–Not, clear 55
Compote, cov, Shell and Tassel, clear, 9" h 150
Compote, cov, Swag Block, clear, Duncan, 8" d 95
Compote, cov, Texas, clear, scalloped lid, 6" d 250
Compote, cov, Wildflower, blue, high standard, 8" d 125
Compote, open, Basketweave, clear, patent date June 30th '74, age cracks
    around top 40
Compote, open, Butterfly and Flower, etched, 8¹/₂" w 37
Compote, open, Cable, clear, flint 50
Compote, open, Chain with Star, clear, 7" h, 9" d 20
Compote, open, Champion, ruby stained, 5¹/₂" h, 5¹/₂" d 80
Compote, open, Diamond and Daisy, purple carnival, US Glass 70
Compote, open, Diamond Point, clear, high standard 145
Compote, open, Diamond Thumbprint, clear, high standard, 8" d 125
Compote, open, Diamond Thumbprint, plain foot 95
Compote, open, Diamond Thumbprint, scalloped foot 110
Compote, open, Eyewinker, clear, 7" d 85
Compote, open, Eyewinker, fluted, clear, low standard 95
Compote, open, Goose Girl, clear 225
Compote, open, Heart with Thumbprint, high standard, clear, 8¹/₂" d 100
Compote, open, Heart with Thumbprint, ruby stained, 8¹/₂" d 185
Compote, open, Horn of Plenty, clear, low standard, 7" d 125
Compote, open, Jenny Lind, amber, 8³/₈" w 90
Compote, open, King's Crown, ruby stained, scalloped edge, 8" d 65
Compote, open, Long Thumbprint, green carnival, Dugan 40
Compote, open, Millard, ruby stained, 8¹/₄" h, 7¹/₂" d 250
Compote, open, Nail, clear, etched floral dec, 8" d 85
Compote, open, Palace, clear, 8" d 60
Compote, open, Pressed Block, clear, high standard 110
Compote, open, Reverse Torpedo, clear, high standard, 8" d 110
Compote, open, Sailboats, marigold carnival, Fenton 65

Compote, open, Shrine, clear **20**
Compote, open, Teepee, clear, 9" d **40**
Compote, open, Thumbprint, clear, low standard, 9¼" d **115**
Compote, open, US Coin, clear, small chip, 7" d **125**
Compote, open, Zipper, clear, high standard **65**
Creamer, Heart with Thumbprint, clear **65**
Creamer, Heart with Thumbprint, ruby stained **175**
Creamer, Leaf Tiers, ftd, marigold carnival, Fenton **85**
Creamer, Lustre Rose, purple carnival, Imperial **55**
Creamer, Swan, clear **55**
Cream Pitcher, Classic, clear **40**
Cream Pitcher, Goats Head, frosted and clear **55**
Cream Pitcher, Holly Amber, 4½" h **450**
Cream Pitcher, Jumbo, etched, Jumbo with PT Barnum, Barnum head design
   at handle base, slight base rim roughness **90**
Cream Pitcher, Lion and Baboon, clear **125**
Cream Pitcher, Oaken Bucket, vaseline **100**
Cruet, Block and Triple Bars, clear **50**
Cruet, Double Circle, blue **175**
Cruet, Empress, green **375**
Cruet, Esther, green, short **125**
Cruet, Flora, green, gold trim **200**
Cruet, Idyll, blue **175**
Cruet, Paneled Thistle, clear **50**
Cruet, Portland, clear **75**
Cruet, Shoshone, clear **65**
Cruet, Shoshone, green **125**
Goblet, Actress, clear **55**

Left: Butter Dish, cov, Jumbo, clear, round PT Barnum head, trunk separation, $330. Photo courtesy Gene Harris Auction Center.

Right: Condiment Set, Maize, clear, consisting of salt and pepper shakers, mustard, and glass base, Libbey, 5³/₄" h, 6" w, $200.

Goblet, Argus, clear 75
Goblet, Ashburton, clear 50
Goblet, Baby Thumbprint, clear 100
Goblet, Ball and Swirl, clear 25
Goblet, Barred Oval, clear 35
Goblet, Bellflower, clear 50
Goblet, Bird and Roses, clear, etched 25
Goblet, Classic, clear, log foot 300
Goblet, Curtain Tieback, clear 25
Goblet, Dahlia, clear 50
Goblet, Dakota, clear, fern and berry etching 25
Goblet, Dewdrop, blue 25
Goblet, Excelsior, clear 75
Goblet, Galloway, clear 100
Goblet, Garfield Drape, clear 50
Goblet, Gothic, clear 65
Goblet, Heart with Thumbprint, clear 60
Goblet, Heart with Thumbprint, ruby stained 115
Goblet, Horn of Plenty, clear 65
Goblet, Huber, clear 25
Goblet, Inverted Fern, clear 50
Goblet, Lincoln Drape, clear 150
Goblet, Loop and Dewdrop, clear 30
Goblet, Michigan, clear 45
Goblet, New England Pineapple, clear 70
Goblet, Octagon, marigold carnival, Imperial 65
Goblet, Ostrich Looking at the Moon, clear 140
Goblet, Paneled Forget–Me–Not, amethyst 325
Goblet, Paneled Herringbone, clear 30
Goblet, Pennsylvania, clear, gold trim 20
Goblet, Pigs in Corn, clear 550
Goblet, Pineapple Stem, clear 50
Goblet, Pointed Jewel, clear 30
Goblet, Portland, clear 50
Goblet, Reverse Torpedo, clear 65
Goblet, Ribbed Palm, clear 50
Goblet, Ribbon, clear 30
Goblet, Ribbon, frosted 50
Goblet, Rose in Snow, clear 45
Goblet, Scarab, clear 170
Goblet, Sedan, clear 15
Goblet, Seneca Loop, clear, flint 45
Goblet, Sheraton, amber 50
Goblet, Sheraton, clear 35
Goblet, Shrine, clear 70
Goblet, Snail, clear 110
Goblet, Texas, clear 115
Goblet, Thousand Eye, blue 150
Goblet, Three Panel, blue 45
Goblet, US Coin, clear, 1892 dimes 550
Goblet, Waffle, clear 30

Goblet, Wild Loganberry, peach opalescent carnival, Westmoreland 150
Ice Bucket, Heart with Thumbprint, clear 65
Jelly Compote, cov, Holly Amber, 8" h 850
Milk Pitcher, Grape, green carnival, Imperial 300
Mug, Birds at Fountain, opaque blue, 1^7/$_8$" h 17
Mug, Cleveland–Thurman, light blue 275
Mug, Dogs and Bird, blue, 2^5/$_8$" h 35
Mug, Holly Amber, 4" h 400
Mug, Westward Ho, clear, 1^7/$_8$" h 200
Mustard, Heart with Thumbprint, clear, silverplated cov 95
Mustard, Humpty Dumpty, marigold carnival 75
Mustard, Mortar, amber 10
Nappy, Grape, marigold carnival, Imperial 30
Nappy, Heart with Thumbprint, clear, triangular 30
Plate, Grapevine Lattice, Dugan, 9" d 275
Plate, Heart with Thumbprint, clear, 6" d 25
Plate, Heart with Thumbprint, clear, 10" d 45
Plate, Heart with Thumbprint, ruby stained, 6" d 40
Plate, Heart with Thumbprint, ruby stained, 10" d 75
Plate, Holly Amber, 7^1/$_2$" d 400
Plate, Peacock and Urn, purple carnival, Fenton, 9" d 500
Punch Cup, Heart with Thumbprint, clear 20
Punch Cup, Heart with Thumbprint, ruby stained 30
Punch Cup, Memphis, purple carnival, Northwood 40
Relish Dish, Gibson Girl, frosted and clear 55
Relish Dish, Holly Amber, slight edge roughness, 9" l 375
Relish Dish, Neptune, blue, 6" l 55
Rose Bowl, Floral and Optic, ftd, peach opalescent carnival, Imperial 190
Rose Bowl, Heart with Thumbprint, large, clear 65
Rose Bowl, Heart with Thumbprint, large, ruby stained 95
Salt and Pepper Shakers, pr, Heart with Thumbprint, clear 95
Spooner, Baby Face, frosted and clear 75
Spooner, Classic, clear 75
Spooner, Diamond Point Columns, marigold carnival, Imperial 40
Spooner, Goat's Head, frosted and clear, slight base rim roughness 17
Spooner, Heart with Thumbprint, clear 50
Spooner, Heart with Thumbprint, ruby stained 75
Spooner, Holly Amber, edge roughness, 4" h 850
Spooner, Jumbo, Jumbo with PT Barnum, Barnum–head handle 300
Spooner, Oaken Bucket, blue 35
Sugar, cov, Baby Face, cov, frosted and clear 165
Sugar, cov, Butterfly and Berry, cov, marigold carnival, Fenton 100
Sugar, cov, Classic, cov, clear 250
Sugar, cov, Goat's Head, cov, clear 55
Sugar, cov, Heart with Thumbprint, individual, clear 25
Sugar, cov, Heart with Thumbprint, individual, ruby stained 35
Sugar, cov, Holly Amber, cov, 7^1/$_4$" h 850
Sugar, cov, Jumbo, cov, Jumbo finial, Jumbo with PT Barnum, ring handles,
   Barnum–head design at handle base 315
Sugar, cov, Oaken Bucket, cov, vaseline 115
Toothpick Holder, Bear, blue 65

Toothpick Holder, Beatty Honeycomb, blue 55
Toothpick Holder, Bohemian, green, gold dec 275
Toothpick Holder, Box in Box, green, gold dec 85
Toothpick Holder, Croesus, amethyst, gold dec 150
Toothpick Holder, Daisy and Button, blue 75
Toothpick Holder, Daisy and Button, blue, V ornament 55
Toothpick Holder, Delaware, rose stain, gold dec 175
Toothpick Holder, Dog and Stump, clear 22
Toothpick Holder, Elephant Toe, rose stain 80
Toothpick Holder, Empress, green, gold dec 275
Toothpick Holder, Fancy Loop, green, gold dec 170
Toothpick Holder, Forget–Me–Not, pink 65
Toothpick Holder, Frog and Shell, blue 33
Toothpick Holder, Frog and Shell, clear 27
Toothpick Holder, Frog and Shell, green 38
Toothpick Holder, Gatling Gun, amber 15
Toothpick Holder, Gonterman Swirl, blue 230
Toothpick Holder, Gonterman Swirl, blue, slight opal 330
Toothpick Holder, Grecian Column, blue 120
Toothpick Holder, Hobnail, clear 65
Toothpick Holder, Holly Amber, 2½" h, 3" d 350
Toothpick Holder, Kittens, marigold carnival, Fenton, 3" h 175
Toothpick Holder, Klondike, clear 175
Toothpick Holder, Leaf Umbrella, mauve, cased 375
Toothpick Holder, Minnesota, marigold carnival, US Glass 60
Toothpick Holder, Monkeys on Stump, amber 17
Toothpick Holder, Monkey with Hat, emerald green 55
Toothpick Holder, Nestor, amethyst 120
Toothpick Holder, New York, ruby stained, US Glass 75
Toothpick Holder, Petticoat, vaseline, gold dec 125
Toothpick Holder, Pig on Flatcar, amber 500
Toothpick Holder, Pineapple and Fan, green 190
Toothpick Holder, Priscilla, clear 125
Toothpick Holder, Punty and Diamond Point, clear 270

Loving Cup, Orange Tree, marigold carnival, Fenton, $275.

Toothpick Holder, Ribbed Panels, marigold carnival   300
Toothpick Holder, Ribbed Pillar, pink   90
Toothpick Holder, Royal Ivy, clear   165
Toothpick Holder, Royal Ivy, frosted rubina   175
Toothpick Holder, Royal Ivy, rainbow spatter   325
Toothpick Holder, Texas Star, clear   135
Toothpick Holder, Two Roosters, amber   60
Toothpick Holder, Vermont, blue, flower dec   150
Toothpick Holder, Vermont, opaque ivory   125
Tray, Actress, clear   55
Tray, Columbia, amber   110
Tray, Holly Amber, 8" d   850
Tray, Knights of Labor, vaseline   500
Tray, Studs, round, marigold carnival, Jeannette   65
Tray, Windmill, green carnival, Imperial   65
Tumbler, Banded Rib, marigold carnival   25
Tumbler, Blackberry Block, blue carnival, Fenton   75
Tumbler, Garfield, clear   50
Tumbler, Heart with Thumbprint, clear   45
Tumbler, Heart with Thumbprint, ruby stained   60
Tumbler, Holly Amber, 4" h   300
Tumbler, Holly Amber, beaded rim, 3½" h   600
Tumbler, Pansy, purple carnival, Imperial   90
Vase, Corn, purple carnival, Northwood   800
Vase, Hand, amber   38
Vase, Hand, amber and clear   65
Vase, Heart with Thumbprint, clear, 6" h   40
Vase, Heart with Thumbprint, clear, 10" h   65
Vase, Heart with Thumbprint, ruby stained, 6" h   60
Vase, Heart with Thumbprint, ruby stained, 10" h   85
Vase, Heavy Diamond, green carnival, Imperial   65
Vase, Holly Amber, 6¼" h, 3" w   400
Vase, Star Medallion, marigold carnival, Imperial, 6" h   40
Vase, Wide Panel, blue carnival, Fenton   60
Water Carafe, Heart with Thumbprint, clear   100
Water Pitcher, Camel with Rider, etched   100
Water Pitcher, Classic, clear   300
Water Pitcher, Daisy and Button   40
Water Pitcher, Heart with Thumbprint, clear   200
Water Pitcher, Holly Amber, 9" h 1,500
Water Pitcher, Oaken Bucket, amethyst   220
Water Pitcher, Oaken Bucket, clear   110
Water Pitcher, Owl, amber   330
Water Pitcher, Paneled Forget–Me–Not, clear   65
Water Pitcher, Swan, clear   115

KITCHEN

Family life in rural America focuses around the kitchen. A substantial breakfast at the break of dawn and a robust satisfying meal at the end of a day's hard work were standard fare. At the conclusion of the evening meal, it was not uncommon to sit around the table and converse, often for hours. In an agrarian environment, the kitchen table is as important a social center as the living room or parlor.

The kitchen remained a central focal point in the family environment until frozen foods, TV dinners, and microwave ovens freed the family to congregate in other areas of the house during meal time. Initially, food preparation involved both the long and short term. Home canning remained popular through the early 1950s.

Many early kitchen utensils were handmade and prized by their owners. Next came a period of utilitarian products manufactured of tin and other metals. Design began to serve both an aesthetic and functional purpose. Brightly enameled handles and knobs were made to appeal to the busy housewife. With the advent of Bakelite and plastic even more color found its way into the kitchen.

Multicolored enameled matchsafes, pot scrubbers, and string holders were not only functional, but advertised a product or service. These early advertising giveaways are prized by country collectors.

The newfangled gadgets and early electrical appliances changed the type and style of kitchen products. Many products became faddish. Electric waffle makers were popular in the 1930s and breakfast was served on special waffle dinnerware sets, complete with serving platters and syrup pitchers. Old hand-operated egg beaters were replaced by aerators and mixers.

References: Christina Bishop, *Miller's Collecting Kitchenware*, Millers Publications, 1995; Terri Clemens, *American Family Farm Antiques*, Wallace–Homestead, Krause Publications, 1994; Linda Campbell Franklin, *300 Years of Kitchen Collectibles: An Identification and Value Guide, Fourth Edition*, Krause Publications, 1997; Jan Lindenberger, *Black Memorabilia For the Kitchen: A Handbook and Price Guide*, Schiffer Publishing, 1992; Barbara Mauzy, *The Complete Book of Kitchen Collecting*, Schiffer Publishing, 1997; Kathryn McNerney, *Kitchen Antiques: 1790–1940*, Collector Books, 1991, 1997 value update; Kathryn McNerney, *Primitives: Our American Heritage, First Series* (1979, 1996 value update), *Second Series* (1987, 1996 value update), Collector Books; George C. Neumann, *Early American Country Furnishings: Northeastern America, 1650–1800's*, L–W Book Sales, 1984, 1996 value update; Ellen M. Plante, *Kitchen Collectibles: An Illustrated Price Guide*, Wallace–Homestead, Krause Publications, 1991; Suzanne Slesin, et al., *Everyday Things: Wire*, Abbeville Press, 1994; Diane Stoneback, *Kitchen Collectibles: The Essential Buyer's Guide*, Wallace–Homestead, Krause Publications, 1994.

BAKING ITEMS

The Country kitchen is readily acknowledged as the source of nourishing, hearty meals. A Country kitchen isn't complete without a freshly baked pie cooling on the window sill. The smell of freshly baked goods lingers in the minds of many individuals. Homemade bread is a must. Dessert is an integral part of dinner. In fact, dessert products have a habit of showing up at breakfast as well as in the lunch box.

All items associated with baking are collectible, from ingredient packaging to utensils used to serve the end product. Collectors concentrate on three distinct periods:

1850 to 1915, 1915 to 1940, and 1940 to the present. The presence of the original box is extremely important for items made after 1915.

Pieces containing a manufacturer's or patent date marking and highly decorated pieces, either painted or lithographed, are more highly valued than unmarked or plain examples. Many collectors like to use these old implements. Hence, the desirability of pieces that are in working condition. Finally, the category is subject to crazes. Pie birds are the "hot" collectible of the moment.

References: *Griswold Cast Iron, Vol I,* (1993, 1997 value update), *Vol 2* (1995), L–W Book Sales; Jon B. Haussler, *Griswold Muffin Pans,* Schiffer Publishing, 1997; L–W Book Sales, *Collectors Guide to Wagner Ware and Other Companies,* L–W Book Sales, 1994; *Price Guide to Griswold Mfg. Co,* 1918 Catalog Reprint, L–W Book Sales, 1996; David G. Smith and Charles Wafford, *The Book of Griswold & Wagner: Favorite Piqua, Sidney Hollow Ware, Wapak,* Schiffer Publishing, 1995.

Newsletters: *Cast Iron Cookware News,* 28 Angela Avenue, San Anselmo, CA 94960; *Cookies,* 5426 27th Street NW, Washington, DC 20015; *Kettles 'n Cookware,* Drawer B, Perrysburg, NY 14129; *Piebirds Unlimited,* 14 Harmony School Road, Flemington, NJ 08822.

Collectors' Clubs: Antique Stove Assoc, 5515 Almeda Road, Houston, TX 77004; Cookie Cutter Collectors Club, 1167 Teal Road SW, Dellroy, OH 44620; Griswold & Cast Iron Cookware Assoc, Drawer B, Perrysburg, NY 14129; Kollectors of Old Kitchen Stuff, 501 Market Street, Mifflinburg, PA 17844.

Apple Parer, double wheel, pegged, hand forged and lathe turned parts, mid–19th C, 22" l	$35
Apple Peeler, cast iron, Reading Hardware Co, top painted gold, C clamp base with wing nut, small wood handle on crank, mkd "78" in keystone in circle and "Made Only By The Reading Hardware Co., Reading, Pa., U.S.A.," 12" h	50
Apple Slicer, wood and iron, 6 blades, 19th C, 42" l	150
Baking Pan, cast iron, Wagner #150	250
Beater, Chicago, motor on top, measuring glass bottom	35
Biscuit Board, softwood, rect, breadboard ends, raised at 1 end, sides with arched wood roller mounts, horizontally ribbed wood roller with wood crank handle, 23⅞ x 18½"	50
Biscuit Cutter, tin, Mennonite, cuts fourteen rolls each revolution, 11" l	30
Biscuit Cutter, tin, Rumford Baking Powder adv, single biscuit	15
Biscuit Prick, wood, 8 cut nail prongs, c1870, 4" h	60
Biscuit Stamp, chip carved "Jamaica" imprint, c1850, 4" h	35
Bread Board, wood, round, carved motto "Give Us This Day Our Daily," 9½" d	50
Bread Maker, White House Bread Maker, table clamp, 1902	135
Bread Pan, tin, Ideal, 2 tubes	30
Bread Raiser, tin, stamped, ventilated dome lid, 8 qt	40
Bread Slicing Box, wood, varnished, 19th C, 13½" l, 5¾" h	65
Breadstick Pan, cast iron, Wagner EE	50
Bundt Pan, cast iron, Wagner style B	250
Cake Mold, cast iron, lamb, 2 pcs, 13" l	125
Cake Mold, cast iron, rabbit, Griswold	270
Cherry Pitter, Enterprise, #16	40
Cherry Pitter, Watt, #15	65

Coconut Grater, turned iron shaft, serrated blades, brass and wood handle, mid–19th C, 7" h 100

Cookie Board, beech, chip carved letters, old patina, worm holes, some edge damage, 4⅝ x 21" 200

Cookie Board, birch, double sided, carved man on horseback with flag 1 side, other with rooster and hen, initialed "F.E.," old varnish finish, age cracks, few worm holes, 9¾ x 6" 475

Cookie Board, mahogany, carved man on horse, stamped "J. Conger" 2,500

Cookie Board, maple, carved cornucopia, fish, flower basket, woman at well, rose, and knight on horseback, cherry colored old finish, minor age cracks, 6⅓ x 11¼" 800

Cookie Board, pewter, wood backing, 6 designs of flowers, fish, and bird, 3⅞ x 4¾" 50

Cookie Cutter, tin, dancing Dutchman, 9¼" h, 6⅝" w 55

Cookie Cutter, tin, deer, stylized antlers, 1 section at back of neck loose, 6½" l 150

Cookie Cutter, tin, dog, rusted, 10" l 95

Cookie Cutter, tin, eagle, 4" h 100

Cookie Cutter, tin, heart and hand, cylindrical handle, 3⅛" l 475

Cookie Cutter, tin, leaping deer, 8" l 195

Cookie Cutter, tin, lovebirds on heart, 7" h 1,200

Cookie Cutter, tin, man and woman, standing, hands on hips, 11½" h, price for pair 145

Cookie Roller, wood, acorns, old patina, 6¾" l 100

Corn Bread Skillet, Wagner 25

Corn Stick Pan, cast iron, 7 cavities, Griswold, #79 40

Corn Stick Pan, cast iron, 7 cavities, Wagner B 50

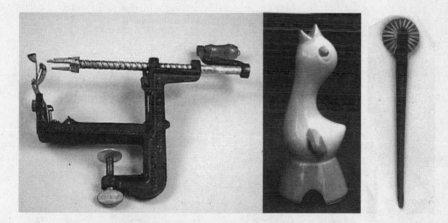

Left: Apple Peeler, table clamp, mkd "Apple Parer, Corer, Slicer, Made in USA, White Mountain Freezer, Inc.," painted green, red wood knob, 11" l, $35.

Center: Pie Bird, Shawnee, white, green eyes and wings, pink beak and base, glossy, unmkd, 5" h, $35.

Right: Pie Crimper, bone wheel, wood handle, 1850–70, $75.

Dough Box, poplar, dark reddish brown graining, 2 board top, dovetailed box, mortised and pinned apron, splayed turned legs, 42" w, 20" d, 29" h . .   635

Dough Box, walnut, dovetailed, splayed base with square tapered legs, refinished, 36½" l, 21½" w, 29" h   375

Doughnut Box, wood, natural finish, minor damage to bottom, PA, c1860, 12½" d, 6" h   100

Doughnut Cutter, wood, c1880, 4" w   60

Dough Scraper, steel and brass, mkd "P.D. 25, 1850" (Peter Derr, PA), 4" l . . .   500

Flour Dredger, tin, dome pierced lid, strap handle, ftd, c1825, 6" h   25

Flour Grinder, cast iron, graniteware hopper, wood pusher, late 19th C   80

Flour Sifter, tin, double ended, yellow wood handle, Kwik, 5 cup   20

Food Mold, copper, round, eagle with arrows and laurel, 7¾" d   385

Fruit Press, cast iron, nickel plated, bowl shaped hopper, table clamp, mkd "Enterprise Mfg. Co., Philadelphia," Sept 30, 1879 patent date, 12" h, 11" l   65

Lemon Reamer, maple, c1910, 6" l   12

Measuring Cup, spun aluminum, Swans Down Cake Flour adv, 1 cup   15

Measuring Spoons, Towles Log Cabin Syrup adv, price for set of 4   45

Mixing Spoon, wood, turned handle   15

Muffin Pan, cast iron, Griswold #8   200

Muffin Pan, cast iron, John Wright, alternating lion and lamb heads, mkd "Lion & Lamb Popover Pan" and "C 1904 John Wright Cast in USA," 6½ x 10¾"   200

Muffin Pan, cast iron, Wagner, Turk's head, 6 cups   275

Nut Grinder, cast iron and tin, glass jar, screw–on tin hopper, Climax, 1940s .   15

Nutmeg Grater, iron, wood handle, c1880, 5" l   75

Pastry Blender, wire, Omar Wonder Flour adv   10

Pastry Board, rect wood board with tin cov, rounded rim, small round hole and wire loop for hanging, bottom of board with applied wood shelf with rounded corners, 2 tin brackets mounted on front hold maple rolling pin with traces of green paint on turned wood handles, 22⅛" w, 21½" h   200

Pastry Brush, turned wood handle, Shaker, 8¼" l   125

Pastry Crimper, aluminum, Just Right Pie Sealer   10

Pastry Crimper, brass, black wood handle   15

Pastry Cutter, 2 blades, 1 steel, 1 wedge, red handle   15

Pastry Roller, turned wood, vining design, soft patina, minor chips on edge of cylinder, 14" l   250

Left: Cookie Cutter, tin, woman's profile, 6 air holes, 3 x 4⅛", $8.

Right: Cookie Cutter, tin, horse, 2 finger holes, 7½ x 5½", $35.

Peach Parer, cast iron, wood board base, 2 opposing forks, David H
  Whittemore, 1860s **100**
Pie Bird, ceramic, bird, pink, yellow, and turquoise, Morton Pottery **20**
Pie Bird, ceramic, duck, long neck, blue and black, 1950s **25**
Pie Bird, ceramic, rooster, Cleminson Pottery, 1940s **20**
Pie Crimper, carved bone, crown top, cookie cutter end, Lancaster County,
  PA, c1820, 5" l **300**
Pie Fork, wood handle, 2 iron tines, late 19th C, 16" l **25**
Pie Lifter, brass ferule, turned wood handle, Shaker **50**
Pie Pan, tin, Knotts Berry Farm adv **6**
Popover Pan, cast iron, Erie **20**
Poppyseed Mill, cast iron, painted turquoise, spun brass hopper, table
  clamp, Standard, 1890s, 9¼" h **45**
Pudding Mold, copper, melon shaped, 2 pc, oval hinged handles on top and
  bottom, mkd "50," 7⁹/₁₆ x 5¹³/₁₆", 3½" h **25**
Pudding Mold, tin, round with rounded bottom and tall tapered center cone,
  sides flare slightly toward rim, supported by 3 ring shaped feet, lid with
  slightly rounded top and 2 ring shaped handles, 8½" d, 8¼" h **25**
Raisin Seeder, cast iron, mkd "Ezy Raisin Seeder, Pat May 21, 1895" and
  "Scald the Raisins," 6" l **125**
Rolling Pin, curly maple, 18" l **115**
Rolling Pin, glass, fiery opalescent, red, green, and olive gold enameled
  house, dec border, mkd "Union," 14" l **135**
Sifter, round, bentwood sides, fitted with wire mesh with 3 metal crossed
  support rods, early red paint, 17³/₄" d, 4¼" h **25**
Spatula, curly maple, refinished, 13½" l **100**
Vienna Roll, cast iron, Wagner, 6 cup **125**
Wafer Iron, round cast iron wafer mold with eagle and shield design and "E
  Pluribus Unum," scissor-form wrought iron handles, 27" l **450**
Waffle Iron, cast iron, Griswold #8, finger hinge **125**
Waffle Iron, cast iron, Wagner #8, high base **50**
Whole Wheat Pan, Griswold #28 . . . .   **225**

CANNING ITEMS

The bountiful harvest is a common theme in Country collecting. However, a bountiful harvest meant plenty of hard work, especially for the country housewife. The
products of one harvest had to last until the next harvest was gathered. Further, one
had to plan ahead, laying away extra in case the next year's returns were insufficient.

Canning, also known as jarring, is labor intensive. Time passed quicker and more
was accomplished when extra hands were available. Canning bees, similar to quilting
bees, were common occurrences. Most canning parties consisted of the women from
one's extended family. Often the group moved from one home to another during a harvest season.

An innovative Philadelphia glass maker, Thomas W. Dyott, began promoting glass
canning jars in 1829. John Landis Mason patented the screw-type canning jar on
November 30, 1858. The progress of the American glass industry and manufacturing
processes can be studied through fruit jars. Early handmade jars show bits of local
history.

Many ways were devised to close the jars securely. Lids of fruit jars can be a separate collectible, but most collectors feel it is more desirous to have a complete fruit

jar. Closures can be as simple as a cork or wax seal. Other closures include zinc or glass lids, wire bails, metal screw bands, and today's rubber sealed metal lids.

Many fruit jar collectors base their collections on a specific geographical area, others on one manufacturer or one color. Another way to collect fruit jars is by patent date. Over fifty different types bear a patent date of 1858. Note: The patent date does not mean the jar was made in that year.

Most canning collectors do not limit their focus to fruit jars. Canners, funnels, sealing equipment, and cooking thermometers also are sought.

References: Douglas M. Leybourne, Jr., *The Collector's Guide to Old Fruit Jars: Red Book No. 8,* published by author, 1997; Jerry McCann, *The Guide to Collecting Fruit Jars: Fruit Jar Annual, Vol 3–1998,* Phoenix Press, 1997; Dick Roller (comp), *Fruit Jar Patents: Vol II, 1870–1899,* Phoenix Press, 1997; Dick Roller (comp), *Fruit Jar Patents: Vol III, 1900–1942,* Phoenix Press, 1996; Dick Roller, *Indiana Glass Factories Notes,* Acorn Press, 1994; Bill Schoeder, *1000 Fruit Jars: Priced and Illustrated,* 5th Edition, Collector Books, 1987, 1996 value update.

Newletter: *Fruit Jar Newsletter,* 364 Gregory Avenue, West Orange, NJ 07052.

Collectors' Clubs: Ball Collectors Club, 22203 Doncaster, Riverview, MI 48192; Federation of Historical Bottle Collectors, Inc, 88 Sweetbriar Branch, Longwood, FL 32750; Jelly Jammers, 110 White Oak Drive, Butler, PA 16001; Midwest Antique Fruit Jar & Bottle Club, PO Box 38, Flat Rock, IN 47234.

Note: Fruit Jars listed below are machine made unless otherwise noted.

Canner, Mudge's Patent Canner, tin and copper, Biddle–Gaumer Co, late
  1880s **$225**
Canning Jar, stoneware, medium brown, imp 5–point star on shoulder, tin
  lid and wire closure, c1890–1910, qt **45**
Canning Rack, wire, rect, used in 2 hole boiler **15**
Corn Dryer, twisted wire, hanging ring, c1910 . . . . : **15**
Fruit Dryer, tin frame, wire screen, 3 shelves, removable trays, Arlington
  Oven Dryer, 9" h **135**
Fruit Jar, "Ball Deluxe," clear, glass lid, wire bail, pt **3**
Fruit Jar, "Cleveland Fruit Juice Co, Cleveland, OH," clear, ground lip, glass
  lid, ¹/₂ gal **5**
Fruit Jar, "Cohansey Glass Mf'g Co. Pat. Mch 20 77" on base, bluish aqua,
  barrel shape, smooth base, applied groove ring wax sealer, c1880–90, qt . . **70**
Fruit Jar, "Double Safety," clear, glass lid, wire bail, ¹/₂ pt **5**
Fruit Jar, "Economy," amber, cylindrical, metal lid, spring clip, pt **5**
Fruit Jar, "Hartell's Glass Air Tight Cover" on rim, "Patented Oct, 19 1858"
  on top of lid, pale bluish green, smooth base, ground lip, orig emb glass
  lid, c1865–75, pt **225**
Fruit Jar, "Jumbo Brand Apple Butter, patented June 24, 1930," smooth lip,
  metal lid, painted, 10 oz **20**
Fruit Jar, "Magic TM Mason," clear, emb cup and oz measurements 1 side,
  milliliter measurements other side **1**
Fruit Jar, "Mason," amber, smooth base, smooth lip, zinc screw lid,
  c1910–20, pt **60**
Fruit Jar, "Mason," clear, emb "1776," Liberty Bell, and "1976" **3**
Fruit Jar, "Mason Fruit Jar," medium amber, smooth base, ground lip, zinc lid,
  ³/₁₆" chip on lip, c1875–95, pt **175**

Fruit Jar, Ideal, aqua, quart, $5.

Fruit Jar, Mason Jar Sealer and Opener, cast iron frame, steel blade,
adjustable leather strap, c1912 .... **20**
Fruit Jar, "Mason's Crystal Jar," clear, smooth base, ground lip, zinc screw lid,
c1875–90, midget pt **130**
Fruit Jar, "Mason's (keystone in circle) Patent Nov 30th 1858," cornflower
blue, smooth base, ground lip, zinc screw lid, c1875–95, ½ gal **140**
Fruit Jar, "Mason's Patent Nov. 30th 58," medium yellowish green, smooth
base, ground lip, zinc screw lid, c1875–95, pt **800**
Fruit Jar, "Mastadon," aqua, "I.A. Evans & Co. Pittsburgh PA" on smooth
base, applied groove ring wax sealer, tin lid, 1" chip on side of lip,
c1875–95, qt **170**
Fruit Jar, "Newmark Special Extra Mason," green, metal lid, qt **12**
Fruit Jar, "Red Mason's Patent Nov 30th 1858," aqua, zinc lid, pt **12**
Fruit Jar, "Regal" in oval, clear, glass lid, qt **3**
Fruit Jar, "Security Seal," clear, glass lid, wire bail, qt **7**
Fruit Jar, Simplex, metal, Gorman Mfg Co, late 19th C **15**
Fruit Jar, "Standard From Foote, Baer & Co Cleveland. O. – W. McC & Co,"
bluish aqua, smooth base, applied groove ring wax sealer, tin lid, shallow
¼" flake off lip, c1880, qt **180**
Fruit Jar, "Stevens Tin Top, Patd July 17, 1873," aqua, "S.K. & Co. (around N
within star)" on smooth base, applied groove ring wax sealer, tin lid, shal-
low ⅜" chip on outer edge of ring, c1875–95, qt **50**
Fruit Jar, Sun Trade Mark, aquamarine, clear glass lid, ground mouth, metal
yoke clamp, pt **80**
Fruit Jar, "The Eclipse," bluish aqua, smooth base, applied groove ring wax
sealer, tin lid, 1" iridescent bruise on inside of wax seal ring, qt **45**
Fruit Jar, "Trademark Climax Registered," clear, smooth lip, ½ pt **4**
Fruit Jar, "Trade Mark Lightning," straw yellow with olive tone, "Putnam" on
smooth base, ground lip, orig glass lid and lightning type closure,
c1885–95, qt **125**
Fruit Jar Holder, wire, 6" h **6**
Fruit Jar Lifter, E–Z Lift, iron **5**
Fruit Jar Wrench, Presto, iron, Cupples Co, orig box, 20th C **8**
Fruit Jar Wrench, Speedo, cast metal, geared mechanical, c1900 .... **10**
Fruit Jar Wrench, Wilson's, cast iron, Wilson Mfg Co, early 20th C **15**

Funnel, Enamelware, wide untapered neck, c1900, 5" l . . . . 　**15**
Funnel, tin, ring handle, large mouth, c1900 . . . . 　**8**
Herb Drying Rack, wood, painted blue, 19th C, 28" l . . . . 　**425**
Jelly Glass, pressed glass, clear . . . . 　**3**
Jelly Thermometer, knife shaped, calibrated metal plate, glass tube, tapered
　turned wood handle, hanging loop, Taylor Instrument Co, NY, mid–1930s 　. 　**8**

CLEANING & WASHDAY

Living and working in a rural environment was dirty business. Field work and feeding the animals generated large amounts of dust. Wet weather meant mud and plenty of it.

The housewife faced a never–ending battle to keep things clean. Dusting was a daily chore. Washday was not limited to Mondays on most farms. Rural society always has judged wives on how they kept house and family. Women's liberation may have changed some things, but not this.

Many individuals who decorate in Country favor the weathered look. Cleaning and washday material fits the bill. These implements were meant to be used, used hard, and to last. Try beating a rug with a carpet beater.

Because electricity came late to many rural areas, most pre–1940 implements were hand powered. The number of variants within each product is overwhelming. Mail order catalogs are a great research source to determine what was available during a given time period.

References: Linda Campbell Franklin, *300 Years of Housekeeping Collectibles,* Books Americana, Krause Publications, 1992; David Irons, *Irons By Irons,* published by author, 1994; David Irons, *More Irons By Irons*, published by author, 1997; David Irons, *Pressing Iron Patents: A Pictorial Presentation of Patent Briefs, 1876–1912,* published by author, 1994.

Periodical: *Iron Talk,* PO Box 68, Waelder, TX 78959.

Collectors' Clubs: Club of the Friends of Ancient Smoothing Irons, PO Box 215, Carlsbad, CA 92008; Midwest Sad Iron Collectors Club, 24 Nob Hill Drive, St Louis, MO 63138.

Left: Clothes Sprinkler, clothespin, ceramic, metal stopper, $100.

Right: Trivet, crown, cast iron, Colebrookdale Iron Co, Pottstown, PA, 6" h, $20.

Wash Boiler, cov, Lisk adv, copper, orig paper label, wood handles, 26" w, 12" d, 16" h, $85.

Carpet Beater, wire, intertwined circles design, turned wood handle, c1910, 32" l **$25**

Clothes Dasher, heavy tin, wood handle, Rapid Vacuum Washer, c1920 ..... **45**

Clothes Dryer, wood, folding **25**

Clothespins, wood, suppressed ball shaped flattened tops, simple incised line around side, 4¾" l, price for set of 5 .... **50**

Clothes Sprinkler, ceramic, cat, white, orange glass eyes, mkd "Cardinal," 7½" h **135**

Clothes Sprinkler, ceramic, Dearie is Weary, woman holding iron, yellow dress, head is sprinkler **225**

Clothes Sprinkler, ceramic, mammy, white dress with red trim **250**

Clothes Sprinkler, ceramic, rooster, long neck, plastic cap, 10" h **100**

Clothes Sprinkler, ceramic, sadiron, ivy **40**

Dusting Brush, horsehair, turned wood handle, 9" l **20**

Dust Pan, graniteware, gray speckled **100**

Dust Pan, pine, lollipop handle, painted gray–blue, c1840, 14" w **125**

Ironing Board, poplar, folding, single board top, 4 turned legs, old green paint on base, 59½" l, 30" h **150**

Laundry Basket, woven splint, oblong, ribbed, open rim handles, 24" l, 20" w, 11" h **120**

Plate Drying Rack, softwood, rect box, arched top with oval cutout handle, hinged plate rest, dovetailed construction, bottom nailed, refinished, 27¼ x 5¾" **95**

Sadiron, round back, 5¾" l, 4½" h **20**

Soap Saver, tin frame, twisted wire handle, hanging loop, wire mesh container, 3½ x 2½", 7" l handle **20**

Washboard, wood frame, Midget–Washer, glass scrubber, 8½" l **15**

Washboard, wood frame, yellow ware insert with brown sponging, gray weathered wood, pottery worn and chipped, 12¾" w, 25" h **195**

Washboard, wood frame, Zinc King, zinc scrubber **18**

Whisk Broom, wood, mammy handle, 4½" l **20**

Wringer Washer, square stainless steel tub **125**

COOKBOOKS

Among the earliest Americana cookbooks are *The Frugal Housewife,* or *Complete Woman Cook* by Susanna Carter, published in Philadelphia in 1796 and *American Cookery* by Amelia Simmons, published in Hartford, Connecticut in 1796. Cookbooks of this era are crudely written, for most cooks could not read well and measuring devices were not yet refined.

Other types of collectible cookbooks include those used as premiums or advertisements. This type is much less expensive than the rare eighteenth century books.

References: Bob Allen, *A Guide to Collecting Cookbooks and Advertising Cookbooks: A History of People, Companies, and Cooking,* Collector Books, 1990, 1995 value update; Mary Barile, *Cookbooks Worth Collecting,* Wallace–Homestead, Krause Publications, 1994; Linda J Dickinson, *Price Guide to Cookbooks and Recipe Leaflets,* Collector Books, 1990, 1997 value update; Barbara Jane Gelink, *Collectible Old Cookbooks With Values, Second Edition,* Onento, 1997.

Periodical: *Cookbook Collectors' Exchange,* PO Box 32369, San Jose, CA 95152.

Newsletter: *Cook Book,* PO Box 88, Steuben, ME 04680.

Collectors' Club: Cook Book Collectors Club of America, PO Box 56, St James, MO 65559.

Museums: Culinary Institute of America, Hyde Park, NY; Home Economics Library, Ohio State University, Columbus, OH; Library of Congress, Rare Books & Special Collections Division, Washington, DC; Schlesinger Library at Radcliffe College, Cambridge, MA.

356 Ways to Prepare Chicken, Doubleday, orig edition, green cloth, 1974, 232 pp	**$15**
Adventures in Good Cooking, Duncan Hines, Bowling Green, KY, 1939	**30**
American Cooking "In Der Kuche," Sadie Summers, NY, 1948, 324 pp	**18**
American Everyday Cookbook, Agnes Murphy, NY, second printing, 1955, 200 pp	**12**
American Housewife Cookbook, Miss T S Shute, Lewis & Menzies Co, Philadelphia, 1878, 384 pp	**140**
American Regional Cookery, Sheila Hibben, Boston, 1946, 354 pp	**30**
Americana By Choice, Angelo M Pellegrini, NY, first edition, 1946, 240 pp	**25**
Amish Way Cookbook, KY, first edition, wraps, 1981, 196 pp	**12**
Apple Cooking: Recipes for Every Month of the Year, Gertrude Mann, NY, 1954, 92 pp	**15**
Baking Book, Ann Pillsbury, includes Bake–off #1, NY, first edition, 1950, 372 pp	**50**
Campbell's Book: Canning Preserving & Pickling, Clyde Campbell, revised, NY, 1937, 860 pp	**50**
Centennial Cookbook & General Guide, Ella E Myers, Philadelphia, engravings, 1876	**300**
Cheese Making, John Decker, Ohio, 1905, 202 pp	**25**
Chosen Sweets, P R Short, Donnelly Co, Chicago, first edition, 1923, 63 pp	**30**
Clementine in the Kitchen, S Chamberlain, first edition, illus, 1943	**30**
Coffee: From Plantation to Cup, Francis Thurber, NY, 1886, 416 pp	**100**
Compilation of Household Science, Mary Ryan, 1913, 168 pp	**35**

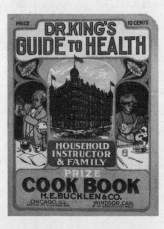

Left: Dr. King's Guide to Health, *34 pp, 9¹/₈ x 6³/₄",* **$15.**

Right: Kitchen Magic, *Larabee's Best Flour, recipe foldout, 5 folds, color cov and illus, 1920s, 3⁵/₈ x 6" closed, 18 x 6" open, $12.*

Good Housekeeping Everyday Cookbook, Isabel Curtis, Phelps Pub, NY, 1903, 320 pp **60**

Grape Juice As a Therapeutic Agent, Welch Juice Co, NY, 1921, 28 pp **20**

Grocer's Window Book, R E Taylor, Chicago, 1919, 192 pp **45**

Hay Dieting, Josephine Boyer, Scribner, first edition, 1934, 384 pp **20**

Help for the Marthas, arranged by the young ladies of Class #9, St Paul Sunday School, Reading, PA, Daniel Miller printer, stiff wrappers, 1892, 66 pp **50**

History of Quaker Oats, Harrison Thornton, 1933, 279 pp **35**

Home Baked Bread and Cakes, Mary Norwak, Hamlyn, 1966 .... **10**

Home Cook Book, Tried & True Recipes From Ladies of Chicago and Other Cities, IL, brown pictorial cloth stamped in black and gold, yellow end papers, 1875, 336 pp **50**

Home Grown, Della T Lutes, Little, Brown, Boston, first edition, 1937, 272 pp **25**

Homemaker's Cookbook, Esther Gardner, Vegetarian, fourth printing, 1946, 573 pp **15**

Household Cookbook, Isabel Lord, Harcourt, Brace, first edition, 1936, 490 pp **25**

House–Keeping Made Easy, Mrs A P Hill, NY, illus, 1867, 427 pp **100**

How to Cook Meat and Poultry, Myrtle Reed, Putnam's NY, volume 6 of 10–volume set, 1908, 504 pp **50**

How to Keep a Husband or Culinary Tactics, San Francisco: Cubery, first edition, wraps, 1872, 76 pp **55**

Ice Cream Industry, Grover Turnbow, NY, 1949, 654 pp **24**

It's Fun to Cook, Lucy Maltby, Philadelphia, Ruth King illus, 1938, 397 pp ... **65**

Kitchenette Cookbook, Ruth Taylor, NY, first edition, 1936, 299 pp **20**

Let's Cook It Right, Adelle Davis, NY, 1947, 626 pp **20**

Let's Stand to Cook Farm Journal, Nell Nichols, tall, 1966 .... **10**

Magic Chef Cooking, Dorothy Shank, American Stove Co, St Louis, first edition, 1934, 204 pp **18**

Maple Sugar Cookbook, Brattleboro, VT, wraps, c1890, 43 pp **50**

Mary At the Farm and Book of Recipes, Edith Thomas, first edition, 1915 .... **150**

Mary Land's Louisiana Cookery, Mary Land, Baton Rouge, LA, first edition, hard cov, 376 pp **35**

May Irwin's Home Cooking, May Irwin, NY, first edition, 1904, 268 pp **30**

Meats, Poultry, & Game, Edouard Panchard, NY, 1919, 134 pp **45**

Miss Parloa's New Cook Book, Miss Maria Parloa, Boston, first edition, 1880, 430 pp **125**

Modern Housewife, Alexis B Soyer, Appleton, NY, first American edition, 1850, 364 pp **175**

Modernistic Recipe Menus, Jessie De Booth, Chicago, 1929, 318 pp **30**

Most Nearly Perfect Food: Milk, S Crumbine, 1929 .... **15**

Mrs. Anna J Peterson's Simplified Cookery, Anna J Peterson, People's Gas Light & Coke, Chicago, illus, 1924, 255 pp **35**

Mrs Gilpin's Frugalities, Susan Anna Brown, NY, cloth cov, pictorial label, 1883, 102 pp **100**

Mrs Hill's New Cook–Book, Mrs A P Hill, enlarged edition, cloth, 1898, 416 pp **65**

Mrs Owen's Illinois Cook Book, Mrs T J V Owen, Springfield, IL, J H Johnson printer, cloth, 1871, 360 pp **50**

Left: My Meat Recipes, *The National Live Stock and Meat Board, color cov, black and white illus, 1926, 48 pp, 5¹/₂ x 8",* $15.

Right: Tested Recipes with Blue Ribbon Malt Extract, *color covers and illus, 1927, 28 pp, $12.*

Toll House Tried & True Recipes, Ruth Wakefield, Barrows Co, NY, eighth
   edition, 1939, 214 pp **50**
Twentieth Century Cookbook, Chicago, 1921, 182 pp **20**
Universal Cook Book, Mary Ellen Quinlan, World Publishers, revised, 1937,
   250 pp **20**
Universal Recipe Book, H W Harper, Boston, blue boards, 1869, 292 pp **75**
Vermont Maple Recipes, Mary Pearl, VT, third printing, wraps, 1956, 87 pp ..   **12**
Virginia City Cookbook, Helen Brown, pictorial wraps, 1954 ....   **20**
Virginia House–Wife, Mrs Mary Randolph, Washington, fourth edition with
   amendments and additions, rebound, 1830, 180 pp **175**
What Mrs. Dewey Did With the Jello!, Jell–O, color illus, mother and daugh-
   ter tasting Jell–O on cov, wraps, 1933, 23 pp **8**
When Mother Lets Us Cook, Constance Johnson, 1908 ....   **20**
Wilson's Meat Cookery, George Rector, illus, 137 pp **15**
You Must Eat Meat, Max Jutte, NY, 1936, 164 pp **20**

COOKIE JARS

   Cookie jars, colorful and often whimsical, are one of the fastest growing categories
in the collectibles field. Many cookie jars have been made by more than one company and as a result can be found with different marks. This resulted from mergers or
splits of manufacturers, e.g., Brush–McCoy which is now Nelson McCoy. Molds were
also traded and sold among companies.

   Cookie jars often were redesigned to reflect newer tastes. Hence, the same jar may
be found in several different style variations.

   Cookie jars are subject to chips and paint flaking. Collectors should concentrate
on jars which have their original lid and are in very good or better condition. Learn to
identify makers' marks and codes. Do not fail to include some of the contemporary
manufacturers in your collection.

References: John W. Humphries, *Humphries Price Guide to Cookie Jars,* published by
author, 1997; *1996 Cookie Jar Express Pricing Guide to Cookie Jars,* Paradise
Publications, 1996; Fred Roerig and Joyce Herndon Roerig, *The Collector's
Encyclopedia of Cookie Jars* (1991, 1997 value update), *Book II* (1994, 1997 value
update), *Book III* (1998), Collector Books; Mike Schneider, *The Complete Cookie Jar
Book,* Schiffer Publishing, 1991; Mark and Ellen Supnick, *The Wonderful World of
Cookie Jars,* L–W Book Sales, 1995, 1997 value update; Ermagene Westfall, *An
Illustrated Value Guide to Cookie Jars, Book I* (1983, 1997 value update), *Book II*
(1993, 1997 value update), Collector Books.

Newsletters: *Cookie Jar Collectors Express,* PO Box 221, Mayview, MO 64071; *Cookie
Jarrin',* RR 2, Box 504, Walterboro, SC 29488; *Crazed Over Cookie Jars,* PO Box 254,
Savanna, IL 61074.

Collectors' Club: Cookie Jar Club, PO Box 451005, Miami, FL 33245.

Museum: The Cookie Jar Museum, Lemont, IL.

Apple, California Originals **$75**
Apple, Hull, matching grease jar and salt and pepper shakers, price for 4 pc
   set **65**
Apple, McCoy, yellow **40**
Apple, Metlox, deep burgundy **110**

Apple, Treasure Craft, large **35**
Asparagus, McCoy **60**
Baby Pig, Clay Art **45**
Baking Time Mammy, Clay Art **28**
Bananas, Red Wing, turquoise **170**
Barnyard Pig, Clay Art **45**
Barrel of Apples, Metlox **125**
Basket of Potatoes, McCoy **60**
Basket of Strawberries, McCoy **48**
Basset Hound, Metlox **650**
Bean Pot, McCoy, hp flowers **30**
Bear on Beehive, McCoy **40**
Bear with Cookie, American Bisque **75**
Bell Pepper, Doranne, green **55**
Betsy Ross, Enesco **150**
Betty Crocker **125**
Blue Bird on Pine Cone, Metlox **95**
Blue Bonnet Sue, Nabisco, 1989 .... **65**
Blue Daisy, Metlox, cylinder **70**
Bowl of Peaches, Robinson Ransbottom **75**
Broccoli, Metlox **140**
Brown Peasant, Red Wing **70**
Calico Cat, Metlox **145**
Carousel, Shawnee, cold paint **140**
Cat, Pacific Stoneware, orange **30**
Cat on Coal Bucket, McCoy, brown cat **200**
Cats on Churn, Twin Winton **95**
Chef, Pearl China **650**
Chick, American Bisque **75**
Churn, American Bisque, 1958 .... **25**
Churn Boy, American Bisque **135**
Coffee Grinder, California Originals **25**
Coffeepot, McCoy, Pennsylvania Dutch Treat **60**
Cookie Barrel, American Bisque **25**
Cookie Cottage, McCoy **110**
Cookies 'N Milk Wagon, American Bisque **165**
Cook Stove, McCoy, white **35**
Corn King, Shawnee **190**
Cottage, Shawnee **1,500**
Country Girl, Metlox **45**
Covered Wagon, Brush **500**
Cow, Brush, brown, cat finial **145**
Cow, Metlox, purple **425**
Crowing Rooster, American Bisque **60**
Dancing Pig, American Bisque **195**
Darner Doll, Hedi Schoop, blue and green **250**
Diaper Pin Pig, Regal **450**
Dog, California Originals **35**
Dog, Doranne **30**
Dog, Weiss **20**
Dog on Basket, McCoy **70**

Dog on Drum, Twin Winton   225
Donkey and Cart, American Bisque   75
Donkey and Cart, Brush   350
Drum Major, Shawnee   475
Duck, Hull   33
Duck with Corn, Doranne   35
Dutch Girl, Pottery Guild   60
Egg Basket, Metlox   185
Elsie the Cow in Barrel, Pottery Guild   465
Farmer Cow, Treasure Craft   30
Fat Pig, McCoy   40
Feed Bag, American Bisque   130
Fireplace, McCoy   70
Formal Pig, Brush   225
Frog, California Originals   60
Frontier Family, McCoy, cylinder   35
Fruit, McCoy, cylinder   25
Gingerbread Boy, Hull, beige   400
Gingham Dog, Metlox   85
Goldilocks, Regal   300
Granny, American Bisque, green dress   135
Grapefruit, Metlox   170
Harvest Farm Pig, Fitz & Floyd   130
Hen, Doranne, blue   45
Hen, Treasure Craft   25
Hen on Nest, McCoy   65
Hermoine Heifer, Fitz & Floyd   75
Hey Diddle Diddle, Shirley Corl, flasher   275
Hobby Horse, Abingdon   375
Hootie Owl, Robinson Ransbottom   100

Left: Mammy, McCoy, imp script "McCoy," 10¹/₂" h, $100.

Right: Smiley Pig, Shawnee #60, bank, butterscotch bottom, 11¹/₄" h, $500. Photo courtesy Ray Morykan Auctions.

Horse Doctor, AMC 75
Hound Dog, Doranne 65
Humpty Dumpty, Abingdon 295
Humpty Dumpty, Brush, peak hat 295
Humpty Dumpty, McCoy 95
Ice Wagon, Treasure Craft, brown 85
Jack, Shawnee, gold dec 325
Jack, Shawnee, striped pants 150
Jack, Shawnee, yellow pants 75
Jack Tar, gold trim, black hair 900
Jill, Shawnee, tulip 165
Jill, Shawnee, tulip, gold dec 350
Jill, Shawnee, yellow skirt 75
Jo Jo, Shawnee, gold dec 350
Kettle, Doranne, green 20
Kittens and Yarn, American Bisque 100
Kittens and Yarn, McCoy, maroon 110
Lady Pig, American Bisque 175
Lady with Apron, Hedi Schoop 195
Lamb, Treasure Craft 25
Lamb, Twin Winton 35
Lazy Pig, McCoy 75
Lemon, Doranne 60
Little Red Riding Hood, Hull, poinsettia 950
Little Red Riding Hood, Weiss 310
Mail Box, Doranne 35
Mammy, Brayton Laguna, red 595
Mammy, Mosaic Tile, blue 575
Mammy, Pearl China 710
Mammy, Shirley Corl 125
Meat and Vegetable Truck, Henry Cavanaugh 275
Milk Can, McCoy, brown 40
Milk Carton, Doranne 45
Milkmaid Mammy, Carol Gifford McCalip 275
Milk Wagon, American Bisque 50
Morning Glory Crock, Red Wing 900
Mother Goose, Doranne 150
Mother Goose, Metlox 185
Muggsy, Shawnee, gold dec 850
Muggsy, Shawnee, plain 425
Noah's Ark, Metlox 295
Oaken Bucket, American Bisque, with dipper 400
Oaken Bucket, McCoy 30
Old MacDonald's Cow, Fitz & Floyd 85
Old Woman and the Shoe, Pfaltzgraff 400
Orange, Metlox 85
Owl, Shawnee, gold dec 275
Pear, Red Wing, aqua 90
Pear and Apple, Hull, cylinder 25
Pepper, McCoy, green 55
Picnic Basket, McCoy 40

Pig Head, Cardinal **95**
Pig Head, DeForrest, "Make a Pig of Yourself" **135**
Pillsbury Flour Sack **50**
Pot Belly Stove, McCoy, black **30**
Pot Belly Stove, Treasure Craft **35**
Puss 'N Boots, Shawnee, plain **225**
Puss 'N Boots, Shawnee, red bow **150**
Puss 'N Boots, Shawnee, red and gold bow, gold dec **600**
Quaker Oats, Regal **100**
Rabbit, California Originals **50**
Rag Doll, Metlox **115**
Raggedy Andy, Maddux **95**
Raggedy Ann, Brush **450**
Raggedy Ann, California Originals **100**
Raggedy Ann, Metlox **170**
Red Riding Hood, Brush **750**
Red Riding Hood, Pottery Guild **135**
Ribbon Geese, Treasure Craft **25**
Rocking Horse, McCoy **80**
Rooster, American Bisque, multicolor **45**
Rooster, California Cleminson **40**
Rooster, Sierra Vista, cylinder **75**
School House, American Bisque **50**
Scottie Dog, Metlox, white **175**
Sheriff Pig, Robinson Ransbottom, red hat **70**
Sir Francis Drake, Metlox **50**
Smiley, Shawnee, blue cold paint neckerchief **100**
Smiley, Shawnee, blue neckerchief, gold dec, decals **110**
Smiley, Shawnee, green cold paint neckerchief **80**
Smiley, Shawnee, red cold paint neckerchief **80**
Smiley, Shawnee, shamrock **250**
Smiley, Shawnee, tulip, plain **450**
Smiley, Shawnee, white **75**
Smiley, Shawnee, yellow neckerchief, gold dec, decals **300**
Squash, Metlox **140**
Squirrel, Sierra Vista **225**
Squirrel, Starnes **85**
Squirrel on Log, Brush **100**
Squirrel on Pine Cone, Metlox **60**
Squirrel on Stump, California Originals **120**
Stacking Animals, Clay Art **14**
Stove, California Cleminson **150**
Stove, McCoy, black **35**
Strawberry, Metlox **55**
Sunday Cow, Clay Art **20**
Three Bears, Abingdon **145**
Tomato, California Originals **75**
Wheat Shock, House of Webster **15**
Winking Pig, McCoy **235**
Winnie, Shawnee, blue **250**

EGG & DAIRY

Most farms were self–sufficient. Even grain farmers kept a cow and flock of chickens to meet their need for dairy products. What was not used on the farm was sold for extra income. Many a farming wife bought Christmas presents with the egg money.

Egg and dairy products were both primary and secondary food stuffs. They were an important ingredient in baking. It was necessary to process many products before use. Churning butter was an after–dinner task that often fell to young children. Of course, there was a pleasurable side, especially when the ice cream freezer was brought out.

Butter prints are divided into two categories: butter molds and butter stamps. Butter molds are generally of three–piece construction—the design, the screw–in handle, and the case. Molds both mold and stamp the butter at the same time. Butter stamps are of one–piece construction, sometimes two pieces if the handle is from a separate piece of wood. Stamps are used to decorate the top of butter after it is molded.

References: Brenda C. Blake, *Egg Cups: An Illustrated History and Price Guide*, Glass Press, 1995; Paul Dickson, *The Great American Ice Cream Book*, Galahad Books, 1972; Paul Kindig, *Butter Prints and Molds*, Schiffer Publishing, 1986; Ralph Pomery, *The Ice Cream Connection*, Paddington Press, 1975; Wayne Smith, *Ice Cream Dippers: An Illustrated History and Collector's Guide to Early Ice Cream Dippers*, published by author, 1986; Pat Stott, *The Collectors Book of Egg Cups*, published by author, 1993; Don Thornton, *Beat This: The Eggbeater Chronicles*, Off Beat Books, 1994.

Newletters: *Creamers*, PO Box 11, Lake Villa, IL 60046; *The Udder Collectibles*, HC 73, Box 1, Smithville Flats, NY 13841.

Collectors' Clubs: Cream Separator Assoc, Route 3, Box 189, Arcadia, WI 54612; Eggcup Collectors Club, 67 Stevens Avenue, Old Bridge, NJ 08857; The Ice Screamers, PO Box 465, Warrington, PA 18976.

Museum: The New York State Historical Assoc and The Farmer's Museum, Cooperstown, NY.

Additional Listings: See Country Barn, Dairy Collectibles.

Butter Churn, electric, Dazey, 4 qt **$90**
Butter Churn, rocker type, wood churn and cradle, red milk paint 300
Butter Churn, wood, dasher type, barrel shape, stave construction, metal
    bands turned lid, old dark finish, dasher, some edge damage, 26" h plus
    handle 275
Butter Churn, wood, dasher type, brass hoops, North Andover, MA, 19th C,
    18½" h 250
Butter Churn, wood, dasher type, stave constructed, steel bands, lid and
    dasher, old red paint, 24" h 200
Butter Cutter, cast iron, nickel plated, painted, table mount, wire cutter,
    early 20th C 50
Butter Fork, wood, painted, 5 tines, "Mrs Bragg's Butter Fork," late 19th C,
    6" l 20
Butter Merger, Mak–Mor Butter Machine, tabletop glass jar, cast iron frame
    and gears, metal blades, NY, May 30, 1911 patent date 65
Butter Mold, fish, round, scrubbed finish, cracked case, 3¾" d 350
Butter Mold, pomegranate, round, cased, 4¾" d 45
Butter Mold, rose, rect, old varnish finish, 5 x 8" 75

Butter Print, goat, elliptical, chip carved tulips, $192. Photo courtesy Aston Macek.

Butter Mold, roses and cherries, rect, old patina, age cracks, 4 x 7" **100**
Butter Paddle, burl bowl, some brown paint, edge damage to bowl, 8½" l . . . **60**
Butter Paddle, curly maple, cutout handle with hook finial, worn bowl and
finish, 9½" l **150**
Butter Paddle, maple, some figure, carved hook handle, old finish, 10½" l . . . **225**
Butter Print, compass star flower, round, smooth back, scrubbed finish, 5" d . . **110**
Butter Print, crown, round, 1 pc, turned handle, scrubbed finish, 4¼" d **110**
Butter Print, double print, tulips 1 side, star flower other side, round,
scrubbed finish, age cracks, 4¾" d tulips, 3¾" d star flower **385**
Butter Print, eagle, with branch and star, round, self–turned handle, old pati-
na, minor edge damage, 4¼" d **200**
Butter Print, 4 hearts, lollipop type, old patina, 9⅜" l **275**
Butter Print, pineapple and foliage, round, 1 pc, turned handle, old finish,
small hole in center, 4¼" d **185**
Butter Print, stylized tulip, with hearts and leaves, walnut, round, scrubbed
finish, inserted handle missing, 4½" d **135**
Butter Print, sunburst floral, semi–circular, inserted handle, 7" l **275**
Butter Print, swan, round, deeply carved, old finish with varnish, edge
damage, age cracks and small hole, found in PA, 5½" d **135**
Butter Print, tulip and star, round, 1 pc, turned handle, old dark finish,
4⅞" d **225**
Butter Print, tulip and star, with other flowers, round, 1 pc, turned handle,
scrubbed finish, 4⅜" d **275**
Butter Worker, 2 pc, softwood, large oblong board with sides tapering
toward front, applied gallery rails on sides, splat on underside slants board
forward, long flat paddle with turned handle attached to board with iron
hook and eye, 15 x 24¼" board **45**
Cheese Drainer, basket, round top, tightly woven sides, square bottom, 2
handles, 19th C, 12½" d, 6" h **275**
Cheese Ladder, wood, pegged, 2 rungs, c1820, 22" l, 8" w **80**
Cheese Mold, pig, carved wood, round, 19th C, 12" d **85**
Cheese Press, tin, cylindrical, pierced bottom and lower sides, 3 legs, ring
handle, handmade, 19th C, 6⅜" d, 7⅛" h **150**
Cheese Sieve, bentwood and woven splint, round, 23" d **125**
Cheese Sieve, tin, heart shaped, hanging ring resoldered, 6" h **350**
Cheese Sieve, woven splint, round, good age and patina, 27" d **475**
Curd Whipper, spring steel blades, wood handle, c1880, 24½" l **75**

Egg Basket, wire, c1905, 8" d 25
Egg Beater, Aug 22, 1899 patent date, Holt 75
Egg Candler, The Family Egg–Tester, pierced tin cylinder, strap handle,
    Mar 13, 1876 patent date 30
Egg Lifter, wire 8
Egg Scale, cast iron, weight and balance, red and blue, aluminum pan, brass
    pointer, Zenith Egg Grader #1002, early 20th C 35
Egg Timer, Alarm Whistle, aluminum insert, orig box and instructions 15
Ice Cream Carrier, Bradley Ice Cream Cabinet, oak box, zinc lining, side
    door for ice cream storage, lift–off top for ice, late 19th C, 8½" 250
Ice Cream Dipper, Mosteller #79 200
Ice Cream Disher, adjustable shank, Mayer 250
Ice Cream Freezer, Kwik Freeze, galvanized tin, blue, paper label 50
Ice Cream Mold, pewter, basket, #598, 3 part, early 20th C 40
Ice Cream Mold, pewter, eagle with shield, full figure, 5" h 135
Ice Cream Mold, pewter, George and Martha Washington, full figure,
    5½" h, price for pair 250
Ice Cream Scoop, Dover #20, nickel plated brass, round bowl, turned wood
    handle, lever activated scraper, 1930s, 10½" 50
Ice Cream Scoop, Indestructo #30, nickel plated brass, round bowl, wood
    handle, Benedict Mfg Co, 1920s, 10½" l 65
Ice Cream Scoop, Quick and Easy #486, nickel plated brass, cone shaped
    bowl, thumb lever, turned wood handle, Erie Specialty Co, c1910 75

FOOD PREPARATION

A country housewife cooked, and cooked, and cooked. Just as farming was a seven–day–a–week occupation, so too was cooking. The country cook was willing to try any labor–saving device at least once. This explains why so many mint examples remain with their original box. Not every device worked well.

Many of these implements were mechanical. Collectors prefer examples in working order. Value decreases rapidly if an object is rusted or pitted.

Look for unusual shapes, highly decorated pieces, and examples that obviously have been used but carefully cared for. A marked piece is a plus. Most collections focus on one form and its many variations.

References: *Griswold Cast Iron, Vol I*, (1993, 1997 value update), *Vol 2* (1995), L–W Book Sales; L–W Book Sales, *Collectors Guide to Wagner Ware and Other Companies*, L–W Book Sales, 1994; *Price Guide to Griswold Mfg. Co*, 1918 Catalog Reprint, L–W Book Sales, 1996; David G. Smith and Charles Wafford, *The Book of Griswold & Wagner: Favorite Piqua, Sidney Hollow Ware, Wapak*, Schiffer Publishing, 1995; Don Thornton, *Apple Parers*, Off Beat Books, 1997.

Newsletters: *Cast Iron Cookware News*, 28 Angela Avenue, San Anselmo, CA 94960; *Kettles 'n Cookware*, Drawer B, Perrysburg, NY 14129.

Collectors' Clubs: Antique Stove Assoc, 5515 Almeda Road, Houston, TX 77004; Griswold & Cast Iron Cookware Assoc, Drawer B, Perrysburg, NY 14129; International Society for Apple Parer Enthusiasts, 17 East High, Mount Vernon, OH 43050; Kollectors of Old Kitchen Stuff, 501 Market Street, Mifflinburg, PA 17844.

Applebutter Kettle, copper, slightly rounded bottom, sides flare toward rolled rim, cast iron rect hand mounts applied to sides, hand wrought iron bail handle, hand wrought iron tripod with round top and 3 splayed flattened legs, surface pitting, 17³/₈" d kettle **$120**

Apple Roaster, tin, double, New England, c1830–40, 10" l **400**

Apple Roaster, tin, wrought iron frame, single, 12" l, 8" h **250**

Bean Dryer, tin, rect **10**

Bone Marrow Scoop, iron, key handle, c1780, 7" l **80**

Broiler, rotating, cast iron, round, sgd "WJ" on handle, replaced legs, minor early repairs, c1800, 22" l **70**

Cider Press, Buckeye, Dewey and Able Bros, Buffalo, NY, late 19th C, 32" l, 45" h **450**

Coffee Grinder, cast iron, gold paint accents, red, gold, and black decal on front of hopper, iron crank with turned wood knob, C–clamp base with wing nut, mkd "Universal 010 Coffee Mill, Landers, Frary & Clark, New Britain, Conn., U.S.A., Pat. Feb. 14, 1905," 12³/₈" h **100**

Coffee Grinder, cast iron, hinged top, hopper, crank, and mechanism, square wood base with drawer, ebonized wood handle, crank and top painted gold, mkd "Imperial, Arcade Manufacturing Company" around rim, 7" sq, 10³/₈" h **65**

Coffee Grinder, cast iron, wood base with drawer, worn old black paint with traces of gold, mkd "Enterprise Mfg. Co., Philadelphia, Pa. No. 1," 11½" h . **165**

Coffee Grinder, cast iron, wrought iron, walnut, and pine, mushroom shaped handle, circular bean receptacle above molded box with drawer and shaped foot, C Meyer, PA, 19th C, 10" h **350**

Coffeepot, tin, copper bottom, sides taper toward rim, simple stamped band dec, applied spout with strainer, small arched ribbon handle at base, wire bail with turned wood handle, lid with arched tin handle, 9³/₄" d, 9³/₄" h ... **25**

Coffee Roaster, stove top, tin, crank type, wood handle, c1885, 16" l **60**

Colander, copper, round with pierced rounded bottom, rolled rim, applied copper mount on side with round iron ring for hanging, 11³/₁₆" d, 3" h **70**

Cutting Board, wood, round with lollipop handle, 20" d **25**

Dipper, polished brass bowl, wrought iron handle, 14¼" l **95**

Dipper, wood, long handled, old dark finish, 45" l **250**

Dutch Oven, cov, cast iron, Griswold, #6, smooth top, block emblem **175**

Dutch Oven, cov, cast iron, Griswold, #7, raised lettering on cov, applied handle **65**

Dutch Oven, cov, cast iron, Griswold, #8, Tite Top **45**

Dutch Oven, cov, cast iron, Griswold, #10, lettering on cov **125**

Dutch Oven, cov, cast iron, Wagner, #7, 4 ring **50**

Dutch Oven Trivet, cast iron, Griswold #9 .... **30**

Egg Skillet, cast iron, Griswold #53 .... **35**

Food Chopper, copper, steel, and wood, horse shaped body, 12½" l **250**

Food Chopper, wrought iron, rect blade with applied iron tapered shaft extending up and fitted with round turned wood handle with incised line designs, heart shaped iron mounts, minor surface pitting, 6" w, 6½" h **20**

Food Chopper, wrought steel, decorative blade mkd "P. Cutlani," turned wood handle, 6⁵/₈" w **135**

Food Grinder, Keen Kutter #K110, tinned cast iron, Simmons Hardware **35**

Food Mold, ear of corn, copper and tin, 4 x 6" **120**

Food Mold, redware, Turk's head, Rockingham glaze **65**

Food Mold, sheaf of wheat, copper and tin, 4½ x 6" **100**

Frying Pan, graduated set of 5, cast iron, spider type, similar but not matched
   set, 6" to 12" d, price for set **250**

Griddle, Wagner, #7, oval, mkd "Wagner" **75**

Griddle, Wagner, #8, Wardway **15**

Griddle, Wagner, #9, round **35**

Herb Grinder, hardwood, mortar and pestle type, mortar built into large
   wood table clamp, old varnish finish, worm holes in mortar, 5¾" h plus
   thumb screw **300**

Kettle, cast iron, Griswold #8, 3 legs **45**

Kitchen Saw, Keen Kutter, carbon steel blade, wood handle, Simmons
   Hardware, 13½" l **15**

Kraut Cutter, hardwood, with chip carved flowers, heart, and initials, diagonal steel blade, wire nails in strips holding blade, old finish with worm
   holes, 12" l **250**

Kraut Cutter, walnut, rect, shaped crest with cutout heart handle, attached
   side rails, diagonal steel blade, PA, 19th C, 21½" l **575**

Ladle, Griswold Erie **95**

Maple Sugar Mold, cast iron, series of thirteen small star, heart, round, and
   round with scalloped design molds arranged in rect cast iron pan, "Reids
   Pan, Dec. 1870" cast on rounded handles, 16½" l, 8¹³⁄₁₆" w, ¾" h **65**

Maple Sugar Mold, tin and wood, curved heart shaped wood bottom with 4
   small carved star designs, galvanized tin sides overlapped at bottom and
   secured with wood clothespin–type pin, 3¼" w, 5" l, 1½" h **30**

Maple Sugar Mold, wood, hand carved, oblong, curved heart design at
   either end flanking spade shaped center design, brass hanger added to
   top, 4¾ x 16⅛" **200**

Meat Fork, wrought iron, flattened tapered handle, terminating in hanging
   loop, 2 tines, handle mkd "P.E. Will," 2¹⁄₁₆" w, 13⅞" l **160**

Meat Fork, wrought iron, scrolled end, 3 tines, 12⅞" l **225**

*Left: **Batter Pitcher**, stoneware, cobalt blue, **$35.*** Photo courtesy Ray Morykan Auctions.

*Right: **Cabbage Cutter**, mkd "Arcadia Manufacturing Co., Newark, New York, Pat'd 1885–1891," adjustable blade, iron handle, fold–down locking legs, 9¾ x 21¾", **$85.***

Meat Tenderizer, stoneware, wood handle, mkd "Pat'd Dec 25, 1877," 9½" l .   85
Noodle Cutter, The Ideal, rolling type, wire handle and frame, 14 blades,
    Toledo Cooker Co, c1910   15
Patty Iron, cast iron, Griswold #2, orig box   40
Peel, wrought iron, ram's horn handle, pitted, 46" l   110
Reflector Oven, iron, porcelain door knob, 22" l, 10" w, 17" h   125
Roaster, cast iron, Wagner, #7, full writing on cov   325
Roasting Fork, wrought iron, 2 tines, flat handle turning back into hook, PA,
    early 19th C, 15" l   50
Sauce Pan, sheet iron, cylindrical, old black finish, 13" l plus handle   60
Sauce Pans, cast brass, graduated set of 3, wrought iron tubular handles,
    5¾" d, 6¾" d, and 8¼" d plus handles, price for set   90
Sauce Pans, copper, graduated set of 3, cast iron handles, worn tin lining,
    2⅝" d, 3¼" d, and 4" d plus handles, price for set   40
Sauce Pans, dovetailed, applied hand wrought tapered copper handles with
    small hole for hanging, heart shaped handle mount attaches to side of pan
    with 3 copper rivets, pans with flat bottoms and straight sides, 6½" d,
    8½" d, and 9¼" d plus handles, price for set   110
Sausage Stuffer, cherry and other hardwoods, metal teeth, refinished, 17" l . . .   50
Sieve and Ladle Set, wrought iron, deep bowls, engraved vine dec flat han-
    dles with rounded handgrip sections, ends turned back for hanging, PA,
    c1835, 19" l   80
Skillet, cast iron, Griswold, #4, slant, small logo   2
Skillet, cast iron, Griswold, #5, slant "Erie, Pa. USA"   35
Skillet, cast iron, Griswold, #6, block, smoke ring   100
Skillet, cast iron, Griswold, #9, block "Erie, Pa. USA," deep smooth bottom . .   100
Skillet, cast iron, Griswold, #11, block "Erie, Pa. USA"   195
Skillet, cast iron, Griswold, #12, small emblem, smoke ring   35
Skillet, cast iron, Wagner, #2   125
Skillet, cast iron, Wagner, #4, script logo, with O and smoke ring   65
Skillet, cast iron, Wagner, #5, pattern #1055   20
Skillet, cast iron, Wagner, #7, mkd "Wagner"   30
Skillet, cast iron, Wagner, #9, pattern #1069   50
Skillet, cast iron, Wagner, #10, pattern #1070   75
Skillet, cast iron, Wagner, #12, mkd "Wagner"   90
Skillet, cast iron, Wagner, #13, pie logo   800
Skillet Cov, Griswold #8   35
Skillet Rack, cast iron, Griswold   300
Skimmer, large copper bowl, wrought iron handle, some old alterations and
    repair, 24½" d bowl   100
Spatula, brass blade, wrought iron handle, 17¾" l   80
Spatula, wrought iron, rounded blade, flattened tapered handle terminating
    in hanging loop, handle stamped "P.E. Will," 14½" l   210
Spoon, wood, turned handle   20
Taster, brass bowl, wrought iron handle, polished bowl, 9¾" l   150
Utensil Rack, wrought iron, scrolled crest, 5 hooks with acorn terminals,
    minor brazed repair, 10¾" l   750
Utensil Set, plain, wrought iron bar with 4 hooks holds dipper with brass
    bowl, spatula with brass blade, fork, and skimmer with pierced brass
    bowl, simple tooling on handles, 24¾" l bar, price for set   27

GRANITEWARE

Graniteware is the name commonly given to iron or steel kitchenware covered with an enamel coating.

The first graniteware was made in Germany in the 1830s. It was not produced in the United States until the 1860s. At the start of World War I, when European manufacturers turned to the making of war weapons, American producers took over the market.

Colors commonly marketed were white and gray. Each company made their own special colors, including shades of blue, green, brown, violet, cream, and red. Because graniteware is still manufactured, the earliest pieces are in greatest demand among collectors.

Old graniteware is heavier than new graniteware. Pieces with cast iron handles date from 1870 to 1890; wood handles date from 1900 to 1910. Other dating clues are seams, wood knobs, and tin lids.

References: Helen Greguire, *The Collector's Encyclopedia of Graniteware: Colors, Shapes & Values, Book I* (1990, 1994 value update), *Book II* (1993, 1997 value update), Collector Books.

Collectors' Club: National Graniteware Society, PO Box 10013, Cedar Rapids, IA 52410.

Angel Food Pan, cobalt swirl	$175
Angel Food Pan, lava	175
Ant Trap, gray, "Royal" paper label	300
Ashtray, end of day, Kerr Range Co	35
Baking Pan, Chrysolite	150
Baking Pan, red swirl, white int, oblong, 2 handles, rolled lip	4,000
Berry Bucket, cov, blue swirl, granite lid	325
Berry Bucket, cov, blue swirl, tin lid	200
Berry Bucket, cov, brown swirl, granite lid	275
Berry Bucket, cov, chrysolite, granite lid with strap handle, wire bail handle with turned wood grip	600
Berry Bucket, cov, chrysolite, tin lid	375
Berry Bucket, cov, cobalt swirl, granite lid	925
Berry Bucket, cov, columbian, granite lid	575
Berry Bucket, cov, Dutchessware, tin lid	300
Berry Bucket, cov, emerald swirl, granite lid	325
Berry Bucket, cov, emerald swirl, tin lid	200
Berry Bucket, cov, red swirl, wire bail handle with turned wood grip, tin lid with turned wood knob finial, hole in lid	2,000
Berry Bucket, cov, Thistleware, granite lid	150
Biscuit Cutter, gray	400
Biscuit Tray, onyx	45
Bowl, ftd, gray, pewter trim	225
Bucket, gray, miniature	300
Bundt Pan Carrier, gray swirl	60
Butter Churn, floor model, wood, gray drum	1,350
Butter Dish, gray, pewter trim, with insert	350
Candlestick, cobalt swirl, fluted	200
Candlestick, gray, dish base, strap finger hold	60

Candlestick, gray, pewter trim **450**
Canister Set, Snow on the Mountain, 6 pc **140**
Chicken Feeder, gray speckled, 2 pc, cone top, 4 openings **150**
Cocoa Dipper, gray, wood handle **350**
Coffee Boiler, Chrysolite **185**
Coffee Boiler, Columbian, 10" h **215**
Coffee Carrier, cov, gray, tin lid **650**
Coffeepot, blue relish, tilt pot and tray with pewter trim **300**
Coffeepot, blue swirl **175**
Coffeepot, Chrysolite **275**
Coffeepot, Columbian, 7" h **300**
Coffeepot, Dutchessware, 7" h **625**
Coffeepot, emerald swirl, 8" h **600**
Coffeepot, emerald swirl, 10" h **650**
Coffeepot, gray, miniature, straight spout **850**
Coffeepot, gray, ornate pewter trim, ftd **3,000**
Coffee Roaster, onyx **140**
Colander, brown swirl **125**
Colander, Chrysolite **375**
Colander, cobalt swirl **165**
Colander, gray, salesman's sample **550**
Cream Can, cov, blue swirl, granite lid **350**
Cream Can, cov, Chrysolite, tin lid with strap handle, wire bail handle **2,500**
Cream Can, cov, cobalt swirl, tin lid **750**
Cream Can, cov, Columbian, tin lid, wire bail handle with wood grip **750**
Cream Can, cov, emerald swirl, granite lid **825**
Cream Can, cov, emerald swirl, tin lid **625**
Cream Can, cov, iris swirl, granite lid **1,150**
Creamer, blue swirl **175**
Creamer, emerald swirl **850**
Creamer, gray, pewter trim, ewer shaped **300**
Cup, emerald swirl **300**
Cup, gray, Army **400**
Cup, gray, canted sides, ftd base, pewter trim **575**
Dipper, red swirl, curved hook handle **500**
Dish Pan, emerald swirl **200**
Double Boiler, red swirl, granite lid with turned wood finial, black handles . .   **3,500**
Egg Pan, emerald swirl, 2 handles **400**
Flask, gray, "Graystone" paper label **200**
Funnel, brown swirl, 3" d **200**
Funnel, cobalt swirl, 5" d **400**
Funnel, emerald swirl, 5" d **400**
Liquid Measure, emerald swirl, small **1,200**
Liquid Measure, blue swirl, stacked, iron rack, chips on dish rims, 11⅛" h . . .   **45**
Liquid Measure, brown swirl, oval, 3 pc, granite lid **1,800**
Liquid Measure, gray, ⅛ qt **750**
Liquid Measure, gray, oval, canted sides, wood lid **750**
Liquid Measure, gray, round **225**
Muffin Pan, cobalt swirl, 8 cavities **200**
Mug, railroad, blue swirl, mkd "G.N.R.Y." **135**
Mush Mug, red swirl **550**

Pan, light blue swirl, round, slightly flared sides, rounded rim, white int, black rim, chip and some wear on bottom, slight nicks on rim, 5³/₄" d, 2" h   5

Percolator, light blue swirl, hinged rounded lid with glass dome top, aluminum coffee basket, black handle and rims, flat bottom with rounded base and straight sides, 5³/₈" d, 8¹/₄" h   45

Pitcher and Wash Bowl, blue swirl   650

Roaster, Columbian, emb "Columbian"   450

Roaster, iris swirl, with insert   80

Salt Box, hanging, gray   950

Salt Shaker, iris swirl   500

Scoop, cobalt swirl, strap handle   250

Soap Dish, emerald swirl, granite insert   215

Soap Dish, End of Day, red, with insert   200

Spittoon, Columbian   475

Spittoon, emerald swirl, 2 pc   170

Spoon, end of day, yellow, black, and red   90

Spooner, brown swirl   325

Sugar Bowl, cov, cobalt swirl, granite lid   400

Sugar Bowl, cov, emerald swirl, granite lid   675

Sugar Bowl, cov, gray, pewter trim   370

Sugar Shaker, gray, tin top 1,000

Syrup, Chrysolite   775

Tea Kettle, gooseneck, Columbian   950

Teapot, cov, gooseneck, cobalt swirl, 10"   250

Teapot, cov, gooseneck, Columbian   500

Teapot, cov, gooseneck, Dutchessware, 7"   600

Teapot, cov, gooseneck, emerald swirl, 10" 1,800

Teapot, cov, gooseneck, gray, granite biggen and lid   700

Teapot, cov, gooseneck, gray, miniature, pewter trim, 5"   700

Teapot, cov, gooseneck, gray, pewter trim, 9"   200

Teapot, cov, gooseneck, iris swirl, granite lid with knob finial   750

Left: Coffeepot, robin's egg blue, speckled, $45. Photo courtesy Ray Morykan Auctions.

Right: Utensil Set, rack and 4 ladles, white with cobalt blue trim, 18" h, 13³/₄" w, $50.

Teapot, cov, gooseneck, lava, 7" 275
Teapot, cov, gooseneck, onyx, 5" 125
Teapot, cov, gooseneck, shaded blue 165
Tea Set, tilt teapot, sugar, and creamer, gray, pewter trim 3,000
Tea Steeper, cov, Chrysolite, granite lid with knob finial, white int, strap side
   handle 275
Tea Steeper, cov, lava, granite lid 225
Tray, Columbian, oval, 18" l 400
Tray, gray, pewter trim, square 875
Utensil Rack, with onion holder, Snow on the Mountain 195
Wash Basin, salesman's sample, blue swirl 125
Wash Basin, salesman's sample, Chrysolite 625
Washtub, gray, child's 350
Waste Jar, gray, pewter trim, 5" d 600
Water Carrier, cov, cobalt swirl, granite lid 325
Water Filter, light blue swirl, lava, 3 pc, granite lid with strap handle 250
Water Pitcher, Bluebelle Ware 170
Water Pitcher, Chrysolite 600
Water Pitcher, Columbian, 1 gal 600
Water Pitcher, iris swirl 225
Water Pitcher, light blue swirl 275
Weather Vane, rooster silhouette, letter directionals, gray 300
Windsor Dipper, blue swirl 140
Windsor Dipper, cobalt relish 60

STRING HOLDERS

    The string holder developed as a utilitarian tool to assist the merchant or manufacturer who needed tangle–free string or twine to tie packages. Early holders were made of cast iron, some patents dating to the 1860s.

    When the string holder moved to the household, lighter and more attractive forms developed, many made of chalkware. The string holder remained a key kitchen element until the early 1950s.

Reference: Sharon Ray Jacobs, *A Collector's Guide to Stringholders*, L–W Book Sales, 1996.

Cast Iron, ball, wire hanger, 6" d $12
Cast Iron, beehive, dated "Apr 1865," 6" h 60
Cast Iron, Dutch girl 25
Cast Iron, fish 60
Cast Iron, gypsy kettle 125
Ceramic, black porter, wearing gold cap, string emerges from mouth, mkd
   "Fredericksburg Art Pottery USA," 6³/₄" h 9
Ceramic, cat head, white cat, red, white, and black plaid collar, string
   emerges from mouth, mkd "Holt Howard 1958," 5" h 25
Ceramic, girl, wearing bonnet and dress with flounced white skirt with green
   floral dec, holding basket of flowers, string emerges from basket,
   stamped "Made in Japan," 6¹/₄" h 35
Ceramic, kitten with yarn, white kitten with blue eyes, white ball of yarn,
   string emerges from kitten's mouth, 5¹/₂" h 35

Ceramic, mammy, wearing blue turban, blue and white dress and apron, holding flowers, mkd "Japan, Fred Hirode," 1940s 80

Ceramic, mammy, wearing red turban, red and white checkered dress 120

Ceramic, mammy, wearing white dress with green and yellow dec, white apron and kerchief, string emerges from Mammy's folded hands, 7" h 150

Ceramic, 3 girls, 1 facing forward and holding floral bouquet, other 2 facing to sides and holding handbag and parasol, wearing bonnets and dresses with flounced white skirts with green floral dec, string emerges from bouquet, Japan, 6" h 40

Ceramic, 2 ladies and man, man facing forward wearing top hat and tuxedo and holding floral bouquet, flanked by ladies wearing bonnets and flounced white skirts with green floral dec, 1 lady holding parasol, other holding handbag, string emerges from bouquet, Japan, 6¼" h 40

Chalkware, apple, red and yellow, green leaves, brown tree branch, string emerges from base of apple, 8" h 40

Chalkware, chef, red hat, green collar, string emerges from mouth, 8" h 45

Chalkware, chef, white hat, string emerges from mouth, mkd "Plasto Mfg. Co., Chicago," 7½" h 45

Chalkware, Dutch girl, string emerges from mouth, 7" h 40

Chalkware, elderly woman, in rocking chair 35

Chalkware, girl, wearing blue bonnet 45

Chalkware, kitten with yarn, comical black and white smiling kitten, red ball of yarn, string emerges from yarn, 6¾" h 45

Chalkware, realistic black and white kitten, red ball of yarn, string emerges from yarn, 6½" h 45

Chalkware, mammy, wearing white turban with red polka dots, c1920, 5" h . . 150

Chalkware, peach 30

Chalkware, pear 30

Redware, lady with curly hair 125

Tin, woman knitting, cat playing with yarn 25

 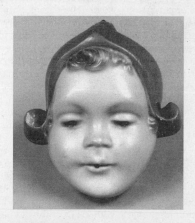

Left: Beehive, cast iron, 6½" d, 4½" h, $60.

Right: Dutch Girl, plaster, green hat, blue eyes, 7" h, 6⅜" w, $40.

LEISURE & PLAY

Life in rural America is hard and repetitive. Members of the agrarian community work hard and play hard. They are believers in the adage that "all work and no play makes Jack a dull boy."

Farming is a seven–day–a–week occupation. It is difficult to escape for an extended vacation. As a result, leisure activity often centered around day–long or half–day events. Extended leisure time was possible only when someone stayed behind to do the chores.

Leisure activities and social interaction are closely linked. Rural America is held together by its strong sense of community. It is only natural to spend time with family and friends during holidays, outings, and religious events.

A day away from the daily routine is a day from which memories are created. Souvenirs, mementos, and photographs document and rekindle the event. These treasured keepsakes grace the parlor or a favored corner of the bedroom chest of drawers.

Not all leisure and play is socially interactive. Some allows individuals a little time to themselves. Until the post–World War II era, rural families were large, often nucleated. Finding one's own space (to use a modern phrase) was difficult. The means to achieve that space, whether toy or hunting rifle, is among the most cherished of possessions.

The Country decorator too often misses the leisure and play side of country life. The tendency is to stress decorative elements that convey hard work and products derived from that work. A true Country decorating scheme never fails to illustrate the agrarians' ability to celebrate life itself.

AMUSEMENT PARKS, CARNIVALS, CIRCUSES, COUNTRY FAIRS, & WILD WEST SHOWS

The biggest social events in the lives of most agrarians were the county and state fairs. Participation often occurred on two levels—through membership in a local agrarian organization, usually The Grange, and individually. One planned for the fair for a year. For many, it was their one trip away from home.

A trip to the fair usually resulted in many keepsakes. First, there were the prizes ranging from trophies and ribbons that were won. Second, manufacturers often handed out premiums such as bookmarks, calendars, and sewing implements to help remind individuals of their products. Finally, there were the souvenirs from a pinback button to a pennant.

Although most county and state fairs contained a midway, the primary reason for going was business and education. Pleasure came only after the business at hand was concluded. Rest assured that entering a pie in the pie contest was serious business. Local reputation stood or fell on the results of the judging.

When the agrarian family simply wanted to get away from it all, they went to an amusement park, carnival, or circus. These were purely social events.

Carnivals normally were sponsored by a local group, ranging from the church to a fire company. Often they contracted with professional groups to provide rides and booths featuring games of chance. Food was provided locally. The most commonly found memento is a piece of carnival chalkware.

Carnival chalkware, cheerfully painted plaster of Paris figures, was manufactured as a cheap, decorative, art form. Doll and novelty companies mass produced and sold chalkware pieces for as little as a dollar a dozen. Many independents, mostly immigrants, molded chalkware figures in their garages. They sold directly to carnival booth owners.

Carnival chalkware was marketed for a nominal price at dime stores. However, its prime popularity was as a prize at games of chance located along carnival midways. Some pieces are marked and dated; most are not. The soft nature of chalkware means it is easily chipped or broken.

By the mid–nineteenth century the tent circus with accompanying side shows and menagerie became popular throughout America. There were hundreds of circus companies, varying in size from one to three rings. The golden age of the tent circus was the 1920s to the 1940s when a large circus would consist of over 100 railroad cars.

Almost every rural town of any size was visited by a circus. It was a day eagerly anticipated by the local youth who would gather at the rail siding to watch the circus unload, follow it to the field where it set up, and hang around until performance time.

The most commonly found circus souvenir is the program. A few individuals saved the large promotional broadsides. Country collectors often incorporate the circus theme into their settings through games, puzzles, and toys. Although not obtained at a circus, they capture the excitement that the circus creates.

A trip to the amusement park meant a trip to the big city. It was quite common for a town or township to have "community" or "church" day at an amusement park. Mothers and their children arrived in the morning. Fathers joined the festivities when work was done. Of all the features, it is the amusement park carousel which is best remembered.

By the late seventeenth century carousels were found in most capital cities of Europe. In 1867 Gustav Dentzel carved America's first carousel. Other leading American manufacturers include Charles I. D. Looff, Allan Herschell, Charles Parker, and William F. Mangels. The price of carousel figures skyrocketed in the 1980s when folk art collectors took the market for themselves. Today most Country collectors who want a carousel figure as an accent piece utilize a modern reproduction.

References: Charlotte Dinger, *Art of the Carousel*, Carousel Art, 1983; Tobin Fraley, *The Carousel Animal*, Tobin Fraley Studios, 1983; Tobin Fraley, *The Great American Carousel: A Century of Master Craftsmanship*, Chronicle Books, 1994; Frederick Fried, *The Pictorial History of the Carousel*, Vestal Press, 1964; *Price Guide to Carnival Chalkware, Giveaways and Games*, L–W Book Sales, 1995; William Manns, Peggy Shank, and Marianne Stevens, *Painted Ponies: American Carousel Art*, Zon International Publishing, 1986; Thomas G. Morris, *The Carnival Chalk Prize*, Prize Publishers, 1994.

Periodicals: *Carousel Shopper*, PO Box 6459, Santa Fe, NM 87502; *The Carousel News & Trader*, 87 Park Avenue West, Suite 206, Mansfield, OH 44902.

Newsletters: *Carousel Collecting & Crafting*, 3755 Avocado Boulevard, Suite 164, La Mesa, CA 91941; *Circus Report*, 525 Oak Street, El Cerrito, CA 94530.

Collectors' Clubs: American Carousel Society, 3845 Telegraph Road, Elkton, MD 21921; Circus Fans Assoc of America, 1544 Piedmont Avenue NE, Suite 41, Atlanta, GA 30324; Circus Historical Society, 3477 Vienna Court, Westerville, OH 43081; Historic Amusement Foundation, 4410 North Keystone Avenue, Indianapolis, IN 46205; National Amusement Park Historical Assoc, PO Box 83, Mount Prospect, IL 60056; National Carousel Assoc, PO Box 4333, Evansville, IN 47724.

Museums: American Carousel Museum, San Francisco, CA; P. T. Barnum Museum, Bridgeport, CT; Carousel World Museum, Lahaska, PA; Circus City Festival Museum, Peru, IN; Circus World Museum, Baraboo, WI; Heritage Plantation of Sandwich,

Sandwich, MA; Herschell Carousel Factory Museum, North Tonawanda, NY; Indianapolis Children's Museum, Indianapolis, IN; International Museum of Carousel Art, Hood River, OR; Emmett Kelley Historical Museum, Sedan, KS; Knoebels Amusement Park & Carousel Museum, Elysburg, PA; Merry Go Round Museum, Sandusky, OH; New England Carousel Museum, Bristol, CT; John and Mable Ringling Circus Museum, Sarasota, FL.

Business Card, "Miss Cresey Russell The Expert Rifle Shot Who Will Give A Free Exhibition of Her Fancy Rifle Shooting," black and white, 2³/₈ x 4" **$40**

Carousel Figure, carved wood, painted, dog, Herschell–Spillman, jumper, sweet expression, c1905, 54" l **7,000**

Carousel Figure, carved wood, painted, goat, PTC, jumper, animated pose, heavily carved fur, layered trappings, c1906, 45" l **6,000**

Carousel Figure, carved wood, painted, horse, Carmel, outside row lead stander, wildly flowing mane, draped forelock, jeweled trappings, full sword and scabbard, fish–scale armor, fringed fabric, layered straps, Herman's Park, Caroga Lake, NY, c1915, 64" l **30,000**

Carousel Figure, carved wood, painted, horse, Dentzel, prancer, alert expression, intricately carved mane, layered straps, rippled blanket, western saddle, c1900, 64" l **13,500**

Carousel Figure, carved wood, painted, horse, Illions, jumper, slim tapered head, spirited expression, full reverse swept mane, c1910, 52" l **5,500**

Carousel Figure, carved wood, painted, horse, Looff, Brooklyn, NY, inside row stander, alert expression, flowing mane, applied with pressed brass and jeweled trappings, scrolled saddle with double eagle cantle, worn paint, c1895, 60" l, 56¹/₂" h **18,500**

Carousel Figure, carved wood, painted, horse, Looff, Brooklyn, NY, Prancer, gentle expression, full mane, checkered blanket, double eagle cantle, c1895, 66" l **8,000**

Carousel Figure, carved wood, painted, horse, Parker, Leavenworth, KS, jumper, racing pose, head lunging forward, forelegs up, hind legs back, long full windswept mane, dog's head saddle cantle, repainted, c1917, 57" l, 26" h **5,000**

Carousel Figure, carved wood, painted, horse, PTC, jumper, Muller period, sensitive expressive face, parted and curled mane, fancy forelock, jeweled trappings, c1905 . . . .**10,000**

Carousel Figure, carved wood, painted, horse, PTC, outside row stander, Zalar style, gentle expression, full flowing mane, long draped forelock, tucked head, layered straps with star motif, large jewel at bridle rosette, PTC Carousel #49, Clementon Park, NJ, c1919, 65" l **22,000**

Carousel Figure, carved wood, painted, horse, Spillman, jumper, layered and jeweled trappings, fringed blanket, large single rose on breast strap, c1924, 58" l **6,000**

Carousel Figure, carved wood, painted, mule, Herschell–Spillman, jumper, animated pose, pleasant expression, folded blanket, Rocky Point Park, RI, c1914, 52" l **7,000**

Carousel Figure, carved wood, painted, pig, tongue lolling to side, red ribbon and bow at neck and tail, red and cream saddle and stirrups, 64" l, 28" h **4,625**

Carousel Figure, carved wood, painted, stag, Muller, leaping pose, forelegs up, hind legs down, scrolled saddle, no paint, from Willow Grove Park, PA, c1906, 51" l, 26" h **14,300**

Carousel Figure, carved wood, painted, zebra, PTC–Morris, outside row stander, layered blanket, ornate fringed straps, Lakemont Park, Altoona, PA, c1903, 46" l 22,000

Carousel Rounding Board, canopy or fersard–type top with scene of 2 people walking up dirt road toward home, 96" l, 44" h 775

Circus Wagon Wheel, sunburst 550

Diecut, standup, Willimantic Thread Circus, pig riding tricycle 50

Envelope, Cumins Indian Congress and Wildest West, "42 Different Savage Tribes," Indian image, cancelled 135

Letterhead, Ringling Brothers, chromolithographed colors, gold letters, 1911 . 50

Photograph, Barnum & Bailey, "Congress of Nations," black dancers, 1896 .. 35

Pinback Button, Annual Fair, farm animals, horse race, c1900, 1¼" d 5

Pinback Button, Coney Island, NY, "The Great Coal Mine, Coney Island," mule pulling cart and miner swinging ax at mine shaft, c1905, 1¼" d 20

Pinback Button, Steeplechase Park, NY, "Steeplechase Funny Place," smiling man, 1910s, ⅞" d 20

Postcard, Atlantic City, NJ, "Famous Old Landmark, The Elephant at South Atlantic City," photograph, Chilton Pub Co #9 5

Postcard, The Great Allentown Fair, Allentown, PA, Dan Patch race horse, undivided back, 1906 75

Poster, Barnum & Bailey Greatest Show on Earth, "Exciting Hurdle and Jockey Races," jockeys jumping hurdles under big top, Strobridge, 1903, 18 x 28" 975

Poster, Carson & Barnes Circus, performing clowns, removable date sheet, 1950s, 42 x 36" 75

Poster, Cole Bros Circus, "Miss Allen with Her Five Gaited Palominos," close–up of Allen and palomino, removable date sheet, 1945, 21 x 35" ... 165

Poster, Ringling Bros and Barnum & Bailey Combined Circus, "Miss Dorothy Herbert World's Most Daring Rider," Herbert hanging upside down from rearing horse, 1934, 27 x 40" 275

Program, Buffalo Bill's Wild West Show Company, "Buffalo Bill Bids You Good Bye, The Wild West and Far East, A Life Story and Book of Brave Deeds" 275

Left: Booklet, Barker's "Komic" Picture Souvenir, Part 2, Barker's Liniment adv, color litho cov, black and white illus, 52 pp, 9½ x 6", $35.

Right: Poster, Ringling Bros Barnum & Bailey Circus, litho clown, red, white, and blue, 28 x 41", $140.

Souvenir Glass, ruby stained, butter dish, cov, Lancaster Fair, Button Arches pattern, 1916 .... **150**

Souvenir Glass, ruby stained, tumbler, "Carnival, July 29, 1904, J. M. Craig," Button Arches pattern, 3⅞" h **35**

Souvenir Spoon, "Goin' to the Fair," Chicago Children's Home, young girl, 1892 .... **40**

Stereograph, Asbury Park, NJ, buildings, G W Pach, 1870s **10**

Stereograph, Bostock Wild Animal Show, lion tamer and lions, Whiting #74 .. **25**

Target, ball toss, screened canvas, clown faces, lamb's wool fringe, 12" h, price for set of 4 .... **25**

Target, shooting gallery, cast iron, bird, spring base, worn silver paint, 4½" h plus wood base **100**

Target, shooting gallery, cast iron, eagle, wings spread, looking left, center bull's eye, missing feet, 13" h **300**

Target, shooting gallery, cast iron, 2 chickens, steel frame, bull's eye below, worn red, white, and black paint, 18¾" h **250**

Ticket, PT Barnum, reverse with Sudine Washing Powder adv **35**

Wheel of Fortune, painted wood, horses and jockeys, with orig hardware, 24" d **200**

BIRD CAGES

During the Victorian era, the keeping of exotic pets, such as parrots and other types of birds, was common among the middle and upper classes. A standing bird cage often graced a solarium or living room. Well–to–do farmers and small town merchants imitated their big city counterparts.

Bird cages were constructed from a variety of materials ranging from wire and wood to wicker. Few period cages survive in good condition.

Bird cages became a "hot" decorator item in the late 1980s. Although primarily associated with the Victorian revival, they quickly found a place in the Country community. The most decorative examples made from natural materials also attracted the attention of the folk art collector.

Reference: Leslie Garisto, *Birdcage Book: Antique Birdcages for the Contemporary Collector,* Simon & Schuster, 1992.

Reproduction Alert: The vast majority of the bird cages being offered for sale today are reproductions. Before buying any bird cage become familiar with the Victorian Fantasies catalog from J. K. Reed.

Bamboo, 3 rooms with peaked roofs, 16" h **$75**

Brass Plated, cylindrical, dome top, gooseneck floor stand, replated, 24" d, 66" h **500**

Pine, carved, paint dec, demilune shaped top fitted with hanging ring, 1 side with sliding door, int fitted with 2 paint dec carved wood birds, 1875–95, 9¾" w, 16" h **1,375**

Pine, carved and painted, house shape, rect with 6 mansard roofs and wire towers above crenulated border with gilded turrets and finials, 6 doors, perforated sides, painted green, yellow, red, and gold, probably PA, late 19th C, 29" w, 21" d, 27" h **2,500**

Tin, cylindrical, dome top, old blue paint, 13½" d, 20½" h **200**

Left: Wood, Tramp Art, painted black with gold and green trim, 10¹/₂ x 15¹/₂ x 20¹/₂" h, $750.

Right: Wicker, hanging, painted white, $200.

Tin, cylindrical, flat top, tubular bars, hanging ring and chain, traces of green paint, 20" h **100**

Wicker, round cage with conical roof, stand with double cage supports and spreading circular foot, painted white **200**

Wire, rect, domed roof with turned wood baluster–form finial, flanked by 2 arched towers, sponge painted green and brown, 32" w, 16" d, 32¹/₂" h . . . **750**

Wood and Wire, cylindrical, dome top, dangling spring toys attached in spoke fashion around top, 23" h **300**

Wood and Wire, house shaped, wood frame with molded cornice and turned posts and feet, wire bars, pullout tray in base, old green paint with brown glaze, clear clown glass water fountain, 10¹/₄ x 15", 18" h **300**

Wood and Wire, pagoda shaped, ornate scrolling, white repaint trimmed in blue, 25¹/₂" h **115**

CHILDREN'S RIDE–ON TOYS

Many toys found in agrarian homesteads were handmade. Among the most common were children's ride–on toys, especially rocking horses. Since rural families were large, especially during the nineteenth and first half of the twentieth centuries, ride–on toys were made to survive. Repainted and repaired examples are typical.

During the late nineteenth century, mass–produced riding vehicles and wagons arrived upon the scene. Many were made by the same companies that manufactured larger vehicles. Wood was the most commonly found construction element.

By the 1920s pressed metal riding vehicles appeared. Many of these automobiles, fire trucks, and planes mimicked their real–life counterparts. Pedal cars from the 1920s through the 1950s are one of the "hot" collectibles in today's market.

References: Marguerite Fawdry, *An International Survey of Rocking Horse Manufacture,* New Cavendish Books, 1992; Andrew G. Gurka, *Pedal Car Restoration and Price Guide,* Krause Publications, 1996; L–W Book Sales (ed), *Riding Toys With Price Guide,* L–W Book Sales, 1992; Patricia Mullins, *The Rocking Horse: A History of Moving Toy Horses,* New Cavendish Books, 1992; Joan Palicia, *Flexible Flyers and Other Great Sleds for Collectors,* Schiffer Publishing, 1997; Neil S. Wood (ed),

Evolution of the Pedal Car and Other Riding Toys, Vol 1 (1989, 1997 value update), *Vol 2* (1990, 1997 value update), *Vol 3* (1992), *Vol 4* (1993), L–W Book Sales.

Newsletters: *The Peddler,* 5415 East 65th Street, Indianapolis, IN 46220; *The Wheel Goods Trader,* PO Box 435, Fraser, MI 48026.

Collectors' Club: National Pedal Vehicle Assoc, 1720 Rupert NE, Grand Rapids, MI 49505.

Bear, tan mohair, shoe button eyes, iron frame, ears missing, moth and fiber damage, Steiff, c1908, 18" l **$175**
Bicycle, boneshaker, wood spoke wheels, forged rims, c1860, 35½" front wheel **2,500**
Bicycle, Colson Firestone Bullnose, girl's, Firestone whitewall tires, orig paint, c1939 . . . . **775**
Bicycle, Colson Packard, girl's, streamline, saddle seat, snap–in 3 rib tank, headlight, drop rack, c1939 . . . . **450**
Bicycle, Columbia, 2–tone red, leather saddle, locking spring fork, front drum brake, Goodyear whitewall tires, c1948 . . . .**1,500**
Bicycle, Crescent No. 1, man's, safety pneumatic, wood handlebars and rims, orig Crescent logo seat, Western Wheel Works, Chicago, IL, 19th C . . **600**
Bicycle, Elgin Blackhawk, speedometer, c1934 . . . .**2,000**
Bicycle, Firestone Pilot, boy's, red and white, basket, chrome carrier, 26" **175**
Bicycle, Firestone Super Cruiser, girl's, blue and white, c1947, 26" **100**
Bicycle, Fitchburg Model C, woman's, Iver Johnson Arms & Cycle Works, c1890 . . . . **400**
Bicycle, I J Lovell, cushion tire safety, cantilever drop frame, 1890 patent date, 28" **1,700**
Bicycle, Iver Johnson, cushion tire safety, J P Lovell Arms Co, Boston, MA, 1890 patent date, 28" **900**
Bicycle, J C Higgins, girl's, cream, gray, and red, c1948–50, 26" **85**
Bicycle, Pierce Arrow "Tried & True," woman's, orig tool bag, Geo N Pierce Co, Buffalo NY, c1898, 28" **500**
Bicycle, Rambler #7, Gormully & Jeffery Co, Mfg, Chicago, 1891 patent date . **825**
Bicycle, Rover Tandem, c1900 . . . . **300**
Bicycle, Schwinn Mini–Twin Tandem, Schwinn burnt orange, 20" **1,100**
Bicycle, Schwinn Whizzer, maroon, Stewart–Warner speedometer, steering lock and key, 1948 . . . .**6,500**
Bicycle, Shelby Flyer, boy's, 4 rib horn tank, "air flo" chain guard, red, black, and white, 26" **725**
Bicycle, Silver King Monark, stepped stainless steel fenders, lobdell saddle, headlight, 1936 . . . . **300**
Bicycle, Silver King Wingbar, man's, stainless steel fenders, working speedometer, hex bars, tool box seat, Carlisle whitewall tires, 1938 . . . . . .**2,300**
Bicycle, Spaulding, man's, chainless shaft drive, A G Spaulding & Bros, Chicopeed Falls, MA, c1890, 28" **1,000**
Bicycle, Westfield 50th Anniversary, girl's headlight, full coverage chain guard and drop stand, c1937 . . . . **175**
Bicycle, White Sewing Machine Co, Cleveland, OH, orig paint, tool bag, and brakes, c1895, 28" **1,150**
High Wheeler, Aeolus, wood rim pneumatic ordinary with planetary gear drive and mustache handlebars, front wheel bearing mkd "The Aeolus Pat. #3531 1877 W. Brown Maker J," 35" front wheel **15,500**

High Wheeler, American Champion, radially spoked ordinary with ram's horn handlebars and wood saddle, Gormully & Jeffery, 54" **2,850**

High Wheeler, Columbia, open head radially spoked ordinary, straight bars, Pope Mfg Co badge, 50" front wheel **1,925**

High Wheeler, Columbia, radially spoked ordinary with brake, oversprayed with aluminum paint, spade handlebar grips, 52" front wheel **2,100**

High Wheeler, Columbia "All Bright," ordinary with dropped handle bars, brake hardware, pedals, and seat, c1885, 52" front wheel **4,000**

High Wheeler, Otto, ordinary, cast seat with "Otto" cutout, wood spokes, 19th C **1,875**

High Wheeler, Star, safety ordinary with brake, seat mounted above high wheel, G W Pressey, Hammonton, NJ, H B Smith Machine Co, NJ, c1888, 52" back wheel **5,000**

Horse, carved wood horse with saddle, glass eyes, and hair tail, walking rocker feet, small wheels on back rockers 275

Lamb, wood and steel frame with natural white woolly coat with felt and glass eyes, red embroidered nose and mouth, missing ear button, minor wear, Steiff, 14¹/₂" l, 14¹/₂" h **1,200**

Pedal Boat, restored, Murray Jolly Roger, c1960 950

Pedal Car, American National, Stutz model, with oil can, bulb type horn, windshield, chrome headlights and bumpers, light green with orange striping, blue fenders and running boards, blue, orange, and green wheels, restored, c1932–33, 5" l, 30" h **3,250**

Pedal Car, American National, with windshield, hand brake, horn, side light, and hub wheels, maroon with gold and black trim, 46" l, 29" h **4,000**

Pedal Car, Farmall Tractor, red, white, and black, hard rubber wheels, 38" l . . 100

Pedal Car, Murray Fireball, sheet steel, red and white, chrome trim, 40" l 275

Pedal Car, Murray Torpedo, 4 portholes on sides at motor, chrome windshield, headlights, bumpers, and squeeze type horn, 1950, 38" l, 20" h . . . 950

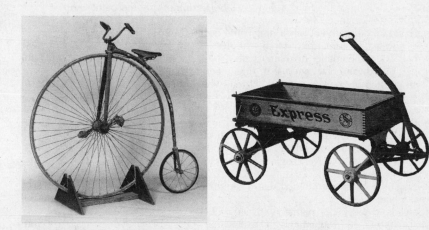

Left: Bicycle, high wheeler, wire spoke wheels, c1800, $1,750. Photo courtesy Copake Auction.

Right: Wagon, wood, dovetailed, wood spoke wheels, $125.

Rocker, duck, chair mounted between 2 duck silhouettes, platform base, turned spindle sides, orig ivory paint with black, gold, and red trim, missing seat upholstery, worn paint, 30" l **175**

Rocker, rooster, bench seat mounted between 2 rooster silhouettes, dark red, green, and yellow paint, seat adjusts, fitted with rockers and folding wheels, partial paper label on bottom, 39½" l **715**

Rocking Horse, carved wood, brown hide covered horse with glass eyes and hair tail, with saddle and stirrups, red painted wood frame with black and white stenciling, cast iron brackets mkd "Mallable, Unbreakable" **475**

Rocking Horse, carved wood, gray dappled horse with glass eyes and darkened brown varnish, worn orig saddle and stirrups, wood platform base, 40" l, 34" h **575**

Rocking Horse, carved wood, gray dappled horse with hair tail and horseshoes on extended legs, wood and iron frame, leather saddle **375**

Rocking Horse, carved wood, gray dappled horse with yarn tail, red stenciled frame **450**

Rocking Horse, carved wood, hide covered horse with white mane and patch on face, posed with 1 front leg up and supported by 3 decorative balls, leather harness, 38" l, 29" h **115**

Rocking Horse, carved wood, white with glass eyes and rear horseshoes, painted wood frame with stenciling, saddle needs repair **325**

Seal, steel frame, worn ivory colored mohair, salmon colored embroidered nose and mouth, nylon filament whiskers, straw stuffing, button on tail flipper, rubber tread wheels, eyes missing, 28" l **200**

Sled, wood, galloping horse, decorated, polychrome painted in red, black, and white with yellow highlights, red ground, poplar and oak, shaped deck, peaked runners joined by turned frontal stretcher, rect legs with chamfered corners, metal braces added, PA, 19th C, 34" l **975**

Sled, wood, "Grant," painted red and black, pinstriping and floral dec, iron tipped looped fronts on wooden runners, missing 1 brace, 37½" l **450**

Sled, wood, "King of the Hill," stenciled label, striping, orig red paint and varnish, steel runners, 39" l **275**

Sleigh, wood, painted red, pinstriping, hide covered horse head with glass eyes and leather trim, upholstered seat, 40" l, 24" h **525**

Tricycle, Adult Pneumatic, Tinkham Cycle Co, NY, c1900, 28" **1,000**

Tricycle, Boardwalk, oak caned seat, tiller steering, hand crank drive, built to be pushed or cranked, c1880, 27" rear wheel **110**

Tricycle, Columbia Light Roadster, orig finish with name plate "Pope Mfg. Co., pat. Nov. 1885," missing seat, pedals, 1 coaster peg, head lamp, and some spokes, 19th C, 39" front wheel, 23" rear wheels **7,700**

Tricycle, Homer Benedict, invalid, pneumatic rear wheels, hard tire front wheel, 19th C, 14" front wheel, 26" rear wheels **325**

Tricycle, Horse, chain drive, cast iron frame, full bodied wood horse, leather strapping, 36" l, 31" h **850**

Tricycle, Tiller, cushioned bench seat, restored, c1900, 9" front wheel, 19" rear wheels **300**

Velocipede, wood, coach painted with star motif on rear seat brackets, wood seat, 19th C, 28" front wheel, 23" rear wheels **1,100**

Velocipede, wood, red with black pinstriping, carpet covered seat, 19th C, 23" front wheel, 20" rear wheels **1,000**

Velocipede, wood, Velocipede Horse, wood rocking horse with glass eyes, steel frame with wire wheels, old repaint with deep golden tan horse and blue–green frame, harness and saddle refurbished, 39" l **550**

Wagon, Badger Coaster, wood body, wood spoked wheels with steel bands, 42" l **375**

Wagon, Buckboard, wood body, wood wheels with steel bands, wood seat, 48" l **825**

Wagon, Buckboard, wood stake body, wire wheels with hard rubber tread, painted red and black, 39" l bed **650**

Wagon, Lightning Wheel Coaster, wood body, wood spoke wheels, 42" l **400**

Wagon, Pioneer Coaster, wood body, wood artillery wheels, 1900, 43" l **500**

Wagon, Wire Haired Fox Terrier, mohair plush, ear button, glass eyes, steel frame and wheels, moth and fiber damage, growler not functioning, Steiff, 20" l, 17" h **450**

FIREPLACE EQUIPMENT

The fireplace was a gathering point in the colonial home for heat, meals, and social interaction. In the urban environment, it maintained its dominant position until the introduction of central heating in the mid–nineteenth century. In the countryside, the fireplace as a heat source remained dominant well into the twentieth century.

Even after central heating was introduced, the rural farmhouse retained working fireplaces. There was something nostalgic, comfortable about a roaring fire.

The open fireplace was one of the most popular decorating motifs of the early American decorating revival of the 1920s and 1930s. When Country became popular in the 1970s and 1980s, the living room and parlor fireplace became a major decorative focus.

Because of the continued popularity of the fireplace, accessories still are manufactured, usually in an early American motif. In the 1970s the folk art community developed a strong interest in fireboards, a device put in front of the fireplace to hide the opening when it was not in use during the late spring, summer, and early fall. It was not long before several reproduction craftspersons began providing contemporary copies of old fireboards.

References: Rupert Gentle and Rachael Feild, *Domestic Metalwork 1640–1840, Revised,* Antique Collectors' Club, 1994; George C. Newmann, *Early American Antique Country Furnishings: Northeastern America, 1650–1800's,* L–W Book Sales, 1984, 1996 value update.

Reproduction Alert: Modern blacksmiths are reproducing many old iron implements.

Andirons, pr, acorn finials above turned standard on circular pedestal base with hipped cabriole legs ending in flattened penny feet, brass, Chippendale, Philadelphia, PA, c1800, 17" h **$550**

Andirons, pr, ball and spire finials, spire–form finial above turned ball–form standard and faceted support on downswept hipped legs ending in pointed pad feet, brass, Chippendale, NY, 18th C, 22" h **800**

Andirons, pr, ball and steeple finials, vase shaped standards, scrolled arched supports, brass and wrought iron, old repairs, second half 17th C, 25½" l, 25½" h **2,500**

Andirons, pr, basket shaped ember support at top, shaft fitted with 4 spit hooks, arched base, wrought iron, late 17th/early 18th C, 32⅛" h **1,000**

Andirons, pr, black man cast in half round in squatting position with hands resting on outturned knees, wearing jacket, waistcoat, and pants, cast iron, early 20th C, 16¾" h **575**

Andirons, pr, cat cast in half round seated on its haunches on scrolled plinth, molded fur detail, inset green glass eyes, retains traces of black paint, cast iron, early 20th C, 16⅜" h **1,000**

Andirons, pr, cooking, faceted ball finial above gooseneck support, shaft mounted with spit hooks on arched legs ending in penny feet, billet bars fitted with mushroom form log stops, wrought iron, New England, 18th C, 16" w, 27½" d, 37" h **1,500**

Andirons, pr, floral bouquet, cast iron, attributed to New Haven Iron Works, Cincinnati, OH, 12" h **100**

Andirons, pr, Indian warrior with bow and arrows, cast iron, rusted surface, attributed to New Haven Iron Works, Cincinnati, OH, 13" h **225**

Andirons, pr, knife blade form with urn finials and arched supports ending in penny feet, wrought iron with brass finials and trim, 19½" h **725**

Andirons, pr, owl cast in half round and perched on arched branch, inset amber glass eyes, brass, early 20th C, 13" h **1,150**

Andirons, pr, soldier with pointed hat, blue coat, and black boots, painted cast iron, 19th C, 20" h **700**

Andirons, pr, spiral finial on urn form support, plinth below columnar standard, arched spurred cabriole legs ending in claw and ball feet, cast brass and wrought iron, Philadelphia, c1780, 22" h **2,875**

Apple Roaster, wrought iron, hinged apple support, heart–pierced end on slightly twisted projecting handle, late 18th C, 34¼" l **1,650**

Ash Shovel, wrought iron, handle stamped "G. McRoberts," 18" l **325**

Bellows, decorated, painted black with yellow striping and 2–tone gilt vintage designs, brass nozzle, worn orig leather, matching hearth brush, 20th C, 17½" l bellows, 22" l brush, price for set **75**

Bellows, decorated, painted red with gold and black vintage design, sheet brass nozzle, worn releathering, 17¾" l **225**

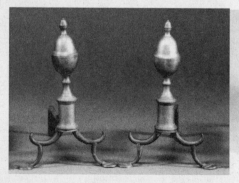 

Left: Andirons, Chippendale, turned acorn finials on pedestal base, hipped cabriole legs ending in flattened penny feet, Philadelphia, c1800, 17" h, $546. Photo courtesy Sotheby's.

Right: Bellows, orig red and gold paint dec on worn leather, 14¾" l, 7½" w, $150.

Bellows, decorated, smoked yellow paint, stenciled and freehand fruit and
foliage dec in gold, green, black, and red, brass nozzle, releathered, 18" l . **875**
Bellows, decorated, turtle back, orig cream colored paint with stenciled and
freehand fruit and foliage dec in various shades of bronze powder with gilt
and black, brass nozzle, releathered, 18¼" l **350**
Bird Roaster, tin reflector, 4 hooks, 1870s **175**
Broiler, wrought iron, rect, attached drip pan, heart handle, 10½ x 16" **525**
Cauldron on Stand, copper cauldron with hinged bail handle and riveted
tabs, circular wrought iron stand with 3 splayed legs, 9" h, 12" d **350**
Chestnut Roaster, pierced iron, heart shaped, long twisted handle, 18th C,
28½" l **1,000**
Coal Grate, wrought and cast iron, brass finials and trim, attached andirons,
removable bottom grate, 23¼" h **185**
Coal Hod, sheet steel, painted gold, green, and red dec on black ground,
with 3 brass handled tools, 24" h, price for set **375**
Coals Carrier, wrought iron, sliding lid, 31" l **225**
Coffee Roaster, down–hearth, sheet metal, iron rod, wood handle, late
18th/early 19th C, 51" l **150**
Crane, wrought iron, scrolled detail, 38½" l **100**
Ember Tongs, wrought iron, scissor extension, 14½" l **150**
Fire Back, cast iron, rect, minister in pulpit with German inscription below,
painted black, PA, 18th C, 29¼" w, 26¾" h **1,850**
Fire Back, cast iron, rect, Tree of Life, Lancaster, PA, 18th C, 24" w, 21" h **400**
Fire Board, geometric design, painted blue, yellow, green, sienna, black, and
white, 22¾ x 36¼" **2,000**
Fire Cover, wrought iron, gooseneck, penny feet, 18th C, 9½" h **150**
Fire Fender, brass, wrought iron, and wirework, curved sides, brass top rail
with 3 bulbous brass finials, full–length scrolling wirework design, repairs . **650**
Fire Fender, brass, wrought iron, and wirework, serpentine front, surmount
ed by 3 double lemon form finials, fender below with scrolling wirework
design, Federal, NY, c1800, 62" w, 17" d, 21" h **3,500**
Fire Mark, cast iron, oval, eagle, traces of old paint, dated 1792, 3¹⁄₁₆" h **50**
Fire Screen, folding, wrought iron, brass, and wirework, rect central panel
flanked by hinged wings surmounted by convex brass cap and dec with
wire swags and scrolls, conformingly shaped wrought iron base, NY,
c1800, 40" w, 20" d, 24" h **2,150**
Flue Cover, cast iron, plain **20**
Flue Cover, tin, emb border, painted ground, paper litho farm scene, c1900 .. **18**
Hearth Brush, baluster turned wood handle, grain painted, smoke dec,
leaves and flowers on gray and yellow ground, c1830, 27" l **450**
Kettle Shelf, wrought iron, hanging, pitted, 16½" h **75**
Kettle Tilter, wrought iron, acorn finial on swivel ring, c1810, 14" w **375**
Mantel, quarter sawn oak, double decker with molded cornice, rect beveled
mirror plate, pillars with scrolled capitals, mirror damage, 61½" w, 85" h .. **275**
Match Box, toleware, hanging, trefoil crest, crimped edge, orig red, green,
yellow, and white floral dec on black ground, 6" h **65**
Match Holder, wood, Scottie dog image **15**
Match Safe, brass, figural milk pail **175**
Match Safe, cast iron, figural horseshoe, antlered stag crest, knob finial on
lid **40**

Match Safe, wood, heart shaped, chip carved edges, angled pocket, white
sanded paint, gold trim **75**
Roasting Spit, brass and wrought iron, 12" l **40**
Rotary Broiler, round, wrought iron, tooled handle with initials "P.B.," small
welded repair, 12½" d, 21¾" l **135**
Stove Plate, cast iron, stylized floral designs with hearts in double arch, emb
"Henrich Wilhelm, Elisabeth Furnace," HW Stiegel Foundry, 25½" w,
23½" h **250**
Tool Set, brass, tongs, hearth brush, ash shovel, and poker, matching stand,
price for set **125**
Tool Set, wrought iron, shovel and tongs, brass handles with ball finials,
31½" l, price for pair **250**
Trammel, narrow shaft with double ring hanger and 3–prong hook, 24½" h . .   **200**
Trammel, sawtooth shaft with heart cutout and faintly engraved with tulip
design, surmounted by large hanging ring, 50¾" h **875**
Trammel, wrought iron, central standard dec with bird above scrolled heart
surmounted by ring support, shaft pierced with diamond, spade, heart,
and club, incised on lower section of shaft "Belpa Lime L1837," PA, dated
1837, 42" unextended height **11,500**
Trivet, wrought iron, heart shaped, scrolled and tooled detail, flattened han-
dle with hanging ring, spade feet, 9¾" l **250**
Trivet, wrought iron, triangular, tooled stylized leaf design in center, looped
handle, turned–up feet, 10½" l **325**

FISHING

Water is a precious commodity in rural America. The location of a stream often
dictated the site of a town or farmstead. The farm pond, usually stocked with a variety
of fish, provides a hedge against drought.

Fishing was more a means of relaxation than sport for the farmer. Many a cartoon
of "the lazy farmer" pictured him asleep with his back against a tree while fishing
along the bank of a stream that ran through his farm.

Early man caught fish with crude spears and hooks made of bone, horn, and flint.
By the middle 1800s metal lures with hooks attached were produced in New York
State. Later, the metal was curved and glass beads added for greater attraction.
Spinners with wood–painted bodies and glass eyes appeared around 1890. Soon after,
wood plugs with glass eyes were being produced by many different makers. A large
number of patents were issued in this time period covering developments of hook
hangers, body styles, and devices to add movement to the plug as it was drawn
through the water. The wood plug era lasted up to the mid–1930s when plugs constructed of plastic were introduced.

With the development of casting plugs, it became necessary to produce fishing
reels capable of accomplishing that task with ease. Reels first appeared as a simple
device to hold a fishing line. Improvements included multiplying gears, retrieving line
levelers, drags, clicks, and a variety of construction materials. The range of quality in
reel manufacture varied considerably. Collectors are mainly interested in reels made
with quality materials and workmanship, or those exhibiting unusual features.

Early fishing rods were made of solid wood which were heavy and prone to break
easily. By gluing together strips of tapered pieces of split bamboo a rod was fashioned
which was lighter in weight and had greatly improved strength. The early split bam-

boo rods were round with silk wrappings to hold the bamboo strips together. With improvements in glue, fewer wrappings were needed, and rods became slim and lightweight. Rods were built in various lengths and thicknesses, depending upon the type of fishing and bait used. Rod makers' names and models can usually be found on the metal parts of the handle or on the rod near the handle.

The fishing collectibles category has broadened significantly beyond rod, reel, and lure to include landing nets, minnow traps, bait boxes, advertising signs, catalogs, and fish decoys used in ice spearing. Items in original containers and in mint condition command top prices. Lures that have been painted over the original decoration or rods that have been refinished or broken have little collector value.

References: Bruce Boyden, *Fishing Collectibles: Identification and Price Guide,* Avon Books, 1995; Jim Brown, *Fishing Reel Patents of the US, 1838–1940,* published by author; Silvio Calabi, *The Collector's Guide to Antique Fishing Tackle,* Wellfleet Press, 1989; Ralf Coykendall, Jr., *Coykendall's Complete Guide to Sporting Collectibles,* Wallace–Homestead, Krause Publications, 1996; Clyde A. Harbin, *James Heddon's Sons Catalogues,* CAH Enterprises, 1977; Art and Scott Kimball, *Collecting Old Fishing Tackle,* Aardvark Publications, 1980; Art and Scott Kimball, *Early Fishing Plugs of the USA,* Aardvark Publications, 1985; Art and Scott Kimball, *The Fish Decoy, Vol I* (1986), *Vol II* (1987), *Vol III* (1993), Aardvark Publications; Carl F. Luckey, *Old Fishing Lures and Tackle: Identification and Value Guide, Fourth Edition,* Books Americana, Krause Publications, 1996; Albert J. Munger, *Those Old Fishing Reels,* privately printed, 1982; Dudley Murphy and Rick Edmisten, *Fishing Lure Collectibles: An Identification and Value Guide to the Most Collectible Antique Fishing Lures,* Collector Books, 1995, 1997 value update; Donald J. Peterson, *Folk Art Fish Decoys,* Schiffer Publishing, 1996; Harold Smith, *Collector's Guide to Creek Chub Lures & Collectibles,* Collector Books, 1997; J. L. Smith, *Antique Rods and Reels,* Gowe Printing, 1986; Richard L. Streater, *Streater's Reference Catalog of Old Fishing Lures, Volumes I and II;* Donna Tonelli, *Top of the Line Fishing Collectibles,* Schiffer Publishing, 1997; Steven K. Vernon, *Antique Fishing Reels,* Stackpole Books, 1984; Karl T. White, *Fishing Tackle Antiques and Collectables: Reference and Evaluation of Pre–1960 Tackle,* Holli Enterprises, 1990.

Periodicals: *American Angler,* PO Box 4100, Bennington, VT 05201; *Fishing Collectibles Magazine,* 2005 Tree House Lane, Plano, TX 75023; *Sporting Collector's Monthly,* PO Box 305, Camden Wyoming, DE 19934.

Newsletter: *The Fisherman's Trader,* PO Box 203, Gillette, NJ 07933

Collectors' Clubs: American Fish Decoy Assoc, 624 Merritt Street, Fife Lake, MI 49633; National Fishing Lure Collectors Club, 22325 B Drive South, Marshall, MI 49068; Old Reel Collectors Assoc, 849 NE 70th Avenue, Portland, OR 97213.

Reproduction Alert: Lures and fish decoys.

Bobbers, pr, wood, tapered, turned knobs on ends, multicolored stripes, 12" l   **$80**
Canoe, wood and canvas, Hunter Model, Penn Yan, 1955, 15' **715**
Canoe Seat, folding, wood frame, caned seat and back, sled style base,
    stamped on underside "Vermont Tubbs–Forestdale VT" **200**
Catalog, Creek Chub Bait Co, color, 1947, 22 pp **250**
Catalog, Pflueger Fishing Tackle, 1929, 152 pp **150**
Creel, Adirondack style, splint, pot–bellied, pine lid with center hole, combination leather hinges and carrying strap, orig wood latch **150**

Creel, A E Nelson, Salem, OR, split willow and hand tooled leather, old style snap closure, hanging handle, tooled leather harness, large size **500**

Creel, Brady, whole willow, leather harness and shoulder strap, canvas cover, large front pocket, 2 pouches, trout size **165**

Creel, brook trout, split willow, 6" ruler attached to top, leather latch strap and hinges, classic shape **60**

Creel, Ed Cumings, Flint, MI, fly fisher's landlock salmon creel, whole willow, orig sliding wood latch mkd with J F Anderson's 1937 patent number 2,085,564, curved back, leather and web harness, 13" l **115**

Creel, George Lawrence, Portland, OR, #5A, split willow and tooled leather, leather hanging handle and harness, paper label on bottom reads "Best–Made–Reg. U.S. pat. Off," large size **550**

Creel, Hardy, wicker, leather edged canvas pouch on front, leather straps, fish opening at corner of lid, lid opens away from angler, leather harness, leather and web shoulder strap, rubber liner **125**

Creel, Indian, reversed white birch bark, dyed fish and flower images on lid, flowers, bird, and rabbit on sides, 10" h **300**

Creel, Maine, guide's, splint, pot–bellied, wood lined oval center hole, wood reinforced edges, figure 8 latch strap with peg latch, c1900 .... **400**

Creel, Oregon style, split willow and tooled leather, leather knife sheath on underside of lid, hanging handle, leather harness, classic shape, large size . **750**

Creel, trout, split willow, tooled leather, hanging handle, leather and web harness, classic shape **450**

Creel, turtle trademark, trout creel, whole willow, rattan wrapped lid edge, 11" ruler on lid, leather and web harness, hand carved turtle sliding latch, old paper label **1,650**

Decoy, Bruce Wakefield, St Cloud, MN, wood, custom made, yellow and black with silver flakes, metal fins, belly weight, 7" l **60**

Decoy, Heddon Metal Fish Decoy, metal, white body, red nose, mkd "Pat. Pending" under dorsal fin, 4½" l **200**

Decoy, ice spearing, carved bone, exaggerated pointed tail and carved mouth and gill detail, "MS" carved on belly, 1940s, 7" l **150**

Decoy, MI, pike, carved wood, plastic eyes, green, yellow, and cream, metal fins, sgd "J.M.," 10½" l **70**

Left: Lure, Hansen Michigan, Minnow, 3–hook model, aluminum body, speckled iridescent blue back, 1908, $880.

Right: Reel, American Trout Reel, maker marking "T. H. Bate – N.Y." on handle crank, German silver, c1860, 2¼" d, 1" w spool, $1,265.

Photos courtesy Lang's Sporting Collectables.

Decoy, Vernon Baggs, Kalkaska, MI, ice spearing, carved wood, metal fins
and tail, blue body with silver and red trim, 10" l **100**

Flies, Frances Stearns, 30 salmon hair flies in frame, patterns include Orange
Blossom, Gary Yellow Dog, Frazier Spec, Downeaster, and Silver Satan . . . **550**

Gaff, spring loaded, mkd "Norlund's, Williamsport, PA. U.S.A.," some pit-
ting, 56" l handle **80**

Line Drier, brass and iron construction mounted on paddle shaped wood
base with sliding rings to hold reel, folding, mkd "C. Farlow & Co. Ltd." . . . **225**

Lure, Calkin, glass, salesman's sample, bulbous midsection, raised rings front
and rear to retain line tie and tail hook hangers, wired–on metal band mkd
"LCSMIASMI–2," sgd "Lowell Calkin–Millville, N.J.–One A Day Mino,"
hole in front, large hole in rear **1,000**

Lure, CCBC, sucker, wood, natural blue sucker scales, glass eyes, belly age
lines, minor chips, c1932 . . . . **325**

Lure, Hastings, frog, hollow rubber, hp, thick line tie wire follows body into
external belly weight, 2 tail hooks and weed guard wires enter rear of
belly weight, c1895, 3½" l **175**

Lure, Heddon, #170 SOS Wounded Minnow, L–rigs, early shiner finish with
red color, glass eyes, finish age lines, tiny chip at tail end, minor chips at
l hook rig, 4½" l **90**

Lure, North Coast Minnow, green back with age yellowed body, round end
tail prop mkd "Pat. Pen.," glass eyes, single trailing hook, 3 belly weights,
c1909, 3" l **125**

Lure, Pflueger, Monarch Underwater 5–hook minnow, green back, white
belly, V–shaped body, hp gill marks, glass eyes, see through wire hangers,
3⅝" l **275**

Lure, Pflueger, Neverfail Minnow, 3 hook, early perch finish, hp gill marks,
large glass eyes, unmkd props, Neverfail hook hangers, 2¾" l **285**

Lure, Shakespeare Revolution, hollow aluminum, prop mkd "Pat. Appl'd
For," trailing feathered double hook, 3⅛" l **90**

Lure, South Bend Truck–Oreno, red and white wood body with wood prop,
large feathered trailing treble hook, 5" l **450**

Lure, Stump Dodger, wood, green back, red lateral stripe, white belly, tacked
eye, name stenciled on top, 2 treble hooks, 3¾" l **80**

Lure, Weller Simplex Wiggler, orig box mkd "Weller's Classic
Minnow–Junior Size–No. 3," chub finish, hp gill marks, glass eyes, early
1–pc lip and line tie, 3⅛" l **160**

Minnow Bucket, tin, painted green, fish decal and "Falls City Jones" on front,
oblong, screened lift–out int, heavy rod carrying handle, lift–out inner
bucket with air valve **200**

Reel, "A. Coats Pat. Mar. 20th, 88, Watertown, N.Y.," side mount combination single action or multiplying trout reel, spool reel, rotary click, double
line guides, threaded filler plug for unused post, 2" d, ¾" w **400**

Reel, "Blue Grass Reel–Made By B. F. Meek & Sons, Louisville, Ky., No. 3,"
bait casting reel, handmade, German silver, click and drag switches, seri-
al number stamped at end of foot **300**

Reel, Bogdon No. 0 salmon reel, handmade, engraved owner's name,
3⅛" d, 1⅛" w **875**

Reel, "Conroys Makers, NY," trout reel, handmade, German silver, raised
rear click housing, ivory handle, offset foot, c1850, 2" d, 1⅛" w **650**

Trophy, salmon, Maine Hooked Jaw Landlocked, painted background scene, sgd "Mounted by Billy Hatch, Cornish, Me. – Dec. 28, 1928" on back, walnut frame, 30" fish, 29 x 46" frame, $440. Photo courtesy Lang's Sporting Collectables.

Reel, Coxe Model No. 25–w, bait casting reel, nickel silver, cross bolt construction, no–tools take apart, mkd leather case with papers, late 1940s . . . **115**

Reel, Cozzone, 60–yard trout reel, dark and light marbleized plates, German silver and hard rubber, click switch, wear compensating rear bearing cap, 2¼" d, 1" w **375**

Reel, Farlow Ambassador, single action salmon reel, back plate drag adjustment, strong click, 4" d, ¾" w **80**

Reel, Hardy Special Perfect trout reel with "Duplicated Mark II Stamp," raised front plate click housing, orig natural aluminum color handle plate, 90% orig blued finish, 3¼" d, 1" w **875**

Reel, Hardy St George trout reel, agate line guide, 3–screw latch, orig box, 3⅜" d **575**

Reel, Heddon Pal P–41, bait casting reel, black plates, jeweled bearing caps, orig box, bag, booklet, and retailer hanging tag, 1950s **95**

Reel, "J. B. Moscrops Patent, Manchester," fly reel, brass, black finish, foot ends filed, 1 shortened, 3⅛" d, 1" w **50**

Reel, J C Arsenault, Canada, machined trout click reel, S–handle, aluminum, 1⅜" d, 1" w **190**

Reel, "Orvis Magnalite Multiplier" fly reel, multiplying reel with exposed rim and drag switch, 3⅛" d, ⅞" w **55**

Reel, Perfection Model 360, No. 1/0 size trout reel, handmade, German silver and hard rubber, click switch, aluminum spool ends, under handle drag adjusting knurled ring with early arrowhead point, red drag setting indicator dots, mkd "Edw. Vom Hofe, N.Y. Pat. Jan 23, 83," 3⅛" d, 1⅛" w . **2,750**

Reel, Shakespeare 1740 Free Spool Tournament reel, Model FK, jeweled nickel silver, old silk tournament line **80**

Reel, "T. H. Bate, N.Y.," trout reel, German silver, maker marking on handle crank, 1 foot end flattened, c1860, 2¼" d, 1" w **1,265**

Reel, W A Adams, traditional trout reel, click reel with adjustable drag, exposed rim spool, right or left hand wind, labeled leather zippered case, 2¾" d, ¾" w **275**

Reel, Wm Mills & Son, NY, trout reel, raised pillar, crank handle, thick German silver plates, 1–pc solid foot without hole, back frame engraved in tiny old script "Newt Earle," rubber plates browned, some age tarnish, 2⅜" d, ⅞" w **385**

Rod, Constable Fine Fly trout rod, 2 pc, 1 tip, #7 weight line, ferrule plug, orig bag, 8' l **125**

Rod, Dickerson 761510 R B trout rod, 3 pc, 2 tip, agate stripper guide, nicely figured walnut reel seat spacer, orig bag and tube, 7½' l **3,350**

Rod, Edwards Quadrate Special Luxor medium fresh water action spinning rod, 2 pc, full length, 7' l **55**

Rod, Edwards Special trout rod, Edwards Sons, Bristol, CT, 3 pc, 2 tip, medium fast action, fine tips, agate stripper, tip top guides, orig bag and tube, 7½' l **350**

Rod, E F Roberts trout rod, 2 pc, 2 tip, #5 weight line, orig bag, labeled tube, 7' l **275**

Rod, F E Thomas Browntone Special trout rod, Top of the Line Model, Bangor, ME, 3 pc, 1 tip, agate stripper, tip top guides, blued hardware, long cork handle with thumb depression, bag and tube, 8½' l **175**

Rod, G H Howells trout rod, 2 pc, 2 tip, 3¼ oz, #5 line, flawless glass–like finish, orig bag and labeled tube, 7½' l **1,800**

Rod, Green Mountain Special Back Packer #4/5 impregnated trout rod, Vivian R Shoker maker, 4 pc, 1 tip, 21" l sections, agate stripped guide, orig bag and tube, 7' l **350**

Rod, H R Sedgwick trout rod, Hartford, CT, 3 pc, 2 tip, 3.3 oz, agate stripper guide, intermediate wraps, intricate signature winds, 7½' **700**

Rod, Orvis Midge trout rod, 2 pc, 2 tip, Wes Jordan type handle with thumb depression, orig tube, 7½' l **475**

Rod, Payne Parabolic trout rod, 2 pc, 2 tip, 3⅛ oz, ink owner's initials at base of cork reel seat, ferrule plug, orig bag with tag, tube labeled with owner's initials and 1958 date on cap, 7' l **4,500**

Rod, W E Carpenter #80570 trout rod, 2 pc, 2 tip, slightly swelled butt, deep flamed cane with complimentary wraps, agate stripper guide, ferrule plug, orig bag and labeled tube, 1980, 7' l **2,000**

Skinning Board, wood, hp fish on back, sgd "A. Deaver L.R.," chipped work surface **45**

Tackle Box, cedar, homemade, divided section in bottom, lift–down lid revealing slots for lures, brass handle, corner reinforcements, and hasp–type lock, 25" l **95**

Trophy, rainbow trout, attached to wood plaque hand carved to simulate stony stream bed with sculptured back splash, 25" l fish **150**

HOLIDAYS

Holidays provided a welcome break from the tedious daily chores that were a constant in country living. Work could not be totally ignored. The cows had to be milked and the animals fed, holiday or not. The rural community followed a Sunday, rather than a weekday schedule.

Religious holidays tended to be family oriented and personal. Coming together was achieved at the traditional church service. Patriotic holidays were community celebrations, a time when frivolity prevailed.

Many holidays such as Christmas, St. Patrick's Day, Easter, and Halloween have both religious and secular overtones. National holidays such as the Fourth of July and Thanksgiving are part of one's yearly planning. There are regional holidays. Fastnacht Day in Pennsylvania–German country is just one example.

Some holidays are the creation of the merchandising industry, e.g., Valentine's Day, Mother's Day, Father's Day, etc. The two leading forces in the perpetuation of holiday gift giving are the card industry and the floral industry. Through slick promotional campaigns they constantly create new occasions to give their products. Other marketing aspects follow quickly. Holiday items change annually. Manufacturers constantly must appeal to the same buyer.

Collectors tend to specialize on one holiday. Christmas, Halloween, and Easter are the most popular. Christmas collectors split into two groups—those who collect material associated with the Christmas tree and those who collect Santa Claus related material. Halloween and Easter collectors tend to be generalists, albeit some Easter collectors limit their collection to Easter bunnies. New collectors still can find bargains, especially in the Thanksgiving and Valentine's Day collectibles.

Many holiday collectibles were manufactured abroad. Germany and Japan are two of the leading exporters of holiday items to the United States. German items from the turn of the century are highly prized.

It is possible to build a holiday collection around a single object. Two possibilities are postcards and papier–mâché candy containers. Among contemporary material, it is possible to find one or more limited edition collectors' plates issued for most holidays.

One of the most overlooked holiday collectibles is the greeting card. A greeting card's message and artwork is an important reflection of the values of the time the card was printed. With the exception of Valentines, most examples, even those from the early decades of the twentieth century, are priced under two dollars.

References: Pamela E. Apkarian–Russell, *Collectible Halloween,* Schiffer Publishing, 1997; Robert Brenner, *Christmas Past, 3rd Edition,* Schiffer Publishing, 1996; Robert Brenner, *Christmas Through the Decades,* Schiffer Publishing, 1993; Robert Brenner, *Valentine Treasury: A Century of Valentine Cards,* Schiffer Publishing, 1997; Juanita Burnett, *A Guide to Easter Collectibles,* Collector Books, 1992; Dan and Pauline Campanelli, *Halloween Collectables: A Price Guide,* L–W Books, 1995; Pauline and Dan Campanelli, *Holiday Collectables: A Price Guide,* L–W Book Sales, 1997; Dan and Pauline Campanelli, *Romantic Valentines,* L–W Book Sales, 1996; *Favors & Novelties: Wholesale Trade List No. 26, 1924–1925,* L–W Book Sales, 1994–95 value update; Helaine Fendelman and Jeri Schwartz, *The Official Price Guide to Holiday Collectibles,* House of Collectibles, 1991; George Johnson, *Christmas Ornaments, Lights, and Decorations,* Collector Books, 1987, 1995 value update; Polly and Pam Judd, *Santa Dolls and Figurines Price Guide: Antique to Contemporary, Revised,* Hobby House Press, 1994; Chris Kirk, *The Joy of Christmas Collecting,* L–W Book Sales, 1994; Jeanette Lasansky, *Collecting Guide: Holiday Paper Honeycomb, Cards, Garlands, Centerpieces, and Other Tissue Paper Fantasies of the 20th Century,* published by author, 1993; Ruth Webb Lee, *A History of Valentines,* reprinted by the National Valentine Collectors Assoc; Robert M. Merck, *Deck the Halls,* Abbeville Press, 1992; Mary Morrison, *Snow Babies, Santas and Elves: Collecting Christmas Bisque Figures,* Schiffer Publishing, 1993; Margaret Schiffer, *Christmas Ornaments: A Festive Study,* Schiffer Publishing, 1984, 1995 value update; Margaret Schiffer, *Holiday Toys and Decorations,* Schiffer Publishing, 1985; Stuart Schneider, *Halloween in America: A Collector's Guide With Prices,* Schiffer Publishing, 1995; Margaret and Kenn Whitmyer, *Christmas Collectibles, Second Edition,* Collector Books, 1994, 1996 value update.

Newsletters: *Boo News,* PO Box 143, Brookfield, IL 60513; *Creche Herald,* 117 Crosshill Road, Wynnewood, PA 19096, *I Love Christmas,* PO Box 5708, Coralville, IA 52241; *Trick or Treat Trader,* PO Box 499, Winchester, NH 03470.

Collectors' Clubs: Golden Glow of Christmas Past, 6401 Winsdale Street, Minneapolis, MN 55427; International Creche Festival Assoc, 1421 Cornwall Avenue

#B, Bellingham, WA 98225; National Valentine Collectors Assoc, PO Box 1404, Santa Ana, CA 92702.

CHRISTMAS

Candle Lights, red and blue, miniature base, Mazda, boxed set of 10, working **$65**

Candy Container, basket, colored wrapping paper and tinsel, chromolith graph Santa, Sears adv, USA, early 1920s, 3" h **100**

Candy Container, boot, red and gold chenille, holly sprig on side, Japan, 6" h **80**

Candy Container, cornucopia, red and silver foil, mesh drawstring top, Santa face dec, Japan, 4" h **40**

Candy Container, Santa, figural, carrying pack, papier–mâché, 9" h **70**

Candy Container, Santa, figural, riding in sleigh, papier–mâché, painted, 7¹⁄₂" l **85**

Candy Container, Santa, figural, riding rocking horse, painted glass **75**

Candy Container, Santa, figural, sitting on cotton snowball, cotton body, slide in bottom, 5" h **165**

Candy Container, Santa, figural, wearing pointed hat, squatty body, Western Germany, 10" h **50**

Candy Container, Santa, figural, tree, goose feather, spring type candle clips, holly dec flower pot, 6" h **100**

Chocolate Mold, Santa, tin, 4 cavities, Germany **235**

Color Wheel, 4 colored gel panels, orig box **30**

Cookie Cutter, Father Christmas, tin, 19th C **600**

Diecut, winter church scene and "Merry Christmas," Germany, 13" w **50**

Left: Candy Container, belsnickle, papier–mâché, gold mica coat, red piping around hood, black base, missing feather tree and stopper, Germany, 5" h, $400.

Center: Candy Container, molded plastic face, white mesh body, red fabric hood and arms, silver stars and trim on molded cardboard car, Japan, 1930s, 5¹⁄₂" h, 6" l, $95.

Right: Ornament, angels, scrap and tinsel, 1890–1910, $15.

Doorstop, Santa, cast iron, early 20th C, 10½" h **350**
Figure, Frosty the Snowman, plastic, holding broom, illuminated, Miller **60**
Figure, Santa, clay face, cloth pack on back, Occupied Japan, 5½" h **135**
Figure, Santa, cotton body, cardboard sleigh and deer, 9" l **50**
Figure, Santa, papier–mâché, wearing suit and cape, holding tree, 41" h **550**
Lantern, metal, double–faced glass Santa head, battery operated, orig box ... **60**
Light Bulb, figural, miniature base, baseball player, clear, Japan **300**
Light Bulb, figural, miniature base, Punch, clear, pointed cap, ruffled collar
 and cuffs, rosy cheeks, Germany **130**
Nativity Figure, composition, dog, shepherd, 2–tone brown, 2½" h **4**
Nativity Figure, donkey, hide covered, wood legs, Germany, 5" l **25**
Nativity Figure, Joseph, kneeling, Japan, 2⅛" h **3**
Nodder, bisque, boy holding flower, head held with string, Germany, 3" h ... **35**
Stocking, fabric, St Nicholas with toys on 1 side, smiling moon over city on
 reverse, "'Twas the Night Before Christmas" verse, 30" l **135**
Toy, Santa in sleigh, 4 reindeer, pull toy, hard plastic, orig box, 10½" l **95**
Toy, Santa in sleigh, 1 reindeer, windup, celluloid Santa and reindeer, metal
 sleigh, 7½" l **150**
Toy, Santa on tricycle, windup, celluloid Santa, metal tricycle, "Merry
 Christmas" on bell, orig box, Japan **75**
Tree, chenille, green, orig box, 1920, 7'h **300**
Tree, goose feather, green, sq base with stenciled holly, Germany, 38" h **200**
Tree Ornament, angel, blown glass, Dresden wings, clip–on, c1920, 4" h **150**
Tree Ornament, angel, scrap, emb, spun glass halo and skirt, 5" h **25**
Tree Ornament, angel, wax, flying, 4" l **75**
Tree Ornament, ball, blown glass, wire wrapped, 3" d **35**
Tree Ornament, bell, blown glass, emb Santa, 1920s, 2½" h **85**
Tree Ornament, boot, c1960, 3" h **4**
Tree Ornament, candy cane, blown glass, c1950, 6½" l **8**
Tree Ornament, candy cane, chenille, 12" l **8**
Tree Ornament, Christmas tree, plastic, green, 3¾" h **5**
Tree Ornament, church, blown glass, 1920s, 4⅛" h **15**
Tree Ornament, clown playing banjo, blown glass, 1930s, 4½" h **30**
Tree Ornament, cornucopia, scrap angel dec, tinsel outline, wire coil, 9" h .. **50**
Tree Ornament, cottage, mica coated cardboard, 2¾" h **18**
Tree Ornament, ear of corn, blown glass, c1930, 4¾" h **40**
Tree Ornament, Father Christmas, scrap, spun glass robe, 9" h **65**
Tree Ornament, fish, blown glass, wire wrapped, 1920s **20**
Tree Ornament, french horn, blown glass, pre–1940, 4" h **15**
Tree Ornament, Graf Zeppelin, blown glass, 1920s, 5" l **200**
Tree Ornament, grape cluster, blown glass, blue, early 1900s, 7" h **175**
Tree Ornament, kite, glass beads, Czechoslovakia **20**
Tree Ornament, man in the moon, blown glass, crescent, c1930, 3½" h **75**
Tree Ornament, mushroom, blown glass, red and white, clip–on, c1930 .... **40**
Tree Ornament, parakeet, blown glass, spun glass tail, clip–on, c1930 ...... **40**
Tree Ornament, pine cone, blown glass, red, c1940, 3½" h **5**
Tree Ornament, Santa, celluloid **50**
Tree Ornament, Santa, clay face, chenille body, Occupied Japan, 6" h **20**
Tree Ornament, Santa, cotton body, Japan, 5" h **35**
Tree Ornament, Santa, plastic, red, white fur trim, 4½" h **8**
Tree Ornament, Santa holding bag, blown glass, clip–on, 1920s, 6" h **100**

Lights, figural, Germany, 1915–20s, $40 to $55 each. Left to right: Father Christmas, cat with mandolin, songbird, monkey, and clown.

Tree Ornament, sedan, blown glass, 1920s, 3¼" l	135
Tree Ornament, sheep, cotton body, wood legs, red ribbon around neck, Germany, c1910	35
Tree Ornament, snowman, blown glass, 1930s, 3½" h	25
Tree Ornament, star, glass beads, Occupied Japan, 1950s	20
Tree Ornament, swan, celluloid	40
Tree Stand, cast iron, relief Santa head and beard, painted red, green, and gold, 11" d	275
Tree Topper, angel, blown glass, c1935, 5" h	125
Tree Topper, angel, plastic, opening for bulb, 1950s	25
Tree Topper, ball with spire top, blown glass, wire wrapped	40
Tree Topper, Santa, blown glass, c1930, 4¼" h	125
Tree Topper, wreath, wire frame, felt holly leaves, composition berries, 12" d	35

EASTER

Basket, twig, grass and chenille chicks, early 20th C	$75
Basket, wood, painted flowers, "Made in Germany" paper label on base, 6" d, 10" h with handle	20
Candy Box, litho cardboard, square, bunnies and carrots	10
Candy Container, chick, papier–mâché, glass eyes, wire spring feet, c1930	175
Candy Container, chicken, composition, dressed as man, 4" h	150
Candy Container, duck, composition, 1920s	125
Candy Container, egg, papier-mâché, litho of boy golfer on front, separates at middle, mkd "Germany," 4" l	35
Candy Container, gentleman rabbit, composition, wearing yellow jacket, Germany, 4" h	150
Candy Container, rabbit, composition, fur covered, carrot in mouth, c1900	235
Candy Container, rabbit, papier–mâché, white, open back, Germany	40
Candy Container, rabbit, papier–mâché body, wood legs, mkd "Germany"	100
Candy Container, rooster, composition, metal feet, removable head, "Germany"	75
Chocolate Mold, standing rabbit, tin, 2–part mold with separate 2–part molds for ears and forelegs, mkd "Anton Reiche, Dresden, Germany," 18½" h	225
Cookie Cutter, egg shape, tin, late 19th C	5
Figure, rabbit emerging from egg, composition, 6½" h	60
Mask, rabbit, heavy papier–mâché, 11" h	20
Nodder, rabbit, chalkware, brown flocking, mkd "USA," 1950s, 5" h	15

Roly Poly, rabbit, celluloid, dressed in purple, standing on ball, Japan, 4½" h .   25
Toy, rabbit, windup, fur covered, hops, mkd "Japan," 5" h   60

HALLOWEEN

Candy Container, cat, papier–mâché, painted black, 7" h $125
Candy Container, pumpkin, molded cardboard, 1940   65
Candy Container, witch, composition, Germany, 4" h   250
Chocolate Mold, witch, 4 cavities, Germany, early 20th C   150
Diecut, black cat face, emb   20
Figure, black cat with arched back standing on die, celluloid, Japan, 3½" h . .   75
Figure, owl, papier–mâché, orange and black, glass eyes, 10" h   100
Figure, witch on pumpkin, papier–mâché, black, orange, and pink, 5⅝" h
    plus stand   250
Ice Cream Mold, witch, pewter, 5½" h   150
Lantern, papier–mâché, cat head, orange, paper face, 5" h   100
Lantern, papier–mâché, jack–o'–lantern, red, paper face, 5" h   100
Light Set, center 5½" w jack–o'–lantern and six 4" w jack–o'–lanterns, cellu-
    loid, Noma, 1920s   800
Noisemaker, wood, ratchet, small black composition cat on top, 5½" l   75
Tambourine, litho tin, black cat face, orange ground   40
Toy, witch and jack–o'–lantern on motorcycle, hard plastic, black accents . . .   100
Whirligig, witch on broomstick, polychrome painted wood, 13½" l   55

INDEPENDENCE DAY

Bank, mechanical, Uncle Sam, late 19th C $1,500
Candy Container, Liberty Bell, blue glass, early 20th C   75
Candy Container, Uncle Sam, composition, removable base, 1930s   85
Embroidered Panel, eagle and American flag, shades of brown, white, black,
    red, and blue, overall wear, fading, stained background, 25¼" sq   200
Figure, Uncle Sam with Flag, wood silhouette, screened red, blue, black,
    and white paint, printed cloth flag, 12¾" h   200
Flag, 38 stars, silk–screened paint on gauze, framed, c1885, 32¾ x 49"   475
Ice Cream Mold, eagle with shield, pewter, 5" h   125

Right: Candy Container, turkey, painted papier–mâché body, lead feet, 3¾" h, $45.

Left: Chocolate Mold, rabbits playing drums, 3 cavities, tin, hinged, Anton Reiche, Dresden, #26024, 10⅝" w, 6" h, $150.

NEW YEAR'S DAY

Banner, fabric, "Out With the Old—In With the New," 1935 . . . . **$25**
Candy Container, champagne bottle, cardboard, paper label, 1920 . . . . **125**
Handkerchief, cotton, bell and "Happy New Year Greetings," 1940 . . . . **6**
Hat, top hat shape, foil covered cardboard, 1960s **5**
Noisemaker, horn, litho tin, New Year's baby, red, yellow, and blue, wood
    mouthpiece, 1920 . . . . **12**
Noisemaker, snapper, cardboard, crepe paper dec, glitter "Happy New Year" . **5**
Noisemaker, whistle, paper and cardboard, feather blow–out, 1930 . . . . **7**

THANKSGIVING

Candy Container, turkey, composition, metal feet, Japan **$60**
Chocolate Mold, turkey, tin, Germany, 8" h **35**
Dishes, turkey set, ironstone, dark blue transfer of tom turkey and farmyard
    scene, mkd "Florence Bistro, England," 19³/₈" l platter and six 10¹/₄" d
    plates, price for set **375**
Figure, turkey, composition, folded tail, green base, mkd "Japan," 6" h **35**

VALENTINE'S DAY

Ice Cream Mold, entwined hearts and "Love," pewter, early 20th C **$30**
Valentine Card, carriage, children, and flowers, honeycomb foldout, 1910 . . . **150**
Valentine Card, Colonial dancers, emb, poem inside, 2³/₄ x 4¹/₄" **6**
Valentine Card, delivery boy on motorbike holding red hearts, "A Valentine
    Specially For You," mkd "Germany," 4" h **8**
Valentine Card, winter scene with children ice skating, Grace Drayton illus,
    easel back, 20th C **25**

HUNTING

    There is a strong linkage between the country community and firearms. Almost every farmer owns one or more rifles. These weapons provide self–preservation and sport.

    Varmints from rats to groundhogs plague the farmer. Some attack small domesticated animals, eat harvested grain, or cause damage that can lead to accidents. The standard means of ridding the farm of varmints is to shoot them.

    Hunting also plays an important role in the agrarian community. In lean times, it provides all–important food for the table. In good times, it provides sport and a means of escape from daily chores.

    The fifteenth century arquebus was the forerunner of the modern firearm. The Germans refined the wheel lock firing mechanism during the sixteenth and seventeenth centuries. English settlers arrived in America with the smoothbore musket; German settlers had rifled arms. Both used the new flintlock firing mechanism.

    A major advance was achieved when Whitney introduced interchangeable parts into the manufacturing of rifles. The warfare of the nineteenth century brought continued refinements in firearms. The percussion ignition system was developed by the 1840s. Minie, a French military officer, produced a viable projectile. By the end of the nineteenth century cartridge weapons dominated the field.

Two factors control the pricing of firearms—condition and rarity. The value of any particular antique firearm covers a very wide range. For instance, a Colt 1849 pocket model revolver with a 5" barrel can be priced from $150 to $750, depending on whether or not all the component parts are present and original, how much of the original finish (bluing) remains on the barrel and frame, how much silver plating remains on the brass trigger guard and back strap, and the condition and finish of the grips. Be careful to note any weapon's negative qualities. Know the production run of a firearm before buying it.

Muzzle loading weapons of the eighteenth and early nineteenth centuries varied in caliber and required the owner to carry a variety of equipment with him, including a powder horn or flask, patches, flints or percussion caps, bullets, and bullet molds. In addition, military personnel were responsible for bayonets, slings, and miscellaneous cleaning equipment and spare parts.

In the mid–nineteenth century, cartridge weapons replaced their black powder ancestors. Collectors seek anything associated with early ammunition from the cartridges themselves to advertising material. Handling old ammunition can be extremely dangerous due to decomposition of compounds. Seek advice from an experienced collector before becoming involved in this area.

References: Robert H. Balderson, *The Official Price Guide to Antique and Modern Firearms, Eighth Edition,* House of Collectibles, 1996; Ralf Coykendall, Jr., *Coykendall's Complete Guide to Sporting Collectibles,* Wallace–Homestead, Krause Publications, 1996; Norman Flayderman, *Flayderman's Guide to Antique American Firearms...and Their Values, Sixth Edition,* DBI Books, Krause Publications, 1995; Howard Harlan, *Duck Calls: An Enduring American Folk Art,* published by author, 1988; Howard Harlan, *Turkey Calls: An Enduring American Folk Art,* published by author, 1994; Jim and Vivian Karsnitz, *Sporting Collectibles,* Schiffer Publishing, 1992; Joseph Kindig, Jr., *Thoughts On the Kentucky Rifle in Its Golden Age,* 1960, available in reprint; Russell and Steve Quetermous, *Modern Guns: Identification & Values, Eleventh Edition,* Collector Books, 1997; Ned Schwig, *Standard Catalog of Firearms, Seventh Edition,* Krause Publications, 1997; Gordon L. Stetser, Jr., *The Complete Muzzleloader,* Mountain Press, 1992; Bob and Beverly Strauss, *American Sporting Advertising Vol I* (1987, 1992 value update), *Vol 2* (1990, 1992 value update), published by authors.

Periodicals: *Gun List,* 700 East State Street, Iola, WI 54990; *Sporting Collector's Monthly,* PO Box 305, Camden Wyoming, DE 19934; *The Double Gun Journal,* 5014 Rockery School Road, East Jordon, MI 49727; *The Gun Report,* PO Box 38, Aldeo, IL 61231.

Collectors' Clubs: Call & Whistle Collectors Assoc, 2839 East 26th Place, Tulsa, OK 74114; Callmakers and Collectors Assoc of America, 137 Kingswood Drive, Clarksville, TN 37043; Winchester Arms Collectors Assoc, Inc, PO Box 6754, Great Falls, MT 59406.

Museums: National Firearms Museum, Washington, DC; Springfield Armory National Historic Site, Springfield, MA.

Reproduction Alert: The number of reproduction and fake powder horns is large. Be very cautious!

Ammunition Box, cardboard, Clinton Cartridge Co Mallard Loaded Shells,
2–pc box, 16 gauge, multicolor label with flying mallard, empty **$65**
Ammunition Box, cardboard, Eley Special Quail Cartridges, 2–pc box, 12
gauge, No. 10 shot size, multicolor label with flushing quail on front, mkd
"Smokeless Diamond Cartridges" on side panel, empty, 2½" **250**

Ammunition Box, cardboard, Federal Monark Trap Shells, 2-pc box, 16
gauge, red shooter, black and red print, yellow ground, empty **265**
Ammunition Box, cardboard, Peters HV "Blue Bill," 2-pc box, 12 gauge,
No. 6 shot size, multicolor labels with flying mallard, empty **75**
Ammunition Box, cardboard, Western Xpert Shotgun Shells, 2-pc box, 12
gauge, blue, yellow, red, and white label with pointer, empty, 2⁵/₈" **95**
Ammunition Dispenser, Winchester, tin, wall hanging, holds 10 boxes of .22
ammo, 1950s **250**
Bird Call, crow, walnut barrel, stamped "Mfg. by Charles H. Perdew, Henry,
Ill," silver band, 4¹/₄" l **235**
Bird Call, duck, horn and walnut, E I Quinn, New Burn, TN, walnut stopper
both ends, sgd and dated "12-23-93" **150**
Booklet, Dupont, *Important American Game Birds,* compiled by E G
Forbush, illus by Lynn Bogue Hunt and others, over 40 color plates of
ducks, shorebirds, geese, turkey, etc., 1917, 56 pp **60**
Bow, handmade, takedown, recurve, maple riser, laminated limbs, +/– 35
lbs **50**
Bow, Hoyt, recurve, leather "Bear" quiver, 3 wood arrows with field points,
handle needs recovering **25**
Bowie Knife, blade mkd "J. A. Brown, Pulaski," stag handle with .31 cal per-
cussion gun barrel with spring loaded hammer mounted flush in grip, dull
gray blade, 13¹/₄" l, 8" blade **200**
Bullet Mold, .560 cal ball, no maker's name, brown patina **28**
Bullet Mold, Hensley and Gibbs, .50 cal, round, single cavity, scissors type,
brown finish, wood handles **50**
Bullet Mold, Winchester .38 WCF, wood handles, orig black finish **50**
Canister, Volcano Smokers, smoking cartridges for driving animals from their
dens, green and black paper label image of hunter using product, contains
15 cartridges **70**
Catalog, Remington, red leatherette hard covers with gold print, features
arms and ammo, 1923 . . . . **70**
Catalog, Savage No. 61, multicolor covers with screaming Indian on front,
features guns, ammo, and accessories, 1920, 76 pp **120**
Catalog, Stoeger Arms Corp, New York, NY, "The Shooter's Bible" No. 36,
arms, ammunition, and equipment, rifles and shotguns, pistols and
revolvers, policemen's supplies, target practice materials, traps and skeet,
cartridges, sportsmen's outdoor clothing, animal scents, 1945, 512 pp,
8 x 10" **45**
Decoy, crow, papier–mâché, glass eyes, repairs to hook on back **15**
Hand Trap, Western "White Flyer," orig box **25**
Kentucky Long Rifle, percussion, maple stock, silver star on cheek pc,
matching bird in front, silver and brass ramrod pipes, incised molding
along ramrod channel and comb, engraved and pierced silver and brass
patch box with bird finial, 60¹/₂" l **1,450**
License, pinback button, California, 1934–35, Resident Citizen's Hunting
License, no paper **60**
License, pinback button, Connecticut, 1927, Resident Combination Hunting
and Fishing License **100**
License, pinback button, Delaware, 1936, Resident Hunting & Trapping
License **75**
License, pinback button, Hawaii, 1939–40, County Hunting License **1,500**

License, pinback button, Michigan, 1929, Resident Deer License **110**

License, pinback button, New York, 1917, Hunting and Trapping License, white with blue print, celluloid, screw type pin latch **100**

Loading Tool, Winchester .38 WCF, orig black finish **60**

Musket, Brown Bess, engraved Tower lock with crown mark and "G.R.," browned 42" barrel with replaced breech plug, walnut stock with brass fittings, pinned repairs at fore–end, 58" l **1,650**

Musket,, Flintlock, cherry full stock with brass hardware and iron sling swivels, 42" l browned barrel fitted for lug bayonet, engraved lock sgd "Ashmore," with bayonet, age crack in butt stock **1,000**

Musket, Providence Tool Co, Model 1861, percussion, .58 cal, 39" l barrel, eagle stamp with "US" and "1864" on lock, faint inspector's mark, rear sight missing, 55" l **775**

Musket, Springfield, percussion, lock stamped "U.S. Springfield" and "1861," with bayonet, light pitting to breech area and lock, bayonet pitted, 56" l **1,325**

Oil Bottle, Remington, blue tinted glass, emb front reads "Rem–Oil, Remington–UMC, Powder Solvent, Lubricant, Rust Preventative," paper label on back, orig cork stopper, c1912 .... **100**

Pellet Rifle, Winchester, .177 .... **225**

Pistol, Balthaser Auer, Kentucky percussion derringer, .55 cal, $3^3/4$" sighted barrel rifled with 6 grooves and stamped "B. Auer, Louisville, Ky." continuing over breech, breech dec with star on percussion and opposing false bolster, sighted long tang extending over full butt length, plain lock, engraved hammer, walnut stock, strongly lipped fore–end and butt, engraved iron trigger guard, small plain silver mounts, c1859–69, $7^1/4$" l ...**2,400**

Pistol, Blunt & Syms, percussion single shot side hammer pistol, .44 cal, 6" heavy octagonal sighted rifled barrel stamped "B & S, New York, Cast Steel," blued finish, plain rounded box–lock action with traces of finish, varnished walnut grips, trigger guard formed in 1 with rear ramrod pipe, ramrod replaced, c1845, 10" l **975**

Pistol, Haviland & Gunn, percussion single shot gallery pistol, .17 cal, all metal, barrel, frame, and butt cast in 1 pc, nickel plated finish, top of breech with 2–line stamp "Remington Ilion N.Y.," and patent date, narrow trigger guard forming mainspring, c1875, 8" l **1,375**

Pistol, Remington–Rider, rimfire 5–shot magazine pistol, .32 cal, plain nickel plated extra short barrel, magazine, and frame, standard barrel marking, frame numbered "2" beneath left grip, nickel plated hammer, cartridge carrier, and trigger, ivory grips, period leather holster, c1871–88, $5^3/4$" l **1,375**

Pistol, Slotter & Co, percussion derringer, .41 cal, $2^3/8$" sighted barrel rifled with 5 grooves, stamped "Wart Steel" on right and "Kittredge, Cin. O." in arc, breech struck with Deringer sunburst proof mark and stamped "J. Deringer, Philadela.," engraved sighted tang, walnut stock, engraved German silver mounts, c1860, 5" l **1,850**

Pistol, Woodward, English rimfire turn–over pistol, .43 cal, Birmingham proof marks, No. 900, hand rotated case hardened sighted barrels rifled with 6 wide grooves, blued border engraved frame grooved for loading on right, maker's signature and "Feby 4, 1863" patent date in hand engraved oval on left, spur trigger, blued safety catch, checkered walnut grips, lanyard ring, c1863–65, $7^7/8$" l **1,000**

Rifle, American, percussion, half–stock, fancy grade with brass and silver inlays in tiger maple stock, c1830, 34¹/₈" l, $1,000.

Powder Flask, cork, "Safety First" emb on bottom, jug shaped, painted white, replaced stopper, c1870 .... **25**

Powder Flask, glass, mold blown, emb scene with 3 birds on either side, cork stopper, wire hanger **60**

Powder Flask, horn and brass, Wheelock, reinforced brass and iron wrench hole near bottom, wood replacement stopper, c1780, 7¹/₂" l, 3¹/₂" w at base **315**

Stag Antler, made from fork of antler, hollow with 3 protruding ends capped with bone covers, allover floral scrimshaw, iron hardware made by black-smith, spring loaded spout with turned lever, fitted with iron belt hook with ring at end, 1 end cap missing, 10" h, 4" w at base **385**

Rifle, Springfield, Model 1873, trap door, 32¹/₂" l barrel with dark brown fin-ish, 6 groove rifling, walnut stock with dark finish, shallow chip near lock, areas of pitting **325**

Rifle, Winchester, Model 1873, lever action, .44 cal, 24¹/₄" l octagonal bar-rel, full magazine tube, walnut stock stamped "A.G.Z." and "S.H.," mag-azine tube end cap missing **875**

Shipping Box, wood, Remington–UMC "Kleanbore," .22 LR, dovetailed, green and red stenciled labels **40**

Shipping Box, wood, Winchester Model 12, dovetailed, contained 10 shot-guns, hinged lid, clasp, stenciled labels, c1920s, 33 x 16¹/₂ x 11" **350**

Shipping Box, wood, Winchester No. 4 Primers, 25 bricks of 10/100 packs, handle cutouts on sides, complete with contents **430**

Shooting Gallery Target, cast iron, center bull's eye flanked by squirrel on either side, painted black, mounting bracket attached **85**

Shotgun, American Gun Co, double hammer, 20 gauge, 27¹/₂" l barrels with worn bluing, checkered walnut stock **225**

Shotgun, Stevens, double barrel, 16 gauge, 28" l blued barrels, good case colors and simple engraving on receiver **225**

Shotgun, Winchester, Model 1897, 12 gauge, full choke, worn bluing on receiver **275**

Sizing Die/Loading Tool, Winchester 40–65, dark age patina, mkd with logo and March 17, 1891, patent date, 9" l **160**

Sizing Gauge, brass, used by inspectors at Winchester or Western, gauges shot shells and primers, unmkd, early 19th C, 11 x 2¹/₂" **45**

Snowshoes, pr, ash wood frames, rawhide stringing, unmkd **75**

Target, Pope, paper, printed by P J O'Hare, Maplewood, NJ, 9¹/₂ x 12¹/₂" **35**

Target, Quakenbush No. 2, iron, 1 to 10 concentric circles for scoring, spring loaded red bird pops up when bull's eye is hit, painted red and black, 12" d **325**

Target Ball, glass, NB Perth Glass Works, light green, fishnet design, slightly
chipped neck **235**
Target Ball, glass, Van Custem, cobalt blue, fishnet design, mkd "Van
Custem, a St. Quientin," lightly chipped neck **140**
Trophy, Eastern Canada Moose, full shoulder mount, 49" spread, mounted
on wood plaque **500**
Trophy, White Tail Buck, 7 point, full shoulder mounted, 23" spread, mount-
ed on wood plaque **150**

MUSICAL INSTRUMENTS

Music played an important role in rural life. A parlor organ and/or piano was found
in most well–to–do homes. Family singing as a form of social interaction was common.
In addition, farmers and housewives sang aloud, often to themselves, to pass the time
of day.

Within the agrarian community, love of music enhanced social contact. Many individuals sang in church and secular choirs. "Barber Shop" harmony was practiced
informally.

Most individuals were proficient on a musical instrument. Community bands flourished. Most rural town parks had a band stand. Many fraternal associations, fire companies, and veteran organizations had their own bands to provide marching music for
members during community and regional parades.

Brass instruments such as trumpet, trombone, and tuba were among the most popular. Many communities had an all brass band, albeit most had a few percussion players for marching purposes.

Live music was required for hoe–downs and community dances. The country fid-
dler enjoyed a prominent position. He was often joined on stage by a bass, guitar, and
banjo player.

The more traditional musical instruments were often supplemented by a host of
folk and improvised instruments, many of which were handmade. The best known of
the folk instruments is the dulcimer. Improvised instruments range from the washboard
to the boom–bas, a virtual one–person band.

The most valuable antique instruments are associated with the classical
music period of 1650 to 1900, e.g., flutes, oboes, and violins. Few of these are found
in the countryside. Most country instruments, e.g., trumpets and guitars, have more
value on the "used" market than they do as antiques.

Periodicals: *Concertina & Squeezebox,* PO Box 6706, Ithaca, NY 14851; *Vintage
Guitar Magazine,* PO Box 7301, Bismarck, ND 58507.

Collectors' Clubs: American Band Organ Assoc, 3766 Mann Road, Blacklick, OH
43004; American Musical Instrument Society, RD 3, Box 205–B, Franklin, PA 16323;
Automatic Musical Instrument Collectors Assoc, 919 Lantern Glow Trail, Dayton, OH
45431; Fretted Instrument Guild of America, 2344 South Oakley Avenue, Chicago, IL
60608.

Museums: Miles Musical Museum, Eureka Springs, AR; Museum of the American
Piano, New York, NY; Musical Museum, Deansboro, NY; Smithsonian Museum,
Division of Musical History, Washington, DC; Shrine to Music Museum, Vermillion,
SD; Streitweiser Foundation Trumpet Museum, Pottstown, PA; University of Michigan,
Stearns Collection, Ann Arbor, MI; Yale University Collection of Musical Instruments,
New Haven, CT.

Banjo, Dandy, maple, 16 hooks, 17 frets, F hole resonator, replaced nut, 11" head **$85**

Banjo, Gibson, trapdoor, 24 hooks, 20 frets, orig pick guard, 10½" head **250**

Banjo, homemade, folk banjo, 8 hand forged hooks, 18 frets, metal rim, open metal resonator, carved pegs, inlaid with maker's initials, orig arm guard, tail pc, and bridge, torn head, c1900, 12½" h **75**

Banjo, Orpheum No. 1, #6394, 24 hooks, tone ring, thick wood pot, ornate inlay, 2 hooks missing, 11¾" head **225**

Banjo, Regina, 18 hooks, 17 frets, peghead and fingerboard inlaid with mother–of–pearl crescent moons, double thick wood and metal rim, tone ring, metal resonator, 1920 patent date, 11" head **125**

Banjo, S S Stewart, student's, maple hoop, 20 hooks, all orig **150**

Banjo, unknown maker, 11 frets, snake skin head, aluminum hoop, fancy cutouts in aluminum resonator and armrest, torn head, c1950, 10" head . . **50**

Banjo Ukulele, Pennant, 12 hooks, spruce hoop and resonator, ebony fingerboard, laminated neck **95**

Banjo Ukulele, unknown maker, 12 hooks, maple hoop and neck, metal strings, set up like tenor **85**

Baritone Ukulele, Regal, spruce top, edge binding around top and back, zippered bag **125**

Baritone Ukulele, Wabash, mahogany **85**

Drum, Boy Scout, tin with japanned band, scouts in uniform and "Boy Scout Band" in black, white, blue, and gold on red ground, wood bands repainted, rope replaced, worn heads, with 2 drum sticks, 12" d **385**

Drum, Carl Fischer, NY, transfer dec of eagle and shield, rope and leather binding, worn orig varnish, ropes and leather replaced, 1 head split, with 2 drum sticks, 16½" d **325**

Left: Music Box, Regina, mahogany case, 15½" disc player, c1900, $4,000.

Right: Drum, wood, military type, made by Frank Mehman, 1892, 13½" h, 18" d, $195.
Photo courtesy Collectors Auction Services.

Drum, child's, tin, emb with thirteen stars and flags in gold japanning, red, and blue, wood band with orig 2–tone finish, small tears in worn heads, dated "1887," 13" d 375

Dulcimer, pine, paint dec, black and white sound board with 8–petaled flowers and geometric musical notes, grain painted case, trapezoidal beveled frame fitted with tuners holding wire strings on pierced sound board, PA, 19th C, 41" w, 14³/₄" d, 3¹/₈" h 400

Guitar, C F Martin and Co, Nazareth, PA, Model 0–28K, stamped "C. F. Martin & Co., Nazareth, P.A., 31225," 2–pc back and sides of strongly figured koa wood with dec inlaid center strip, top similar, with herringbone purfling, body bound in faux ivory, mahogany neck, ebony fingerboard with diamond shaped pearl inlay, with case, 1927, 19¹/₁₆" l back, 13³/₄" w bottom bout 4,500

Guitar, Herk Favilla Workshop, classical, labeled "Made in USA est. 1890 original Favilla Guitars Inc., Herk Favilla, Ser No. 101223 style C–8 solo," 1–pc mahogany back, similar sides and neck, medium grain spruce top, rosewood fingerboard, with case, 18¹⁵/₁₆" l back 285

Mandolin, Gibson Mandolin Guitar Co, Kalamazoo, labeled "Gibson Mandolin Style F4, Number 33785, is hereby guaranteed...," 2–pc maple back and sides with strong curl, medium grain spruce top, fully bound in ivoroid, cedar neck with bound ebony fingerboard with pearl eyes, peg head inlaid "The Gibson," with case, 12⁷/₈" l back 1,725

Mandolin, Standard Rex, bowl back, labeled "This Instrument is Warranted...No. 162585 Standard Rex, Mandolins, Banjos, Guitars, Zithers," 34 stave back, medium grain spruce top bound in faux ivory and dec wood inlay, cedar neck, bound fingerboard with floral pearl inlay, with case 375

Melodeon, Dreher Kinnard & Co, Cleveland, OH, rosewood veneer case, ivory and ebony keyboard, glued break in music stand, minor veneer damage, working, 45³/₄" w, 22" d, 31¹/₂" h 600

Music Box, Criterion, upright, mahogany floor model cabinet, double comb, 2 broken teeth, needs damper work, fifteen discs, 20¹/₂" h 10,000

Music Box, Lochmann Original, tubular bells, single disc, upright box, needs restoration, 10 discs, 24¹/₂" disc box 13,500

Music Box, Perfection, single comb, felt dampering system, fully restored, 4 discs, 14" 2,150

Music Box, Regina, automatic changer, dragon front style, home model, solid wood lower front, piano sounding board style back, oak finish, all orig, eighteen discs, 27" 21,500

Music Box, Regina, folding top, oak casket model, double comb, coin operated, some excess governor noise, all orig 10,500

Music Box, Regina, Style 50, serpentine mahogany case, matching disc cabinet with serpentine top, curved front and sides, dec legs, 15¹/₂" 6,750

Music Box, Stella, single comb, mahogany case, unrestored, needs cleaning and adjusting, 13 discs, 9¹/₂" 950

Music Box, Symphonion, double comb, coin operated, American model, New York bedplate, orig condition, needs regulation, 14³/₄" 3,500

Phonograph, Brunswick, floor model, japanned cabinet 1,000

Phonograph, Columbia, AS Graphophone, coin operated, new horn 6,275

Phonograph, Columbia, Baby Grand 3,025

Phonograph, Columbia, HJ Graphophone, front mount disc 900

Phonograph, Columbia, Q Graphophone **415**
Phonograph, Edison, Home Phonograph, oak case, repainted, replaced
    chain,16" l **575**
Phonograph, Edison, Opera, oak, horn, no lid **3,850**
Phonograph, Edison, Triumph B, cygnet wood horn **2,750**
Phonograph, Edison, Triumph D2, external oak horn, domed lid **2,900**
Phonograph, Fairy Phonograph, octagonal lidded case with black fringe and
    gold tassels, copper and brass ftd base, Burns & Pollack Electrical Mfg Co . **3,250**
Phonograph, Victor, II, oak horn **3,850**
Phonograph, Victor, III, golden oak case, spear tip horn **3,575**
Phonograph, Victor, IV, mahogany spear tip horn **5,225**
Phonograph, Victor, V, external oak spear tip horn **2,200**
Phonograph, Victor, MS, ornate case, oak spear tip horn **4,125**
Phonograph, Victor, R Talking Machine, pre–Nipper **1,450**
Phonograph, Victor, Zonophone, mahogany horn **2,100**
Pump Reed Organ, Kimball, oak case with Eastlake detail, backboards
    incomplete, stop knob labels missing, not working, worn finish, 43" w,
    22³/₄" d, 74" h **30**
Reed Organ, mechanical, walnut case with gold dec, labeled "Mechanical
    Orginette Co. New York," working, 26¹/₂" w **500**
Tambourine, hp landscape with tree on canvas cover, wear, small hole,
    10" d **50**
Ukulele, Favilla Tear Drop **125**
Ukulele, Martin Style O **165**
Ukulele, Milton G Schiller, friction, koa wood **85**
Ukulele, The Serenader, B&G, New York, double binding around edge and
    hole, celluloid fingerboard and head, needs bridge and keys **75**
Zither, pine case with worn rosewood graining, white striping, red designs,
    and yellow stars, 45" l **275**

TOYS, DOLLS, & GAMES

Toys, dolls, and games were a favorite pastime in rural America. Games that
involved all members of the family were popular. Many of the toys found in the agrarian household were handmade.

The first manufactured toys in America were imported from Europe. The first toys
manufactured in America were made of cast iron, appearing shortly after the Civil War.
Leading nineteenth–century manufacturers include Hubley, Dent, Kenton, and
Schoenhut. In the first decades of the twentieth century, Arcade, Buddy L, Marx, and
Tootsie Toy joined the earlier firms.

The importation of toys never ceased. German toys dominated until World War I.
After World War II, Japanese imports flooded the market. Today, many "American" toys
are actually manufactured abroad.

During the fourteenth through the eighteenth centuries doll making was centered
in Europe, mainly Germany and France. The French dolls produced in the era repre-
sented adults and were dressed in the latest couturier designs. They were not children's
toys.

During the mid–nineteenth century, child and baby dolls made in wax, cloth,
bisque, and porcelain were introduced. Facial features were hand painted; wigs were
made of mohair and human hair. They were dressed in baby or children's fashions.

Doll making in the United States began to flourish in the 1900s with names like Effanbee, Madame Alexander, Ideal, and others.

Teddy bears are rapidly increasing as collectibles and their prices are increasing proportionately. As in other fields, desirability should depend upon appeal, quality, uniqueness, and condition.

The first American board games have been traced back to the 1820s. Mass production of board games did not begin until after the Civil War. Firms such as Milton Bradley, McLoughlin Brothers, and Selchow and Righter were active in the 1860s. Parker Brothers began in 1883. Milton Bradley acquired McLoughlin Brothers in 1920.

Every toy, doll, teddy bear, and game is collectible. The key is condition and working order if mechanical.

References: There are a wealth of books devoted to the subject of toys, dolls, and games. A basic reference is *Harry L. Rinker's A Collector's Guide to Toys, Games, and Puzzles* (Wallace–Homestead, 1991). The following references are merely starting points. Their bibliographies will point you in additional directions.

Toys: Graham Claytor, Jr., Paul A. Doyle, and Carlton Norris McKenney, *Greenberg's Guide to Early American Toy Trains,* Greenberg Publishing, 1993; Terri Clemens, *American Family Farm Antiques,* Wallace–Homestead, Krause Publications, 1994; Joe and Sharon Freed, *Collector's Guide to American Transportation Toys 1895–1941,* Freedom Publishing, 1995; Richard Friz, *The Official Identification and Price Guide to Collectible Toys, Fifth Edition,* House of Collectibles, 1991; Morton A. Hirschberg, *Steamtoys: A Symphony in Motion,* Schiffer Publishing, 1996; Sharon and Bob Huxford, *Schroeder's Collectible Toys: Antique to Modern, Second Edition,* Collector Books, 1996; Charles M. Jacobs, *Kenton Cast Iron Toys: The Real Thing in Everything But Size,* Schiffer Publishing, 1996; Sharon Korbeck (ed), *Toys & Prices, 5th Edition,* Krause Publications, 1997; David Longest, *Antique & Collectible Toys, 1870–1950: Identification & Values,* Collector Books, 1994; Richard O'Brien, *Collecting Toys: A Collectors Identification and Value Guide, 8th Edition,* Krause Publications, 1997; Richard O'Brien, *Collecting Toy Trains: Identification and Value Guide, No. 4,* Books Americana, Krause Publications, 1997; Sharon and Bob Huxford (eds), *Schroeder's Collectible Toys: Antique to Modern Price Guide,* Collector Books, 1998; Linda Garland Page and Hilton Smith (eds), *The Foxfire Book of Appalachian Toys & Games,* University of North Carolina Press, 1993; Glenda Thomas, *Toy and Miniature Sewing Machines* (1995, 1997 value update), *Book II* (1997), Collector Books.

Dolls: Kim Avery, *The World of Raggedy Ann Collectibles: Identification & Values,* Collector Books, 1997; Linda Edward, *Cloth Dolls: From Ancient to Modern,* Schiffer Publishing, 1997; Jan Foulke, *12th Blue Book Dolls and Values,* Hobby House Press, 1995; Susan Ann Garrison, *The Raggedy Ann and Andy Family Album,* Schiffer Publishing, 1989; Patricia Hall, *Johnny Gruelle: Creator of Raggedy Ann and Andy,* Pelican Publishing, 1993; Dawn Herlocher, *200 Years of Dolls: Identification and Price Guide,* Antique Trader Books, 1996; Dee Hockenberry, *Enchanting Friends: Collectible Poohs, Raggedies, Golliwoggs & Roosevelt Bears,* Schiffer Publishing, 1995; Jan Lindenberger, *Raggedy Ann and Andy Collectibles,* Schiffer Publishing, 1995; Patsy Moyer, *Doll Values: Antique to Modern,* Collector Books, 1997; Joyce Rinehart, *Wonderful Raggedy Anns,* Schiffer Publishing, 1997.

Games: Lee Dennis, *Warman's Antique American Games, 1840–1940, Current Market Values,* Wallace Homestead, 1991; Harry L. Rinker, *Antique Trader's Guide to Games & Puzzles,* Antique Trader Books, 1997; Bruce Whitehill, *Games: American Games* *and Their Makers, 1822–1992, with Values,* Wallace–Homestead, Krause Publications, 1992.

Teddy Bears: Kim Brewer and Carol–Lynn Roussel Waugh, *The Official Price Guide to Antique & Modern Teddy Bears,* House of Collectibles, 1990; Pauline Cockrill, *Teddy Bear Encyclopedia,* Dorling Kindersley, 1993; Pam Hebbs, *Collecting Teddy Bears,* Pincushion Press, 1992; Dee Hockenberry, *Bear Memorabilia: Reference & Price Guide,* Hobby House Press, 1992; Dee Hockenberry, *The Big Bear Book,* Schiffer Publishing, 1996; Margaret Fox Mandel, *Teddy Bears and Steiff Animals* (1984, 1997 value update), *2nd Series* (1987, 1996 value update), Collector Books; Linda Mullins, *American Teddy Bear Encyclopedia,* Hobby House Press, 1995; Linda Mullins, *4th Teddy Bear & Friends Price Guide,* Hobby House Press, 1993; Gustav Severin, *Teddy Bear: A Loving History of the Classic Childhood Companion,* Running Press, 1995.

Periodicals: *Antique Doll World,* 225 Main Street, Suite 300, Northport, NY 11768; *Antique Toy World,* PO Box 60641, Chicago, IL 60641; *Doll Castle News,* PO Box 247, Washington, NJ 07882; *Dolls: The Collector's Magazine,* 170 Fifth Avenue, 12th Floor, New York, NY 10010; *National Doll & Teddy Bear Collector,* PO Box 1032, Portland, OR 97208; *Teddy Bear & Friends,* 741 Miller Drive SE, Suite D2, Harrisburg, PA 20175; *Teddy Bear Review,* 170 Fifth Avenue, 12th Floor, New York, NY 10010; *Toy Farmer,* 7496 106th Avenue SE, LaMoure, ND 58458; *Toy Shop,* 700 East State Street, Iola, WI 54990; *Toy Tractor Times,* RR 3, Box 112–A, Osage, IA 50461; *Toy Trader,* PO Box 1050, Dubuque, IA 52003; *Tractor Classics CTM,* PO Box 489, Rocanville, Saskatchewan, S0A 3L0 Canada.

Newsletters: *Farm Toy Shopper,* PO Box 398, Ash Grove, MO 65604; *Rags,* PO Box 823, Atlanta, GA 30301; *Spec Tacular News,* PO Box 368, Dyersville, IA 52040.

Collectors' Clubs: American Game Collectors Assoc, PO Box 44, Dresher, PA 19025; Antique Engine, Tractor & Toy Collectors Club, Inc, 5731 Paradise Road, Slatington, PA 18080; Farm Toy Collectors Club, PO Box 38, Roxholm, IA 50040; Teddy Bear Boosters Club, 19750 SW Peavine Mountain Road, McMinville, OR 97128; Train Collectors Assoc, PO Box 248, Strasburg, PA 17579; United Federation of Doll Clubs, 10920 North Ambassador, Kansas City, MO 64153.

Museums: Checkers Hall of Fame, Petal, MS; Enchanted World Doll Museum, Mitchell, SD; Essex Institute, Salem, MA; Mary Merritt Doll Museum, Douglasville, PA; Museum of the City of New York, NY; National Farm Toy Museum, Dyersville IA; Smithsonian Institution, Washington, DC; Margaret Woodbury Strong Museum, Rochester, NY; Teddy Bear Museum of Naples, Naples, FL; University of Waterloo Museum & Archive of Games, Waterloo, Ontario, Canada; Victorian Doll Museum, North Chili, NY; Washington Dolls' House & Toy Museum, Washington, DC; Yesteryears Museum, Sandwich, MA.

Bank, cast iron, "Always did 'Spise a Mule," mechanical, polychrome paint, missing mule's tail, back legs brazed, trap replaced, $10^{1}/_{8}$" l **$200**
Bank, cast iron, bank building with cupola, still bank, painted red and green, $3^{1}/_{2}$" h **100**
Bank, cast iron, Darktown Battery, mechanical, polychrome paint, $9^{3}/_{4}$" l **1,700**
Bank, pottery, dog head, white clay, dark green glaze, $2^{1}/_{2}$" h **110**
Bank, pottery, sitting pig, painted black and white, 6" l **125**
Bank, pottery, standing pig, brown and blue marbleized glaze, $6^{1}/_{2}$" l **75**
Bank, yellow ware, house shaped, molded detail trimmed in black, "For My Dear Girl" on roof, firing crack at 1 chimney, $3^{5}/_{8}$" h **650**

Barn, R Bliss, wood, chromolitho paper covering and paint, 15" h **300**

Bird Whistle, porcelain, brown glaze, 2⅝" l **45**

Bird Whistle, white metal, cast, traces of blue paint, 2¼" l **20**

Blocks, wood, alphabet letters, multicolor paper litho coverings, American
Spelling Blocks, 6" sq dovetailed wood box with lid, price for set of 64
with box **95**

Blocks, wood, alphabet letters and other designs, die stamped, emb, and
painted, price for set of 26 . . . . **80**

Blocks, wood, birds, children, animals, and alphabet letters, nesting blocks,
multicolor litho paper covering, 3¼ x 3¼ x 3½", price for set of 6 . . . . **115**

Blocks, wood, figural children, chromolitho paper coverings, 5" h, price for
set of 33 . . . . : **325**

Blocks, wood, letters, animals, and Egyptian hieroglyphics, stacking blocks
form obelisk, chromolitho paper covering, edge damage, 26½" h obelisk,
price for set of 6 . . . . **425**

Buffalo, Schoenhut, carved wood, painted eyes, carved mane, leather ears
and tail, 7⅝" l **375**

Bulldog, Schoenhut, wood, painted eyes, leather ears, collar, and tail, 6¼" l . **135**

Carpet Ball, ironstone, red spatter dec, 3" d **150**

Circus Bear, gold mohair, amber glass eyes, red harness with chain, hollow
body, 10" l **110**

Circus Performers, Schoenhut, painted wood, 7" ringmaster with molded top
hat, 8" lady bareback rider, and 6⅜" lady bareback rider, price for set **250**

Circus Wagon, Kenton, Overland Circus, cast iron, painted, wagon, caged
animal, driver, and 2 horses with riders, orig box, 14" l **275**

Constellation Viewer, Clarke's Astronomical Lantern, D C Heaty & Co,
Boston, tole, painted black and gold, 2 candle sockets, frosted glass, 13
cards punched with constellations, orig wood box, 12" l **400**

Coupe, Arcade, cast iron, painted blue, nickel plating, decal, 5" l **175**

Covered Wagon, Kenton, cast iron, painted, wagon, driver, and 2 horses,
orig cloth top in sealed envelope, orig box, 15¼" l **385**

Cribbage Board, carved bone, reticulated board with hearts and compass
stars, small compartment with 2 red and 2 white pins, 7" l **215**

Croquet Set, wood, worn polychrome paint, 4 mallets, four balls, 2 stakes,
wire wickets, and stand **65**

Croquet Wickets, cast iron, figural jockeys, old polychrome repaint, light
rust, some wear, 17½" h, price for set of 9 . . . .**2,500**

Doll, Amish, white cotton and navy blue wool body, green cotton dress,
early 20th C, 13¼" l **150**

Doll, black, cotton body and stuffing, 4–seam rounded head, no hair, penciled facial features, blue and white dress, white bonnet and apron, sepa-
rately stitched fingers, stub feet, late 1800s, 18" l **350**

Doll, leather, M S Davis Co, painted hair and features, laced up body, 1903
Gussie Decker patent, 12" h **125**

Doll, Missionary Rag, Beecher, needle sculpted stockinet body, jointed
knees, hips, and shoulders, sparse wool yarn hair, needle sculpted and
painted facial features, blue eyes, closed mouth, white baby dress and
bonnet, stitched fingers and toes, c1900, 23" h **2,500**

Doll, Moravian Rag, cotton body, jointed hips, knees, and shoulders, no hair,
hand drawn and painted facial features, lace ruffle sewn around face, blue

Left: Bank, pig, painted pottery, cracked, $99. Photo courtesy Aston Macek.

Right: Bank, St Bernard, glazed and slip dec red earthenware, 19th C, $3,738. Photo courtesy Sotheby's.

and white gingham dress and bonnet, white apron, stitched fingers and separate thumbs, stub feet, early 1900s   900

Doll, Presbyterian Rag, unbleached cotton body, cotton stuffing, jointed shoulders and hips, oil painted facial features on flat face, ankle length dress and matching prairie bonnet, white underclothes, long black stockings and black leather shoes on stub feet, stitched fingers, separate thumbs, late 1800s, 17" l 1,000

Doll, rag, Art Fabric Mills, NY, girl, printed cotton, wearing white dress, patented 1900, 25" h   150

Doll, Raggedy Ann, Gruelle, unbleached cotton, cotton stuffing, brown wool yarn hair, hp facial features, shoe button eyes, blue dress, white apron, wood heart hidden in chest, 1915, 15" h   500

Doll, wax and cloth, girl, wax covered head and bodice, cloth body, glass eyes, brown hair, kid forearms and hands, long blue and white print dress, repairs and repaint to wax, 15¼" h   225

Doll, wood, Schoenhut, boy, walking, painted, mohair wig, character face with sober expression, jointed shoulders and hips, non–mechanical, free swinging joint at hips, 1911–20, 16½" h   275

Doll Carriage, folding steel frame, painted black, brown leatherized fabric covering, replaced spoke wheels, 22" h   50

Doll Furniture, cabinet, pine and oak, painted dark red, molded cornice, full length glazed door, int shelving, molded base, porcelain knob, 19" h   500

Doll Furniture, candlestand, curly maple, oblong top, turned column, tripod base with spider legs, natural varnish finish, handmade reproduction, 8 x 14" top, 14¼" h   165

Doll Furniture, cradle, cherry dovetailed case, shaped canted sides, arched ends with handle cutouts, pine rockers, 27¾" l   250

Doll Furniture, cupboard, step back, pine, square nail construction, molded cornice, pair glazed doors with int shelving, pair paneled cupboard doors, molded base, old dark finish, porcelain knobs, 19" h   400

Doll Furniture, desk, school master's, pine, old brown graining over yellow repaint, orig red stain int, shaped crest, slanted lift lid writing surface, 3 int drawers, turned legs, dec brass trim, restored, 14½" w, 9" d, 12¼" h . .   415

Doll Furniture, pewter cupboard, hardwood, wire nail construction, flat top, 2 open shelves, pair cupboard doors, bracket legs, old pale green repaint, 1 door hinge broken, 11½" w, 12⅝" h   25

Doll Furniture, rocker, wicker, woven wicker back, bamboo bowed crest, arms, legs, and stretchers, 15" h **150**

Doll Furniture, rocker, wood, ball finials on canted posts, 3–spindle back, straight spindle arms, stretcher base, painted red with gold finials, 12¼" h .. **200**

Doll Furniture, rope bed, birch, cannonball finials, shaped headboard, turned posts, mattress made from old ticking, glued break in headboard, old natural finish, 19½" l **250**

Doll House, wood, homemade, 2 rooms, with 3 corn cob dolls, furniture, curtains, rugs, bedding, and accessories, 19th C, 26½" l, 12½" d, 10⅞" h .. **250**

Doll House, wood, Whippany, NJ, 3 story, 9 rooms, pierced glazed windows, hinged front door, stairs, lattice work dec, orig wallpaper, carpets, and lace curtains, includes furniture and accessories, electric lights and doorbell, 1901, 45 x 48", 16" h **8,250**

Dominoes, ebony and bone dominoes, 12¾" l wood box with replaced sliding lid, price for set of 50 .... **200**

Dominoes, ebony and ivory dominoes, 8¼" l wood box with sliding lid, price for set of 28 .... **70**

Drum, tin sides with polychrome litho eagle and shield on blue ground, wood bands, cord and leather binding, cord, leather, and heads replaced, with 2 drumsticks, 8" d **300**

Dust Pan, toleware, green ground, gold stenciled floral design **35**

Elephant, Schoenhut, painted wood, glass eyes, worn tusks **125**

Felix the Cat, Schoenhut, painted wood, c1920, 3¾" h **150**

Finger Toy, pecking hens, wood, 2 carved hens with wire legs mounted on either side of bowl on sliding wood platform base, 9¾" l **175**

Fire House, wood, polychrome painted brick ext, 2 hinged doors, 13½" w, 18" d, 17½" h **160**

Fire Truck, Arcade, cast iron, painted red with blue and silver trim, Arcade balloon wheels, decal label, nickel plated ladders and grill, 9¾" l **200**

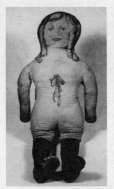  

Left: Doll, painted and stuffed cloth, long curls, c1900, $85.

Center: Pull Toy, horse, dappled, horsehair tail, orig wooden base and wheels, $578. Photo courtesy Aston Macek.

Right: Teddy Bear, golden mohair, jointed, button eyes, American, early 20th C, 27" h, $325. Photo courtesy Aston Macek.

Fire Wagon, cast iron, 3 horses, 2 drivers, 2 ladders, painted, rear steering wheel missing, drivers replaced, 31½" l **800**

Game Board, checkers, inlaid wood, maple, cherry, walnut, and rosewood, scratch carved numbers on squares, multiple border frame, 17¼" sq **325**

Game Board, checkers, pine, worn green, orange, and white repaint, recessed tray edge for checkers, 21" sq **175**

Game Board, checkers, poplar, painted black and cream squares, green border, 14¼ x 17 ¾" **300**

Game Board, Checkers/Backgammon, walnut with cherry and maple inlay checkerboard, reverse with red, yellow, black, and green painted backgammon board, 16½" sq **450**

Game Board, Checkers/Parcheesi, painted wood, 1 wide with red, black, and green painted checkerboard, other with multicolor Parcheesi design, 16" sq **575**

Game Board, Parcheesi, plywood board, pine frame, polychrome painted playing surface, 31" sq **415**

Goat, Schoenhut, wood, painted eyes, black and white coat, leather horns and tail, leatherette ears, 8¼" l **175**

Hansom Cab, Kenton, cast iron, painted, cab, driver, and horse, orig box, 16" l **550**

Horse, Schoenhut, wood, painted eyes, dapple gray with platform saddle, leather harness, leatherette ears, yarn tail, 9½" l **125**

Jack–in–the–Box, pine, paper covering, wood clown with cloth costume trimmed with lace and printed round cardboard head, full figure pops to upright position when activated, 6½" l box **475**

Jumping Jack, composition head, articulated wood body, natural patina with painted blue and white stripes, 15" h **35**

Kaleidoscope, C C Bush, Providence, RI, turned walnut, 1870s, 13¾" h **925**

Marble, sulphide, pig, 1⅞" d **125**

Noah's Ark, 11 carved wood animals and 1 person with worn polychrome paint, 6¼" l ark painted red and pink with black windows, price for set . . . **465**

Noah's Ark, 14 carved wood animals with natural patina and traces of red and white paint, 21¼" l wood ark with cut paper detail and dark brown finish, Germany, price for set **525**

Noah's Ark, 37 carved wood and polychrome painted animals and 2 women, wood ark with worn straw inlay, 8" l ark, price for set **325**

Nodder, kitten, carved pine, painted black, seated articulated figure bobs head and tail when weighted string is pulled, late 19th C, 6" l, 3½" h **350**

Ox–Drawn Wagon, with driver, cast iron, painted red, yellow, brown, black, and maroon, 16" l **575**

Pecking Bird, carved and painted pine, stylized bird with hinged neck, long beak, large upcurved wings, and tail back, painted dark red with black and white spots, mounted on rect wood base with rounded corners, chip and loss to beak, PA, late 19th/early 20th C, 10¼" l, 4½" h **500**

Piano, Schoenhut, grained wood with litho paper on front panel, early 20th C, 17¼" w, 8" d, 11½" h **30**

Pipsqueak, animated, cat, wood and composition, worn white flannel coat, painted brown and gray, white button eyes with painted pupils, opens mouth and squeaks when head is pushed, not working, 7¼" h **110**

Pipsqueak, animated, dog, wood and composition, white flannel coat, glass eyes, worn whiskers, 1 leg broken, voice box silent, 7" h **150**

Pull Toy, cow, composition, brown and white, wood base, 12" l **300**

Pull Toy, dog, platinum and gold mohair, glass eyes, embroidered nose, fabric collar, straw stuffing, steel frame and spoke wheels, 12" l **60**

Pull Toy, donkey, Steiff, worn platinum mohair coat, button eyes, black mane and tail, worn red felt blanket, ear button, steel frame, wooden wheels attached to feet, 1 wheel replaced, 13½" l **300**

Pull Toy, elephant, Steiff, worn platinum mohair coat, bead eyes, ring pull voice box, steel frame, wood platform and wheels, unmkd, voice box silent, 16" l **275**

Pull Toy, geese, 3 papier–mâché geese on wood platform base with cast iron spoke wheels, orig polychrome paint, 10¼" l **850**

Pull Toy, horse, papier–mâché, painted dapple gray, fiber tail, tin spoke wheels, wood base painted red and black, ears missing, 9½" l, 10" h **300**

Pull Toy, horse, papier–mâché, painted dapple gray, red wood base, small cast metal spoke wheels, mkd "Germany," missing mane and tail, 8" l **165**

Pull Toy, horse, wood, black fabric covering, hair mane and tail, leather harness and saddle, wood base with red edge stripe and cast iron spoke wheels, loose legs, mane, tail, harness, and saddle restored, 24" h **450**

Pull Toy, horse, wood, smoked dapple gray paint, worn red paper blanket, leatherized cloth harness, wood base with red wood wheels, 5¾" l **75**

Pull Toy, horse, wood, worn black mohair covering, orange harness, wood base with red trim and steel spoke wheels, mkd "Made in Germany," 9½" l, 11" h **200**

Pull Toy, lamb, Steiff, curly white wool coat, 2 ear buttons, bead eyes, green and red ribbons with bells, wood wheels attached to feet, 11" l, 11¾" h . . . **385**

Pull Toy, lamb, Steiff, curly wool coat, ear button, felt face, ears, and legs, glass eyes, excelsior stuffing, metal frame and wheels, c1913, 12½" l, 11⅛" h **1,600**

Punch Bowl Set, doll size, clear pressed glass, Near Cut pattern, ftd bowl and 8 cups, minor chips, 4¼" h bowl **75**

Puzzle, White Sewing Machines adv, paper cov wood, 2 sided, int Victorian home 1 side, US map other side, 11 x 16" **125**

Santa in Sleigh, pulled by 2 reindeer, cast iron, painted red and white with gold trim, 16¼" l **450**

Left: Milk Wagon, cast iron, emb lettering, scratches, soiling, paint chips, wagon wheels repainted, driver missing, 13" l, $190. Photo courtesy Collectors Auction Services.

Right: Trolley, Marklin, 859 Third Avenue RR Co, 4 volt, $14,500. Photo courtesy James D. Julia.

Sewing Machine, Betsy Ross, model #707, electric, hammertone green finish, red simulated leather carrying case, chain stitch, 8¾" h   100

Sewing Machine, Casige, Germany, sheet metal body, table clamp, black, gold scroll design on base, sunflowers dec, chain stitch, 7" h   100

Sewing Machine, Delta Specialty Co, American Girl, metal, wood base, hand operated, chain stitch, 6¼" h   125

Sewing Machine, Ernst Plank, Germany, Victoria, black metal, gold stenciling, hand operated, pre–1940, 6½" h   135

Sewing Machine, Gateway Engineering Co, Jr model NP–1, red metal, hand operated, 1940s–50s, 7" h   45

Sewing Machine, KAYanEE, US Zone, Germany, Sew Master, metal, floral design, hand operated, 7" h   90

Sewing Machine, Lindstrom, litho metal, light blue with flowers, mkd "Made in USA," 7¼" h   55

Sewing Machine, Muller, model #15, cast iron, black, replaced driving handle, 7" h   300

Sewing Machine, Singer, Great Britain, beige metal, gear driven hand wheel with wood handle, seam gauge, stitch length, tension regulator, chain stitch, 6½" h   60

Stagecoach, R Bliss, Pawtucket, RI, coach mkd "Pansy," 4 horses and 2 drivers, wood with chromolitho paper covering, some glued repairs, 29" l . . .   75

Steam Engine, Avery, cast iron, painted black with red and gold trim, 4½" l . .   200

Stereo Viewer, Universal View Co, Philadelphia, PA, Triumph, with 35 stereo cards   75

Stuffed Animal, dachshund, Steiff, black and brown wool, jointed, black shoe button eyes, embroidered nose, mouth, and claws, c1930, 18" l   350

Stuffed Animal, fox, Steiff, mohair, fully jointed, glass eyes, embroidered nose, mouth, and claws, excelsior stuffing, ear button missing, c1913, 10¼" l, 5½" h   425

Stuffed Animal, rabbit, Steiff, sitting up, blonde mohair, fully jointed, pink glass eyes, excelsior stuffing, c1913, 12" h   800

Stuffed Animal, rabbit, velveteen, ear button, cream with rust markings, black bead eyes, 1908, 5" h   350

Stuffed Animal, squirrel, Steiff, blonde mohair, fully jointed, black steel eyes with felt backing, embroidered nose, mouth, and claws, excelsior stuffing, 1920, 7½" h   400

Teddy Bear, gold mohair, fully jointed, bead eyes, embroidered features, paw pads recovered, 12½" h   275

Teddy Bear, gold mohair, fully jointed, glass eyes, embroidered features, straw stuffing, 19" h   250

Teddy Bear, Ideal, blonde mohair, fully jointed, accentuated hump, shoe button eyes, rust broadcloth and embroidered nose, embroidered claws, excelsior stuffing, early 20th C 1,250

Teddy Bear, reddish mohair, fully jointed, replaced button eyes, embroidered features, felt paw pads, straw stuffing, repairs, straw stuffing exposed in places, limp muzzle, 18" h   50

Teddy Bear, Steiff, blonde mohair, fully jointed, ear button, shoe button eyes, embroidered features and claws, excelsior stuffing, c1906, 11" h   575

Teddy Bear, Steiff, blonde mohair, fully jointed, steel eyes, embroidered snout and claws, felt pads, ear button missing, c1904, 13" h 1,100

Teddy Bear, Steiff, curly mohair, fully jointed, shoe button eyes, excelsior
stuffing, ears, nose, and pads replaced with brown corduroy, c1910, 19" h   .   **850**
Teddy Bear, Steiff, honey mohair, fully jointed, black button eyes, embroidered nose, mouth, and claws, excelsior stuffing, ear button missing,
1906–10, 27" h **10,350**
Teddy Bear, Steiff, light apricot mohair, fully jointed, blank ear button, shoe
button eyes, embroidered nose, mouth, and claws, 1903–04, 15" h **1,500**
Teddy Bear, Steiff, long gold mohair, fully jointed, glass eyes, embroidered
nose, mouth, and claws, felt pads, straw stuffing, ear button missing,
1950s, 19½" h **500**
Train, American Flyer, S gauge, #285 C&NW Pacific steam locomotive, 1952 .   **30**
Train, American Flyer, S gauge, #928 New Haven flatcar with log load, 1954 .   **12**
Train, American Flyer, S gauge, #954 Grand Canyon observation car,
1953–56 . . . .   **60**
Train, American Flyer, S gauge, #24077 Northern Pacific stock car, red,
1959–62 . . . .   **75**
Train, Ives, #17 locomotive, cast iron, clockwork, litho name plates, cast
iron 10–spoke wheels, c1912 . . . .   **100**
Train, Ives, #25 Silver Ives NYC & HR tender, O gauge, 8 wheel **150**
Train, Ives, #121 caboose, red with green cupola, late automatic couplers . . .   **45**
Train, Ives, #125 merchandise car, type IV–D trucks, dark red roof **300**
Train, Ives, #700 passenger set, outline 3235R electric locomotive, 184 club
car, 186 observation car, dark red with brass plates, orig box **500**
Train, Ives, #12578 Union Pacific boxcar, orange sides, red roof, automatic
couplers, type III trucks, 9" l **1,100**
Train, Ives, #12584 Salt Lake boxcar, tuscan sides, white lettering, light gray
roof, type IV–B trucks, 9" l **850**
Train, Lionel, #0016 South Pacific hopper and dump car, 1938–42 . . . .   **60**
Train, Lionel, #60 trolley, yellow, red roof, blue lettering, 1955–58 . . . .   **65**
Train, Lionel, #310 baggage car, 1926 . . . .   **65**
Train, Lionel, #2025 locomotive and tender, #2454, #2257, #2452x, and
#2465 cars, O gauge, with controls and box of track, damaged caboose . . .   **115**
Train, Marx, #54 diesel locomotive, litho tin, red, yellow, and black with yel-
low and white lettering **30**
Train, Marx, #652 Shell tank car, litho tin, 8 wheels, orange with red letter-
ing, 3/16 scale **8**
Train, Marx, #817 Colorado & Southern box car, tin, 4 wheels, yellow with
black lettering **12**
Train, Strombecker, wood, engine and 5 cars, 1930s **75**
Train, unknown maker, cast iron, CB&QRR, engine, tender, and open freight
car, painted black and red, 10" l engine **350**
Ventriloquist Dummy, handmade, papier–mâché head, wood and cloth
body, 39" h **75**
Village, carved and painted pine, comprised of houses grouped around
green, cast iron trees, wire vegetation, late 19th C **450**

LIGHTING

Country life cannot stop because the day is cloudy or the electric power fails. Daily chores need to be done daily. Rural America required cheap, dependable lighting.

The key concerns were utility and durability. Form did follow function—simple design, easy to service; less joints and edges, least likely to snag; and plain surface, less maintenance. Lighting devices, especially those used in barns and fields, were expected to withstand rough treatment and last for years. The ability to interchange parts was essential. Repairs often had to be made on the spot.

Until the arrival of electricity, the kerosene lamp was king. Lamps burn fuel and generate heat. Heat attacks surfaces. This is why tin, which was painted and repainted to preserve it, and glass were favored. Fuel oil lamps also generate soot. To work effectively, they have to be cleaned regularly, a chore generally assigned to the children.

Decorative lighting was confined to the household with the best examples located in the dining room and parlor. Among the forms with the widest variety of pattern and color are miniature lamps and fluid lamps. They are important decorative accents in any Country setting.

The arrival of electricity changed life in rural America. Most initial electrical lighting and many appliances were purchased via mail order or at the general store. The arrival of a specialized electrical store in a rural community often was ten to fifteen years behind the arrival of electricity.

Because members of the agrarian community are "savers" by nature, rural basements, attics, sheds, and barns are major sources for early electrical lighting. There is a strong tendency to put an old lamp or appliance in storage just in case the new one breaks.

The current Country craze focuses heavily on the kerosene lamp era. However, change is in the wind. There is a growing interest in the rural farmstead of the 1920s through the 1950s. When this period becomes fashionable, electric lighting will play a major role in any decorating scheme.

References: Nadja Maril, *American Lighting: 1840–1940,* Schiffer Publishing, 1995; Jo Ann Thomas, *Early Twentieth Century Lighting Fixtures,* Collector Books, 1980.

Collectors' Club: The Rushlight Club Inc, 8312 Vera Drive, Brecksville, OH 44141.

Museum: Winchester Center Kerosene Lamp Museum & Lighting Emporium, Winchester Center, CT.

CANDLE HOLDERS

The candle, whether homemade or commercially produced, was one of the major lighting sources in rural America prior to electrification. A host of devices from candlesticks to fairy lamps were created to utilize this important lighting source.

The domestic candlestick arrived on the scene in the fourteenth century. Picket, named for the sharp point used to hold the candle, and socket were in use by the mid–seventeenth century.

Beginning in the eighteenth century, candlestick design began to mirror furniture design as decorative accessories became part of a unified room setting. In the late seventeenth century, baluster stem candlesticks replaced Doric or clustered stem candlesticks in popularity. Elaborate rococo motif candlesticks arrived in the mid–eighteenth century followed by neoclassical styles as the century ended.

Some candlestick styles, e.g., the brass baluster stem stick, became so popular that they never lost favor. This is why manufacturing methodology is critical to dating. Twentieth–century examples are often dated much earlier by inexperienced sellers and buyers.

Candlestick are made in a wide variety of materials ranging from metal to wood. Early rural examples were frequently handmade, the local blacksmith and tinsmith being the source of many. The commercial production of candlesticks was prevalent by the end of the eighteenth century. Most imported examples were mass produced.

The fairy lamp, a candle–burning night light used in nurseries, hallways, and dim corners of the home, was developed in England in the 1840s. Two leading candle manufacturers, the Price Candle Company and the Samuel Clarke Company, promoted fairy lamps as a means to sell candles. Both contracted with other manufacturers of glass, metal, and porcelain to produce the needed shades and cups. For example, Clarke purchased products from England's Worcester Royal Porcelain Company, Stuart & Sons, and Red House Glass Works as well as firms in France and Germany. Clarke's trademark was a small fairy with a wand surrounded by the words "Clarke Fairy Pyramid, Trade Mark."

Fairy lamps were produced in two pieces (cup and shade) and three pieces (cup with matching shade and saucer). Fittings were made in a wide variety of styles. Shades ranged from pressed to cut glass, from Burmese to Nailsea. Cups are found in brass, glass, nickel, porcelain, and silver plate.

American firms selling fairy lamps included Diamond Candle Company of Brooklyn, Blue Cross Safety Candle Company, and Hobbs, Brockunier & Company of Wheeling, West Virginia.

References: Margaret and Douglas Archer, *The Collector's Encyclopedia of Glass Candlesticks,* Collector Books, 1983, out of print; Ronald F. Michaelis, *Old Domestic Base–Metal Candlesticks,* Antique Collectors' Club, 1978; Kenneth Wilson, *American Glass 1760–1930: The Toledo Museum of Art, 2 vols,* Hudson Hills Press and The Toledo Museum of Art, 1994.

Candlestand, wrought iron, adjustable height, 2 sockets on tapered rod with
  baluster ornament, arched tripod base with penny feet, light rust, 22¼" h .**\$3,500**
Candlestand, wrought iron and brass, 2 light, ball finial above flaring shaft,
  adjustable T–shaped arm with scroll terminals surmounted by circular
  brass drip pans and candle sockets, arched tripod base ending in penny
  feet, repairs to drip pans, 20th C, 18" d, 56" h **2,875**
Candlestick, brass, baluster stem above octagonal stepped base, 9" h   275
Candlestick, brass, baluster stem above square base with invected corners,
  5⅛" h   275
Candlestick, brass, baluster stem above square base with short feet, 6¼" h . . .   225
Candlestick, brass, neoclassical, flared socket, straight stem with side
  push–up, stepped circular base, 8½" h, price for pair   385
Candlestick, brass, octagonal with floral engraving, domed and stepped
  base, 1 stem soldered to base, 9⅛" h, price for pair   550
Candlestick, brass, Queen Anne, turned socket and stem, petal base, maker's
  stamp on 1 corner of underside "Joseph Wood," 7⅜" h, price for pair **3,750**
Candlestick, brass, Queen Anne, wide flaring lip, baluster stem, square base
  with invected corners, 6¾" h, price for pair   600
Candlestick, brass, removable bobèche above elaborately shaped stem and
  scalloped base, c1770, 9⅝" h, price for pair **3,165**

Left: Fairy Lamp, end-of-day shade in red, pink, green, yellow, and white, clear patterned base, unsgd, 3³/₄" h, $250. Photo courtesy James D. Julia.

Right: Candle Holder, graniteware, base mkd "OGGA," handle and rim chips, 2¹/₂" h, 6¹/₂" d, $25. Photo courtesy Aston Macek.

Candlestick, brass, turned candle socket mounted to domed base, 4³/₈" h **300**

Candlestick, brass, turned socket and narrow stem, drum base, 5" h, price for pair **2,250**

Candlestick, brass, Victorian, push–up, beehive and diamond quilted detail, 10" h, price for set of 4 . . . .   **300**

Candlestick, glass, Sandwich, canary, hexagonal socket, square base with extended round corners, c1830–45, 5" h **350**

Candlestick, glass, Sandwich, canary, Petal and Loop, c1840–60, 7" h **650**

Candlestick, glass, Sandwich, clambroth, hexagonal socket, loop base, tiny fleck under base rim, c1840–60, 7" h **175**

Candlestick, glass, Sandwich, clambroth and blue, petal socket, columnar, c1850–65, 9" h **700**

Candlestick, glass, Sandwich, clear, dolphin stem, small fleck on 1 sharp point of base, c1855–70, 7" h **150**

Candlestick, glass, Sandwich, clear, hexagonal socket, square base with extended rounded corners, c1830–45, 6" h **200**

Candlestick, glass, Sandwich, lime green, petal socket, columnar, wafer separating socket and column, shedding, 9" h, price for pair **900**

Candlestick, glass, Sandwich, opaque blue and white, blue socket, white stick, acanthus leaf dec, crack in socket, c1840–65, 7¹/₂" h **225**

Candlestick, glass, unknown maker, clear flint, flared deep socket with wafers, hollow blown stem, pressed base with reeded circular steps, 10¹/₂" h, price for pair **465**

Candlestick, iron, Hogscraper, push–up, lip hanger, brass trim on base, 7³/₈" h, price for pair **185**

Candlestick, iron, Hogscraper, push–up mkd "Shaw," lip hanger, pitted, 7¹/₄" h **125**

Candlestick, iron, thin spiral stem, adjustable height, turned wood base, 7³/₄" h **85**

Candlestick, iron, wide spiral stem, adjustable height, turned wood base, 7¹/₈" h **175**

Candlestick, pewter, Endicott & Sumner, New York, NY, 1846–51, 8³/₈" h **350**

Candlestick, pewter, Flagg & Homan, 7⅝" h, price for pair   425
Candlestick, pewter, Gleason, Roswell, Dorchester, MA, c1840, 6½" h   250
Candlestick, pewter, Henry Hopper, NY, straight line touchmark, 10" h   275
Candlestick, pewter, Ostrander & Norris, New York City, saucer base, resol-
    dered, 1848–50, 4" h   150
Candlestick, pewter, Rufus Dunham, Westbrook, ME, straight line touch-
    mark, c1840, 6" h, price for pair   950
Candlestick, pewter, Sellew & Co, Cincinnati, OH, removable bobèche,
    baluster stem, stepped circular base, mkd, 8" h   250
Candlestick, pewter, Smith & Co, Boston, MA, curved line touchmark, mid–
    19th C, 6⅛" h   175
Candlestick, pewter, Thomas Wildes, Philadelphia, PA and New York City,
    NY, straight line touchmark, complete with bobèche, 1829–40, 10" h   200
Candlestick, silver, James Deakin & Sons, England, hexagonal, removable
    bobèche, weighted base, Sheffield hallmarks, 1920, 7" h, price for pair . . .   110
Candlestick, tin, Hogscraper, brass trim, flared socket with lip hanger,
    push–up stem, slightly domed circular base, 8½" h, price for pair   500
Candlestick, tin, Hogscraper, plume–like push–up knob, 6½" h   80
Chamberstick, brass, circular bobèche and push–up on rect foot, molded
    rect drip pan fitted with scrolling handle with shaped terminal and coni-
    cal snuffer, 5¼" h   250
Chamberstick, brass, threaded stem, loose drip pan, long handle, 9½" l, 4" h .   60
Chamberstick, pewter, Meriden Britannia Co, gadrooned rim on saucer
    base, 1850, 4¼" h   225
Chamberstick, pewter, turned stem, circular dish base, strap handle, mkd "S.
    Rusts Patent New York," 19th C, 8⅝" h, price for pair   500
Chamberstick, silver, Coin, Jacobi and Jenkins, repoussé, mkd "A. Jacobi," 5
    troy oz, 5½" d base   385
Chamberstick, silver, English, J Cafe, London, George II, knopped stem,
    square shell and scroll base, engraved crest, 1751–52, 66 troy oz, 8¼" h,
    price for set of 4 4,350
Chamberstick, silver, English, W Hutton & Son, London, Victorian, stop flut-
    ed, weighted stepped base, slight dents, 1899–1900, 5½" h, price for pair .   625
Chamberstick, silver, sterling, Shreve Crump and Low, Queen Anne style, 22
    troy oz, 7" h, price for pair   575

*Left: Candlesticks, pr,
attributed to Boston and
Sandwich Glass Co, electric
blue, pressed petal socket
attached by wafer to
hexagonal base, 1 stick
glued beneath wafer, 7½" h,
$1,200.*

*Right: Candlestick,
Bennington, Rockingham
glaze, minor base chips,
8" h, $70.* Photo courtesy
Collector's Sales & Service.

Fairy Lamp, Burmese shade, clear pressed base, mkd "S. Clarke's, Patent, Trademark, Fairy," 4½" h   325
Fairy Lamp, Burmese shade, ruffled base, ⅜" notch in base bottom   100
Fairy Lamp, Cottage, pottery, orange roof, pierced windows and doors, green saucer base, England, 4¾" h   120
Fairy Lamp, Diamond Quilted, blue mother–of–pearl shade and base, clear insert sgd "S. Clarke Pat'd trademark Fairy," minor shade edge roughness, shade darker than base, 5½" h   225
Fairy Lamp, kitten head, bisque, figural, gray, blue collar, green eyes   500
Fairy Lamp, Nailsea type, opaque white loopings on citron shade, clear base mkd "Clarke Cricklite," 4¾" h   175
Fairy Lamp, owl, bisque, figural, brown and gold, mkd "Noritake Hand Painted Made in Japan," 7¼" h 1,350
Fairy Lamp, Peach Blow shade, ivy dec, clear glass candle cup, base sgd "Clarke," tiny chip on base, 5" h   400
Fairy Lamp, ribbed dome, vaseline, pressed green base mkd "Clarke," 3½" h . .   175
Fairy Lamp, spatter, gold, white, and pink, swirl shade with white int, clear peg type base mkd "Clarke," brass candlestick, 14" h   425
Fairy Lamp, swirled, white on amber shade, clear base, mkd "Clarke," 3⅝" h .   100
Fairy Lamp, 3 panel, colored lithophane shade, cloisonné bamboo motif base, sgd "LONGWI," 8" h   550
Loom Light, wrought iron, sawtooth trammel, oval shelf with 2 candle sockets with push–ups and splint holder, 27" h   200
Loom Light, wrought iron, spring trammel with scrolled detail, splint holder and single candle socket, 24" h   775
Rush Light, wrought iron, candle socket counter balance, twisted detail, ring base, 12¼" h   350
Sconce, tin, crimped circular crest, rect back panel, circular shelf, 11¼" h . . .   250
Sconce, tin, oval fluted sunburst reflectors, S–curve arms, crimped drip pans, 13" h 1,000
Sconce, tin, simple star flower tooling, 10¾" h   135
Sconce, tin, tombstone shaped, punched dec around edge, 11¼" h   80
Sticking Tommy, wrought iron, single socket, looped handle, 12½" l   275
Taper Jack, silver plated, urn finial, snuffer cap on chain, mkd "Exeter," red taper, worn silver, 5½" h   275
Taper Sticks, miniature, fiery opalescent glass, spiral ribs, circular ribbed base, late 19th/early 20th C, 3¼" h, price for pair   50

LAMPS

An agrarian life means rising at first light and going to bed when the sun sets. While this is the ideal, many a farmer and small town merchant rose before the sun came up and went to bed long after it set. Lamps and lighting were cherished and well–cared–for possessions.

It was not until the late 1930s and in some areas the early 1950s that rural electrification was accomplished. As a result, the kerosene oil lamp survived in the countryside long after it was banished from urban America.

The kerosene oil lamp is an important decorative element in any Country decor. Variety was achieved through a wealth of glass patterns and colors as well as ornately decorated shades. The best, i.e., most decorative, lamps graced the parlor and dining room. Large lamps used in the kitchen and upstairs tended to be plain and highly utilitarian. On the other hand, miniature lamps were highly decorative, often adding a splash of color to a room.

Lighting devices have evolved from simple stone age oil lamps to the popular electrified models of today. Aimé Argand patented the first oil lamp in 1784. Around 1850 kerosene became a popular lamp burning fluid, replacing whale oil and other fluids.

Miniature oil and kerosene lamps, often called "night lamps," are diminutive replicas of larger lamps. Simple and utilitarian in design, miniature lamps found a place in the parlor (as "courting" lamps), hallway, children's rooms, and sickrooms.

Miniature lamps are found in many glass types from amberina to satin glass and measure 2½ to 12 inches in height. The principal parts are the base, collar, burner, chimney, and shade. In 1877 both L. J. Atwood and L. H. Olmsted patented burners for miniature lamps. Their burners made the lamps a popular household accessory.

References: J. W. Courter, *Aladdin Collectors Manual & Price Guide #17: Kerosene Mantle Lamps,* published by author, 1997; J. W. Courter, *Aladdin Electric Lamps Collectors Manual #3,* published by author, 1997; J. W. Courter, *Aladdin: The Magic Name in Lamps, Revised Edition,* published by author, 1997; Robert De Falco, Carole Goldman Hibel, John Hibel, Larry Freeman, *New Light on Old Lamps,* American Life Foundation, 1984; Marjorie Hulsebus, *Miniature Victorian Lamps,* Schiffer Publishing, 1996; L–W Book Sales (ed), *Better Electric Lamps of the 20's & 30's: Moe Bridges, Pittsburgh and Others,* L–W Book Sales, 1997; Ann Gilbert McDonald, *Evolution of the Night Lamp,* Wallace–Homestead, 1979, out of print; Richard C. Miller and John F. Solverson, *Student Lamps of the Victorian Era,* Antique Publications, 1992; Bob and Pat Ruf, *Fairy Lamps,* Schiffer Publishing, 1996; Frank R. and Ruth E. Smith, *Miniature Lamps,* Schiffer Publishing, 1981; Ruth E. Smith, *Miniature Lamps–II,* Schiffer Publishing, 1982; John F. Solverson, *"Those Fascinating Little Lamps"/Miniature Lamps Value Guide* (includes prices for Smith numbers), Antique Publications, 1988; Catherine M. V. Thuro, *Oil Lamps II,* Collector Books, 1983, 1994 value update; Catherine M. V. Thuro, *Oil Lamps: The Kerosene Era in North America,* Wallace–Homestead, Krause Publications, 1976, 1992 value update; Kenneth Wilson, *American Glass 1760–1930: The Toledo Museum of Art,* 2 vols, Hudson Hills Press and the Toledo Museum of Art, 1994.

Newsletter: *Light Revival,* 35 West Elm Avenue, Quincy, MA 02170.

Collectors' Clubs: The Aladdin Knights of the Mystic Light, 3935 Kelley Road, Kevil, KY 42053; Historical Lighting Society of Canada, PO Box 561, Postal Station R, Toronto, Ontario, M4G 4E1 Canada; Night Lights, 38619 Wakefield Court, Northville, MI 48167.

Museums: Sandwich Glass Museum, Sandwich, MA; Winchester Center Kerosene Lamp Museum & Lighting Emporium, Winchester Center, CT.

Reproduction Alert: Reproductions of miniature abound. Study these lamps carefully. Married pieces are common.

Astral, frosted cut to clear glass shade, clear cut prisms, brass font mkd "Cornelius & Baker, Philadelphia," stepped square marble base, electrified, needs rewiring, 19½" h **$600**

Baker's, tin, rect, 2 burners, tin shade, wire hanger, 7" l, 9½" h **200**

Banner Electric Lamp, nickel plated brass, triangular punched design around base, kerosene burner, mkd on flame spreader, c1880, 11½" h **150**

Banquet, Rochester Lamp Co, New Rochester Banquet Lamp, brass and brass plated, acid cut fleur–de–lis design on frosted globe, c1890, 28" h . . . **500**

Betty, copper, hinged lid, 4¹/₄" h plus hanger **135**

Betty, wrought iron, semicircular crest, hinged lid with well–detailed fasten-
er, hook hanger, missing pick, 3³/₄" h plus hanger **225**

Betty, wrought iron and brass, shield shaped brass medallion inscribed "J.D."
with crossed hammers below and mounted with shaped hook, fluid
receptacle below shaped lid, wood stand with circular lamp support and
base and ring turned standard, PA, 19th C, 4" h lamp, 10¹/₄" h stand **2,250**

Boudoir, Handel, dome shade painted on ext with winter landscape scene
of bare trees and snow covered ground, orange and green vegetation in
background, golden amber sky, bronzed metal base naturalistically modeled as gnarled tree trunk with roots spreading across circular foot, 7" d
shade sgd "Handel 5624," artist initialed "M," 16" h **2,500**

Bracket, Buckeye Glass Co, Optic Rib pattern on sapphire blue patent dated
font with threaded ext, Swirled Optic pattern on matching shade, orig
black and gold finish on iron bracket and mount, J F Miller patent, c1880,
15" h **700**

Chandelier, Bradley & Hubbard, cast iron openwork frame, 12 arm, clear
glass fonts and crimped chimneys, brass burners, mkd with 4 patent dates,
c1870, 40" d, 58" h **1,250**

Chandelier, Handel, large dome central globe with fish scale leaded panels
in caramel colored glass, surrounded by 5 sgd Handel tulip shades in
caramel glass with geometric overlay **3,500**

Chandelier, tin, six S–shaped arms with candle sockets, shades with
punched design, PA, c1850 .... **600**

Left: Fluid Lamp, amberina, threaded, 3 clear applied feet, $1,800.

Center: Fluid Lamp, carnival glass, Zippered Loop pattern, marigold, Imperial, $1,500.

Right: Fluid Lamp, miniature, Log Cabin, amber, hornet burner, 3⁵/₈" h, $500. Photo
courtesy James D. Julia.

Chandelier, wood and tin, cut nail construction, 4 S–shaped arms with candle sockets, PA, c1850 . . . . **500**

Desk, brass, old dark patina, white ruffled glass shade, adjustable gooseneck, column with sphere above domed circular base, 22" h **225**

Desk, polished brass, conical cased green glass shade, adjustable gooseneck, stepped circular base, 24" h **450**

Double Astral, brass urn shaped font centered above brass arm mounted with 2 frosted cut to clear glass shades and clear prisms, reeded brass stem on stepped square marble base, electrified, 20³/₄" h **1,000**

Double Crusie, wrought iron, chicken finial, wire hanger, 6¹/₄" h **350**

Double Torch, cast iron, mkd "PZL" in high relief both sides, remains of orig wicks inside, 19th C, 7³/₈" h **125**

Factory, mkd "Bradley's Security Factory Lamp" in raised letters on font bottom and brass plate inside tin holder, yellow dec on black ground, c1870, 3³/₈" h **125**

Finger, glass, flat base, bull's eye, emerald green, No. 1 burner and chimney, 3¹/₂" h **75**

Finger, glass, flat base, Coinspot, blue opalescent, applied blue handle, Zero burner and chimney, 3³/₈" h **925**

Finger, glass, flat base, Coolidge Drape, cobalt blue font and tulip top chimney, No. 1 burner, 3¹/₂" h **385**

Finger, glass, flat base, Heart, yellow custard, No. 1 burner and chimney, 3¹/₄" h **275**

Finger, glass, flat base, Hobbs Coindot, cranberry opalescent, Zero burner and chimney, 3" h **600**

Finger, glass, flat base, Markham Swirl Band, clear opalescent, Zero burner and chimney, 3³/₄" h **165**

Finger, glass, flat base, plain, pale green translucent, Zero burner and chimney, 3¹/₂" h **100**

Finger, glass, flat base, Snowflake, blue opalescent, Zero burner and chimney, 3" h **450**

Finger, glass, flat base, Star, light sapphire blue, emb stars, applied handle, No. 1 burner and chimney, 3³/₄" h **165**

Finger, glass, flat base, Swirl, light blue opalescent, Zero burner and chimney, 3¹/₂" h **350**

Floor, Handel, dome shade with chipped sand finish, reverse painted with lakeside landscape in green, black, and pink, crimson trees in background silhouetted against golden orange sunset, shade suspended in bronze metal harp frame with tulip shaped socket, plain standard with bud terminal and molded circular foot, 10" d shade sgd "Handel 6893," 60" h . . .**3,500**

Fluid, brass, alcohol, mkd "Made in United States of America" on bottom, 3¹/₂" h **15**

Fluid, brass, lemon shaped font, deep saucer base, ring handle, japanned and gilt finish, alcohol burner, Bradley & Hubbard, c1900, 4¹/₄" h **225**

Fluid, brass, vase lamp, nickel plated brass and iron, floral dec opaque white shade, ornate emb dec, ftd, sgd 3 places, 5 patent dates, Bradley & Hubbard, c1890, 15" h to top of shade **300**

Fluid, glass, clear American shield font, canary square base, minor chips on underside, Sandwich, c1840–60, 3¹/₂" w, 8" h **325**

Fluid, glass, clear blown globular font with vertically cut bands mounted above circular drip pan, pressed and frosted figural stems of man and woman, each holding arm above head to support font, spreading circular foot, 11³/₄" h, price for pair   225

Fluid, glass, clear blown pear shaped font above ribbed knop, square lacy base, brass collar with insert, minor chips on base, 8¹/₈" h   200

Fluid, glass, clear flint globular font, hollow blown stem with wafers above and below, pressed waterfall base with square foot, whale oil burner, chips on base, 9³/₈" h plus burner, price for pair   500

Fluid, glass, clear flint with gilded dec, pressed comet font, baluster stem, hexagonal foot, 9⁷/₈" h   165

Fluid, glass, clear pressed globular font, Rockingham base with spreading circular foot, brass collar and connector, 9⁷/₈" h   400

Fluid, glass, Coolidge Drape, cobalt blue font and tulip top chimney, ftd, No. 1 burner, 6" h   450

Fluid, glass, cranberry cut to clear font, matching stem mounted on double step marble foot, P & A Victor burner and ring with frosted and cut 5³/₄" ball shade, prism ring contains 12 fancy cut flat 5" prisms, Sandwich, 21" h 2,500

Fluid, glass, cut double overlay white to ruby quatrefoil font, pressed opal No. 40 base, opal globe shade dec with pink roses, Sandwich, c1860–70, 4" d font, 3⁷/₈" sq base, 10¹/₂" h, price for pair   550

Fluid, glass, cut overlay dark emerald green to clear font, marble base with gilt brass fittings, patented kerosene burner with shade ring, Sandwich, c1850–70, 4¹/₂" d, 11³/₄" h 1,500

Fluid, glass, Eason, clear opalescent, black foot and handle, No. 1 burner and chimney, 5³/₈" h   385

Fluid, glass, Empress, green, ftd, No. 1 burner and chimney, 5¹/₄" h   135

Fluid, glass, Erin Fan, emerald green, ftd, No. 1 burner and chimney, 5¹/₄" h . .   75

Fluid, glass, Grange Twelve Panel, green, molded handle, ftd, No. 1 burner and chimney, 5¹/₄" h   100

Fluid, glass, Heart, yellow custard, ftd, No. 1 burner and chimney, 5" h   300

Fluid, glass, milk glass font and domed shade with yellow and gold enameling and blue, yellow, and red transfer of birds, cast iron and brass fittings, kerosene burner, minor flakes, 16¹/₄" h   55

Fluid, glass, pink cut to white cut to clear font, white milk glass stem and foot, gold trimmed font, scenic dec double ring Sandwich shade with pink band and house and fence beside pond scene, worn gold trim, minor surface stress lines at top of stem, Sandwich, 12" h 1,250

Fluid, glass, Prince Edward, white milk glass, ftd, No. 1 burner and chimney, 5¹/₈" h   225

Fluid, glass, Sheldon Swirl, blue opalescent, ftd, No. 1 burner and chimney, 5³/₄" h   425

Fluid, glass, Snowflake, cranberry opalescent, ftd, No. 1 burner and chimney, 5¹/₈" h 1,450

Fluid, glass, Turkey Foot, sapphire blue, ftd, No. 1 burner and chimney, 6³/₄" h   175

Fluid, glass, Windows, blue opalescent, molded handle and foot, No. 1 burner and chimney, 5" h   775

Gas Light, hanging, inverted green glass shade with oval Hobnail pattern and goffered rim, metal frame, c1870–80, 29" h **100**

Grease, brass and steel, Peter Derr, PA, pointed and spurred hanger above arched support inscribed "P.Derr 1840," ovoid hinged font below opening to reservoir with projecting spout, mounted on contemporary turned and incised baluster form walnut stand, repair to underside of font, 14½" h with stand **1,500**

Grease, wrought iron, twisted link hanger, 4 spout, 4½" h plus hanger **60**

Hand, glass, emerald green, Loop pattern, attached ear handle, brass collar, 3⅜" h **875**

Hanging, fluid, brass, Bradley & Hubbard, emb font, opaque white glass domed shade, company name stamped on shoulder and filler cap, c1890, 13⅝" d shade, 52" h **600**

Hanging, fluid, cast iron, ornate frame with top hanging bracket, clear glass font, milk glass shade and smoke bell with applied mahogany colored rim, 13¾" d shade **165**

Hitchcock, brass, mkd "Improved Hitchcock Lamp," sidewinder motor stamped with patent dates from Nov 30, 1880, to Feb 28, 1899, 11⅞" h .. **175**

Jeweler's, amber glass font, tin egg cup shaped base, alcohol burner, 2 patent dates on shoulder, 1880–90, 3¼" h **30**

Kitchen, Union Glass Co, clear Lomax font, 1870 patent date on underside, 6⅜" h **75**

Lace Maker's, globular blown glass font, fluted clear stem, scalloped diamond point base, 9¾" h **750**

Lard, toleware, cylindrical font, saucer pan, worn black and gold repaint, 6¾" h **75**

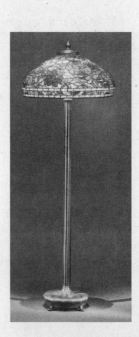

Left: Pan Lamp, hanging type, wrought iron, 16¾" h, $475.

Right: Floor Lamp, Tiffany, favrile glass, red peonies on mottled green ground, gilt bronze ribbed standard with stylized foliate base, shade stamped "Tiffany Studios N.Y. 150," base stamped "Tiffany Studios New York 379," 22" d shade, 64" h, $63,000.

Lecturer's, bell in base, orig black paint with gold striping, pricket for
candle, 10" h   250
Library, brass, cut and frosted glass font with brass shoulder and drip trough,
brass crown on wide conical opaque white glass shade, brass hanger with
chain, c1880, 13³/₈" d shade, 25" h   650
Marriage, Ripley, opaque white and blue glass, pair of opaque blue glass
fonts above brass threaded connector dated 1868, opaque white glass
stem and base with stepped circular foot, brass collar, lamp mkd "D. C.
Ripley, Patent Pending," 11¹/₂" h plus burner   875
Mercury, brass, opaque white glass Vienna shade, font mounted higher than
reservoir, fuel level maintained by hydrostatic pressure, reservoir floats on
mercury, burner mkd "Waterbury," c1880, 22" h   500
Miniature Lamp, Acanthus, pink milk glass, emb   125
Miniature Lamp, Amberina, tiny nicks to shade edge, flake on fitter edge, 9" h   500
Miniature Lamp, Artichoke, white milk glass painted pink and green, 7³/₄" h . .   300
Miniature Lamp, Basket, pink satin glass, flakes at shade bottom, shade
much lighter than base, 7" h   500
Miniature Lamp, Basket, white milk glass, emb   90
Miniature Lamp, Beaded, green   125
Miniature Lamp, Beaded Drape, butterscotch satin, white lined, 9" h   100
Miniature Lamp, Beaded Drape, green satin, 9¹/₂" h   250
Miniature Lamp, Beaded Drape, red satin, flake to shade edge, 9¹/₂" h   100
Miniature Lamp, Beaded Heart, clear glass, emb   115
Miniature Lamp, Beaded Heart, clear glass, emb, 6–toed, 5¹/₄" h   275
Miniature Lamp, Beauty Night Lamp, nickel   55
Miniature Lamp, Bohemian Cut, cobalt blue on clear glass, applied clear
glass handle, 9" h   450
Miniature Lamp, Bull's Eye pattern, clear glass stem   45
Miniature Lamp, cabbage design, frosted   50
Miniature Lamp, cased glass, emb dec, pink, 8" h   650
Miniature Lamp, cased glass, pink glossy, 7" h   225
Miniature Lamp, cased glass, pink satin, medium to very light pink shade,
medium pink base, 7" h   275
Miniature Lamp, cased glass, yellow satin, 7¹/₄" h   500
Miniature Lamp, Cathedral, clear, 8³/₄" h   200
Miniature Lamp, China boy, pushing wheelbarrow   200
Miniature Lamp, Christmas tree, white milk glass, gold trim   110
Miniature Lamp, Cone pattern, yellow cased glass, minor roughness to
shade edge, 8" h   500
Miniature Lamp, Cosmos, white milk glass, emb, pink bands, multicolored
floral dec, 7³/₄" h   250
Miniature Lamp, crackled overlay glass, blue, clear applied shell feet,
smooth base, molded rib shade, 1 rough foot, 8" h   700
Miniature Lamp, cranberry, 2 nicks to top edge of shade, 8¹/₂" h   250
Miniature Lamp, Daisy and Cube, emb, clear, 8" h   250
Miniature Lamp, delft, blue and gray dec, white milk glass, Pairpoint, 8¹/₄" h .   600
Miniature Lamp, delft, blue dec, white milk glass shade, porcelain base,
6¹/₄" h   350
Miniature Lamp, Diamond Quilted, mother–of–pearl, dark to light blue,
frosted applied petal feet, flake to inside top edge of shade, staining in air
channels, 9³/₄" h   450

Miniature Lamp, Diamond Quilted, mother–of–pearl, green satin, $1/4$" bruise on side of base, color difference between shade and base   150

Miniature Lamp, Diamond Quilted, mother–of–pearl, pink to apricot satin, burner ring damaged 1,050

Miniature Lamp, Drape pattern, pink and white milk glass   75

Miniature Lamp, "Eagle," emb white milk glass, pink and blue painted dec, $7^3/4$" h   300

Miniature Lamp, emb, blue milk glass, 8" h   550

Miniature Lamp, emb, green milk glass, $8^1/4$" h   500

Miniature Lamp, emb, white and green   95

Miniature Lamp, End of Day, beaded and ribbed, pink, white, and green, minor fitted edge roughness, $9^1/4$" h   750

Miniature Lamp, End of Day, Beaded Swirl   300

Miniature Lamp, End of Day, cased glass, red, yellow, green, and white, clear applied petal feet, small chip on 1 foot, $9^1/4$" h 1,050

Miniature Lamp, End of Day, yellow and red, minor roughness to top edge of shade, $8^1/4$" h   200

Miniature Lamp, finger lamp, Atterbury Head pattern, clear, crack in bottom of handle, 4" h   225

Miniature Lamp, finger lamp, blue   95

Miniature Lamp, finger lamp, blue with stars, emb "Wide Awake"   115

Miniature Lamp, finger lamp, custard font, applied amber feet and handle, minor chip on foot, $4^1/2$" h   325

Miniature Lamp, finger lamp, green milk glass   65

Miniature Lamp, finger lamp, pink melon ribbed and swirled font, applied clear handle, enameled orange, white, and blue painted flowers, crack in handle, $4^1/4$" h   25

Miniature Lamp, floral, blue and white milk glass, painted dec   100

Miniature Lamp, floral, blue satin, emb, minor roughness to bottom edge of shade, 8" h   800

Miniature Lamp, floral, flared shade, painted dec   400

Miniature Lamp, floral, green and white, painted and emb   50

Miniature Lamp, floral, white milk glass, emb, multicolor dec, $7^3/4$" h   150

Miniature Lamp, floral, white milk glass, emb, red and green dec, 8" h   250

Miniature Lamp, floral, white milk glass, emb, red and lavender dec, yellow bands, 8" h   95

Miniature Lamp, floral, yellow cased glass, gold enameled floral dec, wear to base dec, 8" h   700

Miniature Lamp, Floral and Fishnet, emb, $7^1/2$" h   350

Miniature Lamp, Floral with Ribbing, emb, blue opaline   350

Miniature Lamp, geometric design, emb, milk glass   45

Miniature Lamp, girl with cart, bisque, peach, blue, and brown with gold highlighting, wicker shade with pink lining, wear to gold, minor damage to beads on 1 wheel, 9" h   250

Miniature Lamp, glow lamp, pink and butterscotch base 1,200

Miniature Lamp, glow lamp, white milk glass, flower dec   30

Miniature Lamp, Grand Vals Time Lamp, clear base, cobalt blue beehive shade, $6^3/4$" h   145

Miniature Lamp, Grand Vals Time Lamp, clear base, white milk glass beehive shade, $6^3/4$" h   150

Miniature Lamp, Grecian Key, white milk glass   50

Miniature Lamp, green, metal hanger and reflector **50**
Miniature Lamp, green, milk glass, 6½" h **175**
Miniature Lamp, Handle Lamp, brass and blue base **60**
Miniature Lamp, Hobnail, vertical ribs **5**
Miniature Lamp, Iris, emb, white milk glass **80**
Miniature Lamp, Liberty Bell, clear glass **200**
Miniature Lamp, Log Cabin, amber, 3⅝" h **500**
Miniature Lamp, Log Cabin, blue, handles **1,100**
Miniature Lamp, Medallion Pattern, emb, white milk glass **45**
Miniature Lamp, Melon Ribbed, pink cased glass, flake on edge of shade,
7¼" h **250**
Miniature Lamp, opalescent, amber–pink feet **3,000**
Miniature Lamp, opalescent, blue, applied blue feet, ¼" chip to top edge of
shade, 7" h **1,050**
Miniature Lamp, opalescent, cranberry, clear stem and foot, 7¾" h **2,300**
Miniature Lamp, opalescent, pink, clear applied feet, minor roughness,
7½" h **1,300**
Miniature Lamp, owl, white milk glass, emb, 8" h **1,450**
Miniature Lamp, owl, white milk glass, green fired–on paint, minor paint
wear, 8" h **800**
Miniature Lamp, "Pan–American Exposition," white milk glass, bluish green
background, 3 flakes on shade edge, 8¾" h **450**
Miniature Lamp, Paneled, amber, 3½" h **115**
Miniature Lamp, Pond Lily, emb inside painting **180**
Miniature Lamp, Quilted Phlox, green cased glass, 7" h **650**

Left: Student Lamp, pewter and brass, glass font, patented June 14, 1870, new chimney, 20¼" h, $450.

Center: Boudoir Lamp, custard glass shade, metal base, beige with multicolored floral dec, 16" h, $85.

Right: Table Lamp, Bradley & Hubbard, ivory slag glass panes, brass–washed metal frame, emb floral pattern, base lights up, 18" d shade, 22" h, $600. Photo courtesy David Rago Auctions.

Miniature Lamp, Raindrop, blue mother–of–pearl satin, applied blue feet, cobalt blue chimney, shade lighter than base, 8" h **550**

Miniature Lamp, Santa Claus, red and black painted dec, 9½" h **2,300**

Miniature Lamp, satin glass, blue, emb, 2 flakes to top inside shade edge, 9" h **800**

Miniature Lamp, satin glass, blue, flake to shade edge, mfg blemish in base, 8¼" h **100**

Miniature Lamp, satin glass, dark apricot to light pink to white shading, emb, 11¼" h **1,500**

Miniature Lamp, satin glass, green, brass foot, 10" h **700**

Miniature Lamp, satin glass, green, mfg roughness to shade edge, 8¼" h **345**

Miniature Lamp, satin glass, pink and butterscotch, glossy **1,550**

Miniature Lamp, satin glass, pink cased glass, shade slightly darker than base, 8½" h **175**

Miniature Lamp, satin glass, red, minute flakes on shade edge, 8¾" h **325**

Miniature Lamp, satin glass, rose, flared shade **1,000**

Miniature Lamp, satin glass, white, emb with painted flowers **95**

Miniature Lamp, scrolling and flowers, emb, clear **85**

Miniature Lamp, shoe, amber glass, 3" h **900**

Miniature Lamp, Skeleton, white bisque, lavender and blue trim, green glass eyes, 5½" h **4,000**

Miniature Lamp, Snowflake, clear opalescent, silver filigree, 7" h **1,050**

Miniature Lamp, Spanish Lace, filigree **750**

Miniature Lamp, Swirl, amber with opalescent honey swirls of various widths, applied peach colored feet, ribbed base, smooth shade, 7¾" h **900**

Miniature Lamp, Swirl, clear opalescent, 6¼" h, minor mfg roughness at shade edge **350**

Miniature Lamp, Swirled and Ribbed, blue milk glass, shade darker than base, 7¾" h **175**

Miniature Lamp, Swirled and Ribbed, cranberry, 8½" h **425**

Miniature Lamp, Thumbprint, cranberry **200**

Miniature Lamp, "Twinkle" Lamp, dark amethyst, 7" h **225**

Peg, clear glass blown spherical font, angled on forked stem, square base, tin drop whale oil burners, 4¼" h, price for pair **500**

Left: Lard Lamp, tin, 2–handled skillet, $85.

Right: Fluid Lamp, toleware, orig pick, 19th C, 8" h, $468. Photo courtesy Aston Macek.

Peg, clear glass paneled font, fastened into pewter chamber stick, brass cou-
lar and fluid burners with snuffer cap on chain, 7" h, price for pair **560**

Petticoat, japanned tin, candlestick peg, whale oil burner, 1850–60, 4⅛" h . .   **40**

Railway Car, Adams & Westlake, hanging, cast bronze and brass, orig white
enameled metal shades, double font, maker name mkd on fonts, c1890,
30" w, 32" h **1,325**

Railway Car, Williams & Page Co, Boston, MA, bracket, brass, glass font, cast
brass bracket, 1870–80, 7" h **150**

Safety, hand lamp, brass, Perkins & House, custom made burner, early chim-
ney, c1860 . . . .   **375**

Safety, hand lamp, tin, E Miller & Co, c1890, 5½" h **50**

Ship's, gimbaled, brass, glass font, lead weighted base, free standing or wall
mount, c1860, 6¾" h **85**

Spout, brass, funnel shaped base, removable font, minor battering, polished,
11" h **80**

Stand, Atterbury Swan, pink clambroth #2 font with emb swan, blue clambroth figural swan on stepped hexagonal base, 10⅝" h **3,000**

Student, brass, Bridgeport Brass Co, fluid burning, nickel plated, opaque
white glass shade, clear chimney, c1880, 14¼" h to top of shade **400**

Student, brass, Manhattan Brass Co, ribbed green cased glass shade, electri-
fied, mkd on chimney ring, 20½" h **325**

Student, tin, Mason's Factory, built–in reflector, painted green, paper label,
11½" h **100**

Suspension, rect tin shade, glass font, kerosene burner, c1860–70, 25" h **50**

Table, Handel, bell shaped shade with chipped lightly sanded finish, ext
painted with evergreen trees against sky shading clear to amber, bronzed
metal vase with vertically ribbed baluster stem raised on molded square
pedestal foot, 14" d shade sgd "Handel 5478," artist initialed "L," 21" h . . .**1,850**

Table, Pittsburgh, textured domed glass shade reverse painted with grist mill
scene, obverse painted in leafy trees with dark coloration, 2–socket metal
base with floral medial band, 14" d shade, 22" h **2,100**

LANTERNS

A lantern is an enclosed, portable light source, hand carried or attached to a bracket or pole to illuminate an area. Many lanterns can be used both indoors and outdoors
and have a protected flame. Fuels used in early lanterns included candles, kerosene,
whale oil, coal oil, and later gasoline, natural gas, and batteries.

Lanterns designed for use on the farm often had special safety features such as a
filling cap lock or special base to prevent tipping. When collecting farm lanterns, do
not overlook vehicle lanterns and the small hand–held lanterns used to walk to the
barn or privy.

References: *Collectible Lanterns,* L–W Book Sales, 1997; Anthony Hobson, *Lanterns
That Lit Our World,* published by author, 1991; Neil S. Wood, *Collectible Dietz
Lanterns, 1917 Catalog,* Reprint, L–W Books, (1997).

Barn, wood frame, square, ash and other hardwoods with old dark patina,
mortised and pinned construction, old glass in 3 sides, solid wood panel
in door, tin chamberstick with push–up inside, wire bail handle, age crack
in top, 10¾" h plus bail **$475**

Barn, wood frame, square, cherry with old dark patina, molded edge top and bottom, mortised and pinned construction, glass panes all 4 sides, old glass in 3 sides, glass missing from door, wire bail handle, age crack and slight warp in top, 11¾" h plus bail **350**

Barn, wood frame, square, pine and beech frame, square, glass panes and door, handmade iron fittings, strap handle, wire bail, glued age cracks, 7½" h plus bail **450**

Bicycle, 20th C Lamp Co, kerosene, red and green lens, curved head lens, nickel plated, mkd "Pat. 1895, U.S.A.," 19th C **225**

Bicycle, Edward Miller & Co, The Everlit, kerosene, red and green jewels, curved head lens, nickel plated, 19th C **110**

Bicycle, Hub lamp, black, kerosene, unmkd, c1880s **1,000**

Bicycle, Lucas "Calcia–Club," carbide, brass, 19th C **95**

Bicycle, Powell & Manmer "Duplex," right angle, carbide, nickel plated, 19th C **350**

Buggy, E T Wright & Co, painted black, late 19th C, 9" h **100**

Campaign, tin, 2 spouts, replaced bamboo handle, wire wrap and cradle, 48" l **35**

Candle, tin, semi–circular, punched design on pyramidal roof, hinged glass door, ring hanger, light rust, 13" h **375**

Candle, tin, semi–circular, punched vents on conical roof, hinged glass door, strap handle attached to back, ring handle on top, 12" h plus ring ... **275**

Candle, tin, square, star design punched in pyramidal top, glass panes all 4 sides, four wire guards, worn dark brown japanning, large ring handle, patent label with "Boston, Mass," soldered repairs, 11½" h plus ring **165**

Candle, tin, triangular, conical roof, glass on 2 sides, wire guards, ring hanger, 12½" h **350**

Dashboard, Kemp Mfg Co, painted red, reflector, spring clips, brass label, c1900, 15" h **150**

Dietz Sport, tin, clear glass globe, wire bail handle, frame and globe mkd "Dietz Sport," 7¾" h **200**

Fireman's, Eclipse, green over clear globe, mkd "American La France Fire Engine Company" **1,000**

Fireman's, Ham's, Boston Woven Hose Co, brass and nickel, wire slide, water shield **275**

Hurricane, Hurricane Lantern Co, brass, chain hanger, sgd, 1860–70, 8⅞" h . **475**

Kerosene, tin, brass trim, clear glass globe, kerosene burner, wire bail handle, 12½" h **125**

Marine, Wilcox, Crittendon & Co, Middletown, CT, wire chimney guards, wire bail handle, late 19th C, 10½" h **225**

Miner's, iron, chicken finial, wick pick, 8" h **250**

Paul Revere Type, punched tin, cylindrical, hinged door, punched design all around, conical roof with ring handle, black repaint, 15" h plus ring **125**

Pierced Tin, conical form with ring finial, cone top pierced with stripes and bands and "H. Howard," sides pierced with allover geometric design of circles, ovals, and bands, early 19th C, 20" h **1,500**

Railroad, Adlake Reliable, horizontal wire guard, bellbottom frame, clear globe and frame mkd "KCSRY," May 9, 1922 patent date, wire bail handle, 5⅜" h **250**

Railroad, Armspear Mfg Co, NY, trouble lantern, red globe mkd "B & O RR, Armspear Mfg. Co. New York 1925," 2 detonators attached to frame, weighted iron base, wire bail handle, 10" h **200**

Railroad, Dietz & Co, inspector's lantern, New York Central System logo on lobe, "Ideal Inspector Lamp" imp on back and "B.R.&P.Ry" on front label, traces of silver paint on reflector, hanging ring, wire bail handle, late 19th C, 11" h **185**

Railroad, Dietz & Co, polished brass bellbottom frame, crossed wire guards, red globe, wire bail handle, mkd "Dietz Victor," kerosene burner, minor soldered repair, 13¼" h plus handle **600**

Railroad, Keystone Lantern Co, The Casey, single horizontal wire guard, twist wick raiser, 5⅛" h amber globe, frame mkd "NYP&N R CO," Dec 30, 1902 patent date **850**

Railroad, N L Piper Railway Supply Corp, tin, S Sargent label, brass top, glass globe, 1861 and 1866 patent dates, 13" h **175**

Railroad, unmkd, tin, cylindrical, conical roof with large ring handle, cranberry glass globe engraved "C.R.R." and with clear applied ring at top and bottom, replaced brass font with burner, 12½" h **1,100**

Skater's, tin, glass globe, circular font base, wire bail handle amethyst globe, 7" h **525**

Skater's, tin, glass globe, circular font base, wire bail handle, aqua globe, 6¼" h **300**

Skater's, tin, glass globe, circular font base, wire bail handle, cornflower blue globe, 7⅛" h **300**

Skater's, tin, glass globe, circular font base, wire bail handle, electric blue globe, frame painted black with gold dec, 7" h **325**

Skater's, tin, glass globe, circular font base, wire bail handle, emerald green globe, 6½" h **450**

Skater's, tin, glass globe, circular font base, wire bail handle, light green globe, 6⅝" h **275**

Tin, pyramid shaped, tin frame with punched circle designs in top sides, strap handle and wire bail attached to top, beveled glass panes all 4 sides, brass kerosene burner, crack in 1 pane filled with solder, 8¾" h **250**

Tin and Brass, cylindrical tin top and bottom, brass dome with ring handle and vent holes around collar, large clear blown glass spherical globe, removable font with whale oil burner, missing wire globe guards, 13½" h plus ring **350**

SHADES & ACCESSORIES

Lamp shades were made to diffuse the harsh light produced by early gas lighting fixtures. This was achieved by a variety of methods—using an opaque glass such as milk glass, frosting the glass, painting the glass, or developing a mold pattern that scattered the light. In addition to being functional, they often were highly decorative.

During the "golden age" of American art glass in the last quarter of the nineteenth century and the first quarter of the twentieth century, many manufacturers including Durand, Quezal, Steuben, Tiffany, and others made shades for lamps and gas fixtures. Most shades are not marked. Examples did work their way into the countryside.

The popularity of these "high style" designs quickly led to the manufacture of inexpensive copies. These copycats also are collectible. Lamp and gas shades can provide an important color highlight in a Country setting.

The most highly prized shades are those in stained glass. Beware of signed "Tiffany" examples. Over the years unscrupulous individuals have added Tiffany markings to many lesser quality shades.

One of the most overlooked collecting categories are electric lamp shades. The agrarian housewife was often a skilled handcrafter, especially in sewing. Many added a personal touch to their home by designing and making their own lamp shades. Shades were made to match draperies or furniture upholstery. The variety was endless. Often the frilliest examples were reserved for the guest bedroom.

Should you decide to take up lamp shade collecting, do not overlook the mass–produced shades. Many featured ornately printed designs and patterns on translucent material ranging from stiff paper to celluloid.

References: Larry Freeman, *New Light on Old Lamps, 7th ed,* American Life Foundation, 1984; Jo Ann Thomas, *Early Twentieth Century Lighting Fixtures,* Collector Books, 1980, out of print.

Chimney, clear glass, beaded rim	**$8**
Chimney, clear glass, fluted rim, cut floral dec on frosted bands, c1900, 4³/₄" d, 6" h	**45**
Chimney, clear glass, plain	**5**
Globe, glass, green, late 19th C, 3³/₄" d, 2³/₄" h	**50**
Globe, glass, ruby, late 19th C, 3¹/₄" d, 1³/₄" fitter	**45**
Lamp Filler, polished brass, gooseneck spout, strap side handle, 4⁷/₈" h	**75**
Lamp Hook, cast iron, mounted on board, c1875, price for set of 9	**450**
Lamp Mantle, Welsbach Junior J Mantle, orig box, early 20th C	**50**
Lantern Globe, pale amber glass, fluted, 19th C, 4¹/₂" d, 5³/₄" h	**12**
Oil Container, Ohio Lantern Co, clear blown glass jar, metal container, wire mesh guard mkd "Made by Ohio Lantern Co. Tiffin" on 1 side, 1889 patent dates on other, 12¹/₂" h	**150**
Shade, glass, clear, acid etched floral design, onion shaped, late 19th C, 7¹/₄" d, 4¹/₂" h	**60**

Left: Shade, carnival glass, Soda Gold, 2" fitter, $25.

Right: Shade, Quezal, pulled feather dec, gold, green, and white, gold iridescent int, sgd, c1910, $145.

Shade, glass, clear and frosted, engraved flowers, onion shape, late 19th C, 7" d, 4½" h 45

Shade, glass, frosted, chimney shaped, turned down rim, cut floral design, 1850–1900, 4½" d, 6" h 100

Shade, glass, gold iridescent, tulip form with 10 vertical ribs, sgd "L.C.T. Favrile," slight edge roughness, 5" h 450

Shade, glass, gold iridescent with blue, ribbed tulip form, sgd, Quezal, 12" h, price for pair 275

Shade, glass, leaded, green slag segments, broad border of flying ducks, hanging dome, 25" d, 8½" h 650

Shade, glass, opalescent, Swirl pattern, angle lamp, c1890, 8½" h 150

Shade, glass, pink and white cased, domed, Sandwich, c1865–70, 10" d 125

Shade, glass, pulled feather, deep green with oyster white ground and iridescent surface, sgd, Steuben, 5" h, 2¼" fitter, price for set of 4 650

Shade, glass, white, dome shape, 7¾" d, 6" h 50

Shade, glass, white, flat, fluted, late 19th C, 9½" d, 2" h 12

Shade, glass, white morning glories and large lavender butterfly on rust orange ground, conical, Sandwich, c1875, 10" d 500

METALS

In a life filled with uncertainties, the agrarian community welcomed something associated with strength and permanence. Objects made of metal fit the bill. As a result, metal implements and household appliances were among the most treasured possessions.

Wrested from the earth, metals symbolize man's ability to conquer and tame nature. Raw elements were transformed into useful products. Much of the success of working with metals during the eighteenth and nineteenth centuries was achieved through trial and error, a concept that stressed mankind's innovative nature.

The presence of an individual who could work metal was critical to a rural community's survival. In most cases, this task fell to the blacksmith who knew his own craft and dabbled in some of the other metal trades as well. The blacksmith worked at an anvil. His most important roles were the manufacture of tools and hardware along with keeping farm machinery operational.

The role of shoeing horses in agrarian America fell to the farrier. The farrier obtained his horseshoes from the blacksmith. Few farmers had the time nor wished to incur the expense of bringing their horses to the village smith. The farrier with his portable forge was a welcome visitor. Because he traveled a wide circuit, he was also a major source of "outside" news.

As a community grew, additional metal workers arrived. Some brought a combination of skills. The rural silversmith manufactured flatware and an occasional hollow piece. Often he acted as a jobber for a silversmith from a larger town or a silver plate manufacturer. A rural silversmith earned the bulk of his income as a jeweler and repairer of clocks, guns, and watches.

Tinsmiths tended to concentrate solely on their craft. Their products, ranging from dinner plates to coffeepots, were easily transportable and durable. Holes and cracks that did appear could be easily repaired. More difficult metal repairs were done by the tinker, a mobile sales and repair service specializing in brass, copper, and tin.

By the mid–nineteenth century industrial production reached the point where most of the metal product needs of the rural community were not manufactured locally. The repair function far outweighed the production function of the local craftsman. A repair business was a viable business. Metal products were expected to last for generations provided they were well cared for and kept in good repair.

As times changed, so did the rural metal craftsperson. The blacksmith became the auto mechanic. Many silversmiths opened a jewelry store. Others, such as the tinsmith, entered the mercantile community. The farrier shifted his portable forge from the back of a wagon to a pickup truck.

Most of the metal products that are encountered in a Country setting are utilitarian in nature and found in a patinated finish. There was enough to do without having to spend time keeping an item polished. Of course, there were a few pieces that were "kept for nice," but these were brought out only on special occasions.

Most metal products in a Country setting are displayed out of context. Few individuals want to recreate a "shop" within their home environment. Shop settings are frequently found at farm museums.

The crafts revival of the 1970s and 1980s witnessed a rebirth of many of the metal crafts. Blacksmiths and tinsmiths abound. Their products often are exact duplicates of their historic counterparts. Most are unmarked. In time, the only way to distinguish them from period pieces will be to analyze the metal content.

Museum: National Ornamental Metal Museum, Memphis, TN.

BRASS

Brass is a durable, malleable, and ductile metal alloy consisting mainly of copper and zinc. It achieved its greatest popularity for utilitarian and decorative art items in the eighteenth and nineteenth centuries.

When collecting brass, check to make certain that the object is not brass plated. This can be done with a magnet. A magnet will not stick to brass. If a magnet sticks to a "brass" item, it is plated.

References: Mary Frank Gaston, *Antique Brass and Copper,* Collector Books, 1992, 1996 value update; Rupert Gentle and Rachael Feild, *Domestic Metalwork 1640–1820, Revised,* Antique Collectors' Club, 1994; Henry J. Kauffman, *Early American Copper, Tin & Brass: Handcrafted Metalware From Colonial Times,* Astragal Press, 1995; Peter, Nancy, and Herbert Schiffer, *The Brass Book,* Schiffer Publishing, 1978.

Reproduction Alert: Many modern reproductions of earlier brass forms are being made, especially in the areas of buckets, fireplace equipment, and kettles.

Bed Warmer, engraved rooster on lid, turned cherry handle, 44½" l **$475**
Bed Warmer, engraved stylized bird and leaves dec on lid, red and ocher
   grain painted ring turned birch handle, late 18th C, 45½" l 1,250
Bed Warmer, pierced floral design on lid, turned wood handle with old dark
   finish, 44" l 250
Bed Warmer, punched geometric design on lid, turned chestnut handle, 42" l . 275
Bed Warmer, tooled lid with flowers and peacock, turned wood handle, 43" l 375
Boot Scraper, brass lyre, cast iron pan, 15" l, 12" h 300
Door Bell, metal netting hung with small spheres, larger center sphere, orig
   mounting bracket 85
Door Knocker, architectural, engraved "J. Frey. 1805," 7¾" h 80
Door Knocker, dog head, 7" h 75
Door Knocker, eagle, 8½" h 70
Door Knocker, horse head, 5½" h 135
Door Knocker, lion head, ring knocker, c1880, 5" h 80
Doorstop, cast, pineapple shape, 13" h 125
Flagpole Finial, figural spread–winged eagle, 7" w 35
Inkwell, hinged well, sides flaring to tray edges, etched stylized tree motif,
   sgd "WD," stamped "709," 5¼" l, 9" d 150

Bar Rail Hardware, cast, 6½" h, $45.

Bed Warmer, incised floral dec, turned wood handle, 10¹/₂" d, 41" l, $225.

Inkwell, Victorian, pierced scrolled back plate, 2 ink pots, pen tray, 11" l	**125**
Jamb Hook, scroll detail, 19th C, 6" h, price for pair	**80**
Kettle Stand, reticulated top, wrought iron base, 10" h	**125**
Letter Clip, cast, figural owl, painted red, c1900, 4¹/₂" h	**60**
Match Holder, pig shape, 2" l	**175**
Nutcracker, figural alligator	**35**
Pail, spun brass, American Brass Kettle label, wrought iron bail handle, 22¹/₂" d, 15" h	**150**
Pail, spun brass, Haydens Patent label, iron bail handle, 9¹/₂" d, 6" h	**85**
Pen Tray, sgd "Bradley & Hubbard"	**50**
Plate, hammered, 5¹/₂" d	**10**
Salt, cov, paw feet, 3" d, 4³/₄" h	**75**
School Bell, No. 7, turned wood handle	**40**
Stencil, rooster pattern, mkd "HA&Co 56 Boston," 13¹/₂" sq	**200**
Tinder Lighter, candle socket on lid, brass damper, with flint and steel, old resoldering, 5" d	**325**
Trolley Car Bell	**125**
Umbrella Stand, Victorian, demilune, urn finials, 4 partitions, painted tin undertray, 19th C, 25" h	**425**
Warming Pan, turned wood handle	**175**
Wick Trimmer Holder, hexagonal base, 4¹/₄" h	**75**
Wick Trimmer Scissors, with tray, 9³/₄" l	**150**

COPPER

Copper objects, such as kettles, warming pans, measures, etc., played an important part in the nineteenth century household. Outdoors, the apple butter kettle and still were the two principal copper items. Copper culinary objects were lined with a thin protective coating of tin to prevent poisoning. They were relined as needed.

Great emphasis is placed by collectors on signed pieces, especially those by American craftsmen. Since copper objects were made abroad as well, it is hard to identify unsigned examples.

References: Mary Frank Gaston, *Antique Brass and Copper,* Collector Books, 1992, 1996 value update; Henry J. Kauffman, *Early American Copper, Tin & Brass: Handcrafted Metalware from Colonial Times*, Astragal Press, 1995.

Reproduction Alert: Reproductions, especially those made thirty years ago and longer, are extremely difficult to distinguish from their historical counterparts without electrospectography analysis.

Bed Warmer, engraved peacock on lid, turned wood handle with hanging ring, 31" l **$525**

Bed Warmer, tooled floral design on lid, turned wood handle, 44" l **100**

Bed Warmer, tooled geometric design on lid, turned wood handle with worn black and red grain painting, 42" l **350**

Bowl, hammered, wrought handles, 10" d **75**

Box, oblong, enameled fighting cock birds on lid **275**

Box, oval, enameled hunter and dog design, repaired **175**

Chafing Dish, supported by 3 realistically modeled rabbits, mkd "Black, Starr & Forest," wood base, 11" h **450**

Chestnut Roaster, wriggle work dec, 19th C, 23" l, 11½" d **175**

Coal Hod, brass handles, 19th C, 17" h **175**

Hot Water Bottle, mkd "WAFAX," 8½" h **75**

Jar, hammered, dovetailed seams, 11¼" d, 9" h **40**

Measure, cylindrical, brass rim, "Fairbanks & Co US Standard New York" label, 5" d, 3⅞" h **300**

Measure, Haystack, dovetailed seams, flange base, handle mkd "J. Sykes, Cin.," 8¼" h **250**

Milk Pail, stamped "1070," bail handle, 12" h **500**

Mitten Warmer, copper pan, brass ferrule, turned wood handle, 9" l **125**

Mug, wrought iron handle, 18th C, 7½" h **60**

Pitcher, hammered, square strap handle, brown–green patina, imp "AG Barton," 7½" h **85**

Planter, hammered, flaring bowl, applied ivy dec, brown–green patina, orig liner, metal tag imp "L LaGatta," 9¼" d, 3" h **550**

Post Lamp, polished copper, 4 glass panes, wrought iron mounting bracket, 45" h **450**

Scoop, turned wood handle, lip split, old soldered reinforcement, 14½" l **75**

Still, sour mash whiskey, 3 pc, boiler, extended spout, and coiled condenser . **200**

Tea Kettle, dovetailed construction, gooseneck spout, large swivel strap handle stamped "5," soldered repair on bottom, minor dents, 7½" h plus handle **85**

Teapot and Burner, cov, wood handle, tarnished, 11¼" h, 8½" w, $50. Photo courtesy Collectors Auction Services.

Tea Kettle, straight sided, stepped lid with strap ring finial, gooseneck spout, large swivel handle riveted to body and stamped "1840," 8¼" h plus handle **200**

Umbrella Stand, hammered, flared rim, cylindrical body, 2 strapwork loop handles, repoussé medallion dec, riveted flared foot, c1910, 25" h **675**

Vase, hammered, baluster form, waisted neck, flared mouth, brown patina, imp "Jauchens, Old Copper Shop, 36," c1915, 11¾" h **400**

Wall Sconce, concave crimped top, c1830, 12¼" h, price for pair **650**

Wash Boiler, cov, oval, turned wood handles **85**

Watering Can, long spout, "Joseph Breck & Sons, Boston" label **150**

IRON

Iron, a metallic element that occurs abundantly in combined forms, has been known for centuries. Items made from iron range from the utilitarian to the decorative. Early hand–forged iron wares are of considerable interest to Country collectors.

The malleability of iron appealed to farmers. It could be shaped by hand into a wealth of useful products. When broken, it was easily repaired. It weathered well when properly cared for.

References: Frank T. Barnes, *Hooks, Rings & Other Things: An Illustrated Index of New England Iron, 1660–1860,* The Christopher Publishing House, 1988; Jeanne Bertoia, *Doorstops: Identification & Values,* Collector Books, 1985, 1996 value update; Douglas Congdon–Martin, *Figurative Cast Iron: A Collector's Guide*, Schiffer Publishing, 1994; Gerald McBride, *A Collector's Guide to Cast Metal Bookends,* Schiffer Publishing, 1997; Kathryn McNerney, *Antique Iron,* Collector Books, 1984, 1995 value update; George C. Neumann, *Early American Antique Country Furnishings: Northeastern America, 1650–1800's,* L–W Book Sales, 1984, 1996 value update; James Rollband, *American Nutcrackers: A Patent History and Value Guide,* Off Beat Books, 1996; Herbert, Peter, and Nancy Schiffer, *Antique Iron,* Schiffer Publishing, 1979.

Collectors' Club: Doorstop Collectors of America, 1881–G Spring Road, Vineland, NJ 08630.

Additional Listings: See Kitchen, Baking Items and Food Preparation; Leisure & Play, Fireplace.

Architectural Ornament, cast, eagle on sphere, gold repaint, 14" h **$250**

Bathtub, cast, claw and ball feet **75**

Bookends, pr, cast, basket of flowers, worn polychrome paint, 5¼" h **60**

Bookends, pr, cast, Indian chief, painted, late 19th C, 6" h **125**

Bookends, pr, cast, oval, painted farmhouse, trees, and bridge over stream . . .   **120**

Bootjack, cast, beetle, painted black, 9¼" l **40**

Bootjack, cast, open heart and circle, scalloped sides, 13" l **225**

Bootjack, cast, pair of pheasants, 19" l **225**

Bootjack, cast, V–shaped, ornate **45**

Boot Scraper, cat, cast, walking with tail extended, 17¾" l **300**

Boot Scraper, double scroll ram's horn finials, wrought, weathered white stone base, 15" h **385**

Boot Scraper, lyre shape, cast, diamond shaped base, old green paint, 12" w, 8½" h **150**

Boot Scraper, pecking rooster, cast, traces of polychrome paint, 19th C,
14" l, 9" h **1,500**
Boot Scraper, ram's horn, wrought, 13" l 275
Bottle Opener, figural, cockatoo, polychrome paint, 5" h 85
Bottle Opener, figural, squirrel, tail up, polychrome paint 75
Church Bell, cast, emb "C.S. Bell & Co., Hillsboro, O.," large clapper, yoke,
c1900, 24" d **1,000**
Door Knocker, cast, Amish man, movable eyes 35
Door Knocker, cast, fruit cluster 25
Door Knocker, cast, hand, worn black repaint, 7" l 95
Door Knocker, cast, rooster 75
Door Knocker, cast, spider, hanging from web, bee caught in web, 3½" l 100
Doorstop, cast, basket of flowers, mkd "John Wright," polychrome paint,
9¾" h 75
Doorstop, cast, Boston Terrier, black and white polychrome paint, 9¾" h 60
Doorstop, cast, Boxer, facing forward, brown with tan markings, 8½" h 175
Doorstop, cast, cat, sitting, Hubley, white repaint, some rust, 9" h 95
Doorstop, cast, Colonial woman, Hubley, 8" h 125
Doorstop, cast, cottage, mkd "Eastern Specialty Mfg Co," blue roof, flowers,
fenced garden, 14" h 150
Doorstop, cast, duck, looking up, worn black paint, 11½" h 575
Doorstop, cast, eagle, standing on platform base with stars, looking over
right shoulder, wings spread, traces of old reddish brown paint, 6¾" h 275
Doorstop, cast, eagle, standing on rocks, looking back over left shoulder,
wings spread, old gold repaint, 13¾" l 135
Doorstop, cast, eagle, standing on rocks, looking over right shoulder, wings
spread, old black paint, 7" h 275
Doorstop, cast, goldenrod, sgd "Hubley 268," natural color, 7⅛" h 150
Doorstop, cast, horse and jockey, jumping fence, sgd "Eastern Spec Co
#790," 7⅞" h 185
Doorstop, cast, jonquils, sgd "Hubley 453," yellow with red and orange
cups, 7" h 150
Doorstop, cast, lighthouse, 3-dimensional buildings and lighthouse,
Highland, 7¾" h 275

Left: Bottle Opener, cast, figural squirrel, painted, 3" l, 1⅞" h, $35.

Right: Doorstop, cast, Persian cat, cream with black highlights, mkd "Hubley," 11" l, $100.

Doorstop, cast, mammy, wearing blue dress, white apron, and red and white polka dot handkerchief, sgd "copyright Hubley" inside, 12" h **300**

Doorstop, cast, parrot, old worn polychrome repaint, 7⅝" h **275**

Doorstop, cast, pheasant, brown with bright markings and green grass, sgd "Fred Everett" on front and "Hubley" on back, 8½" l **200**

Doorstop, cast, Pointer, worn orig paint, 15½" l **100**

Doorstop, cast, rabbit, sitting up, yellowed fur, black eyes, mkd "Hilltop," worn paint, 7⅝" h **135**

Doorstop, cast, ram, standing on rockwork base, small casting flaw in base, no paint, 10½" l, 8" h **225**

Doorstop, cast, rooster, black with red comb and yellow beak and feet, 12" h **350**

Doorstop, cast, Sea Captain, standing at ship's wheel, hand blocking sun from eyes, wearing rain gear, 6¼" h **165**

Doorstop, cast, squirrel holding nut, old worn layers of paint, 8⅜" h **150**

Doorstop, cast, 3 kittens in basket, mkd "M Rosenstein, Lancaster, PA," c1932, 7" h **325**

Doorstop, cast, tulips, polychrome paint, 13" h **450**

Doorstop, cast, twin doormen in livery, mkd "Fish," worn paint, Hubley, 12" h **1,750**

Ember Carrier, wrought, sliding lid, 31" l **250**

Fence Section, wrought, 19th C, 47" l, 41" h **450**

Hat Rack, cast, painted flower basket form, late 19th C, 33" w, 40½" h **800**

Hook, wrought, spike ends, scroll finials, price for set of 4 .... **100**

Lock, wrought, scrolled detail, old paint, 10" l **85**

Match Box, cast, grotesque man's head with comic nose, hat is lid, worn black paint over rust, 5¼" h **165**

Mortar and Pestle, cast, urn shaped mortar with pedestal base, late 1800s, 4" h **75**

Nutcracker, cast, elephant, worn red and black paint, 9¾" l **225**

Nutcracker, cast, man with long nose, worn green paint, 7" l **250**

Paperweight, cast, black man's head, worn gold paint, 3¼" h **65**

Paperweight, cast, frog, black spots on green, worn paint, 4" l **60**

Left: Bootjack, cast, filigree center, double–ended, patented May 18, 1869, 12" l, $40.

Right: Trivet, cast, "Jenny Lind," $45.

Paperweight, cast, pig, mkd "A. Pluemer & Co. Cin'ti., O.," worn gold paint,
2¼" h 75
Shelf Bracket, cast, ornate scrolled design, 6½" h, price for pair 20
Shoe Last, cobbler's, cast, 1850–90 15
Shutter Dog, cast, girl's head, "Brevete SGDG" anchor mark, 8⅝" l extend-
ed, price for set of 4 150
Skillet, cast, Wapak Indian Head, #9 150
Snowbird, cast, eagle, 5¼" h, price for pair 140
Spill Holder, wrought, circular stepped wood base, 11¼" h 150
Spittoon, cast, granite lined, 9¾" d, 10" h 35
Spring Latch, with keeper, wrought, mounted on block of wood, PA, 8½" l ... 165
Stove, cast, Burnside No. 20A, Enterprise, pot bellied, name emb on door,
48" h 400
Stove, cast, Peoria, parlor, round, emb stylized leaf and swirl designs, name
on side 500
Stove, cast, Station Agent, Union Stove Works, NY, name emb on circular
top rim, 25½" d, 56½" h 400
Stove Lid Lifter, Jewel, emb name, openwork handle, c1890 15
Stove Plate, cast, emb wild turkey and trees, 5" d 35
Strap Hinges, wrought, horseshoe shaped pintles, 23" l, price for pair 150
Trivet, cast, rect with setter within wreath of vines and leaves, heart shape
handle, pitted, old break, 9" l 140
Trivet, wrought, triangular with tooled leaf detail, turned up feet, 10½" l 325
Watch Hutch, cast, leafy scrollwork supported by spread–winged eagle,
traces of black paint, light rust, 10¼" h 85

PEWTER

Pewter is a metal alloy, consisting mostly of tin with small amounts of lead, copper, antimony, and bismuth added to improve malleability and hardness. The metal
can be cast, formed around a mold, spun, easily cut, and soldered to form a wide variety of utilitarian articles.

Pewter ware was known to the ancient Chinese, Egyptians, and Romans. English
pewter fulfilled most of the needs of the American colonies for nearly 150 years before
the American Revolution. The Revolution ended the embargo on raw tin and allowed
the small American pewter industry to flourish. This period lasted until the Civil War.

Pewter fits more easily into the early American decorative motif than it does in a
Country decor. Wooden and tin utensils were far more common in the countryside
than was pewter. However, since Country decorators like the patinated look of unpol-
ished pewter, it is included in this book.

The listing concentrates on the American and English pewter forms most often
encountered by the collector.

References: Donald L. Fennimore, *The Knopf Collectors' Guides to American
Antiques, Silver & Pewter,* Alfred A. Knopf, 1984; Henry J. Kauffman, *The American
Pewterer: His Techniques & His Products,* Astragal Press, 1994.

Collectors' Club: Pewter Collectors Club of America, 504 West Lafayette Street,
Westchester, PA 19380.

Museum: The Currier Gallery of Art, Manchester, NH.

Basin, Belcher, Joseph, faint touchmark, pitting and scratches, 8" d **$650**
Basin, Ellis, Samuel, London, 18th C, 9⅛" d **200**
Basin, Hamlin, Samuel, partial touchmark, 5¾" d, 2" h **250**
Basin, Jones, Gershom, Providence, RI, c1800, 8" d **100**
Basin, Lee, Richard, Springfield, VT, 1795–1815, 5¾" d **300**
Basin, Mabberley, Stephen, England, old repair in bottom, c1670, 9" l **75**
Basin, Stafford, Spencer, Albany, NY, c1820, 7¾" d **300**
Basin, unknown maker, unmkd, 6" d, 2" h **100**
Beaker, J B Woodbury, Beverly, MA and Philadelphia, PA, good touchmark,
   handle, 1830–38, 3" h **400**
Bedpan, Thomas Danforth Boardman, Hartford, CT, triple touchmarks,
   c1820, 10½" l **400**
Bowl, American, unmkd, ftd, 6" d **250**
Bowl, Danforth, T, Philadelphia, eagle touchmark, mkd "T. Danforth,
   Philada," wear, scratches, 11⅝" d **385**
Box, "AG" touchmark, hinged lid, divided int, engraved bottom reads "V W
   Alford," 4½" d **225**
Candle Mold, 6 tubes, 2 rows of 3 tubes, walnut bench–form frame with
   bootjack ends and scrubbed finish, 1 edge strip poplar and probably an
   old replacement, 5½ x 9¾", 12½" h **1,295**
Candle Mold, 24 tubes, 3 rows of 8 tubes, pine and poplar bench–form
   frame with bootjack ends and stenciled label "W. Humiston, Maker, Troy,
   N.Y. Warranted, Premium," 6⅞ x 21⅛", 17¼" h **1,375**
Candle Mold, 24 tubes, 2 rows of 12 tubes, pine frame with old worn pati-
   na and steel rods for tying wicks, tubes with cast label "W. Webb N.Y.,"
   minor age cracks in wood, 6¼ x 22", 17½" h **825**
Castor Set, Eben Smith, Beverly, MA, 4 clear glass bottles, 1813–56 . . . . **375**
Chamber Lamp, American, unmkd, whale oil burner, minor dents, collar
   replaced, 5¼" h plus burner **115**
Charger, Austin, Nathaniel, MA, c1800, 13½" d **650**

Left: Plate, Thomas Danforth, Philadelphia, 8¾" d, $150.
Right: Spittoon, D Curtis, Albany, NY, 7⅞" d base, 2½" h, $275.

Charger, Danforth, Samuel, Hartford, CT, faint touchmark, wear and pitting, 13¼" d 225
Charger, Eadem, Samuel, scratches and pitting, 15" d 250
Charger, Hamlin, Samuel, Providence, RI, c1800, 13½" d 650
Charger, Hunter, William, touchmarks, 15" d 200
Charger, Jones, Gershom, Providence, RI, late 18th C, 14½" d 725
Charger, Townsend, John, Fen Church Street, London touchmark, 16½" d 325
Chocolate Pot, William Calder, Providence, RI, "Calder" touchmark, wood handle, 11" h 375
Coffeepot, Broadhead, R & Co, Sheffield, England, minor repair, 6½" h 60
Coffeepot, Calder, William, Providence, RI, lighthouse shape, c1839, 11" h .. 650
Coffeepot, Danforth, Josiah, Middletown, CT, dome lid, early 19th C, 11" h ..1,250
Coffeepot, Dixon, James & Sons, England, octagonal, wood handle, 10½" h .. 200
Coffeepot, Dunham, Rufus, Westbrook, ME, gooseneck spout, ftd, mid–19th C, 12" h 300
Coffeepot, Gleason, Roswell, Dorchester, MA, wood handle and finial, 10" h . 325
Coffeepot, Griswold, Ashbill, Meriden, CT, pyramid shaped, 10½" h 350
Coffeepot, Homan & Co, Cincinnati, OH, cast foliage finial, engraved floral design, mkd "H Homan," 10¼" h 250
Coffeepot, Lewis, Isaac C, Meriden, CT, 19th C, 11½" h 175
Coffeepot, Porter, Freeman, Westbrook, ME, pear shaped, mkd "F Porter No. 2, Westbrook," c1840, 10¾" h 250
Coffeepot, Richardson, George, Boston, MA and Cranston, RI, "G Richardson, Warranted" touchmark, 1818–45, 11" h 525
Coffeepot, Smith & Co, Boston, MA, pedestal base, wood handle, 10" h 275
Coffeepot, Trask, Israel, Beverly, MA, lighthouse shape, bright cut engraved band, c1830, 11" h 350
Coffeepot, unknown maker, unmkd, cylindrical, flared base, 10" h 325
Creamer, American, unmkd, cast ear handle, 5⅝" h 175
Creamer, Joseph, Henry, London, 3 small feet, mkd "HJ," 1740–85 2,500
Deep Dish, Danforth, Samuel, Hartford, CT, c1800, 12¼" d 250
Deep Dish, Hamlin, Samuel, Hartford, CT, late 18th C 600
Deep Dish, Melville, David, Newport, RI, late 18th C, 14" d 250
Flagon, Boardman & Hart, NY, domed lid, shaped thumb rest and handle, tapering sides, stepped circular base, Laughlin touchmark, c1835, 12½" h .1,350
Flagon, English, unmkd, dated "1718," 10¾" h 175
Food Cover, James Dixon & Sons, Sheffield, oval, beaded handle and rim, traces of silver plating, 1 nut holding handle missing, 16½" l 110
Food Mold, English registry mark, detailed fruit design on top, removable base mkd "1 Quart," 6⅝" d 200
Hot Water Warming Platter, Compton, London, England, touchmark, wood handles, wear and scratches, 20" l 200
Hot Water Warming Platter, Dixon & Sons, England, touchmark, tree and well, repairs, 19" l 250
Inkwell, American, unmkd, 5 quills, 6⅞" d 150
Ladle, unknown maker, touchmark, turned wood handle, 15" l 150
Ladle, Yates, John, Birmingham, England, minor pitting on bowl, c1835, 13½" l 80
Lamp, double spout fluid burner, American, unmkd, cylindrical font, turned stem, circular pedestal base, fluid burner with brass tubes, pewter snuffer caps, and chain, repair on base, 7¾" h 250

Teapot, cov, Savage, Middletown, CT, 10" h, $250.

Lamp, double spout fluid burner, Yale & Curtis, NY, cylindrical font, turned stem, circular pedestal base, whale oil burner, 8¼" h plus burner **225**

Measure, James Yates, England, bellied, 1 qt, 6⅛" h **85**

Muffineer, 7½" h **200**

Mug, Hamlin, Samuel, Hartford and Middletown, CT and Providence, RI, dent at base, 1767–1801, 1 qt, 5⅞" h **600**

Mug, Whitmore, Jacob, Middletown, CT, fair touchmark, 1758–90, 1 qt **1,750**

Petticoat Lamp, mkd "Morey & Smith, Warranted, Boston" touchmark, double spout fluid burner, battered burner, 4" h plus burner **100**

Pitcher, American, unmkd, hinged lid, cast ear handle, some battering, 6¼" h **200**

Pitcher, Dunham, Rufus, Westbrook, ME, cider type, c1845, 2 qt, 6½" h **350**

Pitcher, Gleason, Roswell, Dorchester, MA, cov, c1840, 12" h **650**

Pitcher, unmkd, hinged lid, cast ear handle, some battering, 6¼" h **200**

Plate, Boardman, Thomas Danforth, Hartford, CT, 2 eagle touchmarks, wear and scratches, 7¾" d **165**

Plate, Calder, William, Providence, RI, eagle touchmark, c1840, 8⅜" d **375**

Plate, Danforth, Samuel, Hartford, CT, eagle touchmark, wear and pitting, 7⅞" d **135**

Plate, Danforth I, Thomas, MA and CT, rampant lion touchmark, wear and scratches, 8" d **225**

Plate, Danforth III, Thomas, Philadelphia, PA, eagle touchmark, very worn with dents, 7¾" d **135**

Plate, Lightner, George, Baltimore, MD, "G Lightner, Baltimore" touchmark, 7⅞" d **225**

Plate, unknown maker, "Love" touchmark, some wear and dents, 7⅞" d **165**

Porringer, Green, Samuel, Boston, MA, cast crown handle, 5½" d **550**

Porringer, New England, unmkd, cast crown handle, 5" d **175**

Porringer, Salt, Parks Boyd, Philadelphia, PA, beaded rim and base, ftd, 1795–1819 . . . . **950**

Spoon, Bradford, William, New York City, NY, round bowl, 1719–85, 6⅝" l . . **1,600**

Spoon, LB touchmark, cast handles, wire rack, price for set of 21 . . . . **250**

Sugar Bowl, cov, Sheldon & Feltman, Albany, touchmark, scrolled handles with spurred thumb rests, hexagonal stepped base, 7⅝" h **95**

Syrup, American, unmkd, miniature lighthouse coffeepot shape, lid resoldered to hinge, 5½" h **225**

Syrup, Hall & Catton touchmark, hinged lid, 6¹/₈" h **650**
Tall Pot, cov, Munson, J, touchmark, handle repainted black, minor dents,
 small nick, 11³/₈" h **225**
Tall Pot, cov, Porter, K Westbrook touchmark, lid finial pushed in, finial wafer
 missing, 10³/₄" h **115**
Tall Pot, cov, Richardson, G, Boston, flower finial, scrolled wood handle
 with spurred thumb rest, gooseneck spout, ftd, 10¹/₂" h **300**
Tankard, unmkd, tulip shape, 3³/₄" h **60**
Teapot, cov, American, unmkd, wood handle, minor damage to hinge, some
 resoldering, 6⁵/₈" h **150**
Teapot, cov, Boardman, Thomas D and Samuel, Hartford, CT, cast acorn
 finial, copper bottom mkd "TD & SB," 8³/₈" h **100**
Teapot, cov, Dixon, James & Sons, England, octagonal, wood handle and
 finial, 8" h **175**
Teapot, cov, Griswold, Ashbil, Meriden, CT, touchmark, mkd "J#154," finial
 wafer missing, 7¹/₄" h **85**
Teapot, cov, Putnam, James, Walden, MA, mkd "Putnam," 7⁵/₈" h **300**
Teapot, cov, Savage, William, Middletown, CT, "Savage, Midd Ct." touch-
 mark, flower finial, scrolled handle with spurred thumb rest, gooseneck
 spout, pedestal base, 7³/₄" h **250**
Teapot, cov, Sellow & Co, Cincinnati, OH, touchmark, finial wafer missing,
 8" h **175**
Teapot, cov, Smith & Co, Albany, NY, touchmark, 7³/₄" h **150**
Teapot, cov, Townsend & Compton, England, touchmark, pear shaped, 7" h .. **400**
Tea Set, unmkd, miniature, cov teapot, creamer, open sugar, and 4 cups and
 saucers, damage and repairs, 2¹/₂" h teapot **70**
Water Pitcher, Boardman, lion touchmark, battered, 8¹/₄" h **250**

SILVER & SILVERPLATE

Sterling silver never enjoyed great popularity in the agrarian community. If a farmer or small town merchant hoarded anything, the preferred metal was gold. When a touch of class was needed, elaborately decorated silverplate was more than adequate.

Most pieces of silver and silverplate appeared only on special occasions. The rural housewife simply did not have the time or help to keep them polished. The best pieces were displayed on the dining room buffet when company came and then stored inside for the balance of the time.

The natural beauty of silver lends itself to the designs of artists and craftsmen, often pricing it out of reach for most members of the country community. Pure silver is too soft to be fashioned into strong, durable, and serviceable utensils. Alloys of copper, nickel, and other metals are added to give silver its required degree of hardness.

Plated silver production by an electrolytic method is credited to G. R. and H. Ekington, England, in 1838. In electroplating silver, the article is completely shaped and formed from a base metal, then coated with a thin layer of silver. In the late nineteenth century, the base metal was Britannia, an alloy of tin, copper, and antimony. Other bases are copper and brass. Today the base metal is nickel silver.

In 1847 the electroplating process was introduced in America by Rogers Bros., Hartford, Connecticut. By 1855, a number of firms were using the method to mass produce silver plated items. The quality of plating is important. Extensive use or polishing can cause the base metal to show through. Silverplate has enjoyed a revival due to the Victorian decorating craze of the late 1980s.

References: Frederick Bradbury, *Bradbury's Book of Hallmarks,* U. W. Northend, 1987; Maryanne Dolan, *1830's–1990's American Sterling Silver Flatware: A Collector's Identification and Value Guide,* Books Americana, Krause Publications, 1993; Rachael Feild, *Macdonald Guide to Buying Antique Silver and Sheffield Plate,* Macdonald & Co, 1988; Donald l Fennimore, *Silver & Pewter,* Alfred A. Knopf, 1984; Nancy Gluck, *The Grosvenor Pattern of Silverplate,* Silver Season, 1996; Nancy Gluck, *The Vintage Pattern of Silverplated Flatware,* Silver Season, 1995; Lillian Gottschalk and Sandra Whitson, *Figural Napkin Rings,* Collector Books, 1996; Tere Hagan, *Silverplated Flatware: An Identification and Value Guide, Revised Fourth Edition,* Collector Books, 1990, 1998 value update; Richard Osterberg, *Sterling Silver Flatware for Dining Elegance,* Schiffer Publishing, 1995; Dorothy T. Rainwater, *Encyclopedia of American Silver Manufacturers, 3rd Edition,* Schiffer Publishing, 1986; Dorothy T. and H. Ivan Rainwater, *American Silverplate,* Schiffer Publishing, 1988; Harry L. Rinker, *Silverware of the 20th Century: The Top 250 Patterns,* House of Collectibles, 1997; Jeri Schwartz, *The Official Identification and Price Guide to Silver and Silver–Plate, Sixth Edition,* House of Collectibles, 1989; Peter Waldon, *The Price Guide to Antique Silver, Second Edition,* Antique Collectors' Club, 1982 (price revision list 1988); Seymour B. Wyler, *The Book of Old Silver, English, American, Foreign,* Crown Publishers, 1937 (available in reprint).

Periodical: *Silver Magazine,* PO Box 9690, Rancho Santa Fe, CA 92067.

Museums: Bayou Bend Collection, Houston, TX; Boston Museum of Fine Arts, Boston, MA; Currier Gallery of Art, Manchester, NH; Wadsworth Atheneum, Hartford, CT; Yale University Art Gallery, New Haven, CT.

COIN SILVER, AMERICAN

Bowl, Joseph Richardson Sr, Philadelphia, PA, circular, flaring sides, molded rim, molded circular foot, base engraved "IM," mkd twice on base, 1740–1775, 17 oz, 6³/₄" d, 3³/₈" h **$27,500**

Creamer, neoclassical, monogrammed, 5³/₈" h **225**

Creamer, urn shaped, mkd "Coin, Boston," 4.5 troy oz, 5³/₄" h **500**

Pepper Box, Cooney, John, Boston, MA, cylindrical, low domed pierced lid, double molded rim, double scrolled and beaded handle, bottom engraved with contemporary initials, mkd on side and base, repair to handle, 1700–20, 2 oz, 10 dwt, 2¹/₂" h **9,350**

Pepper Box, Palletreau, Elias, Southampton, NY, octagonal, faceted domed pierced lid, baluster finial, S–scrolled handle, contemporary engraved initials on base, mkd on base, c1760, 3 oz, 10 dwt, 3⁷/₈" h **13,250**

Porringer, Boelen, Henricus, New York, NY, circular bowl, everted rim, pierced handle, mkd on base with conjoined "HB" struck over center punch, 1661–91, 7 oz, 10 dwt, 5" d, 7⁵/₈" l **3,850**

Porringer, Winslow, Edward, Boston, MA, circular, everted rim, pierced keyhole handle engraved "DRW," date "1760" engraved later in bowl, mkd near rim, minor repairs to rim and base, 1725–53, 8 oz, 10 dwt, 5" d **1,750**

Punch Strainer, Daniel Parker, Boston, MA, circular bowl, decorative piercing, molded rim flanked by 2 open handles with stylized leafage and terminals, engraved on back, mkd on back of handle, 1755–75, 4 oz, 10 dwt, 10³/₈" l **6,750**

Salver, Chaundrons & Rasch, Philadelphia, PA, molded border, band of cast anthemia centering plain surface, 3 tapering legs, leaf dec, stippled ground, early 19th C, 11.2 oz, 8" d **600**

Left: Porringer, George Hanners, Boston, MA, twice mkd, small dent, c1720, 4³/₄" d, $2,650.

Right: Porringer, Daniel Van Voorhis, NY, angular rim, open strapwork handle, engraved monogram and later name, c1769, 7" l, 7 oz, $862. Photo courtesy Sotheby's.

Sauce Boat, Holland, Littleton, Baltimore, MD, oval, strap handle with bifurcated leaf terminal, oval molded foot, rim and foot with reeded molding, engraved monogram, mkd on foot, c1805, 7 oz, 5¹/₂" h, 6¹/₂" l 3,520

Sauce Ladle, rat tail handle, mkd "E. & D. Kinsey," monogrammed, 7" l 150

Sugar Sifter, Charles L Boehme, Baltimore, MD, pierced oval bowl, rounded end handle, engraved script monogram, 1799–1812, 2 oz, 7" l 825

Sugar Tongs, shell jaws, "E. Cook," 6" l   40

Tablespoon, Duhme & Co, bright cut engraving and name, 7.9 troy oz, 8⁵/₈" l, price for a pcs 225

Tea Caddy, Joseph Richardson Jr, Philadelphia, PA, oval, flat hinged lid, urn finial, beaded borders, center keyhole, engraved oval cartouche with script initials, int with later brass lock, mkd on base, 1790–1810, 12 oz, 10 dwt, 4¹/₄" h, 5¹/₂" w 18,750

Teapot, Aiken, George, Baltimore, MD, oval, domed lid, urn shaped finial, S–scrolled spout, borders on lid and body, engraved shield in wreath, script monogram, mkd on base, 1790–1810, 29 oz, 10 dwt, 6³/₄" h 1,650

Teapot, Lincoln & Reed, hammered construction, mkd "Lincoln & Reed Pure Silver Coin, Boston," c1835, 7¹/₄" h 500

Tea Service, Joel Sayre, NY, teapot, stand, cov sugar, creamer, and waste bowl, Neoclassical style, canoe form cross section, molded lid and cave to engraved with cut floral bands, monogrammed wreath, early 19th C . . .6,500

Water Pitcher, Gorham, Providence, RI, baluster, chased medallion, floral and shell design, 1848–65, 33 oz, 10¹/₈" h 1,000

Water Pitcher, Richards, Thomas, New York, NY, baluster, squared handle, gadroon moldings at rim, shoulder, and foot rim, engraved with later coat of arms, mkd on base, c1810, 31 oz, 10 dwt, 9¹/₄" h 3,850

SILVER, AMERICAN, MOSTLY STERLING

Basket, unmkd, reticulated rim, swivel handle, 17 troy oz, 12¹/₄" l $400

Beaker, unmkd, engraved initials within wreath of flowers, 3¹/₄" h   75

Bowl, George Jensen, cov, oval, knopped standard formed as grape cluster raised on stylized leaves, ring handles set with grape clusters, 47 oz, 11" l .6,325

Bowl, Kirk, S & Sons, engraved garlands, circular foot, mkd "S. Kirk & Sons Co. 925," 20 troy oz, 9³/₈" d, 4" h 225

Bowl, Lunt, Revere copy, circular foot, mkd "Sterling," 12.9 troy oz, 7" d,
3¹/₂" h **110**

Bowl, Serpico & Laind, oval, ruffled rim, hammered finish, mkd "Sterling
925, Serpico & Laind," 25 troy oz, 15¹/₈" h **400**

Bowl, Tiffany & Co, Chrysanthemum pattern, everted foliate rim, 17 oz,
10¹/₂" d **925**

Bowl, unknown maker, unmkd, oval, urn and swag border, reserve mono-
gram, 16 oz, 12¹/₂" l **150**

Bowl, Wooley, James, Boston, MA, deeply fluted, banded foot, imp conjoined "JW" and "Sterling," early 20th C, 6 oz, 5¹/₂" d, 2¹/₂" h **325**

Box, unmkd, teardrop shape, engraved floral design, reticulated sides and
lid, 5¹/₄" l **50**

Butter Dish, unmkd, shell shape, folding, 13" l **525**

Cake Stand, J E Caldwell, Philadelphia, PA, oval, scrolling branch form loop
handles, center molded cavetto, repoussé band of flowers enclosing dia-
pered ground, monogrammed, late 19th C, 43 oz, 15" l, price for pair **1,500**

Center Bowl, Gorham, shallow, engraved with foliage, gadrooned border,
35 oz, 12¹/₂" d **750**

Center Bowl, Tiffany & Co, oval, undulating rim with pierced foliate motifs
and shells, 33 oz, 14¹/₂" l **2,750**

Center Bowl, unknown maker, unmkd, molded husk border, lobed reserve,
10 oz, 10" d **80**

Cigar Box, Tiffany & Co, New York, NY, rect, hinged domed cov, etched cactus and palm, center cast silver finial, sides etched with palm trees,
applied cast elephants on 4 sides, four massive cast silver cactus legs with
elephant feet, gilt cov int, 3–part mahogany lined case, mkd, attributed as
presentation piece to Theodore Roosevelt, 13¹/₄" w, 9" h **15,500**

Coffeepot, Gorham, gooseneck spout, scrolled wood handle, mono-
grammed "S," mkd "Gorham, Sterling," 8⁵/₈" h **250**

Coffee Set, 3 pcs, William B Durgin Co, Concord, NH, coffeepot with ivory
finial and wooden handle, open sugar, and creamer, hammered pattern,
band of geometric devices, mkd with logo and "Sterling," 24 oz **700**

Compote, George Jensen, raised on standard of alternating stylized leaves
and berried branches, spreading circular foot, 10 oz, 5¹/₂" h **1,000**

Compote, Reed & Barton, repoussé floral rim, mkd "Reed & Barton Francis
I Sterling," 25.7 troy oz, 11⁵/₈" d, 5¹/₂" h **625**

Creamer, George Jensen, carved ivory handle flanked by squash blossoms,
raised on spreading circular base, 11 oz, 4¹/₂" h **2,000**

Creamer and Sugar, lion head and paw feet, 11 troy oz, 3⁷/₈" h **115**

Cup, William Homes, Jr, Boston, MA, molded rim, gadrooned foot, mono-
grammed, c1800, 3¹/₄" h **450**

Decanter, Shreve & Co, San Francisco, CA, hammered globular body, long
neck, matching stopper, applied flowers, 11 oz, 8¹/₂" h **1,500**

Dish, Gorham, shell shaped, monogrammed, 9¹/₄" d **250**

Dish, Paval, Phillip Kran, rect rim on round bowl asymmetrically balanced
on base, large "C" curve handle attached to bowl rim, applied small strap
handle, imp "Paval Sterling," 5.5 oz, 6³/₈" l, 3" h **400**

Dish, Tiffany & Co, heart shaped, mkd "Tiffany & Co Sterling," 8.4 troy oz,
6" l, price for pair **200**

Dresser Set, Tiffany & Co, mirror, 2 brushes, cov round box, and hatpin pin-
cushion, price for set **1,150**

Flatware, Gorham, Buttercup pattern, service for 12 composed of 12 each
dinner forks, salad forks, soup spoons, teaspoons, dinner knives, and but-
ter spreaders, 70 oz, price for 72 pcs **975**

Flatware, Gorham, La Scala pattern, service for 9 and serving pcs, incom-
plete, 77 troy oz total, price for 59 pcs **900**

Flatware, Gorham, Lyric pattern, service for 8, incomplete, 75 troy oz, price
for 79 pcs **600**

Flatware, Gorham, Melrose pattern, service for 12, incomplete, approx 72
troy oz, price for 56 pcs **775**

Flatware, International, service for 9 and serving pcs, floral scroll handles,
70 troy oz total, price for 66 pcs **900**

Flatware, Kirk, service for 12 and serving pcs, price for 108 pcs **2,500**

Flatware, Reed & Barton, Francis I pattern, service for 8 and serving pcs,
missing 1 dinner knife, 100 troy oz total, price for 70 pcs **1,750**

Flatware, Tiffany & Co, Chrysanthemum pattern, service for 12 plus extras,
16 each dinner forks, salad forks, and soup spoons, 32 teaspoons, 14 dinner knives, and 6 serving pcs, 174 oz, price for 100 pcs **8,625**

Flatware, Towle, Old Master pattern, service for 8 with extra knives, forks,
and spoons, 6 serving pcs, approx 58 troy oz, price for 50 pcs **975**

Flatware, Wallace, Stradivarius pattern, service for 12, 12 each dinner forks,
salad forks, soup spoons, dinner knives, and butter spreaders, 24 tea-
spoons, 11 serving pcs, 91 oz, price for 95 pcs **700**

Fruit Bowl, black, Starr & Frost, NY, shaped and dec everted rim, low foot,
24 oz, 12¾" d **450**

Fruit Bowl, Gorham, everted rim with reticulated foliate border, 32 oz,
12½" d **1,275**

Ice Cream Spoons, Gorham, Providence, RI, Florentine pattern, gold washed
bowls, monogrammed, 15 oz, 5¼" l, price for set of 12 . . . .   **325**

Jug, Jones, Low & Ball, Boston, MA, baluster shape, repoussé body with
chased Rococo cartouche, molded spout with mask, foliate knop, c1840,
10¼" h **1,725**

Left: Napkin Ring, sterling, cat, $175.

Right: Sugar Urn, cov, Joseph Lownes, Philadelphia, stepped cover with urn–form finial, engraved monogram, square base, beaded rims, cov repaired, c1785, 10" h, 14 oz, $1,380.
Photo courtesy Sotheby's.

Kettle and Stand, Tiffany & Co, shouldered, ovoid, neck set with stylized band of leaves, swing handle, 50 oz, 12" h **1,725**

Mug, Whiting Mfg Co, cylindrical, deep repoussé sides, chased with putti and scrolling acanthus, acanthus terminals on handles, base inscribed, dated 1892, 8 oz, 4$^1/_8$" h **1,325**

Pitcher, Gorham, Providence, RI, mkd "Gorham Sterling," 21 troy oz, 8$^3/_4$" h . **385**

Plate, Stieff, repoussé floral rim, engraved monogram, mkd "Stieff Sterling," 16.8 troy oz, 12$^1/_8$" d **385**

Platter, Gorham, ornate repoussé rim, mkd "Sterling," dents in center, 87 troy oz, 25" l **1,800**

Presentation Bowl, Tiffany & Co, presentation inscription dated 1920, mkd "Tiffany & Co, Sterling," 20 troy oz, 9$^1/_4$" d, 3$^1/_2$" h **450**

Punch Bowl, Adelphi, NY, cut glass bowl, cut in star and crosshatch design, everted, beaded, and engraved silver rim, c1905, 13$^1/_2$" d, 6$^1/_2$" h **1,000**

Punch Ladle, Shreve Crump & Low, engraved monogram, 7.5 troy oz, 12" l . . **200**

Salad Set, Arthur Stone, Gardner, MA, fork and spoon, engraved and pierced thistle dec, imp shopmarks and craftsman's initial "B" for Charles W Brown, early 20th C, 7 oz, 9$^3/_8$" l **850**

Sauce Boat, Kirk, Baltimore, MD, repoussé, chased floral dec, 1903–07, 9 oz, 8$^5/_8$" l **400**

Service Plate, unmkd, wide border of repoussé with flowers, 245 oz, 10$^1/_2$" d, price for set of 12 .... **6,600**

Stand, S Kirk & Son, Baltimore, MD, oval form, gadrooned rim, 4 gadrooned feet, monogrammed, c1850, 13" l **875**

Stuffing Spoon, Jones, Shreve, Brown & Co, olive pattern, monogrammed, 19th C, 4 troy oz, 13" l **185**

Tablespoon, engraved "PAR," mkd "SNR," late 18th C, 9" l, price for pair **125**

Tea and Coffee Service, Tiffany & Co, teapot, coffeepot, cov sugar, creamer, and waste bowl, pyriform, engraved with foliate motifs, handles cast as branches, 10$^1/_2$" h coffeepot, price for 5 pcs **9,250**

Tea and Coffee Service, comprising coffeepot (illus), teapot, cov sugar urn, waste bowl, and cream jug, each with lobed oval section, conforming foot, and engraved monogram, hinged cov with urn–form finial, Samuel Williamson, Philadelphia, c1795, 11$^1/_4$" h, price for set, $6,325. Photo courtesy Sotheby's.

Tea Service, comprising cov teapot (illus), cov 2–handled sugar bowl, and cream jug, each of urn form with lobed lower body and circular base, flower basket–form finial, William Thomson, NY, c1810, 9¼" h, price for set, $1,840. Photo courtesy Sotheby's.

Teapot, Gorham, gooseneck spout, floral finial, scrolled handle, chased floral dec, mkd "Sterling," crooked finial, 29 troy oz, 8¼" h 325

Teapot, Kirk, S, Baltimore, MD, inverted pear shape, repoussé body with chinoiserie scene, domed cov, floriform knop, mid–19th C, 7¾" h 925

Tea Set, Gorham, Plymouth pattern, teapot, sugar, creamer, and silver plated tray, 62 troy oz, 21½" l tray, price for 4 pcs 1,000

Tray, unknown maker, unmkd, pierced ribbon and foliate border, monogrammed, 20 oz, 11½" d 200

Tray, Warner, Andrew E, Baltimore, MD, beaded and molded rim, engraved dot pattern center and foliate border, monogrammed, c1835, 11¾" d 975

Trophy Cup, Gorham, goblet form, scrolling handles, 48 oz, 10" h 1,000

Tureen, Whiting Co, bombé form, chased and repoussé body with flowers and foliage above gadrooning, chased flower, foliage, and spiral pattern cov with ball shape knop, 4 bracketed ball feet, c1880, 11" w 2,500

Vase, Gorham, cylindrical, flaring, scrolls and flowers dec, lattice ground, 20 oz, 12" h 650

Waiter, William Gale & Son, NY, oval, engraved bead molded rim, crest engraved on brim, mkd on base, 1856, 17 oz, 12" l, 8⅛" w 675

Water Pitcher, John B Jones, Boston, MA, vase shape, gadrooned rim, lobed body, molded circular foot, c1835, 9½" h 1,000

SILVER, CONTINENTAL

Basket, boat form, reticulated sides, cupid and foliage dec, swing handle, 36 oz, 17½" h $1,375

Bowl, engraved birds and scrolling cartouches, 5 troy oz, 5⅛" d 350

Box, cov, square, repoussé with flowers and scrolls, 17 oz, 5" l 450

Cigarette Case, engraved Biblical scenes, gold washed int, 5 troy oz, 4⅞" l, 3⅛" w 125

Decanter, glass, silver mounted, stoppered, rect, pierced figural and foliate
dec, 10½" h, price for pair **1,275**
Dish, round, pierced leaf and flower motif, 7 oz, 9½" d **575**
Ladle, engraved, shell shape bowl, maker's mark "JS," early 19th C, 14" l **250**
Stuffing Spoon, Scottish, mkd "Alt" and "HG," 19th C, 14⅜" l **400**
Teapot, cov, globular form, engraved with flowers and scrolls, raised on
reticulated circular base, 25 oz, 7½" h **600**

SILVER, ENGLISH

Beaker, Daniel & Charles Houle, London, Victorian, tapered cylindrical,
bright cut engraving, floral festoons between stylized foliate bands, gilt
liners, 1865, 12 oz, price for pair **$1,325**
Castor, Boardman, Glossop & Co, Ltd, London, Edward VII, vase shape,
pierced partly domed cov with baluster finial, rising circular base, 3 angular handles, 2 applied leaves, 1904, 8¼" h **350**
Coffee Set, mkd "A E J," Birmingham, George V, after dinner, coffeepot,
creamer, and sugar, classical form, olive branch band, hammered texture,
maker's marks, 1929–30, 23 oz **600**
Creamer, Emes and Barnard, monogrammed "F," molded leaf handle,
1813–14, 6.3 troy oz, 3⅜" h **175**
Fish Server, pierced engraved blade, wood handle, London hallmarks, 14½" l **125**
Punch Ladle, Eley and Fearn, London hallmarks, 5.9 troy oz, 12½" l **225**

*Left: Mug, George III, Adam Graham, Glasgow, engraved stylized monogram, leaf–capped
scroll handle, c1765, 4¼" h, 10 oz, $805.*

*Right: Tea Caddy, cov, Edward Dowdall, London, engraved monogram within oval
cartouche, mansard cov with pinecone finial, beaded rims, bracket feet, 1783, 5" h, 12 oz,
$2,070.*

Photos courtesy Sotheby's.

Left: Bowl, Elkington & Co, Birmingham, shaped rim, lion's mask and ring handles, 4 leaf–capped feet, 1919, 14¹/₂" l handle to handle, 59 oz, $1,610.

Right: Box, wolfhound head form, gilt int, maker's mark "WH," London, 1909, 7¹/₂" l, 7 oz, $4,025.

Photos courtesy Sotheby's.

Punch Ladle, Higgins, Francis, London hallmarks, 9 troy oz, 13³/₈" l **175**

Salver, William Stevenson, London, Regency, molded circular rim shaped by scrolls with shells at intervals, 4 scroll feet, int later chased scrolling foliage, engraved crest, 1815–16, 136 oz, 21¹/₂" d **5,500**

Sauce Tureen, cov, Joseph Angell, London, George IV, molded oval, applied rocaille and foliate scroll rim, foliate ring handle with cast tied anchor oop handles, 4 lion's paw feet with acanthus joints, 1835, 35 oz, 9" l **1,250**

Snuff Box, engraved swags, tassel, and urn on top, coat of arms and initials on bottom, maker's mark "IP," dated 1793 . . . . **475**

Tankard, William Shaw II & William Priest, London, George II, cylindrical, applied reeded band, double scroll monogrammed handle, heart shaped terminal, domed cov with openwork thumbpiece, short spreading foot, 1732, 25.5 oz, 8" h **3,250**

Teapot, cov, Boyton, Charles, Victorian, ridged globular body, floral finial, 22 oz. **400**

Teapot, cov, Robins, John, domed cov, fluted ovoid body, looped treen handle, ivory disc finial, 1795 . . . . **450**

Tea Set, Wakely & Wheeler, London, George I style, teapot, cream jug, sugar bowl, circular, molded spreading foot, wooden scroll handle, paneled curved spout, wooden button finial, 1946, 41 oz, 6¹/₄" h teapot **1,000**

Tray, oval, Peter and William Bateman, George II, 4 feet, engraved lion carrying flower, 10¹/₈ x 8" **800**

Wick Scissors, engraved dog's head, mkd "TR," 19th C, 5" l **125**

SILVER, ENGLISH SHEFFIELD

Coaster, wood base, early 19th C, 5¹/₄" d, price for pair **$325**

Creamer, trifid feet, 1898–99, 3¹/₂" h **100**

Tea Set, 2 teapots, creamer, and sugar, hand engraved, price for 4 pcs **75**

Tray, ftd, cast rim, 1905–06, 6.19 troy oz, 10¹/₄" d **275**

Water Pitcher, Atkin Brothers, Edward VII, urn finial over narrow waisted neck, globular body with stylized scroll and paw feet, monogram, handle dent, minor imperfections, 1907–08, 23 troy oz, 9" h 275

SILVER, PLATED

Bun Warmer, Victorian, oval body, rolled cov with paneled border and wriggle work foliate dec, down curved legs, lion paw feet, 8½" h $250
Butter Dish, oval, engraved floral design, retracting lid, 8¾" l 125
Cache Pot, reeded, swag dec, rolled rim, ftd, 5½" h, price for pair 375
Compote, Derby Silver Co, Derby, CT, circular, fluted rim, applied frog, stem support, circular foot, dish and base with Japanese taste relief dec, late 19th C, 7" d, 5¾" h 200
Flatware, English, luncheon service, 12 knives, 11 forks, 2 crumbers, serving knife and fork, engraved blades, ivory handles, price for 27 pcs 125
Inkstand, rect, 2 rect reeded bottle frames, cut glass bottles, cylindrical chamberstick holder, 2 pen trays, dentil borders, wooden stand with drawer, plated ball handle, 4 ball feet, c1810, 9" l 825
Kettle and Stand, Victorian, lobed, scrolling and foliate motifs, raised on tripod base, legs in form of griffins, 17½" h 650
Mint Julep Cup, Homan & Co, Cincinnati, silver plating over pewter, 3⅛" h .. 85
Punch Bowl Set, bowl with applied fruit and foliage within strapwork, 24 cups with flaring rims, foliage scroll handles, 15½" d bowl 350
Serving Tray, Regency style, oval, pierced gallery, cutout handles, bun feet, 23½" l 450
Snuff Box, commemorative, oval, engraved view, titled "Tomb of Washington," dated 1860, 3¼" l 85
Tea and Coffee Service, E G Webster and Son, teapot, coffeepot, cov sugar, and creamer, baluster body, C–scroll and floral dec, acorn finial 850
Tea Tray, 2–handled with foliate dec, 28" l, price for set of 4 750
Tray, International Silver Co, grape and vine dec, monogrammed, 19th C, 17¾" d 100
Tray, unknown maker, oval, broad border applied and engraved with scrolling foliage, flowerheads, and rocaille, 2 upturned handles, stamped "Mounts stamped from the Original Boulton & Watt Dies," c1774, 30" l ... 275
Tureen, oval, beaded and Greek fret borders, 19th C, 13½" l 525
Wine Cooler, fluted tapered ovoid form, egg and dart border, applied grape and grape leaf dec, scrolling feet, 2 handles, 19th C, 8" h, 8" d 550

TIN

Beginning in the 1700s many utilitarian household objects were made of tin. Tin is non–toxic, rust resistant, and fairly durable. It can be used for storing food and often was plated to iron to provide strength. Because it was cheap, tinware and tin plated wares were within the price range of most people.

Almost every small town and hamlet had its own tinsmith, tinner, or whitesmith. Tinsmiths used patterns to make items. They cut out the pieces, hammered and shaped them, and soldered the parts. If a piece was to be used with heat, a copper bottom was added because of the low melting point of tin. The Industrial Revolution brought about machine–made, mass–produced tinware pieces. The handmade era ended by the late nineteenth century.

In addition to utilitarian tinware, the Country look also focuses on decorated tinware. Decorating sheet iron, tin, and tin–coated sheet iron dates back to the mid–eighteenth century. The Welsh called the practice pontipool, the French To'le Peinte. In America the center for tin–decorated wares was Berlin, Connecticut.

Several styles of decorating techniques were used—painting, japanning, and stenciling. Designs were created by both professionals and itinerants. English and Oriental motifs strongly influenced both form and design.

There were two periods of revival of handcrafted painted tin—1920 to 1940 and 1950 to the early 1960s. The easiest way to identify later painted pieces is by color tone and design.

Pennsylvania tinsmiths are noted for their punch work on unpainted tin. Forms include foot warmers, spice boxes, lanterns, and pie safe panels.

Reference: Henry J. Kauffman, *Early American Copper, Tin & Brass: Handcrafted Metalware From Colonial Times,* Astragal Press, 1995.

Museum: Cooper–Hewitt Museum, National Museum of Design, New York, NY.

ABC Plate, "Who Killed Cock Robin...," worn yellow varnish, 8" d	**$30**
Candle Box, hanging, cylindrical, int compartments, hinged door, 18" l	**250**
Candle Mold, 2 tubes, miniature, petticoat base, ear handle, 5" h	**350**
Candle Mold, 6 tubes, arranged in circle tapering from top to bottom to form cone, 2 ear handles, 4 splayed conical feet, some rust damage and resoldering, 11¾" h	**375**
Candle Mold, 6 tubes, 2 rows of 3 tubes, rect, half candle size, ear handle, some rust damage on top rim, 6" h	**200**
Candle Mold, 11 tubes, single row of tubes, rect, ear handle, curved foot, 14¾" l, 12" h	**300**
Candle Mold, 12 tubes, arranged in circle, conical finial with punched design and ring handle, some battering, old splits in base, 12" h plus ring	**500**
Candle Mold, 12 tubes, 2 rows of 6 tubes, rect, large ear handle, 8⅛" h	**275**
Candle Mold, 16 tubes, 4 rows of 4 tubes, rect, silver painted tin tubes in pine bench–form frame with bootjack ends, old paint, 8½ x 12½", 14" h	**875**
Candle Mold, 20 tubes, 2 rows of 10 tubes, wood frame with adjustable height for wick holders and tubes, turned feet, tin strap handle, 1 foot missing, 1 adjusting screw broken, some rust damage, 28" h	**135**
Candle Mold, 24 tubes, 4 rows of 6 removable tubes, rect, ftd tin carrier with wire bail handle, soldered repair, some tubes mismatched, 7¾ x 11½", 16¼" h	**225**

Candle Mold, 6 tubes, strap handle, $150.

Candle Mold, 24 tubes, 4 rows of 6 tubes, rect, half candle size, ear handle, light rust, 6" h **400**

Candle Mold, 24 tubes, 4 rows of 6 x tubes, rect, pine bench form frame with cutout feet, applied molding, and orig red paint with gold stenciled label "J. Walker, Livonia, N.Y.," wood top with tin lining, wire wick tying rods, 7³/₄ x 13", 11" h **1,600**

Candle Mold, 24 tubes, 4 rows of 6 tubes, rect, top edge with notches for wick rods, double ear handles, 11³/₄" h **300**

Candle Mold, 30 tubes, 3 rows of 10 tubes, rect, cast pewter top and bottom, minor damage, 5³/₄ x 16", 12³/₄" h **85**

Candle Mold, 36 tubes, 4 rows of 9 tubes, cherry bench–form frame with bootjack ends and old dark worn patina, wire rods for tying wicks, ends have ghost lines and nail holes indicating some other attachments at 1 time, 14 x 23", 16" h **1,500**

Candle Mold, 36 tubes, 6 rows of 6 tubes, rect, pine bench–form frame with bootjack ends and old red paint with black stenciled "J. Walker, E. Bloomfield," label, recessed wood top lined with tin, wire rods for tying wicks, 11 x 13¹/₄", 11" h **2,250**

Candle Mold, 50 tubes, 5 rows of 10 tubes, cherry bench–form frame with bookjack ends, 7³/₈ x 17¹/₄", 10¹/₄" h **1,000**

Candle Mold, 72 tubes, 8 rows of 9 tubes, rect, 2 ear handles, 10¹/₂" h **950**

Canister Set, graduated set of 5, worn orig white paint with black smoked graining, light rust, sizes range from 6" d, 8¹/₂" h to 21" d, 34" h, price for set of 5 .... **200**

Coffeepot, cov, parrot beak spout, replaced pewter finial, 10¹/₂" h **200**

Comb Case, emb tooled eagle on crest, light rust, 7¹/₄" l **75**

Food Warmer, white ironstone insert, brass label and burner with ironstone pan and candle, all parts mkd "Clarke's patent, Pyramid Food Warmer," ironstone has crazing and minor damage, 12¹/₄" h **160**

Foot Warmer, mortised hardwood frame, red stained with turned corner posts, punched tin panels with circles and arcs, wire bail handle, 8 x 8³/₄" . **180**

Foot Warmer, mortised walnut frame, with turned corner posts and old dark worn finish, punched tin panels with circle within a circle and heart designs, rust damage, 7³/₄ x 9" **135**

Kerosene Jug, emb brass label "W. S. Miley & Son...shoe findings and kerosene goods...Haverhill Mass," black repaint, repairs, 11" h **60**

Lunch Pail, oval, cast pewter finial, bail handle, 9¹/₂" l **35**

Pail, cov, worn old white paint, black smoked graining, 9¹/₂" d, 7¹/₄" h **105**

Shelf, lighting, holds candlesticks and betty lamps, punched design with large star on back, wear and some rust, 13¹/₂" w, 15" h **275**

Tall Pot, pewter fittings, wood handle, damage, 11¹/₂" h **35**

Tinder Box, circular, candle socket on lid, strap handle, int holds flint, steel, and damper, 4¹/₂" d **375**

Toleware, apple tray, quatrefoil shaped, white rim band with ornate yellow comma designs and red, green, and black floral and leaf dec, dark brown japanning over crystallized surface, some wear, old revarnishing, 12" l, 11¹/₂" w **650**

Toleware, bookends, pr, cutout silhouette, fruit basket shape, worn orig paint, 9¹/₄" w, 5³/₄" h **725**

Toleware, box, book shaped, red, white, and green floral dec, initial "W" on back, worn orig yellow paint, 3¹/₄" l **200**

Toleware, bread tray, oval dished form, black paint with floral dec in yellow, green, red, and white, minor wear, 14" l, 7" w 775

Toleware, candlestick, hogscraper, pushup and lip hanger, red and yellow floral design and striping, black ground 300

Toleware, coffeepot, cov, cylindrical tapering body, black painted and dec with bands of green stylized leaves, red berries, yellow fruit, hinged dome lid, swan's neck spout, strap handle, PA, 19th C, 11" h 4,600

Toleware, coffeepot, cov, cylindrical tapering body, black painted and dec with stylized red and yellow flower issuing 2 buds and green foliage on taupe circular medallion with yellow highlight fillips, hinged lid, straight spout, strap handle, PA, 19th C, 7¾" h 3,450

Toleware, coffeepot, cov, cylindrical tapering body, red painted and dec with red and brown fruit and flowers issuing foliage, yellow fillips, hinged lid, straight spout, strap handle, PA 19th C, 8¾" h 5,175

Toleware, deed box, dome top, oval ring handle, dark brown japanning with floral dec in red, yellow, white, and faded green, minor wear, 10" l 925

Toleware, match box, hanging, crimped edge trefoil crest, black paint with floral dec in red, green, yellow, and white, 6" h 65

Toleware, mug, cylindrical tapering form, strap handle, black painted and dec with red and yellow stylized flowers within a taupe medallion surrounded by yellow fillips, PA, 19th C, 5⅞" h 275

Toleware, mug, strap handle, black ground dec with stylized red fruit and yellow and green foliage, int rim dec with yellow fillips, PA, 19th C, 5" h .. 2,750

Toleware, mug, tankard shape, strap handle, dark brown japanning with large single flower in red, yellow, and white, 5¾" h 965

Toleware, needle case, yellow and orange dec, worn orig black japanning, 9" l 35

Toleware, shaker, red, green, and white floral dec, orig brown japanning, 3¼" h 25

Toleware, bread basket, rect dish form, crystalline int enclosed by conforming yellow and black dec band, raised sides dec with yellow, red, green, and blue fruit, flowers, and foliage, Philadelphia, attributed to Louis (c1825) or Frederick (c1875) Zeitz, 19th C, 12½" w, $4,370. Photo courtesy Christie's New York.

*Toleware, tea canister, tiger lilies, bottom sgd "Sawyer,"
7¹/₂" h, $375.*

Toleware, spice box, round, 6 int canisters and grater, brown japanning with
gold stripe, 7¹/₄" d **100**

Toleware, syrup, cylindrical tapering body, hinged lid, strap handle, red
painted ground dec with stylized red flowers and brown leaves within
taupe semi–circular cartouche, yellow fillips, possibly Berks County,
PA, 19th C, 4" h **12,650**

Toleware, tea canister, ovoid, black ground dec with red and yellow flowers
issuing green foliage and yellow fillips, PA, 19th C, 4¹/₂" h **350**

Toleware, tea canister, ovoid, black ground dec with red flower issuing green
and yellow highlighted fillips, PA, 19th C, 5³/₄" h **1,000**

Toleware, tea canister, ovoid, red ground dec with band of stylized fruit in
yellow, blue, and red with brown and green flowers and yellow fillips,
attributed to Louis (c1825) or Frederick (c1875) Zeitz, Philadelphia, PA,
5¹/₄" h **3,675**

Toleware, tray, hexagonal, yellow, red, and green feathery wide border
design, worn orig brown japanning, some flaking down to bare metal, 9" l .   **450**

Toleware, tray, octagonal, red, black, and white stylized floral dec, worn orig
red ground, scratches, 17³/₄" l **140**

Toleware, tray, rectangular, conforming crystalline int surrounded by meandering tulips and leaves on taupe ground, conforming raised sides with
yellow painted leaf dec, rolled edges and canted corners, PA, 1820–40,
12¹/₄" l, 8¹/₂" w **1,375**

PAPER EPHEMERA

Maurice Rickards, author of *Collecting Paper Ephemera*, suggests that ephemeras are the "minor transient documents of everyday life," material destined for the wastebasket but never quite making it. This definition is more fitting than traditional dictionary definitions that stress length of time, e.g., "lasting a very short time." A driver's license, which is used for a year or longer, is as much a piece of ephemera as is a ticket to a sporting event or music concert. The transient nature of the object is the key.

Collecting ephemera has a long and distinguished history. Among the English pioneers were John Seldon (1584–1654), Samuel Pepys (1633–1703), and John Bagford (1650–1716). Large American collections can be found at historical societies, libraries, and museums across the country, e.g., Wadsworth Antheneum, Hartford, CT, and Museum of the City of New York.

When used by collectors, "ephemera" usually means paper objects, e.g., billheads and letterheads, book plates, documents, labels, stocks and bonds, tickets, valentines, etc. However, more and more ephemera collectors are recognizing the transient nature of some three–dimensional material, e.g., advertising tins and pinback buttons. Today's specialized paper shows include dealers selling both two– and three–dimensional material.

References: Ron Barlow and Ray Reynolds, *The Insider's Guide to Old Books, Magazines, Newspapers, Trade Catalogs*, Windmill Publishing, 1995; Anne F. Clapp, *Curatorial Care of Works of Art on Paper*, Nick Lyons Books, 1987; Joseph Raymond LeFontaine, *Turning Paper to Gold*, Betterway Publications, 1988; John Lewis, *Printed Ephemera*, Antique Collectors' Club, 1990; Norman E. Martinus and Harry L. Rinker, *Warman's Paper*, Wallace–Homestead, Krause Publications, 1994; Robert Reed, *Paper Collectibles: The Essential Buyer's Guide*, Wallace–Homestead, Krause Publications, 1995; Maurice Rickards, *Collecting Paper Ephemera*, Abbeville Press, 1988; Demaris C. Smith, *Preserving Your Paper Collectibles*, Betterway Publications, 1989.

Periodicals: *Paper & Advertising Collector (P.A.C.)*, PO Box 500, Mount Joy, PA 17552; *PCM (Paper Collector's Marketplace)*, PO Box 128, Scandinavia, WI 54977.

Collectors' Clubs: Ephemera Society of America, Inc, PO Box 95, Cazenovia, NY 13035; Ephemera Society of Canada, 36 Macauley Drive, Thornhill, Ontario, L3T 5S5 Canada.

Museum: Crane Museum, Dalton, MA.

ALMANACS, BIBLES, BOOKS, & OTHER LITERATURE

The agrarian community enjoyed a relatively high reading level due in part to their desire to read almanacs, the Bible, and books. Every rural farmstead had a minimum of one bookcase filled with books. The family Bible was given a prominent place in the parlor or sitting room. Children's books were a means of education as well as enjoyment.

Practical books ranging from accounting to home medicine were prevalent, the latter serving as a reference in cases of emergency. Picture books also were found. The agrarian community did a great deal of traveling with their imaginations.

Most books were ordered through the mail. Literature sets were popular since many publishers sold them on a one–book–a–month basis.

Eighteenth– and early nineteenth–century almanacs contain astronomical data, weather forecasts, and agricultural information carefully calculated to the area of publication. They are a combination of things reasoned and things mystic—showing the dualistic nature of early rural America.

As important documents of early printing in the United States, their value increases when they contain woodcuts such as the astrological man, ships, exotic animals (elephants, tigers, etc.), and genre scenes. The Pennsylvania almanacs were among the first to label Washington as "Father" of this country and hence are eagerly sought by collectors.

By the mid–nineteenth century, almanacs became a compendia of useful information—stagecoach routes, court schedules, business listings, humorous stories and jokes, health information, and feature articles. Their emphasis became strongly rural–agricultural. Businesses also began to issue almanacs to help advertise and promote their products.

The Bible, in its many early editions, versions, languages, and translations, is the most popular and widely published book in the world. Recently Bible collecting has gained wider appreciation with a corresponding increase in prices.

King James version English Bibles printed after 1800 are common, not eagerly sought, and command modest prices. Fine leather bindings and handsome illustrations add to value. Check for ownership information, family records, and other ephemera concealed within the pages of a Bible. These items may be worth more than the Bible itself.

References: American Book Prices Current, Bancroft–Parkman, published annually; *Huxford's Old Book Value Guide, Ninth Edition,* Collector Books, 1997; Marie Tedford and Pat Goudey, *The Official Price Guide to Old Books,* House of Collectibles, 1994; Nancy Wright, Books, *Identification and Price Guide,* Avon Books, 1993.

Children's Books: Barbara Bader, *American Picture Books From Noah's Ark to the Beast Within,* Macmillan, 1876; E. Lee Baumgarten (comp), *Price Guide and Bibliographic Checklist for Children's & Illustrated Books for the Years 1880–1960, 1996 Edition,* published by author, 1995; Richard E. Dickerson, *A Brownie Bibiography: The Books of Palmer Cox, 1840–1924, Second Edition,* Golden Pippin Press, 1995; Margery Fisher, *Who's Who In Children's Books: A Treasury of the Familiar Characters of Childhood,* Holt, Rinehart and Winston, 1975; Virginia Haviland, *Children's Literature, A Guide to Reference Sources,* Library of Congress, 1966; first supplement 1972, second supplement 1977, third supplement 1982; Bettina Hurlimann, *Three Centuries of Children's Books in Europe,* (tr and ed by Brian W. Alderson), World, 1968; Diane McClure Jones and Rosemary Jones, *Collector's Guide to Children's Books, 1850 to 1950: Identification & Values,* Collector Books, 1997; Cornelia L. Meigs (ed), *A Critical History of Children's Literature, Second Edition,* Macmillan, 1969; Edward S. Postal, *Guide & Bibliography to Children's & Illustrated Books,* M. & P. Press, 1995.

Periodicals: *AB Bookman's Weekly,* PO Box AB, Clifton, NJ 07015; *Bookseller,* PO Box 8183, Ann Arbor, MI 48107; *Book Source Monthly,* 2007 Syossett Drive, PO Box 567, Cazenovia, NY 13035; *Firsts: The Book Collector's Magazine,* PO Box 65166, Tucson, AZ 85728.

Newsletters: *Martha's KidLit Newsletter,* PO Box 1488, Ames, IA 50010; *Rare Book Bulletin,* PO Box 201, Peoria, IL 61650.

Collectors' Club: Antiquarian Booksellers Assoc of America, 50 Rockefeller Plaza, New York, NY 10020.

Museum: American Antiquarian Society, Worcester, MA; American Bible Society, New York, NY; Free Library of Philadelphia, Philadelphia, PA; Library of Congress, Washington, DC; Lucile Clarke Memorial Children's Library, Mount Pleasant, MI; Toledo Museum of Art, Toledo, OH.

ALMANAC

1796, *Poor Will's Almanack for...1796*, Philadelphia, printed and sold by
Joseph Crukshank, woodcut of the astrological man, 40 pp **$40**
1822, *Poor Richard's Almanac...New York*, David Young, printed by S Marks
for Daniel D Smith, 36 pp **25**
1877, *Clarks ABC Almanac*, black and yellow, 32 pp **20**
1880, *Ayers Almanac*, yellow cov, printed color **6**
1882–83, *Greens Diary Almanac*, color, 32 pp . . . ./. . . . **15**
1883, *New Favorite Cooking Receipts of the Shakers and Illustrated Almanac
for 1883*, black and white, 6 x 7³/₄" **40**
1884, *The Michigan State Almanac Diary and Gazeteer*, Wells, Richardson
& Co, Burlington, VT, color **25**
1892, *Shaker Almanac*, testimonials and adv, blue and gray, 32 pp **75**
1893, *Hazeltine's Pocket Book Almanac*, color **8**
1894, *The Ladies Birthday Almanac for 1894*, Wine of Cardui, Thedfords
Black Drought, color **15**
1895, *Wright's Pictorial Family Almanac*, yellow and black, 24 pp **8**
1902, *Dr Morse's Indian Root Pills Almanac*, color **8**
1905, *Marshall's Almanac*, color illus, 48 pp **6**
1913, *Flying Dutchman Almanac and Farmer's Catalog*, Moline Plow Co,
yellow and black, 32 pp **25**

Left: Studebaker Farmers' Almanac and Weather Forecast, 11th Edition, *1910, 44 pp, $25.*

Right: Uncle Arthur's Bedtime Stories, *Arthur S Maxwell, Review and Herald Publishing Assoc, Tacoma, Washington, black and white illus, 1941, 96 pp, 5¹/₄ x 7¹/₂", $8.*

BIBLE

1805, Reading PA, *Biblia, Das Ist: Die Ganze Gottliche Heilige Schrift...Erste Auflage,* Gottlob Jungmann, contemporary polished calf binding, 1,235 pp, 8 x 10" **$125**

1846, New York, *The Illuminated Bible,* morocco gilt, 2 engraved titles, 1,600 plates, 8 x 10" **250**

1850, Philadelphia, PA, *Bible,* woodcut illus, English medical recipe (Pow–Wow) broadside on rear paste down, Petre family record **35**

1854, Philadelphia, PA, *Holy Bible: Comprehensive Bible...,* gilt emb leather cov **35**

1866, *23rd Psalm,* Hurd Houghton, NY, 7 chromolithographs, gilt binding ... **45**

CHILDREN'S BOOK

Alcott, L M, *Little Women,* A B Stephens illus, Little, Brown pub, 1914, 15 black and white plates, 617 pp **$45**

Bader, Barbara, *American Picture Books From Noah's Ark to the Beast Within,* Macmillan, NY, 1976, 1st ed, illus, dj, 10½ x 7¾" **50**

Bambi's Children, Whitman Better Little Books #1497, 1943 .... **35**

Barringer, M, *Martin the Goose Boy,* Petershams illus, Doubleday pub, 1932, 1st ed, black cloth cov, 8 color plates, dj **60**

Baum, Frank L, *Glinda of Oz,* John R Neill illus, Reilly & Lee, Chicago, 1920, 1st ed, red cloth, pictorial cov label, black and white pictorial endpapers, 2 color plates and black and white drawings **400**

Brown, E, *Manni the Donkey in the Forest World,* Walt Disney Studio illus, Disney Little Golden Book #D75, c1959 .... **5**

Burgess, T, *Farmer Brown's Boy Becomes Curious,* N Jordan illus, Whitman pub, 1929, illus boards, color illus, 24 pp **40**

David Copperfield, Whitman Big Little Book #1148, 1934 .... **85**

The Pronouncing Edition of the Holy Bible, AJ Holman & Co, Philadelphia, c1900, 10 x 12³⁄₄", $45. Photo courtesy Ray Morykan Auctions.

Dickens, Charles, *Mr Pickwick's Christmas,* G A Williams illus, Baker/Taylor pub, 1st ed, 6 color plates, 149 pp 60

Farjeon, E, *Old Nurse's Stocking Basket,* E H Whydale illus, Stokes pub, 1931, 1st American illus ed, 154 pp 35

Frost, S Annie, *Tiny Books,* American Tract Society, NY, 1881, 1st eds, 4 vols, gilt tooled cloth, chromolithograph pictorial cov labels, 2¼ x 1½" 95

Gene Autry, Cowboy Detective, Whitman Better Little Books #1494, 1940 ... 40

Gilbert, W S, *Pinafore Picture Book,* A B Woodward illus, G Bell pub, 1908, 1st ed, 16 color plates 75

Gottlieb, Gerald & J H Plumb, *Early Children's Books and Their Illustration,* Pirpont Morgan, NY, 1975, 1st ed, cloth cov, illus with color plates, dj, 11¾ x 8¾" 45

Grey, Heraclitus, *Playing Trades,* Cassell, NY, 1892, 1st ed, chromolithograph boards, 16 color plates of children performing various chores, rubbing to cov and extremities, chipping to spine ends, hinges cracked, paper browning 65

Hill, William L, *Jackieboy in Rainbow Land,* Fanny Y Cory illus, Rand McNally, Chicago, 1911, 1st ed, gilt lettered cloth, pictorial cov label, whimsical color plates, soiled dj, 9 x 6½" 75

Hough, E, *Singing Mouse Stories,* W Bradley illus, Forest/Stream pub, 1895, 1st ed, 182 pp 100

Just Kids, Whitman Big Little Book #1401, 1937 45

Kipling, R, *Just So Stories,* R Kipling illus, Macmillan pub, 1902, 1st ed, red cloth cov, 22 black and white plates, 249 pp 225

Lee, E D, *Ever Living Fairy Tales,* E D Lee illus, NY, 1924, green cloth cov, 18 color plates 50

Lenski, L, *Alphabet People,* L Lenski illus, Harper pub, 1928, 1st ed, blue cloth cov, 104 pp 45

Lockwood, H, *The Golden Book of Birds,* Feodor Rojankovsky illus, Little Golden Book #13, c1943, dj 20

McEvoy, J P, *Bam Bam Clock,* J Gruelle illus, Volland pub, 1st ed, illus boards, color illus, 38 pp 70

Moffat, A, *Our Old Nursery Rhymes,* H W LeMair illus, Augener pub, 1911, 1st ed, color illus, 63 pp 150

Mother Goose, K Greenaway illus, McLoughlin pub, 1882, illus boards, color illus, 48 pp 150

Nast, E R, *Our Puppy,* Feodor Rojankovsky illus, Little Golden Book #56, c1948 10

Nicholson, Wm, *Square Book of Animals,* W Nicholson illus, Russell pub, 1900, 1st American ed, illus boards, 12 color plates 300

Polly and Her Pals on the Farm, Saalfield Little Big Books #1060, 1934 32

Pool, M L, *Red–Bridge Neighborhood,* C Carleton illus, Harper pub, 1898, 1st ed, 13 black and white plates, 369 pp 30

Pyle, K, *Tales of Two Bunnies,* K Pyle illus, Dutton pub, 1913, 1st ed, red cloth cov, black and white illus 45

Rollins, P A, *Jinglebob,* N C Wyeth illus, Scribner pub, 1st ed, 7 color plates, 263 pp 125

Shute, H A, *Farming It,* R Birch illus, Houghton pub, 1909, 1st ed, 16 black and white plates 35

Three Little Kittens, K Wiese illus, Macmillan pub, 1928, 1st ed, illus boards, 40 pp 30

Uncle Ray's Story of the United States, Whitman Big Little Book #722, 1934 . **60**

Werner, J, *Animal Friends,* Garth Williams illus, Little Golden Book #167, c1953 .... **5**

White, E O, *When Molly Was Six,* K Pyle illus, Houghton pub, 1894, 1st ed, cloth cov, 3 black and white plates, 133 pp **45**

Wood, Robert Williams, *How to Tell the Birds From the Flowers: A Manual of Fornithology for Beginners (1907),* and *Animal Analogues (1908),* Paul Elder, San Francisco, 1st eds, 2 vols, illus, humorous comparisons of birds to flowers and animals to animals, cloth backed pictorial boards, 7½ x 5⅓" **45**

Yonge, C, *The Little Duke,* B Stevens illus, Duffield pub, 1923, 1st ed, 4 color plates **35**

NON-FICTION

Anderson, R C, *The Rigging of Ships in the Days of the Spritsail Topmast, 1600–1720,* Salem, 1927, cloth cov **$45**

Arms, Dorothy Noyes, *Fishing Memories,* William J Schaldach illus, New York, 1938, cloth cov, dj **45**

Bantock, Miles, *On Many Greens: A Book of Golf and Golfers,* Grosset & Dunlap, NY, 1901, 1st ed, intro by Findlay S Douglas, illus include frontispiece of the Shinnecock Hills Golf Club club house, pictorial cloth, minor rubbing to spine ends **375**

Bewick, Thomas, *A General History of Quadrupeds. The Figures Engraved on Wood By...,* Newcastle Upon Tyne, 1824, 8th ed, re-backed using orig leather cov, 526 pp **85**

Bigelow, Horatio, *Flying Feathers, A Yankee's Hunting Experiences in the South,* Richmond, 1937 .... **45**

Bishop, Robert E, *Bishop's Wildfowl,* text and stories by Earl Prestrud and Russ Williams, illus from etchings and oil paintings by Bishop, Brown & Bigelow, St Paul, 1948, 1st ed, pictorial, padded leather, gilt edges, 12 x 8¾" **100**

Choules, John Overton, *The Cruise of the Steam Yacht North Star: A Narrative of the Excursion of Mr. Vanderbilt's Party to England, Russia, Denmark, France, Spain, Italy, Malta, Turkey, Madeira, etc.,* Boston, 1854, cloth cov **75**

Custer, Elizabeth, *Boots & Saddles, or Life in Dakota with General Custer,* Norman, University of Oklahoma Press, 1961, map and illus, part of Western Frontier Library series, 280 pp, 12mo **15**

Davison, Gideon M, *Fashionable Tour in 1825. An Excursion to the Springs, Niagara, Quebec and Boston, Saratoga Springs, 1825, 2nd ed,* leather-backed marbled boards, 169 pp **40**

Eaton, Elon Howard, *Birds of New York,* Albany, 1910 and 1914, 1st ed, 2 vols, green cloth cov, color plates **145**

Everitt, Simon W, *Tales of Wild Turkey Hunting,* William C Hazelton, Chicago, 1928, cloth cov **300**

Gibson, William H, *The Complete American Trapper; or The Tricks of Trapping and Trap Making,* New York, 1876, cloth cov, wood engraved frontispiece, divisional titles, plates, and text illus **150**

Gilmor, Colonel Harry, *Four Years in the Saddle,* New York, 1866, 1st ed, blue cloth cov, engraved frontispiece, 291 pp **225**

Gilmore, Parker ("Ubique"), *Prairie and Forest: A Description of the Game of North America, with Personal Adventures in Their Pursuit,* Harper, NY, 1874, 1st ed, brick red cloth, gilt lettered and dec spine, wood engraved plates   80

Hallock, Charles, *The Sportsman's Gazetteer and General Guide. The Game Animals, Birds and Fishes of North America: Their Habits and Various Methods of Capture...,* Forest & Stream NY, 1880, 5th ed, illus with 3 folding hand colored maps, red cloth, gilt lettered spine, 1 map missing . . .   60

House, Homer D, *Wild Flowers of New York,* Albany, 1923, 2nd printing, 2 vols, green cloth cov, color plates   110

Hubert, Philip G, *Liberty and a Living. The Record of an Attempt to Secure Bread and Butter,* Sunshine and Content, by Gardening, Fishing, and Hunting, New York, 1889, cloth cov, frontispiece   75

Hurd, D Hamilton, comp, *History of New London County, Connecticut, with Biographical Sketches,* Philadelphia, 1882, gild dec leather–backed cov, 678 pp   70

Jeffries, Richard, *The Gamekeeper at Home: Sketches of Natural History and Rural Life,* wood engravings by Charles Whymper, Smith, Elder, London, 1892, new ed, gilt lettered and dec green cloth, rubbing to joints and spine ends, scattered foxing   35

Kippis, Andrew, *A Narrative of the Voyages Round the World Performed by Captain James Cook,* NY, c1870   55

Marshall, John, *Life of George Washington,* Philadelphia, 1804–07, 1st ed, 5 vols, gilt spines, red leather spine labels, some foxing   165

Merrill, Samuel, *The Moose Book: Facts and Stories From Northern Forests,* New York, 1916, plates reproducing photos and paintings by Carl Rungius and others, cloth cov, dj   145

Neihardt, John G, *The Song of the Indian Wars,* Allen True illus, NY, 1925, 1st ed, publisher's slipcase, cloth cov, author sgd, limited to 500 numbered copies   45

Oliphant, J Orin, ed, *On the Arkansas Route to California in 1849. The Journal of Robert B Green of Lewisburg, Pennsylvania,* Bucknell U Press, 1955, 1st ed, glassine wrapper   100

Peake, Ora, *The Colorado Range Cattle Industry,* Arthur Clark, Glendale, 1937, 1st ed, orig cloth cov, gilt top edges, maps and illus, 357 pp, 8vo . . .   150

Periam, et al., *The American Farmer's Pictorial Cyclopedia of Live Stock,* St Louis, 1890, black and white engravings, 8 animal chromolithographs, 7 x 10"   60

(Pike) Coues, Elliott, *Expeditions of Zebulon Montgomery Pike, To the Headwaters of the Mississippi River, Through Louisiana Territory, & in New Spain, During the Years 1805-6-7,* Harper, NY, 1895, new ed, 3 vols, reprinted from orig 1810 edition, orig cloth, maps, #842 of 1,150 copies . .   600

Pollard, Edward A, *The Lost Cause; A New Southern History of the War of the Confederates,* NY, 1867, cloth cov, 6 plates, faded spine, 752 pp   925

Reynolds, Harry S, *Diet and Care of Children: Questions Mothers Ask the Doctor,* Laird & Lee, Chicago, 1924, 1st ed, slightly soiled and stained cov, 154 pp   16

Roosevelt, Theodore, *Outdoor Pastimes of an American Hunter,* New York, 1905, 1st ed, pictorial cloth cov   55

Scudder, Horace E, *American Commonwealths,* Boston, 1888, 12 vols representing 11 states, cloth cov, frontispiece maps, ex–library ed   250

Seton, Ernest Thompson, *Lives of Game Animals,* Garden City, 1925, limited
1st ed, 4 vols, illus, cloth cov, unsgd, publishers 2–pc boxes **415**
Sewell, William, *A History of the Rise, Increase and Progress of the Christian*
People called Quakers Intermixed with Several Remarkable Occurences.
To Which is Prefixed a Brief Memoir of the Author Compiled From Various
Sources, Baker & Crane, NY, 1844, 1st ed, 2 vols bound as 1, 422 pp and
465 pp **1,350**
The Fishermen's Own Book, Procter Brothers, 1882, illus, list of men and
vessels lost from the Port of Gloucester, MA, from 1874 to Apr 1, 1882 . . .   **85**
Walsh, John Henry, *The Dog in Health and Disease...by Stoneheng...Third*
Edition, London, 1879, illus, cloth cov **100**
Wheeler, Colonel Homer W, *Buffalo Days. Forty Years in the Old West: The*
Personal Narrative of a Cattleman, Indian Fighter and Army Officer,
Indianapolis, 1925, 1st ed, cloth cov, 18 plates **150**

CERTIFICATES

Carefully stored in a trunk or bureau drawer were the documents that chronicled the life of a member of the agrarian community—birth certificate, baptismal certificate, diploma, marriage certificate, professional appointments, and rewards of merit. Few were framed to hang on the wall. The major exception was an appointment document.

These certificates record the evolution of American printing. The wood block certificates of the early nineteenth century were replaced by lithographed examples in the 1870s and 1880s. The presentation was often elaborate.

In addition, many of these certificates are very colorful and decorative. This is the feature that attracts the Country collector. Today these certificates are no longer hidden. They are framed and prominently displayed as major accent pieces.

References: Patricia Fenn and Alfred P. Malpa, *Rewards of Merit...,* The Ephemera Society of America, 1994; Lar and Sue Hothem, *School Collectibles of the Past,* Hothem House, 1993.

Baptismal, 1873, Currier & Ives, 14 x 10" **$15**
Baptismal, 1925, Aldine May Sittler, PA, printed, pink flowers, white dove,
cream to blue–green ground, Abingdon Press, New York and Cincinnati,
No. 60, 11½ x 16" **8**
Bond, 1862, Chicago & Alton Railroad, issued and canceled, $500, 3
vignettes including train, rect cancel in corporation seal, sgd by Samuel
Tilden, US statesman **85**
Bond, 1868, Rockford, Rock Island & St Louis Railroad, issued and can-
celed, $1,000 (or 200 English pounds) gold bond with 3 scarce imprinted
revenue stamps, 2 train vignettes **125**
Bond, 1874, Oregon Steam Navigation Company, issued, not canceled,
black, white, and red, early steamship vignette **185**
Bond, 1878, International & Great Northern Railroad, issued and canceled,
Palestine, TX, green engraved certificate with vignette of cowboys roping
cattle **165**
Bond, 1881, Carolina Central Railroad, issued, not canceled, engraved,
$1,000 gold bond with coupons, vignette of trains passing through pas-
toral landscape with cows and farmer in foreground **125**

Birth and Baptism, mkd "Lith. & Pub. by Currier & Ives, 152 Nassau St., New York," 1873, 14 x 10", $15.

Bond, 1884, Broadway & Seventh Avenue Railroad, NYC, issued and canceled, $1,000, eagle and flag vignette, "V" hole cancellation 55

Bond, 1890s, Pittsburgh, McKeesport & Youghiogheny Railroad, issued and canceled, engraved, green, mine int vignette 35

Bond, 1893, Columbus & Ninth Avenue Railroad, NYC, issued and canceled, crown, engraved, $5,000 gold bond, ornate company name and coupons 65

Bond, 1900–02, Fairmount Park Transportation Co, issued and canceled, green, Philadelphia trolley company 20

Bond, 1905, Consolidated Railway Company, unissued, $10,000, brown printing, horse–drawn trolley vignette 25

Bond, 1910s, Lehigh Valley Transit Company, issued and canceled, colorful engraved certificate with PA state seal vignette 8

Bond, 1912, Twenty–Third Street Railway, NYC, issued and canceled, orange engraved $1,000 gold bond with coupons and trolley vignette 45

Bond, 1920s, New York Railways, issued and canceled, engraved, trolley vignette 18

Bond, 1924, Toledo, St Louis & Western Railroad, unissued, engraved pink $5,000 gold bond with ornate train vignette 18

Bond, 1929, City of Fort Wayne, Paul Baer Field Aviation, $1,000, early plane vignette, brown border, coupons, issued 45

Bond, 1940s, Canada Southern Railway, issued, engraved with 1880s steam train vignette 20

Bond, 1947, Southern Bell Telephone & Telegraph, issued, $1,000, vignettes of rural landscapes and telephone, coupons 15

Confirmation, 1877, Samuel W Gerhab, PA, black etching, gold printing, red and gold Bible verses, framed, 8 x 11" 12

Cradle Roll, 1912, Providence Litho, 8 children around end of cradle, 10½ x 13½" 18

Customs, 1804, Benjamin Lincoln, Boston, emb seal, 5 x 9½" 55

Deed, 1856, Pike County, IL, receipt, emb seals 18

Honorable Discharge, Vicksburg Muster–Out Roll, Aug 1, 1863, Lt Joseph Treadway, 23rd Wisconsin Volunteers, sgd by officers 30

Inspection Certificate, bark, Carolina of NY, inspection for hidden slaves, sgd by Inspector Gibson, 4½ x 7" 75

Land Grant, 1815, parchment, Tuscarawas County, OH, sgd "James Madison" with seal, faded ink, damage at fold lines, old grained frame, 17" w, 13" h **350**

Marriage, 1898, E A Strohl and Matilda C Hahn, PA, 6 vignettes of different stages of married life, Bible verses, multicolored, Ernst Kaufmann, NY, No. 105, 12³/₄ x 17" **15**

Membership, 1882, Members Exchange of St Louis Certificate of Membership, engraved, exchange and 3 buildings, 11¹/₂ x 9¹/₂" **10**

Membership, 1898, Association of Descendants of Edward Foulke, Martha Kinsey, commemorates 200th anniversary of landing of Edward and Eleanor Foulke, multicolored emb coat of arms, framed, 8¹/₄ x 7" **8**

Membership, 1898, Trinity Reformed Church, Sarah Ann Fried, PA, hymn verse, decorative border, gold and red lettering, Daniel Miller pub, Reading, PA, 8¹/₂ x 11¹/₂" **5**

Membership, 1899, American Flag House & Betsy Ross Memorial Association, numbered and sgd, 11 x 14" **25**

Membership, 1898, 1900s, Merchants Exchange of St Louis Certificate of Membership, waterfront vignette, 11¹/₂ x 10" **5**

Membership, 1898, 1908, Francis Scott Key Memorial Association, Charles H Weigerber, 14¹/₂ x 11¹/₂" **25**

Membership, 1898, 1926, Stockman Protective Association, OK, farm scene vignette **6**

Membership, 1898, 1937, Oak Park Republican Committeemen's Organization, IL, Office of Secretary of State, engraved, 8¹/₂ x 14" **25**

Occupational, 1905, Teacher's Elementary School Certificate, Perry County, OH, sunrise over mountain vignette, 9¹/₄ x 13" **15**

Reading Circle, 1896, Indiana Young People's, organized by the State Teachers' Association, ornate, 5³/₄ x 3¹/₄" **10**

Reward of Merit, 1871, Card of Approbation, 50 tokens of merit, Swiss landscape litho on back **5**

Reward of Merit, 1872, Testimonial of Approbation, black and white, 8¹/₂ x 10¹/₄" **12**

Reward of Merit, 1876, Toledo Public Schools Grade One Card of Worth, blue and red **8**

Reward of Merit, 1879, Card of Honor, Diligency—One Hundred tokens of Merit, multicolored chromolithograph **15**

Stock, 1870, Chicago Cotton Manufacturing Co, unissued, ornate design, brown center, factory vignette **10**

Stock, 1873, Santa Clara Valley Mill & Lumber Co, CA, unissued, lumber mill vignette **15**

Stock, 1883, Providence, Boston Railroad Co, boats, factories, and train vignette **25**

Stock, 1900, Fairview Golden Boulder Mining Co, NV, unissued, brown, gold nugget vignette **12**

Stock, 1903, Ishpeming Livery Co, Ltd, MI, unissued, horse vignette **6**

Stock, 1911, North Butte Mining Co, miners working in mine vignette **7**

Treasury, dated Jan 1, 1780, Revolutionary War, MA, payable to John Bradford **400**

MAPS

Most agrarian libraries contained copies of world and county atlases. They provided a means of keeping in touch with the world and one's local community. County atlases from the nineteenth century often contained the names of individual property owners. When county directories arrived upon the scene in the mid–twentieth century, county atlases disappeared.

Maps provide one of the best ways to study the growth of a country or region. From the sixteenth to the early twentieth centuries, maps were both informative and decorative. Engravers provided ornamental detailing which often took the form of bird's–eye views, city maps, and ornate calligraphy and scrolling. Many maps were hand colored to enhance their beauty.

Maps generally were published in plate books. Many of the maps available today result from these books being cut apart and the sheets sold separately.

In the last quarter of the nineteenth century, representatives from firms in Philadelphia, Chicago, and elsewhere traveled the United States preparing county atlases, often with a sheet for each township and a sheet for each major city or town. Although mass produced, they are eagerly sought by collectors. Individual sheets sell for $25 to $75. The atlases themselves can usually be purchased in the $200 to $400 range. Individual sheets should be viewed solely as decorative and not as investment material.

Periodical: *Mercator's World,* 845 Williamette Street, Eugene, OR 97401.

Newsletter: *Antique Map & Print Quarterly,* PO Box 254, West Simsbury, CT 06070.

Collectors' Clubs: Cartomania, 8 Amherst Road, Pelham, MA 01002; The Chicago Map Society, 60 West Walton Street, Chicago, IL 60610.

Museum: Heritage Map Museum, Lititz, PA; Hermon Dunlap Smith Center for the History of Cartography, Newberry Library, Chicago, IL 60610.

ATLAS

Beers, Ellis & Soule, Atlas of Hampden County, MA, 1870, NY, disbound
sheets, 48 pp, folio **$200**
Beers, F W & Co, Atlas of Bristol County, MA, 1871, NY, disbound sheets,
few edges frayed, 48 of 54 pp, folio **160**
Beers, J B & Co, County Atlas of Middlesex, MA, 1875, NY, leather backed
cloth, 2 large folding maps, spine chipped, minor margin leaves damaged,
large torn Boston map, 164 pp, folio **425**
Cary, John, Cary's New Universal Atlas, London, 1811, 19th C cloth, 55
engraved double page maps, hand colored in outline, folio **4,400**
Cornell, S S, Cornell's Grammar–School Geography, New York, 1864, hand
colored maps, tall 8vo **120**
Harper's School Geography, New York, 1894, color, small 4to **50**
Home Knowledge Atlas...Showing the Greatest Number of Maps of Any
Atlas Published in the World, c1899, Toronto, Canada, 79 inserted pp,
leather backed cloth, worn, 657 pp, folio **250**
Johnson & Ward, Johnson's New Illustrated (Steel Plate) Family Atlas, 1862,
NY, leather backed cloth, engraved title page, 61 hand colored maps, 2
maps with centerfold splits, some damp staining to text leaves, folio **675**

Johnston, Alex K, Handy Royal Atlas of Modern Geography, W & AK Johnston, 1880, Edinburgh, 45 double maps, half leather, gilt dec boards, inked number on spine, front cover with bookplate and charge slip, blind stamp in top corner of each map, 102 pp, folio **110**

Manhattan Land Book, New York, 1934, 188 color street plans, some with overlays updating from an earlier edition, cloth covers, oblong 4to **190**

Mitchell, S Augustus Jr, New General Atlas, 1868, Philadelphia, leather backed cloth, 58 colored maps (5 double paged), extremities worn, folio . . **600**

Morse, Jedidiah and Sidney, A New Universal Atlas, 1822, New Haven, 20 hand colored engraved maps, contemporary ¼ morocco cov, small 4to . . . **450**

New Historical Atlas of Rockland County, New York, 1876, New York, 21 litho maps, some double page and linen backed, missing title and preliminaries, folio **120**

Ogle, George A & Co, Standard Atlas Of Lincoln County Nebraska Including A Plat Book Of The Villages, Cities And Townships Of The County, 1907, Chicago, some color maps, orig binding reinforced with library tape, 81 pp and supplement, folio **140**

Raleigh, Sir Walter, The History of the World, 1614, London, engraved double page maps, contemporary calf, rebacked, missing letterpress title, thick large folio **525**

Rand McNally & Co's New Family Atlas of the World, c1891, Chicago, cloth, slightly worn, both inner hinges cracked, 321 pp, folio **80**

Sherman, W A, Comstock, and Cline, Atlas of Norfolk County, MA, 1876, NY, disbound sheets, several leaves frayed at edges, 114 of 138 pp, folio . . **150**

Smith, C, Smith's New General Atlas, Being A Reduction Of His Large Quarto Atlas, Containing Maps Of All The Empires, Kingdoms & States Throughout The World, 1820, London, leather backed marble boards, engraved title page, table of contents, 33 hand colored maps, marble boards slightly worn, 4to **350**

Smith, Charles, New English Atlas, London, 1808, 2nd ed, 46 double page maps, hand colored, contemporary ½ calf, folio **2,850**

The Times Atlas, London, 1895, 117 double page color maps, ½ morocco, small folio **165**

Walker, Geo H, Atlas of New Bedford City, MA, 1881, Boston, leather backed cloth, 16 maps, 12 plates, extremities worn, 79 pp, folio **140**

MAP

"An Accurate Map of New Hampshire in New England," c1795, folding, engraved, hand colored in outline, margins trimmed within plate mark, 335 x 295mm **$190**

Anville, Jean Baptiste Bourguignon d', "Amerique Septentrionale," 1746, Paris, engraved 2–sheet map joined, wide margins, hand colored in outline, 460 x 870mm **250**

Bowen, Emanuel, "A New Map or Chart of the Western or Atlantic Ocean, with part of Europe, Africa & America," 1740, London, engraved folding map, ample margins as issued, extracted from *Gentleman's Magazine*, 360 x 306mm **70**

Brookes, R, "A New Map of the World with the New Discoveries by Capt. Cook," 1817, London, engraved rolled wall map, hand colored background with land areas in outline, double hemispheric map surrounded

by numerous smaller spheres picturing planets, comet, peninsula, etc,
linen backed, wood supports top and bottom, early varnish, some disruption
to map surface with minor loss, 475 x 820mm **2,185**

Burr, David, "Map of the State of New–York with parts of the adjacent
Country," 1834, New York, large engraved 24–section map, hand colored,
linen backed, orig 4to cloth portfolio case, minor separation at few intersecting
folds, 1205 x 1455mm **6,450**

Colton, G W and C B, "Map of the State of North Carolina," 1866, New York,
2 folding hand colored litho maps, each pictures ¹/₂ of state, orig 8vo cloth
folder, each measures 850 x 760mm **525**

Colton, J H, "Colton's New Topographical Map of the States of Virginia,
Maryland and Delaware," 1862, New York, issued soon after start of Civil
War, 21–section engraved map, hand colored, linen backed, minor separation
where few sections meet, 830 x 1175mm **975**

Ensign, Thayer & Co, "The Empire State," 1851, New York, engraved, hand
colored in outline, expertly closed tears, 555 x 745mm **325**

Faden, William, "The United States of North America," 1785, London, double
page engraved map, hand colored, offsetting from cartouche on facing
portion of map, side margins wide, top and bottom margins trimmed
to platemark, scattered browning and soiling, cellotape stains along fold
on verso, 540 x 640mm **750**

Hinton, J, "A New And Accurate Map Of The Province Of Georgia In North
America," 1779, London, engraved, published in *The Universal
Magazine*, 12³/₄ x 10³/₄" **300**

Homan, Johann Baptist, "Totius Americae Septentrionalis et Meridionalis,"
c1730, Nuremberg, double page engraved map, hand colored, wide margins,
490 x 580mm **1,265**

Ingell, Sally B L, "The United States drawn by Sally B L Ingell, aged 10 yrs,
Saunton, August 23, 1819, Private School," eastern states from Maine to
Georgia, west to Louisiana territory, hand drawn, pen and ink and watercolor
on paper, matted and framed, 34¹/₄ x 28¹/₄" **750**

*"Nova Totius Terrarum
Orbis Geographica ac
Hydrographica Tabula,"
1630s, Amsterdam,
double–page engraved
world map, wide
margins, hand colored
vignettes and outline,
small stain near
Scandinavia, scattered
minor soiling,
410 x 540mm, $9,200.*
Photo courtesy Swann
Galleries.

Kilborne, John, "Map of Ohio," 1822, Columbus, engraved, hand colored, framed, 31 x 32" **650**

Kitchin, Thomas, "A Map of the Seat of War in the Southern Part of Virginia, North Carolina, and Northern Part of South Carolina," 1781, London, engraved, linen backed, ample margins, 285 x 355mm **250**

Kitchin, Thomas, "A New and Accurate Map of the British Dominions in America according to the Treaty of 1763," c1766, London, engraved folding map, wide margins, scattered browning, principally along several folds, some weakness or thins at several intersecting folds, 535 x 630mm .. **485**

Kitchin, Thomas, "Map of the World," 1783, London, engraved folding map, hand colored, ample margins, 360 x 525mm **375**

Kitchin, Thomas, "Mitchell's National Map American Republic," 1844, 28 eastern states, Indian Territories with tribal claims, 32 cities detailed, population charts, color, 41 x 49" **135**

Moll, Herman, "A General Chart of the Sea Coast of Europe, Africa & America," c1720, London, engraved folding map, wide margins, 360 x 285 .... **80**

Moll, Herman, "A New and Exact Map of the Dominions of the King of Great Britain on ye Continent of North America," 1715, London, engraved 3–sheet map, hand colored in outline, margins trimmed close, 190mm closed tear with some minor loss in area of Gulf of Mexico, abrading and some disruption near margins where joined in several places, scattered browning, faded coloring, 1020 x 620mm **1,500**

Moll, Herman, Montresor, John, "Province de New York," 1777, Paris: Chez le Rogue, French version of eastern seaboard from Monmouth County, NJ up to Lake George, NY, large engraved 4–sheet map (vertical sheets joined, horizontal sheets unjoined), hand colored in outline, inconsistent margins, tears and discoloration along some creases, tears and paper loss in margins, 1460 x 930mm **1,850**

Morse, Jedidiah, "A Map of Northern and Middle States," 1792, London: Stockdale, double page engraved map, hand colored, wide margins, right margin soiled, 335 x 410mm **230**

"New York State, Railroad, Post Office, Township, and County," 1901–02, lists 71 railroad lines with mileage between junctions, terminals, 71 steamship lines, details major cities of New York, Jersey City, and Hoboken, 42 x 48" **125**

Nicollet, J N, "Hydrographical Basin of the Upper Mississippi River," 1843, Washington, shows Mississippi northward from its confluence with the Missouri into Iowa and Wisconsin Territories and the Missouri westward into Indian Territory, large folding engraved map, few short tears at folds principally restricted to margins, very short separation at few intersecting folds, 965 x 850mm **375**

Page, H R, "Map of Iowa," 1879, Chicago, large folding litho map, loose, hand colored, orig 12mo cloth folder, few short tears at intersecting folds, small hole at fold repaired on verso, 710 x 1090mm **575**

Phelps, Humphrey, "Ornamental Map of the United States & Mexico," 1846, New York, large wood engraved map, hand colored, ornamental border encloses portraits of Cortes, Montezuma, Zach Taylor, and Santa Anna, coloring on Texas portion separates it from both the United States and Mexico, 750 x 560mm **800**

"Railroad Map of Illinois," 1891, Rand McNally, Chicago, color, folding, folds into orig 12mo letterpress wrappers **100**

Sauthier, CJ and Matthaeus Albert Lotter, "A Map of the Provinces of New–York and New–Jersey, with a part of Pennsylvania and the Province of Quebec," 1777, Augsburg: Lotter, 2–sheet engraved map joined, hand colored in outline, trimmed to platemark or engraved borders, some disturbance, small stains and soiling on image, remargined right and left, 780 x 560mm **485**

Sayer, Robert, "A New Map of the Whole Continent of America," 1786, London, taken from Anville's map of the Americas, 4–sheet engraved map, horizontal sheets joined, hand colored in outline, margins trimmed generally to outer border or rule, some browning, several small holes in ocean portion with minor loss, 1060 x 1215mm **1,100**

Schenk, Peter, "America Septentrionalis—America Meridionalis," c1730, Amsterdam, shows California as an island, engraved, double page, hand colored in outline, top margin trimmed to plate mark, 500 x 565mm **1,000**

Scherer, Heinrich, untitled double page engraved world map, from Part 4 of Scherer's Atlas Novus, c1700, Munich, wide margins, some browning along vertical fold, 235 x 355mm **800**

Schraembl, Franz, "Generalkarte Nordamerica," 1788, Vienna, engraved 4–sheet folding map, unjoined, hand colored in outline, wide margins, minor damp staining on several sheets, 1085 x 1280mm **1,500**

Senex, John, "A New Map of the English Empire in America," 1719, London, engraved double page, hand colored in outline, wide margins, slight scattered browning, 505 x 595mm **1,875**

"Sketch of the Public Surveys in Iowa," c1846, McClelland, Washington, shows area between the Mississippi and Missouri Rivers, folding, engraved, wide margins, 480 x 605mm **50**

Smith, J L, "Smith's New Map of Philadelphia and Vicinity," 1881, Philadelphia, large folding hand colored litho map, linen backed, folds into orig small 12mo cloth folder, some minor separation at intersecting folds, 685 x 1080mm **70**

Tiddeman, Mark, "A Draught of New York from the Hook to New York Town," 1729, London: Mount and Page, rendering of Manhattan, part of Long Island, Staten Island, and portion of New Jersey, double page engraved map, hand colored, trimmed to border in top margin with some minor loss, other margins ample, minor soiling and browning, 455 x 565 .. **1,380**

White, John, "Americae pars Nunc Virginia," 1590, first separate map of Virginia, engraved double page, hand colored, ample margins, extensive repairs and restoration in 3 margins on verso, several tears in image neatly closed, 325 x 430mm **2,425**

Wilson, Joseph S, "Map of the United States and Territories," 1866, Washington, 48–section engraved map, hand colored in outline, linen backed, soiling, some bent corners where paper is lifting from linen, 1 section along left border lacking about half the paper (of the Pacific Ocean only), 725 x 1440mm **230**

Young, J H, "Map Of The State Of Texas From The Latest Authorities," c1852, Thomas Cowperthwait publisher, Philadelphia, Galveston City and Northern Texas inset, multicolored, 17 x 14" **150**

PHOTOGRAPHS, PHOTO ALBUMS, & PHOTOGRAPHIC PRINTS

Next to the Bible, the most important book a rural family owned was the nucleated family photo album. Filled primarily with individual head and shoulder photographs, it provided a visual chronicle of the family's ancestry.

The chief problem is that most photographs are unidentified. The individual who received them knew who they were. This information was passed orally from generation to generation. Most of it was lost by the third and fourth generations.

The principal photographs are Cartes de Visite and Cabinet Cards. It is also common to find memorial cards and mass–produced photographs of important military and historical figures. Pictures that show a person in a working environment, identifiable building or street scene, or a special holiday, e.g., Christmas, are eagerly sought. Most studio shots have little value.

Many of the albums were ornately decorated in velvet and applied ormolu. Some covers contained celluloid pictures, ranging in theme from a beautiful young woman to the battleship *Maine*. The Victorian decorating craze drew attention to these albums in the late 1980s. Prices have risen significantly over the last several years.

Cartes de Visite, or calling card photographs were patented in France in 1854, flourished from 1857 to 1910, and survived into the 1920s. The most common Carte de Visite was a $2^1/4$ x $3^3/4$" head and shoulder portrait printed on albumen paper and mounted on a $2^1/2$ x 4" card. Multi–lens cameras were used by the photographer to produce four to eight exposures on a single glass negative plate. A contact print was made from this which would yield four to eight identical photographs on one piece of photographic paper. The photographs would be cut apart and mounted on cards. These cards were put in albums or simply handed out when visiting, similar to today's business cards.

In 1866 the Cabinet Card was introduced in England and shortly thereafter in the United States. It was produced similar to Cartes de Visite, but could have utilized several styles of photographic processes. A Cabinet Card measured 4 x 5" and was mounted on a $4^1/2$ x $6^1/2$" card. Portraits in cabinet size were more appealing because of the larger facial detail and the fact that images could be retouched. By the 1880s the Cabinet Card was as popular as the Carte de Visite and by the 1890s was produced almost exclusively. Cabinet Cards flourished until shortly after the turn of the century.

Tintypes, another photographic form, are also utilized in a Country decor. Sometimes called ferrotypes, they are positive photographs made on a thin iron plate having a darkened surface.

Rural America relied heavily on the formal portrait as a means of documenting family lineage. By the end of the nineteenth century, most towns and villages had one or more photography studios. Far too few of these early professional and semi-professional photographs documented everyday life. Store interior and exterior photographs are the major exception.

Rural America immediately fell in love with Kodak's inexpensive box camera. Early camera owners continued to take primarily family and homestead exterior photographs. However by the 1920s and 30s, amateur photographers became much more adventuresome. Photograph albums containing pictures of daily farm and village life remain strongly undervalued in respect to the historical documentation contained within them.

Most buyers and sellers describe Wallace Nutting colored photographs as prints. They are photographs not prints, which is why they and Wallace Nutting–style colored photographs are included in this category.

Wallace Nutting (1861–1941) was born in Rockingham, Massachusetts. He attended Harvard University from 1883 to 1886 and the Hartford Theological Seminary and Union Theological Seminary between 1886 and 1888. He retired from the ministry in 1904 and opened a photography studio in New York.

Nutting took all his own pictures. Over 10,000 photographs in an assortment of sizes have been identified. By 1913 Nutting's operation was located in Farmingham, Massachusetts, and employed over 200 colorists, framers, salesmen, and support staff. Printing, coloring, framing, and even signing Nutting's name was done by his employees. Business declined sharply in the 1930s. In the early 1970s most of Nutting's negatives were destroyed.

The commercial success of Wallace Nutting's hand-colored, framed photographs spawned a series of imitators. David Davidson (1881–1967), Charles Higgins (1867–1930), Charles Sawyer (born 1904) and his Sawyer Picture Company, and Fred Thompson (1844–1923) are only a few of the dozens of individuals and businesses that attempted to ride Nutting's coattails.

Most of these photographers followed the same procedure as Nutting. They took their own photographs, usually with a glass plate camera. Upon returning to the studio, prints were made on special platinum paper. Substitute paper was used during World War I. Each picture was titled and numbered, usually by the photographer. A model picture was colored. Colorists then finished the remainder of the prints. Finally, the print was matted, titled, signed, and sold.

References: Stuart Bennett, *How to Buy Photographs,* Salem House, 1987; Paul Berg, *Nineteenth Century Photographic Cases and Wall Frames,* published by author, 1995; William C. Darrah, *Cartes de Visite in Nineteenth Century Photography,* William C. Darrah, 1981; B. E. C. Howarth–Loomes, *Victorian Photography: An Introduction for Collectors and Connoisseurs,* St. Martin's Press, 1974; Michael Ivankovich, *Collector's Guide to Wallace Nutting Pictures: Identification & Values,* Collector Books, 1997; Michael Ivankovich, *The Guide to Wallace Nutting–Like Photographers of the Early 20th Century,* Diamond Press, 1991; O. Henry Mace, *Collector's Guide to Early Photographs,* Wallace–Homestead, Krause Publications, 1990; Lou W. McCulloch, *Card Photographs, A Guide to Their History and Value,* Schiffer Publishing, 1981; Floyd and Marion Rinhart, *American Miniature Case Art,* A. S. Barnes, 1969; Susan Theran, *Prints, Posters & Photographs: Identification and Price Guide,* Avon Books, 1993; Susan Theran (ed), *Leonard's Annual Price Index of Prints, Posters & Photographs,* Auction Index, published annually; John Waldsmith, *Stereoviews: An Illustrated History and Price Guide,* Wallace–Homestead, Krause Publications, 1991.

Periodicals: *On Paper,* 39 East 78th Street, #601, New York, NY 10021; *Military Images,* RD 1, Box 99A, Henryville, PA 19332.

Newsletter: *The Photograph Collector,* 301 Hill Avenue, Langhorne, PA 19047.

Collectors' Clubs: American Photographical Historical Society, 1150 Avenue of the Americas, New York, NY 10036; The Daguerreian Society, 3045 West Liberty Avenue, Suite 7, Pittsburgh, PA 15216; National Stereoscopic Assoc, PO Box 14801, Columbus, OH 43214; Photographic Historical Society, Inc, PO Box 39563, Rochester, NY 14604; Photographic Historical Society of Canada, PO Box 54620, Toronto, Ontario, M5M 4N5 Canada; Photographic Society of America, 3000 United Founders Boulevard, Suite 103, Oklahoma City, OK 73112; Wallace Nutting Collectors Club, 186 Mountain Avenue, North Caldwell, NJ 07006.

Note: Prices listed are for cards in excellent condition. Cards with soiling, staining, tears, or copy photographs are worth about half the prices listed. The categories on the list are for the most common or collectible types; other collecting categories do exist.

ALBUM

Leather Cov, emb, presented to Gracie by Mrs. Roger, 1882, 44 tintypes of
  Gracie at ages 4 to 11 with her family, friends, dolls, and pet chicken **$750**
Red Velvet Cov Front and Back, emb scroll design trim on front cov, emb
  brass clasp, gold–edged heavy cardboard pages, 10½ x 14½" **55**

CABINET CARD, BLACK & WHITE

Boy, sitting on tricycle, Kansas **$15**
Fireman, Chicago, 4¼ x 6½" **12**
Girl, standing with bicycle **12**
Howe Sewing Machines Adv, large porcelain doll sitting at small sewing
  machine, text on back **60**
Tom Thumb and Wife, with other unidentified man **20**
Two Women, holding violins, Springfield, NY **8**
Woman, seated, looking at her reflection in mirror, E W Lyon, Maple Rapids,
  MI **10**
Young Girl, studio pose, meadow flowers, doll hanging from rustic fence,
  Gibson, Norwalk, OH **35**

CARTE DE VISITE

All Mine, child surrounded by toys, black and white **$15**
Beating Grandpa, grandfather playing game with grandson, printed, hand
  colored, 1860s **8**

Left: Album, holds cabinet cards, emb lettering and floral dec on celluloid front cov, orange, red, and green velvet back cov, emb brass closure, 8½ x 10¾", $60. Photo courtesy Ray Morykan Auctions.

Right: Daguerreotype, 1½ x 1¼" image, 2 x 1½" red velvet–lined case, $35.

Christmas Tree, boy and girl carrying tree, printed, hand colored, 1860s   12
His Only Pair, grandmother mending grandson's pants, printed, hand
    colored, 1860s   5
Kittens at Peace, 3 kittens, black and white   6
Pool Player, holding cue stick, outdoors, backdrop hung on wall behind   50
Red Riding Hood, in woods, printed, hand colored, 1860s   15
Sinking the Alabama, boy urinating on boat, printed, black and white   20
Tea Party, 2 boys and 2 girls at tea party, girls holding dolls, older boy read-
    ing book, small stove at right, Merz, NY, c1865   100
The Little Barber, girl and cat, printed, hand colored, 1860s   10
Untitled, Civil War Soldier, seated, black and white   10
Untitled, Post Mortem, deceased child in mother's arms, black and white   20
Untitled, Young Dressmaker, 3 girls holding dolls, black and white   12

DAGUERREOTYPE

Elderly Woman, seated at table with book, wearing white bonnet and
    capelet collar, split leather case, 6th plate $30
Girl, wearing gold highlighted jewelry, portrait by A Boisseau, Cleveland,
    velvet emb pad, mat stamped "1856," repaired case, 6th plate   100
Man, wearing eye patch, early mat form, split leather case, pad missing, 6th
    plate   385

PHOTOGRAPH

A February Morning, Charles Sawyer, brook winding through snow covered
    ground and trees, 13 x 16" $200
A Maine Coast Sky, Wallace Nutting, ominous clouds above rocky Maine
    coastline, 13 x 16"   350
An Oak Palm Drive, Wallace Nutting, California road running beneath large
    oak and palm trees, 12 x 16"   350
An Old Drawing Room, Wallace Nutting, girl playing piano, overmat,
    12 x 16"   45
Apple Blossom Lane, Charles R Higgins, country road running between
    blossom trees and orchard walls, 7 x 11"   25
A Puff or Two, Villar, kneeling girl using fireplace bellows near spinning
    wheel, 11 x 14"   75
A Puritan Lady, David Davidson, girl at spinning wheel beside fireplace, 9 x
    12"   70
A Winding Stair, Charles R Higgins, girl climbing hallway stairs near spin-
    ning wheel, 7 x 14"   35
Baseball Player, Kalkaska, MI, black and white, 6 x 9"   10
Birch Brook, Wallace Nutting, autumn birches beside leaf covered pond,
    13 x 16"   85
Boat, *Maid of the Mist*, Niagara Falls, black and white, close–up, 5½ x 6" . . .   15
Charles Lindbergh, standing in front of *Spirit of St Louis*, black and white,
    close–up, 8 x 10"   20
Christmas Day, David Davidson, close–framed snow scene with tracks in
    snow running between snow covered trees and wire fence, signature and
    title, orig label on back, 12 x 16"   16
Christmas Tree, decorated branches, on table, gifts on table and floor, child
    sitting in rocker, black and white, 10 x 12"   25

"Toiler of the Sea," Fred Thompson, hand colored, 13 x 16", $578. Photo courtesy Michael Ivankovich Auction Co.

Civil War Theme, inscribed "Nineteenth Regiment, Iowa Vol. Inf. as they appeared on the 24th day of July at New Orleans, La. after an imprisonment of 10 months in the State of Louisiana and Texas," black and white .. **60**

Day Dreams, Villar, girl sitting on porch chair beneath vine covered porch, 11 x 14" **35**

Fabric Store, Welsh, int of store, black and white, photographer, 10 x 12" **20**

Family Reunion, large family posed on lawn before large house, black and white, 8 x 10" **12**

Fireside Fancy Work, Fred Thompson, girl sewing beside large fireplace, taken in parlor of Wallace Nutting's Southbury, CT, home, 16 x 20" **140**

Gosport Church, Charles Sawyer, hilltop church, 4 x 5" **90**

Homeward Bound, David Davidson, sailing ship at dusk, 4 x 6" **45**

Horse and Buggy, decorated for parade, black and white, close–up, 10 x 12" .. **10**

Knitting for the Boys, Fred Thompson, 2 girls sewing while sitting on front porch beneath large American flag, 14 x 17" **16**

Lumber Camp, mkd "Redy's Camp #2," black and white, 8 x 10" **2**

Lumberjacks, standing on mountain of cut logs, winter view, black and white, 7 x 9" **12**

Mary's Little Lamb, Wallace Nutting, lamb drinking from stream, 13 x 16" ... **200**

Memorial, "The Maine as she Lay in Havana Harbor," statistics on back, black and white, 5 x 7" **10**

Minstrels, 9 men, 6 with black faces, black and white, 8 x 9¾" **20**

President and Mrs Harding, black and white, price for pair **8**

Railroad Men at New Camp B. Oct., 21st 1909, 27 men posed outside building, black and white, 8 x 10" **12**

Road Crew, horse–drawn road graders, black and white, 7 x 9" **10**

School Children, standing in front of school, oak leaves cover bare feet, black and white, 8 x 9½" **15**

Ship, Great Lakes ship *D.C. Kerr*, black and white, glued to cardboard, 4 x 6" .. **8**

Six Master, Fred Thompson, 6–masted sailing ship, 11 x 14" **100**

Spring Delights, sheep grazing beside stream, 11 x 14" **45**

Steamboat, "The Quincy on Mississippi River," black and white, close–up, 5½ x 6½" **15**

Street Car, conductors standing outside, black and white, 5½ x 6½" **10**

Theater Players, man and woman, Keene, NH, black and white, 5³/₄ x 7³/₄" . . .   10
The Fair at Barryton Mich., Oct. 11th 1909, horses and buggies, black and
    white, 9 x 12"   40
US 4th Cavalry, men, wagon, horses, and tents, black and white, 11 x 13" . . .   25
Ye Old Time Call, Florence Thompson, woman in horse–drawn carrriage
    calling on friend at large home, 7 x 9"   100

TINTYPE

Boy, wearing Confederate uniform $80
Civil War Soldier, seated, holding sword, dressed in uniform, in case, 1860s .   150
Girl, doll in doll bed, 2³/₄ x 3¹/₄"   10
Little Girl, sitting on chair, holding dark–haired porcelain doll, album size . . .   35
Outdoor View, house and people, 3¹/₂ x 5"   6
Post Mortem, child, doll under arm, in case, 1860s   60
Two Black Women   20
Two Firemen, wearing dress uniforms, parade ribbons, and hats, "I" on hats
    and belt buckles, posed with draped US flag, album size   18
Woman, Civil War, wearing fancy dress with stars on blouse, holding striped
    shield, 5 x 7"   85

POSTCARDS

America went postcard crazy in the first decades of the twentieth century. Sending postcards to friends and relatives became a national pastime. "Postal" exchanges involving sending packs of unused cards were commonplace.

Special albums were developed to store and display postcards. These quickly found their way onto library shelves and parlor tables. A typical album held between one and two hundred cards. In the past, collectors and dealers stripped the cards from these albums and discarded them. Now they are beginning to realize that there is value in the albums themselves as well as the insight that can be achieved from studying the postcard groupings.

The golden age of postcards dates from 1898 to 1918. While there are cards printed earlier, they are collected for their postal history. Postcards prior to 1898 are called "pioneer" cards.

European publishers, especially in England and Germany, produced the vast majority of cards during the golden age. The major postcard publishers were Raphael Tuck (England), Paul Finkenrath of Berlin (PFB–German), and Whitney, Detroit Publishing Co., and John Winsch (United States). However, many American publishers had their stock produced in Europe, hence, "Made in Bavaria" imprints.

Styles changed rapidly, and manufacturers responded to every need. The linen postcard which gained popularity in the 1940s was quickly replaced by the chrome cards of the post–1950 period.

The more common the holiday, the larger the city, or the more popular the tourist attraction, the easier it will be to find postcards about these subjects because of the millions of cards that still remain in these categories. The smaller runs of "real" photo postcards are the most desirable of the scenic cards. Photographic cards of families and individuals, unless they show occupations, unusual toys, dolls, or teddy bears, have little value.

Stamps and cancellation marks rarely affect the value of a card. When in doubt, consult a philatelic guide.

Postcards fall into two main categories: view cards and topics. View cards are easiest to sell in their local geographic region. European view cards, while very interesting, are difficult to sell in America.

It must be stressed that age alone does not determine price. A birthday postcard from 1918 may sell for only ten cents, while a political campaign card from the 1950s may bring ten dollars. Every collectible is governed by supply and demand.

References: Many of the best books are out of print. However, they are available through libraries. Ask your Library to utilize the Inter–library loan system.

Diane Allmen, *The Official Price Guide to Postcards,* House of Collectibles, 1990; J. L. Mashburn, *The Postcard Price Guide, Third Edition,* Colonial House, 1997; Frederic and Mary Megson, *American Advertising Postcards—Set and Series: 1890–1920,* published by authors, 1985; Susan Brown Nicholson, *The Encyclopedia of Antique Postcards,* Wallace–Homestead, Krause Publications, 1994; Dorothy B. Ryan, *Picture Postcards in the United States, 1893–1918,* Clarkson N. Potter, 1982; paperback edition; Jack H. Smith, *Postcard Companion: The Collector's Reference,* Wallace–Homestead, 1989; Jane Wood, *The Collector's Guide to Post Cards,* L–W Promotions, 1984; 1997 value update.

Periodicals: *Barr's Post Card News,* 70 South 6th Street, Lansing, IA 52151; *Postcard Collector,* PO Box 1050, Dubuque, IA 52004.

Barr's Post Card News and the *Postcard Collector* publish lists of over fifty regional clubs in the United States and Canada.

Collectors' Clubs: Deltiologists of America, PO Box 8, Norwood, PA 19074; Postcard History Society, PO Box 1765, Manassas, VA 22110.

Museum: Curt Teich Postcard Archives, Lake County Museum, Wauconda, IL.

ADVERTISING

BPD Gunshot, hunting dog and equipment	**$50**
Chas F Broadwater Hardware Store, baseball theme, Outcault illus, 1913	50
Cherry Smash, black servant serving George and Martha Washington, "Cherry Smash" spelled out on lawn	100
Chick Golf Balls, "On The Lynx," animals playing golf, sgd "Albertine Randall Wheelan," 1907	40
Continental Rubber Heels, crow looking at box of heels, Germany	65
Dinger & Conard Co, Leading Rose Growers of America, West Grove, PA, undivided back, 1901–07	8
Gaumont Chocolates, "Do You Like Chocolate Drops?," dapper black man, emb, yellow ground	40
Gold Medal Flour, lighthouse at Nice, France, adv for free cookbook, c1905	45
Goodrich Tires, "Best in the Long Run," auto racing donkey on dirt road, 1915	85
Jack Dempsey's Restaurant, printed, black and white, white border	10
La Moreaux Nursery Co, seed catalog, printed, color, divided back, 1913	9
Lasha Bitters, view of lower New York from airship, printed, color, divided back, copyright 1911	10
Lindsay Gas Lights and Gas Mantels, the Lindsay Girl, printed, color, divided back, 1907–15	8
Prudential Insurance, groceries and grocery receipt	40

ARTIST SIGNED

Clapsaddle, Ellen, Halloween, mechanical, black child in white robe, pumpkin in arm moves, #1236, emb, divided back, 1907–15 .... **$150**

Clapsaddle, Ellen, St Patrick's Day, #1249, emb, divided back, 1907–15 8

Fidler, Alice Luella, Utah State Girl, printed, color, divided back, 1907–15 ... 12

Gassaway, Katherine, "What are little boys...," printed, color, undivided
back, 1901–07 10

Gibson, Charles Dana, "In Days to Come the Churches will be Fuller," #103,
pictorial comedy, printed, black and white, divided back, 1907–15 8

Grzeiner, M, Christmas Bear under mistletoe, #791, emb, divided back,
1907–15 8

Kirchner, Raphael, girl, looking at butterfly on flower, Tuck Continental series
4025, printed, color, gilt trim, white border, undivided back, 1901–07 50

Kirchner, Raphael, woman with insects, printed, color, gilt trim, undivided
back, 1901–07 45

Leach, B K, San Francisco fire, comic, printed, color, undivided back, ©1906 . 10

McClure, "On the Golf Links," rabbits playing golf, printed, black and white,
undivided back, 1901–07 ....

O'Neill, Rose, Santa being lowered by Kewpies, Gibson #86180, printed,
color, divided back, 1907–15 45

Outcault, R F, "A Quiet Day in Town," #1, comic souvenir, printed, color,
undivided back, P C Co, 1901–07 10

Outcault, R F, Tige and bees, "Don't Be Surprised," printed, color, undivided
back, J Ottmann Lithograph, 1901–07 8

Price, Mary Evans (MEP), "Christmas Wishes," 2 stockings, baby on pillow,
series 875–C, emb, divided back, 1907–15 8

Twelvetrees, Charles, black girl, series 658, printed, color, divided back,
1907–15 10

GEOGRAPHICAL/SOUVENIR

Columbian Exposition, Manufacturers and Liberal Arts, Transportation, and
Federal buildings, 1893 .... **$125**

Davenport, IA, "Night View Municipal Stadium," linen, printed, color 15

Hot Springs disaster, "Central Ave. looking South from Goddard Hotel after
the fire, Sept. 6, 1913," black and white, divided back, 1907–15 12

New York World's Fair, "The Royal Visitors, King George & Queen Elizabeth,"
Miller Art Co, linen 6

Ohio–Columbus Centennial, 1912 45

St Louis World's Fair, Palace of Arts building, emb, 1904 85

Tonapab, NV, The Bottle House, house made out of bottles, printed, black
and white, divided back, E Mitchell, Publisher, 1907–15 10

Virginia City, MN, bird's–eye view, printed, black and white, divided back,
Stern Publisher, 1907–15 6

HOLIDAY

Christmas, girl holding small dec tree, star background, "A Joyful Christmas,"
hold–to–light, diecut, 1980 .... **$150**

Christmas, Santa and sleeping child, Santa wearing red silk suit, emb, 1909 .. 40

Christmas, Santa in car, wearing red suit, emb, divided back, Winsch, 1913 . .   **30**
Christmas, Santa walking in snow, wearing maroon suit, emb, divided back . .   **15**
Christmas, Tree, child, and toys, photographic, divided back, 1915 . . . .   **20**
Easter, rabbit and girl leaning on tree dec with colored eggs, hold–to–light,
    diecut **60**
Halloween, "A Joyful Halloween," 3 witches riding brooms, man in the
    moon, emb, divided back, Whitney **15**
Halloween, "Hallowe'en," witch and verse, H L Woehler **35**
Halloween, "May Halloween bring you a joy like this," boy, girl, and
    jack–ó–lanterns, series #188, emb, divided back, Tuck, 1907–15 . . . .   **8**
Halloween, "The Halloween Spirit," cat and witch riding broom and bat in
    front of full moon, series 80, emb, divided back, 1909 . . . .   **10**
Halloween, "With Hallowe'en Wishes," man reading book to 2 children,
    ghosts rising from book, emb **85**
St Patrick's Day, Irish girl in front of shamrock, emb, Winsch, 1911 . . . .   **60**
Thanksgiving, Indian couple with turkey, emb, dark green border, divided
    back, Winsch, 1907–15 . . . .   **20**
Valentine's Day, valentine, Japanese girl with cupid, emb, divided back,
    Winsch, 1910 . . . .   **20**
Valentine's Day, valentine, mushroom, large, 1 in installment set, #353,
    emb, divided back, 1907–15 . . . .   **15**

NOVELTY

Copper Harbor, MI, copper, moose, poem, divided back, 1924, 3 x 5¼" **$8**
Empire State Building, card opens, building rises from city, printed, color,
    white border, Sherwin Baas & Co, 1931 . . . .   **12**
Farmer, leather, printed, color, undivided back, 1901–07 . . . .   **6**
Magic Moving Pictures, mechanical, pull tab, man kisses woman, printed,
    black and white, divided back, G Felsenthal & Co, Chicago, Aug 1906 . . . .   **15**
Your Fortune Teller, Oracle, emb, divided back, Charles Gerlach, 1910 . . . . .   **8**

*Left: Holiday,
"A Merry Christmas
to All," emb, divided
back, c1920, $3.*

*Right: Novelty,
"Wish Winter Was
Over," Rotograph Co,
New York City,
divided back, $4.*

PHOTOGRAPHIC, BLACK & WHITE

Colonel W F Cody and his Group of Sioux Indians, divided back, trimmed
on 2 ends, 1907–15 .... **$50**
Deptartment Store, int view 8
Douglas Fir Log Truck, Seattle 20
Electric Trolley, stopped at small shelter with adv for local store, rural area,
used, 1910 25
Harvesting Tobacco, Weston, MO, tobacco drying in field, undivided back,
1901–07 6
Indians, attacking white men, staged, divided back, 1907–15 8
Man and Boy, on horse–drawn ice cream wagon, soft drink and ice cream
signs hanging on sides, parked in front of classic billboards, P. M.
Ashtabula, OH, 1911 95
Masqueraders, 5 people costumed for Halloween, 1 with black face, 1
woman dressed as man, divided back, 1907–15 5
Performing Bears, standing on hind legs, Main St, divided back, 1907–15 ... 35
Pool Hall, int, cigars, tables, divided back, 1907–15 25

POLITICAL

Abraham Lincoln, "Log Cabins to the White House," printed, black and
white, undivided back, 1905 .... **$8**
Charles E Hughes, 1916 campaign 30
Ohio's Seven Presidents, photos of McKinley, Hayes, Harrison, Grant,
Garfield, Harding, and Taft 85
Republican National Convention, Chicago, June 7, 1916, no women, black
and white, divided back 15
Taft for President, elephant with "GOP" on its side, inset black and white
photo, 1908 85
The Prohibition Nominees, Chafin and Watkins, brown and white, 1908 85
Win With Willkie, real photo, 1940 60
Woodrow Wilson, addressing Congress, sepia, divided back, 1907–15 12

TRANSPORTATION

Airplane, "Lincoln Beachy, The World's Greatest Aviator, Souvenir of
Oakland–San Francisco Aviation Meet, Feb 17 to 25, 1912," aeroplane
station and aviation field, black and white, divided back with cancellation . **$40**
Automobile, auto dealer card, 1936 Hudson Super Straight Eight, printed,
color, white border 10
Dirigible, *Goodyear*, linen 8
Great Lake Ship, Clarence A Black, black and white, white border 10
Motor Car, "San Diego & La Jolla Motor Car, San Diego, CA," printed, color,
divided back 6
Motorcycle, attached sidecar, black and white, divided back 12
Paddle Wheeler, Mt Washington on Lake Winnepesaukee, NH, black and
white, divided back, 1907–15 12
Railroad Depot, Gaylord & Alpena Depot, Boyne City, MI, printed, black
and white, divided back, 1907–15 10
Sight–Seeing Car, "Seeing Sandusky, OH," printed, color, divided back,
1907–15 12

PRINTS

Every room in a country home had several wall decorations, the vast majority of which were prints. Several themes dominated—historic, panoramic, nostalgic, patriotic, and religious. In almost every instance, color was the key—the more colorful, the better.

Prints were inexpensive, meaning that they could be changed every few years. Instead of throwing them out, they went into storage. Most prints were framed. In today's market, check the frame. It could be more valuable than the print.

Prints serve many purposes. They can be reproductions of an artist's paintings, drawings, or designs, original art forms, or developed for mass appeal as opposed to aesthetic statement. Much of the production of Currier & Ives fits this last category. Currier & Ives concentrated on genre, urban, patriotic, and nostalgic scenes.

References: William P. Carl and William T. Currier, *Currier's Price Guide to American and European Prints at Auction, Third Edition,* Currier Publications, 1994; Victor J. W. Christie, *Bessie Pease Gutmann: Her Life and Works,* Wallace–Homestead, 1990; Frederic A. Conningham and Colin Simkin, *Currier & Ives Prints, Revised Edition,* Crown Publishers, 1970; Patricia L. Gibson, *R. Atkinson Fox, William M. Thompson: Identification & Price Guide,* Collectors Press, 1995; Martin Gordon, *Gordon's Print Price Annual,* Gordon & Lawrence Art Reference, published annually; William Keagy, et al., *Those Wonderful Yard–Long Prints and More, #3,* published by authors, 1996; Robert Kipp, *Currier's Price Guide to Currier & Ives Prints, Third Edition,* Currier Publications, 1994; Craig McClain, *Currier & Ives: An Illustrated Value Guide,* Wallace–Homestead, 1987; Rita C. Mortenson, *R. Atkinson Fox: His Life and Work, Revised,* L–W Book Sales, 1991; Rita C. Mortenson, *R. Atkinson Fox, Book Two,* L–W Book Sales, 1992; Susan Theran, *Prints, Posters & Photographs: Identification and Price Guide,* Avon Books, 1993; Susan Theran (ed), *Leonard's Annual Price Index of Prints, Posters & Photographs,* Auction Index, published annually.

Periodicals: *Journal of the Print World,* 1008 Winona Road, Meredith, NH 03253; *On Paper,* 39 East 78th Street, #601, New York, NY 10021.

Collectors' Clubs: American Antique Graphics Society, 5185 Windfall Road, Medina, OH 44256; American Historical Print Collectors Society, PO Box 201, Fairfield, CT 06430.

Museums: American Museum of Natural History, New York, NY; John James Audubon Museum, Henderson, KY; Museum of Prints & Printmaking, Albany, NY; Museum of the City of New York, New York, NY.

Reproduction Alert: Reproductions are a problem, especially Currier & Ives prints. Check the dimensions before buying a print.

Audubon, John James, "American Badger," Plate 47, Philadelphia: Bowen, 1844, hand colored litho from folio edition of *Audubon's Viviparous Quadrupeds,* snarling badger protecting recently killed bird **$1,000**
Audubon, John James, "Downy Squirrel," Plate 25, New York, 1845–48, hand colored litho from folio edition of *Viviparous Quadrupeds,* 2 smiling squirrels, light soiling along edge 315
Bachelder, John Bader, publisher, Henry Bryan Hall, Jr, engraver, "Gettysburg," engraving on paper, identified within matrix, framed, sheet size 18½ x 37¼" 325

Bartlett, William Henry, "View from Mt Holyoke," hand colored litho, 8" w, 6" h **65**

Baumann, Gustave, "Big Timber Upper Pecos," color woodblock on laid paper, sgd "Gustave Baumann" in pencil with hand in heart chop lower right, titled in pencil lower left, numbered "15 of 100" in pencil lower center, identified on labels on back, framed, 9³/₄ x 11¹/₄" **1,100**

Besler, Basilius, "Solanum Pomiferum with a sprig of Amaracus Vulgaris," Eichstadt and Nuremberg, 1613, hand colored engraved plate from Besler's *Hortus Eystettensis*, full folio sheet, clean, expertly matted **2,300**

Bodmer, Karl, "Indians Hunting the Bison," London: Ackermann, 1839–44, etched, engraved, and aquatint plate from *Maximilian, Prince zu Weid's Travels in the Interior of North America*, wide margins, plate size 400 x 535mm **860**

Bradford, LH and Co, lithographers, "To the Firemen and Citizens of Troy N.Y....Presented by Union Fire Company No. Three of Providence, R.I.... 1854," chromolitho with hand coloring on paper, identified within matrix, staining and scattered foxing, period frame, sheet size 19¹/₄ x 14¹/₂" **325**

Brookshaw, George, London, 1807, hand colored aquatint plate of a pineapple, from Brookshaw's *Pomona Britannica*, full folio sheet, matted, framed . **5,500**

Calder, Alexander, "Spider's Nest," color litho, sgd in pencil lower right, numbered 25/95, 29¹/₂ x 43¹/₄" **500**

Left: Prideaux Selby, "Peregrine Falcon, Plate XV," Edinburgh, 1819, hand colored engraved plate, from Selby's **Illustrations of British Ornithology,** *wide margins, archivally matted, 410 x 265mm, $805.*

Right: Karl Bodmer, "Junction of the Yellow Stone River with the Missouri, Tableau 29," London: Ackermann, 1839–44, etched, engraved, and aquatint plate, from **Maximilian, Prince zu Weid's Travels in the Interior of North America,** *wide margins, emb Bodmer stamp beneath publisher's imprint, 415 x 545mm, $1,092.*

Photos courtesy Swann Galleries.

Currier and Ives, publishers, 1857–1907, "American Homestead Summer," minor stains in margins, repaired tear in top margin, matted and framed, c1868, 15³/₄" h, 19¹/₂" w **225**

Currier and Ives, publishers, 1857–1907, "Bombardment & Capture of Fort Henry Tennessee," ironclads firing on fort in distance, small folio, some stains in margin, 9" h, 13" w **200**

Currier and Ives, publishers, 1857–1907, "George M Matchen, Brown Dick and Millers Damsel," 3 racing sulkies with riders, fenced and wood background, large folio, foxing lines and areas, some scrapes in sky, oak frame, sight size 21" h, 29¹/₄" w **800**

Currier and Ives, publishers, 1857–1907, "Pacing Horse 'Billy Boyce' of St. Louis," racing horse with jockey, large folio, foxing, 1 vertical line and spots, stains to bottom margin, sight size 21" h, 29" w **600**

Currier and Ives, publishers, 1857–1907, "Siege And Capture Of Vicksburg, Mississippi, July 4th, 1863," soldiers attacking hill, large explosion in background, small folio, some spots, sight size 9¹/₂" h, 13¹/₂" w **175**

Currier and Ives, publishers, 1857–1907, "The American Fireman, Facing The Enemy," fireman hosing down flames, discoloration to border, tear 2¹/₂" from top, corner tip missing, 22³/₄" h, 17³/₄" w **650**

Currier and Ives, publishers, 1857–1907, "The Burning Of Chicago," view from water of raging fire through city with ships and train in foreground, small folio, some minor discoloration, sight size 12¹/₂" h, 16¹/₂" w **325**

Currier and Ives, publishers, 1857–1907, "The Celebrated Boston Team Mill Boy and Blondine...," chromolitho on paper, fully identified in inscription lower margin, staining, losses, stray pencil marks, 1882, framed, sheet size 24¹/₂ x 36⁵/₈" **325**

Currier and Ives, publishers, 1857–1907, "The Express Train," hand colored litho on paper, touches of gum arabic, red pencil inscription in lower left margin corner, slight soiling, sheet size 10 x 14" **1,760**

Currier and Ives, publishers, 1857–1907, "The Fall Of Richmond Virginia On The Night Of April 2, 1865," Richmond ablaze with carriages and people fleeing city over bridge, small folio, border obscured by white mat, sight size 9" h, 13" w **150**

Currier and Ives, publishers, 1857–1907, "The Fight At Charleston South Carolina April 7, 1863," 9 ironclads firing on Fort Sumter, small folio, white mat obscures border, 3 rect areas of discoloration, possible tape marks, sight size 9³/₄" h, 13¹/₂" w **250**

Currier and Ives, publishers, 1857–1907, "The Great Ocean Yacht Race between the Henrietta, Fleetwing and Vesta...," Charles Parsons lithographer, printed color, additional hand coloring, heavy paperboard, fully identified in inscriptions in lower margin, label from the Old Print Shop, NY, on back, framed, sheet size 23¹/₈ x 32³/₄" **2,200**

Currier and Ives, publishers, 1857–1907, "The Ivy Bridge," pen and ink presentation inscription in border, stains, framed, 17" w, 12³/₄" h **75**

Currier and Ives, publishers, 1857–1907, "The Miniature Ship Red, White and Blue," hand colored litho on paper, fully identified in inscriptions in lower margin, toning, minor wrinkles, framed, sheet size 12 x 16" **150**

Currier and Ives, publishers, 1857–1907, "The US Sloop of War, Kearage Seven Guns, sinking the Pirate Alabama Eight Guns," hand colored litho heightened by gum arabic on paper, fully identified in inscriptions in lower margin, matted, unframed, 1864, sheet size 13¹/₂ x 17¹/₄" **225**

Currier, Nathaniel, publisher, "American Country Life/May Morning,"
Frances Flora (Fanny) Palmer lithographer, printed color on paper, additional hand coloring, fully identified in lower margin, period frame, 1855,
sheet size 20¼ x 26¾"   650

Currier, Nathaniel, publisher, "Clipper Ship Nightingale," Charles Parsons
lithographer, hand colored litho on paper, fully identified in inscription in
lower margin, label from Old Print Shop, NY, on reverse, framed, 1854,
sheet size 18¾ x 25" 3,000

Currier, Nathaniel, publisher, "The Sinking of the Cumberland [sic] by the
Iron Clad Merrimac off Newport News, VA, March 8th 1862," hand colored litho, fully identified in inscription in lower margin, framed, sheet
size 12 x 15½"   450

Currier, Nathaniel, publisher, Elliot, Daniel Giraud, "Dusky Grouse/
Hartlaub's Spruce Grouse," New York, 1864–65, pair of hand colored
litho plates, from Elliot's A Monograph of the Tetraoninae, large folio
sheets, archivally matted   575

Endicott & Co, "New York Clipper Ship Challenge...," litho, printed color,
additional hand coloring, fully identified in inscription beneath image,
label from Old Print Ship, NY on reverse, framed, 1852, sheet size
23½ x 32½" 3,300

Endicott & Co, "View of Newburyport, Massachusetts," after John Badger
Bachelder, hand colored litho, gum arabic, heavy paper, identified in
inscription on reverse, framed, sheet size 22¾ x 29½"   400

Gearhart, Frances Hammel, "Incoming Fog," color woodblock on Japan
paper, sgd "Frances H. Gearhart" in pencil lower right, titled in pencil
lower left, minor creasing, tape to edges, matted and framed, 10 x 11" 1,430

*Left: Basilius Besler, "Tulipa lutea maculis aspersa minutis and friends," Eichstadt and
Nuremberg, 1613, hand colored engraved plate from Besler's Hortus Eystettensis, full folio
sheet, text visible from verso, archivally matted, $2,300.* Photo courtesy Swann Galleries.

*Right: Nathaniel Currier, publisher, "American Farm Scene No. 1," c1853, hand colored
lithograph, slight discoloration, soiled margins, framed, 16¹⁵/₁₆ x 23⁷/₈" image, $1,725.*
Photo courtesy William Doyle Galleries.

Grant Wood, "Seed Time and Harvest," dated 1937, artist sgd, $1,900.

Gould, John, "Gallinula Chloropus/Podiceps Nigricollis," London, 1860s, pair of hand colored litho plates of waterfowl, from Gould's *Birds of England*, folio sheets, slight mat burn at edges, price for pair **750**

Illman & Sons, publisher, "The Declaration of Independence and Portraits of the Presidents," Philadelphia, c1858, engraved, wide margins, portraits of presidents through Buchanan surround engraved text of Declaration, 505 x 405mm **250**

Low, David, 8 hand colored plates of farm animals, from Low's *Breeds of the Domestic Animals of the British Isles*, London, 1840–42, small folio sheets, each slightly toned, scattered foxing, price for 8 . . . . **750**

Mayer and Stetfield, lithographers, "Built by the Amoskeag Manufacturing Co, Manchester, NH," printed litho on paper, black and tan, identified within the matrix, staining, foxing, minute abrasions, period frame, sheet size 19½ x 27½" **465**

Norton, Elizabeth, "Library Step, Stanford University," color woodblock on Japan paper, sgd and dated "E. Norton 1922" in pencil lower right, monogrammed in block lower right, annotated "del. sc et imp" lower left, 5½ x 4½", framed **500**

Pennant, Thomas, "The Little Owl," London, 1761–66, hand colored engraved plate from Pennant's *British Zoology*, folio sheet, scattered light browning, archivally matted **125**

Selby, Prideaux, "Common Buzzard, Female," Plate VI, Edinburgh, 1819, large hand colored plate from Selby's *Illustrations of British Ornithology*, wide margins, archivally matted, 545 x 410mm **450**

Thayer & Co, Boston, Lithographers, "View of the Grand Mass Washingtonian Convention on Boston Common on the 30th of May, 1844," hand colored litho on paper, full typographical inscription below image, 8½ x 13½" image, period burl walnut frame, staining and fading . . **175**

Unknown Artist, "Birdseye View, Centennial Buildings, Phila 1876," chromolitho, shadowbox frame with gilt liner, 30¼" w, 24" h **50**

Unknown Artist, "G Washington," black and white litho, eglomise glass and gilt frame, 7⅝" w, 9½" h **38**

Unknown Artist, "Landscape, Bethlehem, Pennsylvania," hand colored engraving, stains, small tears and repairs in margins, framed, 24" w, 18¼" h **110**

Unknown Artist, "Red Peony," Pratt, chromolitho, matted and framed, 9⅞ x 12⅞" **100**

SHEET MUSIC

The parlor piano played a major role in the social life of the country homestead. Family members could often play one or more musical instruments. Families kept abreast of the latest tunes through the purchase of sheet music. Catalogs were the principal source of supply.

Sheet music often was exchanged among friends, thus accounting for the large number of sheets found with an individual's name added in pencil or ink on the cover. Music sheets frequently were bound in volumes. A young bride took her volumes with her when establishing a new home. Based upon the quantity and variety of sheet music found at country auctions, rural Americans were musically literate.

Sheet music, especially piano scores, dates to the early nineteenth century. Early music sheets contain some of the finest examples of American lithography.

Sheet music covers chronicle the social and political trends of any historical period. The golden age of the illustrated cover dates from 1885. Leading artists such as James Montgomery Flagg used their talents in the sheet music industry. The cover frequently sold the song.

Once radio and talking pictures became popular, sheet music covers featured the stars. A song sheet might be issued in as many as six different cover versions depending on who was featured. When piano playing lost popularity in the 1950s, the market for sheet music declined. Further, song sheets failed to maintain their high quality of design. There is little collector interest in sheet music issued after 1960 unless associated with a famous personality or rock group.

Center your collection around a theme—show tunes, songs of World War I, Sousa marches, black material, songs by a particular lyricist or composer—the list is endless. Beware of dealers who attach a high price to subject theme sheets based upon the concept that the specialized collector will pay anything to get what they want. Learn the value of a sheet to a sheet music collector and buy accordingly.

Be careful about stacking your sheets on top of one another. Cover inks tend to bleed. The most ideal solution is to place acid free paper between each cover and sheet. Unfortunately, people used tape to repair tears in old sheet music. This discolors and detracts from value. Seek professional help in removing tape from rarer sheets.

References: Debbie Dillon, *Collectors Guide to Sheet Music,* L–W Promotions, 1988, 1995 value update; Marie–Reine A. Pafik and Anna Marie Guiheen, *The Sheet Music Reference and Price Guide, Second Edition,* Collector Books, 1995; Marion Short, *The Gold in Your Piano Bench: Collectible Sheet Music,* Schiffer Publishing, 1997; Marion Short, *More Gold in Your Piano Bench: Collectible Sheet Music,* Schiffer Publishing, 1997.

Note: It is the author's opinion that the pricing in the Pafik and Guiheen guide is inaccurate and highly manipulative. The book has been roundly criticized, and rightly so, within the sheet music community.

Periodical: *Sheet Music Magazine,* PO Box 58629, Boulder, CO 80321.

Newsletter: *The Rag Times,* 15522 Ricky Court, Grass Valley, CA 95949.

Collectors' Clubs: City of Roses Sheet Music Collectors Club, 13447 Bush Street SE, Portland, OR 97236; National Sheet Music Society, 1597 Fair Park Avenue, Los Angeles, CA 90041; New York Sheet Music Society, PO Box 354, Hewlett, NY 11557; Remember That Song, 5623 North 64th Avenue, Glendale, AZ 85301; Sonneck Society for American Music & Music in America, PO Box 476, Canton, MA 02021.

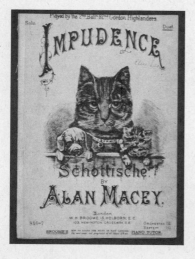 

Left: Impudence, *Alan Macey, $12.*

Right: On the Honeymoon Express, *Lou Klein, James Kendis, and Frank Stilwell, 1913, $10.*

Just a Lonely Hobo, Cole, Autry cov, 1932 20
Lay Him Low Dirge, dedicated in memory to Gen'l Philip Kearny, 1863,
    10 x 13" 50
Lincoln Centennial March, E T Paull, New York, 1909, 11 x 14" 65
Listen to the Mocking Bird, Drumheller, 1908 8
Little Orphan Annie 15
Meet Me in St Louis, Louis, 1904 5
Moonbeams and Dreams of You, 1907 4
Mother O'Mine, Rudyard Kipling, 1903 10
Mrs Casey Jones, Newton, 1915 30
Muzzle the Back Seat Driver & Drive Wherever You May, McDermott, 1928 .. 12
My Prairie Songbird, Indian girl cov, 1909 3
Oh How I Hate to Get Up in the Morning, Irving Berlin, 1914 7
Oh Susanna, 1923, 9 x 12" 45
Oh Susanna, 1935, Foster 4
On the Atchinson, Topeka & Santa Fe, Judy Garland cov, 1945 25
Our Flag & Freedom, 1917 3
Over the Rainbow, whole cast pictured on cov 30
Paul Revere's Ride, E T Paull, black and white 30
Red River Valley, Gene Autry cov, 1935 10
Rockaway—Or On Old Long Island's Sea Girt Shore, Geo P Reed, Boston,
    1860, 10 x 14" 65
Rosey's Scorcher, George Rosey, 1897, 11 x 14" 70
Saratoga Schottisch, Horace Waters, New York, 1851, 13 x 10" 85
Scorcher, Popular Bicycle Song, Willis Woodward, 1897, 11 x 14" 95
Silver Sleigh Bells, E T Paull color illus, 1906 30
Skating Rink Girl, W Woodward & Co, New York, 1907, 11 x 14" 45
Texas—Where the Mockin' Bird Is Singin', Passenger Department, Texas &
    Pacific Railway, 1898, 11 x 14" 100
That International Rag, Irving Berlin, Uncle Sam cov 10
The Banjo Pickers, Frederic Groton, Carl Fisher Inc, green illus, white back-
    ground, 1929 20
The Baseball, Johann C Schmid, published by United States Music Co, blue
    on yellow, 1915 50
The Dying Drummer, Thomas Manahan & Mrs Parkhurst, 1864, 10 x 14" 35
The Grandpappy Polka, Johnny Giacoma, Gordon Jennings, 1947 5
The Light of Western Stars, Zeke Williams, 1945 5
The Little Ford Rambled Right Along, C R Foster, 1914, 11 x 14" 50
The Midnight Fire Alarm, E T Paull, minor wear 25
The Trolley Song, Judy Garland, 1944 35
Union Soldier's Battle Song, Oliver Ditson & Co, Boston, 1864, 10 x 13" 35
When I Dream About the Wabash, Roy Rogers, 1945 10
When It's Circus Day Back Home, c1917 8
White Christmas, Irving Berlin, 1924 7
You're the Top, Cole Porter, 1934 5

POTTERY & PORCELAIN

Rural housewives liked their pottery and porcelain to be decorative, functional, and durable. While the family may have owned a set of bone china to use on holidays and when special guests visited, their ordinary dinner service was a modestly priced set of American dinnerware.

Use was heavy, breakage inevitable. Replacement pieces had to be readily available. An everyday dinner service lasted between ten and fifteen years before needing to be replaced. When acquiring a new service, the rural housewife wanted the latest pattern.

American dinnerware manufacturers made patterns that appealed strongly to the rural family. Designs were simple and colorful. Bodies and glazes were thick. Fruits and animals often were part of the pattern. Colors were vivid, albeit several patterns stressed pastels and earth tones.

Occasionally sets were assembled through premium offers from a manufacturer, grocery store, or movie theater. The premiums normally provided only place setting pieces. Serving pieces were sold during the premium giveaway period.

Pottery storage vessels were common during the nineteenth century. Redware had to be glazed on the interior to prevent it from leaking. Pottery baking molds were an important kitchen utensil.

Every rural housewife kept a stash of pottery vases. Flower beds and gardens were a source of pride and accomplishment. Products from Roseville and Weller were highly favored. Occasionally an art pottery piece joined the stash.

Among the pottery in a rural homestead were family heirlooms, objects that belonged to grandparents and great grandparents. Most of these were English in origin since "English" pottery was perceived to be more valuable. English softpaste, especially pieces decorated in gaudy patterns, flow blue, historical Staffordshire, and Staffordshire chimney ornaments are a few of the most commonly found forms.

Finally, do not overlook the souvenir china, ranging in form from plates to vases. This category is still surprisingly affordable. Many pieces sell for under twenty–five dollars despite the fact that they date from the turn of the century.

References: Susan and Al Bagdade, *Warman's American Pottery and Porcelain,* Wallace–Homestead, Krause Publications, 1994; Susan and Al Bagdade, *Warman's English & Continental Pottery & Porcelain, Second Edition,* Wallace–Homestead, Krause Publications, 1991; Jo Cunningham, *Collector's Encyclopedia of American Dinnerware,* Collector Books, 1982, 1995 value update; Jo Cunningham, *The Best of Collectible Dinnerware,* Schiffer Publishing, 1995; Gerald DeBolt, *DeBolt's Dictionary of American Pottery Marks: Whiteware and Porcelain,* Collector Books, 1993; Harvey Duke, *The Official Identification and Price Guide to Pottery and Porcelain, Eighth Edition,* House of Collectibles, 1995; Paul Evans, *Art Pottery of the United States,* Feingold & Lewis Publishing Corp, 1987; Joanne Jasper, *Turn of the Century American Dinnerware 1880s to 1920s,* Collector Books, 1996; William C. Ketchum, Jr., *American Pottery and Porcelain,* Avon Books, 1994; Ralph and Terry Kovel, *Kovels' American Art Pottery: The Collector's Guide to Makers, Marks and Factory Histories,* Crown Publishers, 1993; Lois Lehner, *Lehner's Encyclopedia of US Marks on Pottery, Porcelain & Clay,* Collector Books, 1988.

Periodical: *The Daze,* PO Box 57, Otisville, MI 48463.

Collectors' Clubs: American Art Pottery Assoc, 125 East Rose Avenue, St Louis, MO 63119; American Ceramic Circle, 419 Gate Lane, Philadelphia, PA 19119; Pottery

Lovers Reunion, 4969 Hudson Drive, Stow, OH 44224; Southern Folk Pottery Collectors Society, 1828 North Howard Mill Road, Robbins, NC 27325.

Museums: Everson Museum of Art of Syracuse and Onondago County, Syracuse, NY; George Gardiner Museum of Ceramic Art, Toronto, Canada; Museum of Ceramics at East Liverpool, East Liverpool, OH; National Museum of American History, Washington, DC; National Museum of Ceramic Art, Baltimore, MD; The Jones Museum of Glass & Ceramics, East Baldwin, ME.

ABINGDON

The Abingdon Sanitary Manufacturing Company, Abingdon, Illinois, was founded in 1908 for the purpose of manufacturing plumbing fixtures. Sometime during 1933–34 Abingdon introduced a line of art pottery ranging from decorative pieces to vases. The company produced over 1,000 shapes and used over 150 colors to decorate their wares. In 1945 the company changed its name to Abingdon Potteries, Inc. Production of the art pottery line continued until 1950 when fire destroyed the art pottery kiln.

After the fire, the company placed its emphasis once again on plumbing fixtures. Eventually, Abingdon Potteries became Briggs Manufacturing Company, a firm noted for its sanitary fixtures.

Reference: Joe Paradis, *Abingdon Pottery Artware: 1934–1950,* Schiffer Publishing, 1997.

Collectors' Club: Abingdon Pottery Club, 210 Knox Highway 5, Abingdon, IL 61410.

Bookends, pr, cactus, #370	$65
Bookends, pr, fern leaf, #428, 5½" h	45
Bookends, pr, horse head, #441, white	70
Bookends, pr, quill, #595, black and white	125
Bowl, oval, #547, blue	18
Bowl, ripple, #644, 6" h	22
Bowl, scallop, #564, pink	15
Bowl, shell, #501, pink	25
Box, candy cane, #607D, 4½" d	95
Box, rosebud, #585D, 4½" d	80
Bud Vase, #483, 8" h	35
Cache Pot, #558, floral design, 4¾" h	25
Candle Holders, pr, daisy, #384, 4½" d	20
Candle Holders, pr, sunburst, #447, 8" h	50
Console Bowl, #125, 11 x 6¼" h	50
Console Bowl, #180, scalloped, 17" d	40
Console Bowl, #532, dark blue	25
Console Bowl, #532, gold trim dec	40
Console Bowl, #532, light blue	25
Cookie Jar, "Choo Choo" Locomotive, #651	175
Cookie Jar, Cutie Pie, blue	185
Cookie Jar, floral plaid, #697, 8½" h	110
Cookie Jar, hobbyhorse, #602	450
Cookie Jar, jack–ó–lantern	350
Cookie Jar, Mother Goose, #695	325

Cookie Jar, pumpkin, #674 .... **385**
Cookie Jar, rocking horse **75**
Cookie Jar, sitting baby, on lid, #561, 11" h **600**
Cookie Jar, windmill, #678 .... **275**
Cornucopia, single, floral design, #220, 7" h **25**
Cornucopia, single, white, #303, 7½" h **60**
Creamer, Daisy **12**
Figure, Goose, #571, 5" h **35**
Flowerpot, Le Fleur, nesting, set of 4, #149, 3" h **15**
Flowerpot, Le Fleur, nesting, set of 4, #149D, 4" h **25**
Flowerpot, Le Fleur, nesting, set of 4, #150, 4" h **15**
Flowerpot, Le Fleur, nesting, set of 4, #150D, 5" h **30**
Jam Jar, Daisy, strawberry lid **15**
Planter, donkey, #669, blue **35**
Planter, fan, #484, dark green, raised bow at base, 4¾" h, 9" l ... **12**
Planter, gourd, #667, 5½" h **30**
Planter, puppy, #652D, 6¾" l **45**
Urn, Regency, #539, white **15**
Vase, #101, mint green, glazed, mkd "Abingdon USA" in stamped block on
  2 lines, and imp "101" on bottom, 9½ h, 6" d at top ... **20**
Vase, #324, scalloped edges, 6" h **35**
Vase, Hollyhock, #496, 7½" h **30**
Vase, Morning Glory, #391 .... **40**
Vase, Tulip, #654 .... **25**
Vase, Wreath, #467, 8" h **30**
Wall Pocket, butterfly, 9" h **65**
Wall Pocket, carriage, #711, white **5**
Wall Pocket, cookbook, #676D **50**
Wall Pocket, Dutch boy, #489, 10" h **125**
Wall Pocket, fern leaf, #431 .... **110**
Wall Pocket, ivy hanging basket, #590D **65**
Wall Pocket, leaf, #724 .... **35**
Wall Pocket, shell, #508 .... **90**
Window Box, #498, Han L G, 14½" l **20**

Left: Abingdon, vase, #550, fluted, white, stamped "Abingdon U.S.A." in rectangle, 1941–50, 11¾" h, $30.

Right: American Bisque, cookie jar, churn, mkd "USA," $25.

AMERICAN BISQUE

The American Bisque Company, founded in Williamstown, West Virginia, in 1919, first manufactured china head dolls. Within a few years, the company expanded its line to include ashtrays, cookie jars, giftware, planters, salt and pepper shakers, and serving dishes.

B. E. Allen, founder of the Sterling China Company, was a heavy investor, eventually purchasing the company's entire stock. In 1982 the company changed hands, operating briefly as the American China Company. Operations ceased in 1983.

American Bisque Company products are found with a variety of markings. "Sequoia Ware" is usually found on items manufactured for sale in gift shops. The Berkeley trademark was used on pieces sold in chain stores. A stack of three baby blocks with the letters "A," "B," and "C" is the most commonly found mark.

American Bisque Company's figural cookie jars and planters, because of their whimsical, child-like designs executed in pastel and earth tones, are extremely popular with Country collectors. Avoid examples with glaze or paint loss. Do not buy until you find an example in fine condition or better.

Reference: Mary Jane Giacomini, *American Bisque: A Collector's Guide With Prices,* Schiffer Publishing, 1994.

Cookie Jar, animal crackers **$40**
Cookie Jar, barrel, mkd "Cookie Barrel" on side, 9½" h **40**
Cookie Jar, basket, cookie dec on lid, mkd "USA," 11¼" h **65**
Cookie Jar, beehive, flower and butterfly dec, applied kitten on lid, 11¾" h .. **35**
Cookie Jar, carousel, knob finial **50**
Cookie Jar, cat in basket **50**
Cookie Jar, chef, 11¼" h **40**
Cookie Jar, churn, fruit and leaf dec, brown lid, "USA" imp mark, 10¾" h ... **25**
Cookie Jar, coffeepot, pine cone dec, 9½" h **35**
Cookie Jar, "Cookies & Milk" Wagon, horse wearing blue hat and pulling
    wagon, 9" h **55**
Cookie Jar, cowboy boots, some int crazing **100**
Cookie Jar, Davy Crockett **350**
Cookie Jar, granny **125**
Cookie Jar, hobo, holding chalkboard, 14" h **125**
Cookie Jar, jack-in-the-box, yellow and blue, 12" h **50**
Cookie Jar, lantern, 13" h **60**
Cookie Jar, merry-go-round, mkd "USA" on side, 9¼" h **35**
Cookie Jar, milk can, bell on lid, "After School Snacks" in black **35**
Cookie Jar, pig, brown ruffle at neck, hands in pockets, 8¾" h **45**
Cookie Jar, potbellied stove, 11¼" h **25**
Cookie Jar, rabbit in hat, blue **45**
Cookie Jar, recipe jar, hexagonal shape, 9½" h **45**
Cookie Jar, rooster, multicolored, 11¼" h **45**
Cookie Jar, sadiron, yellow and white rooster dec on front, figural black iron
    lid, 11½" h **55**
Cookie Jar, sitting horse **150**
Cookie Jar, striped cat, pink bow, applied tail handle on lid, 10½" h **65**
Cookie Jar, The Cow Jumped Over the Moon, mkd "806 USA" on back, 11" h ... **120**
Cookie Jar, thread spool, applied yellow spool on lid, 10¾" h **75**

Cookie Jar, water bucket, brown, applied dipper on lid, "USA" imp mark on
back, 9³/₄" h **50**
Planter, bears at tree, 5¹/₂" h **12**
Planter, cat with fish bowl, 5³/₄ x 7" **20**
Planter, Dutch girl with tulips, 7¹/₂" h **15**
Planter, farmer pig with corn, 6¹/₈" h **8**
Planter, Little Davy Crockett, 5" h **45**
Planter, parakeet on stump, 6¹/₂" h **12**
Planter, pushcart man, 5⁷/₈" h **15**
Planter, rearing circus horse, 6³/₄" h **30**
Planter, reclining horse, 6¹/₂" l **12**
Planter, wailing kitten **20**
Salt and Pepper Shakers, pr, churn **65**
Salt and Pepper Shakers, pr, Figaro **75**

AUTUMN LEAF

The Hall China Company of East Liverpool, Ohio, developed the Autumn Leaf pattern as a premium line for the Jewel Tea Company in 1933. Mixing bowls and other kitchenware were the first items produced. Hall introduced Autumn Leaf dinnerware in 1936 when it manufactured a decal–decorated breakfast set. The demand for Autumn Leaf was so great during the 1930s that it is credited with keeping The Hall China Company in business during the Depression.

As the popularity of the Autumn Leaf pattern spread, Hall licensed the decorative use of the Autumn Leaf pattern to manufacturers of glass, metal, and textiles for the kitchen. Several other ceramic manufacturers, including American Limoges and Harker, also made products using an Autumn Leaf motif.

Pieces were continually added and dropped from the line. Those produced for a short period of time are harder to find and usually have the highest value. Hall ceased production of Autumn Leaf in 1978.

The pattern's appeal to Country collectors is twofold. First is the pattern's muted, fall, earth tones. Second is the memories of the pattern actually being used in grandmother's or mother's kitchen.

References: C. L. Miller, *Jewel Tea: Sales and Houseware Collectibles,* Schiffer Publishing, 1995; C. L. Miller, *The Jewel Tea Company: Its History and Products,* Schiffer Publishing, 1994; Margaret and Kenn Whitmyer, *The Collector's Encyclopedia of Hall China, Second Edition,* Collector Books, 1994, 1997 value update.

Collectors' Club: National Autumn Leaf Collectors Club, 62200 East 236 Road, Wyandotte, OK 74370.

Ball Jug, #3 . . . . **$45**
Berry Bowl **5**
Bowl, Radiance, #5, 9" d **25**
Bowl, Sunshine, #4 . . . . **20**
Bread and Butter Plate, Ruffled–D, 6" d **5**
Bread Box, tin **150**
Bud Vase **200**
Butter Dish, 1 lb **500**
Cake Plate, metal stand **145**

```
Cake Server .................................................... 525
Candlesticks, pr ................................................. 75
Candy Dish, metal base .......................................... 430
Clock, battery operated ......................................... 250
Coffee Canister, tin, 4" h ........................................ 35
Coffeepot, drip coffee, all china ................................ 250
Coffeepot, electric, Rayed, 9 cup ................................ 65
Cookie Jar, Rayed ............................................... 175
Cookie Jar, Zeisel .............................................. 175
Creamer .......................................................... 5
Creamer and Sugar ............................................... 45
Cream Soup ...................................................... 30
Cup, St Denis ................................................... 22
Cup and Saucer .................................................. 12
Custard, Radiance ................................................ 6
Dinner Plate, 10" d ............................................. 20
Drip Jar ........................................................ 15
Dutch Oven, 5 qt ............................................... 100
Flour Sifter, tin ............................................... 350
Flute French Baker, 2 pt ........................................ 145
Fondue Set ..................................................... 200
Gravy Boat ...................................................... 30
Luncheon Plate, 9" d ............................................ 12
Marmalade, 3 pc ................................................ 125
Marmalade, with underplate ...................................... 90
Mayonnaise, with underplate, cov ................................ 50
Mug, Conic ...................................................... 50
Mug, Irish coffee .............................................. 110
Mustard and Underplate .......................................... 45
Pickle Dish, Ruffled–D .......................................... 35
Pie Plate ....................................................... 40
Platter, oval, 11³/₈" l ........................................... 8
Reamer, orange .................................................. 80
Salad Bowl ...................................................... 20
Salad Fork ..................................................... 500
Salt and Pepper Shakers, pr, handle ............................. 50
Sauce Pan, 2 qt ................................................. 60
Saucer ........................................................... 2
Skillet, 9¹/₂" d ................................................. 90
Stack Set, 4 pc ................................................ 125
Sugar, 1940 ..................................................... 30
Tea Canister, tin, copper lid, 4" h ............................. 35
Teapot, Aladdin ................................................. 75
Tidbit, 3 tier, Ruffled–D ...................................... 120
Tidbit, 2 tier .................................................. 75
Tumbler, frosted, 5¹/₂" h ....................................... 20
Utility Jug ..................................................... 20
Vegetable Bowl, oval, divided .................................. 125
Warmer, oval ................................................... 140
Warmer, round .................................................. 225
```

Left: Autumn Leaf, gravy boat, $30.

Right: Bauer, Ring mixing bowl, yellow, imp "Bauer 18," 8¹/₂" d, $40. Photo courtesy Ray Morykan Auctions.

BAUER

In 1909 John Andrew Bauer established the Bauer Pottery in Los Angeles, California by relocating workers from the former family owned Paducah Pottery, Paducah, Kentucky. Carloads of machinery were shipped from the Kentucky factory to the new plant.

Production included utilitarian items and an artware line. At one point Bauer was the only California pottery manufacturing red clay flowerpots, which accounted for half the company's sales. The Bauer family sold their interest before the incorporation of the firm in 1922–23. The firm was sold to the Batchelder Tile Co. around 1933. The plant closed in 1938 and reopened in 1948. The firm closed for the last time in 1962.

Colored dinnerware was introduced in 1930. A line of art pottery, mainly in Art Deco shapes featuring pastel matte glazes or dark high fired glazes, also was produced. The popularity of this dinnerware pattern kept Bauer alive. New patterns were added in the 1940s, including Monterey and La Linda, but they did not surpass the popularity of the original pattern, Ring.

The wares made in the art line were mostly molded and are usually found with molded marks. Other pieces of Bauer pottery have cobalt blue imprinted marks. Many items were not marked, or were simply stamped "Made In USA."

Reference: Jack Chipman, *Collector's Encyclopedia of Bauer Pottery: Identification & Values,* Collector Books, 1998; Mitch Tuchman, *Bauer: Classic American Pottery,* Chronicle Books, 1995.

Newsletter: *Bauer Quarterly,* PO Box 2524, Berkeley, CA 94702.

Art Pottery, ewer, turquoise, 10" h	$50
Art Pottery, figure, duck, head up	25
Art Pottery, figure, pony, on base	175
Art Pottery, figure, Scottie, sitting, white, matte glaze	200
Art Pottery, flowerpot, applied lion dec, turquoise, 10" h	150
Art Pottery, oil jar, #100, orange–red, 22" h	750
Art Pottery, rose bowl, white, 5¹/₂ x 6¹/₂"	400
Art Pottery, vase, applied handles, blue, 17" h	450
Brusche Contempo, butter dish, yellow speck	40

Brusche Contempo, dinner service, service for 4 plus serving pcs, pink speck . 95
Brusche Contempo, gravy boat, pink speck 20
Brusche Contempo, tea set, teapot and 4 #46 mugs, spice green 45
Brusche Contempo, vegetable bowl, indigo brown, 7½" d 20
Gloss Pastel Kitchenware, batter bowl, green, 2 qt 55
Gloss Pastel Kitchenware, casserole, in metal holder, 1 qt 40
Gloss Pastel Kitchenware, coffeepot, individual, canary yellow 35
Gloss Pastel Kitchenware, cookie jar, blue, matte 90
Gloss Pastel Kitchenware, jug, 1 qt 40
Gloss Pastel Kitchenware, mixing bowl, orange, #18 25
Gloss Pastel Kitchenware, mixing bowl, yellow, 1 qt 40
Gloss Pastel Kitchenware, teapot, canary yellow, 8 cup 55
La Linda, ball jug, ice lip, gray 95
La Linda, carafe, chartreuse, glossy, wood handle 20
La Linda, cookie jar, jade 85
La Linda, cookie jar, plain 70
La Linda, creamer, turquoise 20
La Linda, cup and saucer, ivory, glossy 18
La Linda, cup and saucer, pink, matte 15
La Linda, fruit bowl, canary yellow 10
La Linda, plate, chartreuse, 9" d 15
La Linda, plate, dark brown, glossy, 7½" d 20
La Linda, plate, green, matte, 6½" d 9
La Linda, plate, ivory, glossy, 9½" d 10
La Linda, ramekin, pink, glossy 8
La Linda, shaker, tall, turquoise, glossy 15
La Linda, teapot, olive green, 8 cup 35
La Linda, tumbler, burgundy, glossy, metal handle 20
Monterey Moderne, berry bowl, burgundy 18
Monterey Moderne, berry bowl, orange 18
Monterey Moderne, beverage server, cov, orange–red 125
Monterey Moderne, chop plate, California orange–red 50
Monterey Moderne, chop plate, canary yellow, 13" d 35
Monterey Moderne, coffee server, wood handle, 8 cup 35
Monterey Moderne, creamer and sugar, midget, canary yellow 55
Monterey Moderne, creamer and sugar, midget, orange 55
Monterey Moderne, fruit bowl, ftd, yellow, 13" d 60
Monterey Moderne, gravy boat, canary yellow 33
Monterey Moderne, plate, Monterey blue, 6" d 10
Monterey Moderne, plate, turquoise, 9½" d 15
Monterey Moderne, plate, white, 7½" d 18
Monterey Moderne, platter, canary yellow, 17" l 45
Monterey Moderne, soup bowl, blue, 7½" d 30
Monterey Moderne, teapot, cov, canary yellow, 6 cup 65
Monterey Moderne, tumbler, orange–red, 9 oz 20
Monterey Moderne, vegetable bowl, divided, Monterey blue 45
Ring, baking dish, cov, black, 4" h 50
Ring, ball jug, turquoise 75
Ring, batter bowl, #18, orange 125
Ring, beater pitcher, cov, orange 120

Ring, berry dish, green 35
Ring, berry dish, orange ....) 35
Ring, berry dish, white 12
Ring, berry dish, yellow 25
Ring, butter dish, orange 150
Ring, candlesticks, pr, spool, cobalt blue 295
Ring, carafe, canary yellow, metal handle 60
Ring, casserole, canary yellow, in metal rack, 7¹/₂" d 60
Ring, casserole, orange, individual, 4" h 70
Ring, cereal bowl, turquoise 20
Ring, chop plate, delph blue, 12" d 55
Ring, chop plate, orange, 17" d 225
Ring, cigarette jar, blue 85
Ring, coffeepot, 8 cup 150
Ring, cookie jar, cov, orange 125
Ring, creamer, orange 15
Ring, creamer and sugar, yellow, midget 55
Ring, cup, yellow 25
Ring, cup and saucer, blue 40
Ring, custard cup, "Hi–Fire" style 10
Ring, egg cup, turquoise 85
Ring, goblet, turquoise 55
Ring, jug, ice lip, with metal handle, 2 qt 95
Ring, lug soup, cov, orange, 5¹/₂" d 90
Ring, mustard jar, orange 80
Ring, nappy, #5, black 65
Ring, pickle dish 20
Ring, pie baker, 9" d 25
Ring, plate, canary yellow, 6" d 12
Ring, plate, canary yellow, 10¹/₂" d 75
Ring, plate, turquoise, 10¹/₂" d 25
Ring, plate, white, 10" d 20
Ring, platter, oval, 12" l 45
Ring, punch bowl 300
Ring, ramekin, orange 15
Ring, refrigerator jar, open, turquoise 25
Ring, refrigerator stack set, turquoise, orange, canary yellow, in metal rack ... 90
Ring, relish, 5 part 95
Ring, salt and pepper shakers, pr, jade, low 15
Ring, salt and pepper shakers, pr, orange 12
Ring, shaker, sugar 140
Ring, sherbet 65
Ring, souffle dish 175
Ring, soup bowl, burgundy, 7¹/₂" d 25
Ring, soup plate, 7¹/₂" d 25
Ring, spice jar, #3, orange 75
Ring, teapot, canary yellow, wood handle, 6 cup 55
Ring, tumbler, barrel shape, metal handle 55
Ring, vegetable bowl, oval, 8" 45
Ring, vegetable bowl, oval, 10" 60
Ring, water bottle, cov 275

BENNINGTON & BENNINGTON–TYPE

In 1845 Christopher Webber Fenton joined Julius Norton, his brother–in–law, in the manufacture of stoneware in Bennington, Vermont. Fenton sought to expand the company's products and glazes; Norton wanted to concentrate solely on stoneware. In 1847 Fenton broke away and established his own factory.

Fenton introduced the famous Rockingham glaze, developed in England and named after the Marquis of Rockingham, to America. In 1849 he patented a flint enamel glaze, "Fenton's Enamel," which added flecks, spots, or streaks of color (usually blues, greens, yellows, and oranges) to the brown Rockingham glaze. Forms included candlesticks, coachman bottles, cow creamers, poodles, sugar bowls, and toby pitchers.

Fenton produced the little known scroddled ware, commonly called lava or agate ware. Scroddled ware is composed of different colored clays, mixed with cream colored clay, molded, turned on a potter's wheel, coated with feldspar and flint, and fired. It was not produced in quantity, as there was little demand for it.

Fenton also introduced Parian ware to America. Parian was developed in England in 1842 and known as "Statuary ware." Parian is a translucent porcelain which has no glaze and resembles marble. Bennington made the blue and white variety in the form of vases, cologne bottles, and trinkets.

Five different marks were used, with many variations. Only about 20% of the pieces carried any mark; some forms were almost always marked, others never. Marks: (a) E. Fenton's Works, 1845–47, on Parian and occasionally on scroddled ware; (b) 1849 mark (four variations) for flint enamel and Rockingham; (c) U.S. Pottery Co., ribbon mark, 1852–58, on Parian and blue and white porcelain; (d) U.S. Pottery Co., lozenge mark, 1852–58, on Parian; and (e) U.S. Pottery, oval mark, 1853–58, mainly on scroddled ware.

The hound handled pitcher is probably the best known Bennington piece. Hound handled pitchers were also made by some thirty other potteries in over fifty-five variations. Rockingham glaze was used by over 150 potteries in eleven states, mainly the Mid–West, between 1830 and 1900.

References: Richard Carter Barret, *How to Identify Bennington Pottery,* Stephen Greene Press, 1964; Laura Woodside Watkins, *Early New England Potters and Their Wares,* Harvard University Press, 1950.

Museum: Bennington Museum, Bennington, VT 05201.

Book Bottle, Parted Spirits, flint enamel, corner chip, $7^7/8$" h **$450**
Book Flask, Departed Spirits G, brown and yellow Rockingham glaze, small
   edge chips, $5^1/2$" h **290**
Book Flask, Ned Buntline's Bible, flint enamel glaze, Fenton's "1849" mark,
   6" h **2,500**
Book Flask, Rockingham glaze, edge chips, 11" h **775**
Bowl, shallow, brown and yellow Rockingham glaze, Fenton's "1849" mark,
   $7^1/8$" d **775**
Candlestick, $6^7/8$" h **715**
Candlestick, $7^3/4$" h, Rockingham glaze **350**
Candlestick, 8" h, Rockingham glaze, black flecks **465**
Chamber Pot, flint enamel, Scalloped Rib pattern, $9^1/8$" d **600**
Churn, ovoid, cobalt slip stylized flower, imp "E. Norton & Co. Bennington,
   Vt 4" mark on neck, $17^1/2$" h, chips and flakes **170**

Coffeepot, cov, flint enamel glaze, olive and mottled amber glaze, fluted finial, 1849–58, 12³/₄" h **1,700**

Creamer, Rockingham glaze, ribbed, Fenton's "1849" mark, pinpoint flakes, short rim hairline at handle, 5¹/₂" h **1,100**

Crock, cobalt bird on branch with dots below, imp "E. & L. P. Norton, Bennington, Vt" mark, and cobalt "6," 13" h 600

Crock, cobalt slip feather design, imp "E. & L. P. Norton, Bennington, Vt. 3," 10¹/₂" h 230

Figure, poodle, flint enamel, 1 leg repaired, half of basket handle missing, 9¹/₂" l, 8¹/₄" h, price for pair **5,500**

Goblet, Rockingham glaze, 4¹/₂" h 275

Jar, cov, ovoid, blue double handles, imp blue "L. Norton 2," mark, c1830, 12" h 250

Jug, cobalt quill bird on branch, imp "J. & E. Norton, Bennington, Vt," mark, 11¹/₄" h 400

Jug, cobalt slip stylized floral design, pebble glaze imp label "J. Norton, Bennington, Vt. 4," 18" h 570

Nameplate, Rockingham glaze, white letter "F," scrolling shape 245

Picture Frame, Rockingham glaze, oval, old repairs, 8³/₄ x 9³/₄", price for pair . 325

Pie Plate, Rockingham glaze, yellow highlights, "1849" mark, 11" d 715

Pipkin, Rockingham glaze, curved handle, minor wear, short hairlines in rim, 5¹/₂" plus handle 350

Pitcher, cobalt quill bird on branch design, imp label "F. & E. Norton, Bennington, Vt," repaired, 12¹/₂" h 220

Pitcher, molded hunt scenes and vintage, Rockingham glaze, hound handle, c1850, 9" h 175

Pitcher, molded vintage, hounds, and stag, Rockingham glaze, hound handle, 9¹/₂" h 600

Pitcher, Parian, Cascade pattern, imp label "United States Pottery Co. Bennington, VT.," 10" h 150

Pitcher, scalloped ribs, 12¹/₂" h 770

Pitcher, swirled ribs, chip at end of handle, 9¹/₂" h **1,800**

Pitcher, white, tulip and sunflower, US Pottery ribbon mark, 8³/₄" h **1,300**

Snuff Jar, toby hat, Rockingham glaze, Fenton, "1849" mark, 4" h 400

Soap Dish, cov, flint enamel glaze, Alternate Rib pattern, "1849" mark, 5⁵/₈" l 880

Left: Book Bottle, stoneware, yellow–green mottled glaze, small area of glaze restored at top edge, 5¹/₂" h, 4¹/₄" w, $65. Photo courtesy Collectors Auction Services.

Right: Pitcher, hunter and hounds, Rockingham glaze, Fenton, 9" h, $175.

Pie Plate, brown and yellow Rockingham glaze, Fenton's "1849" mark, 11³/₄" d, $825. Photo courtesy Garth's Auction.

Soap Dish, cov, flint enamel glaze, olive brown and cream, glazed, green flecks, dated "1849" on bottom, 5¼" l **125**

Spittoon, diamond pattern, brown and yellow flint enamel glaze, 8½" d **275**

Spittoon, flint enamel glaze, "1849" mark, 9½" d **450**

Sugar Bowl, Parian, Repeated Oak Leaves pattern, blue and white, raised grapevine dec lid, 3³/₄" h **125**

Syrup Pitcher, cov, Spinning Wheel pattern, white glaze, c1850, 7¼" h **230**

Teapot, cov, Alternate Rib pattern, flint enamel, pierced pouring spout, period lid **400**

Toby Jug, Coachman, Rockingham glaze, honey colored, "1849" mark, 10³/₈" h **475**

Toby Jug, General Stark, Rockingham glaze **1,200**

Toothbrush Holder, cov, Alternate Rib pattern, flint enamel glaze **500**

Vase, tulip, black olive flint enamel glaze, 10" h **900**

Whiskey Jug, cobalt abstract floral design, imp "Julius Norton Bennington, Vt. 2" mark, 14" h **165**

Whiskey Jug, cobalt painted jumping deer, imp "Norton & Fenton, East Bennington, Vt. 2" mark, c1845, 13¼" h **570**

Whiskey Jug, ovoid, 3 blue flowers, imp "L. Norton & Son Bennington 2" mark, 14" h **140**

BLUE RIDGE

Blue Ridge dinnerware was produced by Southern Potteries of Erwin, Tennessee, from the late 1930s until 1956. The company used eight shapes and over 400 different patterns. Reasons for the company's success included cheap labor, easily changed and decorated patterns, and the use of dinnerware as premiums. Many a set of Blue Ridge china was accumulated by going to the theater or using a particular brand of gasoline. Sales of this popular dinnerware were through Sears and Montgomery Ward in the 1950s.

Blue Ridge Pottery is especially appealing to the Country decorator and collectors because of its simple designs. Flowers, roosters, and similar designs grace the patterns. Bright, cheery, colors predominate.

Southern Potteries products, including the Blue Ridge patterns, are identified by a variety of marks, ranging from simple script names to elaborate marks featuring rocky landscapes and trees.

References: Winnie Keillor, *Dishes, What Else? Blue Ridge of Course!,* privately printed, 1983; Betty and Bill Newbound, *Collector's Encyclopedia of Blue Ridge Dinnerware* (1994), *Vol II* (1988), Collector Books; Betty Newbound, *Southern Potteries, Inc. Blue Ridge Dinnerware, 3rd Edition,* Collector Books, 1989, 1996 value update; Frances and John Ruffin, *Blue Ridge China Today,* Schiffer Publishing, 1997.

Periodical: *Blue Ridge Beacon Magazine,* PO Box 629, Mountain City, GA 30562.

Newsletter: *National Blue Ridge Newsletter,* 144 Highland Drive, Blountville, TN 37617.

Collectors' Club: Blue Ridge Collectors Club, 208,Harris Street, Erwin, TN 37650.

Apple Jack, tidbit tray, 3 tier	**$25**
Autumn Apple, plate, 10½" d	**20**
Beaded Apple, plate, 10¼" d	**5**
Beaded Apple, saucer	**3**
Becky, cup and saucer	**30**
Bellemeade, creamer and sugar, cov	**20**
Bellemeade, fruit bowl	**20**
Bellemeade, soup plate	**12**
Bluebell Bouquet, bread and butter plate, 6" d	**3**
Bluebell Bouquet, dinner plate	**8**
Bluebell Bouquet, fruit bowl	**3**
Bluebell Bouquet, platter, 15" d	**20**
Bluebell Bouquet, sugar	**6**
Brittany, demitasse cup and saucer	**40**
Buttercup, fruit bowl, 6" d	**10**
Calico, candy box	**175**
Calico, salt and pepper shakers, pr, blossom top	**35**
Carnival, Candlewick blank, cereal bowl	**8**
Carnival, Candlewick blank, dinner plate, 9¼" d	**8**
Carnival, Candlewick blank, saucer	**3**
Cherries, dinner plate	**5**
Cherries, sauce dish	**4**
Cherries, soup bowl	**6**
Cherry Bounce, dinner service, 45 pcs	**200**
Chick, jug	**100**
Chintz, celery	**20**
Chintz, chocolate pot	**160**
Chintz, pitcher, Milady shape, 8¼" h	**100**
Colonial, creamer	**12**
Colonial, demitasse cup and saucer	**15**
Colonial, dinner plate, 9¼" d	**10**
Colonial, salt and pepper shakers, pr	**15**
Crab Apple, creamer and sugar, cov	**16**
Crab Apple, demitasse cup and saucer	**30**
Crab Apple, plate, 9" d	**10**
Crab Apple, plate, 10" d	**12**
Crab Apple, teapot, Colonial shape	**55**
Daffodil, cup and saucer	**5**
Daffodil, plate, 6" d	**5**
Daffodil, plate, 10¼" d	**10**

Daffodil, sugar **12**
Emalee, cup and saucer **30**
Fairmeade Fruits, eggcup **18**
Fantasia, teapot, Skyline shape **65**
Folklore, plate, 7¼" d **4**
Folklore, platter, 13¼" d **8**
French Peasant, chocolate pot **300**
French Peasant, creamer and sugar **125**
French Peasant, pitcher, 8¼" h **375**
French Peasant, platter, 13" d **120**
French Peasant, vase, handled **70**
French Peasant, vegetable bowl **80**
Fruit Fantasy, butter pat **15**
Fruit Fantasy, cup and saucer **12**
Fruit Fantasy, plate, 9¼" d **8**
Fruit Fantasy, vegetable bowl **20**
Gladys, vase, boot shape, 8" h **100**
Greenbriar, fruit bowl **3**
Greenbriar, gravy boat **10**
Greenbriar, plate, 9¼" d **10**
Mountain Ivy, creamer **3**
Mountain Ivy, dinner plate **8**
Mountain Ivy, sugar bowl **8**
Mountain Ivy, vegetable bowl **10**
Nocturne, Colonial shape, creamer, wide **15**
Nocturne, Colonial shape, flat soup, 8" d **15**
Nocturne, Colonial shape, teapot, yellow **10**
Nove Rose, bonbon, shell shape **45**
Poinsettia, lug soup bowl **5**
Poinsettia, soup bowl **15**
Poinsettia, soup plate **5**
Provincial Farm Scenes, plate, 6" sq **55**
Quaker Apple, cup and saucer **8**
Quaker Apple, dinner service for 4 . . . .   **150**
Quaker Apple, plate, 6" d **8**
Red Barn, plate, 9" d **22**
Ribbon Plaid, cereal bowl **10**

Left: Berry Bowl, blue flower, 5½" d, $5.
Right: Cup and Saucer, red and blue flowers, $10.

Ridge Daisy, relish dish, 4 part, top handle 55
Rock Rose, eggcup 20
Rooster, cigarette set, cov box and 4 ashtrays 180
Rooster, platter 100
Rooster, salt and pepper shakers, pr, toe flake 90
Rustic Plaid, dinner plate 5
Rustic Plaid, salad plate, 6¹⁄₄" d 5
Rustic Plaid, sugar 5
Spray, cup and saucer 8
Strawberry Sundae, cup and aucer 5
Strawberry Sundae, dinner plate 5
Sunflower, plate, 10" d 10
Sungold #2, eggcup 15
Sunny, cereal bowl 8
Valley Violet, cup and saucer 25
Valley Violet, salt and pepper shakers, pr 40
Valley Violet, sugar bowl 35
Whirligig, bread and butter plate 6
Whirligig, soup bowl 15
Winnie, berry bowl 5
Winnie, bread and butter plate, 6" d 5
Winnie, creamer 10
Winnie, cup and saucer 10
Winnie, dinner plate 15
Winnie, platter, 13" l 25
Winnie, soup bowl 10
Winnie, sugar, cov 15
Woodcrest, butter dish 60
Yellow Nocturne, creamer 10
Yellow Nocturne, cup and saucer 8
Yellow Nocturne, teapot 15

CAMARK

Samuel Jack Carnes founded Camark Pottery, Camden, Arkansas, in 1926. The company produced art pottery, earthenware, and decorative accessories. John Lessell, previously employed at Weller, and his wife were among the leading art potters working at Camark.

After Carnes sold the plant in 1966, Mary Daniels ran it primarily as a retail operation. In January 1986 Gary and Mark Ashcraft purchased the Camark Pottery building with the expectation of re–establishing a pottery at the site. At the time of the purchase, they stated that they did not intend to reissue pieces using the company's old molds. Good intentions aside, the Ashcrafts were unable to reopen the plant, and it continues to remain idle.

Be very careful to not confuse Camark Pottery's art ware with its utilitarian household decorative wares. The majority of the listings are art pottery. Most household pieces, especially vases, are valued between $10 and $25.

References: David Edwin Gifford, *Collector's Encyclopedia of Camark Pottery: Identification & Values,* Collector Books, 1997; Letitia Landers, *Camark Pottery: An Identification and Value Reference, Vol 1* (1994), *Vol 2* (1996), Colony Publishing.

Collectors' Club: Arkansas Pottery Collectors Society, PO Box 7617, Little Rock, AR 72217.

Ashtray, leaf shape, frosted green, 7¼" l	$25
Ashtray, round, 5¾" d	10
Ashtray, sunburst	15
Ball Jug, brown and blue speck, 8" h	245
Ball Jug, brown stipple, gold Arkansas ink stamp, 6¼" h	300
Basket, handled, orange, unmkd, 3¾" h	15
Batter Pitcher, cat handle, green, "USA, Camark 088," mold mark, 7¼" h	95
Batter Pitcher, parrot handle, blue, gold Arkansas ink stamp, 6¼" h	175
Batter Pitcher, parrot handle, ivory crackle bright, gold Arkansas ink stamp, 9" h	300
Batter Pitcher, parrot handle, sea green, gold Arkansas ink stamp, 6¼" h	175
Batter Pitcher, parrot handle, yellow, gold Arkansas ink stamp, 6¼" h	175
Bottle, figural, frog, olive green, light overflow, first block letter, 4 x 3"	95
Bottle, figural, pig, orange, first block letter, 9 x 3"	245
Bowl, blue and white stipple, gold Arkansas sticker, 5¼" h	245
Bowl, pumpkin, small	15
Box, frosted green, second Arkansas inventory sticker "s–948a," and "f–70," 2¼ x 4¼"	75
Casserole, cov, chicken lid	40
Dresser Tray, white	30
Figure, wistful kitten, 8¼" h	40
Flower Bowl, Aztec Red Mottled, Arkansas die stamp, 5¼" h	175
Flower Frog, swans	25
Ginger Jar, mirror black, brown Arkansas sticker, 9" h	245
Humidor, brown stipple, first block letter, 5¼" h	135
Humidor, delphinium blue, first block letter, 6¼" h	95
Jug, "Arkansas Pure Corn, RCA," black Arkansas ink stamp, 5¼" h	75
Jug, "Pure Iowa Corn," black Arkansas ink stamp, 5" h	75
Lamp Base, mulberry, green overflow, unmkd, 5" h	175
Lamp Base, olive green, black overflow, unmkd, 6" h	175
Miniature Pitcher Vase, #674, burgundy glaze	18
Pitcher, Barcelona/Spano Ware, sea green, ribbed, unmkd, 8¼" h	220

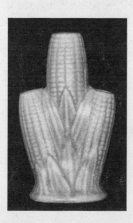

Left: Vase, corn, matte solid color, frosted green, 8½" h, $90.

Right: Vase, handled, matte combination colors, orange green overflow, 4½" h, $70.

Pitcher, brown stipple, gold Arkansas ink stamp, 6¼" h 245
Pitcher, bulbous, cat handle, 8¼" h 50
Planter, rolling pin, N1–51 8
Planter, rooster 20
Planter, shot glass, orange, green overflow, unmkd, 2" h 25
Vase, Aztec Red Mottled, brown Arkansas sticker, 6" h 220
Vase, brown stipple, mkd "Compliments, B. P. W. Club, Camden, Ark.," gold
    Arkansas ink stamp, 7¼" h 135
Vase, celestial blue, black overflow, Arkansas die stamp, 10¾" h 275
Vase, coraline, incised "JL," 6" h 450
Vase, frosted green, "783, USA," mold mark, 3¾" h 15
Vase, green Crackle, gold Arkansas ink stamp, 12¼" h 850
Vase, morning glory, 11" h 50
Vase, Old English Rose, sgd "LeCamark," 8" h 900
Vase, orange, green, and red swirl design, unmkd, 4¼" h 95
Vase, orange, green overflow, ribbed, 2 handles, unmkd, 7¼" h 115
Vase, rose, green overflow, unmkd, 4" h 55
Vase, silver luster, sgd "LeCamark," 10¼" h 1,000
Vase, Venetian Jonquil, gold Camark script, 9" h 850
Vase, wedding vase, green, ribbed, 6¾" h 75

CHALKWARE

William Hutchinson, an Englishman, invented chalkware in 1848. It was a substance used by sculptors to imitate marble. It was also used to harden plaster of Paris, creating a confusion between the two products.

Chalkware often copied many of the popular Staffordshire items of the 1820 to 1870 period. It was cheap, gaily decorated, and sold by vendors. The Pennsylvania German "folk art" pieces are from this period.

Carnivals, circuses, fairs, and amusement parks awarded chalkware pieces as prizes during the late nineteenth and early twentieth centuries. They were often poorly made and gaudy. Don't confuse them with the earlier pieces. Prices for these chalkware items range from ten to fifty dollars.

References: Thomas G. Morris, *The Carnival Chalk Prize,* Prize Publishers, 1994; *Price Guide to Carnival Chalkware, Giveaways and Games,* L–W Book Sales, 1995.

Bird, perched on spherical plinth, old dark yellow paint with red and black,
    7⅞" h $165
Cat, nodder, black, red, and yellow dec, worn dark gray patina, wear, dam-
    age to side of head, 8½" l 210
Cat, pipe in mouth, 10¼" h 240
Cat, reclining, black and white stripe paint, colorful bow, 12" l 165
Cat, seated, black and red details 250
Deer, reclining, head turned to side, one leg slightly raised, molded collar,
    painted ocher brown with black spots, red ears, ocher eyes, on rect grassy
    base, mid–19th C, 9⅞" h, price for pair 400
Dog, seated, on haunches, head turned to side, molded fur detail, painted
    brown with black spots and red collar 200
Dog, seated, painted red, green, and brown, 6" h 360
Dog, seated, worn black, red, green, and yellow, 6¼" h 110

Dog, standing, with open legs, worn red, black, yellow, and green, 7⅞" h . . . 245
Doves, perched side by side on circular base, kissing, red, green, and dark
   brown molded feather detail, mid–19th C, 5⅝" h 425
Ewe and Lamb, reclining, molded fur detail, oblong grassy base with yellow
   border, 1 ear repaired 650
Fruit and Foliage, orig green, yellow, orange, and black polychrome paint,
   14" h 1,760
Garniture, basket of fruit, pair of lovebirds above, yellow, red, and black,
   7¾" h 390
George Washington on Horseback, George Washington holding saber,
   astride white horse, star dec oval base, inscribed "K 347," 19th C 1,000
Girl, bust, polychrome paint, pedestal base, old touch–up repairs, 11" h 200
Kissing Lovebirds, polychrome paint, 5" h 300
Old Woman, holding parasol, polychrome paint, 9¼" h 230
Parrot, yellow, green, and black polychrome paint, emb feather detail, ball
   base, 7¾" h 275
Poodle, seated on haunches, head turned to left, molded stippled fur, brown
   ears, red dotted collar, red and green rect base, mid–19th C, 6¼" h 575
Rabbit, nodder, reclining, black and red, neck chip 950
Rabbit, seated, yellow and black highlights, 10" h 200
Ram, standing, with open legs, red, olive yellow, and black, chip on base,
   flakes on ears, unfilled bubble on chin, 9" h 940
Ram, yellow, black, and red polychrome paint, worn, 5¼" h 680
Robin, red, black, brown, and gold, old touch–up repairs, 6¾" h 535
Rooster, full bodied, standing, modeled with comb, wattle, feather, and tail
   detail, inset glass eyes, on quatrefoil base with scrolled acanthus support,
   repaired base, 20" h 550
Rooster, standing, molded wing, tail, wattle, and comb, painted ocher,
   brown, and red, circular base, 4⅝" h 400
Rooster, yellow, black, and red polychrome paint, worn, 5¼" h 675
Sheep, reclining, molded fur detail, red and black painted spots, oblong base   675
Squirrel, hollow, worn red, black, orange, and green paint, hollow, 1 with
   closed base, 6¼" h, price for pair 330
Squirrel, polychrome paint, 6¼" h 300
Squirrel, solid cast body, old yellow tinted varnish finish, wear and old chips,
   8" h   70
Stag, polychrome paint, smoke dec, PA, c1850, 6 x 9¼" h 400
Stag, reclining, red, black, and yellow details, oblong base 500

CLARICE CLIFF

   Clarice Cliff (1899-1972) joined A. J. Wilkinson's Royal Staffordshire Pottery at
Burslem, England, in the early 1910s. In 1930 she became the company's art director.
   Cliff is one of England's foremost twentieth–century ceramic designers. Her influ-
ence covered a broad range—shapes, forms, and patterns. Her shape lines include
Athens, Biarritz, Chelsea, Conical, Iris, Lynton, and Stamford. Appliqué, Bizarre,
Crocus, Fantasque, and Ravel are among her most popular patterns.
   In addition to designer shape and pattern lines, Cliff's signature also appears on a
number of inexpensive dinnerware lines manufactured under the Royal Staffordshire
label. Several of these patterns, especially Celtic Harvest and Tonquin, appeal strongly to the Country collector.

Reference: Pat and Howard Watson, *The Clarice Cliff Colour Price Guide,* Francis Joseph Publications, 1995, distributed by Krause Publications.

Collectors' Club: Clarice Cliff Collector's Club, Fantasque House, Tennis Drive, The Park, Nottingham, NG7 1AE, UK.

Cabbage Flower, condiment set, conical shape	**$300**
Celtic Harvest, plate, raised colored fruit, tan ground, c1935, 8³/₄" d	100
Celtic Harvest, vegetable bowl, raised colored fruit forms handles, tan ground, c1935, 11¹/₂" d	230
Fruit and Berries, raised design, pitcher, brown and yellow leaves, twisted rope band, green int, 7³/₄" h	435
Fruit and Berries, raised design, tray, brown and yellow leaf, green ground, Newport Pottery Co mark, 13" l, 5¹/₄" w	185
My Garden, pitcher, brown and orange on gray, flower handle, 9" h	375
My Garden, vase, pink melon sectioned scalloped top, emb painted flowers at base, 7" h, 5" d	110
Tonquin, ashtray, Royal Staffordshire Pottery, Wilkinson, Ltd	45
Tonquin, bone dish, brown transfer, Royal Ironstone mark, 6³/₄" l	18
Tonquin, bone dish, green transfer, 7" l	15
Tonquin, bowl, purple transfer, 5" d	5
Tonquin, bowl, purple transfer, 9" d	20
Tonquin, dinner service, 46 pcs, brown, eight 10" d dinner plates, 8 dessert plates, seven 6¹/₂" d salad plates, 6 cups, 8 saucers, creamer and sugar, round bowl, and oval platter	125
Tonquin, gravy boat and underplate, purple	25
Tonquin, plate, blue transfer, 8" d	8
Tonquin, plate, pink transfer, 6¹/₂" d	5
Tonquin, plate, red transfer, 12" l	15
Tonquin, platter, purple transfer, 11¹/₂" l	25
Tonquin, platter, red transfer, 12" l	20
Tonquin, sauceboat and underplate, brown transfer	20
Tonquin, soup plate, pink transfer, 8" d	20
Tonquin, teapot, cov, reddish brown transfer	100

COORS

Coors Pottery was manufactured in Golden, Colorado. Adolph Coors founded both the Coors Porcelain Company and the Coors Brewing Company. By 1914, the war and Prohibition caused the Coors family to concentrate on pottery production. A close alliance with the Herold China and Pottery Company was established. In 1920, the Herold company became part of the Coors Porcelain Company. The demand for good quality American–made pottery continued after the war. Coors eagerly tried to fill the need.

Coors produced high gloss, brightly colored dinnerware several years before Fiesta became the rage. Dinnerware lines contained standard table settings as well as casseroles, teapots, coffeepots, waffle sets, and other essentials for the homemakers of the 1930s and 40s. Rosebud is the most widely collected Coors pattern.

Government orders caused the factory to discontinue dinnerware production during World War II. Expansion of other lines caused large quantities of dinnerware to be given to major customers who often used it as premiums. After World War II, a variety of wares, including ovenware, teapots, beer mugs, ashtrays, and vases were made. By the 1980s, all tableware and ovenware lines had been discontinued.

Coors' glazes and colors were industry leaders. Because of this, many companies hired Coors for commemorative pieces. Limited edition items served as employee gifts or giveaways. These are eagerly sought by collectors.

The Coors Porcelain Company continues, but no longer produces the vibrant dinnerware known to Country collectors.

References: Carol and Jim Carlton, *Colorado Pottery: Identification and Values,* Collector Books, 1994; Robert H. Schneider, *Coors Rosebud Pottery,* Busche–Waugh–Henry Publications, 1984.

Newsletter: *Coors Pottery Newsletter,* 3808 Carr Place North, Seattle, WA 98103.

Coorado, casserole, cov, individual, maroon, 2 x 2"	**$15**
Coorado, custard set, 6 custards, metal holder	45
Coorado, dinner plate, yellow	10
Coorado, pitcher, maroon	32
Coorado, salt and pepper shakers, pr, green	22
Coorado, teapot, yellow	175
Mello–Tone, bread and butter plate, yellow, 4" d	8
Mello–Tone, cup and saucer, blue	15
Mello–Tone, gravy boat with underplate, green	20
Mello–Tone, platter, green, 15" l	20
Mello–Tone, vegetable bowl, blue, 9" d	20
Rosebud, baking pan, 12¼ x 8¼ x 2¼"	20
Rosebud, bean pot, cov, yellow	18
Rosebud, cake knife, maroon, yellow rosebud, 3 green leaves, 10" l	20
Rosebud, casserole, triple, red	95
Rosebud, cereal bowl, yellow, 6" d	10
Rosebud, cookie jar, deluxe	140
Rosebud, creamer	45

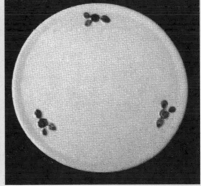

Left: Rosebud, bean pot, cov, green, 4½" d top, 2½ pt, $18.
Right: Rosebud, cake plate, 11" d, $15.

Rosebud, cream soup, blue, 4" d   12
Rosebud, cream soup, rose   20
Rosebud, cup and saucer, green   8
Rosebud, custard   20
Rosebud, deep plate   50
Rosebud, dinner plate, green, 9¹/₂" d   12
Rosebud, honeypot, cov, maroon   20
Rosebud, honeypot spoon, orange   320
Rosebud, mixing bowl, 10" d   80
Rosebud, pie baker, yellow   15
Rosebud, pudding bowl, blue   65
Rosebud, ramekin   55
Rosebud, salad plate, yellow, 7" d   10
Rosebud, salt and pepper shakers, pr, blue   18
Rosebud, shaker, tall   65
Rosebud, utility jar, cov, yellow   25
Rosebud, vase, peach, 6" h   50
Rosebud, vase, white, 8" h   75
Rosebud, water server with cap, green   250

CREAMWARE

Creamware is not porcelain. It is a cream colored earthenware. It is characterized by its thin body and brilliant glaze.

Creamware arrived on the ceramic scene early in the eighteenth century. In 1740 Enoch Booth of Tunstall, Staffordshire, perfected a fluid glaze that resulted in a brilliant, transparent cream color. Booth's glaze was quickly utilized by other Staffordshire potters including Thomas Whieldon and Josiah Wedgwood. By 1760 creamware pieces were being decorated with enamel and production had spread to Derbyshire, Liverpool, Swansea, and Yorkshire.

In 1786 the basic formula of creamware was altered. China clay and china stone from Cornwall were added to the body and glaze.

The golden age of period creamware is 1760 to 1820, the period during which most of the pieces in the listings were made. However, the creamware proved so popular that it never went out of production. Wedgwood and other dinnerware manufacturers still make a variety of creamware dinnerware and giftware products.

Basket, oval, loop handle, brown rope border, Wedgwood, 6" l $90
Bowl, reticulated, with ladle, molded fiddleback handle, "Wedgwood" imp
  mark, 8¹/₈" l   165
Charger/Platter, emb magenta feather edge, scalloped rim, imp "Wedgwood
  3" on reverse, 16" d   325
Child's Mug, brown cylindrical transfer on front with Great Seal of the
  United States beneath 15 stars, "May Success Attend Our Agriculture
  Trade Manufactures And Sailors Rights" below eagle's tail, brown enamel
  band on rim, Staffordshire, c1820, 2" h   600
Cups and Saucers, handleless, set of 6, black transfer portraits of Washington
  and Lafayette on cups, "Washington, his Country's Father" on saucer,
  price for 12 pcs   990
Dish, Ferrara pattern, leaf form, dark blue "Wedgwood" mark, 10" l, 8" w . . .   230

Dish and Underplate, oval, reticulated borders, 9⅞" l **275**

Pitcher, globular shape, cream spout, olive green bottom, green, rust, and cream border, c1810, 4½" h **700**

Pitcher, molded, house and flowers in purple and pink luster, wear, stains, short hairline, 6" h **250**

Pitcher, Oriental holding parasol on front, and holding parasol and child on reverse, brick red, yellow, green, purple, and black, professional restoration to tip of spout, c1770, 5⅞" h **160**

Plate, brown, green, and yellow Whieldon–type tortoise shell glaze, scalloped rim with molded design, crazing, small chips, 8" d, price for pair ... **375**

Plate, florets, cream glazed surrounded by green glazed leaves, 1765, Wedgwood, 9½" d **200**

Plate, flower, red and black enameled, geometric border, 8⅛" d **185**

Plate, molded flutes, edge design with reticulated rim, 2 with "Leeds Pottery" imp mark, two 10" d, six 9⅜" d, price for 8 ....**1,100**

Plate, Royal Crest of England, black transfer, scalloped rim with floral dec, 9¾" d **280**

Plate, scenes, polychrome enamel, floral rims, inscriptions in Dutch, 10" d, price for 4 ....**1,980**

Plate, ship in water, flying American flag, black transfer, green enamel highlights on water, 9¾" d, price for pair **440**

Table Set, set of six 9¾" polychrome plates with figures dec, inscribed "Denverloorenzoon Zynafschyd Znarmoe," 5" h bulbous teapot with bird finial, branch form handle, and spout supported on 3 paw feet, marriage plate depicting portrait bust of lady and gentleman, initialed "PVOR," large serving plate with feather dec scalloped border, and creamware chamber stick, "LEEDS POTTERY" imp on underside, price for 10 pcs **4,000**

Tea Caddy, floral, red and green enamel dec, 5¼" h, price for pair **1,400**

Tea Caddy, rect, Macaroni figures highlighted in blue with touch of pale yellow and pale green, blue leaf and vine dec on sides and shoulder, fluted cov with blue highlight, 6¼" h **1,000**

Left: Platter, oval, alternating basketweave and scroll lattice border, 16⅝ x 13⅜", $75.

Right: Teapot, Jack the Sailor red transfer, unmkd, c1890, 9" l, 8" h, $475.

Tea Caddy, thin black and white checkerboard band between 2 wide blue
　bands, 19th C, 4³/₈" h **180**
Teapot, burner base, imp "Wedgwood," mismatched lid, 11⁵/₈" h overall **180**
Teapot, molded acanthus spout, ribbed handle, 4³/₄" h **385**
Teapot, Prince of Orange portraits, polychrome enameled, molded spout,
　intertwined ribbed handle, restored mismatched lid, 5" h **440**
Teapot, Rose, polychrome enameled, intertwined ribbed handle, molded
　floral ends, flower finial, 4³/₄" h **3,025**

CROOKSVILLE

　　The Crooksville China Company, Crooksville, Ohio, was founded in 1902 for the
manufacture of artware such as vases, flowerpots and novelties. Dinnerware soon
became its stock in trade. Crooksville made a good grade of semi–porcelain that
rivaled more expensive vitrified ware. The factory continued until 1959 and employed
over 300 people for many years.

　　Crooksville China produced several patterns. The decoration of their wares was
primarily achieved through the use of decals. These detailed decals are very colorful
and durable. Silhouette was one of the most popular patterns. The Silhouette decal is
in black on a yellow glaze ground and shows two men sitting at a table with a dog
looking up at them, waiting for food. Other patterns feature country–type decorations.

　　Crooksville answered the need for practical, attractive, utilitarian pieces. Earliest
production included teapots, waffle sets, jugs, spice jars, and covered baking sets.
Dinnerware followed this line of interestingly shaped pieces.

　　The Crooksville China Company used over fifteen different marks. Some contain
pattern names and dates, others were simply the company name.

Autumn, casserole, 8" d **$15**
Autumn, coffeepot **25**
Autumn, pie baker, 10" d **8**
Autumn, plate, 9³/₄" d **4**
Autumn, sugar **10**
Autumn, vegetable bowl, 9¹/₄" l **9**
Dartmouth, cookie jar **50**
Dartmouth, creamer **8**
Dartmouth, cup **5**
Dartmouth, mixing bowl, 8" d **12**
Dartmouth, mixing bowl, 9" d **15**
Dartmouth, plate, 10" d **12**
Dartmouth, sugar **15**
Dartmouth, syrup jug **30**
Dartmouth, teapot **50**
Dawn, bowl, 5¹/₄" d **3**
Dawn, casserole **22**
Dawn, plate, 6"d **2**
Dawn, plate, 9¹/₄" d **10**
Dawn, saucer **2**
Euclid, casserole, 8" d **20**
Euclid, coffeepot **45**
Euclid, custard **6**
Euclid, pie baker, 10" d **12**

Apple Blossom, bean pot, cov, $25.

Euclid, plate, 6¾" d	3
Euclid, tray, batter set	15
Harmony, casserole	25
Harmony, creamer	6
Harmony, plate, 9" d	8
Harmony, sugar	10
Ivora, gravy boat	15
Ivora, plate, 6" d	3
Ivora, saucer, 6" d	2
Ivora, soup bowl, 8¼" d	12
Ivora, teapot	30
Petit Point House, berry bowl	5
Petit Point House, casserole, 7" d	15
Petit Point House, cup and saucer	8
Petit Point House, pie server	20
Petit Point House, plate, 7" d	5
Provincial Ware, casserole	25
Provincial Ware, gravy boat	15
Provincial Ware, plate, 6" d	3
Provincial Ware, platter, 11½" d	12
Quadro, eggcup	12
Quadro, plate, 8" d	2
Quadro, saucer	3
Quadro, sugar	12
Quadro, vegetable bowl	12
Rust Bouquet, coffeepot	25
Rust Bouquet, pie baker	15
Rust Bouquet, platter, 11½" l	8
Silhouette, batter jug, bulbous	40
Silhouette, cookie jar, flat lid, rattan handle	50
Silhouette, creamer	12
Silhouette, mixing bowl, 8" d	18
Silhouette, pie baker, Pantry Bak–In	20
Silhouette, plate, 8" d	12
Silhouette, plate, 10" d	10

Silhouette, platter	20
Silhouette, saucer, 6" d	4
Silhouette, serving tray, handled, 11¾" l	25
Silhouette, soup bowl, 7¼" d	20
Silhouette, tumbler, 8 oz	20
Trellis, batter pitcher, cov, duckbill shape, 8" h	50
Trellis, cup and saucer	15
Trellis, plate, Iva–Glo, 8" d	10
Trellis, syrup pitcher, cov, duckbill shape, 6" h	40
Trellis, utility tray, 11¼" l	25

DEDHAM

Alexander W. Robertson established the Chelsea Pottery in Chelsea, Massachusetts, in 1860. In 1872 it was known as the Chelsea Keramic Art Works.

In 1895 the pottery moved to Dedham, and the name was changed to Dedham Pottery. Their principal product was gray crackleware dinnerware with a blue decoration, the rabbit pattern being the most popular. The factory closed in 1943.

The following marks help determine the approximate age of items: (1) Chelsea Keramic Art Works, "Robertson" impressed, 1876–1889; (2) C.P.U.S. impressed in a cloverleaf, 1891–1895; (3) Foreshortened rabbit, 1895–1896; (4) Conventional rabbit with "Dedham Pottery" stamped in blue, 1897; (5) Rabbit mark with "Registered," 1929–1943.

Reference: Lloyd E. Hawes, *The Dedham Pottery and the Earlier Robertson's Chelsea Potteries*, Dedham Historical Society, 1968.

Collectors' Club: Dedham Pottery Collectors Society, 248 Highland Street, Dedham, MA 02026.

Museum: Dedham Historical Society, Dedham, MA.

Bacon Rasher, Rabbit pattern, crackled white ground, ink mark, imp rabbits, 9½ x 6"	$175
Bowl, Chick pattern, #6, blue stamp, 2 hairlines, 4½" d, 2" h	800
Bowl, Lotus pattern, raised fluted emb design, blue embellishments, 5½" d	700
Bowl, Rabbit pattern, cov, blue rabbit stamp, 5¾" d	180
Bowl, Rabbit pattern, crackleware, ink stamped, 4¾ x 8"	325
Candle Snuffer, rabbit border, 2" h	645
Celery Tray, Rabbit pattern, 10" l	320
Chop Plate, Lobster pattern, imp marks and stamp, glaze bursts, 12" d	870
Chop Plate, Rabbit pattern, imp mark twice and stamp, 12" d	280
Coffeepot, Rabbit pattern, blue rabbit stamp on bottom, 8" h	180
Creamer and Sugar, Rabbit pattern, stamped mark	345
Demitasse Cup and Saucer, Rabbit pattern, blue "Dedham Pottery, Registered," and 2 imp rabbits on saucer bottom, 2½" h cup	430
Dinner Plates, set of 2, white crackleware, 1 in dolphin and baby emb mark, mkd "C.P.U.S.," other painted in duck pattern, registered mark and 2 bunnies, 10¼" d, price for pair	225
Eggcup, Grape pattern, dark blue, 2 blue bands above design, mkd "D. P.," 2½" h	250
Humidor, 2 elephants, inscribed "Dedham, Pottery/May 1917#79," 7" h	1,975

Luncheon Plate, Grape pattern, cobalt grapes on crackled white ground, small glaze flake to back of 1 plate, chip repair to back of other, each with ink mark and imp rabbit, 8½" d, price for pair **175**

Luncheon Plate, Mushroom pattern, blue mushrooms on crackled white ground, rabbit stamp and ink stamp, 8½" d **200**

Pitcher, Butterfly pattern, blue ink mark, imp rabbit, 8¾" d **420**

Pitcher, Crab pattern, blue and white, imp rabbit mark, rim chip, small surface flakes, 6¼" d **165**

Pitcher, Duck pattern, imp and stamped marks, 8⅝" d **370**

Pitcher, Elephant pattern, baby elephant, "Dedham Pottery, Registered," 5" h .**2,110**

Pitcher, Floral pattern, blue and white, 6" d, price for 6 .... **2,145**

Pitcher, Golden Gate, San Francisco, inscribed on reverse to "M Sheperd," artist's cipher for Hugh C Robertson, enhanced blue stamp, imp mark, glaze bursts, chip on foot, 10" d **2,765**

Pitcher, Grape pattern, ink mark, imp rabbit, chip repair to back, 8½" d **175**

Pitcher, Grape pattern, stamped and imp rabbit marks, early 20th C, 9¾" h .. **80**

Pitcher, Horse Chestnut pattern, stamped mark, 2 imp marks, base chip, early 20th C, 7½" d **130**

Pitcher, Iris pattern, blue and white, imp rabbit mark, 2 rim hairlines, 6⅛" d .. **165**

Pitcher, Lion pattern, blue and white, 8¾" d, price for pair **2,310**

Pitcher, Lion and Owl pattern, bisque, dark pattern, imp mark, artist initials of Hugh C Robertson, c1900, 10" d **1,545**

Pitcher, Lobster pattern, imp and stamped marks, foot chip, 8¾" d, price for set of 5 .... **1,645**

Pitcher, Lotus Water Lily pattern, "Dedham Pottery, Registered," 8¼" d **195**

Pitcher, Moth pattern, imp and stamped marks, 6¼" d **370**

Pitcher, Mushroom pattern, crackled white ground, rabbit and ink stamp, 8½" d **200**

Pitcher, Owl and Chicken pattern, "Night and Day," crackleware, blue, white ground, 5 x 5¼" **425**

Pitcher, Owl and Roosters pattern, "Night and Day," crackleware, blue, white ground, blue ink mark, 5 x 5½" **375**

Pitcher, Poppy pattern, crackleware dec surrounded by poppy pods, ink and die stamp, 8½" d **350**

Left: Creamer, Elephant pattern, 1929–43, 5" h, $500.

Right: Bread and Butter Plate, Azalea pattern, 6" d, $40.

Pitcher, Poppy pattern, imp mark, stamp and inscribed cross, 8½" d **500**
Pitcher, Rabbit pattern, blue and white crackle glaze, rim chip, 11⅞" d **135**
Pitcher, Rabbit pattern, dark blue, band on rim, mkd "Dedham Pottery Registered," 5¼" h **700**
Pitcher, Rabbit pattern, rabbit leaping over lower handle, initialed "P," imp and stamped marks, 8⅜" h **1,320**
Pitcher, Swan pattern, blue rabbit stamp and 2 incised rabbits, 6⅛" d **245**
Pitcher, Turkey pattern, blue and white, 8⅝" d, price for pair **495**
Plate, Azalea pattern, blue rabbit mark, 9¾" d **50**
Plate, Birds, in Potted Orange Trees pattern, blue and white, imp rabbit, 8¾" d **465**
Tea Bowl, dripping mossy green glaze over crackled ground, blue rabbit mark, 2½ x 4½" **450**
Vase, baluster shape, textured dark green, yellow, and rouge glaze, incised "Dedham Pottery/HCR/BW," 10 x 4½" **325**
Vase, bulbous, blue, plume design, white crackle ground, mkd "Dedham 38," 5 x 4½" **1,600**
Vase, bulbous, blue and cafe–au–lait luster glaze, incised "Dedham Pottery," 7½ x 4¾" **750**
Vase, bulbous, crackleware, painted blue with plume design, mkd "DEDHAM 38," 5 x 4½" **1,600**
Vase, bulbous, cylindrical neck, crackled dark green glaze over yellow, dark green textured glossy ground, incised "Dedham Pottery/B. W./HCR," 9 x 6" **400**
Vase, bulbous, frothy blue and clear green glaze, incised mark, 10 x 8" **800**
Vase, bulbous, iris blossoms, hp in cobalt and medium blue on crackled ground, painted "Dedham/TT/34," 7¼ x 4¾" **1,800**
Vase, bulbous, textured red and deep brown glaze, incised "Dedham Pottery/HCR," 8¼ x 6" **2,700**
Vase, bulbous, thick curdled volcanic moss and brown glaze, incised "DEDHAM POTTERY/HCR," 11 x 7½" **2,200**
Vase, Chelsea Keramic Art Works, center cylindrical neck surrounded by 4 smaller necks, bulbous body, circular foot, mustard glaze, "Hugh C Robertson" imp mark, c1880, 6⅝" h **830**
Vase, Chelsea Keramic Art Works, dragon's blood and olive green irid gloss glaze, imp "CKAW," base pulls, crazing, c1888, 9½" h **1545**
Vase, Chelsea Keramic Art Works, 8 recesses framed and accented by incising, bisque, imp "CKAW," c1880, 4½" h **280**
Vase, Chelsea Keramic Art Works, gray crackle glaze, peppering, imp mark, c1886, 6¾" h **170**
Vase, Chelsea Keramic Art Works, rounded shoulder, incised shadowing, 4 square sides, circular ftd base, bisque, imp "CKAW," c1880, 4½" h **280**
Vase, dripping glaze, brown, dark brown, and green, incised "Dedham Pottery," short firing lines at rim and base, 9 x 7" **700**
Vase, dripping glaze, green over red, incised "Dedham," 9 x 5" **800**
Vase, dripping glaze, oxblood and gunmetal, 9 x 4½" **1,300**
Vase, luster glaze, blue and café–au–lait, incised "Dedham Pottery," 7½ x 4¾" **750**
Vase, luster glaze, garnet to green, incised "DEDHAM, POTTERY/HCR," 6½ x 5" **1,200**

Vase, ovoid, glossy mottled gray–green glaze, incised "Dedham
Pottery/HCR," 6½ x 4½" **700**
Vase, ovoid, snag–de–boeuf glaze, incised "Dedham Pottery," 5 x 3½" **750**
Vase, ovoid, textured, red and brown, incised Dedham Pottery, 8¼ x 6" **2,700**

EDWIN KNOWLES

In 1900 Edwin M. Knowles established the Edwin M. Knowles China Company in Chester, West Virginia. Company offices were located in East Liverpool, Ohio. The company made semi–porcelain dinnerware, kitchenware, specialties, and toilet wares and was known for its commitment to having the most modern and best equipped plants in the industry.

In 1913 a second plant in Newell, West Virginia, was opened. The company operated its Chester pottery until 1931, at which time the plant was sold to the Harker Pottery Company. Production continued at the Newell pottery. Edwin M. Knowles China Company ceased operations in 1963.

The Edwin M. Knowles Company name resurfaced in the 1970s when the Bradford Exchange acquired rights to the company's name. The Bradford Exchange uses the Knowles name to front some of its collector plate series. The name also has been attached to Rockwell items. Bradford Knowles–marked pieces are made by offshore manufacturers, not in the United States at either of the old Knowles locations.

Do not confuse Edwin M. Knowles China Company with Knowles, Taylor, and Knowles, also a manufacturer of fine dinnerware. They are two separate companies. The only Edwin M. Knowles China Company mark that might be confusing is "Knowles" spelled with a large "K."

Knowles dinnerware lines enjoyed modest sales success. No one line dominated. The more popular lines among general collectors are: Deanna, a solid color line found occasionally with decals and introduced in 1938; Esquire, designed by Russel Wright and manufactured between 1956 and 1962; and Yorktown, a modernistic line introduced in 1936 and found in a variety of decal patterns such as Bar Harbor, Golden Wheat, Penthouse, and Water Lily.

Country collectors concentrate on Daisy, Fruits, Poppy, Tulip, Tuliptime, Wheat, and Wildflower decal patterns. The patterns are colorful, light, and airy. Most are commonly found on plain white pieces with little or no border decoration.

When collecting decal pieces, buy only pieces whose decals are complete and still retain their vivid colors. Edwin M. Knowles China Company did make a Utility Ware line that has found favor with kitchen collectibles collectors. Prices for Utility Ware are comparable to prices for similar pieces in the dinnerware patterns.

Alice Ann, bowl, oval, 8" d	**$12**
Alice Ann, creamer	5
Alice Ann, gravy boat	20
Alice Ann, plate, 8" d	8
Alice Ann, saucer	5
Arcadia, casserole	25
Arcadia, platter	10
Beverly, casserole	22
Beverly, cup	5
Beverly, eggcup, double	12
Beverly, plate, 8½" d	6

Beverly, teapot 30
Deanna, bread and butter plate, yellow, 6" d 8
Deanna, butter dish, open, dark blue 15
Deanna, coffee server, green 38
Deanna, coffee server, stripes 35
Deanna, creamer, red 10
Deanna, cup and saucer, yellow 12
Deanna, dinner plate, dark blue, 10" d 15
Deanna, gravy boat 15
Deanna, lug soup, yellow 6
Deanna, platter, Daisies 12
Deanna, vegetable bowl, orange–red, 8" d 22
Diana, creamer 8
Diana, cup 5
Diana, gravy boat 22
Diana, plate, 6" d 3
Diana, plate, 9" d 10
Diana, soup bowl 15
Esquire, bread and butter plate, Botanica, beige ground, 6¼" d 8
Esquire, creamer 12
Esquire, cup and saucer, Snowflower 22
Esquire, fruit bowl, Snowflower, 5½" d 12
Esquire, platter, Queen's Lace, 13" l 25
Esquire, saucer 5
Esquire, vegetable bowl, divided, Seeds 70
Fruits, batter pitcher, cov 30
Fruits, pie server 22
Fruits, syrup, cov 22
Fruits, utility plate 18
Marion, ribbed, creamer 8
Marion, ribbed, cup 8
Marion, ribbed, plate, 7" d 6
Marion, ribbed, platter, 13¾" l 22
Marion, ribbed, vegetable bowl 15
Potomac, butter dish, open 22
Potomac, chop plate 15
Roslyn, casserole 28
Roslyn, cup 8
Roslyn, gravy boat 22
Roslyn, plate, 7" d 10
Roslyn, sugar 12
Sylvan, casserole 30
Sylvan, plate, 9" d 10
Sylvan, saucer 2
Sylvan, sugar 12
Tulip, Utility Ware, cookie jar 40
Tulip, Utility Ware, pie plate 20
Williamsburg, creamer 8
Williamsburg, saucer 2
Yorktown, bread and butter plate, yellow, 6" d 8
Yorktown, chop plate, burgundy, 10¾" d 20

FIESTA

The Homer Laughlin China Company introduced Fiesta dinnerware in January, 1936, at the Pottery and Glass Show in Pittsburgh, Pennsylvania. Fredrick Rhead designed the pattern; Arthur Kraft and Bill Bensford molded it. Dr. A. V. Bleininger and H. W. Thiemecke developed the glazes.

The original five colors were red, dark blue, light green (with a trace of blue), brilliant yellow, and ivory. A vigorous marketing campaign took place between 1939 and 1943. In 1938 turquoise was added; red was removed in 1943 because of the war effort and did not reappear until 1959. In 1951 light green, dark blue, and ivory were retired and forest green, rose, chartreuse, and gray were added to the line. Other color changes took place in the late 1950s, including the addition of a medium green.

Fiesta ware was redesigned in 1969 and discontinued in 1972–73. In 1986 Fiesta was reintroduced by Homer Laughlin China Company. The new china body shrinks more than the old semi-vitreous and ironstone pieces, thus making the new pieces slightly smaller than the earlier pieces. The modern colors also differ in tone. The cobalt blue is darker than the old blue. Other modern colors are black, white, apricot, and rose.

Fiesta is one of the most widely recognized dinnerware patterns. During its heyday it was probably the most popular dinnerware made in America. Original production began with fifty–four items. Several specialized pieces and sets were made in the 1940s as sales stimulators. These limited production items, such as handled chop plates, covered refrigerator jars, and French casseroles are highly prized today. Millions of pieces of Fiesta dinnerware were manufactured during its forty years of production.

The molds used originally had the name molded into the base of the piece. The new 1986 line is made from original molds but also carries a stamped mark making them easily recognizable.

There is some concern today over the red glaze. Uranium oxide was used as a base for this bright glaze. During World War II this glaze was suspended and the popular color did not reappear until May of 1959. Production of this uranium oxide glaze continued until 1972. Some radiation can be detected on the red glazed pieces and these should not be used. Care should be taken when storing and displaying them as well.

References: Linda D. Farmer, *The Farmer's Wife Fiesta Inventory and Price Guide,* published by author, 1984; Sharon and Bob Huxford, *The Collectors Encyclopedia of Fiesta, Seventh Edition,* Collector Books, 1992, 1996 value update; Harry L. Rinker, *Dinnerware of the 20th Century: The Top 500 Patterns,* House of Collectibles, 1997; Jeffrey B. Snyder, *Fiesta: Homer Laughlin China Company's Colorful Dinnerware,* Schiffer Publishing, 1997.

Collectors' Clubs: Fiesta Club of America, Inc, PO Box 15383, Machesney Park, IL 61115; Fiesta Collectors Club, PO Box 471, Valley City, OH 44280.

Ashtray, gray	$65
Ashtray, red	45
Ashtray, rose	85
Ashtray, yellow	40
Berry Bowl, cobalt blue, large	45
Bowl, chartreuse	40
Bowl, gray	40
Bowl, turquoise	40
Bowl, yellow	18
Bread and Butter Plate, 6", chartreuse	8
Bread and Butter Plate, 6", gray	8
Bread and Butter Plate, 6", medium green	25
Bread and Butter Plate, 6", yellow	3
Bud Vase, cobalt blue	95
Bud Vase, yellow	90
Butter Dish, cobalt blue, ½ lb	225
Cake Server, Kitchen Kraft, cobalt, orig label	275
Cake Server, Kitchen Kraft, red	150
Cake Server, Kitchen Kraft, yellow	150
Candlesticks, pr, cobalt blue, tripod	850
Candlesticks, pr, red, bulb	125
Carafe, cobalt blue	375
Carafe, red	375
Carafe, turquoise	245
Casserole, cov, chartreuse	325
Casserole, cov, cobalt blue	30
Casserole, cov, medium green	1,100
Casserole, cov, rose	325
Casserole, French, yellow	345
Casserole, open, ivory	125
Chop Plate, chartreuse, 15" d	135
Chop Plate, cobalt blue, 13" d	35
Chop Plate, forest green, 13" d	95
Chop Plate, medium green, 13" d	275

Left: Ashtray, turquoise, unmkd, 5⁷/₁₆" d, $30.
Right: Dinner Plate, light green, 10³/₈" d, $40.

```
Chop Plate, red, 15" d ...........................................    40
Chop Plate, rose, 13" d ..........................................    95
Chop Plate, turquoise, 15" d .....................................    50
Coffeepot, cov, cobalt blue ......................................   175
Coffeepot, cov, ivory ............................................   225
Coffeepot, cov, red ..............................................   225
Coffeepot, cov, rose .............................................   450
Coffeepot, cov, turquoise ........................................   210
Coffeepot, cov, yellow ...........................................   200
Compote, ivory, 12" d ...........................................   195
Cream Soup, chartreuse ..........................................    90
Cream Soup, cobalt blue .........................................    30
Cream Soup, forest green ........................................    90
Cream Soup, ivory ...............................................    75
Cream Soup, red .................................................    75
Cream Soup, yellow ..............................................    45
Creamer, stick, cobalt blue ......................................    55
Creamer, stick, turquoise ........................................    95
Creamer, stick, yellow ...........................................    45
Creamer, table size, chartreuse ..................................    35
Creamer, table size, red .........................................    32
Creamer, table size, rose ........................................    40
Cup and Saucer, cobalt blue ......................................    25
Cup and Saucer, red .............................................    25
Cup and Saucer, yellow ..........................................    25
Deep Plate, chartreuse ..........................................    50
Deep Plate, forest green ........................................    50
Deep Plate, red .................................................    45
Deep Plate, rose ................................................    50
Deep Plate, turquoise ...........................................    40
Demitasse Cup and Saucer, forest green ..........................   625
Demitasse Cup and Saucer, ivory .................................    65
Demitasse Cup and Saucer, rose ..................................   625
Demitasse Pot, red ..............................................   500
Demitasse Saucer, red ...........................................    12
Dessert Bowl, 6" d, chartreuse ...................................    45
Dessert Bowl, 6" d, forest green .................................    50
Dessert Bowl, 6" d, gray .........................................    50
Dessert Bowl, 6" d, ivory ........................................    30
Dessert Bowl, 6" d, red ..........................................    40
Dessert Bowl, 6" d, rose .........................................    50
Dessert Bowl, 6" d, turquoise ....................................    30
Dessert Bowl, 6" d, yellow .......................................    30
Dinner Plate, 10" d, chartreuse ..................................    50
Dinner Plate, 10" d, cobalt blue .................................    35
Dinner Plate, 10" d, gray ........................................    50
Dinner Plate, 10" d, ivory .......................................    32
Dinner Plate, 10" d, turquoise ...................................    22
Dinner Plate, 10" d, yellow ......................................    32
Dish, divided, chartreuse ........................................    85
Dish, divided, light green .......................................    40
```

Eggcup, chartreuse **125**
Eggcup, gray **130**
Eggcup, red **90**
Eggcup, rose **130**
Eggcup, turquoise **50**
Eggcup, yellow **45**
Fruit Bowl, chartreuse, 4³/₄" d **25**
Fruit Bowl, dark green, 4³/₄" d **25**
Fruit Bowl, forest green, 5¹/₂" d **32**
Fruit Bowl, gray, 4³/₄" d **25**
Fruit Bowl, ivory, 4³/₄" d **20**
Fruit Bowl, light green, 5³/₄" d **22**
Fruit Bowl, red, 4³/₄" d **25**
Fruit Bowl, rose, 5¹/₂" d **32**
Fruit Bowl, yellow, 4³/₄" d **20**
Gravy Boat, red **65**
Grill Plate, cobalt blue, 10¹/₂" d **65**
Grill Plate, turquoise, 10¹/₂" d **40**
Jug, chartreuse, 2 pt **145**
Jug, forest green, 2 pt **145**
Jug, ivory, 2 pt **95**
Jug, ivory, 3 pt **65**
Jug, light green, 2 pt **95**
Jug, rose, 2 pt **145**
Jug, turquoise, 2 pt **95**
Juice Pitcher, gray **2,200**
Juice Pitcher, yellow **55**
Juice Set, pitcher and 6 tumblers, yellow **350**
Juice Tumbler, cobalt blue **45**
Juice Tumbler, ivory **45**
Juice Tumbler, red **45**
Juice Tumbler, rose **55**
Luncheon Plate, 9" d, chartreuse **15**
Luncheon Plate, 9" d, forest green **18**
Luncheon Plate, 9" d, gray **15**
Luncheon Plate, 9" d, ivory **15**
Luncheon Plate, 9" d, light green **12**
Luncheon Plate, 9" d, rose **50**
Luncheon Plate, 9" d, yellow **30**
Marmalade, red **325**
Mixing Bowl, cobalt blue, #2 . . . . **190**
Mixing Bowl, cobalt blue, #5 . . . . **240**
Mixing Bowl, cobalt blue, #7 . . . . **625**
Mixing Bowl, light green, #2 . . . . **115**
Mixing Bowl, red, #1 . . . . **225**
Mixing Bowl, turquoise, #1 . . . . **225**
Mixing Bowl, yellow, #2 . . . . **95**
Mixing Bowl, yellow, #6 . . . . **225**
Mug, chartreuse **95**
Mug, light green **55**
Mug, red **70**

Mug, turquoise 50
Mug, yellow 50
Mustard, light green 250
Nappy, chartreuse, 5½" d 32
Nappy, chartreuse, 8½" d 50
Nappy, dark green, 5½" d 32
Nappy, dark green, 8½" d 75
Nappy, light green, 8½" d 40
Nappy, medium green, 5½" d 110
Nappy, medium green, 8½" d 195
Nappy, red, 8½" d 65
Nappy, rose, 8½" d 65
Nappy, turquoise, 8½" d 40
Onion Soup, cov, ivory 750
Onion Soup, cov, yellow 600
Onion Soup Lid, red 450
Pepper Shaker, cobalt blue 10
Pie Plate, cobalt blue 65
Pitcher, disc, chartreuse 225
Pitcher, disc, gray 365
Pitcher, disc, medium green 1,700
Pitcher, disc, turquoise 100
Pitcher, disc, yellow 75
Pitcher, ice lip, red 195
Platter, forest green 65
Platter, gray 60
Platter, ivory 40
Platter, medium green 35
Platter, red 40
Platter, turquoise 90
Relish, divided, cobalt, missing center 150
Relish Set, ivory 350
Salad Bowl, ftd, light green 575
Salad Bowl, ftd, red 600

Left: Coffee Server, cov, Amberstone, $40.

Right: Teapot, cov, cobalt blue, $195.

Salt and Pepper Shakers, pr, light green 15
Salt and Pepper Shakers, pr, medium green 175
Salt Shaker, red 10
Sauce Boat, chartreuse 70
Sauce Boat, cobalt blue 55
Sauce Boat, rose 70
Sauce Boat, turquoise 30
Soup Plate, flat, yellow 30
Stack Set, cobalt blue 35
Sugar, cov, chartreuse 65
Sugar, cov, cobalt blue 20
Sugar, cov, forest green 65
Sugar, cov, gray 75
Sugar, cov, light green 45
Syrup, ivory 650
Syrup, light green 585
Teapot, large, light green 200
Teapot, large, red 295
Teapot, large, yellow 200
Teapot, medium, chartreuse 250
Teapot, medium, cobalt blue 195
Teapot, medium, medium green 1,550
Tom and Jerry Set, bowl and 8 mugs, ivory 750
Utility Tray, cobalt blue 30
Utility Tray, light green 40
Utility Tray, yellow 40
Vase, cobalt blue, 12" h 1,295
Vase, gray, 10" h 800
Vase, ivory, 10" h 975
Vase, yellow, 12" h 1,095
Water Tumbler, light green 65
Water Tumbler, red 75

FLOW BLUE

Flow blue, or flowing blue, is the name applied to a cobalt blue and white china, whose color, when fired in a kiln, produced a flowing or smudged effect. The blue varies in color from dark cobalt to a grayish or steel blue. The flow varies from very slight to a heavy blur where the pattern cannot be easily recognized. The blue color does not permeate through the china.

Flow blue was first produced around 1835 in the Staffordshire district of England by a large number of potters including Alcock, Davenport, J. Wedgwood, Grindley, New Wharf, and Johnson Brothers. Most early flow blue, 1830s to 1870s, was ironstone. The late patterns, 1880s to 1910s, and modern patterns, after 1910, were usually a more delicate semi–porcelain variety. Approximately 95% of the flow blue was made in England, with the remaining 5% made in Germany, Holland, France, Belgium, and the United States. American manufacturers included Mercer, Warwick, and Wheeling Pottery companies.

References: Mary F. Gaston, *The Collector's Encyclopedia of Flow Blue*, (1983, 1996 value update), *Second Series*, (1994, 1996 value update), Collector Books; Ellen R.

Hill, *Mulberry Ironstone, Flow Blue's Best Kept Little Secret,* published by author, 1993, (1996 revision); Jeffrey B. Snyder, *Fascinating Flow Blue,* Schiffer Publishing, 1997; Jeffrey B. Snyder, *Flow Blue: A Collector's Guide to Pattern, History and Values, Revised,* Schiffer Publishing, 1996; Jeffrey B. Snyder, *Historic Flow Blue,* Shiffer Publishing, 1994; Petra Williams, *Flow Blue China—An Aid to Identification, Revised Edition,* Fountain House East, 1981; Petra Williams, *Flow Blue China II, Revised Edition,* Fountain House East, 1981; Petra Williams, *Flow Blue China and Mulberry Ware—Similarity and Value Guide, Revised Edition,* Fountain House East, 1993.

Collectors' Club: Flow Blue International Collectors' Club, 11560 West 95 Street, #297, Shawnee Mission, KS 66214.

Museum: Hershey Museum of American Life, Hershey, PA 17033.

Berry Bowl, Alaska, W H Grindley, 5¼" d	**$35**
Berry Bowl, Gironde, W H Grindley, 6" d	**35**
Berry Bowl, Iris, Wilkinson, 5¼" d	**15**
Berry Bowl, Roses and Ribbons, John Maddock & Sons, gold trim, gold sponged work on body, 7½" dish, 8¾" drainer	**270**
Bowl, oval, Alaska, W H Grindley, 9" l	**120**
Bowl, oval, Astoria, Upper Hanley Pottery, 11½" l, 6½" w	**145**
Bowl, oval, cattle scene, W Adams & Sons, c1800s, 19" l, 14" w	**950**
Bowl, round, Bay, Ford & Sons, Ltd	**75**
Bowl, round, Norfolk, Doulton, 8" d	**70**
Bread and Butter Plate, Waverly, WH Grindley	**65**
Butter Dish, cov, Oregon, Mayer, 12 panel lid, c1845	**450**
Butter Dish, cov, Touraine, Stanley, with drain, tiny chip on rim of base, c1898	**200**
Butter Pat, Daisy, Burgess & Leigh, c1896	**35**
Butter Pat, Oakland, John Maddock & Sons, 2¾ x 2⅞"	**45**
Butter Pat, Stanley, Johnson Brothers, 4¼" h, 8" d	**465**
Butter Pat, Virginia, John Maddock, set of 10	**120**
Cake Plate, Pansy, Warwick China Co, gold trim, 10" d	**170**
Cake Stand, Delph, unmkd, pedestal base, gold trim, 7½" d	**300**
Cake Stand, Persian Spray, Doulton, gold designs, 3" h, 9" d	**300**
Cereal Bowl, Harvest, Alfred Meakin, Ltd, 7⅞" d	**50**
Cereal Bowl, Meissen, T Furnival, J R Gibney printed mark	**45**
Chamber Pot, cov, Campion	**400**
Chamber Pot, cov, Doreen, W H Grindley	**425**
Chamber Pot, open, attributed to Ashworth, Hizen, Mason's, snake shape handle, 5½" h, 8½" d	**420**
Cheese Dish, Iris, Doulton, 9½" h, 9" d	**600**
Cheese Dish, Mixed Flower, Doulton, gold trim 7½" h, 11½" l	**520**
Chocolate Pot, Abbey, George Jones, 10" h	**200**
Compote, Roseville, John Maddock & Sons, gold trim 4" h, 9" d	**400**
Creamer, Alton, W H Grindley, 3½" h	**110**
Creamer, Chapoo, Wedgwood, primary shape, 5"	**400**
Creamer, Ning Po, Hall, primary shape, c1845, 5"	**200**
Creamer, Pelew, Challinor, lighthouse shape, c1840, 5¼"	**100**
Cup, Bay, Ford & Sons, Ltd, ships in water	**45**
Cup, Norfolk, Doulton, buildings and windmill scene	**100**
Cup and Saucer, Brunswick, New Wharf Pottery, 3½" h cup, 5¾" d saucer	**90**

Cup and Saucer, cattle scene, unmkd, beaded border 95
Cup and Saucer, Iris, Arthur J Wilkinson, Royal Staffordshire, gold outline,
  2¼" h cup, 3" d saucer 80
Cup and Saucer, Lakewood, Wood & Son, overlaid pattern, gold designs 95
Cup and Saucer, Morning Glory, unmkd, handleless cup, pedestal base 145
Cup and Saucer, Oregon, Johnson Brothers, gold trim, 2⅜" cup, 6" d saucer .. 95
Cup and Saucer, Pekin, Thomas Dimmock, 2¾" h handleless cup, 5¾" d
  saucer 155
Cup and Saucer, Touraine, Stanley, c1898, price for 4 sets 125
Cup Plate, Scinde, J & G Alcock 150
Demitasse Cup and Saucer, Ashburton, W H Grindley 65
Demitasse Cup and Saucer, Canton, John Maddock, 2½" h 115
Dresser Set, Corey Hill, polychromed, 12½" l tray, candle holder, 2 cov
  boxes, hair receiver, pin tray, and ring tray, tray mkd "England" 1,000
Fruit Bowl, Blue Rose, W H Grindley, 5" d 30
Fruit Compote, Cleopatra, E Walley, 9" h, 13" w 1,000
Gravy Boat, Beatrice, John Maddock, gold trim, 9" l 95
Gravy Boat, Burslem Berries, Newport Pottery Co, Ltd, pedestal base 90
Gravy Boat, Chapoo, Wedgwood, c1850 225
Gravy Boat, Ford & Sons, Watford 75
Gravy Boat, Osborne, WH Grindley, gold trim, 6½" l 110
Gravy Boat with Underplate, Ladas, Ridgways, gold trim, gold outline on
  emb body design, 8¾" l 180
Gravy Boat with Underplate, Rose, W H Grindley, gold trim 145
Gravy Boat with Underplate, Touraine, Stanley, c1898 150
Jardiniere, large open petaled flowers design, Thomas Forester & Sons,
  9⅜" h, 8½" d 550
Ladle, Coburg, Barker & Kent, 7" l 135
Ladle, Luzerne, Mercer Pottery Co, gold trim 295
Milk Pitcher, Chapoo, Wedgwood, bulbous shape, c1850, 6" h 600

Left: Platter, Scroll, mkd "F.M.," 14¾" l, 12" w, $250.

Right: Plate, Chapoo, mkd "Ironstone / J. Wedgwood," 9" d, $80.

Mitten Relish, Chapoo, Wedgwood, c1850 50
Pitcher, Amoy, unmkd, attributed to Adams, 19th C, 7" h 650
Pitcher, Astoria, New Wharf Pottery, 6³/₄" h 360
Pitcher, Cavandish, Keeling, c1910, 7" h 195
Pitcher, Celestial, John Ridgway & Co, initials "J. R." in oval shape with
    crown, c1800s, 7" h 650
Pitcher, Chapoo, Wedgwood, lighthouse shape, partial restoration to handle
    and rim, c1850 1,200
Pitcher, Chusan, C Collinson & Co, pedestal base, 11" h 900
Pitcher, Ferrara, Wedgwood, 6" h 325
Pitcher, Monarch, Myott, Son, & Co, 5" h 245
Pitcher, Poppy, Doulton, 7³/₄" h 300
Pitcher, Verona, Wood & Son, 8¹/₂" h 450
Plate, Bisley, W H Grindley, 9" d 80
Plate, Cauldon, England, sponged gold work around fluted border, 10" d 95
Plate, Chiswick, Ridgways, scalloped edge, 10" d 80
Plate, Claremont, Johnson Brothers, 10" d 80
Plate, Coburg, John Edwards, imp "JE" and "Warranted," 8" d 125
Plate, Fulton, Johnson Brothers, 10" d 85
Plate, Greville, Bishop & Stonier, 10¹/₄" d 95
Plate, Halford, Ford & Sons, Ltd, 10" d 70
Plate, Iris, Cauldon, England, sponged gold work on body and fluted border,
    10" d 85
Plate, Old English Rural Scenes, William Adams & Sons, 10" d 110
Plate, Onion, Allertons, 8" d 85
Plate, Pekin, Davenport, gold accents, 10¹/₂" d 150
Plate, Poppy, New Wharf Pottery, 8³/₄" d 75
Plate, Portsmouth, New Wharf Pottery, gold work around outer border, 9" d .. 90
Plate, Sutton, Ridgways, gold outline on floral design, 9" d 75
Plate, Swallow, Grove & Stark, 10" d 80
Plate, The Bolingbroke, Ridgways, gold embellished design, 10" d 75
Plate, The Holland, Alfred Meakin, gold trim, 10" d 85
Plate, Tonquin, W Adams & Sons, 8¹/₂" d 145
Platter, Bourne & Leigh, Albion Pottery, 14" l 300
Platter, Chapoo, Wedgwood, c1850, 13³/₄ x 10¹/₂", chip on underside 150
Platter, Chapoo, Wedgwood, c1850, 15³/₄ x 12¹/₄" 350
Platter, Chinese, Well and Tree, Dimmock, c1845, 15³/₄ x 12" 350
Platter, Coburg, mkd "B & K," attributed to Barker & Kent, 13" l, 10¹/₂" w 300
Platter, Coburg, Edwards, c1860, 10 x 7³/₄" 100
Platter, Doric, unknown mfgr, 19³/₄ x 15⁵/₈" 575
Platter, Indian, Pratt, c1840, 15 x 11¹/₂" 150
Platter, Jeddo, W Adams, c1845, 18 x 14" 200
Platter, Kiswick, New Wharf Pottery, 14" l 320
Platter, Oregon, T J and J Mayer, 18 x 14" 500
Platter, Pekin, Royal Staffordshire, border pattern, 8" d 60
Platter, Savoy, Empire Porcelain Co, 13¹/₂" l, 10¹/₂" w 245
Platter, Turkey/Wild Turkey, "Cauldon England" printed in blue, 23¹/₄" l,
    19¹/₂" w 950
Platter, Whampoa, Mellor & Venables, c1840, 21 x 17¹/₄" 900
Rose Bowl, Morning Glory, Thomas Hughes & Son, gold trim, 6" d 165
Salad Bowl, Arundel, Doulton, silver rim 240

Salad Fork and Spoon, Arundel, Doulton   275
Saucer, Navarre, Wedgwood & Co, Ltd, gold trim, 6½" d   35
Saucer, Neopolitan, Johnson Brothers, gold designs superimposed over printed pattern, 6" d   30
Saucer, Rock, E. Challinor   50
Sauce Tureen, open, Anemone, Lockhart & Arthur, pedestal base, 2 handles . .   425
Sauce Tureen and Underplate, cov, Burleigh, Burgess & Leigh, gold trim, 5 x 8" tureen, 7¾ x 5¼" underplate   550
Sauce Tureen and Underplate, cov, Chapoo, Wedgwood, c1850 1,100
Sauce Tureen and Underplate, cov, Oregon, Mayer, with ladle, finial reattachment to lid, restoration to base, c1845   600
Serving Dish, open, Leipsic, J Clementson, rect, 10½" l, 8" w   375
Serving Tray, Hauge, Josiah Wedgwood, 17½" l, 8" w   475
Shaving Mug, Stratford, Burgess & Leigh, Middleport Pottery, 54¼" h   92
Soap Dish, cov, Doreen, W H Grindley   320
Soup Bowl, Clayton, Johnson Brothers, 7½" d   55
Soup Plate, Crescent, W H Grindley, gold luster designs   80
Soup Plate, Eileen, W H Grindley, 10" d   75
Soup Tureen, cov, Hindustan, Maddock, with white Staffordshire ladle, 14" w, 8" d, 9" h   600
Soup Tureen, open, W H Grindley, gold embellishments, 7" h, 14" l   550
Sugar, cov, Amoy, Davenport, 8½" h   650
Sugar, cov, Chapoo, Wedgwood, primary shape, restoration to foot of base and rim, c1850   475
Sugar, cov, Columbia, Clementson & Young, pedestal base   525
Sugar, cov, Dahlia, unmkd, attributed to Edward Challinor, 7½" h   450
Sugar, cov, Kaolin, Podmore, Walker & Co, pedestal base   650
Sugar, cov, Temple, Podmore, Walker & Co, gothic shape, lion head handles, finial reattached, c1850   300
Teapot, cov, Cabul, Challinor, lighthouse shape, hairlines, c1847   700

Left: Sugar Bowl, cov, Tonquin, c1850, 8" h, $350.
Right: Sauce Dish, Amoy, Davenport, 5¼" d, $60.

Teapot, cov, California, unmkd, attributed to Podmore, Walker & Co, unmkd except for registry mark of April 2, 1849, 8½" h **850**

Teapot, cov, Chapoo, Wedgwood, primary shape, restoration to teapot and lid, c1850, 9" h **400**

Teapot, cov, Countryside, H J Wood, rural buildings and man feeding chickens **490**

Teapot, cov, Nankin, unmkd, attributed to Cauldon, pedestal base, c1800s ... **900**

Teapot, cov, Peking, Ridgeway, primary shape, rosebud finial, partial restoration on spout, c1845, 8¾" h **650**

Teapot, cov, Scinde, Alcock, pumpkin shape, minor restoration to lid, small chip on spout, c1840, 8½" h **725**

Teapot, cov, Shell, E Challinor **850**

Toothbrush Holder, Doreen, W H Grindley **255**

Toothbrush Holder, Marguerite, H Brothers, gold sponged work **300**

Vase, Clematis, Barker & Kent, 8" h **425**

Vegetable Bowl, cov, Claremont, Johnson Brothers, floral designs, gold outline **320**

Vegetable Bowl, cov, Douglas, Ford & Sons, 11" l, 8" d **320**

Vegetable Bowl, cov, Floral, Thomas Hughes & Son, rect **295**

Vegetable Bowl, cov, Le Pavot, W H Grindley, 11" l, 7" d **320**

Vegetable Bowl, cov, Oregon, Mayer, pedestal, c1845, 9½ x 9½" **625**

Vegetable Bowl, cov, Touraine, Stanley, c1898, 11 x 6½" **225**

Vegetable Bowl, open, Chapoo, Wedgwood, c1850, 9½ x 7" **200**

Wash Bowl and Pitcher, Belmont, W H Grindley **1,500**

Wash Bowl and Pitcher, Doreen, W H Grindley **1,200**

Wash Bowl and Pitcher, Hong Kong, Meigh, bulbous pitcher, 6 concave panels, partial restoration to bowl, c1845 .... **650**

Wash Bowl and Pitcher, Ormonde, Alfred Meakin, Ltd **1,500**

Wash Bowl and Pitcher, Salisbury, Ford & Sons **2,200**

Waste Bowl, Celeste, unknown mfg, 5¾" d, 5½" h **220**

Waste Bowl, Chapoo, Wedgwood, 14 panels, restored, c1850, 5⅜" d, 3¼" h **150**

FRANCISCAN

Franciscan Ware was manufactured by Gladding, McBean and Company, located in Glendale and Los Angeles, California. Charles Gladding, Peter McBean and George Chambers organized the firm in 1875. Early products included sewer pipes and architectural items.

Production of dinnerware and art pottery began in 1943. The dinnerware was marketed under the trademark Franciscan and first appeared in plain shapes and bright colors. Soon, skillfully molded underglaze patterns were developed. Patterns like Desert Rose, Ivy, Autumn, and Apple are eagerly sought by Country collectors. Numerous setting and service pieces allow collectors to assemble large collections. More pieces are seen at flea markets and antique shows.

Franciscan Ware has been marked with over eighty different marks. Many contain the pattern name, patent numbers or dates.

References: Delleen Enge, *Franciscan Ware: Embossed Hand Painted, Made In California Only,* published by author, 1992; Delleen Enge, *Plain and Fancy Franciscan Made in California,* published by author, 1996; Harry L. Rinker, *Dinnerware of the*

20th Century: The Top 500 Patterns, House of Collectibles, 1997; Jeffrey B. Snyder, *Franciscan Dining Services,* Schiffer Publishing, 1996.

Collectors' Club: Franciscan Collectors Club, 8412 5th Avenue NE, Seattle, WA 98115.

Apple, ashtray **$20**
Apple, baker, rect **225**
Apple, berry bowl **4**
Apple, bread and butter plate, 6" d **5**
Apple, bread and butter plate, 6½" d **4**
Apple, butter dish, cov, ¼ lb **45**
Apple, cake plate, 12½" d **35**
Apple, casserole, cov, 1½ qt **85**
Apple, casserole, individual, with handle **75**
Apple, cereal bowl, 6" d **10**
Apple, child's plate **125**
Apple, chocolate mug **100**
Apple, chop plate, 12" d **55**
Apple, chop plate, 14" d **100**
Apple, cigarette box **110**
Apple, coaster **50**
Apple, cookie jar, cov **250**
Apple, creamer **15**
Apple, cream soup **8**
Apple, cup **10**
Apple, demitasse cup **50**
Apple, dinner plate, 10½" d **20**
Apple, fruit bowl **10**
Apple, gravy boat and underplate **35**
Apple, grill plate **135**
Apple, juice tumbler, 5 oz **45**
Apple, jumbo cup **65**
Apple, luncheon plate, 9½" d **18**
Apple, milk pitcher **110**
Apple, mixing bowls, set of 3 . . . . **275**
Apple, mug **125**
Apple, pepper mill, cylindrical **165**

Apple, compote, 4" h, 5" d, $65.

Apple, pie server 30
Apple, platter, 14" l 45
Apple, platter, 19" l 295
Apple, relish 30
Apple, salad bowl, large 145
Apple, salad plate, 8½" d 12
Apple, salad plate, Crescent 35
Apple, serving platter, 14" l 25
Apple, sherbet 22
Apple, soup bowl, 8½" d 15
Apple, soup bowl, ftd 32
Apple, soup plate, flanged rim 20
Apple, soup tureen, small 425
Apple, steak plate, coupe shape 130
Apple, sugar, cov 40
Apple, sugar, open 20
Apple, syrup jug, tall 85
Apple, teapot, cov 95
Apple, tidbit server, 2 tier 45
Apple, tumbler 40
Apple, vegetable bowl, divided 45
Apple, water pitcher 120
Bountiful, cereal bowl 20
Bountiful, creamer 35
Bountiful, creamer and sugar 65
Bountiful, cup and saucer 18
Bountiful, fruit bowl 25
Bountiful, sugar 45
Cafe Royal, baker, square, 1 qt 160
Cafe Royal, dinner plate 10
Cafe Royal, dish, heart shaped 100
Cafe Royal, mug, bulbous 40
Cafe Royal, platter, small 32
Coronado Swirl, chop plate, 12" d 50
Coronado Swirl, dinner plate, 10½" d 20
Coronado Swirl, gravy boat and underplate, yellow, satin 25
Coronado Swirl, sherbet, ftd 20
Coronado Swirl, vegetable bowl, oval, yellow, satin 25
Daisy, bread and butter plate 5
Daisy, cup 12
Daisy, dinner plate 15
Daisy, lug soup bowl 15
Daisy, saucer 5
Desert Rose, ashtray, oval 85
Desert Rose, bread and butter plate 5
Desert Rose, bud vase 85
Desert Rose, butter pat 18
Desert Rose, candlesticks, pr 85
Desert Rose, casserole, cov 85
Desert Rose, cereal bowl 12
Desert Rose, child's plate, divided 150

Desert Rose, chop platter, 12" l   32
Desert Rose, chop platter, 14" l   125
Desert Rose, cigarette box   85
Desert Rose, coffeepot, cov, green trim lid   125
Desert Rose, creamer and sugar, cov   50
Desert Rose, cup   10
Desert Rose, cup and saucer   12
Desert Rose, demitasse cup and saucer   30
Desert Rose, dinner plate, 10½" d   12
Desert Rose, eggcup   35
Desert Rose, goblet   250
Desert Rose, gravy boat   35
Desert Rose, juice tumbler   55
Desert Rose, luncheon plate, 9½" d   15
Desert Rose, milk pitcher   85
Desert Rose, mixing bowl, set of 3   500
Desert Rose, mug, tall   40
Desert Rose, pepper mill   125
Desert Rose, pepper mill set   250
Desert Rose, pitcher, ½ qt   100
Desert Rose, pitcher, 1 qt   70
Desert Rose, platter, 14½" l   40
Desert Rose, relish, divided   65
Desert Rose, salad bowl   100
Desert Rose, salad plate   8
Desert Rose, salt and pepper shakers, pr, large   35
Desert Rose, saucer   45
Desert Rose, soup bowl   15

Left: Ivy, dinner plate, 10³/₈" d, $45.
Right: October, dinner plate, brown trim, $45.

Desert Rose, sugar, individual **145**
Desert Rose, syrup pitcher **75**
Desert Rose, vegetable bowl, divided **35**
Desert Rose, water pitcher **100**
Desert Rose, water tumbler **12**
Duet, bread and butter plate, 6" d **8**
Duet, butter dish, cov **30**
Duet, creamer and sugar, cov **25**
Duet, salt and pepper shakers, pr **20**
Duet, vegetable bowl, divided **28**
Forget–Me–Not, cereal bowl **20**
Forget–Me–Not, dinner plate **20**
Forget–Me–Not, salt and pepper shakers, pr **35**
Forget–Me–Not, vegetable bowl, large **35**
Fresh Fruit, cup **8**
Fresh Fruit, dinner plate **25**
Fresh Fruit, platter, 14" l **40**
Ivy, bread and butter plate **8**
Ivy, casserole **165**
Ivy, chop platter, 14" l **185**
Ivy, flat soup bowl **40**
Ivy, gravy boat and underplate **12**
Ivy, luncheon plate **30**
Ivy, oatmeal bowl, ftd **35**
Ivy, platter, 12" l **35**
Ivy, platter, 14" l **45**
Ivy, platter, 19" l **225**
Ivy, salt and pepper shakers, pr **35**
Ivy, sherbet **45**
Ivy, sugar, cov **40**
Ivy, tumbler, Libbey, hp dec **20**
Meadow Rose, baker, rect **145**
Meadow Rose, baker, square **110**
Meadow Rose, bread and butter plate **5**
Meadow Rose, bud vase **75**
Meadow Rose, butter dish **65**
Meadow Rose, candle holder **125**
Meadow Rose, coffee mug, tall **45**
Meadow Rose, compote **150**
Meadow Rose, creamer and sugar **42**
Meadow Rose, cup and saucer **12**
Meadow Rose, dinner plate **15**
Meadow Rose, eggcup **35**
Meadow Rose, goblet **100**
Meadow Rose, gravy boat **65**
Meadow Rose, milk pitcher **85**
Meadow Rose, pepper mill set **175**
Meadow Rose, platter, 14" l **34**
Meadow Rose, relish, divided **85**
Meadow Rose, salad bowl **225**
Meadow Rose, salt and pepper shakers, pr **35**

Meadow Rose, snack plate **95**
Meadow Rose, syrup jug **95**
Meadow Rose, tumbler **35**
Meadow Rose, water pitcher **185**
Mesa, bread and butter plate, 6¼" d **20**
Mesa, creamer and sugar, cov **100**
Mesa, cup and saucer **40**
Mesa, dinner plate, 10½" d **40**
Mesa, salad plate, 8⅛" d **25**
October, creamer and sugar, cov **40**
October, creamer and sugar, open **35**
October, platter, 14" l **35**
Old Fruit, cup and saucer **35**
Old Fruit, gravy boat **130**
Old Fruit, salad plate **35**
Poppy, cereal bowl **45**
Poppy, cup and saucer **35**
Poppy, dinner plate **40**
Poppy, gravy boat and underplate **145**
Starburst, ashtray, individual **25**
Starburst, bread and butter plate, 6" d **12**
Starburst, butter dish, cov **35**
Starburst, fruit bowl **18**
Starburst, relish, divided, triangular, 6½" w **30**
Starburst, salt and pepper shakers, pr **65**
Strawberry Fair, bread and butter plate **8**
Strawberry Fair, cereal bowl **12**
Strawberry Fair, cup **45**
Strawberry Fair, salt and pepper shakers, pr **40**
Trio, dinner plate, 10" d **20**
Trio, platter, 14" l **20**
Trio, vegetable bowl, open **22**
Twilight Rose, platter, 14" l **85**
Wildflower, bread and butter plate **35**
Wildflower, cereal bowl **70**
Wildflower, chop plate, 12" d **350**
Wildflower, creamer **150**

FRANKOMA

John Frank, a ceramics instructor at Oklahoma University, established Frankoma in 1933. In 1938 he moved his commercial production from Norman to Sapulpa. When a fire destroyed the plant in 1939, he rebuilt immediately.

A honey–tan colored clay from Ada was used to make Frankoma pieces prior to 1954. After that date the company switched to red brick clay from Sapulpa. Today some clay is brought into the plant from other areas.

Fire again struck, destroying the Sapulpa plant in September 1983. By July 1984, a new plant was opened. Since the early molds were lost, new molds were designed and made.

Much has changed at Frankoma during the last few years. Native Oklahoma clay is no longer used for some production. The current Frankoma ownership in league with select dealers has made new molds of historic pieces and issued limited edition castings. Finally, many pieces have remained in production for decades. Beware of paying premium prices for a modern piece.

References: Phyllis and Tom Bess, *Frankoma and Other Oklahoma Potteries, Revised,* Schiffer Publishing, 1997; Gary V. Schaum, *Collector's Guide to Frankoma Pottery 1933 Through 1990: Identifying Your Collection Including Gracetone,* L–W Sales, 1997.

Collectors' Club: Frankoma Family Collectors Assoc, PO Box 32571, Oklahoma City, OK 73123.

Ashtray, #914, Dutch shoe, desert gold, red clay, 6"	$25
Aztec, creamer and sugar, cov, #7A&B, prairie green	40
Batter Creamer and Sugar, mini, #504, desert gold, Ada	30
Batter Pitcher, #87, qt, desert gold, Ada	30
Bowl, #45, slender, desert gold, Sapulpa, 12"	30
Bowl, #202, carved, desert gold, Sapulpa, 11"	30
Bud Vase, #32, modern, prairie green, Sapulpa	12
Bud Vase, #43, crocus, prairie green, Sapulpa	15
Clam Shell Dish, #T10, 13½"	35
Cornucopia, #57, brown satin, Sapulpa, 7"	10
Cornucopia, #222, desert gold, Ada, 12"	20
Eagle Pitcher, mini, #555, desert gold, Ada	25
Flower Bowl, prairie green, Sapulpa	25
Gracetone, cup, pink champagne glaze, chipped	2
Gracetone, dinner plate, pink champagne glaze	15
Guernsey Pitcher, cov, #93	15
Honey Jug, #8, prairie green, Sapulpa	15
Honey Jug, #833, brown satin, Sapulpa	15
Horseshoe, salt and pepper shakers, pr, #94L, prairie green, Ada	25
Indian Head, #135, onyx black, 4"	30

Lazybones, creamer, #4A, clay blue, 1953–61, $8.

Juice Jug, #90, no stopper, 1942 mark 75
Lazy Susan, #818, ball bearing base, desert gold, Sapulpa 40
Lazybones, cereal bowl, #4X, brown satin 5
Lazybones, mug, #4M, 16 oz 5
Lazybones, soup cup, #4SC, brown satin, Sapulpa 5
Lazybones, vegetable bowl, #4N, prairie green 10
Match Holder, #89A, royal blue 40
Mug, #C2, flame, Sapulpa 5
Plainsman, baker and warmer, #5W, prairie green, 3 qt 15
Plainsman, creamer, #5A, flame 5
Plainsman, dinner plate, #5F, desert gold, 10½" 12
Plainsman, mug, #5M, desert gold, 16 oz 10
Plainsman, plate, #5G, desert gold, 8" 5
Plainsman, platter, #5P, royal blue 60
Plainsman, platter, #5Q, desert gold, 13" 20
Plainsman, salad bowl, #5X, brown satin 5
Plainsman, salad plate, #5G, desert gold, 8" 5
Plainsman, salt and pepper shakers, pr, #5H, prairie green 5
Plainsman, sauce boat, #5S, prairie green 25
Plainsman, soup cup, #4SC, brown satin 8
Plainsman, teacup, #5CC, 5 oz, prairie green 8
Plainsman, vegetable bowl, #4N, prairie green 10
Planter, duck #208A, prairie green 12
Planter, mallard, #208, royal blue, 1942 40
Vase, #19, fan, prairie green, Sapulpa 30
Vase, #23A, pedestal, brown satin, Sapulpa 8
Vase, #54, fan shell, prairie green, Ada 40
Vase, #228, swan, prairie green, Sapulpa 15
Vase, #272, ringed, brown satin, Sapulpa 8
Vase, #F36, orbit, brown satin, Sapulpa 10
Wagon Wheel, bean pot, individual, #94U, desert gold, Sapulpa 40
Wagon Wheel, casserole, #94V, desert gold, Sapulpa 35
Wagon Wheel, creamer and sugar, #94A & B, desert gold, Sapulpa 25
Wagon Wheel, dessert bowl, #94XO, desert gold, Ada 8
Wagon Wheel, fruit bowl, small, #94XS, desert gold, Ada 10
Wagon Wheel, pitcher, #94D, desert gold, Sapulpa 25
Wagon Wheel, plate, dinner, #94FL, desert gold, 10", Ada 10
Wagon Wheel, plate, dinner, #94FL, desert gold, 10", Sapulpa 10
Wagon Wheel, plate, luncheon, #94F, desert gold, Ada, 9" 10
Wagon Wheel, plate, salad, #94G, desert gold, Ada, 7" 10
Wagon Wheel, platter, #94Q, 13" l, desert gold, Ada 25
Wagon Wheel, platter, #94Q, 13" l, prairie green, Sapulpa 15
Wagon Wheel, salt and pepper shakers, pr, #94H, prairie green, Ada 15
Wagon Wheel, saucer, #94E, desert gold, Ada 6
Wagon Wheel, server, divided, #94QD, desert gold, Sapulpa 25
Wagon Wheel, serving dish, #94N, desert gold, Sapulpa 15
Wagon Wheel, sugar, mini, #510, prairie green, Ada 10
Wagon Wheel, teapot, #94J, 2 cup, desert gold, Sapulpa, no lid 10
Westwind, chili bowl, #6X, prairie green, 14 oz 5
Westwind, cup, #6, prairie green 5
Westwind, teapot, cov, #6J, 2 cup, brown satin 12

FULPER

The American Pottery Company, Flemington, New Jersey, manufactured Fulper Art Pottery, beginning around 1910 and ending in 1930. All pieces were molded. Pieces from the 1930s tend to be of higher quality due to less production pressures.

Pieces exhibit a strong Arts and Crafts and/or Oriental influence. Glazes differ tremendously as Fulper experimented throughout its production period.

Fulper pieces with basic geometric shapes and earth tone glazes are favored by Country collectors. Both matte and high gloss glazes were used. Greens and blues are among the most commonly found glaze colors.

In the late 1990s a number of one–of–a–kind Fulper fakes appeared on the market. While none of the shapes and glazes found on these pieces were part of the Fulper vocabulary, the mark was close enough to the correct Fulper mark to fool many collectors and dealers.

Collectors' Club: Stangl/Fulper Collectors Club, Box 538, Flemington, NJ 08822.

Reproduction Alert.

Artichoke Bowl, leopard's skin crystalline flambé glaze, unmkd, 8¼ x 3¾" h . **$350**
Bowl, blue, ivory, and brown flambé glaze, imp mark, 11½" d **225**
Bowl, blue dip glaze, beige and green int, 9½" d **225**
Bowl, blue green drip, 7½" d **20**
Bowl, leopard skin crystalline glaze, flaring rim, vertical ink racetrack marks,
2" h, 5" d, price for set of 6 . . . . **465**
Bud Vase, blue–green frothy glaze, classic shape, vertical ink racetrack mark,
6¾ x 2" **200**
Bud Vase, cat's eye flambé glaze, squat base, vertical rect ink mark, 5¼
x 3¾" **150**
Cabinet Vase, dark brown and gray matte crystalline glaze, vertical rect ink
mark, 4" h, 3" w **375**
Cabinet Vase, Wisteria matte glaze, slender ovoid body, flared rim, short
pedestal, domed, ringed foot, vertical ink mark **95**

Vase, green matte to wisteria flambé glaze, vertical ink racetrack mark, 4¾" d, $192. Photo courtesy Jackson's Auctioneers & Appraisers.

Centerpiece Bowl, ftd, mirrored black glaze, lotus shaped, incised vertical mark, 6 x 11" **325**

Effigy Bowl, cat's eye flambé glaze, int forming peacock feather effec, ext in mustard matte and brown, vertical rect ink mark, 7½" h, 10½" w **750**

Effigy Bowl, cat's eye glaze, peacock feather effect, matte mustard and café–au–lait ext, 3 crouching figurines holding low bowl, rect ink mark, 7½ x 10½" **750**

Effigy Bowl, frothy butterscotch flambé glaze over mustard matte, speckled dark brown matte glaze base, 3 squat figurines supporting flat, curl rimmed bowl, early ink mark, 7½ x 10¾" **800**

Flower Frog, flambé glaze, mushroom shaped **18**

Jar, #564, matte green glaze, 5¼" h **270**

Table Lamp, ceramic and leaded glass, red jewels and flambé slag glass set into ceramic shade, cat's eye and flemington green flambé finish, early Vasekraft marks, 22" h, 17" d **1,300**

Urn, black and silver cucumber crystalline green flambé glaze, imp geometric dec, 4 sided, tapering, early ink mark, 8 x 4" **475**

Urn, blue crystalline glaze, 4 handled, incised vertical racetrack mark, 13 x 11½" **1,300**

Urn, blue–green and blush flambé glaze, pear shaped, 2 buttressed handles, raised racetrack mark, 9½ x 8" **425**

Urn, Grecian, cobalt and periwinkle blue glaze, 2 handles, ink racetrack mark, 10¾ x 6" **200**

Vase, cat's eye to Chinese blue flambé glaze, bell pepper shaped, vertical rect ink mark, 4¼ x 4¾" **385**

Vase, copperdust crystalline to Flemington green flambé glaze, corseted, 2 handled, raised vertical racetrack mark, 10" h, 6¾" w **600**

Vase, cucumber crystalline to cucumber matte glaze, tall and tapering form, 2 handled, ink racetrack mark, 13" h, 7½" w **1,000**

Vase, elephant's breath flambé glaze, bulbous, collar rim, early Prang mark, 4¼ x 6¼" **450**

Vase, Flemington green and gun metal flambé glaze, Pilgrim flask shaped, scrolled handles, early ink mark, 10 x 8" **750**

Vase, Flemington green flambé glaze, reticulated mushroom shaped, emb mushrooms and 2 square holes, early ink mark, Jordan–Volpe label, 10 x 4½" **1,100**

Vase, green to cobalt crystalline flambé glaze, ovoid, 2 handled, incised racetrack mark and paper label, 7¾" h, 5¾"w **325**

Vase, ivory, mahogany, and mirrored black flambé glaze, bulbous, ribbed, 2 small handles, incised vertical racetrack mark and paper label, 12" h, 7½" w **1,000**

Vase, ivory to Chinese blue to mirrored black flambé glaze, tear drop shaped, 3 curving horns on sides, early ink mark, 6½ x 6¼" **1,100**

Vase, mahogany and elephant's breath flambé glaze, bullet shaped, 3 handles, early ink mark, 6½ x 4¼" **550**

Vase, mauve, mustard, and leopard skin crystalline flambé glaze, bottle shaped, vertical rect ink mark, 11¼" h, 6½" w **2,700**

Vase, metallic trailing blue snowflake crystalline base, rust and mahogany undertones, tapered, 2 ring handles, vertical ink racetrack mark, 13 x 7¼" .. **1,100**

Vase, mirrored black to copperdust crystalline flambé glaze, baluster shaped, raised dots on shoulder, unmkd, 7" h, 4½" w **650**

Vase, mirrored black to Flemington green flambé glaze, gourd shaped, vertical rect Prang mark, 5½" h, 3" w **450**
Vase, silvery Flemington green glaze, bottle shaped, early ink mark, 5 x 3½" . **375**
Vessel, blue and rose famille glaze, matte green, spherical, closed–in rim, rect ink mark, 5½ x 7" **400**
Vessel, cat's eye to Chinese blue flambé glaze, bell pepper shaped, vertical rect ink mark, 4¼" h, 4¾" w **350**
Vessel, leopard skin crystalline glaze, 2 angular buttressed handles, vertical rect ink mark, 6½" h, 8" w **550**

GAUDY WARES

Gaudy Ware is the name used by many collectors and dealers to describe a particular type of pottery. This white bodied ware usually sports stylized floral, luster, and enamel under–the–glaze decorations. Gaudy Ware is made up of three basic types—Gaudy Dutch, Gaudy Ironstone, and Gaudy Welsh.

Gaudy Dutch is an opaque, soft–paste ware made between 1790 and 1825 in England's Staffordshire district. Most pieces are unmarked; marks of various potters, including the impressed marks of Riley and Wood, have been found.

Pieces were first hand decorated in an underglaze blue, then fired, and finally they received additional decoration over the glaze. This overglaze decoration is extensively worn on many pieces. Gaudy Dutch found a ready market within the Pennsylvania German community because it was inexpensive and intense with color. It had little appeal in England.

Gaudy Ironstone was made in England around 1850. Most pieces are impressed "Ironstone" and bear a registry mark. Ironstone is an opaque, heavy–bodied earthenware which contains large proportions of flint and slag. Gaudy Ironstone is decorated in patterns and colors similar to Gaudy Welsh.

Gaudy Welsh is a translucent porcelain that was originally made in the Swansea area of England from 1830 to 1845. Although the designs resemble Gaudy Dutch, the body texture and weight differ. One distinguishing factor is the gold luster on top of the glaze.

All of the Gaudy Wares are welcome additions in a Country setting. Their brightly colored decorations add an interesting dash to cupboards and shelves. The patterns are fun to identify. Variety can also be achieved through shapes and sizes.

Reference: John A. Shuman III, *The Collector's Encyclopedia of Gaudy Dutch and Welsh,* Collector Books, 1991, 1998 value update.

Collectors' Club: Gaudy Collector's Society, PO Box 274, Gates Mills, OH 44040.

Reproduction Alert: Gaudy Dutch cup plates, bearing the impressed mark "CYBRIS," have been reproduced and are collectible in their own right. The Henry Ford Museum has issued pieces in the Single Rose pattern, although they are porcelain rather than soft–paste.

GAUDY DUTCH

Bowl, Dahlia, 6¼" h **$360**
Bowl, Flower Basket, 10½" d **340**
Bowl, Grape, lustered rim, 6½" d **375**
Bowl, Oyster, 6½" d **650**

Bowl, Straw Flower, 6½" d 500
Bowl, Urn, 6¼" d 350
Bowl, Zinnia, 6¼" d 360
Coffeepot, Sunflower, 9½" h 1,650
Creamer, Butterfly, 3½" h 700
Creamer, Dover, 4⅞" h 450
Creamer, Flower Basket 400
Creamer, Grape, 4" h 600
Creamer, Single Rose, 4¾" h 500
Creamer, Sunflower, 9½" h 1,650
Creamer, Urn, 4½" h 880
Creamer, War Bonnet, 4⅜" h 460
Creamer, Zinnia, 4½" h 750
Cup, Butterfly, 2½" h 250
Cup, Sunflower, 2⅜" h 120
Cup, Urn, 2½" h 135
Cup, Zinnia 175
Cup and Saucer, handleless, Butterfly, minor enamel flaking, small chips on
　table rings 660
Cup and Saucer, handleless, Carnation, 2½" h cup, 5½" d saucer 100
Cup and Saucer, handleless, Dove, scalloped edges, salmon rims 550
Cup and Saucer, handleless, Oyster, cup broken and reglued 70
Cup and Saucer, handleless, Sunflower 350
Cup and Saucer, handleless, Urn, wear and scratches 300
Cup and Saucer, handleless, War Bonnet 370
Cup and Saucer, handleless, Zinnia 325
Dish, deep well, Butterfly, 9⅞" d 1,000

Left: Gaudy Dutch, shallow bowl, cobalt blue, green, brown, and yellow dec, incised mark "Clews Warranted Staffordshire" around crown on bottom, 6" d, 1¼" h, $350.

Right: Gaudy Dutch, handleless cup and saucer, Single Rose, blue, rust, yellow, and green, $525.

Dish, deep well, Oyster, 9½" d **700**
Dish, deep well, Single Rose, 7⅞" d **370**
Dish, deep well, War Bonnet, 9½" d **830**
Jug, Double Rose, mask spout with light beard, 6¼" h **575**
Jug, Grape, 6¼" h **600**
Jug, Single Rose, 6¼" h **550**
Jug, Zinnia, 6¼" h **625**
Pitcher, Dove, 8" h **2,500**
Pitcher, Grape, 8" h **2,400**
Pitcher, Zinnia, 8" h **2,500**
Plate, Butterfly, chip on back of rim, wear, repair, retouched enamel colors,
  8⅜" d **375**
Plate, Carnation, 8¼" d **220**
Plate, Double Rose, 10" d **940**
Plate, Grape, wear, stains, faded enamel, 8¼" d **300**
Plate, Oyster, 6½" d **450**
Plate, Primrose, 4¾" d **425**
Plate, Rose, 9⅞" d **550**
Plate, Single Rose, 8⅛" d **400**
Plate, Straw Flower, 5½" d **400**
Plate, Sunflower, 6½" d **750**
Plate, Urn, 8¼" d **900**
Plate, War Bonnet, 8⅛" d **880**
Plate, War Bonnet, 9¾" d **550**
Plate, Zinnia, 8¼" d **600**
Platter, Double Rose, 15" l **3,650**
Platter, Grape, 15" l **1,700**
Platter, Straw Flower, 14" l **2,500**
Saucer, Grape and Oyster, price for pair **220**
Saucer, Urn **320**
Saucer, War Bonnet **250**
Soup Bowl, Carnation, 8⅜" d **430**
Soup Bowl, War Bonnet, 8⅛" d **730**
Soup Plate, Double Rose, 9⅝" d **650**
Soup Plate, Oyster, 10" d **800**
Soup Plate, War Bonnet, red, yellow, green, and black, blue underglaze,
  8⅛" d **725**
Sugar Bowl, cov, Dove, 5⅜" h **360**
Sugar Bowl, cov, Flower Basket **375**
Sugar Bowl, cov, Oyster, very worn, enamel flakes, hairlines, chips, 5⅝" h . . . **380**
Sugar Bowl, cov, Urn, shell handles, 5½" h **350**
Teapot, cov, Carnation, 6½" h **650**
Teapot, cov, Double Rose, flower finial, 6½" h **750**
Teapot, cov, Grape, old yellowed repairs, 6¼" h **1,950**
Teapot, cov, Urn, shell handles, 6½" h **500**
Teapot, cov, War Bonnet, repairs, 5¾" h **80**
Toddy Plate, Carnation, 6½" d **930**
Toddy Plate, Double Rose, 3½" d **1,000**
Toddy Plate, Grape, 6½" d **800**
Toddy Plate, Oyster, 6½" d **825**
Toddy Plate, Zinnia, 3½" d **750**

Waste Bowl, Dove, 6³/₈" d 650
Waste Bowl, Dove, 6¹/₂" d 825
Waste Bowl, Oyster, 5³/₈" d, 2¹¹/₁₆" h 700
Waste Bowl, Single Rose, wear, hairlines, and stains with flake on table ring
  and glaze flakes on rim, 5¹/₂" d 350
Waste Bowl, Sunflower, 6¹/₂" d, 3³/₁₆" h 575
Waste Bowl, Urn, some discoloration, 6¹/₄" d, 3" h 600

GAUDY IRONSTONE

Chop Plate, 9 rabbits, 4 frogs, and flowers in black transfer, circular center,
  minor crazing, 12³/₄" d $990
Creamer, Floral, molded, polychrome enamel, blue underglaze 125
Creamer, Morning Glory, paneled, foliage handle, 6¹/₂" h 150
Cup and Saucer, handleless, Floral, red, blue, green, and black, price for pair 120
Cup and Saucer, handleless, Strawberry, flower dec on saucer 165
Dinner Service, 7 pcs, one 8" d plate, 6 handleless cups and saucers, red,
  green, blue, and black floral dec, lion and unicorn mark, "England" 225
Dinner Service, 33 pcs, Oriental, polychrome enameling, 13¹/₂" l large
  tureen and undertray, sauce tureen, seven 9³/₈" d plates, six 8" d plates,
  two 11³/₄" l cov vegetable bowls, 6 cups and saucers, 2 large saucers, and
  2 platters, one 13" l, other 15" l, mkd "Ashworth Bros. Hanley England" ... 725
Pitcher, Floral, molded design, blue and luster highlights, 7⁷/₈" h 175
Pitcher, lion head handle, red, blue, and green, by Mason's, mkd "Patent
  Ironstone China," 7¹/₂" h 325
Plate, 8 rabbits in black transfer, circular design center, 9³/₈" d 28

Left: Gaudy Ironstone, plate, blue with copper luster trim, 9¹/₂" d, $155.
Right: Gaudy Ironstone, teapot, Strawberry, 10¹/₄" h, $250.

Plate, Floral dec, blue, green, red, and worn purple luster, imp "Ironstone,"
8¹/₂" d, price for pair 275
Plate, Floral, blue and luster underglaze, imp "Ironstone," wear, 8³/₄" d 130
Plate, Morning Glory, blue and green, wear, crazing, 1 has hairline, 8¹/₂" d,
price for pair 450
Plate, 9 rabbits, 3 cabbages, 3 frogs, and 3 trees in black transfer, 9³/₈" d 385
Plate, 6 rabbits, 3 frogs, and flowers in black transfer, 9³/₈" d 465
Plate, Strawberry, polychrome enamel and luster, blue underglaze, wear and
chip on table ring, 8¹/₂" d 155
Plate, Strawberries and Flowers, imp "Thos Walker," 9⁷/₈" d 275
Plate, Sunflower, yellow, green, and black, 6³/₄" d 65
Plate, Tulips and Berries, red, green, and black enamel, blue underglaze,
stains, 8³/₄" d 160
Plate, Urn, stains, enamel wear, 8⁵/₈" d, price for 6 870
Plate, Urn and Flowers, blue, red, pink, and green, 12 sides, 9³/₄" d 135
Plate, Vase of Flowers, polychrome enamel, blue and luster underglaze,
8⁵/₈" d, price for pair 385
Platter, oval, Adam's Rose, red, green, and black, imp "Adams," 19¹/₂" l 320
Platter, oval, 8 rabbits, 4 frogs, and flowers in black transfer, stains and craz-
ing, 14⁷/₈" l 1,100
Platter, oval, floral rim, gold touch–up repair, 25" l 385
Serving Dish, cov, Urn and Flowers, minor wear, 9¹/₂" d, 7³/₄" h 780
Sugar, cov, Urn and Flowers, stains, damage, finial glued, 7³/₈" d 170
Teapot, floral, luster trim, fruit finial, mkd "Walley" and English registry
mark, 9¹/₂" h 240
Tureen with Underplate, floral dec, green, red, and blue, stains, hairlines in
tray and plate, 14³/₄" l 135

GAUDY WELSH

Bowl, floral dec, red and green enamel with purple luster and blue under-
glaze, "Be Canny with the Sugar," small flowers ext dec, 5¹/₈" d, 2³/₄" h $385
Bowl, single flower, ftd, round with side flaring toward rim, some discolor-
ing, chip on base, flaking to green polychrome on back side, 6⁵/₁₆" d,
3⁵/₁₆" h 350
Bowl, Wagon Wheel, 7¹/₂" d 325
Creamer, Lotus, polychrome enamel, luster trim, 4³/₄" h 130
Creamer, single flower, oval, arched handle, discoloring and glaze wear,
5¹¹/₁₆" l, 4" h 110
Cup, Wagon Wheel 65
Cup and Saucer, Grape, scalloped edges, "Wedgwood" imp mark on reverse . 500
Cup and Saucer, Lotus, polychrome enamel, blue underglaze 115
Cup and Saucer, Violet 400
Loving Cup, 4" h 260
Mug, Grape, c1840, 2" h 150
Pitcher, Anglesey, 4¹/₄" h 95
Plate, Columbine, 5¹/₂" d 85
Plate, Daisy and Chain 90
Plate, floral dec, blue, red, purple, and 2 shades of green enamel, 9" d 165
Plate, Lotus, polychrome enamel, blue underglaze, luster trim, 9" d, price for
pair 200

Gaudy Welsh, mug, Grape, 3¹/₂" h, $150.

Plate, Oyster, wear, 8¹/₂" d **110**
Plate, Single Flower, scalloped rim, chip on base, 9³/₈" d **70**
Plate, Wagon Wheel, 5¹/₂" d **95**
Plate, Wagon Wheel, 8³/₄" d **110**
Soup Plate, Strawberry, 9" d **115**
Sugar, cov, Daisy and Chain **210**
Sugar, cov, Flower Basket, lion head handles, luster trim **165**
Teapot, cov, Peach, crow's foot, 6" h **325**
Teapot, cov, single flower, ftd, scrolled handle, curved spout, deep flared
    gallery type rim, oval finial, end of spout broken, chip on rim of shoulder,
    glaze wear, 10³/₈" l, 7¹/₂" h **10**
Teapot, cov, Vine, stains, chips, and short hairlines, 9¹/₄" h **230**
Toddy Plate, single flower, scalloped rim, some discoloring, 5¹/₈" d **85**

GEORGE OHR

George E. Ohr of Biloxi, Mississippi, is responsible for Ohr pottery. While experts disagree on the exact date Ohr started making pottery (some say 1878, others 1883), Ohr did exhibit over 600 examples of his work in 1884.

Ohr's pottery is characterized by crinkled, crushed, dented, folded and/or twisted bodies of thin-walled clay resulting in grotesque, odd, and sometimes graceful forms. Most early pieces are signed with an impressed stamp that included his name and location in block letters. Later he most often used a flowing script "G E Ohr" signature.

Ohr ceased operations in 1906 and turned his inventory of 6,000 pieces over to his family in hopes that they would sell the collection intact to the United States Government. It never happened. The collection remained in storage until 1972 when it was rediscovered and entered the secondary collecting market.

Beware of unglazed pieces that have been covered with poor-quality glazes in an effort to enhance their value. These pieces usually have the flowing script mark and do not have stilt marks on the bottom.

Reference: Garth Clark, Robert Ellison, Jr., and Eugene Hecht, *The Mad Potter of Biloxi: The Art & Life of George Ohr,* Abbeville Press, 1989.

Bowl, 4–sided, pinched corners and dimpled sides, mottled gunmetal glaze
over green ground, die stamped "G. E. OHR/Biloxi, Miss.," 3½ x 4½" . . .$1,000

Bowl, low, 4–lobed, crimped, speckled green glaze over orange clay, mkd
"GEO.E.OHR/BILOXI, MISS," 2 x 3¾" 850

Bowl, open, oval, brown and speckled green glaze, ruffled body, mkd "GEO
E OHR/BILOXI, MISS.," restoration to rim, 7½ x 5" 1,400

Bud Vase, conical base, in–body twist, cupped top, dead matte black crystalline glaze, die stamped "G. E. Ohr/Biloxi," 5¼" h 1,400

Candle Holder, organic, pinched ribbon handle, in–body twist, ribbed base,
yellow, green, and raspberry matte mottled glaze, script mark, small chip
to base, 6½" h 3,300

Chamberstick, deep in–body twist, folded handle, bisque clay, script signa-
ture, 5½ x 4¾" 375

Chamberstick, flattened bulbous base, deep red, green, and yellow matte
mottled glaze, hand incised "GE Ohr," stilt pulls to bottom, 4" h, 3¾" d . . .1,500

Demitasse Cup, green, cobalt, and raspberry marbleized glazed ext,
sponged cobalt and raspberry volcanic glazed int, die stamped "G. E. Ohr,
Biloxi, Miss," 2½" h 1,500

Jar, cov, spherical, gunmetal and green glaze dripping over mottled raspberry ground, die stamped "G. E. Ohr, Biloxi, Miss," shallow abrasion ring
around pot from orig storage, 4¼" h, 5" d 1,500

Moustache Cup, occupational, hand built as shirt cuff with ribbon handle,
sponged blue glazes, die stamped "G. E. Ohr, Biloxi, Miss," 2¾" h, 4" d . . .2,000

Mug, protruding handle, notches all over dimples, 3–part glaze, gunmetal
and green, gunmetal and brown, and peacock blue, script signature, 5¼
x 6½" 850

Pitcher, bulbous, medium and light green, gunmetal, and blood red glaze,
mkd "G.E. OHR, Biloxi, Miss.," 5¼ x 6" 1,700

Pitcher, cupped top, flaring base terminating in a ruffle, light clay, script signature, 4¾ x 4¾" 500

Pitcher, dimpled body, bulbous and squat, gunmetal over dark green glaze,
crimped rim, die stamped "G. E. Ohr, BILOXI," 2¼ x 3¾" 1,000

Pitcher, pinched, cut–out handle, vulvic opening, gunmetal glaze, mkd "G.
E. OHR, Biloxi, Miss," 3¾ x 4¾" 1,700

Pitcher, pinched and folded, marbleized brick and putty, scroddled bisque
clay, incised "GEOhr," 4¼ x 6" 1,500

Vase, bottle shaped, brown, green, and amber speckled lustered glaze, die
stamped "G. E. Ohr, Biloxi, Miss.," restoration to tiny rim chip, 8½" h 1,200

Vase, corseted, 2 looping ribbon handles, mottled dark green, amber, and
gunmetal glaze, random red spots, mkd "GEO.OHR, Biloxi, Miss.," 7¾ x
5½" 3,750

Vase, crimped rim, dimpled body, bulbous and squat, gunmetal over dark
green glaze, die stamped "G. E. Ohr, BILOXI," 2¼ x 3¾" 1,000

Vase, cupped top, deep in–body twist, pinched ribbon handles, green and
purple mottled glaze, die stamped "G. E. Ohr/Biloxi, Miss," 4¾" h 4,250

Vase, cylindrical, deep in–body twist, khaki green speckled glaze, "G. E.
OHR/Biloxi, Miss." imp mark, 6¾ x 3¾" 1,600

Vase, deep in–body twist, ruffled and pinched rim, bulbous, speckled metallic dark amber and gunmetal glaze, repair to rim chip, 6 x 5¼" 1,500

Vase, deep in–body twist near rim, bulbous, speckled gunmetal and khaki
glaze, mkd "G. E. OHR/Biloxi, Miss," 6¼ x 5½" 2,400

Vase, Easter Egg design, corseted, semi–matte spotted green, dark blue, and purple glaze on lavender–gray ground, "G. E. OHR/Biloxi, Miss" imp mark, 10³/₄ x 5" **9,000**

Vase, flaring, 2 asymmetrical handles, gunmetal and sponged yellow blotches on matte pink ground, mkd "GEORGE. E. OHR/Biloxi, Miss," professional repair to rim and top of 1 handle, 3³/₄ x 4³/₄" **1,200**

Vase, flaring folded rim, corseted, blue–green glaze top, bottom with added motttled raspberry glaze, die stamped "Biloxi, Miss/Geo. E. Ohr," minor abrasion to rim, 4" h, 3³/₄" w **4,250**

Vase, folded rim, dimpled body, bulbous and squat, buff clay, bisque–fired, incised "GE Ohr," 4 x 5¹/₄" **700**

Vase, folded top, dimpled body, bulbous and squat, semi–volcanic gray and pink glaze, mkd "GEORGE E. OHR/Biloxi, Miss.," repair to rim, 4³/₄ x 5" ..**1,200**

Vase, ovoid, ftd, deep in–body twist, speckled brown glaze, "G. E. OHR/Biloxi, Miss." imp mark, 5¹/₄ x 3¹/₂" **2,000**

Vase, ruffled and pinched rim, dimples, bulbous, metallic brown and gunmetal mirrored finish, mkd "GEORGE E. OHR/Biloxi, Miss.," 6³/₄ x 6¹/₂" ...**2,750**

Vase, twisted and compressed base, semi–matte speckled mustard glaze, stove pipe top ending in folded rim, matte gunmetal glaze, "BILOXI, MISS./GEO. E. OHR" imp mark, 6³/₄ x 7" **4,750**

Vessel, bulbous, severely folded and pinched top, leathery gunmetal glaze over amber base, die stamped "G. E. Ohr, Biloxi, Miss.," 5¹/₂" h, 4¹/₄" w ...**2,400**

Vessel, corseted middle with exaggerated flat in–body twist, bisque and scroddled clay, script signature, 3¹/₄ x 4" **800**

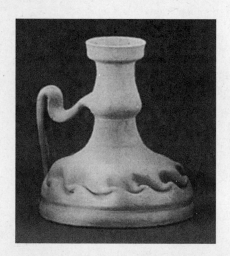

Left: Chamberstick, deep in–body twist, folded handle, bisque clay, script signature, 5¹/₂ x 4³/₄", $375.

Right: Vessel, folded crinolated rim, bisque and scroddled clay, script signature, 4 x 4³/₄", $1,100.

Photos courtesy David Rago Auctions.

Vessel, deep in–body twist, mirrored mottled gunmetal brown glaze, script
  signature, 2³/₄ x 4" 1,200
Vessel, dimpled and folded 4–sided rim, gunmetal and khaki speckled glaze,
  "G. E. OHR/Biloxi, Miss" imp mark, 4 x 4¹/₂" 900
Vessel, flat shoulder, indigo and green sponged pattern on raspberry ground,
  white overglaze, die stamped "GEO. E. OHR/BILOXI, MISS.," 3 x 4" 2,400
Vessel, folded and pinched, gunmetal glaze, "G. E. OHR/BILOXI" imp mark,
  3 x 4¹/₂" 2,500
Vessel, folded base and rim, bisque and red clay, script signature, 2³/₄ x 3³/₄" . 200
Vessel, folded crinolated rim, bisque and scroddled clay, script signature,
  4 x 4³/₄" 1,000
Vessel, folded rim over dimpled body, gunmetal glaze, mkd "G. E. OHR,
  Biloxi, Miss.," 3¹/₄ x 3³/₄" 850
Vessel, gourd shaped, closed–in rim, pink, blue, and green mottled glossy
  glaze, "G. E. OHR/Biloxi, Miss." imp mark, 4³/₄ x 3³/₄" 1,300
Vessel, heavily dimpled front and back, folded rim, green speckled glossy
  glaze, die stamped "G. E, Ohr, Biloxi, Miss," 5¹/₂" h, 4³/₄" w 3,000
Vessel, long vertical flutes, bisque and buff clay, script signature, 5³/₄ x 4¹/₂" .. 650
Vessel, loosely folded body, tightly folded rim, bisque and red clay, "G. E.
  OHR/Biloxi, Miss." imp mark, 2¹/₂ x 5¹/₂" 1,400
Vessel, ovoid, closed–in dimpled rim, mirrored black and brown glaze, "G.
  E. OHR/Biloxi, Miss" imp mark, 3 x 5 ¹/₄" 850
Vessel, pinched wave–like folds, unglazed scroddled clay, script mark,
  4¹/₂" h, 6¹/₂" w 8,750
Vessel, scalloped rim, dimpled, glossy raspberry ext glaze, shimmering gun-
  metal int, die stamped "G. E. OHR, BILOXI," 2¹/₂ x 3¹/₂" 1,600
Vessel, straight sides, folded rim, mahogany, aventurine, and gunmetal
  glaze, incised "Biloxi" in script, 5 x 4¹/₂" 850
Vessel, tapered neck, squat base, gunmetal over mottled raspberry glaze,
  script signature, 4¹/₄" h, 3³/₄" d 1,500

GRUEBY

After spending a number of years in the ceramic industry, William Grueby founded the Grueby Faience Company in Boston, Massachusetts, in 1897. In 1910 the firm
split into the Grueby Pottery Company and the Grueby Faience and Tile Company. Art
pottery production was the responsibility of the Grueby Faience and Tile Company.
Operations ceased in 1908 when the company declared bankruptcy.

Country collectors are attracted to Grueby pottery because of its matte-glaze finish
and the use of earth–tone color glazes, singly or in combination. Green is the most
commonly found glaze color. Grueby produced his wares using a variety of techniques
including molding, throwing, and tooling.

Bowl, applied leaves dec under curdled matte light green glaze, raised on
  circular foot, imp mark, 4³/₈" d, 3" h $345
Bowl, overlapping leaves in low relief dec, matte green glaze, "10/30" imp
  marks, and incised artist's initials "ER," 6¹/₄" d, 3¹/₄" h 1,380
Bowl, spherical shape, rounded rim imp mark, incised "DEW," 7 x 9¹/₂" 1,500
Cabinet Vase, matte green glaze, bottle shaped, paper label over imp mark,
  repair to rim nick, 3 x 2¹/₄" 250

Candle Holder, stacked, applied leaves under thick dark blue matte glaze, unmkd, 8³/₄ x 3³/₄" **1,400**

Jardiniere, tooled and applied full length leaves under curdled matte green glaze, circular mark "WP/7/2/7," restoration to small rim chips, 5 x 8¹/₄" ...**1,800**

Lamp, Tiffany Lemon Leaf leaded glass shade with band of yellow leaves on green and white slag glass grid, yellow jonquils and green leaves against green ground base, orig fittings, "Tiffany Studios New York" imp on shade, base mkd "Grueby Pottery," minor resoldering to small section of shade, some color run to flowers, 22 x 18" **12,000**

Lotus Bowl, stacked tooled and applied leaves under mattte green glaze, crackled white glaze int, imp "WP" circular mark, minor glaze nicks to edges, restoration to small rim chip, 3¹/₄ x 7¹/₂" **2,700**

Paperweight, scarab, matte mustard glaze, circular "Grueby Faience" imp mark, 4 x 2³/₄" **750**

Tile, emb stylized cupid in matte oatmeal glaze on green matte ground, letters "EROS" emb on front, flat chips to corners on sides, 6" sq **325**

Tile, emb stylized design of knight in caramel brown, blue ground, sgd "DC" on back, 6" sq **250**

Tile, 4 penguins on iceberg, brown, green, blue, and ivory, paper label, 4" sq **600**

Tile, pines and landscape, curdled matte green, blue, and brown, mkd "E.A.," 6" sq **1,800**

Tile, Spanish galleon dec, ivory, brown, amber, and green on green ground, "AS/GM" painted on back, orig price tag and paper label, 6" sq **1,300**

Tile, water lilies in ivory, orange, and light green, dark green ground, designed by Addison le Boutillier, unmkd, burst bubble and glaze chip to edge, 6" sq **1,300**

Tile, Faience, horses with blue eyes, green grass, pale blue sky, cream and pale brown matte glaze, inscribed artist's initials "DC," 6" sq **635**

Tile, Faience, mermaid, No. 657, red terra–cotta form, matte ochre glaze in cloisonné manner with dec in low relief, imp "657," 6" sq **285**

Tile, Faience, sailing ship, yellow, cream, green, and blue matte glaze, outlined in black/mauve, raised architectural mark, inscribed "MD" in glaze, 4¹/₄" l **250**

Left: Vase, 6–sided, tooled and applied yellow daffodil dec, matte green enamel, mkd with circular stamp and "ER," 11¹/₄ x 5¹/₄", $7,750.

Right: Vase, tooled leaves, matte green finish, mkd with imp pottery mark and "RE" (Ruth Erikson), 5¹/₄ x 3", $1,200.

Photos courtesy David Rago Auctions.

Tile, Faience, turtle in brown and cream matte glaze under green leaves, yellow ground, artist's initials "KC," 6" d **805**

Vase, alternating leaf blade and bud on stem in low relief dec, matte green glaze, modeled by Ruth Erickson, "160" imp mark, incised artist's initials, 11¾" h, 5½" d **2,645**

Vase, curdled matte blue glaze, bulbous, 4½ x 4" **550**

Vase, emb 5–petal flowers alternating with broad flat leaves design, dark green matte glaze with blue–green flowers, bulbous, imp stamp mark, artist's cipher, restoration to small rim chip, 6 x 9" **4,100**

Vase, full height tooled and applied leaves alternating with 4 scrolled handles, matte mauve glaze, modeled by Wilhelmina Post, Vase, "Grueby Faience/W.P." imp mark, hairlines **5,000**

Vase, full length leaves interspersed with buds, curdled matte green glaze, "Grueby Pottery" circular mark, short hairline at rim, 9 x 4½" **1,600**

Vase, matte green drip glazing, ovoid, red bisque body, "3032" imp mark, repair to small rim chip, 9 x 5½" **600**

Vase, matte green glaze, bulbous, squat, ribbed, corseted neck, obscured imp mark, 3¾ x 3¼" **500**

Vase, matte green glaze, imp mark, 6⅞" h, 3⅝" d **545**

Vase, matte ocher glaze, unsgd, 7" h, 3½" d **460**

Vase, matte pale blue glaze, imp mark, 4½" h, 3⅜" d **345**

Vase, overlapping leaves in high relief dec, matte green glaze, rolled rim over slightly tapering cylindrical neck on swollen squat body, modeled by Ruth Erickson, imp marks and incised artist's initials, 12¾" h, 8" d **2,760**

Vase, tooled and applied leaves, covered in organic matte green glaze, gourd shaped, modeled by Marie Seaman, "Grueby Faience" imp mark, 8¼ x 4½" **7,000**

Vase, tooled and applied leaves, feathered cucumber green matte finish, bulbous, cylindrical neck, "Faience" imp mark, 7 x 4½" **2,000**

Vase, tooled and applied leaves, matte green glaze, bulbous, circular mark, 4½ x 3¼" **2,400**

Vase, tooled and applied rounded leaves around base, matte leathery glaze, bulbous, circular Faience mark "WP," restoration to glaze chips at rim, 7½ x 4½" **1,500**

Vase, wide leaf blades in high relief dec, matte green glaze, modeled by Wilhelmina Post, imp marks and incised artist's initials, 7¾" h, 3¼" d **1,955**

Vase, yellow buds and molded spade shaped leaves, matte green glaze, squat, "Grueby Faience" circular mark, 7 x 12" **14,000**

HAEGER

In 1871 David H. Haeger established a brickyard on the banks of the Fox River in Dundee, Illinois. He was succeeded in 1900 by Edmund H. Haeger, his son. Edmund introduced an art pottery line in 1914. Within a short period of time, Haeger became a leading manufacturer of artware, characterized by a lustrous glaze and soft glowing pastels. The company built and operated a complete working pottery at the 1933–34 Chicago World's Fair.

The company introduced its Royal Haeger line in 1938. The Royal Haeger Lamp Company was formed in 1939, the same year the company purchased the Buckeye Pottery building in Macomb, Illinois, for the purpose of manufacturing its art line for the florist trade.

In 1954 Joseph F. Estes, Edmund's son–in–law, assumed the presidency. Nicholas Haeger Estes and Alexandria Haeger Estes, son and daughter of Joseph, continue the tradition of family leadership for the company.

Reference: David D. Dilley, *Haeger Potteries,* L–W Book Sales, 1997.

Collectors' Club: Haeger Pottery Collectors of America, 5021 Toyon Way, Antioch, CA 94509.

Ashtray, #109–S, gold tweed, 7" sq **$20**
Ashtray, #127, gold tweed, triangular, 10¼" l 20
Ashtray, #128, mandarin orange, triangular, 13¼" l 10
Ashtray, #2145, square leaf with acorns, green, 9¾" sq 15
Ashtray and Cigarette Holder, #702, mandarin orange, 10¼" l 20
Bookends, pr, #R–475, calla lily, amber, "Royal Haeger R475 U.S.A." mold-
 ed on bottom, 4½ x 4½ x 6⅛" h 65
Bookends, pr, #R–638, panther planters, ebony, c1950s 135
Bookends, pr, #R–641, stallion, chartreuse, unmkd, 5½ x 3½ x 8¾" h 55
Bookends, pr, #R–718, ram heads, oxblood, 5½" h 55
Bookends, pr, #R–1144, water lilies, green with white flowers, c1952, 7½" h . 60
Bowl, #25, 3 ftd, dark and light blue, diamond shaped "Haeger" molded on
 bottom, c1914, 6" d, 3¼" h 65
Bowl, #352, ftd, black mystique, rect, 14½" l 40
Bowl, #863, round, diamond pattern, tan with white int, "Haeger, ©, USA,
 863," 9¾" d, 2¾" h 20
Bowl, #R–333, lilac, 16¼" l 40
Bowl, #R–373, applied flowers, cloudy blue and white, unmkd, 19 x 6 x
 6½" h 80
Bowl, #R–442, floral relief, mauve agate ext, mauve int, 18¼" l 50
Bowl, #R–967, starfish shaped, pearl gray drip, "Royal Haeger–R 967 USA"
 molded on bottom, "Royal Haeger–Dundee, Illinois" foil label,
 14½" l, 2⅜" h 50
Candle Holder/Planter, #R–458, double light, chartreuse, c1946, 7½" l 20
Candle Holders, pr, #R–203, standing double fish, mauve agate, unmkd,
 5" h 80
Candle Holders, pr, #R–243, twisted stem, peach agate, unmkd, c1927, 4¼"
 base, 7½" h 110
Candle Holders, pr, #R–304, fish, mauve agate, 4¼" h 50
Candle Holders, pr, #R–437, leaf, ebony, 2¾" h 15

Beaded Bowl, #R–476, Green Briar color, 14¾" l, 7¼" w, 4¾" h, $25. Photo courtesy Ray Morykan Auctions.

Candy Dish, #8044–H, 4 bowls, center handle, mandarin orange, 8³/₄" w **20**
Candy Dish, #R–459, triple bowl, fish handle, blue, c1946, 8¹/₂" l **50**
Canister, #726–H, horse dec, "Haeger 726–H USA" molded on bottom,
   c1967, 4¹/₄" h **40**
Compote, #3003, white ext, turquoise int, 12" l, 4¹/₂" h **25**
Dish, #3961, blue with black specks, c1967, 8" sq **10**
Figure, #612, rooster, burnt sienna, c1973, 11" h **50**
Figure, #649, dove, 8¹/₂" h **55**
Figure, #F–3, duck, white, c1941, 5" h **20**
Figure, #F–17, wild goose, white matte glaze, c1941, 6¹/₄" l, 6¹/₂" h **20**
Figure, #R–103, green briar, unmkd, 8¹/₄" h **40**
Figure, #R–130, pheasant, green agate, crown foil label mkd "Royal Haeger–
   Dundee, Illinois," 11¹/₄" l, 6" h **35**
Figure, #R–412, standing fawn, pink, 1950, 11³/₄" h **45**
Figure, #R–777, cocker spaniel, brown, black tail, c1950s, 5¹/₂" l, 3" h **55**
Figure, #R–784, elephant, chartreuse and honey, 8¹/₄" l **40**
Flower Frog, #57, swan, green, white, and beige, unmkd, c1918, 4" h **30**
Flower Frog, #R–359, 2 birds, cloudy blue, c1940s, 5" d base, 8³/₄" h **95**
Goblet, #3928, gold, "Haeger–USA ©," stamped on bottom, c1962–69,
   3⁵/₈" d base, 4¹/₂" d top, 9³/₈" h **20**
Lamp, #5190, bucking bronco, cactus finial, 26" h **230**
Lamp, #5473, 2 deer, abstract, 15¹/₂" h **180**
Lamp, #6204, stallion head, oxblood and white, "Royal–Haeger–Dundee,
   Illinois" crown foil label, 36" h overall **220**
Planter, #508, donkey, red transparent, 9¹/₄" h **40**
Planter, #3311, cat, blue, c1946, 5³/₄" l, 7" h **35**
Planter, #3314, standing horse, white, unmkd, 7¹/₂" l, 6" h **50**
Planter, #3318, Colonial flower girl, chartreuse, unmkd, 9" h **40**
Planter, #3910, clown jack–in–the–box, pink, 8¹/₂" h **20**
Planter, #8008–H, blue bird, blue crackle, "Haeger–© 8008H–USA" mold-
   ed on bottom, "H" designed foil label reads "Haeger," 7³/₄" h **20**
Planter, #R–1761, turkey, red and black, "Royal Haeger–R1761 U.S.A."
   molded on bottom, 14" l, 12" h **155**
Planter, #R–1844, duck, jade crackle, "Royal Haeger R1844 USA" molded
   on bottom, 8" l, 6¹/₂" h **35**
Serving Plate, chicken shaped, yellow, brown, "Royal Haeger 873 © U. S.
   A." molded on bottom, 14³/₄" l, 10³/₄" w **80**
Table Lighter, #812–H, fish, jade crackle blue, c1960, 10" h **35**
Table Lighter, #889, ribbed, mandarin orange, c1950s–60s, 3" d, 5" h **15**
TV Lamp, #6140, sailfish, silver spray, 9¹/₄" l **40**
Vase, #R–321, shell shaped, chartreuse, white int, "Royal Haeger–USA 321"
   molded on bottom, 7³/₄" h **30**
Vase, #S–447, oblong, thumbprint design, incised lines, "Haeger © USA" ink
   stamped on bottom, "Craftsman for a Century" label, c1952, 8" h **30**
Wall Lamp, #5240, horse head, ebony, crown foil label, c1947, 5¹/₄" d base,
   9¹/₄" l **220**
Wall Pocket, #R–745, grape vine, purple and green, molded "Royal Haeger
   R–745 USA" **110**
Wall Pocket, #R–16275, fish, antique white, "Royal Haeger ©" crown label,
   13¹/₄" l **110**

HALL

Robert Hall founded the Hall China Company in 1903 in East Liverpool, Ohio. He died in 1904 and was succeeded by his son, Robert Taggart Hall. After years of experimentation, Robert T. Hall developed a leadless glaze in 1911, opening the way for production of glazed household products.

The Hall China Company made many types of kitchenware, refrigerator sets, and dinnerware in a wide variety of patterns. Some patterns were exclusive, such as Heather Rose for Sears.

Hall's most popular pattern was Autumn Leaf, an exclusive premium designed in 1933 for the Jewel Tea Company by Arden Richards. Still a Jewel Tea property, Autumn Leaf has not been listed in catalogs since 1978 but is produced on a replacement basis with the date stamped on the back.

Like Homer Laughlin's Fiesta pattern, Autumn Leaf is recognized as a separate collecting category independent of its manufacturer.

References: Harvey Duke, *Hall Price Guide Update, Two,* ELO Books, 1995; Harvey Duke, *Hall 2,* ELO Books, 1985; Harvey Duke, *Superior Quality Hall China,* ELO Books, 1977; Margaret and Kenn Whitmyer, *The Collector's Encyclopedia of Hall China, Second Edition,* Collector Books, 1994, 1997 value update.

Collectors' Club: Hall Collector's Club, PO Box 360488, Cleveland, OH 44136.

Blue Bouquet, ball jug, #3	**$80**
Blue Bouquet, casserole, thick rim	50
Blue Bouquet, cereal bowl, 6" d	12
Blue Bouquet, custard, thick rim	12
Blue Bouquet, fruit bowl, 5½" d	8
Blue Bouquet, gravy boat	35
Blue Bouquet, leftover, rect	50
Blue Bouquet, plate, 6" d	5
Blue Bouquet, plate, 8¼" d	12
Blue Bouquet, plate, 9" d	15
Blue Bouquet, salad bowl, 9" d	12
Blue Bouquet, saucer	3
Blue Bouquet, soup tureen	245
Cameo Rose, butter dish, ¼ lb	55
Cameo Rose, creamer	8
Cameo Rose, flat soup, 8" d	15
Cameo Rose, gravy boat and underplate	30
Cameo Rose, plate, 7¼" d	8
Cameo Rose, plate, 9¼" d	10
Cameo Rose, platter, oval, 11¼"	15
Cameo Rose, tidbit tray, 3 tier	40
Cameo Rose, vegetable bowl, 9" d	25
Carrot, casserole, Radiance	60
Casual Living, bean pot, brown	15
Colonial, creamer, green	7
Crocus, ball jug	195
Crocus, cake plate	30
Crocus, casserole, cov	60
Crocus, creamer, Medallion	60

Crocus, cup, St Denis 45
Crocus, cup and saucer 18
Crocus, custard 15
Crocus, gravy boat 35
Crocus, mixing bowl 50
Crocus, pie baker 35
Crocus, plate, 8¼" d 10
Crocus, plate, 9" d 12
Crocus, plate, 10" d 35
Crocus, platter, oval, 13¼" l 35
Crocus, soup tureen 425
Crocus, sugar, cov, Meltdown 70
Crocus, tidbit, 3 tier 55
Fantasy, ball jug, #2 100
Game Bird, bowl, oval 32
Game Bird, coffee mug 15
Game Bird, cookie jar, Zeisel 160
Game Bird, creamer 15
Game Bird, platter 35
Game Bird, sugar, cov 30
Heather Rose, cake plate 15
Heather Rose, cookie jar, flared shape 15
Heather Rose, creamer 10
Heather Rose, flat soup, 8" d 12
Heather Rose, gravy boat and underplate 20
Heather Rose, pie baker 20
Heather Rose, plate, 10" d 8
Heather Rose, platter, oval, 13¼" d 15
Heather Rose, salad bowl, 9" d 15
Heather Rose, sugar, cov 15
Homewood, bowl, Radiance, 6" d 12
Homewood, bowl, Radiance, 9" d 25
Homewood, cup 8
Homewood, fruit bowl, 5½" d 6
Homewood, salt and pepper shakers, pr, handled 20
Homewood, saucer 2
Mums, bowl, oval, 10¼" d 25
Mums, cup 25
Mums, drip jar, open, #1188 35
Mums, flat soup, 8½" d 15

Red Poppy, salt and pepper shakers, pr, range size, 5" h, $22.

Mums, gravy boat 25
Mums, jug, Simplicity 130
Mums, plate, 8¼" d 6
Mums, plate, 9" d 12
Mums, stack set, Radiance 80
Mums, sugar, cov, Medallion 25
No. 488, butter dish, Zephyr, 1 lb 425
No. 488, casserole, thick rim 40
No. 488, creamer, Meltdown 30
No. 488, cup 15
No. 488, flat soup, 8½" d 25
No. 488, leftover, square 70
No. 488, pretzel jar 130
No. 488, soup tureen 245
No. 488, sugar, cov, modern 20
Orange Poppy, bowl 12
Orange Poppy, canister, Radiance 275
Orange Poppy, casserole, cov, oval, 8" l 65
Orange Poppy, casserole, 9" l 55
Orange Poppy, coffeepot, S lid, hairline 50
Orange Poppy, creamer 7
Orange Poppy, leftover 75
Orange Poppy, plate, 6" d 6
Orange Poppy, plate, 9" d 15
Orange Poppy, salt and pepper shakers, pr, handled 50
Orange Poppy, sugar, cov 25
Pastel Morning Glory, cake plate 20
Pastel Morning Glory, cereal bowl, 6" d 12
Pastel Morning Glory, creamer, New York 15
Pastel Morning Glory, cup 10
Pastel Morning Glory, drip jar, open, #1188 30
Pastel Morning Glory, gravy boat 25
Pastel Morning Glory, plate, 8¼" d 6
Pastel Morning Glory, plate, 10" d 30
Pastel Morning Glory, saucer 3
Pastel Morning Glory, shaker, open, Teardrop 15
Pastel Morning Glory, tea tile 50
Primrose, creamer 7
Primrose, fruit bowl, 5¼" d 4
Primrose, jug, Rayed 15
Primrose, pie baker 20
Primrose, plate, 7¼" d 5
Primrose, plate, 10" d 8
Primrose, sugar, cov 15
Radiant Ware, nesting bowls, #1 to 4, set of 4 175
Red Poppy, ball jug, #3 40
Red Poppy, cake plate 30
Red Poppy, cup 10
Red Poppy, custard 20
Red Poppy, drip jar 30
Red Poppy, mixing bowl, #5, Radiance 10

Red Poppy, pie baker   30
Red Poppy, plate, 9" d   7
Red Poppy, salad bowl, 9" d   15
Red Poppy, salt and pepper shakers, pr   22
Red Poppy, tumbler, frosted, 5¼" h   22
Serenade, bowl, Radiance, 7½" d   15
Serenade, creamer, New York   15
Serenade, drip jar, cov, Radiance   20
Serenade, fruit bowl, 5½" d   5
Serenade, gravy boat   30
Serenade, plate, 9" d   8
Serenade, saucer   2
Serenade, sugar, cov, New York   15
Silhouette, ball jug, #3   90
Silhouette, bean pot, #4, New England   120
Silhouette, bowl, flared, 7¾" d   30
Silhouette, bowl, oval   25
Silhouette, casserole, Medallion, 6" d   15
Silhouette, cereal bowl, 6" d   10
Silhouette, clock, electric   70
Silhouette, drip jar, cov, Medallion   30
Silhouette, jug, Simplicity   125
Silhouette, plate, 6" d   6
Silhouette, plate, 8¼" d   8
Silhouette, platter, oval, 11¼" l   20
Silhouette, salt and pepper shakers, pr, 5 bands   30
Silhouette, saucer, St Denis   10
Silhouette, vegetable bowl, round, 9¼" d   30
Springtime, ball jug, #3   50
Springtime, cake plate   15
Springtime, casserole, thick rim   25
Springtime, cereal bowl, 6" d   8
Springtime, cup   7
Springtime, custard   6
Springtime, flat soup, 8½" d   12
Springtime, gravy boat   20
Springtime, plate, 7¼" d   6
Springtime, plate, 9" d   9
Springtime, platter, oval, 13¼" l   22

Teapot, Aladdin, cobalt blue, gold trim, flame finial, infusor, 3 pcs, $40.

Springtime, saucer **3**
Teapot, Boston, brown with gold **40**
Teapot, Flare–Ware, white with gold **35**
Teapot, Los Angeles, white, orchid, and black, large chip inside rim **60**
Teapot, Manhattan, blue **65**
Teapot, Melody, Chinese Red **180**
Teapot, Moderne, marine blue with gold, 6 cup **90**
Teapot, Nautilus, 6 cup **125**
Teapot, Newport, pink with floral decal, 5 cup **50**
Teapot, New York, cobalt with gold palm trees **225**
Teapot, Ohio, brown with gold, 6 cup **170**
Teapot, Rhythm, canary with gold, 6 cup **110**
Teapot, Sundial, canary with gold **130**
Teapot, Surfside, ivory and gold, 6 cup **100**
Teapot, Wildflower, Aladdin, oval lid and insert, chip on lid finial **90**
Teapot, Windshield, cobalt with gold roses, 6 cup **205**
Teapot, Zeisel, gold, "In Honor Of Golden Anniversary Of Tea Bag,
  1904–1954," lid repaired **300**
Terrace, coffeepot, white, green, and platinum **22**
Terrace, Drip–O–Lator, floral design, 2 cup **15**
Tulip, bowl, oval, 10¼" d **35**
Tulip, creamer **15**
Tulip, cup and saucer **15**
Tulip, fruit bowl, 5½" d **10**
Tulip, mixing bowl, 6" d **28**
Tulip, mixing bowl, 7½" d **35**
Tulip, nested bowls, thick rims, set of 3 .... **75**
Tulip, platter, oval, 13¼" l **42**
Tulip, sugar, cov **25**
Wildfire, bowl, straight sides, 6" d **12**
Wildfire, cake plate **20**
Wildfire, casserole, tab handled **30**
Wildfire, drip jar, cov, thick rim **25**
Wildfire, eggcup **55**
Wildfire, flat soup, 8½" d **15**
Wildfire, jug, #5, Radiance **35**
Wildfire, plate, 9" d **10**
Wildfire, platter, oval, 13¼" l **30**
Yellow Rose, cup **25**
Yellow Rose, custard **10**
Yellow Rose, gravy boat **30**

***Wildfire, gravy boat, #85, Ruffled–D
shape, gold trim, 9" l, $20.*** Photo
courtesy Ray Morykan Auctions.

HARKER

The Harker Company was established in 1840 when Benjamin Harker, an English slater turned farmer in East Liverpool, Ohio, built a kiln and began making yellow ware products from clay deposits on his land. The business was managed by members of the Harker family until the Civil War when David Boyce, a brother–in–law, took over. Although a Harker resumed management after the war, members of the Boyce family assumed key roles within the firm; David G. Boyce, a grandson of David, served as president.

In 1879 the first whiteware products were introduced. A disastrous flood in 1884 caused severe financial problems which the company overcame. In 1931 the company moved to Chester, West Virginia, to escape the flooding problems. In 1945 Harker introduced Cameoware made by the engobe process. The engobe or layered effect was achieved by placing a copper mask over the bisque and sand blasting to leave the design imprint. The white rose pattern on blue ground was marketed as "White Rose Carv–Kraft" in Montgomery Ward stores.

The Harker Company used a large variety of backstamps and names. Hotoven cookware featured a scroll draped over pots, with a kiln design at top. Columbia Chinaware had a circular stamp with the Statue of Liberty.

Harker made a Rockingham ware line in the 1960s. The hound handled pitcher and mugs were included. The Jeannette Glass Company purchased the Harker Company and the plant was closed in March, 1972. Ohio Stoneware, Inc., utilized the plant building until it was destroyed by fire in 1975.

In 1965 Harker China had the capacity to produce 25 million pieces of dinnerware each year and many patterns also were kept in production for decades. Hence, there is a great deal of Harker material available at garage sales and flea markets.

Between 1935 and 1955 the Harker Company organized Columbia Chinaware, a sales organization used to market Harker products in small towns across the country. The line included enamel ware, glass, and aluminum products. One pattern of Columbia Chinaware was "Autumn Leaf," eagerly sought by Autumn Leaf collectors.

There are dozens of Harker patterns involving flowers, foliage, and fruit that will work well in any Country decorating scheme. Some patterns are relatively simple, others quite elaborate. When selecting a pattern to collect, make certain that the pattern contains a large number of forms so that an elegant, full table can be set.

Also consider focusing on Harker patterns by famous designers. Among these are Russel Wright's White Clover and George Bauer's Cameoware. Many patterns will be found with different color grounds. Other patterns were designed to have mass appeal. Colonial Lade was popular at "dish nites" at the movies or other businesses.

Shapes and forms did change through the decades. An interesting collection might focus on one object, e.g., a sugar or creamer, collected in a variety of patterns from different historical periods. Watch for unusual pieces. Harker produced rolling pins in many patterns including Amy, Fruit Basket, and Petit Point Rose. The Countryside pattern features a rolling pin, scoop, and cake server.

Reference: Nava W. Colbert, *The Collector's Guide to Harker Pottery USA: Identification and Values,* Collector Books, 1993.

Newsletter: *The Harker Arrow,* 69565 Crescent Road, St Clairsville, OH 43950.

Amy, bean pot **$12**

Amy, cup and saucer, 6¼" d **8**

Amy, pepper shaker **12**

Amy, plate, 6¼" d **5**

Amy, Birds and Flowers, pitcher, Regal shape, 8" h **35**

Amy, Birds and Flowers, utility plate, 12" d **15**

Cameoware, berry bowl **4**

Cameoware, casserole, cov **15**

Cameoware, cup and saucer **10**

Cameoware, dinner plate, 10" d **10**

Cameoware, salt and pepper shakers, pr **15**

Colonial Lady, bowl, tab handle **8**

Colonial Lady, bread and butter plate **8**

Colonial Lady, cereal bowl **15**

Colonial Lady, cookie jar, cov **35**

Colonial Lady, rolling pin **125**

Colonial Lady, salad plate **10**

Colonial Lady, salt and pepper shakers, pr **25**

Colonial Lady, soup bowl **22**

Countryside, pepper shaker **15**

Countryside, pie server **18**

Countryside, utility jug, arches shape, 5½" h **30**

Deco–Dahlia, cake lifter **30**

Deco–Dahlia, pie baker, 9" d **20**

Deco–Dahlia, utility plate, 12" d **20**

Ivy, pitcher, Regal shape, 7" h **32**

Ivy, serving plate, 12" d **15**

Laurelton, bread and butter plate **5**

Laurelton, creamer and sugar **22**

Laurelton, vegetable bowl **25**

Left: Colonial Lady, mixing bowl, pour spout, $25. Right: Countryside, scoop, $20.

Mallow, bowl, 5" d **20**
Mallow, jug, cov **18**
Mallow, lard jar, cov **22**
Mallow, plate, 8" d **15**
Mallow, serving spoon **25**
Pansy, cereal bowl **15**
Pansy, cup **15**
Pansy, dinner plate **15**
Petit Point Rose, bowl, 8³/₄" d **20**
Petit Point Rose, cake plate **15**
Petit Point Rose, casserole, cov, 7" d **35**
Petit Point Rose, pie baker **15**
Petit Point Rose, plate, 8¹/₂" d **10**
Red Apple, custard **10**
Red Apple, pie server **25**
Red Apple, serving plate, 12" d **20**
Red Apple, spoon **30**
Red Apple, sugar, no lid **10**
Red Apple, vegetable bowl, 9" d **30**
Rose Spray, breakfast plate, 9" d **8**
Rose Spray, creamer, 10" d **12**
Rose Spray, salad plate, 7" sq **5**
Rose Spray, serving bowl, tab handle **8**

HOMER LAUGHLIN

Homer Laughlin and his brother, Shakespeare, built two pottery kilns in East Liverpool, Ohio, in 1871. Shakespeare withdrew in 1879, leaving Homer to operate the business alone. Laughlin became one of the first firms to produce American made whiteware. In 1896, William Wills and a Pittsburgh group led by Marcus Aaron bought the Laughlin firm.

Expansion followed. Two new plants were built in Laughlin Station, Ohio. In 1906, the first plant (#4) was built in Newall, West Virginia. In 1923 plant #6 was built at Newall and featured a continuous tunnel kiln. Similar kilns were added at the other plants. Other advances included spray glazing and mechanical jiggering.

In the 1930 to 1960 period several new dinnerware lines were added, including the Wells Art Glaze line. Ovenserve and Kitchen Kraft were the cooking ware lines. The colored glaze lines of Fiesta, Harlequin and Rhythm captured major market shares. In 1959 a translucent table china line was introduced. Today, the annual manufacturing capacity is over 45 million pieces.

The original trademark from 1871 to 1890 merely identified the products as "Laughlin Brothers." The next trademark featured the American eagle astride the prostrate British lion. The third marking featured a monogram of "HLC" which has appeared, with slight variations, on all dinnerware since about 1900. The 1900 trademark contained a number which identified the month, year and plant at which the product was made. Letter codes were used in later periods.

So much attention has been placed on Fiesta that other interesting patterns have not achieved the popularity which they deserve. Prices still are moderate. Some of the patterns from the 1930s and 1940s have contemporary designs that are highly artistic.

There are dozens of Homer Laughlin patterns that would fit comfortably in any Country decorating scheme. Collectors are advised first to select a shape they like, e.g., Virginia Rose or Yellowstone octagonal, and then the decal pattern. Virginia Rose is a shape, not a pattern name. Several different decals can be found, with delicate pink flowers the most common.

Like Hall's Autumn Leaf pattern, Fiesta is recognized as a separate collecting category independent of its manufacturer.

References: Joanne Jasper, *The Collector's Encyclopedia of Homer Laughlin China: Reference & Value Guide,* Collector Books, 1993, 1997 value update; Richard G. Racheter, *Collector's Guide to Homer Laughlin's Virginia Rose: Identification & Values,* Collector Books, 1997.

Newsletter: *The Laughlin Eagle,* 1270 63rd Terrace South, St Petersburg, FL 33705.

Reproduction Alert: Harlequin and Fiesta lines were reissued in 1978 and marked accordingly.

Amberstone, butter dish, cov, 1/4 lb	**$32**
Amberstone, coffee server	**30**
Amberstone, cup	**7**
Amberstone, dessert plate, 6" d	**5**
Amberstone, sauce boat	**20**
Amberstone, tray, center handle	**25**
American Provincial, plate, 7" d	**4**
Eggshell Theme, cup and saucer	**15**
Eggshell Theme, gravy boat and underplate	**18**
Eggshell Theme, salad plate	**7**
Harlequin, ball jug, gray, 22 oz	**55**
Harlequin, ball jug, rose	**45**
Harlequin, bowl, maroon, 5½" d	**12**
Harlequin, bowl, red	**8**
Harlequin, bread and butter plate, maroon, 6" d	**7**
Harlequin, butter dish, cov, maroon	**100**

Apple Blossom: berry bowl, $5; bread and butter plate, $5; cup and saucer, $12; dinner plate, $10; flat soup, $12; salad plate, $8; vegetable bowl, $15.

Harlequin, candle holders, pr, maroon 190
Harlequin, casserole, cov, medium green 140
Harlequin, cereal bowl, turquoise 8
Harlequin, creamer, individual, maroon 25
Harlequin, creamer, large, medium green 45
Harlequin, cream soup, turquoise 18
Harlequin, cup, mauve blue 20
Harlequin, cup and saucer, yellow 6
Harlequin, demitasse cup and saucer, yellow 35
Harlequin, eggcup, double, turquoise 15
Harlequin, eggcup, single, mauve blue 25
Harlequin, gravy boat, maroon 15
Harlequin, nappy, yellow 35
Harlequin, nut dish, 3 part, mauve blue 8
Harlequin, plate, rose, 7" d 10
Harlequin, salad plate, individual, chartreuse 22
Harlequin, teapot, medium green 65
Harlequin, water pitcher, medium green 75
Jubilee, coffee server, shell pink 40
Jubilee, dinner plate, cream beige 8
Jubilee, mayonnaise and underplate, shell pink 75
Jubilee, saucer, celadon green 5
Kitchen Kraft, salt and pepper shakers, pr 32
Mexicana, cup and saucer 15
Priscilla, casserole, cov 30
Priscilla, creamer 12
Priscilla, pie baker 20
Priscilla, sugar, cov 18
Priscilla, teapot, cov 35
Priscilla, utility bowl, large 35
Rhythm, bowl, maroon, 5" d 5
Rhythm, cup and saucer 15
Rhythm, dinner plate, 10" d 8
Rhythm, fruit bowl, gray 4
Rhythm, gravy boat, turquoise 9
Rhythm, plate, maroon, 7" d 12
Rhythm, platter, forest green, 11½" l 15
Rhythm, soup bowl, chartreuse, 8" d 10
Rhythm, sugar, cov 10
Rhythm, teapot, cov 32
Riviera, bowl, blue 7
Riviera, cream soup, yellow 35
Riviera, cup, mauve blue 8
Riviera, cup and saucer, yellow 12
Riviera, nappy, yellow 20
Riviera, plate, green 10
Riviera, sugar, cov, mauve blue 12
Riviera, sugar, red 15
Royal Harvest, bread and butter plate 4
Royal Harvest, platter, oval 12
Royal Harvest, vegetable bowl, round 8

Angelus, platter, floral decal, emb scalloped rim, 14¹/₄" l, $20.

HULL

In 1905 Addis E. Hull purchased the Acme Pottery Company, Crooksville, Ohio. In 1917 the A. E. Hull Pottery Company began making a line of art pottery, novelties, stoneware, and kitchenware, later introducing the famous Little Red Riding Hood line. Most items had a matte finish with shades of pink and blue or brown predominating.

After a disastrous flood and fire in 1950, J. Brandon Hull reopened the factory in 1952 as the Hull Pottery Company. Newer, more modern styles, mostly with a glossy finish, were introduced. The company currently produces pieces, e.g. the Regal and Floraline lines, for sale to florists.

Hull pottery molds and patterns are easily identified. Pre–1950 vases are marked "Hull USA" or "Hull Art USA" on the bottom. Many also retain their paper labels. Post–1950 pieces are marked "Hull" in large script or "HULL" in block letters.

Each pattern has a distinctive number, e.g., Wildflower with a "W" and number, Water Lily with an "L" and number, Poppy with "600" numbers, and Orchid with "300" numbers. Early stoneware pieces have an "H."

References: Barbara Loveless Gick–Burke, *Collector's Guide to Hull Pottery: The Dinnerware Lines: Identification and Values,* Collector Books, 1993; Joan Gray Hull, *Hull: The Heavenly Pottery, Fifth Edition,* published by author, 1997; Brenda Roberts,

Roberts Ultimate Encyclopedia of Hull Pottery, Walsworth Publishing, 1992; Brenda Roberts, *The Collectors Encyclopedia of Hull Pottery,* Collector Books, 1980, 1997 value update; Brenda Roberts, *The Companion Guide to Roberts' Ultimate Encyclopedia of Hull Pottery,* Walsworth Publishing, 1992; Mark E. Supnick, *Collecting Hull Pottery's "Little Red Riding Hood": A Pictorial Reference and Price Guide,* L–W Book Sales, 1989, 1992 value update.

Newsletters: *Hull Pottery Newsletter,* 11023 Tunnel Hill NE, New Lexington, OH 43764; *The Hull Pottery News,* 466 Foreston Place, St Louis, MO 63119.

Ashtray, Butterfly, B–3, 7" d	**$40**
Ashtray, Continental, 8" d	**40**
Basket, Blossom Flite, T–44, 8½" h	**90**
Basket, Bow Knot, B–25, 6½" h	**330**
Basket, Ebb Tide, E–11, 16½" h	**200**
Basket, Magnolia, 10, matte, 10½" h	**550**
Basket, Mardi Gras/Granada, 32, 8" h	**200**
Basket, Tokay/Tuscany, 6, 8" h	**75**
Basket, Tulip, 102–33, 6" h	**230**
Batter Pitcher, Little Red Riding Hood	**400**
Bookends, pr, Orchid, 316, 7" h	**1,350**
Bowl, Calla Lily, 500–32, 8" d	**125**
Bowl, Iris, 412, rose, 4" d	**70**
Bowl, Open Rose/Camellia, 113, low, 7" d	**100**
Bud Vase, Butterfly, B–1, 6¼" h	**25**
Bud Vase, Iris, 410, 7½" h	**100**
Bud Vase, Orchid, 306, 6¾" h	**45**
Bud Vase, Orchid, 309, 8" h	**165**
Bud Vase, Woodland, W–15, double, post–1950 gloss, 8½" h	**35**
Bud Vase, Woodland, W–15, double, pre–1950 matte, 8½" h	**95**
Butter Dish, cov, Little Red Riding Hood	**350**
Candle Holder, Bow Knot, B–17, 4" h	**125**
Candle Holder, Calla Lily, unmkd, 2¼" h	**100**
Candle Holder, Dogwood, 512, 3¼" h	**130**
Candle Holder, Ebb Tide, F–13, 2¾" h	**30**
Candle Holder, Iris, 411, 5" h	**130**
Candle Holder, Orchid, 315, 4" h	**140**
Candy Dish, cov, Tokay/Tuscany, 9–C, 8½" d	**100**
Canister, flour, Little Red Riding Hood	**650**
Casserole, open, Blossom, Cinderella Kitchenware, 21, 7½" h	**40**
Console Bowl, Calla Lily, 590–33, 4 x 13"	**180**
Console Bowl, Magnolia, 12½" h	**165**
Console Bowl, Orchid, 314, 13" h	**375**
Console Bowl, Tokay/Tuscany, 1, 6½" h	**35**
Console Bowl, Woodland, W–10, 11" h	**45**
Cookie Jar, barefoot boy	**400**
Cookie Jar, Debonair, Kitchenware, O–8, 8¾" h	**125**
Cookie Jar, Little Red Riding Hood, open basket, gold stars on apron	**400**
Cornucopia, Dogwood/Wild Rose, 522, 4" l	**55**
Cornucopia, Open Rose, 101, 8½" h	**170**
Cornucopia, Rosella, R–13, 8½" l	**150**
Cornucopia, Tokay/Tuscany, 1, 6½" l	**30**

Cornucopia, Water Lily, L–7, 6½" l 75
Cracker Jar, Little Red Riding Hood 575
Creamer, Little Red Riding Hood, head pour 400
Creamer, Little Red Riding Hood, top pour, tab handle 350
Double Cornucopia, Magnolia, 6, matte, 12" h 200
Ewer, Calla Lily, 506, 10" h 425
Ewer, Dogwood, 520, 4¾" h 150
Ewer, Mardi Gras/Granada, 31, 10" h 150
Ewer, Wild Flower, 63, 4½" l 95
Flower Arranger, colt, gray 40
Flower Bowl, Capri, C–47, round, 5¼ x 8" 40
Flower Pot, Sunglow, 97, 5½" h 35
Grease Jar, Bouquet, Cinderella Kitchenware, 24, 32 oz 50
Grease Jar, Floral, 43, 5¾" h 120
Hanging Basket, Open Rose, 132, 7" h 200
Hanging Basket, Woodland, W–17, 7½" h 150
Jardiniere, Orchid, 310, 6" h 100
Jardiniere, Poppy, 603, 4¾" h 70
Jardiniere, Water Lily, L–24, 8½" h 200
Jardiniere, Wild Flower, 64, 4" h 70
Kitchenware, Sunglow, salt and pepper, 54 28
Match Box, Little Red Riding Hood 900
Milk Pitcher, Little Red Riding Hood 300
Mixing Bowl, Blossom, Cinderella Kitchenware, 20, 7½" h 40
Pitcher, Blossom, Cinderella Kitchenware, 29, 16 oz 45
Pitcher, Bouquet, Cinderella Kitchenware, 29, 32 oz 55
Pitcher, Poppy, 610, 13" h 650
Pitcher, Tropicana, 56, 13½" h 550
Pitcher, Water Lily, L–3, 5½" h 55

Left: Jardiniere, 536, green and brown glaze, 9", $85.

Right: Pie Baker, Mirror Brown, 566, mkd "Hull Oven Proof U.S.A.," 9⅜" d, $6. Photo courtesy Ray Morykan Auctions.

Pitcher, Woodland, W–3, 5¹/₂" h **40**
Planter, baby and pillow, 92, blue **30**
Planter, Blossom Flite, 10¹/₂" l **100**
Planter, Capri, C–81, twin swan **80**
Planter, Continental, C–68, ftd, rect, 8¹/₂ x 4¹/₂" **25**
Planter, elephant **35**
Planter, lamb **45**
Planter, Mardis Gras/Granada, 204, 6" h **45**
Planter, Parchment & Pine, S–5, scroll, 10¹/₂" h **90**
Planter, Rose Bowl, Iris, 412, 4" h **120**
Planter, swan, 69, lime green **35**
Planter, unicorn, 98, 10" h **50**
Salt and Pepper Shakers, pr, Little Red Riding Hood, 3¹/₄" h **140**
Salt and Pepper Shakers, pr, Little Red Riding Hood, 5¹/₂" h **225**
Salt and Pepper Shakers, pr, Sunglow, Kitchenware, 54 .... **30**
Serving Tray, Butterfly, B–23, matte white and turquoise, gold trim, 11¹/₂" d ... **100**
Shaker, Floral, Kitchenware, 44, 3¹/₂" h **20**
Sugar, cov, Little Red Riding Hood **300**
Sugar, open, Butterfly, B–20 .... **55**
Sugar, open Rose/Camellia, 112, 5" h **85**
Sugar, Water Lily, L–20 .... **55**
Teapot, cov, Bouquet, Cinderella Kitchenware, 26, 42 oz **150**
Teapot, cov, Bow Knot, B–20, 6" h **500**
Teapot, cov, Magnolia, H–20, gloss, 6¹/₂" h **150**
Teapot, cov, Wildflower, 72, 8" h **800**
Vase, Blossom Flite, T–7, handled, 10¹/₂" h **55**
Vase, Bow Knot, B–10, 10¹/₄" h **350**
Vase, Butterfly, B–9, 9" h **45**
Vase, Calla Lily, 502/33, 6¹/₂" h **75**
Vase, Calla Lily, 520/33, 8" h **200**
Vase, Continental, C–53, 8¹/₂" h **40**
Vase, Dogwood/Wild Rose, 504, 8¹/₂" h **95**
Vase, Dogwood/Wild Rose, 517, 4³/₄" h **55**
Vase, Ebbtide, E–2, twin fish, 7" h **65**
Vase, Iris, 407, 7" h **100**
Vase, Iris, 414, 10¹/₂" h **300**
Vase, Jack–in–the–Pulpit, 501–33, 6" h **70**
Vase, Jack–in–the–Pulpit, 510–33, 8" h **100**
Vase, Little Red Riding Hood **375**
Vase, Magnolia, 7, matte, 8¹/₂" h **60**
Vase, Magnolia, 17, winged, 12¹/₂" h **230**
Vase, Magnolia, H–1, pink gloss, 5¹/₂" h **15**
Vase, Magnolia, H–7, gloss, 6¹/₂" h **20**
Vase, Magnolia, Open Rose/Camellia, 118, swan, 6¹/₂" h **85**
Vase, Magnolia, Open Rose/Camellia, 126, hand, 8¹/₂" h **160**
Vase, Orchid, 309, 8" h **165**
Vase, Parchment and Pine, S–1, 6" h **20**
Vase, Parchment and Pine, S–4, 10" h **100**
Vase, Rosella, R–1, 5" h **40**
Vase, Sunglow, 91, 6¹/₂" h **40**
Vase, Thistle, 51, 6¹/₂" h **110**

Vase, Tropicana, T–53, flat sided, 8½" h 385
Vase, Water Lily, 6½" h 60
Vase, Water Lily, 8½" h 100
Vase, Wildflower, 60, 6¼" h 85
Vase, Wildflower, W–13, 9½" h 120
Vase, Woodland, W–18, post–1950 gloss, 10½" h 55
Vase, Woodland, W–18, pre–1950 matte, 10½" h 175
Wall Pocket, Little Red Riding Hood 450
Wall Pocket, Poppy, 609, 9" h 350
Wall Pocket, Rosella, R–10, 6½" h 150
Wall Pocket, Sunglow, 82, whisk broom, 8½" h 65
Window Box, Butterfly, 12¾ x 4¾" 50
Window Box, Serenade, 12½" l 28

IRONSTONE

White patterned ironstone is a heavy earthenware, first patented in 1813 by Charles Mason, Staffordshire, England, using the name "Patent Ironstone China." Other English potters soon began copying this opaque, feldspathic, white china.

White ironstone dishes first became available in the American market in the early 1840s. The first patterns had simple Gothic lines similar to the shapes used in transfer wares. Pattern shapes, such as New York, Union, and Atlantic, were designed to appeal to the American housewife. Embossed designs, inspired by the American western prairie, included wheat, corn, oats, and poppy motifs. Eventually over 200 shapes and patterns, with variations of finials and handles, were made.

White patterned ironstone is identified by shape names and pattern names. Many potters named only the shape in their catalogs. Pattern names usually refer to the decoration motif.

There is something elegant about these all–white ironstone pieces. Country collectors and decorators alike eagerly seek this ware. Large, crisp, white tureens look quite at home in the country setting.

References: Anise Doring Heaivilin, *Grandma's Tea Leaf Ironstone: A Study of English and American Potteries,* L–W Book Sales, 1981, 1996 value update; Dawn Stolzfus and Jeffrey B. Snyder, *White Ironstone: A Survey of Its Many Forms,* Schiffer Publishing, 1997; Jean Wetherbee, *White Ironstone: A Collector's Guide,* Antique Trader Books, 1997.

Collectors' Clubs: Mason's Ironstone Collectors' Club, 542 Seskeyon Boulevard, Medford, OR 97504; Tea Leaf Club International, 324 Powderhorn Drive, Houghton Lake, MI 48629; White Ironstone China Assoc, Inc, RD 1, Box 23, Howes Cave, NY 12092.

Tea Leaf Lustre, cake plate, handled, mkd "Mellor, Taylor & Co., England,
    Warranted Stone China," 11⅞ x 9" $75
Tea Leaf Lustre, coffeepot, cov, rect, vertical ribbing on corners, mkd "Royal
    Ironstone China, Alfred Meakin, England," 8¾" h 40
Tea Leaf Lustre, creamer and sugar, cov, rect, vertical ribbing on corners,
    mkd Royal Ironstone China, Alfred Meakin, England," 6⁵⁄₁₆" h creamer,
    6½" h sugar 25
Tea Leaf Lustre, dinner plate, mkd "Royal Ironstone China, Alfred Meakin,
    England," 8¾" d, price for pair 10

Tea Leaf Lustre, dinner plate, mkd "Royal Stone China, Wedgwood & Co., England," price for pair   5

Tea Leaf Lustre, fruit bowl, square, pleated corners, mkd "Royal Ironstone China, A. J. Wilkinson, England," 4¼" sq, price for 7   20

Tea Leaf Lustre, fruit compote, pedestal base, mkd "Royal Ironstone China, Alfred Meakin, England," 8⁷/₁₆" d at rim, 5½" h   310

Tea Leaf Lustre, gravy boat and underplate, oblong, vertical pleating on sides, mkd "Warranted Stone China, Mellor, Taylor & Co., England"   20

Tea Leaf Lustre, platter, oblong, mkd "Royal Ironstone China, A. J. Wilkinson, England," 14 x 10" . . . . \ 20

Tea Leaf Lustre, platter, oval, mkd "Royal Ironstone China, Alfred Meakin, England," 11 x 7⁷/₈"   12

Tea Leaf Lustre, relish tray, rect, scalloped rim, handles, mkd "Royal Stone China, Wedgwood & Co., England," 7³/₄ x 4½"   12

Tea Leaf Lustre, sugar bowl, cov, oblong, arched handles, mkd "Royal Ironstone China, Alfred Meakin, England," 6¼" h   25

Tea Leaf Lustre, teapot, cov, square, mkd "Royal Ironstone China, A. J. Wilkinson, England," professional repair to base, spout, and lid, 7³/₄" h   15

Tea Leaf Lustre, tureen, cov, handled, mkd "Royal Ironstone China, A. J. Wilkinson, England," 7 x 5³/₈ x 4½" h   135

Tea Leaf Lustre, vegetable bowl, scalloped rim, mkd "Royal Ironstone China, Alfred Meakin, England," 2½" h   7

Transfer, cake plate, 10 sided, molded floral design handles, "Bridgwood & Son" imp mark, 10⅛" d   7

Transfer, plate, Buda, mkd "Buda, England," "W" in diamond within trad mark, 8³/₄" d   8

Transfer, plate, corn design in bottom, fluted design sides, gallery type foot, 8⁵/₈ x 5¹³/₁₆ x 3⁷/₈" h, some discoloring   20

Transfer, plate, Genoa, mkd "Genoa, W. Adams & Sons," 8⁷/₈" d   6

Transfer, plate, Gypsy, 10¼" d   35

Transfer, plate, scenic view, "Wedgwood & Co.," imp mark, 5³/₈" d   8

Transfer, plate, Seine, mkd "Seine, Wedgwood," 9½" d   8

Left: Platter, purple flowers and green leaves on emb scroll rim, gold trim, mkd "Excelsior Porcelain, TSC Co," 17³/₄" l, $25. Photo courtesy Ray Morykan Auctions.

Right: Vegetable Tureen, cov, Wheat and Leaf, mkd "Stone China (W Taylor) Hanley," 11½" l, $70.

Transfer, plate, Tyrol, blue, green, and red accents, mkd "Ironstone China, Tyrol, J. Wedgwood," 6⁷/₁₆" d 8

Transfer, pudding mold, floral rosette design in bottom, leaf shaped designs around sides, 6 x 5 x 4¹/₈" h 30

Transfer, pudding mold, floral spray design in bottom, vertical fluting around sides, oval gallery type foot, imp "10," 6³/₈ x 5 x 2¹¹/₁₆" h 20

Transfer, toothbrush box, cov, elongated oval shape, foliage design, mkd "Clementson Brothers, Hawley, Royal Patent Stone Ware," 8¹/₂ x 3³/₄ x 3¹/₂" h 20

White Patterned, bowl, cov, Leaf Fan, Alcock, 7⁷/₈" d 110

White Patterned, cake plate, Brocade, handled, Mason, 9" w 130

White Patterned, chamber pot, Wheat and Blackberry, Meakin 45

White Patterned, coffeepot, pear shaped, rounded lid with scrolled finial, mkd "Ironstone China, F. D.," 9¹/₄" h 20

White Patterned, compote, German, round scalloped foot pedestal base, scalloped rim, unidentified beehive shaped imp mark, "857" and "61," 11⁵/₈" d, 4³/₄" h 25

White Patterned, creamer, Ceres, Wheat, mkd "Royal Patent Ironstone, Turner, Goddard & Co.," 5" h 15

White Patterned, creamer, Fig, Davenport 65

White Patterned, cup, handleless, Sydenham, price for pair 2

White Patterned, cup, Wheat and Clover 2

White Patterned, cup and saucer, handleless, President, Edwards 50

White Patterned, dinner plate, Atlantic shape, "T. & R. Boote, Atlantic Shape" imp mark, registry dated 1861, 9⁵/₈" d, price for pair 4

White Patterned, food mold, oval, geometric design, 6" l 570

White Patterned, funnel, bowl shaped top, small loop shaped handle, mkd "Sanitary Fruit Jarv Funnel" in green on side, 4³/₄" d, 2⁷/₁₇" h 20

White Patterned, funnel, conical shaped, German, rounded rim, small ring shaped handle on side below rim, imp unidentified eagle trademark on rim, 3⁷/₈" d, 6" h 20

White Patterned, pitcher, Berlin Swirl, Mayer and Elliot 120

White Patterned, pitcher, Sydenham, T and R Boote, 7⁷/₈" h 190

White Patterned, plate, Corn, Davenport, 10¹/₂" d 25

White Patterned, plate, Prairie Flowers, Powell and Bishop, 8¹/₂" d 20

White Patterned, plate, Scalloped Decagon, Davenport, 1852, 9¹/₄" d 5

White Patterned, platter, Basketweave with Band, rect, mkd "Royal Ironstone China, Alfred Meakin, England," 5³/₄ x 11³/₄" 27

White Patterned, platter, Columbia, octagonal, 20" l 130

White Patterned, platter, Wheat, mkd "Ironstone China, J. F.," glaze wear on rim, slight discoloring, 13¹/₄ x 10" 5

White Patterned, platter, Wheat, Meakin, 20³/₄" l 55

White Patterned, punch bowl, Berry Cluster, J Furnival 130

White Patterned, relish dish, Ceres, Elsmore and Forster, 1860 45

White Patterned, relish dish, oval ftd base, mkd "Buffalo China, 1918, Q. M.," 8⁵/₈ x 5 x 1³/₈" h 8

White Patterned, soap dish, cov, round, removable insert, mkd "Geo. S. Harker & Co., E. Liverpool, Ironstone China," 6" d, 5¹/₂" h 7

White Patterned, soup plate, Ceres, Wheat, round, unmkd, age lines on bottom, slight nick on base, 5¹/₈" d, 3³/₄" h 15

White Patterned, soup tureen, Lily of the Valley, Shaw 230

White Patterned, sugar, Ceres, Elsmore and Forster 75
White Patterned, sugar, paneled, T J and J Mayer 50
White Patterned, sugar, round body, molded ear shaped handle, scrolled lid
finial, "Ironstone China, B. & C. Challinor" imp mark, 6³/₄" h 5
White Patterned, syrup pitcher, Paneled Columbia, 1850s, 5" h 65
White Patterned, teapot, Ivy, William Adams, 10" h 80
White Patterned, teapot, Trent, T and R Boote 95
White Patterned, toothbrush holder, Bell Flower, Burgess 50
White Patterned, tray, Moss Rose, handled, gold trim, Wedgwood, 9" w 20
White Patterned, vegetable bowl, Blackberry, cov, unmkd 50
White Patterned, vegetable bowl, Corn and Oats, open, "Davenport
Ironstone China" imp mark, registry mark dated 1861, nick on underside
of rim, 11³/₁₆ x 8¹/₄ x 2³/₈" 5
White Patterned, vegetable bowl, cov, Fluted Pearl, open scrolled handles,
entwined branch–like finial, "J. Wedgwood, Ironstone China" imp mark,
13¹/₈ x 9³/₄ x 7¹/₄" h 50
White Patterned, water pitcher, Chinese shape, mkd "Stone China, Anthony
Shaw, Burslem," 9³/₄" h 85
White Patterned, water pitcher, Columbia, unmkd, 4¹/₈ x 6³/₈" 80

JOHNSON BROTHERS

Johnson Brothers was established in 1883. Three brothers, Alfred, Frederick, and Henry Johnson, purchased the bankrupt J. W. Pankhurst Company, a tableware manufactory in Hanley, Staffordshire, England. Although begun on a small scale the company prospered and expanded.

In 1896 Robert, a fourth brother, joined the firm. Robert, who lived and worked in the United States, was assigned the task of expanding the company's position in the American market. By 1914 Johnson Brothers owned and operated five additional factories scattered throughout Hanley, Tunstall, and Burslem.

Johnson Brothers continued to grow throughout the 1960s with acquisitions of tableware manufacturing plants in Hamilton, Ontario, Canada, and Croydon, Australia. Two additional English plants were acquired in 1960 and 1965. Johnson Brothers became part of the Wedgwood Group in 1968.

Johnson's transfer patterns of idyllic and romantic English scenery, e.g., Coaching Scenes and Old Britain Castles, complement any formal Country table.

References: Mary J. Finegan, *Johnson Brothers Dinnerware: Pattern Directory & Price Guide,* published by author, 1993; Harry L. Rinker, *Dinnerware of the 20th Century: The Top 500 Patterns,* House of Collectibles, 1997.

Coaching Scenes, blue, bread and butter plate, 6" d $5
Coaching Scenes, blue, creamer and sugar 25
Coaching Scenes, blue, cup and saucer 8
Coaching Scenes, blue, dinner plate, 10" d 15
Coaching Scenes, blue, platter, oval, 12" l 35
Coaching Scenes, blue, platter, oval, 14" l 45
Coaching Scenes, blue, vegetable bowl, 8¹/₂" d 30
Coaching Scenes, pink, plate, 6" d 8
Coaching Scenes, pink, plate, 7³/₄" d 12
Coaching Scenes, pink, soup bowl, 8¹/₂" d 15

Coaching Scenes, pink, vegetable bowl, 8½" d   35
English Chippendale, bread and butter plate   8
English Chippendale, cereal bowl, lug handle   15
English Chippendale, cup and saucer   20
English Chippendale, dinner plate   17
English Chippendale, gravy boat   50
English Chippendale, luncheon plate   12
English Chippendale, salad plate, 7½" sq   10
English Chippendale, sugar, cov   30
English Chippendale, vegetable bowl, round   40
Forest Green, punch bowl, base, 12 cups   70
Friendly Village, bread and butter plate, 6" d   3
Friendly Village, cereal bowl, sq   5
Friendly Village, dinner plate, 10" d   8
Friendly Village, milk pitcher, 5½" h   30
Friendly Village, salt and pepper shakers, pr   28
Friendly Village, vegetable bowl, round   15
His Majesty, dinner plate   35
Old Britain Castles, blue, coffeepot, cov   80
Old Britain Castles, blue, dinner plate   15
Old Britain Castles, blue, gravy boat   45
Old Britain Castles, blue, plate, 6" d   8
Old Britain Castles, blue, platter, 15" l   75
Old Britain Castles, blue, soup bowl, 8½" d   15
Old Britain Castles, pink, berry bowl, 5" d   10
Old Britain Castles, pink, creamer and sugar   12
Old Britain Castles, pink, dinner plate, 10" d   15
Old Britain Castles, pink, platter, oval, 12" l   40
Old Britain Castles, pink, vegetable bowl, 8½" sq   40
Old English Countryside, brown, cup and saucer   18

Left: Barnyard King, turkey platter, 20½" l, 16" w, $75. Photo courtesy Ray Morykan Auctions.

Right: Heritage Hall, dinner plate, 9¾" d, $12.

Old English Countryside, brown, platter, oval, 12" l   35
Old English Countryside, brown, vegetable bowl, cov, round   100
Willow Blue, dinner plate   8
Willow Blue, gravy boat and underplate   30
Willow Blue, salt and pepper shakers, pr   28
Willow Blue, vegetable bowl, oval   18

KNOWLES, TAYLOR & KNOWLES

Knowles, Taylor & Knowles made ceramics in East Liverpool, Ohio, from 1854 to 1931. The firm began when Isaac Knowles and Isaac Harvey built a plant to manufacture yellow ware in 1854. Knowles bought out Harvey's interest in 1856. When John W. Taylor, Knowles' son-in-law, and Homer Knowles, Knowles' son, joined the firm in 1870, it became Knowles, Taylor & Knowles.

A new plant was built and opened in 1888. In 1889 the company introduced its famed Lotus Ware, a translucent, artistically designed, superior grade of art china. In 1901 the Knowles plant included 35 kilns and employed 7,000 workers.

In 1929 Knowles, Taylor & Knowles joined seven other companies as part of the American China Corporation. This new company failed, one of the many victims of the Great Depression of the early 1930s.

References: Mary Frank Gaston, *Collector's Encyclopedia of Knowles, Taylor & Knowles China: Identification & Values,* Collector Books, 1996; Timothy J. Kearns, *Knowles, Taylor & Knowles: American Bone China,* Schiffer Publishing, 1994.

America, bouillon cup, 7 oz $12
America, butter dish, cov   50
America, coffeepot, individual   30
America, cream soup   7
America, custard, handled   12
America, eggcup   13
America, fruit bowl, 5" d   5
America, mayonnaise   40
America, plate, 9" d   10
America, salad bowl   35
America, teapot   40
Lotus, baker, 11" d   25
Lotus, bread and butter plate, 6" d   6
Lotus, casserole, cov, 9" d   40
Lotus, chop plate   35
Lotus, demitasse saucer   7
Lotus, nappy, 8½" d   15
Lotus, sauce boat   16
Lotus, sugar, cov   15
Lotus, teapot   50
Niana, casserole, cov   40
Niana, cream soup   18
Niana, eggcup   12
Niana, mayonnaise   35
Niana, plate, 10" d   12
Niana, sauce tureen   40

Niana, sugar, cov	20
Plymouth, baker, 10" d	25
Plymouth, butter pat, individual	6
Plymouth, demitasse cup	10
Plymouth, fruit bowl, 5" d	7
Plymouth, jug, 3½ pt	35
Plymouth, plate, 9" d	10
Plymouth, rim soup, 10" d	12
Plymouth, spoon holder	37
Plymouth, teapot	70
Portland, bone dish	10
Portland, bowl, deep, 1 pt	12
Portland, bread and butter plate, 6" d	6
Portland, cake plate	35
Portland, demitasse cup	15
Portland, ladle	25
Portland, plate, 9" d	10
Portland, sauce tureen	32
Portland, sugar, cov	20
Ramona, baker, 7" d	15
Ramona, butter dish, cov	70
Ramona, chop plate	35
Ramona, demitasse cup	15
Ramona, fruit bowl, 5" d	7
Ramona, nappy, 6½" d	10
Ramona, plate, 8" d	8
Ramona, plate, 9" d	10
Ramona, platter, 11½" l	15
Ramona, ramekin	12
St. Louis, baker, 8" d	18
St. Louis, bouillon cup	15
St. Louis, bowl, deep, 1 pt	15
St. Louis, butter dish, cov	50
St. Louis, cake plate	20
St. Louis, casserole, cov, 8" d	38
St. Louis, fruit bowl, 6" d	10
St. Louis, nappy, 9" d	20
St. Louis, plate, 8" d	8
St. Louis, platter, 8½" d	15
St. Louis, sauce boat	25
St. Louis, sugar	20
St. Louis, tureen, cov	60
Traymore, butter dish, cov	45
Traymore, fruit bowl, 5" d	7
Traymore, jug, 4 pt	45
Traymore, nappy, 7" d	15
Traymore, plate, 9" d	9
Traymore, sugar, cov	15
Traymore, vegetable bowl, cov, 10" d	45
Victory, butter dish, cov	60
Victory, celery tray	12

Victory, demitasse cup	15
Victory, eggcup, double	15
Victory, jug, 15 oz	20
Victory, plate, 6" d	7
Victory, plate, 9½" d	10
Victory, sugar, cov	20
Victory, teapot	60

LIBERTY BLUE

In 1973 the Grand Union Company, a retail supermarket chain based in New Jersey, commissioned Liberty Blue dinnerware to be offered as a premium in grocery stores throughout the eastern United States. Ironically, though intended to celebrate America's independence, the dinnerware was produced in Staffordshire, England, the home of hundreds of potteries from the early 1700s to the present.

Liberty Blue dinnerware, introduced in 1975, was produced of ironstone and portrayed patriotic scenes in blue on a white background. It combined several elements of traditional Staffordshire dinnerware while remaining unique. The Wild Rose border was reproduced from a design dating back to 1784. Original engravings featured events from the American Revolutionary period, including Paul Revere's Ride, Washington's Farewell to the Continental Army, and the Boston Tea Party. Others portrayed historic buildings such as Monticello, the Governor's House at Williamsburg, and Independence Hall.

Liberty Blue dinnerware is easy to identify. Most of the dishes contain the words "Liberty Blue" on the underside and all are marked "Made in England." The back of each dish also contains information about the scene illustrated on it.

Berry Bowl, 5" d	$5
Bread and Butter Plate, 6" d	3
Casserole, cov	75
Cereal Bowl	12
Coaster	12
Creamer	15
Creamer and Sugar, cov	45

Dinner Plate, 10" d, $6.

Cup and Saucer	5
Flat Soup	15
Gravy Boat	35
Gravy Boat and Underplate	45
Gravy Underplate	15
Luncheon Plate, 8½" d	12
Mug	10
Platter, 12" l	50
Platter, 14" l	60
Salad Plate, 7" d	10
Salt and Pepper Shakers, pr	25
Soup Tureen	250
Sugar	20
Teapot	75
Vegetable Bowl, oval	40
Vegetable Bowl, round	45

MAJOLICA

Majolica, an opaque, tin–glazed pottery, has been produced by many countries for centuries. It originally took its name from the Spanish Island of Majorca, where figuline (a potter's clay) is found. Today majolica denotes a type of pottery which was made during the last half of the nineteenth century in Europe and America.

Majolica designs frequently depict elements in nature: leaves, flowers, birds, and fish. Human figures were rare. Designs were painted on the soft clay body using vitreous colors then fired under a clear lead glaze to impart the characteristically rich brilliant colors.

English majolica manufacturers who marked their works include Wedgwood, George Jones, Holdcraft, and Minton. Most of their pieces can be identified through the English Registry mark and/or the potter/designer's mark. Sarreguemines in France and Villeroy and Boch in Baden, Germany, produced majolica that compared favorably with the finer English majolica. Most Continental pieces had an incised number on the base.

Although 600–plus American potteries produced majolica between 1850 and 1900, only a handful chose to identify their wares. Among these manufacturers were George Morely, Edwin Bennett, the Chesapeake Pottery Company, the New Milford–Wannoppee Pottery Company, and the firm of Griffen, Smith, and Hill. The others hoped their unmarked pieces would be taken for English examples.

References: Leslie Bockol, *Victorian Majolica*, Schiffer Publishing 1996; Helen Cunningham, *Majolica Figures*, Schiffer Publishing, 1997; Nicholas M. Dawes, *Majolica*, Crown Publishers, 1990; Marilyn G. Karmason and Joan B. Stacke, *Majolica: A Complete History and Illustrated Survey*, Abrams, 1989: Mariann Katz–Marks, *The Collector's Encyclopedia of Majolica*, Collector Books, 1992, 1998 value update; D. Michael Murray, *European Majolica*, Schiffer Publishing, 1997; *Price Guide to Majolica*, L–W Books Sales, 1997; Mike Schneider, *Majolica*, Schiffer Publishing, 1990, 1995 value update; Jeffrey B. Snyder and Leslie B. Bockol, *Majolica: European and American Wares*, Schiffer Publishing, 1994.

Collectors' Club: Majolica International Society, 1275 First Avenue, Suite 103, New York, NY, 10021.

Etruscan, bowl, Classical, multicolor, 10" d **$250**
Etruscan, bowl, Shell and Seaweed, 7" with hairline and rim chip, 8½" with
   rim chip, price for pair **525**
Etruscan, butter pat, Geranium **120**
Etruscan, butter pat, Shell and Seaweed, rim wear and nick **80**
Etruscan, cake stand, Maple Leaves, pink ground **190**
Etruscan, cake stand, Morning Glory, white ground **200**
Etruscan, compote, Daisy, cobalt blue, hairlines, repairs, price for pair **275**
Etruscan, compote, Maple Leaf, rim repair, 8" h, 10" d **130**
Etruscan, cup and saucer, Shell and Seaweed, rim nicks **190**
Etruscan, mug, Pineapple, base nick **100**
Etruscan, pitcher, Corn, rim repair, hairline **140**
Etruscan, pitcher, Fern, rim chip, 8" h **250**
Etruscan, pitcher, Rustic, rim chip, 7½" h **55**
Etruscan, plate, Cauliflower, surface wear, 9" d **225**
Etruscan, plate, Maple Leaf on Basket, 1 with rim repair, 9" d, price for 3 . . . . **400**
Etruscan, plate, Shell and Seaweed, 8" d **375**
Etruscan, platter, Geranium **350**
Etruscan, salad bowl, Lily, cobalt blue, rim chip repairs **775**
Etruscan, syrup, Sunflower, cobalt blue **550**
George Jones, biscuit barrel, Daisy and Wheat, handle **650**
George Jones, butter dish and underplate, Floral, cobalt blue, no lid **275**
George Jones, centerpiece, man and dolphin supporting shell, 16" h **2,500**
George Jones, condiment dish, 2 part, fawn, fawn's ears restored, early repair
   on 1 side, 16" l **1,300**
George Jones, condiment dish, 2 part, thrush, tip of beak repaired, 13½" l . . .**1,600**
George Jones, nut dish, fox, nick to ear, hairline **1,000**
George Jones, oyster plate, center shell, white **950**
George Jones, pitcher, rustic, 7½" h **550**

Left: Etruscan, teapot, cov, Cauliflower, 4¼" h, $350.

Right: Wedgwood, dish, Strawberry, 3 molded compartments, leaf molded handle, cobalt ground, yellow rim, imp "Wedgwood," year code, and registration mark, restored hairline crack, c1871, 10½" l, $402. Photo courtesy Sotheby's.

Left: Minton, jug, Pineapple, imp marks, 1862 date code and registry mark, 8" h, $1,495.

Right: George Jones, cheese stand, cov, Apple Blossom, basketweave and apple blossom branches on pale blue ground, c1875, 12¹/₂" h, $2,760.

Photos courtesy Wm. Doyle Galleries.

George Jones, sardine box and underplate, cov, pointed leaves, turquoise ...**1,300**
George Jones, strawberry server, basket, repair to sugar well **900**
George Jones, strawberry server, napkin on pink ground, with creamer and
  sugar, rim nick and glaze imperfection to creamer **1,100**
Minton, ewer, heron standing among reeds and lily pads, fish in beak, mul-
  ticolored, dated 1876, 21³/₄" h **2,500**
Wedgwood, bowl, Bird and Fan, ftd, c1870, 10" d, 5" h, price for pair **850**
Wedgwood, cake stand, Bird and Fan, c1870, 9" d, 3" h **250**
Wedgwood, cup and saucer, Cauliflower, blue ground, imp "Wedgwood" ... **125**
Wedgwood, plate, Bird and Fan, blue fans, c1870, 8" d **100**
Wedgwood, plate, Fruit, c1870, 7" d **90**
Wedgwood, serving plate, Strawberry, center well, c1870, 7" d **125**

McCOY

The J. W. McCoy Pottery Co. was established in Roseville, Ohio, in September, 1899. The early McCoy Co. produced both stoneware and some art pottery lines, including Rosewood. In October, 1911, three potteries merged creating the Brush–McCoy Pottery Co. This company continued to produce the original McCoy lines and added several new art lines. Many early pieces are not marked.

In 1910, Nelson McCoy and his father, J. W. McCoy, founded the Nelson McCoy Sanitary Stoneware Co. In 1925, the McCoy family sold their interest in the Brush–McCoy Pottery Co. and concentrated on expanding and improving the Nelson McCoy Co. The new company produced stoneware, earthenware specialties, and artware. Most pottery marked McCoy was made by the Nelson McCoy Co.

McCoy Pottery is best known for its cookie jars, kitchenwares, tablewares, and florist pieces. Bright colors and Country motifs abound. Several types of glazes were used. The highly glazed utilitarian wares are valued as they stand the test of time and hard use. One of the most widely recognized McCoy pieces is a small brown glazed mustard jar which was made for the Heinz Company.

Over twenty different marks have been identified.

References: Bob Hanson, Craig Nissen and Margaret Hanson, *McCoy Pottery: Reference & Value Guide,* Collector Books, 1997; Sharon and Bob Huxford, *The*

Collectors Encyclopedia of McCoy Pottery, Collector Books, 1980, 1997 value update; Martha and Steve Sanford, *Sanfords Guide to Brush–McCoy Pottery, Book 2,* Adelmore Press, 1996; Martha and Steve Sanford, *The Guide to Brush–McCoy Pottery,* published by authors, 1992.

Newsletter: *The NM Express,* 3081 Rock Creek Drive, Broomfield, CO 80020.

Ashtray, arrowhead shape, green	$20
Ashtray, yellow, 8" sq	20
Baby Planter, lamb, white, blue bow	10
Baby Planter, stork, green	10
Ball Jug, yellow, unmkd, 1950s	25
Bank, happy face	25
Bank, pig	45
Basket, basketweave, green and white ext, white int, mkd "McCoy USA," 1952	35
Bookends, pr, birds, 6" h	95
Bookends, pr, lily, 1948	55
Cat Dish	60
Cereal Bowl, individual, brown drip, 12 oz	5
Console bowl, leaf, brown, 1960s	12
Console bowl, tulips, blue, 8³⁄₄" d	10
Cookie Jar, apple, red	45
Cookie Jar, brown drip	5
Cookie Jar, cat, pink basketweave base	50
Cookie Jar, cookie kettle	25
Cookie Jar, picnic basket	40
Corn Dish, brown, 9 x 3¹⁄₄"	10
Creamer, brown drip	5
Dog Feeder, "Man's Best Friend," brown, 7¹⁄₂" d	45
Dresser Organizer, figural buffalo	15
Figure, lamb, white	25
Figure, scottie dog and cat, price for pair	45
Flower Holder, figural, fish, yellow	50

Mixing Bowls, nesting, shield in circle mark, 1926.
Left: green, mkd "4," 9⁵⁄₈" d, $25. Right: yellow, #4, 11¹⁄₂" d, $30.
Photos courtesy Ray Morykan Auctions.

Mug, stoneware, Vintage pattern, green glaze, 5" h, $15. Photo courtesy Ray Morykan Auctions.

Flower Holder, figural, swan, yellow 55
Flowerpot and Saucer, paneled, slightly flared top, pink, mkd "McCoy USA," 1959 8
Gravy Boat, Rooster on Nest 60
Hanging Basket, white matte glaze 30
Hanging Bird Feeder, brown, 1975 15
Jardiniere, Pine Cone, 7½" w, 6½" h 25
Pie Baker, Brown Drip, 9" d 20
Pitcher, old crow 18
Pitcher, vegetable design 40
Pitcher and Wash Bowl, white, blue trim, 1967 15
Planter, Blossomtime, yellow 8
Planter, cat face, black, 5 x 6" 25
Planter, deer, white, dec, 4" h 20
Planter, duck, holding umbrella 80
Planter, fish shape, brown drip, 18" l 35
Planter, frog 10
Planter, hunting dog, Sidney Cope design 80
Planter, liberty bell, green, 10 x 8¼" 170
Planter, quail 30
Planter, rabbit, ivory 8
Planter, rooster, gray, 1951 20
Planter, springwood, ftd, pink matte, white flowers 8
Planter, wishing well 10
Snack Dish, 3 leaves, rustic glaze, 1952 10
Soup Bowl, Brown Drip 6
Sprinkler, figural turtle 50
Teapot, brown drip, long spout, 6 cup 22
Teapot, daisies, #140, white ground 15
Teapot, pine cone 22
Vase, Blossomtime, 2 handled, mkd "McCoy," 1946 25
Vase, Butterfly, blue 45
Vase, Magnolia, mkd "McCoy USA," 1953 35
Vase, Pink Hyacinth, 8" h 12
Vase, Sunflower, 1954 35

Wall Pocket, apple, 1953 .... **40**
Wall Pocket, butterfly, white, 7 x 6" **175**
Wall Pocket, flower, rustic glaze, 1946 .... **15**
Wall Pocket, leaf, pink, blue, 7 x 5½" **35**
Wall Pocket, lily bud, 8" h **150**
Wall Pocket, mailbox, blue, mkd "McCoy USA," 1951 .... **50**

METLOX

In 1921 T. C. Prouty and Willis, his son, founded Proutyline Products, a company designed to develop Prouty's various inventions. In 1922 Prouty built a plant in Hermosa Beach to manufacture decorative and standard wall and floor tiles.

Metlox (a contraction of metallic oxide) was established in 1927. Prouty built a modern all–steel factory in Manhattan Beach to manufacture outdoor ceramic signs. The Depression impacted strongly on the sign business. When T. C. Prouty died in 1931, Willis reorganized the company and began to produce a line of solid color dinnerware similar to that produced by Bauer. In 1934 the line was fully developed and sold under the Poppytrail trademark. The poppy is the official state flower for California. Fifteen different colors were produced over an eight–year period.

Other dinnerware lines produced in the 1930s include Mission Bell, sold exclusively by Sears & Roebuck, Pintoria, based on an English Staffordshire line, and Yorkshire, patterned after Gladding–McBean's Coronado line. Most of these lines did not survive World War II.

In the late 1930s Metlox employed the services of Carl Romanelli, a designer whose work appeared as figurines, miniatures, and Zodiac vases. A line called Modern Masterpieces featured bookends, busts, figural vases, figures, and wall pockets.

During World War II Metlox devoted its manufacturing efforts to the production of machine parts and parts for the B–25 bombers. When the war ended, Metlox returned its attention to the production of dinnerware.

In 1947 Evan K. Shaw, whose American Pottery in Los Angeles had been destroyed by fire, purchased Metlox. Dinnerware production with hand–painted patterns accelerated. The California Ivy pattern was introduced in 1946, California Provincial and Homestead Provincial in 1950, Red Rooster in 1955, California Strawberry in 1961, Sculptured Grape in 1963, and Della Robbia in 1965. Bob Allen and Mel Shaw, art directors, introduced a number of new shapes and lines in the 1950s among which are Aztec, California Contempora, California Free Form, California Mobile, and Navajo.

When Vernon Kilns ceased operation in 1958 Metlox bought the trade name and select dinnerware molds. A separate Vernon Ware branch was established. Under the direction of Doug Bothwell the line soon rivaled the Poppytrail patterns.

Artware continued to flourish in the 1950s and 60s. Harrison McIntosh was among the key designers. Two popular lines were American Royal Horses and Nostalgia, scale model antique carriages. Between 1946 and 1956 Metlox made a series of ceramic cartoon characters under license from Walt Disney.

A line of planters designed by Helen Slater and Poppets, doll–like stoneware flower holders, were marketed in the 1960s and 70s. Recent production includes novelty cookie jars and Colorstax, a revival solid color dinnerware pattern.

Management remained in the Shaw family. Evan K. was joined by his two children, Ken and Melinda. Kenneth Avery, Melinda's husband, eventually became plant manager. When Evan K. died in 1980, Kenneth Avery became president. In 1988 Melinda Avery became the guiding force. The company ceased operations in 1989.

The choices of patterns and backstamps is overwhelming. Collectors should concentrate on one specific line and pattern. Among the most popular Poppytrail patterns are California Ivy, Homestead Provincial, and Red Rooster.

The recent cookie jar craze has attracted a number of collectors to Metlox's cookie jar line. Most examples sell within a narrow range. The Little Red Riding Hood jar is an exception, often selling at two to three times the price of other cookie jars.

Reference: Carl Gibbs Jr., *Collector's Encyclopedia of Metlox Potteries: Identification and Values,* Collector Books, 1995.

Antique Grape, bread and butter plate, 6³/₈" d	**$10**
Antique Grape, butter dish, cov, ¼ lb	**60**
Antique Grape, coffeepot, cov	**80**
Antique Grape, dinner plate	**25**
Antique Grape, platter, oval, 12¹/₂" l	**45**
Antique Grape, relish, 2 part, 9" l	**50**
Antique Grape, sugar, cov	**35**
Aztec, fruit bowl	**10**
Aztec, platter, 13" l	**35**
Aztec, sugar, cov	**40**
California Ivy, bowl, 9" d	**30**
California Ivy, bread and butter plate, 6" d	**5**
California Ivy, chop plate, 13¹/₄" d	**50**
California Ivy, creamer and sugar, cov	**12**
California Ivy, cup and saucer	**17**
California Ivy, demitasse cup and saucer	**20**
California Ivy, gravy boat and underplate	**50**
California Ivy, pitcher, ice lip	**40**
California Ivy, platter, oval, 13³/₈" l	**50**
California Ivy, saucer	**3**
California Ivy, serving bowl, round	**40**
California Ivy, sugar, cov	**25**
California Ivy, vegetable bowl, divided	**40**
California Provincial, bread and butter plate, 6" d	**5**
California Provincial, bread tray, 9³/₄" d	**75**
California Provincial, dinner plate, 10" d	**12**
California Provincial, flat soup, 8¹/₂" d	**8**
California Provincial, fruit bowl, 6" d	**15**
California Provincial, gravy boat	**18**
California Provincial, platter, oval, 11¹/₄" l	**45**
California Provincial, salt and pepper shakers, pr	**30**
California Provincial, vegetable bowl, divided, rect, 8⁵/₈" l	**50**
California Strawberry, canister, coffee	**12**
California Strawberry, creamer	**20**
California Strawberry, dinner plate, 10³/₈" d	**17**
California Strawberry, pitcher, 4¹/₂" h	**30**
California Strawberry, sugar, cov	**25**
Colorstax, dinner service, 4 each dinner plates, salad plates, and mugs, and 3 cereal bowls, fern green, price for 15 pcs	**100**
Della Robbia, bread and butter plate, 6¹/₂" d	**7**
Della Robbia, creamer	**22**
Della Robbia, fruit bowl, 6¹/₂" d	**12**

Della Robbia, platter, oval, 14½" l 45
Della Robbia, sugar, cov 32
Homestead Provincial, ashtray, 4⅝" d 15
Homestead Provincial, bread and butter plate, 6⅜" d 4
Homestead Provincial, bread server 50
Homestead Provincial, cereal bowl 15
Homestead Provincial, chop plate, 12" d 60
Homestead Provincial, coffeepot, 42 oz 80
Homestead Provincial, creamer 25
Homestead Provincial, cup 8
Homestead Provincial, cup and saucer 10
Homestead Provincial, dinner plate 10
Homestead Provincial, flowerpot, chip to bottom rim 50
Homestead Provincial, fruit bowl, 6" d 10
Homestead Provincial, gravy boat 40
Homestead Provincial, jam 15
Homestead Provincial, lug soup 22
Homestead Provincial, mug 22
Homestead Provincial, rim soup, 8½" d 15
Homestead Provincial, salad plate, 7½" d 8
Homestead Provincial, salt and pepper shakers, pr, handled 30
Homestead Provincial, soup tureen 300
Homestead Provincial, sugar, cov 40
Homestead Provincial, turkey platter 200
Homestead Provincial, wall pocket 45
Homestead Provincial Blue, bread server 50
Homestead Provincial Blue, candle holder, ring handle 25
Homestead Provincial Blue, casserole, hen, large, blind chip 150
Homestead Provincial Blue, chop plate 70
Homestead Provincial Blue, coffeepot, cov 95
Homestead Provincial Blue, creamer, cov 25

*Left: **Homestead Provincial Blue**, dinner plate, 10" d, $18.*
*Right: **Red Rooster**, dinner plate, 10" d, $15.*

Homestead Provincial Blue, cruet set with stand, #519 .... **100**
Homestead Provincial Blue, cup **8**
Homestead Provincial Blue, cup and saucer **15**
Homestead Provincial Blue, fruit bowl **15**
Homestead Provincial Blue, lug soup **22**
Homestead Provincial Blue, marmalade, cov **80**
Homestead Provincial Blue, mug **22**
Homestead Provincial Blue, platter, oval, 13½" l **55**
Homestead Provincial Blue, rim soup, 8½" d **20**
Homestead Provincial Blue, salt and pepper shakers, pr, cone shape **35**
Homestead Provincial Blue, saucer **5**
Homestead Provincial Blue, shaker **12**
Homestead Provincial Blue, sugar, cov **25**
Homestead Provincial Blue, vegetable bowl, medium, small chip **10**
La Mancha Gold, cup and saucer **10**
La Mancha Gold, platter, oval, 11¾" l **25**
La Mancha Gold, vegetable bowl, 8" d **25**
Navajo, bowl, 13" d **42**
Navajo, chop plate, 12" d **35**
Navajo, creamer and sugar, cov **35**
Navajo, gravy boat and underplate **32**
Navajo, platter, 11¾" l **35**
Navajo, teapot **45**
Pintoria, bread and butter plate **25**
Pintoria, fruit bowl **32**
Pintoria, serving plate **75**
Pintoria, sugar **70**
Provincial Blue, batter pitcher **75**
Provincial Blue, coaster **15**
Provincial Blue, dinner plate **20**
Provincial Blue, gravy boat **50**
Provincial Blue, salad plate **12**
Provincial Blue, vegetable bowl, cov **80**
Provincial Blue, vegetable bowl, open, round **40**
Provincial Fruit, bowl, tab handled, 5" d **5**
Provincial Fruit, bread and butter plate, 6½" d **5**
Provincial Fruit, butter dish **30**
Provincial Fruit, cup and saucer **8**
Provincial Fruit, dinner plate, 10½" d **10**
Provincial Fruit, gravy boat, handled **15**
Provincial Fruit, relish, divided, rect, handled **15**
Provincial Fruit, salt and pepper shakers, pr **8**
Provincial Fruit, vegetable bowl, 10" d **20**
Red Rooster, ashtray, 4½" sq **25**
Red Rooster, bread and butter plate **5**
Red Rooster, canister, flour **75**
Red Rooster, casserole, small **75**
Red Rooster, coffee carafe **100**
Red Rooster, cruet **55**
Red Rooster, dinner plate, 10" d **15**
Red Rooster, eggcup **20**

MOCHA

Mocha decoration usually is found on utilitarian creamware and stoneware pieces and is produced through a simple chemical action. A color pigment of brown, blue, green, or black is made acidic by an infusion of tobacco or hops. When the acidic colorant is applied in blobs to an alkaline ground, it reacts by spreading in feathery, seaweed–like designs. This type of decoration usually is supplemented with bands of light colored slip.

Types of decoration vary greatly, from those done in a combination of motifs, such as "Cat's Eye" and "Earthworm," to a plain pink mug decorated with green ribbed bands. Most forms of mocha are hollow, e.g., mugs, jugs, bowls, and shakers.

English potters made the vast majority of the pieces. Marked pieces are extremely rare. Collectors group the ware into three chronological periods: 1780–1820, 1820–1840, and 1840–1880.

Country collectors treasure mocha ware. Warm colors and interesting designs lend themselves well to Country collections.

Bowl, black and white checkered band on top, medium blue glaze, 4⅛" d . . . **$75**
Bowl, cup shape, blue seaweed dec on white band, hairline, 4¼" h **200**
Bowl, emb green band, marbelized black, white, blue, and orange dec,
    4¾" d, 2¼" h **625**

Bowl, brown, cream, and orange earthworm dec on tan ground, raised green border, c1790–1820, 6¼" d, $600.

Bowl, green band, canary yellow ground, yellow and black earthworm dec, "CL & Mont" partial imp mark, chips and repair, 4³/₄" d, 3¹/₂" h **100**

Bowl, orange band, blue, white, and brown cat's–eye dec, black stripes **200**

Bowl, pale blue and black earthworm design on orange–tan ground, tooled rim, black and green stripes, 8¹/₄" d, 4" h **620**

Bowl, white wavy lines on dark brown band, tan ground, 5⁵/₈" d, 3" h **380**

Castor, cat's–eye dec, 4¹/₂" h **425**

Chamber Pot, blue on white band, seaweed dec, brown stripes **250**

Chamber Pot, miniature, blue seaweed dec on white band, yellow ware, 2¹/₄" h **120**

Chamber Pot, tan band, blue and black stripes, blue, white, and black earthworm dec, repair, handle replaced, 8¹/₂" h **100**

Creamer, black and white checkered band around shoulder, medium blue glaze, 5¹/₄" h **200**

Creamer, blue and white stripes, stains, chipped spout, 3³/₄" h **30**

Creamer, emb green band, brown and light blue stripes, spout, and leaf handle, 3¹/₂" h **170**

Cup and Saucer, handleless, black and white checkered band on rim, white fluted band at base, matching saucer **130**

Cup and Saucer, handleless, black seaweed design on orange ground, emb blue rim **1,300**

Cup and Saucer, handleless, blue and white stripes **35**

Cup and Saucer, handleless, green, black seaweed dec, orange ground, tooled rims, hairlines on saucer **550**

Flowerpot, blue bands, blue, white, brown, and ocher earthworm design, ocher and brown stripes, tooled blue lip, no saucers, 4¹/₄" h, price for pair . **3,200**

French Jaspé Bowl, multicolored on red, 6" d **50**

Jar, cov, pale blue band, black stripes, white, black, and blue earthworm and cat's–eye dec, repairs, hairline in lid, 5" h **500**

Jar, open, white band, chocolate brown stripes, blue seaweed dec, hairlines, replaced wooden lid, 7" d, 5¹/₂" h **100**

Jug, Liverpool shape, 2 black and white checkered bands, medium blue glaze, foliate handle and spout, 8¹/₂" h **350**

Jug, 2 blue bands, blue and white raised earthworm design, 6⁵/₈" h **680**

Milk Pitcher, blue band, black and blue stripes, earthworm dec, brown, blue, and black, repairs, 4⁷/₈" h **200**

Milk Pitcher, dark bluish gray band, black stripes, emb green and black seaweed band, leaf handle, 4⁵/₈" h **450**

Mug, barrel shape, checkered bands, black and white, medium blue glaze, 3³/₄" h **175**

Mug, black and white checkerboard band around rim, gray–green ground, tan stripes, leaf handle, wear chips, hairline, 5⁵/₈" h **180**

Mug, black, blue, and white rope design on emb bands, green, black, brown, and tan stripes, emb leaf handle, hairline, 5⁵/₈" h **800**

Mug, brown and white geometric design bands, blue and brown stripes, white ground, leaf handle, 4⁵/₈" h **150**

Mug, dark brown, blue, and white stripes, blue bands, white ground, brown and blue foliage design, emb rim band and leaf handle, wear, rim chips, hairline, 5⁷/₈" h **225**

Mug, emb green band and leaf handle, dark brown, orange, and white stripes, chips and repair, 3⁵/₈" h **475**

Mug, gray band, dark brown stripes, earthworm dec, emb leaf handle, 4¼" h 325

Mug, pale blue band, brown stripes, white ground, blue earthworm dec, leaf handle, hairline and flake on bottom, 3⅛" h 300

Mug, teal band, black seaweed dec, blue band around top, black stripes, white ground, 5" h 200

Mug, white band, blue stripes, blue seaweed dec, leaf handle, 3½" h 425

Mug, wide brown band, blue stripe top and bottom, emb leaf handle, some crazing, 5" h 130

Mug, yellow ocher and dark brown bands, blue, white, and brown earthworm dec, black stripes, leaf handle, 3½" h 350

Mustard Pot, cov, blue and black stripes, seaweed dec, brownish gray lid with black stripes, leaf handle, wear and small chips, 2⅞" h 330

Mustard Pot, cov, tan band with black stripes, white, yellow, and black earthworm dec, chip on rim, small repair to lid, 2½" h 600

Pepper Pot, brown, black, and cream, geometric design, engine turned, 4" h .. 650

Pepper Pot, brown, light blue, and yellow scroddled design, white ground, 3½" h 525

Pepper Pot, pale blue, brown, and yellow, white ground, scroddled design, 3½" h 550

Pitcher, applied leaf handle, black and white on blue bands, cat's–eye design, black stripes, 6¼" h 425

Pitcher, applied leaf handle, blue bands, blue, brown, and white earthworm dec, gray green ground, slight loss of glaze, 7¼" h 500

Pitcher, applied leaf handle, blue bands, white and dark brown stripes, yellow ground, 7½" h 450

Pitcher, applied leaf handle, light grayish blue band, brown stripes, brown cat's–eye dec, 7" h 200

Pitcher, applied leaf handle, pale yellow band, running dots in blue, white, and dark brown, blue band, dark brown stripes, stains, old professional repair, 7" h 190

Pitcher, applied leaf handle, 2–tone blue band, blue, tan, and black earthworm design and stripes, white ground, emb bands, small chips, hairline in spout, poorly repaired chip on lip, 6¾" h 400

Salt, blue and brown bands, ocher ground, earthworm dec, rim flake, 2¼" d .. 130

Salt, gray band, black stripes, white wavy lines, stains in foot, hairline in rim, 3" d, 2⅛" h 325

Left: Mug, earthworm and cat's–eye dec, shades of brown, 6" h, $350.

Right: Mug, seaweed design, wide blue band, black ribbon bands, ½ pt, $325.

Shaker, black, tan, and blue stripes, 4⁷/₈" h 350
Shaker, black and white checkered band around center, medium blue speckled glaze, pedestal base, 4⁷/₈" h 80
Shaker, blue band, black stripe, brown, black, and white earthworm dec,
repair, 4⁷/₈" h 300
Shaker, dark brown band, slate blue, tan, olive gray, and dark brown stripes,
tan cat's–eye dec, white ground, damage and repair, 4¹/₄" h 350
Shaker, deep orange band, emb green band, foliage design, blue, white, and
brown stripes, 4" h 800
Shaker, orange band, dark brown stripes, black seaweed dec, stains, 4¹/₈" h .. 460
Shaker, tan bands, brown stripes, black seaweed dec, chips, 4¹/₈" h 225
Spill Holder, dark brown stripes, green glaze, machine tooled, short hairline,
small chips, glued flake, 4³/₈" h 150
Tankard Measure, blue, black, and tan seaweed dec, 1 with "Imperial Pint"
applied white label, other with "Quart" label, minor stains, wear, and
crazing, price for 3 450
Tea Caddy, cov, black, tan, and blue geometric design, 4⁷/₈" h 530
Tea Caddy, cov, marbleized brown, sienna, and white, small nicks, 5¹/₄" h ...1,600
Teapot, cov, globular, black and white checkered band around shoulder,
medium blue glaze, acorn finial, 5¹/₂" h 1,000
Teapot, cov, marbleized brown, sienna, and white, green Leeds rim, minor
nicks on cov and bottom, 4¹/₂" h 1,200
Waste Bowl, amber band, black seaweed dec separated into 5 segments by
squiggly lines, green molded lip band, stains and hairlines, 4³/₄" d 275
Waste Bowl, green molded rib rim, blue, white, black, and tan marbleized
dec, leaf handle, wear and small chips, 2⁷/₈" h 55
Waste Bowl, orange band, black stripes, white, blue, and black earthworm
dec, wear, stains, and hairlines, 5³/₈" d, 2⁷/₈" h 250
Waste Bowl, orange–tan band, dark brown stripes, emb green band, blue,
white, and dark brown earthworm dec, repairs, 5⁵/₈" d, 2⁷/₈" h 550
Waste Bowl, pale orange band, light blue stripes, brown and white cat's–eye
dec, hairline, 5¹/₂" d, 2⁷/₈" h 100
Waste Bowl, tan band, black stripes and seaweed dec, repaired, 6¹/₄" d,
3¹/₄" h 55

NILOAK

The Niloak Pottery was located near Benton, Arkansas. Charles Dean Hyten, Niloak's founder, sought to preserve clay's natural colors in his finished wares. In 1911 he developed Mission Ware, a pottery featuring marbleized layers of predominately brown and cream colors. Niloak is kaolin spelled backwards. Kaolin provided the clay base for Niloak pottery.

A fire destroyed the pottery. It was rebuilt and renamed Eagle Pottery. In 1929 a novelty pottery line was introduced. Early novelty pieces were usually marked Hywood-Niloak. The Hywood portion of the mark was dropped in 1934.

Hyten ended his association with Niloak in 1941. The pottery ceased operations in 1946.

Mission Ware with its Southwest American Indian feel remains the central focus of most Niloak collectors. Although more in tune with Country tastes, Niloak figural pieces and planters are valued far below Mission Ware.

Reference: David Edwin Gifford, *The Collector's Encyclopedia of Niloak: A Reference and Value Guide,* Collector Books, 1993.

Collectors' Club: Arkansas Pottery Collectors Society, PO Box 7617, Little Rock, AR 72217.

Bowl, Mission Swirl	**$200**
Bowl, Peter Pan figure on rolled scalloped rim, blue glaze, 7½" h	**150**
Bud Vase, Hywood Line, leaf blue glaze, 6" h	**15**
Bud Vase, Ozark Dawn II, 4" h	**25**
Candlesticks, pr, double cornucopia, Hywood Art Pottery, unmkd, 6¾" h	**100**
Console Set, Mission Ware, center bowl and pr candlesticks, bowl and 1 stick mkd, 10" d bowl, 8½" candlesticks, price for set	**300**
Cornucopia, cream, 6" h	**20**
Cornucopia, light pink, 3" h	**5**
Ewer, matte blue, emb cameos on sides, 10" h	**45**
Figure, canoe, brown, 8" l	**35**
Figure, frog	**20**
Figure, horse, gloss rust glaze with drips, 4" h	**50**
Figure, squirrel	**20**
Humidor, Mission Swirl, 5" h	**450**
Pitcher, ball shape, Ozark Dawn II, 7¾" h	**130**
Pitcher, Bouquet pattern, blue, 7" h	**30**
Pitcher, Ozark Dawn, "Niloak" imp mark, 4" h	**15**
Pitcher, yellow, 3¼" h	**15**
Planter, boxing kangaroo, tan, 5" h	**30**
Planter, Duck, pink and white, 5" h	**20**
Planter, rabbit, green, 3" h	**15**
Planter, swan, pink, 6½" h	**35**
Pot, Mission Swirl, 2¾" h	**100**
Strawberry Jar, Ozark Dawn II, 7" h	**40**
Table Clock, semi–circular, clay swirl case, orig works, die stamped mark, 4 x 5"	**600**
Vase, bulbous, broad flaring rim, swirling clays of dark brown, dark blue, and brick red, imp mark, 16½ x 7½"	**800**

Left: Vase, Mission Ware, cream, blue, and brown swirl, imp "Niloak," 9¼" h, $195.

Right: Vessel, Mission Ware, blue, rust, and cream swirl, unmkd, 6" h, $165.
Photo courtesy Jackson's Auctioneers & Appraisers.

Vase, maroon, handles, 7" h 15
Vase, Mission Swirl, 3½" h 55
Vase, Mission Swirl, 6" h 85
Vase, molded swirl, 2 handles on rim, matte green, 6½" h 30
Vase, Ozark Dawn II, overlapping leaves, 7" h 45
Vase, shoe, figural, blue, 2½" h 25
Vase, wing handles, green, 6" h 30

NORTH DAKOTA SCHOOL OF MINES

In 1898 Earl J. Babcock, a chemistry instructor at the North Dakota School of Mines, received funding to determine if North Dakota clay had commercial possibilities. While he was impressed by the high purity of the state's clay, he met with limited success.

In 1910 Babcock was instrumental in establishing a Ceramics Department at the school. Margaret Cable, a student of Charles Binns and Frederick H. Rhead, was named department head, a position she retained until her retirement in 1949.

Cable and her students produced a wide range of pottery. While native themes, e.g., animals and flowers, prevail, pieces also were executed in Art Nouveau, Art Deco, and generic shapes and decorative motifs.

An underglaze cobalt blue "University of North Dakota / Grand Forks, N.D. / Made at School of Mines / N.D. Clay" in a circle is the most commonly found mark. Some early pieces are marked only with "U.N.D. / Grand Forks, N.D."

Accurate production records were kept. Pieces were numbered and signed by the instructor and students. Most can be located in the production records. Pieces bearing Cable's signature bring a premium.

References: Darlene Hurst Dommel, *Collector's Encyclopedia of the Dakota Potteries: Identification & Values,* Collector Books, 1996; *University of North Dakota Pottery: The Cable Years,* Knight Publishing, 1977.

Collectors' Club: North Dakota Pottery Collectors Society, PO Box 14, Beach, ND 58621.

Bowl, daffodils and leaves, carved, mustard color on cream ground, Julia
    Mattson "JM" circular ink mark, 5½ x 5" **$700**
Bowl, florals, carved, gray–green matte finish, 5½" d 150
Bowl, flowers, stylized black and green on light blue ground, low, rolled
    edge, incised "MK" circular ink mark, 1¼ x 7¼" 950
Bowl, jonquil and leaves, brown and green, soft blue ground, curled edge,
    "D. Kane, 1925" circular ink mark, 2½ x 8" 700
Bowl, meadowlarks and rushes, closed–in, lime green matte finish, "M.
    Cable, Meadow Lark, 155" circular ink mark, 3¼ x 6¼" 650
Bowl, poppies, excised on top band, olive green finish, 4½" h 450
Ginger Jar, burgundy finish, sgd "Middleton" 75
Paperweight, 4–H design, raised, green gloss finish, 3" d 80
Paperweight,"Parent's Day, 1938," deep blue, 3½" d 100
Pitcher, floral, painted dec, sgd "Mattson," 6" h 280
Pot, wheat, carved dec, light green on cream ground, sgd "Huckfield,"
    3¼" d 180
Tray, leaf shape, shades of blue and green, sgd by artist, 6" d 150

Vase, bulbous, carved daffodils and leaves, mustard and cream ground, circular "JM" (Julia Mattson) ink mark, 5¹/₂ x 5", $700. Photo courtesy David Rago Auctions.

Vase, apple blossoms, incised and painted, pink on cream to pink ground, 8¹/₄" h 850
Vase, apple blossoms and leaves, incised, dark pink and green on gloss pink to cream ground, cylinder shaped, small flared top, incised "Huck #5087 Apple Blossoms," 8¹/₂" h 1,000
Vase, blue, shaded ground, bulbous, sgd "Huck," 4" h 200
Vase, blue, squat shape, 3" h 100
Vase, cowboy and lasso, carved, "Why Not Minot," blue gloss glaze, stamped "JTT," 5³/₄" h 300
Vase, fish, swimming, incised, green on gunmetal ground, bulbous, flaring neck, incised "Marie," 8¹/₂" h 1,400
Vase, flowers, carved stylized band, matte ivory to turquoise glaze, bulbous, 7" h 280
Vase, rings, imp on shoulder, green matte finish, 6¹/₂" h 325
Vase, tulips, incised, stylized tulips under apple green glaze, Elizabeth Bradley, c1933, 9¹/₂" h 600
Vase, tulips, purple with brown Huckfield dec, dark blue ground, cylinder shaped, rolled rim and base, "FLH8/Huck" circular ink mark, 5 x 4" 850
Vase, violets, tooled, white ground, bulbous and squat, "Huck/Jill/670" circular ink mark, 3¹/₂ x 3³/₄" 450
Vase, wheat stacks, carved band, brown shades, bulbous, straight neck, sgd "Huck," 4³/₄" h 380
Vessel, birds on branch, incised, green matte glaze, barrel shaped, stamped "University Of North Dakota Grand Forks, N.D./Made At School Of Mines/N.D. Clay," 4" h 850
Vessel, girls holding hands, carved ring, light and dark brown matte finish, tapered body, M Knutson, dated 1946, 2¹/₂" h, 5¹/₂" d 300

PADEN CITY

Paden City Pottery, located near Sisterville, West Virginia, was founded in September 1914. The company manufactured high quality, semi-porcelain dinnerware. The quality of Paden City's decals was such that the company's wares often were assumed to be hand painted.

The company's Shenandoah Ware shape line was made with different applied patterns. Sears Roebuck featured Paden City's Nasturtium pattern in the 1940s. Bak-Serv, a 1930s' kitchenware line, was produced in solid colors and with decal patterns. Paden City also made Caliente, a line of single-color glazed ware introduced in 1936.

Russel Wright designed the company's Highlight pattern. It was manufactured in five different colors between 1951 and 1952.

Paden City ceased operations in November 1963. Many backstamps were used to mark pieces.

When buying a piece of Paden City decaled ware look for decals that retain their brightness and feature undamaged decals. Washing and exposure to sunlight can cause decals to fade. Decals are often marred by knife cuts.

Berry Bowl, Patio	$3
Carafe, Bak–Serv, ceramic lid, wooden handle	25
Casserole, cov, Caliente, cobalt blue	10
Casserole, cov, Manhattan	20
Casserole, cov, Papoco	20
Casserole, cov, Patio	15
Casserole, cov, Shell Crest, ftd	30
Chop Plate, 12³/₄" d, Blue Willow	15
Chop Plate, 12³/₄" d, Elite	15
Creamer, Far East	5
Creamer, Sally Paden	4
Creamer and Sugar, Jonquil	10
Cup, Elite	4
Cup, New Virginia	5
Cup, Regina	5
Cup, Shell Crest	6
Cup, Shenandoah	6
Cup and Saucer, Spinning Wheel	5
Dinner Plate, Blue Willow, 9" d	10
Dinner Plate, Elite, 9¹/₄" d	8
Dinner Plate, Papoco, 9³/₄" d	8
Dinner Plate, Sally Paden, 9¹/₄" d	8
Dinner Plate, Shell Crest, 8¹/₂" d	6
Dinner Plate, Shenandoah, 9" d	9
Gravy Boat, Manhattan	12
Gravy Boat, New Virginia	12
Gravy Boat, Shenandoah	13
Gravy Boat Underplate, Shenandoah, 9" l	10
Jug, ftd, Bak–Serv	15
Mixing Bowl, Caliente, 9¹/₈" d	18
Platter, oval, Highlight	35
Platter, oval, Patio	10
Platter, oval, Sally Paden, 11¹/₂" l	10
Platter, oval, Shell Crest, 16¹/₂" l	25
Salad Bowl, oval, Caliente, 10" d	20
Saucer, Blue Willow	2
Saucer, Manhattan	2
Saucer, Papoco	1
Saucer, Regina	1
Soup Bowl, Far East	5
Soup Bowl, Regina, 8" d	10
Teapot, Caliente, blue	28

*Soup Bowl, Shenandoah, Poppy,
hp red flowers and green leaves,
mkd, 8" d, $8.*

Teapot, New Virginia	25
Teapot, Jonquil	12
Teapot, Shenandoah	32
Vegetable Bowl, oval, Highlight	35
Vegetable Bowl, oval, Regina, 9" l	10

PAUL REVERE

Paul Revere Pottery, Boston, Massachusetts, was an outgrowth of a club known as "The Saturday Evening Girls." The S.E.G. was a group of young female immigrants who met on Saturday nights for reading and crafts such as ceramics.

Regular production began in 1908. The name Paul Revere was adopted because the pottery was located near the Old North Church. In 1915 the firm moved to Brighton, Massachusetts. Known as the "Bowl Shop," the pottery grew steadily. In spite of popular acceptance and technical advancements, the pottery required continual subsidies. It finally closed in January 1942.

Items produced range from plain and decorated vases to tablewares to illustrated tiles. Many decorated wares were incised and glazed either in an Art Nouveau matte finish or an occasional high glaze.

In addition to the impressed mark, paper "Bowl Shop" labels were used prior to 1915. Pieces also can be found dated with P.R.P. or S.E.G. painted on the base.

Bookends, pr, pastoral river view scenes, sloping blue blocks, imp Revere circular mark, sgd "F2 24," 4" h, 4³/₄" l	$800
Bowl, geese and trees, incised and painted, gunmetal, dark green blue, and frothy white, flaring sides, orig paper label, 5 x 11¹/₂"	1,500
Bowl, Landscape Medallion, cuerda seca dec, green, blue, and yellow, "5–26/EB/JMD" imp mark, 6" d	200
Creamer, wild rose border, white on blue and gray ground, black matte outlines, white int, sgraffito dec, sgd "FR/255–6–09/SEG," 2⁷/₈" h	350
Cup and Saucer, light blue and narrow black band, medium blue ground	45
Demitasse Cup and Saucer, trees, painted bright green against blue sky band, circular ink stamp, 5"d	350
Jar, cov, purple moths border, blue and green stylized band, white ground, sgd by Sara Galner and Ida Goldstein, 1911, 5" d, 4¹/₂" h	1,500

Jardiniere, tulip border, repeating yellow, green, and blue, matte black outlines, yellow ground, flared, sgd on back "11–26 PRP," X in circle artist cipher **350**

Luncheon Set, tree and sky border, repeating blue and green, black outlines, cream ground, sgd and numbered, 5 cups, luncheon plates, and dessert plates, price for 15–pc set **1,600**

Milk Pitcher, lotus blossoms, white with band of green leaves, bright yellow ground, 1935, mkd "P.R.P./12–35," small nick to tip of spout, 4³/₄ x 6" **750**

Mug, strolling rabbit, matte brown and blue, blue band, cream ground, inscribed "John Fisk/Zueblin" below rim, and "Xmas/1914/S.E.G.," hairline, 3" h **400**

Mug, tree filled landscape, incised, green, brown, blue, cream, and yellow glazes, solitary nightingale over inscription "In the forest must always be a nightingale and in the soul a faith so faithful that it comes back even after it has been slain," dec by Sara Galner, incised artist's initials and marks, c1915, 4" h **1,400**

Pitcher, singing chickens, white, black matte outlines, wide white and yellow border, white and yellow int, sgd "SEG/JT/MD/9–19," 1919 .... **300**

Pitcher, tulips, incised and dec yellow stylized tulips, brown leaves, black outlines, yellow ground, white horizontal ring below spout, sgd "SEG/AM," spout loss, hairline, 7³/₄" h **650**

Planter, landscape, white and yellow, stylized brown and tan tree clusters border, black matte outlines, yellow ground, shallow, sgd "SEG/FL/1–23" .. **1,900**

Plate, running pigs border, bands of brown, yellow, and green, dec by Lily Shapiro and Rose Bikini, artists' ciphers, Helen Osbourne Storrow monogram incised at center, numbered, and mkd "SEG," 3¹/₂" d, price for pair .. **3,200**

Plate, star filled sky, quarter moon, lakeside cottage, tall trees, flowering daffodils, black matte outlines, dark and light shades of blue, green, brown, and yellow, sgd "SEG/SG/11–15, 1915" **11,000**

Tankard, snow capped mountain on top, blue–green glaze, 5" h **300**

Teapot, cov, repeating yellow crocus border, black matte outlines, white ground, sgd "196–EG/SEG," small glaze chip on spout, 1912 .... **200**

Tile, cottage by lake, green, brown, white, and orange, black outlines, light blue ground, sgd and numbered, 5³/₄" d **450**

Trivet, Goose on Hill Medallion, dark blue ground, imp mark, 1924, 5¹/₂" d .. **600**

Jug, Rabbit Medallion, yellow–brown ground, "David, His Jug," 4¹/₂" h, $350.

Trivet, House and Setting Sun Medallion, blue–green ground, imp mark,
   5½" h **600**
Urn, mustard colored glaze, 4½" h **175**
Vase, blue–gray gloss glaze, dark blue specks, pot shaped, #924, 3½" h **100**
Vase, floral, stylized, matte yellow, brown, and green band, black outlines,
   matte white–yellow band at shoulder and rim, matte yellow glaze body,
   inscribed marks, 2 hairlines at top, 9⅛" h **530**
Vase, flowers, stylized gray and brown, black outline, dark blue ground, sgd
   "FCN–LY," restored, 4½" h **280**
Vase, flying ducks, band of ducks over blue water, yellow and blue sky, hori-
   zon of green land, black outlines, light blue ground, inscribed marks, rem-
   nants of paper label, rim peppering, 8⅜" h **1,300**
Vase, pink crystals, on light purple, green, blue, and pink glaze, blue–green
   ground, 5" h **250**
Vase, red drip, blue–green ground, teardrop shaped, chips, 6½" h **280**
Vase, slate blue gloss glaze, rust int, flared top, 3½" h **180**
Vase, trees, green band on satin blue–gray ground, ovoid, imp circular mark,
   small glaze bubble on body, 1924, 6¼ x 3½" h **1,400**
Vase, trees, stylized, black outlines, gray–green glaze, flaring cylindrical
   shape, sgd "SEG," 7¼" h . . . .) **450**
Vase, tulips, yellow, mottled dark, light, and teal blue, mkd "P.R.P./11–26/
   JMD," 9" h **2,200**

PENNSBURY

   Henry and Lee Below established Pennsbury Pottery in 1950. The pottery was
named for its close proximity to William Penn's estate "Pennsbury," three miles west
of Morrisville, Pennsylvania. Henry, a ceramic engineer and mold maker, and Lee, a
designer and modeler, had previously worked for Stangl Pottery in Trenton, New
Jersey.
   Many of Pennsbury's forms, motifs, and manufacturing techniques have Stangl
roots. A line of birds similar to those produced by Stangl were among the earliest
Pennsbury products. The carved design technique is also Stangl in origin.
   Pennsbury products are easily identified by their brown wash background. The
company also made pieces featuring other background colors. Do not make the mis-
take of assuming that a piece is not Pennsbury because it does not have a brown wash.
   Pennsbury motifs are heavily nostalgia, farm, and Pennsylvania German related.
Among the most popular lines were Amish, Black Rooster, Delft Toleware, Eagle,
Family, Folkart, Gay Ninety, Harvest, Hex, Quartet, Red Barn, Red Rooster,
Slick–Chick, and Christmas plates (1960–70). The pottery also made a large number of
commemorative, novelty, and special order pieces.
   In the late 1950s the company had sixteen employees, mostly local housewives
and young girls. In 1963 employees numbered forty-six, the company's peak. By the
late 1960s, the company had just over twenty employees. Cheap foreign imports cut
deeply into the pottery's profits.
   Marks differ from piece to piece depending on the person who signed the piece or
the artist who sculptured the mold. The identity for some initials has still not been
determined.
   Henry Below died on December 21, 1959, leaving the pottery in trust for his wife
and three children with instructions that it be sold upon the death of his wife. Lee
Below died on December 12, 1968. In October 1970 the Pennsbury Pottery filed for

bankruptcy. The contents of the company were auctioned on December 18, 1970. On May 18, 1971, a fire destroyed the pottery and support buildings.

Since the pieces were hand carved, aesthetic quality differs from piece to piece. Look for pieces with a strong design sense and a high quality of execution. Buy only clearly marked pieces. Look for decorator and designer initials that can be easily identified.

Pennsbury collectors are concentrated in the Middle Atlantic states. Many of the company's commemorative and novelty pieces relate to local businesses and events, thus commanding their highest prices within this region.

References: Lucile Henzke, *Pennsbury Pottery,* Schiffer Publishing, 1990; Mike Schneider, *Stangl and Pennsbury Birds,* Schiffer Publishing, 1994.

Ashtray, Amish	**$12**
Ashtray, Don't Be so Doppich, 5" d	25
Ashtray, Doylestown Trust	12
Ashtray, Such Schmootzers	18
Ashtray, The Solebury National Bank of New Hope Pa, 5" d	30
Ashtray, What Giffs?	18
Beer Mug, Amish	20
Beer Mug, Eagle, 5" h	30
Beer Mug, Gay Ninety, 5" h	40
Bread Tray, Wheat	30
Butter Dish, Folkart, 5 x 4"	45
Butter Dish, Hex, 5 x 4"	50
Cake Stand, Two Birds Over Heart, 11" d	80
Candle Holder, Red Rooster, 5" h	40
Candle Holder, Tulip, 5" h	40
Candy Dish, Hex Sign, 9" d	40
Casserole, cov, Black Rooster, 10½ x 8¼"	100
Chip and Dip Set, Red Rooster	90
Cigarette Box, Eagle, 3½ x 5"	40
Coaster, Barber Shop Quartet, 5" d	30
Coaster, Fisherman, 4½" d, price for set of 4	100
Coaster, Schultz	20
Coffee Mug, 3¼" h, Amish	20
Coffee Mug, 3¼" h, Barber Shop Quartet	35
Coffeepot, Black Rooster, 8" h	90
Creamer, Amish Woman's Head	15
Cup and Saucer, Black Rooster	15
Cup and Saucer, Hex Sign	30
Cup and Saucer, Red Rooster	18
Desk Accessory, bucket, National Exchange Club	20
Dinner Plate, Blue Dowry, 10" d	35
Dinner Plate, Harvest, 11" d	80
Dinner Plate, Hex Sign, 10" d	15
Dinner Plate, Red Rooster, 10" d	20
Eggcup, Red Rooster, 4" h	22
Luncheon Plate, Hex Sign, 8" d	20
Pie Plate, Apple Tree	90
Pie Plate, Black Rooster, 10" d	35
Pie Plate, Folkart, 9" d	50

Vegetable Dish, divided,
Rooster, 9¹/₂" l, 6" w, 2¹/₂" h,
$35.

Pie Plate, Mother Serving Pie, 9" d 85
Pitcher, Amish Man, miniature, 2" h 15
Pitcher, Barber Shop Quartet, 7¹/₂" h 90
Pitcher, Eagle, 5¹/₄" h 60
Pitcher, Red Barn, 6¹/₄" h 100
Pitcher, Red Rooster, 4" h 30
Plaque, Farm Scene, 6" d 50
Plaque, NFA Centennial 25
Pretzel Bowl, Eagle, 8 x 11" 55
Pretzel Bowl, Gay Ninety, 8 x 12" 90
Salt and Pepper Shakers, pr, Amish Heads 50
Salt and Pepper Shakers, pr, Red Rooster, 2¹/₂" h 25
Snack Tray and Cup, Red Rooster 25
Teapot, Red Rooster 60
Vegetable Bowl, divided, Red Rooster 35

PFALTZGRAFF

Pfaltzgraff is named after a famous Rhine River castle, still standing today, in the Pfalz region of Germany.

In 1811 George Pfaltzgraff, a German immigrant potter, began producing salt glazed stoneware in York, Pennsylvania. The Pfaltzgraff Pottery Company initially produced stoneware storage crocks and jugs. When the demand for stoneware diminished, the company shifted its production to animal and poultry feeders and red clay flower pots. The production focus changed again in the late 1940s and early 1950s as the company produced more and more household products, including its first dinnerware and giftware lines.

In 1964 the company became The Pfaltzgraff Company. Over the next 15 years, Pfaltzgraff expanded through the construction of a new manufacturing plant and distribution center in Thomasville, North Carolina, the purchase of the Stangl Pottery of Trenton, New Jersey, and the acquisition of factories in Aspers, Bendersville, and Dover, Pennsylvania. Retail stores were opened in York County, Pennsylvania; Flemington, New Jersey; and, Fairfax, Virginia.

In the 1960s and 70s Pfaltzgraff stoneware bowls, crocks, and jugs, especially those featuring cobalt blue folk art drawings, were the principal focus of Country collectors. As the 21st century nears, collectors now concentrate on seeking pieces from Pfaltzgraff's 1950s, 60s, and 70s dinnerware patterns.

Reference: Harry L. Rinker, *Dinnerware of the 20th Century: The Top 500 Patterns,* House of Collectibles, 1997.

America, baker, rect, 14¹/₈" l	$30
America, creamer and sugar, cov	22
America, salad plate	4
Christmas Heirloom, cup and saucer	8
Christmas Heirloom, salt and pepper shakers, pr	12
Gourmet, ashtray, 9¹/₄" d	5
Gourmet, creamer and sugar, cov	15
Gourmet, mug	3
Gourmet, tray, 14⁵/₈" l	17
Heritage, baker, rect, 14³/₈" l	10
Heritage, cup and saucer	7
Heritage, gravy boat and underplate	12
Heritage, platter, oval 12" l	10
Heritage, soup bowl, 8⁵/₈" d	8
Village, creamer	10
Village, salad plate, 7" d	4
Village, sugar, cov	12
Windsong, bread and butter plate	6
Windsong, dinner plate	12
Yorktowne, baker, individual	10
Yorktowne, baker, rect	20
Yorktowne, baker, square	25
Yorktowne, bean pot, cov	35
Yorktowne, bowl, heart shaped	15
Yorktowne, butter dish, cov, ¹/₄ lb	10
Yorktowne, candle holder	12
Yorktowne, canister, cov, coffee	12

Left: America, dinner plate, $7. Right: Village, dinner plate, brown, $8.

PORCELIER

The Porcelier Manufacturing Company was incorporated on October 14, 1926, with business offices in Pittsburgh, Pennsylvania, and a manufacturing plant in East Liverpool, Ohio. In 1930 Porcelier purchased the vacant plant of the American China Company in South Greensburg, Westmoreland County, Pennsylvania.

Porcelier began as a manufacturer of light fixtures. Electrical kitchen appliances were added by the mid-1930s. Some credit Porcelier with making the first all-ceramic electrical appliances. During its distinguished history, Porcelier made over 100 patterns of kitchenware and over 100 different light fixtures.

Sears Roebuck and Company and Montgomery Ward were among Porcelier's biggest customers. As such, many products appear with brand names such as Heatmaster and Harmony House.

The company was unionized in the late 1930s, remaining a union shop until it closed. In March 1954 Pittsburgh Plate Glass Industries bought the Porcelier plant and adjacent land. The company was dissolved in the summer of 1954.

Porcelier used decals to decorate most of its wares. Floral motifs in spring and fall tones are a natural for a Country table setting.

Reference: Susan E. Grindberg, *Collector's Guide to Porcelier China*, Collector Books, 1996.

Collectors' Club: Porcelier Collectors Club, 21 Tamarac Swamp Road, Wallingford, CT 06492.

Ball Jug, Beehive Crisscross **$60**
Ball Jug, Mexican 70
Casserole, cov, Basketweave Cameo, 8½" d 45
Creamer, Antique Rose Deco 6
Creamer, Basketweave Wild Flowers 8
Creamer, Cattail 8
Creamer, Double Floral 8
Creamer, Flamingo 6
Creamer, Fleur–de–Lis 8
Creamer, Flower Pot 10
Creamer, Golden Fuchia Platinum 12
Creamer, Lavender Bluebell 4
Creamer, Scalloped Wild Flowers 10
Creamer, Silhouette 8

Creamer, White Flower Platinum 4
Electric Percolator, Black–Eyed Susan 65
Electric Percolator, Golden Wheat 60
Electric Percolator, Leaf and Shadow, short handle 75
Electric Percolator, Orange Poppy 60
Electric Percolator, Starflower, #120 60
Pretzel Jar, Barock–Colonial, gold 85
Spaghetti Bowl, Basketweave Wild Flowers 75
Sugar, Basketweave Wild Flowers 8
Sugar, Field Flowers 8
Sugar, Floral Panel 8
Sugar, Lavender Bluebell 4
Sugar, Mexican 8
Sugar, Rope Bow 6
Sugar, Scalloped Wild Flowers 10
Sugar Canister, Barock–Colonial, #2016, gold 25
Teapot, 8 cup, double floral 25
Teapot, 8 cup, Nautical 25
Tray, Silhouette, #2611, wood 40

PURINTON

Bernard Purinton founded Purinton Pottery in 1936 in Wellsville, Ohio. In 1941 the pottery relocated to Shippensville, Pennsylvania. The plant ceased operations around 1959. William H. Blair and Dorothy Purinton were the chief designers.

Purinton Pottery did not use decals as did many of its competitors. All slipware was cast. Greenware was hand painted by locally trained decorators who then dipped the decorated pieces into glaze. This demanded a specially formulated body and a more expensive manufacturing process. Hand painting also allowed for some of the variations in technique and colors found on Purinton ware today.

References: Jamie Bero–Johnson and Jaime Johnson, *Purinton Pottery,* Schiffer Publishing, 1997; Pat Dole, *Purinton Pottery, Book I* (1985) and *Book II* (1990), Denton Publishing, Susan Morris, *Purinton Pottery: An Identification and Value Guide,* Collector Books, 1994.

Newsletter: *Purinton Pastimes,* PO Box 0394, Arlington, WA 22215.

Apple, bowl, 12" d $25
Apple, candy dish, 2 part, center loop handle, 6¼" h 50
Apple, canister set, cov, flour, sugar, coffee, and tea, price for set 100
Apple, casserole, cov 25
Apple, cereal bowl 8
Apple, coffeepot, cov 30
Apple, creamer and sugar, cov 35
Apple, Dutch jug 30
Apple, fruit bowl, scalloped border, 12" d 45
Apple, grill platter, 12" d 50
Apple, juice tumbler 10
Apple, kent jug, 1 pt 20
Apple, luncheon plate, 9" d 20
Apple, marmalade jar 45

Apple, mug	30
Apple, platter, 12" l	25
Apple, range shaker	15
Apple, salad bowl, ftd, 11" d	35
Apple, salad plate, 8" d	10
Apple, salt and pepper shakers, pr, jug shape, small	25
Apple, sugar, cov	20
Apple, tumbler, 5" h	22
Apple, vegetable bowl, 8½" d	22
Fruit, canister, sugar, red or blue trim, 9" d	70
Fruit, chop plate, 12" d	70
Fruit, creamer and sugar, cov	22
Fruit, cup and saucer	12
Fruit, dinner plate, 9¾" d	15
Fruit, kent jug, 1 pt	32
Fruit, lazy susan canister set, triangular	90
Fruit, range salt and pepper shakers, pr	20
Fruit, relish dish, 3 part, handled	22
Fruit, teapot, 2 cup	30
Fruit, water pitcher	35
Heather Plaid, beer mug	45
Heather Plaid, bread and butter plate, 6¾" d	8
Heather Plaid, canister, coffee, square, 7½" h	45
Heather Plaid, casserole, 9" d	32
Heather Plaid, coffeepot, 9" h	50
Heather Plaid, dinner plate, 9¾" d	15
Heather Plaid, fruit bowl	8
Heather Plaid, grease jar, cov, 5½" h	65
Heather Plaid, mug, 4" h	28
Heather Plaid, party plate, 8½" d	20
Heather Plaid, relish dish, 3 part	30
Heather Plaid, salad bowl, 11" d	30
Heather Plaid, tumbler, 6 oz	15
Heather Plaid, tumbler, 12 oz	20
Heather Plaid, vegetable bowl, divided	30

Apple, teapot, cov, stamped "Purinton Slip Ware," 2 cup, 6¼" h, 7½" w, $25.

Heather Plaid, wall pocket, 3½" h 35
Intaglio, baker, 7" d 25
Intaglio, bean pot, 3¾" h 50
Intaglio, casserole, 9" d 60
Intaglio, chop plate, 12" d 30
Intaglio, cookie jar, oval shape, 9½" h 75
Intaglio, cup and saucer 10
Intaglio, dinner plate 15
Intaglio, fruit bowl, ftd, 12" d 65
Intaglio, salad plate 10
Intaglio, tea and toast set 20
Ivy, drip jar, cov 25
Ivy, jug, 1 pt 15
Ivy, juice tumbler 10
Maywood, bread and butter plate, 6¾" d 12
Maywood, casserole, 9" d 60
Maywood, cereal bowl, 5¼" d 15
Maywood, chop plate, 12" d 60
Maywood, fruit bowl, ftd, 12" d 65
Maywood, party plate, 8½" d 20
Maywood, pickle dish, oblong, 6" l 20
Maywood, platter, oblong, 12" l 45
Maywood, teapot, cov, 6 cup 80
Normandy Plaid, chop plate, 12" d 30
Normandy Plaid, dessert bowl, 4" d 10
Normandy Plaid, dinner plate 8
Normandy Plaid, fruit bowl 20
Normandy Plaid, mug, jug shape 6
Normandy Plaid, pepper shaker, jug shape 7
Normandy Plaid, tumbler, 5" h 22
Normandy Plaid, vegetable bowl, 8½" d 22
Pennsylvania Dutch, bread tray 35
Pennsylvania Dutch, canister set, cov, flour, sugar, coffee, and tea, price for
  set 180
Pennsylvania Dutch, casserole, 9" d 45
Pennsylvania Dutch, cereal bowl 15
Pennsylvania Dutch, chop plate, 12" d 32
Pennsylvania Dutch, creamer, individual 15
Pennsylvania Dutch, creamer and sugar, cov, individual 25
Pennsylvania Dutch, creamer and sugar, cov, large 40
Pennsylvania Dutch, dinner plate, 9¾" d 20
Pennsylvania Dutch, luncheon plate, 8½" d 15
Pennsylvania Dutch, pickle dish, 6" d 12
Pennsylvania Dutch, platter, 12" l 32
Pennsylvania Dutch, salad bowl, ftd, 11" d 45
Pennsylvania Dutch, sugar, individual 12
Pennsylvania Dutch, teapot, 2 cup 35
Pennsylvania Dutch, vegetable bowl, divided 35
Pennsylvania Dutch, vinegar and oil jugs, pr 50
Petals, casserole, 9" d 80
Petals, cup 15

Petals, dessert dish, 4" d **15**
Petals, dinner plate, 9³/₄" d **45**
Petals, pickle dish, oblong, 6" l **30**
Turquoise, baker, 7" d **40**
Turquoise, fruit bowl, 12" d **45**

REDWARE

The availability of clay, the same used to make bricks and roof tiles, accounted for the great production of red earthenware pottery in the American colonies. Redware pieces are mainly utilitarian—bowls, crocks, jugs, etc.

Lead glazed redware retained its reddish color, but a variety of colored glazes were obtained by the addition of metals to the basic glaze. Streaks and mottled splotches in redware items resulted from impurities in the clay and/or uneven firing temperatures.

"Slipware" is a term used to describe redwares decorated by the application of slip, a semi–liquid paste made of clay. Slipwares were made in England, Germany, and elsewhere in Europe for decades before becoming popular in the Pennsylvania German region and elsewhere in colonial America.

"Sgraffito" is a term used to describe redware that has a unique decoration. The entire surface is covered with a thick yellow glaze and the design is scratched into it, removing thin lines to create stylized decorations. Other colors may be added as highlights. Sgraffito ware is time consuming to produce and the glaze often flaked. Pieces in good condition command high prices. Sgraffito ware makes an excellent display piece and new reproductions should not be overlooked.

References: Kevin McConnell, *Redware: America's Folk Art Pottery,* Schiffer Publishing, 1988; *The Potters Medinger: The Last of the Traditional Pennsylvania German Potters,* Philip and Muriel Berman Museum of Art, 1992.

Applebutter Crocks, one 4¹³/₁₆" h with rounded sides and rim and overall
  orange ground glazing, other 4³/₈" h with rounded sides, sloped rounded
  rim, and overall dark brown ground glazing, price for pair **$45**
Bank, apple, red and yellow paint, 3¹/₄" h **150**
Bank, face, painted, "Josephine Chute Age 1," inscribed on reverse, late
  19th/early 20th C, 3" h **230**
Basket, crimped rim, rope twist handle, marbleized brown and white slip,
  5¹/₄" h **8,250**
Bean Pot, dark brown glazed int, 2 rim chips, 5⁵/₈" h **230**
Birdhouse, ovoid, incised shoulder, overhanging knob with hooded perch,
  inscribed "Made in Stahl's Pottery Zionsville PA for MARGARET
  Buchanan 11–26–38," 7³/₄" h **350**
Birdhouse, ovoid, opaque cream colored glaze with yellow highlights, craz-
  ing, 7¹/₂" h **50**
Bottle, pinched sides and tooling, green glaze, brown flecks, green striping,
  "Made by I S Stahl, 11–1–1939" incised label, 5³/₄" h **60**
Bowl, coggled rim, shallow, worn yellow slip dec, inscribed "Cake," worn,
  chipped, 12" d **275**
Bowl, European, yellow slip dec with "Lucia," 8¹/₂" d, 3¹/₄" h **70**
Bowl, flaring rim with swags, concentric line dec below, floral sprig within
  base, tones of green, cream, and yellow on reddish base, 13¹/₂" d **3,400**

Bowl, incised ribbing around sides, coggled dec on side of rim, sgd "Who Shall Live When I am Dead Write My Wishes Quick, Talk of The Good Not The Bad I Did, Made By I. S. Stahl, Jan. 31, 1939, S. P.," 8⅝" d 275

Bowl, rounded sides flaring toward rounded rim, orange–green mottled ground, 8¾" d 80

Bowl, shallow, bird on branch int, yellow slip edge design, green and brown glaze, very worn int, chips, 12½" d 250

Bowl, sides flare toward flared collar with rounded rim, orange ground, 10¼" d, 3¹⁵⁄₁₆" h, rim chip 140

Bucket, pierced cylindrical body, strap handle, 20" h 90

Butter Pourers, set of 4, pinched spout on rim, round stick–type handle, incised line designs on sides, sgd "Made In Stahl's Pottery By Thomas Stahl, 1/2/39," 3¾" d, 1¾" h 230

Cake Mold, incised, PA, 19th C, 7½" d 150

Candlestick, molded candle socket on flaring support with incised base and circular molded drip pan mounted with rope twist handle, cobalt and slip dec, inscribed "Made by I.S. Stahl/May 13–1938," 5" h 575

Carafe, cov, pinched ovoid body, similarly molded foot, removable hourglass form lid with molded foot doubling as drinking cup revealing slender spout and incised shoulder, cobalt blue dec, inscribed "Made by I.S. Stahl 4–24 / 1938," 7¼" h 750

Chamberstick, brown glaze, dark trim, bottom incised inscription "Made by I.S. Stahl, Dec. 6, 1938, S.P.," 7" d 27

Creamer, strap handle, cream colored slip with brown, 3½" h 200

Cream Jar, cov, globular shape, rounded gallery–type rim, arched handle on side, knob shaped finial on lid, orange–brown ground, 6" d, 6¼" h 50

Crock, incised line design around side below rim, "W. Smith, Womelsdorf" imp mark on bottom, 5½" h 30

Crock, incised line design on rim and side, brown ground, mica flakes, "W. Smith, Womelsdorf" imp mark on bottom, 5⅜" h 75

Crock, rounded sides with flared rounded rim, incised double band around side top and bottom, orange–brown ground int, "HF" imp mark on bottom, 5¼" d at rim, 5⅜" h 40

Left: Cup, lug handle, green mottled glaze, Thomas Stahl, 3¾" d, 1⅞" h, $85.
Right: Bank, tomato, painted, $93. Photo courtesy Aston Macek.

Crock, tall, rounded sides and rim, arched handle on side, 6⁷/₈" d, 6⁷/₈" h **35**
Cup, oversized, strap handle, brown splotches, edge wear, chips, 3¹/₂" h,
  5¹/₄" d **120**
Cup, strap handle, bottom incised "J. 1850," attributed to Chambersburg,
  3¹/₄" h **160**
Dish, coggled rim, yellow slip dec, orange, 7¹/₄" d **190**
Dish, oblong, deep green glaze, orange spots, wear, 11¹/₂" l **280**
Dish, round, concentric circles slip dec, notched rim, chips, 19th C,
  11¹/₂" h **1,000**
Figure, baby deer, dark stain finish, incised initials "C. T." and "Porky," 10" h .   **160**
Figure, squirrel, early 20th C, 7¹/₂" h **170**
Flowerpot, flaring side, rounded rim, flat bottom, incised line dec around
  rim, brown mottled ground ext glaze, small drainage hole in bottom,
  7³/₄" d, 6¹/₂" h **100**
Flowerpot, tapering line incised conical body, flaring drip plate, overlapping
  molded rim pierced for hanging, tones of green, yellow, and brown,
  glaze worn on bottom, minor chips to rim, 10¹/₂" d **900**
Flowerpot, tooled and finger-crimped rim, brown sponged glaze, mis-
  matched saucer, 8³/₄" h **230**
Food Mold, ear of corn, oval, arched sides, crimped edge, clear glaze with
  sponging on rim, 4 applied feet, 7⁷/₈" h **450**
Food Mold, ear of corn center, rect, scalloped sides, rounded corners, dark
  brown glaze with black sponging, wear and chips, 7" l **125**
Food Mold, Turk's head, clear glaze, brown flecks, chips and hairlines, 6" d . .   **35**
Food Mold, Turk's head, flared sides, ruffled rim, dark brown ground, 6" d,
  2¹/₂" h **65**
Food Mold, Turk's head, fluted, scalloped rim, greenish glaze, amber spots,
  brown splotches, small edge flakes, 6¹/₄" d, 1¹/₂" h **90**
Food Mold, Turk's head, molded leaf design, amber glaze, 8¹/₂" d **35**
Food Mold, Turk's head, round, swirled and fluted, scalloped rim,
  orange–green mottled ground, 9" d, 3¹/₈" h **65**
Food Mold, Turk's head, round with flared sides, ruffled rim, flat bottom, thin
  center cone, 6" d **65**
Food Mold, Turk's head, swirled and fluted, scalloped rim, orange–brown
  ground, manganese mottling on rim, 8¹/₂" d **45**
Food Mold, Turk's head, swirled design, brown sponging, "John Bell
  Waynesboro" imp mark, minor flakes, 8¹/₄" d **1,200**
Inkwell, ruffled edge, incised chain design, applied pheasant handle cov,
  clear lead glaze, head of pheasant glued, 3¹/₂" d, 3¹/₂" h **350**
Jar, cylindrical, incised double line dec around sides and shoulder, man-
  ganese mottling, 6¹/₂" h **120**
Jar, flared base, doubled incised line dec around neck, green and orange
  mottled ground, 8³/₈" h **35**
Jar, flared lip, tooled bands, amber glaze with brown vertical brush marks,
  chips and hairline in bottom, mismatched lid, 7" h **275**
Jar, miniature, marbleized slip, imp "Gay Head Clay," 1⁷/₈" h **55**
Jar, ovoid, cov, applied shoulder handles, red–amber glaze, chips on lip and
  lid, 12" h **100**
Jar, ovoid, cov, dark brown glaze, glaze flakes, 5³/₈" h **30**
Jar, ovoid, cov, ribbed strap handle, dark orange glaze, brown splotches,
  5³/₄" h **55**

Jar, pinched handle, mica flecks, lid glazed on bottom, unglazed on top, lid
    glued, 6⁵/₈" h **65**

Jar, sloping shoulder, flared lip, light green glaze with amber spots, small
    flakes, hairline in bottom, 8" h **50**

Jar, straight sides, sloping shoulder, gallery lip, green glaze with overall
    orange spots and dark brown sponging in top half, minor glaze wear,
    7³/₄" h **200**

Jug, ovoid, bulbous lip, ribbed strap handle, clear shiny deep orange colored
    glaze, handle chipped, 6¹/₂" h **75**

Jug, ovoid, clear glaze, black splotches, small chip on lip, glaze flakes, 9" h .. **120**

Jug, ovoid, green speckled glaze, hairlines, 5¹/₂" h **100**

Jug, ovoid, incised lines at shoulder, strap handle, light green glaze with
    amber spots, wear, glaze flaking, minor crazing, 8¹/₂" h **125**

Jug, ovoid, strap handle, brown splotches, wear and chips, 7" h **100**

Jug, ovoid, tooled lines at shoulder, ribbed strap handle, green–amber glaze
    with brown flecks, 6³/₄" h **375**

Loaf Pan, oblong, coggled rim, 4–line yellow slip dec, wear, chips and hair-
    lines, 16" l **375**

Loaf Pan, oblong, coggled rim, 3–line yellow slip dec, worn, old chips and
    scratches, 13" l **425**

Meat Roaster, scoop shaped, applied finger–crimped rim, strap handle, end
    spout, green–amber glaze, 12" l **225**

Milk Pan, amber glaze, brown flecks, dark brown daubs, hairline and wear,
    10¹/₂" d, 3³/₄" h **65**

Milk Pan, rim spout, 8" d **150**

Milk Pitcher, oval, arched handle, molded flower design on sides, orange–
    brown ground, manganese mottling, 6⁵/₈" h **60**

Milk Pitcher, tooled and imp dec bands, clear glaze, running brown splotch-
    es, edge wear, small flakes, 4⁵/₈" h **80**

Muffin Pan, green glaze, 12" l, 15¹/₂" w **35**

Mug, flared lip, strap handle, greenish amber glaze, 4" d **40**

Nesting Bowls, set of 3, rounded sides, incised horizontal ribbing, overall
    glazing except for bases, sgd "No. 41–A, Made By I. S. Stahl, April 20,
    1939," some glaze crazing in bottom, price for set **400**

Pan, round, low straight sides, vertically ribbed handle, brown ground, over-
    all manganese mottling on sides, chips and glaze wear on rim, 5⁷/₈" d,
    2⁷/₈" h **140**

Pie Plate, coggled rim, "ABC" and flourish in flaked yellow slip, 11¹/₄" d **190**

Pie Plate, coggled rim, 4–line yellow slip dec, 9¹/₄" d **230**

Pie Plate, coggled rim, yellow slip "X" dec, crazing and rim chips, 7¹/₂" d **150**

Pie Plate, dark brown fleck glaze, 7⁷/₈" d **80**

Pie Plate, folded rim, white slip, green and brown plaid design, 8" d **570**

Pie Plate, sgraffito peacock, yellow slip, "I am not a shame that Peacock is
    my name. Made in Stahl's Pottery, Sept. 20, 1934" rim dec, green glaze,
    10¹/₄" d **125**

Pitcher, globular shape, flared rim, arched handle with vertical ribbing,
    pinched spout, incised line designs around shoulder, sgd "Made In Stahl
    Pottery By Thomas Stahl, Sept. 14th, 1938," 5³/₄" h **70**

Pitcher, mottled dark brown metallic glaze, 6¹/₈" h **60**

Pitcher, white slip with marbleized red, green, and brown, some edge wear,
    glaze flakes, 6³/₄" h **50**

Plate, coggled rim, dark brown glaze, 6¼" h 150

Plate, crimped rim, sgraffito dec, shallow, spreadwing eagle wearing breast plate and clutching olive branches, incised with inscription "In Liberty," dated "1809," green and white on brown field, chips to rim, early 20th C, 8¾" d 1,850

Plate, incised distlefink, flowers, German inscription, and name, dark amber glaze, 10½" d 200

Plate, shallow bowl form, slip dec, stylized flower and flowerpot dec, tones of white and brown on orange field, 8¼" d 800

Plate, 3 yellow slip dec double musical note designs separated by 3 small yellow slip dots, 8³⁄₈" d 70

Plate, 3 yellow squiggled slip dec lines flanked by series of yellow ship darts and darts on sides, round yellow dots at both ends, 8⁵⁄₈" d 100

Plate, white slip, brown combed dec, 8¼" d 400

Plate, yellow slip, green wavy line on rim, brown polka dots, 7¾" d 200

Platter and Bowl, America, platter with dished sides and trailed wavy slip dec, green border and yellow center section, bowl with German inscription on rim, late 19th C, 11½" l, price for pair 11,000

Pot, cov, pouring spout, strap handle, dark brown glaze, brown splotches, mismatched lid, chips, 5" h.. 80

Preserving Jar, glazed, mottled green and brown dec, attributed to southern US, 19th C, 4⁵⁄₈" h 900

Preserving Jar, ovoid, yellow glaze, minor glaze flakes on lip, 7" h 50

Salt, ftd, greenish brown mottled glaze, 3" d, 2" h 55

Shaving Cup, strap handle, brown–green mottled glaze, 5¾" h 275

Spittoon, flared and rounded top, rounded rim, Albany slip glaze, 3⁷⁄₈" h 20

Storage Jar, ovoid, double incised line dec around neck, green and orange mottled ground, 8³⁄₈" h 35

Storage Jar, ovoid, straight plain rim, arched ear handles on sides of shoulder, 2 bands of incised line dec around side, dark brown ground with manganese splotches, chipping around base, chips and glaze flaking around rim, 8" d, 10³⁄₈" h 100

Left: Flowerpot, attached saucer, crimped edges, green and brown glaze, Stahl, 1938, 4¹⁄₂" d, 2¹⁄₂" h, $100.

Right: Food Mold, Turk's head, Midwest, late, 10" d, $65. Photo courtesy Ray Morykan Auctions.

Tobacco Jar, cov, cylindrical, sgraffito dec, coggled band dec on top and sides, pair of clay pipes, cannon, rifle, and maple leaves on sides, fitted lid with ball finial, some chips, 5½" h **1,700**

Tobacco Jar, cov, cylindrical, sgraffito dec, flared rim fitted with domed lid with flattened ball finial, sides dec with incised pair of clay pipes, flowers, and leaves, and "J. S." on yellow ground, attributed to Jacob Scholl, Pennsylvania, lid chipped and cracked, early 19th C, 5¾" h **3,400**

Toddy Plate, yellow slip dec, green wavy line rim, 5⅝" d **500**

Urn, ovoid, circular fluted rim, incised body, mounted opposing ribbed handles on circular foot, tones of green, yellow, and brown, 11" h **1,300**

Urn, ovoid, circular overhanging fluted rim, incised body with circular foot, tones of green, yellow, and brown, 11¼" h **900**

Urn, ovoid, flared rim, high arched handles, green flower slip dec, 19" h **120**

Vase, bulbous base, sgraffito dec birds and flowers, tri–color, mkd "DDR, June 5. 1828, PA," 3⅝" h **1,500**

Washboard, poplar frame, 7 x 13½" **325**

RED WING

The Red Wing pottery category covers several potteries from Red Wing, Minnesota. In 1868 David Hallem started Red Wing Stoneware Co., the first pottery with stoneware as its primary product and with a red wing stamped under the glaze as its mark. The Minnesota Stoneware Co. started in 1883. The North Star Stoneware Co., 1892–1896, used a raised star and the words Red Wing as its mark.

The Red Wing Stoneware Co. and the Minnesota Stoneware Co. merged in 1892. The new company, the Red Wing Union Stoneware Company, made stoneware until 1920 when it introduced a pottery line which it continued until the 1940s. In 1936 the name was changed to Red Wing Potteries, Inc. During the 1930s it introduced several popular lines of hand–painted pattern dinnerware which were distributed through department stores, Sears, and gift stamp centers. Dinnerware production declined in the 1950s, being replaced by hotel and restaurant china in the early 1960s. The plant closed in 1967.

Red Wing stoneware is the most commonly pictured Red Wing in Country magazines. While it is true that the utilitarian and advertising stoneware pieces played a major role in the small towns and rural communities of the Midwest, so also did Red Wing dinnerware patterns, a fact often overlooked. Red Wing's Bob White pattern, designed by Charles Murphy, is touted by some as the most popular dinnerware pattern of the 1950s. Those desiring a solid color ware that was a bit more traditional than modern designs such as Fiesta often chose Red Wing's Village Green or Village Brown pattern. Each was available in thirty–six different forms.

References: Stanley Bougie and David Newkirk, *Price Guide & Supplement for Red Wing Dinnerware (1990–1991 Edition),* published by authors, 1990; Dan and Gail DePasquale and Larry Peterson, *Red Wing Collectibles,* Collector Books, 1990, 1997 value update; Dan and Gail DePasquale and Larry Peterson, *Red Wing Stoneware,* Collector Books, 1983, 1997 value update; David A. Newkirk, *A Guide to Red Wing Markings,* Monticello Printing, 1979; Ray Reiss, *Red Wing Dinnerware: Price and Identification Guide,* Property Publishing, 1997; Gary and Bonnie Tefft, *Red Wing Potters and Their Wares, Second Edition,* Locust Enterprises, 1987, 1995 value update.

Collectors' Club: Red Wing Collectors Society, Inc, 624 Jones Street, Eveleth, MN 55734.

GIFTWARE

Ash Receiver, pelican	$75
Basket, white	25
Bowl, spongeware, 7¼" d	90
Bowl, stoneware, blue dec, Greek Key border, mkd "Luhman & Sanders, Pottsville, Iowa," 8" d	80
Butter Crock, stoneware, gray stripe	180
Console Set, 6 pcs, deep green, 3 holes on rim hold 2" h white baby birds on branch, mother and father birds sit inside bowl, orig label, 12" d bowl, price for set	70
Cornucopia, burgundy, leaf dec	20
Figure, cowboy, hp	165
Figure, man with accordion, solid color	50
Jar, stoneware, Kansas Druggist adv	110
Planter, guitar	35
Planter, rabbit	30
Planter, swan	15
Vase, aqua, brown sprinkle ext, ivory int, V designs, 10½" h	15
Vase, chartreuse, stylized leaves on vertical strips, handled, 8" h	12

DINNERWARE

Bob White, bread and butter plate, 6" d	$7
Bob White, bread tray	80
Bob White, butter dish	70
Bob White, casserole, 2 qt	30
Bob White, cereal bowl, 6½" d	15
Bob White, fruit bowl, 5½" d	12
Bob White, lazy susan, with stand	90
Bob White, platter, 13" l	20
Bob White, soup bowl	15
Bob White, vegetable bowl, divided	25
Chevron, dinner plate, 8" d	5
Chevron, drip jar	25
Chevron, saucer	3
Chevron, sugar	20
Country Garden, dinner plate, 10½" d	20
Country Garden, gravy boat	25
Country Garden, salad plate, 8" d	15
Country Garden, vegetable bowl, divided	25
Driftwood, cup and saucer	7
Driftwood, nappy, 6½" d	20
Driftwood, salad plate, 8" d	12
Fondoso, bread and butter plate, 6½" d	5
Fondoso, creamer, small	8
Fondoso, syrup jug	30
Fruit Service, casserole, pineapple, large	35
Fruit Service, marmalade, apple	25
Fruit Service, salad bowl, pear, large	20
Iris, bowl, 5½" d	10
Iris, creamer	8

Iris, relish, 3 part, 12" l	20
Labriego, French casserole, oval, small	30
Labriego, creamer	15
Labriego, mug	20
Lute Song, celery tray, 16" l	8
Lute Song, vegetable bowl, divided	18
Magnolia, cup and saucer	7
Magnolia, saucer	2
Reed, ball jug, 16 oz	25
Reed, casserole, 7½" d	30
Reed, cup	15
Reed, demitasse saucer	8
Reed, eggcup	25
Reed, platter, oval, 12" l	20
Reed, syrup jug, 19 oz	30
Reed, teapot, 8 cup	55
Round Up, creamer	40
Round Up, dinner plate, chuckwagon, 10½" d	55
Round Up, salad bowl, 10½" d	80
Round Up, vegetable bowl, divided	65
Smart Set, butter dish, cov	250
Smart Set, casserole, 4 qt	65
Smart Set, cruets, pr, with stoppers and stand	165
Smart Set, dinner plate, 7½" d	8
Smart Set, relish tray, 3 part	55
Town and Country, cruet, with stopper	50
Town and Country, cup	8
Town and Country, dinner plate, 8" d	10
Town and Country, teapot	150
Village Green/Brown, casserole, 1 qt	15
Village Green/Brown, mug	20
Village Green/Brown, platter, tree–in–well, 13" l	22
Village Green/Brown, sauce dish	12
Village Green/Brown, teapot, 6 cup	30

REGAL

Regal China Corporation, Antioch, Illinois, was established in 1938. In the 1940s, the Royal China and Novelty Company, a distribution and sales organization, purchased Regal China. Royal used Regal to make the ceramic products that it sold.

In 1948 Ruth Van Tellingen Bendel designed Snuggle Hugs in the shape of bears, bunnies, pigs, etc. She also designed cookie jars, other figurines, and salt and pepper shaker sets.

Regal did large amounts of decorating for other firms, e.g., Hull's Red Riding Hood pieces. Regal has not sold to the retail trade since 1968, continuing to manufacture on a contract basis only. In 1976 Regal produced a cookie jar for Quaker Oats. 1983 products include a milk pitcher for Ovaltine and ship decanter and coffee mugs for Old Spice. Regal currently is a wholly owned subsidiary of Jim Beam Distilleries.

Only a limited number of Regal products have Country appeal. Look for items from Regal's Alice in Wonderland, Old MacDonald, and Snuggle Hugs series.

Alice in Wonderland, creamer, White Rabbit **$400**
Alice in Wonderland, salt and pepper shakers, pr, Alice, white and gold **500**
Old MacDonald, butter dish, cov, cow head on lid, ¼ lb **225**
Old MacDonald, canister, cereal, medium **200**
Old MacDonald, canister, peanuts **350**
Old MacDonald, canister, popcorn, large **280**
Old MacDonald, canister, pretzels, large **290**
Old MacDonald, canister, sugar, medium **200**
Old MacDonald, canister, tea, medium **250**
Old MacDonald, creamer, rooster **85**
Old MacDonald, ginger jar **90**
Old MacDonald, grease jar, pig **150**
Old MacDonald, salt and pepper shakers, pr, boy and girl **75**
Old MacDonald, salt and pepper shakers, pr, feed sack **180**
Old MacDonald, salt and pepper shakers, pr, flour sack, emb sheep **140**
Old MacDonald, teapot, duck head on lid **280**
Peek–A–Boos, shaker, white and red, small **250**
Snuggle Hugs, salt and pepper shakers, pr, bear, brown and pink **15**
Snuggle Hugs, salt and pepper shakers, pr, boy and dog, white **65**
Snuggle Hugs, salt and pepper shakers, pr, bunny, yellow, painted clothes . . . **45**
Snuggle Hugs, salt and pepper shakers, pr, Dutch boy and girl, white **40**
Snuggle Hugs, salt and pepper shakers, pr, Mary and lamb, yellow, black tail . **45**

ROCKINGHAM

Rockingham ware can be divided into two categories. The first consists of the fine china and porcelain pieces made between 1826 and 1842 by the Rockingham Company of Swinton, Yorkshire, England, and its predecessor firms: Swinton, Bingley, Don, Leeds, and Brameld.

The second category of Rockingham ware includes pieces produced in the famous Rockingham brown glaze, that became an intense and vivid purple–brown when fired. It had a dark, mottled tortoise shell appearance. The glaze was copied by many English and American potteries. American manufacturers who used Rockingham glaze include D. & J. Henderson of Jersey City, New Jersey, United States Pottery in Bennington, Vermont, potteries in East Liverpool, Ohio, and several potteries in Indiana and Illinois.

Rockingham glazed pieces are eagerly sought by Country collectors and decorators. The warm brown glazes blend with earth tones and similar color palettes. Rockingham ware is also found in unusual forms, such as foot warmers, bedpans, and spittoons.

Reference: Mary Brewer, *Collector's Guide to Rockingham: The Enduring Ware,* Collector Books, 1996.

Bank, opossum, 5⅝" h **$245**
Bank, pig, 2¾" h **45**
Bedpan, 17" l **12**
Bottle, figural, donut, molded ivy and foliage, 8¾" h **50**
Bottle, figural, hand, 6" h **105**
Bottle, figural, shoe, emb, "Ann Reid 1859," 6" h **245**
Bottle, figural, shoe, old gold paint on sole, 5¾" h **70**

Bowl, leaf design, emb ext, imp "Fire Proof, J. E. Jeffords & Co., Phila.,"
11½" d, 3" h   180
Bowl, monogram mark "SVPNT," 12¾"   65
Bowl, panel design, molded, plaint collar, scalloped bottom panels, brown
mottled ground, 6¼" d, 4⁹⁄₁₆" h   50
Bowl, shallow, 8¾" d, 3¼" h   70
Bowl, shallow, 10½" d, 2¾" h   80
Bowl, shallow, 11¾" d, 3¼" h   80
Bowl, shallow, 12³⁄₈" d, 4½" h   120
Bowl, shallow, 13" d, 3⁷⁄₈" h   35
Creamer, oval, molded floral designs, brown ground, arched handle, nick on
rim spout, 6⁷⁄₁₆" h   10
Crock, cov, emb peacocks, 6½" d, 5" h   70
Cuspidor, molded eagles dec, 6" d   60
Dish, round, 7" d, 2" h   35
Dish, square, emb rim, 9" sq   50
Dish, square, glazed, 8" sq   130
Figure, cat, seated, chipped ears, reglued at base, 11" h   100
Figure, dog, green and brown running glaze, 9¾" h   330
Flask, molded floral dec, band, 8" h   40
Food Mold, Turk's head, paneled sides, plain rim, fluted design bottom and
cone, brown mottled ground, 8⅛" d, 3¼" h   60
Food Mold, Turk's head, spiraled flutes, 9¼" d   50
Food Mold, Turk's head, straight tapered sides, blue flecks in glaze, 10½" d,
4" h   150
Jar, cov, 12" h   180
Jar, cov, leaf handle, 8" h, 8" d   90
Jar, cov, paneled sides, rounded rim on base and top, molded ring–shaped
handles, brown ground, 8¹⁄₁₆" d at rim, 5¼" h   45
Mixing Bowl, rounded flared sides and rim, brown mottled ground,
10⅝" d, 4½" h   30
Muffin Tray, 19th C, 14¾" h   110
Mug, cuspidor shape, 3½" h   190
Mush Bowl, round, flat bottom, sides flaring toward rim, brown mottled
ground, 9½" d at rim, 2½" h   40
Mustache Cup, toby, 4¼" h   120
Nesting Bowls, emb ext design, price for set of 3   80
Pie Plate, 9½" d, 19th C, price for set of 4   115
Pie Plate, 9⅝" d   80
Pie Plate, 10⁷⁄₈" d   90
Pitcher, deer, molded, brown and green variegated glaze, 9" h   50
Pitcher, hunt scenes, emb, 7" h   145
Pitcher, miniature, hound handle, pinpoint edge flakes, 3⅛" h   275
Pitcher, ovoid, flared foot, 7¼" h   160
Pitcher, panels, molded, 10¼" h   50
Pitcher, peacock, molded, 8½" h   80
Pitcher, shoulder rings, strap handle, 11¼" h   130
Pitcher, squatty, C–scroll handle, 4³⁄₈" h   75
Pitcher, swan in cattails, molded, 7" h   125
Pitcher, tulips, molded, 9" h   50
Plate, brown mottled ground, 9" d   85

Plate, mottled design, 9⅛" d **25**
Plate, 10½" d **100**
Platter, oval, 13¾" l **100**
Platter, oval, 15" l **175**
Presentation Pitcher, side medallion portraits, glaze frog figure on bottom
    int, mkd "Mrs. John Webb," 10" h **220**
Preserving Jar, keg shaped, 5½" h **25**
Salt Box, emb peacocks, crest, hanging hole, 6" d **50**
Soap Dish, leaf design, molded, 6" l **50**
Soap Dish, oval, 4⅞" l **55**
Soap Dish, round, rim chip, 5½" d **30**
Spittoon, American Eagles, emb, 6½" sq **70**
Spittoon, raised medallion, 7½" d **50**
Spittoon, shells, molded, surface flake, 7½" d **40**
Sugar Bowl, cov, 5⅞" h **280**
Teapot, cov, fern and foliage, molded, 8⅜" h **125**
Teapot, cov, leaf designs, molded, 8" h **45**
Teapot, cov, ribs and acanthus leaves, emb, 7¼" h **125**
Toby Jug, cov, man with spout, 10¼" h **190**
Toby Jug, cov, woman with flask and cup, 8½" h **60**
Tub, molded cherub heads, brown and blue variegated glaze, 4" h, 6⅜" d ... **190**
Vegetable Bowl, octagonal, spotted glaze, 11½" l **180**
Vegetable Bowl, oval, flared sides, rounded rim, brown mottled ground, 7⅞
    x 5½ x 1⅞" **20**
Washboard, pine frame, Rockingham scrubber insert, 12¾" w, 25½" h **520**
Water Pitcher, cylindrical, molded peacock and flowering tree on sides,
    molded beaded bands around sides, arched handle, brown mottled
    ground, 8⅛" h **45**
Water Pitcher, oval, molded acanthus leaf design below spout and handle,
    molded arched brown handle, chip on rim of spout, 9⅜" h **40**

ROSEVILLE

In the late 1880s a group of investors purchased the J. B. Owens Pottery in Roseville, Ohio, and made utilitarian stoneware items. In 1892 the firm was incorporated and joined by George F. Young who became general manager. Four generations of Youngs controlled Roseville until the early 1950s.

A series of acquisitions began: Midland Pottery of Roseville in 1898, Clark Stoneware Plant in Zanesville (formerly used by Peters and Reed), and Muskingum Stoneware (Mosaic Tile Company) in Zanesville. In 1898 the offices moved from Roseville to Zanesville.

In 1900 Roseville introduced its art pottery—Rozane. Rozane became a trade name to cover a large series of lines. The art lines were made in limited amounts after 1919.

The success of Roseville depended on its commercial lines, first developed by John J. Herald and Frederick Rhead in the first decades of the 1900s. In 1918 Frank Ferrell became art director and developed over eighty lines of pottery. The economic depression of the 1930s brought more lines, including Pine Cone.

In the 1940s a series of high gloss glazes were tried to revive certain lines. In 1952 Raymor dinnerware was produced. None of these changes brought economic success. In November 1954 Roseville was bought by the Mosaic Tile Company.

Country collectors are fond of Roseville pottery. Large collections of interesting patterns, shapes, and colors may be easily acquired. Baskets, urns, and vases readily lend themselves to Country settings as accent pieces. Because most Roseville pieces are marked, identification is easy and accurate.

References: Virginia Buxton, *Roseville Pottery: For Love or Money,* Tymbre Hill Publishing, 1996; John W. Humphries, *A Price Guide to Roseville Pottery By the Numbers,* published by author, 1997; Sharon and Bob Huxford, *The Collectors Encyclopedia of Roseville Pottery, First Series* (1976, 1997 value update), *Second Series,* (1980, 1997 value update), Collector Books; Randall B. Monsen, *Collectors' Compendium of Roseville Pottery, Vol I* (1995), *Vol II* (1997), Monsen and Baer.

Collectors' Club: Roseville's of the Past Pottery Club, PO Box 656, Clarcona, FL 32710.

Ashtray, Imperial II, blue	**$250**
Ashtray, Pine Cone, blue	**125**
Ashtray, Pine Cone, brown	**140**
Ashtray, Zephyr Lily, blue	**75**
Basket, Bittersweet, green, 810–10	**180**
Basket, Columbine, brown	**150**
Basket, Foxglove	**90**
Basket, Freesia, blue, 391–8	**100**
Basket, Freesia, brown, 390–7	**80**
Basket, Lustre, 8 x 5"	**90**
Basket, Magnolia, brown, 384–8	**80**
Basket, Montacello, brown, 632	**550**
Basket, Peony, pink, 278–10	**140**
Basket, Poppy, blue–green	**185**
Basket, Silhouette	**135**
Basket, Snowberry, blue	**150**
Basket, White Rose, pink, 363–10	**120**

Left: Vase, Bleeding Heart, 961–4, 4¹/₈" h, $75.
Right: Pitcher, juvenile, sitting bunnies, unmkd, 4" h, $125.

Basket, Zephyr Lily, brown **90**
Bookends, pr, Apple Blossom, green, 326–6 . . . .   **125**
Bookends, pr, Freesia, green **75**
Bookends, pr, Gardenia **165**
Bookends, pr, Pine Cone, blue **145**
Bookends, pr, Wincraft, blue **50**
Bowl, Baneda, pink **175**
Bowl, Carnelian I, pedestal, blue **60**
Bowl, Clematis, brown, 459–10 . . . .   **80**
Bowl, Columbine, blue, 402 . . . .   **80**
Bowl, Ferella, 12" d **700**
Bowl, Florentine, 7" d **75**
Bowl, Fuschia, green, 847–8 . . . .   **100**
Bowl, Imperial I, ftd **60**
Bowl, Jonquil, 621 . . . .   **50**
Bowl, Mostique, ivory, 6" d **25**
Bowl, Pine Cone, blue, 179–9 . . . .   **145**
Bud Vase, Peony, handles, 173, 7¼" h **80**
Bud Vase, Pine Cone, 7½ x 5" **375**
Bud Vase, Zephyr Lily, 7" h **90**
Candle Holders, pr, Carnelian II **130**
Candle Holders, pr, Cherry Blossom, yellow and white flowers, cream and
    brown ground **450**
Candle Holders, pr, Clematis, brown, 1154–2 . . . .   **50**
Candle Holders, pr, Cosmos **50**
Candle Holders, pr, Fuschia, green, 1133–5 . . . .   **160**
Candle Holders, pr, Lily, 1161–2 . . . .   **45**
Candle Holders, pr, Panel, brown **50**
Candle Holders, pr, Tourmaline, dark pink and turquoise **100**
Candle Holders, pr, White Rose **75**
Candle Holders, pr, Zephyr Lily, green, 1163 . . . .   **80**
Centerpiece Bowl, oval, Ferella **700**
Centerpiece Bowl, oval, Topeo **100**
Compote, Florentine **35**
Console Bowl, Fuschia, green, 353–14 . . . .   **145**
Console Bowl, Teasel, beige, 345–12 . . . .   **50**
Console Bowl, White Rose, blue, 393–12 . . . .   **100**
Console Set, Calla Lily, 7" d bowl, pr candle holders **100**
Console Set, Columbine, blue, 10" d bowl, pr 2½" h candle holders **175**
Cornucopia, Bleeding Heart, green, 141-6 . . . .   **85**
Cornucopia, Columbine, 7" h **70**
Cornucopia, Foxglove, blue, 166–6 . . . .   **50**
Cornucopia, Peony, tan, 171–8 . . . .   **125**
Cornucopia, Snowberry, 6" h **50**
Creamer and Sugar, Zephyr Lily, brown **95**
Dish, cov, Volpatto, ftd **275**
Double Cornucopia, White Rose, blue, 145–8 . . . .   **90**
Ewer, Clematis, 18–15 . . . .   **300**
Ewer, Foxglove, blue, 5–10 . . . .   **150**
Ewer, Fuschia **275**
Ewer, Gardenia, tan, 618, 15" h **230**

Ewer, Magnolia, brown, 15–15 250
Floor Vase, Azurean, Claud Leffler, fish dec on shaded blue ground, sgd by
   artist, 12½ x 3" 3,500
Floor Vase, Bushberry, brown, 12½" h 230
Floor Vase, Carnelian II, 16 x 11" 2,400
Floor Vase, Freesia, 2 handled, 19 x 8¼" 600
Floor Vase, Wisteria, bottle shaped, 2 handled, 15½ x 7" 2,500
Floor Vase, Zephyr Lily, 18" h 850
Flowerpot and Saucer, Bushberry, 5" h 180
Flowerpot and Saucer, Poppy 250
Gravy Boat, Raymor, terra cotta 20
Hanging Basket, Bushberry, pink 145
Hanging Basket, Fuschia, brown 200
Hanging Basket, Ixia, yellow 190
Hanging Basket, Mostique, 6½ x 6½" 350
Hanging Basket, White Rose, blue 150
Jardiniere, Baneda, pedestal, 24½ x 11" 2,100
Jardiniere, Columbine, blue, 655–4 70
Jardiniere, Dahlrose, pedestal, unmkd, 30½ x 14" 950
Jardiniere, Donatello, pedestal, 22" h 600
Jardiniere, Futura, pedestal, unmkd, small repair, 28 x 15" 1,000
Jardiniere, Rozane, pedestal, 29 x 14" 400
Jardiniere, Sunflower 80
Jardiniere, Water Lily, pedestal, pink 700
Lamp, white, pink, yellow, and blue flowers on shaded orange, green, and
   blue ground, complete with fittings, unmkd, 10½ x 6½" 650
Pitcher, Colonial, 8¼" h 50
Pitcher, Holland, 6½" h 225
Pitcher, Magnolia, 388–6 115
Planter, Magnolia, green, 183–6 45
Planter, Peony, 387, 8" l 90
Planter, Poppy, blue 50
Planter, Vista, round, 449–6, 3½ x 7" 150
Planter, Water Lily, hanging, brown 165

Left: Basket, Freesia, 390–7, small handle flake, 7" h, $80. Photo courtesy Collectors Auction Services.

Right: Wall Pocket, Dahlrose, 8⅛" h, $325.

Jardiniere and Pedestal, Freesia, brown, raised mark, minor chip to jardiniere foot ring, 24¹/₂" h, 12" d, $425. Photo courtesy David Rago Auctions.

Umbrella Stand, Chloran, octagonal, raised floral dec, matte green glaze, c1907, 23¹/₄" h	280
Umbrella Stand, Sunflower, yellow flowers, brown, green, and blue ground, 20¹/₄ x 11"	6,000
Urn, Cherry Blossom, brown, 7" h	180
Urn, Florentine, brown, 463–5	85
Vase, Baneda, pink, 4¹/₂" h	165
Vase, Blackberry, beehive, 5¹/₂" h	240
Vase, Carnelian II, red, 5" h	100
Vase, Clematis, brown, 128–8	45
Vase, Ferella, bulbous, 5¹/₂ x 6¹/₂"	550
Vase, Foxglove, green and pink, 53–14	280
Vase, Fuschia, blue, 895, 7" h	120
Vase, Futura, balloon shape, unmkd, 8¹/₂ x 6³/₄"	1,300
Vase, Futura, fan shape, blue, 6" h	375
Vase, Iris, 917–6	80
Vase, Jonquil, 9¹/₂" h	450
Vase, Laurel, yellow, 6" h	95
Vase, Luffa, 2 handled, 12¹/₄ x 7¹/₄"	700
Vase, Mayfair, 10" h	70
Vase, Pine Cone, blue, 711–10	430
Vase, Pine Cone, fan shape, tan gloss, 272–6	70
Vase, Primrose, brown, 767–8	85
Vase, Rosecraft, black, 5¹/₂" h	50
Vase, Savona, green, 12" h	145
Vase, Tourmaline	50
Vase, Tuscany, gray, 8" h	90
Vase, White Rose, blue, 147–8	80
Vase, Wincraft	30
Vase, Windsor, spherical, 2 handled, 7¹/₂ x 7³/₄"	400
Vase, Zephyr Lily, green, 131–7	45
Vessel, Rozane Crystallis, squat, flaring base, 3 buttresses, green and sand mottled microcrystalline glaze, unmkd, 6 x 7¹/₂"	1,000

Wall Pocket, Bittersweet, green **300**
Wall Pocket, Carnelian I, pink and blue **175**
Wall Pocket, Cherry Blossom, 8 x 5¼" **1,600**
Wall Pocket, Clematis, brown **100**
Wall Pocket, Dahlrose, 10" h **325**
Wall Pocket, Imperial II, 7½ x 9" **600**
Wall Pocket, Lotus, burgundy **150**
Wall Pocket, Mostique, 10½" l **150**
Window Box, Dahlrose, 6¼ x 16" **450**

ROYAL CHINA

The Royal China Company, located in Sebring, Ohio, utilized remodeled facilities that originally housed the Oliver China Company and later the E. H. Sebring Company. Royal China began operations in 1934.

The company produced an enormous number of dinnerware patterns. The back of the piece usually contains the names of the shape, line, and decoration. In addition to many variations of company backstamps, Royal China also produced objects with private backstamps. All records of these markings were lost in a fire in 1970.

The company's Currier and Ives pattern, designed by Gordon Parker, was introduced in 1949–50. Early marks were date coded. Other early 1950s patterns include Colonial Homestead and Old Curiosity Shop.

In 1964 Royal China purchased the French–Saxon China Company, Sebring, which it operated as a wholly owned subsidiary. On December 31, 1969, Royal China was acquired by the Jeannette Corporation. When fire struck the Royal China Sebring plant in 1970, Royal moved its operations to the French–Saxon plant.

The company changed hands several times, being owned briefly by the Coca–Cola Company, the J. Corporation from Boston, and Nordic Capitol of New York, New York. Production continued until August 1986 when operations ceased.

Country collectors concentrate on specific patterns. Among the most favored are Bluebell (1940s), Currier and Ives (1949–50), Colonial Homestead (c1951–52), Old Curiosity Shop (early 1950s), Regal (1937), Royalty (1936), blue and pink willow ware (1940s), and Windsor.

Royal China patterns were widely distributed. Colonial Homestead was sold by Sears through the 1960s. The result is that pieces are relatively common and prices moderate.

Because of the ease of accessibility, only purchase pieces in fine to excellent condition. Do not buy pieces whose surface is marked or marred in any way.

Reference: Eldon R. Aupperle, *A Collector's Guide for Currier & Ives Dinnerware,* published by author, 1996.

Collectors' Club: Currier & Ives Dinnerware Collectors Club, RD 2, Box 394, Hollidaysburg, PA 16648.

Colonial Homestead, bread and butter plate, 6" d **$3**
Colonial Homestead, casserole, cov **35**
Colonial Homestead, cup and saucer **5**
Colonial Homestead, dinner plate **4**
Colonial Homestead, fruit bowl, 5½" d **4**
Colonial Homestead, salad plate, 7" d **3**
Colonial Homestead, vegetable bowl, 9" d **8**

Currier & Ives, ashtray   10
Currier & Ives, baker   15
Currier & Ives, berry bowl   3
Currier & Ives, bread and butter plate, 6" d   3
Currier & Ives, cake plate, 10" d   25
Currier & Ives, casserole, cov   85
Currier & Ives, cereal bowl, 6½" d   6
Currier & Ives, chop plate, 12" d   17
Currier & Ives, chop plate, 13" d   25
Currier & Ives, coffee mug   22
Currier & Ives, creamer   10
Currier & Ives, creamer and sugar, cov   12
Currier & Ives, cup and saucer   4
Currier & Ives, custard, milk glass   5
Currier & Ives, dinner plate, 10½" d   5
Currier & Ives, flat soup, 8½" d   12
Currier & Ives, fruit bowl   3
Currier & Ives, Hostess Set, 9 pcs   100
Currier & Ives, luncheon plate, 9" d   15
Currier & Ives, platter, oval   17
Currier & Ives, salad plate, 7¼" d   8
Currier & Ives, salt and pepper shakers, pr   20
Currier & Ives, soup bowl   12
Currier & Ives, sugar, cov   12
Currier & Ives, tumbler, milk glass   5
Currier & Ives, vegetable bowl, open, 9" d   12
Memory Lane, bread and butter plate, 6" d   4
Memory Lane, cake plate, handled   15
Memory Lane, cup and saucer   6
Memory Lane, dinner plate, 10" d   8
Memory Lane, fruit bowl, 5½" d   2
Memory Lane, gravy boat and underplate   20
Memory Lane, luncheon plate, 9" d   7
Memory Lane, salad plate, 7" d   6
Memory Lane, saucer   1

*Currier & Ives, pie plate, mkd
"Royal China Jeannette Corp,
Conventional and Microwave Oven
Approved, Dishwasher Safe, USA,"
10" d, $15.*

Memory Lane, soup bowl, 8¼" d 8
Memory Lane, vegetable bowl, 10" d 25
Old Curiosity Shop, bread and butter plate 3
Old Curiosity Shop, cereal bowl, tab handles 10
Old Curiosity Shop, creamer and sugar, cov 12
Old Curiosity Shop, flat soup, 8½" d 7
Old Curiosity Shop, platter, oval, handled, 10" l 15
Old Curiosity Shop, salt and pepper shakers, pr 12
Old Curiosity Shop, vegetable bowl, open, 9" d 13
Regal, butter dish 25
Regal, creamer 6
Regal, gravy boat 15
Regal, sugar 12
Regal, teapot 25
Royalty, bread and butter plate, 6¼" d 6
Royalty, casserole 30
Royalty, gravy boat 15
Royalty, saucer 3
Windsor, casserole 28
Windsor, coffeepot 38
Windsor, gravy boat 18
Windsor, platter, oval, 8¼" l 9
Windsor, soup bowl, 7¾" d 15

ROYAL COPLEY

Royal Copley and Royal Windsor are trade names of the Spaulding China Company. Royal Copley, representing approximately 85% of all Spaulding production, was sold through chain stores such as Grants, Kresges, Murphys, and Woolworth along with an occasional gift or department store. Royal Windsor items were sold to the florist trade.

Spaulding China, Sebring, Ohio, was founded in 1942. Initially located in the abandoned plant of the Alliance Vitreous China Company, Spaulding eventually acquired and renovated the Sebring Rubber Company plant. Morris Feinberg served as president; James G. Eardley as plant manager.

Initially a straight tunnel kiln and low-temperature decorating kiln were used for decal and gold decorated wares. In 1948 the tunnel kiln was replaced by a continuous circular kiln. Daily production was 18,000 pieces.

The company deliberately chose names with an English air, e.g., Spaulding not Spalding. Royal Copley and Royal Windsor were chosen because they sounded regal and fine. Even marketing terms such as Crown Assortment and Oxford Assortment continued this English theme. The company's motto was "Gift Shop Merchandise at Chain Store Prices." Pieces were marked with a paper label.

Birds, ducks, piggy banks, Oriental boy and girl wall pockets, and roosters were among Royal Copley's biggest sellers. The smaller birds originally retailed for 25¢.

Cheap Japanese imports and labor difficulties plagued Spaulding throughout the post-war period. In 1957 Morris Feinberg retired, contracting with nearby China Craft to fill Spaulding's remaining orders. Spaulding was sold to a Mr. Shiffman, who made small sinks for mobile homes. After being closed for several years, Eugene Meskil of Holiday Designs bought the plant. The company made accessories, canisters, cookie jars, and teapots. Richard C. Durstein of Pittsburgh bought the plant in 1982.

Reference: Mike Schneider, *Royal Copley: Identification and Price Guide*, Schiffer Publishing, 1995.

Newsletter: *The Copley Courier,* 1639 North Catalina Street, Burbank, CA 91505.

Ashtray, leaf and bird, 5½" d	$20
Bank, rooster, 7½" h	50
Bank, teddy bear, 7½" h	60
Figure, cat, 8" h	25
Figure, cockatoo, 7¼" h	25
Figure, deer on sled, 6½" h	25
Figure, parrot, yellow, 5" h	12
Figure, rooster, white, green base, 8" h	50
Figure, swallow, 8" h	20
Figure, warbler, 5" h	12
Lamp, Colonial gentleman, orig shade	40
Pitcher, daffodil, yellow and pink, 8" h	32
Pitcher, floral, pink, blue ground, 8" h	30
Planter, apple and finch, 6½" h	18
Planter, cocker spaniel head, 5" h	10
Planter, dog and mailbox, 7¾" h	18
Planter, girl with pigtails, 7" h	20
Planter, hummingbird, 5¼" h	30
Planter, ivory dec, paper label, 4 x 7"	12
Planter, kitten with yarn, yellow	30
Planter, pony, 5½" h	12
Planter, rooster and wheelbarrow, paper label, 8" h	55
Planter, sitting mallard, 5" h	20
Vase, cornucopia, gold trim, 8¼" h	20
Vase, leaf, stylized design, paper label, 5½" h	8
Vase, trailing leaf and vine, 8" h	15
Wall Pocket, apple	15
Wall Pocket, cocker spaniel head	18
Wall Pocket, mill	70

Planter, kitten in basket, pastel colors, glossy, unmkd, 1950s, 8" h, 8½" l, $35.

SHAWNEE

In 1937 brothers Malcolm A. and Roy W. Schweiker acquired the 650,000–square–foot plant that formerly housed the American Encaustic Tiling Company. Addis E. Hull, Jr., ceramic engineer and president/general manager of the A. E. Hull Pottery Company, was hired as president. Louise Bauer, the in–house designer, developed a company logo consisting of an arrowhead inside of which was a profile of a Shawnee Indian head.

Shawnee Pottery produced its first wares in August 1937. Dinnerware production was targeted toward companies such as S. S. Kresge, McCrory Stores Corporation, Sears Roebuck and Company, and F. W. Woolworth. In 1938 Rum Rill Pottery Company moved its production of art pottery from its Red Wing, Minnesota, location to Shawnee.

Between 1942 and July of 1946 over 90% of Shawnee's production was related to war contracts. Realizing that the war would soon end, Shawnee hired designer Robert Heckman in 1945. Heckman was responsible for the King Corn line, Pennsylvania Dutch line, and numerous figurine, planter, and vase designs.

Like many potteries, Shawnee experienced major financial difficulties following World War II. The wholesale market was simply not lucrative enough. During this period Shawnee sold vast quantities of pieces to small sales outlets. Many of these individuals added decals and gold paint to Shawnee factory stock. Financial difficulties continued. Record losses were witnessed in 1953.

When John F. Bonistall became president in 1954, he eliminated hand–painted decoration in favor of spray–painted motifs. He also shifted emphasis from the dinnerware to decorative items. The Queen Corn line replaced the King Corn line. The company survived until 1961.

Shawnee can be found marked "Shawnee," "Shawnee U.S.A.," "USA—," "Kenwood," or with character names, e.g., "Pat. Smiley," "Pat. Winnie," etc. Many pieces are unmarked.

Many Shawnee pieces came in several color variations. Some pieces also contained both painted and decal decorations. The available literature will indicate some, but not all of these variations. Because of limited collector interest, Shawnee dinnerware lines such as Cameo, Cheria (Petit Point), Diora, and Touche (Liana) remain modestly priced.

References: Pamela Duval Curran, *Shawnee Pottery: The Full Encyclopedia*, Schiffer Publishing, 1995, Jim and Bev Mangus, *Shawnee Pottery: An Identification and Value Guide*, Collector Books, 1994, 1996 value update; Mark Supnick, *Collecting Shawnee Pottery: A Pictorial Reference and Price Guide*, L–W Book Sales, 1989, 1997 value update; Duane and Janice Vanderbilt, *The Collector's Guide to Shawnee Pottery*, Collector Books, 1992, 1996 value update.

Collectors' Club: Shawnee Pottery Collectors Club, PO Box 713, New Smyrna Beach, FL 32170.

Additonal Listings: See Kitchen, Cookie Jars.

Bank, Smiley Pig, dark brown base	**$365**
Bud Vase, swan, gold trim	18
Coffeepot, large emb flower, #54	100
Creamer, tulips	35
Figure, dog, gold trim	80
Figure, rabbit	35

Grease Jar, White Corn, gold **150**
King Corn, casserole, cov, #74 .... **85**
King Corn, cereal bowl, #94 .... **55**
King Corn, creamer, #70 .... **30**
King Corn, mixing bowl, #5 .... **40**
King Corn, mixing bowl, #6 .... **40**
King Corn, mug, #69, 8 oz **45**
King Corn, platter, #96, 12" l **30**
King Corn, relish tray, #79 .... **40**
King Corn, salad plate, #93 .... **40**
King Corn, salt and pepper shakers, pr, large **35**
King Corn, sugar, cov **25**
King Corn, teapot, individual **250**
Pitcher, Bo Peep, blue bonnet **80**
Pitcher, grist mill, #35 .... **15**
Planter, bird and cup, #502 .... **12**
Planter, boy at high stump **8**
Planter, boy with wheelbarrow, #750 .... **15**
Planter, children on shoe **15**
Planter, coal bucket **12**
Planter, conestoga wagon, green, 6 x 9½" **20**
Planter, doe and fawn, #669 .... **15**
Planter, fawn, yellow, #624 .... **25**
Planter, girl with flower basket, #616 .... **15**
Planter, man with pushcart, #621 .... **15**
Planter, rabbit at stump, #606, green **10**
Planter, skunk, #512, pink **30**
Planter, 2 coolies carrying basket, #537 .... **5**
Queen Corn, butter dish, cov, #72 .... **35**
Queen Corn, dinner plate, #68, 10½" d **10**
Queen Corn, fruit bowl, #92, 6" d **15**
Queen Corn, mixing bowl, #5, 5" d **20**

Left: Teapot, Tom the Piper's Son, #44, mkd "U.S.A.," $450.

Right: Creamer, elephant, mkd "USA," 4¼" h, $12. Photo courtesy Ray Morykan Auctions.

Queen Corn, mixing bowl, #6, 6½" d 25
Queen Corn, mixing bowl, #8, 8" d 30
Queen Corn, mug, #69, 8 oz 30
Queen Corn, platter, #79, 12" l 30
Queen Corn, salt and pepper shakers, pr, small 20
Queen Corn, shaker, #76, 3¼" h 5
Queen Corn, shaker, #77, 5¼" h 8
Queen Corn, teapot, cov 75
Queen Corn, vegetable bowl, #95, 9" d 35
Salt and Pepper Shakers, pr, chanticleers, large 55
Salt and Pepper Shakers, pr, Jack/Jill, large 100
Salt and Pepper Shakers, pr, Muggsy, large 170
Salt and Pepper Shakers, pr, Smiley, peach bib, large 125
Salt and Pepper Shakers, pr, White Corn, gold trim, large 150
Salt and Pepper Shakers, pr, Boy Blue/Bo Peep, small 25
Salt and Pepper Shakers, pr, chef, S & P, small 20
Salt and Pepper Shakers, pr, ducks, small 40
Salt and Pepper Shakers, pr, flower/fern, turquoise, small 25
Salt and Pepper Shakers, pr, flower cluster, small 32
Salt and Pepper Shakers, pr, flowerpots, small 22
Salt and Pepper Shakers, pr, fruit, small 25
Salt and Pepper Shakers, pr, milk cans, small 20
Salt and Pepper Shakers, pr, owls, blue eyes, small 15
Salt and Pepper Shakers, pr, owls, gold trim, small 35
Salt and Pepper Shakers, pr, owls, green eyes, small 23
Salt and Pepper Shakers, pr, Puss 'N Boots, small 40
Salt and Pepper Shakers, pr, Smiley/Winnie, blue, small 50
Salt and Pepper Shakers, pr, White Corn, small 25
Spoon Rest, flower, yellow and green 20
Sugar, cov, Granny Anne 60
Sugar Shaker, White Corn, gold trim 150
Teapot, emb rose, gold trim 35
Vase, cornucopia, #865 20
Vase, dove, #829, yellow 30
Vase, leaf 30
Vase, swan, yellow, gold trim 35
Wall Pocket, birds at birdhouse 25
Wall Pocket, Bo Peep, #586 25
Wall Pocket, telephone, #529 22
Wall Pocket, wheat 35

SPATTERWARE

Spatterware is made of common earthenware, although occasionally creamware was used. The earliest English examples were made about 1780. The peak period of production was 1810–1840. Marked pieces are rare. Firms known to have made spatterware are Adams, Barlow, and Harvey and Cotton.

The amount of spatter decoration varies from piece to piece. Some objects simply have decorated borders. These often are decorated with a brush, requiring several hundred touches per square inch to achieve the spatter effect. Other pieces have the entire surface covered with spatter. Aesthetics of the final product is a key to value.

Collectors today focus on the patterns—Cannon, Castle, Fort, Peafowl, Rainbow, Rose, Thistle, Schoolhouse, etc. On flat ware the decoration is in the center. On hollow pieces it occurs on both sides.

Color of spatter is another price key. Blue and red are most common. Green, purple, and brown are in a middle group. Black and yellow are scarce.

Like any soft paste, spatterware was easily broken or chipped. Prices are for pieces in very good to mint condition.

References: Kevin McConnell, *Spongeware and Spatterware,* Schiffer Publishing, 1990; Carl and Ada Robacker, *Spatterware and Sponge,* A. S. Barnes & Co, 1978.

Creamer, Flower, faded red and green, blue spatter, glaze flakes on rim, 4¼" h **$465**

Creamer, Fort, gray, black, red, and green, blue spatter, repair and short hairlines, 4½" h **190**

Creamer, Peafowl, black, yellow ocher, and blue, green spatter, black edge stripe, leaf handle, 3¾" h **500**

Creamer, Peafowl, blue, red, yellow, and black, blue spatter, stains, small chips, repaired handle, 5⅛" h **190**

Creamer, Peafowl, octagonal, red, yellow, green, and black, blue spatter, repaired handle, 5½" h **330**

Creamer, Rainbow, red, yellow, and green, hairline in cup **95**

Creamer, Rose, red, black, and green, brown and black spatter, 4" h **250**

Creamer, Rose and Cornflower, paneled, red, blue, green, and black, red and blue spatter, stains and hairlines, 5⅛" h **150**

Creamer, School House, red, yellow, green, and black, blue spatter, damage and glued repair, 4" h **300**

Creamer, Thistle, red and green, blue spatter, 4½" h **440**

Cup, handleless, miniature, Christmas Balls, red and green, chip on table ring of cup **1,050**

Left: Pitcher, Rainbow Loop, green and red spatter, 6" h, $1,100. Photo courtesy Jackson's Auctioneers & Appraisers.

Right: Teapot, cov, Peafowl, red, blue, yellow, and black peafowl, blue spatter, 1830–50, 6" h, 10½" w, $250.

Cup, handleless, miniature, Primrose, purple, green, black, and yellow, red
   spatter **220**
Cup, handleless, miniature, Rooster, black, yellow, blue, and red, red spatter . **95**
Cup, handleless, miniature, Tree, green and black, brown spatter **135**
Cup and Saucer, handleless, Black Dots, blue spatter **3,250**
Cup and Saucer, handleless, Flower, blue, black, and red, brown spatter **470**
Cup and Saucer, handleless, Peafowl, black, red, blue, green, and yellow
   ocher, green spatter, glazed over chip on table ring **1,600**
Cup and Saucer, handleless, Peafowl, blue, green, red, and black open body,
   green tree, red spatter **1,700**
Cup and Saucer, handleless, Peafowl, miniature, red, blue, yellow, and
   black, green spatter **330**
Cup and Saucer, handleless, Plaid, blue, red, and green **530**
Cup and Saucer, handleless, Rainbow, red and blue, green dots, molded
   panels, wear and minor stains, hairline in foot of cup **465**
Cup and Saucer, handleless, Rooster, red, blue, yellow ocher, and black,
   blue spatter, pinpoint flake on rim of cup **360**
Cup and Saucer, handleless, Rose, red, green, and black, purple spatter, pin-
   point flake on saucer table ring **245**
Cup and Saucer, handleless, School House, red, green, and brown, red
   spatter **80**
Cup and Saucer, handleless, Star, red, green, and yellow, blue spatter, minor
   damage and light overall stain **330**
Cup and Saucer, handleless, Thistle, red and green, purple spatter **520**
Cup and Saucer, handleless, Tulip, red, green, yellow, and black, blue spat-
   ter, stains, hairline on cup **100**
Dish, Rose, oblong, octagonal, red, green, and black, repair, 6³/₄" l **165**
Inkwell, figural shoe, red, black, and green, stick spatter, edge chip, small
   hole, 4¹/₂" l **60**
Mug, blue spatter, wear, stains and flakes on rim, 3⁷/₈" h **40**
Mug, maroon and green, 2³/₄" h **245**
Mug, Peafowl, red, yellow ocher, green, and black, leaf handle, hairlines,
   stains, poorly repaired chips, 3¹/₈" h **65**
Pepper Pot, pierced domed cov, Peafowl, blue, ocher, rose, and black, yel-
   low spatter, mkd "Staffordshire," c1840, 4³/₄" h **1,200**
Pitcher, Flower, white reserves with green, pink, yellow, and black flower on
   front and back, blue spatter, stains and wear, 7⁵/₈" h **330**
Pitcher, Fort, gray, black, red, and green, blue spatter, molded handle and
   spout, damage and old yellow repairs, 7³/₈" h **385**
Pitcher, House, purple, brown, and green, light blue spatter, leaf handle, pin-
   point flakes, 5¹/₈" h **3,000**
Pitcher, Rainbow, red, blue, green, yellow, and black, 7¹/₂" h **580**
Pitcher and Bowl Set, Peafowl, red, green, blue, and black, imp "Adams,"
   11" h pitcher, 13¹/₂" d bowl **630**
Pitcher and Bowl Set, Rose, red, green, and black, blue spatter, hairlines,
   small chips, 12" h pitcher, 13¹/₂" d bowl **630**
Plate, Bull's Eye, red spatter, 9¹/₄" d, price for 6 .... **600**
Plate, Castle, brown spatter, minor wear and crazing, 8¹/₂" d **340**
Plate, Castle, green spatter, 8³/₈" d **245**
Plate, center swag design, red, blue, green, purple, and yellow, red spatter
   border, crazing, 9¹/₄" d **2,500**

Platter, yellow and blue flowers, green leaves, cream ground, red and black sponged border design, 13½" l, 11" w, $175.

Plate, Floral, Gaudy polychrome, red stick spatter, mkd "Scotch Ivory," 10" d **200**

Plate, Flower, red with black stem and green leaves, blue spatter design border with red stripes, "Cotton and Barlow" imp mark, minor stains, 9⅞" d .. **145**

Plate, Peafowl, blue, orange, red, and black, red spatter, small unglazed area below peafowl head, 8¼" d **550**

Plate, Pomegranate, red, blue, green, and black, blue spatter, wear and rim chips, 8½" d **385**

Plate, Rose, red, green, and black, blue spatter, Adams, 7½" d **330**

Plate, Snowflake, red, blue, and green, stick spatter, chip on underside of lip, 7¾" d **110**

Plate, Star, red, green, and yellow, blue spatter, 8¼" d **600**

Plate, Thistle, red and green, red spatter, 8¼" d **140**

Plate, Tulip, red, green, and black, yellow spatter, crazing, stains, and repair, 8½" d **135**

Platter, Holly Berry, purple spatter, 10⅞" d **175**

Sauce Bowl, Peafowl, red, blue, green, and black, blue spatter, imp "Adams," 5¼" d **80**

Soup Plate, Dahlia, red, blue, and green, blue spatter, wear and some glaze wear on flower, 9⅜" d **525**

Soup Plate, Peafowl, blue, yellow ocher, red, and black, 10½" d **2,100**

Soup Plate, Peafowl, red, blue, green, and black, green spatter, chips, 4⅜" h **1,550**

Soup Plate, Tulip, red, blue, green, and black, purple spatter, "Barber & Till, Opaque China" imp mark, 10½" d **230**

Sugar, cov, Fort, black, green, and red, blue spatter, crazing and wear, lid edges and finial are chipped, 4½" h **360**

Sugar, cov, Peafowl, paneled, blue, green, red, and black, red spatter, stains, edge damage and crazing, finial and rim poorly repaired, 7¾" h **165**

Sugar, cov, Peafowl, red, 2 shades of blue, yellow, green, and black peafowl in tree, red and blue rainbow spatter rim and lid, rim and lid repairs, crow's foot in bottom, 4⅞" h **330**

Sugar, cov, Pinwheel Flower, blue spatter, 4½" h **550**

Sugar, cov, Rainbow, red and blue spatter, stains, wear, some damage, glued
    break in lid, 4³/₈" d **145**
Sugar, cov, Rainbow, red, blue, and green, Adam's Rose in red, green, and
    black, scalloped rim, imp "Adams," minor glaze wear on rim, 9" d **500**
Sugar, cov, Rose, brown spatter, crow's foot and minor edge wear, 5" h **300**
Sugar, cov, Tulip, blue, red, green, and black, red spatter, yellowed repairs,
    4¹/₂" h **165**
Teapot, cov, Acorn and Oak Leaf, green, black, teal, and yellow ocher, red
    spatter, 8¹/₄" h **550**
Teapot, cov, blue and white spatter, 5¹/₂" h **200**
Teapot, cov, Peafowl, blue, yellow, green, and black, red spatter, several
    chips on lid, spout repair, 7¹/₄" h **1,650**
Teapot, cov, Rooster, red, blue, yellow, and black, blue spatter, 5³/₄" h **275**
Teapot, cov, Rose, red and green spatter, 6¹/₄" h **275**
Teapot, cov, Tree, green and black, blue spatter, molded flower finial and
    handle, minor stains, 6" h **330**
Tea Set, miniature, blue and white spatter, 5³/₄" h teapot, creamer, sugar, and
    2 handleless cups, chips, price for set **120**
Toddy Plate, Tulip, red, green, and black, blue spatter, 6¹/₂" d **630**
Vase, molded swirled ribs, blue and white sponge spatter, 5¹/₂" h **165**
Vegetable Bowl, open, Fort, gray, black, red, and green, blue spatter, repair,
    10¹/₂" l **550**
Vegetable Bowl, open, Rose, red, green, and black, blue spatter, 8³/₈" l **250**
Waste Bowl, Eagle and Shield, blue transfer, blue spatter, hairline on base,
    6¹/₂" d **130**
Waste Bowl, Fort, gray, black, red, and green, blue spatter, repair, foot has
    stains and small chips, 5⁵/₈" d, 3¹/₂" h **300**
Waste Bowl, House, red, yellow, black, and green, blue spatter, 5³/₄" d, 3" h ..**1,375**

SPONGEWARE

Spongeware is a specific type of decoration, not a type of pottery or glaze.

Spongeware decoration is found on many types of pottery bodies—ironstone, red-ware, stoneware, yellow ware, etc. It was made in both England and the United States. Marked pieces indicate a starting date of 1815, with manufacturing extending to the 1880s.

Decoration is varied. In some pieces the sponging is minimal with the white under-glaze dominant. Other pieces appear to be sponged solidly on both sides. Pieces from 1840–1860 have sponging which appears in either a circular movement or a streaked horizontal technique.

Examples are found in blue and white, the most common colors. Other prevalent colors are browns, greens, ochers, and greenish blue. The greenish blue results from blue sponging which has been overglazed in a pale yellow. A red overglaze produces a black or navy color.

Other colors are blue and red (found on English creamware and American earth-enware of the 1880s), gray, grayish green, red, dark green on stark white, dark green on mellow yellow, and purple.

References: Kevin McConnell, *Spongeware and Spatterware,* Schiffer Publishing, 1990; Earl F. and Ada Robacker, *Spatterware and Sponge,* A. S. Barnes & Co, 1978.

Bank, bottle shaped, blue polka dots on neck, stenciled blue initials "J.W.B.,"
lip chips, 6" h **$750**
Bank, eagle, teal sponging, Roseville, 1900–10 .... **225**
Bank, pig, brown and blue sponging **70**
Bean Pot, blue sponging **450**
Bean Pot, blue and white sponging, 4⅝" h **400**
Bowl, blue and white sponging, stains and crazing, 6½" d, and 7¼" d, price
for pair **55**
Bowl, blue sponge int, oval, ironstone, 7" w **200**
Bowl, blue sponging, 8½" sq, 2⅜" h **350**
Bowl, gray and blue sponging, white ground, hairlines, 9½" d, 4" h **55**
Bowl, red sponging, paneled, Cobb, WI adv, 12¼" d **130**
Butter Crock, cov, blue and white sponging, molded pinwheels, wire bail
with wooden handle, 7½" d **220**
Butter Crock, cov, dark blue sponging, molded rim, 3 rim hairlines, 5½" h ... **110**
Butter Crock, open, blue and white sponging, "Butter" on front, wire bail,
wooden handle, 6" d **80**
Butter Crock, open, blue and white sponging, center white band with dark
blue label "Butter" on front and "Village Farm Dairy" on back, hairlines,
5¾" h **165**
Butter Crock, open, blue and white sponging, molded fruit, wire handle
missing, minor edge chips and crazing, 7" h **135**
Chamber Pot, blue sponging, salesman's sample **100**
Cookie Jar, sponging on band, barrel shaped, Red Wing **130**
Cooler, cov, blue and white sponging, mkd "5," has bung hole but no spig-
ot, chip on 1 handle, 14¾" h **150**
Creamer, figural cat, polychrome sponging, 4¼" h **35**
Creamer, green sponging, waisted, 4" h **70**
Creamer, Old Sleepy Eye, blue and gray sponging, small flakes on bottom,
3⅞" h **450**
Crock, blue and white sponging, 7⅝" d, 7⅜" h **75**
Cup and Saucer, blue sponging, c1840 .... **135**

*Creamer, Cow and Maid, Staffordshire,
earthenware, stylized cow with
manganese sponged body, early 19th C,
$293.* Photo courtesy Sotheby's.

Teapot, cov, blue and green sponged dec, white ground, unmkd, 1830–50, 6" h, 10¹/₂" w, $200.

Cuspidor, miniature, blue and white sponging, blue stripes, repaired rim chips, 3¹/₄" d 275
Dish, cov, blue and white sponging, 3¹/₄" d 950
Food Mold, Turk's head, brown and green sponging, imp "Upton M Bell, Waynesboro, PA," 5³/₄" d 330
Ink Pot, blue sponging, stoneware 70
Jar, blue and white sponging, blue stripes, cylindrical, hairlines, 15¹/₂" h 775
Jug, blue sponge bands, cream ground, flared top, applied handle, 7¹/₄" h . . . 130
Milk Pitcher, dark blue sponging, stain, 5³/₄" h 330
Milk Pitcher, dark bluish gray sponging, bulbous base, molded swirled ribs, 5⁵/₈" h 400
Mixing Bowl, blue and white sponging, stripes, wear and old rim repair, 12¹/₂" d, 5⁵/₈" h 55
Mug, blue sponging, 4" h 165
Pitcher, beige and blue sponging, white ground, edge chips and hairlines, 10" h 130
Pitcher, blue sponging, yellow ware, 8¹/₄" h 140
Pitcher, blue and white sponging, 9" h 330
Pitcher, blue and white sponging, curved shoulders, small rim flake, 8¹/₄" h . . 470
Pitcher, blue and white sponging with stripes, barrel shaped, hairlines, 8⁵/₈" h 300
Pitcher, brown and green sponging, yellow ground, 4¹/₂" h 70
Plate, blue sponging, white ground, emb scalloped edge, 10¹/₄" d 180
Platter, dark blue and white sponging, 13³/₈" l 50
Salt and Pepper Shakers, pr, green and amber sponging, white ground 90
Salt Box, with crest, blue and white sponging, chips on back of hanger hole, small rim flake and 2 hairlines, 3" d, 3³/₈" h 325
Spittoon, blue and white sponging, brass top, 1880–1900, 10" d, 4" h 115
Syrup Jug, green and rust sponging 400
Teapot, miniature, blue and white sponging, small flakes, handle has professional repair, 4¹/₄" h 575
Teapot, olive green and white sponging, 7¹/₄" h 320
Umbrella Stand, Dutch boy and girl transfer design, blue and white sponging, blue stripes, hairlines, 2¹/₄" h 825

STAFFORDSHIRE

The Staffordshire district of England is the center of the English pottery industry. There were eighty different potteries operating there in 1786, with the number increasing to 179 by 1802. The district includes Burslem, Cobridge, Etruria, Fenton, Foley, Hanley, Lane Delph, Lane End, Longport, Shelton, Stoke, and Tunstall. Among the many famous potters were Adams, Davenport, Spode, Stevenson, Wedgwood, and Wood.

In historical Staffordshire the view is the most critical element. American collectors pay much less for non–American views. Dark blue pieces are favored. Light views, e.g., light blue, pink, green, continue to remain undervalued. Among the forms, soup tureens have shown the highest price increases.

A wide variety of ornamental pottery items originated in England's Staffordshire district, beginning in the seventeenth century and extending to the present. The height of production was from 1820 to 1890.

These naive pieces are considered folk art by many collectors. Most items were not made carefully; some were even made and decorated by children.

The types of objects varied, e.g., animals, cottages, and figurines (chimney ornaments). The key to price is age and condition. Generally, the older the piece, the higher the price.

References: David and Linda Arman, *Historical Staffordshire: An Illustrated Check List,* published by author, 1974, out of print; David and Linda Arman, *Historical Staffordshire: An Illustrated Check List, First Supplement,* published by author, 1977, out of print; Ada Walker Camehl, *The Blue China Book,* Tudor Publishing Co, 1946, (Dover, reprint); A. W. Coysh and R. K. Henrywood, *The Dictionary of Blue and White Printed Pottery, 1780–1880,* Antique Collectors' Club, 1982; Pat Halfpenny, *English Earthenware Figures, 1740–1840,* Antique Collectors' Club; Adele Kenny, *Staffordshire Spaniels,* Schiffer Publishing, 1997; Ellouise Larson, *American Historical Views on Staffordshire China, 3rd Edition,* Dover Publications, 1975; P. D. Gordon Pugh, *Staffordshire Portrait Figures of the Victorian Era,* Antique Collectors' Club; Dennis G. Rice, *English Porcelain Animals of the 19th Century,* Antique Collectors' Club, 1989; Jeffrey B. Snyder, *Historical Staffordshire: American Patriots and Views,* Schiffer Publishing, 1995, Jeffrey B. Snyder, *Romantic Staffordshire Ceramics,* Schiffer Publishing, 1997.

Museum: Hershey Museum of American Life, Hershey, PA.

Basket, East Cowes, Isle of Wight, dark blue, open work, professional restoration to crack off rim, replacement of 1 handle, 11½" l **$200**

Stirrup Cup, figural fox head, black muzzle, yellow eyes, black facial details and collar, iron–red sponged fur, minor wear, 19th C, 5" l, $500.

Basket, Wild Rose, ftd, dark blue, open work, pierced rim with open chain design, dark blue branch–like handles, 4" h, 12" l **500**

Basket and Stand, salt glazed, basket has scrolled handles with press molded and pierced basketweave rim, stand has basketweave border, slight rim chips, c1760, 9" l **975**

Coffeepot, cov, creamware, molded cream colored florets over green glazed leaves dec, leaf molded spout with serpent head nozzle, 2 rim chips to cov restored, c1770, 10" h **7,475**

Coffeepot, cov, lady with a scythe, dark blue, Prince of Wales Feather border, 10" h **325**

Cream Jug, pear shaped, salt glazed, polychrome enamel floral dec, c1760, $2^{7}/_{8}$" h, rim nick **690**

Creamer, English scene, dark blue, imp "Wood," $7^{7}/_{8}$" d **135**

Creamer, horse–drawn sleigh, dark blue, imp "Wood," $5^{3}/_{4}$" h **550**

Creamer, Mt Vernon, The Seat of the Late Gen'l Washington, dark blue, $4^{3}/_{4}$" h **600**

Cup, Commodore MacDonnough's Victory, dark blue, Wood **300**

Cup and Saucer, handleless, Commodore MacDonnough's Victory, dark blue, pinpoints on table ring of cup, imp "Wood & Sons" **600**

Cup and Saucer, handleless, floral, dark blue transfer, small flakes, Adams ... **165**

Cup and Saucer, handleless, shepherd and sheep, dark blue transfer, imp "Clews," small chips on cup **80**

Cup and Saucer, handleless, ship with American flag, imp "Wood & Sons" .. **775**

Cup and Saucer, handleless, 3 children, dog in basket, dark blue transfer, pinpoint flakes and stains, Stevenson Stone China **110**

Cup and Saucer, handleless, Vase of Flowers, dark blue transfer, small flakes . **50**

Cup Plate, Quadrupeds with Hyena, dark blue transfer, 4" d **365**

Cup Plate, The Landing of the Fathers, dark blue, Wood, $4^{5}/_{8}$" d **200**

Cup Plate, Woodlands Near Philadelphia, dark blue, spread eagle border, Stubbs, $3^{1}/_{4}$" d **100**

Left: Plate, View of Liverpool, dark blue, 10" d, $425.

Right: Soup Tureen, Village of Cedars, blue, Francis Morley & Co, Hanley, 11" d, $1,000.

Photos courtesy Jackson's Auctioneers & Appraisers.

Left: Toby Jug, Martha Gunn, pearlware, puce blouse, yellow bodice, red skirt, blue apron, c1825, 5⅝" h, $1,093.

Right: Figure, recumbent sheep on grassy mound, pearlware, hollow–molded, brown and ocher border, dark brown facial details, hairline crack in base, ears restored, c1790, 5¾" l, $518.

Photos courtesy Sotheby's.

Dinner Service, partial, William Penn's Treaty, 9 cups, 11 saucers, and eight 7½" d plates, brown transfer, chips and minor hairlines, Thomas Green, Fenton, England, mid–19th C **545**

Dish, leaf shaped, salt glazed, emb bird perched on leafy branch, circle and dot ground, feathered rim, c1760, 9½" l **1,725**

Figure, peasant woman, lead glazed creamware, translucent brown and green, foot rim chips, c1755, 4¼" h **345**

Jug, bear, brown slip eyes, collar, and paws, salt glazed, allover dec with shreds of clay, repaired collar hairlines, slight line at shoulder, c1740, 10" h **2,200**

Plate, America and Independence, dark blue, imp "Clews," minor surface flakes, 10⅝" d **275**

Plate, Australia, blue transfer, 10¼" d **15**

Plate, Boston State House, medium blue, imp "Wood & Sons," 10¼" d **165**

Plate, Chase, blue transfer, 10¾" d **15**

Plate, Entrance of the Erie Canal into the Hudson at Albany, 6" d **690**

Plate, Harvard College, medium blue, minor edge roughness and light stains, 10⅛" d **100**

Plate, India, red transfer, matching floral border, 9" d, and 10½" d, price for pair **110**

Plate, Junction of the Sacandaga & Hudson River, black transfer, small rim glaze defect, 7" d **95**

Plate, Klosterneuburg, Germany, dark blue, minor wear and scratches, 9⅞" d **100**

Plate, leaf shaped, press–molded, bird on leafy branch, veined ground, rim chips, c1760, 9⅝" d **1,150**

Plate, Park Theatre, New York, dark blue, minor stains, 10⅛" d **330**

Plate, Seal of the United States, dark blue, Adams, 6" h **650**

Plate, The Baltimore & Ohio Railroad, dark blue, imp "Enoch Wood," 9¼" d . **770**

Plate, The Capitol Washington, dark blue transfer, shell border, imp "Wood & Sons," 7⅝" d **940**

Plate, View of London, medium blue transfer, 9⅞" d **135**

Platter, Landing of General Lafayette, dark blue transfer, imp "Clews," scratches and wear, 17" l **1,100**

Platter, molded leaves with circle and dot dec, scalloped rim, salt glazed, c1760, 13½" l **1,725**
Platter, Sheltered Peasants, dark blue transfer, 17" l 950
Platter, Ships in Water, dark blue transfer, "Sandusky," 16⅝" l **8,525**
Sauce Boat, Fruit and Flowers, dark blue, molded feet and handle, rim chips, 7⅞" l 325
Sauce Boat, Octagon Church Boston, dark blue, Ridgway, 9⅞" d 325
Soup Plate, Antelope, dark blue, Quadrupeds series, Hall, 10" d 50
Soup Plate, Picturesque Views, Hudson, Hudson River, black transfer, imp "Clews," 10½" d 165
Soup Plate, rococo paneled cartouches, bordered in reedwork, 1 panel depicting sheep grazing, reverse depicting cows grazing, salt glazed, c1760, 2⅜" h... 800
Soup Plate, View of Liverpool, dark blue transfer, 8⅜" d 300
Soup Plate, Windsor Castle, dark blue, acorn and oak leaves border, RSW, 18½" l 650
Soup Plate, Winter View of Pittsfield, Mass, dark blue, imp "Clews," 10⅜" d . 450
Soup Tureen, cov, Belleville on the Passaic River, eagle at bottom, cov with different view, blue transfer, imperfections, Enoch Wood & Sons, 14½" l ... **4,700**
Soup Tureen, cov, shells, dark blue, scroll finial, scroll handle, Rogers, 8¼" h, 15¼" l 500
Soup Tureen and Underplate, cov, Classic Ruins, black transfer, chips, matching ladle broken in 3 pcs, 6⅝" h 90
Soup Tureen and Underplate, cov, Landing of Lafayette, rect, dark blue, imp "Clews," restoration 500
Soup Tureen and Underplate, cov, Sheltered Peasants, dark blue, Hall 550
Sugar, cov, Mt Vernon, The Seat of the Late Gen'l Washington, dark blue, 5⅝" h 700
Sugar, cov, Wadsworth Tower, rect, dark blue, shell border, Wood, 5¾" h 725
Tea Canister, cut corner rect form, molded panels of Chinese figural, floral, and landscape designs, 1765, 4⅜" h **2,500**

Left: Pitcher, Newburgh, Hudson River, blue, HS Clews, 9" h, $400.
Right: Soup Bowl, Italian Villa, blue, J H & Co. (J. Heath), 7¾" d, $75.

Platter, Scenes After Constable, The Glebe Farm, blue, Grindley, 1936–64, 14" l, $65.

Teapot, cov, Camel, figural with howdah on its back, paneled sides with Chinese subjects, fruiting vine handle, rect base, salt glazed, rim chips on cov and pot, c1750, 5" h 5,450

Teapot, cov, floral and vinework, applied dec, lead glazed creamware, leaf molded handle, bird finial, mounted on 3 lion mask and paw feet, restorations, small chip to spout and foot rim, 5³/₈" h 2,300

Teapot, cov, globular, riverbank scene, enameled dec with house and yard, salt glazed, crabstock handle and spout, c1760, 4¹/₄" h 2,200

Teapot, cov, melon–form body with paneled veining and raised leaves, green glazed, crabstock handle and finial, c1760, 3³/₈" h 6,325

Toddy Plate, scene of ruins, dark blue transfer, Clews, 5¹/₂" d 180

Toddy Plate, ship scene, shell border, dark blue, imp "Wood," 5³/₄" d 325

Underplate, Boston State House, oval, dark blue, Rogers, 8" l 325

Underplate, Landing of Lafayette, dark blue, Clews, 9³/₄" l 200

Vegetable Bowl, Bank of England, dark blue, Regent's Park series, Wood, 11¹/₂" l 475

Vegetable Bowl, Quebec, square, dark blue, regular shell border, shallow chips on underside of ground rim, overall mellowing, Wood, 2" h, 8¹/₈" l .. 100

Wash Bowl, Upper Ferry Bridge over the River Schuylkill, dark blue, Stubbs, 4⁵/₈ x 12¹/₂" 750

Waste Bowl, birds and flowers, medium blue transfer, wear, pinpoint flakes, 3" d, 3¹/₂" h 120

STANGL

The Stangl Pottery, located in Trenton and Flemington, New Jersey, was founded in 1930 by J. M. Stangl, formerly of Fulper Pottery. In 1978 it was purchased by the Pfaltzgraff Company. The Flemington factory currently serves as a Pfaltzgraff factory outlet. One of the original kilns remains intact to exemplify the hard work and high temperatures involved in the production of pottery.

Stangl Pottery produced several lines of highly collectible dinnerware and decorative accessories, including the famed Stangl birds. The red bodied dinnerware was produced in distinctive shapes and patterns. Shapes were designated by numbers. Pattern names include: Country Garden, Fruit, Tulip, Thistle, and Wild Rose. Special Christmas, advertising and commemorative wares were also produced.

Bright colors and bold simplistic patterns have made Stangl Pottery a favorite with Country collectors. Stangl's factory sold seconds from its factory store long before outlet malls became popular. Large sets of Stangl dinnerware currently command high prices at auctions, flea markets, and even antique shops.

Stangl's ceramic birds were produced from 1940 until 1972. The birds were manufactured at Stangl's Trenton plant, then shipped to the Flemington plant for hand painting.

During World War II the demand for these birds and Stangl pottery was so great that forty to sixty decorators could not keep up with the demand. Orders were contracted out to private homes. These pieces were then returned for firing and finishing. Colors used to decorate these birds varied according to the artist.

As many as ten different trademarks were used. Dinnerware was marked and often signed by the decorator. Most birds are numbered; many are artist signed. However, signatures are useful for dating purposes only and add little to values.

Several birds were reissued between 1972 and 1977. These reissues are dated on the bottom and worth approximately one half the value of the older birds.

References: Harvey Duke, *Stangl Pottery,* Wallace–Homestead, Krause Publications, 1993; Joan Dworkin and Martha Horman, *A Guide to Stangl Pottery Birds,* Willow Pond Books, Inc, 1973; Norma Rehl, *The Collectors Handbook of Stangl Pottery,* Democrat Press, 1982; Mike Schneider, *Stangl and Pennsbury Birds,* Schiffer Publishing, 1994.

Collectors' Club: Stangl/Fulper Collectors Assoc, PO Box 538, Flemington, NJ 08822.

BIRD FIGURES

#3250A, Standing Duck, 3¼" h **125**
#3250F, Quacking Duck, 1⅝" h **125**
#3273, Rooster, hollow base, orig label, glued tail, 5¾" h **275**
#3275, Turkey **375**
#3276, Bluebird **70**
#3276D, Bluebirds, 1978 .... **200**
#3404D, Kissing Lovebirds, light turquoise crackle **275**
#3407, Terra Rose Blue Owl, small glaze chip on head **200**
#3443, Flying Duck, teal **225**
#3444, Cardinal, red matte finish, paint missing under tail, 6¾" h **130**
#3446, Hen, yellow **185**
#3450, Passenger Pigeon **1,100**
#3451, Willow Ptarmigan, 11" h **2,500**
#3453, Mountain Bluebird **1,100**
#3454, Key West Quail Dove **800**
#3490D, Redstarts **210**
#3518D, White Headed Pigeons, 7⅞ x 12½" **600**
#3580, Cockatoo **110**
#3581, Chickadees, group, black and white, orig price tag **350**
#3582D, Parakeets, green **250**
#3599D, Hummingbirds, 1973, orig price tag, 8¾" h **275**
#3627, Rivoli Hummingbird, pink flower **175**
#3628, Rieffers Hummingbird, 1972, orig price tag **80**
#3635, Goldfinch, group **250**
#3715, Bluejay, with peanut, antique gold, repaired beak **95**
#3717D, Bluejays, 13" h **3,700**

Sandwich Plate, Fruit, center handle, $8.

#3725, Redheaded Woodpecker, porcelain, leaf repaired 1,250
#3749, Western Tanager 325
#3750D, Western Tanagers 425
#3752D, Redheaded Woodpeckers, pink gloss finish, 7³/₄" h 325
#3754D, White Winged Crossbills, red matte, factory–repaired base flaw
    crack 400
#3755, Audubon Warbler, orig price tag, 4¹/₂" h 425
#3852, Cliff Swallow 185
#3853, Golden Crowned Kinglets, group 600
#3868, Summer Tanager 425
#3923, Vermilion Flycatcher, small chip on back of leaf, 5³/₄" h 850
#3924, Yellow Throated Warbler, 5³/₄" h 350

DINNERWARE & ACCESSORIES

Amber Glo, butter dish $25
Amber Glo, cereal bowl, 5¹/₂" d 5
Amber Glo, chop plate, 12¹/₂" d 15
Amber Glo, vegetable bowl, divided 25
Americana, creamer 4
Americana, dinner plate, 10" d 6
Americana, sugar, open, individual 6
Antique Gold, bowl, 8" d 30
Antique Gold, bud vase, 6¹/₂" h 30
Antique Gold, candy dish, cov, #3676, 5¹/₂" l 32
Antique Gold, server, center handle 20
Apple Delight, cake stand 25
Apple Delight, cereal bowl, 5¹/₂" d 2
Apple Delight, gravy boat and underplate 40
Apple Delight, salad bowl, 10" d 30
Apple Delight, salad plate, 8" d 15
Apple Delight, saucer 3
Apple Delight, snack plate, 8¹/₄" d 4
Ashtray, apple tree, 5" d 20
Ashtray, flower, 5" d 15

Ashtray, Sportsman, oval, pheasant, 10⅝" l **40**
Bella Rosa, bread and butter plate, 6" **4**
Bella Rosa, casserole, individual, stick handle **12**
Bella Rosa, fruit bowl, 5½" d **8**
Blueberry, casserole, 8" d **70**
Blueberry, creamer, individual **10**
Blueberry, salad bowl, 10" d **35**
Chicory, casserole, 8" d **22**
Chicory, chop plate, 12½" d **25**
Chicory, salad bowl, 10" d **35**
Cigarette Box, cov, rect, heart, 7¼ x 3⅜" **40**
Colonial, bean pot, individual, persian yellow **22**
Colonial, creamer **7**
Colonial, cup **5**
Colonial, eggcup, colonial blue **12**
Colonial, salad plate, silver green, 8" d **12**
Colonial, vegetable bowl, oval, tangerine, 10" l **20**
Country Garden, coaster **15**
Country Garden, cup and saucer **20**
Country Garden, gravy boat and underplate **35**
Country Garden, pitcher, 2 qt **50**
Country Life, eggcup, chick **40**
Country Life, fruit dish, pony, 5½" d **70**
Country Life, shaker, duckling **30**
Fruit, bean pot, 2 handles **75**
Fruit, cake stand **20**
Fruit, coffeepot, 4 cup **65**
Fruit, mixing bowl, 7" d **30**
Fruit, relish dish **30**
Fruit, server, 2 tier **25**

Left: Vase, green matte glaze, mkd "STANGL 3110," 7⅛" h, $30.

Right: Food Molds, 2 with grape clusters, 2 with peach, brown ground, 4⅝" l, 3½" w, 2" h, price for set of 4, $35. Photo courtesy Ray Morykan Auctions.

Fruit, teapot, individual 22
Garden Flower, casserole, balloon flower, 8" d 50
Garden Flower, chop plate, tiger lily, 12½" d 45
Garden Flower, creamer, individual, Rose 12
Garden Flower, cup and saucer, rose cup, leaves saucer 20
Garden Flower, pitcher, sunflower, 2 qt 45
Garden Flower, saucer, leaves 3
Garden Flower, teapot, sunflower 50
Golden Harvest, casserole, 6" d 15
Golden Harvest, creamer 5
Golden Harvest, mug, 2 cup 30
Golden Harvest, salad plate, 8" d 10
Golden Harvest, sugar 10
Golden Harvest, vegetable bowl, divided 40
Magnolia, butter dish 40
Magnolia, creamer and sugar 25
Magnolia, pitcher, 1 qt 35
Magnolia, salt and pepper shakers, pr 15
Planter, pig, #1745, medium blue, 1½" h 30
Planter, swan, platina, 6¾" h 25
Rooster, cup 12
Rooster, pitcher, 1 pt 20
Rooster, saucer 5
Salt and Pepper Shakers, pr, hen and rooster 130
Thistle, chop plate, 14½" d 35
Thistle, creamer, individual 10
Town and Country, bowl, blue, 26 oz 30
Town and Country, ladle 20
Tulip, casserole, 8" d 40
Tulip, vegetable bowl, divided, round, 10" d 35
Vase, figural horse head, #3611, blue, white trim, mkd "Stangl Terra Rose
    Made In Trenton, U.S.A." 700
Vase, Terra Rose, tulip 50
Wall Pocket, Cosmos, green matte, 1937 45
Wild Rose, creamer 15
Wild Rose, eggcup 10
Wild Rose, salad bowl, 12" d 50

SYRACUSE

Syracuse China traces its origins to W. H. Farrar who established a pottery in Syracuse, New York, in 1841. The plant moved from Genesee Street to Fayette Street in 1855 and operated as the Empire Pottery. The Empire Pottery became the Onondaga Pottery Company after a reorganization in 1871, retaining the name until 1966 when the company became the Syracuse China Company. Few noticed the change because Onondaga Pottery had marketed its dinnerware under a Syracuse China brand name as early as 1879.

Onondaga introduced a high–fired, semi–vitreous ware in the mid–1880s that was guaranteed against crackling and grazing. In 1888 James Pass introduced Imperial Geddo, a translucent, vitrified china. By the early 1890s, the company offered a full line of fine china ware.

Onondaga made commercial as well as household china. In 1921 a new plant, devoted exclusively to commercial production, was opened. In 1959 Onondaga Pottery acquired Vandesca-Syracuse, Joliette, Quebec, Canada, a producer of vitrified hotel china. In 1984 Syracuse China absorbed the Mayer China Company.

After manufacturing fine dinnerware for ninety–nine years, Syracuse China discontinued its household china line in the 1970s, devoting its production efforts exclusively to airline, commercial, hotel, and restaurant china.

References: Cleota Reed and Stan Skoczen, *Syracuse China,* Syracuse University Press, 1997; Harry L. Rinker, *Dinnerware of the 20th Century: The Top 500 Patterns,* House of Collectibles, 1997.

Bracelet, bread and butter plate, 6¼" d	$5
Bracelet, creamer	25
Bracelet, cup and saucer, ftd	18
Bracelet, dinner plate, 9¾" d	12
Bracelet, platter, oval, 14" l	40
Bracelet, vegetable bowl, open, oval, 10¼" l	35
Briarcliff, creamer	18
Briarcliff, demitasse cup and saucer	12
Briarcliff, flat soup, 8" d	10
Briarcliff, fruit bowl, 5⅛" d	8
Briarcliff, salad plate, 8" d	7
Coralbel, bread and butter plate, 6¼" d	5
Coralbel, cereal bowl, 6⅜" d	15
Coralbel, chop plate, 12½" d	35
Coralbel, gravy boat and underplate	35
Coralbel, salad plate, 8" d	8
Coralbel, vegetable bowl, 9" d	30
Minuet, bread and butter plate, 6¼" d	8
Minuet, creamer	20
Minuet, gravy boat and underplate	60

Left: Briarcliff, dinner plate, 10" d, $10.   Right: Stansbury, dinner plate, 10" d, $15.

Minuet, soup bowl, 7⁵/₈" d **18**
Stansbury, berry bowl, 7¹/₈" d **15**
Stansbury, cereal bowl, 5" d **10**
Stansbury, cup and saucer, ftd **20**
Stansbury, gravy boat and underplate **45**
Stansbury, salad plate, 8" d **12**
Stansbury, sugar, cov **20**
Stansbury, vegetable bowl, oval, 10⁵/₈" l **30**
Sweetheart, creamer **22**
Sweetheart, dinner plate, 10¹/₂" d **15**
Sweetheart, sugar, cov **30**
Sweetheart, vegetable bowl, open, oval, 10" d **45**
Wayside, butter dish, cov, ¹/₄ lb **22**
Wayside, creamer **15**
Wayside, dinner plate, 10¹/₈" d **10**
Wayside, platter, oval, 12¹/₂" l **25**

TAYLOR, SMITH & TAYLOR

C. A. Smith and Colonel John N. Taylor founded Taylor, Smith & Taylor in Chester, West Virginia, in 1899. In 1903 the firm reorganized and the Taylor interests were purchased by the Smith family. The firm remained in the family's control until it was purchased by Anchor Hocking in 1973. The tableware division closed in 1981.

Taylor, Smith & Taylor started production with a nine–kiln pottery. Local clays were used initially. Later only southern clays were used. Both earthenware and fine china bodies were produced. Several underglaze print patterns, e.g. Dogwood and Spring Bouquet were made. These prints, made from the copper engravings of ceramic artist J. Palin Thorley, were designed exclusively for the company.

Taylor, Smith & Taylor also made LuRay, produced from the 1930s through the early 1950s. Available in Windsor Blue, Persian Cream, Sharon Pink, Surf Green, and Chatham Gray, their coordinating colors encourage collectors to mix and match sets.

Competition for a portion of the dinnerware market of the 1930s through the 1950s was intense. LuRay was designed to compete with Russel Wright's American Modern. Vistosa was Taylor, Smith & Taylor's answer to Homer Laughlin's Fiesta.

Taylor, Smith & Taylor used several different backstamps and marks. Many contain the company name as well as the pattern and shape names.

Reference: Kathy and Bill Meehan, *Collector's Guide to Lu–Ray Pastels: Identification and Values*, Collector Books, 1995.

Autumn Harvest, platter, oval, 13¹/₂" l **$20**
Beverly, bread and butter plate, 6¹/₄" d **2**
Beverly, platter, oval, 11¹/₂" l **10**
Break O'Day, cereal bowl **5**
Break O'Day, cup and saucer **4**
Break O'Day, salad plate **2**
Courting Couple, gravy boat **30**
Courting Couple, vegetable bowl **25**
Daylily, dessert bowl **5**
Daylily, serving bowl **17**
Ever Yours, bread and butter plate **3**

Ever Yours, cup and saucer 4
Ever Yours, salad plate 3
Garland, cup 5
Garland, saucer 2
Golden Button, bread and butter plate 2
Golden Button, creamer 3
Golden Button, cup and saucer 5
Golden Button, platter, oval 4
Golden Button, salt and pepper shakers, pr 8
Laurel, casserole 20
Laurel, saucer 2
Laurel, sugar 8
LuRay, bowl, 36's, Windsor Blue 22
LuRay, bread and butter plate, Sharon Pink, 6½" d 5
LuRay, bud vase, Surf Green 145
LuRay, cake plate, lug handle, Windsor Blue, 11" d 28
LuRay, chop plate, Persian Cream, 14" d 30
LuRay, creamer, Windsor Blue 7
LuRay, cup and saucer, Chatham Gray 30
LuRay, demitasse cup and saucer, Chatham Gray 20
LuRay, dinner plate, Persian Cream, 10" d 12
LuRay, eggcup, Persian Cream 15
LuRay, flat soup, Persian Cream 20
LuRay, flat soup, Windsor Blue 15
LuRay, grill plate, Persian Cream 25
LuRay, juice tumbler, Persian Cream 40
LuRay, juice tumbler, Sharon Pink 40
LuRay, mixing bowl, Surf Green, 8¾" d 75
LuRay, nut dish, Sharon Pink 80
LuRay, platter, oval, Chatham Gray, 13" l 30
LuRay, platter, oval, Persian Cream, 12" l 12
LuRay, platter, oval, Persian Cream, 13½" l 15
LuRay, salad bowl, Surf Green 45
LuRay, salad bowl, Windsor Blue 60
LuRay, salad plate, Chatham Gray, 8" d 22
LuRay, salad plate, Surf Green, 8" d 18
LuRay, teapot, Persian Cream, curved 65
LuRay, teapot, Windsor Blue 30
LuRay, vegetable bowl, cov, oval, Windsor Blue, 10" l 13
LuRay, water pitcher, Sharon Pink 50
Marvel, eggcup 10
Marvel, salad bowl, 9½" d 15
Marvel, vegetable bowl, oval, 9¼" l 10
Paramount, butter pat 6
Paramount, casserole, ftd, rattan handle, 11 x 8¼" 20
Paramount, saucer 2
Pebbleford, butter dish, ½ lb 20
Pebbleford, casserole 20
Pebbleford, vegetable bowl, divided 15
Petit Point Bouquet, cake plate, tab handled, 11" d 12
Petit Point Bouquet, dinner plate 8

Bowl, ftd, orange and green floral dec, green ink stamped "Taylor Smith Taylor" in wreath above "1478," 5¹³/₁₆" d, $5.

Petit Point Bouquet, platter, tab handled, 12½" l	15
Plymouth, casserole	20
Plymouth, sugar	8
Rooster, custard cup	3
Rooster, fruit dish	4
Rooster, soup bowl	5
Silhouette, butter dish, cov	145
Silhouette, salad bowl, 8¾" d	20
Silhouette, salt and pepper shakers, pr, 5" h	70
Summer Rose, dinner plate, 10" d	6
Summer Rose, sauce bowl, 5¼" d	3
Taverne, bowl, 36's	20
Vistosa, chop plate, yellow, 11" d	25
Vistosa, creamer, light green	20
Vistosa, flat soup, mango red	25
Vistosa, flat soup, yellow	25
Vistosa, gravy boat, cobalt blue	150
Vistosa, jug, mango red	50
Vistosa, teacup, cobalt blue	10
Vistosa, teapot, mango red	80
Vogue, casserole	20
Vogue, creamer	4

TORQUAY

In 1869 G. J. Allen discovered red terra–cotta clay on the Watcombe House grounds, just north of Torquay, England, and established the Watcombe Pottery. Skilled workers were recruited from the Staffordshire district by Charles Brock, the company's manager. Watcombe was the first of several potteries founded near Torquay.

The years 1870 and 1900 marked the high–point of the English art pottery movement. The innovative shapes and natural terra–cotta products of Watcombe found a ready market. Initially Watcombe pieces mirrored classical forms. Later busts of contemporary and historical celebrities, architectural and garden wares, terra–cotta plaques, and tea services were added to the product line.

In 1875 Dr. Gillow founded the Torquay Terra–Cotta Company at Hele Cross, just north of Torquay. It produced utilitarian ware along with busts, figurines, plaques, and statues. The plant closed in 1905 as the Arts and Crafts movement reached its end. In 1908 Enoch Staddon reopened the plant to produce terra-cotta wares. It ceased operations during World War II.

John Phillips directed the operations of the Aller Vale Pottery, founded in 1881 to make terra–cotta and other art wares. By 1890 its production had shifted to souvenir items featuring designs painted on thick colored slip. Rhymes or proverbs were scratched through the slip so the lettering featured the dark red body color of the base clay. This ware became known as "Motto Ware" and is the first style individuals think of when Torquay pottery is mentioned.

Watcombe Pottery and Aller Vale merged in 1901 to become the Royal Aller Vale and Watcombe Art Potteries. "Devon Motto Ware" or "Cottage Ware," featuring a thatched cottage between trees, was introduced. Place names replaced rhymes and proverbs. Commemorative pieces also were made. Operations ceased in 1962.

Burton, Daison, and Longpark are some of the other small potteries located in or near Torquay. Most were started by individuals who worked for one of the larger firms.

Far too many Country collectors think of Torquay only in terms of "Motto Ware." Many other products from Torquay potteries also work well within the Country decorating motif.

Collectors' Club: North American Torquay Society, 12 Stanton, Madison, CT 06443.

Biscuit Barrel, pink roses, streaked mauve ground, wicker handle, Longpark
   Torquay mark, 8" h **$145**
Cake Stand, fruit, "He is Well Paid Who is Well Satisfied," 9" d **100**
Chamberstick, black cockerel, "Snore and You Sleep Alone," stamped
   "Longpark Torquay," 4" h **85**
Condiment Set, cottage, "Actions Speak Louder Than Words" salt, "Good
   Examples Are Best Sermons" pepper, and "Speak Little Speak Well" sugar . . **40**
Creamer, Cockington Church, Cockington, Watcombe Torquay mark, 2" h . . . **45**
Creamer, Kerswell Daisy, "Straucht Frae The Coo," imp "Aller Vale," 3" h **70**
Creamer, Scandy, "Take a Little Cream," scalloped edge, 3½" h **55**
Cup and Saucer, black cockerel, "Dauntee Be Fraid Au't Now," Longpark
   Torquay mark **65**
Eggcup, cottage, "Fresh Today," Longpark Torquay mark, 2½" h **50**
Eggcup and Saucer, cottage, "Fine Words Will Not Fill," 3" h **40**
Mug, cottage, "When Day Breaks Make the most of the Pieces," mkd
   "Longpark," 5" h **120**
Pitcher, Cottage, "Good Morning, Never Say Die, Up Man And Try," 4½" h . . **70**
Pitcher, Flying Seagull, blue ground, "Bigbury On Sea," stamped "Royal
   Watcombe Torquay," 3" h **30**
Pitcher, Sailboat, 2¼" h **35**
Plate, Cottage, "Better To Sit Still Than Rise To Fall," Watcombe Torquay
   mark, 6½" d **50**
Plate, Cottage, "Home Well and Have Well," mkd "Royal Watcombe
   Pottery," 5" d **45**
Plate, Cottage, Sailboat, "Torquay, Say Little But Think Much," stamped
   "Watcombe Torquay," 5" d **50**
Plate, Cottage, Scandy, blue rim, "We're Not the Only Pebbles on the
   Beach," Aller Vale mark, 5¼" d **45**
Pot, story house, "If You Can't Fly Climb," 3½" h **35**

Scent Bottle, Devon Violets, 2" h **30**
Sugar Bowl, Cottage, scalloped edge, "Elp Yerzel Tu Sugar," stamped
"Longpark Torquay," 1³/₄" h **55**
Sugar Bowl, Snow Cottage, "Take a Little Sugar," Watcombe Torquay mark,
1³/₄" h **45**
Teapot, Primrose, "Now Ladies All I Pray Make Free and Tell Me How You
Like Your Tea," 4¹/₂" h **100**
Teapot, Scandy, "Elp Yerzels Cum Me Artiez," 4" h **85**
Tray, "A Reminder of a Visit to the English Lake District," coronation year
1937, stamped "Watcombe Torquay England," 5" l, 3" w **70**
Vase, Black Cockerel, "Du All Tha Gude Ur Kin in Every Wey Ye Kin," 3 han-
dles, mkd "Longpark Torquay," 3¹/₂" h **75**
Vase, Daffodil, 3 handles, mkd "Royal Torquay Pottery," 6¹/₂" h **140**
Vase, Diving Kingfisher, with water lilies, 3 handles, mkd "Watcombe
Torquay England," 9³/₄" h **225**
Vase, Scandy, "Life is mostly Froth and Bubble, Two Things Stand as Stone,
Kindness in Another's Trouble, Courage in Your Own," 2 handles, mkd
"Longpark Torquay," 9¹/₂" h **200**
Vase, White Flowers, green leaves, terra cotta, imp "Terracotta Works
Longpark Torquay," c1883–95, 4¹/₄" h **80**

UNIVERSAL

In 1934 The Oxford Pottery Company created Universal Potteries of Cambridge, Ohio, and purchased the Atlas–Globe plant properties. The Atlas–Globe operation was a merger of the Atlas China Company (formerly Crescent China Co. in 1921, Tritt in 1912 and Bradshaw in 1902) and the Globe China Company.

Even after the purchase, Universal retained the Oxford ware, made in Oxford, Ohio, as part of their dinnerware line. Another Oxford plant was used to manufacture tiles. The plant at Niles, Ohio, was dismantled.

The most popular lines of Universal were "Ballerina" and "Ballerina Mist." The company developed a detergent–resistant decal known as permacel, a key element in keeping a pattern bright. Production continued until 1960, when all plants were closed.

Not all Universal pottery carried the Universal name as part of the backstamp. Wares marked "Harmony House," "Sweet William/Sears Roebuck and Co.," and "Wheelock, Peoria" are part of the Universal production. Wheelock was a department store in Peoria, Illinois, that controlled the Cattail pattern on the Old Holland shape.

Like many pottery companies Universal had many shapes or styles of blanks, the most popular being Camwood, Old Holland, and Laurella. The same decal might be found on several different shapes. Decals with an appeal to the Country collector include Hollyhocks, Iris, Largo, Rambler Rose, and Red Poppy. Universal's booster Woodvine line, often used as a premium by grocery stores to stimulate business, is readily available and attractive to a collector willing to blend Country and modern themes.

The Cattail pattern had many accessory pieces. The 1940 and 1941 Sears catalogs listed an oval wastebasket, breakfast set, kitchen scale, linens, and bread box. Calico Fruits is another pattern with accessory pieces.

The Calico Fruits decal has not held up well over time. Collectors often have to settle for less than perfect pieces.

Ballerina Mist, canister set, 3 pcs, light aqua with cream, silver trim lids,
   price for set **$20**
Bittersweet, drip jar, cov **20**
Bittersweet, platter **30**
Bittersweet, salad bowl **32**
Bittersweet, salad plate, 7" d **12**
Bittersweet, stack set **35**
Calico Fruit, batter jug **28**
Calico Fruit, bread and butter plate, 6" d **4**
Calico Fruit, chop plate, 11½" d **25**
Calico Fruit, cookie jar, cov **50**
Calico Fruit, cup and saucer **8**
Calico Fruit, custard cup, 5 oz **5**
Calico Fruit, dinner plate, 10" d **9**
Calico Fruit, jug, cov **50**
Calico Fruit, salt and pepper shakers, pr **18**
Calico Fruit, soup bowl, tab handle **7**
Calico Fruit, stack set **45**
Calico Fruit, utility plate, 11½" d **20**
Cattail, batter jug, metal lid **85**
Cattail, bowl, tab handle, 6" d **12**
Cattail, bowl, 8½" d **15**
Cattail, bread and butter plate **4**
Cattail, bread box, double compartment **30**
Cattail, butter dish, cov **40**
Cattail, cake lifter **20**
Cattail, casserole, cov, 8¼" d **20**
Cattail, dinner plate, 9" d **8**
Cattail, gravy boat **25**
Cattail, luncheon plate, 9½" d **15**
Cattail, pie baker **20**
Cattail, platter, small **18**
Cattail, salad plate, 7" d **6**
Cattail, salt and pepper shakers, pr **20**
Cattail, syrup, metal lid **70**
Cattail, teapot **35**
Cattail, tea set, 4 pcs **50**
Cattail, vegetable bowl, oval, 10" l **20**
Largo, bread and butter plate, 6" d **4**
Largo, creamer and sugar **18**
Largo, pie baker **12**
Largo, salt and pepper shakers, pr **7**
Rambler Rose, gravy boat **10**
Rambler Rose, salt and pepper shakers, pr **18**
Three Red Roses, casserole, cov, tab handles, 5¼" d **20**
Three Red Roses, casserole, cov, tab handles, 8½" d **28**
Three Red Roses, flat soup **12**
Three Red Roses, pie plate **15**
Woodvine, creamer and sugar, cov **20**
Woodvine, mixing bowl, 4" d **20**
Woodvine, mixing bowl, 7½" d **25**

VAN BRIGGLE

After a highly successful career at Rookwood, where he successfully reproduced the Ming dynasty matte glaze. Artus Van Briggle moved to Colorado Springs, Colorado, and established Van Briggle Pottery Company in 1900. Van Briggle continued his glaze experiments at Colorado Pottery.

Shortly after arriving in Colorado, Van Briggle married Anne Gregory, an artist who worked with him. His pottery won numerous awards including one from the 1903 Paris Exhibition. Artus Van Briggle died in 1904.

Anne became president of Van Briggle Pottery, reorganized the company, and built a new plant. Van Briggle produced a wide range of products including art pottery, garden pottery, novelty items, and utilitarian ware such as decorative tiles. Artware pieces produced between 1901 and 1912 are recognized for the high quality of their design and glaze. Van Briggle's Lorelei vase is a classic.

Anne remarried in 1908. A reorganization in 1910 produced the Van Briggle Pottery and Tile Company. By 1912 the pottery was leased to Edwin DeForest Curtis who in turn sold it to Charles B. Lansing in 1915. The plant was destroyed by fire in 1919. Lansing sold the company to I. F. and J. H. Lewis in the 1920s who renamed the company Van Briggle Art Pottery.

The company survived a major flood in 1935. In 1953, Van Briggle purchased the Midland Terminal Railroad roundhouse for use as an auxiliary plant.

Kenneth Stevenson acquired the company in 1969. He continued the production of art pottery, introducing some new designs and glazes. Upon his death in 1990, Bertha (his wife), and Craig (his son) continued production.

The Stevensons use a mark that is extremely close to the interlocking "AA" mark used by Artus and Anne. Because they also make the same shapes and glazes, novice collectors frequently confuse newly made ware for older pieces. Because the Stevensons only selectively release their wholesale list, discovering what older shapes and glazes are in current production is difficult.

All pieces had the "AA" mark and "Van Briggle" prior to 1907. These marks also were used occasionally during the 1910s and 20s. "Colorado Springs" or an abbreviation often appears on pieces made after 1920. Some early pieces were dated. Value rises considerably when a date mark is present.

References: Carol and Jim Carlton, *Colorado Pottery,* Collector Books, 1994; Richard Sasicki and Josie Fania, *Collector's Encyclopedia of Van Briggle Art Pottery,* Collector Books, 1993, 1997 value update.

Collectors' Club: American Art Pottery Assoc, PO Box 525, Cedar Hill, MO 63016.

Reproduction Alert: Van Briggle pottery is still being produced today, Modern glazes include Midnight (black), Moonglo (off–white), Russet, and Turquoise Ming.

Bookends, pr, pug dog, mulberry, 1920s	**$175**
Bowl, Lotus, white, with flower frog	45
Bowl, Mulberry, #903D, with flower frog, 1920s	250
Bowl, Persian Rose Leaf, 8½" d, 4¾" h	150
Bowl, squat, emb poppy blossoms around rim, mottled blue over white matte glaze, incised "AA Van Briggle/Colo. Spgs," c1906, 2 x 5½"	275
Bud Vase, emb leaves, matte brown glaze, incised "AA/Van Briggle/1902/III/104," 4¾ x 4"	5,500
Cowboy Hat, turquoise and dark blue, 5½" w	125
Creamer, #291, melon ribbed body, turquoise, 1970s	15

Ewer, #71, turquoise, c1955 . . . .   **30**
Lamp, bird, white, no shade **85**
Lamp, butterfly **150**
Night Light, owl, mulberry **400**
Paperweight, rabbit, maroon, c1925, 3" d **125**
Planter, emb tulips under dark blue matte glaze, incised "AA/Van Briggle/
    Colo. Spgs./725," 1908–11, 5 x 6" **750**
Vase, #645, blue, 1920s, 5" d **150**
Vase, #838, 1920, 6" d **125**
Vase, baluster shaped, #430, matte mottled turquoise, green, and purple
    glaze, incised "AA/430/Van Briggle/1903/III," 6¹/₂ x 3¹/₂" **575**
Vase, bulbous, 2–handled, emb leaves under rose–pink glaze, incised
    "AA/Van Briggle/1904/232/90–10," 10 x 6" **1,800**
Vase, corseted, #671, emb stylized iris under microcrystalline French blue
    matte glaze, incised "AA/Van Briggle/Colo.Spgs.671," 1908–11, 10 x 4" . . .   **850**
Vase, cylindrical shaped, #62, emb blue peacock feather against medium
    green ground, incised "AA/Van Briggle/1903/III/62C," 12 x 3¹/₂" **1,600**
Vase, cylindrical shaped, "Climbing for Honey," 2 figural bears at opening,
    dark green to brown matte finish, mkd "AA/1918," 14¹/₂ x 5¹/₂" **5,700**
Vase, daffodils, emb under frothy periwinkle blue glaze, mkd "AA/Van
    Briggle/1903/III/100," 14 x 5¹/₂" **4,750**

Left: Vase, emb iris dec, dark blue matte glaze with light blue mottling, incised Van Briggle logo, name, date "1904," shape "167," and "V," 13¹/₄" h, $3,850.

Center: Vase, emb stylized birds in deep mulberry, medium blue matte glaze, incised Van Briggle logo, name, "Colorado Springs," date "1907," and shape "498," 9¹/₂" h, $4,070.

Right: Vase, tulips and leaves, eggplant matte glaze, design #503, c1918, 9¹/₄" h, $450.

Photos courtesy Jackson's Auctioneers & Appraisers.

Vase, Dos Cabezas, Art Nouveau style, 2 emb women with flowing hair and
garments, matte light green glaze, 3 lines in base, incised "AA/Van
Briggle/1902/III," 7½ x 5" **19,000**

Vase, dragonfly, blue **95**

Vase, ovoid, 2–handled, incised trefoils, smooth matte brown–green glaze,
incised "AA/Van Briggle/1904/III/229," 16¼ x 6¾" **5,500**

Vase, peacock feathers, stylized and emb, mottled blue–green matte glaze,
incised "AA/1911," 14½ x 7" **1,900**

Vessel, Lorelai, figure of woman draped around rim, turquoise and blue
matte glaze, incised "AA Van Briggle/USA," 1920–25, 10 x 4½" **700**

Vessel, spherical, dark green mottled matte glaze, incised "AA Van Briggle/
1903/III," 5½ x 6" **600**

Vessel, squat, band of leaves, stylized and emb, curdled mustard matte
glaze, incised "AA Van Briggle/Colo.Spgs/64–4," 1908–11, 3½ x 6¼" **700**

Vessel, squat, daisies, emb under leathery green and rose–pink glaze,
incised "AA/Van Briggle/V/1904/283," 5 x 10½" **1,000**

Vessel, squat, thistle, stylized and emb, medium curdled green matte glaze,
protruding shoulder, tapering neck, incised "AA/Van Briggle/461/Col.
Spring/1906," 8½ x 6½" **850**

VERNON KILNS

During the Depression, many small potteries flourished in southern California.
One of these, Poxon China, was founded in Vernon, California, in 1912. Faye G.
Bennison purchased this pottery in 1931 and renamed it Vernon Kilns. It also was
known as Vernon Potteries, Ltd. Under Bennison's direction, the company became a
leader in the pottery industry.

The high quality and versatility of its wares made it very popular. Besides a varied
dinnerware line, Vernon Kilns also produced Walt Disney figurines, and advertising,
political, and fraternal items. One popular line was historical and commemorative
plates, which included several series featuring scenes from England, California mis-
sions, and the West.

Vernon Kilns survived the Depression, fires, earthquakes, and wars. However, it
could not compete with the influx of imports. In January 1958, the factory was closed.
Metlox Potteries of Manhattan Beach, California, bought the trade name and molds
along with the remaining stock.

Like many pottery companies, Vernon Kilns developed a number of dinnerware
lines and then offered them in a wide variety of decal and hand–painted decorations.
Decorative motifs varied from extremely traditional, e.g., Romantic Staffordshire–style
transfer patterns on a line of traditional English forms, to post–World War II modern.
Country collectors might consider the San Fernando shape line with the R.F.D. pattern
(featuring a rooster weathervane) or one of the four hand–tinted patterns: 1860,
Hibiscus, Vernon Rose, and Desert Bloom.

Vernon Kilns used forty–eight different marks during its period of operation.

Reference: Maxine Nelson, *Collectible Vernon Kilns,* Collector Books, 1994.

Newsletter: *Vernon Views,* PO Box 945, Scottsdale, AZ 85252.

Anytime, pitcher, streamline, 2 qt **$35**
Anytime, relish, divided **25**
Anytime, tumbler **28**

Arcadia, bread and butter plate 6
Arcadia, gravy boat 22
Arcadia, luncheon plate 12
Bell–Aire, creamer 12
Bell–Aire, dinner plate 12
Bell–Aire, salt and pepper shakers, pr 20
Bell–Aire, tumbler 20
Brown Eyed Susan, bread and butter plate 3
Brown Eyed Susan, cup and saucer 6
Brown Eyed Susan, dinner plate, 9³/₄" d 6
Brown Eyed Susan, dinner plate, 10¹/₄" d 8
Brown Eyed Susan, salt and pepper shakers, pr 10
Camelia, chop plate, 14" d 35
Camelia, dinner plate 12
Camelia, flat soup 15
Camelia, sugar, cov 18
Country Cousins, cereal bowl, lug handle, 6" d 4
Country Cousins, creamer 4
Country Cousins, dinner plate, 10" d 8
Country Cousins, fruit bowl, 5¹/₂" d 3
Country Cousins, salad plate, 7¹/₂" d 3
Early California, creamer, ice lip, pink 3
Early California, cup and saucer, turquoise 6
Early California, demitasse cup and saucer, orange 30
Early California, dinner plate, turquoise, 10¹/₂" d 4
Early California, platter, orange, 12" l 20
Early California, vegetable bowl, orange, 8¹/₂" d 12
Gingham, bread and butter plate 3
Gingham, bulb jug, 1 pt 25
Gingham, carafe 30
Gingham, casserole, cov 45
Gingham, chicken pot pie, cov 30
Gingham, chop plate, 12¹/₄" d 12
Gingham, creamer 10
Gingham, cup and saucer 7
Gingham, dinner plate, 9¹/₂" d 5
Gingham, dinner plate, 10¹/₂" d 8
Gingham, flat soup 13
Gingham, mixing bowl, 8" d 25
Gingham, pitcher, 2 qt 35
Gingham, range salt and pepper shakers, pr 40
Gingham, saucer 1
Gingham, sugar, open 4
Gingham, teapot, cov 22
Gingham, vegetable bowl, 9" d 10
Heavenly Days, butter dish, cov 15
Heavenly Days, dinner plate, 10" d 4
Heavenly Days, vegetable bowl, 7¹/₂" d 6
Homespun, chop plate, 12¹/₄" d 15
Homespun, coaster, 3⁷/₈" d 9
Homespun, eggcup 25

Homespun, fruit bowl, 5½" d	5
Homespun, pitcher, 8½" h	20
Homespun, salt and pepper shakers, pr	15
Homespun, sauce boat, 6½" l	12
Homespun, saucer	2
Homespun, tumbler	28
Modern California, bowl, azure blue, 9" d	40
Modern California, bread and butter plate, azure blue, 6¼" d	7
Modern California, cup and saucer, pistachio green	15
Modern California, dinner plate, orchid, 9¾" d	15
Modern California, mug, azure blue	35
Organdie, butter dish	38
Organdie, chop plate, 12" d	15
Organdie, eggcup	28
Organdie, flat soup	8
Organdie, platter, oval, 14" l	18
Organdie, tidbit tray, 2 tier	25
Raffia, bread and butter plate	5
Raffia, eggcup	18
Raffia, tumbler	20
Tam O'Shanter, butter pat	30
Tam O'Shanter, casserole, cov	45
Tam O'Shanter, chicken pot pie, cov	30
Tam O'Shanter, coaster	30
Tam O'Shanter, coffee carafe	40
Tam O'Shanter, eggcup	25
Tam O'Shanter, flat soup	13
Tam O'Shanter, salad bowl, individual	20
Tam O'Shanter, teapot	55

WATT

Watt Pottery, founded in 1922 in Crooksville, Ohio, was well known for its stoneware. The pottery occupied the site of the former Globe Stoneware Company (1901–1919) and the Zane W. Burley Pottery (1919–1922). Local Crooksville clay was used. Kitchenware production began in 1935. The plant was destroyed by fire in 1965 and never rebuilt.

It is the color tones and patterns of Watt Pottery that appeal to Country collectors and decorators. The background consists of earth tones of off–white and light tan. It is similar in feel to many patterns from Pennsbury, Pfaltzgraff, and Purinton as well as the English Torquay pieces.

Most Watt Pottery features an underglaze decoration. The Red Apple pattern was introduced in 1950, the Cherry pattern in 1955, and the Star Flower in 1956. Other popular patterns include Pennsylvania Dutch Tulip and Rooster. Examples with advertising are highly collectible.

References: Sue and Dave Morris, *Watt Pottery: An Identification and Value Guide,* Collector Books, 1993, 1996 value update; Dennis Thompson and W. Bryce Watt, *Watt Pottery: A Collector's Reference with Price Guide,* Schiffer Publishing, 1994.

Collectors' Clubs: Watt Collectors Assoc, PO Box 1995, Iowa City, IA 52244; Watt Pottery Collectors, PO Box 26067, Cleveland, OH 44126.

Apple, baker, open, #96 .... **$100**
Apple, baking dish, oblong, #85, 1 qt **60**
Apple, canister, #81, 6" h **80**
Apple, casserole, cov, #19 .... **200**
Apple, chop plate, #49 .... **300**
Apple, creamer, #62 .... **110**
Apple, drip jar, #01 .... **60**
Apple, mixing bowls, nesting set of 4, #04, 05, 06, and 07 .... **130**
Apple, mug, #121 .... **325**
Apple, nappy, cov, #05 .... **325**
Apple, pitcher, 3 leaf, #16 .... **135**
Apple, platter, #31 .... **500**
Apple, teapot, #112, 1 1/2 qt **295**
Bleeding Heart, bean pot **130**
Bleeding Heart, creamer **75**
Bleeding Heart, pitcher, #15 .... **55**
Cherry, berry bowl, #4 .... **30**
Cherry, cereal bowl, #52 .... **25**
Cherry, mixing bowl, #8 .... **50**
Cherry, salt shaker **55**
Commemorative, grease jar, 1995 .... **150**
Commemorative, sugar, Green Apple, 1995 .... **150**
Dutch Tulip, creamer, #62 .... **350**
Dutch Tulip, pitcher, #15 .... **225**
Open Apple, mixing bowl, #6 .... **85**
Open Apple, mixing bowl, #7 .... **100**
Pansy, dinner plate, 10" d **70**
Pumpkin, casserole, loops, #8 .... **40**
Rooster, bowl, #05, PA Dutch Days adv **400**
Rooster, bowl, #73, open **80**
Rooster, creamer, #62 .... **100**
Rooster, sugar, cov, #98 .... **155**

Left: Apple, ribbed bowl, #60, $125; Center: Apple, salad bowl, #73, $85; Right: Apple, ribbed mixing bowl, #7, $55. Photo courtesy Ray Morykan Auctions.

Rooster, pitcher, 6¹/₄" h, 7" w, $125.

Starflower, bean pot, handled, #76   95
Starflower, mug, #501   90
Starflower, platter, #31   145
Starflower, salt and pepper shakers, pr, barrel shaped   155
Tear Drop, bean pot, cov, #76   125
Tear Drop, bowl, #66   50
Tear Drop, cheese crock, #80   280
Tear Drop, mixing bowl, ribbed, #7   45
Tear Drop, pitcher, #16   80
Tulip, creamer, #62   250
Tulip, pitcher, #16   200

WELLER

In 1872 Samuel A. Weller opened a small factory in Fultonham, Ohio, to produce utilitarian stoneware, e.g. milk pans and sewer tile. In 1882 he moved his facilities to Zanesville. In 1890 Weller built a new plant in the Putnam section of Zanesville along the tracks of the Cincinnati and Miskingum Railway. Additions followed in 1892 and 1894.

In 1894 Weller entered into an agreement with William A. Long to purchase the Lonhuda Faience Company, which had developed an art pottery line under the guidance of Laura A. Fry, formerly of Rookwood. Long left the company in 1895 and this line was renamed Louwelsa. Charles Babcock Upjohn became the new art director. He, along with Jacques Sicard, Frederick Hurten Rhead, and Gazo Fudji, developed Weller's art pottery lines.

At the end of World War I, many high prestige lines were discontinued and Weller concentrated on commercial wares. Rudolph Lorber joined the staff and designed the Roma, Forest, and Knifewood lines. In 1920 Weller acquired Zanesville Art Pottery and claimed to be the largest pottery in the country.

Art pottery enjoyed a revival in the 1920s and 30s with the introduction of the Hudson, Coppertone, and Graystone Garden lines. However, the Depression forced the closing of the Putnam and Marietta Street plants in Zanesville. Following World

War II, cheap Japanese imports took over Weller's market. In 1947 Essex Wire Company of Detroit bought the controlling stock. Early in 1948 operations ceased.

References: Sharon and Bob Huxford, *The Collectors Encyclopedia of Weller Pottery*, Collector Books, 1979, 1998 value update; Ann Gilbert McDonald, *All About Weller: A History and Collectors Guide to Weller Pottery*, Zanesville, OH, Antique Publications, 1989.

Bowl, Dickensware II, 4 lobed, red and green flowers on dark blue ground,
    imp mark, 4 x 8" **$475**
Bowl, florala, 8" d **165**
Bowl, wide flared rim, hp red and yellow crazed designs on sides, ftd base,
    unsgd, 7^{15}/$_{16}$" d, 3^5/$_8$" h **20**
Bud Vase, Woodcraft, tree trunk with berries and foliage in brown, green,
    and red, 6^3/$_4$" h **60**
Candle Holder, Sydonia, double, green **25**
Centerpiece Bowl, Glendale, frog with birds and nest against molded
    foliage, green, blue, red, and brown, 3^1/$_4$ x 16" **700**
Chamberstick, Louwelsa, handled, bulbous top, flaring base, gold and
    brown pansies on gold to dark brown ground, imp "Louwelsa," 7^1/$_4$ x 5" .. **150**
Console Bowl, Hobart, boy with goose flower frog, 9" d, 3" h **140**
Console Bowl, Hobnail **75**
Console Bowl, Silvertone, with flower frog **475**
Console Bowl, Wild Rose, 7^1/$_2$" d **35**
Cookie Jar, mammy, incised "Weller," 11" h **1,800**
Ewer, Dickensware **450**
Figure, white spaniel with brown ears and eyes, unmkd, 11 x 14" **2,200**
Flask, Order of Moose **100**
Flower Frog, Moskota, boy fishing, unmkd, 6^1/$_2$ x 4^1/$_4$" **75**
Hanging Basket, creamware **125**
Humidor, Dickensware II, Turk's head shape, brown, blue, white, and black,
    7^1/$_4$ x 6^1/$_2$" **375**
Jardiniere, cream, molded entwined rose designs on 4 side panels, with
    stand, imp "Weller," 13" d, 11^7/$_8$" h **110**
Jardiniere, Forest, brown int, 11^1/$_2$" h **950**
Jardiniere, Glasgow roses and foliage, 2 handled, matte green, die stamped
    "Weller," 6 x 7" **400**
Jardiniere, Jap Birdimal, blue trees and moon on gray–blue ground, die
    stamped "Weller," 5^1/$_2$ x 7" **250**
Jardiniere, Klyro, square, fence–like sides, flowers and fruit dec, imp
    "Weller," 6^1/$_2$" sq **60**
Jardiniere, Louwelsa, orange, brown, green, and gold, 9" h **130**
Jardiniere, Muskota, continuous raised frieze of children walking in woods,
    7^1/$_4$" h **600**
Jardiniere, Selma, emb squirrels, owls, birds, and foliage, green and tan on
    brown and green ground, 8^1/$_4$ x 9" **500**
Lamp, Blue Ware, 10^1/$_2$" h **250**
Lamp, horse's head against brown and green ground on marble base,
    32^1/$_2$" h **1,000**
Lamp Base, trefoil, foliage design, imp "Dicken's Ware, Weller," profession-
    ally repaired, 10" w, 7^1/$_4$" h **55**
Mug, Eocean, mushrooms, 5^3/$_4$" h **150**

Mug, Jap Birdimal, black rooster under squeezebag trees on green ground,
  incised "Weller Faience," 5¼ x 4¾" **450**
Mug, Louwelsa, cherries and leaves on dark brown ground, imp "Louwelsa
  Weller," artist mark at handle, 6⅛" h **90**
Pitcher, Eocean, blackberries on shaded ivory to green ground, stamped
  "Weller," incised "Eocean," 12¼" h **150**
Planter, Burntwood, Knifewood mold swan, 5" h, 6" w **150**
Planter, Pastel, P–5, 8" l, 4" h **30**
Planter, Woodcraft, log, 11" l, 5" h **55**
Syrup Pitcher, mammy, incised "Weller," 6¼" h **700**
Table Clock, Louwelsa, yellow wild rose by W.Y. in slip on shell shaped
  blank, brown and dark brown tones, artist sgd, and Louwelsa stamp,
  7 x 5¼" **400**
Teapot, Forest **245**
Umbrella Stand, Ardsley, 19" h **550**
Umbrella Stand, Arts & Crafts, 2 handles, flaring rim, 2 stylized bushes with
  Glasgow rose covered in dark matte green glaze, unmkd, 20 x 10½" **1,100**
Umbrella Stand, Claywood, 19½" h **150**
Umbrella Stand, Griffins and Arabesques, stylized and emb under green
  matte glaze, 21 x 10¾" **125**
Umbrella Stand, Zona, Weller kiln stamp, 19¾" h **425**
Urn, ftd, Sabrinian, shell shaped body, 2 seahorse handles, ink stamped,
  12" h **300**
Vase, Alvin, 7½" h **125**
Vase, Arts and Crafts, tapering, emb beetles and leaves, glossy dark purple
  glaze, 4¾" h **400**
Vase, Baldin, bulbous, 2 handled, blue with emb apples, 10¼" h **500**
Vase, Chase, fan shaped, white hunter on horseback with dog, blue ground,
  incised "Weller Pottery," 8½" h **250**

Left: Flowerpot and Saucer, Bonito, stamped mark, artist sgd, 4½" h, 5" d, $75.

Right: Jardiniere, Forest, int hairline, glued body chip, 7½ x 9", $80. Photo courtesy David Rago Auctions.

Left: Ewer, Cameo, salmon and white, 9³/₄" h, $80.

Right: Vase, Abe Lincoln, Dickensware, 9" h, $880. Photo courtesy Gene Harris Auction Center.

Vase, Chengtu, orange, 7" h	75
Vase, Drapery, blue, 8" h	50
Vase, Eocean, bulbous, mauve and gray leaves on shaded ivory to charcoal ground, incised "Weller Eocean," 6¹/₂" h	375
Vase, Eocean, flowers, berries, and green leaves on shaded dark green to ivory ground, incised "Weller Eocean," and artist's signature, 10¹/₄" h	600
Vase, Eocean, tapering, 4 sided, irises, incised "Eocean," 10¹/₄" h	475
Vase, Eocean, Etna, corseted, grapes and leaves on shaded blue to pink ground, stamped "Weller Etna," 15¹/₂" h	700
Vase, Eocean, Glendale, 8" h	400
Vase, Hudson, bulbous, lotus flower on white ground, stamped "Weller," 10" h	150
Vase, Hudson, classic shape, nasturtium on shaded blue–green and pink ground, by McLaughlin, ink stamped "Weller" and signature, 11³/₄" h	950
Vase, Hudson, cylindrical, pink roses on blue ground, stamped "Weller," 13¹/₂" h	475
Vase, Hudson, tapering, hp swans and lake scene on white ground, incised "Weller" and artist's cipher, 7" h	450
Vase, Irises, emb in polychrome on blue matte ground, stamped "Weller," 10" h	850
Vase, La Sa, classic shape, tree and landscape dec, sgd "Weller," Weller Ware paper label, 8¹/₂" h	325
Vase, Louwelsa, bulbous, roses, stamped "Weller Louwelsa" and artist's signature, 8¹/₂" h	150
Vase, Neiska, #11, 7" h	85
Vase, Patra, polychrome art deco design, incised "Weller Pottery," 4⁷/₈" h	50
Vase, Sicard, tapering, fig shaped, sgd "Weller Sicard," 4" h	400
Vase, Sicard, 2 handled, daisies in purple, green, and blue nacreous glaze, scalloped rim and body, sgd "Sicard," 5¹/₂" h	1,500
Vase, Sicard, Woodcraft, cylindrical, squirrel on tree limb handles, stamped "Weller," 17³/₄" h	1,500
Vessel, frosted matte, feathered green glaze, unmkd, 11¹/₄ x 7¹/₂"	850

Vessel, Knifewood, barrel shaped, emb hunting dogs under glossy finish, ink
    stamped, 5" h **375**
Vessel, Lonhuda, 3 ftd, three handled, green dogwood dec, die stamped
    "Weller" and artist's cipher, 7 x 8" **200**
Vessel, Sicard, acorn shaped, stylized mistletoe on burgundy ground, mkd
    "Weller Sicard," 4 x 3³/₄" **450**
Wall Pocket, Glendale **225**
Wall Pocket, Marvo, brown fern on green ground, 7¹/₂ x 4¹/₂" **150**
Wall Pocket, Wild Rose **80**
Wall Pocket, Woodland, azaleas **140**

YELLOW WARE

Yellow ware is a heavy earthenware of differing weights and strengths. Yellow ware varies in color from a rich pumpkin to lighter shades which are more tan than yellow. Although plates, nappies, and custard cups are found, kitchen bowls and other cooking utensils are most prevalent.

The first American yellow ware was produced at Bennington, Vermont. English yellow ware has additional ingredients which make its body much harder. Derbyshire and Sharp's were foremost among the English manufacturers.

Yellow ware has long been a favorite of Country collectors. Large bowls, unusual molds, and other household items are cornerstone collection pieces and desirable decorative accents.

References: John Gallo, *Nineteenth and Twentieth Century Yellow Ware,* Heritage Press, 1985; Joan Leibowitz, *Yellow Ware: The Transitional Ceramic,* Schiffer Publishing, 1985, 1993 value update; Lisa S. McAllister, *Yellow Ware Book II: An Identification & Value Guide,* Collector Books, 1997; Lisa S. McAllister and John L. Michael, *Collecting Yellow Ware,* Collector Books, 1993, 1995 value update.

Bank, dog, sitting, green and brown running glaze, rect base, coin slot in
    center of bottom, chips on base and coin slot, 7¹/₂" h **$1,000**
Bank, house, molded black detail, "For My Dear Girl" on roof, 3⁵/₈" h **650**
Bank, pig, black and brown sponging, amber glaze, 3³/₄" h **100**
Bowl, blue and brown sponging, mkd "Red Wing Saffron Ware," 9³/₄" d **45**

Bowls, brown bands, minor edge wear and chipping. Left: 5" h, 9¹/₂" d; Right: 5¹/₂" h, 10¹/₂" d; price for pair, $35. Photo courtesy Collectors Auction Services.

Bowl, brown spatter dec border on scalloped rim, 9³/₈" d, 2¹/₄" h **10**
Bowl, brown spatter dec, rounded sides and rim, 8⁵/₈" d, 3⁵/₈" h **35**
Butter Tub, pale blue glaze on molded staves, 4³/₄" d, 4" h **190**
Canning Jar, barrel shaped, 7" h **100**
Casserole, cov, brown sponging, 7¹/₄" d **50**
Creamer, black stripes, white band, and green seaweed dec, hairline at han-
    dle base, 3⁷/₈" h **160**
Creamer, brown stripes, white band, and blue seaweed dec, 4³/₄" h **440**
Creamer, tavern scenes, molded, brown Rockingham glaze, 4¹/₄" h **20**
Crock, flat bottom with rounded base, sides flaring slightly toward a round-
    ed rim with flattened top, overall blue spatter dec, 6¹/₂" d, 6¹/₂" h **20**
Cuspidor, green, blue, and tan sponging, 5 x 7¹/₂" **65**
Food Mold, corn, oval **95**
Food Mold, pinwheel **100**
Food Mold, Turk's head, brown sponging, 9" d **110**
Grease Lamp, bluish green running glaze, rayed circle with "W," 14¹/₂" h **60**
Jar, cov, cylindrical, white band, brown stripes, very minor flakes, 8³/₄" d,
    6¹/₄" h **200**
Jar, cov, cylindrical, white bands, blue seaweed dec, mismatched lid has
    blue stripes and black seaweed, chips and hairlines, 5¹/₄" d **135**
Match Holder, white sanded finish, 2 playing kittens with stumps for match-
    es, imp "Tschinkel," 6" h **190**
Milk Pitcher, squat shape, sides taper toward rim, overall variegated blue,
    red and brown spatter dec on ext, 5¹/₄" d, 5" h **115**
Mixing Bowl, blue and white stripes, mkd "Warranted Fireproof," int wear,
    12¹/₄" d, 5³/₄" h **75**
Mixing Bowl, blue band, molded rim, 12¹/₂" d **85**
Mixing Bowl, brown and white stripes, wear and stains, 13³/₄" d **40**
Mixing Bowl, molded scene of girl with watering can, chips and hairlines,
    10¹/₄" d, 5³/₈" h, price for nesting set of 3 . . . . **80**

Left: Mug, brown and white banding, 2¹/₄" h, 3" d, $20.

Right: Bowl, molded design, unmkd, 6³/₈" d, $15. Photo courtesy Ray Morykan Auctions.

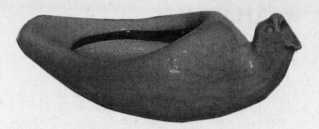

Urinal, bird motif, chips at mouth, c1850, 6¹/₂" h, $30. Photo courtesy Collectors Auction Services.

Mush Bowl, round with flat bottom, sides flare toward rim, brown sponge dec, 6¹³/₁₆" d   30

Nappy, 8" d   100

Pie Funnel, 2¹/₄" h   125

Pie Plate, molded rim design, mkd "Oven Serve," 9" d   65

Pitcher, brown, black, and green sponging, 6³/₄" h   200

Pitcher, paneled, emb floral designs, amber glaze, imp "Norton & Fenton, East Bennington Vt.," hairlines, old spout and rim repair, 10" h   250

Pitcher, squat form, brown, Rockingham glaze, 4¹/₂" h   80

Pitcher, white band, blue seaweed dec, brown stripes, ribbed strap handle, handle glued in 3 places, 8³/₄" h   750

Serving Bowl, brown spatter border on rim, scalloped rim, 9³/₈" d, 2¹/₄" h   10

Serving Bowl, brown spatter ext dec, 8⁵/₈" d at rim, 3⁵/₈" h   35

Soap Dish, round, 5¹/₂" d   175

Vegetable Bowl, open, oval, brown sponging, 8³/₄" l   30

Water Pitcher, cylindrical, overall brown and green spatter dec, molded diamond–like design around sides, 5¹/₄" d   100

SHAKER

When looking for an elegant, but handcrafted look, Country collectors and decorators turn to Shaker. The look has a natural and utilitarian emphasis. Warm earth tones dominate.

'Because the Shakers were self–sufficient, they developed products for all aspects of daily living. Individuals who are only familiar with Shaker furniture are missing much of the picture. The Shaker way of life is understood only in totality.

The Shakers, so named because of a dance used in worship, are one of the oldest communal organizations in the United States. This religious group was founded by Mother Ann Lee, who emigrated from England and established the first Shaker community near Albany, New York, in 1784. The Shakers reached their peak in 1850 with 6,000 members.

Shakers lived celibate and self–sufficient lives. Their philosophy stressed cleanliness, order, simplicity, and economy. Highly inventive and motivated, the Shakers created many utilitarian household forms and objects. Their furniture reflected a striving for quality and purity in design.

In the early nineteenth century, the Shakers produced many items for commercial purposes. Chair making and the packaged herb and seed businesses thrived. In every endeavor and enterprise, the members followed Mother Ann's advice: "Put your hands to work and give your heart to God."

References: Charles R. Muller and Timothy D. Rieman, *The Shaker Chair,* The Canal Press, 1984; Timothy D. Rieman and Jean M. Burks, *The Complete Book of Shaker Furniture,* Harry N. Abrams, 1993; June Sprigg and David Larkin, *Shaker Life, Work, and Art,* Stewart, Tabori & Chang, 1987; June Sprigg and Jim Johnson, *Shaker Woodenware: A Field Guide,* Berkshire House, 1991.

Periodical: *Shakers World,* PO Box 1276, Manchester, CT 06045.

Collectors' Club: Shaker Heritage Society, Albany–Shaker Road, Albany, NY 12211.

Museums: Hancock Shaker Village, Pittsfield, MA; Shaker Historical Museum, Cleveland, OH; Shaker Village of Pleasant Hill, Harrodsburg, KY; The Shaker Museum and Library, Old Chatham, NY.

Apple Corer/Slicer, riveted construction, 4 quarter–round cutting blades surround hollow stem handle, circular brown leather guard, round base, Canterbury, NH, 5" h, 4⅝" d **$90**

Basket, ash, round, straight sides, single wrap over shaped rims, double bottom, wrapped ear handles, "For the Meeting Room in the Meeting House" in ink script on outside of basket, "Office" and "F.L." inscribed in pencil on weavers, 12½" d, 8½" h **400**

Basket, black ash, oval top, rect bottom, shaped handle, "C.S.F." painted in 2" letters on side, initialed "CSF" on handle and bottom, single wrap rim, 1" w uprights, narrow weavers, 17" l, 11½" w, 5¾" h **475**

Bed, walnut, refinished, Pleasant Hill Community, c1850, 33" h, 34" w, 76" l **850**

Bench, seat, pine, grain–painted, red over olive green, single board seat with legs set into dado, foot cut in bootjack pattern, half–dovetailed braces, braces replaced at 1 end, possibly Harvard, MA, 81¼" l, 9¼" w, 5½" h . . . **550**

Bench, kneeling, poplar, old natural patina, underside stenciled "J. E. Andrews," attributed to Union Village Shakers, 6³/₄ x 36"   300

Blanket Chest, pine, painted, 2 graduated thumb–molded drawers, old red wash, orig wood pulls, replaced lock, Canterbury, NH, c1820, 39¹/₄" w, 19¹/₄" d 1,200

Blanket Chest, pine, red paint, lift top, int with 2 lift top tills, single long drawer, bootjack ends, handmade metal escutcheon plate, Canterbury, NH, c1840, 35" w, 17" d, 25³/₄" h 1,600

Blanket Chest, red paint, applied edge molding to top, dovetailed case and bracket feet, stenciled label on back reads "H.B. Bear," some wear and edge damage, 1 back foot replaced, attributed to Ohio Community, 48¹/₂" w, 23³/₄" d, 29¹/₂" h   775

Bootjack, natural "Y" with chamfered edges, old red finish, 20¹/₂" l   100

Box, cov, bentwood, cov, old dark bluish green paint, round, stationary wire bail and wood handle, bottom loose, minor edge damage, attributed to Enfield, CT, 9¹/₂" d   525

Box, cov, bentwood, cov, 3 finger base, 1–finger lid, oval, copper tacks, old worn red paint, 11¹/₂" l 1,425

Box, cov, bentwood, cov, 2 finger base, 1–finger lid, oval, iron tacks, worn old bluish greenish gray paint, 6⁵/₈" l   650

Box, cov, bentwood, cov, varnish finish, swivel handle, copper tacks, 7¹/₄" d . .   135

Box, cov, handkerchief, poplar, kidskin trim, yellow ribbons and satin lining, orig cardboard box inscribed "Manufactured by the Canterbury Shakers, East Canterbury, New Hampshire"   635

Box, cov, round, pine top and bottom, ash or hickory sides, blue–green paint, straight seam, iron tacks, 8³/₈" d, 4" h   230

Box, cov, seed, unfinished pine, black and white paper label reads "Shakers" Garden Seeds, Raised at New Lebanon, N.Y.," leather hinges broken, 14³/₄" l 1,100

Box, cov, sewing, cherry, maple, and mahogany with old finish, top compartment for thread spools with bone or ivory eyelets and turned pincushion, drawer in base, minor edge damage, small area of veneer missing on drawer, cushion cover missing, 6" h   140

Box, oval, painted lamb in grass and tree dec, pine top and bottom, 3–finger construction, copper tacks, "In love from your sister Abigail Crosman 1868" inscribed inside top, 1¹/₂" h, 3¹/₂" w, 2¹/₂" d, $1,500.
Photo courtesy James D. Julia.

Box, cov, sewing, hardwood, 2–tier with drawer, spool compartment and pincushion, worn fabric on cushion, age cracks, damage to bottom back corner, 7" h **165**

Box, cov, sewing, oval with side pockets, 3½ x 11¼" **25**

Brush, wood and horsehair, red paint, swelled handle with 2 scribe lines around widest section and narrow section below knob, 1 scribe line around ball end, probably Canterbury, NH, 14¼" l **1,850**

Carpet and Runner, wool carpet with red, blue, green, and white weft and dark green cotton warp, 1 end overcast by hand and the other finished with overcasting into ⅜" band of dark green cotton, wool runner with 2 twist woven strips of light blue, gold, red, orange, and green plied weft and black/dark green cotton warp, wear along edges of carpet, runner has unraveled facing and mended holes, Sister Jennie Wells of Mount Lebanon, NY, 20' 10" l x 26¾" w carpet, 19" l x 26" w runner **600**

Carrier, bentwood, oval, 4–finger, copper tacks, bentwood handle, old refinishing with traces of red, minor break in handle, 11" l **275**

Carrier, pine, oval, 4–finger (left–handed), yellow paint, copper nails, shaped maple and ash handle, bottom inscribed "Ministry Shop," break in handle, 3⅝" h carrier, 11" l, 8" d, 7⅝" h overall **875**

Carrier, tin, rect, handle set at midpoint, Canterbury, NH, 11¼" l, 8" d, 3" h . . **350**

Chair, armchair, maple, 3–slat back, splint seat, old brown stain, c1930, Mount Lebanon, NY, 18⅞" h seat, 41⅛" h overall **700**

Chair, side, #3, ladder back, imp "3" on top slat, orig dark finish, "Mt. Lebanon, N.Y.," label on bottom slat, replaced blue and gray woven tape seat, 33½" h **475**

Chair, #3, orig dark brown finish, gold stenciled label on back leg reads "Shaker's Trade Mark, Mt. Lebanon, N.Y. No.3," replaced paper rush seat and back, 33¾" h **275**

Chair, ladder back, 3 slats, turned finials, old dark finish, woven split cane seat, attributed to South Union, KY, 38" h **85**

Chair, on tilters, maple, 3 arched slats with acorn finials, dark red–brown stain, rush seat, Mount Lebanon, NY, 16" h seat, 41¼" h overall **1,050**

Chest, 4 graduated dovetailed drawers with center knobs, cut base with angled cutout legs, natural finish, filled escutcheon holes, paint surface stripped, Canterbury, NH, 30 x 16" base, 36½" h **1,000**

Sewing Box, red and black grain painted, 3–finger construction, copper tacks, brown pincushion attached with wood disc, cushion detached, replaced disc screw, minor roughness, 7½" w, 4¾" d, 5" h with cushion, $450. Photo courtesy James D. Julia.

Chest and Cupboard, 1 pc, pine, old refinish with varnish ext, salmon wash on back, red wash int, brass hardware, old varnish finish, cupboard has molded cornice and 2 paneled doors, each with sliding spring latch and orig lock and different sized key, double arched skirt, lift–top chest with molded overhanging rim on 2 sides, dovetailed ends front and back, applied ogee shape brackets on end and backboard, single board bottom to entire pc, star shaped paper tag reads "$20," hinges replaced, brackets missing from front legs, Canterbury, NH, c1840, 63⅝" h cupboard section, 56⅝" l chest, 23¼" d, 81" l overall **4,600**

Chip Box, pine, red stain, dovetail construction with nailed bottom, copper tacks, shaped and tapered ash handle, "Pegs" in faint chalk on end, small chip in handle, 15" l, 9⅜" w, 9¼" h **1,850**

Creamer, tin, hinged lid, some resoldering and light rust, 4¼" h 70

Cream Pitcher, cylindrical, sides taper inward toward rim, thin ribbed handle with cut edges soldered over seam, broad flaring spout, Canterbury, NH, 2⅞" d at base, 3¼" h 175

Cup, cov, painted black, domed lid with turned wooden knob, Canterbury, NH, 4¼" d, 2⅞" h 260

Cupboard, butternut and pine, shellac or varnish finish, slight overhang at top, 2 large symmetrical doors over 2 small doors, wooden pulls and iron hinges, upper int compartment with 3 shelves, paneled sides, feet formed by sides of case, damage to lower right case and door, Mount Lebanon, c1860, 49" w, 19½" d, 60¼" h **2,775**

Cupboard, pine, old blue paint over red, single board overhanging top with fine molding on 3 sides, single 23 x 15½" raised panel door with brass pull and iron hinges, unpainted int with single central shelf, pegged case, back notched on bottom, probably Sabbathday Lake, ME, c1790, 36½" w at base, 17⅛" d, 37¼" h **17,250**

Cupboard, red wash, door over door, 2 raised panel doors double pinned through mortise with 2 H–hinges, lock, and wooden knob, toggle clasps on cupboard close over brass plates tacked to doors, 1 shelf in each cupboard compartment, beaded corner case, ship–lapped back boards, applied bracket base with mitered and nailed corners and arched cutouts, ogee molding form on cornice and base, Mount Lebanon, NY, c1800, 49¼" w, 21" d, 77" **17,250**

Cupboard, yellow stain, single door with 2 flat panels, two int shelves set in dadoes in ends, Canterbury, NH, c1870, 25½" w, 27½" h **2,000**

Desk, lap, butternut, cherry, and poplar, old varnish finish, dovetailed slant–top writing surface with breadboard end, case has pencil till with ink compartment and hidden compartment beneath, opposing drawers, turned hardwood pulls on drawers and till lid, 21" w, 17¾" d, 3½" h **3,800**

Desk, school, pine, grain painted red–orange, slant top, lift top fitted with leather straps each side and with remnants of oilcloth covering, int with center divider and narrow shelf, dovetailed upper case with center front lock secured to base with applied cove molding, apron front and sides, 4 square tapered legs, repairs to mortised leg joints, section of front apron and cove molding replaced, possibly Harvard, MA, 66" l, 31¼" w, 31⅝" h . **1,150**

Desk, sewing, pine, fruitwood pulls, salmon paint, plank side case with ogee shaped base, recessed upper gallery with 2 small drawers above sliding work surface, 4 graduated drawers with nailed construction and bottoms chamfered in at front, each drawer has single fruitwood pull, drawer

blades set in with half dovetails, scrolled side panels, work surface
repaired, 1 drawer blade replaced, Canterbury, NH, c1840, 26" w, 18" d,
36" h **8,700**

Dipper, tin, heavy gauge, straight sides, flat bottom, rolled rim, hollow handle attached with supporting bracket ending in D–shaped ring, "S 20"
stamped near rim, Canterbury, NH, 3" h x 4¼" d bowl, 12¾" h overall **350**

Dipper, tin, triangular bowl, wire encased tapering handle, 14¼" l **30**

Dust Pan, folded corners, rolled top rim, finely turned birch handle with
scribe lines and red painted knob, "Harriet Johns 1880" inscribed on bottom, small split in side of pan, Canterbury, NH, 13" l, 5" w **3,700**

Firkin, pine bottom and V–shaped tongue–and–groove joined staves, orig
blue paint, diamond shaped bail plates, iron hoops with V–shaped ends,
hardwood concave turned red stained handle with scribe line at center,
bottom installed several inches from base, Canterbury or Enfield, NH,
11¼" d top, 12⅞" d bottom, 11" h **1,650**

Food Warmer, sheet steel, rect box shape, riveted construction, worn bluing
with light rust, 11¼" l **45**

Food Warmer, tin, oval dome shape, 12½" l **80**

Footstool, pine, brown stain, nailed 5–board construction, slight overhang
on top, sides have semi–circular cutouts at feet, bottom step set into dado
in sides, 14¾" w, 8" d, 9½" h **750**

Footstool, worn dark finish, "Mt. Lebanon, N.Y." label, edge wear and minor
corner damage, 11½ x 11¾" **300**

Foot Warmer, soapstone with 3–layer cotton cov, navy blue, windowpane
plaid outer layer, beige interlining, white on blue striped lining, 2 blue
buttons and handmade buttonholes, lining torn and hole in outer cover,
9¾ x 5¾ x 1¼" soapstone, 13 x 6½" cover **60**

Foot Warmer, soapstone with 3–layer cotton cov, olive green, pattern–woven
outer layer, pink interlining, blue and white print lining, 2 white buttons
with concentric rings of dark turquoise and handmade button holes, small
burn mark, Canterbury, NH, 10 x 5½ x 1" soapstone, 12 x 6½" cover **60**

Grain Measure, round, oak and pine, natural color, bottom stenciled "Shaker
Society, Sealed, W. Gloucester, ME." in black, c1880–96, 7½" d, 4" h **230**

Herb Infuser, tin, spherical, 5" d **20**

Labels, canned goods, chromolithographic, "Butter Beans" and "Fresh
Tomatoes," "Anna Case Trustee South Family Shakers. West Albany,"
matted and framed, 20" w, 15" h **300**

Medicine Bottle, aqua, "Shaker Digestive Cordial, A.J. White, New York,"
5⅝" h **35**

Pail, miniature, blue paint, turned wood and wire bail handle with diamond
plate attachments, newer overpaint, 4½" h, 5½" w **225**

Pail, miniature, stave construction, deep blue over white ext, worn white
paint int, metal bands and diamond handle attachments in black, wire
bail and wooden handle, branded label on bottom reads "W. B. Va," worn
white paint int, 4½" h, 5¾" d **780**

Pail, pine staves and bottom, square tongue–and–groove joints, orig
ocher–orange paint, iron hoops with clipped ends, coffin shaped bail
plates, hardwood shaped handle stained brown, possibly New Lebanon,
NY, 9¼" h, 12" d **1,400**

Pail, pine staves and bottom, V–shaped tongue–and–groove joints, orig
chrome yellow paint ext and white paint int, iron hoops with V–clipped

ends, diamond shaped bail plates, hardwood handle with 3 scribe lines, bottom has imp "8" and "E H/5" (East House) painted in black, Canterbury or Enfield, NH, 5³/₈" h, 7" d 1,050

Pail, wood, cov, stave construction, tongue–and–groove joints, red painted ext, heavy wire bail, wooden handle, recessed knob in center of lid, 7⁵/₈" h, 9³/₄" d 230

Peg Board, pine and cherry, old patina, 1 peg missing, 38³/₄" l 50

Picnic Hamper, woven, double lid top, old color, small pcs of weaving unwrapped, 17¹/₂" l, 10¹/₂" w, 16" h 75

Quilt Rack, mortised and pinned construction, nailed semi–circular top rail, 47¹/₂" w, 38" h 330

Rocker, #3, ladder back, 3 slats, imp "3" on top slat, orig dark brown finish, rush seat, Mount Lebanon, NY, 15" h seat, 34¹/₂" h overall 300

Rocker, #4, maple, 3 slats, "4""on back of slat, ebony stain, red and olive tape seat with olive velveteen cov, rockers pinned through legs, Mount Lebanon, NY, 15" h seat, 34³/₄" h overall 400

Rocker, #6, mushroom type arms, orig finish, seat replaced, 17" h seat, 42" h overall 850

Rocker, #7, armchair, ladder back with shawl bar, imp "7" on back of top slat, worn orig dark finish, replaced maroon and beige tape seat, traces of Mount Lebanon label inside 1 rocker, 41" h 675

Rulers, pr, wooden, 1 with brown stain, hand–stamped numbers right to left in ¹/₈" segments, stamped "AD 1865" on verso, 12" l, ³/₄" w, other with orange stain, hand–stamped numbers on both sides, 12" l, 1" w, price for pair 525

Scoop, tin, 10¹/₄" l 50

Shovel, carved from single pc of wood, 35¹/₂" l, 11¹/₄" w 325

Sorting Tray, cherry, 4–sided, kidney shaped cutout handles, 33" w, 20" d, 4¹/₂" h 150

Left: Rocker, slat back, branded "3" on top slat, dark brown finish, rush seat, Mount Lebanon, NY, 15" h seat, 34¹/₂" h, 19" w, $300.

Right: Wide Chair, curved slats, turned finials, contemporary cloth taped seat, 16" h seat, 40" h, $125.

Photos courtesy James D. Julia.

Spool Rack, maple and fruitwood, 2 rows of 6 hand carved spindles pegged through base, rect base with dark stain, 9 turned wooden spools, 1 with "M.O." paper label, probably Canterbury, NH, 7½" l, 3" w, 4" h **1,100**

Spools, various hardwoods, 1 with yellow wash, 1 with salmon wash, ranging in size from ¾" to 2¼" h, price for 10 . . . . **700**

Stand, Elder's lift top, tiger maple square top, hinged rear with locking wood clasp, tapered square legs, wood pegged, missing spline, possibly Pleasant Hill Community, 18½ x 18" top, 27¾" h **800**

Stool, 2 step, pine, red paint, nailed construction, L–shape board sides with steps nailed through top, 2" w brace nailed to rabbet at floor level front, 1" w brace set into back, 12⅝" w, 11⅛" d, 14¾" h **90**

Stove, cast iron, 4 legs, hinged door with latch, turned wooden knob handle, circular hearth, canted sides, 28¾" l, 12" w, 16⅜" h **475**

Stove, cast iron, 3 legs, penny feet, hinged door with latch, turned wooden knob handle, circular hearth, canted sides, crack on side, 33" l, 12¾" w, 17½" h **800**

Stove Tools, shovel and tongs, iron, shovel shaft swelled below knob, half domed knob at ends, wear, 21½" l shovel, 21¾" l tongs, price for pair **140**

Stove Tools, shovel and tongs, wrought iron, attributed to Canterbury, NH, 22" l shovel, 17½" l tongs, price for pair **500**

Strainer, formed flared bowl with integral punched screen bottom, turned handle painted black, handle and handle flange may be replacements, Canterbury, NH, 4¼" d bowl, 9⅛" h **45**

Sugar, cov, lid finial, some resoldering and light rust **100**

Swift, collapsible, pine and maple, yellow wash, wooden thumbscrew, ink "Laundry No.12," on base, dated "1852" on blade, 25½" h **1,850**

Swift, collapsible, worn yellow varnish, minor crack in table clamp, attributed to Hancock, MA, 15" h **225**

Tailor's Counter, 6 dovetailed lip–molded drawers, walnut mushroom shaped pulls,
$24,150. Photo courtesy James D. Julia.

Table, drop leaf, pine, ash, and birch, traces of red paint, boldly turned legs, height modified, Canterbury, NH, 72½ x 41½" top extended, 27½" h **2,075**

Table, pine, red paint, 2–board top, mortised case with single drawer with turned knob, Canterbury tag with "$10" in faded script attached to knob, turned tapered legs, major repair to right rear leg, Canterbury, NH, c1850, 60¾" l, 35⅝" d, 30¾" h **2,300**

Table, red paint, single board top, single drawer with molded face and turned wooden knob, tapered leg, horizontal crack through center of top, 42¼" x 27½" top, 29¾" x 21½" base, 29" h **1,500**

Table, work, 2–board top with rounded corners, hardwood base with old red and pine top with scrubbed finish, square tapered legs with mortised and pinned apron, attributed to Enfield, NH, 37½" x 48¾" top, 27¼" h **950**

Teapot, tin, side spout, 8½" h **175**

Tool Cabinet, pine, gray paint, tool cabinet, top finished with quarter–round molded edge and secured by screws and nails, dovetailed case, single door with 6 panels, wooden pull, and later iron hardware, int contains 2 rows of dovetailed drawers with walnut fronts, dovetailed shelf bracket on inside of door, and 4 shelves, incised "E.W." above drawer fronts, Harvard, MA, c1875, 38¾" w, 12⅝" d, 44⅝" h **2,000**

Trundle Bed, oak, dark olive green paint, solid headboard panel between side rails drilled for roping, headboard tapered at front, posts at foot chamfered to octagonal shape at top, height modified by reduction of legs and addition of wooden–wheeled casters with iron brackets, Mount Lebanon, NY, 68" l, 30½" w **400**

Wheelbarrow, green paint, removable sides, large 8–spoke wooden wheel, metal supporting rods and detail work, curved handles with mortise and tendon joints, 81" l, 27" w, 32½" h **600**

Wood Bin, pine, bin top with hinged lid with breadboard ends, old mellow finish, square single dovetailed overlapping drawer, corner posts with chamfered feet, int has red stain and wear, old pieced repair to 1 end of drawer front, Canterbury, NH, 37½" w, 21" d, 31" h **875**

STONEWARE

Slip and sgraffito decorated redware dominate the early American look. The pottery of choice for the Country collector and decorator is stoneware.

Made from dense kaolin clay and commonly salt–glazed, stonewares were hand–thrown and high–fired to produce a simple, bold vitreous pottery. Stoneware crocks, jugs, and jars were produced for storage and utility purposes. This use dictated shape and design—solid, thick–walled forms with heavy rims, necks, and handles with little or no embellishment. When decorated, the designs were simple: brushed cobalt oxide, incised, slip trailed, stamped, or tooled.

Stoneware has been made for centuries. Early American settlers initially imported stoneware items but soon began producing their own. Two major North American traditions emerged based only on the location or type of clay. North Jersey and parts of New York comprise the first area; the second was eastern Pennsylvania spreading westward and into Maryland, Virginia, and West Virginia. These two distinct locations, style of decoration, and shape are discernible factors in classifying and dating early stoneware.

By the late eighteenth century, stoneware was manufactured in all sections of the country. During the nineteenth century, this vigorous industry flourished until glass "fruit jars" appeared and the use of refrigeration became widespread. By 1910, commercial production of salt–glazed stoneware came to an end.

References: M. H. Alexander, *Stoneware in Blue and White: An Identification and Value Guide, Revised,* published by author, 1993; Dan and Gail DePasquale and Larry Peterson, *Red Wing Stoneware,* Collector Books, 1983, 1997 value update; Georgeanna H. Greer, *American Stoneware: The Art and Craft of Utilitarian Potters, Revised,* Schiffer Publishing, 1996; Steven B. Leder and Fred Cesana, *The Birds of Bennington,* Stoneware Publications, 1991; Jim Martin and Betty Cooper, *Monmouth–Western Stoneware,* published by authors, 1983, 1993 value update; Don and Carol Raycraft, *American Stoneware,* Wallace–Homestead, Krause Publications, 1995; Don and Carol Raycraft, *Collector's Guide to Country Stoneware and Pottery* (1985, 1995 value update), *Second Series* (1990, 1996 value update), Collector Books; George Sullivan, *The Official Price Guide to American Stoneware,* House of Collectibles, 1993; Terry G. Taylor and Terry and Kay Lowrance, *Collector's Encyclopedia of Salt Glaze Stoneware: Identification & Value Guide,* Collector Books, 1997; Kathryn McNerney, *Blue & White Stoneware,* Collector Books, 1981, 1996 value update; Elinor Meugniot, *Old Sleepy Eye,* published by author, 1979.

Collectors' Clubs: American Stoneware Assoc, 208 Crescent Court, Mars, PA 16066; Old Sleepy Eye Collectors Club of America, PO Box 12, Monmouth, IL 61462; Stoneware Collectors Society, PO Box 281, Bay Head, NJ 08742.

Museums: The Bennington Museum, Bennington, VT; Museum of Ceramics at East Liverpool, East Liverpool, OH.

Applebutter Crock, ½ gal, unknown maker, semi–ovoid, flanged rim, cobalt
   blue brushed "½" and stenciled maple leaf dec **$85**
Bank, jug shaped, 4" h, blue band around shoulder **125**
Bank, jug shaped, 6³⁄₈" h, brown Albany slip **175**

Batter Pail, 4 qt, unknown maker, semi–ovoid, flanged rim, lug handle at base, wire bail handle with turned wood grip, imp "4," brown Albany slip inside and out **75**

Batter Pail, 1 gal, Cowden & Wilcox, Harrisburg, PA, cov, bulbous, lug handle at base, wire bail handle with turned wood grip, cobalt blue brushed vining flower with large blossoms all around, blue at ears and lug handle, orig tin lids **4,500**

Batter Pail, 1 gal, E & L P Norton, Bennington, VT, cov, lug handle at base, wire bail handle with turned wood grip, imp label, cobalt blue "4," tin cap on spout, minor chips **175**

Batter Pail, 1 gal, F H Cowden, Harrisburg, cov, wire bail handle with turned wood grip, imp label, cobalt blue brushed 5–bloom flower dec front and back, blue at ears and lug handle, orig tin lids on spout and top, minor chips **1,500**

Batter Pail, 1 gal, Sipe & Sons, Williamsport, PA, semi–ovoid, lug handle at base, wire bail handle with turned wood grip, cobalt blue brushed flourish, blue at ears, spout, and lug handle, some chips at spout and rim **400**

Batter Pail, 1 gal, Sipe, Nichols & Co, Williamsport, PA, semi–ovoid, lug handle at base, wire bail handle with turned wood grip, imp label, cobalt blue brushed flower, blue at ears, spout, and lug handle, some chips at spout and rim **500**

Batter Pail, 1½ gal, Evan R Jones, Pittston, PA, ovoid, lug handle at base, wire bail handle with turned wood grip, imp label, large cobalt blue brushed flower and stenciled "1½," blue at ears and spout, 2 small chips on lug handle **400**

Batter Pail, 1½ gal, Sipe & Sons, Williamsport, PA, semi–ovoid, lug handle at base, wire bail handles with turned wood grip, imp "1½" and label, cobalt blue brushed flower, cobalt blue at ears and lug handle, some repair around spout **300**

Bean Pot, cov, unknown maker, molded dec and figures, emb "Boston Baked Beans," int crazing, 6³/₈" h **185**

Bean Pot, cov, unknown maker, semi–ovoid, flared rim, strap handle, brown Albany slip inside and out, minor glaze flake **25**

Batter Pail, 4 qt, Evan R Jones, Pittston, imp label, cobalt blue long–nosed man in the moon dec, cobalt blue at ears and around spout, wire bail handle, small rim chips, $2,530. Photo courtesy Arthur Auctioneering.

Bean Pot, cov, Whites, Utica, coggle wheel dec around neck, handle with thumb rest, raised "Boston Baked Beans" label, cobalt blue at handle, label, and all around, chip on lid **200**

Bedpan, brown Albany slip **35**

Bottle, 1 qt, D W Defreest, cylindrical, conical top with molded lip, stamped label, cobalt blue slip script "R," small chips on lip **110**

Bottle, 1 qt, Krebs & Knorr, cylindrical, conical top with molded lip, cobalt blue band below lip, stress line on side **90**

Bowl, ½ gal, Rabb & Rehm, Bloomsburg, PA, flanged rim, brown Albany slip **85**

Brandy Pig, 1½ gal, cobalt blue scalloped, feather, and leaf bands around ...**1,200**

Butter Churn, 1 gal, unknown maker, flared rim, sloping shoulder, large lug handles, tobacco spit glaze at handles, minor chips around bottom, 13¼" h **85**

Butter Churn, 2 gal, Lyons, table top, flanged rim, sloping shoulder, lug handles, imp label, strong cobalt blue brushed flower with leaves, 2 cobalt blue brushed "2"s, rim chip **350**

Butter Churn, 3 gal, unknown maker, ovoid, lug handles, imp "3," cobalt blue brushed flourish, 15¼" h **325**

Butter Churn, 4 gal, E Norton & Co, Bennington, VT, straight sided, imp label, cobalt blue slip stylized flower, chips and flaking, 17½" h **165**

Butter Churn, 4 gal, New Geneva, tan clay, tooled bands, 2–tone amber and brown slip, cobalt blue stenciled design, wear and chips, 18¾" h **150**

Butter Churn, 4 gal, unknown maker, ovoid, red clay body, gray salt glaze, brushed cobalt blue "4" and floral dec, 16½" h **85**

Butter Churn, 5 gal, Macomb Stoneware & T C Co, Macomb, IL, molded rim, slightly rounded shoulder, lug handles, cobalt blue stenciled "5" and label, tight crack at top edge, small inner rim chip **225**

Butter Crock, 1 qt, unknown maker, straight sided, lug handles, incised "F. L. Burber" **30**

Butter Crock, 1 gal, Old Sleepy Eye, straight sided, lug handles, cobalt blue band at rim, cobalt blue molded Indian design **575**

Butter Churn, 6 gal, Whites, Utica, imp label, cobalt blue large fantail bird in floral and fern dec, cobalt blue at label, crack through dec, $1,045. Photo courtesy Arthur Auctioneering.

Butter Crock, 1 gal, P Herman, cov, straight sided, lug handles, cobalt blue brushed feathery leaf and floral dec all around lid and crock, inner rim chip on lid 325

Butter Crock, 1 gal, unknown maker, straight sided, lug handles, incised lines top and bottom, cobalt blue brushed leafy dec around, tight glued cracks on side 150

Butter Crock, 1 gal, unknown maker, straight sided, lug handles, cobalt blue brushed leafy vine and blossom dec all around, tiny chip on bottom edge .. 250

Butter Crock, 1 gal, unknown maker, straight sided, molded with rose bouquets on crosshatched ground all around, cobalt blue band at top and bottom, blue at bouquets, salt glazed 110

Butter Crock, 1½ gal, Hamilton & Pershing, Johnstown, PA, lug handles, cobalt blue feather dec around 500

Butter Crock, 1½ gal, unknown maker, covered, straight sided, lug handles, cobalt blue brushed floral dec, imp "1½," hairline in base and minor chip on inside of lid flange, 12" d 425

Butter Crock, 1½ gal, unknown maker, straight sided, lug handles, cobalt blue quillwork "6 Butter 1870" and flourish, 13¾" d 375

Cake Crock, 2 gal, A Conrad, New Geneva, PA, straight sided, lug handles, cobalt blue stenciled and freehand "2" and label 300

Cake Crock, 2 gal, Cowden & Wilcox, Harrisburg, PA, straight sided, lug handles, imp label, strong cobalt blue brushed leaf and "2," blue at label, small stone ping on side 650

Cake Crock, 2 gal, T F Reppert, Greensboro, PA, straight sided, lug handles, cobalt blue stenciled label, freehand "2" and sheaf design 425

Cake Crock, 4 gal, Haxstun & Co, Fort Edward, NY, straight sided, lug handles, imp "4" and label, cobalt blue bird on branch, tight 2" crack at top edge, glaze flaking on back 175

Cake Crock, 4 gal, NY Stoneware Co, Ft Edward, NY, straight sided, lug handles, imp label, cobalt blue quillwork flower, tight glued crack on side, minor chips, some glaze flaking 125

Cake Crock, 4 gal, P Herman, attributed to, straight sided, lug handles, cobalt blue brushed floral dec all around, cinnamon colored, minor rim chips 450

Canning Jar, 1 pt, Jas Hamilton & Co, Greensboro, PA, cobalt blue stenciled and freehand label, minor rim chips 150

Cake Crock, 2 gal, unmkd, lug handles, cobalt blue floral dec around, tight crack on side and across bottom, $250. Photo courtesy Arthur Auctioneering.

Canning Jar, 1 qt, A P Donaghho, Parkersburg, WV, incised lines around shoulder, cobalt blue stenciled label **100**

Canning Jar, 1 qt, Excelsior Works, Isaac Hewitt, Jr, Rices Landing, PA, incised lines around neck, cobalt blue stenciled label, wax seal, minor inner rim chips **450**

Canning Jar, 1 qt, Hartford City Salt Co, Dealers in Salt & General Merchandise, Hartford City, WV, cobalt blue stenciled label, chips and hairlines, 6³/₄" h **275**

Canning Jar, 1 qt, Lock Haven, PA, imp label, brown color **100**

Canning Jar, 2 qt, A Conrad, New Geneva, PA, cobalt blue stenciled label, 8¹/₂" h **225**

Canning Jar, 2 qt, Hamilton & Jones, Greensboro, PA, wax seal, flanged rim, sloping shoulder, cobalt blue stenciled and freehand label **145**

Canning Jar, 2 qt, New Geneva Pottery, cobalt blue wavy lines, stenciled label, small flake on lip, 9¹/₂" h **275**

Canning Jar, 2 qt, unknown maker, straight sides taper slightly from top to bottom, 5 cobalt blue brushed bands, wax seal, very minor flake off inner rim, 9¹/₄" h **140**

Canning Jar, 1 gal, unknown maker, cobalt blue stenciled and freehand "S & L Vickers Dealers in Dry Goods & Groceries & C Loydsville, O" **475**

Canning Jar, 1 gal, Wilkinson & Fleming, Shinnston, WV, cobalt blue stenciled label with rose, 10" h **275**

Canning Jar, 1¹/₂ gal, unknown maker, imp "1¹/₂," cobalt blue brushed floral dec, lime deposits, 11" h **45**

Chamber Pot, child's, flared rim, spurred ear handle, blue and white salt glazed, small age lines **35**

Cheese Crock, 1 qt, unknown maker, cobalt blue stenciled adv label "Vanity Fair, Wm. S. Kimball & Co., Rochester, NY" **50**

Chicken Fountain, 1 gal, A L Hyssong, Bloomsburg, attached underplate, cobalt blue brushed flower **450**

Chicken Fountain, 1 gal, unknown maker, tan colored, no underplate **25**

Crock, 2 qt, unknown maker, semi–ovoid, imp adv label "D. P. Hobart, Agent, Williamsport, PA," minor rim chip **65**

Crock, 1 gal, A L Hyssong, Bloomsburg, semi–ovoid, flanged rim, cinnamon colored, rim chip, tightly glued crack **75**

Crock, 1 gal, Brady & Ryan, Ellenville, NY, straight sided, molded rim, lug handles, imp label, cobalt blue slip leaf with flower buds **175**

Crock, 1 gal, Cowden & Wilcox, Harrisburg, PA, semi–ovoid, flanged rim, imp label, cobalt blue brushed flower **350**

Crock, 1 gal, D Ack, Mooresburg, PA, semi–ovoid, flanged rim, imp label, cobalt blue brushed snapping turtle, rim chips, tight crack at top edge **750**

Crock, 1 gal, D P Shenfelder, PA, semi–ovoid, flanged rim, incised lines around shoulder, cobalt blue brushed feather dec all around, very tight crack at top edge, spider line crack in bottom **100**

Crock, 1 gal, Evan R Jones, Pittston, PA, semi–ovoid, flanged rim, cobalt blue brushed flower, rim chip **300**

Crock, 1 gal, F T Wright & Son, Stoneware, Taunton, Mass, straight sided, flanged rim, lug handles, stenciled label, cobalt blue stenciled grape cluster, rim chips, tight cracks around top **45**

Crock, 1 gal, I Seymour & Co, Troy, semi–ovoid, lug handles, imp label, blue at label and handles, minor rim chips **50**

Crock, 1 gal, Ithaca, NY, semi–ovoid, lug handles, incised rim band, imp label, cobalt blue brushed flower, blue at label, crack in back 75

Crock, 1 gal, John Burger, Rochester, straight sided, lug handles, imp label, cobalt blue brushed flower, tight crack on side 400

Crock, 1 gal, N A White & Co, Binghamton, ovoid, flanged rim, lug handles, imp label, cobalt blue slip flower, blue at label, very tight crack in back . . . 55

Crock, 1 gal, Sipe & Sons, Williamsport, PA, straight sided, lug handles, imp label, cobalt blue brushed single spike flower, tight crack at back base, minor rim chips 125

Crock, 1 gal, Sipe, Nichols & Co, Williamsport, ovoid, flanged rim, imp label, cobalt blue brushed drooping bellflower, blue at label 165

Crock, 1 gal, T D Metcalf, Sunbury, PA, semi–ovoid, imp label, simple cobalt blue brushed leafy flourish, rim chip 225

Crock, 1 gal, unknown maker, flared lip, open loop handles, cobalt blue slip 2–bloom flower within wreath, 3 cobalt blue stripes, dots on handles, 10¼" h 250

Crock, 1 gal, Whites, Utica, straight sided, lug handles, cobalt blue slip "1863," rim chip on back 150

Crock, 1½ gal, Evan R Jones, Pittston, PA, semi ovoid, lug handles, flanged rim, imp "1½" and label, cobalt blue brushed flower, blue at label, minor rim chip 300

Crock, 1½ gal, F T Wright & Son, Taunton, Mass, straight sided, flanged rim, lug handles, imp label and "1½," very elaborate cobalt blue slip bird perched on stump, blue at label, professional rim chip repair 550

Left: Crock, 3 gal, H Weston, Honesdale, PA, semi–ovoid, lug handles, imp label, cobalt blue bird on branch, $1,183.

Right: Crock, 4 gal, unknown maker, cobalt blue pecking chicken dec, $575.

Photos courtesy Arthur Auctioneering.

Crock, 1½ gal, G Apley & Co, Ithaca, NY, straight sides taper to base, lug handles, imp label, cobalt blue brushed double blossom flower, blue at label, large chip at base edge **60**

Crock, 1½ gal, John B Claire & Co, Main St, Poughkeepsie, NY, straight sided, imp label, cobalt blue slip stylized flower, glaze flakes, 10½" h **325**

Crock, 1½ gal, Lewistown Pottery, ovoid, flanged rim, cobalt blue brushed drooping tulip, tight crack, some discoloration, small rim chip **125**

Crock, 1½ gal, Sipe & Sons, Williamsport, PA, semi–ovoid, flanged rim, imp label, strong cobalt blue brushed bellflower dec, blue at label, large chips on outer rim **65**

Crock, 1½ gal, Sugar Valley, PA, semi–ovoid, imp label, cobalt blue brushed floral dec, minor spider line crack at bottom **650**

Crock, 1½ gal, unknown maker, semi–ovoid, urn shaped, ear handles, incised lines around shoulder, cobalt blue brushed feather leaf dec all around, small rim chip, sealed crack on side **200**

Crock, 2 gal, A O Whittemore, Havana, NY, straight sided, lug handles, imp label, cobalt blue bird on branch, cracks on back **150**

Crock, 2 gal, Burger & Co, Rochester, NY, straight sided, imp label, ornate cobalt blue fan shaped flower with 2 serrated leaves, blue "2" in flower center, blue at label **300**

Crock, 2 gal, Cowden & Wilcox, Harrisburg, PA, semi–ovoid, flanged rim, lug handles, imp "2" and label, cobalt blue brushed man in the moon dec, blue at handles **5,600**

Crock, 2 gal, Cross Bros, Sterling, PA, straight sided, lug handles, imp label, cobalt blue brushed and slip flower, some fry, 9½" h **150**

Crock, 2 gal, E S Fox, Athens, NY, semi–ovoid, lug handles, imp label, incised line around shoulder, cobalt blue "2" and date "1833," blue at label and handles, minor chips **175**

Crock, 2 gal, Evan R Jones, Pittston, PA, straight sided, flanged rim, lug handles, imp "2" and label, strong cobalt blue brushed horizontal flower, blue at label **175**

Crock, 2 gal, I Seymour, Troy, semi–ovoid, lug handles, imp label, incised lines around shoulder, cobalt blue brushed feather dec, blue at label, minor chips at top and bottom edges **75**

Crock, 2 gal, J M Mott & Co, Ithaca, NY, semi–ovoid, lug handles, imp "2" and label, cobalt blue brushed double bloom flower with leafy stems, minor spider line crack on side **150**

Crock, 2 gal, Lyons, straight sided, lug handles, imp label, incised lines at rim, 2 cobalt blue slip "2"s, strong cobalt blue brushed leafy design, blue at label and handles, inner rim chip, chip on bottom edge **200**

Crock, 2 gal, N Clark Jr, Athens, NY, semi–ovoid, lug handles, imp label, cobalt blue "2" and brushed double blossom flower, blue at handles and label, minor rim chips **125**

Crock, 2 gal, N White & Co, Binghamton, semi–ovoid, lug handles, incised line around shoulder, imp label, cobalt blue "2" and large poppy, very tight crack on side **175**

Crock, 2 gal, Union Pottery Stoneware, slightly concave side, flanged rim, lug handles, imp label, cobalt blue brushed script "2 G" and triple bloom flower **225**

Crock, 2 gal, unknown maker, flared rim, lug handles, cobalt blue brushed leaf dec, blue at handles, tight crack at top edge, chips around **55**

Crock, 3 gal, C Hart, Sherburne, semi–ovoid, lug handles, imp "3" and label, cobalt blue brushed plow flower, blue at label, spider line cracks in back, minor rim chips **150**

Crock, 3 gal, Cowden & Wilcox, Harrisburg, PA, semi–ovoid, flanged rim, lug handles, imp label, cobalt blue brushed cherry branch, blue at handles, minor flake on inner rim **600**

Crock, 3 gal, Cowden & Wilcox, Harrisburg, PA, semi–ovoid, flanged rim, lug handles, imp "3" and label, cobalt blue slip bird in wreath, blue at label and handles, stone ping in making, small rim chip **4,675**

Crock, 3 gal, E B Hissong, Cassville, PA, semi–ovoid, lug handles, flared rim, cobalt blue flowering branch, minor rim chip **2,000**

Crock, 3 gal, Evan R Jones, Pittston, PA, straight sided, lug handles, imp "3" and label, cobalt blue brushed drooping flower, tight spider line cracks on side **175**

Crock, 3 gal, F B Norton & Co, Worchester, MA, straight sided, lug handles, imp label, cobalt blue bird in tree, chip on bottom edge **575**

Crock, 3 gal, F H Cowden, Harrisburg, semi–ovoid, flanged rim, lug handles, imp label, cobalt blue stenciled diamond shaped dec, tight crack on bottom edge **175**

Crock, 3 gal, Fulper Bros, Flemington, NJ, straight sided, lug handles, imp label, incised rim band, strong cobalt blue slip stylized triple leaf design, rim chips, repaired **175**

Crock, 3 gal, Hubbell & Chesebro, Geddes, NY, straight sided, lug handles, imp "3" and label, cobalt blue stylized branch with flower and leaves, rim chip **125**

Crock, 3 gal, J H Dipple, Lewistown, PA, straight sided, lug handles, imp label, cobalt blue brushed feathery dec, rim chip, crack on back **275**

Crock, 3 gal, J Swank & Co, Johnstown, PA, semi–ovoid, lug handles, imp label, cobalt blue feathery dec all around, cinnamon tan color **350**

Crock, 3 gal, Seymour & Bosworth, Hartford, straight sided, flanged rim, lug handles, imp label, faded cobalt blue slip bird on stump dec, spider line crack on side **120**

Crock, 5 gal, J Norton & Co, Bennington, VT, lug handles, imp early Norton stamp, cobalt blue basket of flowers, cobalt blue at label, minor handle chip, $1,430. Photo courtesy Arthur Auctioneering.

Crock, 3 gal, Sipe & Sons, Williamsport, PA, semi–ovoid, flanged rim, lug handles, imp label, cobalt blue brushed bellflower, blue at handles, small chips **130**

Crock, 3 gal, T Harrington, Lyons, straight sided, lug handles, imp label, cobalt blue "3" and tulip, blue at handles, crack at left of flower, inner rim chip. **125**

Crock, 3 gal, Thomas & Bros, Huntingdon, PA, straight sided, lug handles, imp "3" and label, cobalt blue brushed flower **625**

Crock, 4 gal, Adam Caire, PO'Keppsie [sic], NY, straight sided, flanged rim, lug handles, imp label, cobalt blue slip stylized flower, professionally repaired top edge **85**

Crock, 4 gal, Brady & Ryan, Ellenville, NY, straight sided, lug handles, imp label, cobalt blue bird on branch **450**

Crock, 4 gal, Cowden & Wilcox, Harrisburg, PA, semi–ovoid, lug handles, imp "4" and label, incised lines around shoulder, cobalt blue brushed floral bouquet, blue at label, tight spider line crack on side **650**

Crock, 4 gal, E W Farrington, Elmira, NY, straight sided, flanged rim, lug handles, imp "4" and label, cobalt blue brushed robin on branch, blue at label, tight cracks on side and back **165**

Crock, 4 gal, F H Cowden, Harrisburg, semi–ovoid, flanged rim, lug handles, imp label, cobalt blue stenciled geometric design, rim chip on back, tight crack bottom edge **65**

Crock, 4 gal, Fulper, attributed to, straight sided, flanged rim, lug handles, unmkd, cobalt blue slip Fulper style bird on branch, very tight 2" hairline on top edge **385**

Crock, 4 gal, John Burger, Rochester, semi–ovoid, molded rim, lug handles, imp label, strong cobalt blue slip "4" with fern leaves, tight crack in back, small rim chip **165**

Crock, 4 gal, Johnson & Knapp, Olean, NY, straight sided, imp "4" and label, cobalt blue brushed double daisy, blue at label, tight crack at top back . . . **200**

Crock, 4 gal, M & T Miller, Newport, PA, semi–ovoid, flanged rim, lug handles, imp label, elaborate cobalt blue brushed double bloom floral dec, blue at handle, crack in back, rim chip **750**

Crock, 4 gal, Millburn, BC, semi–ovoid, straight sided, lug handles, imp label, incised band at rim, cobalt blue leafy floral bouquet, 14" h **425**

Crock, 4 gal, Morgan, David, NY, incised and cobalt blue floral dec front and back, early 19th C, 12" h **1,100**

Crock, 4 gal, N W White & Son, Utica, NY, straight sided, lug handles, imp label, cobalt blue compote and flowers **450**

Crock, 4 gal, NY Stoneware Co, Ft Edward, NY, straight sided, lug handles, imp label, cobalt blue bird on branch, repair on side, glued crack, glaze flaking around bottom **100**

Crock, 4 gal, Ottman Bros, Fort Edwards, NY, straight sided, imp "4" and label, cobalt blue slip bird on branch, crack in back, 11¼" h **200**

Crock, 4 gal, R S Rand, Portland, ME, straight sided, lug handles, imp "4" and label, cobalt blue grape cluster, 1 handle replaced, tight crack in back **150**

Crock, 5 gal, Cowden & Wilcox, Harrisburg, PA, semi–ovoid, imp "5" and label, cobalt blue brushed feathery fan shaped flower, blue at handles, rim chip, tightly glued crack on side **325**

Crock, 5 gal, Evan R Jones, Pittston, PA, straight sided, lug handles, imp "5" and label, cobalt blue bird on stump, blue at label, tight crack bottom back edge **525**

Crock, 5 gal, J Burger, Jr, Rochester, NY, straight sided, molded rim, lug handles, imp label, strong cobalt blue slip "5" and stylized double blossom flower, some fry, very tight crack in center of dec **400**

Crock, 5 gal, Riedinger & Caire, Poughkeepsie, NY, straight sided, lug handles, cobalt blue fancy bird on stump, glaze flaking, handles replaced **150**

Crock, 5 gal, W H Farrar & Co, Geddes, NY, semi–ovoid, lug handles, incised band around shoulder, cobalt blue slip triple bloom stylized floral bouquet, minor rim chips **425**

Crock, 6 gal, Cowden & Wilcox, Harrisburg, PA, semi–ovoid, flanged rim, lug handles, large cobalt blue grape cluster and vine dec, blue at handles, some fry **685**

Crock, 6 gal, Evan R Jones, Pittston, PA, straight sided, molded rim, lug handles, imp "6" and label, strong cobalt blue brushed leafy flower, blue at label, spigot hole below flower, tight crack on left side **265**

Crock, 6 gal, J H Dipple, Lewistown, straight sided, lug handles, imp label, cobalt blue daisy and leaves, tight crack bottom back **575**

Crock, 20 gal, William Lintons Pottery and Sales Room, Corner of Lexington and Pine Streets, Baltimore, MD, straight sided, lug handles, imp label front and back, cobalt blue brushed dandelions all around, gray with tan speckles, salesroom showpiece, glued crack on side, 24" h **3,075**

Crock Lid, 9" d, cobalt blue floral band around rim, 7" d inner rim **50**

Crock Lid, 12" d, cobalt blue brushed "X" on flat finial and flower bud dec around rim, 10¼" d inner rim **110**

Crock Lid, 12½" d, unglazed, minor chip, 10½" d inner rim **40**

Cup, child's, incised checkerboard design all around, alternating cobalt blue squares, minor chip bottom edge **75**

Dish, coggle wheel dec rim, minor chip, 8" d **45**

Figure, lion, standing, salt glazed, 7½" l, 6" h **75**

Figure, pig, Macomb Pottery Co, 1 leg glued **300**

Grotesque Jug, possibly Meanders Pottery, GA, green glaze, 20th C, 7½" h, $400.

Flowerpot, 1 gal, Wm Everson, incised script label, mkd "Patented April 27, 1875," brown and gray color **50**

Food Mold, Turk's head, rim chips **60**

Foot Warmer, Goodwill's Bed & Foot Warmer and Water Carrier. Pat. August 20, 1895, cylindrical, ftd, cobalt blue stamped label, missing wire bail handle **70**

Grotesque Jug, David Meanders, GA, inserted eyes, green ash glaze, 6" h . . . **165**

Grotesque Jug, Lanier Meanders, GA, 2 face jug, double ear handles, inserted eyes and stone teeth, green ash glaze, 9³/₄" h **875**

Inkwell, N Boors, Vanport, PA, incised "Union," cobalt blue stars, early 20th C, 1¹/₂" h **875**

Inkwell, unknown maker, round, dark color, tight spider line crack on side, 4" d **50**

Jar, 1 qt, unknown maker, molded rim, sloping shoulder, simple cobalt blue brushed double leaf dec all around, 6³/₄" h **225**

Jar, 2 qt, A P Donaghho, Parkersburg, WV, cobalt blue stenciled label, 8¹/₂" h **100**

Jar, 2 qt, New York, incised lines at shoulder, cobalt blue brushed tadpole–like design, dark color **75**

Jar, 2 qt, Shenfelder, incised rings around neck, cobalt blue brushed flower . . **225**

Jar, 2 qt, Sipe, Nichols & Co, Williamsport, PA, ovoid, imp label, cobalt blue brushed flourish, glaze flakes, 8" h **275**

Jar, 2 qt, unknown maker, molded rim, sloping shoulders, cobalt blue brushed leaves around shoulder, tiny flakes at top edge, 8³/₄" h **110**

Jar, 1 gal, A Conrad, New Geneva, PA, flanged rim, rounded shoulder, cobalt blue stenciled label and rose, crack on top **55**

Jar, 1 gal, Cowden & Wilcox, Harrisburg, PA, covered, flaring neck, sloping shoulder, lug handles, imp label, cobalt blue brushed double blossom bellflower and leaf spray, blue at label, small flakes off edge of lid **500**

Jar, 1 gal, Cowden & Wilcox, Harrisburg, PA, flanged rim, sloping shoulder, lug handles, imp label, cobalt blue brushed drooping bellflower, blue at label and handles, tight crack along side **190**

Jar, 1 gal, Hamilton & Jones, Greensboro, PA, semi–ovoid, flanged rim, cobalt blue stenciled and freehand label with tulips **230**

Jar, 1 gal, Hamilton & Pershing, Johnstown, PA, semi–ovoid, raised ring around neck, cobalt blue brushed feathery dec around shoulder **250**

Jar, 1 gal, James Hamilton & Co, Greensboro, PA, cobalt blue stenciled label and rose **175**

Jar, 1 gal, N Clark & Co, Lyons, ovoid, lug handles, incised lines around shoulder, cobalt blue slip "1" and leaf, minor rim chips **200**

Jar, 1 gal, Nichols & Co, Williamsport, PA, flared rim, incised lines around shoulder, imp label, cobalt blue brushed floral dec, minor rim chip, di colored spot on side **75**

Jar, 1 gal, P Herman, cobalt blue brushed feathery dec all around, very tight crack at bottom edge **100**

Jar, 1 gal, Sipe & Sons, Williamsport, PA, flanged rim, rounded shoulder, imp label within incised bands, cobalt blue brushed flourish **200**

Jar, 1 gal, unknown maker, possibly unmkd H Glazier, semi–ovoid, flanged rim, sloping shoulder, hood handles, cobalt blue slip flower dec all around, small chip on handle **275**

Jar, 1 gal, Whites, Utica, lug handles, imp label, cobalt blue bird looking back, perched on twig **225**

Jar, 1½ gal, C Boynton & Co, Troy, ovoid, lug handles, imp label, cobalt blue brushed flourish, blue at handles and label, small chips, 10¾" h **250**

Jar, 1½ gal, Hamilton & Jones, Greensboro, PA, ovoid, cobalt blue stenciled label, 9¼" h **115**

Jar, 1½ gal, unknown maker, semi–ovoid, flared rim, lug handles, cobalt blue brushed leafy dec, blue at handles, 2 tiny rim chips **325**

Jar, 1½ gal, unknown maker, semi–ovoid, molded rim, lug handles, strong cobalt blue brushed leafy dec all around shoulder, minor flake off rim, age line on bottom edge **220**

Jar, 1½ gal, W Flesher, imp label, cobalt blue brushed flourish front and back, stains, 11¼" h **200**

Jar, 2 gal, Burger & Co, Rochester, NY, molded rim, sloping shoulders, lug handles, imp label, cobalt blue slip "2" within fern leaves, blue at label, professionally sealed crack at back top edge **85**

Jar, 2 gal, Clark & Fox, Athens, ovoid, lug handles, imp label, incised lines around neck and shoulder, cobalt blue slip date "1834," blue at label and handles, minor chips on handles, some tight spider line cracks **300**

Jar, 2 gal, Cortland, flared rim, sloping shoulder, lug handles, imp label, cobalt blue slip "2" and vining double blossom flower, blue at label, some chips on handles, small rim chip **100**

Jar, 2 gal, Cowden & Wilcox, ovoid, imp label, cobalt blue brushed floral dec, 10" h **450**

Jar, 2 gal, Fulper Bros, Flemington, NJ, flared rim, sloping shoulders, imp label, cobalt blue slip stylized flower **325**

Jar, 2 gal, Hamilton & Jones, Greensboro, PA, semi–ovoid, incised ring at shoulder, cobalt blue stenciled and freehand label, dark color, small inner rim chip **110**

Jar, 2 gal, John Burger, Rochester, lug handles, imp label, cobalt blue brushed leafy dec, small discolorations **250**

Jar, cov, 2 gal, John Burger, Rochester, cobalt blue stylized flower dec, $650. Photo courtesy Arthur Auctioneering.

Jar, 2 gal, Lyons, cov, lug handles, imp label, cobalt blue brushed flower flanked by two "2"s, 4 feathery leaves at corners, lid stamped "2," minor chip on lid **725**

Jar, 2 gal, N A White & Son, Utica, NY, straight sided, flanged rim, long neck, incised band on sloping shoulder, lug handles, imp label, cobalt blue brushed flower, rim chip repair **85**

Jar, 2 gal, N Clark & Co, Lyons, ovoid, lug handles, imp label, cobalt blue brushed flower, blue at label **175**

Jar, 2 gal, N White & Co, Binghamton, lug handles, imp "2" and label, cobalt blue feathery bird on branch, tight crack in back, minor chips **325**

Jar, 2 gal, P H Smith, imp label, cobalt blue splotch at label **75**

Jar, 2 gal, Union Pottery, Newark, NJ, molded flaring rim, sloping shoulders, lug handles, cobalt blue slip "2. g" and fern leaf with brushed bird perched on top, tight spider line cracks in back **200**

Jar, 2 gal, unknown maker, semi–ovoid, flanged rim, cobalt blue stenciled adv label reads "B. F. Hetzel & Co. Groceries, Cumberland, MD, 2," dark color **300**

Jar, 2 gal, unknown maker, straight sided, flanged rim, rounded shoulder, strong cobalt blue brushed trailing tulips all around shoulder, minor rim chip, gray color **195**

Jar, 3 gal, Cowden & Wilcox, Harrisburg, PA, bulbous, flanged rim, lug handles, imp "3" and label, very strong cobalt blue brushed floral dec with 3 blooms and leaves, blue at handles **1,700**

Jar, 3 gal, E & L P Norton, Bennington, VT, semi–ovoid, flanged rim, sloping shoulder, lug handles, imp label, strong cobalt blue slip stylized flower and brushed band around bottom, early blacksmith repair on bottom, later professional repair around **65**

Jar, 3 gal, H Glazier, Huntingdon, PA, urn shaped, wide loop handles, cobalt blue brushed flower within wreath–like leaves on front and back, blue at rim and handles, minor rim chip **1,850**

Jar, 3 gal, James Ryan, Pittston, PA, semi–ovoid, flanged rim, sloping shoulder, lug handles, cobalt blue slip dec of chicken pecking corn, tight crack down back **525**

Jar, 3 gal, J F Ack & Bro, Mooresburg, PA, lug handles, imp "3" and label, incised lines around neck, simple cobalt blue brushed leafy flourish, minor chips on handle, stone ping on side, tight crack at top edge **350**

Jar, 3 gal, Norton & Fenton, Bennington, VT, ovoid, imp circular label, cobalt blue brushed floral dec, 12³/₄" h . . . . : **400**

Jar, 3 gal, W R F Weimer & Bro, Snydertown, PA, lug handles, imp label, cobalt blue flourish, professionally repaired **475**

Jar, 4 gal, I M Mead, Portage Co, OH, cov, ovoid, lug handles, imp label, cobalt blue brushed flower, hairlines and shallow chips on jar and lid, 15¹/₂" h **275**

Jar, 4 gal, unknown maker, semi–ovoid, hood handles, strong cobalt blue vine with blossoms and leaves all around shoulder, some fry, tight crack running down from top edge **190**

Jar, 4 gal, White & Wood, Binghamton, NY, imp label, cobalt blue quil work bird on branch, hairlines, 13³/₄" h **425**

Jar, 6 gal, D Albright, ovoid, lug handles, imp label, tooled lines, mottled grayish tan glaze with tan spots, 17" h **175**

Jar, 6 gal, E Lauersweiler, Empire City Pottery, 517 & 519 W 27th Street, straight sided, flanged rim, sloping shoulder, lug handles, imp "6" and label, large cobalt blue slip stylized flower, blue at label, rim chip on side .. **165**

Jar, 8 gal, Hamilton, Greensboro, PA, ovoid, lug handles, imp label, cobalt blue brushed floral dec, badly cracked, 18½" h **850**

Jug, miniature, Gold Star Whiskey, bulbous, molded lip, strap handle, incised label and star, brown Albany slip, minor wear flakes on lip, 3" h ... **40**

Jug, 1 pt, unknown maker, strap handle, blue ink stamped label "Pure Old Rye Whiskey, Salzman & Spiegelman, Brooklyn, NY" in rect, brown top, gray bottom **25**

Jug, 1 qt, unknown maker, ovoid, strap handle, cobalt blue blobs around neck **75**

Jug, 2 qt, A P Donaghho, Parkersburg, WV, strap handle, cobalt blue stenciled label, strong blue at handle **75**

Jug, 2 qt, Connell & Son, Newport, strap handle, imp label, cobalt blue script "Vinegar," spout chip, crack on side **35**

Jug, 2 qt, G C Kirk & Co, semi–ovoid, molded lip, sloping shoulder, long strap handle, stamped label, brown Albany slip, fingerprints around bottom **100**

Jug, 2 qt, Hamilton & Jones, Greensboro, PA, strap handle, cobalt blue stenciled label, minor chips on bottom **150**

Jug, 2 qt, J J O'Connor, strap handle, cobalt blue script label and splotches, minor chip at lip **90**

Jug, 2 qt, Sipe & Sons, Williamsport, PA, strap handle, imp label, brown color, lip chip **35**

Jug, 1 gal, A L Hyssong, Bloomsburg, semi–ovoid, sloping shoulder, strap handle, imp label, brown Albany slip **70**

Jug, 1 gal, Brewer & Halm, Havana, NY, semi–ovoid, strap handle, imp label, cobalt blue brushed flower, blue at label, small repair 1 side **75**

Jug, 1 gal, Clark & Co, Rochester, ovoid, strap handle, imp label, cobalt blue brushed leafy dec **125**

Jug, 1 gal, C McArthur & Co, Hudson, NY, straight sided, molded lip, sloping shoulder, strap handle, imp label, cobalt blue brushed flower, blue at label and handle **275**

Jug, 1 gal, Cowden & Wilcox, Harrisburg, PA, molded lip, rounded shoulder, strap handle, imp label, strong cobalt blue brushed flower, blue at label and handle **450**

Jug, 1 gal, Evan R Jones, Pittston, PA, semi–ovoid, molded lip, sloping shoulder, strap handle, imp label, cobalt blue slip 3–blossom flower, blue at label, some fry to dec **225**

Jug, 1 gal, F H Cowden, Harrisburg, semi–ovoid, molded lip, sloping shoulder, strap handle, imp label, cobalt blue stenciled geometric design, blue at handle, dark spot on back **100**

Jug, 1 gal, H Heilbronmer & Co, Schenectady, NY, straight sided, sloping shoulder, strap handle, incised label, brown Albany slip **35**

Jug, 1 gal, James Ryan, Pittston, PA, strap handle, imp label, cobalt blue stenciled adv label "Drink '67' Rye, P. J. Conway, Pittston, PA," rim chip **35**

Jug, 1 gal, J Fisher, Lyons, NY, straight sided, sloping shoulder, strap handle, imp label, cobalt blue script "Smith & Brown, 40 Charlotte St., Utica, N.Y." adv label **90**

Jug, 1 gal, J Hayes & Co, Manchester, NH, strap handle, imp label with cobalt blue highlight, minor lip flakes, 9½" h **175**

Jug, 1 gal, J W Cowden, semi–ovoid, molded lip, strap handle, imp label, cobalt blue brushed flower and leaves, early Cowden mark, spider line crack in back **385**

Jug, 1 gal, Moyer, Harrisburg, lug handles, imp label, cobalt blue brushed feathery dec, blue at label and handles **475**

Jug, 1 gal, N A White & Son, Utica, strap handle, imp label, cobalt blue slip pine tree **175**

Jug, 1 gal, North Bay, strap handle, cobalt blue slip eagle on branch **350**

Jug, 1 gal, Park & Tilford, New York, straight sided, molded lip, rounded shoulder, strap handle, imp label, cobalt blue brushed maple leaf, chip at mouth **175**

Jug, 1 gal, Penn Yan, strap handle, imp label, cobalt blue brushed feather design, strong blue at handle **200**

Jug, 1 gal, Rabb & Rehm, Bloomsburg, PA, straight sided, flanged lip, sloping shoulder, strap handle, stamped label, large opening **100**

Jug, 1 gal, Shenfelder, Reading, PA, attributed to, straight sided, molded lip, sloping shoulder, strap handle, cobalt blue brushed vining flower all around, blue at handle **165**

Jug, 1 gal, Sipe & Sons, Williamsport, PA, straight sided, molded lip, sloping shoulder, strap handle, imp label, simple cobalt blue brushed flower, blue at handle and label, dark color **110**

Jug, 1 gal, T O Goodwin, spherical, molded lip, strap handle, cobalt blue slip "1849," small bump on side with spider line crack **165**

Jug, 1 gal, unknown maker, molded lip, sloping shoulder, strap handle, cobalt blue wash incised swan **175**

Jug, 1 gal, Whites, Utica, straight sided, molded lip, sloping shoulder, strap handle, imp label, cobalt blue slip roadrunner on branch, replaced handle **300**

Jug, 1 gal, Wm E Warner, West Troy, straight sided, molded lip, sloping shoulder, strap handle, imp label, cobalt blue brushed long stemmed flower, blue at label, small stress line in front **75**

Left: Jug, 2 gal, OL&AN Ballard, Burlington, VT, strap handle, imp label, cobalt blue dancing 10–point buck, couple stone pings in making, some fry in dec, $660. Photo courtesy Arthur Auctioneering.

Right: Jug, 2 gal, unsgd, possibly NY, cobalt blue bird on branch, $150.

Jug, 1 gal, Wm Moyer, semi–ovoid, molded lip, strap handle, imp label,
  cobalt blue brushed leafy branch, blue at label and handle   550
Jug, 1 gal, W Roberts, Binghamton, NY, strap handle, imp label, cobalt blue
  bird on branch, bird looking back, dark color, crack in back   125
Jug, 1½ gal, J & E Norton, Bennington, strap handle, imp label, cobalt blue
  slip stylized flower, minor wear, small chips, 10½" h   350
Jug, 2 gal, Boston, MA, ovoid, ribbed strap handle, imp label, tooled lines,
  2–tone brown and gray salt glaze, 14½" h   700
Jug, 2 gal, Boston, MA, ovoid, strap handle, incised bands at neck, cobalt
  blue fish and foliage dec, some chips and abrasions, 15" h 1,500
Jug, 2 gal, Clark & Fox, Athens, ovoid, strap handle, imp label, cobalt blue
  feather dec, blue at handle   275
Jug, 2 gal, Cowden & Wilcox, Harrisburg, semi–ovoid, strap handle, imp
  label, cobalt blue brushed fan shaped leaf, blue at handle   300
Jug, 2 gal, Γ B Norton & Co, Worcester, Mass, straight sided, molded lip,
  sloping shoulder, strap handle, large cobalt blue slip stylized flower, chips
  around spout, some glaze flaking on back   120
Jug, 2 gal, Γ H Cowden, Harrisburg, strap handle, imp label, cobalt blue
  stenciled flower, blue at handle   125
Jug, 2 gal, Fort Edward, NY, strap handle, imp label, cobalt blue brushed
  rose, fitted as lamp, 14½" h   200
Jug, 2 gal, Fulper, NJ, attributed to, straight sided, sloping shoulder, strap
  handle, strong cobalt blue slip Fulper bird dec, tight crack on side   225
Jug, 2 gal, Harrington & Burger, Rochester, semi–ovoid, strap handle, imp
  label, strong cobalt blue brushed flower   250
Jug, 2 gal, I M Mead & Co, ovoid, strap handle, imp label, cobalt blue at
  label, 13" h   175
Jug, 2 gal, James Ryan, Pittston, PA, strap handle, imp label, cobalt blue
  script adv label "S J Freeman, Pittston, Pa," minor chip on bottom   175
Jug, 2 gal, J Burger Jr, Rochester, NY, strap handle, cobalt blue slip "2" and
  polka dot flower, minor lip chips   300
Jug, 2 gal, J J Lawlow, Albany, NY, strap handle, imp label, large cobalt blue
  stylized flower   200

Left: Jug, 3 gal, Moore, Nichols & Co, Williamsport, PA, semi–ovoid, imp label and "3," cobalt blue flowers, blue at handle and label, chip on back bottom edge, $523.

Right: Jug, 4 gal, West Troy Pottery, imp label, cobalt blue "1880," $440.

Photos courtesy Arthur Auctioneering.

Jug, 2 gal, J Mantell, Penn Yan, strap handle, imp label, cobalt blue brushed triple bloom flower, blue at label 325

Jug, 2 gal, John Burger, Rochester, strap handle, imp label, cobalt blue "2" and quillwork flower, lip chip, glaze flake repair on back 325

Jug, 2 gal, Lehman & Riedinger, Poughkeepsie, NY, bulbous, molded lip, sloping shoulder, strap handle, imp label, cobalt blue brushed double bloom floral dec, tiny chips around base 350

Jug, 2 gal, M & T Miller, Newport, PA, straight sided, molded lip, sloping shoulder, strap handle, imp label, very strong cobalt blue slip leaf, blue at handle 2,300

Jug, 2 gal, Moyer, Harrisburg, semi–ovoid, strap handle, simple cobalt blue feather dec, blue at handle, small spider line crack on side 325

Jug, 2 gal, N A White & Son, Utica, NY, strap handle, imp label, cobalt blue brushed flower, short hairline crack in base, 14" h 300

Jug, 2 gal, N Clark & Co, Lyons, ovoid, strap handle, imp "2" and label, cobalt blue floral dec, chips on bottom 200

Jug, 2 gal, Nichols & Boynton, Burlington, VT, straight sided, molded lip, sloping shoulder, strap handle, imp "2" and label, cobalt blue slip stylized flower, blue at label, small chips at lip 145

Jug, 2 gal, NY Stoneware Co, Ft Edward, NY, strap handle, imp "2" and label, cobalt blue script and printed adv label "M. A. Ingalls, Liquor Dealer, Little Falls" 125

Jug, 2 gal, Thomas D Chollar, Cortland, ovoid, strap handle, imp label, cobalt blue "2" and feathery leaf, blue at label and handle 275

Jug, 2 gal, unknown maker, straight sided, molded lip, rounded shoulder, strap handle, brown Albany slip, tight crack at handle 20

Jug, 2 gal, unknown maker, straight sided, molded lip, rounded shoulder, strap handle, cobalt blue slip "2" above flourish, shiny glaze 120

Jug, 2 gal, West Troy Pottery, straight sided, sloping shoulder, strap handle, imp label, cobalt blue slip bird on branch, tiny flake at spout 685

Jug, 2 gal, White & Wood, Binghamton, NY, straight sided, sloping shoulder, strap handle, imp label, cobalt blue slip and brushed paddletail bird perched on branch, chip at spout 465

Jug, 2 gal, W Roberts, Binghamton, NY, strap handle, imp label, cobalt blue polka dot roadrunner and foliage, blue at label, minor lip chip 575

Jug, 3 gal, Bergan & Foy, strap handle, imp label, cobalt blue quillwork bird on branch, 15" h 1,100

Jug, 3 gal, Clark & Fox, Athens, ovoid, strap handle, imp label, cobalt blue brushed double bloom flower, blue at label and handle, discoloration 250

Jug, 3 gal, Cowden & Wilcox, Harrisburg, PA, semi–ovoid, strap handle, imp label, cobalt blue sunflower in wreath, blue at handle, tight crack near lip 525

Jug, 3 gal, F H Cowden, Harrisburg, semi–ovoid, molded lip, strap handle, imp label, cobalt blue brushed floral dec, blue at label and handle, part of handle missing 90

Jug, 3 gal, H & G Nash, Utica, ovoid, strap handle, imp label, simple cobalt blue flower and "3," dent on side in making 225

Jug, 3 gal, J & E Norton, Bennington, VT, strap handle, imp label, strong cobalt blue quillwork floral dec, blue at label, glaze flake repair on back, stone ping in dec 250

Jug, 3 gal, John Young & Co, Harrisburg, PA, strap handle, imp label, cobalt blue quillwork stylized double bloom flower, 17" h **925**

Jug, 3 gal, M & T Miller, Newport, PA, strap handle, elaborate allover cobalt blue floral leaf design, tight crack through dec **2,500**

Jug, 3 gal, Moore, Nichols & Co, Williamsport, PA, semi–ovoid, strap handle, imp "3" and label, cobalt blue floral dec **550**

Jug, 3 gal, N A White & Son, Utica, NY, straight sided, sloping shoulder, strap handle, strong cobalt blue slip and brushed stylized flower, small chips in blue and inside spout **110**

Jug, 3 gal, Perry, S S & Co, West Troy, strap handle, imp "3" and label, cobalt blue brushed triple bloom flower, blue at label, tight crack at top, some repair on bottom edge **125**

Jug, 3 gal, unknown maker, ovoid, molded lip, strap handle, cobalt blue brushed tulip, blue at handle **350**

Jug, 3 gal, W E Welding, Brantford, ovoid, strap handle, imp label, cobalt blue brushed floral dec, 16¼" h **375**

Jug, 3 gal, W Roberts, Binghamton, NY, strap handle, imp "3" and label, cobalt blue slip double bloom polka dot flower with spiky leaves, dark color, chip on bottom edge **200**

Jug, 4 gal, Cowden & Wilcox, Harrisburg, PA, semi–ovoid, molded lip, strap handle, imp "4" and label, strong cobalt blue bellflower dec with large leafy branch, blue at label and handle **625**

Jug, 4 gal, Cowden & Wilcox, Harrisburg, PA, semi–ovoid, molded lip, strap handle, imp label, very large and elaborately detailed cobalt blue slip floral bouquet in urn dec, blue at label **18,700**

Jug, 4 gal, Nichols & Boynton, Burlington, VT, strap handle, imp label, cobalt blue quillwork stylized floral dec, large chip on lip, hairline in handle, flake on base, 17¼" h **125**

Jug, 4 gal, unknown maker, ovoid, molded lip, strap handle, large cobalt blue brushed flower on shoulder, blue at handle **275**

Jug, 4 gal, Whites, Utica, strap handle, imp "4" and label, ornate cobalt blue design with 2 peafowl perched in tree, bodies crossed, and both looking back at the other, minor chip on lip, some fry on blue **550**

Match Holder, cobalt blue at incised lettering and dec, 5" h, 6½" d, $425.
Photo courtesy Arthur Auctioneering.

Jug, 5 gal, I M Mead, Mogadore, OH, ovoid, double ear handles, imp label, cobalt blue brushed "5" and floral dec, professionally restored, 18½" h . . .   **375**

Jug, 5 gal, Penn Yan, ovoid, strap handle, imp label, cobalt blue quillwork "5" and 2 polka dot birds, minor wear, short hairlines, 18½" h **2,500**

Jug, 10 gal, NY Stoneware Co, Fort Edward, NY, ovoid, strap handle, imp label, cobalt blue bird holding banner dated "1876" in its beak, glaze flakes, 19½" h **1,500**

Jug, 10 gal, W Lunn, ovoid, double ear handles, cobalt blue brushed "10" and "1882" on 1 side, "W. Lunn" on other, lip and one handle glued, 19½" h **200**

Match Holder, GAR Buckingham Post No. 12, Nov. 21, 1883, jar shaped, semi–ovoid, flanged rim, incised label, brown Albany slip, 2¾" h **80**

Milk Pan, 1 gal, Moore, Nichols & Co, Williamsport, PA, bowl shaped, flanged rim with pour spout, imp label, simple cobalt blue brushed flower, large rim chip, glaze flaking **90**

Milk Pan, 1 gal, Sipe, Nichols & Co, Williamsport, PA, bowl shaped, flanged rim with pour spout, imp label, cobalt blue brushed bellflower, blue at label, rim chips **175**

Milk Pan, 1 gal, unknown maker, tapered sides, flanged rim with pour spout, cobalt blue brushed leaves alternating with flourishes all around, dark color **450**

Mixing Bowl, 1 gal, Thomas D Chollar, Homer, lug handles, imp label, minor chips **85**

Molasses Jug, 1 gal, I Seymour, Troy, ovoid, cobalt blue brushed feather, blue at label, spout chip **625**

Mug, C N Y Pottery, Utica, NY, straight sided with tooled rings and band near base, stamped label, imp inscription "25 Bezirks Turnfest, West New York, FFTS/SII/Dolgeville, NY 1894," cobalt blue at rings and inscription **90**

Mug, Old Sleepy Eye, molded and cobalt blue Indian head, cobalt blue handle, bottom mkd "W. S. Co., Monmouth, Ill.," tight age line at top edge, small chip bottom edge **200**

Left: Milk Pan, 1 gal, PA, cobalt blue feather dec around rim, cobalt blue at lug handles, small rim chips, $385.

Right: Milk Pan, 1 gal, PA, handled, pour lip, cobalt blue floral and leaf dec all around, bottom chip, $410.

Photos courtesy Arthur Auctioneering.

Spittoon, Cowden & Wilcox, imp label, cobalt blue leaf dec all around, rim and base chips, $250. Photo courtesy Arthur Auctioneering.

Mug, unknown maker, cov, straight sided, ear handle, cobalt blue brushed stripes and incised rings, hinged pewter lid, 5" h **80**

Mug, Whites, Utica, No. 39, straight sided, molded tavern scene, bulbous base with molded crosshatched design, pedestal foot, cobalt blue band at top and bottom and highlights on handle and molded designs, tiny glaze chip on handle **65**

Pitcher, 1 pt, Old Sleepy Eye, molded and cobalt blue Indian head, bottom mkd "W. S. Co., Monmouth, Ill.," age lines at top edge, 4" h **125**

Pitcher, 1 pt, unknown maker, raised ring around rim and shoulder, cobalt blue brushed leaf design, 6½" h **425**

Pitcher, 1 pt, White's, Utica, attributed to, bulbous, ear handle, large molded floral design highlighted with cobalt blue both sides, blue at handle, 6¼" h **130**

Pitcher, 1 pt, White's Pottery, squat shape, strap handle, molded hunting scene with bull elk, unmkd, all–over cobalt blue highlighting, 6½" h **450**

Pitcher, 1 qt, F & E Norton, Bennington, VT, ovoid, imp label, cobalt blue quillwork bird on branch, extensive professional repair, 12½" h **175**

Pitcher, 1 qt, Remmey, PA, attributed to, cobalt blue leafy flower dec, minor outer rim chip **725**

Pitcher, 1 qt, unknown maker, bulbous, strap handle, cobalt blue brushed flourishes at rim and all around shoulder, blue at handle, rim chips, 13½" h **250**

Pitcher, 1 qt, unknown maker, bulbous, strap handle, strong cobalt blue brushed floral dec all around, blue at handle, tight crack through dec, chip on rim, 8½" h **200**

Pitcher, 1 qt, White's, Utica, attributed to, tankard shape, ear handle, all–over molded design with tavern scene and leafy bands at rim and foot, cobalt blue at molded dec, minor rim chip repair, 9¼" h **75**

Pitcher, 1 qt, White's, Utica, bulbous, spurred handle, alternating coggle wheel and cobalt blue brushed bands at top and bottom, molded warrior with shield and little dancing girl, both highlighted in blue, 9" h **55**

Pitcher, 1 qt, Williamsport potter, attributed to, cobalt blue brushed leafy dec, blue at handle **375**

Pitcher, 2 qt, unknown maker, bulbous, strap handle, strong cobalt blue brushed flower and fern leaf at shoulder, blue at spout and handle, gray color, 9" h **500**

Pitcher, 1 gal, Lyons, imp label, cobalt blue double tulip, blue at handle, professional rim chip repair **350**

Rolling Pin, cobalt blue flowers and adv label "Compliments of D. C. Struthers, Phillipsburg, NJ," replaced wood handle 300

Salt Crock, Old Sleepy Eye, molded Indian head, cobalt blue band and highlights 725

Spigot, General Ceramics Company, NY, brown Albany slip, crack in T handle, 15" l 65

Spittoon, waisted, coggle wheel dec, cobalt blue bands 100

Tenderizer, round stoneware mallet with pyramid shaped knobs all around, turned wood handle, dated "1877" 110

Vase, Sleepy Eye, cobalt blue brushed band at top and bottom, molded Indian bust highlighted in blue, 8¹/₂" h 300

Vase, unknown maker, semi–ovoid, ruffled rim, circular openings around shoulder, cobalt blue at rim and around each opening 100

Vase, Whites Pottery, vasiform shape, molded band of flowers around shoulder and foot and elongated vertical sprays around body, highlighted with cobalt blue, Bristol glaze, 2 small glaze chips, 6¹/₈" h 90

Water Cooler, cov, 2 qt, unknown maker, barrel shaped, cobalt blue bands, mkd "A. A. Co. Patent Applied For," minor chip on end 185

Water Cooler, cov, 2 gal, unknown maker, barrel shaped, cobalt blue bands, blue ink stamped "2" within crown, blue stripes on lid 55

Water Cooler, cov, 3 gal, S S Reilly, 400 & 409 Canal St, New York, barrel shaped, imp label, blue bands, tight crack on side 65

Water Cooler, cov, 3 gal, unknown maker, barrel shaped, cobalt blue bands, blue ink stamped "3" within crown, blue stripes on lid 65

Water Cooler, cov, 10 gal, unknown maker, ovoid, high neck, lug handles, coggle wheel bands, remains of applied decorative detail on shoulder between handles, cobalt blue quillwork flourishes, old chips and firing cracks, 21¹/₂" h 350

Water Cooler, cov, 16 gal, Alderman and Scott, Belpre, OH, ovoid, ear handles, applied tooled ornaments around bung hole, cobalt blue stenciled label and "16" in wreath, hairlines and repair, 23¹/₂" h 825

Water Jug, 4 gal, W H Farrar, Geddes, NY, imp label, cobalt blue slip "4" and tornado–like designs, spout chip 325

Water Crock, barrel shaped, incised bands and label, cobalt blue florals, bands, and Northwind face, $990. Photo courtesy Aston Macek.

TEXTILES

Thrift was a way of life in agrarian America. Few people had money to waste. Textiles were purchased that would wear well. When something did "wear out," it was recycled. Patchwork quilts and hooked rugs are the final resting place for many a shirt and dress. Feed bags wound up as dresses and shirts when times were lean.

Textiles are cloth or fabric items, especially anything woven or knitted. Those that survive usually represent the best since these were the objects that were used carefully and stored by the housewife.

Textiles helped brighten life in rural America. Red and blue are dominant colors with block, circle, and star pattern motifs the most common. Colorful window curtains were changed seasonally. The same held true for bedspreads. A party dress or shirt was a welcome respite from the pastel colors of daily work clothes.

Textiles are collected for many reasons—to study fabrics, understand the elegance of an historical period, and for decorative and modern use. The renewed interest in clothing has sparked a revived interest in textiles of all forms.

References: Alda Horner, *The Official Guide to Linens, Lace, and Other Fabrics,* House of Collectibles, 1991; Florence Montgomery, *Textiles in America: 1650–1870,* W. W. Norton & Co, 1984; Betty King (ed), *Needlework: An Historical Survey, revised edition,* The Main Street Press, 1984.

Museums: Cooper–Hewitt Museum, New York, NY; Currier Gallery of Art, Manchester, MN; Museum of American Textile History, Lowell, MA; Museum of Art, Rhode Island School of Design, Providence, RI; National Museum of American History, Washington, DC; Philadelphia College of Textiles & Science, Philadelphia, PA; Shelburne Museum, Shelburne, VT; Textile Museum, Washington, DC; Valentine Museum, Richmond, VA.

CLOTHING

Farm clothing can be divided into two groups—workday and Sunday. Within each group, clothing is further divided into manufactured and homemade. The agrarian housewife was usually an expert seamstress.

Most collectors of vintage clothing and accessories have focused on high style items. Only in the last few years have some collectors begun to focus on clothing used in rural America. While Country decorators have used clothing as decorative highlights within room settings for years, emphasis has fallen largely on accessories such as aprons and infant wear.

"Vintage clothing" is a broad term used to describe clothing manufactured from the late Victorian era (1880s) to the end of the psychedelic era (1970s). While purists would prefer a cutoff date of 1940, clothing from World War II, the fifties, and sixties is also highly collectible. In reality, vintage clothing is defined by what is available and current collecting trends.

A few clues to dating clothing are: (1) do not depend on style alone; (2) check labels; (3) learn which fabrics and print patterns were popular in each historical period; and, (4) examine decorative elements.

Clothing is collected and studied as a reference source in learning about fashion, construction and types of materials used. Collecting vintage clothing appears to have reached a plateau. Although there are still dedicated collectors, the category is no longer attracting a rash of new collectors annually.

The hot part of the clothing market in the 1990s is accessories. Clothing collectors acquire everything from hats and shoes to handbags and jewelry to accessorize their garments. However, because many clothing accessories are collectibles in their own right (compacts, hatpins, purses, etc.), collectors of clothing often find themselves competing with these specialized collectors.

Country auctions are usually rich in clothing accessories. Hand–me–down was a way of life. However, many items in the hand–me–down pile never made it to their next owner, winding up in long–time storage instead.

References: Maryanne Dolan, *Vintage Clothing, 1880–1980, Third Edition,* Books Americana, Krause Publications, 1995; Ellen Gehret, *Rural Pennsylvania Clothing, Liberty Cap Books,* 1976; Kristina Harris, *Victorian and Edwardian Fashions for Women, 1840–1910,* Schiffer Publishing, 1995; Kristina Harris, *Vintage Fashions for Women: 1920s–1940s,* Schiffer Publishing, 1996; Tina Irick–Nauer, *The First Price Guide to Antique and Vintage Clothes,* E. P. Dutton, 1983; Susan Langley, *Vintage Hats & Bonnets, 1770–1970: Identification & Values,* Collector Books, 1997; Terry McCormick, *The Consumer's Guide to Vintage Clothing,* Dembner Books, 1987; Diane McGee, *A Passion For Fashion,* Simmons–Boardman Books, Inc, 1987; Desire Smith, *Hats,* Schiffer Publishing, 1996; Diane Snyder–Haug, *Antique & Vintage Clothing: A Guide to Dating & Valuation of Women's Clothing 1850–1940,* Collector Books, 1997; Meredith Wright, *Everyday Dress of Rural America: 1783–1800,* Dover Publications, 1992.

Periodical: *Lady's Gallery,* PO Box 40443, Bay Village, OH 44140.

Newsletters: *Lill's Vintage Clothing Newsletter,* 19 Jamestown Drive, Cincinnati, OH 45241; *The Glass Slipper,* 653 South Orange Avenue, Sarasota, FL 34236; *The Vintage Connection,* 904 North 65th Street, Springfield, OR 97478; *Vintage Gazette,* 194 Amity Street, Amherst, MA 01002.

Collectors' Clubs: Federation of Vintage Fashion, 401 Dan Gabriel, Vallejo, CA 94590; The Costume Society of America, PO Box 73, Earleville, MD 21919.

Museums: Black Fashion Museum, New York, NY; Boston Museum of Fine Arts, Boston, MA; Costume and Textile Department of the Los Angeles County Museum of Art, Los Angeles, CA; Fashion Institute of Technology, New York, NY; Fullerton Museum Center, Fullerton, CA; Levi Strauss & Co Museum, San Francisco, CA; Metropolitan Museum of Art, New York, NY; Museum of Vintage Fashion, Lafayette, CA; The Museums at Stony Brook, Stony Brook, NY; Wadsworth Atheneum, Hartford, CT; Western Reserve Historical Society, Cleveland, OH.

Apron, blue and white check, machine sewn, small repairs, 33½" l	**$65**
Apron, muslin, ruffled sleeve and trim, buttons down back and ties, 1880s	**150**
Baby Dress, crocheted, flounce and upper part of skirt attached at waist, 1912	**500**
Baby Shoes, pr, black leather, ankle strap	**35**
Bib, linen, white embroidery	**30**
Blouse, woman's, handkerchief linen, ¾–length sleeves, handmade, c1900	**1,000**
Boots, pr, boy's, leather, cowboy style, capped toes, 1 stamped on sole "A.A. Shumway & Co., Warranted," each stamped "7" on heel, some wear	**245**
Cap, boy's, wool, c1930	**20**
Christening Gown, cotton, embroidered sleeves and bodice, c1825	**185**
Christening Gown, cotton, long sleeves, embroidered hem and yoke, lace trim and tucking, c1900	**85**

Christening Gown, cotton, pin tucks along sleeves, bodice, and skirt, edged
with lace, c1880s 125
Christening Gown, cotton, trimmed with handmade Buckinghamshire lace
along bodice, sleeves, and hem, c1830 325
Coat, woman's, light wool, ecru, ornate braid trim, wool flannel lining 700
Coat, Vest, and Hat, man's, black wool, Amish 125
Dress, girl's, calico, blue, 2 pc, matching bonnet, c1900 165
Dress, girl's, wool, high waisted, puffy sleeves, hem ruffle 400
Dress, woman's, cotton, black and white dots, c1863 150
Dress, woman's, muslin, V–neck, tiered flounces on skirt, bell sleeves, hand
sewn, c1853 190
Dress, woman's, wool, black and green, ornate black glass buttons, center
front pleats, gathers at back, c1868 250
Jumper, girl's, cotton, brown, red, blue, and white, 3 glass buttons on front,
19th C 220
Nightgown, woman's, cotton, crochet straps and bodice, c1885 180
Nightcap, woman's, cotton, ruffled 45
Nightshirt, man's, cotton, pearl buttons down front, front and sleeves with
crocheted edging, c1880 180
Petticoat, girl's, cotton, lace edging, 1880 165
Petticoat, woman's, cotton, white, crocheted insert, wide crocheted hem 50
Petticoat, woman's, quilted cotton and linsey woolsey, printed and colored
calico and linsey woolsey fabric, reversible to contrasting color with fab-
ric waistband, sizes 10–12, PA, 19th C, price for 5 230
Purse, drawstring, cotton homespun, pen and ink floral dec, "Mary Littlefield
1816" poem on 1 side, landscape on rev, fragile, wear, stains, small tears,
9" h, 10½" w 230
Shawl, black lace, flowers, scalloped hem, 112" w, 54" l 35
Shawl, wool, paisley, 70 x 70" 300
Shawl, woven, paisley, orange, blue, green, and gold, black center 170
Shirt, man's, homespun, red silk cross stitching, mkd "SHL" 200
Shoes, pr, man's, black leather, felt top, buttons 100

Left: Baby's Jacket, cotton, handmade, c1900, $35.
Right: Sun Bonnet, cotton, calico, Pennsylvania Dutch, $25.

Shoes, pr, woman's, canvas, white, high top style, spool heel, cotton laces,
early 1900s **95**
Waistcoat, boy's, wool, front and collar embroidered in silk with green leafy
sprigs, front with 2 pockets and 4 brass buttons, 19th C **225**
Walking Skirt, woman's, overshot, slate blue, adjustable 24" waist **35**

COVERLETS

A loom in every country home is a myth. Most coverlets were woven by a semi–professional (a farmer who supplemented his income by weaving in the winter months) or a professional weaver.

A coverlet is made by weaving yarns together on a loom. A quilt, made by sewing together layers of fabric, is an entirely different textile.

The earliest coverlets are overshot. The double weave dates from 1725 to 1825. Single weave, double face coverlets (winter/summer) were popular in the first quarter of the nineteenth century.

The Jacquard loom arrived upon the scene in the early 1820s. It allowed the manufacture of wide, single piece coverlets. However, the pieced coverlet tradition continued well into mid–century.

Natural dyes in soft hues were made from animal, mineral, and plant matter and used prior to 1820. Mineral dyes made between 1820 and 1860 are harsher in color. Synthetic dyes, which retain a bright, permanent color, were in use by the early 1860s.

By the 1860s, commercially made blankets replaced coverlets and quilts as the principal bed covering. While quilt making survived, coverlet production ceased.

References: Harold and Dorothy Burnham, *'Keep Me Warm One Night': Early Handweaving in Eastern Canada,* Toronto Press, 1972; Judith Gordon, *American Star Work Coverlets,* Design Books, 1995; John W. Heisey, *A Checklist of American Coverlet Weavers,* The Colonial Williamsburg Foundation, 1978; Carleton Safford and Robert Bishop, *America's Quilts and Coverlets,* Bonanza Books, 1985.

Collectors' Club: Colonial Coverlet Guild of America, 5617 Blackstone, La Grange, IL 60525.

Museums: Abby Aldrich Rockefeller Folk Art Center, Williamsburg, VA; University of Maryland Historical Textile Data Base, College Park, MD.

Bedspread, candlewick, cotton, natural white, floral medallion center
enclosed by geometric designs, stylized floral swag border, initialed
"SSF12," old mends, imperfections, c1830 . . . . **$80**
Blanket, wool, bright green, indigo, and rose madder plaid twill, full fringe
on 3 sides, 2 pc, 78 x 82" **250**
Blanket, wool, indigo, ocher, and brown plaid, 67 x 80" **100**
Blanket, wool, madder, blue plaid twill, 2 pc, 72 x 90" **525**
Blanket, wool and linen, homespun, madder and black wool, natural linen,
3 pc, 70 x 86" **225**
Blanket, woven, line, broken twill check pattern, squash and cream colors,
some fiber loss, 98 x 88" **150**
Coverlet, Snowball and Pine Tree, 2 pc, double weave, summer/winter, navy
blue, red, and natural white, minor wear and repair, 64 x 78" **150**
Jacquard, 1 pc, central floral medallion, single weave, capitol buildings border, red, green, and natural white, overall and edge wear, 77 x 81" **175**

Coverlet, 2 pc, geometric design, red, white, and blue, applied fringe, 72 x 94", $275.

Jacquard, 1 pc, floral, single weave, Oriental buildings in borders, black, pale yellow, salmon, and natural white, wear, salmon wool very worn, some fringe damage, 75 x 98" 100

Jacquard, 1 pc, foliage medallions, single weave, busts of presidents border, red, olive green, and natural white, wear, fringe is incomplete, small holes, and 1 repair, 82 x 86" 175

Jacquard, 1 pc, 4 rose medallions, double weave, corners mkd "Double Rose," red and white, top is frayed and turned and rebound, faded and worn, 72 x 78" 150

Jacquard, 1 pc, geometric floral medallions, single weave, floral border, corners dated "1854," olive gold, deep blue, deep pink, and natural white, worn fringe incomplete and stains, 71 x 87" 275

Jacquard, 1 pc, sawtooth, woven, tulips, acorns, and leafage border, PA, 19th C, 37 x 31" 400

Jacquard, 1 pc, star and flower medallions, single weave, vintage border, corners labeled "W. in Mt. Vernon Knox County, Ohio by Jacob and Michael Ardner 1852," rust red and natural white, edge wear, small holes, incomplete fringe, 76 x 82" 475

Jacquard, 1 pc, stars and flowers, single weave, bird borders, corners dated 1857, blue and natural white, 66 x 90" 575

Jacquard, 1 pc, star center, double weave, floral border, corners labeled "Made by E. Hausman, Trexlertown, Pa. 1851," red, green, and blue, 79 x 99" 625

Jacquard, 1 pc, vintage center, single weave, Christian and Heathen side border, bird border on end, corners labeled "Daniel Bury Cornersburgh, Ohio, 1850," purple, gold, blue, black, and natural white, 76 x 90" 850

Jacquard, 2 pc, bird and flowers, double weave, corners labeled "Bird of Paradise," navy blue and natural white, very worn, holes, and repairs, 81 x 82" 275

Jacquard, 2 pc, blossoms and pinwheels, horizontal and vertical stripes, 19th C, 88 x 100" 525

Jacquard, 2 pc, bold floral design, double weave, Greek key border, corners dated 1848, navy blue and natural white, minor wear, 70 x 84" 500

Jacquard, 2 pc, bold geometric floral, double weave, navy blue and natural white, overall and edge wear, no fringe, 82" sq 200

Jacquard, 2 pc, Christian and Heathen, double weave, blue and natural white, small holes and repairs, 74 x 100" 325

Jacquard, 2 pc, floral, double weave, compotes of fruit borders, eagles in corners with "E Pluribus Unum," and "Mary A Martin, Jefferson Co, NY, 1847," navy blue, black, and natural white, no fringe, 86 x 92" **1,700**

Jacquard, 2 pc, floral, double weave, corners dated "1850," navy blue and natural white, 78 x 92" **550**

Jacquard, 2 pc, floral, single weave, double vintage border, navy blue and natural white, worn and holes, 76 x 90" **200**

Jacquard, 2 pc, floral, single weave, eagle corners, labeled "Knox County, Ohio, 1847," red, teal, blue, and natural white, incomplete fringe, halves not sewn, 66 x 79" **425**

Jacquard, 2 pc, floral, single weave, turkey in tree corners, "Manufactured by Henry Oberly, Womelsdorf, Penn," tomato red and natural white, overall wear, fringe removed, ends rebound, 78 x 90" **550**

Jacquard, 2 pc, floral and star flower medallions, single weave, bird borders, corners labeled "Peace and Plenty 1847," navy blue and white, fringe, top edge turned and rebound, 76 x 79" **600**

Jacquard, 2 pc, floral medallions, single weave, eagle and shield border, bird in wreath corners initialed "F.B.," dark and light olive, red, and natural white, faded, stains, and wear, some missing fringe, 70 x 94" **275**

Jacquard, 2 pc, floral medallions, single weave, 9 large medallions with diamonds in between, single weave, navy blue, salmon red, and natural white, wear and stains, 82 x 90" **275**

Jacquard, 2 pc, flowers, single weave, vintage, corners labeled, "Samuel Meily, Mansfield, Richland, Ohio, 1844," blue, teal, red, and natural white, very worn, holes, no fringe, 66 x 70" **150**

Jacquard, 2 pc, Foliage and Star Flower, vintage border, corners labeled "Made by W. Fasic Clark Co. Ills. 1851," navy blue and white, 72 x 80" . . . **775**

Jacquard, 2 pc, 4 rose medallions, single weave, bird and rose borders, corners with "E. Spitler Fancy Coverlet Woven by G. Heilbronn Lancaster, O. 1848," navy blue, bluish green, deep red, and natural white, 70 x 91" **650**

Jacquard, 2 pc, 4 rose medallions, single weave, eagle and tree borders, corners with "The Property of Ann Dobbs, D.P. Johnson Weaver, Orleans County, N.Y. 1847," salmon and natural white, stains, 69 x 91" **450**

Left: Jacquard, blue and white, labeled "Samuel Meily, Mansfield, Richland, Ohio, 1852" 72 x 85", $375.

Right: Jacquard, floral medallions, bird and tree border, corners labeled "Made by J Lutz, E Hempfield Township, for Rebacca Hershey, 1839," 99 x 77" with 4 1/2" fringe, $650.

Jacquard, 2 pc, 4 rose medallions, single weave, pots of flowers, building borders, corners labeled "J. Swank, Hancock County, Ohio, 1848," navy blue, red, and white, 72 x 82" 385

Jacquard, 2 pc, geometric floral center, single weave, rose border at bottom edge, corners labeled "W. Minster, Allen Co. 1848" with rooster, navy blue, red, olive green, and natural white, minor wear and stains, small holes in top edge, 62 x 86" 475

Jacquard, 2 pc, geometric floral medallions, double weave, lily border, bird corners with "1869," red, and navy blue, fringe on 1 end, 80 x 86" 1,000

Jacquard, 2 pc, geometric floral medallions, single weave, trellis and bird borders, corners labeled "John Rick in Rome. S.C., Ohio, 1854," navy blue, red, and natural white, wear, top edge worn, fringe is incomplete, 69 x 82" 400

Jacquard, 2 pc, peacock and young, single weave, urns of flowers, vintage and floral border, corners mkd "Made 1862," attributed to Bucyrus, Crawford County, Ohio, red, navy blue, and natural white, 70 x 88" 500

Jacquard, 2 pc, snowflakes, double weave, pine tree border, navy blue and natural white, some wear, 67 x 77" 125

Jacquard, 2 pc, star and flower, double weave, bird and rose borders, corners labeled "G. Stich, Newark, Ohio, 1839," navy blue, tomato red, and natural white, worn, very worn fringe, small holes and stains, 70 x 84" 325

Jacquard, 2 pc, star medallions, single weave, floral border, corners labeled "Margret Snuder, 1867," navy blue, deep red, green, and natural white, small holes in blue wool, some fringe loss, 76 x 92" 250

Jacquard, 2 pc, turkeys and peacocks in trees, double weave, vintage border, navy blue and natural white, wear, small holes, stains, top edge very worn, 78 x 84" 125

Jacquard, 2 pc, urns of fruit and flowers, double weave, birds, peacocks feeding young, buildings border, corners with "Manufacd by Jay A Vanvleck, Gallipolis, O," navy blue and natural white, 82" sq 500

Overshot, 2 pc, Bow Ties and Diamonds, red, blue, teal, and natural white, minor wear, 66 x 93" 225

Overshot, 2 pc, Chariot Wheel, cotton and wool, blue and natural white, 74 x 90" 100

Overshot, 2 pc, Diamonds and Crosses, wavy line borders, blue and white, PA, early 19th C, 94 x 80" 525

Overshot, 2 pc, Frenchman's Fancy variation, navy blue, salmon, and natural white, no fringe, some wear, 62 x 94" 135

Overshot, 2 pc, geometric pattern, linen and wool, bittersweet colored wool, natural linen, 86 x 92" 275

Overshot, 2 pc, Goose Eye and Check, red and teal wool yarns, some discoloration at ends, 80 x 90" 80

Overshot, 2 pc, grid pattern, geometric motif, double weave, red, green, and cream, PA, early 19th C, 80 x 94" 575

Overshot, 2 pc, Optical, woven, olive green, navy blue, salmon red, and natural white, applied fringe on 3 sides, 78 x 92" 275

Overshot, 2 pc, Optical, woven, olive green, red, and natural white, 64 x 82" 200

Overshot, 2 pc, Optical, woven, red, blue, and white, 68 x 86" 125

Overshot, 2 pc, Optical, woven, red, 2 shades of blue, 76 x 94" 225

Overshot, 2 pc, Optical, woven, salmon pink, bluish black, and natural white, minor wear, 66 x 94" **225**

Overshot, 2 pc, Optical, woven, tan, natural white, single weave, woven fringe on 3 sides, 85 x 95" **275**

Overshot, 2 pc, Pine Tree, light blue, dark brown, and natural white, no fringe, edge wear, 68 x 82" **150**

Overshot, 2 pc, small stars, pine tree border, navy blue, olive, gold, and natural white, wear and moth damage, worn fringe on 1 end, bare thread spots, 70 x 92" **225**

Overshot, 2 pc, Snowflake and Pine Tree, deep navy blue, natural white, some edge wear, holes and stains, 74 x 88" **250**

Overshot, 2 pc, stars, trees, flowers, and stick soldiers, navy blue, salmon red, gold, and natural white, wear, edge damage, missing fringe, 70 x 89" . . **325**

Overshot, 2 pc, stars and flowers, navy blue, red, olive, and natural white, worn, fringe, 65 x 80" **100**

Overshot, 2 pc, stripes, band of white alternating with red, blue, and white, 69 x 98" **175**

Overshot, 3 pc, maroon, natural white, and salmon, tied fringe on ends, some wear and damage, 60 x 88" **100**

FEED & GRAIN BAGS

The first cotton grain bags appeared in the early 1800s and were used as an alternative to the barrel. They were handmade and not widely used.

The invention of the sewing machine and machines expressly designed to manufacture flour sacks opened the door to the daily use of textile bags in areas such as the packaging of feed, grains, sugar, and fertilizer. Feed bags reached the peak of their popularity from the 1930s through the 1950s.

The original sizes of bags corresponded to barrel measurements. One barrel of flour weighed 96 lbs, a half barrel weighed 48 lbs, and so forth down to ⅛ barrel at 12 lbs. In 1943 the War Production Board standardized weights at 100, 50, 25, 10, 5, and 2 lb sizes.

The first manufactured bags were solid colors, usually white. Labels were either printed directly on the bag or paper labels were sewn or pasted to the front. Bags printed with floral or striped designs or doll and clothing patterns were introduced during the late 1920s and early 1930s. The rural housewife made clothing, dish towels, quilts, and toys from them.

Reference: Anna Lue Cook, *Textile Bags,* Books Americana, 1990.

Collectors' Club: The Feedsack Club, 25 South Starr Avenue, Apt, 16, Pittsburgh, PA 15202.

American Beauty Flour, Russell–Miller Milling Co, Minneapolis, MN, rose illus, 25 lbs, 24 x 13" **$20**

Archer Brand Poultry Feeds, Archer–Daniels–Midland Co, Minneapolis, MN, archer in center circle, issue date of June 2, 1942, printed on textile bag, 100 lbs, 39 x 23" **25**

B–B Poultry Ration, Maritime Mfg Co, Buffalo, NY, floral print textile bag, 100 lbs, 38 x 23" **50**

Birchmont Flour, St Cloud Milling Co, St Cloud, MN, Fulton Bag Co, building illus front, eagle over "Fulton seamless A junior size" in circle on back,
white, 98 lbs, 36 x 20" **80**

C and H Pure Cane Berry Granulated Sugar, California and Hawaiian Sugar
Refining Corp, San Francisco, CA, Pure Cane Berry Granulated inside tri-
angle illus, 2 lbs, 5 x 10" **15**

Corazon Oro, Russell–Miller Milling Co, Minneapolis, MN, heart design
with product name, 200 lbs, 40 x 29" **25**

Domino Pure Grain Sugar, American Sugar Refining Co, New York, NY,
product name on front, 25 lbs, 19 x 12½" **20**

Easter Lily Wheat Gray Shorts, Trenton Milling Co, Trenton, IL, "Easter Lily"
in circle with white lilies, white, 100 lbs, 38 x 21" **25**

Elmore Growing Mash, Elmore Milling Co, Inc, Oneonta, NY, boy feeding
chicken illus, white, 100 lbs, 36 x 22" **25**

Franklin Cane Sugar, Franklin Sugar Refining Co, Philadelphia, PA, Ben
Franklin illus, 10 lbs, 15½ x 9½" **22**

Fuzzy Mulch, Southern Cotton Oil Division, Hunt Foods and Industries, Inc,
Memphis, TN, Colonel "Sco–Co" illus on front, white, 100 lbs, 39 x 27" .. **20**

Graham Flour, Sperry Flour Co, San Francisco, CA, "Sperry Flour" in circle
with barn on front, white, 9 ⁹/₁₀ lbs, 14 x 10" **25**

Indian Girl Pure Wheat Flour, Williamsville Roller Mill Co, Williamsville,
MO, Indian girl inside tree illus, white, 24 lbs, 25 x 12" **25**

Lady Clair Self–Rising Flour, Cumberland Valley Flour Co, Nashville, TN,
running horse illus, 24 lbs, 26 x 12½" **30**

McCahan's Sunny Cane Sugar, W J McCahan Sugar Refining and Molasses
Co, Philadelphia, PA, sun illus in 2 corners on front, "The best cooks are
generous with sugar" printed on back, white, 10 lbs, 16 x 9" **15**

*Left: Quaker Pure Cane Sugar, Pennsylvania Sugar Co, Philadelphia, PA, Quaker woman in
keystone, red and blue printing on white, 5 lbs, 7¼ x 12", $18.* Photo courtesy Ray
Morykan Auctions.

*Center: Bambino Pinto Beans, Babe Ruth image, yellow, red, and black on burlap, 17½ x
35¼", $15.*

Right: Sunnyfield Family Flour, blue and yellow on white, 98 lbs, 34 x 15¾", $28.

Merit Poultry Feed, Clark–Burkle and Co, Memphis, TN, rooster, hen, and chick illus, white, 100 lbs, 33 x 17½" **45**

Pearl White Sugar, Matanzas Sugar Estates, Inc, Cuba, crown illus, white, 100 lbs, 34 x 18" **45**

Poultry Feed, Quaker Oats Co, Chicago, clock with roman numerals and turkey illus, 100 lbs, 38 x 18" **40**

Pure Granulated Sugar, Central Santa Isabel, Fomento, Las Villas, Cuba, palm trees illus on front, 100 lbs, 34 x 18" **40**

Rose Self–Rising Flour, All Star Mills, Inc, Albemarle, NC, rose illus on striped ground, white, 50 lbs, 30 x 16½" **20**

Russell's Best Enriched Flour, Russell Milling Co, Russell, KS, letter "R" on front with wheat illus, "Handi Work Tea Towel Design" to be embroidered on back, white, 50 lbs, 30 x 17" **30**

Scott's Auburn Leader Soft Winter Wheat Shorts, Auburn Mills, Inc, Auburn, KY, sailboat in water illus, 100 lbs, 38 x 22" **15**

Sea Island Sugar, Western Refinery, San Francisco, CA, clouds, trees, and waves illus, 25 lbs, 20 x 13" **10**

Sea Island Sugar, Western Sugar Refinery, San Francisco, CA, doll pattern back, white, copyright 1936, 10 lbs, 16 x 10½" **45**

Snow Lily Flour, green strips at top and bottom, 10 lbs, 17 x 9½" **10**

Southern Queen Self–Rising Flour, Fulton Bag Co, St Louis, long–haired woman and printed floral design, 10 lbs, 17 x 10½" **30**

Spreckels Sugar, Spreckels Sugar Co, San Francisco, CA, Honey–Dew Brand inside diamond, 100 lbs, 34 x 18½" **15**

Sterling Quality Pure Cane Sugar, Sterling Sugars Inc, Franklin, LA, handled sugar bowl with spoon inside circle, white, 100 lbs, 34 x 17" **20**

Valiant Winter Wheat Flour, Pillsbury Co, Minneapolis, MN, warrior with shield inside octagonal illus, white, 100 lbs, 33½ x 20" **20**

Wayne Hog Supplement, Allied Mills, Inc, Chicago, IL, man on horse illus, white, 100 lbs, 38 x 21" **25**

White Frost Shorts, Model Milling Co, snow capped mountains illus, white, 100 lbs, 35 x 19" **15**

White Gold Pure Cane Sugar, South Coast Corp, New Orleans, product name inside scroll illus on back, 10 lbs, 15½ x 10" **12**

White Ring All Purpose Flour, H C Cole Milling Co, Chester, IL, plate with biscuits inside floral banded ring, "All Purpose Flour" beneath, camera, clock, radio, and percolator illus on printed bag, 10 lbs, 18 x 10" **15**

HOMESPUN, LINENS, & DOILIES

Homespun is a loosely hand–woven fabric, usually of handspun linen or wool yarns. Flax was an important secondary crop on many agrarian farmsteads of the eighteenth and first half of the nineteenth centuries. During this period, the rural housewife often spun her own linen thread. However, once spun, the housewife took the thread to a semi–professional or professional weaver to have it woven into cloth.

The mass production of inexpensive cloth by the 1840s and 50s meant that the rural housewife could store the spinning wheel up in the attic for good. Time devoted to spinning was rechanneled into sewing and handcrafting decorative textile pieces.

In Pennsylvania a unique textile form known as the show towel developed. These long, narrow towels of white homespun linen were gaudily decorated with colorful embroidery and drawn–thread panels. They were generally worked by adolescent girls for pastime and pleasure. They hung on the door between the sitting room and kitchen in the Pennsylvania German household. The golden age of the show towel was between 1820 and 1850.

The literature explosion, especially in the first quarter of the twentieth century, included a number of magazines devoted to sewing and needlework. The rural housewife was an eager subscriber. Among the most popular handcrafted needlework was crocheting.

Most fine crochet was done during the period between 1850 and 1950, almost exclusively by women. Crochet is done by hand using a crochet hook and varying sizes of cotton thread. Occasionally linen or wool threads are used. The thread came in a variety of colors. The most widely used were white, cream, and ecru. Among the most popular patterns are filet work, pineapple, and Irish.

The country wife believed in the adage of "waste not, want not." Textiles used for one purpose were recycled for something else. The rural housewife was decades ahead of her time.

References: Maryanne Dolan, *Old Lace & Linens Including Crochet: An Identification and Value Guide,* Books Americana, Krause Publications, 1989; Ellen J. Gehret, *This Is the Way I Pass My Time: A Book About Pennsylvania German Decorated Hand Towels,* The Pennsylvania German Society, 1985; Frances Johnson, *Collecting Antique Linens, Lace & Needlework: Identification, Restoration and Prices,* Wallace Homestead, Krause Publications, 1991; Frances Johnson, *Collecting More Household Linens,* Schiffer Publishing, 1997; Elizabeth M. Kurella, *Everybody's Guide to Lace and Linens,* Antique Trader Books, 1997; Marsha L. Manchester, *Vintage White Linens: A to Z,* Schiffer Publishing, 1997; Elizabeth Scofield and Peggy Zalamea, *20th Century Linens and Lace: A Guide to Identification, Care and Prices of Household Linens,* Schiffer Publishing, 1995.

Periodical: *The Lace Collector,* PO Box 222, Plainwell, MN 49080.

Collectors' Club: International Old Lacers, Inc, PO Box 481223, Denver, CO 80248.

Museums: Henry Morrison Flagler Museum, Palm Beach, FL; Ipswich Historical Society, Ipswich, MA; The Lace Museum, Sunnyvale, CA.

Antimacassar, filet crochet, cream colored, reclining cat design, scroll work
  around border, 3–pc set, 12 x 15" **$40**
Bed Tick, homespun, blue, red, green–blue, and cream plaid, New England
  or PA, 19th C, 75 x 58" **250**
Crib Sheet, white muslin, embroidered animals, blue top band, matching
  pillowcase, 48 x 52" **40**
Dish Towel, white textile bag, embroidered designs and day of week on each
  towel, 38 x 18", price for set of 7 .... **30**
Doily, cotton, embroidered, 12 x 14" **5**
Doily, ecru linen, painted floral and leaf design, embroidered, lace edging,
  24" d **20**
Doily, white muslin, embroidered red silk roses and green leaves, scalloped
  green silk floss edge, 18" d **20**
Handkerchief, cotton, red on white, printed bird design **20**
Hand Towel, wool on linen, plain woven ground, peacocks, 2 small, and 2
  large, "1850" above stylized vases of flowers centering third group of
  flowers emanating from heart above "Jacob Buch," small peacocks above
  double fringed edge and pink border bottom, rect cross–stitched border,
  PA, 57 x 18½" **575**

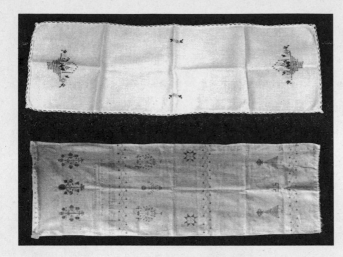

Top: Dresser Scarf, cross–stitch embroidered baskets of flowers, $15.

Bottom: Show Towel, rose–red color, 16¹/₂ x 50¹/₂", $175.

Hand Towel, wool on linen, plain woven ground, pink flowering tree, pink and white birds, "18/SH/24" in pink cross stitch, centered by small stylized flowers above drawn open panel with flowers and central diamond over fringed base, applied hanging loops at each top corner, 52 x 15¹/₂" . . .   **285**

Mattress Cover, homespun, blue and white, 1 seam, white homespun backing, minor wear and age stains, 60 x 104" **115**

Mattress Cover, homespun, blue and white plaid, white backing, 52 x 68" . . .   **150**

Pillow Case, homespun, blue and white, 21 x 32" **40**

Pillow Case, white muslin, 3" crocheted and tatted edging, unused, 21 x 35", price for pair **25**

Pillow Sham, brown, pink, and white printed calico sham with embroidered birds, initialed "CT," and dated "1829," PA, early 19th C **200**

Place Mats, linen, woven red and tan checks, fringe, matching napkins, 12 x 18", price for set of 4 . . . .   **22**

Remnant, homespun, 14 pcs, brown and white, blue and brown, blue and yellow checks and plaids, 18th/19th C **1,250**

Remnant, homespun, 6 pcs, blue and white, brown and white, brown and red checks and plaids, 18th/19th C **860**

Sheet, cotton homespun, 2 pc, center seam, hand–sewn hem, 77 x 78" **65**

Sheet, cotton textile bags, white, crib size, 54 x 40" **10**

Sheet, linen homespun, 2 pc, hand hemmed, Ephrata, PA, 76 x 100" **45**

Show Towel, cotton homespun, 2 compotes with fruit, red embroidery, diamond bird's–eye weave with woven red stripes, crocheted lace, 11 x 86" . .   **70**

Show Towel, linen homespun, hearts, flowers, birds, stars, and "Anne Gibbel 1849" in silk cross–stitch embroidery, 55 x 19" **135**

Show Towel, linen homespun, stylized flowers, birds, and tulip tree, diamond bird's–eye weave with cut and drawn work panel, crocheted lace with fringe, stains, 59 x 13¹/₂" **115**

Show Towel, linen homespun, stylized flowers, geometric stripes, and initials in silk cross–stitch embroidery, cut work design of star and 2 women, minor wear and light stains, 59¹/₂ x 18" **350**

Show Towel, linen homespun, stylized flowers, stars, birds and initials "F.H."
   in silk cross–stitch embroidery, 3 rows of fringe, some wear and stains, ½"
   tear in top edge, 56½ x 17" **50**
Show Towel, linen homespun, stylized star flowers, tulips, and checkerboard
   band, white on white woven pattern, cut and drawn work panel, strip of
   machine–made lace between towel and cut work, stains, 53 x 16" **50**
Tablecloth, homespun, blue and white plaid check, minor stains, small
   holes, 33 x 52" **85**
Tablecloth, homespun, cotton, woven geometric design, "Fanny Erb A.D.,
   1843," faded red, 2–pc construction, edge fringe, minor soiling and small
   stains, 51 x 70" **75**
Tablecloth, linen, cut work, filet lace inserts, 12 matching napkins, 76 x
   116", price for set **300**
Tablecloth, linen, woven bird's–eye diamond pattern, hand–sewn hem and
   center seam, 52 x 74" **55**
Tablecloth, machine woven, blue and white check, hand–sewn hem 1 edge,
   basted selvage other, 54 x 76" **130**
Tablecloth, overshot, tones of beige and oyster, PA, mid–19th C **55**
Table Runner, linen homespun, natural, brown pinstripe, 2 pc, hand–sewn
   seam, hand hemmed, embroidered initials, stains, 66 x 85" **50**
Ticking, cotton, light blue, red, green, and cream plaid, PA, 19th C **130**
Ticking, linen, butternut and cream check, New England, 19th C **125**
Towel, linen homespun, coarsely woven, hand–sewn hem, 13½ x 40" **25**
Towel, linen homespun, natural and white embroidery, 11½ x 32" **25**
Towel, linen homespun, overshot woven design, applied cotton fringe and
   embroidered "S.M.1" in olive, 17 x 45" **10**
Towel, linen homespun, woven stripes, red, embroidered "WH9," 18 x 66" .. **15**
Vanity Set, 4 pcs, white linen, bonnet girls in royal blue embroidery, 10 x
   20", price for set **30**

NEEDLEWORK & SAMPLERS

Finding time to do needlework in rural America was a luxury. It was an art form
that was centered along the eastern seaboard, primarily in urban areas. Needlework is
found in many forms: clothing, embroidered pictures, fire screens, pocketbooks, samplers, and seat coverings.

Country collectors and decorators have romanticized needlework. They have formulated an idyllic image of a woman sitting in front of a blazing fireplace at the end
of day, happily doing needlework as a means of relaxation. If this were true, tens of
thousands more examples would have survived. Executing a needlework picture was
time consuming and required great skill. Few were trained and capable of doing it.

English needlework has flooded the American market. The following clues will
help you distinguish American examples from their English counterparts. Identify the
maker and check vital statistic records in the region of the needlework's origins. Do
not rely on town names. Many English and American town names are identical. By
1750 American needlework was more naturalistic in style and often contained a
greater variety of stitches than its English counterpart. British samplers are usually
more balanced and possess brighter colors because of better dyes. By 1800 Americans
favored the pictorial approach to the more formal, horizontal band style. When doubt
exists, assume the piece is English.

Samplers, a needlework form, served many purposes. For a young child they were a practice exercise and permanent reminder of stitches and patterns. For a young woman they demonstrated her skills in a "gentle" art and preserved key elements of family genealogy. For the mature woman they were a useful occupation and functioned as gifts or remembrances, e.g., mourning pieces.

Schools for young ladies of the early nineteenth century prided themselves on the needlework skills they taught. The Westtown School in Chester County, Pennsylvania, and the Young Ladies Seminary in Bethlehem, Pennsylvania, are two examples. These schools changed their teaching as styles changed. Berlin work was introduced by the mid–nineteenth century.

Examples of samplers date back to the 1700s. The earliest ones were long and narrow, usually done only with the alphabet and numerals. Later examples were square. At the end of the nineteenth century, the shape tended to be rectangular.

Simialr motifs were used throughout the country. The name is a key element in determining the region. Samplers are on linen unless otherwise indicated.

References: Tandy and Charles Hersh, *Samplers of the Pennsylvania Germans, The Pennsylvania German Society,* 1991; Glee Krueger, *A Gallery of American Samplers: The Theodore H. Kapnek Collection,* Bonanza Books, 1984 edition; Betty Ring, *American Needlework Treasures; Samplers and Silk Embroideries From the Collection of Betty Ring,* E. P. Dutton, 1987; Anne Sebba, *Samplers: Five Centuries of a Gentle Craft,* Thames and Hudson, 1979.

Collectors' Club: Stumpwork Society, 55 Ferncrest Avenue, Cranston, RI 02905.

NEEDLEWORK PICTURE

1790, "To the Memory of Esther Derby Obt. June 13 1790 AE 14 Months and 14 Days," silk stitches and watercolor on silk, woman standing next to monument, "ED" monogram and verse below willow tree, 18¾ x 14¾" . . **$7,000**

1800, "Wrought by Penelope Howland in the 9th year of her age, and sacred to the memory of seven, small Brother's, and Sister's," silk threads and ground, triptych monument surmounted by 7 urns below willow trees, gold, green, blue, gray, brown, and black, imperfections, 8 x 8¼" **7,000**

1804, "Sacred to the Memory of John & Martin Sanger deceased April 25 1799 aged 5 months & 3 days," silk stitches, watercolor and ink on satin, woman placing blossoms on monument with verse, smaller monument on left inscribed "Irana Sanger Oct. 19, 1798 aged 7 days" beneath 2 willow trees, rising sun and leafy tree in background, inscribed "Wrought by Olive Sanger, Bridgewater Academy, 1804," 15¾ x 19½" **6,900**

1836, "Elizabeth Moyer Wismers neadlework [sic] made in the year of my lord 1836," silk threads, woman seated on chair with sheep, trees, bird, dog "Rover," and cat "Cubit," wear and fading edges tattered, floss inscription incomplete, mahogany frame with half turnings and old dark finish, 15⅜ x 21⅜" **825**

Undated, flowers and birds, silk and metallic thread on linen homespun, minor damage, framed, 14¾ x 18¾" **140**

SAMPLER

1748, "Anna Gould Her Sampler Made in the Year 1748," silk on linen, bands of alphabets and stylized meandering floral vines within zigzag border, 11½ x 8¼" **$5,750**

1785, "Elizabeth Wells Was Born September the 5 in the Year of Our Lord 1776, John Wells Was Born May the 3 in the Year of Our Lord 1784/Finished in the Year of Our Lord 1785," linen ground, lower section with initials "GW" centering a basket of fruit, 21 x 11⁷/₈" 700

1785, "Margaret Summers her work done in the thirteenth year of her age," silk on linen, alternating rows of alphabets and flowering vines above verse and potted flower, vining floral border, framed, scattered stains, 17 x 15¹/₂" 2,200

1792, "Abigail Wingate wrought this in the 13 year of her age and in the year...1792," rows of alphabets above verse and inscription, floral border, framed, 16¹/₂ x 13³/₄" 7,500

1793, "Mary Steel in the 6th year of her age 1793," silk on linen homespun, alphabets, numerals, crows, trees, birds, and inscription, gold, green, and gray, 9¹/₂ x 13¹/₂" 1,125

1796, "Polly Wilde Sampler Wrought in Salem, June 1796," and "Massachusetts State Salem...," silk threads, rows of alphabets, 2 floral urns in middle section, center lion, lower section of 2 ladies seated facing, trees, birds, florals, and animals, pyramid shaped devices on 2 inner borders, framed, 12¹/₂ x 13³/₄" 8,800

1798, "Ann Lunn her sampler aged 6 years 1798," silk on linen homespun, rows of alphabets and verse, framed, 12³/₄ x 11" 525

1799, "Charlotte Hough Daughter of Samuel and Susannah Hough Aged 10 Years 1799 Sarah Shoemaker," silk on linen, bands of alphabets and numerals, pine trees, birds, meandering verse flanked by pots of flowers and deer, floral vine and strawberries outer border, green, red, brown, blue, peach, orange, and white, 16¹/₂ x 15" 11,000

1799, "John Field and Dianna Field Married July 21st, Elizabeth Field, born December 25th 1779, finished sampler at Chesterfield, October 18th, 1799," silk on linen homespun, alphabets, "The Ten Commandments in Verse," stylized house, trees, pots of flowers, and birds, flowering and geometric borders, stains, some floss missing with several words missing letters, framed, 19 x 22¹/₂" 825

1799, "Rosamond Lamb her sampler in the year of our Lord 1799," polychrome silk on linen homespun, rows of alphabets and numerals above inscription, surrounded by floral vine border, framed, minor discoloration and fiber loss to ground, 15 x 12³/₄" 1,000

1800, "Suzanne Smith born July 16 1792 aged 8 years 1800," silk on linen, Washington memorial, American eagle above wreathed urn with initials "GW," centering inscriptions commemorating Washington, rows of alphabets above, surrounded by floral vining border, cream, brown, and green, framed, discoloration, 20 x 15¹/₂" 3,200

1802, "Harriot King Work'd this Sampler 1802 Aged thirteen," silk on linen, alphabet and signature above urn surmounted by American eagle on plinth inscribed "GW," flanked by trees, memorial verse below within sawtooth borders, stylized floral vines on outer border, green, gold, brown, and white, 17¹/₄ x 13³/₁₆" 3,450

1802, "June Potter, Dec The 7th 1802, aged 8 years," silk and wool on linen homespun, alphabet, rows of trees, flowers, strawberries, and birds, red, pink, shades of green, blue, white, and gold, some wear, stains, small holes, 13¹/₄ x 15¹/₂" 450

1803, "Elisabeth Hoover made this sampler in Harrisburg in Mrs. Leah Bratten School in the year of our Lord 1803 Susanna Hoover and Hannah Hoover my sis...," and "Elisabeth Hoover was born in Northampton County Obermilford Township, on the 18 day of September 1787," silk on linen homespun, blue, green, gold, pink, brown, and white, 16¼ x 15⅛" . . **7,500**

1805, "Amelia A age 10, 1805," silk on linen homespun, stylized trees, flowers, house, birds, and butterflies, vining border, faded, worn, stained, with holes and missing floss, framed, 16¾ x 14¼" **325**

1806, "West–Town Boarding School. Anna Pancoast. 1806," black silk on linen gauze, verse within vine and leaf border, minor staining, 10¼ x 13" . **8,000**

1807, "Ann Cornells Sampler 1807," silk on linen homespun, alphabets and verse, framed, stained, 12¼ x 18¼" **775**

1810, "Abigail Cool born Feb. 6th, 1796, Abigail Cool is my name and with my needle I wrought the same for I was by my parents taught not to spend my time for naught. 1810," silk on linen homespun, alphabets, stylized floral band, zigzag border, green, blue, pink, rust red, and white, unframed, 14¼" sq **2,150**

1812, "Julia O'Brien Washington City June the 4th 1812," polychrome silk threads on green linen, verse above landscape with house, flowering vining border, framed, minor losses to ground, minor discoloration, 18 x 18½" **34,500**

1813, "Sarah Mingin's Easton School, 1813," silk on linen, alphabets enclosed in vine and leaf oval, meandering floral vines and birds border, ribbon rosettes in upper corners, initialed "EC, IM/CM," green, gold, brown, and white, some staining and discoloration, 16⅜ x 12½" **3,000**

1815, "Mary Owen AE 12 Portland June 19 1815," silk on linen, alphabet above verse, lower section with landscape and 2 houses, trees, and fence, outer borders with rose vines tied by a bow, some discoloration, 16½ x 11½" **7,500**

1817, "Mary Ann Jewell finished this work, April 24th, 1817 at Mrs. Venthams Boarding School, Winton, Aged – Years," intricate silk stitches on linen homespun, verse, cottage, barn, farm, people, and wild animals, vining border, brown, gold, green, white, black, and light blue, framed, 12¾ x 17" **1,600**

1818, "Wrought by Hannah F. Thayer Randolph Aged 11 Years 1818," silk threads, applied paper cutouts on linen, bands of alphabets above village scene with figures of gentlemen and ladies, a barking dog, and a bird in tree, meandering floral border tied by a blue bow, scattered staining and discoloration, 16⅞ x 15½" **6,900**

1820, "Worked by Olive Handley, aged 11 years, 1820," linen ground, alphabet and verse, floral and vine border, discoloration, fading, framed, 16¼ x 17¼" **1,100**

1821, "Abigail Whiting, Franklin, September, AD 1821," silk on linen homespun, alphabets, house, and tree, vining floral border, 18½ x 11¾" **1,100**

1822, "Margaret Warnes work done in the 14th year of her age September 14, 1822," silk on linen, floral swags above alphabet, verse, and inscription, landscape with house, trees, and flower baskets below, framed, tack holes, 18¾ x 17" **1,400**

1822, "Mary Elizabeth Ellington, Aged 11 Years 1822," silk on cotton, flower vase surrounded by crosses, budding vine border, initialed "EG," pink, blue, yellow, green, white, and brown, 17⅜ x 14¼" **6,300**

1823, "Ann Drinkwater Age 12 1823," silk on linen, verse over large pot of flowers, trees and baskets of flowers, meandering floral vine outer borders, green, yellow, brown, and white, staining, 21³/₄ x 17⁷/₈" 5,750

1823, "Catharine Foster, Aged 12, 1823," silk on linen homespun, verse, birds, angels, and flowers, flowering border, pink, olive, ivory, gray, green, and gold, some moth damage, orig molded black frame, 15 x 15¹/₂" 700

1824, "Susan Parker her work anno Domini 1824, aged 11," silk on linen homespun, stylized flowers, Adam and Eve, serpent in tree, strawberry border, framed, 10¹/₂ x 8" 1,750

1825, "Catherine Kellar worked this in the twelve year of her age 1825," linen homespun, alphabets, stylized pots of strawberry–like flowers, matted, gilt frame, 21¹/₄ x 28" 250

1826, "Catharina Borgholder, 1826," silk on linen, alphabet bands and numerals above vases of stylized flowers, peacocks, and animals, 16" sq . .3,450

1827, "Ann Mayron aged 13 Edmond Iley School 1827," silk on linen, rows of alphabets, flowering vine, tree of life surrounded by potted plants, birds, and animals, inscription, framed, 16" sq .2,000

1827, "Fliza J. McGilvreay, Aged 9 Years, E. M. Westin Inst," and "Merrimack Sept. 21 AD 1827," silk on linen, bands of alphabets over verse, outer border with meandering floral vine, lower section with cottage, trees, and grazing cow, peach, green, yellow, brown, cream, and black, discoloration, 17¹/₈ x 18³/₈" 2,850

1828, "Mary Ann Smith aged 7 Y 7 M, Sept. 2nd 1828," silk and linen homespun threads, rows of alphabets, stylized flowers, and birds with verse, vining floral border, green, tan, yellow, white, black, and beige, stains, some fading, matted and framed, 11¹/₂ x 13¹/₂" 500

1830, "Betsy Archer Ivinghoe School May 26, 1830," silk threads, homespun, alphabets, verse, flowers, buildings, and inscription, vining border, framed, stained, minor holes, edge damage, 16¹/₂" sq 875

1831, "Mary Ann Scott and George Town, March 23, 1831," variety of silk stitches on linen homespun, baskets of fruit, bands of alphabets, pious verse, and baskets of flowers over brick house flanked by birds perched on trees, black dogs, stylized rosebud border, green, blue, gold, brown, and white, 20³/₄ x 17¹/₂" 8,100

1834, "Mary Collier Aged 9 1834," verse above lower panel with Adam and Eve, framed, 14¹/₂ x 12" 975

1835, "Angela Nicholas Aged 9 years, 1835," silk on linen homespun, flowers, birds, animals, house, and crowns, vining border, shades of blue, green, gold, white, brown, and black, wear and stains, holes in linen, poorly glued repairs, framed, 17¹/₂ x 19" 325

1835, "Thomas Lenn, aged 10 years 1835," silk on linen homespun, baskets of flowers, animals, crowns, and verse, flowering border, shades of red, pink, orange, green, light blue, brown, and black, wear, stains, damage to 1 border, modern frame, 16 x 21¹/₂" 225

1837, "Wealthy A. Gregory Aged 12 years, 1837," silk on linen homespun, side by side design with rows of alphabets and numerals on left half, right side with memorial to Sidney J Gregory, verse, stylized people, trees, and church scene of Sidney ascending to heaven, attributed to Pembrook, MA, minor stains, framed, 17³/₄ x 19¹/₄" 1,300

1841, "Mary A Moore's work done in the 12 year of her age 1841," silk on linen homespun, alphabets, birds, and flowers, framed, 17 x 11" 400

1837, Sarah Jane Rest, multicolor threads, vining border, $525.

1842, "Emma Ann Gould, age 8 years 1842," silk on natural linen homespun, alphabets, birds, heart, and vining border, blue, green, red, black, and pink, stapled to cardboard, unframed, 10¹/₂ x 15¹/₄" **600**

1844, "Elizabeth Durrant, Aged 11, May 29, 1844," silk on linen homespun, alphabet, birds, flowers, people, and crowns, vining border, shades of green, brown, and gold, holes in linen, framed, 15³/₄ x 13¹/₂" **325**

1845, "Ellen Sullivan, her work age 11 years, 1845," silk on dark linen homespun, stylized Adam and Eve, church, windmill, angels, flowers, animals, trees, and verse, strawberry border, shades of green, brown, gold, and blue, small holes, brown marker used to highlight some designs, modern frame, 12⁵/₈ x 17¹/₄" **700**

1852, "Emily Miller, May 1852," alphabets and verse, strawberry border, minor stains and color bleeding, walnut molded frame, 22³/₈ x 21" **375**

1856, "Elizabeth Dock Stader," silk on linen homespun, geometric borders, alphabets, flowers, and scene with house and dog, gilt frame, 9¹/₂ x 11¹/₂" .   **250**

1858, "Fannie Cary's Sampler, Richfield, March 22, 1858, Aged 7 years," silk on linen homespun, alphabets and verse, framed, 8 x 14" **225**

1860, "Harriet Adams, March 13, 1860," silk on linen homespun, baskets of flowers, floral bouquets, vining floral border, green, brown, gold, and red, beveled bird's–eye veneer frame, 15 x 17¹/₂" **475**

Undated, "Ages Roberts Aged 9," homespun, alphabets, hearts, crowns, and sheep, red, pink, white, black, and green, framed, 18 x 9¹/₄" **225**

Undated, "Ann Frith, aged 9 years," wool on linen homespun, alphabets, numerals, house, animals, and flowers, linen slightly puckered, minor wear, small holes, some stitches missing, beveled walnut frame, 12¹/₄ x 15⁷/₈" **825**

Undated, "Catherine Margret Martens Age 9," silk on linen homespun, strawberries, alphabets, house, trees, and stag, flowering border, stains, faded scene of house and deer, framed, 18¹/₂" sq **300**

Undated, "George Colson & Mary is the name my parents have and I do hope to honour them till I'm laid in the grave. Mary Colson her work wrought in the 14 year of her age," silk on linen homespun, alphabets, verse, and flowers, vining floral borders, framed, 16 x 13¹/₂" **275**

Undated, "Lucy P. Sewall, Age 9 years," silk on linen homespun, rows of alphabets in several different stitches, satin stitch floral border, blue–green, beige, and white, minor stains, attributed to ME, modern frame, 18⅝ x 20" **700**

QUILTS

In the agrarian household a quilt combined beauty with function. Most were not show pieces. They were used. Quilts varied in weight. It was customary to change quilts with the season.

The quilting bee, a group of women working together to quilt a pieced top to its backing, was an important form of social interaction. Almost every rural farmstead, especially in the nineteenth century, had a quilting frame set up in a room corner. When another woman came to call, it was common for them to spend some time talking over the quilting frame.

Quilts have been passed down as family heirlooms for many generations. Each is an individual expression. The same pattern may have hundreds of variations in both color and design.

The advent of the sewing machine increased, not decreased the number of quilts being made. Quilts are still being sewn today.

The key considerations for price are age, condition, aesthetic beauty, and design. Prices are now at a level position. The exceptions are the very finest examples which continue to bring record prices.

References: American Quilter's Society, *Gallery of American Quilts, 1849–1988,* Collector Books, 1988; Suzy Anderson, *Collector's Guide to Quilts,* Wallace–Homestead, 1991; Cuesta Benberry, *Always There: The African–American Presence in American Quilts,* The Kentucky Quilt Project, 1992; Barbara Brackman, *Clues in the Calico: A Guide to Identifying and Dating Antique Quilts,* EPM Publications, 1989; Barbara Brackman, *Encyclopedia of Pieced Patterns,* Prairie Flower Publications, 1984; Rachael Cochran, et al., *New Jersey Quilts: 1777 to 1950,* American Quilter's Society, 1992; Liz Greenbacker and Kathleen Barach, *Quilts: Identification and Price Guide,* Avon Books, 1992; Carter Houck, *The Quilt Encyclopedia Illustrated,* Harry N. Abrams and The Museum of American Folk Art, 1991; William C. Ketchum, Jr, *The Knopf Collectors' Guides to American Antiques: Quilts,* Alfred A. Knopf, 1982; Jean Ray Laury and California Heritage Quilt Project, *Ho for California: Pioneer Women and Their Quilts,* E. P. Dutton, 1990; Patsy and Myron Orlofsky, *Quilts in America,* Abbeville Press, 1992; Lisa Turner Oshins, *Quilt Collections: A Directory For the United States and Canada,* Acropolis Books, 1987; Rachel and Kenneth Pellman, *The World of Amish Quilts,* Good Books, 1984; Carleton L. Safford and Robert Bishop, *America's Quilts and Coverlets,* Bonanza Books, 1985; Schnuppe von Gwinner, *The History of the Patchwork Quilt,* Schiffer Publishing, 1988; Thos K. Woodard and Blanche Greenstein, *Classic Crib Quilts and How to Make Them,* Dover Publicaitons, 1993.

Periodical: *The Quilt Journal,* 635 West Main Street, Louisville, KY 40202.

Newsletters: *Quilter's Newsletter Magazine,* PO Box 4101, Golden, CO 80401; *Vintage Quilt Newsletter,* 1305 Morphy Street, Great Bend, KS 67530.

Collectors' Clubs: American Quilt Study Group, 660 Mission Street, Suite 400, San Francisco, CA 94105; American Quilter's Society, PO Box 3290, Paducah, KY 42001; The National Quilting Assoc, Inc, PO Box 393, Ellicott City, MD 21043.

Museums: Doll & Quilts Barn, Rocky Ridge, MD; Museum of the American Quilter's Society, Paducah, KY; New England Quilt Museum, Lowell, MA; Quilters Hall of Fame, Marion, IN 46952.

APPLIQUÉD

Album, 16 different stylized designs including flowers, eagle, heart, hands, wreaths, and arrows, embroidered highlights, red, green, and yellow calico, white ground, minor stains, 76" sq **$875**

Baskets of Tulips, red, green, and goldenrod, corners embroidered "Mrs. Saiddie Ford age 67 years, Sept 15, 1882, West Hope, Henry Co., Ohio," feather quilting, minor wear and fading, 70 x 88" **550**

Dogwood Blossoms, white, brown, and goldenrod on medium green ground, light stains, 74 x 82" **275**

Eagle and Flowers, central eagle in shield surrounded by vining flowers, vining floral border, solid red and teal, yellow, calico, 79 x 93" **475**

Floral Medallion, 9 puffed floral medallions, matching edge leaves, red, goldenrod, and green, high relief puff work, wear and stains, 82 x 86" **825**

Floral Medallion, 9 red, green, yellow–green, and blue stylized floral medallions on white ground, green binding, some age stains, 86" sq **400**

Floral Medallion, 15 red and green stylized flowers, crib size, red swag border, white ground, 44 x 69" **800**

Floral Medallion, red and green calico, crib size, yellow center, feather quilting, 36½ x 38½" **700**

Floral Medallion, red, green, and goldenrod, crib size, 28½" sq **30**

Floral Medallion, teal green and red, puffed berries, 86 x 92" **165**

Floral Sprays, cotton, 30 appliquéd chintz squares on cream colored ground, gold and red paisley intersecting gold and red millefiori print sashing, paisley inner border, chintz floral spray print outer border, quilted in alternating herringbone pattern, bound in red millefiori printed cotton, plain cream cotton backing, Philadelphia, late 18th C, 88 x 101½" **2,500**

Flowers, 18 stylized single head flowers, meandering vine with flowers border, yellow, red, and brown calico, wear, edge damage, stains, and 3" l oval patch, 72 x 83" **350**

Flowering Cacti, green and red, white ground, green and red banded borders, late 19th/early 20th C, 69½ x 76½" **310**

Flowers and Eagle, teal and yellow calico, solid red, red backing, 80 x 94" .. **550**

Folky, wool, crib size, patch work center, appliquéd animals, people, ladder, house, scissors, and "Baby" in center, red, blue, olive green, orange, white, and gray, attributed to the Midwest, some wear, moth damage, and repair, 32 x 46" **2,800**

Friendly Cow, cotton and wool, red, brown, green, ocher, and beige patches, a cow, an apple tree, and scattered blossoms between 2 fences on white ground, inscribed "The Friendly Cow, The freindly [sic] cow all red and white, I love with all my heart, She gives me cream with all her might, To eat with apple tart," reverse of red, ocher, green, purple, and blue flannel and cotton printed and solid patches, c1928, 64 x 76½" **1,600**

Fruit Basket, with butterflies, red and pink, white muslin ground, red stripe around border, 70 x 80" **65**

Ice Cream Cones, strawberry, tan, and white, 30 x 40" **235**

Log Cabin Variation, cotton, 36 red, blue, green, orange, purple, brown, yellow, and black blocks, each with center rectangle with signature sur-

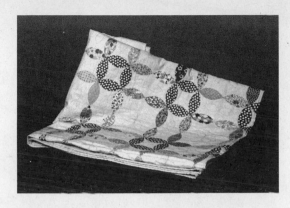

Appliquéd, Melon Patch, multicolored on natural ground, vining and floral border quilting, pencil pattern intact, early 20th C, 92 x 80", **$300.** Photo courtesy Ray Morykan Auctions.

rounded by bars of plaids, calicos, and other prints, green, purple, black, and white stripped borders, brown binding, reverse with brown and white printed checkerboard patterns surrounded by similar border, Pennsylvania, late 19th C, 75½ x 86½" **460**

Morning Glories, purple, violet, and green, embroidered name and date "Sylvia Harris 1936," 67 x 82" **200**

Orchids, with ribbon and other flowers, lavender, pale green, pink, gray, and periwinkle on white ground, overall wear and stains, 73 x 91" **100**

Pinwheel, 9 oak leaf pinwheels, red, green, and goldenrod, similar border design, 70 x 71" **160**

Pinwheel, large center pinwheel with deep pink and white corner plumes, 77 x 81" **380**

Pinwheels, with star centers, plume pinwheels, red and khaki stars and grid, white ground, Eureka, MO origin, stains, 80 x 83" **625**

Poinsettia, potted poinsettias, multifloral border, solid red and green, yellow calico, white ground, old paper label reads "Made in 1844," stains and minor wear, some color loss, 84 x 86" **1,400**

Star of the East Variant, cotton, red, blue, brown, and pink patches, white field with pink border, late 19th/early 20th C, 68 x 84" **170**

Trefoil and Diamond, crib size, red and yellow–green calico on white ground, geometric quilting, 42½ x 48" **380**

Tulip, multicolored prints on white ground, violet border, overall wear, fabric is puckered, 64 x 80" **85**

Tulip and Oak Leaf, teal blue and red on white, meandering tulips in scalloped border, 90 x 92" **1,700**

PIECED

9–Patch, cotton, red, blue, yellow, pink, and white printed calico patches, lightning dividers, white and red banded border, PA, 19th C, 72 x 80" **$520**

12 Black Children, crib size, multicolored prints, white, and beige, embroidered faces, red border, stains, 24 x 32" **190**

35 Stars, multicolored prints in grid, navy and light blue borders, red binding, 76 x 92" **90**

Adirondack Log Cabin, blue, red, yellow, brown, maroon, and black, machine sewn, 78 x 90" **220**

Album Blocks, cotton, red, brown, blue, and yellow calico patches, shell quilting, c1878, 66 x 74" **450**

Alphabet, crib size, pink, embroidered letters, 35 x 50" **380**

Around the World, cotton, multicolored printed calico and solid patches, yellow, red, and green banded borders, PA, late 19th C, 84" sq **460**

Baby Blocks, crib size, blue, outline quilting of blocks, 36 x 45" **115**

Basket, 36 squares in multicolor and white alternate with grayish beige, wear and stains, small hole in 1 corner, 72 x 81" **165**

Baskets of Flowers, beige and red on white ground, feather wreath, meandering feather border, overall wear and stains, 82 x 85" **330**

Bird in Flight, pink, blue, green, brown, yellow, purple, and brown printed patches within wide green calico border, rope quilting, American, c1900, 76" sq **1,000**

Bird Medallions, navy blue print on white, feather designs and hearts, stains, 64 x 72" **220**

Blazing Star, bright yellow, green, rose, maroon, blue, and pink calico patches, wide border of yellow, rose, green, and red fruit and flower printed polished chintz, diagonal line quilting, mid–19th C, 92" sq **2,750**

Bow Tie, navy blue print, and white, machine sewn binding, 70 x 88" **275**

Broken Star, cotton, orange, yellow, red, green, brown, blue, and white printed calico patches, red and white calico Flying Geese border, PA, 19th C, 76 x 80" **460**

Checkerboard, maroon and white calico, minor age stains, 20 x 23" **230**

Checkerboard, pink, white, and blue squares in prints and solids, machine sewn binding, 79" sq **60**

Chinese Lanterns, cotton, green, red, blue, yellow, and white printed calico and solid patches, blue and white ground, red border, diamond and rope quilting, PA, late 19th/early 20th C, 82 x 84" **1,500**

Cobweb, cotton, multicolored printed calico triangular patches, yellow, red, and green banded borders, inscribed "A Present from Grandmother, Mary Elizabeth Weider, To Charles Joel Weider 1886," verso composed of calico patches arranged in 9–patch pattern, 84 x 104" **750**

Pieced, Diamond, multicolor, Amish, Lancaster County, PA, c1925, $875.

Comforter, pieced and knotted, 4 square basket patches, shades of red, pink, goldenrod, and orange, 66 x 76" **100**

Compass Stars, cotton, 9 yellow and red stars on green ground, red and yellow sawtooth sashing and inner border, green outer border, self–bound, pieced yellow and red calico stripped back, diamond and rope–twist quilting, Lebanon County, PA, 19th C, 86 x 88¼" **2,750**

Courthouse Steps, cotton, red, pink, brown, blue, green, and peach printed calico bars and patches, diagonal patch border, PA, late 19th C, 74 x 73" .. **920**

Crazy Quilt, velvet, 16 black, burgundy, purple, red, gold, green, gray, and brown solid and printed patches, velvet border, late 19th C, 72 x 74" **805**

Crosses and Losses, white and lavender, blue–green ground, Amish, Mary Ann Miller, Holmes County, OH, c1935 .... **430**

Delectable Mountain, cotton, brown and white printed calico triangular patches on white ground, diamond, rope, and zigzag quilting within sawtooth border, PA, 19th C, 92" sq **2,100**

Diamond–in–the–Square, silk damask, red, blue, gold, and orange, teacup quilting, bound in salmon silk, backed in brown silk, Germantown, PA, early 19th C, 96½ x 104" **7,100**

Double Irish Chain, cotton, rust, teal, orange, and green, double border of orange and rust, orange binding, diamond and princess feather quilting, Mennonite, PA, c1880, 83½ x 95" **2,300**

Drunkard's Path, navy blue print and solid white, edge wear and light stains, 76" sq **325**

Fans, colored prints on 2–tone pink satin ground, 86 x 94" **350**

Floral, cotton, red, yellow, and green patches arranged in 5 clusters of blossoms alternating with stylized flowerheads on blue calico ground, red and yellow zigzag border, verso with red and blue calico bars, PA, late 19th C, 86 x 88" **1,250**

Flower Garden, brown, brick red, golden yellow, and peach printed calico and solid patches, banded borders, each corner stamped "John Hyman," Mennonite, 74 x 90" **1,050**

Flower Garden, red, white, and brown on grayish green ground, red backing, 83 x 86" **165**

Friendship Quilt, red, blue, green, yellow, and brown printed calico, solid white and chintz patches arranged in squares with star, floral, patchwork, and pinwheel dec, sgd and stamped with signatures of Hicksite Quaker members throughout, blue–green and white chintz zigzag borders, Middletown, Bucks County, PA, dated 1845–49, 100 x 102" **3,000**

Grandmother's Flower Garden, multicolored prints on white ground, 78 x 90" **190**

House, pink and white, 72 x 79" **165**

Irish Chain, olive and red on white ground, initial "CK" in 1 square, wear and light stains, 79" sq **600**

Joseph's Coat, cotton, dark blue, teal, ruby, orange, and yellow stripes, shell quilting, self–bound, PA, late 19th C, 82 x 86" **1,500**

Leaf, blue and white, wear, light stains, and minor damage, attributed to OH, 71 x 72" **380**

Lone Star, multicolored solids on white ground, light blue border stripe, unused, 20th C, 88" sq **430**

Lone Star, pink, blue, lavender, and salmon horses and flowers on blue ground, minor stains, Mennonite **650**

Optical Star, crib size, cotton, red, brown, beige, and turquoise blue patches, reverse in red and brown calico fabric, crisscross quilting, Pennsylvania, early 20th C, 35 x 41" **290**

Orange Slices, cotton, brown, white, and blue printed calico and solid patches on blue and white calico ground, Mennonite, PA, 19th C, 80" sq .. **280**

Philadelphia Pavements, cotton, blue, red, orange, and white square printed and solid patches, orange and red banded borders, feather and floral vine quilting, PA, late 19th/early 20th C, 80 x 84" **800**

Pine Tree, cotton, coral and white patches, leaf quilting, c1900, 72" sq **400**

Puss in the Corner, multicolored prints and calico, beige gingham print ground, red floral strip print backing, PA, 86 x 95" **375**

Rainbow, cotton, green, blue, orange, and brown patches, diagonal line and cable quilting, PA, c1859, 70 x 84" **750**

Sailboats, pastel, pink, and lavender double border, embroidered, 77 x 96" .. **110**

School House Blocks, brown, rust, blue, and tan, tan muslin sashing border, 70 x 84" **80**

Single Star Variant, navy blue and white print on white ground, pencil quilt pattern intact, minor age stains, 25½" sq **400**

Snowball, pastel colors, black and gray segments, Amish, 78 x 86" **75**

Snow Crystal, triangular and hexagonal patches, multicolored prints, yellow ground, Elta Hargie, Kansas City, KS **400**

Spider Web, cotton, pink, red, blue, purple, green, peach, and brown printed calico patches, wide purple calico border, diagonal line quilting, PA, late 19th C, 80 x 82" **800**

Squares, multicolored postage stamp size concentric squares, 88 x 92" **275**

Star and Flying Geese, crib size, cotton, brown, white, orange, pink, and blue printed calico patches, reverse with black, white, brown, and beige checked and printed calico, crisscross quilting, PA, 19th C, 33 x 46" **750**

Star of Bethlehem, cotton, 16 green, red, and brown diamond blocks with alternating green and white triple borders with domino square blocks enclosing a rainbow Star of Bethlehem variation pattern, enclosed by alternating green and white triple border, diamond and ocean waves quilting, 19th C, 116 x 118" **2,200**

Stars, red, white, and calico, 70 x 71" **400**

Pieced, Star of the East, navy blue and white print stars and border, red and white print ground and backing, geometric quilting, $275.

Stars and Squares, cotton, brown, red, blue, and yellow printed calico patches, banded border, PA, 19th C, 76 x 87" **630**

Stripes, brightly colored stripes, red and yellow calico bar back, 3 quilting
patterns, 85 x 87" **1,300**

Sunburst, crib size, cotton, pink, red, green, navy blue, and orange cotton
patches, reverse in paisley fabric, PA, early 20th C, 40 x 41" **860**

Sunflower, red, yellow, brown, navy blue, and green calico flowers on white
ground, red and blue printed sashings, batting, PA, 19th C, 92 x 104" **2,650**

Sunshine and Shadows, pink, beige, red, black, blue, green, yellow, and
lavender patches, wide purple border, meandering floral vine quilting, PA,
20th C, 73 x 80" **1,000**

Trapunto Design, with feather wreaths and flowers, light blue and white,
66" sq **600**

Triangles, shades of blue print, worn faded, stains, 68 x 81" **380**

Trip Around the World, cotton, crib size, red, blue, white, and yellow patches, red and yellow backing, crisscross quilting, PA, late 19th/early 20th C,
35 x 36" **350**

Tulips in Square, red, green, and yellow printed calico patches, broad
brown, red, green, and white Coronation chintz and rose vine border, PA,
19th C, 91 x 94" **900**

Tumbling Blocks, bright solid colors, orange border, 63 x 88" **165**

Tumbling Blocks, multicolored silk, satin, and velvet, 62 x 82" **480**

Wild Goose Chase, 2 shades of blue print and white, 76 x 84" **220**

Windmill, cotton, yellow, red, green, and blue printed calico patches, wide
red calico border with swag quilting, PA, late 19th C, 76 x 86" **700**

Zigzag Bars, red, gray, and white zigzag designs, bluish purple print diamonds, chintz back with brown, green, and white flowers on lilac ground,
78 x 106" **165**

PIECED AND APPLIQUÉD

2 Deer, cotton, brown and white, 2 deer with locked horns flanked by stars,
1 side depicting mountains with hunter, 2 bears, and tree, other side
depicting house, 2 guns, saw, tree, and bear, with princess feather, diamond, and clover quilting, Armstrong County, PA, c1910, 74 x 76" **$2,800**

Alphabet, cotton, 30 squares of green, teal, and orange, each square worked
in orange with a letter of the alphabet with orange corner blocks, each
corner with diamonds, enclosed by green border, with diamond quilting,
Lancaster County, PA, c1870, 76½ x 91" **1,725**

American Flag, cotton, blue, red, green, mustard, white, yellow, pink, and
cotton calicos and chintzes around American flag with sawtooth border,
Kansas sunflower pattern border surrounded by dotted red and green diamond border, alternating pinwheel and sunflower pattern surround,
c1865, 83 x 90¼" **20,700**

Blazing Star, red, ocher, green, and white printed and solid calico patches,
large central star surrounded by clusters of buds, trailing vines border,
shell quilting, OH, late 19th/early 20th C, 90 x 96" **1,600**

Eagle, cotton, crib size, red, blue, white, brown, and yellow, center profile
of eagle head in red, blue, and white diamond surround, white ground,
corner stars, red border, ocean waves and diamond quilting, c1940,
27 x 38" **2,300**

Floral Circles, cotton, circles of blue and yellow flowers and teal leaves on rust ground, double border of teal and rust, blue binding, borders quilted with ocean waves variation, central field quilted with flowers and medallions, PA, 19th C **5,175**

Floral Pinwheels, cotton, 9 squares in red, green, pink, orange, and beige on yellow ground, surrounded by continuous meandering floral vine with star in each corner, bound in red, Lancaster County, PA, 1820–50, 84" sq .. **4,000**

Flower Baskets, green and pink calico, goldenrod flower centers, pink calico borders, overall wear, light stains, 82" sq **425**

Fruit, yellow, white, deeper yellow and green fruit appliqués, stains and small holes, 66 x 82" **275**

Log Cabin, cotton, crib size, 16 squares of brown, pink, red, gray, yellow, orange, magenta, and blue calicoes, chintzes, flannels, twills, satins, and solid cotton, green calico border with chain pattern quilting, black and red plaid cotton binding and backing, Berks County, PA, 1820–50, 33" sq . **460**

Log Cabin, wool, 12 squares of brown, teal, olive, salmon, purple, and magenta, brown calico border with dark brown binding, ocean waves quilting, Berks County, PA, c1890, 67 x 85" **3,200**

Mariner's Compass, blue, yellow, green, red, and pink printed calico patches, borders with scrolling and blossoming vines, some discoloration, patches on reverse, 19th C, 83 x 99" **1,500**

Martha and George Washington, cotton, blue, white, and red in bars pattern, center printed portraits of Martha and George Washington each within white banner with diamond and blue border inscribed in ink "Memorial 1876, Memorial 1776," and "Centennial" twice, beige binding, c1876, 55¼ x 75¼" **4,500**

Ocean Waves, white, navy blue print, appliquéd border, 70 x 80" **275**

Sampler, cotton, 25 red, blue, yellow, orange, and green blocks of stylized stars, trees, flowers, or geometric patterns, many with stamped or cross–stitched names and moneys collected, green sashing, red flowered border, cotton paisley backing, Frenchtown, NJ, dated 1908, 84 x 88" **1,600**

Pieced and Appliquéd, Floral Pinwheels, cotton, 9 pinwheel squares surrounded by meandering floral vine, red, green, pink, orange, and beige on yellow ground, star in each corner, bound in red, Lancaster County, PA, 1820–50, 84" sq, $4,025. Photo courtesy Christie's New York.

Sampler, cotton, blue, green, brown, red, cream, pink, and yellow printed glazed cotton chintz patches with central rectangular panel appliquéd with flowers, birds, and animals on cream ground, surrounded by smaller blocks decorated with figures, fruits, flowers, animals, and cottages, Eliza and Jane Vial, Boston Massachusetts, c1790, 64 x 86½" **3,200**

Star, red, blue, green, white, pink, and rose solid, printed, and damask patches, center hexagonal panels appliquéd and embroidered in wool with colorful floral wreaths, rose wool backing with diagonal line and trailing vine quilting, discoloration, staining and losses, wear, edges trimmed, c1830, 72 x 95" **2,600**

Star of Bethlehem, cotton, blue, yellow, red, pink, orange, and light blue, central star surrounded by pieced yellow stars enclosed by yellow border, oak leaf and feather quilting, pink and white oak leaf pattern printed backing, PA, late 19th C, 82 x 83" **1,400**

Star of Bethlehem, cotton, red, pink, yellow, orange, and teal central star surrounded by 6 smaller pierced stars in yellow and pink on dark blue ground, appliquéd red, orange, and pink inner border, red outer border with ocean wave quilting, pink binding, 84" sq **3,000**

Stylized Floral Medallions, brown and teal vining border, bright yellow ground, 84" sq **250**

Tulips, solid and printed cotton patches, red, green, and cream, parallel line quilting, imperfections, 40 x 42" **165**

Turkey Tracks, red and pale green, machine sewn border stripes, attributed to Amanda Baker, Sevier County, TN, 68 x 84" **325**

Urns, sprouting tiers of blossoms, with buds and berries, green, red, and yellow solid and printed calico patches on white cotton field, channel and diamond quilting, mid–19th C, 80 x 82" **1,500**

QUILT TOP

Pomegranate and Blossom, cotton, pieced and appliquéd, red, yellow, pink, and green patches, pieced and reverse appliquéd and mounted on white cotton ground, Arthur Schuman, Berne, Berks County, PA, late 19th C, 80" sq **$450**

Rose Medallions, appliquéd, vining bud border, red and green solids, and pink calico, 78 x 86" **165**

Tulips, appliquéd, 13 stylized tulips, red, goldenrod, and teal blue, white ground, matching pillow cover, some blues faded, 60" sq **55**

RUGS

Although American mass–produced rugs were available as early as 1830, many agrarian families made due with handmade examples during much of the nineteenth century. Yarn–sewn rugs, constructed with two–ply yarn on a homespun linen backing or a two–grain sack, were popular between 1800 and 1840. Popular patterns were patriotic, nautical, animal, floral, and geometric motifs.

The importation of burlap to America in the 1850s opened the door for the hooked rug. The hooked rug tradition began in New England, quickly spreading throughout the country. The rug was made by pulling narrow stripes of fabric up through holes in the burlap. Most of the early designs were free–form. By 1900 preprinted patterns were available from Diamond Dye Co. and Montgomery Ward Co.

Rug hooking enjoyed a revival in the 1920s and 1930s when the early American decorating craze dominated. In the 1970s the folk art community discovered hooked rugs and turned them into an art form. Design motif and artwork was stressed. Many collectors and dealers failed to realize that factory production of hooked rugs was well established by the 1930s. Examples that can be easily confused with handworked pieces have been found marked "MADE IN OCCUPIED JAPAN."

Three other types of rugs also appeared in the rural homestead—woven, braided, and penny. Woven rugs, also called rag rugs, were done on simple wooden hand looms. Braided rugs became popular in the 1830s and have continued ever since. Penny rugs date from the 1880 to 1915 period.

Prosperous members of the agrarian community liked to demonstrate their wealth and good taste by placing an oriental rug in their parlor and/or dining room. Hall runners were another favorite way of introducing oriental rugs to a rural home.

Oriental rugs first appeared in the west in the sixteenth century. The rugs originated in the regions of Central Asia, Iran (Persia), Caucasus, and Anatolia. Early rugs can be classified into basic categories: Iranian, Caucasian, Turkoman, Turkish, and Chinese. Later, India, Pakistan, and Iraq produced rugs in the oriental style.

The pattern name is derived from the tribe which produced the rug, e.g., Iran is the source for Hamadan, Herez, Sarouk, Tabriz, and others.

When evaluating an oriental rug, age, design, color, weave, knots per square inch, and condition determine the final value. Silk rugs and prayer rugs bring higher prices.

Native American Indian rugs are also commonly found in Country settings. Many examples of these colorful woven rugs have been brought back east by visiting tourists. Others were purchased and used as accent rugs to brighten Country homes. Today these rugs can be identified by tribes or region and may command high prices.

References: Murray Eiland, *Oriental Rugs: A New Comprehensive Guide,* Little, Brown and Company, 1981; H. L. James, *Rugs and Posts,* Schiffer Publishing, 1988; Linda Kline, *Beginner's Guide to Oriental Rugs,* Ross Books, 1980; Ivan C. Neff and Carol V. Maggs, *Dictionary of Oriental Rugs,* Van Nostrand Reinhold Company, 1979; Marian Rodee, *Weaving of the Southwest,* Schiffer Publishing 1987; Helene von Rosenstiel, *American Rugs and Carpets; From the Seventeenth Century to Modern Times,* William Morrow and Company, 1978; Jessie A. Turbayne, *Hooked Rugs: History and the Continuing Tradition,* Schiffer Publishing, 1991; Jessie A. Turbayne, *Hooked Rug Treasury,* Schiffer Publishing, 1997; Jessie A. Turbayne, *The Hooker's Art: Evolving Designs in Hooked Rugs,* Schiffer Publishing, 1993; Joyce C. Ware, *The Official Price Guide to Oriental Rugs, Second Edition,* House of Collectibles, 1996.

Periodical: *Rug Hooking,* 500 Vaughn Street, Harrisburg, PA 17110.

HOOKED

2 Black Dogs, white picket fence, green and red flowers, blue sky, red and
black border, wear, faded, 26 x 47½" $330
2 Cats and Birds, primitive design, pale blue, tan, white, black, and olive,
mounted on stretcher, 16¼ x 37" 700
3–Masted Ship, with American flag, wool, black, shades of blue, yellow, and
white, red, white, and blue flag, purple, beige, and red, with pink stars in
corners border, some stains, 40 x 59" 1,200
Angel, slaying devil, cross and eye above, shield with "Quis ut Deus,"
shades of brown, blue, purple, yellow, and black on light ground, wear
and fading, 29 x 40" 500
Animals, multicolored, brown ground, mounted on stretcher, 26 x 41" 300

Floral, vining floral border, shirred wool fabric, blue, red, green, brown, and cream, 19th C, 62 x 29", ***$2,750.*** Photo courtesy Skinner, Inc., Boston, MA.

Baby Blocks, wool and cotton, shades of blue, green, purple, red, and brown, multicolored border with purple corner blocks, bound in black cotton twill, late 19th/early 20th C, 21¼ x 57½" **400**

Basket of Flowers, Waldoboro type sculptured flowers, elaborate scroll border, red, pink, yellow, blue, and green, beige ground, olive border, minor wear, damage, slight fading, 30 x 60" **200**

Birds and Flowers, sculptural sheared yarn, red, orange, pink, brown, and shades of green on dark ground, 30 x 41" **225**

Cat, wool, cream with black spots, gray–green ground, black border, late 19th/early 20th C, 21 x 32" **3,000**

Cat, wool, gray on gold, yellow half circle, half border with multicolored polka dots, 20 x 33" **400**

Cat and Dog, brown, gray, magenta, black, blue, and orange, bluish black ground, brown and gray border, dated "1938" in white, 28 x 38½" **350**

Cobbler, woman spinning, fireplace, and cat, multicolored, yellow ground, 19 x 69" **575**

Cottage and Hollyhocks, wear, some edge damage, rebacked, 24 x 33" **30**

Cow and Landscape, foliage in spandrels and edge stripes, red, brown, blue, gray, olive, and white, rows of scalloped gray felt and brown wool have moth damage, 25 x 38" **600**

Deer, with floral cornucopias and landscape, multicolored wool yarn on canvas, rebacked, edge damage, repaired, 27 x 62" **575**

Dog, leaf border, attached to larger pc of wool felt, some minor damage, 25 x 40½" **175**

Evergreen Tree, stylized, gold and orange, blue, gray, and green geometric ground, 18 x 28" **60**

Ewe and 3 Lambs, orange, red, yellow, green, blue, and brown, PA, 20th C, 28½ x 41" **400**

Fish, birds, 2 squirrels, flowers, and circles, wool, white, red, yellow, green, and blue, black ground, fish scale edges, white floss embroidery, wear, moth damage, repairs, mounted on fabric covered foam core, 22 x 43" ... **1,900**

Fish Scale Design, red, green, brown, and black, 31 x 63" **750**

Floral, alternating pink blossoms on pale green grounds and multicolored blocks, green, blue, beige, red, pink, and brown, bands of blue and beige pinwheels on ends, early 20th C, 51 x 37" **900**

Floral, stylized, red, tan, pale green, and gray, black ground, red and white border stripe, 22 x 37" **300**

Flowerhead, circular, beige, gray, green, red, blue, pink, purple, yellow, and orange, scalloped borders, frayed edges, late 19th/early 20th C, 93" d **5,200**

Flying Geese, pine trees, tan, blue, green, black, and yellow, black border, labeled "Green Labrador Industries," wear, edge damage on top corners, 27¼ x 38½" **700**

Geometric, multicolored, burlap back, damage, 115 x 144" **2,750**

Geometric, red, blue, brown, and green, olive and brown ground, yarn and rag on canvas, on stretcher frame, worn edges, 24 x 42" **150**

Hearts, wool, 15 triangular blocks in black and light blue, each centering alternating upside up and upside down red hearts on cream bound, later backing and velcro frame, early 20th C, 19 x 32" **2,200**

Horse, brown and black, blue, brown, and beige ground, braided border with camel, 24½ x 26" **550**

Horse, running, brown, beige, cream, and peach, beige and cream striped ground, sides with scrolled leafage, 19th C, 29 x 58" **4,500**

Horse and Bird, black and red, light brown ground, black border, 22 x 31" . . **300**

Horse and Cart, with boy driver, black, gray, blue, beige, and brown, red and purple detail, gray ground, brown crocheted yarn binding, 17 x 33¾" **40**

Hunter, dog, and deer, blue, brown, and beige on orange ground, wear and fading, 19 x 36" **275**

Leopard, crouched on branch, blue and purple, red tropical fruit, green leaves, gray ground, 24 x 44" **175**

Long Tailed Blue Bird, in flowering tree, red and pink ground, gray stripe, 26 x 40" **110**

Man, with horse, colt, and barn, multicolored, 18½ x 34½" **190**

Peacock, wool and cotton, circular, green and taupe striped base, multicolored tail feathers in full plume, black ground, early 20th C, 35½" d **4,400**

Ring Design, multicolored, 15 x 15½" **80**

Rooster, crowing, multicolored, 19 x 33½" **220**

Rooster, pale yellow, cream, lavender, red, gray, and black, corners with stars, black ground, wear and minor repairs, late 19th c, 24¾ x 43¾" **1,250**

Roosters, pr, centering inverted heart, olive green brown, blue, red, and black, top and sides bordered with band of blocks, dated 1896, 16¾ x 30¼" **2,200**

Roosters, pr, crowing, white, brown, yellow, and red, brown ground, border with segments of bright colors, 19 x 34" **500**

Sailboat, shades of blue, white, gray, tan, green, and pink, black border, labeled "Greenfell Labrador Industries," 10½ x 14" **350**

Squirrel and Scrolls, brown, gray, green, maroon, and black, scalloped black felt border, minor damage and fading, 21 x 37" **150**

Men and Oxen in Field, sgd "RL," Maine origin, $303.
Photo courtesy Aston Macek.

Standing Bears Playing with Red Ball, yellow, white, and blue stacked balls, double red and black border, early 20th C, 43 x 29", $1,320. Photo courtesy Aston Macek.

Stag, in almond reverse, oak leave and acorns border, wooden stretcher, 33½ x 59" 330

Steamboat in Harbor, shoreline with scattered cottages, trees and dog, red, green, orange, blue, brown, beige, and gray, mounted on stretcher, some wear, holes, late 19th C, 23½ x 39½" 2,300

Tumbling Block, browns, blue, and gray, 26 x 70" 230

Urn of Flowers, semi–circular shape, green, red, and yellow, gray ground, black border, edges rebound, mounted on board, 23 x 40" 220

US Seal with Eagle, round, 49" d 50

Winter Scene, multicolored, wear and fading, 12 x 16" 100

Wreath of Poinsettias, 2 shades of red on gray and brown striped ground, green leaves, black border, frayed edges, 25 x 38" 30

Young Girl, wool, wearing blue dress with pink sash and roses, green, blue, white ground, shadowbox frame, 20 x 17½" 150

NAVAJO

2 Gray Hills, Spirit Line break, hand–carded wool, black, gray, tan, and natural colors, 1960s, 30 x 58" $325

6–Pointed Star, dark red center, whirling log design with arrows at top and bottom, gray ground, stains, 23 x 25½" 75

Cross, red, brown, orange, gray, black, and natural, 46 x 70" 175

Cross and Terrace, red, browns, and natural, small holes, stains, bleeding, and wear, Ganado, c1930, 36 x 59" 300

Diamond, central diamond design, red, black, gray, brown, and natural white, West Reservation border, Klagetoh, 39 x 68" 280

Diamond, serrate diamond, red, brown, and natural, c1920, 46 x 72" 440

Diamond, step terrace diamond, hand–spun and carded wool, white, orange, gray, black, and red, 30 x 58" 325

Diamond, triple diamond design in double eye red, gray, black, and white, traditional black and white stripe background, Klagetoh, 38 x 68" 450

Diamond, whirling log centers, stepped border, dark red, dark brown, and natural, carded gray ground, West Reservation area, 55 x 92" 850

Diamond, floral, multicolored, red ground, Sparta, c1930, 91 x 116" 450

Geometric, black triangular design, tan ground, red border, warp breaks, holes, selvage damage, some color bleeding, Ganado area, c1920, 27 x 49" 140

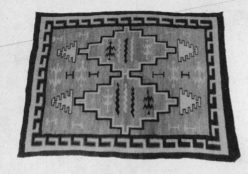

*Navajo, black, white, red, and gray,
minor stains, 73 x 54", $2,100.*
Photo courtesy James D. Julia.

Geometric, brown, black, red, and white, 54 x 76" **600**
Hourglass, central design, serrate border diamonds with old style cross
   design, hand–carded wool in tan, black, red, and natural white, stains,
   damage, poorly repaired corner, c1950, 37 x 60" **75**
Star, multicolored, gray ground, c1970s, 27 x 38" **60**
Storm, dark brown, gray, natural, and faded red, minor wear at edges,
   c1940, 36 x 63" **160**
Storm, rust, brown, and white, 53 x 77" **90**
Stripes and Rhomboids, carded gray, black, double dye red, and white, edge
   damage, 19 x 36" **100**
Stylized Chief's Blanket Motifs, red, black, ivory, and shaded brown, natural
   and aniline dyed homespun wool, dye runs, wool loss, 37 x 52" **500**
Sunrise, shades of tan, gray, and black with double eye red outlining,
   "W""and star element with West Reservation selvage edge pattern,
   Klagetoh, 32 x 49" **200**
Triangles, longitudinal bands in red, natural, and brown, black outlining on
   carded gray ground, natural border, stains, soiled, warp break at edge,
   29 x 58" **120**

ORIENTAL

2 Hexagonal Medallions, inset with cloudbands in abrashed navy blue,
   ivory, gold, and blue–green on red field, ivory border, overall wear, 50 x
   90" **$400**
2 Serrated Diamond Medallions, and scattered geometric motifs in navy
   blue, brown, rose, and gold, sky blue border, even wear to center, Kazak,
   Southwest Caucasus, late 19th C, 38 x 44" **700**
3 Hooked Diamond Medallions, red, sky blue, ivory, plum, and blue–green
   on midnight blue field, multiple narrow borders, Southwest Persia, early
   20th C, 62 x 104" **1,600**
Afghanistan Pattern, red, ivory, gold, and teal green on gold ground, 51 x 79"   **190**
Bijar Pattern, shades of blue and pink on red ground, 48 x 74" **150**
Deer, rabbits, and birds, ivory foliage, blues, tans, pink, and green, black
   ground, Pakistan Tabriz, 121 x 172" **3,000**
Dense Floral Sprays, midnight, navy, and royal blue, rose, gold, olive, and
   blue–green on red field, midnight blue border, small areas of slight wear,
   Sarouk, West Persia, second quarter 20th C, 105 x 141" **3,300**

Floral Designs, shades of blue, ivory, pink, and tan on red ground, dark blue
border, 45 x 69" **200**

Gabled Square Medallion, blossoming vines, navy and sky blue, rose,
tan–gold, red–brown, and blue–green on terra–cotta red field, navy blue
border, Heriz, Northwest Persia, early 20th C, 98 x 132" **2,200**

Gabled Square Medallion, floral motifs, midnight, sky, and ice blue, rose,
pale gold, and blue–green on terra–cotta red field, sky blue spandrels,
midnight blue border, small areas of minor wear, Heriz, Northwest Persia,
early 20th C, 102 x 132" **3,500**

Geometric Motifs, narrow horizontal bands, navy and sky blue, rust, rose,
ivory, and olive, ivory border, slight wear, Anatolian kelim, early 20th C,
65 x 124" **800**

Hexagons, 3 columns flanked by paired flowerheads in sky blue, red, rust,
gold, apricot, and aubergine on dark brown field, ivory border, small
repairs, Central Anatolian kelim, early 20th C, 62 x 156" **1,500**

Indented Diamond Medallion, matching spandrels, midnight and sky blue,
red, tan, dark brown, and blue–green on rust field, midnight blue "turtle"
border, Northwest Persia, early 20th C, 53 x 84" **1,600**

Large Circular Flowerhead Medallion, leafy vines in rosy red, sky blue, ivory,
and camel on midnight blue field, brown palmette and vine border,
Malay, West Persia, late 19th C, 60 x 80" **1,400**

Large Flowerheads, 8 in dark red, coral, and blue–green on royal blue field,
ivory meander border, Kazak, Southwest Caucasus, late 19th C, 50 x 90" . .**1,800**

"Memling" Guls, 2 columns in navy and sky blue, red, gold, and ivory on
dark brown field, ivory border, even wear to center, Kurd, Northwest
Persia, late 19th C, 42 x 84" **550**

Mythological Animals, green, orange, white, red, and black, dark blue
ground, 45 x 83" **720**

Notched Flowerheads, diagonal rows in navy blue, rust, dark red, and dark
brown on camel field, red border, Baluch, Northeast Persia, late 19th C,
30 x 52" **1,000**

Octagonal Medallion, small bird and geometric motifs in midnight and sky
blue, gold, red–brown, ivory, and blue–green on abrashed red field, midnight blue spandrels, multicolored border, Khamseh, Southwest Persia,
early 20th C, 45 x 82" **1,150**

*Hamadan Carpet, medallion
center with rosettes on ivory
field, pear motif border,
c1920, 80 x 51", $605.*
Photo courtesy Jackson's
Auctioneers & Appraisers.

Octagonal Turret Guls, Turkoman style, 8 in red, ivory, and navy blue on dark
aubergine field, red star border, Baluch, Northeast Persia, early 20th C,
36 x 66" **630**

Prayer Rug, large flowering shrub in cochineal, rose, apricot, gold, and soft
brown on ivory field, cochineal spandrels, ivory border, areas of wear,
Kerman, Southeast Persia, late 19th C, 108 x 136" **5,750**

Scalloped Diamond Medallion, blossoming vines in navy and ice blue, red,
rose, gold, tan, and light blue–green on ivory field, navy blue spandrels,
dark brown border, slight even wear, small repair, Malay, West Persia, late
19th/early 20th C, 52 x 80" **1,800**

Staggered Dyrnak Guls, midnight and sky blue, red, apricot, and green on
rust field, ivory border, rust elems, Yomud, West Turkestan, late 19th C,
46 x 74" **450**

Turkish Caucasian Pattern, pastels with ivory border on blue ground,
38 x 55" **50**

PENNY RUG

Circles, dark red, blue, gray, and black, wool, appliquéd, white cotton
ground, black velvet binding, 35 x 66" **$120**

Circles, gray wool and olive twill, red felt centers on white flannel ground,
tab border, 27½ x 51½" **150**

Concentric Diamonds, wool, rect, olive, gray, and maroon, red outer corners
with floral embroidery, worn, holes and repair, 28 x 46" **200**

RAG

Compass Star, round, red, gray, black, blue, and yellow, 55" d **$400**

Geometric, olive, red, and maroon earth tones, corners and center with
checkerboard type design, 25½ x 34½" **150**

Stripes, multicolored, square blocks, minor wear, 33 x 56½" **250**

Stripes, red, purple, yellow–green, white, and lavender, 2 strips joined make
rug, replaced binding at 1 end, PA, 70 x 75" **150**

Stripes, red and green on beige ground, wear, stains, and soiling, 37 x 158" .. **35**

SEWING & WEAVING IMPLEMENTS

A wide variety of sewing items were found in almost every rural home. Necessity
required that rural housewives were skilled in dress making, sewing, and sewing
repairs. Just as the farmer valued his tools, the rural housewife treasured her favorite
sewing implements.

Many implements served special functions. Sewing birds, an interesting conve-
nience item, were used to hold cloth (in the bird's beak) while sewing. Made of iron
or brass, they could be attached to table or shelf with a screw–type fixture. Later models featured a pincushion.

Sewing implements were frequently received as gifts and passed down from generation to generation. Many manufacturers used sewing implements as giveaway premiums. Advertising needle threaders and needle holders are two examples.

Although large–size weaving was left to professionals, many rural housewives did
have small tape and ribbon looms. Also found along with sewing implements are tools

associated with carding and spinning. Although no longer used, they tended to be saved for nostalgic reasons.

References: *Advertising & Figural Tape Measures,* L–W Book Sales, 1995; Elizabeth Arbitter et al., *Collecting Figural Tape Measures,* Schiffer Publishing, 1995; Carter Bays, *The Encyclopedia of Early American Sewing Machines,* published by author, 1993; Victor Houart, *Sewing Accessories: An Illustrated History,* Souvenir Press (London), 1984; Bridget McConnel, *The Story of the Thimble: An Illustrated Guide For Collectors,* Schiffer Publishing, 1997; Wayne Muller, *Darn It!, The History and Romance of Darners,* L–W Book Sales, 1995; Gay Ann Rogers, *American Silver Thimbles,* Haggerston Press, 1989; Gay Ann Rogers, *An Illustrated History of Needlework Tools,* Needlework Unlimited, 1983, 1989 price guide; Glenda Thomas, *Toy and Miniature Sewing Machines* (1995), *Book II* (1997), Collector Books; Helen Lester Thompson, *Sewing Tools & Trinkets: Collector's Identification & Value Guide,* Collector Books, 1997; Estelle Zalkin, *Zalkin's Handbook of Thimbles & Sewing Implements,* Warman Publishing, Krause Publications, 1988.

Newsletters: *That Darn Newsletter,* 461 Brown Briar Circle, Horsham, PA 19044; *Thimbletter,* 93 Walnut Hill Road, Newton Highlands, MA 02161.

Collectors' Clubs: International Sewing Machine Collectors Society, 1000 East Charleston Boulevard, Las Vegas, NV 89104; The Thimble Guild, PO Box 381807, Duncanville, TX 75138; Thimble Collectors International, 8289 Northgate Drive, Rome, NY 13440.

Museums: Fabric Hall, Historic Deerfield, Deerfield, MA; Sewing Machine Museum, Oakland, CA.

Additonal Listings: See Shaker; Wood and Natural Materials, Baskets, Boxes.

Bobbins, lace maker's, turned wood, orig box **$45**
Booklet, *How to Make Children's Clothes,* Singer, 1930 . . . . **8**
Catalog, *The Fashion World,* New York, NY, 42 pp, 1925, 9¼ x 21½" **20**
Catalog, *Needlework Star Journal,* Vol 6, No 4, American Thread Co, New York, NY, 20 pp, 1921, 8½ x 11¾" **19**
Catalog, *Singer Manufacturing Co,* New York, NY, 16 pp, c1870, 3¼ x 5½" . . **27**
Chatelaine Hook, silver, inverted heart form hook with bright cut engraved border, initialed "MR," repaired at neck, John Adam Jr, Alexandria, VA, c1800, 2⅛" l **800**
Embroidery Frame, bird's–eye maple, rect, adjustable, studded with iron nailheads, 19th C, 17¼" l **460**
Embroidery Hoop, wood, round, handmade, 16" d **6**
Hatchel (flax comb), cherry, chestnut, and walnut, chip carved dec, sheet metal trim, steel spikes, old patina, 16" l **85**
Hatchel (flax comb), Treenware, simple scratch carved dec, cutout handle, 11½" l **9**
Magazine, *Home Needlework Magazine,* Florence Publishing Co, Florence, MA, April, Vol 1, No 2, 176 pp, 1899, 5½ x 8" **17**
Magazine, *The Ladies Standard Magazine,* New York, NY, August, 66 pp, 1893, 8 x 11" **19**
Manual, Howe Sewing Machine, NY, 20 pp, 1872, blue printed wrapper **25**
Needle Book, Army and Navy **15**
Needlecase, carved ivory, figural woman wearing bonnet and dress with apron, flat oval base, French, probably Dieppe, c1790, 3" h **1,100**

Needlecase, carved ivory, umbrella shaped, screw–off handle/lid, 4" l **130**
Needlecase, celluloid, silver overlay design, c1920 .... **12**
Needlecase, wood, bullet shaped, turned, holds tatting needles, threaded
    lid, early 1800s, 2" d, 6½" h **50**
Niddy–Noddy, cherry, turned detail, old dark finish, 9" l **200**
Niddy–Noddy, wood, turned, bentwood brace is old replacement, 18½" l ... **30**
Pincushion, dog on ball, red corduroy dog, tape measure, 4" h **55**
Pincushion, fish, carved ivory, scale and fin detail engraving on both sides,
    mid–section fitted with green velvet pincushion, 19th C, 2⅝" l **500**
Pincushion, heart, red satin, colored–head pins dec, 6¼" h **50**
Pincushion, mallet, carved ivory, turned handle, barrel form head fitted on
    each end with blue velvet emery and pincushion, 19th C, 2½" l **525**
Pincushion, oval, knitted silk, red, yellow, and white silk stitching with
    crown head hearts, sgd and dated "Sarah Hockey 1796," reverse with styl-
    ized ship surrounded by stippled dec, fading, PA, 2" l **700**
Pincushion, star, chintz and silk covering, PA, late 19th C **80**
Pincushion, strawberry, folk art, red and green, large inverted strawberry on
    pressed glass base, 4 smaller hanging needle–sharpener strawberries, 8" h . **200**
Pincushion, tomato, satin **7**
Quilting Template, tin, 6–point starflower, set of 5 range in size from 5" to
    7¼" d **60**
Reel Stand, brass, painted cast iron, baluster with pierced flower shaped col-
    lar and 6 vertical reel holders, surmounted by bulbous pincushion cov-
    ered in worn red velvet, on green, red, blue, and yellow painted cast iron
    flower shaped base with 3 leaf shaped feet, late 19th C, 8" h **200**
Sewing Basket, woven splint, dish shape, stand–up handles, center beehive
    basket with lid, Shaker, 19th C, 4¼" h, 7½" d **1,400**

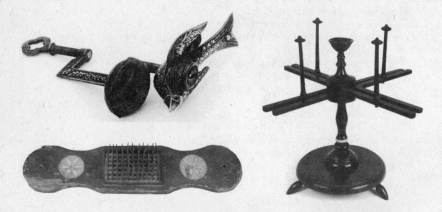

Left Top: Sewing Bird, silver plated, 1853 patent date, one pincushion missing, 5¼" h, 3⅝" l, $135.

Left Bottom: Hatchel (flax comb), carved wood, painted pinwheels, sgd "HV," Lancaster Co, dated 1869, $330. Photo courtesy Aston Macek.

Right: Swift, burl and ivory banded collar, cup finial, $660. Photo courtesy Aston Macek.

Sewing Bird, brass, worn silvering, missing pincushion, 5" l   55
Sewing Bird, cast and wrought iron, heart shaped thumb screw, 4" h   150
Sewing Bird, gilded brass, salmon pink corduroy pincushions, c1850, 4½" h .   230
Sewing Bird, silver plated brass, large and small pincushions, table clamp,
   5¼" h   130
Sewing Box, hardwood and pine, primitive, 1 drawer, tiered thread caddy,
   wooden pins, traces of old finish, 12" h   30
Sewing Box, ivory, rect, inlaid with silver and ivory bands, center rect silver
   plaque, hinged lid opens to light blue silk int fitted with various ivory and
   wood needleworking tools, early 19th C, 2½" h, 8⅞" l 2,300
Sewing Box, pine, sliding lid, lollipop crest, filled with knitting or tatting
   needles, old worn brown finish, 13" l   600
Sewing Box, pine and mahogany veneer, inlaid ivory escutcheon and geo-
   metric veneer on beveled edge lid, calico and paper lined int with mirror
   and liftout tray, soft old patina with water spots on lid, 11⅛" l   95
Sewing Box, poplar, decorated, 1 drawer, gold stenciling, turned feet, orig
   black paint, 7 x 8", 6½" h   350
Sewing Box, poplar, hanging, natural and ebonized finish, cut out and chip
   carved designs, hinged lid compartment in base, 2 semi–circular shelves,
   crest with worn pincushion, 20¾" h   777
Sewing Box, rosewood veneer, cov, rect, inlaid brass and wood floral
   designs, fitted red satin and gold star patterned red paper int, 10" l   130
Sewing Case, silver plated, fish shaped, scale fin, eye, and mouth detail, blue
   velvet int with metal scissors, bodkin, stiletto, fish form thread winder, and
   silver thimble, E Bonhemme, Palais Royale, Paris, c1820, 4" l   975
Sewing Kit, J P Coats, 6 spools, aluminum thimble, 2 needles, c1930   20
Sewing Kit, nut shaped, hinged lid, gilded, 1¾" l   225
Sewing Roll, cylindrical, black leather, fitted on each end with velvet pincushion, unrolling to purple striped satin underside fitted with a pocket, 3
   graduated wool needle holders, and metal thimble, probably Shaker,
   19th C, 7⅛" l   230
Sewing Set, carved wood, cylindrical tape measure, flattened rect needle
   case, and stiletto, carved wood case with fluting, leaf, and floral dec, stippled with nailheads, c1790, price for 3–pc set 1,380
Spinning Wheel, cast iron, table clamp, hand crank, orig yellow striping on
   black paint, old welded repair, 19¼" l   90
Spinning Wheel, hard and softwoods, old dark patina, 20" d wheel, 38" h . . .   190
Spinning Wheel, wood, red painted flywheel, 12 turned spokes above 2
   black painted reel, ring, and ball turned supports, slanted trapezoidal
   table with sawtooth, notched and molded edges, table fitted with a reel
   and columnar, turned support with red painted pointed distaff, all on 3
   black painted reel, ring, and swell turned legs, PA, 19th C, 49½" h   750
Spinning Wheel, wood, 2 spindles, turned members, old patina, age cracks
   in wheel, 32½" h   150
Swift, hard and soft woods, 2 squirrel cages, adjustable reel, 4 legs, old dark
   patina, 47" h   100
Swift, hardwood and pine, 4 squirrel cages, vertical adjustable post, old pati-
   na, 39½" h   50
Swift, wood, carved, slightly tapered cage top with acorn finial, mounted on
   turned cylindrical clamp with wood key, inscribed "Tr. Br/g. U.S.," prob-
   ably Shaker, 19th C, 11½" l   170

Needle Book, The Army and Navy Needle Book, printed color cov, warship on front, eagle on reverse, Japan, 1930s, 5 x 2³/₄", $12.

Tape Loom, hard and soft woods, leather and metal fittings, 2 heddles, 21¹/₂" l, 12¹/₂" w **150**

Tape Loom, oak, poplar, and maple, ratcheted cylindrical bobbin and shaped trough centering pierced panel, shaped crest and ratcheted gathering wheel on rect plank and faceted splayed legs, PA, 19th C, 25" h **900**

Tape Loom, pine, dovetailed box, 2 ratchet spindles, cracked heddle frame, old patina, 19" l, 10" w **280**

Tape Measure, celluloid, hen and chicks, Japan, c1920 .... **55**

Tape Measure, celluloid, pig, mkd "Occupied Japan," c1947 .... **25**

Thimble, brass, Clark's O.N.T. adv, "Our New Thread" **25**

Thimble, glass, crystal, enameled blue and white cornflower, 1" h **5**

Thimble, spun crystal, hummingbird and blossom finial, gold trim **10**

Thimble Holder, crystal, figural acorn, top with scrolls and foliage dec, American, late 19th/early 20th C **170**

Thimble Holder, silver, cylindrical, scrolls and foliage dec, American, late 19th/early 20th C **190**

Thread Holder, barrel form, ivory, turned, with bands, arched swivel bracket, oval hook with scrolls, trellis, and rocaille dec, German, Nuremburg, c1750, 5" h **2,700**

Thread Holder, basket shaped, silver, fitted with 8 filigree tongues worked with sunflower dec, swing handle suspended from wrist bracket with matching dec, early 19th C, 7¹/₄" h **700**

Thread Holder, cylindrical, silver, cover initialed "KM," American, late 19th/early 20th C **200**

Thread Holder, wool wheel, various hardwoods, turned legs and detail, accessories, worn finish, 45" d **160**

Yarn Winder, black painted box, housing counting mechanism, chamfered top, sawtooth edging, ext with inscribed circular dial and hand–fitted painted sheet metal, red painted turned 6–arm winding wheel above rect plinth with sawtooth and molded edges, 4 turned and splayed legs, 42³/₄" h **700**

Yarn Winder, hard and soft woods, chip carved detail, turned legs, branded label "N. Lindsaey, Reading," old dark patina, wear and edge damage, gear box housing damaged and renailed, 30" h, 24" d **100**

Yarn Winder, hardwood, geared counting mechanism, good patina, 32" h, 26" d **80**

Yarn Winder, pine, primitive, turned post, 4–part int in dovetailed box base, scalloped dividers, 37" h **150**

VEHICLES & ACCESSORIES

While Country collectors and decorators emphasize the vehicles and accessories from the horse–drawn vehicle era, there is growing collector interest in steam and gasoline powered equipment.

The decorating community views vehicles and vehicle accessories primarily as accent pieces. They frequently can be found in department store window displays. Favorite forms include sleighs and surreys. Animal–drawn children's carts are also popular. Since decorators want the vehicles for effect, they are willing to accept defects.

Individuals who collect and restore vehicles for display or use are much more demanding. They want the vehicles in working order with as many original parts as possible. Just as in the automobile field, there is a strong tendency to overrestore, i.e., make the vehicle look as though it just left the carriage shop or factory.

The formation of collectors' clubs contributed significantly to the preservation of farm equipment. These clubs, along with specialized periodicals, allowed a network to be established for the exchange of information and parts. You will find them exhibiting at most farm shows and state agricultural fairs.

References: Bristol Wagon & Carriage Works, Ltd, *Bristol Wagon & Carriage Illustrated Catalog 1900,* Dover, 1994; David Erb and Eldon Brumbaugh, *Full Steam Ahead: J I Case Tractors & Equipment, 1842–1955,* American Society of Agricultural Engineers, 1993; Carol Belanger Grafton (ed), *Horses and Horse–Drawn Vehicles: A Pictorial Archive,* Dover, 1994; Susan Green (comp), *Conservation and Restoration of Horse Drawn Vehicles,* The Carriage Museum, 1997; Susan Green (comp), *Horse Drawn Sleighs,* Astragal Press, 1995; Chuck Wendel, *Encyclopedia of American Farm Implements,* Krause Publications, 1997.

Periodicals: *Antique Power,* PO Box 838, Yellow Springs, OH 45387; *The Belt Pulley,* PO Box 83, Nokomis, IL 62075; *Farm Antique News,* 812 North Third Street, Tarkio, MO 64491; *Gas Engine Magazine,* PO Box 328, Lancaster, PA 17603; *Iron Man Album,* PO Box 328, Lancaster, PA 17608; *Polk's,* 72435 SR 15, New Paris, IN 46553; *Rusty Iron Monthly,* PO Box 342, Sandwich, IL 60548; *The Tractor Magazine,* PO Box 424, Rush Springs, OK 73082; *The Tractor Trader Magazine,* 300 North Elm Street, Graham, TX 76450.

Collectors' Clubs: American Wagon Assoc, PO Box 436, Ronceverte, WV 24970; Antique Engine, Tractor & Toy Club, 5731 Paradise Road, Slatington, PA 18080; Carriage Assoc of America, 177 Pointers–Auburn Road, Salem, NJ 08079; Cast Iron Seat Collectors Assoc, PO Box 14, Ionia, MO 65335; Early American Steam Engine & Old Equipment Society, PO Box 652, Red Lion, PA 17356; Early Day Gas Engine & Tractor Assoc, Route 2, Box 167A, Republic, MO 65738.

Museums: Antique Gas & Steam Engine Museum, Inc, Vista, CA; Billings Farm & Museum, Woodstock, NY; Carriage Museum of America, Bird In Hand, PA; John Deere Historic Site, Dixon, IL; Landis Valley Farm Museum, Lancaster, PA; Living History Farms, Urbandale, IA; Makoti Threshers Museum, Makoti, ND; Mifflinburg Buggy Museum, Mifflinburg, PA; The Museum at Stony Brook, Stony Brook, NY; National Agricultural Center Hall of Fame, Bonner Springs, KS; Ontario Agricultural Museum, Milton, Canada.

Note: Consult *Maloney's Antiques & Collectibles Resource Directory* by David J. Maloney, Jr at your local library for collector clubs and periodicals on the individual tractor manufacturers.

Stage Coach Chest, dovetailed, 3 drawers, yellow stenciled labels list stage stops, orig red paint, replaced hardware, New England, 19th C, 32¹/₄" w, 15¹/₄" d, 39¹/₄" h, $1,650.

ACCESSORIES

Buggy Seat, child–size buggy, wood plank seat and back, wrought iron frame, 27¹/₂" l **$375**

Buggy Step, cast iron, rect foot plate attached to angled support, ornamental treads, price for pair **30**

Carriage Step, cast iron, cutout plate on U–shaped support, c1870 .... **25**

Carriage Trim, from horse–drawn carriage, cast iron, ornamental cross designs, 19th C **25**

Coach Lamp, brass, beveled glass panes, eagle finial, converted to electric lamp, 29" h **50**

Conestoga Wagon Box, pine, slant top, wrought iron strap hinges, decorative hardware, traces of old paint, 17" w, 21" h **300**

Conestoga Wagon Seat, hard and soft woods, cutout ends, chamfered edges, shoe feet, old worn red repaint over black, 30¹/₂" w **575**

Sleigh Bells, twenty 2¹/₂" h numbered brass bells, wide leather strap, orig red paint, geometric dec, 1880, 8' l strap **135**

Sleigh Seat, hardwood, bench style, 33" w **70**

Wagon Jack, wood and wrought iron, good iron work with tooled design and "1814, P. Ordver," adjustable lift bar, traces of old red paint, 19¹/₂" h **100**

Wagon Seat, double ladder back, pointed finials, turned, woven splint seat, old finish, 22¹/₄" h **650**

Wagon Seat, double ladder back, turned front legs, replaced woven splint seats, 32¹/₄" h, 33¹/₂" w **550**

Wagon Seat, pine, bootjack ends, old refinishing, 40" w **250**

Wagon Tool Box, wood, cast iron oil spout dome and cutout end panels, mkd "Whitely," 16' l, 5¹/₄" w, 8 ¹/₂ h **150**

HORSE–DRAWN VEHICLE

Albany Cutter, Charles Schlosser, 03 Loch St, Syracuse, NY, black, maroon panels and runners, striping, burgundy upholstery, shafts, restored **$2,100**

Albany Cutter, C T Nevens, Auburn, ME, striping, artist sgd paint "G. Gisgen, Pntr.," shafts, c1865 .... **1,000**

Albany Cutter, Flandrau & Co, NY, 4 passenger, black body, gold striping, red
runners, decorative plumes attached to dash, shafts **1,400**

Albany Cutter, 4 passenger, dark green and maroon, brushed striping and
scroll work, scene on back, triple striping, maroon mohair upholstery,
pole, restored **3,100**

Albany Cutter, H Murray, Niles, MI, burgundy, green, and black, striping,
shafts **2,500**

Albany Cutter, R Millers Son, Kutztown, PA, Brewster green and burgundy
body, tufted upholstered seat, shafts with shaft bells **2,000**

Albany Cutter, William Winter, Schoharie, NY, carved eagle heads on dash
ironwork, orig paint and striping **1,500**

Bob Sleigh, black, red trim and runners, collapsible driver's seat swings both
directions, brakes, pole, 12 volt headlight **750**

Bob Sleigh, J Colyer & Co, Newark NJ, pony size, 4 passenger, black body,
red bob runners **2,100**

Bob Sleigh, T C Sawyer, South Amesbury, MA, red and black body, black
leatherette upholstery, shafts, restored **400**

Bronson Wagon, Clark Coach Co, black and maroon, ivory striping, maroon
upholstery, cut under with reach, wheels on rubber, pole, shafts, lamps,
restored **3,500**

Bronson Wagon, natural wood finish, cut under with reach, driver's wedge
seat, wheels on rubber, shafts **2,500**

Brougham, Demarest & Co, dark blue body, blue suede upholstery, wheels
on rubber, orig front wheel brakes, pole, restored **4,100**

Brougham, Healey & Co, NY, serial #2590, ¾ size, equipped with brakes,
wheels on rubber **5,700**

Brougham, Henry Killam, Broadway, NY, serial #3259, mkd on hubcaps **1,100**

Buckboard, black body, stick seat, burgundy running gear and upholstery,
brass trim, cargo rack on back, removable back seat, wheels on rubber,
shafts **2,800**

Buckboard, J J Haydock Carriage Co, Cincinnati, OH, natural wood body,
burgundy wheels and shafts, stick seat, shafts **1,650**

Buggy, A P Stevens, Athens, PA, midnight blue, white stick seat, leather sides,
pole, shafts, restored **2,300**

Buggy, Clarence Lowell, New Bedford, MA, side spring, black top, shafts **750**

Buggy, doctor's, painted, gold leaf trim, shafts, 50" wheels **1,800**

Buggy, H H Babcock Co, side bar, dark green body, white stick seat, gold
trim, wire spoke wheels **900**

Buggy, pony size, wicker sides, fenders, wheels on rubber, shafts, pole,
restored **3,000**

Buggy, W A Patterson, Flint, MI, Concord type, folding top, side springs,
wheels on rubber, shafts, restored **1,800**

Buggy, W F Whiton & Co, Bangor, ME, doctor's, pneumatic tires, shafts **325**

Calliope Wagon, Gus Kelting, Germany, pony size, carved and painted, circle gear, tongue pole, body pole for 6–up hitch, red sunburst wheels,
114" l, 69" w hub to hub, 91" h to top of flare board **1,500**

Carriage, Amish, brakes, lights, shafts **300**

Carriage, C L Stone & Sons, Hartford, CT, child's, black, red and green striping, red striped wheels, fold–down top, black tufted upholstery, maker's
name stamped under seat **1,000**

Cart, pony size, D & J Furniture Co **775**

Coach, Brewster & Co, New York, NY, The Outlaw, pole, serial #22800, black and yellow body, yellow striping, wheels on rubber, brakes, boxes in rear boot, crab end **50,000**

Coach, pony size, black and yellow body, black striping, red running gear, brakes, crab end pole, leader bars **15,500**

Explosives Wagon, parasol top, black body, "Explosives" painted on sides, red running gear, side springs, brakes, wheels on steel **2,300**

Express Wagon, C Eastman & Sons, West Concord, NH, former fire wagon from South Berwick, ME, brass rails on sides of body, gold striping, pole, shafts **3,500**

Farm Wagon, high box body, stenciled sideboards, metal wheels, handset brake, cast iron step **225**

Farm Wagon, Studebaker, green, red gear, spring seats, brakes, pole **575**

Gig, Brewster & Co, NY, Stanhope, serial #24788, Brewster green and black, leather dash and fenders, wheel wrench, shaft stand, mkd on brass wheel hub **5,000**

Gig, wicker body and dash, woven diamond design on sides, C–spring **2,700**

Governess' Cart, Brewster & Co, Broome St, NY, small horse size, mkd on brass wheel caps **400**

Governess' Cart, pony size, maroon and black body, wicker basket, gray upholstery, wheels on rubber, restored **2,900**

Governess' Cart, Van Tassell and Kearney, NY, 4 wheels, black body, yellow wicker basket, wheels on rubber **700**

Hansom Cab, black body, red tufted upholstered int **400**

Buggy, E Hayward & Son, Hacketstown, NY, fold–down top, wood spoke wheels, tufted leather upholstery, cast iron steps, 63" l, 37" w, 82" h, $1,000. Photo courtesy Ray Morykan Auctions.

Hay Wagon, Gruber Wagon Works, 14' hay bed, pole, hay rack, serial #1116 running gear, 1¾" axle **4,500**

Hay Wagon, stake body, rect hardwood bed, iron–rimmed wheels **150**

Hearse, bowed front, full fifth wheel cut under, wheels on steel, pole **2,400**

Hearse, C P Kimball & Co, Chicago, IL, black, ornately carved wood, lamps, shafts, hub wrench, plated cross, wheels on rubber, removable sleigh runners, funeral establishment name painted both sides **5,800**

Hearse, Jenny Lind, side springs, stick seat, side curtains **850**

Hearse Sleigh, bob runners **850**

Hitch Wagon, red, white wheels, gold trim, full fifth wheel cut under, brakes, brass trim, pole, restored **1,800**

Huckster Wagon, "W. Steigerwalt, Bowmanstown, PA" painted on sides, brakes, pole, lamps **5,200**

Ice Wagon, stenciled sideboards **550**

Mail Wagon, red and blue body, "Rural Delivery Route No. 2, U. S. Mail" and American flag painted on sides, red running gear, shafts, restored **725**

Pall Bearer's Coach, Cunningham, maroon and black body, beveled glass windows, wheels on rubber, pole **10,000**

Phaeton, American Stanhope, folding top, royal blue, camel hair cloth upholstery, cut under with reach, wheels on rubber, shafts **3,500**

Phaeton, Brewster & Co, NY, serial #18301, drop front, burgundy and natural wood finish, black folding top, wheels on rubber, shafts **5,500**

Phaeton, Ferd F French & Co, Ltd, Boston, MA, doctor's, folding top **1,500**

Phaeton, gentleman's, green, yellow striping, wicker seat, dash, and groom's seat, cut under, wheels on rubber, shafts **6,500**

Phaeton, J E Guyer, Waverly, NY, serial #3711, lady's, parasol top, burgundy, black, and wicker body, wicker dash, fenders, and groom's seat, wheels on rubber, tan Bedford cord upholstery, shafts, shaft stand, pole, yoke, tag located under toeboard, restored **7,200**

Phaeton, J M Quimby, Newark, NJ, lady's, parasol top, Webster green, yellow striping, wicker seat, groom's seat, and dash, whipcord cushioned seats, shafts with patent leather, restored **5,700**

Phaeton, Kimball, Boston, MA, folding top, wheels on rubber, shafts, old restoration **2,150**

Phaeton, Studebaker, gentleman's, black body, carmine gear, tuckaway groom's seat, cut under with reach, wheels on rubber, shafts, restored **7,700**

Phaeton, T W Lane Carriage Co, Amesbury, MA, lady's, drop front, blue and black, auto folding top, fenders, shafts, wrench **3,000**

Phaeton, William R Bishop, 36 Warren St, NY, lady's, wicker, natural finish, shafts **2,000**

Popcorn Wagon, Cretors, cut under, adv painted on sides **2,000**

Portland Cutter, Blackhall & Co, Troy, NY, black and red body, red runners . . . **700**

Portland Cutter, S B Wise & Sons, Orrstown, PA, shafts, late 1800s **450**

Portland Cutter, Sturtevant & Larrabee Co, Binghamton, NY, Welsh pony size, black, red runners and shafts, lambs wool seat cover **575**

Rockaway, S E Bailey Co, Lancaster, PA, curtain, dark green and wine, leather upholstery, cut under with reach, pole, shafts, c1910 . . . . **2,500**

Rockaway Coupe, H H Babcock Co, Watertown, NY, black, red, and natural body, natural finish wheels, wheels on rubber, shafts, whipple tree, old restoration **2,500**

Runabout, black body, tulip seat, restored black upholstery, yellow wheels, wheels on rubber, shafts **900**

Runabout, Columbus Carriage & Harness Co, Columbus, OH, spindle seat, shafts, bicycle axle **1,200**

Runabout, John Moore & Co, Warrent St, NY, pony size, wheels on rubber, shafts **550**

Runabout, Van Tassell & Kearny, 130–132 E 13th St, NY, pony size, natural wood finish, cut under with reach, wheels on rubber, shafts and pole **3,500**

Showman's Wagon, Smith & Sons Carriage Co, Barnesville, GA, louvered racks on back hold circus tent, brakes, c1880 .... **2,100**

Sleigh, butcher's, "E. L. Whitcomb" painted on canvas sides, bob runners, orig butcher block and tools **3,400**

Sleigh, cabriolet, black body, gold striping, ornate ironwork **1,500**

Sleigh, Charles Childs & Co, Utica, NY, squareback cutter, black body, tan upholstery, yellow runners **625**

Sleigh, child's, cutter style, wood, metal fittings, old red repaint, old damage and repair, 36" l **190**

Sleigh, child's, primitive, wood and tin, old red repaint, black and yellow striping, upholstered seat, black leatherized fabric, 38" l **100**

Sleigh, country cutter, red body, gray tufted upholstered seat, rein rail, restored **550**

Sleigh, John S Wilber, Sandy Hill, NY, squareback cutter, black body, gold striping, red upholstery **550**

Sleigh, "Manufactured for Wise Bros., Lewisberry, PA" tag, pony size, removable sleigh body, shafts **700**

Sleigh, racing, black body, maroon undercarriage, gold striping, maroon tufted upholstery, restored **2,200**

Western Stage Coach, "Mudwagon," from private collection of Gene Autry, $7,150. Photo courtesy Butterfield & Butterfield.

Sleigh, swell body cutter, dark green and maroon, striping, maroon mohair
    upholstery, shafts, restored 3,000
Spray Rig, NY, wood plank platform, cast iron axles, cast iron and forged
    spoked wheels, 1890–1900 150
Spring Wagon, Studebaker, 6 passenger, brakes, pole 1,800
Spring Wagon, upholstered seats, steel leaf springs, cast iron steps, painted,
    faded stenciling 450
Spring Wagon, Wright Bros, Deckertown, NJ, 4 passenger, canopy top,
    Brewster green body, red gear, wheels on rubber, brakes, pole, shafts,
    restored, c1890 2,700
Stage Coach, Abbott & Downing, serial #339, red body, yellow gear, leather
    slung, side curtains, brakes, pole 11,000
Sulky, cob size, natural finish, cane seat, shaft irons, black hickory shafts,
    c1891 425
Surrey, 4 passenger, canopy fringe top, side spring, natural wood finish, tan
    upholstery, brakes, wheels on rubber, shafts 1,500
Surrey, Michigan Buggy Co, pony size, 4 passenger, canopy fringe top, whip
    holder, cut under with reach, shafts 1,600
Surrey, Studebaker, 4 passenger, auto top, black body, striping on side enclo-
    sures, maroon wheels, shafts, mkd on step treads, new top and sides 2,000
Surrey Sleigh, 4 passenger, bob runners 550
Tandem Cart, Columbia Buggy Co, Detroit, MI, black and maroon, ivory
    wicker sides and back, driver's wedge, wheels on rubber, 2 sets of shafts,
    product #976 mkd under seat, restored 3,100
Trap, A T Demarest, side bar, natural wood finish, beige upholstery, rear seat
    reverses to face forward or backward, wheels on rubber, pole, yoke,
    restored 2,800
Trap, back–to–back seating, black body, maroon undercarriage, natural
    wicker sides, striping on siding, cut under with reach, wheels on rubber,
    shafts, restored 3,200
Trap Sleigh, oak, burgundy body, striping, gray wool upholstery, spindled
    sides, front seat moves back and forth for easy entry, fold–down back seat,
    shafts 3,400
Viceroy, natural wood finish, stick seat, wire spoke pneumatic wheels, 2 sets
    of shafts 300
Victoria Sleigh, Brewster & Co, Broome St, NY, panel boot, pole 3,400
Village Cart, Van Tassell & Kearney, NY, burgundy body, yellow running gear,
    black upholstery, wood hub, wheels on rubber, Dennet 3–spring suspen-
    sion, wooden dash and fenders, fulcrum shafts, height adjustment
    at rear, 2 rear steps, restored, c1905 1,100
Vis–a–Vis Sleigh, Heiko Wurhmann, 6 to 8 passenger, burgundy, navy uphol-
    stery, hand–carved lion heads both sides, brass trim, hand crank brake,
    brass heads on pole, restored 2,900
Vis–a–Vis Sleigh, black body, yellow runners, 2 screens in front of coach-
    man's seat, doors on both sides of passenger's seats 3,300
Vis–a–Vis Sleigh, wicker cutter, dark green and yellow platform and runners,
    wicker body, restored 400
Wagon, Amish, Harper, sliding doors, 1920s 2,500
Wagon, Democrat, natural wood finish, oak shadow box side panels,
    adjustable seats, 5 sets of springs, new foam rubber cushions, restored,
    c1870 2,000

Water Wagon, Studebaker, yellow, black trim, wheels on steel, brakes, full
    fifth wheel cut under, meter on top of tank, sprinkler on rear, restored **7,500**

TRACTOR

Case, 1921, 10–18 . . . . **$2,000**
Case, 1925, cross motor, restored **6,000**
Case, 1935, model C, rubber, spokes **2,400**
Case, 1937, model L, on steel, runs **825**
Case, 1950, model SC **675**
Farmall, 1930, regular **900**
Farmall, 1938, model F–14, rubber **1,750**
Farmall, 1940, model B, mower **1,900**
Farmall, 1946, model M, restored **2,300**
Farmall, 1949, model MD, complete, runs **600**
Ford, 1953, model NAA **2,250**
Fordson, 1923, on steel, runs **2,300**
Fordson, 1936, rubber, runs **1,100**
Gray, 1916, 3–wheel **15,000**
Hart–Parr, 1925, 28–50 . . . . **2,500**
John Deere, 1931, model GPWT, restored **8,000**
John Deere, 1935, model A, factory round spokes **1,300**
John Deere, 1936, model B, on steel **2,200**
John Deere, 1941, model AR **1,400**
John Deere, 1951, model AR **2,000**
John Deere, 1952, model 50 . . . . **1,100**
John Deere, 1953, model 50 . . . . **2,000**
John Deere, 1955, model 80 . . . . **4,200**
Lawson, 1925, full jeweled **1,500**
Mc–Deering, 1936, model O–12, rubber, runs **2,500**
Mc–Deering, 1952, model WD–6 . . . . **600**
M–H, 1936, Challenger, steel **2,200**
M–M, 1938, model KTA **1,200**
M–M, 1947, model GTA **1,000**
M–M, 1953, model UT **400**
Oliver, 99 GM **3,400**
Silver King, 1946, runs **1,800**

WOOD & NATURAL MATERIALS

Rural America used wood because it was inexpensive and readily available. As land was cleared for settlement and farming, the wood from trees became fuel for heat or lumber for building or manufacturing a host of products ranging from barrels to furniture.

Grain and tone explain the appeal of natural wood. Each piece exhibits individual characteristics. This aspect was understood and admired in an agrarian society. Natural wood has an earthy tone, strong yet subdued.

Over the years wood patinates and oxidates. These two forces create a feel to wood that is impossible to duplicate. Only time can accomplish the effect.

Many wooden forms were grained, painted, or stenciled. Because this was done by hand, they also exhibit strong individual characteristics. In the 1950s it was common practice to strip painted pieces and refinish them to expose the natural wood grains. The folk art revival of the late 1960s through the early 1980s focused interest on painted pieces, showing that the painting is an integral part of the piece.

Painted pieces now have strong appeal among Country collectors as well. Tastes range from ornately decorated blanket chests to the warm milk paint tones often found on pie safes. Painted wooden pieces have found a permanent place in Country homes.

BASKETS

The Country look focuses on baskets made of splint, rye straw, or willow. Emphasis is placed on handmade examples. Nails or staples, wide splints which are thin and evenly cut, or wire bail handles denote factory construction which can date to the mid–nineteenth century. Painted or woven decorated baskets rarely are handmade, unless American Indian.

Baskets are collected by (a) type– berry, egg, or field, (b) region—Nantucket or Shaker, and (c) composition—splint, rye, or willow. Stick to examples in very good condition; damaged baskets are a poor investment even at a low price.

References: Don and Carol Raycraft, *Collector's Guide to Country Baskets,* Collector Books, 1985, 1994 value update; Nancy N. Schiffer, *Baskets, Revised,* Schiffer Publishing, 1996; Martha Wetherbee and Nathan Taylor, *Legend of the Bushwhacker Basket,* published by author, 1986; Christoph Will, *International Basketry For Weavers and Collectors,* Schiffer Publishing, 1985.

Museums: Maryhill Museum of Art, Goldendale, WA 98620; Old Salem, Inc, Winston-Salem, NC; The Heard Museum, Phoenix, AZ.

Additional Listings: See Shaker; Textiles, Sewing & Weaving Implements.

Apple, oak staves, solid turned pine bottom, bentwood bail handle, overlapping rim strip, wire reinforcement around lower section, 15" d, 9" h . . . **$150**
Apple, split wood, rounded bottom, bentwood swivel handle, hanging strap and hook, c1915, 16" d **75**
Berry, picket fence, wood, wire, and tin, wood and wire bail handles, old dark finish, 6½" l **275**
Berry, split wood, crisscross bands, 7" d, 5¾" h **45**
Berry Carrier, turned handle, square tray, 4 stapled machine–cut softwood berry baskets **25**
Burden, woven splint, square bottom, round rim, old patina, 14" sq, 16" h . . . **45**

Bushel, stave construction, wrapped with wire bands, wooden rim, bentwood rim handles, old varnish finish, 18 x 11" **150**

Buttocks, woven splint, bentwood handle, 14 ribs, Eye of God design woven at handle, good color, some damage, 16½ x 15", 6½" h plus handle **70**

Buttocks, woven splint, bentwood handle, 14 ribs, old brown patina, minor damage, 5½ x 5", 3" h plus handle **300**

Buttocks, woven splint, bentwood handle, 20 ribs, old patina, some damage, 15 x 14", 9" h plus handle **65**

Buttocks, woven splint, bentwood handle, 22 ribs, blue and black stripes woven in at rim and center, 16½ x 13½", 8½" h plus handle **135**

Buttocks, woven splint, bentwood handle, 22 ribs, old thick blue paint, 5 x 4¼", 2¼" h plus handle **575**

Buttocks, woven splint, bentwood handle, 26 ribs, faded red and green strips woven in, natural patina, 7¼" sq, 4¼" h plus handle **225**

Buttocks, woven splint, bentwood handle, 26 ribs, tightly woven, good color, some damage, 14½ x 12", 7" h plus handle **100**

Buttocks, woven splint, bentwood handle, 28 ribs, good color, some damage, 16½ x 12", 7¼" h plus handle **70**

Buttocks, woven splint, bentwood handle, 28 ribs, 2–tone with dark varnish finish, minor damage, 8½ x 7", 4½" h plus handle **200**

Buttocks, woven splint, bentwood handle, 30 ribs, painted floral dec in red, orange, and green, minor damage, 10½ x 10", 5" h plus handle **450**

Buttocks, woven splint, bentwood handle, 32 ribs, miniature, tightly woven, well shaped, old patina, 4½ x 4", 2" h plus handle **635**

Buttocks, woven splint, bentwood handle, 32 ribs, old worn and weathered gray scrubbed finish, attributed to western NC, 13½ x 12½", 8" h plus handle **100**

Buttocks, woven splint, bentwood handle, 38 ribs, natural patina, 7½ x 7", 4" h plus handle **135**

Buttocks, woven splint, bentwood handle, 40 ribs, old gray paint, 14 x 13½", 7" h plus handle **650**

Buttocks, woven splint, bentwood handle, 58 ribs, old orange–tan pigmented varnish, twisted detail at handle, 12½" sq, 6½" h plus handle **550**

Cheese, round, hexagonal weave, woven splint, good age and color, minor damage, 21" d, 7" h **275**

Cheese, round, hexagonal weave, woven splint, gray scrubbed finish, 21½" d, 8" h **275**

Cheese, round, hexagonal weave, woven splint, openwork X's below wrapped rim, 9¼" d **135**

Clothespin, willow, early 20th C, 14¼ x 12½" **85**

Cotton Picking, woven splint, old worn blue paint, leather shoulder strap, 18" h **325**

Dough Rising, rye straw, hickory splint binding, shallow, PA, late 19th C, 23" d **125**

Drying, woven splint, open weave wire bottom, bentwood handle branded "Dr. Webb," 15 x 14½" **70**

Egg, woven splint, bentwood handle, handle sgd "Haver," good patina, 7¼" d, 4½" h **250**

Egg, woven splint, bentwood handle, old green paint, 8½" d **225**

Egg, woven splint, bentwood handle, weathered gray scrubbed finish, 17 x 15" **55**

Feather, ash splint, New England, early 19th C, 20" d, 26" h **275**

Field, woven splint, oval, oak splint, bow handles, ftd, carved oak runners reinforced bottom, c1875, 28 x 17", 12" h **135**

Field, woven splint, oval, oak splint, rib construction, wrapped bentwood handle, 19th C, 29½ x 17" **265**

Field, woven splint, rect, ash splint, CT, 19th C, 42 x 26", 12" h **350**

Field, woven splint, round, ash and hickory splint, loosely woven, c1900, 29" d **325**

Field, woven splint, round, bentwood rim handles, good color, minor damage, 18" d, 12¾" h **85**

Field, woven splint, round, oak splint, rib construction, carved handles, c1880, 30" d, 15¾" h **225**

Field, woven splint, round, rib construction, bow handles, New England, c1850, 32" d, 16½" h **275**

Field, woven splint, round, wood bottom, old natural patina, "H.S.B." painted in red, 15" d, 11½" h **60**

Flower, ash splint, round, tightly woven, extra long carved handle, New England, 1800s, 10½" d **110**

Fruit, pierced, contrasting woods, ftd, attributed to North Andover, MA, 19th C, 7¾" h **250**

Game, woven splint, hanging, 2 part, loom crest, 21" h **200**

Garden, woven splint, round, carved handle continues to bottom, VA, 19th C, 11½" d, 6½" h **190**

Gathering, woven splint, bentwood handle, oval, flared sides, traces of old red paint, some damage, 13½ x 10½", 5" h plus handle **85**

Gathering, woven splint, bentwood handles, radiating ribs, old varnish, 16 x 15", 6½" h plus handle **200**

Gathering, woven splint, bentwood handles, weathered gray finish, 16 x 11", 8½" h plus handle **60**

Gathering, woven splint, rect, boat shaped, shallow, high handle, 12 x 18½" . **55**

Gathering, woven splint, rect, 2 rim handles, 1 perpendicular handle, 20½ x 15½", 10" h **150**

Gathering, woven splint, round, flat tray, old green paint, 9½" d **150**

Gathering, woven splint, round, scrubbed finish, 17" d, 7¼" h plus handle ... **115**

Gathering, woven splint, round, weathered gray finish, well shaped handle, minor damage, 15" d, 8½" h plus handle **100**

Goose Feather, cov, woven splint, domed lid, bentwood handles covered by lid, good color, rim of lid broken, minor damage, 25" h **80**

Goose Feather, cov, woven splint, oblong, double lids, brushed black paint, wrapped bentwood handle, 18 x 14", 9" h plus handle **250**

Goose Feather, cov, woven splint, round, bentwood handle, 16" d, 24" h **95**

Goose Feather, cov, woven splint, urn shaped, wrapped ear handles, 24" h .. **350**

Half Basket, woven splint, bentwood handle, wall hanging, 12 ribs, 11" l **150**

Half Basket, woven splint, bentwood handle, wall hanging, 13 ribs, 12" l **175**

Herb Drying, woven splint, openwork sides, good age and color, 11¾ x 11", 5¼" h **200**

Herb Drying, woven splint, rect, 20½ x 21" **355**

Herb Drying, woven splint, round, open weave base, bentwood rim handles, minor damage, 16" d, 6³/₄" h **240**

Hourglass Shaped, woven splint, 2 part, 12" d, 22" h **70**

Knife, woven splint, polychrome watercolor floral design, divided int, bentwood handle, 9 x 12", 3¹/₂" h **225**

Laundry, woven splint, oblong, ribbed, open rim handles, damage, 24 x 20", 11" h **95**

Laundry, woven splint, oval, rim hand holds, 22 x 27", 12¹/₂" h **100**

Laundry, woven splint, rect, natural finish, bentwood rim handles, 20¹/₂ x 25¹/₂", 10³/₄" h **75**

Laundry, woven splint, round, bentwood rim handles, 21" d, 10" h **65**

Laundry, woven splint, round, bentwood rim handles, mkd "OHW," 18¹/₂" d, 12" h **55**

Laundry, woven splint, round, rim handles, copper wire woven in bottom, 19" d, 11³/₄" h **95**

Laundry, woven splint, rim handles, dark finish, some damage, 26" d, 16" h . . **50**

Loom, woven splint, hanging, shaped rest, 12" w, 13" h **100**

Loom, woven splint, hanging, 2 section, traces of yellow paint, 10¹/₂" w, 17" h **375**

Lunch, woven splint, oval, ash wrapped handle, 2 lift lids on cross pcs, tightly woven, 1800s, 8 x 6" **165**

Market, cov, woven splint, bentwood handle, rect, damage, 11 x 20", 9" h . . . **75**

Market, woven splint, bentwood handle, rect, natural, red, and black woven design, 8¹/₂ x 14¹/₂", 6¹/₄" h **85**

Market, woven splint, bentwood handle, rect, round, swivel handle, 12" d, 7¹/₂" h **125**

Market, woven splint, bentwood handle, rect, woven center brace, faded green bands, 16 x 23", 11³/₄" h **200**

Melon Rib, woven splint, bentwood handle, 8 ribs, miniature, multicolor strips woven in at handle, 2¹/₄" d, 1³/₈" h plus handle **115**

Left: Easter Basket, braided rim and handle, 10¹/₂" w, 9" h, $25.

Right: Nantucket Basket, cov, carved swing handle, honey patina, slight damage, $715.
Photo courtesy Aston Macek.

Melon Rib, woven splint, bentwood handle, 12 ribs, old patina, 13½" d, 9½" h plus handle 225

Melon Rib, woven splint, bentwood handle, 14 ribs, red strips woven in near handle, Berks County, PA, 6¾ x 6", 3¼" h plus handle 165

Melon Rib, woven splint, bentwood handle, 20 ribs, Eye of God designs woven at handle, old varnish, 12½ x 11¼", 5½" h plus handle 60

Nantucket, woven cane and splint, turned wood bottom, bentwood handle, Boyer, S P, swivel handle, ivory insert in bottom, stamped label "Boyer," partial paper label "Made by S.P. Boyer," old worn patina, 6 x 6½", 4" h plus handle 2,100

Nantucket, woven cane and splint, turned wood bottom, bentwood handle, oval, Ray, Mitchell, swivel handle, orig paper label "Lightship Baskets Made by Mitchell Ray, Nantucket, Mass.," 9 x 8½", 5½" h plus handle 1,300

Nantucket, woven cane and splint, turned wood bottom, bentwood handle, oval, swivel handle, Nantucket Island, MA, early 20th C, 8" l, 4½" h 250

Nantucket, woven cane and splint, turned wood bottom, bentwood handle, round, lightship type, swivel handle, Nantucket Island, MA, early 20th C, 6" d, 8" h 1,100

Nantucket, woven cane and splint, turned wood bottom, bentwood handle, round, old worn patina, swivel handle, stains, minor damage, 8½" d, 3¾" h plus handle 750

Nantucket, woven cane and splint, turned wood bottom, bentwood handle, round, out of round, swivel handle, 6¼" d, 4½" h plus handle 385

Nantucket, woven cane and splint, turned wood bottom, bentwood handle, round, rim handles, 14" d, 6¾" h plus handles 2,400

Nantucket, woven cane and splint, turned wood bottom, bentwood swivel handle, round, Nantucket Island, MA, early 20th C, 8¾" d, 10¼" h 325

Native American, Algonquin, storage, birch bark, negative scraped leaf designs, wear and breaks in bottom, 24½ x 16½", 13" h 200

Native American, Apache, tray type, willow and martynia, round, eighteen figures, painted rim, small rim breaks, 5" tear, c1920, 20½" d, 4¾" h 1,000

Native American, Astugewi, Hot Creek, northern CA, round, turned base changes to full twist overlay of beargrass and redbud, lattice twined band, checkerboard design, 6½" d, 5" h 250

Native American, Cahvilla, southern CA, round, natural and dyed juncus design, rim wear, 11½" d, 3¾" h 225

Native American, Chemehuevi, polychrome basketry olla, round, brown and purple geometric design on natural ground, attributed to Ann Land, c1900, 5¾" d, 4¾" h 3,500

Native American, Chippewa, woven cane, multicolored, 11" h 140

Native American, Eskimo, grass, round, knobbed lid, polychrome design, c1900, 7¼" d, 7¾" h 115

Native American, Hopi, coil, tri–color check design in rust, black, and nat- ural, rim and outer body stitches missing, wear to bottom, 9½" d, 5⅝" h . . 80

Native American, Hupa, acorn storage, round, half and full twist twined beargrass and woodwardia design, heavy reinforced rim, 2 holes at base, 1 warp break at top spacing, 10" d, 7½" h 75

Native American, Jicarilla Apache, deep oval, faded aniline red and green zigzag design, minor wear mainly in bottom, 19¼" l, 8½" h 225

Native American, Macha, cov, twined, whaling ships and birds, minor rim damage, 3" d, 2" h 125

Native American, Makah, storage, leaf design between double bands, 10 x 12", 4³/₄" h **100**

Native American, Mission, juncus design, rim damage, 9¹/₂" d, 2³/₄" h **175**

Native American, Navajo, wedding tray, finely woven, rich patina, somewhat faded design, orig early collection tag, c1890, 14" d, 3⁵/₈" h **650**

Native American, Papago, bowl type, martynia and yucca, stepped zigzag design, 7³/₄ x 10", 4¹/₂" h **175**

Native American, Papago, tray, martynia and willow, stepped whirling fret design, minor rim damage, 14" d, 3¹/₂" h **150**

Native American, Pima, tray, martynia and willow, whirling fret design, holes at center for hanging, 11" d, 2¹/₂" h **250**

Native American, Pima/Papago, bowl type, martynia and yucca, round, woman design, some stitch damage, 7¹/₂" d, 3" h **150**

Native American, Piute, seed storage, twined, jar shaped, round, plant cordage lugs, 9¹/₂" d, 6¹/₂" h **350**

Native American, Salishan, berry, bowl shaped, round, braided rim, beargrass spot design, loose rim end, 6" d, 4¹/₂" h **85**

Native American, Western Apache, bowl type, willow and martynia, round, 3 circular bands of men and women figures, drips of green paint on rim and bottom, 11³/₄" d, 3¹/₄" h **1,500**

Native American, Woodlands, woven splint, round, watercolor dec, 2 shades of green, some damage, 14¹/₂" d **40**

Peanut Gathering, factory made, machine–cut wide splint, painted white, VA, 19³/₄" l, 3¹/₄" h **75**

Pea Picking, oval, wide overlapping split wood, attached feet, full circular bentwood handle, 16 x 11", 6" h **75**

Pea Picking, rect, woven splint, red, 10" l **225**

Picket Fence, wood and wire, oblong, old dark finish, wire bail handles, some edge damage to tops of pickets, 33" l, 16³/₄" w **125**

Picnic, woven splint, rect, bentwood handle, covered, swivel handle, 16 x 12¹/₂" **85**

Picnic, woven splint, rect, bentwood handle, double hinged lid, green and natural colored int design, faded ext, 7³/₄ x 15", 7" h **100**

Picnic, woven splint, rect, bentwood handle, red paint over earlier black paint, swivel handle, 9³/₄ x 15", 7" h **65**

Potato, ash splint, round **35**

Round, woven splint, bentwood handle, 14 ribs, old green paint, 13¹/₄" d, 7" h plus handle **450**

Round, woven splint, bentwood handle, 20 ribs, loosely woven, 14" d, 10" h plus handle **70**

Round, woven splint, bentwood handle, 24 ribs, old brown patina, 12" d, 8" h plus handle **200**

Round, woven splint, bentwood handle, 28 ribs, good patina, 10¹/₂" d, 5¹/₂" h plus handle **275**

Round, woven splint, bentwood handle, 30 ribs, red, black, and yellow strips woven in, applied foot, 11 x 10", 6¹/₄" h plus handle **110**

Round, woven splint, bentwood handle, 32 ribs, some damage, 12" d, 9¹/₂" h plus handle **50**

Round, woven splint, bentwood handle, 42 ribs, swivel handle, 7¹/₂" d, 4³/₄" h plus handle **225**

Rye Straw, oval, minor wear, 10³/₄ x 8¹/₂", 4¹/₂" h **50**

Sewing, woven splint, small rim baskets for accessories, woven round at rim to square base, attributed to Shakers, 12" d, 5¼" h 70

Sower's, woven splint, bentwood handle, 12 x 14½", 7" h 50

Storage, rye straw, oval, 10" h 50

Storage, rye straw, round, rim handles, 16" d, 8½" h 85

Storage, woven splint, rect, alternating red potato print design and yellow paint, cov, minor damage, 17¼" l 250

Storage, woven splint, rect, dark patina, bentwood rim handles, 12 x 16¼", 6½" h 75

Storage, woven splint, rect, dark stain with red–orange and blue strips woven in, cov, wear and damage, 19½" l 70

Storage, woven splint, rect, old mustard yellow paint, bentwood swivel handle, 17 x 18", 9" h, ... 1,300

Storage, woven splint, rect, red, black, and green painted dec, 12 x 15", 9½" h 100

Storage, woven splint, rect, red, blue, and yellow watercolor designs, cov, worn, 19 x 20", 11" h 170

Storage, woven splint, rect, teal blue and pink watercolor designs, cov, worn, 15 x 19", 12" h 135

Storage, woven splint, round, rim handles, minor damage, 21" d, 14½" h 145

Storage, woven splint, round rim, square base, twill pattern, old patina, c1910, 14" d, 15¾" h 150

Table, white oak splint, round, loosely woven, 14" d 45

Tobacco, splint, open weave, shallow, 38" l 75

Utility, woven splint, bentwood handle, oblong, 7½ x 12½", 4½" h 75

Utility, woven splint, bentwood handle, oblong, out of round, swivel handle, old varnish finish, old repair in bottom, 15 x 17", 8½" h 130

Utility, woven splint, bentwood handle, oblong, polka dot designs on red and black watercolor and natural ground, worn rim, 13½ x 15½", 9½" h . . 85

Utility, woven splint, bentwood handle, oblong, radiating ribs, old patina, 13 x 17", 7½" h 65

Utility, woven splint, bentwood handle, oval, dark varnish finish, 14½ x 18", 8½" h 65

Utility, woven splint, bentwood handle, oval, double swivel handles, worn finish, 10 x 14½", 7" h plus handle 100

Utility, woven splint, bentwood handle, round, curlicue band, 13" d, 6¾" h . . 150

Utility, woven splint, bentwood handle, round, faded green and purple paint, 12½ x 13½", 10" h plus handle 45

Utility, woven splint, bentwood handle, round, faded red woven design, 9¾" d, 5½" h 150

Utility, woven splint, bentwood handle, round, hickory handle, weathered finish, 8" d, 5" h 100

Utility, woven splint, bentwood handle, round, old varnish finish, 11½" d, 6½" h 100

Utility, woven splint, bentwood handle, round, rim handles, old patina, 9" d, 5" h 175

Utility, woven splint, bentwood handle, round, scalloped rim, 10" d, 4" h . . . 250

Utility, woven splint, bentwood handle, square, natural patina, faded blue paint, 12" sq, 4½" h 200

Vegetable, woven splint, bentwood handle, oval, red, blue, and green pot to print designs, rim handles, 14½ x 11¼", 7¼" h plus handles 500

Vegetable, woven splint, bentwood handle, rect, dark worn finish, stationary
handle, some damage, 8³/₄ x 6¹/₂", 4¹/₂" h plus handle **100**
Vegetable, woven splint, bentwood handle, rect, handle attached length-
wise, c1880, 18 x 14¹/₂", 7³/₄" h **120**
Vegetable, woven splint, bentwood handle, rect, red, blue, and natural, 17
x 10¹/₂", 10¹/₂" h plus handle **75**
Vegetable, woven splint, bentwood handle, rect, yellow bands with blue
potato print designs, swivel handle, minor damage, 23 x 15¹/₂", 10³/₄" h . . .   **275**
Wall Pocket, woven splint, painted yellow over white and red, 19th C, 9" l . .   **110**
Wall Pocket, woven splint, poplar splint, New England, c1850, 12 x 9", 6" h .   **95**
Wine, willow, factory made, divided interior holds 12 bottles, early 20th C,
21³/₄" l **65**
Work, woven splint, light blue paint, bentwood rim handle, attached small
woven oval basket int corner, 11¹/₂ x 18" **110**

BOXES

Boxed storage was commonplace in the rural American home. Although pasteboard boxes were available, most rural individuals preferred boxes made from wood.
There simply was something sturdy and lasting about a wood box.

Boxes were designed for specific tasks. Among the most commonly found forms
are candle boxes, document boxes, jewelry, and knife boxes. Everything imaginable
was stored in boxes—clothing, salt, spices, and trinkets, just to name a few. Often the
family Bible was kept in a Bible box.

The name "band box" came from the utilitarian, lightweight pasteboard boxes
used in England to store men's neckbands and lacebands. During their period of greatest popularity in America, 1820 to 1850, large band boxes were used to store hats and
clothing while smaller boxes held gloves, handkerchiefs, powder, ribbons, and sewing
materials.

Most band boxes were covered with highly decorative wallpaper. Floral, marble,
and geometric designs were commonplace. The most desirable boxes are those covered with paper picturing an historical theme, e.g., the Erie Canal or a balloon ascent.

Individuals, such as Hannah Davis of East Jaffrey, New Hampshire, made a living
as band box makers. A maker's label can double the value of a box. Band boxes also
were sold as sets. A matching set commands a premium price.

The folk art collecting craze of the 1970s and 80s drew attention to the painted
box. A grain painting revival occurred among contemporary craftspersons. The
Country movement became enamored with "primitives," i.e., crudely constructed
boxes. Completely overlooked were the high style and better constructed boxes, many
of which were imported from abroad.

During the early American revival from the 1930s through the 1950s, a great
hoopla was raised over Bride's boxes, ornately painted oval bentwood boxes, many of
which featured a picture of a bride and groom. Many were passed as American in origin. Research has proven that almost all originated in Europe.

In fact, there is a strong painted furniture tradition in a number of European countries—Norway, southwest Germany, and many Slavic countries. Although different in
color tone and design, many novice collectors buy these items believing them to be
American in origin.

References: Arene Burgess, *19th Century Wooden Boxes,* Schiffer Publishing, 1997; Martin and Maryann LaBuda, *Price & Identification Guide to Antique Trunks: Their History & Current Values,* published by authors, 1995.

Additional Listings: See Shaker; Textiles, Sewing & Weaving Implements.

Apple, pine, red, conical feet, 9³/₄ x 10 x 4" **$300**
Apple Shape, turned fruitwood, mirror underside of cover, some losses at
   stem, 19th C, 3" h **425**
Ballot, pine, primitive, red, slant top lid, side hole, iron hasp, 11¹/₂" h **70**
Ballot, poplar, decorated, red and black graining, bird and foliage on front,
   polychrome bronze powder stenciled eagle, shield, and vintage on lid,
   gold striping, ballot slot in lid and bottom, 6" l **165**
Band, bird and flower, wallpaper, repairs and losses, 19th C, 19" l **110**
Band, brick house, with farmyard, trees in background, road in foreground,
   printed wallpaper, red and brown on blue ground, imperfections, c1830,
   11" h **875**
Band, buildings and trees, black, blue, brown, tan, and white, cardboard,
   16" l **500**
Band, buildings and trees, blue, brown, green, and white, bentwood, 19" l . . **400**
Band, Clayton's Ascent, pattern wallpaper, hot air balloon over trees and
   houses, pink, bittersweet, yellow, and white, c1835, 16¹/₂" l, 11" h **500**
Band, decorated, red, white, black, and yellow floral polychrome dec, with
   full figure of man raising glass on lid, pine, bentwood, oblong, laced
   seams, orig blue paint, wear, edge damage, edge of lid band is incom-
   plete, 16¹/₄" l **935**
Band, drapery swag, with 3 roses and vase design, wallpaper, imperfections,
   c1830, 10¹/₂" h **500**
Band, floral, wallpaper, brown and green, off–white ground, bentwood,
   13³/₄" l **175**
Band, floral, wallpaper, red and gold, light blue ground, cardboard, news-
   paper lined, 5" l **325**
Band, floral, wallpaper, seascape and pastoral vignettes, minor imperfec-
   tions, attributed to Hannah Davis, Jaffrey, NH, c1850, 14" h **325**
Band, floral, wallpaper, white and yellow, faded blue ground, cardboard,
   18" l **200**
Band, floral and fruit, printed wallpaper over bentwood, flowers, bowls of
   fruit, and foliage, white, brown, black, and faded red, blue ground, int
   lined with 1835 newspaper, printed label "Warranted Nailed Band–Boxes
   Made by Hannah Davis, Jaffrey N.H.," some wear, edge damage, dam-
   aged lid banding, 20" l **685**
Band, foliage, wallpaper, box, green, red, and brown, off–white ground,
   cardboard, lined with 1839 Hagerstown newspaper, 7³/₄" l **275**
Band, geometric floral, wallpaper, purple, orange, olive green, black, and
   yellow, cream colored ground, bentwood, 19³/₄" l **800**
Band, harbor scene, eagle and foliage scrolls, green, gray, black, and white,
   cardboard, 17¹/₄" l **275**
Band, Heraea Games, wallpaper, c1830, block printed, 14" l, 10³/₄" h **360**
Band, horses and chariots, landscape background, 19¹/₂" l, 13¹/₂" h **350**

Band, "Les Trois Jours," wallpaper, commemorates July 27–29, 1830 restoration of Louis Philippe to French throne, c1830, 19³/₄" l, 15" h 375

Band, peacocks and flowers, wallpaper, pink, green, and white, light blue ground, newspaper lined, c1834, 12" l, 6⁵/₈" h 550

Band, quadriga filled with flowers, wallpaper, couple pulling chariot loaded with flowers, c1830, 19" l, 12" h 550

Band, squirrel, wallpaper, hand blocked, blue, tan, and white, 19th C, 15" l, 12" h 325

Band, swag and tassel, wallpaper, int lined with 1833 and 1834 Patriot Marine Journal, 19¹/₂" l, 12" h 600

Band, The Three Days, wallpaper, repairs and losses, c1830, 17" l 110

Band, Walking Beam Sidewheeler pattern wallpaper, repairs and losses, 19th C, 17¹/₂" l 135

Band, waterfalls, with deer and trees, wallpaper, brown, green, and pale blue, white ground, cardboard, 15¹/₂" l 85

Bible, walnut, poplar, Chippendale, 2–board thumb molded top, dovetailed case, bracket feet, orig lock with brass bird head escutcheon, replaced hinges, 14¹/₄ x 22³/₄ x 8¹/₂" 900

Bird's–Eye Maple, brass bound, fitted int, lower drawer, imperfections, 12¹/₂ x 9 x 5¹/₂" 600

Black Ball, walnut, turned handle, "Parson & Co, Manufactures of Regalia..." partial paper label, old finish, 9¹/₂" h plus handle 110

Bride's, cov, pine, bentwood, oval, polychrome painted, buildings, house, and trees, white ground, damaged lid, 15³/₄" l 225

Bride's, cov, pine, bentwood, oval, polychrome painted, floral decoration, lid with couple and German inscription, blue ground, bottom board and laced seams loose, age crack in side, 20¹/₂" l 1,300

Bride's, cov, pine, bentwood, oval, polychrome painted, floral decoration, lid with equestrian soldier with saber, German inscription, black ground, lid and base repinned, lid seam replaced, 17³/₄" l 1,000

Left: Storage Box, lift–out sectioned tray, $1,980. Photo courtesy Aston Macek.

Right: Band Box, oblong, cardboard, black, brown, and white canal scenes and "Grand Canal" on teal ground, 20¹/₄" l, 12³/₄" h, $700.

Bride's, cov, pine, bentwood, oval, polychrome painted, floral decoration, lid with German inscription "Thou Goest with me and I with thee...," and couple holding hands, black ground, 18³/₄" l **2,300**

Candle, cherry, walnut burl veneer, scalloped crest, 12¼" l **550**

Candle, mahogany, hanging, dovetailed, pine bottom with indistinct inscription "Manufactured by Uncle Daniel St–whot died–1824," old finish, old repair in end, 9³/₄" h **250**

Candle, oak, dovetailed, sliding lid, shaped crest, edge damage, 21¹/₂" h **165**

Candle, pine, incise carved compass red and black flower designs, traces of white, natural dark brown patina ground, 8¹/₄ x 10 x 14" **750**

Candle, pine and poplar, 3–finger hole sliding lid, old red paint, 19¹/₄" l **175**

Candle, tin, hanging, horizontal cylinder, hinged lid, hanging tabs, old black paint, 10¹/₂" l **125**

Carved, allover chip carving, sliding lid, made from single pc of wood, 3¹/₂" l .. **100**

Carved, figural, comical stout man with long coat, brass buttons, and horn eyes, hinged door in back, constructed from single pc of wood with inserted feet, 3³/₈" h **750**

Carved, mahogany, figural 2 stacked books, mirror inletted into sides with spines, sliding door on each flat side, 1 with compartment, other with mirror, orig finish, 4¹/₈" l **3,300**

Carved, pine, old blue, red, yellow, black, and white paint, 7⁷/₈" l **550**

Decorated, black and white graining, pine and poplar, iron lock and hasp, brass keyhole cover, 24" l **1,450**

Decorated, blue vinegar graining, white ground, pine, red and yellow edge stripes, dovetailed, till with lid, orig iron lock, hasp missing, hinges replaced, wear on lid, 29" l **1,000**

Decorated, brown graining, pine, striping in imitation of inlay, yellow painted "Sarah Coher" in oval on lid, minor wear, 18" l **550**

Decorated, brown vinegar graining, poplar, green, yellow, and red multicolored ground, iron lock with key, 8³/₄ x 10¹/₄ x 18" **2,150**

Decorated, floral, black and blue stenciled and freehand dec, poplar, rect, red ground, hinged lid with wire hinges, old hard putty repair to bottom front edge, 10¹/₄" l **525**

Decorated, floral, crewel–like dec in black, blue, white, and pink, oval, bentwood, hardwood, and pine, natural brown patina, dated at bottom center of design "1808," rim of lid damaged, glued, and incomplete, attributed to Old Saybrook, CT, 22¹/₂" l **4,500**

Decorated, floral, stenciled and freehand dec, orig blue green paint, striping and initials "R.M." in red, yellow, white, and black, wrought iron lock with hasp, minor wear, age cracks in lid, bottom reattached, attributed to Cooperstown, New York, 11¹/₄ x 12¹/₂ x 27" **4,600**

Decorated, fruit and flowers, pine, black paint, stenciled fruit and flowers on front panel, lyres on ends in gold, green, silver, and white, silver edging, fruit compote on lid, minor touch–up repair, hinges replaced, 9³/₈" l **1,150**

Decorated, fruits and flowers compotes, gold stenciled designs on 4 sides and inside and outside of lid, old black paint, nailed construction, wear, repairs, and leather hinges replaced, 9¹/₄" l **80**

Decorated, green, red, and black stylized dec, round, bentwood, pine, and hardwood, natural varnished ground, 8¹/₂" d **1,000**

Decorated, house and stars, mahogany, maple, and pine, 1 turned foot replaced, veneer repair, age cracks, and putty repair, 4³/₄ x 7³/₄ x 11³/₄" **450**

Decorated, red, poplar, deep yellow and olive green striping, old worn repaint, plaid printed paper int lining, 17" l **110**

Desk, poplar and pine, square corner posts, tapered feet, applied edge moldings, slant top lid, narrow high shelf int, old cherry colored finish, 12" h . . . **520**

Document, green paint, dome top, early 19th C, 7⁷/₈" l, 4³/₄" d, 5¹/₄" h **475**

Document, pine, mahogany veneer, cross–banded inlay, 2 oval inlaid shell medallions and edge banding, ring brasses with emb urns, 7¹/₄ x 9 x 10¹/₂" . .**1,300**

Document, smoke grained, shaped cov, New England, early 19th C, 13" l, 8¹/₄" d, 6³/₄" h **450**

Dome Top, decorated, brown vinegar graining, pine, dovetailed, black, yellow, and olive initials on painted front panel with olive initials and date "MAB 1822," staple hinges, 12³/₄" l **350**

Dome Top, decorated, floral, polychrome dec, pine, blue green ground, wire hinges and hasp replaced, small chip on front edge, 7" l **300**

Dome Top, decorated, stippling and swirl, freely brushed black dec, poplar, dovetailed, old brown patina, age cracks, 28" l **475**

Dome Top, hide cov, leather binding, brass tacks, brass bail handle, lock and hinges, lined with 1806 NY newspaper, broken hasp, 15" l **80**

Dough, cov, poplar, rect, splayed base, turned legs, old worn red paint, 42 x 19³/₄ x 27³/₄" **825**

Dough, cov, poplar, rect, whittled leg stand, old refinish, 36" l, 27" h **250**

Hanging, cov, walnut, dovetailed, cutout swan's neck crest, 12¹/₂" w, 13" h . . . **930**

Hanging, maple and pine, pierced and chip carved front panel, some curl, old mellow finish, 8¹/₂" w, 4³/₄" d, 14³/₄" h **2,100**

Hat, cov, bent laminated wood, leather strap handle, black painted label, int paper label, 12" d, 16¹/₄" h **70**

Jewelry, 2 drawers, gold painted cutout design with red cloth backing, white porcelain pulls, cigar box back board, 8" l **40**

Knife, bentwood, cutouts and wooden knob fasteners on laminate sides, old varnish finish, 11³/₄" l **45**

Knife, decorated, orig red graining, poplar, dovetailed with cymba curves on sides and divider, yellow striping ext, white int, walnut handle with cross–hatch carving and mortised joints, wear, age crack on 1 side, 13" l **1,000**

Knife, mahogany, chestnut bottom board, center divider with cutout handle, 14" l **400**

Knife, miniature, dovetailed, cutout handle, early 20th C, 2¹/₄" l **200**

Knife, poplar, carved and scalloped crest with handle, worn salmon and red paint, 10 x 13³/₄" **220**

Mail, walnut, screw construction, scrolled edge design, locking compartment, old worn finish, 9¹/₄" w, 21¹/₄" h **100**

Match, pine, hanging, worn orig mustard paint, red, green, and white striping, floral and strawberries dec, wear, edge damage, scrolled edges are incomplete, PA, 11" h **350**

Microscope, walnut, green striping, leather handle, old dark finish, 13¹/₂" l . . . **65**

Painter's, dec, poplar or basswood, blind dovetail construction with divided int, floral and vintage dec, red, gold, green, olive, and black drapery wreath, swags, and classical columns dec on lid, dark blue ground, lighter blue showing beneath, attributed to Rufus Cole, 12" sq **1,750**

Puzzle, curly maple, 3¹/₂" l **525**

Salt, hanging, pine, dovetailed, cutout crest, lift lid, homemade hinges, old dark paint over green, 9¹/₂ x 7 x 8³/₄" **150**

Scouring, pine, scrolled edge detail, old worn patina, age crack in backboard, 14" h **325**

Sewing, hardwood, 2 tier with drawer, spool compartment, and pincushion,
old brown varnish, Shaker, 7" h **160**

Sewing, hexagonal, paper covering with applied beaded velvet flower dec,
purple velvet covered top with white floral beading, worn, 6" l **320**

Shaving, mahogany, geometric inlay, fitted dovetailed case with hinged lid
and orig folding mirror, contains straight razor with celluloid ivory handle,
brush, strop, and accessories, 3 x 6¼ x 9¾" **275**

Snuff, birch bark, oval, hinged lid, engraved designs with German inscriptions, 4" l **100**

Spice, cherry, dovetailed, 4–compartment int, sliding lid, refinished, 9" l **110**

Spice, pine and poplar, hanging, polychrome floral dec on lid, ends, and
front surface, scrolled crest, divided int with hinged lid, 2 nailed drawers
with porcelain pulls, orig salmon pink paint with black, yellow, and red
striping, 13 x 7½ x 15½" **19,250**

Spice, yellow graining, 5 dovetailed drawers, orig black pulls, wire nail construction, 11⅝ x 10" **1,500**

Storage, cherry, sliding lid, dovetailed, old soft finish, 1 edge of lid restored,
9" l **75**

Storage, poplar, molded detail on top edge and lid, divided 3–section int, old
reddish brown stain, sliding lid, 5 x 9" **250**

Treen, round, beech, polychrome floral dec, natural ground, threaded lid,
age crack in lid, 4" d **275**

Treen, round, walnut, elaborately turned spire shaped finial, turned pedestal
base, old soft finish, age cracks, some glued repairs, 12" h **175**

Utility, beech, rect, floral dec, wood pin hinges, orig polychrome paint,
8⅝" l **550**

Utility, pine, orig black paint, orange striping, stenciled "Deborah W
Holway," 12¾" l **110**

Writing, olive wood veneer, mahogany bands, fitted int, brass lock with key,
inlaid medallion on lid replaced, 15¾" l **225**

Writing, poplar, dovetailed, scalloped crest with hanging hole, divided int,
hinged lid, 12½" w **775**

BUCKETS, BARRELS, & BOWLS

Wooden buckets, barrels, and bowls were a necessity in rural America. Barrels
were used to store a variety of materials ranging from fruits to flour to whiskey. Every
medium–size village along a major transportation route had a cooper in residence.

Burl bowls were prized possessions. Owners were captivated by the individuality
of the grain. They wore like iron. Their major problem was that they were subject to
cracking.

Like many other wooden objects, a number of specialized bucket forms developed. The pail is one example. However, the ones most sought by Country collectors
and decorators are sugar buckets and firkins. Many sugar buckets eventually wound
up inside the rural home as sewing baskets or storage containers for objects such as
cookie cutters. Buckets with a manufacturer's mark or period paint bring a premium.

If not properly cared for, buckets, barrels, and bowls will crack and fall apart. Keep
them away from areas of high heat and low humidity. Barrels that were meant to hold

liquid should be filled for a few days several times each year to keep the joints swollen tight. Do not oil bowls. Simply wipe them clean with a damp cloth.

Additional Listings: See Shaker.

Barrel, cov, stave construction, laced wood bands, refinished, 19" h **$100**
Barrel, cov, stave construction, pine, Lebanon, NY, late 18th C, 17½" d, 27" h **350**
Bowl, burl, ash with good figure, oval bowl, shaped cutout rim handles, thin sides, old finish, dark stain, age crack, and wear in bottom, 8⅞" l, 7⅞" w, 2¾" h **2,650**
Bowl, burl, ash with good figure and scrubbed finish, turned rim, some stains, 11" d, 3¾" h **875**
Bowl, burl, ash with soft scrubbed finish, turned rim, 17¼" d, 5½" h **1,425**
Bowl, burl, good figure with old dark finish, thin sides, minor stains, 5¾" d . . **400**
Bowl, burl, oblong, old brown patina, age wear, some rim damage, 16¾" l, 11½" w, 4¾" h **1,100**
Bowl, burl, oval, octagonal base, worn old finish, rim damaged from use, 4⅜" l, 1⅞" h **250**
Bowl, burl, refinished, 4¼" d, 1¾" h **200**
Bowl, burl, refinished ash with densely figured burl, turned rim, minor putty filled holes, 14¼" d, 4⅜" h **1,100**
Bowl, poplar with good old worn gray patina, 14½" l, 5¼" w, 4½" h **135**
Bowl, treen, curly maple with old brown finish, 6½" h **95**
Bucket, decorated, stave construction, grain painted, 19th C, 9¼" h **275**
Bucket, painted blue, porcelain knob on lid, late 19th C, 9" h **225**
Bucket, varnish over worn orange and green paint, primitive, iron bands, wood side handles, 14" d, 10¾" h **100**
Bucket, yellow graining on white ground with green stenciled pony, dog, deer, birds, and scrollwork, metal bands, wire bail handle with turned wood grip, minor wear, 6⅝" d, 5⅝" h **825**
Keg, miniature, cov, turned wood, string handle, worn green paint, 3¼" h . . . **150**
Keg, stave construction, split sapling bands, worn paper label "Rifle P wder, Rustin Powder Co., Cleveland, Ohio" **125**
Oyster Bucket, cov, stave construction, iron bands, bail handle, and hasp closure, sides taper out to base, paint stenciled label "Boston Oyster Company," New England, early 20th C **300**

Bucket, stave construction, metal bands, hp dec, wire bail with turned wood handle, int painted red, 9½" h plus lid, 9⅜" d top, $75.

Pickle Bucket, cov, painted yellow, red bands, black stenciled "Sweet
Pickles," wire bail handle **125**

Piggin, stave construction, 1 stave extended above rim for handle, bottom
stamped "N. Corthell," old worn finish **175**

Sugar Bucket (firkin), cov, stave construction, wood bands, copper tacks,
sides taper out to base, wire bail handle with turned wood grip, blue,
painted, lid edge damaged, 7⅝" h **625**

Sugar Bucket (firkin), cov, stave construction, wood bands, copper tacks,
sides taper out to base, wire bail handle with turned wood grip, gray, old
paint, 6½" h **300**

Sugar Bucket (firkin), cov, stave construction, wood bands, copper tacks,
sides taper out to base, wire bail handle with turned wood grip, red, paint-
ed, 8" h **225**

Sugar Bucket (firkin), cov, stave construction, wood bands, copper tacks,
sides taper out to base, wire bail handle with turned wood grip, red, paint
faded to salmon/gray color, 6½" h **350**

WOODENWARE

Many utilitarian household objects and farm implements were made of wood.
Although they were used heavily, these implements were made of the strongest woods
and well taken care of by their owners.

One of the elements that attracts collectors and decorators to woodenware is the
patinated and oxidated finish on unpainted pieces. The wood develops a mellowness
and smoothness that is impossible to duplicate.

Lehnware is a favorite with folk art collectors because of its polychrome decorations. It blends nicely with the stenciled decorated pieces of the mid–nineteenth century. These collectors have chosen to ignore the fact that most of the pieces are mass
produced.

This category serves as a catch–all for wood objects that do not fit elsewhere.

References: George C. Neumann, *Early American Antique Country Furnishings:
Northeastern America, 1650–1800's*, L–W Book Sales, 1984, 1996 value update;
Carole and Richard Smyth, *The Burning Passion: Antique & Collectible
Pyrography–Burnt Wood*, L–W Book Sales, 1995.

Bank, walnut, turned, hidden swivel coin slot, damaged trick locking mech-
anism, old dark finish, age crack in base, 6" d, 6" h **$165**

Barn Lantern, pine, hinged door, worn red finish, age cracks, 11½" plus wire
bail **440**

Bin, primitive, softwood, worn green repaint, 30" w, 19¾" d **250**

Bookends, woman's head, butterfly on base, gold paint, 7¾" h **60**

Can, "Kerosene Oil," stave construction, worn orig red paint with black
labels, 16¾" h **190**

Candle Drying Rack, hardwood and pine, 8 removable disks with wire
hooks, old patina, 32" d, 40" h **575**

Clothes Tree, ball finial on turned standard, 6 turned pegs, 4 turned legs, ball
feet, worn green paint, 68" h **225**

Compote, burl, varnish, 5" h, 6¼" d **250**

Dipper, burl, curly handle, curved hook and drilled hole for hanging, worn
patina, 10½" l **250**

Dipper, burl, curly handle, old finish, wear at rim, 6" d, 4" handle   275
Drying Rack, hardwood, turned, old red and green paint, late 19th C, 39" h . .   135
Drying Rack, pine, shoe feet, screws added to mortised and pinned joints,
old dark finish, 25" w, 34³/₄" h   80
Finial, circus wagon, worn and weathered polychrome repaint, 7³/₈" h   85
Gate, cherry, turned posts with finials, attributed to Shakers, 30 x 39"   330
Grain Shovel, carved maple, open D–shaped handle, early 1800s, 37" l   150
Hair Receiver, burl, turned detail, threaded lid, age cracks, 4¹/₈" d, 3¹/₄" h   220
Jar, barrel shaped, treen   30
Jar, cov, old varnish, age cracks in lid, Pease, 4" h   100
Jar, cov, polychrome flowers on peach ground, strawberries on lid, ftd,
Lehnware, 5" h   700
Jar, cov, polychrome strawberries on pink ground, Lehnware, 5¹/₈" h   950
Jar, cov, poplar, treen, acorn finial, ftd, thin side with small holes, 6¹/₂" h   95
Jar, cov, wire bail and wooden handle, varnish finish, Pease, 3" h   75
Jug, dog shape, removable head, old finish, black spots, 3⁵/₈" l   95
Jug, turned detail, wire bale with wooden handle, orig varnish, Pease, 3⁷/₈" h .   465
Jug, wire bale with wooden handle, bottom mkd "Mrs, Theobald," old soft
finish, minor age cracks, Pease, 8¹/₂" d, 8¹/₄" h   800
Mantel, pine, country Classical Revival, old tan repaint, 62¹/₄" w, 44¹/₂" h   190
Match Holder, treen, wine glass shaped, 2 free turned rings, black striping,
3¹/₂" h   55
Measure, bentwood, round, turned side handle, varnish over old finish, age
crack in bottom, some edge damage, 5³/₄" d   50
Mortar and Pestle, turned, burl mortar, chestnut pestle, old finish, 6¹/₄" h   200
Mortar and Pestle, turned, maple, 7" h   55
Nightstick, chamfered sides, old patina, 7³/₄" h   150
Nutcracker, carved, figural dog's head, glass eyes, painted detail, 7⁷/₈" l   350
Plate, tiger maple, treen, 19th C, 10" d   525
Sieve, round, late 19th C, 14" d   25
Spoon, burl, soft finish, 5" l   165
Spoon, engraved design in bowl, shaped handle with letter "K," 6¹/₄" l   60
Stocking Stretcher, child size, old patina, 16" h   45
Towel Rack, tiger maple, 19th C, 22¹/₄" l, 2¹/₈" h   250
Tub Stand, mortised construction, 3 arms, pencil post legs, old blue paint
traces, 28 x 36"   30

Left: Saffron Jar, cov, Lehnware, hp, pink ground, stem with leaves, applied rose and fruit decals, pedestal foot, 5¹/₂" h, $350.

Right: Shoe Lasts, pr, Century, size 10D, $30.

INDEX

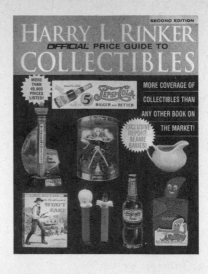